IFIP Advances in Information and Communication Technology 594

Editor-in-Chief

IFIP – The International Federation for Information Processing

IFIP was founded in 1960 under the auspices of UNESCO, following the first World Computer Congress held in Paris the previous year. A federation for societies working in information processing, IFIP's aim is two-fold: to support information processing in the countries of its members and to encourage technology transfer to developing nations. As its mission statement clearly states:

IFIP is the global non-profit federation of societies of ICT professionals that aims at achieving a worldwide professional and socially responsible development and application of information and communication technologies.

IFIP is a non-profit-making organization, run almost solely by 2500 volunteers. It operates through a number of technical committees and working groups, which organize events and publications. IFIP's events range from large international open conferences to working conferences and local seminars.

The flagship event is the IFIP World Computer Congress, at which both invited and contributed papers are presented. Contributed papers are rigorously refereed and the rejection rate is high.

As with the Congress, participation in the open conferences is open to all and papers may be invited or submitted. Again, submitted papers are stringently refereed.

The working conferences are structured differently. They are usually run by a working group and attendance is generally smaller and occasionally by invitation only. Their purpose is to create an atmosphere conducive to innovation and development. Refereeing is also rigorous and papers are subjected to extensive group discussion.

Publications arising from IFIP events vary. The papers presented at the IFIP World Computer Congress and at open conferences are published as conference proceedings, while the results of the working conferences are often published as collections of selected and edited papers.

IFIP distinguishes three types of institutional membership: Country Representative Members, Members at Large, and Associate Members. The type of organization that can apply for membership is a wide variety and includes national or international societies of individual computer scientists/ICT professionals, associations or federations of such societies, government institutions/government related organizations, national or international research institutes or consortia, universities, academies of sciences, companies, national or international associations or federations of companies.

More information about this series at http://www.springer.com/series/6102

Felix Nyffenegger · José Ríos ·
Louis Rivest · Abdelaziz Bouras (Eds.)

Product Lifecycle Management Enabling Smart X

17th IFIP WG 5.1 International Conference, PLM 2020
Rapperswil, Switzerland, July 5–8, 2020
Revised Selected Papers

Springer

Editors
Felix Nyffenegger
University of Applied Sciences Rapperswil
Rapperswil, Switzerland

Louis Rivest
École de Technologie Supérieure
Montreal, QC, Canada

José Ríos
TU Darmstadt
Darmstadt, Germany

Universidad Politécnica de Madrid
Madrid, Spain

Abdelaziz Bouras
Qatar University
Doha, Qatar

ISSN 1868-4238 ISSN 1868-422X (electronic)
IFIP Advances in Information and Communication Technology
ISBN 978-3-030-62806-2 ISBN 978-3-030-62807-9 (eBook)
https://doi.org/10.1007/978-3-030-62807-9

This Springer imprint is published by the registered company Springer Nature Switzerland AG
The registered company address is: Gewerbestrasse 11, 6330 Cham, Switzerland

Preface

The year 2020 will go down in history as the year of the COVID-19 crisis. A global pandemic changed all our lives and restricted our freedom of movement. Eventually, industry was hit hard by lockdowns in many regions of the world. Closed factories, short-time work, and restricted border traffic led to broken supply and demand chains. Our traditional mode of operation could no longer be maintained.

But then again, crisis has always been a driver for innovation. Many parts of our society had to react extremely fast to adopt their daily work to virtual collaboration. Education on every level went online within one or two weeks. Wherever possible, work was shifted to home office. Nobody would have thought that such radical changes in our work culture would be possible in such a short time.

Yet, it was no coincidence that this was possible. Rather it was the result of continuous research and development during the last decades and particularly the efforts to foster digitalization throughout the last years. Since 2003, the IFIP WG 5.1 International Conference on Product Lifecycle Management (PLM) brought together researchers, developers, and users of PLM. This event always aimed to integrate business approaches to the collaborative creation, management, and dissemination of product and process data throughout the extended enterprises that create, manufacture, and operate engineered products and systems. In this context, approaches such as digital and virtual product development, digital twins, smart manufacturing, or artificial intelligence were discussed and developed further. While these ideas seemed vague and visionary at the beginning, the contributions of this year's edition clearly showed that these novel concepts have reached a more mature level and have successfully been implemented in industry. Virtual collaboration, agile supply chains, smart manufacturing, and working interoperability have become vital. The development of PLM systems based on cloud and Web service technologies combined with Internet of Things (IoT) platforms seem to be key enablers of such intelligent or smart solutions for products, processes, and decisions. PLM enables smart X.

The 17th edition of IFIP International Conference on PLM 2020 was organized by the University of Applied Sciences of Eastern Switzerland. Due to the global impact of COVID-19 the conference was held in a virtual edition. This was the first time in the history of PLM conferences. Around 120 delegates from research and industry, originating from 17 nations joined the event. In more than 70 online sessions, 64 papers and 3 keynotes were presented, along with several social activities. Keynotes included speeches from Konrad Wegener of ETH Zurich, Alex Simeon of HSR, and two members of our community that were recently listed among the most influential researchers to achieve the smart factory: Ramy Harik and Thorsten Wuest. Every day was completed with an open industrial webinar, freely accessible to everyone. High ranking representatives from industry such as Buehler Group, Amstein + Walthert, and the DigitalLab@HSR were presenting their experience, followed by intense podium discussions with researchers and participants from industry. In the pre-conference program a PhD workshop was held virtually, dedicated to young researchers.

All submitted papers were reviewed in a double-blind review process by at least 2 reviewers (2.6 reviewers per paper on average). In total, 98 abstracts were submitted, followed by 80 full paper submissions from which 61 were accepted to be presented at the conference. In addition, 3 of the submitted papers that originated from industrial members were selected to be presented in a special, nonscientific track for industrial technical contributions. The proceedings include 63 revised contributions presented at the PLM 2020 conference. The papers are grouped into 14 topical sections:

1. Smart factory
2. Digital twins
3. Internet of Things (IoT, IIoT)
4. Analytics in the order fulfillment process
5. Ontologies for interoperability
6. Tools to support early design phases
7. New product development
8. Business models
9. Circular economy
10. Maturity implementation and adoption
11. Model based systems engineering
12. Artificial intelligence in CAx, MBE, and PLM
13. Building information modeling
14. Industrial technical contributions

This book is part of the IFIP Advances in Information and Communication Technology (AICT) series that publishes state-of-the-art results in the sciences and technologies of information and communication. In addition to this conference, the *International Journal of Product Lifecycle Management* (IJPLM) is the official journal of the WG 5.1. Selected papers of this conference might be published as extended versions in this journal.

It took a lot of effort from many people to organize this conference and its proceedings. We want to thank all the authors, all those listed below, and all those who are not included but contributed to make the PLM 2020 conference a success, particularly under the given circumstances.

November 2020

Felix Nyffenegger
José Ríos
Louis Rivest
Abdelaziz Bouras

Organization

Program Committee Chairs

Felix Nyffenegger	University of Applied Sciences Rapperswil, Switzerland
Abdelaziz Bouras	Qatar University, Qatar
Dimitris Kiritsis	École polytechnique fédérale de Lausanne, Switzerland
Sergio Terzi	Polytechnic University of Milan, Italy
Ralf Gerdes	Inspire, Switzerland

Steering Committee

Alain Bernard	École Centrale de Nantes, France
Clément Fortin	Skoltech, Russia
José Rios	TU Darmstadt, Germany, and Universidad Politécnica de Madrid, Spain
Louis Rivest	École de technologie supérieure Montreal, Canada
Osiris Canciglieri Junior	Pontifical Catholic University of Paraná, Brazil

Scientific Committee

Cordula Dorothea Auth	TU Darmstadt, Germany
Romeo Bandinelli	University of Florence, Italy
M.-Lounes Bentaha	University of Lyon, France
Alain Bernard	École Centrale de Nantes, France
Nikolaos Bilalis	Technical University of Crete, Greece
Abdelaziz Bouras	Qatar University, Qatar
Matthieu Bricogne	Université de Technologie de Compiègne, France
Kay Burow	Bremer Institut für Produktion und Logistik, Germany
Osiris Canciglieri Junior	Pontifical Catholic University of Paraná, Brazil
Paolo Chiabert	Politecnico di Torino, Italy
Christophe Danjou	Polytechnique Montréal, Canada
Frederic Demoly	University of Technology of Belfort-Montbéliard, France
Benoit Eynard	Université de Technologie de Compiègne, France
Clement Fortin	Skolkovo Institute of Science and Technology, Russia
Shuichi Fukuda	Keio University, Japan
Detlef Gerhard	RUHR University Bochum, Germany
Balan Gurumoorthy	Indian Institute of Science Bangalore, India
Mikhail Gusev	Skolkovo Institute of Science and Technology, Russia
Lars Hagge	German Electron Synchrotron, Germany
Peter Hehenberger	University of Applied Sciences Upper Austria, Austria

Hiroyuki Hiraoka	Chuo University, Japan
Hannu Tapio Karkkainen	Tampere University, Finland
Stefan Kehl	Volkswagen Group, Germany
Dimitris Kiritsis	École polytechnique fédérale de Lausanne, Switzerland
Bas Koomen	University of Twente, The Netherlands
Mariangela Lazoi	Università del Salento, Italy
Julien Le Duigou	Université de Technologie de Compiègne, France
Jong Gyun Lim	Samsung Research, South Korea
Wen Feng Lu	National University of Singapore, Singapore
Johan Malmqvist	Chalmers University of Technology, Sweden
Nicolas Maranzana	Arts et Métiers ParisTech, France
Fernando Mas	Comlux America LLC, USA, and University of Seville, Spain
Chris Mc Mahon	University of Bristol, UK
Alison McKay	University of Leeds, UK
Grant McSorley	University of Prince Edward Island, Canada
Mourad Messaadia	Centre d'Etudes Superieures Industrielles, France
Néjib Moalla	Université Lumière Lyon 2, France
Sergei Nikolaev	Skolkovo Institute of Science and Technology, Russia
Frédéric Noël	Grenoble INP, G-SCOP, France
Felix Nyffenegger	University of Applied Sciences Rapperswil, Switzerland
Yacine Ouzrout	University of Lyon, France
Hervé Panetto	University of Lorraine, CNRS, France
Henk Jan Pels	Retired, The Netherlands
Romain Pinquié	Grenoble INP, G-SCOP, UMR, CNRS, France
Sudarsan Rachuri	National Institute of Standards and Technology, USA
José Ríos	TU Darmstadt, Germany
Louis Rivest	École de technologie supérieure Montreal, Canada
Lionel Roucoules	Arts et Métiers ParisTech, France
Nickolas S. Sapidis	University of Western Macedonia, Greece
Michael Schabacker	University of Magdeburg, Germany
Frédéric Segonds	Arts et Métiers ParisTech, France
Vishal Singh	Indian Institute of Science, India
Alexander Smirnov	St. Petersburg Institute for Informatics and Automation of the Russian Academy of Sciences, Russia
Sergio Terzi	Politecnico di Milano, Italy
Nikolay Teslya	St. Petersburg Institute for Informatics and Automation of the Russian Academy of Sciences, Russia
Klaus-Dieter Thoben	Bremer Institut für Produktion und Logistik, Germany
Carlos Vila	Universitat Politècnica de València, Spain
Thomas Vosgien	HILTI Group, Austria
Thorsten Wuest	West Virginia University, USA
Bob Young	Loughborough University, UK
Eduardo Zancul	University of São Paulo, Brazil

Doctoral Workshop Chairs

Yacine Ouzrout — University of Lyon, France
Monica Rossi — Politecnico di Milano, Italy

Local Organization Committee

Felix Nyffenegger — University of Applied Sciences Rapperswil, Switzerland
Florian Fischli — University of Applied Sciences Rapperswil, Switzerland
Nicolas Hofer — University of Applied Sciences Rapperswil, Switzerland
Filiz Varisli-Cizmeci — University of Applied Sciences Rapperswil, Switzerland
Phlipp Steck — University of Applied Sciences Rapperswil, Switzerland

Honorary Chair

Alex Simeon — University of Applied Sciences Rapperswil, Switzerland

Sponsors

Intelliact AG
www.intelliact.ch

PROCAD (Schweiz) AG
www.pro-file.com

CONTACT Software Schweiz AG
www.contact-software.com

PTC (Schweiz) AG
www.ptc.com

Share PLM
www.shareplm.com

Mensch und Maschine Schweiz AG
www.mum.ch

Contents

Ontologies for Interoperability

Tools to Support Early Design Phases

New Product Development

Maturity Implementation and Adoption

Model Based Systems Engineering

Industrial Technical Contributions

Smart Factory

Distributed Scheduling in Cellular Assembly for Mass Customization

Elie Maalouf[1], Julien Le Duigou[2(✉)], Bassam Hussein[1], and Joanna Daaboul[2]

[1] Department of Industrial Engineering, International University of Beirut, Beirut, Lebanon
{elie.maalouf,bassam.hussein}@liu.edu.lb

[2] Roberval Research Center, Université de technologie de Compiègne, CS 60 319, 60203 Compiègne Cedex, France
{julien.le-duigou,joanna.daaboul}@utc.fr

Abstract. Industry 4.0 has many objectives; among them is increasing flexibility in manufacturing, as well as offering mass customization, better quality, and improved productivity. It thus enables companies to cope with the challenges of producing increasingly individualized products with a short lead-time to market and higher quality. In Mass Customization, manufacturers are challenged to produce customized products at the lowest possible cost with minimal lead-time. This increased customization increases complexity in production planning. The main challenge becomes planning production for lots of one and for high product variety and volatile market demand. Moreover, the customer requires real time update on his order status, and is less tolerant for delays. Nevertheless, in a make to order or assembly to order supply chain, many disturbances (supplier delay, machine brake-downs, transportation network disturbance, …) may highly increase the customer order delay. Hence, production planning in this context becomes more complex requiring real-time information exchange with all stages of the supply chain. This paper tries to answer this challenge by proposing a distributed production scheduling approach for mass customization in a cellular assembly layout.

Keywords: Mass customization · Distributed scheduling · Cellular assembly · Smart scheduling

1 Introduction

Most of the research and industrial road maps and directives such as the European Union roadmap project titled "IMS2020", the German Industry 4.0 plan in 2013, the Chinese white paper of "Made in China 2025" [1] aim at producing customized products and offering an individual experience for every customer by using smart, flexible and autonomous manufacturing systems.

Among flexible and autonomous manufacturing layouts, the cellular layout lays half way between the line and job shop process [2]. If well designed, it has the ability to capture the benefits of both systems: large quantities from line or product process, and high variety of job shop process. Hence, it is a suitable layout for mass customization.

Published by Springer Nature Switzerland AG 2020
F. Nyffenegger et al. (Eds.): PLM 2020, IFIP AICT 594, pp. 3–14, 2020.
https://doi.org/10.1007/978-3-030-62807-9_1

To offer Mass Customization (MC), manufacturers are challenged to produce high quality customized products at the lowest possible cost with minimal lead-time. MC manufacturers should set a strategy that makes their production reflect the ever-changing and customized market and should manage the increased manufacturing complexity due to MC. This complexity is induced by a very volatile demand and high product variety, and impacts highly the production planning and scheduling. Moreover, MC requires real-time tracking of the order and quick response to customer order, hence manufacturers need to use digital technology and be connected to the entire supply chain. In MC context, any disturbance in the supply chain whether in the transportation network, production, or replenishment from suppliers, can delay the order and reduce customer satisfaction. About this disturbances and changes, Zhang (2019) mentions that changes to the schedule are inevitable, and become more critical in mass customization and adaptive manufacturing. Changes like emergencies, new orders, cancelled orders, machine failures interrupting the whole system is unacceptable. Therefore, smart factory with smart distributed scheduling is demanded in the future.

The question remains about which information to use in real time, to optimize the scheduling for MC in order to reduce overall generated costs and respect the customer required order delay. This paper is a first attempt to answer this question, by proposing a framework for smart distributed scheduling for MC.

This paper is organized as follows. Section 2 presents a literature review related to mass customization, cellular assembly and scheduling for mass customization and for cellular assembly. Section three presents the proposed framework, and section four concludes this paper and describes the future works related to this research.

2 Background and Related Research

2.1 Mass Customization

Mass Customization (MC) is a major tenet of Industry 4.0. It provides customers with customized features for their goods and services. MC is a trio of product attributes meeting customer needs, robust process design (that can re-use or recombine resources), and supporting customers in finding solution with minimum complexity [5]. MC is applied in many businesses like cars, clothing, and computer manufacturing, food industry, among others [6].

Mass customization is classified based on product life cycle (PLC), from concept to use, in the cyber physical consumer durable (CPCD) environment. [7] defined seven types of MC: (1) Co-customization, (2) Custom-fabrication, (3) Assembly-by-company, (4) Assembly-by-customer, (5) On-delivery-customization, (6) Embedded-customization, and (7) Standard-customization.

In this research, the focus is on assembly-by-company MC. A customer chooses to order from a catalogue of available options. The operation realized after order receipt, is an assembly one, meaning that pre-fabricated parts and components are available, and the value added is in assembling the product using options and adds-on from the catalogue that the customer used to order. In other words, the customer order decoupling point positions just before the assembly activities.

2.2 Cellular Layout

Cellular layout is made up of different cells, and each cell contains several workstations. Orders start in one cell and continue to the other until they finish, depending on the process sequence. [8] discussed the optimum number of cells and number of machines in each cell. Each machine type can perform one or more operations (machine flexibility). Likewise each operation can be done on one or more machine type with different times (routing flexibility).

According to [9] Multi-cell environments include several independent manufacturing cells located in the same plant and they allow high-volume productions or multiple product types by exploiting all the available manufacturing resources. Cellular manufacturing (CM) has many advantages including reduction in material handling costs, setup times, expedition costs, in-process inventories, part makespan, and improvement of human relations and operator expertise [10]. The primary objectives of cell layout are the minimization of movement cost, minimization of backtracking and maximization of throughput [11]. Its ultimate goal is converting the make-to-stock production system (push production) to make-to-order production system (pull production [12].

2.3 Scheduling for Mass Customization and for Cellular Assembly

A production schedule identifies and controls the release of jobs to the shops, ensures required raw materials ordered on time, whether delivery promises can be met, and identifies resource conflicts [13]. Scheduling involves the allocation of the available production resources in a workflow generated in a previous planning stage In a sense, to find a schedule π of jobs over machines yielding an optimal value $F(\pi)$, where F denotes some objective function [14].

There are many types of scheduling problems, including the Job Shop Problem (JSP) defined as an optimization problem in which various manufacturing jobs are assigned to machines at particular times while trying to minimize the makespan [15]. It is classified into basic type JSP, the multi-machine type or flexible job shop scheduling model FJSP, the multi-resource type MrFJSP, the multi-plant and transportation MpFJSP, and finally the Smart Factory SFFJSP which is highly dynamic scheduling, incorporates real time data from all the factory [15]. [14] and [16] defined Dynamic Scheduling as planning for unforeseen events and problems. They divided problems into 1) shop- related (machine breakdowns, operator illnesses, unavailability or tool failures, loading limits, delays in the arrival or shortage of materials and defective materials) and 2) job- related (rush jobs, job cancellations, due date changes, early or late arrival of jobs, changes in job priorities, changes in job processing times). For [16], dynamic scheduling falls under 3 categories:

1. Completely reactive scheduling: A dispatching rule is used to select the next job with highest priority to be processed from a set of jobs awaiting service at a machine that becomes free.
2. Predictive–reactive scheduling: most common dynamic scheduling. Schedules are revised in response to real-time events, by minimizing effects of disruption, in shop efficiency and schedule stability.
3. Robust pro-active scheduling: focus on building predictive schedules which satisfy performance requirements predictably in a dynamic environment. The main difficulty of this approach is the determination of the predictability measures.

According to [15], and under industry 4.0, scheduling problem should shift towards SFFSJP incorporating both a dynamic and a distributed approach with multi-resources, multi-plants, transportation and smart factory. Yet many challenges are still to be overcome to implement SFFSJP [15]. The distributed approach, requires also a set of rules to when to require the centralized approach, and when every sub-system can handle its decentralized dynamic scheduling when disturbances occur. This was discussed by [14], who discussed more precisely the efficient screening procedures, or Tolerance Scheduling, in their approach to Smart Scheduling. Tolerance Scheduling tries to identify the range of scenarios in which a given schedule keeps being optimal or acceptable and hence do not require to go up to the centralized optimization.

Implementing SFFSJP, and according to [15] requires five steps, each with its associated scheduling problem: (1) construction of IoT and network management system associated with its Multi-objective Optimization algorithm, (2) information transfer between smart jobs and the system: each job optimizes separately, (3) information transfer between smart jobs associated: each job optimizes separately and selects its own operation sequence with selected machine according to system rules (4) information is transfer between smart jobs and smart machines: each machine optimizes and selects job by itself (5) information transfer between smart jobs and smart multi-resources, where Each resource optimizes and selects the job by itself. Hence, the traditional centralized system no longer handles alone the effects of schedule changes, but rather the autonomous smart subsystems can adapt and react to and even predict changes, and respond accordingly. The main inconvenience of this proposed approach is the high complexity of its implementation.

In this research we are interested in scheduling for MC and smart cellular assembly. Table 1 summarizes some of the works addressing scheduling either for MC, for cellular assembly, or for both. It shows that the main objective functions for scheduling are reducing cost and meeting due date.

Table 1. Summary of works related to scheduling for mass customization, cellular assembly, and real-time scheduling.

Ref	System description	MC	SCM data	Real-time data	Objective function		Solving method
					Cost	Tardiness	
[8]	Cell formation				X	X	NP
[9]	Flexible cells			X	X		Distributed GA
[11]	Cellular manufacturing				X	X	GT layout
[12]	Cellular manufacturing		X		X	X	Axiomatic design
[13]	Cellular system	X			X	X	Fuzzy Logic-Matlab
[14]	Smart scheduling			X	X	X	Tolerance scheduling
[15]	Smart manufacturing			X	X	X	AI approximate method
[16]	Manufacturing system			X	X	X	Agent-based scheduling
[17]	Cellular network			X	X	X	Bidding
[18]	Manufacturing cells	X		X	X	X	Sequencing part families
[19]	Supply chain scheduling	X	X		X	X	DP
[20]	Network for services	X	X		X		Ant algorithm
[21]	CPSS		X		X		MOO
[22, 23]	Smart manufacturing	X		X			KBE
[24]	Manufacturing	X		X			5-layer framework
[25]	production/fabrication	X		X			NP hard
[26]	Manufacturing	X			X	X	NP
[27]	Cellular manufacturing	X		X		X	Multi-agent system
[28]	Cell formation				X		Hierarchical GA
[29]	Fabrication & Ass.			X		X	Meta-heuristic
[30]	Component manufacturing	X			X		SA
[31]	Manual manufacturing	X				X	Distributed scheduling
[32]	Cellular manufacturing		X		X		Re-scheduling
[33]	Manufacturing	X		X	X		Adaptive scheduling engine

(*continued*)

Table 1. *(continued)*

Ref	System description	MC	SCM data	Real-time data	Objective function		Solving method
					Cost	Tardiness	
[34]	One machine	X		x		X	Combinatorial auction
[35]	Production system	X				X	Combinatorial auction. Bidding
[36]	Manufacturing	X				X	Makespan minimization in a job shop

Ass. = Assembly; CP = Cyber Physical; CPSC = Cyber Physical Social System, CPCD = Cyber Physical Consumer Durables; DP = Dynamic Programming; GA = Genetic Algorithm; GT = Group Technology; MC = Mass Customization; NP = Non-linear Programming; SA = simulated annealing, MOO = constraint Multi-Objective Optimization, KBE = Knowledge Based Engineering.

The table shows how many authors tackled interesting topics such as scheduling for mass customization and supply chain management (SCM) integration like [14–16], or scheduling for mass customization using real-time data such as [15, 17–19]. It also shows the different used methods to solve the scheduling problem, such as genetic algorithm, non-linear programming, simulation annealing, etc. of the proposed approaches [13]. Suggested fuzzy logic technique to select the routes based on WIP, processing time and distance.

Of the works focused on scheduling for cell manufacturing systems, [17] discussed the bidding system that chooses the cell that can finish the job based on earliest finish time. It is made up of four steps for dynamic task assignment: (1) task announcement; (2) bidding (3) bid evaluation; and (4) task awarding. As for types of cell he defined 1) flexible cells (wide range of operations) 2) product-oriented cells (certain type of product made) and 3) robot assembly cell where robots put assemblies together. In task announcement the cells have deadline to respond, bidding depends on processing time, waiting time in queue, and travel time between cells, and awarded based on early finish time. [18] differentiated between cell scheduling CS (where family of parts are assigned to a cell) and group scheduling GS is that in CS the jobs of a part family follow a known order of machines. Whereas in GS jobs can go to all machines, because they don't belong to a family. [22, 23] explored the possibility of determining Cell Formation, Group Layout and Group Scheduling decisions concurrently using genetic algorithm-based procedure. Their computations took long time and needed heuristic mutation to speed up the convergence. But could not find where exactly the proper heuristic knowledge can come into play.

What is noticeable in Table 1, is the lack of literature that covers all the aforementioned parameters (MC, SCM, real-time data) simultaneously. Even though [15] presented a full approach for scheduling in a smart factory, all related mathematical models and implementations were not presented. Also, the whole approach requires that every resource, machine, and job are smart and imbedded with their own optimization and decision capabilities, this is highly complex to implement Conflict can easily be created between the job made decisions and those of the machines and resources which can highly increase computation time and cost as well as the cost of information sharing.

3 Proposed Framework: Distributed Scheduling for Mass Customization

This paper adopts a smart factory flexible job shop scheduling approach for cell manufacturing system and for assembly-by-company mass customization. The cells are flexible, hence offer a wide range of operations.

The system consists of mainly an assembly operation of a menu-driven demand, meaning that some fabrication or machining takes place but mostly assembly. In other words, a job representing an MC customer order, is formed of a sequence of mainly assembly operations that can be done on one or several cells to create the whole product as customized by the customer.

The aim of the smart scheduling approach is to define which machine of which cell will do each of these operations at which time. This while respecting system constraints, and customer requirements in the context of a smart factory. The smart factory job shop scheduling includes real-time data from all the supply chain stages and from each cell within the cellular assembly system. This highly complexifies the already complex mathematical problem of scheduling for mass customization that is usually a job shop problem. Job shop scheduling is NP-hard, especially when three or more machines are assumed [32]. Hence smart scheduling is based on dividing the problem into several subproblems by using a distributed approach. According to [27] the distributed environment leads to better product quality, lower production cost and lower management risks. It also facilitates rescheduling due to disturbances. The smart factory flexible job shop problem is also based on dynamic scheduling.

The distributed model, presented in Fig. 1, is made up of two scheduling modules that are separate yet integrated through real-time feedback. These are master scheduling and cell scheduling.

The master scheduling module is connected in real-time to the different supply chain stages: supplier, distribution, transportation, and customer orders. After the customer customizes his product, the master scheduling module receives the order including chosen product components, quantity per product, and order due date. Since we are in an assembly-by-company customization, it is important to know the current level of inventory per product component. This information is received in real-time from the Warehouse Management System or ERP. It also receives real-time data from the supply chain partners (shipment schedules, quantities) and delays from transportation network. This information is needed to prioritize customer orders depending on supply chain availability. The master scheduling module has access to every product assembly sequence/process, and to assembly related times per product and per cell. The master scheduling module is associated to a multi-objective optimization problem. Its aim is to define which cell will do which operation for each job.

The Master Schedule handles the assignments of jobs to cells. It makes sure there are enough material and are on time and place for the set of jobs for the scheduled period. It uses the cloud and the ERP, as well as the information from suppliers and distributors and the logistics. This schedule allows the distribution of orders on the different cells based on their capacity and availability, in order to reduce total related cost and minimize tardiness. This decision is then communicated to the cell scheduling modules.

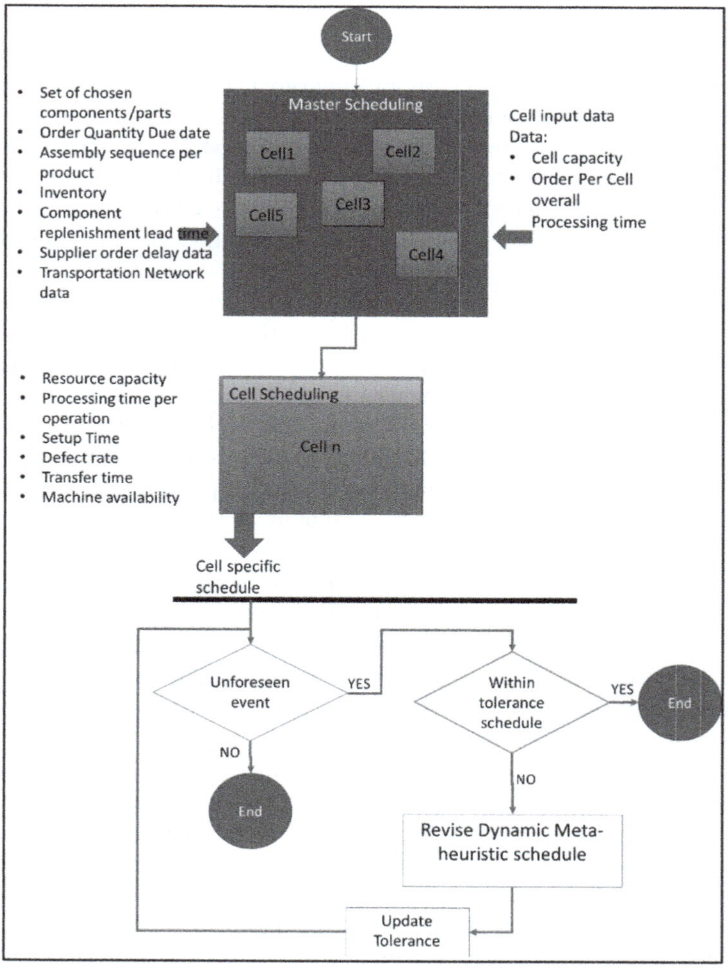

Fig. 1. Distributed scheduling approach for MC in cellular assembly

At the cell level, and for every cell, the master scheduling decision is an input for its specific scheduling module. The cell scheduling module receives input from each machine in the cell regarding its availability, current state, lack of materials, and relates it to the master schedule module. The output of the master schedule module becomes input to the cell schedule. Required inputs are order quantity, due date, assembly sequence by product, machine capacity and assembly processing time, machine setup time, distance and transfer time, machine defect rate and availability. What comes out of every cell is the cell specific schedule. This output is fed back to the master schedule. Figure 2 presents the smart cell scheduling schema.

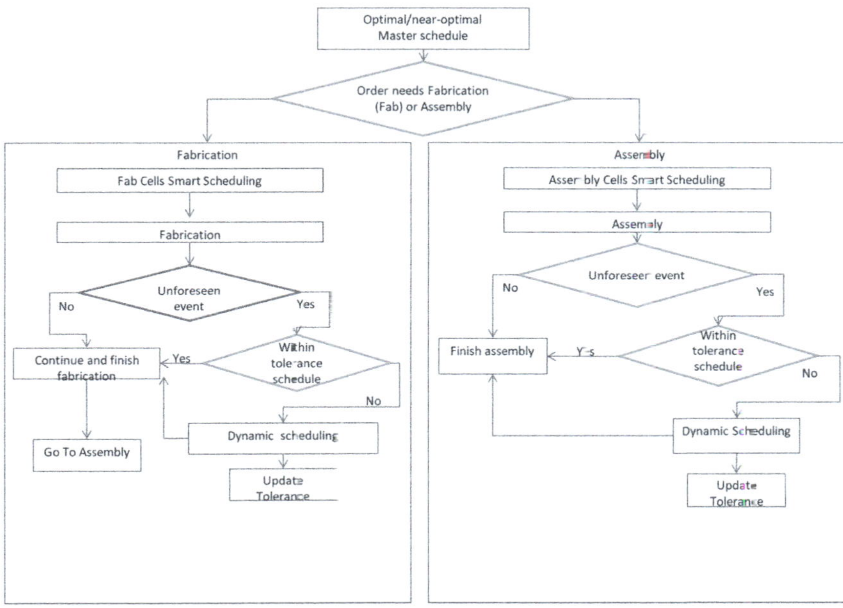

Fig. 2. Cell scheduling schema

The cell schedule starts when the Master Scheduling module sends the order to either the assembly or fabrication local smart scheduling modules. A job could need only fabrication or assembly or both.

Each fabrication cell, named fab cell, is a flexible job shop, made up of clusters of similar machines, laid out by function. Inside each fab cell is a smart scheduler that uses the bidding system to assign jobs and operations among machines, based on processing time (p), queue time (q) and transportation time (t). If an operation needs processing for example on a milling machine, and there are several milling machines, then the bidding system inside the cell chooses the appropriate machine based on (pqt). The same applies if the operation needs a different process like drilling.

When an unforeseen event occurs, then a tolerance scheduling system could take place, based on a weight or inertia, the schedule either is redone or not. if the tolerance scheduler decides to re-run the schedule, then different scenarios can occur, like right-shift schedule repair, or rescheduling within the cell, or rerouting jobs and operations to other fab cells. After finishing fabrication, and the job needs assembly then it is handled by the assembly cell smart scheduler.

Here, each assembly cell has a set of workstations where the job needs to move along. This is due to the fact that this model is about customized assembly, meaning that the master scheduling module receives order from customers based on a menu-driven set of options. Each option has a set of routing and material specific to it. Inside each assembly cell, the job could use all or some of the workstations found, and these workstations are not duplicate, meaning that one operation can be done on only one workstation. Each assembly cell could handle a family of jobs that have a certain commonality to be assigned a cell.

When an unforeseen event occurs, if tolerances are exceeded, a tolerance scheduler, which handles the assembly cells, will decide which dynamic scheduling approach is most suited and if a job is to be assigned on another cell. Afterwards, the assembly finishes, and the tolerance is updated.

The main advantage of this approach is simplifying the mathematical problem by dividing it into two connected problems. This allows to reduce the considered variables per problem. For example, the first integrates supply chain real-time data, whereas the second considers machines availability. The first problem schedules for cells whereas the second schedules for machines within each cell.

4 Conclusion and Perspectives

Mass customization is a reality, and requires flexible manufacturing systems such as cellular ones. It complexifies the production planning and control especially in an industry 4.0 context where the entire supply chain is connected and real-time data can be acquired and integrated. In this context, production scheduling has to evolve to smart scheduling based on distributed and dynamic scheduling. This paper proposed a distributed and dynamic approach for scheduling for MC and cellular assembly in the context of smart factory. This approach divides the problem into two sub-problems: master scheduling and cell scheduling. Future works include developing the mathematical models and choosing the most suitable method for solving the master and cell scheduling problems, and testing this approach on a case study.

References

1. Xu, L.D.: Internet of Things IOT. IEEE (2014)
2. Hayes, R, Wheelwright, S.: Link manufacturing process and product life cycles. Harv. Bus. Rev. (1979)
3. Kusiak, A.: Smart manufacturing. Int. J. Prod. Res. **56**, 1–2 (2017)
4. Aheleroff, S., Philip, R, Zhong, R, Xu, X.: The degree of mass personalisation under industry 4.0. In: 52nd CRP Conference on Manufacturing Systems, Procedia CIRP (2019)
5. Fabrizio, S, de Holan, P.M., Piller, F.: Cracking the code of mass customization. MIT Sloan Manag. Rev. **50**(3) (2009)
6. Anderson-Connell, L.J., Ulrich, P.V., Brannon, E.L.: A consumer-driven model for mass customization in the apparel market. J. Fash. Mark. Manag. Int. J. **6**(3), 240–258 (2002)

7. Pourtaleb, S., Optye, E., Horvath, I.: Multi-aspect study of mass customization in the context of cyber-physical. In: Consumer Durables. Conference: ASME International Design Engineering Technical Conferences and Computers and Information in Engineering Conference, Portland, Oregon, USA (2013)
8. Aryanezhad, M.B., Deljoo, V., Mirzapour, S.M.J.: Dynamic cell formation and the worker assignment problem: a new model. Int. J. Adv. Manuf. Technol. **41**, 329–342 (2009)
9. De Giovanni, L., Pezzella, F.: An improved genetic algorithm for the distributed and flexible job-shop scheduling problem. Eur. J. Oper. Res. **200**, 395–408 (2010)
10. Reene, T.J.: Sadowski PR: A review of cellular manufacturing assumptions, advantages and design technique. J. Oper. Manag. **4**(2), 85–97 (1984)
11. Hassan, M.: Layout design in group technology manufacturing. Int. J. Prod. Econ. **38**, 173–188 (1995)
12. Kulaka, O., Durmusoglua, M.B., Tufekci, S.: A complete cellular manufacturing system design methodology based on axiomatic design principles. Comput. Ind. Eng. **48**, 765–787 (2005)
13. Srinoi, P., Shayan, E., Ghotb, F.E.: Scheduling of flexible manufacturing systems using fuzzy logic. Ind. Res. Inst. (IRIS) (2004). Swinburne
14. Rossit, D.A., Tohme, F., Frutos, M.: 4.0: smart scheduling. Int. J. Prod. Res. **57**(12), 3802–3813 (2019)
15. Zhang, J., Ding, G., Zou, Y., Qin, S., Fu, J.: Review of job shop scheduling research and its new perspectives under industry 4.0 (2019)
16. Ouelhadj, D,. Petrovic, S.,: A survey of dynamic scheduling in manufacturing systems (2009)
17. Shaw, M.J.: A distributed scheduling method for computer integrated manufacturing: the use of local area networks in cellular systems (1987)
18. Neufeld, J.S., Teucher, F.F., Buscher, U.: Scheduling flowline manufacturing cells with intercellular moves: non-permutation schedules and material flows in the cell scheduling problem. Int. J. Prod. Res. (2019)
19. Yao, J., Liu, L.: Optimization analysis of supply chain scheduling in mass customization. Int. J. Prod. Econ. **117**, 197–211 (2009)
20. Yao, J., Deng, Z.: Scheduling optimization in the mass customization of global producer services. IEEE Trans. Eng. Manag. **62**(4), 591–603 (2015)
21. Yilma, B.A., Naudet, Y., Panetto, H.: Introduction to personalisation in cyber-physical-social systems. In: Debruyne, C., Panetto, H., Guédria, W., Bollen, P., Ciuciu, I., Meersman, R. (eds.) On the Move to Meaningful Internet Systems: OTM 2018 Workshops. OTM 2018. Lecture Notes in Computer Science, vol. 11231. Springer, Cham (2019). https://doi.org/10.1007/978-3-030-11683-5_3
22. Zawadazki, P., Zywicki, K.: Smart product design and production control for effective mass customization in industry 4.0. Manag. Prod. Eng. Rev. **7**(3), 105–112 (2016)
23. Zheng, M., Ming, X.: Construction of cyber-physical system–integrated smart manufacturing workshops: a case study in automobile industry. Adv. Mech. Eng. **9**(10), 1–17 (2017)
24. Zhang, Z., Wang, X., Zhu, X., Cao, Q., Tao, F.: Cloud manufacturing paradigm with ubiquitous robotic system for product customization. Robot. Comput. Integr. Manuf. **60**, 12–22 (2019)
25. Chen, Y.J., Zhang, M., Tseng, M.M.: An integrated process planning and production scheduling framework for mass customization. Int. J. Manuf. Sci. Prod. **6**(1–2), 89 (2004)
26. Leusin, M., Kuck, M., Frazzon, E., Maldonado, M., Freitag, M.: Potential of a multi-agent system approach for production control in smart factories. IFAC PapersOnLine **51–11**, 1459–1464 (2018)

27. Wu, X., Chu, C.H., Wang, Y., Yue, D.: Genetic algorithms for integrating cell formation with machine layout and scheduling. Comput. Ind. Eng. **53**, 277–289 (2007)
28. Khodke, P.M., Bhongade, A.S.: Real-time scheduling in manufacturing system with machining and assembly operations: a state of art. Int. J. Prod. Res. **51**(16), 4966–4978 (2013)
29. Bazargan, L., Kaebernick, H.: Intra-cell and inter-cell layout designs for cellular manufacturing. Int. J. Ind. Eng. Appl. Pract. **3**, 139–150 (1996)
30. Barnett, L., Rahimifard, S., Newman, S.: Distributed Scheduling to Support Mass Customization in the Shoe Industry (2004)
31. Chan, F.T.S., Chung, S.H., Chan, P.L.Y.: An adaptive genetic algorithm with dominated genes for distributed scheduling problems. Exp. Syst. Appl. **29**(2), 364–371 (2005)
32. Ariafar, S., Ismail, N., Tang, S.H., Ariffin, M.K.A.M., Firoozi, Z.: Inter-cell and intra-cell layout design in a cellular manufacturing system. In: IEEE Symposium on Business, Engineering and Industrial Applications (ISBEIA) (2011)
33. Mourtzis, D., Vlachou, A., Xanthopoulos, N.: Machine availability monitoring for adaptive holistic scheduling: a conceptual framework for mass customization. Proc. CIRP **25**, 406–413 (2014)
34. Suginoushi, S., Kaihara, T., Kokuryo, D., Kuik, S.A.: Research on optimization method for integrating component selection and production scheduling under mass customization. In: 49th CIRP Conference on Manufacturing Systems (2016)
35. Modrak, V., Soltysova, Z., Semanco, P., Sudhakara, P.: Production Scheduling and Capacity Utilization in Terms of Mass Customization (2019)
36. Mosheiov, G.: Complexity analysis of job-shop scheduling with deteriorating jobs. Discr. Appl. Math. **117**(1–3), 195–209 (2002)

Smart Learning Factory – Network Approach for Learning and Transfer in a Digital & Physical Set up

Roman Hänggi[1(✉)], Felix Nyffenegger[1], Frank Ehrig[1], Peter Jaeschke[2], and Raphael Bernhardsgrütter[3]

[1] Hochschule für Technik (HSR), Rapperswil, Switzerland
{roman.haenggi,felix.nyffenegger,frank.ehrig}@ost.ch
[2] Fachhochschule für Angewandte Wissenschaften (FHS), St. Gallen, Switzerland
peter.jaeschke@ost.ch
[3] Interstaatliche Hochschule für Technik Buchs (NTB), Buchs, Switzerland
raphael.bernhardsgruetter@ost.ch

Abstract. The smart factory promises significant cost savings particularly for high cost labor markets. The challenge in teaching smart factory courses or digitalization of manufacturing is the complexity of the topic. The smart factory is understood as a future state of a fully connected and flexible manufacturing system, operating autonomously or with optimized interaction between humans and machines by generating, transferring, receiving and processing necessary data to conduct all required tasks for producing different types of goods.

Due to this complexity the standard classroom teaching is not achieving satisfactory results. A key element is the understanding of the physical goods process linked to data and IT infrastructure. This digital representation of the physical world is then the base for learning from data for a specific use case for the factory of tomorrow.

This paper describes how the Smart Learning Factory as a sample case at the university of applied sciences OST will be set up as an unique approach with three interconnected locations with a real, daily manufactured product mainly for educational purposes. Over the last years, successful initiatives towards the Smart Learning Factory have been established. This base is the fundament for a significant larger step. We are now approaching this next horizon with strong support by the Canton of St. Gallen and the strategic focus of the entire school. Our goal is to give all students of all technical and economic studies the opportunity to experience the smart factory in the real world. A fully digital twin of the physical world will play a key role in understanding the future of manufacturing. This makes it possible to discuss the conceptual approaches, challenges and success factors to implement a smart factory.

Keywords: Smart factory · Industrie 4.0 · Learning factory · PLM · ERP · Machine learning · OST · HSR · Digital transformation

F. Nyffenegger et al. (Eds.): PLM 2020, IFIP AICT 594, pp. 15–25, 2020.
https://doi.org/10.1007/978-3-030-62807-9_2

1 Challenges and Target for a Smart Learning Factory

1.1 Understanding the Smart Factory

In recent years, the concept of a smart factory has often been seen as an answer to cope with the strong cost pressure in the high cost labor market. There is no general definition of the smart factory. Elements of a characteristics such as "agility", "modularity", "automation", " cyber-physical-systems", "combination of software, hardware and manufacturing technology", "robotics", "digital twin", "IT systems" "collaboration between partners" and "learning from data" are often used [7, 9, 13, 14]. In addition, there is often a focus on the sharing between sensors, machines and production systems [9], partially also with a link to a data cloud. The combination and modeling of sensor data, machine data and production systems data will generate new insights, such as quality prediction of produced parts or preventive maintenance information for a production machine.

Based on all elements, we define the smart factory [12] as a future state of a fully connected and flexible manufacturing system, operating autonomously or with optimized interaction between humans and machines by generating, transferring, receiving and processing necessary data to conduct all required tasks for producing different kinds of goods.

1.2 Learning and Transferring

In our daily work as teachers for our engineering students, we are very challenged explaining the smart manufacturing concept on this theoretical basis. Standard classroom teaching does not meet our goals in developing the appropriate student competences. New ways are needed to digest the breadth of the smart factory topic. We are certain that a learning factory, with its ability of real world teaching and creating personal experience for the students, is our way for future teaching.

It is fundamental for students to understand the complexity of the implementation of a smart factory. These implementation barriers are the outcome of two research projects funded by Innosuisse[1] with 6 industrial companies, the University of St. Gallen and the Hochschule für Technik (HSR) [5, 6, 9, 13]. A total of 8 different levers were identified that have to be overcome for a successful implementation of the smart factory (see Fig. 1). A key topic is selecting the right use case, followed by understanding the existing processes and data management. When the smart factory path is started, the concept of lean and standard production management techniques hopefully is realized in advance. This will plot the base for the digital journey. Before a new IT system with the appropriate security concept is implemented, it must be ensured that the mathematical model for analyzing the data will generate the required insights for continuous improvement for your use case. The people topic is a massive challenge. Job fear as

[1] Innosuisse is a governmental organization that funds applied research projects in Switzerland. It is mandatory in every project that industrial companies join forces with academia. A defined business plan by the industrial companies makes the result tangible.

well as technology and competence gaps need to be addressed early in any smart factory journey.

In the mechanical and industrial engineering curriculum, we have defined that our students need to reach the Bloom taxonomy competence level 6 [2, 3] for the smart factory lectures. The implementation of the smart factory considering the breadth, complexity and barriers require this substantial learning goal for these two studies.

We have decided to convey the topic of smart manufacturing in existing modules in all technical and economic studies at both the bachelor and master level In addition, we aim to offer further specific courses around the smart factory. Every module defines the Bloom taxonomy competence levels for itself. The Smart Learning Factory will also support these studies to reach the appropriate taxonomy levels depending on their specific course curriculum. Specific lectures, exercises and practical work will be created.

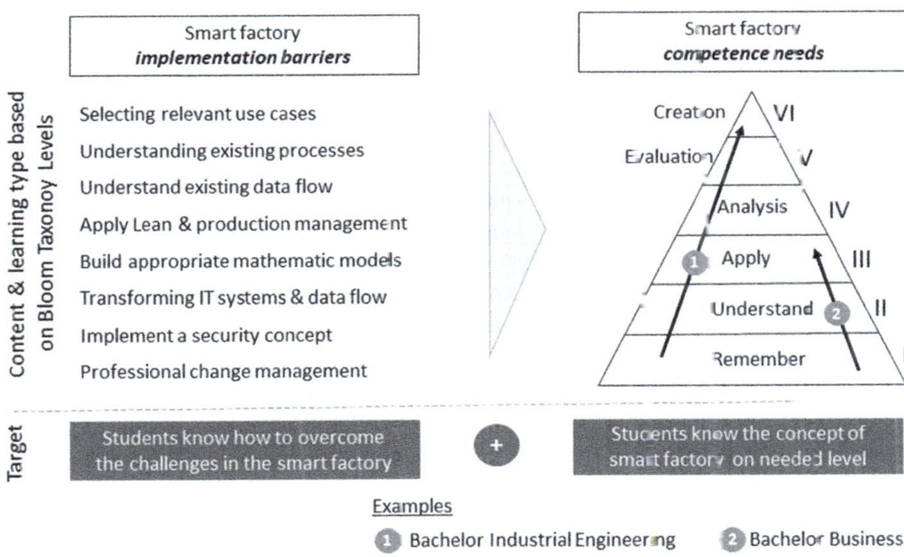

Fig. 1. Smart factory learning targets for the students in regards to competences and implementation barriers for the smart factory

Specifically, the Smart Learning Factory will support the following learning and organizational goals for our school. These goals have been guiding us in defining and building our Smart Learning Factory since 2016.

Learning Goals

1. Students can experience, model and develop the flow of data and materials flow for a smart factory
2. Students can use, configure, implement and further develop the relevant IT systems with their interfaces (IT and Internet of Things) and the required master data

3. Students can understand, model and program data analytics up to machine learning algorithm based on all available data from the Smart Learning Factory
4. Students know how to transform an existing production facility into a smart factory
5. Students will experience failure and can progress successfully in an agile approach
6. The learning goals are relevant for all technical and economic study programs and should allow to tailor different taxonomy levels and smart factory content for the respective course

Organizational Goals

7. Students will be involved in creating the lecture and the future development of the Smart Learning Factory through project work, bachelor and master thesis.
8. The creation of the elaboration examples and the content of lectures are a journey and needs a wide involvement of expertise of many professors

2 First Step Towards the Smart Learning Factory

A learning factory stipulates two directions. Schuh et al. distinguish, based on the definition by the CIRP Collaborative Working Group on learning factories, a learning factory in a narrow and a broader sense. A factory in the narrow sense signifies a real production system and implies the manufacturing of a physical product. The aspect of learning highlights the gain of knowledge as a purpose. Then we talk of a factory in broader sense. Then a physical product is not necessary [15].

Since 2016 we have focused on a model and not a real product. The complexity and investment on the aspect of learning with a Smart Learning Factory were the driver for this decision. We used a pick-and-place LEGO robot as a product. Fradl, Sohrweide and Nyffenegger described the example extensively [4]. The robot sorts LEGO bricks. This LEGO robots exists as a full digital twin. In addition, we have installed different sensors to collect data of the robot in production. A RFID chip identifies all LEGO bricks that we sort. Serialization of the robot with its key components is implemented using a 2D-Matrix code and the link to the ERP system. Specific Kanban processes were set up using ERP-controlled Kanban transparency dashboards. We have designed the full LEGO robot in CAD, then send the data to a PLM system, where we are managing the bill of material and the document change process. This BOM is then transferred into the ERP system, where we have set up a factory to produce the LEGO robot. In addition, we implemented a configurator in the ERP system to sell the different versions based on product management guidelines. Currently, we are extending the IT system landscape into the MES system. This system will then be the central data collector and allows data to be displayed on a dashboard (Fig. 2).

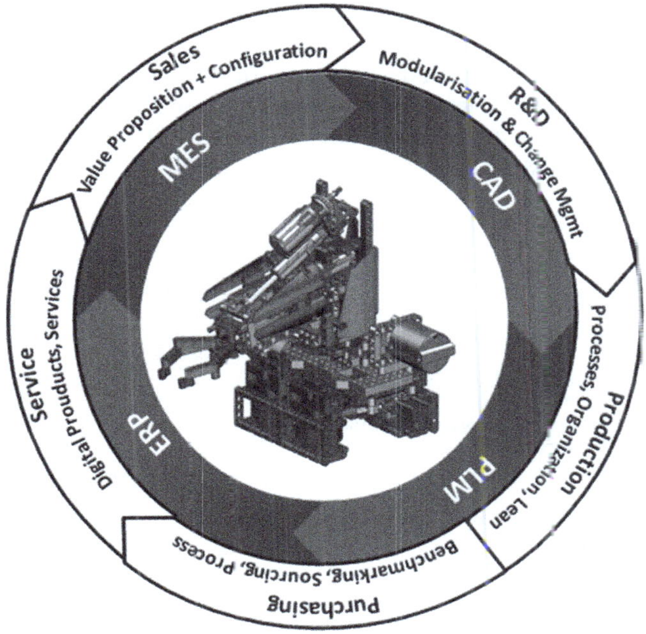

Fig. 2. Elaboration example LEGO pick & place robot

A key topic are the different lectures and practical work with semi – guided exercises along the way. In one course the students work in groups of 5 and have to design and build a production plant to manufacture the pick & place robot. They also have to configure and partially implement the required IT systems. The goal of the course is to configure and issue a real purchase order for their built production plant for one customer order for one pick & place robot. Organizationally the course starts with the R&D process, where the focus lies on modularization and document change management. Then followed by the manufacturing, sourcing and service module. For this course, the LEGO bricks offer a big advantage. You can assemble and disassemble the product. By doing so, you will experience the bill of material, a possible manufacturing and assembly strategy including stock concept. Additionally, two critical parts have to be sourced and a service portfolio including digital services has to be defined. At the end of the course, a sales approach including a digital configuration of the robot completes the lecture.

This elaborations example have been developed and continuously improved by many bachelor and master thesis. Additional funds by the school were highly important. The school sees this elaboration example as a corner stone for the education for the mechanical and industrial engineers.

With this model, we have built a first and comprehensive step of our Smart Learning Factory, primarily focusing on the data flow. The basis for any smart factory is an integrated data flow and processes [10]. In addition, the processes need to follow waste free lean processes as much as possible. Through assembly and disassembly of a

LEGO based product it is very easy to understand certain topics (Bill of material, Kanban flow), but limitations are reached when physical material flow is needed (size, complexity, technology, organizational aspects). The digital twin of the LEGO robot is on the other hand very tangible, and the students can switch easily between the physical and the digital world. The different interfaces between CAD – PLM – ERP – MES can be experienced, discussed and further developed (Fig. 3).

	Achievement with LEGO Robot
Learning Goals	
• Students can experience, model and develop the flow of data and materials flow for a smart factory	• data: yes / material: no
• Students can use, configure and develop the relevant IT systems with its interfaces (IT and Internet of Things) and needed master data	• IT systems: Yes / IoT: partially
• Students can understand, model and program data analytics up to machine learning algorithm based on all available data of the Smart Learning Factory	• no
• Students know how to transform an existing production facility into a smart factory	• partially, primarily on the data side
• Students will experience failure and can progress successfully in an agile approach	• yes
• The learning goals are relevant for all technical and economics studies and should allow tailor different taxonomy level and smart factory content for the respective course	• partially, real factory will help
Organizational Goals	
• Students will be involved in creating the lecture and in the future development of the Smart Learning Factory through project work, Bachelor and Master thesis.	• yes
• The creation of the elaboration examples and the content of lectures are a journey and needs a wide involvement of expertise of many professors	• partially, can be expanded

Fig. 3. Meeting the goals of the Smart Learning Factory with the LEGO robot model

The Lego robot offers a good learning platform for digitalization. The weakness is identified in the area of experiencing the smart factory on a real product, instead of a LEGO example. This is also the biggest criticism by the students. Although the feedback on the quality on learnings is very positive, the students prefer a real product, e.g. it is difficult to source a LEGO motor or the scaled up real motor based on digital LEGO data. Due to the model and its technical capabilities, we cannot run sufficient production quantities. This limits us from modeling a use case for data analytics or machine learning in a real world environment.

3 Approach of a Physical Smart Learning Factory with Digital Representation

Many initiatives at the same time brought a strong force behind a new approach for a Smart Leaning Factory with a real physical product with further expanded digital representation.

Political and Organizational Driver: The Canton of St. Gallen is focusing heavily with its "IT Bildungsinitiative" [8] on the IT competencies which should be taught to all students on all level. In addition, three universities of applied sciences (Rapperswil, St. Gallen, Buchs) merge to one new university of applied science "OST" [11] with in total around 4'000 Students, 400 researchers and around 45 Mio Fr. research and project turnover. The new Smart Learning Factory is one cornerstone in this merger, because the different competences of the original universities complete each other very well and make the concept solid and strong. To do so, a large project is set up and supports the integration into one school through the buildup of the Smart Learning Factory. The fund of these two strategic directions is the financial base for the new Smart Learning Factory.

Clear and Holistic Vision: The school developed jointly a clear and holistic picture to start with. The scope of Smart Learning Factory is not restricted to the manufacturing processes. It will also include the development, purchasing, service and sales processes. In the future, an extension towards integrating partners on the supply chain as well as customers is foreseen in a 2nd step.

Strong Research Departments: The new University of applied science OST has a very strong technical department with around 200 people and 30 professors that focus on their research mainly in industrial companies. The digital transformation is a key topic in their research. In addition, the research departments own many different production machines from different vendors with relevant production technologies from plastic molding, 3D printing, sintering, grinding, milling, robots, adaptive robots, plastic extrusion, assembly, quality control and testing.

LEGO Robot as a Successful First Step: The success by the LEGO robot motivated the involved people to look for the next step. The feedback of the students shows the direction. We need to have a real smart factory.

Three Locations in One School is an Advantage: All three schools have focused in the past four years already on the topic of Learning Factory, e.g. the location Buchs built up a fully integrated electronics manufacturing and assembly line. Some significant investments into hard- und software were made. Due to the different focuses of all three schools, all the past investment is 100% complementary. This brought us to the decision to combine all efforts into one Smart Learning Factory over three locations and produce one physical product.

New Laboratory Building: Due to the significant growth of the University of Applied Sciences HSR in Rapperswil over the past years, the board has decided to build a new 5000 m^2 laboratory building, called TechPark. The focus of this new laboratory building will be on the topic of Smart Learning Factory.

Above six driving forces make the significant path forward realistic. Financial and people resources are available. Figure 4 shows the dimensions according to Abele et al. [1] of the Smart Learning Factory at the newly merged university [11] as a natural progression of existing investments and initiatives.

Dimension of the Smart Learning Factory

Purpose: Teaching, executive programs, (research)
Process: authentic, 3 locations
Setting: changeable, real, vritual
Product: physical, every day production, serial number, batch tracking
Didactic: formal & informal, own action by students (exersize, practical training), on site, classrom, remote access, project work, team work, study work
Operating Model: sustaining plan allows the ongoing operation, infrastructure up to date by institute

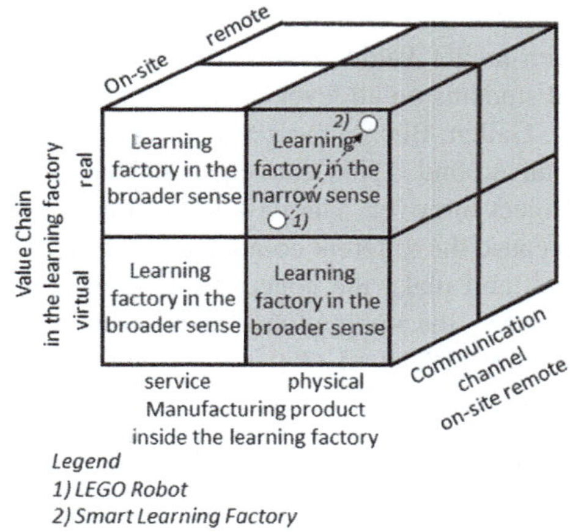

Fig. 4. Dimension of the Smart Learning Factory at OST

The Smart Learning Factory is focusing on producing a physical product daily. The value chain is real and virtual. Teaching is possible on-site and remote. This product will be produced every day. This gives enough production and sensor data. The daily production gives the opportunity for many lectures to involve the Smart Learning Factory in their courses independent from the lecture schedule. In addition, the smart factory will be managed in a production network with three locations in St. Gallen, Buchs and Rapperswil. See Fig. 5 below for the role and focus of research for each location.

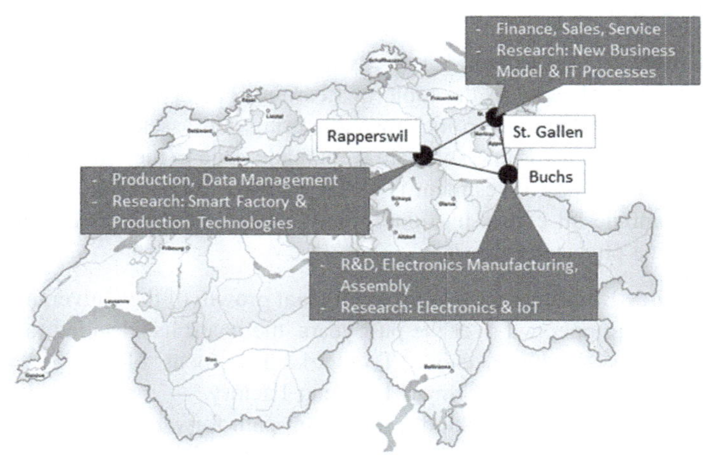

Source: Wikipedia "Datei:Karte Gemeinden der Schweiz 2017.04.02.png", accessed 22.03.2020

Fig. 5. The three connected sites of the Smart Learning Platform with its focus

The nearly 5000 m^2 Rapperswil facility will be connected digitally but also logistically to the different sites in Buchs and in St. Gallen (see Fig. 6). In Rapperswil the different parts of the product will be produced or molded, then shipped to Buchs, where the assembly and sourcing takes place. A physical inventory is located in Buchs. In St. Gallen the headquarter with Finance, Sales and Service is organized.

On the IT side, we run the Smart Learning Factory first on one standard ERP, PLM and MES. Additional further ERP/MES tools will be added over time to be independent. Different CAD System or other data sources provide the necessary input data (e.g. design, simulation) for the Smart Learning Factory. This concept will allow to integrate continuously relevant learnings of different research project into the Smart Learning Factory. So new technologies and approaches can be added.

All finished products are tracked by serial numbers and batch tracking for relevant material is intended. An RFID Chip is integrated during the molding process. A data matrix code is additionally placed on the product for the serial number identification.

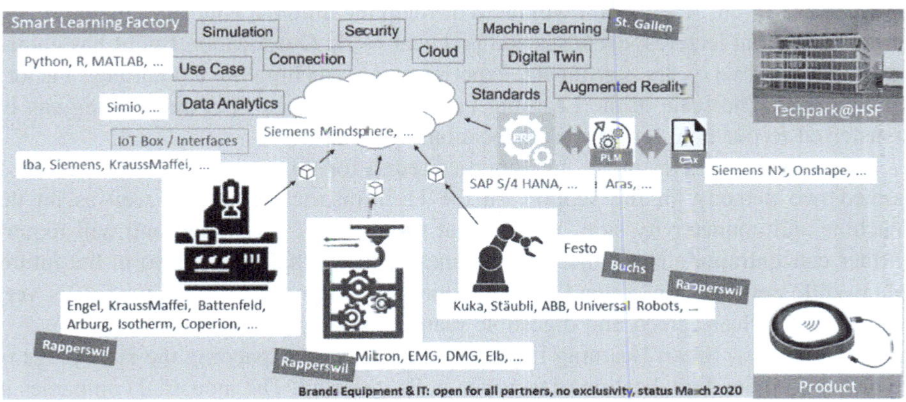

Fig. 6. Technologies used in the Smart Learning Factory @ University of Applied Science OST

The risk and criticism on a Learning Factory in the narrow sense is the complexity, cost and flexibility of needed change [1]. Actual machines and IT tools is a further need. To cope with these challenges, we have set up the following requisites and organizational responsibilities:

- Every institute is responsible for keeping the machines and IT Infrastructure actual and state of the art. It is in their interest to do this as their research also depends on this equipment. Therefore, the infrastructure continues to belong to the institutes.
- Due to the strategic relevance, financial funds are foreseen by the Canton of St. Gallen and OST.
- Since two years, a large project team has been working in implementing the Smart Learning Factory. Specific resources have already be assigned to the project.
- The different competences of the three locations are combined and complement each other. This positive energy is crucial for the success.

- Additional resources for the operation support for the Smart Learning Factory will be assigned.
- Different learning modules will be developed on a central base. This content can then be used by the different lectures in different studies.

4 Project Status, Open Points and Next Steps

The project is in the implementation stage. The new TechPark as a physical building is ready to move in towards June 2020. A key challenge will be setting up the IT infrastructure including all relevant IoT interfaces. We are building up our know how on a frequent basis. Our research activities supporting the connectivity, standardization and integration challenges heavily. Our new Smart Learning Factory is challenging our industrial partners on the machine as well as the IT side. We have included these partners early in the process and therefore support is given. Naturally resource discussions are given. A key point will be to develop the different education modules. We are talking about lectures, exercises and practical work. Our location Buchs has gained over the last two years significant experience on teaching in a Learning Factory environment. The scale of the Learning Factory was different, but the learning can be transferred to our new set up over 3 locations.

We will not underestimate the support needed for this complex set up. We have named two persons for the support on the IT infrastructure side as well as on the machine and connectivity side. We see that this will not be enough and will require further concentration. The project management will be challenging also in the future. Many different ideas on content and strategic direction need to be aligned. It is very critical that a clear agreed and digestible plan is rigorously followed.

With the new Smart Learning Factory, we find a way expanding the knowledge of implementing the digitalization of factories in Switzerland. The industrial companies in high cost countries are very challenged with the high cost structure, therefore, it is fundamental to drive the smart factory content and competences on a next level in education.

References

1. Abele, E., Metternich, J., Tisch, M.: Learning Factories. Concepts, Guidelines, Best-Practice Examples, 1st edn. Springer, Cham (2019)
2. Anderson, L.: Taxonomy of educational objectives. In: Phillips, D.C. (eds.) Encyclopedia of Educational Theory and Philosophy, vol. 1, pp. 790–791. SAGE Publications, Inc., Thousand Oaks, California (2014)
3. Bloom, B.S.: Taxonomy of Educational Objectives: The Classification of Educational Goals. McKay, Longman, New York, London (1956)
4. Fradl, B., Sohrweide, A., Nyffenegger, F.: PLM in education - the escape from Boredom. In: Ríos, J., Bernard, A., Bouras, A., Foufou, S. (eds.) Product Lifecycle Management and the Industry of the Future. PLM 2017. IFIP Advances in Information and Communication

Technology, vol. 517, pp. 297–307. Springer, Cham, Switzerland (2017). https://doi.org/10.1007/978-3-319-72905-3_27
5. Hochschule für Technik: Use-case pattern for autonomous decision-making in production. s. l: Innosuisse, Projektnummer 27399.1 (2017)
6. Hochschule für Technik: Machine Learning basiertes Prozessmanagementsystem zur Optimierung des Spritzgiessprozesses. s.l. : Innosuisse, Projektnummer 29621.1 (2018)
7. Hozdić, E.: Smart factory for industry 4.0: a review. Int. J. Modern Manuf. Technol. **7**(1), 28–35 (2015)
8. Kölliker, S., Trösch, R.: IT Bildungsinitiative (2019). www.sg.ch/bildung-sport/ueberbildung/IT-Bildungsoffensive.html. Accessed 19 Mar 2020
9. Lee, J.: Smart factory systems. Informatik-Spektrum **38**(3), 230–235 (2015). https://doi.org/10.1007/s00287-015-0891-z
10. Nyffenegger, F., Hänggi, R., Reisch, A.: A reference model for PLM in the area of digitization. In: Chiabert, P., Bouras, A., Noël, F., Ríos, J. (eds.) PLM 2018. IAICT, vol. 540, pp. 358–366. Springer, Cham (2018). https://doi.org/10.1007/978-3-030-01614-2_33
11. OST Homepage (2020). www.ost.ch/. Accessed 19 Mar 2020
12. Osterrieder, P., Budde, L., Friedli, T.: The smart factory as a key construct of industry 4.0: a systematic literature review. Int. J. Prod. Econ. **221**, 107476 (2020). https://doi.org/10.1016/j.ijpe.2019.08.011
13. Phillips, D.C. (eds.): Encyclopedia of Educational Theory and Philosophy. SAGE Publications, Inc., Thousand Oaks, California (2014)
14. Radziwon, A., Bilberg, A., Bogers, M., et al.: The smart factory: exploring adaptive and flexible manufacturing solutions. Proc. Eng. **69**, 1184–1190 (2014). https://doi.org/10.1016/j.proeng.2014.03.108
15. Schuh, G., Prote, J.-P., Dany, S., et al.: Classification of a hybrid production infrastructure in a learning factory morphology. Proc. Manuf. **9**, 17–24 (2017). https://doi.org/10.1016/j.promfg.2017.04.007

Towards a Machine Learning Failure Prediction System Applied to a Smart Manufacturing Process

Tainá da Rocha[1], Arthur Beltrame Canciglieri[1], Anderson Luis Szejka[1(✉)], Leandro dos Santos Coelho[1,2], and Osiris Canciglieri Junior[1]

[1] Industrial and Systems Engineering Graduate Program, Pontifical Catholic University of Parana, Curitiba, Brazil
{anderson.szejka, osiris.canciglieri}@pucpr.br

[2] Department of Electrical Engineering (PPGEE), Federal University of Parana (UFPR), Polytechnic Center, Curitiba, Brazil
leandro.coelho@ufpr.br

Abstract. At a time when the competitive market is operating rapidly, manufacturing industries need to stay connected, have interchangeability and interoperability in their factories, ensuring that there is heterogeneous communication between sectors, people, machines and the client, challenging the manufacturing industry to discover new ways to bring new products or improve their manufacturing process. Precisely because of the need to adjust to these new market demands, factories pursue complex and quick decision-making systems. This work aims to propose applications of Machine Learning techniques to develop a decision-making platform applied to a manufacturing line reducing scrap. This goal will be achieved through a literature review in the fields of Artificial Intelligence (AI) and Machine Learning to identify core concepts for the development of a failure prediction system. This research has demonstrated the problems and challenges faced by manufacturing daily, and how, through the application of AI techniques, it is possible to contribute to assist in these problems by improving quality, performance, scrap rates and rework, through connectivity and integration of data and processes. This paper contributes to evaluate the performance of machine learning ensembles applied in a real smart manufacturing scenario of failure prediction.

Keywords: Machine learning · Interoperability · Industry 4.0 · Artificial intelligence · Integration manufacturing

1 Introduction

Performance gains have been discussed lately, not only in the manufacturing perimeter, but also in different areas, especially in the business strategy, which has shown prominence [1]. This theme is increasingly correlated with the Industry 4.0 paradigm, which is supported by nine pillars: Collaborative Robotics, Simulation, Systems Integration, Industrial Internet of Things, Cyber Security, Cloud Computing, Additive

Published by Springer Nature Switzerland AG 2020
F. Nyffenegger et al. (Eds.): PLM 2020, IFIP AICT 594, pp. 26–35, 2020.
https://doi.org/10.1007/978-3-030-62807-9_3

Manufacturing, Augmented Reality and Big Data and Analytics. Its goal is to make processes faster, more flexible and more efficient, promoting the union and/or representation of physical resources with digital ones, connecting machines, systems and assets to produce higher quality, more profitable, lower-cost items resulting in a better performant process [2].

In this context, it is necessary to take as support a combination of these pillars to achieve this result. Currently, these pillars form a strategy for implementing techniques from Industry 4.0, bringing benefits such as manufacturing flexibility, autonomy and intelligent make-decision through the data processing of an integrated manufacturing system and providing data quickly and reliably to assist in faster decision making [3]. Factories must change their physical and procedural structures, integrating horizontally and vertically, concepts and paradigms, respecting the addendums of the third industrial revolution: Automation. At this stage, the manufacturing industries already encounter several problems due to obsolete machinery and systems that need to be automated and connected to a network when possible.

The motivation for this work came from the need to predict and reduce parts failure, optimize performance indicators and reduce scrap costs through a regression approach. In this way, this paper presents an intelligent test system applied to a metal-mechanic assembly line through performance metrics such as Mean Absolute Error (MAE). The main research contribution is the use of artificial intelligence techniques to promote interoperability between machines and systems, reduce the information gap, make improvements in production lines and failure prediction between operations to optimize performance indicators, reduce costs in rework, optimize workflow and increase quality.

The remainder of this work is as follows: Sect. 2 illustrates the problem statement addressed in this work. Section 3 presents the Technological Background with concepts based in the literature. In session 4 exposes the conceptual proposal applied in the case study. Section 5 shows the preliminary results of the application in this case study. Finally, session 6 presents the conclusion and future works.

2 Problem Statement

The lack of communication between manufacturing operations causes many impacts, among them the loss of productivity [4, 5]. In this work, the focus is the integration of data communication of two specific operations in an industry of the metal-mechanical sector, having as objective the improvement of the communication between stations, anticipating through a forecast, under the possible failures in products, consequently reducing the waste of the operation. For reasons of industrial manufacturing secrecy, the data cannot be disclosed in this work and it was uncharacterized both the characteristics and the name of the operation.

A schematic drawing is presented in Fig. 1 to better illustrate the adjustment performed. “X” represents the measurement of the internal dimension of the cylinder. “Y” represents the measurement of the other cylinder’s height, which is fitted to the first cylinder mentioned. “Z” represents the compensation/adjustment washer.

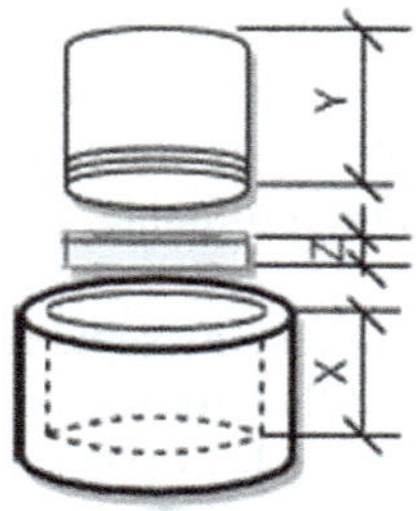

Fig. 1. Product illustration

In this production process, one operation (station D) is responsible for making a mechanical adjustment and another operation ahead (station J) for checking this previously adjusted measurement. The problem between them is that according to process influences, oscillation and deviations as product geometry, machining influences, and so on, it is necessary to perform an adjustment at station "D" according to measurements from station "J". This adjustment is performed manually, using a measurement compensation washer, and has a 15 pieces delay (Fig. 2). Therefore, the purpose of this article is to optimize this adjustment so that it is anticipated by forecasting using Machine Learning techniques.

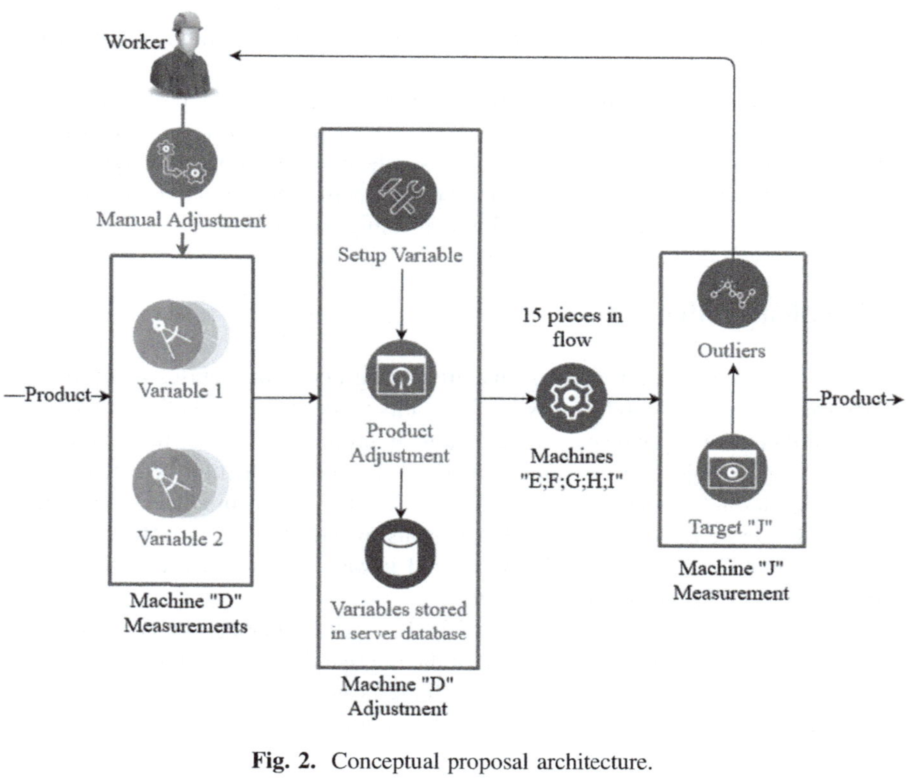

Fig. 2. Conceptual proposal architecture.

3 Technological Background

Nowadays, the information is dynamic, and its complete understanding is essential for quality control of the resulting product. It is necessary to involve a series of sectors from the suppliers to the delivery for a customer, where it goes through several stages consisting of requirements such as quality, personalization, cost, time, budget, for example, that need to be respected, and this is when there are hidden risks due to misinformation, misunderstanding, divergence and indirect information [6]. These risks, also called impacts, arise from heterogeneity in the sector (domain) and its peers semantically.

3.1 Industry 4.0

Industry 4.0, also called "Smart Factory", is the next revolution on the industry scene. According to [7], sensors, machines, workpieces and IT (Information Technology) systems will be connected along the value chain in addition to a single company. This cyber-physical system (CPS), is a set of transforming technologies that allow the connection of physical asset operations between computational resources. The CPS is controlled and monitored by computer-based algorithms and is fully integrated with its users (objects, humans, and machines) via the Internet [8], being able to interact with each other and analyze data to predict failures, configure and adapt changes. Sector 4.0, or I4.0, will make it possible to gather and analyze data between machines, enabling faster, more flexible, and more efficient processes to produce higher-quality goods at a reduced cost.

Also, automatic solutions will adopt versatile operations, consisting of operational components, devices, and analytics, such as "autonomous" manufacturing cells and adjustments that independently control and optimize multi-step manufacturing [9].

3.2 Artificial Intelligent

Artificial Intelligence (AI) enables systems to make decisions independently, supported by digitally established pattern logic, and can thus resemble situations, think about responses, make decisions, or act preventively. Thus, machine learning is a specific strand of AI that trains machines to learn from data, the closer to the data and real scenario, better.

Process management requires, at all levels, access, and display of the data necessary to oversee, diagnose and report the current status of the process [10]. But the existence of this type of technology does not inhibit human capacity because it is dependent on human training, teaching, creativity, and supervision, but it becomes a time optimization tool for repetitive and high-data decision-making activities. The creation of a data processing platform is the product of a group of information and techniques, which are: process data set to be applied, AI method, and, finally, the goal to be achieved. These methods from AI, belong to its subgroup called Machine Learning (ML).

Machine learning focuses on the question of how to build algorithms and computers that improves through experience automatically. It is one of today's trends among data scientists, lying in the intersection of computer science and statistics, within the core of artificial intelligence and data science [11]. ML is a branch of artificial intelligence based on the idea that systems can learn from data, identify patterns, and make decisions with minimal human intervention. Thus, instead of being programmed for specific actions only, machines use complex algorithms to make decisions and interpret data, automatically performing tasks. These programs can learn from the high power of data processing without human intervention. Waze, Netflix, Siri (Apple) are examples of use of the Machine Learning. Below follows a brief explanation of the ML methods used in this paper:

- K-Nearest-Neighbor (KNN)s: It is a classifier where learning is based on analogy [12]. The KNN algorithm is a supervised machine-learning algorithm used for classification and regression problems. Its operating principle is to separate individuals into groups (or classes) according to the existing similarity [13].
- Gradient Boosting Machine (GBM): It is a decision tree-based machine-learning algorithm that uses a gradient boosting framework, thus having several adjustment hyperparameters [14].
- Random Forest (RF): This technique generates several decision trees during training that can be randomly divided from a starting point [15]. This results in a "forest" of generated decision trees where the results are clustered by the algorithm [16]. The RF algorithm presents several advantages; it runs efficiently on large datasets, it is not sensitive to noise or over-fitting, it can handle thousands of input variables without variable deletion, and it has fewer parameters compared and adjustment with that of other machine-learning algorithms [17].
- Cross-Validation: Today's machine learning methods tend to overfit into the large datasets used for training and validating the algorithms. To solve this problem many data scientists have chosen to use cross-validation methods to attempt improving the robustness of the machine learning methods. In [18], indicate that the cross-validation method is one of the best techniques to evaluate the predictive performance of a model involving large samples. The process of Cross-validation is through randomly partition the sample into equally sized subsamples named folds. Finally, it is chosen the parameter with the best estimated average performance increasing the efficiency of the machine learning technic.

4 Discussion

Firstly, it was created a database with 35,634 rows of data to be used in the training and validation steps of the machine learning methods. As previously mentioned, for reasons of signed industrial confidentiality, the data cannot be shown in this work, so the name of the characteristics, as well as the name of the operation. The database includes two product variables, a setup variable, a product adjustment, and the target value of machine "J". The data was normalized between 0 and 1 and is shown in Table 1.

Table 1. Normalized data of test dataset

	Variable 1	Variable 2	Setup variable	Product adjustment	Target "J"
mean	0.2429	0.8656	0.0841	0.5027	0.2966
std	0.0090	0.0162	0.0488	0.1480	0.0662

With the dataset ready, a study of variable correlation between machine "D" and machine "J" was made to understand the linearity of the problem, since machine "D" makes a product adjustment in production and machine "J" measures this adjustment with higher precision, indicating that the variables from both machines should have in theory high linear correlation.

However, it was found that although theoretically there was a high correlation between the two variables (Variable 1 and Variable 2) from machine "D" and the measuring variable from machine "J", there was a correlation of less than 25%. The setup variable had a high correlation of almost 80% because it is a constant that changes only with a manual entry from the programmer and is adjusted within machine "J" parameters. All this information indicates that the automatic adjustment problem was more complex and could not be solved with linear regressions, indicating the need for Machine Learning methods along with improvements in the measurement process for good accuracy.

From this, it was necessary to establish a measurement basis for the accuracy of the methods that would be tested, so that it was possible to compare and validate the result. It was performed a study of the current state of the adjustment of machine "D" it was found that the worker made the adjustment based on the average of 9 measurements of machine "J" and observed the trend of the data and its outliers. Therefore, the worker would adjust downward if the 9 pieces were rising, and up if the 9 pieces were falling. However, this form of measurement is not periodically controlled, due to being checked visually by the operator, which is not exclusive for this task, and the machine operator "J" needed to indicate outliers to the machine operator "D" for an operating adjustment to be made.

Thus, it was seen that the current state of the adjustment process between machines "D" and "J" could be translated by a simple 9-measurement moving average method with 15-piece measurement delay, since there is a delay of 15 pieces between setting machine "D" and measuring it on machine "J".

After understanding the functionality of the process, its measurements and characteristics, the data from a manufacturing period were extracted and mined. At this stage, it was understood that these were non-linear variables. The time applied to understand the reality of production was of fundamental importance, as well as the knowledge of operators, experience of adjustments in "n" types of products, and the difference in how each product behaves in the same production line.

The data were extracted from historical databases, and were manually mined, excluding outliers, duplicate data, columns without information, thus preparing the data to be worked on in the methods to be chosen.

The ML methods used were chosen through trial and error. Method by method was tested, its result, assertiveness, and stability evaluated. It was concluded that the best scenario found was a combination of methods.

The choice of the best model was carried out through the help of programming software for machine learning "H_2O", where combinations of models and ensembles were tested, using the Gradient Boosting Machine (GBM), Random Forest (RF) method as input, General Linear Models (GLM). Through this, it had a product, the best combination indicated for the application according to the problem presented.

Consequently, it was proposed three models of machine learning applied to the problem: Random Forest, Gradient Boosting Machine, and K-nearest neighbor. These models used only two variables of part measurement operation "D" and one set-up variable to obtain a prediction of the measurement result of operation "J" and thus perform the adjustment automatically. The conceptual proposal of horizontal integration of two manufacturing machines through Machine Learning tools can be seen in the figure below (Fig. 3).

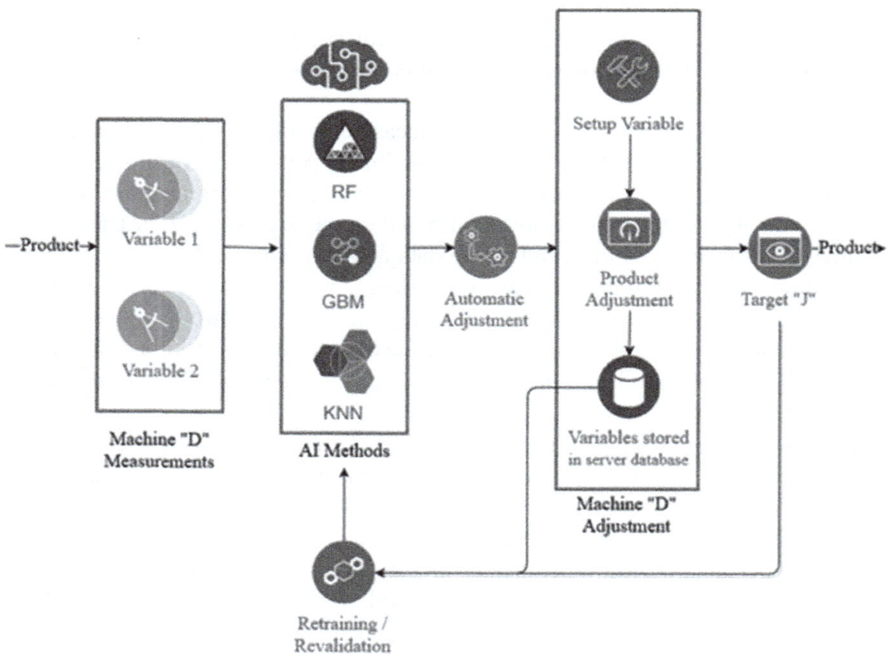

Fig. 3. Proposed automatic adjustment architecture.

Figure 3 shows the desired future scenario, in which machine "D" will perform product measurements (variable 1 and variable 2), then it will send the measurement data for processing in the selected AI method, which will send a signal with Box Magazine, according to the thickness washer that will best approach the chosen target to be reached in the "J" measurement operation. This Fig. 3 states, the moment when AI will be applied, as well as the replacement of the production operator, thus ceasing to be manual, becoming automatic. Another observation to make is that the AI analyzes the trend forecast for each product measurement and no longer as done in the scenario presented (Fig. 2), which waited an average of 9–15 pieces to perform adjustments, if necessary. The problem is that many times this range of parts was outside the established limits, generating rework and scrap.

5 Preliminary Results

In this paper, we present a case study testing the proposed models (Random Forest, Gradient Boosting Machine, and K-nearest neighbor) in the previous item compared with the moving average model that represents the current state of the process. Each test was made using 35,634 test pieces and a cross-validation method of 5 folds to avoid overfitting of the models and that they could forecast with new data and parts without losing its accuracy, avoiding failures/rework, refuse, due to this problem of interoperability between workstations, thus optimizing the production process.

The result of the model validation is presented below in Table 2 with their square mean error, standard deviation of predictions, mean absolute error in microns, and their percentage improvement based on the current state. The ensembles were tested using weighted average from the model's prediction results of Gradient Boosting Machine (GBM), K-nearest neighbor (KNN), and Moving average (MA). The ensembles did not use the Random forest predictions since it had a worse performance than the moving average used as a baseline.

Table 2. Result of proposed ML methods and ensembles

Model	Parameters	Square mean error (Microns^2)	Standard deviation of prediction (Microns)	Mean absolute error (Microns)	Improvement (MAE)
Moving average	n = 9 pieces delay = 15 pieces	16.7993	2.0847	**2.1814**	Base line
Random Forest	estimators = 1000	17.2245	1.9845	**2.3250**	**−6.585%**
K-Nearest Neighbours	neighbours = 100 weights = distance	14.3738	0.8026	**1.9304**	**11.50%**
Gradient Boosting Machine	estimators = 25 max_depth = 6 min_samples_split = 2 learning rate = 0.2 loss = Huber	14.3823	0.7503	**1.8212**	**16.51%**
Ensemble 1	0.5 * GBM + 0.5 * KNN	14.1492	0.6470	**1.8437**	**15.48%**
Ensemble 2	0.9 * GBM + 0.1 * KNN	14.2999	0.7103	**1.8197**	**16.58%**
Ensemble 3	0.4 * GBM + 0.3 * KNN + 0.3 * MA	13.8360	0.7863	**1.8550**	**14.96%**
Ensemble 4	0.85 * GBM + 0.05 * KNN + 0.1 * MA	14.1162	0.6939	**1.8135**	**16.86%**

As can be seen in Table 2, the best result was from model ensemble 4 with an improvement of 16.86% over the baseline model. This represents that the cloud computing with the machine learning models being ensemble could predict the result in machine "J" almost 20% better than the operator could and then make automatically the adjustment for better control of the whole process of manufacture.

6 Conclusion

Throughout this case, we can conclude that the best standalone algorithm with the dataset presented was the Gradient Boosting Machine, and that the boosting technic helped the prediction of values more precisely. Also, the random forest method did not meet the expectation and presented a worse result than a simple moving average, not being able to adapt to the information presented. The ensembles presented were done only with a weighted average from the prediction values, needing more studies for stacked ensembles and more advanced methods of ensembling the machine learning algorithms.

It was also seen that the Industry 4.0 concepts have difficulties to be implemented, even with all its digital transformation over the years, regarding data collection and reliability, machine communication, consistency and stabilization of production processes, and people's resistance to the use of this technology. Throughout the implementation of this case, it was difficult to identify new features to be used, with some not being measurable, or even, stored in a database, by today's process because they deal with external influences such as temperature and humidity, and others are not saved by the database.

We can conclude, after the application of AI, that because it is a nonlinear case, some Machine Learning techniques do not adapt, or do not have good accuracy and estimated error results, so it was used several techniques, from which the best result was almost 17% improvement, according to the current scenario. However, there are other techniques, an ensemble of techniques, of which still do not have much study on, but are demonstrating to be significant, insertion of new features and adjustment of the hyper-parameters that may contribute improving this result, thus being an input for future work (article).

Acknowledgments. The authors would like to thank Pontifical Catholic University of Parana (PUCPR) and Robert Bosch CtP for the financial support to the development of this research.

References

1. Neely, A., Kennerley, M.: Measuring performance in a changing business environment. Int. J. Oper. Prod. Manage. **23**, 213–229 (2003)
2. Zdravković, M., Panetto, H.: The challenges of model-based systems engineering for the next generation enterprise information systems. Inf. Syst. e-Bus. Manage. **15**(2), 225–227 (2017). https://doi.org/10.1007/s10257-017-0353-z

3. Ghobakhloo, M.: The future of manufacturing industry: a strategic roadmap toward Industry 4.0. J. Manuf. Technol. Manage. **29**(2), 910–936 (2018)
4. Szejka, A.L., Aubry, A., Panetto, H., Júnior, O.C., Loures, E.R.: Towards a conceptual framework for requirements interoperability in complex systems engineering. In: Meersman, R., et al. (eds.) OTM 2014. LNCS, vol. 8842, pp. 229–240. Springer, Heidelberg (2014). https://doi.org/10.1007/978-3-662-45550-0_24
5. Szejka, A.L., Canciglieri Jr., O., Rocha Loures, E., Aubry, A., Panetto, H.: Requirements interoperability method to support integrated product development. In. 45th Conference on Computers and Industrial Engineering, Metz, 28–30 October, pp. 1–10 (2015)
6. Karabegovic, I.: The role of industrial and service robots in the 4th industrial revolution industry – 4.0. ACTA Technica Corviniensis **XI**(2), 11–16 (2018)
7. Rüßmann, M., et al.: Industry 4.0: The future of productivity and growth in manufacturing industries, vol. 9, pp. 54–89. Boston Consulting Group (2015)
8. Adamczyk, B.S., Szejka, A.L., Canciglieri, O.: Knowledge-based expert system to support the semantic interoperability in smart manufacturing. Comput. Ind. **115**, 103161 (2020)
9. Lasi, H., Fettke, P., Kemper, H.-G., Feld, T., Hoffmann, M.: Industry 4.0. Bus. Inf. Syst. Eng. **6**(4), 239–242 (2014). https://doi.org/10.1007/s12599-014-0334-4
10. Reis, M.S., Kenett, R.: Assessing the value of information of data-centric activities in the chemical processing industry 4.0. AIChE J. **64**(11), 3868–3881 (2018)
11. Jordan, M.I., Mitchell, T.M.: Machine learning: Trends, perspectives, and prospects. Science **349**(6245), 255–260 (2015)
12. Hadad, H.M., Mahmoud, H.A., Ali Mousa, F.: Bovines muzzle classification based on machine learning techniques. In: International Conference on Communication, Management and Information Technology, vol. 65, pp. 864–871 (2015)
13. Zhu, X., Cheng, D., Zong, M., Li, X., Zhang, S.: Learning k for KNN classification. ACM Trans. Intell. Syst. Technol. **8**(3), 1–19 (2017)
14. Natekin, A., Knoll, A.: Gradient boosting machines, a tutorial. Front. Neurorobot. **7**(21), 1–10 (2013)
15. Andronicus, A.A., Aderemi, O.A.: Classification of phishing email using random forest machine learning technique. J. Appl. Math. **2014**(425731), 1–6 (2014)
16. Lyncha, A.M., et al.: Prediction of lung cancer patient survival via supervised machine learning classification techniques. Int. J. Med. Inform. **108**, 1–8 (2017)
17. Wang, L.A., Zhou, X., Zhu, X., Dong, Z., Guo, W.: Estimation of biomass in wheat using random forest regression algorithm and remote sensing data. Crop J. **4**(3), 212–219 (2016)
18. Pinto, J.M., Marçal, E.F.: Cross-validation based forecasting method: a machine learning approach. CEQEF **49**, 1–18 (2019)

A Method to Gaze Following Detection by Computer Vision Applied to Production Environments

Emannuell Dartora Cenzi and Marcelo Rudek(✉)

Pontifícia Universidade Católica do Paraná PUCPR, Industrial and Systems Engineering Graduate Program – PPGEPS, Curitiba, PR 80215-901, Brazil
emannuellcenzi@gmail.com, marcelo.rudek@pucpr.br

Abstract. The humans have the natural ability of following objects with the head and eyes and identify the relationship between those objects. This daily activity represents a challenge for computer vision systems. The procedure to identify the relationship between human eye gaze and the trackable objects is complex and demands several details. In this current paper we proposed a review of the main gazing following methods, identified the respective performance of them and also proposed an AI based method to estimate the gaze from 2D images based on head pose estimation. The main important details to be recovered from images are scene depth, head position and alignment and ocular rotation. In this approach we perform a track estimation of the gaze direction without the use of the eye position, and also, the face partial occlusion is considered in the analysis. The proposed approach allows low cost in processing with considerable accuracy at low complexity sceneries, because we don't need to extract the facial features. Gaze tracking is important to evaluate employees' attention to specific tasks in order to prevent accidents and improve work quality. The presented method improves the current knowing workflow by applying the head pose estimation instead face detection for training and inference. The promisors results are presented and open points are also discussed.

Keywords: Gaze following · Computer vision · Artificial intelligence · Gaze direction · Artificial neural network

1 Introduction

Following the direction of gaze is an important task to understand the behavior in human-human and human-object interaction. The marketing and sales sectors of retail companies seek to understand the consumer behavior in relationship to the acquisition of goods, taking into account cognitive aspects such as visual and behavioral information of the consumer. In factories production lines, for example, the level of attention on different items or parts can be inferred based on human-object eye contact in real time, seeking to understand human interaction in the production process, measure the time spent on tasks and analyze productivity. For safety, in remote

Published by Springer Nature Switzerland AG 2020
F. Nyffenegger et al. (Eds.): PLM 2020, IFIP AICT 594, pp. 36–49, 2020.
https://doi.org/10.1007/978-3-030-62807-9_4

lifeproof systems (liveness detection), in education and training approaches to determine the level of attention of students on the teacher.

An analysis of where they direct their gaze is an example of this. In this article we propose an analysis of the datasets and previous approaches to propose an end-to-end solution and we apply a study case with the objective of estimating where people are looking.

In order to avoid any misunderstanding, in this work we use the term "focus of attention" to refer to the direction in which the person is looking (the object of gaze fixation), called gaze following [1].

Shared attention is present in every part in our daily life and it can be observed in almost all social interactions. Human beings have the ability to follow another person's gaze naturally. Although this ability is of vital importance and natural to humans, for computer vision it is extremely challenging for three reasons [2]:

1. Deducting the point of view requires information on the depth of the scene, the pose of the head and the movement of the eyeball. However, inferring the depth of the scene with a monocular image is complex and can have a high computational cost. In addition, estimating the position of the head and the movement of the eyeball is often not possible due to occlusion.
2. There may be ambiguity in the focus of gaze estimates as in Fig. 2(a).
3. Gaze following involves understanding the geometric relationship between the target person and the other objects in the scene, as well as understanding the content of the scene, which is a difficult task.

2 Related Works

Although important, a few works in the field of computer vision have explored the subject by limiting the scope of the problem and restricting situations to scenes of people looking at each other [3], in controlled environments or using multiple image sources to determine the target [4]. The literature review was based on the methodology of [5] where the main identified works that use eye-tracking techniques and can be applied to controlled scenarios such as human-computer interaction [6, 7].

Recent works have explored the problem of estimating gaze direction in different ways. Some previously explored approaches are highlighted

- In [3] it was sought to determine whether or not people are looking at each other on television videos.
- An eye-tracking technique that consists of tracking the movements of the eyeball was applied by [8], which predicts the next object of attention in order to improve the recognition of actions.
- Through tracking the eye by monitoring the position of the iris, a set of annotations of facial points is made to perform eye tracking [1].
- Estimating the direction of gaze with only the position of the head, but without the specific target point [9].

- Given an image containing several people, gaze direction is estimated without environmental restrictions, and the target point of the gaze is determined by detecting salient points [4].
- Other works propose approaches for videos in [10, 11].
- 3D images contain information about the depth of the scene and some highlighting contributions are presented in [12–14].

The problem of gaze following was explored by [15] to infer the attention shared among two or more individuals over another object or human.

The current state of the art for monocular images consists of the use of deep neural networks (deep learning). It is a two-stage neural network to predict the gaze direction of the person selected in the scene, where in the first stage, only the image of the head (crop) and its position in the scene are necessary to perform the gaze direction prediction. Then, possible vectors are generated which are used to characterize the distribution of the points of gaze without considering the content of the scene [2].

Shared attention is present in daily life and can be observed in social interactions [15]. Through videos extracted from public television programs with scenes of social interaction, it was possible to automatically determine shared attention. It is a phenomenon where two or more people simultaneously look at a target in the scene that must be analyzed as a third person (outside the scene). The solution was a proposal for a space-time neural network to detect shared attention in videos.

Different approaches have used eye tracking to successfully determine gaze direction [6, 7, 16, 17]. However, [4] observed that these techniques are severely affected by self-occlusion generated by the individual's positioning in the scene. In this way, they propose a neural network architecture divided into two paths with the objective of determining the focus of people's eyes on everyday images without the restriction of the environment. The detection pipeline is divided into two independent neural networks. The image follows a path that discovers the salient points (Saliency Pathway), assuming that they are targets of attention in order to highlight and emphasize certain objects that people tend to look at. The other path (Gaze Pathway) uses an image of the detected face and its position in a neural network model to determine the direction of gaze from the position of the head [4].

The limitation of the proposal by [4] is that the object in the region of eye focus may not always be salient, revealing a difficulty in finding the end point of the gaze directly through salience algorithms. According to [18], the detection of salient points consists of highlighting regions of an image, and can be applied in the segmentation of images and videos, image compression, action recognition, and video summarization, among others.

Given that the works proposed to use the position of the head and the movement of the eyeball separately to determine gaze direction, [12] proposed an approach with multiple cameras using two separate deep neural networks, one for the prediction of the position of the head and another for the movements of the eyeball without using facial points. To connect the two layers, the "gaze transformation" layer was created. The output presents a vector composed of the starting point (eye coordinates) and the direction of the gaze to the target point in 3D space.

The current state of the art for monocular images [2] consists in the use of deep learning. Advances were made by [4] since 2015 with a new approach to determine the focus of gaze suggesting a two-step method inspired by the human behavior of gaze following. Especially when a person outside the scene (third person) analyzes it with the objective of estimating the person's gaze direction, the estimation of the target of the gaze is made based on the image of the head. Thus, the authors propose to use the image of the head and its position in the image to determine the gaze direction in the first stage, and then the gaze direction field is "coded" in three different scales. In the second stage, the gaze direction vectors generated in the previous step are linked with the image to generate a heat map where the point with the highest value represents the target of the gaze.

Heatmap regression is a technique used in many applications such as pose estimation [8] that uses regression models to propose a cloud of possible points to determine the pose of people in videos. In the same way, the point of gaze is predicted based on a heatmap of the content of the scene over the multiple estimated gaze direction vectors.

2.1 Gaze Following and Head Pose Estimation

Estimating the position of a person's head is a problem that has a wide range of applications, such as assisting in gaze following, defining attention, adjusting 3D models (animations or characterization of characters) to the video, performing face alignment, monitoring driver behavior, or associating with other techniques in view of the fact that it is closely related to everyday problems such as gaze following.

Previous approaches have generally used facial point estimation to make a correspondence from 2D to 3D. However [19, 20] argue that relying entirely on the performance of detecting facial points to estimate the position of the head is a fragile method, which involves some steps constructed in the form of a cascade, so if the first stage fails, consequently the rest will be affected. From the face detection, the markings of the reference points in the 2D image are estimated and adapted in an average 3D model of the human face, and with the camera parameters it is possible to calculate corrections to then make the correspondence between the 2D points and the 3D model.

Large face datasets [21, 22] and efficient methods with different approaches have previously been proposed to solve problems related to facial analysis, such as face detection [23–26], face recognition [27], age estimation, detection of facial points and estimation of head position [19, 20].

The head pose estimation problem from a simple 2D image is resolved with the ResNet-50 multi-loss neural network architecture [19], where each loss has a classification and a regression corresponding individually to the three angles of yaw, pitch and roll. Given the position of the head, the product of the proposed method is a 3D vector that contains the yaw, pitch and roll angles. Estimating the pose of the head from an image basically requires learning to map between 2D and 3D spaces. Some methods use 3D images that contain depth information not present in 2D images that are the objective of these approaches.

3 Methodology

In this section it is presented the proposed methodology to determine the direction of gaze. This methodology is based on facial detection and head position estimation, without using the points of the face (markers) in an end-to-end flow. The product of the method consists of a vector connecting the head and the focal point of gaze.

The proposal analyzes the union of face detection techniques and head pose estimation [19] with the gaze following technique proposed by [2]. We joined these methods as presented in Fig. 1.

A close relationship was observed between the two techniques, even if for different purposes. Determining gaze direction necessarily goes through the facial detection process, as it does the head pose estimation that uses a cut-out image of the face to determine the position of the head (yaw, pitch, and roll angles).

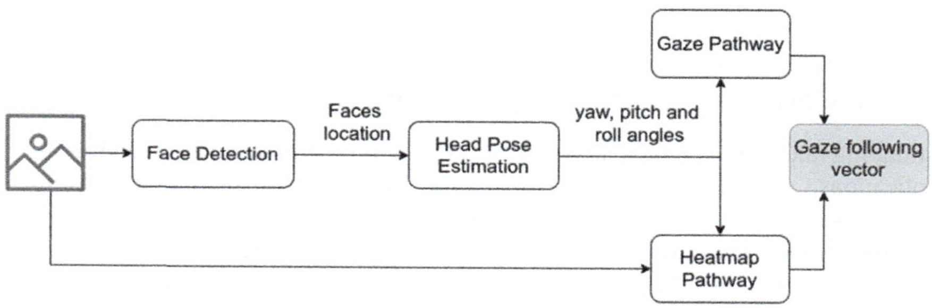

Fig. 1. Proposed detection pipeline.

3.1 Hardware Scheme Configuration

For prototyping, development and training, a computer equipped with Intel Core i5 3.0 GHz with 4 threads, 16 GB of RAM and 1 NVIDIA 1660 GTX GPU with 6 GB of RAM was used. The operating system used was Ubuntu 16.04 LTS. This setup was powerful enough to run the inference tests and training.

4 Training and Testing Dataset

In order to progress in the problem of predicting the gaze direction of one or more people in images, specific datasets must be used. Proposed in 2015, the GazeFollow dataset [4] contains 122,143 images and 130,339 people, with the annotation from the center of the eyes to where the "annotator" believes that the person under analysis is looking, with up to 10 different possible targets of gaze. For this dataset the authors used only images with the aim of looking within the image.

The dataset consists of a selection of images from different sources, such as SUN [28], MS COCO [29], Actions 40 [30], PASCAL [31], ImageNet [32] and Places [33]. This composition of different sources resulted in a large and challenging dataset of images of people in day-to-day activities with diverse scenarios. In Fig. 2, three examples of people engaged in activities and their respective annotations can be seen.

Fig. 2. Examples of images from the GazeFollow dataset [4].

In Fig. 2, examples with one or multiple people can be seen from the GazeFollow dataset, where only one or some but not all have annotations of the direction of gaze (c), even with the target of the gaze within the image or multiple annotations in the same image (b).

Another recent dataset proposal, the Daily GazeFollowing Dataset [2], which analyzes videos of people in everyday scenes interacting with objects and the environment, such as offices and work environments, shared spaces in buildings, interaction between people, etc. The annotations were made by the people in the scene, so they are more reliable according to the authors.

Regarding the dataset, GazeFollowing will be used because it is broader. It is concluded that examples of gaze following in which it is not possible to detect the face are not useful for this study because they are outside the proposed pipeline. In this way, a solution is proposed to repopulate the dataset.

4.1 Repopulation of the GazeFollow Dataset

Divided between training and validation, the dataset proposed by [4] has a large number of images. The annotations maintained the same format, although among the annotations only the gaze vectors originating inside one of the detected face bounding boxes were maintained.

The proposed flow presented in Fig. 3 implies the complete re-processing of the GazeFollow dataset. For each image, the faces are detected with the Dual Shot Face Detector [34] and for each face detected it checks if there is any annotation (ground truth) for this image with the point of origin of the gaze inside the bounding box of the face. If the point of origin of the gaze is related to the detected face, the estimation of the head position is made and the result with the pitch, yaw and roll angles is included in the original annotation of the dataset.

Among the images in which it was possible to detect the face and the origin of gaze direction vector annotations, the head pose estimation was processed. Some examples can be seen in Fig. 8. The result of the head pose estimation has been linked to the dataset as new parameters. These are numbers referring to pitch, yaw and roll angles and Table 1 shows the number of modified images in dataset.

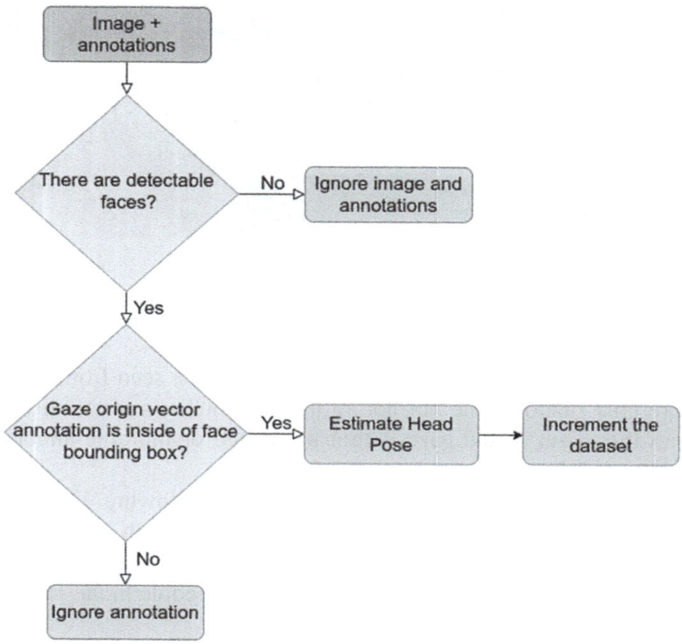

Fig. 3. Flow to repopulate the dataset with head pose estimation. Image elaborated by the author (2020).

Some examples where one or more faces were detected but there are no annotations of the direction of gaze. As presented in Fig. 4, the cyan colored bounding box represent the face annotation and magenta is the not annotated ones.

Fig. 4. Example of face detection without annotation of the gaze directions. Adapted from the *GazeFollow Dataset* [4].

Table 1. Number of images in the datasets.

Dataset	Original	Repopulated
Training	119.125	98.508
Test	4.782	3.883

As presented in Table 1, from 119,125 images for training, 17.3% were discarded because they did not meet the requirements in the repopulation process, whereas in the test dataset after processing, 18.79% of the images were discarded. The images that met the requirements shown in Fig. 3 were included in the new dataset with the head position estimation.

5 Training Strategy with Head Pose Estimation

The network input parameters are originally divided into three parts: head image, head position and the original image. The head and the original image are scaled to 224 × 224 pixels. After the repopulation of the dataset, there is a new parameter with three positions: pitch, yaw and roll.

Used in training, the new parameter "head_pose" has the three angles and is the product of the process of estimating the head position for each face annotated in the dataset.

Our approach does not use head image to determine the direction of the gaze. We changed the input of the neural network, removing the head image from the training process, and fusion layer. The fusion layer combine the eye position and head pose estimation into a sequential linear operation with ReLU activation function.

The outputs of the network remain with the original implementation and consist of two parts: direction of gaze and visual attention. The direction of gaze is the normalized vector from the head position to the point of gaze and the visual attention is a 56 × 56 pixel heatmap whose values indicate the probability of being the point of gaze.

The function that represents the loss is:

$$\iota d = 1 - \frac{\left\{d,\ \widehat{d}\right\}}{\left|d,\ \widehat{d}\right|} \tag{1}$$

Where d represents the ground truth and $\widehat{d}$ is the result of the prediction of the direction of gaze.

To calculate the loss in the heatmap regression, the originally implemented function BCE Loss (Binary Cross Entropy loss) is used, which creates a criterion that measures the binary cross entropy between the ground truth and the output.

Loss functions such as BCE Loss are typically used within the gradient drop, which is an iterative structure for moving parameters (or coefficients) to optimal values. Cross entropy describes the loss between two probability distributions [37].

The implementation is based on the PyTorch framework. To extract the features of the head image, the pre-trained ResNet-50 neural network was used by [2] with the ImageNet dataset [32]. The heatmap is introduced in the training after converging the first training layer, and is generated from the target point of the gaze annotated in the ground truth positioned in the center of the kernel of a Gaussian convolution operation. A sigmoid function was implemented in the output for activation of the heatmap.

Keeping in mind that we are working with the orientation of the head in space, data augmentation functions can be detrimental. Randomly transforming the head pose estimation data (head angles) can cause these to be lost and can confuse the model during training. Therefore, no techniques were used to expand the dataset during training.

6 Metrics and Validation

The classification task can be considered binary when the data input must be classified in only one class [38]. Our assessment compares the annotations (ground truth) of the dataset with the distribution of predictions. Evaluating the performance of different approaches and algorithms to determine gaze direction requires specific metrics for the problem. The following metrics are presented [2]:

- Area Under Curve (AUC) refers to the area under the ROC curve. The higher the value, the better the result.
- L2 or Dist is the Euclidean distance between the focus point of the gaze predicted by the network and the average of the annotation (ground truth).
- Angular error, to be calculated, requires tracing the annotated vectors and the result of the prediction to then calculate the error between them, corresponding to the average between the points of gaze.

Even though the processing cost and time for inference are not the focus of the research, the average time to perform an inference must be taken into consideration when there is a need to embed the solution on IoT devices, or in scenarios with hardware limitation.

7 Results

Hereinafter the results obtained from the implementation of the model to determine gaze direction [2] are presented, as well as the results of the method HopeNet [19] to estimate the position and the angle of the head. Both implementations are available in the Github project repositories [35, 36].

For validation, a 32-s video was recorded at a rate of 30 frames per second (Logitech 12 mp webcam, 1080 $\times$ 720 resolution) to enable comparison and analyze the performance of the application of [2] without annotating the origin of gaze to validate the efficiency of the proposed change. The video has a total of 960 frames, all with the face exposed, without occlusion.

The objective of this experiment is to understand the importance of the face detector in the first stage of the inference pipeline.

Figure 6 on the left shows a positive result of facial detection and heatmap regression to determine gaze direction. On the right side of Fig. 6, the heatmap can be seen linked with the original image to monitor the output of the proposed model. When it is not possible to detect the face (false negative) with the face detector model proposed in this approach, gaze direction cannot be inferred, as in the example in Fig. 7. As shown in Fig. 7(b), the face detection problem directly affects the next stages of the pipeline to determine the gaze direction like as in Fig. 7(a), and exposes the importance of a good face detector to estimate the point of attention in real time.

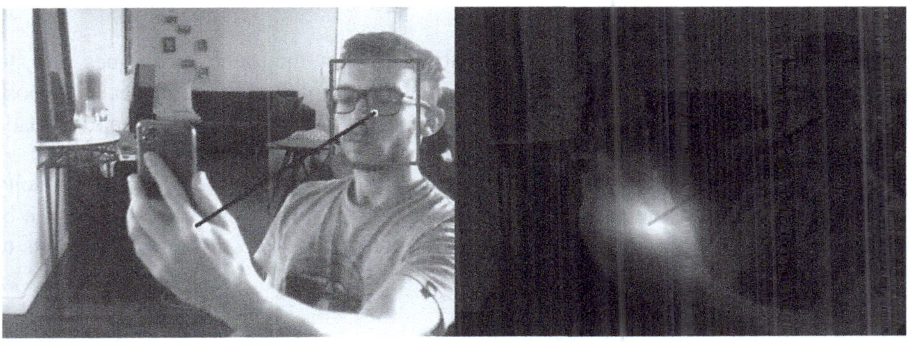

Fig. 6. Example of success in the process of facial detection and gaze following.

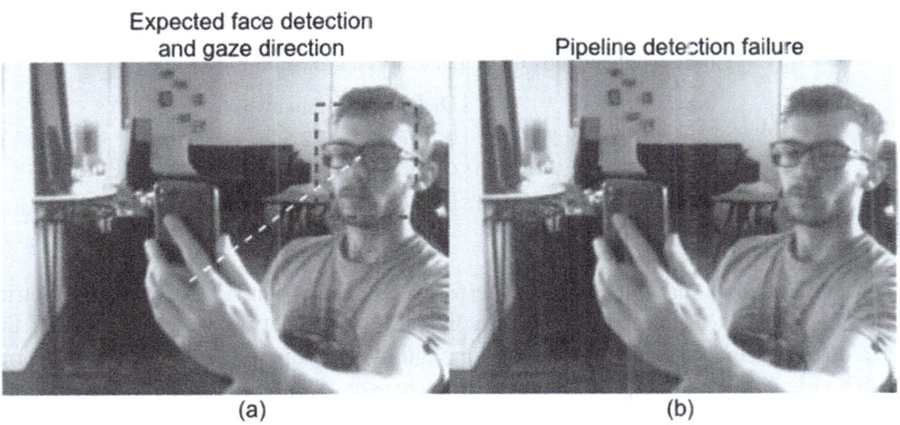

Fig. 7. Example of unsuccessful in face detection and breaking the gaze following frames sequence of the pipeline. (a) expected detection (b) no-detection in consecutive frames.

Fig. 8. Application of head pose estimation in the testing video.

Gaze following and head pose estimation are not the same techniques and no studies were found using both techniques directly coupled. The HopeNet head pose estimation [19] partial tests were performed based on the pre-trained model made available by the authors in the Github repository [36].

As presented by [19] and verified in Fig. 8, HopeNet stood out for its high capacity to determine the head angulation in a wide range of positions and partial occlusion of the face considering the fact that the proposed architecture does not use face points to determine the angulation of the head.

7.1 Results from Proposed Method

The results of the experiments are listed in Table 2. Due to changes in the dataset to include the head position estimate as presented in Sect. 4. The neural network model proposed by [2] was also changed as presented in Session 5.

Table 2. Resultados de treinamento com método proposto.

Methods	AUC	Distance L2	Angular error
Recases *et al.* [4]	0.881	0.175	22.5
Lian *et al.* [2]	0.903	0.156	17.6
Our method	0.911	0.179	20.71

Table 2, shows that our model outperforms [2] and [4] on AUC evaluation metric, and approximates the average of the Euclidean distance between the direction of the gaze direction and ground truth annotation, and average angular error of the direction.

The file with the saved model has an average size 47% smaller (116.5 Mb) than the model made available by [2] (223.4 Mb) for download.

So far, our model does not completely surpass the results obtained by [2], but it presents the model's viability and discusses the use of the gaze direction estimation technique with the head position estimation. Potentially applied in factories environments for production measurement [39], ergonomics systems, classrooms or online teaching softwares, online meetings, or in parallel with other computer vision systems in everyday interactions, web applications and embedded systems.

8 Conclusion

Systems to determine the direction of gaze will be fundamental to improve the human experience when interacting with machines and robots, especially those that seek to imitate human behavior. Based on the results, it is observed that the proposed architecture has the potential to surpass the current state of the art results to determine gaze direction. The proposed method presented in this article has its own characteristics and consists of the connection between the techniques of face detection, head pose estimation and gaze following in a pipeline for inference and training from end to end.

Following the proposed flow does not necessarily imply obtaining the same results, given that there is variation in the results of the head position estimate when repopulating the dataset. This work seeks to determine the gaze direction in 2D images, through a new methodology for training directly with the head pose estimation.

Also, we built a new data structure to the dataset. Changes in the neural network for training will in future be published on Github project repository, along with the new dataset. New discussions and experiments, such as training parameters and transformation functions between layers are necessary to evolve the presented methodology to make it more robust.

References

1. Xiong, X. et al.: Eye gaze tracking using an RGBD camera: a comparison with a RGB solution. In: Proceedings of the 2014 ACM International Joint Conference on Pervasive and Ubiquitous Computing: Adjunct Publication, pp. 1113–1121. ACM (2014)
2. Lian, D., Yu, Z., Gao, S.: Believe it or not, we know what you are looking at! In: Jawahar, C. V., Li, H., Mori, G., Schindler, K. (eds.) ACCV 2018. LNCS, vol. 11363, pp. 35–50. Springer, Cham (2019). https://doi.org/10.1007/978-3-030-20893-6_3
3. Marín-Jiménez, M.J., et al.: Detecting people looking at each other in videos. Int. J. Comput. Vis. **106**(3), 282–296 (2014)
4. Recasens, A. et al.: Where are they looking? In: Advances in Neural Information Processing Systems, pp. 199–207 (2015)
5. Reche, A.Y.U., Canciglieri Jr., O., Rudek, M., Estorilio, C.C.A.: Integrated product development process and green supply chain management: contributions, limitations and applications. J. Cleaner Prod. **249**, 119429–119459 (2019)
6. Krafka, K., et al.: Eye tracking for everyone. In: Proceedings of the IEEE Conference on Computer Vision and Pattern Recognition, pp. 2176–2184 (2016)
7. Aung, A.M., Ramakrishnan, A., Whitehill, J.R.: Who Are They Looking At? Automatic Eye Gaze Following for Classroom Observation Video Analysis. International Educational Data Mining Society (2018)
8. Fathi, A., Li, Y., Rehg, James M.: Learning to recognize daily actions using gaze. In: Fitzgibbon, A., Lazebnik, S., Perona, P., Sato, Y., Schmid, C. (eds.) ECCV 2012. LNCS, vol. 7572, pp. 314–327. Springer, Heidelberg (2012). https://doi.org/10.1007/978-3-642-33718-5_23
9. Pfister, T., Charles, J., Zisserman, A.: Flowing ConvNet for human pose estimation in videos. In: Proceedings of the IEEE International Conference on Computer Vision, pp. 1913–1921 (2015)

10. Recasens, A., et al.: Following gaze in video. In: Proceedings of the IEEE International Conference on Computer Vision, pp. 1435–1443 (2017)
11. Mukherjee, S.S., Robertson, N.M.: Deep head pose: gaze-direction estimation in multimodal video. IEEE Trans. Multimed. **17**(11), 2094–2107 (2015)
12. Zhu, W., Deng, H.: Monocular free-head 3D gaze tracking with deep learning and geometry constraints. In: Proceedings of the IEEE International Conference on Computer Vision, pp. 3143–3152 (2017)
13. Parks, D., Borji, A., Itti, L.: Augmented saliency model using automatic 3D head pose detection and learned gaze following in natural scenes. Vis. Res. **116**, 113–126 (2015)
14. Mora, K.A.F., Odobez, J.-M.: Person independent 3D gaze estimation from remote RGB-D cameras. In: 2013 IEEE International Conference on Image Processing, pp. 2787–2791. IEEE (2013)
15. Fan, L., et al.: Inferring shared attention in social scene videos. In: Proceedings of the IEEE Conference on Computer Vision and Pattern Recognition, pp. 6460–6468 (2018)
16. Vicente, F., et al.: Driver gaze tracking and eyes off the road detection system. IEEE Trans. Intell. Transp. Syst. **16**(4), 2014–2027 (2015)
17. Wang, K., Wang, S., JI, Q.: Deep eye fixation map learning for calibration-free eye gaze tracking. In: Proceedings of the 9th Biennial ACM Symposium on Eye Tracking Research & Applications, pp. 47–55. ACM (2016)
18. Cong, R., et al.: Review of visual saliency detection with comprehensive information. IEEE Trans. Circ. Syst. Video Technol. **29**, 2941–2959 (2018)
19. Ruiz, N., Chong, E., Rehg, J.M.: Fine-grained head pose estimation without keypoints. In: Proceedings of the IEEE Conference on Computer Vision and Pattern Recognition Workshops, pp. 2074–2083 (2018)
20. Yang, T.-Y., et al.: FSA-Net: learning fine-grained structure aggregation for head pose estimation from a single image. In: Proceedings of the IEEE Conference on Computer Vision and Pattern Recognition, pp. 1087–1096 (2019)
21. Yang, S., et al.: Wider face: a face detection benchmark. In: Proceedings of the IEEE Conference on Computer Vision and Pattern Recognition (2016)
22. Jain, V., Learned-Miller, E.: FDDB: A benchmark for face detection in unconstrained settings. Technical report, Technical Report UM-CS-2010-009, University of Massachusetts, Amherst (2010)
23. Chen, Y., Tai, Y., Liu, X., Shen, C., Yang, J.: FSRNet: end-to-end learning face super-resolution with facial priors. In: Proceedings of the IEEE Conference on Computer Vision and Pattern Recognition (2018)
24. Chi, C., Zhang, S., Xing, J., Lei, Z., Li, S.Z., Zou, X.: Selective refinement network for high performance face detection. In: Proceedings of Association for the Advancement of Artificial Intelligence (AAAI) (2019)
25. Li, H., Lin, Z., Shen, X., Brandt, J., Hua, G.: A convolutional neural network cascade for face detection. In: Proceedings of IEEE Conference on Computer Vision and Pattern Recognition (CVPR) (2015)
26. Ren, S., He, K., Girshick, R., Sun, J.: Faster R-CNN: towards real-time object detection with region proposal networks. In: Proceedings of Advances in Neural Information Processing Systems (NIPS) (2015)
27. Yang, J., Luo, L., Qian, J., Tai, Y., Zhang, F., Yong, X.: Nuclear norm based matrix regression with applications to face recognition with occlusion and illumination changes. IEEE Trans. Pattern Anal. Mach. Intell. (TPAMI) **39**(1), 156–171 (2017)
28. Xiao, J., Hays, J., Ehinger, K.A., Oliva, A., Torralba, A.: Sun database: large-scale scene recognition from abbey to zoo. In: 2010 IEEE Conference on Computer Vision and Pattern Recognition (CVPR), pp. 3485–3492. IEEE (2010)

29. Lin, T.-Y., et al.: Microsoft COCO: common objects in context. In: Fleet, D., Pajdla, T., Schiele, B., Tuytelaars, T. (eds.) ECCV 2014. LNCS, vol. 8693, pp. 740–755. Springer, Cham (2014). https://doi.org/10.1007/978-3-319-10602-1_48
30. Yao, B., Jiang, X., Khosla, A., Lin, A.L., Guibas, L., Fei-Fei, L.: Human action recognition by learning bases of action attributes and parts. In: 2011 IEEE International Conference on Computer Vision (ICCV), pp. 1331–1338. IEEE (2011)
31. Everingham, M., Van Gool, L., Williams, C.K., Winn, J., Zisserman, A.: The pascal visual object classes (voc) challenge. Int. J. Comput. Vis. **88**(2), 303–338 (2010)
32. Russakovsky, O., et al.: Imagenet large scale visual recognition challenge. Int. J. Comput. Vis. **115**(3), 211–252 (2015)
33. Zhou, B., Lapedriza, A., Xiao, J., Torralba, A., Oliva, A.: Learning deep features for scene recognition using places database. In: Advances in Neural Information Processing Systems, pp. 487–495 (2014)
34. Li, J., et al.: DSFD: dual shot face detector. In: Proceedings of the IEEE Conference on Computer Vision and Pattern Recognition (2019)
35. GazeFollowing Repository – Github. https://github.com/svip-lab/GazeFollowing. Accessed 2 Mar 2020
36. Deep head pose Hopenet – Github. https://github.com/natanielruiz/deep-head-pose. Accessed 2 Mar 2020
37. Goodfellow, I., Bengio, Y., Courville, A.: Deep Learning. MIT Press, Cambridge (2016)
38. Sokolova, M., Lapalme, G.: A systematic analysis of performance measures for classification tasks. Inf. Process. Manage. **45**(4), 427–437 (2009)
39. Silva, R.L., Rudek, M., Sjeika, A., Canciglieri Jr., O.: Machine vision systems for industrial quality control inspections. IFIP Adv. Inf. Commun. Technol. **540**, 631–641 (2018)

Towards a Knowledge-Based Design Methodology for Modular Robotic System

Lucas Jimenez[1,2(✉)], Frédéric Demoly[1], Sihao Deng[1], and Samuel Gomes[1]

[1] ICB UMR 6303, CNRS, University of Bourgogne Franche-Comté, UTBM, Belfort, France
{lucas.jimenez, frederic.demoly, sihao.deng, samuel.gomes}@utbm.fr

[2] MS-INNOV Company, Belfort, France

Abstract. A particular challenging task in the context of the 4th Industrial Revolution consists in increasing production system automation in European small and medium enterprises (SMEs). However, automation – often addressed with robotization – represents major investments that are not always accessible for SMEs, in which small batch production requires change in an efficient manner. In fact, software programming and hardware (in terms of reachability and maximum payload) are the flexibility barrier of current industrial robots. On the other hand, researchers and industry are currently pushing their efforts to develop modular robots (in terms of hardware and software), which are task-specific computable and changeable. In this context, this paper aims to develop a new design methodology combining both knowledge representation for task definition and computational tools for structural and logical design using modular units. To demonstrate its suitability in an industrial context requiring reconfiguration capabilities, specific developments have been made and tested with a simple case.

Keywords: Modular robotic · Knowledge-based design · Robotic task planning

1 Introduction

Robotic systems are part of the 4th Industrial Revolution and might change the way on which products are designed and manufactured. However, current industrial robots suffer from a lack of reconfiguration capabilities. Actually, they are built for large-scale production and are not suitable enough for small batches with rapid production change as needed in small and medium enterprises (SMEs) [1, 2]. Manufacturing SMEs are indeed dynamic organizations and tend to be more responsive and automated [3]. Past academic and industrial efforts have been made towards the development and integration of more flexible robotic systems, enabling fast physical reconfigurations according to manufacturing strategy changes. Thereby such systems still need additional efforts for easier design, integration, and task programming [4].

Published by Springer Nature Switzerland AG 2020
F. Nyffenegger et al. (Eds.): PLM 2020, IFIP AICT 594, pp. 50–58, 2020.
https://doi.org/10.1007/978-3-030-62807-9_5

Beyond current existing solutions in industry, modular robotics seems to be a promising strategy to address these aforementioned challenges. Over the last two decades, this research field has received huge attention from researchers, especially for developing devices able to evolve in hostile environment. However, their technology readiness levels currently are not enough aligned with industrial requirements [5]. Now modular robotic systems provide more versatility, robustness and are cheapest compared to industrial robots [6]. To ensure an industrial adoption, it is important to develop methods and tools for supporting hardware and software (control system) design [6–8]. Although research works have already been focused on reconfiguration and self-reconfiguration strategies in order to adapt a system to a new task or a new manufacturing environment using different computational procedures [6, 9], efforts still remain on knowledge representation for robotic system design [4].

Therefore, the main research issue consists in capturing and reusing robot task planning knowledge enhanced by computational capabilities for modular robotic design. Actually, developing a knowledge base with reasoning capabilities will facilitate modular robot structure and behaviour generation over embodiment and detailed design stages, especially in SMEs where resources and robotic knowledge are often limited and partial. This structure of the paper is as follows. Section 2 presents a brief literature review on task-specific robot system design and knowledge processing for robotic task definition where motivation is highlighted. Then, in Sect. 3, a knowledge-based methodology for modular robotic design is proposed. Lastly, a case study is introduced with a developed computational layer to illustrate the proposal.

2 Literature Review

This section reports significant research works on task-specific robotic system design and knowledge processing for robotic task definition, on which research motivation has been highlighted.

2.1 Task Specific Robotic System Design

When a new manufacturing instruction is defined, required payload and reachability might change. Using modular elements could then be useful to structurally adapt a robotic system to any task. As modular robots are composed of individual parts, many structural combinations are possible. Selecting the right structure fulfilling a given task is thus a challenging issue. In such a context, Desai *et al.* [10] have developed a tool dedicated to the generation of a heterogenous modular robot structure based on the desired path with a modular robot library [10]. The developed tool uses an A* search algorithm on a weighted tree representing array of structural configurations but does not consider functional specifications (only trajectories). Similarly, Valente [11] has used a stochastic algorithm to support decision during the modular robotic design process. Based on 15 key performance indicators (KPIs) and more than 50 parameters, the developed tool supports robot architecture definition by enabling the robotics engineer to select modules fulfilling multiple tasks. Although this approach seems to be mature, it lacks programming function and is not suitable for a non-robotic expert.

Research efforts become strategic on knowledge representation over the robotic cells design stages to overcome combinatorial complexity of robot structure and robot task planning generation.

2.2 Knowledge Processing for Robotic Design and Task Definition

Knowledge-based design is a research domain that has been widely investigated over the last decades [12]. Such research works – covering knowledge acquisition, representation and reuse – have decreased the required expertise with automation procedures while increasing tasks abstractions level. As an example, a knowledge base describing relationships between robot capabilities, robot structure and robot environment associated to a reasoner can infer new knowledge from a partially defined input problem [13]. From this perspective, ontologies have been developed to capture knowledge related to robot design, robot behaviours in terms of controller programming and trajectories planning. Ontologies are a set of concepts, parameters and relationship belonging to the same domain. Ontologies, among others, have been widely used in Knowledge Base System (KBS), for semantic reasoning in engineering design [15]. If appropriately combined, both ontologies provide assistance in robot architectural design for a specific task. Moreover, efforts have also been made for high abstraction task formalization through the KnowRob framework [17]. It can be seen as an ontology-based framework enabling any robotic system to perform tasks based on abstract instructions.

2.3 Research Issues

The above-mentioned studies have stressed the importance of both designing and programming modular robots for a specific task. Among the research works, two relevant approaches have been highlighted to automatically generate robot architecture and to support robots design and programming via a knowledge base associated to an inference engine. At first glance, these approaches seem to partially tackle fast reconfiguration planning issues in SMEs. The novelty here consists in combining computational tool and multi-perspective knowledge therefore enabling architectural and programming reconfiguration of modular robots.

3 Proposed Methodology

This section gives an overview of the proposed methodology for designing and programming modular robot system based on functional and behavioral specifications, such as pay load or needed tools (functional) and speed or torque (behavioral). In such a routine robotic design context, the proposed framework – illustrated in Fig. 1 – starts by considering the need to implement one or several assembly operations (i.e. manufacturing bill of materials mBOM) defined by the assembly planner in the manufacturing process management (MPM) system. Such information is defined according to the assembly plan that is co-generated with the CAD model of the product and its related engineering BOM (eBOM) stored in the product data management system

(PDM) [16, 17]. Among the defined assembly plan, assembly tasks requiring robotic assistance are elicited for initiating robotics engineer activity. Then, this robotic oriented mBOM is mapped within the proposed ontology. The latter actually requests all surrounding knowledge (i.e. working environment, available tools, initial/final part position, part mass, etc.) in order to infer robot trajectories as functional specifications, and payload and reachability as behavioural specifications with the support of an inference engine. Afterwards, these specifications are used in a computational tool embedding an A* algorithm to generate both modular robot structure (structural design) and programme (logical design).

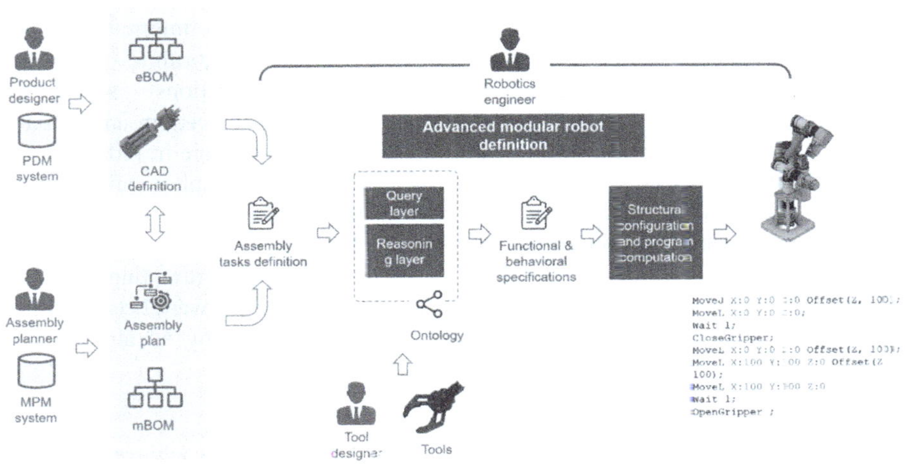

Fig. 1. Proposed knowledge-based methodology for modular robotic system design

3.1 Functional and Behavioural Design

In the preliminary steps of the proposed framework, engineering and manufacturing data from PDM and MPM systems are used and link to an ontology (i.e. knowledge base) that describes relations and rules for robot tasks definitions. The fact of combining ontology and an inference engine ensures the autocompletion of related knowledge of an actual context from an unconstrained problem. As such, Fig. 1 shows how a robotics engineer defines robot tasks such as 'assemble with' or 'move from X to Y'. These descriptive needs are linked to CAD models, e.g. workpieces, working environment, that are also mapping to the ontology in order to infer important parameters for robot structural design. By using the pre-defined requests filled with input data from the robotics engineer and PDM and MPM systems, it is possible to infer, from the ontology, parameters such as the payload, movement range or even working rates and to compute the robot trajectory. This is doable because the ontology capture relations between assembly operations, robotic task, robot environment, robot action and motion planning. For instance, if the robotics engineer defines a task corresponding to the following assembly operation 'Assemble part-1 with part-2',

SPARQL requests will return the data related to the initial position, the assembly information of part-1 and part-2 (e.g. assembly sequence, orientation, etc.), and so on, until defining a set of subsequences of movements needed to achieve the desired task. These subsequences reflect trajectory discretization into points and orientation vectors with action such as closing a gripper or screwing. In addition, data such as mass, part tolerance, maximum distance to reach, are used for the structural configuration and programme computation as shown in Fig. 1.

3.2 Structural and Logical Design

The structural design of the modular robot is then based on a computational algorithm to elaborate a physical configuration, which fulfils the previously inferred functional and behavioural specifications. In such a context, an A* search algorithm – based on a weighted graph which represents all possible module configurations – is proposed. Here each module could have zero or one rotational degree of freedom and a fixture system, allowing modules aggregation. By following the work done in [10], a similar computational strategy has been made, on which the weighted graph is built upon the functional specifications. Indeed, it is essential to adjust weight of the graph to orient A* algorithm towards not only possible solutions, but also efficient solutions for the specific task. In other words, by penalizing some nodes n (i.e. representing a module) of the graph, it is possible to eliminate invalid solutions and put forward better solution. In such a context, nodes that minimize Eq. (1) will be preferred by A* algorithm:

$$f(n) = g(n) + h(n) \tag{1}$$

where $h(n)$ is a heuristic that estimates the final cost of the design to achieve the desired goal (i.e. trajectory). The function $h(n)$ returns the average error of the inverse-kinematic solver of the actual robot structure at node n for the discretized trajectory. The more error is higher, the more the node will be penalized. Collision detection analysis is also processed to check the geometric configuration. Finally, $g(n)$ stands for the cost of a module, computed using a decision matrix (as represented in Table 1), where each criterion is pondered according to robotics engineer's specifications. For instance, the Eq. (2) computes the allocated weight to a module at the tree stage S by dividing the estimated needed static torque for this node by the real static torque of the considered module:

$$A_i(S, M_u, D, \bar{m}, N) = W1 * \frac{M_u * D + (N - S) * \bar{m} * \frac{D}{2}}{T_m} \tag{2}$$

where M_u is the payload, S is the module's stage in the tree,D is the distance from the tested module at the tree stage S and the desired goal, N is the maximum number of joint specified by the robotics engineer, $\bar{m}$ is the average mass of available modules from the MPM system, and T_m is the static torque of the considered module. Therefore, if the real static torque is inferior to the estimated needed torque, the ratio will be superior to 1, then penalizing this module. Finally, once the structural design achieved

Table 1. Decision matrix for the weighted graph computation

Module selection		**Option**				
		Module joint 1 	Module joint 2 	Module arm 1 	Module joint 2 	Module joint 3 
Criteria	**Weight**	**Score**				
Static Torque	W1	A1	B1	X	D1	E1
Accuracy	W2	A2	B2	X	D2	E2
….	…	…	…	…	…	…
Price	W4	A4	B4	C4	D4	E4
Speed	W6	A6	B6	X	D6	E6
	Final Score	$\sum_{i=1}^{n} W_i A_i$	$\sum_{i=1}^{n} W_i B_i$	$\sum_{i=1}^{n} W_i C_i$	$\sum_{i=1}^{n} W_i D_i$	$\sum_{i=1}^{n} W_i E_i$

and checked, the logical design is addressed by synthesizing the trajectory and actions in simple robot instructions such as linear or joint motion with a time discretization.

4 Case Study

To illustrate the proposed methodology, a simple case study is introduced. The objective is to design a modular robot system to ensure a pneumatic linear actuator assembly. In this context, some assumptions have been made, for instance here the robot initial position is predefined, the end-effector orientation will remain constant for all operations.

The product to be assembled and the related working environment are described in Fig. 2. This information is stored in the PDM system (for product information) and the MPM system (for manufacturing information), then mapping within the developed ontology materialized by the concept graph in Fig. 3. According to the tasks' definition, pre-defined SPARQL queries (query language for searching into database) are executed to generate the relevant information such as assembly sequence, position and mass of each object to be assembled in the working environment. Finally, a list of minimal motions is established (i.e. composed of linear motions from point-to-point and actions such as 'close-gripper').

For the sake of clarity, Figs. 4(a) and (b) give an example of SPARQL queries and returned results that are analysed to compute trajectories and parameters used for criteria evaluation using decision matrix describes beforehand. Finally, a weighted graph is pondered and the A* algorithm is executed to generate both a design solution that fulfils functional and behavioural specifications, and a robot programme as illustrated by Fig. 5.

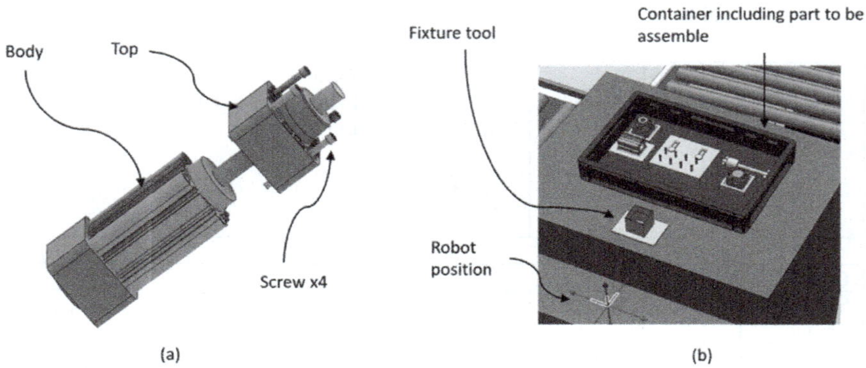

Fig. 2. (a) Product assembly and (b) its working environment

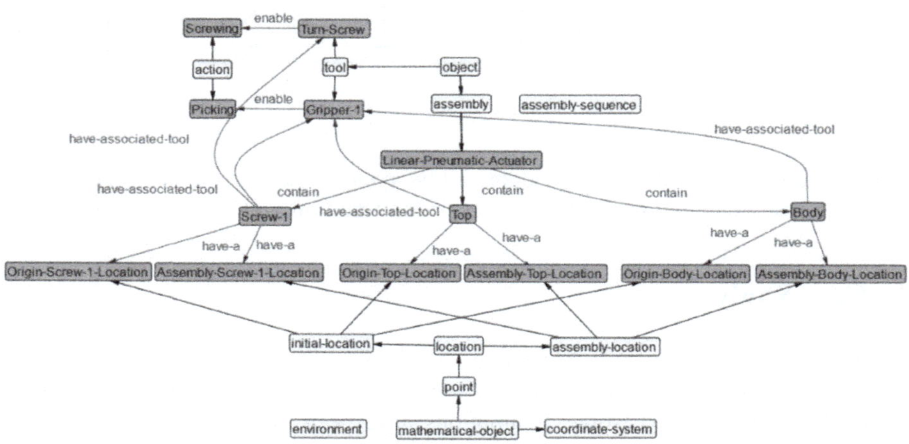

Fig. 3. Concept map and instances extracted from the ontology for robot task definition

(a)

```
select ?Object ?Mass where
{?Object ?MassKg ?Mass.
Filter(?Mass > 0) }
```

Part	Mass (kg)
Screw1	0.05
Top	0.25
Gripper1	0.8
Body	0.75

(b)

```
select ?Part ?Posi-
tion where {?Part
?location ?Position .
```

Part	Position
OriginBodyLocation	X:0 Y:0 Z:0
OriginTopLocation	X:10 Y:0 Z:0
OriginScrew1Location	X: 20 Y: 0 Z: 0
AssemblyBodyLoca-tion	X: 100 Y:100: Z:100

Fig. 4. Example of SPARQL requests about (a) object's mass selection and (b) parts positions

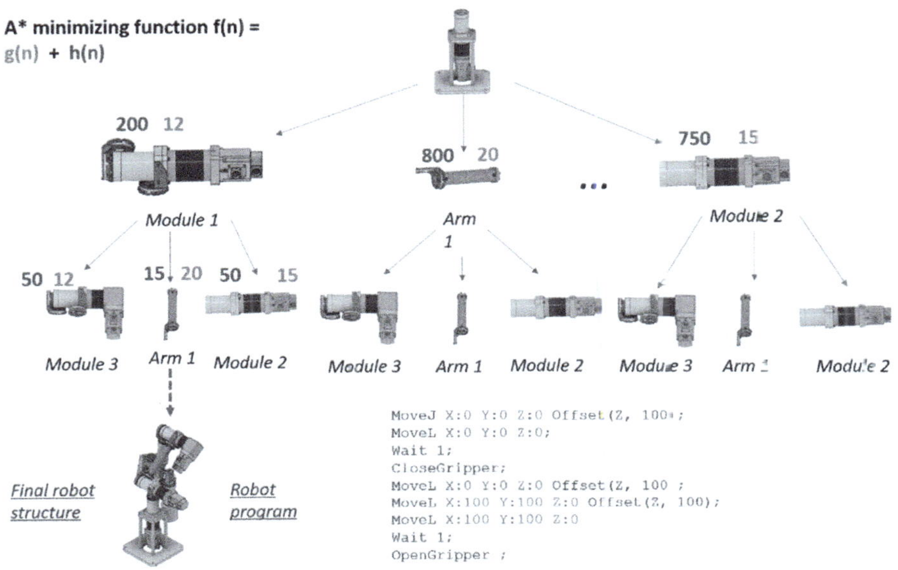

Fig. 5. Weighted graph with preferred path highlighted the final modular robot structure and its related program

5 Conclusion and Perspective

A knowledge-based methodology for modular robot system design has been proposed in this paper. It is built upon two reasoning layers: (1) a knowledge-based processing layer for the identification of functional and behavioural specifications enabling robotics engineer to specify robotic tasks through abstract instructions, and (2) an A* computational algorithm for generating both robot structure and program. Both layers have been implemented in a PLM ecosystem in which an ontology with an inference engine as well as a computational algorithm have been developed to generate robot specifications, structure and programmes. The case study has demonstrated the suitability of the proposed methodology for designing modular robots for task reconfiguration. However, currently, this model is not extensible to real world manufacturing operation. In fact, model information should be filled up to take into consideration important parameters such as assembly constraints, tolerance, robot calibration, etc. Moreover, the proposed methodology needs that all information about product assembly and manufacturing are stored in PLM and PDM systems, but these systems are not always implemented in SMEs and data are often incomplete and\or not up-to-date.

Built on these efforts, future work will be dedicated to the development of an application prototype using Unity 3D engine, ROS (Robot Operating System) and a laboratory prototype PLM system. Additional investigation will be focused on the consideration of robot reconfiguration according to real-time data from manufacturing systems, therefore falling under the umbrella of context-aware cyber-physical systems design.

Acknowledgements. The research activity has been made in collaboration with MS-INNOV company as part of a CIFRE contract (Industrial Standards of Research Training) by the French National Agency for Research and Technology (ANRT). The authors would like to thank all financial supports.

References

1. Gruninger, R., Kus, E., Huppi, R.: Market study on adaptive robots for flexible manufacturing systems. In: IEEE International Conference on Mechatronics, Malaga, Spain, pp. 1–7 (2009)
2. Spena, P.R., Holzner, P., Rauch, E., Vidoni, R., Matt, D.T.: Requirements for the design of flexible and changeable manufacturing and assembly systems: a SME-survey. Procedia CIRP **41**, 207–212 (2016)
3. Matt, Dominik T., Modrák, V., Zsifkovits, H. (eds.): Industry 4.0 for SMEs. Springer, Cham (2020). https://doi.org/10.1007/978-3-030-25425-4
4. Multi-Annual Roadmap for robotics in Europe, ICT24 Horizon 2020 (2015)
5. Hasbulah, M.H., Jafar, F.A., Nordin, M.H.: Comprehensive review on modular self-reconfigurable robot architecture. Int. Res. J. Eng. Technol. **6**(4), 1317–1331 (2019)
6. Yim, M., et al.: Modular self-reconfigurable robot systems. IEEE Robot. Autom. Mag. **14**(1), 43–52 (2007)
7. Spröwitz, A., Moeckel, R., Vespignani, M., Bonardi, S., Ijspeert, A.J.: Roombots: a hardware perspective on 3D self-reconfiguration and locomotion with a homogeneous modular robot. Robot. Auton. Syst. **62**, 1016–1033 (2014)
8. Seeja, G., Arockia Selvakumar, A., Berlin Hency, V.: A survey on swarm robotic modeling, analysis and hardware architecture. Procedia Comput. Sci. **133**, 478–485 (2018). ISSN 1877-0509
9. Aloupis, G., et al.: Linear reconfiguration of cube-style modular robots. Comput. Geom. **42**, 652–663 (2009)
10. Desai, R., Safonova, M., Muelling, K., Coros, S.: Automatic Design of Task-specific Robotic Arms. arXiv preprint: 1806.07419 (2018)
11. Valente, A.: Reconfigurable industrial robots: a stochastic programming approach for designing and assembling robotic arms. Robot. Comput. Integr. Manuf. **41**, 115–126 (2016)
12. Chandrasegaran, S.K., et al.: The evolution, challenges, and future of knowledge representation in product design systems. Comput. Aided Des. **45**(2), 204–228 (2013)
13. Ramos, F., Vázquez, A.S., Fernández, R., Olivares-Alarcos, A.: Ontology based design, control and programming of modular robots. ICA **25**, 173–192 (2018)
14. Tenorth, M., Beetz, M.: Representations for robot knowledge in the KnowRob framework. Artif. Intell. **247**, 151–169 (2017)
15. Demoly, F., Kim, K., Horváth, I.: Ontological engineering for supporting semantic reasoning in design: deriving models based on ontologies for supporting engineering design. J. Eng. Des. **30**, 405–416 (2020)
16. Demoly, F., Yan, X.-T., Eynard, B., Rivest, L., Gomes, S.: An assembly oriented design framework for product structure engineering and assembly sequence planning. Robot. Comput. Integr. Manuf. **27**(1), 33–46 (2011)
17. Demoly, F., Troussier, N., Eynard, B., Falgarone, H., Fricero, B., Gomes, S.: Proactive assembly oriented design approach based on the deployment of functional requirements. J. Comput. Sci. Eng. **11**(1), 014501 (2011)

A Lean Quality Control Approach for Additive Manufacturing

Francesca Sini[1,2], Giulia Bruno[1(✉)], Paolo Chiabert[1], and Frederic Segonds[2]

[1] Politecnico di Torino, Corso Duca degli Abruzzi 24, 10129 Turin, Italy
francesca.sini@studenti.polito.it,
{giulia.bruno,paolo.chiabert}@polito.it
[2] Arts et Metiers Institute of Technology, LCPI, HESAM Université, 75013 Paris, France
frederic.segonds@ensam.eu

Abstract. Additive Manufacturing is becoming more and more popular not just in the manufacturing industry, but also in the consumer market, because it offers a new world of opportunities, starting from the absence of constraints in geometry and the reduction in wastes due to material removal typical of subtractive manufacturing. Moreover, it is able to enhance lean manufacturing objectives of reducing activities that do not add any value for customers. However, a wide application is threatened by the lack of consistent quality. Therefore, it is necessary to further study defects that affect 3D printed products and to propose new manners to control them. This paper proposes to use a low cost, light weight, portable, device as a scanner to rapidly acquire data from 3D printed products and compare it with the original model.

Keywords: Additive manufacturing · 3D printing · Quality control · Lean philosophy

1 Introduction

Additive Manufacturing (AM) is the *"process of joining materials to make objects from 3D model data, usually layer upon layer, as opposed to subtractive manufacturing methodologies"* [1]. AM was born in 1986, and in recent years it is becoming popular both in the industrial and in the consumer market: nowadays, the term "additive manufacturing" is mostly used in industry markets, while "3D printing" mostly refers to the consumer market. The layer by layer production methodology has two main advantages: (i) geometry flexibility, since any geometry can be produced in a single operation without any additional cost or time constraint, and (ii) reduction in consumption of resources, since it enables to use only the precise amount of material necessary to the creation of the final product, avoiding the wastes typical of traditional subtractive manufacturing [2]. There are seven main processes for AM: VAT photopolymerisation, material jetting, binder jetting, powder bed fusion, material extrusion, directed energy deposition, sheet lamination. According to the Wohlers Report, *"Overall the 3D printing industry grew by 21% in the 2017/18 reporting period.*

Published by Springer Nature Switzerland AG 2020
F. Nyffenegger et al. (Eds.): PLM 2020, IFIP AICT 594, pp. 59–69, 2020.
https://doi.org/10.1007/978-3-030-62807-9_6

This figure is an increase on the 17.4% in worldwide revenues from 2016, and is edging closer to the 25.9% growth reported in 2015" [2]. From the industrial point of view, Rapid prototyping (RP) has been the main driver of AM development and, as a consequence, one of its first applications. The evolution of advanced AM techniques has largely proceeded in recent years, leading to broader industry applications [3]. It is vital to consider that AM was born only forty years ago: despite being a quite new technology with respect to traditional manufacturing, AM processes are already a standard for rapid prototyping and have relevant applications in the manufacturing of final products as well. AM is considered as a promising technology that may disrupt the market.

Compared with subtractive manufacturing, AM is particularly suitable for producing low volumes of products, especially for parts with complex geometries. AM processes also offer great potential for customization, such as the fabrication of personalized spared parts, clothes, jewelleries, implants for hip and knee replacements. A further usage that is becoming quite common is the *home fabrication:* users buy the appropriate equipment and directly print objects in their own place [4]. In the past, only very passionate hobbyist owned 3D printing kits, but given the increasing adoption rate, there are some experts announcing that *"desktop manufacturing revolution [...] will change the world as much as the personal computer did"* [5].

Material extrusion, in particular Fused Deposition Modelling (FDM), is the most popular additive manufacturing technique in this field due to the purchase cost of both the printing machine and the materials used [6]. The method consists on the heating of thermoplastic polymer material above its melting point and its extrusion through a nozzle which moves in X and Y directions on a printing platform that moves in the vertical Z-axis each time a layer has been deposited.

Lean manufacturing principles were born in the Toyota company after the Second World War, even if the expression *"lean manufacturing"* was coined only in 1988 by John Krafcik in the article *"Triumph of the lean production system"* [7]. It encompasses a broad array of industrial philosophies, concepts, and strategies thus it is arduous to give a precise definition; though, it can be affirmed with no doubt that its essential aim is to create added value for customers reducing as much as possible the wastes, "doing more with less" [8]. The father of lean manufacturing and Toyota's industrial engineer Taiichi Ohno, defined *muda* (Japanese word for waste) as those activities that do not add any value to the final product and for which the final customer is not willing to pay and identified seven main categories of waste: overproduction, waiting, transporting, over processing, unnecessary inventory, unnecessary motion, defects.

Lean principles aim and succeed to crucially reduce such categories of waste, but some of them cannot be avoided in subtractive manufacturing processes [9]. One of them is the waste of material caused by the production by removal. On the contrary, AM production process consists in the overlapping of different layers and only the exact amount of necessary material is used. The entire production, from the blank to the final product, totally occurs in the 3D printer: this means that there is no components' storage and that the only source of inventory is the raw material. Another example is the waste due to movements of materials and components, which cannot be avoided in a production line. In AM, being the supply chain much shorter, transportation wastes are abated. Waiting times are radically reduced as well: set up times to adapt machineries to production of different parts do not exist in AM, which is also able to reduce time to market thanks to all the advantages it provides in the product development phase. Another important advantage of AM is the possibility to produce by batches of single product.

Lean production is distinguished by mass production for being demand driven and for fosters smaller sized batches in order to minimize final product inventory, however the latter can be eliminated only by producing a part only when demanded by customers. This makes it possible to customize every product without any consequence on the production line thanks to AM design freedom.

Thus, AM is able to enhance lean manufacturing objectives of reducing activities that do not add any value for customers, since it can radically reduce supply chain management costs as it is able to shorten the supply chain and be more proximal to customers. The *muda* that AM is not able to solve yet is the one about defects. In fact, AM technology is not mature enough to grant a consistent quality [10]. Indeed, the most mature AM technologies, such as material extrusion, have a TRL between 6 and 7 [11]. This is the main reason why it has not yet spread. To address this issue, this paper presents a methodology to analyse the defects affecting 3D printed products and to control their quality.

The rest of the paper is organized as follows: Sect. 2 provides a description of defects and quality control proposals for AM, Sect. 3 presents a methodology to perform a quasi-real time quality control through a low-cost, energy efficient, light weight and portable device. The methodology is tested through a use case, described in Sect. 4. Finally, results of the tests and future works are exposed.

2 Quality Control in AM

Quality is defined as *"conformance to requirements or specifications"* [12]. The quality of 3D printed parts can be affected by defects in the following categories: (1) geometry and dimension, (2) surface quality, (3) mechanical properties.

Geometry accuracy is the deviation of the printed object with respect to the form of the CAD model; dimension accuracy is the degree of compatibility between the dimensions of the obtained product and the nominal dimensions foreseen by the CAD model [5]. The most widespread defects affecting geometry and dimensions are shrinkage and warping. The former is a geometric reduction in the size of the product [13] whilst the latter is a change in the nominal shape caused by a non-uniform shrinkage [14].

The surface may present the following criticalities: (i) Staircase effect, a common defect that occurs in the process of slicing when the layer marks become distinctly visible on the surface of the parts [10]; (ii) surface roughness, which deals with the topographical structure of a surface part, which can range from smooth to coarse, depending on build material and printer settings [15]; (iii) Stringing or Oozing, small strands of plastic on places where the printer shouldn't print and the print.

Finally, 3D printed products may present the following mechanical defects: (i) porosity: parts produced with additive manufacturing can present void spaces that, despite being very small, can affect mechanical properties [16]; (ii) low strength and stress behaviour: there may not be high cohesion between layers deposited through FDM may, causing a low resistance to the stress traction.

Another point to take into account is the repeatability, which is the degree of dimensional compatibility of two products of the same nominal geometry, manufactured in the same conditions, with identical values of the process parameters [17].

Quality control in mass manufacturing utilizes the Statistical Process Control, a series of statistical tools to monitor in real time the production process in order to detect any variations that may result into the production of an article that does not meet specifications [18]. Since this method relies on a sufficient sample data, it cannot properly be adapted to AM, which is mostly used to produce a low number of pieces of the same type.

Being AM a relatively recent technology, there is not a consolidated unique methodology for the quality control. In literature, there are several proposals that follow two main approaches: process control and product control.

The former monitors the process parameters and uses statistical and analytical methods to predict the effect they may have on the product quality. Boschetto and Bottini 19] developed a model to predict dimensional deviations of fabricated parts as a function of the process parameters; Rao et al. [19] used statistical analysis and non-parametric sensor-based Bayesian modelling approaches to optimize process conditions for obtaining the best surface roughness and to detect process drifts in real-time; Shirke et al. [20] used Taguchi method to study the effect of process parameters on tensile strength; Mokhtarian et al. [21] proposed a systematic methodology to extract cause-effect relationships among variables to predict the effect of specific design and manufacturing parameters on part defects and to estimate the needed input parameters backwards.

The later directly monitors the piece. Lin [22] simulated an online quality control to detect and identify defects by comparing the surface point cloud obtained by laser scanning with the ideal surface extracted from the CAD model.

The methodologies proposed in literature involve the usage of very expensive equipment (scanner, sensor) with respect to the result and that cannot be generally used by standard consumers. They use 3D printing more like a trial and error process [23] and produce parts with a very low quality, which results in high wastes in material and energy and can be optimized through a MES [24].

For this reason, the aim of our research is to find an alternative methodology that allows consumers to carry out the quality control simply through a new low cost, light weight, portable, device that can be used as a scanner for rapid data acquisitions rather than using sophisticated and expensive equipment. In this manner, it is expected that users are educated to quality control and that there will be a reduction in wastes due to the production of faulty products.

3 Methodological Proposal

The proposed methodology is represented in Fig. 1. AM process starts with a CAD file, which must be converted into a standard 3D format, such as .STL. Successively, slicing process is applied to the 3D file so that it can be manufactured layer by layer. The methodology proposes to pause the process every time that k layers (e.g., k = 15–20) are deposed and verify whether the intermediate product is compatible with the STL model. If it results that the product is not compatible with the model, the production is stopped. In this manner, it is soon understood whether the product will present important defects and wastes in material and energy are prevented.

In order to perform a quasi-real time monitoring, it is necessary that the acquisition process occurs rapidly, otherwise it would be impossible to stop the production so often. However, professional scanners, even though they ensure high accuracy and precision levels, require such long times and complex procedures.

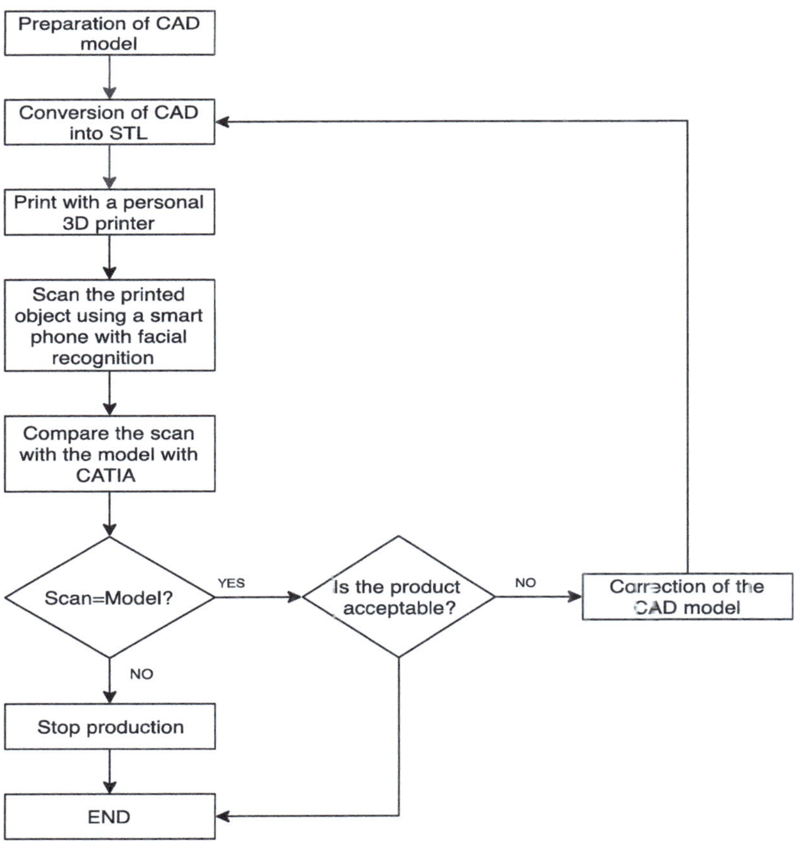

Fig. 1. Methodology for AM quality control

For this reason, it is presented a new low cost, light weight, portable, device that can be used as a scanner for rapid data acquisitions: it is proposed to utilize a last generation iPhone (X models) as a scanner for 3D printed products. Indeed, they are equipped with the TrueDepth Camera, which is the system used as internal frontal camera. Figure 2 shows the so-called notch of iPhone X with the components of the TrueDepth Camera: a part of a traditional 7 MP camera, there are other crucial components. Flood illuminator beams infrared light in order to verify the presence of a face; afterwards the 30,000 points are flashed onto the object surface in front of the device by the dot projector; the light points are received and read by the infrared camera, which is able to create a model of the surface. An infrared radiator ensures accuracy in the detection even when there are poor lighting conditions and a proximity sensor makes the system know when a user is close enough to activate.

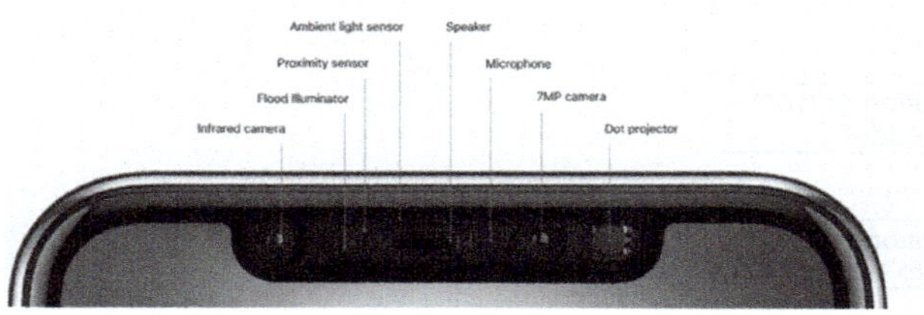

Fig. 2. TrueDepth camera system.

Thanks to this innovative technology, users can unlock the phone, authorize payments and purchases through the facial recognition, but it also opens new doors for several industries. In the interest of this research, it is crucial to explore TrueDepth Camera performance characteristics as a scanner and explore whether it can be used as a portable, light, cheap scanner with rapid acquisition time and low energy consumption. The efficacy of such instrument is tested through a use case, which will be described in the following section.

4 Use Case

The methodology and the idea to use employ the TrueDepth Camera as a scanner are tested through a use case, i.e., the production of a gnome. Gnomes are considered the perfect 3D printing tests as they have some standard characteristics that are suitable to assess printer and scanner features: triangular slouched cap, rounded face and nose, detailed beard, heavy clothes and boots. Among several gnomes that can be found online, Makerbot gnome is undoubtedly the most common and the easiest to find on Thingiverse. Even though it is a simple object, Makerbot gnome presents curves, several surface details, and different types of geometries; at the same time, it does not have any deep depressions or overlapping features that would be difficult to capture even with a professional scanner.

The makerbot gnome has been printed through a FDM technique and it has been scanned with the TrueDepth Camera. The scanning process is extremely fast and easy: it is enough that a person turns the telephone around the object and it takes only a few minutes (6 min). The acquisition process may be further simplified and automatized. It is possible to imagine a tool that make the phone turn around the object so that it is not necessary that a person performs this task.

The point cloud obtained by the scan is transformed into a .stl file and uploaded on CATIA, a software developed by Dassault Systèmes, which supports computer-aided design (CAD) and computer-aided manufacturing (CAM),. The scan allows to perfectly recognize the shape of the gnome, although not all details are accurately detected. However, it is necessary to clean and refine the point cloud because it presents some isolated points and because the TrueDepth Camera detects not just the object of interest but also the surface on which it lays.

Once the scan is clean, it is possible to compare it with the original .STL model. The two point clouds are overlapped and a dimensional deviation analysis is performed. Figure 3 shows the result of such comparison: from the dimensional deviation analysis, it results that there are some areas highlighted with a red colour, which indicates a 2 mm deviations and some area are highlighted for a −1.6 mm difference. Thus, the difference between the scanned object and the original model ranges between −1.6 and 2 mm.

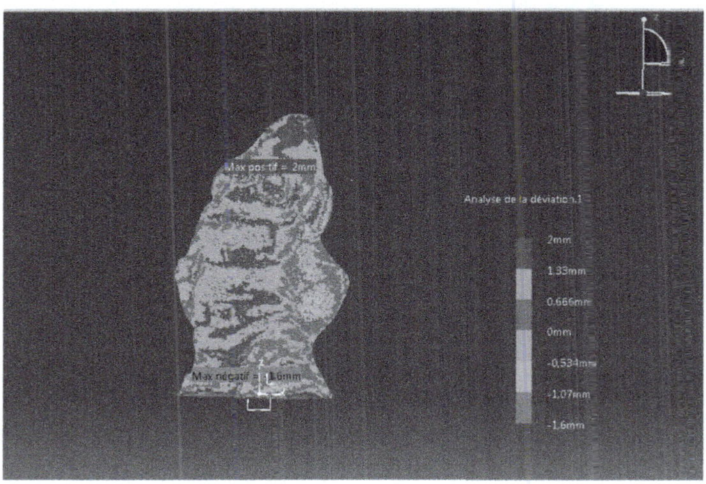

Fig. 3. Comparison between the model and the scan done with the smartphone (Color figure online)

At this point, it is vital to understand whether such difference is due to a defective production of the gnome or it is caused by a systematic instrumental error. In order to investigate on this question, the same printed object has been scanned with the Solutionix D500, a professional scanner which is specialized for small and detailed objects such as jewelleries, the most complex products to scan. It grants the capture even of small details thanks to its accuracy of 0.01 mm and a resolution (point spacing) of 0.056 mm. The result of the comparison between the original model and the point cloud generated by the Solutionix D500 are shown in Fig. 4: it can be appreciated that in this case the deviation ranges from −0.709 to 0.794 mm, against the range −1.6/2 mm. If on the one hand the Solutionix D500 ensures high accuracy, on the other hand the time required to obtain such a good result is way longer that the time required to scan the object through the TrueDepth Camera. Indeed, the scan and the transformation of the point cloud into an.STL file took 1 h and 20 min. Such a long time makes it impossible to consider the idea to use the scanner for a quasi-real time quality control and control the product each 15/20 layers are deposited.

Considering the difference between the results obtained using the TrueDepth Camera and the professional scanner, it can be said that TrueDepth Camera has an accuracy that is suitable for the quality control in 3D printing in case no submillimetre precision is required. Considered that the accuracy of the TrueDepth Camera is way lower than the one of professional scanners, it is necessary to make further analysis on its accuracy, precision and stability as an instrument.

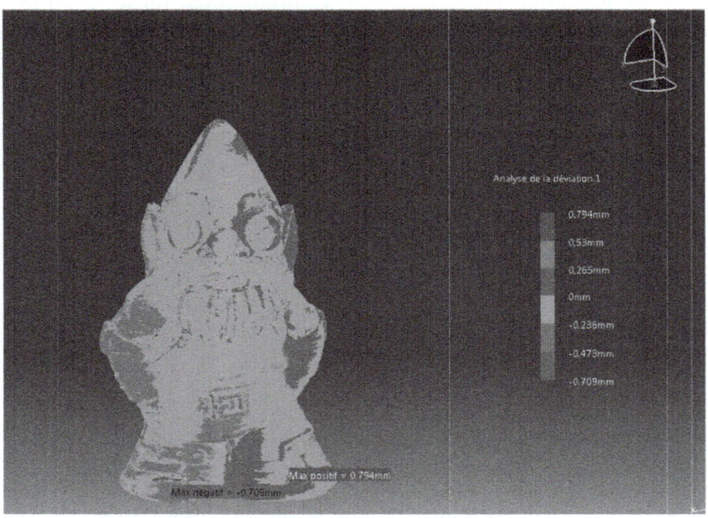

Fig. 4. Comparison between the model and the scan done with the Solutionix D500 scanner

If a more detailed analysis is made on the results obtained with the two instruments, it can be noticed that the areas in which TrueDepth Camera had more difficulties in precisely detecting the details, resulting in a less accurate scanning, is the central part in which there are the recesses. Apparently, the Camera is not able to recognize the differences in depth and measures in such kinds of area. However, there is ground to believe that TrueDepth Camera is able to give more reliable results in case of surfaces without this kind of recessions and irregularities.

Further experiments should be performed in order to confirm this hypothesis. Further studies about the TrueDepth Camera were made in and it is discovered that it is the result of the acquisition by Apple of an Israeli 3D company pioneer in 3D sensor technology, PrimeSense, which developed the system used by Microsoft's Kinect to detect movements and enable users to play Xbox videogames without any controller. The company was acquired by Apple for $360 Million in 2013; therefore, it can be supposed that the technical features are at least as good as Microsoft's Kinect used as a scanner. The accuracy of a Kinect as a scanner for biological science ranged between 2.5 mm and 5.8 mm. Even though a higher experimental sample would be necessary, it is possible to state that TrueDepth Camera has resulted into a better scanning instrument that Microsoft's Kinect.

5 Conclusion and Future Works

Despite being way cheaper than a professional scanner, TrueDepth Camera is able to perfectly recognize the shape of the use case and has the great advantage of guaranteeing a very rapid process acquisition (in the order of minutes) compared to professional scanners (one hour and twenty minutes for the scanner Solutionix D500, whose performance was compared with TrueDepth Camera one). As it can be expected, accuracy level is lower than the one of a professional scanner: indeed, some errors were detected even though there was not any relevant difference between the model and the sample dimensions. However, it is safe to state that TrueDepth Camera can be used as an instrument to perform quality control for 3D printing when no submillimetre precision is needed. Moreover, it is believed that it can represent a tool to educate 3D printer users to take into account how relevant is performing quality control and the wastes in terms of material, energy consumption and costs it can help to minimize. The usage can also be suggested to small and medium enterprises that start their approach toward additive manufacturing technologies and do not want or cannot afford a significant investment in an instrument for quality control. Certainly, more investigations should be made regarding the accuracy of the TrueDepth Camera as an instrument for scanning 3D printed products in order to better define the cases in which it is opportune to use it without any concern: in future, it could be studied whether there exist some shapes that are detected in a better manner or whether there are some parameters that influence positively or negatively the acquisition process.

References

1. International Standards Organisation (ISO), Additive manufacturing. General principles, pp. 1–14 (2015)
2. Strategic Report: Additive & Technology Demonstration EDA AM State of the Art & Strategic Report. Additive Manufacturing Feasibility Study and Technology Demonstration, pp. 1–187 (2018)
3. Guo, N., Leu, M.C.: Additive manufacturing: technology, applications and research needs. Front. Mech. Eng. **8**(3), 215–243 (2013)

4. Rayna, T., Striukova, L.: From rapid prototyping to home fabrication: how 3D printing is changing business model innovation. Technol. Forecast. Soc. Change **102**, 214–224 (2016)
5. Górski, F., Kuczko, W., Wichniarek, R.: Influence of process parameters on dimensional accuracy of parts manufactured using Fused Deposition Modelling technology. Adv. Sci. Technol. Res. J. **7**(19), 27–35 (2013)
6. Masood, S.H.: Advances in fused deposition modeling. In: Comprehensive Materials Processing, vol. 10, pp. 69–91. Elsevier Ltd. (2014). https://doi.org/10.1016/B978-0-08-096532-1.01002-5
7. Krafcik, J.F.: Triumph of the lean production system. MIT Sloan Manage. Revi. **30**(1), 41 (1988)
8. Shah, R., Ward, P.T.: Defining and developing measures of lean production. J. Oper. Manage. **25**(4), 785–805 (2007)
9. Ghobadian, A., Talavera, I., Bhattacharya, A., Kumar, V., Garza-Reyes, J.A., O'Regan, N.: Examining legitimatisation of additive manufacturing in the interplay between innovation, lean manufacturing and sustainability. Int. J. Prod. Econ. **219**, 457–468 (2018)
10. Malekipour, E., El-Mounayri, H.: Common defects and contributing parameters in powder bed fusion AM process and their classification for online monitoring and control: a review. Int. J. Adv. Manuf. Technol. **95**(1), 527–550 (2017). https://doi.org/10.1007/s00170-017-1172-6
11. Lezama-Nicolás, R., Rodríguez-Salvador, M., Río-Belver, R., Bildosola, I.: A bibliometric method for assessing technological maturity: the case of additive manufacturing. Scientometrics **117**(3), 1425–1452 (2018). https://doi.org/10.1007/s11192-018-2941-1
12. Crosby, P.B.: Quality is Free: The Art of Making Quality Certain, vol. 94. McGraw-Hill, New York (1979)
13. Huang, Q., Zhang, J., Sabbaghi, A., Dasgupta, T.: Optimal offline compensation of shape shrinkage for three-dimensional printing processes. IIE Trans. **47**(5), 431–441 (2015)
14. Schmutzler, C., Stiehl, T.H., Zaeh, M.F.: Empirical process model for shrinkage-induced warpage in 3D printing. Rapid Prototyping J. **25**, 721–727 (2019)
15. Leary, M.: Surface roughness optimisation for selective laser melting (SLM): accommodating relevant and irrelevant surfaces. In: Laser Additive Manufacturing, pp. 99–118. Woodhead Publishing (2017)
16. Slotwinski, J.A., Garboczi, E.J.: Porosity of additive manufacturing parts for process monitoring. In: AIP Conference Proceedings, vol. 1581, no. 1, pp. 1197–1204. American Institute of Physics (February 2014)
17. Boschetto, A., Bottini, L.: Accuracy prediction in fused deposition modeling. Int. J. Adv. Manuf. Technol. **73**(5-8), 913–928 (2014). https://doi.org/10.1007/s00170-014-5886-4
18. Colosimo, B.M., Huang, Q., Dasgupta, T., Tsung, F.: Opportunities and challenges of quality engineering for additive manufacturing. J. Qual. Technol. **50**(3), 233–252 (2018)
19. Rao, P.K., Liu, J.P., Roberson, D., Kong, Z.J., Williams, C.: Online real-time quality monitoring in additive manufacturing processes using heterogeneous sensors. J. Manuf. Sci. Eng. **137**(6), 061007 (2015)
20. Shirke, A., Choudhari, C., Rukhande, S.: Parametric optimization of fused deposition modelling (FDM) process using PSO algorithm. In: International Conference on Advances in Thermal Systems, Materials and Design Engineering, ATSMDE 2017 (2017)
21. Mokhtarian, H., Hamedi, A., Nagarajan, H., Panicker, S., Coatanéa, E., Haapala, K.: Probabilistic modelling of defects in additive manufacturing: a case study in powder bed fusion technology. Procedia CIRP **81**, 956–961 (2019)
22. Lin, W., Shen, H., Fu, J., Wu, S.: Online quality monitoring in material extrusion additive manufacturing processes based on laser scanning technology. Precis. Eng. **60**, 76–84 (2019)

23. Garza, J.M.: Understanding the adoption of additive manufacturing (Doctoral dissertation, Massachusetts Institute of Technology) (2016)
24. D'Antonio, G., Segonds, F., Laverne, F., Sauza-Bedolla, J., Chiabert, P.: A framework for manufacturing execution system deployment in an advanced additive manufacturing process. Int. J. Prod. Lifecycle Manage. Indersci. **10**(1), 1–19 (2017). hal-01650891. https://doi.org/10.1504/IJPLM.2017.082996

Integration of PLM, MES and ERP Systems to Optimize the Engineering, Production and Business

Venkat Sai Avvaru(✉), Giulia Bruno, Paolo Chiabert, and Emiliano Traini

Politecnico di Torino, Corso Duca degli Abruzzi 24, 10129 Turin, Italy
{venkat.avvaru, giulia.bruno, paolo.chiabert, emiliano.traini}@polito.it

Abstract. In the era of Industry 4.0, the key factor for the success of a company is the cooperation among its different departments in order to share knowledge and information, thus optimizing time and cost. Three core IT systems are usually present in companies: Product Lifecycle Management (PLM), Manufacturing Execution system (MES) and Enterprise Resource Planning (ERP). PLM manages product and process design information, MES monitors and controls the execution of manufacturing process on the shop-floor, and ERP tracks business resources and the status of business commitments. This paper describes the integration process to optimize the engineering, production, business and management activities in a manufacturing company that operates according to the One-of-a-Kind Production (OKP). It explains the architecture of such integration as well as the methodology applied for the customization of the PLM, MES and ERP systems available in the company. Moreover, the paper highlights the specific solutions developed to integrate the data management of the different systems as well as the IoT technology supporting the data communication.

Keywords: PLM · ERP · MES · REST API

1 Introduction

Most of the large-scale enterprises relay on small and medium-sized enterprises (SMEs) for their products and services. SMEs play a vital role for the growth of industries and the economy of a country [1, 2]. Nowadays demand for customized products has been increasing. In addition to customization, customers also expect the products to be delivered in a short time and approximately same cost as mass-produced product with a relative high quality. This market trend requires manufacturing companies to be able to produce customized products rapidly and cheaply with a required quality level. Customization strategies can be particularly observed in companies whose manufacturing processes are dedicated to manufacture the customized products, as considered to be unique product, by performing customer-order driven engineering known as "one-of-a-kind production", OKP [3, 4].

Published by Springer Nature Switzerland AG 2020
F. Nyffenegger et al. (Eds.): PLM 2020, IFIP AICT 594, pp. 70–82, 2020.
https://doi.org/10.1007/978-3-030-62807-9_7

Being most involved in the production of prototypes, OKP companies is of great importance for the collaboration among all the departments and the sharing of knowledge among the personnel. OKP decision making depends on the past learning experiences based on the similar products and processes which enable the designers and operators to adapt and/or modify the manufacturing process to improve the manufacturing efficiency. According to [1], the main strategy in achieving OKP system is the application of flexible automation and information technologies. The three core IT systems usually present in companies are Product Lifecycle Management (PLM), Manufacturing Execution system (MES) and Enterprise Resource Planning (ERP). PLM is a systematic and controlled method for managing and developing industrial manufacturing products and related information. PLM software offers management and control of the product process and the order-delivery process, the control of the product related data throughout the product life cycle, from the initial idea to the scarp yard [5]. MES is an IT tool that enables information exchange between the organizational level of a company and the control systems for the shop-floor, usually consisting in several, different, very customized software applications [6]. ERP is an enterprise-wide information system that integrates and controls all the business processes in the entire organization. It is an industry-driven concept and systems and it is universally accepted by business and organizational industries as a practical solution to achieve an integrated enterprise information system solution. ERP systems track business resources (e.g., cash, raw materials, production capacity) and the status of business commitments (e.g., orders, purchase orders, and payroll). It facilitates information flow between all business functions and manages connections to outside stakeholders.

One of the pillars of Industry 4.0 is the integration among data coming from different systems. The machines of a manufacturing plant are starting to be connected, following the Industrial Internet of Things (IIoT) paradigm. Currently, the usage of IoT is limited to analyze shop floor behavior by monitoring the environment parameters [7]. However, the most significant challenge is to integrate core IT management systems, to combine the end to end process from the manufacturer to the customer with new advanced business models. This paper proposes a model to integrate the core IT systems with the help of IoT technology to perform the end to end process seamlessly in at most real time.

While there is no particularly extensive literature on this subject, production is concentrated in the last few years. It is clear from this literature that the business strategy of a manufacturing company needs the data that are stored in the PLM, ERP and MES [14]. The MES functions and the MES-PLM data transferring is standardized by the ISA95-IEC62264 [15], and the data from the PLM to MES are classified in CAD model, plans, BOM, manufacturing process, work instructions and machine setup, while the flow from MES to PLM is represented by a report in which the production monitoring activity is summarized. The benefits of such integration are clear in the world of research and are also becoming clear among the industrial players who, however, for example in Italy, struggling to invest in the purchase of these three information systems, see the problem of their integration as a distant issue [16].

The rest of the paper is organized as follows: Sect. 2 explains the functionalities of core IT systems in One-of-a-Kind Production. Section 3 explains the architecture of the Integration of PLM, MES, and ERP with the help of REST API protocol. Section 4 presents the application of the framework in the use case for an Italian automotive prototyping company. Finally, Sect. 5 draws conclusion and future work perspectives.

2 Functionalities of Core IT Systems

The main issues associated with the OKP production are the frequent changes in the customer requirements and the inevitable changes occurring during the project management process that will cause delays in the final delivery [8]. For this reason, it is important to have a way of formally defining the work distribution among the different departments and allow them to communicate to manage the changes occurring during the project. Before defining the architecture of integration of three core IT systems, it is important to know the general functionalities of them which are also commonly seen in OKP. As PLM, MES and ERP are three core IT systems within a company, each of them has its own functionalities which help to flow the data seamlessly.

PLM is a design-level computing solution that looks for implementing an information management strategy generated during the life cycle of a product [9]. PLM is more than a computer system or technology, it is a concept, a strategy, that relies on technology to be applied and whose objective is to control and lead the life cycle of a product. The most important functionality of PLM is to manage the data related to the Product design and Process design. Furthermore, Process planning is another key functionality of PLM. Process planning has been defined as "the subsystem responsible for the conversion of design data to work instruction" [10]. A more specific definition of process planning is given as, "The function within a manufacturing facility that establishes the processes and process parameters to be used as well as those machines capable of performing these processes in order to convert a piece-part from its initial form to a final form which is predetermined on a detailed engineering drawing" [11]. To support the design of process plan, the following functionalities are also used:

- *Project management* is a tool that allows the project manager to control the scope and time of a project. The assignees are given the responsibility for specific activities in the project.
- *Parts and BOM management, Parts* are the basic item of any BOM management application, and can be one of the following classification types: Component, Assembly, Material, or Software. A part can be bought, or made in-house. It can have alternates and substitutes. It can have a Bill of Materials (BOM) associated with it, a list of manufacturers (AML) approved for making this part, a list of vendors (AVL) approved for purchasing this part, a list of documents (such as drawings or specs) associated with the part.
- *Change Management Processes,* is a process by which any required changes to parts or documents are initiated, designed, reviewed and implemented. There are three basic items in Change management i.e., problem report (PR), enterprise change request (ECR) and enterprise change order (ECO).
- *Requirements Management,* is a tool which captures, trace and validate all the requirements throughout the development process.

- *Quality Management,* is a tool encompasses of quality planning and quality systems. Quality planning will cover proactive side of quality i.e., the areas that involve design and/or process planning, risk analysis and risk mitigation. Quality Systems will cover the reactive side of Quality i.e., the areas that involve Issue Identification, Containment and Analysis and Corrective/Preventive Actions (CAPA).

MES system must identify the optimal sequence planning considering the constraints of the process, such as the time for setup and processing and the capacity of the workstations, considering the requirements and the necessities given by the organizational level. MES doesn't have only a single function but it has different ones that support, guide and track each of the primary production activities [12]. Functions of MES in OKP are:

- *Operational Scheduling*: It provides sequencing based on priorities, attributes, recipes associated with specific production unit of an operation.
- *Resource allocation and status*: It is a detailed history of resources and ensures that equipment is properly set up for processing and provides status in real time.
- *Product Tracking*: Monitoring the progress of units, batches or lots of output to create a full history of the product.
- *Performance Analysis*: It provides up-to-the-minute reporting of actual manufacturing operations results as well as comparison to history and expected result.
- *Quality Management:* It's a real-time analysis of measurements collected from manufacturing to ensure correct product quality control and identifies problem. It recommends action to correct the problem, correlating the symptom actions and results to determine the cause.

ERP system includes sales and marketing, finance and accounting, purchasing, storage, distribution, human resources and quality control functions [13]. The main functions of ERP in OKP are:

- *Manufacturing*: It provide tools for planning and scheduling, budgeting, forecasting, procurement and materials management.
- *Accounting:* It support accounts receivable, accounts payable and general ledger functions to manage the finances.
- *Customer Relationship Management:* It helps businesses track campaigns, nurture leads and maintain client information.
- *Inventory Management:* It exchanges data with manufacturing, distribution, sales and customer records. This gives greater visibility of the supply chain and help users to predict issues, such as late delivery due to low inventory levels, with greater accuracy.
- *Distribution:* It involves the processes that get a business's product from the warehouse to its final destination. It manages functions like purchasing, order fulfilment, order tracking and customer support.

3 Architecture of Integration of Core IT Systems

Integration of PLM, MES and ERP systems will give the full control over a product from the Customer order to the delivery of a product. It's an end-to-end process where data will flow seamlessly across different departments within the company, thus breaking the walls between the different functional areas in a company. The proposed Architecture for the integration of PLM, MES and ERP consists of a central Intelligence system called Knowledge Base System (KBS). KBS consists of a database in addition to the individual databases of each system. It is a structured central database in which the IT systems can transfer and withdraw the necessary information. It's a bi-directional dataflow between the IT systems and the KBS as shown in Fig. 1.

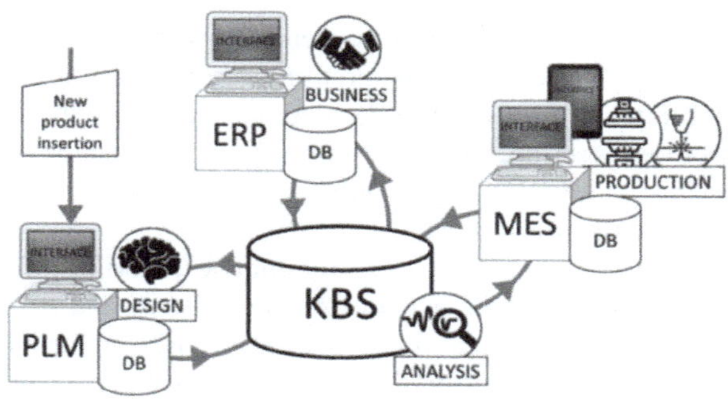

Fig. 1. Conceptual architecture of the knowledge base system

The proposed architecture will allow to collect all the information related to the new component in the KBS system, which helps to perform analysis on a product data. This analysis of product data helps in finding the patterns of different products of a same family, which will reduce the time for the product and process design and able to monitor the performance in the production line. To design such architecture, we have to observe the functional framework in one-of-a-kind production and the data flows among the PLM, MES and ERP.

3.1 Functional Framework in OKP

The generic functional framework in one-of-a-kind production is shown in Fig. 2. The functional framework figure explains that when a new shop order arrives from a customer, ERP as a system will consider and accept the shop order and send the shop order information to PLM to check with the similar Product history thus to interpret the product definition. At this point, KBS as a system plays a key role by providing best possible solution to PLM with similar product history, thus reducing the time in product planning phase. It's a collaborative process of PLM and ERP. Once the product is defined, PLM as a system design the product and processes by comparing with similar product history and share the information with ERP and MES. MES as a system give the command to the shop floor to build a prototype and check for any design modifications. If prototype meet all the constraints of Customer requirements, then MES instruct ERP for the resources allocation as per the demand. ERP instructs the PLM to provide bill of materials (BOM) information and it's a collaborative process of PLM and ERP. Once everything is setup, production process will start and the final product will be controlled by ERP system for the delivery to the customer. KBS as a system gives continuous feedback to the MES for any performance improvement in production line.

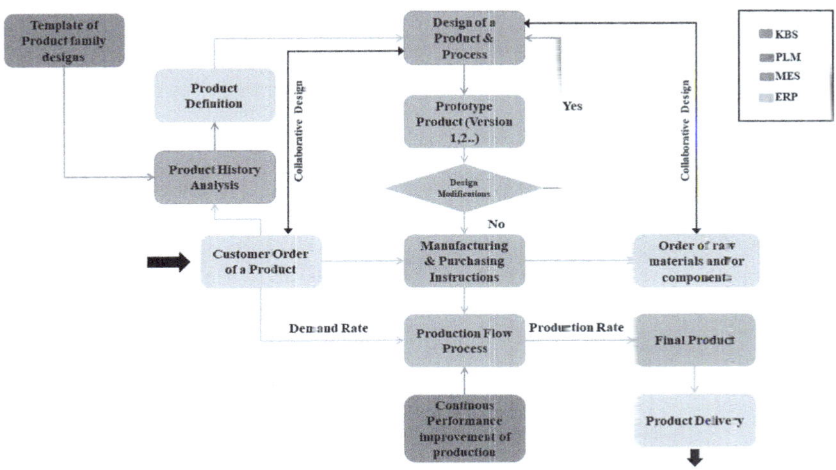

Fig. 2. Functional framework in one-of-a-kind production

As KBS database is a Structural database, it gives full freedom to communicate among the systems. Entity relationship diagram as shown in Fig. 3 explains the data flow among PLM, MES and ERP systems through KBS. When a New shop order arrives from a customer for a specific product, ERP system generate product specifications and store data in the entity called Product. Product Model(s) entity, which is a PLM item, generate one or more models for this product and each model consists of one or more parts (BOM). Manufacturing Process Plan is a PLM entity that defines the parameters of a production cycle for a product model and the corresponding entity called Manufacturing Operations defines the kind of operation, required resources and machines. It shares the relationship with list of operations entity which contains predefined operation details. On the other hand, MES entities called Production Request and Production Planning, help to define the production cycle and can be divided into one or more secondary orders. Production Request contains the data of a production order and Production Planning consists of data to manage the programming of operations of an individual cycle relative to a particular order. One of the key entity of the MES is Production Status because it contains information about the progress of the production. This entity evaluates the data entries to the Physical machine entity. Each one of the Physical Machine entity can have associated at most one Production Status. The Check Start Output entity is linked to the Check Start Machine, which imposes certain controls to monitor before using a machine. Final product entity provides information about the status of a set of by-products and/or final products. This entity evaluates the statements saved in Production Status at time intervals, obtaining result as the status of the articles declared: good, scrap or re-cycle. Final delivery entity, which is a ERP item, stores the data of final products labeled as good and delivered to the customer.

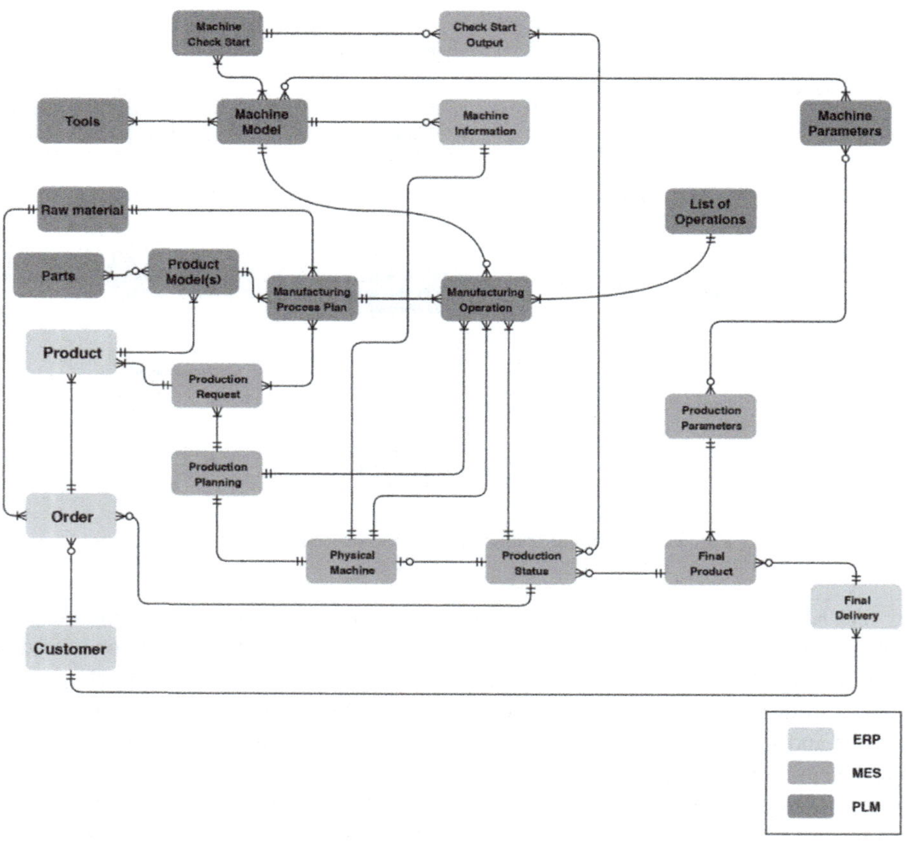

Fig. 3. Entity relationship diagram in KBS DB

3.2 Connectivity

In ground reality, Connectivity is crucial to implement the dataflow among PLM, MES, ERP and KBS. IoT is many things but at the end it's all about connectivity. In 21st century, Application program interface (API) changed the whole concept of connectivity. Currently REST and MQTT API's are predominantly in use. REST (REpresentational State Transfer) is designed as request/response that communicates over HTTP and MQTT (Message Queuing Telemetry Transport) is designed as publish/subscribe that communicates over TCP/IP sockets or WebSockets. MQTT is designed to be a fast and lightweight messaging protocol, and as a result, faster and more efficient than HTTP but MQTT needs a client implementation which is very rare than HTTP client implementation. PLM, MES and ERP are available in the market as an individual software's, so implementation of integration architecture via REST is the best possible choice for now. In REST, requests are made to an application URI and will obtain a response with a payload formatted in HTML, XML, JSON, or some other format. When HTTP is used, most common operations available are GET, HEAD, POST, PUT, PATCH, DELETE, CONNECT, OPTIONS and TRACE. Each application has a specific URL associated with it, that datum can be accessed depending on the syntax of the URL and represented in variety of ways. Each application's REST schema defines the types and specific points of data that can be requested. For example, the PLM schema includes Machine Model, Raw Materials, and so on as a points of data and includes a set of rules about how the request URL must be written in order to access the data. As REST API is a request/response model, we can set the repeat mode to an entity based-on time frame for the request/response depending on the priority. For example, Machine model or Machine Check start entities in PLM are static data to store in KBS which requires less priority compare to Manufacturing Process Plan or Manufacturing Operations.

4 Use Case

Case Study will help researchers to investigate on real world problems and to find solutions for the future progress. This research work will help SME's who follow One-of-a-kind production to integrate the systems in the company for the better efficiency.

4.1 Overview of a Company

The research study was conducted in an Italian company in automotive sector that is dedicated to the design and modifications of mathematical models and fundamentally to the construction of models and prototypes for automobiles. Its main function is to manufacture and assembly of sheet metal and aluminum components for prototypes and small series of automobiles and other road vehicles. The key success factor of this company is producing products which undergo complex manufacturing process in a short time. The company is a tier 2 supplier for global automotive manufacturers. The profile of the company is well suited for One-of-a-kind Production which follows producing customized products as per the customer requirements in a short time.

4.2 Industrial Processes in the Company

Industrial process begins with the new order by a customer who provides CAD Model of a product. The technical department of the company will analyze the CAD model and design the dies, Manufacturing processes and the required material. In the meantime, CAD office will validate the CAD model through simulations. If the Simulations doesn't show any critical issues in the model, it will send to CAM office in order to find the tool paths of milling machines for die construction. In order to accelerate the process and make less mistakes, the company also develop a Styrofoam model as a prototype which meets the requirements. This model will serve as a guide for the next stages. Once the dies are constructed, the metal sheets which are going to use to produce the body part are sent to laser office for trimming with 2D laser machines to obtain exact body outline. Then it will be taken to the sheet metal forming area where it undergoes press operation to acquire the requested shape. The resulting piece will send back to laser office where 3D laser machines cut the metal sheet according to specific laser paths obtaining the final piece. Depending on the complexity of the product, there might be additional operations of pressing and 3D laser cuttings to obtain the perfect finished product as per the customer requirements (Fig. 4).

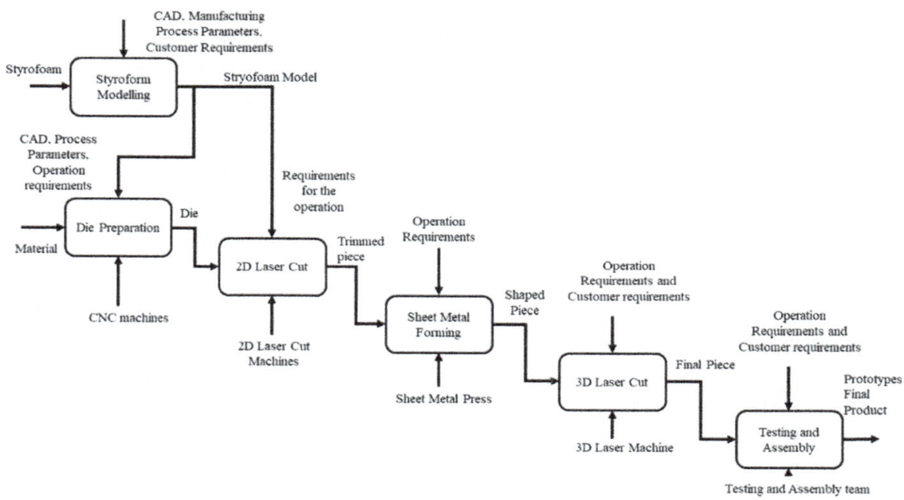

Fig. 4. Industrial process in the company

4.3 Critical Issues in the Company

The production processes performed by the company is extremely variable and difficult: it is difficult to forecast the production trend, problems and misconceptions prevent the plant from having a linear production. The production of prototypes makes the industrial process much more complex compare to the series production. On the other hand, the production of prototypes is characterized by an extremely variable production rate and with high material waste, despite the great experience of the specialized employees. The problems that the company is facing are the type of production (prototype-making) that causes great difficulties in sequencing and scheduling of orders. Another critical issue commonly occurs in the company is the boundaries between departments. For example, in the design phase, role of a designer will end with the design approved by the responsible manager and the designer will not get any feedback on possible problems caused by the design during production. In the same way, shop floor operators will not receive the results of the simulations done by the

CAD office that theoretically indicates the critical issues of the product. The lack of information flow in both directions leads to a lack of continuous learning. Another problem facing by the company is the absence of digital data collection of production systems i.e., no information is collected about the exact number of defectives or material waste. The only relevant data available in the company is the number of pieces produced at the end of the shift. Furthermore, no information is collected regarding the critical issues faced by the operators during the shift which causes dependencies on the experienced professionals of the company. The lack of a structured Knowledge Base System results in production problems and delays when such experienced employees are absent. Another issue commonly seen in OKP is to deal the situation when there are frequent changes in the customer requirements. The proposed architecture solved such problems since the different systems are inter-connected at all the levels and the time to change will be less compare to traditional ways. For example, when the ERP system receives the request for customer change requirements, it asks Manufacturing process plan designer in PLM and Production Manager in MES for the feasibility of customer changes. If it's feasible, changes in the design of product and manufacturing process will be done with a label of new version and the flow of work will be followed as shown in the Fig. 2.

4.4 Implementation of Integrated Architecture

The proposed architecture is an open source data acquisition system able to collect data from multiple applications and provide easy accessibility to such data. Therefore, it is very important to choose software's and the best technology which can give full freedom to the application engineer to create or modify the items and relationship with other items according to the integrated architecture. For this reason, the prototyping system has been developed with the following software's: Aras Innovator is an open source PLM software which gives freedom to customize the PLM platform according to the company needs; JPIANO is an MES application; eSOLVER is an ERP application, Node-RED is an open source application used as a platform to call REST API's, to process the data and push the data to KBS database; PostgreSQL is an open source database used as KBS database.

To implement the complex architecture described in Fig. 3, we used Node-Red application to define the data flow from PLM database to KBS database, from ERP database to KBS database and vice versa. Since Aras PLM software provides 'uri' which is an URL address to a specific item, it gave possibility to extract the data using REST API. In the same way, we can also extract the data from ERP system. The database of MES system is incorporated with KBS database since the data of MES systems are very dynamic in nature. Figures 5 and 6 explain the data flow architecture among the systems. By exploiting the open source Node-Red packages, different nodes are used to serve the purpose. In the presented work, system gets the data via REST API 'GET' request, clean and structure the data as per the KBS database (PostgreSQL) format and sends to the KBS database via 'POST'/'UPDATE' request. As REST API is a request/response based, the system performs several iterations based on time interval and compares the acquired data with the existing data in KBS database. If the data is new, then it will 'POST' the data into the KBS database or, if a value of specific property of an entity is changed, it will perform 'UPDATE' operation. In the same way, another set of nodes will check for new data available in the KBS and perform 'POST'/'UPDATE' operation on the corresponding uri in the application database.

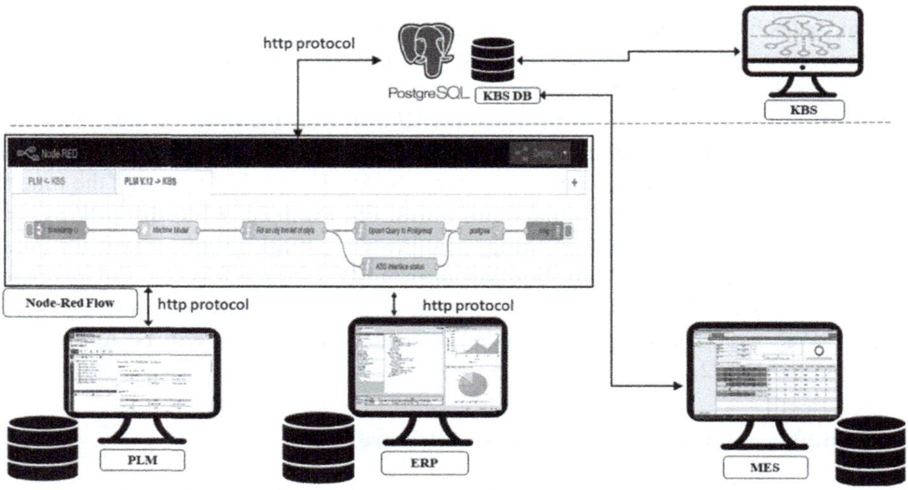

Fig. 5. Data flow architecture among the systems

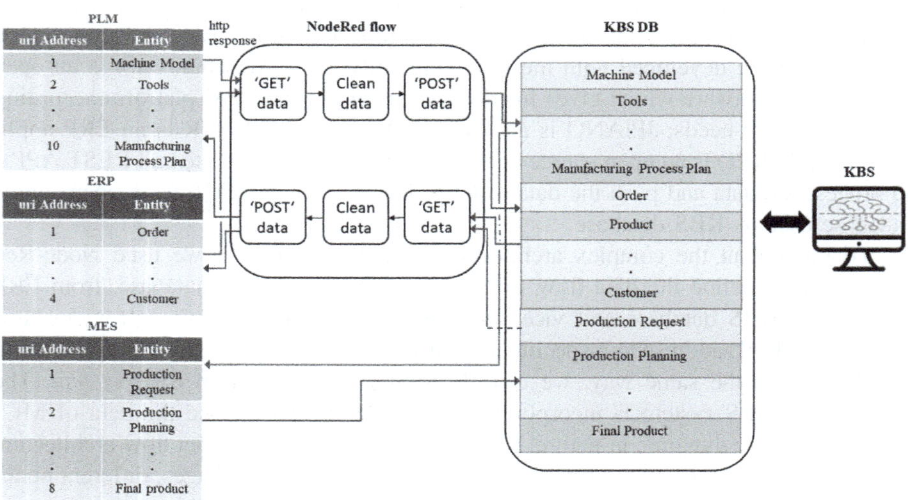

Fig. 6. Detail data flow architecture

5 Conclusion and Future Works

The objective of this paper is to propose a framework to integrate design, production and business systems which helps in reducing the time and cost to produce the product, especially in the companies who follow OKP which usually leads to the inevitable changes occurs in various stages of production. The framework is also an end-to-end process where data will flow seamlessly across different departments within the company, thus breaking the walls between the different functional areas. The system presented in this paper is a Knowledge base system which collects and integrates PLM, MES and ERP data, thus helps to find the uncertainties that occur during the design or production phase. The presented system is installed in the company and it's in a testing phase, which are performing by company design team, operators and other workers.

Our most promising future works will be generating the key performance indicators of various degrees and the application of various Machine Learning techniques to analyze the KBS data which helps in finding the patterns of different products of a same family, which will further reduce the time for the product and process design and able to monitor the performance in the production line.

References

1. Svensson, C., Barfod, A.: Limits and opportunities in mass customization for build-to-order SMEs. Comput. Ind. **49**, 77–89 (2002)
2. Bruno, G., Taurino, T., Villa, A.: An approach to support SMEs in manufacturing knowledge organization. J. Intell. Manuf. **29**(6), 1379–1392 (2016)
3. Wortmann, J.C., Muntslag, D.R., Timmermans, P.J.M.: Customer-Driven Manufacturing. Chapman & Hall, London (1997). ISBN 041-2570-300
4. Traini, E., Bruno, G., Awouda, A., Chiabert, P., Lombardi, F.: Integration between PLM and MES for one-of-a-kind production. In: Fortin, C., Rivest, L., Bernard, A., Bouras, A. (eds.) PLM 2019. IAICT, vol. 565, pp. 356–365. Springer, Cham (2019). https://doi.org/10.1007/978-3-030-42250-9_34
5. Saaksvuori, A., Immonen, A.: Product Lifecycle Management. Springer, Heidelberg (2008). https://doi.org/10.1007/978-3-540-78172-1
6. Meyer, H., Fuchs, F., Thiel, K.: Manufacturing Execution Systems (MES): Optimal Design, Planning, and Deployment. McGraw-Hill Professional, New York (2009)
7. Kambarov, I., D'Antonio, G., Aliev, K., Chiabert, P., Inoyatkhodjaev, J.: Uzbekistan towards Industry 4.0. Defining the gaps between current manufacturing systems and Industry 4.0. In: Chiabert, P., Bouras, A., Noël, F., Ríos, J. (eds.) PLM 2018. IAICT, vol. 540, pp. 250–260. Springer, Cham (2018). https://doi.org/10.1007/978-3-030-01614-2_23
8. Bruno, G., Traini, E., Lombardi, F.: A knowledge-based system for collecting and integrating production information. In: Camarinha-Matos, L.M., Afsarmanesh, H., Antonelli, D. (eds.) PRO-VE 2019. IAICT, vol. 568, pp. 163–170. Springer, Cham (2019). https://doi.org/10.1007/978-3-030-28464-0_15
9. Bruno, G., Korf, R., Lentes, J., Zimmermann, N.: Efficient management of product lifecycle information through a semantic platform. Int. J. Prod. Lifecycle Manag. **9**(1), 45–64 (2016)
10. Link, C.H.: CAPP-CAM-I automated process planning system. In: Proceedings of the 1976 NC Conference (1976)

11. Chang, T.C., Wysk, R.A.: An Introduction to Computer-Aided Process Planning Systems. Prentice Hall, Upper Saddle River (1985)
12. Greeff, G., Ghoshal, R.: Practical E-Manufacturing and Supply Chain Management. Newnes, Oxford (2004). ISBN 9780080473857
13. Sousa, J.E., Collado, J.P.: Towards the unification of critical success factors for ERP implementations. In: Paper Presented in 10th Annual Business Information Technology Conference, Manchester (2000)
14. Joshi, S.: ERP-MES-PLM integration-making information technology strategy compliment business strategy. In: IADIS International Conference on Information System, IS 2009, Barcelona, Spain (2009)
15. ISA-95: Enterprise Control System Integration (2000). http://www.isa-95.com/
16. D'Antonio, G., Macheda, L., Sauza Bedolla, J., Chiabert, P.: PLM-MES integration to support Industry 4.0. In: Ríos, J., Bernard, A., Bouras, A., Foufou, S. (eds.) PLM 2017. IAICT, vol. 517, pp. 129–137. Springer, Cham (2017). https://doi.org/10.1007/978-3-319-72905-3_12

Analyses and Study of Human Operator Monotonous Tasks in Small Enterprises in the Era of Industry 4.0

Paolo Chiabert[1,2] and Khurshid Aliev[1,2](✉)

[1] Politecnico di Torino, Corso Duca degli Abruzzi 24, 10129 Turin, Italy
{paolo.chiabert,khurshid.aliev}@polito.it
[2] Turin Polytechnic University in Tashkent, Kichik Halqa Yuli 17, 100095 Tashkent, Uzbekistan

Abstract. Attraction towards Industry 4.0 is evolving in the academic and industrial communities providing new solutions to reduce the workload of human operators by integrating new technologies into the manufacturing processes. To reduce human operators' time and/or reduce performance of boring tasks, collaborative robots (cobots) can be integrated into workplaces. The term cobots (collaborative robots) designed for cage-free work or that which contains robots that can directly work with human workers without safety barriers on the manufacturing floor. Recent cobots consist of human like arms which can be a supporting tool for the human worker or it can assist him as a co-worker in the same workplace.

This paper provides results of study of human operator's workplaces in small and medium enterprises (SME) to integrate enabling technologies of industry 4.0 and to find new solutions to reduce work load and to increase the productivity of production. In SMEs there are many cases where human operators perform monotonous tasks, implementation of cobots and mobile robots to the workplaces can provide good support for monotonous tasks of human workers, handling the tasks that require high precision or repeatability. The paper describes the integration of cobots into the workplace of a manufacturing company where monotonous, cumbersome and stressing activities affect the wellness of the workers. The paper analyzes the current workflow and the ergonomic load of the worker, further developing the appropriate task distribution between human and robotic operators and demonstrates open source technologies to accomplish human robot collaborative applications.

Keywords: Cobots · Ergonomics · SWOT analyses

1 Introduction

Industry 4.0 (I4.0) is evolving in academics and companies trying to find new solutions to reduce work load and increase productivity of productions by integrating new technologies into the sector. For example, to reduce human operators' process time and/or reduce the burden of tedious tasks, collaborative robots (cobots) could be integrated into workplaces. The term cobots (collaborative robots) designates cage-free

Published by Springer Nature Switzerland AG 2020
F. Nyffenegger et al. (Eds.): PLM 2020, IFIP AICT 594, pp. 83–97, 2020.
https://doi.org/10.1007/978-3-030-62807-9_8

robot that can directly work with human workers without safety barriers on the manufacturing floor. Recent cobots are human like arms which can act as a tool for human worker or as co-worker in the same workplace as shown in Fig. 1. In the following research papers integration of collaborative and mobile robots into human workspaces for repetitive tasks execution have been studied. Automatic progressive framework proposed in [1] where the operator programs a collaborative robot by demonstrating a task in which the robot performs pick and place repetitive movements autonomously after an unknown number of demonstrations. The results of the paper [1] have been demonstrated in laboratory level and have not been implemented in a real industrial case scenario. Task-based programming and task sequence planning method for human robot collaborative assembly was proposed in [2] where the contemporary collaborative work of robots and humans share tasks in the same workspace and executes assembly jobs. Unlike in [3] proposed a multi criteria method for planning of shared human robot collaborative assembly tasks. The product assembly sequence is generated from CAD models. The proposed method has been evaluated in automotive industry based on ergonomics, quality, technical feasibility and productivity criteria. In [4] authors demonstrated collaborative industrial like task execution where the agents are human operator, mobile robot and the manipulator. In case study of [4] robot manipulator finds a workpiece using a camera that is randomly positioned on the mobile robot and executes pick and place tasks. Applicability of commercially available open source components and integration of different technologies belonging to industrial robotics and commercial components into one eco-system is presented in [5] and studied the integration of different I4.0 enabling technologies namely: Robotics, IoT and fog/edge computing.

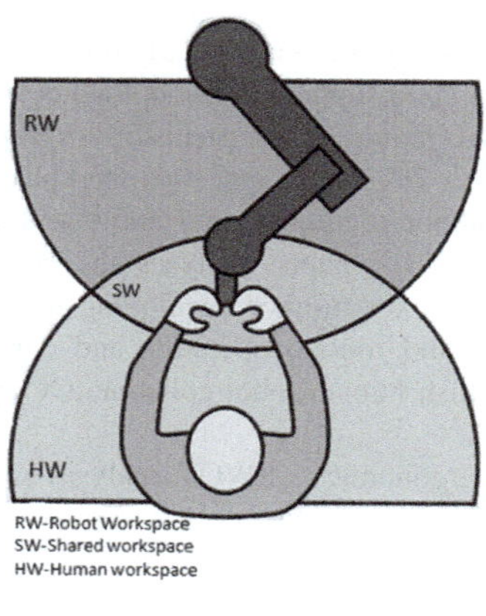

Fig. 1. Human operator and robot workspace's source from [6].

In contrast to the above-mentioned researches, this paper studies current manufacturing processes in an SME by identifying operator tasks workload and operator ergonomics. Further, based on the ergonomic assessment worksheet (EAWS) results, different solutions to reduce human operator workload in repetitive tasks are proposed.

Depending on the workpiece component, different ideas to design the integration of modern robots into the work cell is discussed.

The paper is organized according to the following topics: problem definition and description by analyzing the condition of the SME; human operator's repetitive task analyses using ergonomic evaluation tool and requirements for integrating new technologies; proposed scenarios SWOT analyses and conclusions.

2 Description of the Problem

In spite of I4.0 era, in SMEs there are still situations where human operators perform monotonous tasks. In the company under study, one such tedious task consists of detaching the metal components from the metal sheet after a laser-cut. An example is shown in Fig. 2(A) represents general view of metal sheet and Fig. 2(B) where the metal components that are supposed to be detached after laser-cut have micro joints to avoid their unwanted detachment.

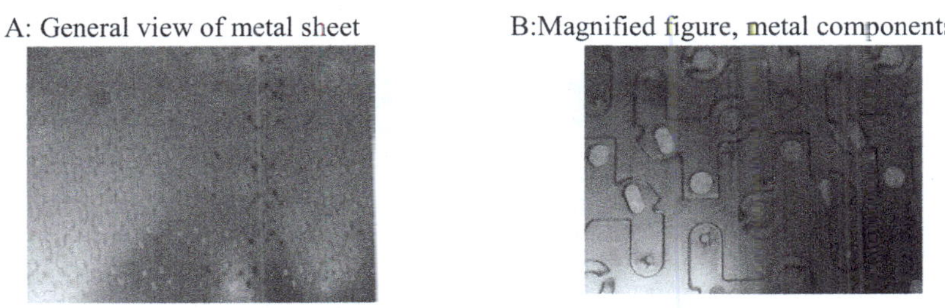

Fig. 2. Detachable metal components in the metal sheet with micro joints

Figure 3 shows laser cut components in the metal sheet. Moreover, the figure depicts the micro joint position and space between the component and metal sheet that is less than 2 mm.

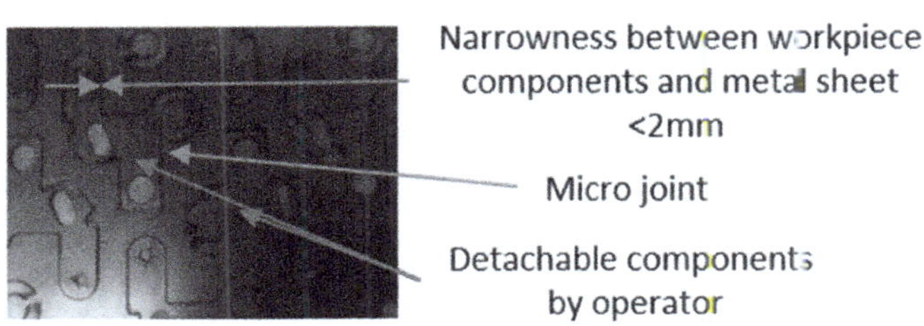

Fig. 3. Detached metal components from the metal sheet by operator.

The detachment tasks are time-consuming and provide stress to the human operator. Moreover, if micro joints are present, the human operator cannot detach workpieces just by hand, he/she usually uses extra forces (using rubber mullet or vibration hammer with air) to detach the workpieces from the metal sheet.

After a few hours of such repetitive work, the human worker gets exhausted and sometimes the workpieces are deformed. Integration of robots into the workplace, could reduce stress and time of the human workers and improve the ergonomics of the workstation.

2.1 Human Operator Workflow to Detach Metallic Components After Laser Cut

In this chapter, a detailed description of the work process is provided. Figure 4 represents a workplace and the work process of the human operator that removes components from the metal sheet after laser-cut. To understand operator monotonous tasks and workplace ergonomics, daily works of the operator have been divided into small parts and analyzed: starting from placing metal sheet after laser-cut to the workplace of the human operator, removing components, sorting and placing removed components to the boxes, transporting packed boxes and removing remained metal sheets from the workplace. Workflow steps of the tasks during the working process are shown in Fig. 5.

Fig. 4. On the left: manual detaching; on the right: detaching with instrument

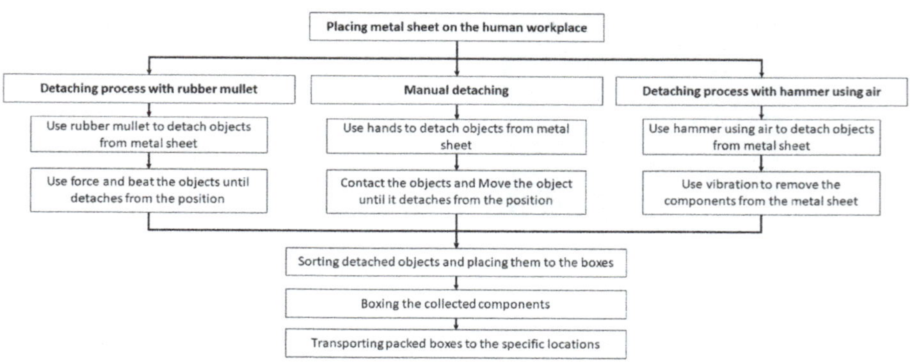

Fig. 5. Process flow of the human operator.

The workflow of the human worker described in Fig. 5 compose of three main detaching methodologies: manual detaching; detaching using rubber mullet and detaching using a vibrating hammer.

Each approach process is described in detail and after removing components a human worker places the components into boxes and transports boxed components to the specific locations.

A repetitive work performance by the operator usually lasts from one to five minutes and duration depends on the size (thickness, width and height) of the metal sheet and a number of components.

To understand the physical tasks of the human operator, five minutes of working time has been recorded, observed and described in the following:

1. Go to laser-cut machine and pick up the metal sheet (5 kg, from 400 mm above floor height, at a horizontal distance of 1000 mm), bring the metal sheet to the workstation (distance <2 m) and place it on the workplace (workplace table size – 1600 × 3300 × 1030 cm).
2. Detach the components by pushing and pulling up and down vertically with a force <0,3 N.
3. Collect all detached components into the boxes.
4. Place boxed components (weight 1–7 kg) to container (distance <2 m).

The process flow and the observed five minutes of working time give a clear view about operator repetitive works and possible integration of new technologies for each phase of the tasks and to develop applications to reduce operator time and remove monotonous works.

2.2 Conditions and Requirements of the Workplace to Integrate Industry 4.0 Components and Tools

Before reorganizing workplace and integrating new types of robots (mainly cobots) with grasping techniques, the condition of the workstation and detaching tasks of the human worker have been studied. The workplace situation and some important features of the detaching components from metal sheet have been identified as follows:

Condition and situation of the workplace of the operator during detaching tasks:

- The gap between workpiece components and the metal sheet is <2 mm: sometimes, the human operator faces complex tasks to enter with finger and detach the component. In this case, he uses external tools such as magnets or vibration hammer using compressed air that is noisy.
- Between workpiece components and metal sheet (blank) might have more than one micro joints.
- The laser-cut metal sheet is on the 2D surface.
- Industrial condition - metal sheet might have dust, burr after laser cut.
- Metal workpiece components might have different holes.
- Different 2D shaped workpiece components in the same metal sheet.

Requirements for the robot in workstation:

- Grasping gripper of the robot must be able to hold metallic components after laser-cutting
- The robot should work in the same workspace with a human operator.

Knowing the situation and workplace condition of the operator, integration of cobots could be a right approach for several reasons:

- Capability to work in the same workplace as a human operator;
- Reduce the workload of the operator by taking dexterity tasks;
- The working duration can be set up longer than the human operator;
- Flexibility and adaptability for different tasks in different workspaces;
- Ability to work in industrial condition including in dust and polluted air;

These working conditions and requirements of the human operator give a better understanding of the workplace constraints before implementing new tools and technologies.

3 Ergonomic Work Assessment of Human Operator

Before implementing new technologies at the workplace of the human operator, the physical workloads of the worker at the workstation have been evaluated.

To perform ergonomic work assessment of the operator there are different screening tools and methodologies. In [7], rapid entire body assessment(REBA) tool is presented. REBA is used to assess selected body posture, forceful exertions, type of movement or action, repetition and coupling of the operator. To evaluate the posture, force and movement associated with sedentary tasks Rapid Upper Limb Assessment (RULA) method is developed in [8]. Ovako Working Posture Analysing System (OWAS) is a method to identify and evaluate poor working postures [9]. OWAS considers factors such as health and safety but mainly focuses on the discomfort caused by the working postures [10]. Unlike abovementioned tools, EAWS [11] is a tool to assess holistic physical workloads. The EAWS tool is developed based on ISO standards [12–14] and it evaluates physical workload only on a three zone (traffic light scheme). In this paper, EAWS tool is selected to assess the physical workload of the operator because it gives a very quick mapping of the different risk areas of all working tasks and to concentrate all the efforts for rapid redesigning.

EAWS tool evaluation is based on printed assessment worksheet paper and pen. Evaluation using EAWS comprehends four sections: evaluation of working postures and movements with low additional physical efforts between 3–4 kg; action forces of the whole body or hand-finger system; manual materials handling and repetitive loads of the upper limbs.

To evaluate the workload of the operator during the removal of metal components from the metal sheet, the process flow described in Fig. 5 and observed five minutes working process in Subsect. 2.2 have been used.

The first assessment using the EAWS tool is estimating the load of the manual material handling per shift (8 h).

First manual detaching of metal components from metal sheet has been evaluated. It is assumed that human operator handles detaching the metal components (<3 kg) by pushing and pulling - 1 point; for the posture is up right and/or not twisted load at the body while detaching – 1 point; holding load manipulation time per shift around 73 min – 5 points. For carrying the load it is assumed that the metal sheet is less than 10 kg – 1.5 points; during loading the metal sheet human operator posture is little trunk bending, sometimes twisted and the component is close to the body – 2 points; duration holding time is less than 2,5 min - 1 point. Manual material handling result for detaching and carrying the load can be estimated as follows:

$$Result = (Load + posture + condition\ points) * duration\ points \quad (1)$$

Afterwards, the sum of all results in 13,5 as shown in line 19 of Fig. 6. Such value is slightly less than 15, which is the maximum cumulative duration point for all manual tasks.

$$Manual\ Handling = \sum line\ 19 \quad (2)$$

Manual material handling assessment shows that the load of the operator can be reduced and could be a reason to redesign the workplace.

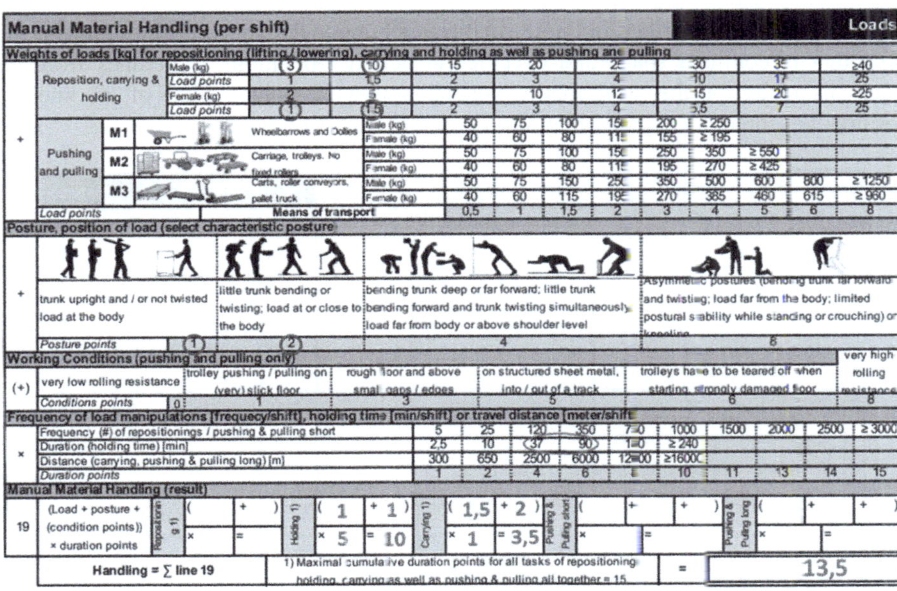

Manual Material Handling (per shift) — Loads

Weights of loads [kg] for repositioning (lifting / lowering), carrying and holding as well as pushing and pulling

Reposition, carrying & holding									
Male (kg)	(3)	(10)	15	20	25	30	35	≥40
Load points	1	1,5	2	3	4	10	17	25
Female (kg)	2	5	7	10	12	15	20	≥25
Load points	(1)	(1,5)	2	3	4	5,5	7	25

Pushing and pulling										
M1 Wheelbarrows and Dollies	Male (kg)	50	75	100	150	200	≥ 250			
	Female (kg)	40	60	80	115	155	≥ 195			
M2 Carriage, trolleys. No fixed rollers	Male (kg)	50	75	100	150	250	350	≥ 550		
	Female (kg)	40	60	80	115	195	270	≥ 425		
M3 Carts, roller conveyors, pallet truck	Male (kg)	50	75	150	250	350	500	600	800	≥ 1250
	Female (kg)	40	60	115	195	270	385	460	615	≥ 960
Load points	Means of transport	0,5	1	1,5	2	3	4	5	6	8

Posture, position of load (select characteristic posture)

	trunk upright and / or not twisted load at the body	little trunk bending or twisting; load at or close to the body	bending trunk deep or far forward; little trunk bending forward and trunk twisting simultaneously; load far from body or above shoulder level	Asymmetric postures (bending trunk far forward and twisting; load far from the body; limited postural stability while standing or crouching) or kneeling
Posture points	(1)	(2)	4	8

Working Conditions (pushing and pulling only)

	very low rolling resistance	trolley pushing / pulling on (very) slick floor	rough floor and above small gaps / edges	on structured sheet metal, into / out of a track	trolleys have to be teared off when starting, strongly damaged floor	very high rolling resistance
Conditions points	0	1	3	5	6	8

Frequency of load manipulations [frequecy/shift], holding time [min/shift] or travel distance [meter/shift]

Frequency (#) of repositionings / pushing & pulling short	5	25	120	350	750	1000	1500	2000	2500	≥ 3000
Duration (holding time) [min]	2,5	10	(37	90)	150	≥ 240				
Distance (carrying, pushing & pulling long) [m]	300	650	2500	6000	12000	≥16000				
Duration points	1	2	4	6	8	10	11	13	14	15

Manual Material Handling (result)

		Repositioning 1)	Holding 1)	Carrying 1)	Pushing & Pulling short	Pushing & Pulling long
19	(Load + posture + condition points))	(+)	(1 + 1)	(1,5 + 2)	(+ +)	(+ +)
	× duration points	× =	× 5 = 10	× 1 = 3,5	× =	× =

Handling = ∑ line 19	1) Maximal cumulative duration points for all tasks of repositioning holding, carrying as well as pushing & pulling all together = 15	=	13,5

Fig. 6. Manual material handling assessment.

Next step is to assess forces applied onto arms and whole body using the EAWS tool. One time detachment of metal component requires 3 s. Force applied onto the arm can be calculated as intensity per duration that is 3 points. Since the operator doesn't apply other forces to the body sum of all actions remain 3 as shown in Fig. 7.

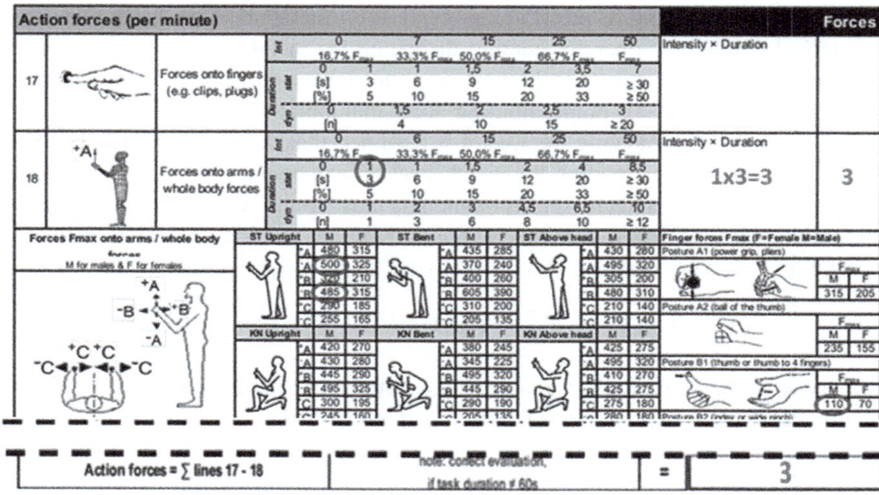

Fig. 7. Action force evaluation.

For the last tasks, 3 and 4 in Subsect. 2.2 that are boxing components and placing boxed components to the container operator uses additional force between 40–70 N and weights below 7 kg. These tasks have been evaluated using postures part of the EAWS worksheet described in Fig. 8. In our tasks operator stands in front of a working table that is confined space and executes detaching operations sometimes from far reach distances for this asymmetric posture assigns 2 points. Sum of all lines of postures is scored 15 points which represents "green" situation.

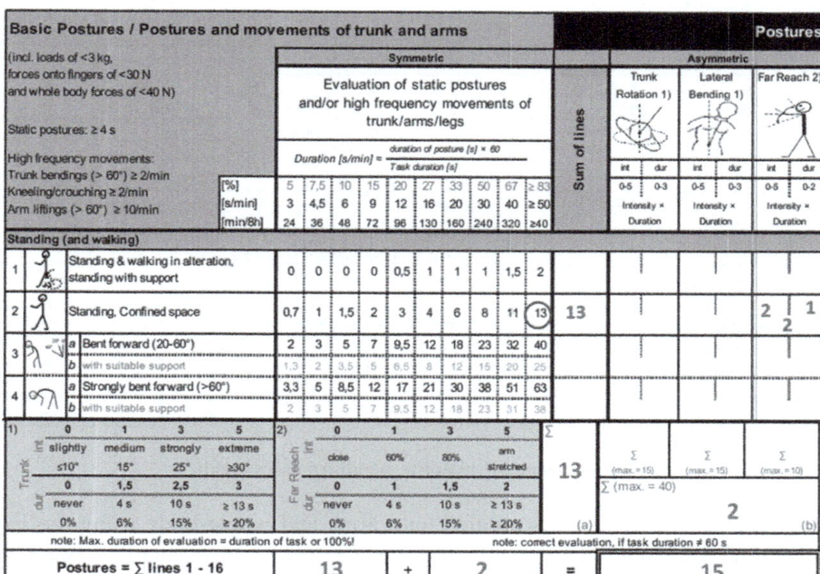

Fig. 8. Postures evaluation.

In Fig. 9, extra points are given for using extra tools depending on tools' weight and frequency of use. Since the operator sometimes uses rubber mullet or vibrating hammer, multiplying intensity and frequency of use those tools assigns 5 points in this section.

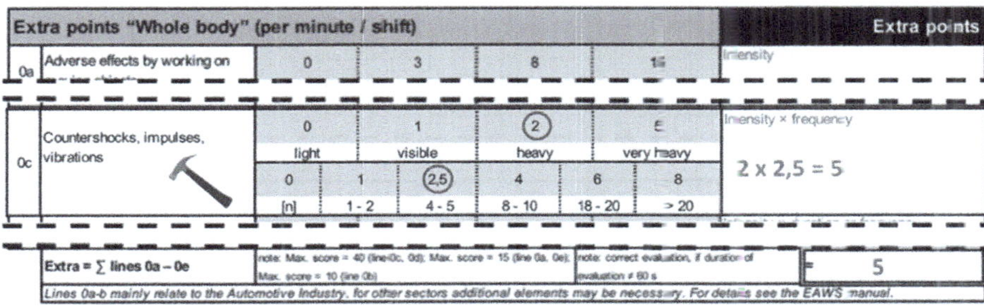

Fig. 9. Extra points for using extra tools.

The final evaluation of the "whole body load" of the operator is estimated by summing all part that is 15 points (working postures) plus 3 points (action forces) plus 13,5 points (manual materials handling loads) plus 5 points (Extra tools) equals 36,5 points that are shown in Fig. 10. This means the overall result is still in the "yellow" road.

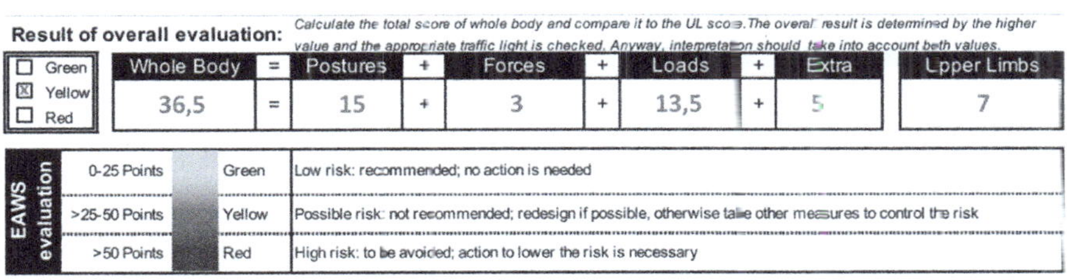

Fig. 10. Assessment of whole body.

To perform a full evaluation, upper limbs load in repetitive tasks have been evaluated in Fig. 11 and scored 7 points that is in "green" road but not added to the whole body.

After evaluations, the results of the EAWS tool showed risky sections such as manual handling and postures that could be reduced by integrating new technologies and that can lead to redesign the workstation.

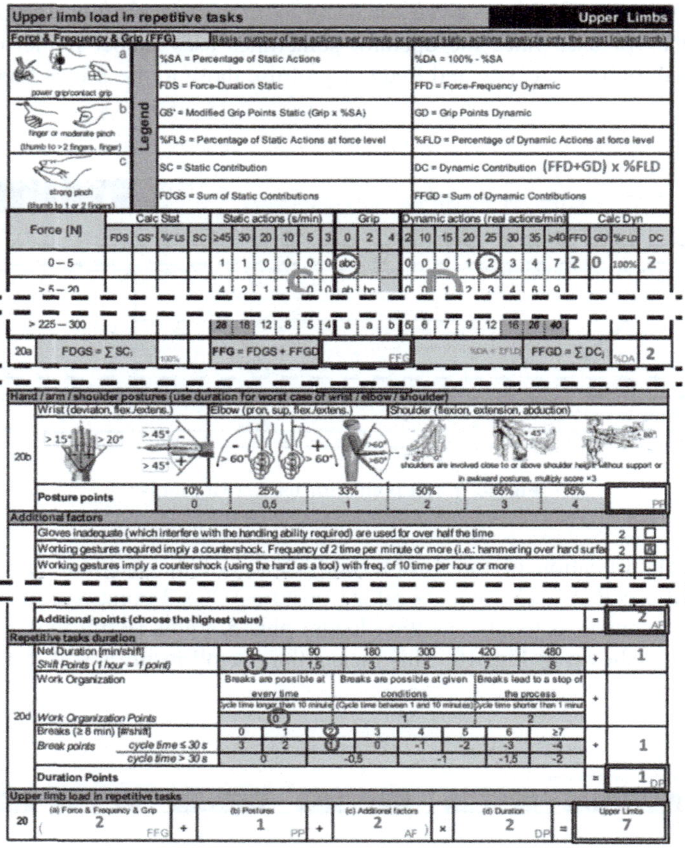

Fig. 11. Upper limbs evaluation section

4 Proposal of Collaborative Robot Integration in Human Operator Workplace

To develop a human-robot interaction system for the detaching of metal components, different levels of interaction in the shared workspace can be defined. In Fig. 12, there are different interaction levels [6] and different integration of cobots into the human workplace:

- the robot is operated in a traditional cage - *cell*;
- human and fence free robot work alongside each other but do not share a workspace - *coexistence*;
- the human worker and the robot share a workspace but only one of the interaction partners is actually present in the workspace at any one time – *synchronized*;

- both interaction partners may have tasks to perform at the same time in the (shared) workspace, but they do not work simultaneously on the same product or component – *cooperation*;
- human worker and robot work simultaneously on the same product or component - *collaboration*.

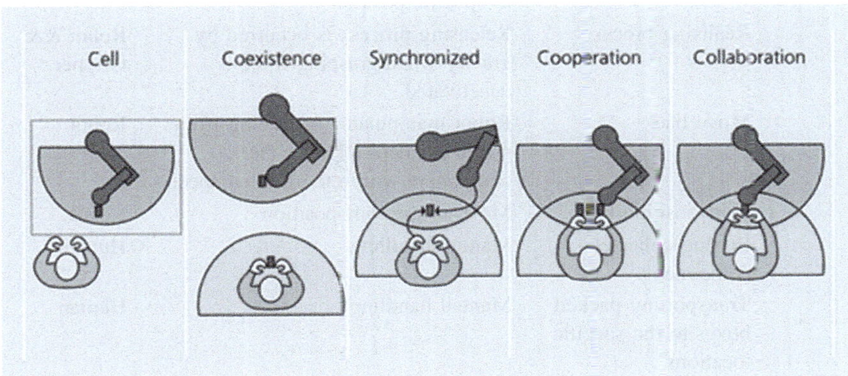

Fig. 12. Different levels of cooperation between a human operator and a robot source from [6].

After the identification of the interaction levels, tasks distribution between human-robot interaction system (HRIS), human operator and robot manipulator has been identified and described in Table 1.

Table 1. Task distribution between human operator, robot manipulator and HRIS.

Processes	Process descriptions	Approach description	Work distribution in processes
1	Placing metal sheet on the workplace	Manual placement into the reference position	Human
2	Get positions and orientations of all target components	Estimate component locations: Using CAD file or vision system	HRIS
3	Approaching to the component	The gripper is positioned near by the target component	Robot
3.1	Coming into contact	Gripper is almost in contact with the target component	Robot && Gripper
3.2	Grasp the component	Contact is achieved	Robot && Gripper
3.3	Detaching action	Moving the gripper in different directions in such a way that detaches the metal component	Robot/Human-Robot/Gripper

(continued)

Table 1. (*continued*)

Processes	Process descriptions	Approach description	Work distribution in processes
3.4	Moving process	The gripper and component are joined and component can be moved to specific position	Robot && Gripper
3.5	Realising process	Releasing process is occurred by gravity when grasping force is deactivated	Robot && Gripper
3.6	Move back	Robot manipulator is moving from position where released the component within the limited speed	Robot
3.7	Start position back	Move to the start position	Robot
4	Boxing collected components	Manual handling	Human
5	Transporting packed boxes to the specific locations	Manual handling	Human

Knowing the interaction levels of human and robot, three ideas have been realized. Short description of the case studies are described as following:

(1) Metal component detaching that has micro joints using *human-robot collaboration approach*: If the metal sheet components have micro joints, human-robot collaboration approach can be used where the tasks are performed in the same time by human and robot. The workflow is the following:
A human operator enters the coordinates of the metal sheet component using the teaching pendant or reading the CAD file; robot holds the workpiece while the human operator detaches the workpiece applying some force to different directions; robot moves the detached workpiece to the target position.
After each detaching task, the human operator enters new coordinates to detach a new workpiece or manipulator reads new coordinates from the CAD file of the metal sheet.

(2) Metal component detaching that has micro joints using *human-robot cooperation approach*: If the metal components have micro joints, human-robot cooperative approach can be used. In this case, a human operator enters the coordinates of the workpieces using the teaching pendant reading the CAD file; a cobot manipulator moves to the workpiece and applies appropriate movements to detach the workpiece; robot moves the detached workpieces to the target position; the human operator waits until robot manipulator finishes its task, then he or she enters new coordinates or reads again coordinates from the CAD file to perform new tasks. For every new component dedicated activity is in a sequence not at the same time.

(3) *Automatic detaching* of metallic components approach can be applied when there are no micro joints in the metal components: robot reads from the CAD file of the metal sheet the coordinates of the metal component; robot reaches the workpiece position, actives the robot gripper to grab the workpiece; robot moves to the stocked position and releases the workpiece;

In the next section, there is a SWOT analysis of the proposed approaches. It provides a valuable description of the processes and contributes to evaluating future strategies.

4.1 SWOT Analysis of Proposed Approaches

Smart selection and integration of robust and inexpensive workstation in a company can support the longevity of production lines and improve financial situation. For proposed approaches, SWOT analyses [15] have been performed as a tool for strategic alternatives. Table 2 shows the SWOT analyses results. The strength of the automatic approach is more than other approaches but it should work for 24 h that means the company has to pay anyways for the electric power and there is no human monitoring during unattended work shifts. On the contrary, the automatic approach can completely reduce operator tasks but the threat in this case operators lose their jobs. Integrating Human-robot collaborative/cooperative approaches lead the integration of new robots to the workstations and operators remain in their positions with robots but they are required to be reskilled.

Table 2. SWOT analyses results

	Strength	Weaknesses	Opportunities	Threats
Human-robot collaboration/cooperation approach	• Robot takes dexterity works of the human • More precise than human • Passing repetitive tasks to robot • Safe approach for operator	• Work duration is equal to human working hour 8 h • Human and robot work simultaneously and in sequence that means more time required to execute tasks compare to automatic approach • Redesign a workstation to integrate cobots	• Integration new enabling technologies • Possible to perform multiple tasks in the same time • Flexibility of robots that can be integrated to other applications • Less risk to lose human operator job. They still work together in these two approaches	• Buying robot and paying salary to operator • Lack of operator skills to work with robots

(*continued*)

Table 2. (*continued*)

	Strength	Weaknesses	Opportunities	Threats
Automatic approach	• Robot works in 24 h autonomously • The same time can perform multiple tasks • More reliable approach compare to other approaches • More safe than other two approaches, no interaction of operator • Robot can work in industrial condition including in dust and polluted air	• Power consumption 24 h • Redesign a workstation to substitute operator with a robot • Lack of monitoring	• Remove risks from operator by integrating automatic detaching system using robots	• High risks to lose jobs for human operators

5 Conclusions and Future Works

Analyses of workflow and ergonomics of physical workloads at the workstation of the human operator during repetitive work to remove components from metal sheet after laser-cut in SME has been evaluated using the EAWS tool. A final evaluation of EAWS worksheet resulted with 36,5 points for "whole body load" of the operator that is the sum of all sections: 15 points (working postures) plus 3 points (action forces) plus 13,5 points (manual materials handling loads) plus 5 points (Extra tools). According to the EAWS tool, the overall result is in "yellow" road that means there is a possible risk and if possible redesign workstation or "manual material handling loads" and "posture" sections points that are high points can be reduced by integrating new I4.0 technologies. For this reason, three ideas have been proposed (human-robot collaborative, human-robot cooperative and automatic detaching approaches). By integrating collaborative robots to the human operator workstation, a company can reduce physical loads of the operator in repetitive works. Afterwards, SWOT analyses of three methods have been performed to choose for the company the best approach to redesign workstation of the operator. The results of SWOT analyses suggest to redesign (if necessary) workplace of the operator by integrating automatic approach that has more strength to detach metallic components. This approach must be considered if there are no micro joints on the components. For the components with micro joints human-robot collaborative or cooperative approach can be implemented. In the future, the redesigned workplace of the operator with cobot and above mentioned approaches will be studied and evaluated.

References

1. Dimeas, F., Fotiadis, F., Papageorgiou, D., Sidiropoulos, A., Doulgeri, Z.: Towards progressive automation of repetitive tasks through physical human-robot interaction. In: Ficuciello, F., Ruggiero, F., Finzi, A. (eds.) Human Friendly Robotics. SPAR, vol. 7, pp. 151–163. Springer, Cham (2019). https://doi.org/10.1007/978-3-319-89327-3_12
2. Aliev, K., Antonelli, D., Bruno, G.: Task-based programming and sequence planning for human-robot collaborative assembly. IFAC-PapersOnLine **52**(13), 1638–1643 (2019)
3. Michalos, G., Spiliotopoulos, J., Makris, S., Chryssolouris, G.: A method for planning human robot shared tasks. CIRP J. Manuf. Sci. Technol. **22**, 76–90 (2018)
4. Aliev, K., Antonelli, D.: Analysis of cooperative industrial task execution by mobile and manipulator robots. In: Trojanowska, J., Ciszak, O., Machado, J.M., Pavlenko, I. (eds.) MANUFACTURING 2019. LNME, pp. 248–260. Springer, Cham (2019). https://doi.org/10.1007/978-3-030-18715-6_21
5. Awouda, A., Aliev, K., Chiabert, P., Antonelli, D.: Practical implementation of Industry 4.0 based on open access tools and technologies. In: Fortin, C., Rivest, L., Bernard, A., Bouras, A. (eds.) PLM 2019. IAICT, vol. 565, pp. 94–103. Springer, Cham (2019). https://doi.org/10.1007/978-3-030-42250-9_9
6. Bauer, W., Bender, M., Braun, M., Rally, P., Scholtz, O.: Lightweight robots in manual assembly—Best to start simply. Frauenhofer-Institut für Arbeitswirtschaft und Organisation IAO, Stuttgart (2016)
7. Hignett, S., McAtamney, L.: Rapid entire body assessment (REBA). Appl. Ergon. **31**(2), 201–205 (2000)
8. McAtamney, L., Corlett, E.N.: RULA: a survey method for the investigation of work-related upper limb disorders. Appl. Ergon. **24**(2), 91–99 (1993)
9. Karhu, O., Kansi, P., Kuorinka, I.: Correcting working postures in industry: a practical method for analysis. Appl. Ergon. **8**(4), 199–201 (1977)
10. Occhipinti, E., Colombini, D.: Proposal of a concise index for the evaluation of the exposure to repetitive movements of the upper extremity (OCRA index). La Medicina del lavoro **87**(6), 526–548 (1996)
11. Schaub, K., Caragnano, G., Britzke, B., Bruder, R.: The European assembly worksheet. Theoret. Issues Ergon. Sci. **14**(6), 616–639 (2013). https://doi.org/10.1080/1463922x.2012.678283
12. Organización Internacional de Normalización, ISO 11226: 2000 (E), Ergonomics: Evaluation of Static Working Postures. ISO (2000)
13. N. ISO 11228-1: Ergonomics-Manual handling-Part 1: Lifting and carrying. International Standard Organization (2003)
14. N. ISO 11228-2: Ergonomics-Manual handling-Part 2: Pushing and pulling. International Standard Organization (2007)
15. Helms, M.M., Nixon, J.: Exploring SWOT analysis–where are we now? J. Strategy Manag. **3**, 215–251 (2010)

Digital Twins

Digital Twin Representations of Concrete Modules in an Interdisciplinary Context of Construction and Manufacturing Industry

Detlef Gerhard(✉), Mario Wolf, Jannick Huxoll, and Oliver Vogt

Institute for Product and Service Engineering, Digital Engineering Chair, Ruhr University Bochum, Universitaetsstr. 150, 44801 Bochum, Germany
{detlef.gerhard,mario.wolf,jannick.huxoll,oliver.vogt}@rub.de

Abstract. Based on the knowledge gained from mechanical engineering and research activities in the context of Industry 4.0, innovative, modular building construction approaches based on flow production methods must be based on a real-time life-cycle-oriented management of information about products, production processes and created systems. To enable rapid, individual, precise, and fault-tolerant production of flexible modules made of free-formable high-performance concrete, data from the ongoing production process and data describing the current status of the module must be continuously collected, combined and made available. Based on this information, the individual production steps can be fine-tuned and the utilization of the machines better planned. Furthermore, it can be verified, whether the current status of a produced module still meets the previously defined requirements from engineering. A state-of-the-art literature review and comparison for digital twin concepts from both involved domains, construction as well as production, is presented in the paper. The contribution gives insights of the requirements elicitation for the formal description of the product requirements in terms of function and quality, considering the possible uncertainties in the course of production. Furthermore, it shows a draft concept for the administration shell for digital twins comprising integrated and adaptable data and interaction models for the industrialized production of high-performance concrete modules.

Keywords: Digital twin · PLM · BIM · Construction industry · Smart manufacturing

1 Introduction

Most construction processes are manually performed by construction workers on site and highly depend on external conditions, often beyond own control, as for instance material supply and weather. This causes inaccuracies regarding geometric requirements, workmanship, and material, which often leads to delays and increased costs. There has been progress in terms of modular building and construction methods for the last decades, together with increased use of high-performance materials such as carbon reinforced concrete. These developments are the key to increase the share of pre-fabrication

Published by Springer Nature Switzerland AG 2020
F. Nyffenegger et al. (Eds.): PLM 2020, IFIP AICT 594, pp. 101–115, 2020.
https://doi.org/10.1007/978-3-030-62807-9_9

in the construction industry and thus tackle the above mentioned challenges. The main idea is to break down each unique building into basic modules that can be pre-fabricated in a highly industrialized manner in order to shift value generation from vulnerable on-site construction to reliable state-of-the-art technology used in manufacturing industry. Furthermore, the idea is to leverage Industry 4.0 approaches, which take advantage of collecting process and operation data by field-sensors at almost any stage of the product lifecycle. Evaluating values with intelligent computer algorithms has become state-of-the-art. A high degree of automation and internet-based communication have established Cyber-Physical Systems (CPS), respectively Cyber-Physical Production Systems (CPPS) [1] if the focus is put on the manufacturing domain.

The project presented in this paper is embedded in the Priority Programme "Adaptive modularized constructions made in a flux: precise and rapid building" [2] of the German Research Foundation and deals with the concept of Digital Twins (DT) in this context. The specific goal of the project is to generate further benefits in terms of digitalization, particularly to enable a digital thread of all planning and building stages, data capturing and processing capabilities, and consistent information flow along the complete lifecycle of a building. Even though DT are considered the virtual counterpart of a physical product, they are more than just data. Digital Twins include algorithms to describe the real product, help to optimize the production process by the processed data, and set the fundamental data basis for operational processes such as predictive maintenance [3]. One major challenge to be tackled in the project is to transfer the concept of CPS, which can describe themselves, are networked, can provide and retrieve services and carry entire data collections over their lifecycle, to the construction industry based on pre-fabricated modules. This includes in particular the representation of specific process modules from concrete construction such as adaptive form-work, reinforcement, concreting and temperature treatment methods with semantic data models.

2 State-of-the-Art and Related Work

2.1 Product Lifecycle View

Comparing construction and manufacturing industry, DT embodies the same thought, but differs in the specific phases of the product lifecycle. The three main phases of the product lifecycle have to be considered adequately for implementing DT concepts. The first phase is the product development phase, or respectively planning phase in construction industry. Here, the focus is put on abstract models on a virtual level, which approximate the real behaviour of a system as accurate as possible. A virtual product model represents the target state and allows early design decisions e.g. through 3D-product review processes. Furthermore, it provides an overview of required materials, estimated costs and time to completion. The most extensive phase with respect to duration is the operation or use of a product respectively building in construction industry. The consideration of the use phase of a product is becoming increasingly important since services in the sense of PSS can leverage additional added value for many companies. In this phase, primarily time series data or sensor-based measured values of a concrete operating state are generated, sometimes with the necessity of real-time data processing. The way in which consistency of information can be ensured, dependencies made transparent and correlations or causal relationships for various issues can be derived, must be conceptually and methodically thought through on a generic level and then implemented in a company-specific manner. In-between planning and operation phase, there is the production respectively building phase, which depicts the transformation from the virtual to the real level. In manufacturing industry, this phase comprises manufacturing an assembly, mostly at a production site, in engineer-to-order processes within plant industry for instance also at customers site. In construction industry, building on-site is predominant but in order to achieve benefits of industrialized production, the share of pre-fabrication is rising.

Even though the product lifecycle is often represented as a linear sequence of successive phases, in reality industrial companies have a multidimensional and complex network of different information processing requirements due to parallel product development projects, parallel customer and production orders in the value-added network or development network and parallel operation of machines or plants in the sense of the PSS concept [4]. With the foundation laid in the early phases of the product lifecycle, the DT particularly serves as a basis for an extended service. Therefore, it is essential, to also have the model representation of the product in operation, i.e. the current usage data and in addition, the continuous documentation of all changes or MRO operations (maintenance, repair, overhaul) of the product or building in operation. This must necessarily happen at the level of the product instance, i.e. a DT exists for each individual product, enhances the digital model representation which is created in the development phase and can be continuously fed and enriched with data from production and later use. In this way, changes in operation and the context of use are taken into account accordingly. One major challenge is to keep the DT permanently up to date over the lifecycle to track changes and enable full traceability. In order to optimize the operation of a product, data is generally recorded by Internet of Things (IoT) devices with sensors or available in the control software used for the DT.

When it comes to planning activities or tasks (engineering phase), e.g. for service operations, for the replacement of plant components, for the introduction of additional safety or supply equipment or for the dynamic simulation of space conditions and collisions with moving parts, sensors and IoT devices are not sufficient for data acquisition. Instead, a spatial representation of the system with its components must be acquired and components must be identified on the basis of geometric or other features. With a lifetime of 30 years or more, this is a permanently recurring task. This is particularly necessary because in industrial practice there are usually deviations between planning and execution, i.e. the information "as designed", "as planned", "as built" and "as maintained" must be compared with each other in order to keep the DT representation up to date.

Building Information Modelling (BIM) is the current state-of-the-art for a digital integration of all relevant information regarding the object, processes and stakeholders in the construction industry. As more than 90% of the value creation within the construction industry takes place on construction sites, digital tools only play a major role for planning and documentation but not during the actual value creation. The guideline

VDI-2552 specifies the fundamentals of BIM, e.g. model-based target-costing, data management, processes and qualification for construction projects [5]. According to this guideline, a usage of a digital representation of a desired product before production helps to reduce project risks and to determine completion date, costs and quality. In particular, visualization and related analyses can optimize operative costs and energy efficiency concepts for the product. The preview of product usage is taken into consideration during early stage of planning and documented within the BIM. This should enable an optimal initial operation of the product and reduce the cost of rework. Moreover, BIM gathers all relevant product information to increase project transparency and is accessible to each project party (Fig. 1).

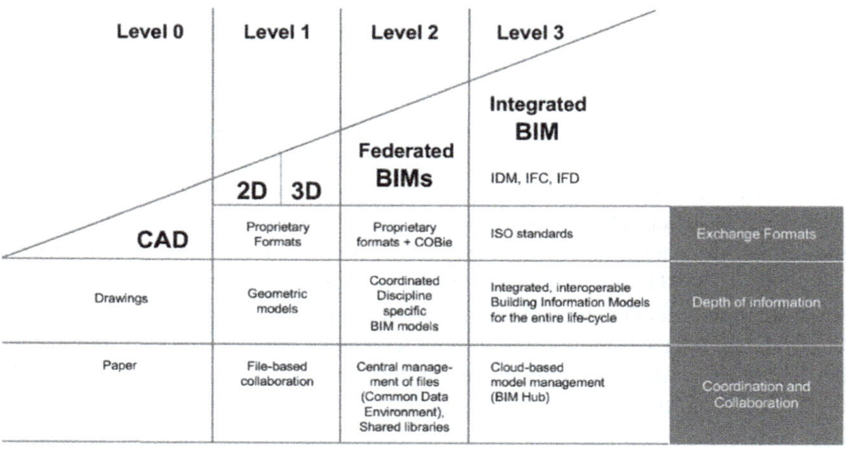

Fig. 1. Performance levels of BIM integration [7]

BIM comprises a set of IT tools and methods to integrate all CAD-design activities, relevant product information like size, material or weight and project parties. However, there are differences regarding the performance level of BIM. VDI-2552 therefore specifies four levels of performance to emphasize the use of different software and data integration intensity. The first level (level 0) stands for cooperation within a project between two or more stakeholders with only individual, data exchange of mainly 2D CAD geometric information without any process tools. Level 1 describes standardized processes regarding the exchange of 2D and 3D geometry as part of a common data environment. In level 2, this 3D-BIM is extended by the information of time (4D) and costs (5D) implemented as attributes within CAD-models. The currently highest performance level of BIM (level 3) represents an integrated digital working environment. That includes a shared model server among all project parties with standardized collaborative digital workflows.

Even though BIM offers a variety of advantages for construction planning, it is also criticized for a need of IT-experts to deal with a high technical burden and a huge amount of work to run these digital tools [6]. BIM is used as a documentation rather than a real time facility management tool. Potential benefits of BIM usage in the operation and maintenance phase have been an unaddressed issue in practical use. Yet, there have been few recent studies about using BIM as a digital basis for facility management. The positive effect of a real time data model for maintenance is shown by an example, where the integration of the internet of things (IoT), BIM and computer aided facility management technologies resulted in better and more intuitive maintenance decisions [8]. Considering that 80% of the total lifecycle costs are generated when the building is in operation [9], this seems to offer an enormous space for improvement.

Process and product data are key to assure a cost-efficient production and high-quality products meeting all predefined requirements. Therefore, gathering data from all phases of the product lifecycle can provide technical insights and act as a starting point for process control and improvement [10]. Product Lifecycle Management (PLM) is a strategic management approach which consists of integrated methods and tools to create, analyze and store all product relevant engineering information along the product lifecycle[11].

At production stage, the state-of-the-art includes two different construction concepts. The first one is the pre-fabrication of modules with simple geometry made out of normal concrete. The second is the construction within the construction zones manually performed by construction workers. The first approach does not apply for complex and unique product structures and modern high-performance materials, whereas the second falls short on using modern production technologies, causes a long time to completion, and relies on factors like weather conditions or personal skill and experience of the workforce. BIM can support this stage by providing all relevant process data. Yet, it cannot directly control the manual process of constructing and is highly dependent on a manual data transfer of current work progress.

Within the phase of product development BIM and PLM are quite similar concepts enabling a common product understanding for design review and decision making. One difference may result from collecting even more data at the stage of production and usage from smart industrial products along the product lifecycle. This allows to optimize production flow and the way a product can be used. From CPPS, insights from production can automatically be transferred to product development. The process of realization thus can become smart and connected – resulting in short production times and reduced loss of production. The concept of modularity is a key factor for modern industrial products and well implemented within the context of Industry 4.0. Many production flows are designed to produce modular products using IoT technologies to establish a real time communication within an autonomous workspace. This allows a pre-fabrication of modules for a final assembly at a later production stage and shortens the lead time for products. Enabling modularity and the technology to manage an intelligent and autonomous production flow, the manufacturing industry seems to be ahead of the construction industry in this regard. An intelligent production system for modular construction products including complex product structures does not exist within the construction industry. By integrating sensors or identification labels to the pre-fabricated modules within the construction industry, the process of assembling will be faster and more structured.

2.2 Digital Twin Model Representation

The fundamental base for digitization of industrial processes is an appropriate information base, respectively a model representation that covers on the one hand side the specifics of particular sub processes and on the other hand side covers the digital thread throughout the lifecycle. The following subsections present the state-of-the-art for the two addressed domains.

Industry Foundation Classes and Model View Definition

In construction industry, the Industry Foundation Classes (IFC) standard DIN EN ISO 16739 [12], specifies schemata developed for exchanging and sharing data for BIM. IFC is not one specific data format but can be encoded in different formats. The IFC schema architecture is divided into Domain layer as the highest layer, Interoperability layer, Core layer and Resource layer, the lowest layer. In the Domain layer, entities are defined that are usually assigned to a specific discipline and used for intra-domain exchange. The Interoperability layer defines entities for products, processes or resource specifications that are used in more than one discipline and exchanged between different domains. The most generic entity definitions are included in the Core layer. A globally unique ID is assigned to every entity that is defined in the Core layer or above. The Resource layer includes all schemata of resource definitions. The standard is continuously updated for a better description of complex buildings or constructions [13]. The current IFC version 4.2 does not include infrastructural constructions like bridges, but IFC5 will support this infrastructural domain as well.

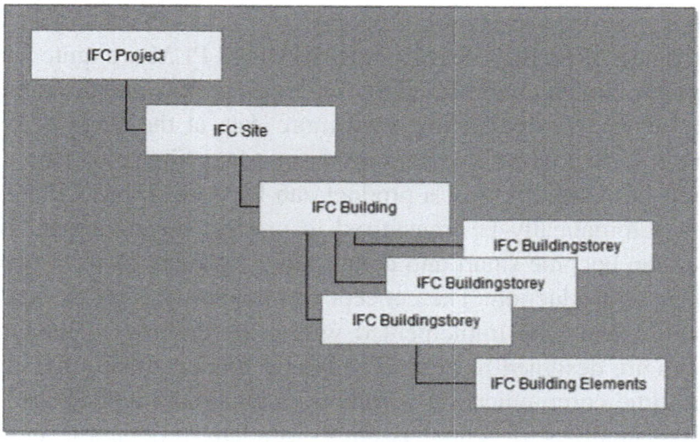

Fig. 2. IFC Tree-View [14]

In an IFC file, a building is structured into subsets. The subsets are arranged in a tree structure (cp. Fig. 2). Every IFC file has to contain one project and at least one site. It is possible to include more than one building in such a structure, but usually there is only one. Every hierarchy element lower than building is project-based and exists in more than one place in the file (for a better overview only one Building Element is pictured).

For each kind of building element, there is an entity that contains standard attributes and relations for describing the element. Due to this semantics, the building is structured and every single element with its attributes can be identified. A transferred or exchanged model cannot be changed or adapted, it is only a reference model. For exchanges, the creator of the IFC-file needs to change the model and export as well as re-distribute the new IFC-file again [15]. To cover prefabricated components IFC4precast [16] was introduced. The ifcElementAssembly is an element aggregated from different ifcElements. ifcElementAssembly includes attributes like the assembly place. With IFC4precast, a strong connection between CAD, MES and the production system can be realized.

When the exchange of models is required, usually the exchange file does not need to include every single information in detail. To limit the exchanged data, the concept of Model View Definition (MVD) defines the required data for a specific use case or workflow. Within MVD exchange specifications for IFC4 are given. There is a limited amount of official MVDs that are used as international standards. For the coordination of design between architects and structural domains there is a different MVD than for estimation of energy usage and costs of the building [17].

Reference Architecture Model for Industry 4.0 (RAMI 4.0)

The RAMI 4.0 standard DIN 91345 [18] specifies all essential terms around the reference architecture model. For a basic understanding, especially the terms asset, administration shell and service are essential. Asset is defined as any uniquely identifiable entity with value to the organization, whether it is an object, software, service or design. Thus, an asset does not have to be a physical object. Every asset in RAMI 4.0 is designed, created, used and disposed of and is therefore subject to a lifecycle according to the common understanding as described in the section above. But in this respect, the definition corresponds to the concept of the unit under consideration from the field of maintenance DIN 13306 [19]. Identification can be performed using indicators according to ISO 29002-5 or as a URI in the URN namespace according to RFC 3986 [20].

The information about an asset is digitally stored and provided in the so-called Asset Administration Shell (AAS), so that an Industry 4.0 (I4.0) component is created as a combination between an asset and its administration shell [21]. This relationship is illustrated in Fig. 3. The administration shell of an asset thus represents the holistic digital representation of an asset. Since the administration shell is also uniquely identifiable, an Industry 4.0 component is also uniquely identifiable as a composition of both elements, whereby a one-to-one relationship exists between the asset and its administration shell. The administration shell is divided into a manifest and a component manager-managed part. The basic idea of recursive asset description is also continued within the administration shell, as each administration shell contains the identifications of the asset and the administration shell itself in the so-called header. In addition, the identification and characteristics list for all submodels are part of the manifest part. Proprietary data models (CAD data, source code, etc.) are managed by the component manager, which can also provide interfaces in the form of services for other I4.0 components based on the submodel manifest.

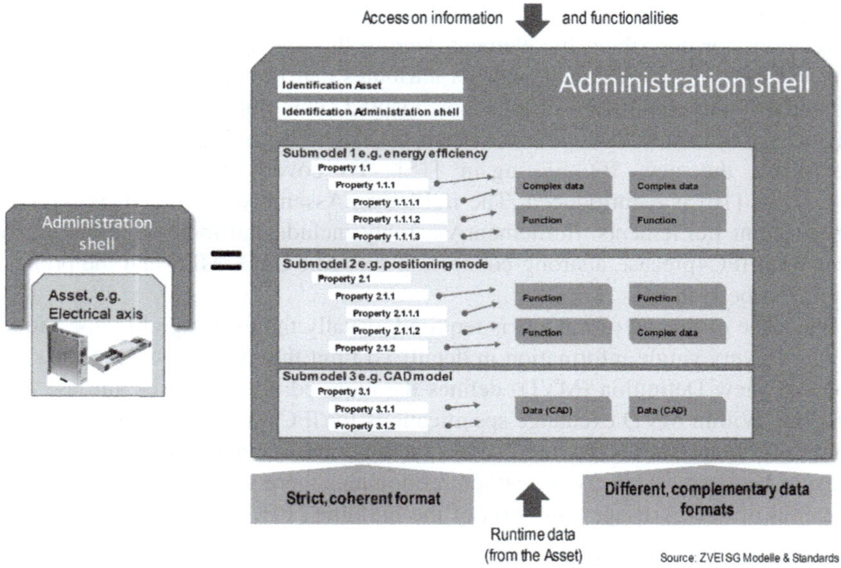

Fig. 3. Basic structure of the Asset Administration Shell - in reference to [22]

In this context, a service is a delimited set of functions that can be offered by an entity or organization via interfaces (APIs) with defined Quality of Service (QoS) properties.

The way an object is managed and thus, its publicity in the information system is independent of the object's ability to communicate. For example, an important device in a system can be managed as an entity even if it is not capable of communication. The tracking of its states in the lifecycle must then be done by external measurement and identification systems or by people themselves and stored in a separate, yet associated way.

Table 1. CP-classification for objects [23]

Communication	Publicity
4 - Service system-compliant communication	4 - administered as an entity
3 - actively able to communicate	3 - known individually
2 - passively able to communicate	2 - anonymously known
1 - not able to communicate	1 - unknown

Following to the notation in Table 1, the Communication/Publicity-classification (CP) of CP33 corresponds to an individually known entity with active communication capability, e.g. a classic field device with fieldbus connection. An entity that is monitored and managed in its lifecycle but has no communication capability whatsoever would have a CP class of CP14. An "I4.0 component" must conform to CP24, CP34 or

CP44. The combination of I4.0 components creates a new I4.0 component with its own comprehensive administration shell. This results in a recursive asset description that is capable of achieving any level of granularity, from simple components to a complete factory plant, as shown in Fig. 4.

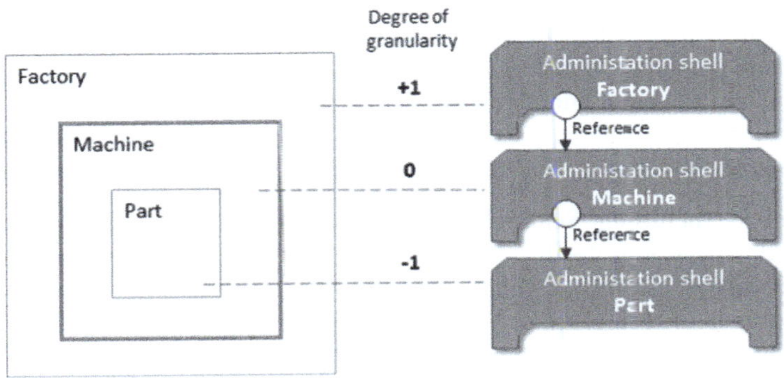

Fig. 4. Work on system design can be started at any level of granularity, structured in reference to RAMI 4.0 [24]

3 Domain-Specific Requirements

Modular construction methods with freely formable high-performance materials are the key to enable integration in industrialized flow process fabrication. Modules have high repetition rates and scalability, making them ideal for industrialized series production in modern flow processes. The advantages of series production known from manufacturing industry can be leveraged. i.e. production speed, geometric and material accuracy, durability and resource conservation through optimization. At the same time, buildings become changeable over their lifetime by exchanging or adding modules. Construction projects that utilize industrialized manufacturing and pre-fabrication processes impose different and extended requirements on DT concepts, particularly model representation and lifecycle information management that go beyond the current scope of BIM in the construction domain and PLM in the manufacturing domain.

Requirements, which have to be regarded and mapped in the sense of a consistent digital thread can be divided into the following categories that reflect the key unique characteristics of the process under consideration:

- Modularity
- Adaptability
- Material
- Manufacturing and pre-fabrication process
- Transport and assembly processes (on construction site)

Modularity: The idea of modularization is based on the possibility of realizing a large number of product variants at low costs using semi-finished components under the criteria of standardization and interchangeability. Modularization brings inherent variability. Modular development attempts to present an external variety of products to the customer, while at the same time limiting the internal variety of product solutions and technical systems. The principle here is the multiple use of subsystems in different configurations. Two approaches are possible: Construction of the structure from known modules (bottom-up) and modularization of the support structure into parametric modules with explicit characteristics (top-down). i.e., either the shape of the overall structure is determined depending on previously defined basic modules or the overall structure is broken down into similar basic elements.

Both ways impose demands on variant management within the DT and require furthermore the implementation of the product type and product instance concept.

Adaptability (Including Scalability and Compatibility Aspects): As mentioned above, modularization is the division of a whole into individual components (modules, segments, building elements), which interact via their interfaces (for building elements: physical points of contact and joints). Modular building structures will become increasingly adaptable over time, i.e., individual elements can be exchanged or maintained. Structures that can be changed by means of minimally invasive structural adjustments according to plan will be created in order to be able to react to changes that were not expectable at the time of planning, e.g. climatic conditions, traffic increases or the necessity for expansion. Equipped with sensory intelligence, these cognitive module systems can for instance communicate their stress or degradation characteristics during use phase. Furthermore, active building structures with the possibility of transient optimization and adaptation over their lifecycle can be created.

The DT has to consider this adaptability aspects, lifecycle spanning in the forward and backward direction. The model representation has to cover both, the prevailing boundary conditions (load assumptions, material properties, manufacturing tolerances, installation quality), which are often subject to uncertainties, as well as the phase time series data capturing actual conditions and reflecting deviations between planning and use phase.

Material: High-performance concretes with carbon or glass fibre reinforcement offer a high potential for freely formed, weight-minimized components and enormous durability high corrosion resistance. Compared to conventional concrete construction, it can take higher loads or save material significantly. Furthermore, improvement strategies are available to do justice to the new material through a targeted material distribution as well as structure or topology optimization. This leads to better material utilization and less waste.

On the other hand, proper material modeling within the DT plays a vital role, since high-performance on the one hand side also means high dependability of the material properties and composition. Quality assurance does not only comprise geometrical aspects but also material micro structure, cavities, particle distribution etc. This has to be reflected in the DT as well as for instance heat treatment.

Manufacturing and Pre-fabrication Process: The state-of-the-art building process has a largely handcraft character. Therefore, it is error prone, associated with long construction times and exposed to high geometrical and material scatter and thus inaccuracies due to weather conditions. Faultless series production with a high degree of individuality of the assembled end product can only be achieved with the consistent digital interlocking of all production steps. The entire value-added chain has to be supported by means of intelligent and digitally networked systems, which also includes the subsequent use phase of the building. CPPS are able to optimize themselves through a continuous flow of information and thus, in complex processes with high tolerance and precision requirements they can recognize errors early on and avoid waste and defective products. Today, BIM and IFC are already frequently used in industrial prefabrication of components in stationary production facilities (e.g. steel construction, form work construction, automatic bending machines, welding robots, etc.). Within Computer Aided Manufacturing (CAM), individual manufacturing steps for automated production are defined on the basis of digital component models.

Nevertheless, a major challenge is the efficient definition of the CAM processes for special and individual components with the required modular precision, particularly the linking of all process steps in the DT, starting at the design level up to production with reduced losses due to manual interfaces. This includes concepts of concreting and form work with high demands on precision and re-usability in production, adaptivity and scalability both at module level and component level (reinforcement). The representation of the required semantics in the DT, based on existing IFC constructs or similar concepts is required.

Transport and Assembly Processes (On Construction Site): As the core idea is to reduce individual building structures to scalable basic modules, i.e. to combine uniqueness with adaptive series production, the construction activity on site should be minimally short and be reduced to the assembly of the modules to the structure. Keeping this in mind, special attention is paid to the interfaces between individual modules, i.e. the formation of joints. Depending on the modularization method, different force transmission requirements are made via these contacts using different geometric shapes (e.g. rectangle, finger joints, undercut toothing (puzzle), etc.) reflecting the particular load and use demands as well as pairing strategies and tolerance compensation approaches.

The geometric definition within the DT has to cover and represent semantics of such joint definitions. Regarding transport, sequencing strategies for component delivery, based on data or the pre-fabrication process is required, taking into account batch and cargo capacities, which are often the limiting factor in construction industry.

4 Draft Concept for the Administration Shell for Digital Twins

As seen in Sect. 2, there has been huge progress regarding standardization in both mentioned industries. On the one hand, the IFC standard for BIM data exchange currently provides four layers for data structuring. Furthermore, the state-of-the-art for BIM data models comprises five dimensions (3D-CAD, time, costs) as shown by the performance levels of BIM integration. On the other hand, RAMI represents a generic approach to cluster technology in the context of Industry 4.0. This reference architectural model is based on a variety of industrial standards. The three-dimensional cube of RAMI characterizes modern industrial technology by different hierarchy levels (IEC 62264, IEC 61512), the lifecycle and value stream (IEC 62890) and six layers to describe the digital information model on an abstract level [21].

The classic product lifecycle in construction industry is a unidirectional approach without digitally providing information from the lifecycle back to the early phase of development. Moreover, the RAMI model differentiates between type data (development) and instance data (after development) in order to establish an efficient flow production by creating many instances from a single type. For construction products this relation is very different. Due to the uniqueness of each project there will usually be only one instance with one type data set of the product itself.

As stated earlier, the goal of the proposed approach is to use a streamlined production for modules made of high-performance concrete that combined form individual structural parts, which would otherwise be produced monolithically on site. Figure 5 shows an example for a wall element ("Building Element 001"), which consists of several concrete modules. Through this approach, each module will have an identifiable type with several unique instances. This way, modularity enables an industrial flow production for individual construction projects.

Yet, the classic PLM approach for construction projects needs to be adapted in order to implement digital consistency through the use of an Asset Administration Shell (AAS).

The AAS must consist of integrated and adaptable data and interaction models, e.g. services, and provide semantics by structured and standardized methods via its component manager (cp. [21]). IEC 61360 specifies four main types of data properties (identification, semantic, value, relational). ZVEI uses these properties to make a proposal for the structure of a digital AAS and defines specific data-wise requirements, e.g. the AAS must consist of a minimum number of properties [21].

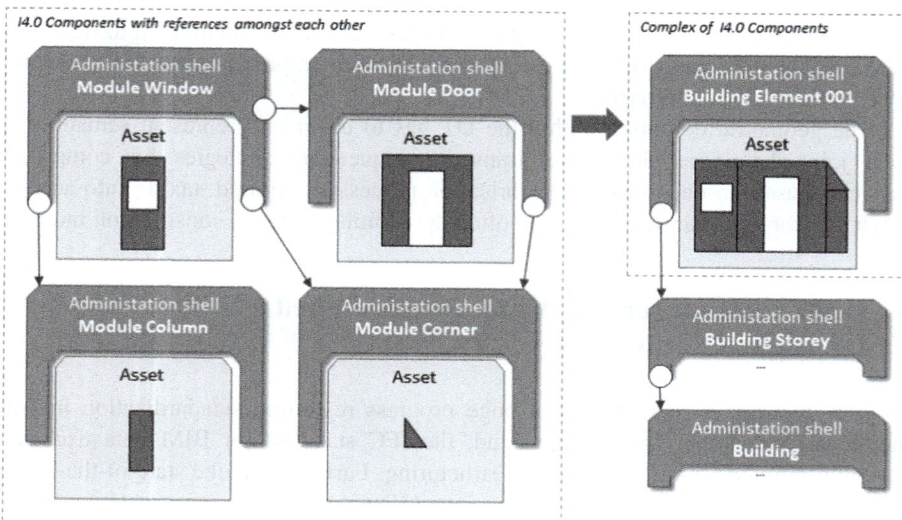

Fig. 5. Exemplary building element made of prefabricated modules - in reference to [24]

To structure data objects, four property classes are derived (basis, obligatory, optional, free) and references from each property to at least the data and functionality within its AAS are mandatory. These ideas act as a set up guideline for an AAS for the DT of construction assets. To manufacture concrete modules efficiently, data properties can be stored in digital containers within their individual AAS. The AAS then contains an arbitrary amount of submodels. These submodels describe different aspects of the asset. The details and information of every submodel is specified by various specifications. To apply the AAS for construction industry, some more specifications need to be considered. IFC with its entities and attributes helps to describe every single element of a building. This information is necessary for different submodels of the AAS. For example, the attributes of a wall specified in ifcWall are relevant for submodels of a building, e.g. energy efficiency, configuration, engineering. All specific attributes need to be considered in submodels.

Each submodel needs to be allocated in the basic's views with attributes, data or functions. The basic views are Business, Constructive, Performance, Functional, Local, Security, Network view, Lifecycle and Human. In construction industry MVD specifies standard views and the attributes, data and functions of every element in construction industry for specific usage. To cover all basic views, MVD needs to be added to the basic views of DIN SPEC 91345 to apply the AAS for construction industry. In Fig. 6, an example of AAS with certain submodels and relevant specifications is shown. Based on ZVEI's figure, the previous mentioned specifications were added.

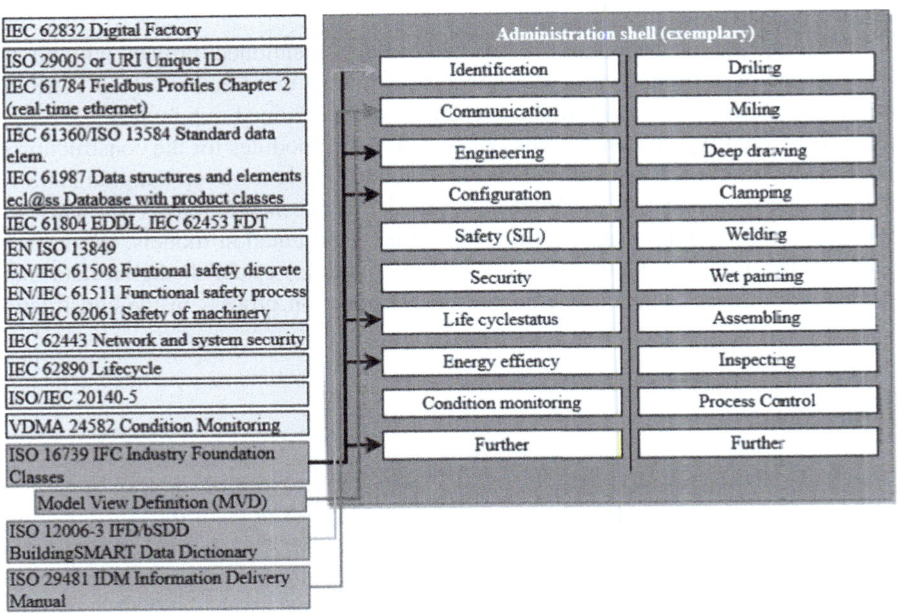

Fig. 6. AAS with submodels and relevant specifications - in reference to [24]

During construction phase, the AAS acts as a reference model to realize a fast and efficient building process in order to save time, foster transparency and reduce costs. At the stage of product usage, the administration shell represents an integrated, updated, digital model of the product, enables a formal and structured way of storing and adapting product data, as well as turning a building or bridge into a cognitive product-service system.

5 Conclusion and Outlook

Industrialized pre-fabrication of modules made from high-performance concrete materials open new opportunities for construction industry in terms of cost and time savings, quality and sustainability. The presented paper provides a technological insight of the construction and manufacturing industry regarding engineering and production processes as well as the product lifecycle management. While construction industry is dominated by individual engineering to order processes, manufacturing industry faces any kind of engineering and production order from one piece to mass production. In order to successfully apply the approach of pre-fabrication of modules from manufacturing to the construction industry, an interdisciplinary technology transfer needs to be considered. Therefore, industrial standards and guidelines for digital information management from both industries must be analyzed from an integrative perspective to set up a modern concept of a DT representation model. More precisely, RAMI and its AAS need to be merged with standards in construction industry like IFC.

One scientific contribution of the work in the mentioned project will be the development of a product lifecycle concept including the creation of an AAS for concrete modules in construction industry under the mentioned requirements. The first step of is to identify a reasonable number of generative modules for the construction of a high number of buildings and bridges. The second step is to set up a digital AAS for each module and establish a digital data transfer between different AAS. This will include the elaboration of an ontology for digital representation models. While modularity allows mass production, the DT of these modules establish digital data management and a more efficient engineering and production process in the construction industry.

References

1. Gerhard, D.: Product lifecycle management challenges of CPPS. In: Biffl, S., Lüder, A., Gerhard, D. (eds.) Multi-Disciplinary Engineering for Cyber-Physical Production Systems, pp. 89–110. Springer, Cham (2017). https://doi.org/10.1007/978-3-319-56345-9_4
2. German Research Foundation: adaptive modularized constructions made in a flux: precise and rapid building. Priority Programme 2187. https://www.ruhr-uni-bochum.de/spp2187/. Accessed 15 Mar 2020
3. Qi, Q., Tao, F.: Digital twin and big data towards smart manufacturing and industry 4.0: 360 degree comparison. IEEE Access **6**, 3585–3593 (2018)

4. Abramovici, M.: Smart products. In: Produ, T.I.A., Laperrière, L., Reinhart, G. (eds.) CIRP Encyclopedia of Production Engineering, pp. 1–5. Springer, Berlin (2014)
5. VDI-2552: Building Information Modeling (BIM). The Association of German Engineers (2019)
6. PricewaterhouseCoopers GmbH, Digitization of the German construction industry. Research study (2019). https://www.pwc.de/de/digitale-transformation/studie-digitales-bauen-nimmt-fahrt-auf.html. Accessed 22 Feb 2020
7. Borrmann, A., König, M., Koch, C., Beetz, J.: Building information modeling: why? what? how? In: Borrmann, A., König, M., Koch, C., Beetz, J. (eds.) Building Information Modeling, pp. 1–24. Springer, Cham (2018). https://doi.org/10.1007/978-3-319-92862-3_1
8. German Facility Management Association: Building Information Modeling im Facility Management. Whitepaper GEFMA 926 Version 1.0 (2017)
9. Rebellius, M.: Creating perfect places with the power of data. In: Building Technology Division. Presentation Paper. Siemens, AG (2017)
10. Eigner, M., Ralph, S.: Product Lifecycle Management. 2nd edn. Springer, Heidelberg (2009). https://doi.org/10.1007/b93672
11. Abramovici, M., Schulte, S., Leszinski, S.: Best practice strategien für die einführung von product lifecycle management. Ind. Manage. **21**(2), 1–10 (2005)
12. DIN EN ISO 16739. Industry Foundation Classes (IFC) für den Datenaustausch in der Bauindustrie und im Anlagenmanagement
13. buildingSMART International. IFC specification database, https://technical.buildingsmart.org/standards/ifc/ifc-schema-specifications/. Accessed 20 Mar 2020
14. buildingSMART International. IFC4 specification. https://standards.buildingsmart.org/ifc/release/ifc4/add2_tc1/html/link/introduction.htm. Accessed 17 Feb 2020
15. buildingSMART International. IFC model implementation guide. https://technical.buildingsmart.org/resources/ifcimplementationguidance/. Accessed 11 Feb 2020
16. buildingSMART Deutschland. IFC4precast, Task Force. https://www.bsde-tech.de/mitarbeiten/projektgruppen/pg-ifc4precast/. Accessed 28 Mar 2020
17. buildingSMART International. MVD database, standard specifications. https://technical.buildingsmart.org/standards/mvd/mvd-database/. Accessed 15 Mar 2020
18. DIN SPEC 91345:2016-04. Referenzarchitekturmodell Industrie 4.0 (RAMI4.0), Deutsches Institut für Normung e. V. (2016)
19. DIN EN 13306. Instandhaltung - Begriffe der Instandhaltung, Deutsches Institut für Normung e. V. (2012)
20. RFC 3986. The Internet Engineering Task Force. Uniform Resource Identifier (2005)
21. Plattform Industrie 4.0 und ZVEI: Struktur der Verwaltungsschale. Fortentwicklung des Referenzmodells für die Industrie 4.0-Komponente, Federal Ministry for Economic Affairs and Energy, Berlin (2016)
22. Plattform Industrie 4.0: Details of the Asset Administration Shell. Part 1-The exchange of information between partners in the value chain of Industrie 4.0 (Version 2.0). Federal Ministry for Economic Affairs and Energy, Berlin (2019)
23. The Association of German Engineers. Industrie 4.0 – Begriffe/Terms, VDI Statusreport Industrie 4.0. VDI/VDE-Gesellschaft Mess- und Automatisierungstechnik (2017)
24. Plattform Industrie 4.0: Relationships between I4.0 Components – Composite Components and Smart Production, Working Paper, Federal Ministry for Economic Affairs and Energy, Berlin (2017)

Middle of Life Digital Twin: Implementation at a Learning Factory

Luiz Fernando C. S. Durão, Matheus Morgado, Roseli de Deus Lopes, and Eduardo Zancul(✉)

University of São Paulo, São Paulo, Brazil
{luiz.durao, roseli.lopes, ezancul}@usp.br, matheus.morgado@alumni.usp.br

Abstract. In recent years, several IT systems have been applied to collect different types of data concerning the full product lifecycle. As a result of Industry 4.0 developments, the amount of product information collected over the entire lifecycle has been growing. Information and communication technology is employed to digitally mirror the lifecycle of a corresponding physical product in Digital Twin applications. These applications are middleware architectures that apply physical world information to support real-time decisions. Therefore, a Digital Twin may be used to enhance simulation, to improve traceability, and to expand the value-added services offering along the lifecycle. However, studies on Digital Twin applications are mainly focused on the beginning of life (BOL) or manufacturing optimization. In this paper, Product Lifecycle Management (PLM) theory and Internet of Things (IoT) solutions and technologies are applied to build a Digital Twin able to collect and cast middle of life (MOL) information to the other lifecycle phases. Based on the scenario implementation in a Learning Factory, the objective is to discuss the information flow that is required for a Digital Twin to be considered for closing the information gap between the product in the use phase and other lifecycle phases. The results show how a middle of life Digital Twin can impact processes and information flow. Future research work should integrate the information of multiple IT systems from the entire product lifecycle in a comprehensive Digital Twin.

Keywords: Digital Twin · Learning Factory · Product Lifecycle Management

1 Introduction

The convergence between physical and virtual spaces has gained wide attention in the digitalization era [1]. To deal with this convergence, the Digital Twin (DT) creates a tunnel between the physical parts and its bytes representation [2]. Therefore, a DT consists of three main components: the physical entities in the physical world, the virtual models in the virtual world, and the connected data that tie the two worlds [1].

Digital Twin application contributes to information transparency and to create a real-time production control [3]. Considering the complexity of data integration, a thoroughly DT implementation is still complicated, and most studies demonstrate partial process views [3]. Several IT systems have been applied to collect different

Published by Springer Nature Switzerland AG 2020
F. Nyffenegger et al. (Eds.): PLM 2020, IFIP AICT 594, pp. 116–127, 2020.
https://doi.org/10.1007/978-3-030-62807-9_10

types of data concerning the full product lifecycle [4]. Examples are related to the integration between PLM (Product Lifecycle Management) and ERP (Enterprise Resource Planning) systems [5]. Indeed, PLM is defined as a systematic concept for the integrated management of all product and process-related information through the entire lifecycle, from the initial idea to end-of-life [6]. However, how to acquire and integrate real-world data in a functional DT is still an open question in the literature.

Digital Twins are used as a tool to shorten time to market and to create further benefits along the entire lifecycle. It is used not only for representation purposes but also for predicting product behavior [7]. Besides, Digital Twin's ability to link enormous amounts of data to simulation makes it possible to perform real-time optimization of products and production processes [8].

Current studies on DT applications are mainly focused on the beginning of life (BOL) or manufacturing optimization. In this paper, Product Lifecycle Management theory and Internet of Things (IoT) solutions and technologies are applied to build a Digital Twin capable of transmitting middle of life (MOL) information back to the beginning of the lifecycle. The purpose of this approach is to propose a flexible data decision interface that closes the PLM information loop.

The paper is structured into five sections. After the introduction of the research topic in Sect. 1, Sect. 2 provides the research approach developed in the paper. In Sect. 3, the requirements brought by literature to the Digital Twin concept are presented. Section 4 presents the scenario implementation. Finally, the conclusion and an outlook on further research needs are discussed in Sect. 5.

2 Methodology

This research started by conducting a literature review [9] on IoT, DT, and PLM (presented in Sect. 3). Based on the gaps from the literature, a middle of life DT model has been implemented in a Learning Factory at the University of São Paulo in Brazil.

A Learning Factory may be defined as a close to real production environment used to perform research, technology tests, teaching, and professional education. Learning Factories usually consider a real physical product to perform its activities and test scenarios. The selected Learning Factory is based on the assembly of a customizable skateboard in the context of Industry 4.0. This Learning Factory features a real IT systems environment, including a PLM, an ERP, and a MES (Manufacturing Execution System) software. Each of these systems is installed in a virtual server at the university cloud services. The existing IT environment provides the ground for analyzing the digital thread related to the Digital Twin. Figure 1 shows a partial view of the Learning Factory assembly line.

This paper focuses on a Digital Twin for the MOL, capable of transmitting middle of life information back to the beginning of the lifecycle. In this paper, the MOL is considered the product usage phase by the client. Data collected during the usage phase can be considered as an input for product development and also for providing value-added services, such as predictive maintenance.

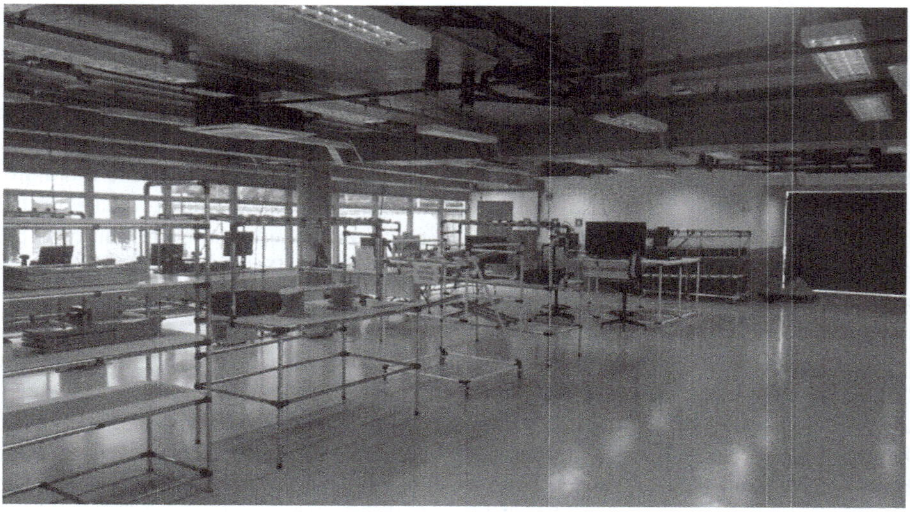

Fig. 1. Learning factory at the University of São Paulo

The research methodology involved three main steps for the DT model deployment: the definition of MOL parameters to be measured based on IoT data collection technologies, the DT construction, and the DT application to decision making (Fig. 2).

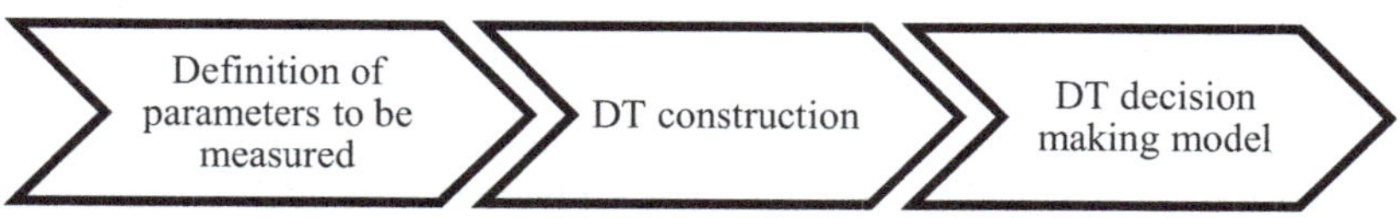

Fig. 2. Research steps

A practical implementation scenario has been constructed presenting a MOL Digital Twin of a connected skateboard (product produced at the Learning Factory). The following requirements and constraints were considered for the DT in this scenario:

- Allow data to be transfer through the internet;
- Measure different parameters of the skateboard;
- Provide alternative information aggregation for different stages of the lifecycle.

The proposed MOL Digital Twin should also be designed to support future integration with PLM, ERP, and MES data in a comprehensive product data aggregation tool.

3 Literature Review

This section presents a discussion on Internet of Things (3.1) and Digital Twin (3.2).

3.1 Internet of Things

Internet of Things can be defined as a mechanism of interaction between physical objects and virtual data environments [10]. It is considered one of the major communication advances in recent years, which offers the basis for the development of independent applications [11]. With IoT technology, a product can be equipped with a uniquely identifiable code that can then be monitored and tracked by using sensors and wireless networks [12].

The implementation of intelligent factories is possible considering the evolution of manufacturing and information technologies, being able to receive different information from multiple sources, and produce items that are more complex in a reduced time and different locations. This change in production technologies requires a new representation of product models and manufacturing processes. This representation would be reached by a Digital Twin.

3.2 Digital Twin and PLM

Digital Twin is a multi-physical, multi-scale, and probabilistic simulation model of a complex product. It uses updated sensors and physical models to mirror physical life in the digital world and vice versa [13, 14].

The Digital Twin is essential to provide the subsystems all required information [15, 16]. It should be able to import background data, component information, and configuration information from the physical component [17–19]. The Digital Twin is used to string different existing IT systems, i.e., Product Lifecycle Management, Manufacturing Execution Systems, among others. It is initiated based on digital knowledge from the product design phase. The physical and environmental knowledge of the product is also embedded in the product 3D model, which forms the initiation of the Digital Twin [20]. The virtual reality-based 3D digital model can meet the intelligent and personalized needs, which is the future of the digital factory [21].

The role of the PLM system is collecting and managing data of product definitions, processes, resources, and decisions across the whole product lifecycle supporting changes and enabling traceability of these changes through a product model [22].

The product model that supports the data interfacing (and then systems interoperability) should describe, with the same semantic, various data. In a low trust level, the product model is used to manage the product information separately in different databases [23]. Therefore, managing the interaction between the physical and digital world starts from the product model. The DT must manage the interaction of the product model and the physical world, and its requirements must reflect that. The question is on how to integrate different types of data to close the PLM loop and connect different stages of the product lifecycle.

4 Results and Applications

This section presents the main research results considering the definition of parameters to be measured (Sect. 4.1), the DT implementation (Sect. 4.2), and the use of the DT as data input for different stages of the PLM (Sect. 4.3).

4.1 Definitions of Parameters to Be Measured

In order to monitor the skateboard use during the middle of life, it was necessary to define the parameters to be measured and to specify how to measure these parameters – transforming a regular skateboard on a connected skateboard.

Considering the skateboard, critical parameters to be measured in the product usage lifecycle phase include the instant speed, the travel distance, and the vibration and position of the board. To measure the speed and the travel distance, the proposal considered counting the number of wheel turns. The Eq. I is applied to calculate the speed, and Eq. II is used to calculate the travel distance.

$$speed = 3600\frac{2\pi r * n_{turns}}{\Delta T} \quad \text{(I)}$$

$$Travel = travel + 2\pi r * n_{turns} \quad \text{(II)}$$

The number of turns in the wheel can be counted by two alternative solutions: the hall effect sensor and the encoder speed. Table 1 presents the strengths and weaknesses of each approach.

Table 1. Strengths and weakness of alternatives for counting wheel turns

	Strengths	Weakness
Hall effect	• Easy to implement • Do not interfere in the skate design	• Electromagnetic interference • Need to use a magnetic
Encoder speed	• High precision measure	• Measure impacted by vibration environments • Need to change skateboard design

By analyzing Table 1, the best option to capture the number of turns and, therefore, the speed and travel distance, was the hall effect sensor.

Two possible alternatives were considered to measure the position/vibration of the board and develop a real-time 3D model to mirror the skate movements: an accelerometer and gyroscope, and the use of the user smartphone sensors to collect the data. Table 2 represents the strengths and weaknesses of each approach.

Table 2. Strengths and weakness of alternatives for position/vibration measurement

	Strengths	Weakness
Accelerometer and gyroscope	• Precise monitoring • Integration with microcontroller	• Small impact resistance
Smartphone integration	• Do not require additional implementation	• Low precision

By analyzing Table 2, the best option to capture the position/vibration was the accelerometer and gyroscope.

Figure 3 shows the initial implementation and tests. The hall effect sensor counts the number of times that the magnetic passes on the sensor, counting the number of times that the wheel turns (Fig. 3 left side). The accelerometer and gyroscope capture the board position (Fig. 3 right side).

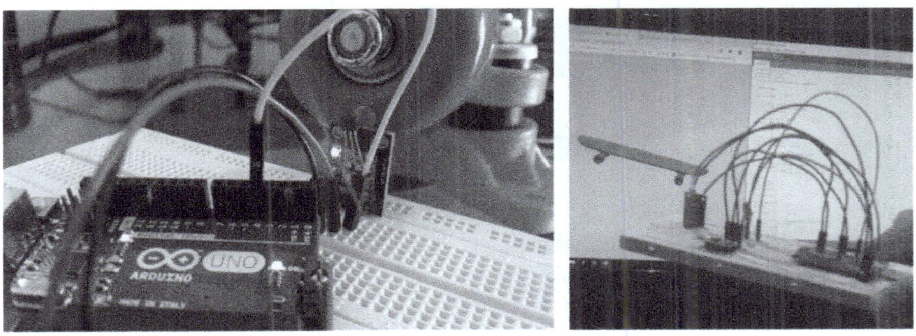

Fig. 3. Hall effect sensor (left side) and accelerometer implementation (right side)

4.2 Digital Twin Implementation

After the sensors' definition, an integrated circuit was developed and installed in the skateboard (Fig. 4), and a digital model was developed to show the movements of the skateboard in real-time. Figure 5 shows the impact of skate movement on the digital model.

Fig. 4. Implementation of sensing technology

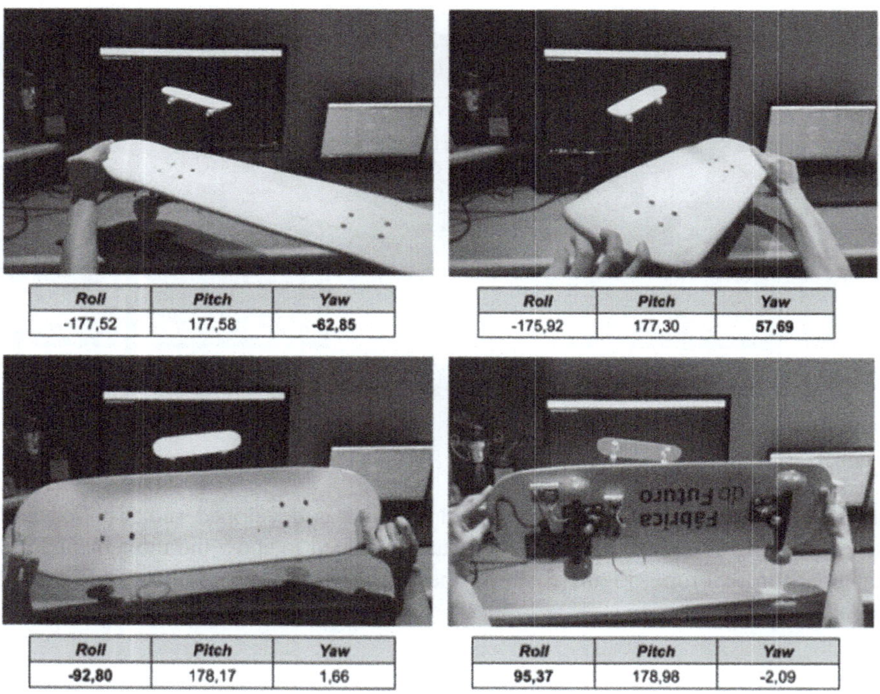

Roll	Pitch	Yaw
-177,52	177,58	-62,85

Roll	Pitch	Yaw
-175,92	177,30	57,69

Roll	Pitch	Yaw
-92,80	178,17	1,66

Roll	Pitch	Yaw
95,37	178,98	-2,09

Fig. 5. Digital model

The implementation was then deployed using C in Arduino ESP8266 and HTML, CSS and Java Script connecting the database and creating a user interface at localhost to perform initial testing. Figure 6 shows a part of Arduino coding (left side) and a part of front-end development (right side). The complete code is available at github. com/duraoluiz.

Fig. 6. Arduino ESP8266 implementation (left side) and front-end coding sampling (right side)

Figure 7 presents the final user interface of the speed and distance monitoring as well as the 3D Digital Twin.

Fig. 7. Digital Twin front-end

With the front-end developed and a back-end running at localhost, it was required to establish a virtual machine to run the Digital Twin and to structure the data. The selected platform to receive the DT was a gcloud Ubuntu 18, and for the back-end, a Firebase was used. Figure 8 shows the Ubuntu server (left side) and the Firebase implementation (right side).

Fig. 8. Server implementation (left side) and Firebase data implementation (right side)

The implementation was then finished as a basic Digital Twin. It can capture real-world information about the product use phase and display this information in real-time in the virtual world. Besides, one can change digital data and impact the real world by turning the skate lights on. Figure 9 presents the physical product and the Digital Twin implementation.

Fig. 9. Digital Twin

4.3 DT Application

Digital Twin implementation enabled analysis of the most important ways to take advantage of the information captured on the product usage phase into the early stages of the product lifecycle. There are different ways to do that, such as anticipating wheels demand for manufacturing, changing the product design considering the most common maneuvers, and the balance of weight, among others. However, for this project, the information that is reused is the speed and average speed by the users. With that information, the manufacturer can suggest the most appropriate wheel diameter for a specific user.

A python script was developed to capture the information from the online database of the user, processing the information, and analyzing the most common acceleration and speed as an input for the manufacturing of new wheels more suitable for the type of use. This information flow closes the information loop from the usage phase to services, using real-time information to improve product use.

Additional value-added services can be derived from the MOL Digital Twin data analysis, such as maintenance and training.

The product usage profile gathered in the Digital Twin database can also serve as a relevant field input to support new product development and product improvement. Therefore, design engineers can analyze detailed user patterns.

5 Conclusions and Future Work

This paper set out to answer if it is feasible to apply Digital Twin concept to connect different stages of the product lifecycle and allow real-time and personalized decision making. In this sense, the role of lifecycle management is collecting and managing data of product definitions, across the whole product lifecycle.

A Digital Twin was developed in a Learning Factory in Brazil. This Learning Factory has as its base product a skateboard. Therefore, all the monitoring and information are related to a skateboard as a scenario reference description for other industries.

The first step was to define the parameters to be measured (speed, distance, and vibration/position) and to define the sensors to be used. The physical product was connected to the internet, providing a real-time digital mirror of the physical world.

Having real-time data is not the final stage of a Digital Twin implementation. The information should be connected to different lifecycle processes and IT systems to follow-up product information. In this paper, an example has been implemented in order to consider real-time data from the usage phase to support decision making on wheels diameter for specific customers based on usage data. The example shows how a middle of life DT can support connecting different stages of the product lifecycle and promote real-time decision making to enhance services.

Current studies in this area usually focus on early product lifecycle phases and on Digital Twin implementation to support simulation. However, the discussion of a multi-phase Digital Twin and the implementation of a Digital Twin on the product use phase is still open in the literature. In this study, we focus on the use phase as a starting point for the Digital Twin deployment.

This research has limitations regarding the use of opensource platforms and a Learning Factory scenario. Future research work should integrate the information of multiple IT systems from the entire product lifecycle in a comprehensive Digital Twin. In this sense, establishing a detailed digital thread to support Digital Twin may be a promising research avenue.

References

1. Vachalek, J., Bartalsky, L., Rovny, O., et al.: The digital twin of an industrial production line within the industry 4.0 concept. In: Proceedings of 2017 21st International Conference on Process Control PC 2017, pp. 258–262 (2017). https://doi.org/10.1109/PC.2017.7976223
2. Qi, Q., Tao, F.: Digital twin and big data towards smart manufacturing and industry 4.0: 360 degree comparison. IEEE Access **6**, 3585–3593 (2018). https://doi.org/10.1109/ACCESS.2018.2793265
3. Uhlemann, T.H., Lehmann, C., Steinhilper, R.: The Digital Twin: Realizing the Cyber-Physical Production System for industry 4.0. Procedia CIRP **61**, 335–340 (2017). https://doi.org/10.1016/j.procir.2016.11.152
4. Cheng, Y., Zhang, Y., Ji, P., et al.: Cyber-physical integration for moving digital factories forward towards smart manufacturing: a survey. Int. J. Adv. Manuf. Technol. **97**, 1209–1221 (2018)
5. Lu, Y., Xu, X.: Resource virtualization: a core technology for developing cyber-physical production systems. J. Manuf. Syst. **47**, 128–140 (2018). https://doi.org/10.1016/j.jmsy.2018.05.003
6. Terzi, S., Bouras, A., Dutta, D., et al.: Product lifecycle management - from its history to its new role. Int. J. Prod. Lifecycle Manag. **4**, 360–389 (2010). https://doi.org/10.1504/IJPLM.2010.036489
7. Schleich, B., Anwer, N., Mathieu, L., Wartzack, S.: Shaping the digital twin for design and production engineering. CIRP Ann. Manuf. Technol. **66**, 141–144 (2017). https://doi.org/10.1016/j.cirp.2017.04.040
8. Zhang, H., Liu, Q., Chen, X., et al.: A digital twin-based approach for designing and decoupling of hollow glass production line. IEEE Access **5**, 26901–26911 (2017). https://doi.org/10.1109/ACCESS.2017.2766453
9. Boote, D.N., Beile, P.: Scholars before researchers: on the centrality of the dissertation literature review in research preparation. Educ. Res. **34**, 3–15 (2005). https://doi.org/10.3102/0013189X034006003
10. Domingos, D., Martins, F., Cândido, C., Martinho, R.: Internet of things aware WS-BPEL business processes - context variables and expected exceptions. J. Univ. Comput. Sci. **20**, 1109–1129 (2014). https://doi.org/10.3217/jucs-020-08-1109
11. Bleda, A.L., Jara, A.J., Maestre, R., et al.: Evaluation of the impact of furniture on communications performance for ubiquitous deployment of wireless sensor networks in smart homes. Sensors (Switzerland) **12**, 6463–6496 (2012). https://doi.org/10.3390/s120506463
12. Fang, C., Liu, X., Pardalos, P.M., Pei, J.: Optimization for a three-stage production system in the Internet of Things: procurement, production and product recovery, and acquisition. Int. J. Adv. Manuf. Technol. **83**, 689–710 (2015). https://doi.org/10.1007/s00170-015-7593-1
13. Tao, F., Cheng, J., Qi, Q., Zhang, M., Zhang, H., Sui, F.: Digital twin-driven product design, manufacturing and service with big data. Int. J. Adv. Manuf. Technol. **94**, 3563–3576 (2017). https://doi.org/10.1007/s00170-017-0233-1
14. Brenner, B., Hummel, V.: Digital twin as enabler for an innovative digital shopfloor management system in the ESB logistics learning factory at Reutlingen - University. Procedia Manuf. **9**, 198–205 (2017). https://doi.org/10.1016/j.promfg.2017.04.039
15. Havard, V., Jeanne, B., Lacomblez, M., et al.: Digital twin and virtual reality: a co-simulation environment for design and assessment of industrial workstations for design and assessment of industrial workstations. Prod. Manuf. Res. **7**, 472–489 (2019). https://doi.org/10.1080/21693277.2019.1660283

16. Barbosa, S., Silva, F.P., Rafael, L., Otto, R.B.: Virtual assistant to real time training on industrial environment (2018). https://doi.org/10.3233/978-1-61499-898-3-33
17. Park, K.T., Nam, Y.W., Lee, H.S., et al.: Design and implementation of a digital twin application for a connected micro smart factory. Int. J. Comput. Integr. Manuf. **32**, 596–614 (2019). https://doi.org/10.1080/0951192X.2019.1599439
18. Liu, J., Zhou, H., Tian, G., Liu, X., Jing, X.: Digital twin-based process reuse and evaluation approach for smart process planning. Int. J. Adv. Manufact. Technol. **100**, 1619–1634 (2018). https://doi.org/10.1007/s00170-018-2748-5
19. Zhuang, C., Liu, J., Xiong, H.: Digital twin-based smart production management and control framework for the complex product assembly shop-floor. Int. J. Adv. Manufact. Technol. **96**, 1149–1163 (2018). https://doi.org/10.1007/s00170-018-1617-6
20. Wang, X.V., Wang, L.: Digital twin-based WEEE recycling, recovery and remanufacturing in the background of Industry 4.0. Int. J. Prod. Res. **57**, 3892–3902 (2019). https://doi.org/10.1080/00207543.2018.1497819
21. Wang, A.X., Wang, X.: Virtual Reality of 3D digital factory based on coastal environment. Coast. Res. **83**, 507–512 (2019). https://doi.org/10.2112/SI83-085 1
22. Wiesner, S., Freitag, M., Westphal, I., Thoben, K.D.: Interactions between service and product lifecycle management. Procedia CIRP **30**, 36–41 (2015). https://doi.org/10.1016/j.procir.2015.02.018
23. Belkadi, F., Bernard, A.: Trust-based patterns for the management of inter-enterprises collaborations in context of extended enterprise. IFAC-PapersOnLine **28**, 1186–1191 (2015). https://doi.org/10.1016/j.ifacol.2015.06.245

A Complete Digital Chain to Enable the Digital Twin of a Shop Floor

Frédéric Noël[(✉)], Gülgün Alpan, and Fabien Mangione

Univ. Grenoble Alpes, CNRS, Grenoble INP (Institute of Engineering Univ. Grenoble Alpes), G-SCOP, 38000 Grenoble, France
{Frederic.Noel,Gulgun.Alpan,Fabien.mangione}@grenoble-inp.fr

Abstract. Digital twins is a recent paradigm. It creates an entangled link between the physical system and its digital twin. The digital twin has obviously no sense without the existence of the physical system, but the physical system highly depends on the digital twin. This concept opens many new challenges and opportunities.

Authors contributed to the construction of a digital twin architecture to manage a shop floor. The experience concerns a complete shop floor. To reach the status of digital twin, it was expected to reach simulation capacities and a complete digital chain to ensure the real time synchronisation of the real world with the underlying model which is the core component of the digital twin. A bottleneck was to create a coherent information system connecting information coming from various sources (MES, Machine Design, ERP, etc.), then to propose first functions to demonstrate the added value of this digital twin; here a production simulation was expected within a visual 3D realistic representation of the shop floor. The simulation uses data directly captured from the shop floor to support better decision making.

This paper presents the developed digital twin and its added value respect to production needs. It focuses on key performance indicators synchronisation as observed in the physical world and the impact on anticipation of the various futures depending on production decisions. It reports a first step of a digital twin deployment.

Keywords: Digital twin · Production flow · Workfloor · Virtual reality

1 Digital Twin Within Product Life Management

The digital twin wording emerged recently [4,7] and acts as a new paradigm for industry of the future. It was indeed introduced first in 2012 [4] and finally adopted by Dr. Grieves in 2014 for PLM, after using various names: Ideal Concept For PLM and Mirrored Spaces [6,8]. Digital Twin concept seems to be adopted by a wide community within academic research and industry. If the digital twin was just a virtual model of the physical world, it would not add value respect to the Digital Mock Up paradigm which appeared in the 1990's [2].

Published by Springer Nature Switzerland AG 2020
F. Nyffenegger et al. (Eds.): PLM 2020, IFIP AICT 594, pp. 128–138, 2020.
https://doi.org/10.1007/978-3-030-62807-9_11

Whenever we mention the development of a digital twin we must consider the type of physical system which is twinned. Apollo XIII spacecraft system is often refereed as a good metaphor to illustrate digital twin concept. Indeed during the Apollo XIII mission an oxygen tank incident [5] stressed the engineers to find solutions to keep the crew alive. By this time, digitisation was still poor and engineers used an earth based physical replica of the aircraft to propose and test problem solving processes. The core idea with the digital twin could be to get a digital model enabling such analysis and decision making about the physical system. Many literature reviews try to define the digital twin concept [9, 17]. They all agree that the digital twin *is required to reach the interaction and convergence between physical and virtual spaces*. Grieves definition was not detailed and remained application dependent; Uhlenkamp and al. [18] proposes dimensions of digital twin applications.

The digital twin is first viewed as a very realistic system simulation to mirror the product during its usage phase. The concept was generalised to any kind of system matching the cyber-physical system [12] definition and adapted to production systems [11, 13, 17]. The digital twin is not only a model, but it is deeply linked to its physical twin. A major point is the synchronization of the model with the real world. The digital twin must maintain a correct representation of the physical world. A supervision system captures the evolution of the physical system. This supervision is stored and versioned all along the system life cycle. Then the digital twin refers a huge amount of information to support decision making to be applied on the physical system.

The digital twin may concern a standard end user product, a manufacturing machine, or any complex system up to a complete production system. It must refer every important information to make decision all along the life cycle. Efforts from the research community to develop such holistic meta-models [3, 15, 16] did not reach a unique model covering every product life cycle. Then the deployment of the digital twin paradigm will lead to the development of partially incomplete digital twins. Within production systems, the distribution of information would be an argue to use big data technologies but they are complementary to the digital twin and do not replace it [14]. Also, the model must be associated to simulation or any other smart system to make decision automatically or to support end-users to make objective decisions [10].

Many papers (as most paper referenced in this section) deeply define the concept and the potential architectures to support the digital twin deployment. The achievement of these architectures faces many challenges within a real shop floor where information is not always digital and seldom integrated. It must also provide direct added value for operators unless it will be abandoned. The authors participated to the development of a digital twin for a shop floor of a first order stakeholder within automotive industry. A complete digital twin cannot be reached in a single step. This paper presents and justifies the key architecture bricks which were developed.

Section 2 describes the various sources of information as found when the project started (ERP, MES, Machine Design models, maintenance documents, etc.). One key point was to rationalize and integrate these sources of information. Section 3 focuses on the triggers used by production engineers to make decisions; these triggers were used to select the information to be managed within the digital twin and led to a distributed digital twin core model. But to become a digital twin, a model must support making decision on every day life. A production simulator was integrated to fill this dimension. At last, but not least the conclusion of the paper discusses the overall process and issues opened via this digital twin experience.

2 Shop Floor Information Sources

2.1 ISA 95: ERP, MES, SCADA: Not yet Fully Deployed

The digitisation of shop floor was standardized with the ISA-95 pyramid [1]. This pyramid builds foundations by automating physical hardware with actuators connected by sensors. SCADA refers the process control system of a limited machine process. At the top of the pyramid the Enterprise Resource Planning (ERP) manages the information system of the complete shop floor. It is usually prescriptive; it models the shop floor as they are expected by the management engineers. MES is often presented to fill the gap between ERP and SCADA; it usually ensures the storage and management of the sensor values; it allows to get operation feedback.

ISA-95 leads to an information system architecture mainly dedicated to manage the manufacturing operations. The process may be either discrete or continuous. Within discrete processes, operations are sequenced on various workstations, while continuous processes are not split on separated workstations. A continuous production line may be huge but should be managed at the SCADA level. ERP and MES are adapted to manage the physical flows among the workstations.

The level of digitisation of shop floor varies from one company to another and even from a factory to another one inside a same company. Even information properly recorded within the ERP is often printed to get rapid access at operational level. In many companies, updating the information system remains a non priority activity. The priority remains the production; the added value of the information system must be properly balanced with respect to the efforts to maintain it up-to-date. Whatever the justifications, it is easily observed that the usage of all the ISA-95 layers remains very incomplete.

The level of digitised detail depends also of every company. KANBAN system are often paper based while in other companies RFID technologies can automate the management of lots. Quality management expects feedback from every workstations that are still reported by hand following either the production line tag time or the work shift while sensors values are reported at various frequencies.

2.2 Shop Floor Evolution

At ramp-up, a new factory is mainly organised to support an estimated demand. Its organisation evolves regarding three main activities.

- production order: whenever a production is launched to answer a client command. It is mainly a definition of parameter values of the process. The frequency of creation of new production orders depends on the product, but even for mass production of rapid production process, the production orders are usually decided daily.
- maintenance: it is triggered on anticipated frequency or by random events The impact of maintenance on the information models may be a simple standby delay information but it may result on modification of a machine and/or the related process parameters but also of the process itself.
- layout reorganisation: it may be due to a performance or quality enhancement (moving machines or integrating new production cells). It may be also driven by a market evolution (observed or anticipated). The frequency of layout reorganisation is seldom less than monthly and can reach several decades for complex equipments (big furnace in a steel production line). In automotive industry the market life cycle of cars is now anticipated from the design stage. Then even stakeholders involved in production of sub-components anticipate the phase-out of references and the layout may be adapted monthly. It was the case in the application where the digital twin was proposed.

The performance of the process depends on layout organisation, on maintenance, on quality processes, and still on the manufacturing process knowledge and know-how. Associated information participate to the digital twin.

2.3 Representations of Factory Components

The global manufacturing process is organised by the physical and information flows between every work station operation. The work station model depends on the expected simulation or survey. Several sources of information about work stations exists. On one side, every workstation is designed by a machine provider or by the company itself. It relies on physics behaviours that must be technically mastered. On an other side machines are issued from another production process. Models were used for the development of manufacturing machines, but the final production of a machine/work station does not directly depends on its own production model. However production is directly impacted by the machine characteristics. There is thus a direct interest to get access to the design models of the machines (specifications, CAD models, etc.). The work station is also modelled by its capacity and performances as reported within a usual ERP. A link between ERP machine structure should be associated with the machine documentation.

When the layout organisation is concerned, all design data is not expected. If the complex geometry impacts the working-station ergonomy and the maintenance process, on the workflow point of view a workstation is mainly a fixed area with material input and output docks. A simplified representation like a footprint is enough for most layout discussions. But some complex layout could be designed and optimised taking advantage of the machine 3D geometry. It is the case if the production lines are stacked up but we must admit that it is not so often. 3D layout is anyhow a real issue for some transfer lines.

It means that it already exists a lot of sources of information about work stations. The impact of every submodel depends on the expected simulations. In addition a model of the factory building is also part of this complete shop floor definition. Most factories do not manage machine models and have basic 2D drawings of buildings. To get access to more complete 3D models, require either a scanning process or a reverse modelling within a CAD modeller. Fortunately for a new machine, a factory should expect its provider to deliver almost a complete CAD model. The 3D model provides a more natural rendering of the factory, which may be an added value to well understand the process for simulations in an immersive modality.

3 Supervision Key Performance Indicators

3.1 A Factory Use Case

The sources of information for a complete factory are widely spread and far from standardisation. But all these models should support making efficient decisions. Decisions take place about production orders, maintenance and layout organisation. This article focuses on production orders. The study is carried out at a first tier automotive supplier. The company produces sub-components in factories. Each factory has about 1000 staff members mainly dedicated to production. Production is organised on 8 h work shift. A factory is hierarchically decomposed into production lines dedicated to a process type. A line is a set working cells which are composed of several workstations.

3.2 Production Order Decisions

In the factory the production orders were decided daily. During a collaborative meeting, every factory line manager is expected to report the current state of his line. Then based on customer commands, and with a more or less formal knowledge of future demand evolution, they can discuss production orders priorities.

The main shared object is a 2D map of the factory layout which is used for sharing the locations of the main current issues. The main triggers for making decisions are the expectation to increase the production performance. They expect to maximise and make uniform the sales revenue associated to every square meter. The machine involvement must be optimised: non productive machine must be minimised taking into account both maintenance periods and ramp-up processes. Launching a new reference into production is not instantaneous and expects a calibration process. Longer production runs for a given reference avoids to stop and re-launch the production line for another reference: it is thus more efficient than a serie of short production runs.

Some objective key performance indicators (KPI) become the main argues for decisions making. KPIS are well known from most production system and may be adapted to any management vision. Here the following KPIs were expected: 1.OEE (Overall Equipment Effectiveness which measures the equipment usage rate), SPA (Sales per unit area which measures the ratio of net sale involving a surface leading), WIP (the work in process which measures output and scrap rate), Total count (of produced item), Bad count (of scrapped items), EFF (efficiency).

These KPIs reflect the global state of the overall factory and indeed integrate various measures. From the standard definition of these KPIs and an analysis of the factory sensors we built the graph of Fig. 1 which defines the dependencies between available measures and the OEE KPI (a complete graph was produced for all the expected KPIs. They are classified as raw parameter (P), raw measures (M) or aggregated values (A). A measure is directly and automatically captured from sensors while raw parameters are data that are set by hand because no direct sensor can capture them. One can note that in our case the number of automated measure remains low.

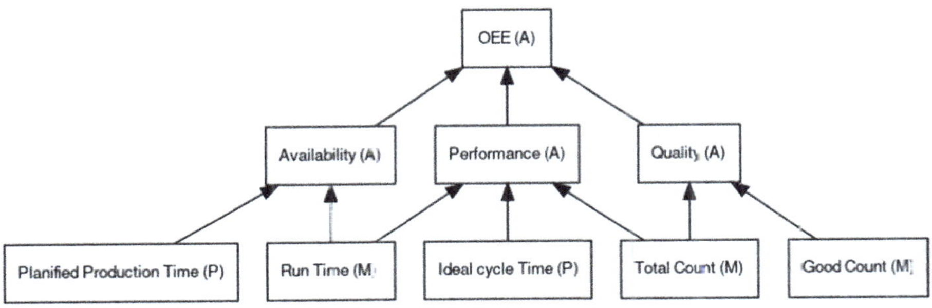

Fig. 1. Links between available measures and the OEE KPI

The supervision from the factory MES is supposed to deliver versioned values of raw parameters. It is also in charge to compute aggregated parameters.

3.3 Shop Floor Structure

The layout organisation has also an impact on the transfer time. To compute transfer times a structural model of the factory is thus expected. In our use case, the factory engineering office has the CAD models of every machine but do not use them. A CAD modeller is also used to maintain the layout definition. But the distance between workstations cannot be directly extracted from this model which was created mainly to get 2D drawings of the layout.

Thus a specific information model is expected. The factory hierarchy can be easily maintained in either a database or a simple excel sheet. A specific process was created to export a 3D wavefront model of every machine plus basic geometric information such as the 2D footprint and the relative position of the machine within its father inside the hierarchy decomposition. Geometric information is exported from a CAD modeller and we create

- one or several obj file (wavefront format) to define various representation of every item at various levels of simplification.
- a structure file (a csv table sheet within our implementation) which decomposes the hierarchy and links to the representation files.

The csv file refers every equipment of the factory, linked to its father (the working cell, the production line, sector up to the facto) and associates every equipment to some basic characteristics: CAD model, OBJ files, 2D footprint, etc. A unique id for every equipment is defined here and every other information source (ERP, MES, etc.) uses refers to this id. The digital twin becomes a distributed model. Specific processes were implemented to keep this model coherent and synchronised with the real world.

4 Production Simulation

4.1 An Enhanced Supervision

The previous model creates a supervision model. It changes the initial state of the art of the company by providing objective KPIs to make decisions. The system was used to create both traditional 2D dashboards but also to experience a full 3D representation of the company with KPIs. Figure 2 shows the 3D system where two complete production lines were modelled. A direct connection to the supervision system in relation with the shop floor structure(csv file) enables to visualise the KPIs and to investigate their evolution along the time. The left picture of Fig. 2 is a picture of the real shop floor while the right snapshot shows the digital twin extended with a direct representation of KPIs (here OEE) on the top of machines. A calendar widget at the bottom of the virtual model allows to navigate along the versioned values of the model.

This digital twin creates a collaborative framework as soon as this vision is shared by several engineers. They have a direct access to objective feedback about the current state of the factory which is in most real situations a real added value since usually the exchange of knowledge about the factory state remains informal through direct discussion. The 3D model makes a realistic framework which makes the framework easy to learn.

The framework enables making decision for production orders, or in few cases layout re-organisation by visualising the main troubles but it does not change drastically the production management. It is expected to go further by providing direct support to make decision through simulation. A simulator was thus integrated to the current system.

4.2 Production Simulator

The simulator is a discrete event based simulator. There exist many industrial well known commercial solution for this type of simulations. Every machine consumes inputs and creates output at every simulation step. The process duration, the type of inputs and outputs depend on machine models that must be defined

Fig. 2. 3D representation of the factory connected to KPI supervision

a priori. Evoluate solutions undertake randomized models based on statistical behavior of machines. Then the simulation result depends on some randomized values. Starting with a given state two simulation occurrences will lead to two different results. For our study a home made simulator was developed. The originality here is that the simulator has a direct access to versioned supervised data. Then the machine input models are continuously updated through the real feedback of the real world.

Figure 3 describes the overall architecture of the digital twin including the simulator:

- The factory digital model merges the 3D geometric model (obj files) exported from the CAD models given by machine providers plus the hierarchical structure which is a simple excel sheet saved as a csv file. All this data can be updated at any time but the real refresh frame-rate is about the month. It is then stored within a shared repository and the information is accessed by network authorisation to the corresponding drive.
- Factory MES is in charge of populating a supervision model. It is also in charge to compute the overall KPIs and to provide them on request through SQL application protocol interface. From the versioned supervision data either the MES or the simulator is able to update statistical models of every machines.
- A specific module must be in charge to export information from ERP system in order for the simulator to get access to the expected physical flow to make any reference product. Such a physical flow is usually made for a given reference and should not evolve frequently. The simulator must also access to production orders which evolve on an every day basis.

- The rendering digital twin system is expected for simulation conditions definition. Indeed engineers expect to simulate various production scenarii depending on:
  1. production orders priority: it is the main job to make decision about the command sequence organisation.
  2. resource assignment. Engineer can decide to assign more or less staff on a given machine or line
  3. layout reorganisation. Even if these decisions are seldom on a daily basis the layout reorganisation is expected
  4. external market information: raw material delivery assumptions, raw material cost evolution, etc.

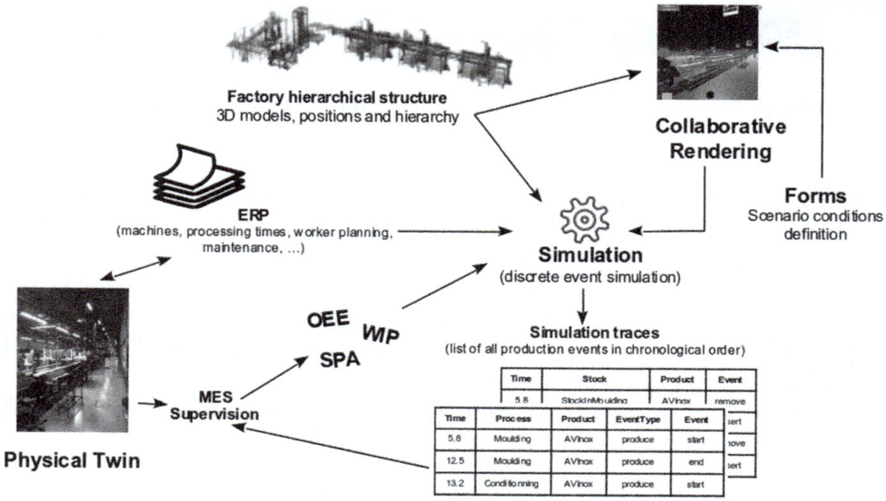

Fig. 3. Simulation information flow

The simulator could used any existing factory simulation software. Here it was encoded based on the open-source DESMO-J library[1]. The behaviour of a given production line is simulated within a few seconds to anticipate several production weeks. From the MES supervision, the simulation is based production order scenarii entered by engineers and on behaviour models directly constructed from the physical world observation. The simulation integrates randomised events following the recent statistical behavior of every machine.

With random event, two consecutive simulations on a same scenario lead to different results. The simulator launches a set of randomized simulations and creates every production events in a simulated period of production. An average answer (in term of KPIs) is created from the set of simulations which is saved

[1] http://desmoj.sourceforge.net/home.html.

in the MES supervision database with a specific status since this data is not historical data but anticipation data for a given scenario. Since it is managed inside the MES, this anticipated scenario is easily displayed on the collaborative rendering digital twin module as a standard supervision. Then Engineers use these results to make comparisons between scenarii and at last to decide which scenario will be executed.

5 Conclusion: Digital Twin Opportunities and Limitations

With the achievement of simulation we reach a first level of the digital twin paradigm. It remains a quite simple simulator but internal behaviors are deduced from the real world. The simulator has access to versioned values of parameters. It can build random models which cover the current risks of real factory because it is not just a model but a more direct physical world measure. It acts as a first step to support Digital Twin deployment.

But new steps with new functions must extend the digital twin usage. As mentioned by Uhlenkamp [18] the digital twin *concept meets the needs and the expectations of people performing different product related tasks.*

Anyhow some questions arise with such a development. The weight to populate the information model then to keep it synchronised with the real world becomes a real challenge which must be discussed regarding the final added value of the complete system. For example the interest of a 3D model must be discussed since most layout are 2D and the decisions do not need 3D simulation and perception. But indeed such a 3D digital twin opens new steps for maintenance or operator training operations where 3D model will be expected. The return on investment will thus depend on the initial simulation added value but also on all the new processes that will be achievable thanks to the digital twin investment.

Aknowledgement. This project was funded by BPI-France through a partnership project. It involved several engineers who participated to some results contributing to this paper. We must thank these engineers; Julian Muller, Gregory German and Bruno Got. We would like to thank Vincent Guizouarn, Pascal Lenormand, and Anthony Compassi from Cooper Standard Vitré for their highly valuable comments and suggestions. We are further grateful for the time our testers have spent evaluating the current prototypes.

The G-SCOP laboratory is member of the Persyval Laboratory of Excellence (French LabEx).

References

1. Brandl, D.: Business to manufacturing (B2M) collaboration between business and manufacturing using ISA-95. Revue De L Electricite Et De L Electronique (8), 46–52 (2002)
2. Drews, P., Weyrich, M.: A system for digital mock-up's and virtual prototype design in industry: 'the virtual workbench'. In: ISIE 1997 Proceeding of the IEEE International Symposium on Industrial Electronics, pp. 1292–1296. IEEE (1997)

3. Foufou, S., Fenves, S., Bock, C., Sudarsan, R., Sriram, R.D.: A core product model for PLM with an illustrative XML ipmlementation. In: Product Life Cycle Management - Emerging Solutions and Challenges for Global Networked Enterprise, vol. 1, pp. 21–32 (2005)
4. Glaessgen, E., Stargel, D.: The digital twin paradigm for future NASA and US air force vehicles. In: 53rd AIAA/ASME/ASCE/AHS/ASC Structures, Structural Dynamics and Materials Conference 20th AIAA/ASME/AHS Adaptive Structures Conference 14th AIAA, p. 1818 (2012)
5. Goodman, J.: Apollo 13 guidance, navigation, and control challenges. In: AIAA Space 2009 Conference & Exposition, p. 6455 (2009)
6. Grieves, M.: Virtually Perfect: Driving Innovative and Lean Products Through Product Lifecycle Management. Space Coast Press, Cocoa Beach (2011)
7. Grieves, M.: Digital twin: manufacturing excellence through virtual factory replication. White Pap. **1**, 1–7 (2014)
8. Grieves, M.W.: Product lifecycle management: the new paradigm for enterprises. Int. J. Prod. Dev. **2**(1–2), 71–84 (2005)
9. Kritzinger, W., Karner, M., Traar, G., Henjes, J., Sihn, W.: Digital twin in manufacturing: a categorical literature review and classification. IFAC-PapersOnLine **51**(11), 1016–1022 (2018)
10. Kunath, M., Winkler, H.: Integrating the digital twin of the manufacturing system into a decision support system for improving the order management process. Procedia CIRP **72**, 225–231 (2018)
11. Lee, J., Lapira, E., Yang, S., Kao, A.: Predictive manufacturing system-trends of next-generation production systems. IFAC Proc. Vol. **46**(7), 150–156 (2013)
12. Monostori, L., et al.: Cyber-physical systems in manufacturing. CIRP Ann. **65**(2), 621–641 (2016)
13. Negri, E., Fumagalli, L., Macchi, M.: A review of the roles of digital twin in CPS-based production systems. Procedia Manuf. **11**, 939–948 (2017)
14. Qi, Q., Tao, F.: Digital twin and big data towards smart manufacturing and industry 4.0: 360 degree comparison. IEEE Access **6**, 3585–3593 (2018)
15. Standard For The Exchange of Product Model Data: (STEP), ISO 10303, A series of documents. Part 42: Geometric and Topological Representation, ISO 10303–42, Available from ISO Secretariat, National Institute Of Standards and Technology (NIST), Gaithersburg, MD (1994)
16. Subrahmanian, E., Rachuri, S., Fenves, S.J., Foufou, S., Siram, R.D.: Product life cycle mangement support: a challenge in supporting product design and manufacturing in a networked economy. Int. J. Prod. Lefecycle Manag. **1**, 4–25 (2005)
17. Tao, F., Zhang, M.: Digital twin shop-floor: a new shop-floor paradigm towards smart manufacturing. IEEE Access **5**, 20418–20427 (2017)
18. Uhlenkamp, J.F., Hribernik, K., Wellsandt, S., Thoben, K.D.: Digital twin applications: a first systemization of their dimensions, pp. 1–8, June 2019. https://doi.org/10.1109/ICE.2019.8792579

Implementation of a Digital Twin Starting with a Simulator

Léandre Guitard(✉), Daniel Brissaud, and Fréderic Noël

G-SCOP Grenoble INP, 46 avenue Félix Viallet,
38041 Grenoble Cedex 1, France
{leandre.guitard,daniel.brissaud,
frederic.noel}@grenoble-inp.fr

Abstract. The term complete Digital Twin describes a digital entity following and taking part in the life of a system, from its design during its regular use, up until its end of life. It is a coherent set of interoperable modules that will be used depending on the state of progress of the system. Since the Digital Twin follows the system from its design to its end of life, it can be a powerful lifecycle management tool.

In this framework, it seems too complicated to try integrating all the modules simultaneously. It's important to prioritize them and build an expandable architecture. One of the major criterion is ensuring the digital continuity in order to implement a sustainable model for the Industry 4.0.

The modules used after-sales, such as the predictive maintenance module, are harder to implement, because the connection/communication with the system after delivery must be managed which is not always possible. Therefore, the modules that are the easiest to implement are the ones before-sales, because they are integrally managed internally.

This study is conducted in a medium size enterprise which allows us to address in a concrete way the deployment of a digital twin in the industrial activities. The deployment strategy needs to be combined in order to prevent the features of the digital twin to be perceived as a hindrance. This study focuses on the development of a simulator that will link up offer design, detailed design and assembly/manufacturing follow up.

Keywords: Digital Twin · Product lifecycle · Cyber-physical systems

1 Digital Twins in the Literature

1.1 State of the Art

With the new technologies that Industry of the future offers us, there is a new tool that we can use to improve our systems; the Digital twin. Even if the wording is relatively recent [1] The concept was first introduced by Dr Grieves in 2005 under the term "Ideal Concept For PLM" [2] where it is described as consisting of three elements; "real space, virtual space(s) and a liking mechanism". Later, the term used to describe this concept became "Mirror Spaces" in 2011 [3] until Dr. Grieves himself adopted the terminology of "Digital Twin" in 2014 [4] where the concept stayed the same, based

Published by Springer Nature Switzerland AG 2020
F. Nyffenegger et al. (Eds.): PLM 2020, IFIP AICT 594, pp. 139–149, 2020.
https://doi.org/10.1007/978-3-030-62807-9_12

around the same three elements. NASA used a similar concept for their Apollo 13 mission [5] where the principle was to build an exact replica of the system to allow diagnosis and scenario testing without the consequences of the real environment. The US Air Force Also worked on the subject of a Digital Twin, by applying it to their aircrafts; the concept goes further in terms of precision, going down to the microstructure of the materials used to build the aircrafts [6].

Since the concept was introduced and developed for NASA and the US Air Force, the Digital Twin has been spreading to numerous other industrial fields such as the manufacturing of civilian ships [7].

In parallel, in 2006 the concept of a product avatar was also mentioned [8]. The concept came from the fact that there was no centralized data relating to a specific product thus making it increasingly complicated when another entity was added to the product's life-cycle. The paper suggested a centralized database relating to each specific product which is very close to the concept of a digital twin as we consider it in this article.

The term Digital Twin is now the one that is used by both, academics and in the industrial sector. The Digital Twin is considered as a virtual model of a physical system, but contrary to a Digital Mockup (Apollo 13 model), the connection with its physical counterpart is much more predominant and crucial.

Out of all these concepts and definitions, the choice relies on the context, in the context of an industrial transfert system, it is not relevant to go down to the microstructure of the aluminum profiles used to build it, but the general concept of the real space, virtual space and a liking mechanism is the foundation upon which to build the structure of a Digital Twin in order to develop and apply it in a real industrial context.

The goal of this study is to validate what an industrial company wants from a Digital Twin, and then suggest and implement a method by which to develop and integrate a Digital Twin to their products.

1.2 Determining Elements

The Digital Twin may be seen as an intelligent database that helps the user to make decisions or directly manages the system it mirrors. The virtual space described by Dr. Grieves is a series of models describing the real world, the corollary to that is that the dimensions of the Digital Twin are defined by two elements; the precision of the models that are attached and if they allow analysis and its connection with its physical brother. We can represent those two factors in a chart (Table 1):

Table 1. Classification of Digital Twins

Precision	Connectivity	
	No connection to field data	Field data available
The models aren't precise enough to make reliable analysis	NA/Not a Digital Twin	Supervision
The models allow for reliable analysis and projections	Apollo 13 like model	Complete Digital Twin

Deriving of that, there are three defining elements:

- **Field data**; they show the current state of the system, how it's evolving, up to in what environment it's evolving (speed, part's temperature, environment's temperature, power consumption, vibration,…) these are the data that will be run through the models to predict and project situations.
- **Configuration data**; they show the structure, the configuration, the program version, all the data that is relevant to show **what** the system **is**. It's on those data that the models will be based, if they aren't precise or reliable the models won't be either.
- **Models** derived from the configuration data, that puts into equations the behavior of the system in order to analyze real time data and predict outcomes.

1.3 Definition of a Complete Digital Twin

In a more tangible way, a functional industrial complete Digital Twin is a set of coherently organized modules, each containing the models and configuration data necessary to address the chosen function. Those modules are made accessible through an interface that can vary depending on the stage at which the system is, that during the normal use of the system is also capable of giving an overview of the system and that is available throughout the life of the system from the first design steps to when parts are reused for other systems (from cradle to cradle).

Figure 1 describes the way this Digital Twin is organized and how it interacts with the user and the physical system.

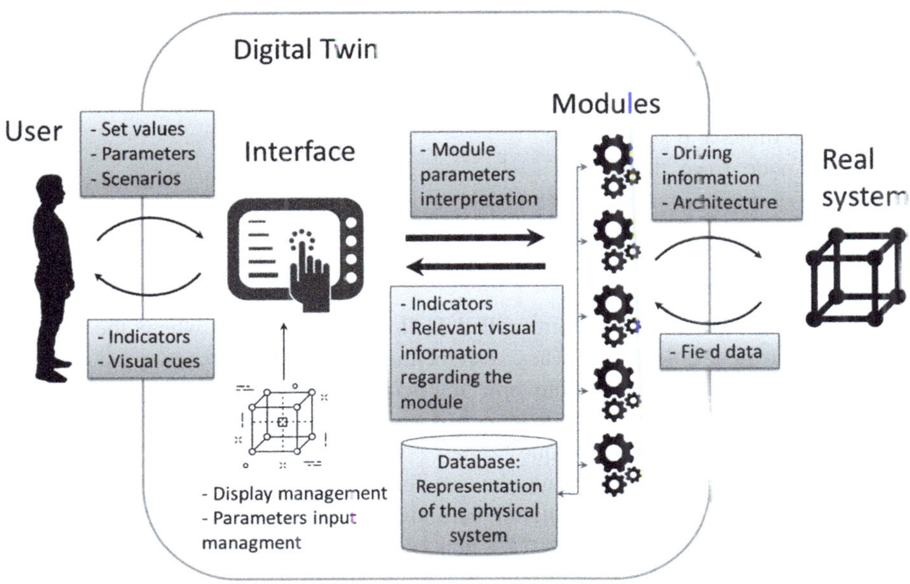

Fig. 1. Synoptic of the Digital Twin

The user will set some values or feed the digital twin with parameters or scenarios via the interface. The interface will then interpret those inputs and send them to the appropriate modules. The modules will process the data and using the field data as well, construct the desired indicators, as well as participate in building the database representing the physical system; the heart of the digital twin.

Once the modules have the indicators, they will be able to send commands to the physical system to adapt its operation. They will also send back to the interface, the relevant indicators and visual cues to tell the user know the conclusions and either suggest actions or show the automated actions that have been taken.

The question that arises now is; how to develop and implement a Digital Twin in a real industrial context?

2 Industrial Context

The company in which this study is conducted is a group called Hellomoov' where these concepts are applied to integrate a digital twin to the product.

2.1 Administrative Description of the Company

Hellomoov' is a French group dedicated to the support of the industry. It has 3 main components; Transept in vendee, Faber in the Ardennes and Elcom in Isère that all together represents around 250 employees. The group has 2 main activities; aluminum profiles and static structures made from them and in-house logistics systems. From conveyors to more complex transfert systems, as shown in Fig. 2.

Fig. 2. A transfert system

There is another office in Isère called Hellomoov' Institute, where the R&D is conducted for the whole group. They oversee the development of new products, new systems by considering innovations and new technologies, for example all the innovations of Industry 4.0. The Institute launched a project that aims at integrating industry 4.0 to in-house logistics; Moovitique®.

Moovitique® "It's the conveying, the transfert and the handling of object, products and containers profiting of all the digital disruption advances, the connected objects and the smart mechatronic applications. This new high stakes discipline will allow to open a whole new field to optimize production lines, conditioning lines in today's and tomorrow".

The Digital Twin integration of the current study must answer this vision.

2.2 Specificities of the Transfert Activity

Our main job today for transfert systems, is to deliver functioning systems that will be able to handle objects and products throughout the factory. Once the systems are delivered, we intervene in case of malfunctions or for regular maintenance. But between maintenance operations, we have almost no contact with the clients or our systems. Besides that, there are other specificities to this type of activity:

The transfert systems are sub-systems of special purpose machines; machines that cannot be standardized, some functions can be, but every project is a new development in a way, which means gain in the design process would be a big gain.

Elcom/Hellomoov' is a supplier of the special purpose machine sector, therefor we are not the first contact with the final customer, which leads to a delay in information and reduces the time that we have.

Elcom/Hellomoov's part in the special purpose machine is to move the client's product along the manufacturing line, but it does not directly bring any added value to the product and therefor have more difficulties convincing the customer to invest in the transfert system.

Those factors are part of the reason why we engaged in the Moovitique® initiative; by that we seek to add functions to our systems that will be able to bring added value to our customers' products and by that we hope to grow in the value chain.

Elcom/Hellomoov' is a rather small company, it works mainly because the product is good and they master it really well, they have a practical and empirical knowledge of their systems, it is highly relying on the knowledge of people that have been in the company for a long time. That can have some impact on assembly quality for new employee that don't have the product background.

2.3 The Digital Twin of a Transfert Product

The Digital Twin is a general concept, it needs to be adapted and applied to the desired technical context, in this case, how to integrate it to Hellomoov's transfert systems.

For this application, there are a series of modules, whit each their specific functions, needing their own models, and data. Also keeping in mind that the Digital Twin needs to follow the digital continuity as a part of Industry 4.0. Every module needs to be able to communicate with rest of the digital environment of the Digital Twin.

The proposed modules are the following:

The design Assistance is the module that seeks to help design a transfert solution. There can be multiple levels of assistance, from designing with a configurator to self-generating algorithms, or from designing a single unit to a complete solution.

The Simulator insures the design is able to meet the requirements. After transferring the data from the design assistant, the simulator is capable of generating a 3D model of that design, and based on a data base of behavior models for each parts of the system, the simulator is then capable of displaying the motion of the relevant parts and generating a summary of the KPIs to validate the design that was proposed. Once the simulation confirms that the design is good, it can communicate with the ERP system to generate a bill of material, an order, …

The Assembly/Manufacturing Assistance is the tool that based on the design, on the types of attachments is able to generate each parts and what operation they require (cutting, drilling,…) as well as propose an order of assembly to help the technicians build the system; based on the bill of material, it can generate an animated 3D representation of the steps to manufacture an assemble the parts. Projected in Augmented reality glasses, it allows to technician to work while keeping in view the steps and how to perform them.

An Industrial Control System; since the Digital Twin is connected with field data from its physical twin, it also allows the monitoring of the system, to be able to know what is the current state of it, and other relevant parameters; such as, the temperature, the speed, the power consumption, … And that even on the other side of the Earth.

The predictive Maintenance Module can, using sensor that are used for process and others specifically designed for maintenance, record, interpret weak signals and generate from them, failure models in order to predict and communicate on what part is going to fail and estimate the time that is left before failure. That will allow the users to anticipate maintenance in order to limit the consequences on production.

The Maintenance Assistance Module will similarly to the assembly/manufacturing assistance module, use assembly models and help the technician replace the required parts by showing him the easiest way to access them and what procedures to use through Augmented reality glasses.

The Reconfiguration Assistance will be able to propose, based on the evolving needs of the user as well as the modularity of the product, an optimized redesign of the system, based not on the theoretical needs of the user, but on the recorded use of the current system.

The End of Life Estimation module will estimate the cumulative cost of foreseen maintenance, based on the predictive maintenance module and price data, and compare it with new systems in order to recommend keeping maintaining or to revamp or replace the system.

The Reuse Module is corollary to the end of life module, once the system is set to be replaced, some parts might be considered not reusable, but for the others, this module will take them into account and targets to reuse them and optimize the design using them as much as possible.

Interfaces that will regroup the most important data. These modules will be made accessible through multiple interfaces. The differences between interfaces will depend on their use, but regardless of the interface, they will all have the same goal; make the relevant models accessible, display a summary of the relevant data at the specific time and place for the specific system.

2.4 Integration and Perspectives

As we can see, the Digital Twin is major tool in the development and life of a system, it can bring numerous benefits, but it also is a complex system, with complex models describing almost everything about the system, which makes it complicated to implement.

As said previously, the company Elcom/Hellomoov' is a rather small company and has a mostly empirical management system, based on the experience of people that works there. The development of such a tool all at once represents a big task and a big paradigm shift that in the structure like this one seems risky. Whereas developing it step by step, function by function will allow to demonstrate the pertinence and the value of each module progressively.

After discussing the advantages and risks of both solutions, the company chose the ramp up approach.

In order to succeed in the deployment of a digital twin, there are global aspects that need the be addressed:

- A digital twin like this generates a lot of data coming from the physical system, all the field data collected can represent an important amount storage. A single source would not necessarily represent an important volume on its own, but multiplied by the number of potential sources on a transfert system, then further multiplied by the number of systems of each of the users will be [9]. The two solutions would be either buying or renting servers or store those data on a cloud. As of today, no decision has been taking yet by the company.
- The models used represents the real added value of a digital, they will help design, operate, integrate weak signals and in general operate the system. The qualifications needed to develop these models and algorithms are crucial and Elcom/Hellomcov' doesn't have them in-house as of today. It is crucial to define the working framework in order to develop them. Define if they will be developed in-house after recruiting or work with a subcontractor/partner. If the models are developed with a subcontractor/partner, it is important de define who will have the ownership of the models.
- Whether it is the models and algorithms or the field data from the client, those pieces of information are sensitive. They could be used in malicious ways and therefor need to be protected. The two main ways to protect them is either by isolating the networks or by encrypting the data flow. As of today the decision has not been taken on which option is chosen, based on the efficiency, the cost and the relevance.

As for a module, the simulator seems to be the ideal starting point because it's a module that can completely stand alone; since to start out with, it can run without any real time data, it is an element that can evolve tremendously; from only validating the design before manufacturing to potentially managing the actual line during its life (based on the ERP data regarding the placed orders and running multiple scenarios and selecting the most optimized: production order sequencing).

Furthermore, the simulator can also have benefits, both in-house and commercially, without the need to modify our products or connect them with IOT systems that can be seen as intrusive to the industrial user. The initial simulation can represent a gain by reducing the number of design iterations in-house and at the same time be used as a commercial tool for the client by visually representing the motion and the workflow of the line.

3 Focus on the Simulator

3.1 Expectations and Requirements

As said previously, the simulator validates the design of a transfert solution, the main target is to verify the flow, making sure that the mobiles don't stay blocked in a particular place, that they are able to complete the cycle in the desired time, that all the station have a sufficient activity, … That would be a potential gain in conception time, by reducing the numbers of design iterations.

In order to obtain that goal the simulator requires a model for each of the elements of a transfert system (mobiles, units, simple cams, diversions, double cams, stoppers, …) with a precision sufficient to analyze predict and thus validate that the system achieves the target.

The first step was to define the requirements specifications in order to see if a commercial solution was available or not.

The simulator on its own needed to allow a client or an in-house technician to design a transfert line and simulate the flow of mobiles in order to validate that the line could answer the need of the client. For that there are a few relevant indicators:

- Highest cycle time: highest time a mobile took to come back to its original position
- Average cycle time: the average of all the mobiles' cycle times
- Longest idle time for a mobile: the longest a mobile didn't move out of a workstation
- Average idle time for a mobile: the average of all the mobiles' idle times
- Longest idle time for a station (workstation and stoppers): the longest a station waited without a mobile to work on, including when a mobile was at the station but the work was done and the mobile couldn't leave
- Average idle time for a station: the average of the stations' idle times

But as a part of the Digital Twin, in the context of Industry 4.0 and digital continuity, the simulator also needs to be able to communicate and interact with other modules and databases representing the physical system thus excluding all commercial solutions that were found during the research; software like Arena Simulation or Visual Components are meant to simulate the flow but as a stand-alone solution, their connectivity or intergrability did not meet the requirements. It was consequently decided to develop an in-house simulator.

The company wanted a development solution that would allow them to retain control over the simulator, therefor an open-source development software was the optimal solution. Godot is open-source development software meant for videogames; it is on that software that the simulator was programmed.

3.2 Architecture and Development

Figure 3. Shows a detailed synoptic of the way the simulator is structured.

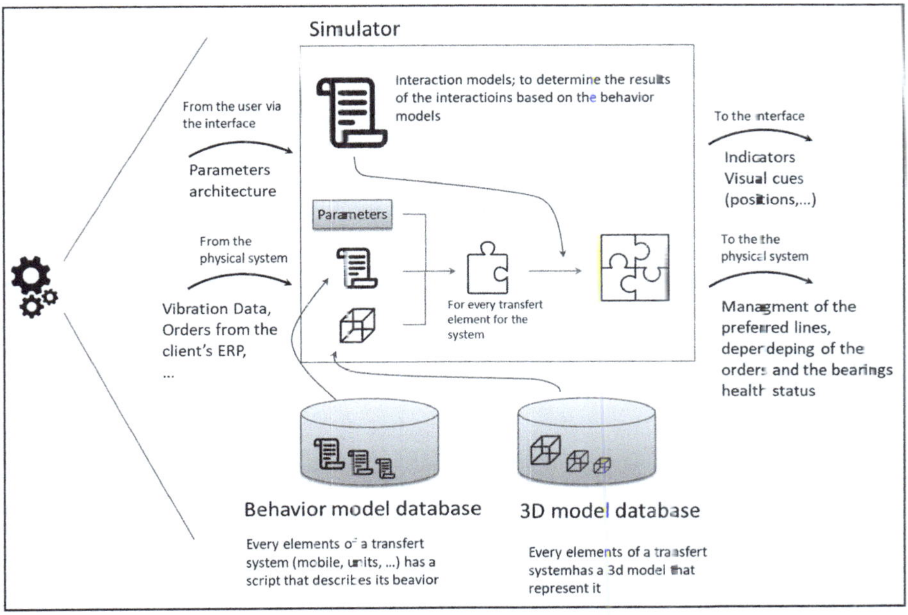

Fig. 3. detailed synoptic of the simulator

The simulator has two external sources of information, the user via the interface and the physical system and its environment. The main data coming from the user are the configuration (which elements and where they are) and the flow data (how long does a mobile need the stay at each stopping points). From the physical system, the simulator uses order data to simulate multiple scenarios and define the most effective way to schedule the production. The simulator can also use vibration data to gage the health status of the system's bearings and favor (if possible) a section over another.

The simulator uses those pieces of information and combines them with two databases; A behavior database, that holds the scripts that describe the way each individual transfert elements behaves and a 3D model database that holds a visual representation of all of these elements. Using the correct user parameters with the correct behavior model and 3D representation, the simulator generates the desired element. After repeating this process for each element of the system, the simulator uses interaction models to describe how all these elements interact. At this point, the user can play the simulation and the simulator will display the movements of the mobiles, and the key indicators.

The behavior models in the database need to be accurate enough. There is a first threshold that represents the minimum accuracy needed to simulate, then, the more accurate they are the least errors there will be and the further in time they will be able to predict satisfactorily. Once the models are recorded in the simulator, and because in the first use the simulator is before the manufacture of the system, there are no field data, the data that is key is the configuration data; the architecture of the system that is up for testing.

Once the simulation has run, what we seek from it is to be able to confirm that the architecture of the system meets the needs of the client, which in turn means that the total cycle time is conform, that the number of mobiles allows the system to work properly and that the system in general is used properly. That comes down to the Key Performance Indicators mentioned previously.

Figure 4 is a display of what the user sees when he uses the simulator. The red boxes are the mobiles and the white squares are stopping points.

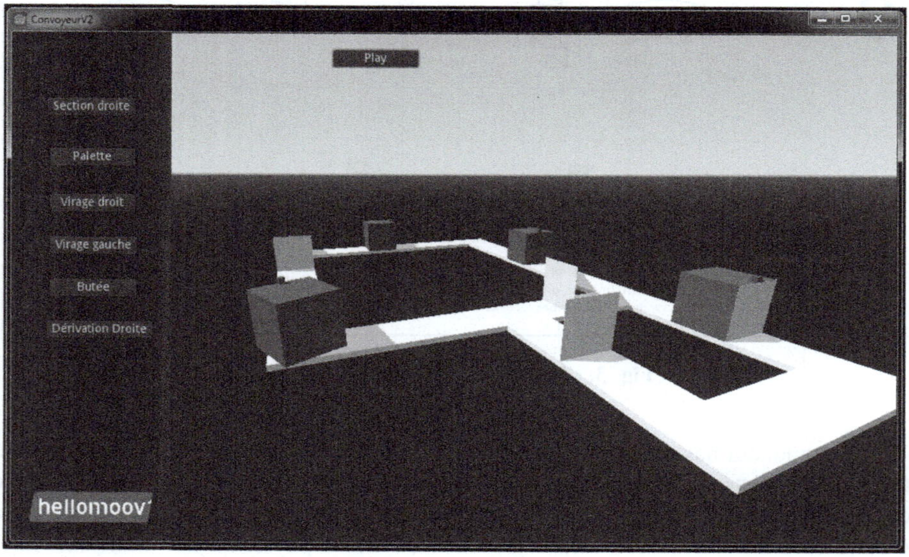

Fig. 4. Rendering of a simulation of a transfert system

4 Conclusion and Perspectives

The perspective is to propose a complete methodology to deploy the digital twin concepts in an SME. Hellomoov's use case will be a validation experience for such a methodology.

For a medium size company, a ramp phase is crucial in order to ensure that the Digital Twin will be accepted and used. At Hellomoov', the choice for the first module to be developed fell on the simulator. It has the advantages to be able to grow relatively easily, it's a module that can stand on its own and it can be a base for a visual representation of the physical twin from the start to the end of the life of the product.

The next step in the development of the Digital Twin in a company is to apply it to a client system use case and make it evolve from there, adapting it along the way. A system that is relatively classic, so that it would represent well what will happen in the future, would be ideal, with a client that we know well in order to ensure a good and easy communication.

But in order to get a complete Digital Twin, it is important not to forget the critical issues that must be overcome; how do to protect the critical data, how to manage the storage of the important mass of data that will be generated by the twins and defining the framework of the interaction and the work with the subcontractor regarding the models that will be at the core of the Digital Twin.

References

1. Glaessgen, E.H., Stargel, D.S.: The digital twin paradigm for future NASA and U.S. Air force vehicles. In: Proceedings of the 53rd AIAA Structures, Structural Dynamics and Materials Conference 2012, Paper no. 1818 (2012)
2. Grieves, M.W.: Product lifecycle management: the new paradigm for enterprises. Int. J. Prod. Dev. **2**(1–2), 71–84 (2005)
3. Grieves, M.: Virtually Perfect: Driving Innovative and Lean Products Through Product Lifecycle Management. Space Coast Press, Cocoa Beach (2011)
4. Grieves, M.: Digital twin: manufacturing excellence through virtual factory replication. White Pap. **1**, 1–7 (2014)
5. Goodman, J.: Apollo 13 guidance, navigation, and control challenges. In: AIAA SPACE 2009 Conference & Exposition (2009). https://doi.org/10.2514/6.2009-6455
6. Tuegel, E.J., Ingraffea, A.R., Eason, T.G., Spottswood, S.M.: Reengineering aircraft structural life prediction using a digital twin. Int. J. Aerosp. Eng. (2011). https://doi.org/10.1155/2011/154798
7. Morais, D., Goulanian, G., Danese, N.: The future reality of the digital twin as a cross-enterprise marine asset. RINA, Royal Institution of Naval Architects. In: 19th International Conference on Computer Applications in Shipbuilding, ICCAS 2019 (2019)
8. Hribernik, K.A., Rabe, L., Thoben, K.D., Schumacher, J.: The product avatar as a product-instance-centric information management concept. Int. J. Prod. Lifecycle Manag. **1**(4), 367–379 (2006). https://doi.org/10.1504/IJPLM.2006.011055
9. Tao, F., Zhang, H., Liu, A., Nee, A.Y.C.: Digital twin in industry: state-of-the-art. IEEE Trans. Ind. Inform. **15**(4), 2405–2415 (2019). https://doi.org/10.1109/TII.2018.2873186

Digital Twin and Product Lifecycle Management: What Is the Difference?

Dmytro Adamenko(✉), Steffen Kunnen, and Arun Nagarajah

University Duisburg-Essen, Lotharstr. 1, 47057 Duisburg, Germany
dmytro.adamenko@uni-due.de

Abstract. With the rapid development of modern information and communication technologies as well as infrastructure, the digital twin approach becomes increasingly popular and widely used throughout the industry and research. The digital twin is considered to be the key technology to realize the comprehensive digital description of components, products and systems including the information from all lifecycle phases. The Product Lifecycle Management (PLM) strategy has been present in the industry for many years and is considered as the most effective way of managing the components, products and systems of a company all the way across their lifecycles from the first idea of the product to its disposal. The digital twin is not yet clearly defined. It can be defined as a set of models, linked with each other as well as with the physical product enabling data storage and real-time processing. In contrast to a digital twin the PLM strategy provides a framework, which serves as single source of truth connecting the partial models, that describe the physical product. The models can receive the data stored in a product data management system (PDM).

The aim of the present paper is to distinguish the characteristics of the digital twin and PLM as well to find similarities and differences in the both approaches. The current development of both strategies is presented, and the answer to the question, where is the difference between digital twin and PLM is given.

Keywords: Digital twin · Product lifecycle management

1 Introduction

The digitization of industry is being driven forward under the term Industry 4.0 and is characterized by two central features such as intelligent components and networking [1]. With increasing globalisation and continually growing individual requirements of customers many companies are coming under increasing competitive pressure. In order to counteract this and improve the industrial competitiveness, companies must offer a broad product portfolio or individual customer-specific solutions due to rapidly changing customer requirements, whereby the quality of the products and the entire process, logistics parameters and costs must not be neglected [2].

The digital existence of products in the network generates large amounts of data over the product life cycle, especially when sensor technologies are used. This data has a value for the user or operator of the product as well as for the developer and manufacturer.

F. Nyffenegger et al. (Eds.): PLM 2020, IFIP AICT 594, pp. 150–162, 2020.
https://doi.org/10.1007/978-3-030-62807-9_13

Companies are constantly trying to further optimise the performance of their products or their own processes. The approach of product data management and the strategy of product life cycle management have established themselves as central solutions for the management of data of complex products and assets in the last decades. However, with development of technologies, the terms are being replaced by new ones.

With the technical progress and the continuous development of information, communication and automation technologies, the possibility of networking different components in real time and gaining an insight into current processes or the current status is being developed. The networked components and machines generate a lot of data that can be used for operation analysis. With the development of the Industry 4.0 the usage gets much better perspectives, because the development of such technologies like Big Data, Machine learning and AI provides the optimization of the usage of the existing product data [3].

The flagship of such targeted use of data is becoming widely known as the digital twin approach, a concept that uses the networking of components and the insights into performance available through the data to represent an actual state of the product at any moment of its life cycle. This approach is gaining more and more interest from companies and its importance in industry but has not yet become fully established. For these reasons, the digital twins will be examined in more detail in the following chapters. The concept and construction possibilities of a digital twin will be presented in detail [3, 4].

The similarities and differences of the PLM and Digital Twin concepts will be presented and discussed in the further course of the paper.

2 Product Lifecycle Management Overview

This section introduces the Product Lifecycle Management approach as well as the core component of PLM the Product Data Management (PDM).

2.1 PLM Theoretical Background

Product lifecycle management strategy can be defined as the product-related and cross-company information management, which comprises the planning, control and organization of the processes required for the generation and holistic management of all data, documents and resources throughout the entire product lifecycle [5].

PLM establishes a continuous flow of information so that current product information and also the previous development and operating statuses are available at all times and to all parties involved in product creation, production and use.

Through transparent processes, PLM ultimately leads to improved product quality, cost and time advantages throughout the entire product life cycle. PLM should be considered as a cross-company approach that also takes into account today's globally distributed processes along the entire product lifecycle [6].

The holistic view of the product life cycle includes all phases of an industrial product. The management of product requirements already supports the early phases of the product life cycle. In the area of capital goods or consumer goods, support of the product life phases after delivery and commissioning as well as product recycling is playing an increasingly important role.

The cycle is closed by the feedback of information from downstream process steps such as product use and product recycling or disposal with the aim of improving product properties. This creates a control loop that enables companies to react more quickly to changing customer requirements and to incorporate experience from product application into the development of new, innovative products [6, 7].

The biggest efficiency with PLM approach can be achieved through so-called top-down strategies involving the company management. The main focus of PLM is the simultaneous, company-wide provision of product data and fast, orderly access to it, as well as the realization of continuous, standardized company processes [7, 8].

PLM provides powerful classification systems for identifying and searching for product data, which facilitate the clear allocation and identification of components and assemblies and support the uniqueness of each component used.

2.2 PDM Systems

The realization of the PLM strategy requires various solution modules, whereby product data management plays a key role in PLM. Product Data Management is considered as essential enabler for PLM and as the technological basis that makes PLM possible [9]. Without a PDM system as the central software component, a PLM strategy cannot be implemented in the company. Conversely, however, a PLM concept is not necessarily required for the productive use of PDM.

The data is collected and linked in a PDM system. PDM systems are used for the management of product-defining data to build a holistic product model, which consists of multiple different linked models in connection with the mapping and management of technical and organizational business processes. Product and process management together allow the complete reconfiguration of any design and manufacturing status over the entire product life cycle [6, 7].

Through the integrated, central view of possibly distributed product data becomes the so-called integrated product model. It consists of the partial models. These models include component information, documents, project-specific configuration data, personnel information, customer data, and much more. A digital product model is defined by logically linking the data with each other. This enables a process-oriented structuring of the data that is generated or required over the entire product life cycle. The most important tasks of the PDM system are to provide the correct data with the correct status and format. Its long-term archiving and support of data exchange via different information channels [7, 12].

2.3 Recent Development of PLM Approach

As technologies evolve, PLM has become a holistic discipline across the entire product lifecycle and across the enterprise - from requirements management to the processing of IoT data. In the classic PLM approach, the document-centered system has been widely used. Modern usage of PLM concept envisions however the data sharing and exchange instead of documents, so that the information out of the documents becomes decomposed and stored as metadata or within specific partial models in database. Critical issue is to ensure that the stored data remains the single source of truth for the product throughout the whole life cycle [10].

Another perspective field is being developed with the evolution of cloud-based data management, which is also emphasizing on information-centered management [11].

This product metadata is defined as the digital information twin of the product and is thus associated with the term digital twin.

3 Digital Twin Overview

There is not yet a standardized definition for a digital twin. There are many different descriptions for a digital twin that differ depending on the purpose and scope. The comparative analyses carried out by Martinez et al. [25] and shows clear differences in the interpretation of the concept of the digital twin and its use as a business model. Small overview of existing concepts and definition is presented in this chapter as well as the most common construction methods.

3.1 Digital Twin Definition

The concept of a digital twin has been developed by Michael Grieves in 2003, as a model consisting of three main components; the physical product in the real world, the virtual product in the digital world and the connection between the real and virtual objects by means of data and information [13].

Digital twin is being widely understood in connection with the rapid acquisition, aggregation and analysis of data from networked technologies and allowing the simulation of possible scenarios for predicting results in the virtual without affecting real production. Great strength of the digital twin lies in the visualization of data: data thus becomes insights into processes that are accessible not only to experts but also to a technically less well-versed audience and is also available independently of location. This data visualization promotes learning and decision-making processes at all levels of the "Connected Enterprise", which is the core of PLM strategy and helps to identify critical areas directly.

Digital twin has several meanings in today industry's context. The digital twin prototype is created within the PLM framework when planning or ordering a physical product, long before the physical twin is even born which is especially crucial for the automation of manufacturing in Industry 4.0 scenarios. With its help, companies can, for example, switch to the individual production of a "lot size 1". The digital twin prototype appears at each production step on the respective machine together with the physical part and controls the processing. At the end of production, the physical twin is born and has all the characteristics of the virtual prototype model.

The digital twin instances, which are created from the image of a finished product and reproduce its continuous configuration or operating data, behave completely differently. In the automotive industry, the DTP reflects the production and the DTI the after-sales processes, such as software updates or operating data such as telematics data [26].

In order to combine the both digital twin meanings in more recent publications, the digital twin is no longer described with the three dimensions already mentioned, but with five dimensions [14]. This model builds on the three-dimensional model introduced by Grieves and adds the data of the digital twin and service as respective dimensions. Figure 2 shows this model in more detail. PE stands for the physical entity, VE for virtual equipment, SS for services, DD refers to digital twin data and CN for the connections [14, 15].

With the digital twin a real object has a digital image that consists of different models. These models have four main functions. The first function is the exact reproduction of the properties, behavior and rules of the physical object to create an accurate image. The second function of the models is that they can be operated autonomously. This means that they simulate different behavior of the object, which can then be used as guidelines for the operation of the physical object. The third function is the ability to predict problems before they occur. The fourth function is fulfilled by validating performance before the product is even finished [15]. The data enables the digital twin to be operated and updated continuously. This data includes information collected by sensors, results of simulations and other knowledge related to the physical object [15] (Fig. 1).

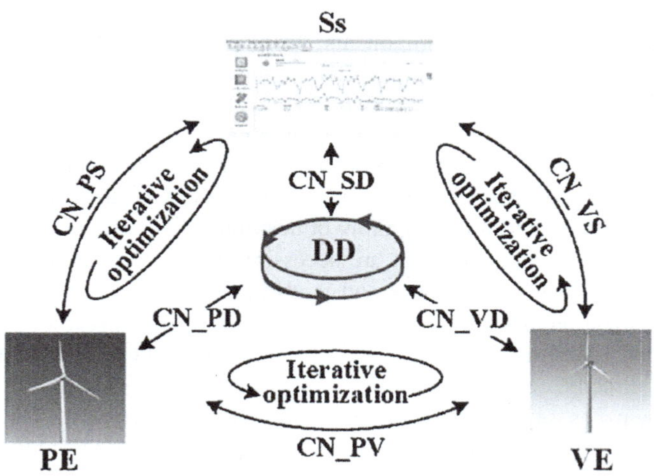

Fig. 1. Five dimensions of a digital twin [14].

Services are used to prepare the functions and information of the digital twin for the general user in such a way that he can access them easily and without much previous knowledge [15]. It can be seen that the digital twin is not a single model, but rather consists of a number of interlinked models [16].

These are based on current and historical information of the object to be depicted [17]. All relevant data generated during the lifecycle are incorporated into the digital twin and continuously developed further [16]. In Fig. 2 the components of a digital twin are presented. It becomes clear that the digital twin does not only consist of models, but also of data, simulations and analyses. It is characterized by its uniqueness, since each digital twin represents exactly one single object. Through the interaction between the digital twin and the real product, the digital twin it is also possible to control the twin and, if necessary, adjust settings and monitor the current status

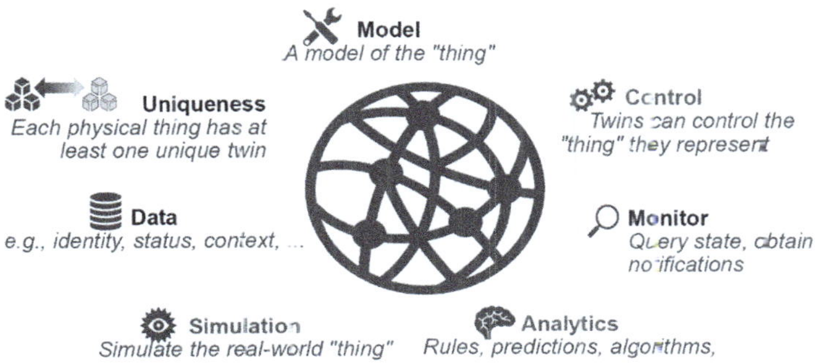

Fig. 2. Digital twin components [18].

For the further course of this work the digital twin is defined as a holistic digital model of a physical object from the real world connected with it. This exact copy contains all properties, information and states of the real object [3].

The general structure of a digital twin first of all includes the question of the complexity of the digital twin. If the complexity and level of detail of the individual models are not high enough, the digital twin will not have any profitable added value for the user. If these are too high, the use of the digital twin becomes too confusing for the system presented [19].

3.2 Digital Twin Construction Methods

Considering actual digital twin construction approaches, digital twin can be built up in main two different ways. One possibility is to create a system model of the physical object to be enriched by real product data. The other possibility is to create a data structure that organizes and links the sensor data and other information. Independent from the creation method, a digital twin is always application-specific and unique and is being created for a specific task. The holistic description of the asset by models up to molecular level cannot be achieved and used because of big volume and high creation and maintenance costs [20].

With a data-based digital twin, the structuring of the data flow is the main focus. Here, the individual instances of the physical object are sorted, for example, according to functionality, in order to gain an insight into the current status and performance of the physical instance. An IoT platform can be used for structuring, for example, which makes various applications for structuring data available to the user. Through these applications the structured data can be stored and analyzed with the tools defined by the user. The advantage of a data-based digital twin is that the physical instance does not have to be virtually visualized for creation and use, but the recorded data sets of the sensors are sufficient for data structuring and analysis. In the building up of such a twin, the data generated from the operation is used (bottom-up). Data-driven models offer less insight into the interior of the system due to their black box type (Fig. 3).

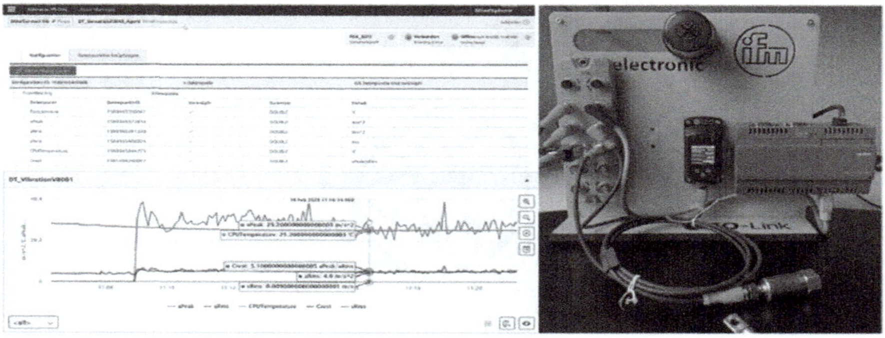

Fig. 3. Data structuring in data-based digital twin [20].

As example a data-based digital twin of a combustion engine constructed in MindSphere can be seen. The data from vibration and temperature sensor as well as alarm switches is being sent in given periods to the IoT platform in order to define the value patterns which lead to alarms and adjust the motor accordingly [3, 20, 21].

The construction method of the system-based digital twin places the physical instance in the foreground. In comparison to the data-based digital twin, not only the data from the sensors are included in the data structuring, but also the entirety of the physical functions of the physical instance.

A PDM system can be used as a skeleton to provide the logic stored in the system model. A complex assembly structure including partial models (geometry, simulation, sensor data models, as can be seen in Fig. 4) can be set up in the common PDM systems. Each change of the entire system model or a single partial model is also documented within the PDM system.

The digital twin should be able to be used by several users. With the help of PDM system the rights and roles of individual users can be set, so that the necessary know-how protection can be guaranteed.

Top-down or system-based concepts offer better insights into the system to be developed and support the maximum possible (and maximum meaningful) parameterization of the system, they are associated with considerable expenditure of time and thus high development costs, since the interfaces between all virtual and real components must be clearly structured and defined. For this purpose, for example, a CAD model of the physical instance can be created, which serves as the basis for the data structure. This partial model can then be implemented in the data structure to link the detailed visualization of the physical instance with the entirety of the recorded data. The digital twin created in this way can be used, for example, for simulations of theoretical scenarios to predict and prevent possible failures of the physical instance.

The advantage of a system-based digital twin is the possibility to use the created data structures and partial models for simulation predictions, which allows a deeper insight into the performance of the object [3, 20].

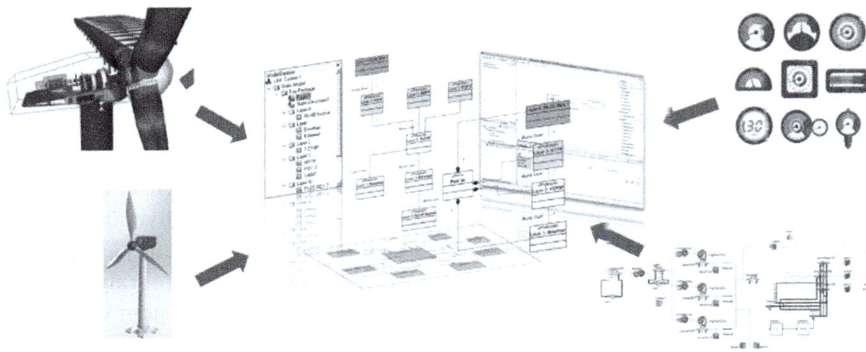

Fig. 4. System-based digital twin [20].

The presented approaches can be combined in the design of the digital twin, which allows the advantages of both approaches to be used.

The biggest challenges of constructing the digital twin are IT infrastructure, data handling, defining a necessary fidelity of a system as well as privacy and security.

The rapid growth of AI needs to be met with high-performance infrastructure in the form of up to date hardware and software, to help execute the algorithms. The challenge with the infrastructure currently is down to the cost of installing and running these systems. From a data point of view, it important to ensure the data is not of inferior quality, it needs to be sorted and cleaned, thereby ensuring the highest quality of data is fed into the AI algorithms. Digital twins can quickly become overloaded and will then never be finished or will not be able to provide the required added value. Therefore, digital twin cannot be provided and held up to date for every application for the smallest element in it. Important is to define the necessary fidelity so that the maintenance of the digital twin does not exceed the added value of its use. Privacy and security are an important issue for anyone concerned with the computing industry and is no different when performing data analytics. Laws and regulation are yet to be established fully because of the infancy of AI. The challenge is more scrutiny, regulation and measures concerning AI in the future as the technology grows. Future regulation ensures the development of algorithms that take steps to protect user data.

3.3 Applications of Digital Twin

The digital twin can map a single element as well as a complete system. The digital twin of a complete system usually consists of several digital twins of subsystems and individual components. Ideally, the digital twin serves several applications that interact with a physical product. However, synergies are only achieved if different physical products also share a twin infrastructure.

The essence of the digital twin is the establishing of connection and real-time synchronization between the data from physical product and the information contained in virtual product model [22].

The digital twin has several advantages. The first major advantage is the significantly increased transparency. Thanks to the various models, which always have up-to-date information, the product or system can be better monitored. Information is presented in such a way that the user can directly and clearly see the current status. Among other things, there is the possibility of 3D visualization of current statuses. Furthermore, maintenance costs and time can be reduced. By continuously collecting and analyzing data and using simulations, future problems can be identified [15]. The simulations are usually based on the entire data history. Maintenance can be planned in advance by predicting the lifetime of individual components. By means of predictive maintenance, these components can be replaced before malfunctions or failures occur [23].

Another advantage of a Digital twin is the reduced time needed to bring a product to market. Simulations can be used to predict how the product or system will behave before it is even finished. In this way, weak points and potential sources of error can be eliminated without much effort.

In addition to the reduced time-to-market, the performance of the product or system can always be maintained at an optimum level. Since product and digital twin exchange data in real time, the current performance can be analyzed. If environmental or operating conditions change, individual parameters are automatically adjusted so that the product or system always behaves as planned.

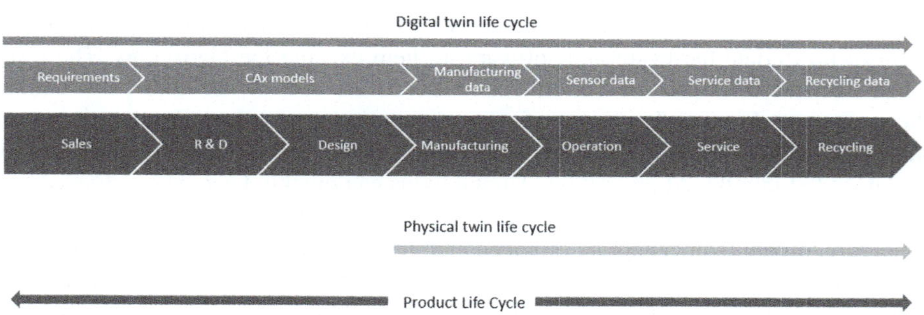

Fig. 5. Product and digital twin life cycle.

The digital twin can be used in different phases of the product life cycle or across different phases. Figure 5 shows the product life cycle. Already during the planning and development of an object or a process, it is possible to predict whether the desired properties and functions will be fulfilled using simulations with the digital twin. Optimizations of design or performance can thus be carried out in advance [3, 24]. Prototype testing can be replaced by simulations on the digital twin, saving costs and time. Digital twin can also influence the planning and development of new products by analysing objects already in use. The data generated by the digital twin can be used to analyse the usage behaviour or operation of products or systems. In this way, improvement possibilities for new products can be identified [15].

The combination of real-time data and simulation models also allows virtual sensors to be placed on the model. This means that data from virtual sensors can be used to generate new insights in places that would not normally be accessible to sensors on the object. Digital twin also allows what-if analyses to be carried out. Changes in environmental conditions or settings can be tested on the digital twin. However, it is also possible to deliberately activate possible errors in the simulation model to generate measurement data for these cases, which can then be used for predictions [3].

4 Comparison of PLM and Digital Twin Approaches

As showed in literature review, core idea of both PLM and digital twin concepts is a holistic product model, which consists of multiple interlinked models to provide different views on the real product. A storage of data, describing the product at any time is also one of important aspects of both approaches.

In order to distinguish the differences between the both approaches, their characteristics according to selected criteria are provided in Table 1.

Table 1. Comparison of PLM and digital twin characteristics.

Criteria	PLM	Digital Twin
Data structure	• Data is stored in the PDM system • Mainly document-centered storage • Model-centered storage evolving • Multiple partial models interlinked	• System-based or data-based structure • Data-centered storage • In case of system-based structure multiple interlinked partial models • In case of system-based structure, a PDM system can provide a platform for models and data storage
Data exchange	• Mainly document exchange • Collaborative access to the documents	• Microservices • Via the IoT-platform
Real-time data usage	• Storage • Simulation within the linked models • Hardly possible in document-centered structure	• Machine learning within IoT-platform • Cross-impact analysis within system model in case of system-based structure • Integration of Big Data algorithms
Product lifecycle coverage	• Whole lifecycle covered	• Coverage of production and service product lifecycle phases • Integration in the development phase only possible for future products
Tracking of individual products	• Big effort in document-centered structure	• Great transparency • Individual for every product in production/in use
Product control	• Defined workflows with defined roles and activities • Defined notification and validation workflows	• Defined workflows, roles etc. within system-based digital twin via PDM system • Defined roles, notifications and workflows within IoT platform for data-based digital twin
Collaboration possibilities	• Full cooperation within a single enterprise • Cooperation between the enterprises mainly limited due to access issues	• Communication between developers, operators and service

5 Conclusions and Outlook

As can be seen in comparative table, both approaches have common characteristics and can be regarded as complements to each other, where having good capabilities within PLM can be applied on a virtual product model and a physical product. Both concepts describe a complete virtual product model from different points of view through integration of different partial models. Both the PLM and digital twin concepts can include process frameworks, so that the different states or life cycles of the products can be processed within firm workflows with integration of defined departments or vendors. The main goal of the digital twin concept is the real-time data processing and exchange between the virtual product model and its physical twin, whereas the PLM concept defines the data processing and exchange in general.

The evolution of PLM approach has led to a migration from document-centred information storage to data-centred and this is a great step towards combination with digital twin approach due to the possibility to use data processing algorithms through the stored data in real time. The digital twin can exist at any stage of the lifecycle and aims leverage aspects of the virtual environment (high-fidelity, multi-physics, external data sources, etc.), computational techniques (virtual testing, optimisation, prediction, etc.), and aspects of the physical environment (historical performance, customer feedback, cost, etc.) to improve elements of the product (performance, function, behaviour, manufacturability, etc.) over it lifecycle. Usage of digital twin approach is at the time suitable for not all the product lifecycle phases (for example sales) but can serve as a value adding service in combination within the defined PLM strategy of an enterprise.

The greatest benefit can be achieved by cleverly combining both approaches. The structure of the digital twin can be built up within the PDM system. The system model can still be used as the "skeleton" of the digital twin with the defined logical links between the partial models stored in PDM system. Also, sensor and simulation data can be stored and linked continuously. Due to the usage of PDM system each adjustment of the entire system and each individual partial model is also documented. The digital twin should be able to be used by several users. With the help of PDM system the rights and roles of individual users can be set, so that the necessary know-how protection can be guaranteed.

For the processing the data in real time and used integration of PDM system with IoT platform is needed. Many of the data platforms also offer interfaces with PDM systems, making it easier to assign data and simulation results to a concrete plant status. Based on the existing data and simulation results, recommendations the benefits of both approaches can be united in single framework.

References

1. Porter, M.E., Heppelmann, J.E.: How smart products change the competition. Harv. Bus. Manag. **36**(12), 34–60 (2014)

2. Schützer, K., de Andrade Bertazzi, J., Sallati, C., Anderl, R., Zancul, E.: Contribution to the development of a Digital Twin based on product lifecycle to support the manufacturing process. In: 29th CIRP Design 2019 (2019). Procedia CIRP 84, pp. 82–87
3. Vogt, O.: Selection of a suitable platform for building up a digital twin. Unpublished master thesis. Duisburg (2019)
4. Mrzyk, P.: Construction of a demonstrator of a digital twin. Unpublished bachelor thesis. Duisburg (2020)
5. Eigner, M., Gerhardt, F., Gilz, T., Mogo Nem, F.: Information Technology for Engineers. Springer, Heidelberg (2012)
6. Eigner, M., Stelzer, R.: Product Lifecycle Management: A guide for Product Development and Life Cycle Management 2nd edn. Springer, Heidelberg (2009)
7. Schilke, M.: Use of product data management systems in special machine construction for the automotive industry. Doctor thesis, Saarbrücken (2010)
8. Abramovici, M.; Schulte, S.: Benefits of PLM: Expert Study, eDM-Report 1, pp. 16–23. Dressler, Heidelberg (2005)
9. Stark, J.: Product Lifecycle Management (Volume 1): 21st Century Paradigm for Product Realisation, 4th edn. Springer, Cham (2020). https://doi.org/10.1007/978-3-030-28864-8
10. Zammit, J.P., Gao, J., Evans, R.: The challenges of adopting PLM tools involving diversified technologies in the automotive supply chain. In: Ríos, J., Bernard, A., Bouras, A., Foufou, S. (eds.) PLM 2017. IAICT, vol. 517, pp. 59–68. Springer, Cham (2017). https://doi.org/10.1007/978-3-319-72905-3_6
11. Khlifi, H., et al.: Towards cloud in a PLM context: a proposal of cloud based design and manufacturing methodology. In: Ríos, J., Bernard, A., Bouras, A., Foufou, S. (eds.) PLM 2017. IAICT, vol. 517, pp. 141–151. Springer, Cham (2017). https://doi.org/10.1007/978-3-319-72905-3_13
12. Stark, R., Pförtner A.: Integrating ontology into PLM-tools to improve sustainable product development. CIRP Ann. Manuf. Technol. **64**, 157–160 (2015)
13. Grieves, M.: Digital twin: manufacturing excellence through virtual factory replication. Whitepaper (2014)
14. Tao, F., Zhang, M.: Digital twin driven prognostics and health management for complex equipment. CIRP Ann. Manuf. Technol. **67**(1), 169–172 (2018)
15. Tao, F., Zhang, M., Nee, A.Y.C.: Digital Twin Driven Smart Manufacturing, 1st edn. Academic Press, Cambridge (2019)
16. Schleich, B., Anwer, N., Mathieu, L., Wartzack, S.: Shaping the digital twin for design and production engineering. CIRP Ann. Manuf. Technol. **66**(1), 141–144 (2017)
17. Kitain, L.: The New Age of Manufacturing: Digital Twin Technology. Seebo Homepage. https://www.seebo.com/digital-twin-technology. Accessed 15 Mar 2020
18. Halpern, M.: Busting the Myth of Digital Twins and Planning Them Realistically. Gartner, Stamford (2017)
19. Cognizant: Study: Is Your Organization Ready to Embrace a Digital Twin? Cognizant (2018)
20. Adamenko, D., Kunnen, S., Pluhnau, R., Loibl, A., Nagarajah, A.: Review and comparison of the methods of constructing the Digital Twin. In: 30th CIRP Design 2020 (2020). Procedia CIRP
21. Adamenko, D., Kunnen, S., Nagarajah, A.: Comparative analysis of platforms for designing a digital twin. In: Ivanov, V., Trojanowska, J., Pavlenko, I., Zajac, J., Peraković, D. (eds.) DSMIE 2020. LNME, pp. 3–12. Springer, Cham (2020). https://doi.org/10.1007/978-3-030-50794-7_1
22. Garetti, M., Rosa, P., Terzi, S.: Life cycle simulation for the design of product-service systems. Comput. Ind.Comput. Ind. **63**(4), 361–369 (2012)

23. Coronado, P.D.U., Lynn, R., Louhichi, W., Parto, M., Wescoat, E., Kurfess, T.: Part data integration in the Shop Floor Digital Twin: mobile and cloud technologies to enable a manufacturing execution system. J. Manuf. Syst. **48**(C), 25–33 (2018)
24. Tchana, Y., Ducellier, G., Remy, S.: Designing a unique Digital Twin for linear infrastructures lifecycle management. In: 29th CIRP Design 2019 (2019). Procedia CIRP 84, pp. 545-549
25. Martinez, V., Ouyang, A., Neely, A., Burstall, C., Bisessar, D.: Service business model innovation: the digital twin. Cambridge Service Alliance (2018)
26. Ried, S.: Digital Twins between expectations and sustainability. Crisp Research (2019)

Internet of Things (IoT, IIoT)

Smart Dust in the Industrial Economic Sector – On Application Cases in Product Lifecycle Management

Manuel Holler[1(✉)], Jens Haarmann[1], Benjamin van Giffen[2], and Alejandro German Frank[3]

[1] Zurich University of Applied Sciences, Theaterstrasse 17, 8400 Winterthur, Switzerland
{manuel.holler,jens.haarmann}@zhaw.ch
[2] University of St. Gallen, Müller-Friedberg-Strasse 8, 9000 St. Gallen, Switzerland
benjamin.vangiffen@unisg.ch
[3] Univ. Federal do Rio Grande do Sul, Av. Osvaldo Aranha 99, Porto Alegre 90035190, Brazil
frank@producao.ufrgs.br

Abstract. Smart dust is an autonomous sensing, computing, and communication system that can be packed into a cubic-millimeter mote to form the basis of integrated, massively distributed sensor networks. The purpose of this manuscript is to identify potential applications of smart dust in product lifecycle management with a focus on the industrial economic sector. Resting upon empirical data from the European DACH region, we describe six applications: (1) Advancement of requirements engineering, (2) Improvement of manufacturing processes, (3) Enhancement of logistics monitoring, (4) Optimization of operations, (5) Ameliorated maintenance and repair processes, and (6) Augmented retirement planning. Bearing the exploratory, qualitative approach and early-stage character of applications in mind, we can reason that smart dust offers great potentials to both product lifecycle management and research on it.

Keywords: Smart dust · Industrial economic sector · Applications · Product lifecycle management · PLM · Case study research

1 Introduction

Product lifecycle management is the common thread of all product- and service-related activities over the lifecycle [1, 2]. As inherently neutral approach, novel technologies have been steadily cultivating product lifecycle management [1, 2]. For instance, the advent of intelligent products led on to closed-loop product lifecycle management [3, 4]. Another example refers to the massive digitization of products and processes, which

Parts of this manuscript draw on modified, updated, and rewritten content from the unpublished research proposal "Smart Dust - Exploring Technology Affordances in the Industrial Economic Sector" of the Swiss National Science Foundation "Spark" program.

Published by Springer Nature Switzerland AG 2020
F. Nyffenegger et al. (Eds.): PLM 2020, IFIP AICT 594, pp. 165–175, 2020.
https://doi.org/10.1007/978-3-030-62807-9_14

gave rise to big data in product lifecycle management [5, 6]. In line with this reasoning, smart dust [7, 8] holds the potential to serve as another powerful technology supporting product lifecycle management. In detail, smart dust is an "autonomous sensing, computing, and communication system that can be packed into a cubic-millimeter mote (…) to form the basis of integrated, massively distributed sensor networks" [8:2].

The past decades have seen a rapid development of technical research to shrink the technology based on few lighthouse applications [9, 10]. In comparison, only few scholars have dealt with systematic research into the role of smart dust for our daily lives [9, 10]. The purpose of this manuscript is to identify potential applications of smart dust in product lifecycle management with a focus on the industrial economic sector. Therefore, we report from a foundational project of the Swiss National Science Foundation and draw on empirical data [11, 12] from the European DACH region. At that, we focus on foundational innovation potentials, ideating value-adding use cases with adopters and placing arising technological impediments back.

In linkage to this prior 'Introduction', the manuscript continues with the 'Background', where the foundations of smart dust and related work are rolled out. The subsequent 'Methodology' unfolds the research strategy and data gathering and evaluation. The 'Findings' in the style of a lifecycle-oriented illustration followed by the 'Discussion' represent the main part. The 'Conclusion' finalizes this manuscript with a summary, contributions, limitations, and an outlook.

2 Background

Foundations. Despite its visionary character, the roots of smart dust reach surprisingly far back into the past [7, 8]. Around the 1990s, Silicon Valley-based UC Berkeley scholars Pister and Kahn coined the term for these miniaturized micro-electro-mechanical systems [9]. Structurally, smart dust is composed of corresponding motes, which in turn are compounded by the sub-components energy supply, sensing elements, computing capacity, and communication capabilities [13]. Regarding this technical anatomy, a spectrum of approaches exists: One-time (e.g., miniaturized batteries) and periodic (e.g., solar cells, energy harvesting) supply provides adequate energy [8]. Sensor modules for almost every physical variable enable the sensing [8]. Traditional methods target to reduce computing times at a given size, whereas down scaled computing focuses on energy reduction, for instance by novel transistors [8]. Optical or communication by radio waves allows for an information exchange with other motes or systems [8]. While smart dust crystallized as main term [10], nearby concepts emerged. Brilliant rocks [9] exhibit externally sensing and reusable character, micro-robots [8] complement their sensing abilities with actuating capabilities, and also communicating materials [14] are known. Upon this interdisciplinary character, scholars revert and contribute to a plethora of research disciplines [10]. We executed a literature review following the advices by Webster and Watson [15] to untangle the relevant body of knowledge. Thereby, we seek to consider both, academia and industry.

Related Work. With regard to the academic status quo, much of the available literature deals with the introduction of the concept and technology itself [7, 8]. In technical terms, authors have been mainly interested in specific questions concerning issues such as communication [16]. With regard to economic aspects, others have highlighted the relevance of applications in general engineering, agriculture and environmental monitoring, civil engineering, as well as health monitoring and surgery, and – as many modern technologies – in the military [10]. For instance, Satyanarayanan [9:2] pictures: “If you added a handful of smart dust to every batch of concrete as it is mixed, the resulting buildings would essentially have a nervous system built into every structural element”. With regard to the industrial status quo, established (e.g., IBM, Hitachi) and aspirant (e.g., AmbiqMicro, CubeWorks) firms develop and manufacture such motes. This increasing feasibility has created an emerging eco in management magazines [17] and the impactful Hype Cycle [18].

Research Gap. Speaking in terms of research gaps, following the work by Müller-Bloch and Kranz [19], a knowledge void emerges. Considering all of this evidence, only few scholars have dealt with systematic research into the role of smart dust for our daily lives [9, 10]. However, both academic and industrial representatives plea for such knowledge and “real life applications” [20:25] for smart dust.

3 Methodology

Research Strategy. Our goal is to identify potential applications of smart dust in product lifecycle management with a focus on the industrial economic sector. Based on the lack of knowledge in this innovative domain, the most popular research strategy for determining such uses is qualitative, exploratory research [11, 12]. In greater detail, we make use of case study research [21, 22], formulated as “empirical inquiry that investigates a contemporary phenomenon within its real-life context, especially when the boundaries between phenomenon and context are not clearly evident” [21:13]. Reverting to Yin’s [21] matrix, we aim for a (1) multiple-case study studying diverse companies and (2) several units of analysis, namely the activities related to product lifecycle management. Contextually, the industrial economic sector with a focus on the European DACH region as fertile, technology-depending and innovation-affine area [23] offers an insightful starting base.

Data Gathering. First, regarding the data gathering, we designed a maximum variation sampling [24]. A key strength of such an approach is to lay down the playfield and illustrate the spectrum of the examined phenomenon [24]. Table 1 demonstrates the empirical data. To maximize the insights, several parameters were varied. First, in terms of cases [21], we included firms from different domains (e.g., transportation), company sizes (e.g., SMEs), manufacturing modes (e.g., ETO), and production foci (e.g., component). Second, regarding the units of analysis [21], we incorporated all stages, from beginning-of-life over middle-of-life to end-of-life [1]. For case study research, Yin [21, 22] suggests a plethora of sources of evidence. Lastly, we selected interviews – well-suited for ideating and discussing the not yet implemented use cases

– and documents (e.g., websites) – ideally for assessing the contextual situation [21, 22]. After the communication of the research goal, we used a questionnaire [25] comprising the sections (1) Introductory questions, (2) Current situation, (3) Ideation of use cases, and (4) Outlook as conversation directive. Across the whole data collection, special emphasis was placed on foundational innovation potentials, ideating value-adding use cases with adopters and placing arising technological impediments back.

Table 1. Empirical data from the DACH region

Case company	Characteristics	Sources of evidence
OpticTech	GER, 5.000 employees	Interview Head of Prod. Design (01/2020), documents
CastingTech	GER, 200 employees	Interview Technical CEO (12/2019), documents
SpaceTech	CH, 10.000 employees	Interview Manager MRO (10/2019), documents
PipeTech	CH, 5.000 employees	Interview Head of Service (12/2019), documents
EnergyTech	CH, 10 employees	Interview CEO (02/2020), documents
TransportTech	AUT, 3.000 employees	Interview Manager MRO (10/2019), documents

Data Evaluation. Second, concerning the data evaluation, we refer to established qualitative examination practices [26, 27]. Both interviews and relevant information from the documents were evidenced by use case formats [28, 29]. Among other elements, a title, description, and sketches were included [28, 29]. Upon the purpose, we furthermore leveraged a lifecycle-oriented theoretical lens. Several decades of research have brought a spread of corresponding lifecycle models [30]. For this manuscript, the well-established model by Terzi et al. [1] is used for systematization. In qualitative investigations, there are more sources for errors than in its quantitative pendent [11, 12]. In order to reduce these uncertainties and augment the quality, we reviewed and applied corresponding recommendations for action (e.g., triangulation, cross-checking [21, 22]).

4 Findings

Figure 1 shows potential applications for smart dust in product lifecycle management with a focus on the industrial economic sector. For a better understanding, we report on the most insightful applications. In what follows, each identified application is described by case company, main challenge, technical solution, obstacles, and generalizability.

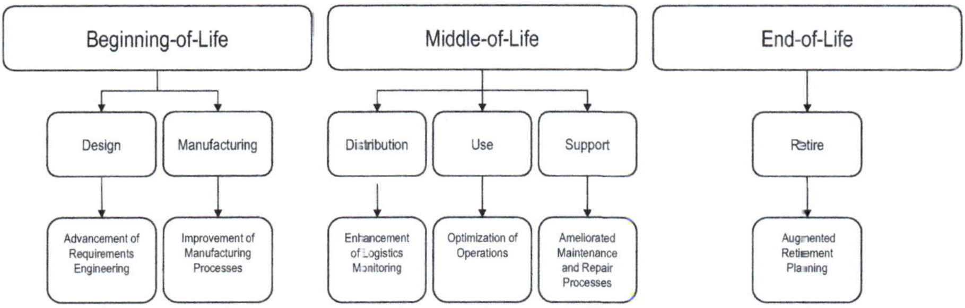

Fig. 1. Potential applications for smart dust in PLM (model by Terzi et al. [1])

4.1 Advancement of Requirements Engineering

OpticTech develops and manufactures opto-mechanics such as spectacles and spectacle frames for the high-end segment. Headquartered in Germany, a global workforce of approximately 5.000 people generates around 500 million EUR sales in B2C (private customers) and B2B (eye shops) markets. A challenge in new product development and product further development is the unknown wearing and usage behavior of spectacles. For example, even after almost 100 years in business, no detailed segment-specific information on the wearing time of glasses is available. A potential technical solution to address this shortcoming refers to the attachment of smart dust motes to the frame to monitor key parameters such as wearing times. A major advantage accrues from both enablement and refinement of design requirements in a real-life setting. The Head of Production Design reported on potential obstacles related to data privacy as glasses are part of all aspects of life. Further challenges referred to the necessary data receiving mechanism. Finally, the expected high costs compared to price of spectacles were named as another criticism. In terms of generalizability, this application seems well-suitable for various consumer and industrial products where requirements are un- or not well-known. Thus, we name a first application of smart dust in beginning-of-life (design): "Advancement of Requirements Engineering".

4.2 Improvement of Manufacturing Processes

CastingTech produces cast pieces made of non-ferrous metals, including pre- and post-activities. As small- and medium-sized enterprise with around 200 employees based in Germany, special engineering, rail transport, and medical technology represent main segments, whereby automotive is explicitly excluded. The Technical CEO reported on unknown rheological behavior during the casting process. These insufficiently transparent material parameters (e.g., flow/cooling rate) lead to varying material properties (e.g., static/dynamic strength). Currently, the engineers apply filling simulations, however their assumptions cannot be validated. A thinkable technical solution describes the infusion of motes into the molten material to sense the casting parameters. Two strategies seem possible, an exploration of parameters in the sense of a pilot, or the continuous monitoring in series production. Critical points are apparently heavy mechanical and thermal stress. Additionally, the communication through the dense material and the impact on the material behavior remained as open points. From a financial perspective in prototypical settings acceptable, casting is named as competitive business. In the narrower sense, the application may be transferred to plastics casting (e.g., injection molding). In a wider sense, a deployment for any primary forming (e.g., 3D printing) seems possible. Hence, we define a second application of smart dust in beginning-of-life (manufacturing): "Improvement of Manufacturing Processes".

4.3 Enhancement of Logistics Monitoring

SpaceTech represents a multi-national technology company (10.000 employees, two billion EUR sales) domiciled in Switzerland. The product and service portfolio encompasses structures and electronics for land and aerospace. Thereby, customers come from both civil and military domains. A prominent obstacle in the internal and external distribution is the transportation of sensitive components to the final assembly location. For example, the fuselage for a plane made from reinforced plastics often needs to be shipped over long distances by road to the original equipment manufacturer for final montage. As potential technological solution, the Manager MRO proposed the embedding of smart dust into the material layers or the direct integration into 3D printed structures. In this way, a granular tracking of stokes or other harmful situations during the transport is made possible. In this scenario, the extensive costs were not perceived as critical. However, concerns were raised with regard to the value-add beyond existing sensor solutions and the sufficient precision for aerospace quality. Such uses seem conceivable for further precious products in the B2B (e.g., airplanes) and B2C (e.g., art) domain. Therefrom, we determine a first application of smart dust in middle-of-life (distribution): "Enhancement of Logistics Monitoring".

4.4 Optimization of Operations

PipeTech is a world-wide leader for industrial piping systems. As part of a larger diversified multi-national, the division offers whole system solutions, individual components, and allied services in domains such as water supply, industrial manufacturing processes, and increasingly data center cooling. For the ambitious data center cooling with guaranteed availabilities close to 100 percent, existing smart connected cooling solutions offer solely limited transparency and control possibility for the critical cooling parameters. According to the Head of Service, the limited number of measuring points causes this weakness. As imaginable technical solution, the infusion of smart dust motes into the pipe material or the transported cooling fluids was proposed. Regarding the former, steady sensing over the pipe length is made possible. Regarding the latter, even more detailed, each volume element of the fluid can be sensed. Depending on the cooling type, both mechanical or/and thermal stress appear on the scene. Generally, such thermo- and fluid-dynamic systems work after complex system dynamics, which in this way even become more intricate. With regard to a wider applicability, vast potentials emerge for further transported fluids or gaseous materials (e.g., process industries). So, we conceptualize a second application of smart dust in middle-of-life (use): "Optimization of Operations".

4.5 Ameliorated Maintenance and Repair Processes

EnergyTech is an emerging clean tech start-up. In the order of ten employees design, assemble, and support renewable energy systems reverting to wind power. Thereby, main customers come from B2C (e.g., private homes and flats) and B2B (e.g., prime contractors, real estate management firms). Such complex industrial assets with long lifecycles bear the necessity of guaranteed availability and optimized maintenance. The CEO reported that unexpected breakdowns are often induced by low-cost parts such as sealing rings. This obstacle may be addressed by the integration of smart dust in these wearing parts. Hence, the progression of wear (e.g., plastics ageing) can be monitored in a more fine grained manner, and when necessary encountered. With regard to the challenges, such an infusion implies heavy compartmentalization and complex system behavior to predict the required maintenance and repair processes. Furthermore, wearing parts at a micro level and power generation at a macro level are considered as heavily price sensitive markets. Referring to the generalizability, this use case seems widely applicable for further mechanically critical components in any maintenance-intensive areas. Consequentially, we name a third application of smart dust in middle-of-life (support): "Ameliorated Maintenance and Repair Processes".

4.6 Augmented Retirement Planning

TransportTech is a market leader for innovative transport systems. The multi-national with several subsidies designs, produces, installs, and maintains ropeways. Approximately 3.000 employees serve touristic mountain regions and increasingly urban areas as main customers, and generate in this way 850 million EUR revenues. In such contexts, the insecure mechanical strength after exceptional events such as storms represents a substantial obstacle. Against the background of human beings as transported good and high investments of the ropeways, it is critical to decide when to retire the ropeway equipment. A potential technical solution may be the infusion of smart dust into mechanical structures as "neural system" to measure the material characteristics at any place at any time. In doings so, a more specific end-of-life prediction can be made, also involving aspects such as local material ageing. Impediments arise from several sides. Although the benefits of traffic safety are non-discussable, an application faces high costs compared to the low occurrence probability of such events. Additionally, according to the Manager MRO, a potential impact on the material behavior seems particular critical. The application is highly generalizable as it can be transferred to any business with safety critical components (e.g., wind turbines, train powertrains). Finally, we introduce an application of smart dust in end-of-life (retire): "Augmented Retirement Planning".

5 Discussion

Two lines are of particular interest for the subsequent discussion. We begin with fundamental discussion including a confrontation with literature, and then pass over to a systematization of the applications.

Fundamental Discussion. First, regarding opportunities, evidence shows that smart dust affords great potential for the lifecycle management of industrial products. In the beginning-of-life stage, smart dust may support design and manufacturing. Distribution, use, and support is facilitated in middle-of-life. And, in the end-of-life stage, this new technology also could augment product retiring. In each stage, we could detect value-add by enabling new or improving existing functions. Second, despite these marvelous chances, a plethora of impediments emerged as well. These range from technical (e.g., mechanical/thermal stress, communication) over financial (e.g., cost/benefit) to social (e.g., data privacy) aspects. In the case of an actual realization, current product lifecycle management organizations, processes, and systems would be impacted profoundly. Contrasting the identified applications with the accomplished literature review [9, 10], we are able to verify, but also to amplify these application possibilities. For instance, compared to the published gaseous uses [9, 10], the field was particularly opened up towards liquid and even solid cases.

Systematization of Applications. Diving more deeply into the diversity, Table 2 shows an initial classification model of smart dust applications in product lifecycle management. Therefore, we used well-established classification methods adopting Nickerson et al. [31]. We assimilate the affordance concept [32] as important meta-characteristic [31], differentiating between material properties ("How can we describe it?") and technology affordances ("What can we do with it?"). More precisely, the dimensions and its characteristics were derived by (1) literature (e.g., [7, 9, 13]) and the (2) empirically collected applications, as advised by Nickerson et al. [31].

Table 2. Classification model of smart dust applications in PLM (model by Chemero [32])

Material properties: How can we describe it?			
Carrier state	Liquid	[Solid]	Gaseous
Distribution	[Fixed]		Loose
Capabilities	[Sensing]		Actuating
Application period	Temporary		[Continuous]
Technology affordances: What can we do with it?			
Value-add scope	[Enhanced product]		Enhanced product management
Value-add level	[Enabler]		Refiner

As we can see, the material properties show a great variety. In terms of carrier state, the smart dust motes may be infused in liquid, solid, or gaseous materials. However, phase transitions (e.g., casting processes) are possible. Looking at the distribution, fixed and loose embedding is suitable to describe this dimension. Regarding the capabilities, only sensing uses appeared, but actuating capabilities (e.g., adaptive pipes) are conceivable as well. In regard to the application period, a temporary or continuous deployment of the motes is possible. Furthermore, also the technology affordances exhibit remarkable variances. In the most simple sense, smart dust affords an enhanced product (e.g., tailored spectacles) or an enhanced product management (e.g., monitored logistics). Describing the value-add level, both enabling and refining opportunities became apparent. For illustrative purposes, we selected an exemplary application ("Advancement of Requirements Engineering" by OpticTech) and highlighted the corresponding characteristics by brackets.

6 Conclusion

The purpose of this manuscript is to identify potential applications for smart dust in product lifecycle management with a focus on the industrial economic sector. Resting upon empirical data from the European DACH region, we describe six applications: (1) Advancement of requirements engineering, (2) Improvement of manufacturing processes, (3) Enhancement of logistics monitoring, (4) Optimization of operations, (5) Ameliorated maintenance and repair processes, and (6) Augmented retirement planning. As bottom line, we can reason that smart dust offers great potentials to both product lifecycle management and research on it.

Up to the authors' knowledge, this contribution is the first time that this technology is proposed for use in product lifecycle management. By overcoming anecdotal use cases (e.g., [9, 10, 33]), this manuscript contributes to a fine-grained, empirically-based, and lifecycle-oriented lineup. We hope that our findings acquire vogue in manifold contexts. For researchers in the scientific community on product lifecycle management as an overview and inspiration [34], for industrial developers and users of product lifecycle management as technology scouting [35], and finally for the society for a sensitization on such disruptive technologies [36].

Despite the valuable results, this manuscript is exposed to limitations, which should be disclosed fairly and squarely. A major limitation emerges from the exploratory, qualitative approach [11, 12] offering deep insights, however no widely generalizable results. Another relevant restriction is associated with the early-stage character, as presently no functional smart dust applications exist where real benefits could be shared to the reader.

Research on smart dust and its relationship to product lifecycle management is by far not depleted. Product lifecycle management and affecting emerging digital technologies are understood as socio-technical phenomenon [37], thus both sides need to be deepened. In terms of social impact, there is great research potential for additional applications of smart dust. For example, diving one level deeper into the lifecycle model (e.g., product design, process design, plant design, [1]) may bring out further uses. With regard to the technical foundation, first applications may be prototyped to collect real-world experiences. As base, however, the feasibility (e.g., energy supply and communication in solids) needs to be evaluated.

Acknowledgements. The authors of this research paper were supported by the Swiss National Science Foundation "Spark" program.

References

1. Terzi, S., Bouras, A., Dutta, D., Garetti, M., Kiritsis, D.: Product lifecycle management – from its history to its new role. Int. J. Prod. Lifecycle Manag. **4**(4), 360–389 (2010)
2. Stark, J.: Product Lifecycle Management: 21st Century Paradigm for Product Realisation. Springer, London (2015)
3. Kiritsis, D.: Closed-loop PLM for intelligent products in the era of the internet of things. Comput. Aided Des. **43**(5), 479–501 (2011)
4. Wuest, T., Schmidt, T., Wei, W., Romero, D.: Towards (Pro-)active intelligent products. Int. J. Prod. Lifecycle Manag. **11**(2), 154–189 (2018)
5. Li, J.R., Tao, F., Cheng, Y., Zhao, L.: Big data in product lifecycle management. Int. J. Adv. Manuf. Technol. **81**(1–4), 667–684 (2015)
6. Zhang, Y., Ren, S., Liu, Y., Sakao, T., Huisingh, D.: A framework for big data-driven product lifecycle management. J. Clean. Prod. **159**, 229–240 (2017)
7. Kahn, J.M., Katz, R.H., Pister, K.S.J.: Emerging challenges: mobile networking for smart dust. J. Commun. Netw. **2**(3), 188–196 (2000)
8. Warneke, B., Last, M., Liebowitz, B., Pister, K.S.J.: Smart dust: communicating with a cubic millimeter computer. Computer **34**(1), 44–51 (2001)
9. Satyanarayanan, M.: Of smart dust and brilliant rocks. IEEE Pervasive Comput. **2**(4), 2–3 (2003)
10. Ilyas, M., Mahgoub, I.: Smart Dust: Sensor Network Applications, Architecture and Design. CRC Press, Boca Raton (2018)
11. Silverman, D.: Doing Qualitative Research. Sage Publications, London (2009)
12. Myers, M.D.: Qualitative Research in Business and Management. Sage Publications, Thousand Oaks (2013)
13. Chong, C.-Y., Kumar, S.: Sensor networks: evolution, opportunities, and challenges. Proc. IEEE **91**(8), 1247–1256 (2003)
14. Kubler, S., Derigent, W., Främling, K., Thomas, A., Rondeau, E.: Enhanced product lifecycle information management using "communicating materials". Comput. Aided Des. **59**, 192–200 (2015)
15. Webster, J., Watson, R.: Analyzing the past to prepare the future: writing a literature review. MIS Q. **26**(2), xiii–xxiii (2002)
16. Kahn, J.M., Katz, R.H., Pister, K.S.J.: Next century challenges: mobile networking for smart dust. In: Proceedings of the 5th Annual ACM/IEEE International Conference on Mobile Computing and Networking, Washington, United States (1999)
17. Forbes Magazine: Smart Dust Is Coming. Are You Ready? https://www.forbes.com/sites/bernardmarr/2018/09/16/smart-dust-is-coming-are-you-ready/. Accessed 05 Mar 2020
18. Gartner: Five Trends Emerge in the Gartner Hype Cycle for Emerging Technologies. https://www.gartner.com/smarterwithgartner/5-trends-emerge-in-gartner-hype-cycle-for-emerging-technologies-2018. Accessed 05 Mar 2020
19. Müller-Bloch, C., Kranz, J.: A framework for rigorously identifying research gaps in qualitative literature reviews. In: Proceedings of the 36th International Conference on Information Systems, Fort Worth, United States (2015)
20. Gaura, E., Girod, L., Brusey, J., Allen, M., Challen, G. (eds.): Wireless Sensor Networks – Deployments and Design Frameworks. Springer, New York (2010). https://doi.org/10.1007/978-1-4419-5834-1
21. Yin, R.K.: Case Study Research – Design and Methods. Sage Publications, London (2003)
22. Yin, R.K.: Validity and generalization in future case study evaluations. Evaluation **19**(3), 321–332 (2013)

23. Statista: Maschinenbau Branchenreport. https://de.statista.com/statistik/studie/id/57556/dokument//. Accessed 05 Mar 2020
24. Coyne, I.T.: Sampling in qualitative research. purposeful and theoretical sampling; merging or clear boundaries? J. Adv. Nurs. **26**(3), 623–630 (1997)
25. Schultze, U., Avital, M.: Designing interviews to generate rich data for information systems research. Inf. Organ. **21**(1), 1–16 (2011)
26. Charmaz, K.C.: Constructing Grounded Theory: A Practical Guide Through Qualitative Analysis. Sage Publications, London (2006)
27. Wiesche, M., Jurisch, M.C., Yetton, P., Krcmar, H.: Grounded theory methodology in information systems research. MIS Q. **41**(3), 685–701 (2017)
28. Carroll, J.M.: Scenario-Based Design: Envisioning Work and Technology in System Development. Wiley, New York (1995)
29. Alexander, I., Neil, M.: Scenarios, Stories, Use Cases: Through the Systems Development Life-Cycle. Wiley, Chichester (2004)
30. Wellsandt, S., Nabati, E., Wuest, T., Hribernik, K.A., Thoben, K.-D.: A survey of product lifecycle models: towards complex products and service offers. Int. J. Prod. Lifecycle Manag. **9**(4), 353–390 (2016)
31. Nickerson, R.C., Varshney, U., Muntermann, J.: A method for taxonomy development and its application in information systems. Eur. J. Inf. Syst. **22**(3), 336–359 (2013)
32. Chemero, A.: An outline of a theory of affordances. Ecol. Psychol. **15**(2), 181–195 (2003)
33. Gorder, P.F.: Sizing up smart dust. Comput. Sci. Eng. **5**(6), 6–9 (2003)
34. Nyffenegger, F., Rivest, L., Braesch, C.: Identifying PLM themes, trends and clusters through ten years of scientific publications. In: Proceedings of the International Conference of Product Lifecycle Management, Columbia, United States (2016)
35. Meier, U., Fischli, F., Sohrweide, A., Nyffenegger, F.: Twenty years of PLM – the good, the bad and the ugly. In: Proceedings of the International Conference of Product Lifecycle Management, Sevilla, Spain (2017)
36. Skog, D.A., Wimelius, H., Sandberg, J.: Digital Disruption. Bus. Inf. Syst. Eng. **60**(5), 431–437 (2018). https://doi.org/10.1007/s12599-018-0550-4
37. David, M., Rowe, F.: Le Management des Systèmes PLM: Un Agenda de Recherche. J. Decis. Syst. **24**(3), 273–297 (2015)

Smart Manufacturing Testbed for the Advancement of Wireless Adoption in the Factory

Richard Candell[1(✉)], Yongkang Liu[1], Mohamed Kashef[1], Karl Montgomery[1], and Sebti Foufou[2]

[1] National Institute of Standards and Technology, Gaithersburg, MD, USA
richard.candell@nist.gov
[2] Universite de Bourgogne, Dijon, France
sfoufou@u-bourgogne.fr
http://www.nist.gov, http://www.u-bourgogne.fr/le2i/sebti.foufou

Abstract. Wireless communication is a key enabling technology central to the advancement of the goals of the Industry 4.0 smart manufacturing concept. Researchers at the National Institute of Standards and Technology are constructing a testbed to aid in the adoption of wireless technology within the factory workcell and other harsh industrial radio environments. In this paper the authors present a new industrial wireless testbed design that motivates academic research and is relevant to the needs of industry. The testbed is designed to serve as both a demonstration and research platform for the wireless workcell. The work leverages lessons learned from past testbed incarnations that included a dual robot machine tending scenario and a force-torque seeking robot arm apparatus. This version of the testbed includes computational and communication elements such that the operation of the physical system is noticeably degraded under the influence of radio interference, competing network traffic, and radio propagation effects applied within the lab. The testbed includes two collaborative grade robot arms, programmable logical controllers, and high-performance computing devices for situational tracking, alerting, and control. The paper is aimed to provide our contribution to the exploration of industrial wireless testbed design while soliciting feedback from fellow researchers.

Keywords: Factory communications · Wireless · Testbed design · Smart manufacturing · Simulation · IIoT

1 Introduction

One method for measuring the physical effects of communication loss and information delay within an industrial wireless network (IWN) on manufacturing processes within a workcell is the creation of a testbed for conducting research

Published by Springer Nature Switzerland AG 2020
F. Nyffenegger et al. (Eds.): PLM 2020, IFIP AICT 594, pp. 176–189, 2020.
https://doi.org/10.1007/978-3-030-62807-9_15

and demonstrating ideas and technologies using real equipment control systems, and processes. Testbeds are useful for investigating cyberphysical systems (CPS) impacts in that physical systems are entirely real or at least partially real. A CPS is a tightly coupled integration of physical, computing, and communications processes. As such, events within the computing and communications processes impact the physical process. Within a testbed, physical processes such as robot dynamics do not have to be simulated because gravity, inertia, and system dynamics are inherently present and measurable. Additionally, within a testbed, the electromagnetic properties are present, and their impacts on the physical networking devices are felt and equally measurable in terms of information loss and delay. These losses and delays influence the performance of the network and lead to abnormalities in the performance of the physical system.

CPS Theoretical Model. Consulting the theoretical model of a CPS shown in Fig. 1, the physical process instrumented with sensors produces one or more sensor outputs, Y, which are transmitted through a network such as an industrial wireless network. Interference and multi-path phenomena may cause losses and delay as the received sensor information $\bar{Y}$ arrives at the control system. The control system then uses $\bar{Y}$ to act upon the physical system by sending commands, U which may arrive as delayed or lost, demoted by $\bar{U}$, at the physical process. The differences between $\bar{Y}$ and Y and between $\bar{U}$ and U cause changes in the behavior of the physical process. The severity of those changes will depend on the resilience of the control system and the properties of the physical system, itself.

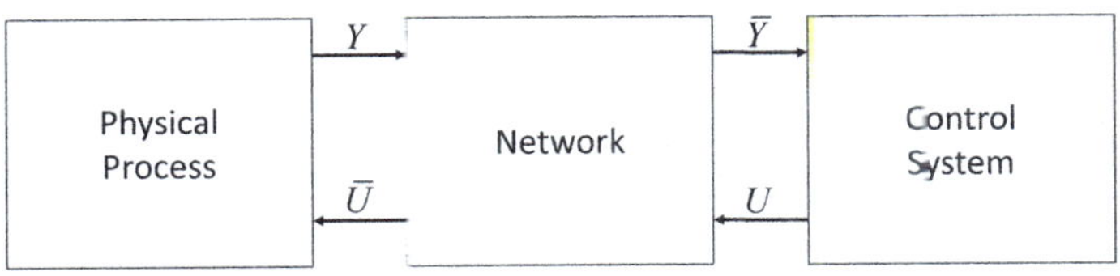

Fig. 1. Theoretical representation of a cyberphysical system.

Motivation. While theoretical modeling and simulation are helpful in understanding CPS behaviour, they lack the accuracy of the real-world systems. Therefore, testbeds are used to reproduce larger physical systems on a smaller scale using computing and communication devices and real physical components such as edge devices and robots. The National Institute of Standards and Technology (NIST) has produced a series of industrial wireless testbeds with use cases ranging from chemical production and confined space sensing to robotic machine tending and force controlled actuation. All of these incarnations of the testbed addressed real needs with use cases of low-rate time considerations on the order of 100 ms or more. However, with the emerging requirement of robotic mobility and remote joint actuation in semi-autonomous robotic systems, a new use case is necessary to conduct future research within the testbed. This use case must be selected such that perturbations within the IWN are rapidly reflected within the physical system. The testbed itself should be implemented to measure in real-time both informational and operational performance commensurate with the use case.

Contributions. The contributions of this work are as follows: 1) We present our lessons learned conducting experimental studies with past incarnations of the NIST industrial wireless testbed; 2) we present our use case requirements and testbed considerations for a general industrial wireless testbed that readily demonstrates cyberphysical effects rapidly in humanly detectable fashion when information loss and delay are introduced; 3) we present the functional design of the testbed which implements our proposed use case.

Paper Organization. The paper is organized as follows: In Sect. 2, previous relevant academic works are presented. Then in Sect. 3, lessons learned from past incarnations of software-based and hardware-in-the-loop testbed simulations are reviewed. Next, in Sect. 4, requirements for the new use case motivated primarily by robotic mobility is addressed along with the requirements for the testbed platform itself. In Sects. 5 and 6, the proposed use case and testbed are elaborated in detail. Concluding remarks are given in the final section.

2 Related Work

Wireless communication technologies have been proactively extending their footprints onto the factory floor from non-critical process monitoring services to more deterministic transmission of mission-critical application data [6]. Standardization bodies have released their own visions of service requirements on industrial wireless communications [1,5]. The European Telecommunications Standards Institute (ETSI) has classified a series of use cases in industrial sectors, mainly as machine-typed communications, and identified corresponding radio transmission requirements on individual classes [5]. The Third Generation Partnership Project (3GPP) has also identified service requirements for industrial wireless use cases and address them in their 5G cellular use scenarios, e.g., massive machine-type communications (mMTC) and ultrareliable and low-latency communications (URLLC) [1]. However, justification of specific values regarding key performance metrics is barely disclosed in these efforts. Recently, there is an ongoing discussion on calibrating wireless service requirements to truly reflect system needs in typical industrial communications scenarios, e.g., factory workcells [12].

Validating industrial wireless requirements and further evaluating candidate solutions have proven challenging. Existing validation approaches can be classified into three main categories: theoretical analysis, software simulation, and hardware testbed. Theoretical analysis has been widely used to showcase performance trend by statistically modelling traffic load and link quality [14].

However, it is very difficult to model complex industrial use cases where factors for both network performance and manufacturing productivity need to be captured thoroughly, especially when transmissions are closely associated with process precision and plant safety. Being widely used to verify theoretical analysis and project system performance, simulation techniques have the flexibility of scaling up and finely tuning the studied use case under different conditions. However, experts in their own domains (e.g., industrial engineers and communications engineers) often find it difficult to select/develop appropriate simulation modules for components that fall out of their expertise, who tend to make over-simplified or erroneous modeling assumptions that deviates the delivery of trustworthy results. Recently co-simulation tools have been developed to jointly mimic behaviors of component systems/networks of CPS in a hierarchical High-Level Architecture (HLA) [13]. Jeng *et al.* introduced a factory co-simulator that jointly considers the production pipeline across multiple workstations and information interaction between them through the network [9]. Such work can also be further extended to the hardware-in-the-loop (HIL) experiments to render more accurate estimation on the performance with tested equipment [3]. Being built upon mathematical models, simulation methods also encounter similar design issues to keep a balance between depiction accuracy and computation efficiency. Besides software-based evaluation, testbeds have been developed to test existing wireless techniques and prototypes in the emulated industrial use cases. Lucas-Estan *et al.* designed experiments to test wireless link redundancy schemes in a multi-robot testbed which is focused on improving reliability of wireless transmissions [11]. Given vast diversity and variability of industrial use cases, the design of effective testbed for individual use cases becomes a key to the success of wireless deployment. NIST engineers have examined the impact of wireless links on industrial system performance through a series of testbeds [2–4,7,8]. Based on lessons learned in these practices, we will examine design principles to highlight industrial wireless requirements in this paper.

3 Lessons Learned from Past Testbed Incarnations

In this section, we discuss the lessons learned from various previous testbeds that have been used in the NIST industrial wireless systems (IWS) lab. These previously developed testbeds and experimental studies can be found in [2–4,7,8].

3.1 Tennessee Eastman Chemical Factory

In [3], industrial wireless communications devices were deployed for pressure, temperature, and flow sensors data transfer for the control of a simulated chemical factory. IEEE802.15.4-based protocols were deployed such as WirelessHART and ISA100.11a. Both simulations and HIL experiments were performed for this application in [10] and [3], respectively. We found that, generally, process control applications with large time constant can be impacted by communications impairments when the wireless channel is poor for an extended period of time. The existing WirelessHART and ISA100.11a can perform adequately for these applications while the wireless sensors are connected to the network. However, we found that networks were not robust to events outside the scheme of information transmission such as the loss of a router node, gateway, etc. due to power loss or similar incidents.

Moreover, comparing simulations to HIL experiments, we found that experimental studies are needed to reflect the more realistic impacts of protocol implementation and higher layer protocol impacts such as by Modbus. We have deployed a channel emulator to replicate the impact of electromagnetic propagation in industrial environments on CPS performance. We have also learned that abstract network performance criteria such as packet loss and packet latency may not reflect the communications impact on the production process and hence physical process related criteria should be evaluated in various experimental studies.

3.2 Confined Space Gas Sensing Testbed

In [7], we performed an experimental study on a testbed which is very similar to the chemical factory use case in Sect. 3.1 such that a similar HIL concept is deployed. The main difference is that different wireless channel models were deployed and different types of information were transferred. In the confined space case, the simulated gas levels at different points of the confined space are transferred over wireless using HIL simulation, and the effectiveness of a safety alerting application is considered. In this setup, we found that the communications protocol implementation could impact the system performance where the implemented Modbus protocol has an update period of 2 s which is much slower than the signal and channel variations. We also found that testing can be performed on the signal-level for sensors and actuators signals in case of unavailability of network-level metrics. However, we concluded that the network-level metrics are needed to further understand the reasons behind the measured performance.

3.3 3D Gantry System Testbed

In [8], a commercial 3D gantry system was deployed where the g-code commands to control the gantry system were streamed using a WiFi network. In this experimental study, we found that while converting an originally wired testbed to a wireless one, a ground truth measuring technique has to exist in order to quantify the system performance and hence the wireless impact on performance. Generally, ground truth measurements can be obtained through instrumented feedback from the system, if exists, or through a remote observer where a vision tracking system was deployed in this testbed.

Similar to previously discussed testbeds, the definitions of physical process metrics are needed where these metrics have to be impacted by wireless communications impairments. In this experiment, where g-code command delays made the 3D gantry to halt at a specific location waiting for the following command, performance metrics, such as dwell time and production rate, were considered. The main lesson learned in this experimental study was that queuing of the control commands can mitigate the impact of rapid changes in the wireless channels i.e., keeping a buffered set of commands at the remote station can help to keep the process running. Buffering is not always a viable solution in latency-sensitive applications.

3.4 Force Seeking Apparatus Testbed

In [4], a force seeking apparatus was built using a robot arm and an attached force-torque sensor (FTS). A single wireless channel is deployed where the FTS transmits the force value to the robot controller which reacts when a specific threshold is reached. A machine learning algorithm is used to estimate the interference level on the wireless channel based on tracking the robot arm movements. In this study, we assessed the impact of interference on the physical performance of a fast process where the direct relation between wireless channel quality and the process is quantified. In single wireless channel scenarios, we study only the impact of external interference while competing traffic scenarios are not considered. Hence, we concluded it would be desirable to have a testbed with multiple deployed wireless nodes allowing us to study channel contention scenarios. We also found that the FTSs are not designed to be used wirelessly where large delays can cause dropping the connection with the robot controller. The dropped connection requires resetting the FTS control box to continue its operation which is not acceptable in industrial processes. We concluded that, in general, the industrial devices should be designed to handle information loss and delay more readily through means of mitigative control system programming or user adjustment of device parameters rather than hard-coding total system failure.

3.5 Dual Robot Machine-Tending Testbed

In [2], a more comprehensive testbed was built where two robot arms, one supervisory PLC, and four machine emulators worked together to perform a pick-and-place task. The supervisory control signals to the robot controllers and the machines were transmitted wirelessly. The data for the network traffic and the status of the machines and robot arms were collected. Although, we were able to show the impact of wireless on the network-level metrics, such as packet latency, the impact of wireless on the physical process was almost negligible because only supervisory commands were transferred wirelessly. The latency of supervisory commands were significantly lower than the scan time of the control loop causing negligible physical impact. We discovered that in-network contention is more impactful than electromagnetic interference. Moreover, we discovered that multiple source of contention impacted the system more compared to a single traffic source.

We have also run experiments using both periodic and event-based Modbus polling for the communications between the supervisor and the robot controllers. We found that periodic Modbus polling is more robust to the channel because no timeout warnings may occur. However, it is less bandwidth efficient than the event-based counterpart. On the other hand, event-based Modbus polling is preferred in wireless communications scenarios not to interfere with other network activities. Moreover, access to the robot arm middleware would allow more control of Modbus polling properties. As a result, a middleware alternative such as robot operating system (ROS) would be suitable.

4 Requirements for New Use Case

To enable adoption of an effective use case for deployment in the NIST industrial wireless testbed, development of clear requirements is a necessary and an essential first step. Using our lessons learned and experience, it was required that the new use case proposed have noticeable physical impact under degraded communications situations, have industry relevance, and have an accessible software middleware.

Noticeable Physical Impact. Learned from Sect. 3.5, the new use case requires noticeable physical impact from the degradation of communication. Such degradation occurs commonly in wireless communications. In the use case, wireless links are used to carry traffic to control the physical action directly; thus, any significant fluctuation in latency or reliability of the wireless link will be immediately noticeable by measurement or observation. In past incarnations, physical manifestations from communication loss and delay were not immediately noticeable because the physical systems were more immune to information disturbances in the wireless network.

Industry Relevance. Constructing a use case that is similar to the types of applications used by industry is required as the findings discovered will be relevant. This requirement suggests that a new use case should perform a similar task or physical operation that is found in industrial applications.

Access to Software Middleware. Many current industrial devices do not support wireless communications in their design. Such devices have proven to have difficulties in compatibility with current wireless solutions, e.g., overly strict timeout thresholds, such as with Modbus client configurations, which may trigger system failures as described in Sects. 3.4 and 3.5. Therefore, it is asserted that the desired industrial wireless testbed provide access to the software residing between applications and the industrial wireless networking stack on each host.

5 Proposed Use Case

In this section, we explain briefly the proposed dual robot leader-follower use case. We first introduce the design of the use case where the major system components are defined. Then, we validate that the proposed use case satisfies the use case requirements in Sect. 4.

5.1 Design

In Fig. 2, the physical process is shown where two robot arms equipped with FTSs are collaborating in lifting a semi-rigid object. Dual robot object lifting is a general industrial approach used for heavy lifting and over-sized material handling. Typically, stationary robots used for lifting communicates through wired technologies. However, the need for flexible manufacturing and mobile robots in future factories requires the deployment of wireless technologies for communications between robots. In the leader-follower schemes, one robot is assigned the rule of the leader to achieve a certain control objective. The other robot, the follower, takes specific actions relative to the leader to maintain a desired relation with the leader with respect to the position or forces on the lifted object. As a result, communications between the leader and the follower plays a crucial role in maintaining the integrity of the lifted object and preventing collisions for the mobile robots.

The control of the leader-follower scenario allows the follower to take decisions based on transferred information about the leader activity. The leader information is transferred using a deployed industrial wireless network. Furthermore, the control of the leader-follower scenario could be done in a centralized approach. In the centralized approach, the centralized controller makes decisions about the follower actions based on the joint state information transferred by the both robots. Moreover, we attach an FTS to the lifted object in order to measure the applied forces and study the impact of wireless communications on the lifted object.

5.2 Requirement Coverage

This proposed use case was selected by incorporating the lessons learned from previous use cases in Sect. 3 and to satisfy the discussed use case requirements in Sect. 4. In the proposed use case, the goal is to get a direct impact of wireless communications on the physical process through having the leader-follower relation between the robots. Any latency or reliability issues in the information transfer between the leader and the follower is expected to affect the desired relation between them. The impact of wireless communications on the physical process can be measured through the position feedback of the robot arms and the FTSs. Capture of network data is made possible through the use of network probes strategically placed throughout the testbed. Similarly, capture of performance data of the physical system is made possible by instrumenting the testbed with ground truth measurement and recording probes such that variables such as forces, torques, positions, velocities, and accelerations are captured independently of the wireless network. We deploy a master clock to synchronize all the collected physical process and network traffic data. Finally, this proposed use case replicates a realistic scenario which can be found in heavy lifting and over-sized material handling.

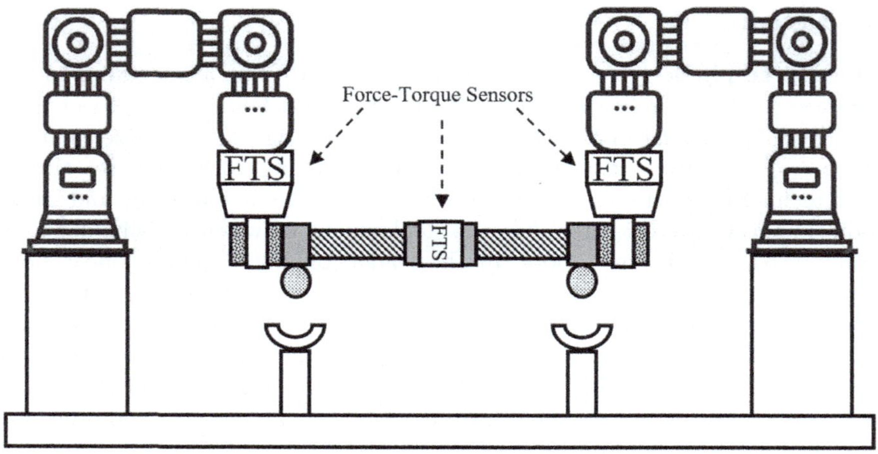

Fig. 2. The leader-follower use case diagram.

6 Proposed Testbed

6.1 Architecture

The testbed serves as an evaluation platform that emulates workcell operations in the proposed use case and measures the impact of node interactions on the production performance. As shown in Fig. 3, it consists of three main subsystems according to their different roles: *workcell modules*, *network components*, and *measurement devices*. In the designed architecture, subsystems are connected with each other through predefined interfaces and integrated as a complete evaluation process. Design details of each one will be elaborated in the following section.

6.2 Components

Workcell modules include testbed components that participate in manufacturing tasks, e.g., robots and their controllers in the leader-follower use case. In the testbed, we deploy two Universal Robots (UR) UR3 CB-series robots that serve as actors in the leader-follower use case. Each UR3 is equipped with a 6 degree-of-freedom (6-DoF) robot arm, one control box, and peripheral devices, known as URCaps, which include a Robotiq gripper and a 6-axis force-torque sensor attached to the end effector. Instead of using proprietary UR programs, the control of robots implements agents atop the robot operating system (ROS) middleware which provides a rich set of options in control functions and peripheral support for UR3. In ROS, robot-oriented processes are identified as separate function nodes which can be distributed across multiple physical machines being connected through the network. As shown in Fig. 3, the testbed hosts three computers running Ubuntu 18.04 with the ROS Melodic distribution. Two of them

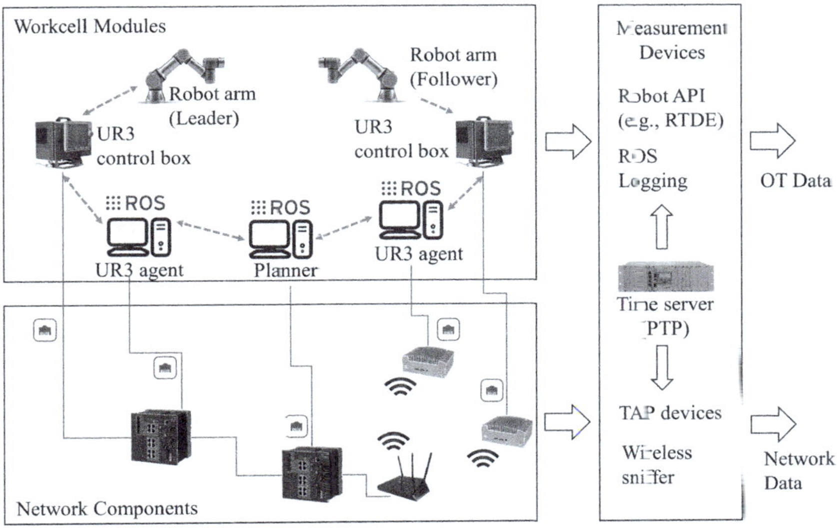

Fig. 3. Workcell testbed architecture

serve as UR3 agents where ROS UR3 drivers are installed to adapt universal ROS functions and commands to UR3 features. The coordination between the leader and the follower can be realized through the peer-to-peer communications between UR3 agents. In this case, the third machine, i.e., the ROS planner, performs motion planning for both robots. There is another feasible approach in which both UR3 agents report to the planner who will resolve their joint trajectory actions and reply to both with respective action commands.

Network components are network devices that enable workcell modules to communicate with each other for job-oriented information exchange and process control. Each workcell module in the testbed contains one or more built-in Ethernet interfaces. Two Cisco IE-4000 industrial gigabit Ethernet switches serve as the wired network backbone. Ethernet-wireless adapters are used to replace wired connections by enabling wireless communications between modules. Figure 3 illustrates an example of connecting to the follower robot through wireless. The testbed uses IPv4 addresses to manage communication devices. Additional network connections are also planned in the testbed that provide measurement data links and other complimentary features, such as time synchronization services.

Table 1. Testbed measurement data collections

Data	Source	Type	Time synced	Format
Actual joint status (e.g., position, velocity, and acceleration)	UR3 joints	Workcell	Yes, PTP	CSV
URCap force and torque	FTSs at UR3 end effectors	Workcell	Yes, PTP	CSV
ROS UR3 control (Leader/follower status)	ROS UR3 agents	Workcell	Yes, PTP	CSV
ROS Motion planning output (target joint status)	ROS master	Workcell	Yes, PTP	CSV
Force and torque (ground truth)	FTS at the lifted object	Workcell	Yes, PTP	CSV
Ethernet packet captures	TAP	Network	Yes, PTP	PCAP
Wireless packet captures	Wireleess sniffer	Network	Yes, PTP	PCAP

Measurement devices collect data including but not limited to manufacturing progress, machine status, link quality, and network health. Table 1 summarizes data to be collected and saved for further analysis. Specifically, production-related workcell data and network data are monitored and captured at different measurement devices. The former ones are usually collected through UR3's API, e.g., the real-time data exchange (RTDE), or saved locally in workcell modules, e.g., the ROS logging at ROS nodes; the latter ones are mainly captured by traffic analysis tools, such as test access point (TAP) devices for real-time traffics in Ethernet links and the wireless sniffer. Note that the testbed uses real-time readings from the FTS at the lifted object as the ground truth for measuring the performance of coordinated operations between the leader and the follower. Besides, timing information is also rendered and embedded into each record so that discrete events can be aligned in time to review the operation logic and network behaviors in future analysis. Therefore, the testbed can implement the precision time protocol (PTP) to provide the sub-microsecond level accuracy across the networked distributed clocks. A Meinberg M900 time server is used as the central PTP master clock that supports the IEEE 1588-2008 (PTPv2) standard.

6.3 Interfaces

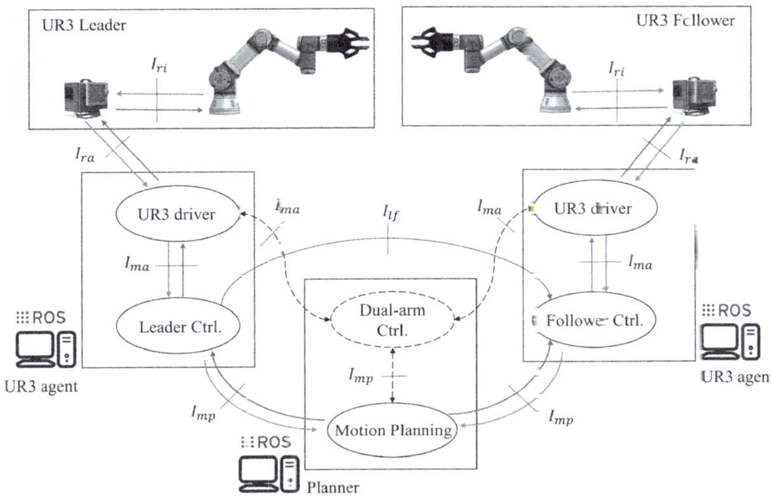

Fig. 4. Testbed interfaces

Figure 4 illustrates interfaces between workcell modules that are used to enable the coordination between the two actors in the proposed leader-follower use case. As data communications are directional, we define the *upstream* data flow to be the one from the end node, i.e. the UR3 robot arm, toward the planner which is denoted by green arrows in the figure. The *downstream* data is reversed and denoted in blue. When the leader (follower) has its own controller residing in the agent machine, the leader will routinely share its motion information to the follower, either as geometrical variables or force-torque readings, which allows the follower to track the leader's trajectory and calculate its own route to keep the metrology bar in the desired state. In another case when the ROS planner also takes over the control mission, a new dual-arm control node will replace the separate controllers in UR3 agents. The flows will be updated accordingly which are illustrated as dashed arrows in Fig. 4.

Table 2 summarizes interfaces defined for data exchanges between different nodes. Note that each interface contains data in both upstream and downstream directions. Except I_{ri} for UR3 internal traffics, the other interfaces are built for communications between ROS nodes. ROS provides three communication styles including synchronous request/reply interactions ("services"), asynchronous data streaming ("topics"), and data storage in a parameter server. We will use the testbed to explore the capability of wireless links in support of different communications styles in selected interfaces. For each interface, a set of protocols is listed for which the use case will be tested. Ethernet is used for baseline performance testing, while wireless local area network (WLAN) protocols

Table 2. Testbed interface specifications

Interface	Protocol	Data		Note
		Upstream	Downstream	
UR3 internal, I_{ri}	Serial	UR3 and URCap status	Joint trajectory action	UR3 proprietary
UR3-ROS, I_{ra}	Ethernet WLAN	Robot status	Joint trajectory action	ROS UR3 driver
ROS master-agent, I_{ma}		Robot status	Joint trajectory action	ROS topics/services
ROS motion planning, I_{mp}		Target trajectory	Joint trajectory action	ROS topics/services
Leader-Follower, I_{lf}		Force-torque-based or geometrical trace		ROS topics/services

such as IEEE 802.11 will be used when a wireless protocol is employed. Fifth generation wireless (5G) is envisioned as well when resources come available.

7 Conclusions

In this paper, we have presented the next evolution of an industrial wireless testbed. The testbed is designed with the goal of investigating use cases that will noticeably degrade under the influence of radio interference, competing network traffic, and radio propagation effects applied within the lab. One specific use case is presented in which two robots perform a coordinated lift operation using either a geometric leader follower or a force-torque minimization control scheme. In the control scheme presented, wireless links are used to carry joint state information such that lost or delayed state information immediately impacts physical action. Capture of performance data of the network and physical systems is made possible by the use of probe devices. Our testbed will serve as a research and demonstration platform for reliable industrial wireless deployment and control system strategies. Finally, our work is presented with lessons learned from past incarnations of our wireless testbed such that our work may help others construct better wireless testbeds by learning from our successes and failures. Once completed, results from our testbed will be made available through reports, papers, and publication of data sets.

Disclaimer

Certain commercial equipment, instruments, or materials are identified in this paper in order to specify the experimental procedure adequately. Such identification is not intended to imply recommendation or endorsement by the National Institute of Standards and Technology, nor is it intended to imply that the materials or equipment identified are necessarily the best available for the purpose.

References

1. 3GPP: Service Requirements for the 5G System. Technical Specification (TS) 22.261, 3rd Generation Partnership Project (3GPP), December 2019. https://portal.3gpp.org/desktopmodules/Specifications/SpecificationDetails.aspx?specificationId=3107. Version 16.10.0

2. Candell, R., Kashef, M., Liu, Y., Montgomery, K., Foufou, S.: A graph database approach to wireless IIoT work-cell performance evaluation. In: Proceedings of the 2020 IEEE International Conference on Industrial Technology, February 2020
3. Candell, R., Lee, K.: Measuring the effect of wireless sensor network communications on industrial process performance. In: 2015 ISA Process Control and Safety Symposium, Houston, TX (2015)
4. Candell, R., Montgomery, K., Kashef, M., Liu, Y., Foufou, S.: Wireless interference estimation using machine learning in a robotic force-seeking scenario. In: 2019 IEEE 28th International Symposium on Industrial Electronics (ISIE), pp. 1334–1341, June 2019. https://doi.org/10.1109/ISIE.2019.8781418
5. (ETSI): ETSI TR 103 588 reconfigurable radio systems (RRS); feasibility study on temporary spectrum access for local high-quality wireless networks. Technical report, European Telecommunications Standards Institute (ETSI), Sophia-Antipolis (2018)
6. Huang, V.K.L., Pang, Z., Chen, C.A., Tsang, K.F.: New trends in the practical deployment of industrial wireless: from noncritical to critical use cases. IEEE Ind. Electron. Mag. **12**(2), 50–58 (2018). https://doi.org/10.1109/MIE.2018.2825480
7. Kashef, M., Candell, R.: Characterization for an industrial wireless network in a gas sensing scenario. In: Proceedings of the 2017 ISA International Instrumentation Symposium (2017)
8. Kashef, M., Candell, R., Foufou, S.: On the Impact of Wireless Communications on Controlling a Two-Dimensional Gantry System. International Manufacturing Science and Engineering Conference, Volume 1: Additive Manufacturing; Manufacturing Equipment and Systems; Bio and Sustainable Manufacturing, June 2019. https://doi.org/10.1115/MSEC2019-2896, v001T02A005
9. Li, H., Geng, J., Liu, Y., Kashef, M., Candell, R., Bhattacharyya, S.S.: Design space exploration for wireless-integrated factory automation systems. In: 2019 15th IEEE International Workshop on Factory Communication Systems (WFCS), pp. 1–8, May 2019. https://doi.org/10.1109/WFCS.2019.8757954
10. Liu, Y., Candell, R., Moayeri, N.: Effects of wireless packet loss in industrial process control systems. ISA Trans. **68**, 412–424 (2017). https://doi.org/10.1016/j.isatra.2017.02.005
11. Lucas-Estañ, M.d.C., Maestre, J., Coll-Perales, B., Gozalvez, J., Lluvia, I.: An experimental evaluation of redundancy in industrial wireless communications, September 2018. https://doi.org/10.1109/ETFA.2018.8502497
12. Montgomery, K., Candell, R., Liu, Y., Hany, M.: Wireless User Requirements for the Factory Work-cell. Technical report (2019). https://doi.org/10.6028/NIST.AMS.300-8. https://www.nist.gov/publications/wireless-user-requirements-factory-workcell
13. Neema, H., et al.: Model-based integration platform for FMI co-simulation and heterogeneous simulations of cyber-physical systems, pp. 235–245, March 2014. https://doi.org/10.3384/ecp14096235
14. Zheng, M., Liang, W., Yu, H., Xiao, Y.: Performance analysis of the industrial wireless networks standard: WIA-PA mobile networks and applications, pp. 1–12 (2015). https://doi.org/10.1007/s11036-015-0647-7

Analytics in the Order Fulfillment Process

Free Text Customer Requests Analysis: Information Extraction Based on Fuzzy String Comparison

Alexander Smirnov[1], Nikolay Shilov[1(✉)], Kathrin Evers[2], and Dirk Weidig[2]

[1] SPIIRAS, St. Petersburg, Russia
{smir,nick}@iias.spb.su
[2] Festo SE & Co. KG, Esslingen, Germany
{kathrin.evers,dirk.weidig}@festo.com

Abstract. Complex systems (such as automation systems), from here on referred as "products" are usually difficult for customers to specify since there are a lot of parameters to be defined and the customer should perfectly know what is really needed and important for the supplier in order to provide for a proper system. As a result, creating forms and templates for the customer request specification entry helps only for relatively simple tasks and the completely digital request acquisition and processing is still a matter of future work. Currently, the original request specification comes from the customer in various ways (texts, images, diagrams, a phone or a direct talk to the company's sales representative) and the results of the analysis of this specification are often forwarded further to the back-office in a form of free or semi-structured text written in natural language. Since this text is the main source of information about the customer request, it is very important to extract as much information from it as possible. The paper reports the research and development work on semantic text analysis for information extraction from customer requests written in natural language. The core of the work is development of methods for finding a pre-defined list of terms (product parameters that are important for the order specification) in a fuzzy (similarity-based) manner with the help of synonym dictionaries. The results are illustrated on a case study from the automation equipment producer Festo SE & Co KG.

Keywords: Free text analysis · Semantic analysis · Fuzzy string comparison

1 Introduction

Today, product lifecycle management (PLM) automation is devoted a significant attention [1–4]. In previous publications we considered intelligent IT support for the entire PLM cycle [5] and the PLM stage of marketing [6, 7]. One of the possible results of this process is "Digital Customer Journey" [8] standing for complete IT support of the customer at all PLM stages from finding the supplier through product configuration and sales to product usage and disposal (Fig. 1).

F. Nyffenegger et al. (Eds.): PLM 2020, IFIP AICT 594, pp. 193–202, 2020.
https://doi.org/10.1007/978-3-030-62807-9_16

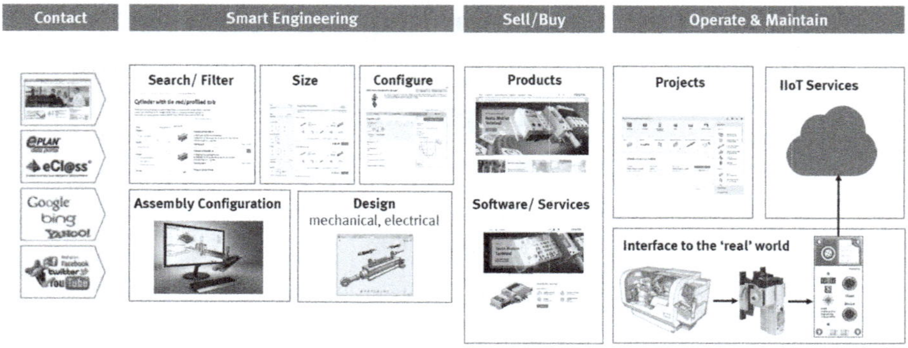

Fig. 1. Digital customer journey [8].

In this paper we would like to concentrate at the early PLM stage of product configuration. Complex automation systems as a rule are sold on the assemble-to-order basis, i.e. the bill of material and is collected out of built to stock (or sometimes built-to-order) [9] components based on the customer's specification. The problem is that such complex systems are usually difficult for customers to specify since there are a lot of parameters to be defined and the customer should perfectly know what is really needed and important for the supplier in order to provide for a proper system. As a result the complete "digital customer journey" from submitting a request and getting the product to its usage and utilisation is currently possible for relatively simple products and systems. For the considered type of products (automation systems) the "journey" starts from submitting a quotation request by the customer in a format that is from the customer's point of view the most convenient and easiest for understanding, including (but not limited to) texts, images, diagrams, or a phone calls.

The request is addressed to a sales representative or application engineer who specifies the customer requirements that are forwarded further to the back-office in a form of free or semi-structured text written in natural language (Fig. 2). For successful customer request fulfilment it is very important to extract as much information from this text as possible. The difficulty of this task is caused by the fact that the texts are filled out manually (sometimes not in native language of the writer), they are very short (e.g., see the text in the tables of Fig. 2), mostly contain specific technical terms, and the training set is relatively small (about 800 samples).

The contribution of this paper is the result of the research and development work on semantic text analysis for information extraction from customer requests written in natural language. The work is split into two parts: development of a method for finding a pre-defined list of terms (parameters of the product, parameters of the automation process the product takes part in, characteristics of objects it has to work with, e.g., workpiece characteristics, and other) from the tables in a fuzzy (similarity-based) manner; and development of a method for extracting information from the longer texts of the requests. While the former task is solved, the latter is still the matter of future research. The report does not discuss typical operations for preparing strings for comparison (deleting special characters, converting all characters to lower case and others),

Your task

Workpiece	Work pieces made of brass	
max. weight	0.02	kg (assumption)
Dimensions workpiece	different	mm (LxWxH)
Stroke Z-Axis	max. 100	mm
Stroke Y-Axis	max. 300	mm
Stroke X-Axis	appro. 0	mm
Cycle time	1.0	s

Notes
The dimensions of the work pieces are diffenrent. In the process of gripping it has to be ensure that the gripper finger can grip all the pieces.

Your task

Pick up of parts from a moving belt with tracking using a camera system and tripod. The parts are detected with a camera system and gripped by a vacuum gripper or a mechanical gripper.
Due to the different shapes of the parts, a tool change might be necessary to have an accurate gripping solution. The parts are aligned with a rotational drive and placed to a defined position.

In this offer is a vacuum gripper included as an example gripping solution. Further details about the parts to handle will be necessary to select an appropriate gripper.

Work piece		
max. weight	0,05	kg
Dimensions work piece	50x[illegible]0x2	mm (LxWxH) approximately
Cycle time	10	s (cycle not defined in inquiry)

Fig. 2. Examples of customer request specification in a form of semi-structured text.

since they are standard. The results are illustrated on a case study from the automation equipment producer Festo SE & Co KG.

The paper is structured as follows. Section 2 discusses the state of the art in the area of semantic analysis of short texts. It is followed by the description of the developed method for extraction of information from very short texts (table cells). Section 4 applies this method to extraction of information from longer texts. The results are summarized in the conclusion section.

2 State of the Art Review

The authors of [10] deal with a similar task, namely understanding of short texts (search requests). The authors analyse different approaches to text analysis taking into account the specifics of short (several words long) texts. Though, this approach seems to be applicable, the authors use the Probase dictionary [11] for reasoning on text semantics. However, this work deals with various technical terms and we could not find any sufficient dictionaries covering the required terminology. As a result it was decided not to continue with approaches relying on dictionaries for their operation.

In [12] the authors have identified and analysed three major directions of text analysis with regard to analysis of short texts, namely:

- Text segmentation – dividing text into a sequence of meaningful components.
- Part of Speech (POS) tagging – identification of the lexical types (parts of speech) of the words in the text.
- Labelling – definition of the most appropriate concepts meant by a word or a phrase within specific context.

Text segmentation approaches [13] can be split into two groups: approaches treating input text as a set of words and approaches considering phrases (e.g., longest matching methods trying to find the longest known (available in a dictionary) phrase in the text). Working with separate words will not be efficient in the considered domain, since they might have different meaning based on the context. For example, “max payload” would usually mean the weight of the workpiece only, and “max payload for

EXCT" would mean the weight of the workpiece together with the weight of the corresponding gripper or other holding device attached to the 2-dimensional linear gantry EXCT. At the same time, the longest matching methods (e.g., [14]) might be of interest since the longer text in this case can be considered as text template (text construction block) with a concrete meaning. Thus, the principles of these methods are partially used in the proposed approach.

POS tagging algorithms can also be split into two groups: rule-based algorithms (based on linguistic rules) and statistical algorithms (based on accumulated statistics including neural networks) [15]. The authors of [12] note that algorithms of both groups assume that the analysed text is properly structured. However, this is not the case for short texts. For example, the following fragments have the same meaning: "max. workpiece weight", "max. weight of workpiece", "max. weight workpiece", "max. weight/workpiece". As a result, POS tagging was not considered as a possible solution for the task set.

Labelling or concept labelling is aimed at identification of certain terms (concepts) in the text. Usually, such methods are built around statistical models [16, 17] or machine learning techniques [18, 19]. The problem with these methods is in extensive usage of available dictionaries and large training sets. However, as it was mentioned, the current research deals with short texts using specific technical terms. Besides, the available training sets were not large enough for training sophisticated AI models. The work by E. Brill [20] is slightly different. Though also based on statistical data, the result of training is a set of rules. An example of such a rule is: *if a word is tagged as the infinitive "to" and the following word is tagged as an article, than the infinitive "to" is replaced with the preposition "to"*. This can be illustrated as follows:

… *to load* the system – "to load" remains an infinitive;
… *to a load* of 1 kg – "to" becomes a proposition and "load" becomes a noun.

Similar rules can be defined for the considered problem in order to better understand the semantic meaning of the words in the short texts analysed.

3 Extraction of Product Parameters from Short Texts

The goal of this task is to set semantic correspondence between texts represented in tables (Fig. 2) with known parameters of the product. The reference parameters were extracted from product datasheets (a fragment is shown in Fig. 3). Such datasheets are used within the company for product description and can be considered as target models for information extraction. As it can be seen in Fig. 2, the text in tables is extremely short and its processing purely by methods described in Sect. 2 would not produce any sufficient results. Experimentation with different algorithms showed that that best results could be achieved via combination of fuzzy (similarity-based) string matching with usage of synonyms supported by pre-defined rules.

There are a number of algorithms for evaluating string similarity measures [21]. One of the most popular is the Levenshtein coefficient. It is based on counting the number of character edits (deleting, inserting or replacing one character) that have to be done to make the compared strings identical. For example, for the strings "max weight

System				
☐ Packaging ☑ Assembly ☐ Hepco ☐ Individual				
Environment				
☐ Mech. production ☐ Assembly ☐ Laboratory ☑ Clean room ☐ Foundr				
Performance				
Production rate			10 (carriers)	pcs./min.
Track length (estimation)			2000	mm
Number of stations			2	Station(s)
Distance between two stations			1500	mm
Accuracy of the system			±0,1	mm
☐ Drawing/sketch/photo in the appendix				
Additional requirements				
Work load				
Mass "holder"	0,3 kg	LxWxH		mm
Mass "product"	0,1 kg	LxWxH		mm
Center of mass		Z/Y/X		mm
Process forces	N	direction		(Z / Y / X)

Fig. 3. Examples of customer request specification in a form of semi-structured text.

of payload" and "max payload weight" (both refer to the weight of the workpiece) the Levenshtein's distance is 16, and for the strings "max weight of payload" and "max payload for EXCT" (the second string refers to the working load of the 2-dimensional linear gantry EXCT) the Levenshtein's distance is also 16. The calculation time for 1000 comparisons of strings "max weight of payload" and "max payload weight" on a computer with Intel Pentium i7 processor is 2.61 ms). The first drawback of this algorithm (difficulty of evaluating/comparing result for strings of different lengths) can be easily overcome, for example, by dividing the result by the length of the larger of the two compared strings (the calculation time increases insignificantly – 3.82 ms under the same conditions). However, the significant drawback demonstrated in the above example is poor results for strings obtained via rearranging words ("max weight of payload" and "max payload weight"), which is a common situation for example for the English language.

As a result of the analysis of existing algorithms for evaluating string similarity, an algorithm was selected based on the calculation of the Sørensen–Dice coefficient for sets [22], which is calculated by the following formula:

$$K = \frac{2|A \cap B|}{|A| + |B|}$$

where A and B are sets consisting of all possible substrings of the strings being compared.

Implementation if this comparison produces the following results:

"max weight of payload" and "max payload weight": 0.37
"max weight of payload" and "max payload for EXCT": 0.23

Obviously, this algorithm handles situations related to word rearrangement better than the Levenshtein algorithm. However, the calculation time is significantly higher than that of the Levenshtein algorithm (106.88 ms for 1000 comparisons). To improve the algorithm, experiments were carried out with a change in the length of the sub-strings being compared, and as a result, an option was chosen with a comparison of only two-letter substrings as having minimal computational complexity but providing sufficient precision and recall for the test set. The result of the operation of this algorithm on the examples above is:

"max weight of payload" and "max payload weight":	0.94
"max weight of payload" and "max payload for EXCT":	0.53

Such result obviously meets the expectations and the calculation time for 1000 comparisons with the improved algorithm is 11.67 ms.

Tests on the available training set showed good results and indicated that spell check was not required (the algorithm processes misspellings by itself). To improve the matching some synonyms had to be added for the situations when the reference parameter text was significantly different from the text in the training set. For example, for the reference parameter name "working load (front unit + workpiece, effective load for Z-axis)" the following synonyms were added: "total load", "moved mass including gripper", "max weight for", "max payload for", "max weight of loading", etc. With 10 synonyms, the rate of 100% hits was achieved for the complete training set with the threshold value of 0.5.

Analysis of the second column (Fig. 2), i.e. extraction of numeric values from texts was done based on pre-defined rules and regular expressions. Since the variety of possible combinations was much smaller, this task did not cause any significant problems, though such cases as "number", "range" (e.g., "3–4"), "box" (e.g., "400 × 250 × 200") and "cylinder" (e.g., "d20 × 100") had to be taken care of. Similar solution was implemented for the column with measurement units.

However, though tables are the easiest parts of the requests for processing, still some significant information is contained within the free text accompanying the tables. The next section describes the approach used to extract information from these.

4 Finding Short Text Fragments in Long Text

Extracting semantic from the longer free text describing the customer request is currently an ongoing work. At the beginning of research, a method for discovering key-words corresponding to the mentioned above reference terms from the product datasheets (Fig. 3) was developed. The aim of the method was finding the reference terms within the text taking into account possible misspellings, different wordings and usage of synonyms. For this purpose the direct search was chosen assuming similarity measurement between the reference term or its synonym and all possible substrings of the considered text. The similarity measurement is done via the same method as used for short text matching (Sect. 3) with the same threshold value of 0.5.

Further in this section we consider an example with the text consisting of 426 symbols. The original text is the following:

All axis could move at the same time up/down. No sidewise movement when Z-axis is in advanced position. Clamping unit required (Pneumatic locking not desired). Sensing required for open clamp. Absolute linear encoder with DRIVE Cliq technology. Color of steel profile: RAL 7035. Manual greasing of roller bearing cassettes needed. Not allowed fall down the grease of any component. No welded parts (or US certificate if welded parts exist).

The cleaned text is as follows:

all axis could move at the same time up down no sidewise movement when z axis is in advanced position clamping unit required pneumatic locking not desired sensing required for open clamp absolute linear encoder with drive cliq technology color of steel profile ral 7035 manual greasing of roller bearing cassettes needed not allowed fall down the grease of any component no welded parts or us certificate if welded parts exist

The method produced expectable results (all keywords were found successfully, and some additional substrings similar to the keywords were found as well), however, the total calculation time for this text on the Intel Pentium i7 computer took 169.383 s. Obviously, this time is too long for daily usage and a search for optimization of the method has been carried out. One can guess that comparing a short reference term with a long text will not result in high similarity. This has led to an effort to study the dependence of the similarity level on the length of the compared strings. The relative length of the compared substring was measured as

$$rl = \frac{length(substring)}{length(ref\_term)}$$

where *ref_term* is reference term being compared, and *substring* is the substring being compared.

The result of experiments with reference terms having different lengths is shown in Fig. 4. The magnified fragment for the relative length between 0 and 10 is shown in Fig. 5. It can be seen that for substrings with relative length more than 3.5 the similarity does not exceed the threshold. This means that limiting the length of the matched substring as 3.5 times the length of the reference term will not cause any loss of

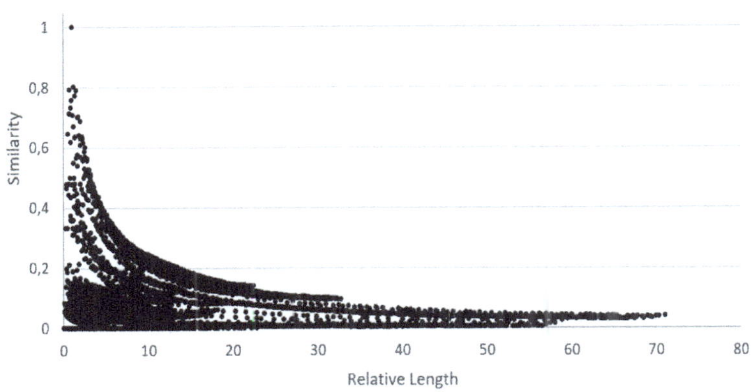

Fig. 4. Dependence of the similarity level on the relative length of the compared text fragment.

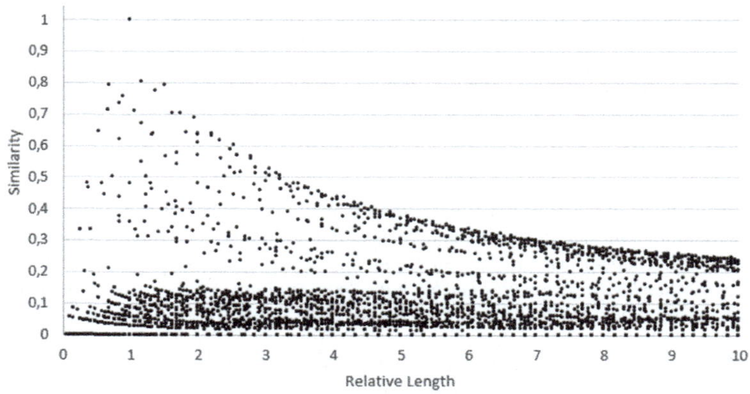

Fig. 5. Dependence of the similarity level on the relative length of the compared text fragment: magnified fragment for relative length between 0 and 10.

possibly matching substrings if the matching threshold is 0.5. On the other hand the calculation time with this limit is 1.469 and the produced result is the same.

As it can be seen, at the moment proposed method is oriented only to one task (finding reference terms in the text) and does not take into account semantics. Planned future work will include using of different semantic-based free text analysis methods including word/phrase labelling.

5 Conclusion and Future Work

The paper considers the problem of customer support at the product configuration PLM stage for assemble-to-order inventory method. Efforts towards achieving a complete support of the digital customer journey (when the customer is supported by IT services at all stages of PLM) have set new problems to be solved. In this paper we consider the problem of semantic text analysis for information extraction from customer requests written in natural language. The work is split into two parts: development of a method for finding matching very short texts (1–5 words) to a pre-defined list of terms (product parameters that are important for the order specification) in a fuzzy (similarity-based) manner; and development of a method for extracting information from the longer texts describing the customer requests.

The first task has been solved through combination of fuzzy (similarity-based) string matching based on the Sørensen–Dice coefficient supported by usage of pre-defined rules and synonyms. The method gave 100% precise matching results on the training set. Achieving such result was possible due to exhaustive analysis of the customer requests and collecting the list of synonyms. Obviously for new requests the matching result will be lower. For this purpose a tool for company experts to evaluate and extend this list of synonyms will be developed.

Tackling the second task has been started with combining the above method with direct search and further optimisation to reduce the calculation time. Planned future work includes using of different semantic-based free text analysis methods including word/phrase labelling.

Acknowledgements. The paper is due to collaboration between SPIIRAS and Festo SE & Co KG (the case study), grant # 18-07-01203 of the Russian Foundation for Basic Research (the framework and methods), and State Research no. 0073-2019-0005 (analysis of customer needs at PLM stages).

References

1. Ferreira, F., Faria, J., Azevedo, A., Marques, A.L.: Product lifecycle management in knowledge intensive collaborative environments: an application to automotive industry. Int. J. Inf. Manage. **37**, 1474–1487 (2017). https://doi.org/10.1016/j.ijinfomgt.2016.05.006
2. Holligan, C., Hargaden, V., Papakostas, N.: Product lifecycle management and digital manufacturing technologies in the era of cloud computing. In: 2017 International Conference on Engineering, Technology and Innovation (ICE/ITMC), pp. 909–918. IEEE (2017)
3. Liu, Y., Zhang, Y., Ren, S., et al.: How can smart technologies contribute to sustainable product lifecycle management? J. Clean. Prod. (2020). https://doi.org/10.1016/j.jclepro.2019.119423
4. Abramovici, M., Göbel, J.C., Savarino, P., Gebus, P.: Towards smart product lifecycle management with an integrated reconfiguration management. In: Ríos, J., Bernard, A., Bouras, A., Foufou, S. (eds.) PLM 2017. IFIPAICT, vol. 517, pp. 489–498. Springer, Cham (2017). https://doi.org/10.1007/978-3-319-72905-3_43
5. Smirnov, A., Shilov, N.: Multi-aspect ontology for semantic interoperability in PLM: analysis of possible notations. In: Chiabert, P., Bouras, A., Noël, F., Ríos, J. (eds.) PLM 2018. IFIPAICT, vol. 540, pp. 314–323. Springer, Cham (2018). https://doi.org/10.1007/978-3-030-01614-2_29
6. Smirnov, A., Shilov, N., Oroszi, A., Sinko, M., Krebs, T.: Changing information management in product-service system PLM: customer-oriented strategy. In: Ríos, J., Bernard, A., Bouras, A., Foufou, S. (eds.) PLM 2017. IFIPAICT, vol. 517, pp. 701–709. Springer, Cham (2017). https://doi.org/10.1007/978-3-319-72905-3_62
7. Krebs, T., Oroszi, A., Sinko, M., et al.: Changing information management for product-service system engineering: customer-oriented strategies and lessons learned. Int. J. Prod. Lifecycle Manage. **11**, 1–18 (2018). https://doi.org/10.1504/IJPLM.2018.10012695
8. Oroszi, A.: Digitalization at Festo - our way in digital transformation. Keynote speech. In: 9th IFAC Conference MIM 2019 (2019)
9. Smirnov, A., Kashevnik, A., Shilov, N., et al.: Changing business information systems for innovative configuration processes. In: Matulevičius, R., Maggi, F.M., Kütgas, P. (eds.) Joint Proceedings of the BIR 2015 Workshops and Doctoral Consortium co-located with 14th International Conference on Perspectives in Business Informatics Research (BIR 2015), pp. 62–73. CEUR (2015)
10. Hua, W., Wang, Z., Wang, H., et al.: Understand short texts by harvesting and analyzing semantic knowledge. IEEE Trans. Knowl. Data Eng. **29**, 499–512 (2017). https://doi.org/10.1109/TKDE.2016.2571687

11. Wu, W., Li, H., Wang, H., Zhu, K.Q.: Probase: a probabilistic taxonomy for text understanding. In: Proceedings of the 2012 International Conference on Management of Data - SIGMOD 2012, p. 481. ACM Press, New York (2012)
12. Hua, W., Wang, Z., Wang, H., et al.: Short text understanding through lexical-semantic analysis. In: 2015 IEEE 31st International Conference on Data Engineering, pp. 495–506. IEEE (2015)
13. Pak, I., Teh, P.L.: Text segmentation techniques: a critical review. In: Zelinka, I., Vasant, P., Duy, V.H., Dao, T.T. (eds.) Innovative Computing, Optimization and Its Applications. SCI, vol. 741, pp. 167–181. Springer, Cham (2018). https://doi.org/10.1007/978-3-319-66984-7_10
14. McDonald, R., Crammer, K., Pereira, F.: Flexible text segmentation with structured multilabel classification. In: Proceedings of the Conference on Human Language Technology and Empirical Methods in Natural Language Processing - HLT 2005, pp. 987–994. Association for Computational Linguistics, Morristown (2005)
15. Kumawat, D., Jain, V.: POS tagging approaches: a comparison. Int. J. Comput. Appl. **118**, 32–38 (2015). https://doi.org/10.5120/20752-3148
16. Zhou, G., Su, J.: Named entity recognition using an HMM-based chunk tagger. In: Proceedings of the 40th Annual Meeting on Association for Computational Linguistics - ACL 2002, p. 473. Association for Computational Linguistics, Morristown (2001)
17. McCallum, A., Li, W.: Early results for named entity recognition with conditional random fields, feature induction and web-enhanced lexicons. In: Proceedings of the seventh conference on Natural language learning at HLT-NAACL 2003, pp. 188–191. Association for Computational Linguistics, Morristown (2003)
18. Song, Y., Wang, H., Wang, Z., et al.: Short text conceptualization using a probabilistic knowledgebase. In: Proceedings of the Twenty-Second International Joint Conference on Artificial Intelligence Short, pp. 2330–2336. AAAI Press (2011)
19. Kim, D., Wang, H.W., Oh, A.: Context-dependent conceptualization. In: Proceedings of the Twenty-Third International Joint Conference on Artificial Intelligence. AAAI Press (2013)
20. Brill, E.: A simple rule-based part of speech tagger. In: Proceedings of the workshop on Speech and Natural Language - HLT 1991, pp. 112–116. Association for Computational Linguistics, Morristown (1992)
21. Kysela, J.: A comparison of text string similarity algorithms for POI name harmonisation. In: Perales, F.J., Kittler, J. (eds.) AMDO 2018. LNCS, vol. 10945, pp. 121–130. Springer, Cham (2018). https://doi.org/10.1007/978-3-319-94544-6_12
22. Udagawa, Y.: Source code retrieval using sequence based similarity. Int. J. Data Min. Knowl. Manage. Process **3**, 57–74 (2013). https://doi.org/10.5121/ijdkp.2013.3404

Data Relevance and Sources for Carbon Footprint Calculation in Powertrain Production

Simon Merschak[1(✉)], Peter Hehenberger[1], Johann Bachler[2], and Andreas Kogler[2]

[1] Research Centre for Low Carbon Special Powertrain, University of Applied Sciences Upper Austria, Wels Campus, Stelzhamerstrasse 23, 4600 Wels, Austria
{simon.merschak,peter.hehenberger}@fh-wels.at
[2] AVL List GmbH, Hans-List-Platz 1, 8020 Graz, Austria
{johann.bachler,andreas.kogler2}@avl.com

Abstract. The purpose of this work is to point out the importance of the production phase for the carbon footprint calculation of powertrain components and to improve the understanding of necessary data for this calculation. Evaluation of lifecycle assessment data from numerous studies showed, that there is often a shift from the emissions in the use phase to emissions in the production phase, when alternative powertrain concepts are used. Therefore, in this work our focus is on the carbon emissions in the production phase of powertrain components. Data of raw materials used, production processes and supply chains is necessary and the uncertainties associated also have to be considered. At present, there is only little sufficient support for design engineers regarding the collection of relevant data for the carbon footprint calculation of powertrain production. In this work a data structure, which supports the collection of relevant data including possible data sources, is presented.

Keywords: Carbon footprint · Powertrain · Data relevance · Data collection · Production phase

1 Introduction

The reduction of lifecycle carbon emissions from powertrains plays an important role towards achieving the ambitious long-term goal of the European Union, a transition to a climate-neutral society [6]. In the past, driven by legislation, the focus was on the emissions deriving from the use phase of powertrains. In the future, a comprehensive assessment of all lifecycle phases will be required to evaluate different powertrain concepts. Especially when alternative powertrain concepts are considered, a shift from the carbon emissions in the use phase to carbon emissions in the production phase can be observed. For example, a vehicle powered by an internal combustion engine (ICE) causes around 16% of its total

Published by Springer Nature Switzerland AG 2020
F. Nyffenegger et al. (Eds.): PLM 2020, IFIP AICT 594, pp. 203–214, 2020.
https://doi.org/10.1007/978-3-030-62807-9_17

carbon emissions in the production phase. For a battery electric vehicle (BEV) this value is about 40%. In addition to the environmental reasons for low CO_2 production, economic reasons will also become more important in the future. Possible carbon taxes or carbon customs duties will increase the demand for low CO_2 production processes. For simplification, in this publication the terms CO_2 and carbon emissions are used instead of the term carbon dioxide equivalent emission (CO_{2eq}), which covers all relevant greenhouse gasses (GHG). For the realization of low carbon powertrains, it will be necessary to include methods for the calculation of the whole lifecycle carbon emissions right from the design phases of a powertrain. In these phases design decisions with a huge impact on the full lifecycle carbon emissions are made and modifications of the design are still possible with moderate effort. A wide range of data is required to calculate the carbon footprint of a powertrain. This work should provide an overview of the required data and possible data sources.

2 Powertrain Components and Their Contribution to the Single Lifecycle Phases

Coming from a fossil fuel propelled past, the technology of powertrains has experienced a significant change in recent years. Today customers can choose between internal combustion engines, fueled by gasoline, diesel or gas, different hybrid configurations (mild hybrid, full hybrid, plug-in hybrid), purely battery-powered vehicles, or fuel cells as a propulsion system for their vehicle. Figure 1 gives an overview of possible powertrain configurations and the main components. For the upcoming years all these configurations will remain on the market, even though the market shares are changing significantly.

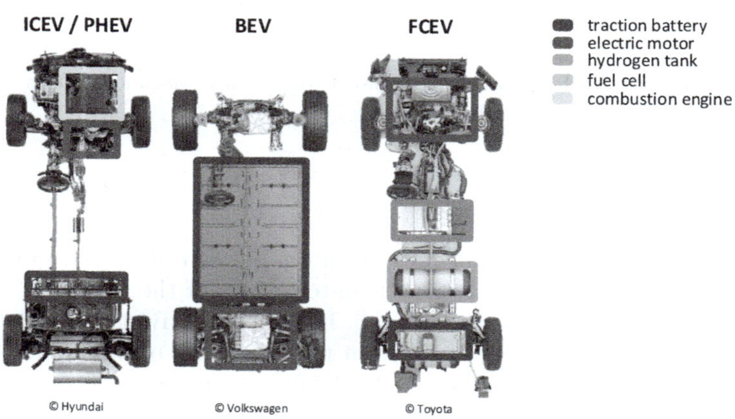

Fig. 1. Main components of different powertrain configurations

While the powertrain of a conventionally powered vehicle consists mainly of the internal combustion engine (ICEV) and the gearbox, the powertrain of a battery electric vehicle (BEV) consists mainly of a high-voltage battery, an electric traction motor and the electronic controller. For a plug-in hybrid electric vehicle (PHEV) all components of the before mentioned powertrain concepts are necessary, of course with different performance characteristics. The powertrain of a fuel cell electric vehicle (FCEV) consists mainly of a fuel cell stack, a hydrogen storage tank, and the electronic components to control the system. Additionally, a battery is necessary as a buffer to compensate for a lower maximum power-output of the fuel cell stack.

Figure 2 gives an overview of the phases that need to be considered in a carbon footprint calculation of an automotive product. The production phase, on which the focus of this paper lies, can be subdivided into the extraction of raw materials, the fabrication of parts, the manufacturing of components, and finally the assembly of the vehicle itself. All these phases are linked by numerous logistics processes. Due to the fact that the high number of parts and components of an automotive powertrain (more than 10,000) are produced and supplied by an extensive global network of suppliers, the overall assessment of the carbon emissions of a vehicle is very difficult, leading to evident differences in the lifecycle results published in various studies. Further factors influencing the results of a holistic approach like a Life Cycle Assessment (LCA) are the different system boundaries and differences in the inventory chosen and assumptions made for materials, production processes and sites, etc. Such an approach is in-line with ISO 14040 [3] and 14044 [4] standard protocols.

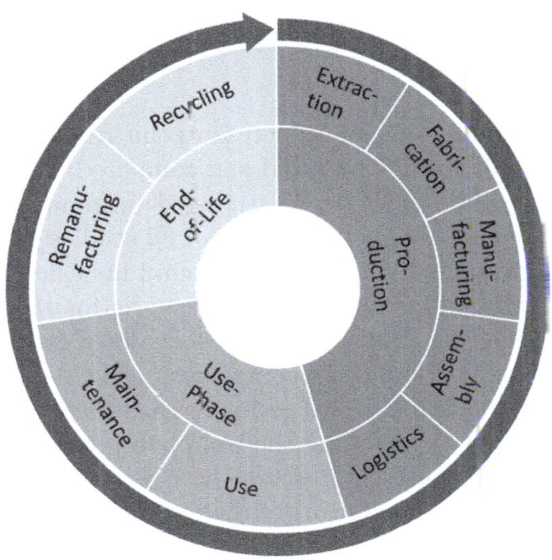

Fig. 2. Major life cycle phases for automotive products

To evaluate the numerous different values defined by already conducted LCAs on ICEVs, BEVs, PHEVs and FCEVs, a survey was executed. The results of this survey on more than 80 publications on vehicle-LCAs, including the standard deviation, min and max values is given in Fig. 3. Apart from the fact that the single production processes are well-known, the studies analyzed show that many assumptions and simplifications had to be made for the production phase. Despite an acceptable standard deviation, the min/max values of the carbon footprint differ by a factor of 3, even for a well-known product like an ICEV (see Table 1). For new powertrain concepts like a BEV or FCEV the differences are even greater. The part 'freight and logistics' is either not considered at all or included as a lump sum. In Europe alone the sector 'Transport' is the second largest contributor of greenhouse gasses with freight and logistics being responsible for a quarter of this amount [7].

Table 1. Carbon emissions for different powertrains and life cycle phases [tCO_{2eq}]

	Production	Use	End of Life	Total	Production	Use	End of Life	Total
	ICEV				PHEV			
MEAN	6,13	30,35	-0,24	36,60	7,53	22,57	0,45	32,03
MEDIAN	5,78	27,75	0,50	35,72	7,38	21,30	0,41	29,16
STANDARD DEVIATION	1,82	14,57	1,28	14,60	1,92	13,14	0,05	13,64
Min	3,08	2,10	-2,63	8,45	5,33	6,33	0,40	11,66
Max	11,25	63,35	1,17	70,95	11,24	43,05	0,50	52,90
N	82	79	38	80	18	15	7	15
	BEV				FCEV			
MEAN	11,08	14,57	0,11	24,49	11,45	14,12	0,65	24,68
MEDIAN	9,79	12,22	0,58	24,15	11,40	15,05	0,50	27,48
STANDARD DEVIATION	4,13	10,58	0,88	11,65	2,35	10,23	1,81	9,80
Min	3,99	0,00	-3,95	3,00	7,17	0,30	-4,61	9,88
Max	19,80	49,27	1,40	62,27	15,28	32,16	0,80	45,00
N	92	83	45	83	16	13	7	12

Table 1 shows the wide range of carbon footprint results of LCAs where "N" stands for the number of studies analyzed and compared. For example the ICEV was analyzed by 82 studies, of those, 79 studies determined the use-phase emissions, but only 38 the end-of-life emissions, and 80 studies gave a total emission figure. Examples of examined studies can be found in [1,5,8]. The complete list of evaluated LCAs may be forwarded on request. As for the production phase, a complete and part specific analysis, which broke down every single component of the vehicle, could not be found. In comparison of LCAs from BEVs, FCEVs and ICEVs the ICEV was less detailed seeing as the others evaluated most of the major components rather than taking the complete powertrain as a single unit. Also, the analysis rarely considered where the components and resources were produced. One of the main contributors of the resulting deviation between all the studies derives from the assumptions made in the use-phase such as e.g. fuel consumption, or vehicle lifetime. Most of the BEV LCAs assumed that the energy demand in the use-phase was supplied by an EU-28 energy-mix but some also assumed, that the energy was completely "carbon neutral", therefore resulting in use-phase emissions of zero CO_2, not considering the carbon footprint of energy production. Another aspect of the use-phase of ICEVs is the fact, that the carbon emissions of this phase are mainly defined in a Tank-To-Wheel (TTW) perspective whereas the other propulsion systems are determined with a Well-To-Wheel (WTW) evaluation. The end-of-life phase also needs further investigation, as this phase depends on the recycling technology used, the amount of material reused and remanufactured and the necessary energy-input for each process-step. All in all, there are multiple aspects that need consideration in an LCA, and these aspects can therefore lead to different total values.

The absolute and relative contribution of the three main lifecycle phases (production, use-phase, end-of-life) to the overall lifecycle carbon emissions depends significantly on the powertrain concept. In the traditional ICEV drivetrain more than 80% of the entire lifecycle emissions (mean values) derive from the use-phase, when fossil fuel is burned, whereas in electrified powertrains around 40% of emissions derive from the production phase (see Fig. 3). This figure can vary significantly (see Table 1), as currently large-scale production processes for new powertrain concepts like BEVs or FCEVs are rather limited and considerable technological progress is constantly being made. In the study performed, literature data gave a value of 1–3.5 t of CO_{2eq} for the production of the fuel cell stack, and 1.2–4 t CO_{2eq} for the hydrogen tank. Despite the existing differences in materials for these components, the major deviations result from the system boundaries chosen, and the assumptions made, due to lack of information on manufacturing processes.

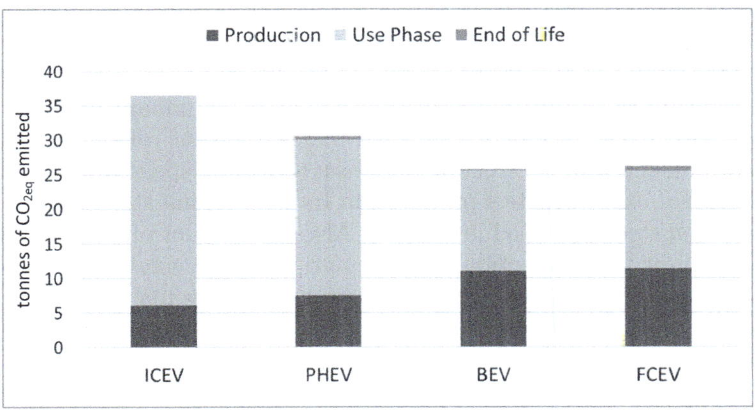

Fig. 3. Mean carbon emissions [tCO_{2eq}] from over 80 LCA studies for different powertrains

As shown in Fig. 3, the carbon emissions from the production of electrified powertrains is twice as high compared to conventional ones. The main influencing factors are the materials used and the energy intensive production processes of batteries, fuel cell stack and hydrogen tank, and – for both powertrain concepts - the energy source used for the production of components. Again, as for all other powertrain concepts, the influence by OEMs on the use-phase are limited (apart from developing a highly efficient powertrain to limit the energy consumption in this phase). Due to the change of ownership at the end of the production phase, as happens in most cases, the vehicle producers have no influence on how a vehicle is used, and how the energy carrier – be it fossil fuel, electric energy or hydrogen – is produced and how it is supplied to the vehicle's tank.

3 Relevant Data for Carbon Footprint Calculation of Powertrain Production

As discussed in Sect. 2 and depicted in Fig. 3, the distribution of the emissions of alternative powertrain concepts across their lifecycle phases is different to classic powertrain concepts. A shift from emissions in the use phase to emissions in the production phase appears. To reach a low-carbon design of future powertrains it is necessary to reduce the carbon emissions of the production processes. Various data is required to calculate the carbon footprint of powertrain production. In this section, the production process, displayed in Fig. 2 with its material flows and energy flows provides guidance for a comprehensive overview of the required data.

Raw Material Extraction and Fabrication Data
The carbon emissions of the raw materials themselves, be it ore mining for raw metal production and crude oil or natural gas extraction for the production of plastics and chemicals must be considered from the very start. In addition to the extraction of the raw materials, the processing of pre-products is also often very energy consuming and has therefore to be considered. Examples of raw material production processes are the production of steel or aluminum profiles or sheet material. The area of production also plays an important role. That is because the energy mix and used production processes strongly depend on the location of production. For example, steel produced in India or China shows higher carbon emissions than steel produced in Austria. Also the amount of recycled material, which is used for the production of the material, has an significant influence on the carbon footprint, especially if the extraction of the raw material is very energy intensive like the production of raw aluminum or the mining of noble metals.

Manufacturing Process Data
Depending on the type of powertrain, the carbon emissions of the manufacturing steps can have a huge share of the total lifecycle carbon emissions. As explained in Sect. 2, particularly the manufacturing process of electric powertrains leads to increased carbon emissions in the manufacturing phase. That is because the production of the battery requires a high amount of energy.

Because of the required robustness or because of other technical requirements, powertrain components are often made of metals like steel, cast iron or aluminum. Typical manufacturing processes for primary shaping of metal parts in powertrain manufacturing are casting and forging. The smelting of the raw material for the casting process requires thermal energy which is either electric energy or fossil fuels. Typical cast parts in powertrains are pistons, casings, engine blocks and cylinder heads. Typical forged powertrain parts are connecting rods, crankshafts and gearbox components.

Other common manufacturing processes in powertrain production are all kinds of cutting processes like turning, milling, cutting, grinding and honing. The electric energy consumption of these processes is dependent on factors such as material parameters, processing time and size of the manufacturing machine. The same part can be processed by hand in a small machine or fully automated in a machining center. In addition to the manufacturing processes, emissions from intralogistics might also have to be considered for the full carbon footprint calculation.

Assembly Data

The assembly of the individual components to produce the final powertrain also leads to carbon emissions. Emissions occur from handling processes where components are moved and from joining processes where components or sub-systems are connected to larger units. Typical handling processes in the industry are carried out either manually by a worker or automated by a robot. Common joining methods for powertrain components are pressing, welding, riveting and screwing.

Logistics Data

The required raw material and vendor parts are often produced all around the globe. Therefore, the transport to the specific production facility also has an impact on the carbon footprint which should not be neglected. Finally, the distribution of the finished product to the customer has to be considered.

Additionally, raw data proprieties such as source reliability, velocity and variety should be provided for all previously mentioned data categories to estimate the data variability impact on the carbon footprint calculation.

4 Data Structure and Data Sources

In this chapter a data structure, which can be filled with required information for the carbon footprint calculation of production processes, is developed. This data structure should provide guidance for the data collection process. It should enable developers to set up a well-formed data model of the production process, which contains all required information for the calculation of the carbon footprint. In this work, the carbon emissions of the production process are assigned to four categories, which are displayed in Fig. 4. These are direct on-site emissions, energy supply emissions, emissions from raw material extraction and emissions from logistics processes. The four categories origin from the observation of typical production processes in powertrain production.

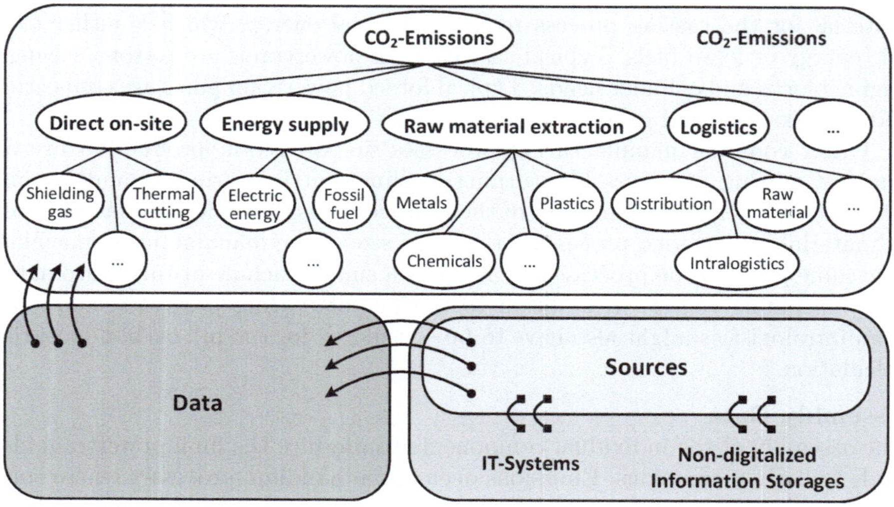

Fig. 4. Data flow and emission categories for carbon footprint calculation

To calculate the carbon emissions, various data from different sources is required. Fortunately, much of the required data is already available in companies. Especially product related data and data of production processes is often digital available. Other required data can be taken from external databases, has to be measured on site or is available in non-digitized form such as handwritten documents or employee knowledge.

4.1 Production Process Data

A possible way to sort the required data of the production process is displayed in Fig. 5. Guidance for the development of a suitable data structure can be found in [10–12]. Data for the description of the manufacturing process can be assigned to the part, to the manufacturing activity or to the machine. Additional data from resource extraction, logistics and general data is required to calculate the full carbon footprint of the product. Typical data of the manufactured part is the raw material, design parameters like surface roughness and functional requirements. Examples of machine data, which have an influence on the carbon emissions, are the power consumption of the machine, the tools required and substances for operation and maintenance. Such substances are e.g. lubricoolant for chipping processes and welding wire for inert gas welding. Activity data is needed to assign the emissions from the machine to the single part. To calculate the carbon emission value, data of resources like electricity generation and raw material extraction is needed. If the production facilities of a company or suppliers are distributed over different countries, emissions from logistics have to be considered for the carbon emission calculation as well.

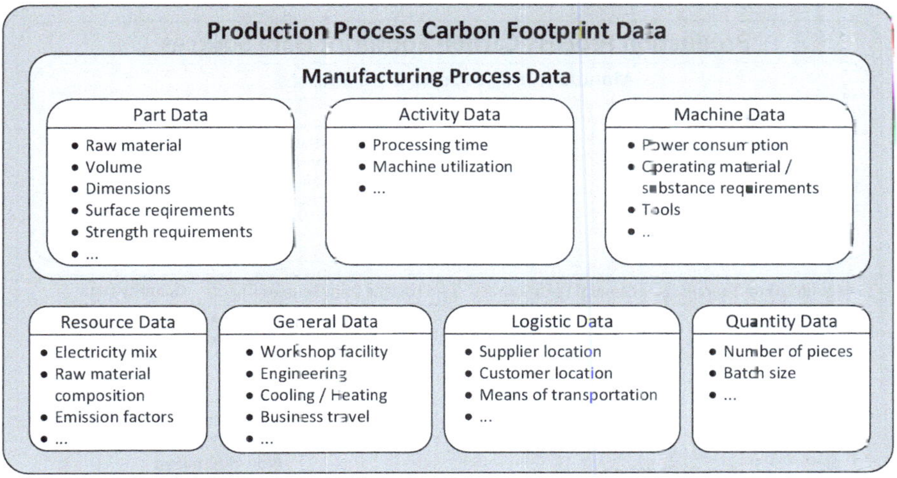

Fig. 5. Data structure for carbon footprint calculation

Finally, quantity data is required to assign the total carbon emissions of the production process to the single product. The data structure in Fig. 5 provides an overview of possibly required data for carbon footprint calculation. It aims to support designers in the data collection process. Another possible classification found in literature is the differentiation between activity data from the production process and emission factors from databases. Here a further fragmentation in primary data, which is measured inside the company, and secondary data from other sources, such as databases and scientific literature, is possible [2]. The data can also be classified according to the location where the emission takes place.

4.2 Data Sources

Depending on the aspect under consideration of the production process, suitable data sources have to be identified. An overview about possible data sources for the different data categories is shown in Fig. 6. In companies, IT-systems like PLM-Systems and ERP-Systems already contain a large number of relevant data sources for the carbon footprint calculation. These sources can be used to speed up the data collection process. In [9], opportunities and limitations of connecting CAD software and PLM systems with ecodesign software tools are assessed and in [13], a methodology to connect a simplified LCA tool with PLM and ERP systems is proposed. If the carbon footprint of a new product should be calculated in the development phase, data from similar products could also be used for a first carbon footprint estimation. To demonstrate the data collection process for carbon footprint calculation, an illustrative case study of a typical powertrain component is presented.

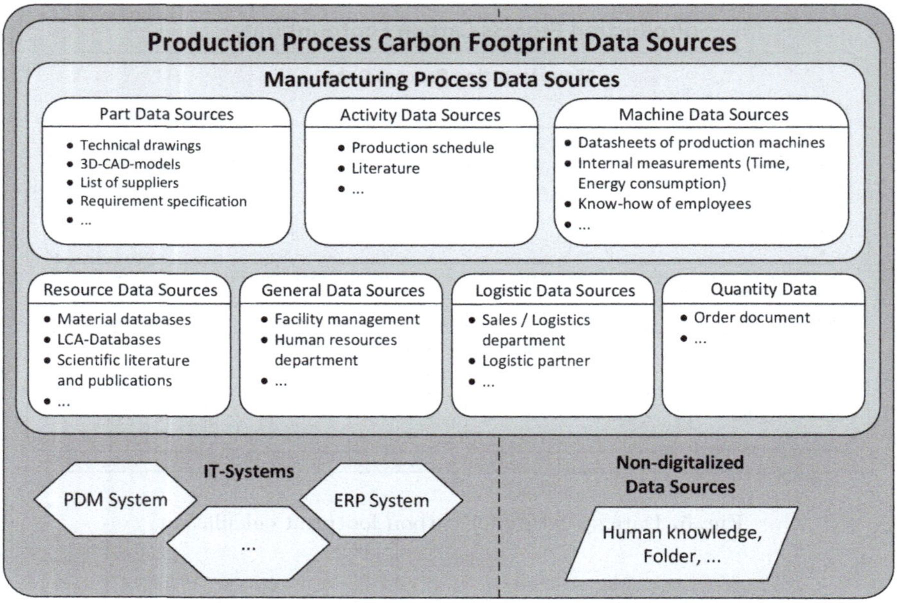

Fig. 6. Data source classification

As an example, the production process of a cast aluminum piston was chosen (Fig. 7). A technical drawing of the piston and a 3D CAD model provide the basis for this case study. The technical drawing contains information about the raw material, heat treatment and surface requirements. The CAD model is used to calculate the amount of required raw material. If a PDM system is implemented in a company, this would be a good source for product related data. Possible sources for data related to the production processes are production plans, which can be found in an ERP system, and non-digitized information sources like knowledge of experienced engineers. For the case study of the piston, information for the calculation of the energy demand of manufacturing machines was found in machine datasheets or was measured like the processing times.

Data of the product and data of the manufacturing processes provide the basis for the carbon footprint calculation of the manufacturing phase. For the calculation of explicit carbon emission values, carbon emission factors are required. They can be found in free emission databases or databases subject to a charge. These databases provide e.g. values for carbon emissions per kg of raw material or carbon emissions per kWh of electric energy. General data can be obtained from facility management and the human resources department. For products with an energy intensive production process, the emissions from company processes which are not directly related to the manufacturing processes, might be neglected. All the previously mentioned data can then be used as input for the calculation of the product carbon footprint.

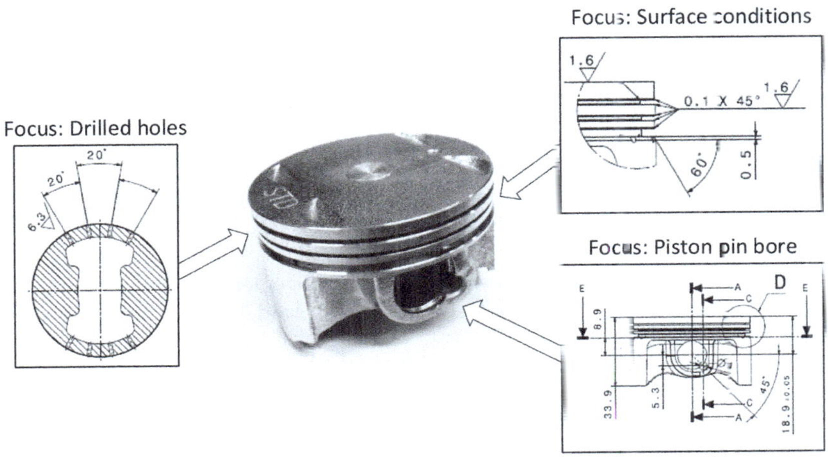

Fig. 7. Illustrative case study of cast aluminum piston

5 Conclusion

This paper points out the importance of the production phase for the total carbon emissions of powertrains. An analysis of 82 studies reveals that especially alternative powertrain concepts show a shift from the carbon emissions in the use phase to emissions in the production phase. With the increasing share of alternative powertrain concepts, the reduction of emissions in the production phase will become an important topic in the future. The calculation of the carbon footprint of production processes requires different types of data from various data sources. Important questions at the beginning of each carbon footprint calculation are, what data must be collected and what are possible sources for the required data? Therefore, in this publication two structures were developed to provide support for the data collection process. One contains the required data and the other one the corresponding data sources. This structures provides the basis for further research and development of a method framework, which can be used for the carbon emission calculation of powertrain component production.

Acknowledgments. The research has been applied for and was granted as COMET project under the guidance of the Austrian Research Promotion Agency FFG and is funded by the Federal Ministry for Transport, Innovation and Technology (BMVIT), the Federal Ministry for Digital and Economic Affairs (BMDW) and the Provinces of Upper Austria and Styria.

References

1. Ager-Wick Ellingsen, L., Hung, C.R.: Research for TRAN committee - Battery-powered electric vehicles: market development and lifecycle emissions (2018)
2. Carbon Trust, Defra, BSI British Standards: Guide to PAS 2050 - How to Assess the Carbon Footprint of Goods and Services (2008)
3. DIN EN ISO 14040:2009-11: Environmental management - Life cycle assessment - Principles and framework (ISO 14040:2006) (2009). https://doi.org/10.31030/1555059
4. DIN EN ISO 14044:2018-05: Environmental management - Life cycle assessment - Requirements and guidelines (ISO 14044:2006 + Amd 1:2017) (2018). https://doi.org/10.31030/2761237
5. Elgowainy, A., et al.: Cradle-to-grave lifecycle analysis of U.S. light duty vehicle-fuel pathways: a greenhouse gas emissions and economic assessment of current (2015) and future (2025–2030) technologies. https://doi.org/10.2172/1254857
6. European Commission: A European strategic long-term vision for a prosperous, modern, competitive and climate neutral economy (2018)
7. European Environment Agency: Greenhouse gas emissions from transport in Europe (2019)
8. Helms, H., et al.: Weiterentwicklung und vertiefte Analyse der Umweltbilanz von Elektrofahrzeugen (2016)
9. Mathieux, F., Lionel, R., Lescuyer, L., Brissaud, D.: Connecting CAD and PLM systems with ecodesign software: current experiences and future opportunities. In: Proceedings of ICED 2007, the 16th International Conference on Engineering Design (2007)
10. Tao, J., Yu, S.: A meta-model based approach for lCA-oriented product data management. Procedia CIRP **69**, 423–428 (2018). https://doi.org/10.1016/j.procir.2017.12.010. 25th CIRP Life Cycle Engineering (LCE) Conference, Copenhagen, Denmark, 30 April–2 May 2018
11. Theret, J.P., Evrard, D., Mathieux, F., Guern, Y.L., Chemla, P.: Integrating CAD, PLM and LCA: new concepts, data model, architecture and integration proposals. In: EnviroInfo (2011)
12. Yang, B., Qiao, L., Zhu, Z., Wulan, M.: A metamodel for the manufacturing process information modeling. Procedia CIRP **56**, 332–337 (2016). https://doi.org/10.1016/j.procir.2016.10.032. The 9th International Conference on Digital Enterprise Technology - Intelligent Manufacturing in the Knowledge Economy Era
13. Yousnadj, D., Jouanne, G., Maranzana, N., Segonds, F., Bouchard, C., Aoussat, A.: Integration of environmental assessment in a PLM Context: a case study in luxury industry. In: Fukuda, S., Bernard, A., Gurumoorthy, B., Bouras, A. (eds.) PLM 2014. IAICT, vol. 442, pp. 201–212. Springer, Heidelberg (2014). https://doi.org/10.1007/978-3-662-45937-9_21

FMECA-Based Risk Assessment Approach for Proactive Obsolescence Management

Imen Trabelsi[1,2(✉)], Marc Zolghadri[1], Besma Zeddini[3], Maher Barkallah[2], and Mohamed Haddar[2]

[1] Quartz Laboratory, SUPMECA, 3 rue Fernand Hainaut, 93407 Saint-Ouen, France
{imen.trabelsi,marc.zolghadri}@supmeca.fr
[2] LA2MP Laboratory, ENIS, Route Soukra Km 3.5, 3038 Sfax, Tunisia
[3] SATIE Laboratory CNRS - UMR 8029, CYTeh ENS Paris-Saclay, Cergy, France
bzi@eisti.eu

Abstract. One of the most critical issues that can affect the useful life of a product is the obsolescence of its components or functionalities. To minimize its effects and bring long-term benefits to systems, obsolescence must be proactively managed. A critical step in the process of proactive obsolescence management is the obsolescence risk analysis of critical components or functionalities. However, estimating the degree of obsclescence of multi-component systems is an area that is still under-explored, particularly when interdependencies exist between components. This estimation can be more complicated where there is no prior knowledge about the interaction between components. We used Weibull's distribution to model the components' interaction and calculate the obsolescence degree of the global system. This approach is evaluated using a numerical example based on a meteorological data acquisition system. The obsolescence of main components of this system is modeled while taking into account the interaction between them. Results are presented and discussed while clarifying the scientific issues that should be tackled in future works.

Keywords: Product Lifecycle Management (PLM) · Proactive obsolescence management · Risk assessment · Weibull

1 Introduction

Nowadays, obsolescence has become an increasingly common problem in all sectors, whether in aeronautics, automotive, home automation, etc. This problem is mainly related to systems with a long-life cycle [13]. The system is designed to operate for a long period while some of its components are exposed to some kind of obsolescence and therefore the vulnerability and exposure to obsolescence of the system increases. Obsolescence or Diminishing Manufacturing Sources and Material Shortages (DMSMS) is defined as "the loss or imminent loss of original manufacturers of items or suppliers of items or raw materials" [2]. In [1], the authors clarified the difference between these two concepts by explaining that "obsolescence does not always lead to

Published by Springer Nature Switzerland AG 2020
F. Nyffenegger et al. (Eds.): PLM 2020, IFIP AICT 594, pp. 215–226, 2020.
https://doi.org/10.1007/978-3-030-62807-9_18

DMSMS problems, and not all DMSMS problems are due to obsolescence". As long as the product is still in production or available to meet future demands, it does not pose a DMSMS problem. But, if the spare parts are obsolete or if the know-how to perform the repair and the possibility to test the system (e.g. test equipment) after repair are not available, this causes a DMSMS problems. The authors in [3] explained the difference between obsolescence and discontinuance. By specifying that obsolescence occurs at a technological level, whereas discontinuance occurs when the manufacturer stops producing an item. However, in the industrial domain, obsolescence includes the cessation of production of a component if there are no other manufacturers for that specific component. This paper deals with the obsolescence problem which can be due to the technological evolution or the absence of support from manufacturers. The objective is to minimize its impact on life cycle costs, system performance, availability, maintainability and safety. Thus, it is necessary to focus on obsolescence management throughout the product life cycle. In [1], the authors present a multidisciplinary process for obsolescence management aimed at identifying the problems resulting from obsolescence; assessing their impacts; analyzing mitigation actions, and finally implementing the most cost-effective strategy.

Obsolescence syndrome concerns all kinds of systems, but its impact is more important in complex systems [17]. Indeed, complex systems are more exposed to obsolescence problems due to their multi-connected components. A complex system can be defined as a coherent set of different interconnected entities [20]. Thus, the study of its obsolescence depends on the obsolescence of each entity and the interactions between them. Components dependency refers to the fact that the obsolescence of one component can influence the life span of the other components of the system. In other words, if a component has become obsolete for various reasons, it may have an impact on the other components, which interact with it, by accelerating their obsolescence. Only a few studies, in the obsolescence literature, have been considered the complexity of systems and the interaction between their components [12, 21]. This problem becomes more difficult when considering the obsolescence evolution over time. Up to our knowledge, conducted works and existing methods in the obsolescence domain do not address the evolution of obsolescence over time. Our research aims to develop an approach to predict system obsolescence over time while taking into account the interactions between its components. To do, the Weibull distribution is used to model the obsolescence evolution of components. Based on these distributions, the system obsolescence degree is calculated while taking into account the interactions of its components.

The remainder of this paper is organized as follows: Sect. 2 presents a brief overview of obsolescence concepts and reviews the different methods of obsolescence management. Section 3 describes the proposed methodology with the necessary assumptions. Under these assumptions, we illustrate our approach in Sect. 4 by an example. Finally, conclusions and perspectives are given in Sect. 5.

2 Obsolescence State of the Art

In this document and in its context, we adopt the definition of obsolescence given as "the loss or imminent loss of system functions due to the loss of items original manufacturers, items or raw materials suppliers, or technical support". The problem of obsolescence is particularly well illustrated by electronic components, but it is not limited to them. Authors in [4] gave a global view of obsolescence, specifying that obsolescence can affect other aspects such as mechanical components, software, materials, skills, tools, and test equipment. Obsolescence goes through different stages; upon notification of change or discontinuity, the company must immediately inform its customers so that they can prepare their obsolescence management plan [5]. Obsolescence can be relative or absolute [6]. When the product stops working (a technical problem), obsolescence is said to be absolute. If it still works and consumers, for example, have chosen to replace it, obsolescence is said to be relative [7].

2.1 Obsolescence Causes

There are many possible reasons for obsolescence. Some of them are related to technological evolution or innovation that makes a component obsolete even though it still works and can be produced and purchased. Other reasons are related to the supplier, such as the disappearance of original suppliers from the market for various reasons [8], or the original component manufacturer or original equipment manufacturer is not willing to continue producing a part for economic reasons for example; when the demand for a component or technology decreases and the manufacturer considers it uneconomic to continue production. Obsolescence can be caused by directives, rules and other laws imposed by governments such as the restriction of the use of certain hazardous substances (RoHS) directive [9] such as the ban on the use of Freon because of its ozone-depleting characteristics. Products may also become obsolete if they are no longer durable due to the ageing process of stored parts, which make their use impossible [10].

2.2 Obsolescence Consequences

Obsolescence is a significant cost generator and can affect products during all their life cycles. Obsolescence consequences can be divided into three main categories: (i) product's requirements, (ii) ecologic and (iii) economic consequences. Requirements consequences imply the no respect of system requirements which can be classified according to [11], in four categories, namely; functional system requirements (the suitability of the component to fulfill its function in its environment); non-functional requirements (maintainability, viability, vulnerability, testability…); performance requirements (efficiency, execution time, transport speed..); constraints (dimensions, supply voltages…). Moreover, obsolescence has strong effects on the environment. In fact, obsolete products result in a huge volume of hazardous waste that intensify the greenhouse gas emissions and pollution. In addition, the replacement of these obsolete products implies an increased use of non-renewable resources. From economical point of view, obsolescence can result in an important life cycle costs that call into question the depreciation of systems. There is a clear evidence that a robust obsolescence management strategy can significantly reduce the impact of these consequences. Thus, many obsolescence management strategies have been proposed in the literature.

2.3 Obsolescence Management

While obsolescence is inevitable [5], its anticipation with a careful planning can minimize its impact and potentially high cost. Sandborn [15] has defined three types for obsolescence management: (i) Reactive management which involves taking action when obsolescence has already occurred, (ii) proactive management is put in place for critical components that are at risk of be- coming obsolete and (iii) strategic management complements proactive and reactive management and includes determining the optimal combination of mitigation approaches and design refreshes.

To carry out these management strategies resolving and mitigating methods are used. Resolving techniques are applied to solve the obsolescence problem when it arises. While mitigation methods are applied proactively to minimize the impact of obsolescence. Table 1 identifies these methods.

Table 1. Methods for resolving and mitigating obsolescence [4].

	Method	Description
Resolution	Redesign	Redesign obsolete parts to improve the performance, reliability, and maintainability of the system
	Last time buy	Purchase and store components following a supplier's product discontinuation notice
	FFF equivalent	Replace the obsolete component with a component that will work fully (in terms of form, fit, and function)
	Emulation	Develop an item with identical form, fit, and function to replace the obsolete parts using advanced technologies
	Cannibalization	Keep products by using components and subassemblies from other unserviceable systems
Mitigation	Lifetime buy	Purchase and store components and spare parts, before production, from the original component manufacturer to meet the system's needs
	Use multi-sourced components	Check that the components included in the BOM can be provided by several suppliers to minimize the number of critical components. Applicable at the design stage
	Technology road-mapping	Help to identify, evaluate and select technological alternatives in order to solve and prevent obsolescence problems caused by technological change

The most commonly used type of management is the reactive one because of its easy implementation and also because companies are often far from being able to implement any proactive or strategic managements. However, it is advisable to use it only if the cost associated to the obsolete component is low [16]. However, if the obsolescence likelihood and the associated costs are high, proactive obsolescence management strategies are recommended to minimize the risk of obsolescence and the associated costs [4, 14]. Various authors [17, 18] have advised the use of obsolescence surveillance to obtain early notification of any risk of obsolescence. For that purpose, in this paper we focus on the proactive obsolescence management by proposing a risk analysis tool to predict the obsolescence over the time.

3 Methodology and Tools

Dealing with obsolescence involves a lot of trade-offs, risk assessment and long-term planning. The key enabler to successful proactive obsolescence management is to predict the exposure degree to obsolescence. The objective of this section is to describe our proposed approach to predicting the evolution of obsolescence over time by taking into account the interactions between components. As shown in Fig. 1, the proposed method consists of three main steps:

1. Obsolescence risk analysis: in this step, the FMECA tool is used to identify main components and their exposure to obsolescence. The FMECA tool is used because it is extremely widespread in all domains that affect the safety, reliability, availability, and maintainability of a product or system [21].
2. Obsolescence modelling: The Weibull distribution is chosen to model the evolution of obsolescence over time because of its generality and flexibility.
3. Manage component interactions.

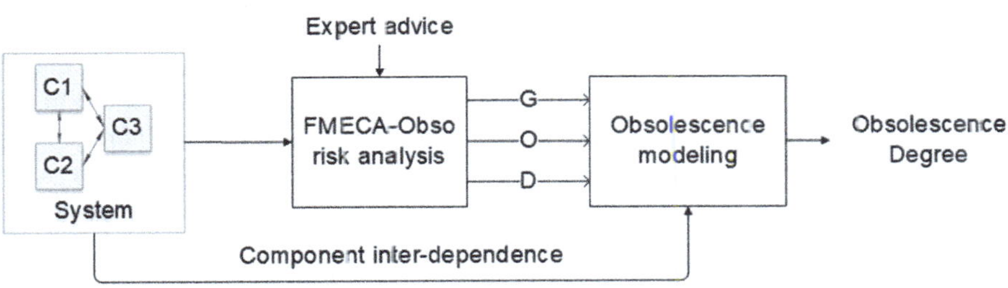

Fig. 1. Illustration of the FMECA-Obso methodology

3.1 FMECA-Obso: Risk Analysis

Obsolescence risk assessment using the Failure Modes, Effects and Criticality Analysis (FMECA-Obso) tool is conducted to analyze the sensitivity of the product to obsolescence and to prioritize risks to manage the components proactively or reactively. Thus, critical entities (components, functions and functionalities) with a high risk of obsolescence are identified, prioritized and managed throughout the system lifecycle. The FMECA-Obso criteria are presented below:

- Gravity: Gravity in this sense refers to the level of risk of the effect of obsolescence. The point here is to prioritize the gravity of the effects of obsolescence.
- Occurrence: The index of occurrence refers to the degree of occurrence of product obsolescence, which depends primarily on the characteristics and functions of the

product. For microelectronic components, the occurrence can be classified as frequent because these components are highly subject to technological development.
- The detection: The assigned index is used to identify the non-detectability of obsolescence.

The evaluation of the obsolescence risks for each entity results in the calculation of the Degree of Obsolescence DO, based on the estimation of the Gravity, Occurrence and Detection indices. An expert on the system domain fixes these parameters.

3.2 Prediction Method

In this part, we are interested in predicting the obsolescence of systems. Predicting is seen as a scientific challenge for the implementation of such a proactive management strategy in which estimating the date of obsolescence is important. To do, we consider the degree of obsolescence (DO) as a Weibull distribution. This probabilistic model is used due to its generality, flexibility and wide applicability in the system life cycle domain [22]. The Weibull probability density function is given by Eq. (1):

$$f(t,\theta,k,\lambda) = \frac{k}{\lambda}\left(\frac{t-\theta}{\lambda}\right)^{k-1} e^{-\left(\frac{t-\theta}{\lambda}\right)^k} \tag{1}$$

where t, θ, k, and λ are strictly positive parameters. k and λ are the shape and scale parameters respectively, and θ presents the position parameter. These parameters define the probability distribution and model component obsolescence. We assume that the predictions were done at the same time for all system components, i.e. θ = 0.

To estimate the Weibull parameters from the FMECA indices, we assume that the shape parameter k is proportional to the indices of gravity and non-detection. In fact, more gravity is high and there is no way to detect the problem (high non-detection index), more the risk of exposure to obsolescence is high: $k = a.G.D$ where a is a constant, G and D are the indices of gravity and detection.

As for the scale parameter λ, it is inversely proportional to the occurrence index; because with more frequent occurrence, the risk of obsolescence is accelerated (λ small): $\lambda = \frac{b}{O}$ where b is a constant and O is the index of occurrence.

The degree of obsolescence DO is therefore given by the following formula:

$$\text{at t} = \text{to};\ DO = \int_0^{to} \frac{k}{\lambda}\left(\frac{t}{\lambda}\right)^{k-1} e^{-\left(\frac{t}{\lambda}\right)^k} dt \tag{2}$$

t_o corresponds to the date of observation.

To analyze the interactions between the components and to correctly monitor their state of obsolescence, it is good practice to represent each component by its cumulative distribution. The cumulative distribution function CDF of Weibull's law is:

$$F(t;k;\lambda) = 1 - e^{-\left(\frac{t}{\lambda}\right)^k} \tag{3}$$

Interaction Rate. The interaction principle considers that the obsolescence of one component induces the obsolescence of the other components that interact with it. The state of obsolescence of the affected component C_a is accelerated with an interaction rate $\rho_{i \to a}$, which generally depends on the state of the influencing component C_i

The interaction rate is given by the following formula:

$$\rho_{i \to a} = 1 + \frac{F_i(t, \lambda_i, k_i)}{1 - F_a(t, \lambda_a, k_a)} \quad (4)$$

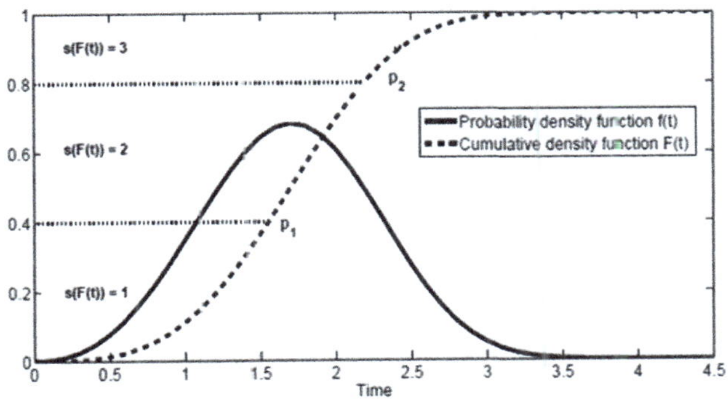

Fig. 2. CDF with different obsolescence states

Consider s(t) the function that indicates the obsolescence status of the component, e.g. "nominal", "critical" or "obsolete" (see Fig. 2) given by:

$$s(F(t)) = \begin{cases} 1 & F(t) < p_1 \\ 2 & p_1 < F(t) < p_2 \\ 3 & F(t) > p_2 \end{cases} \quad (5)$$

Weibull Model Taking into Account Interactions. In characterizing the effects of the interaction between entities in the system, the dependence model is described by the evolution of the obsolescence of the CDF as follows:

$$F(t; k; \lambda) = 1 - e^{-\left(\frac{t}{\lambda'}\right)^k} \quad (6)$$

where $\lambda' = \frac{\lambda}{\rho(t)}$

To set up this model, we consider the following assumptions:

- Without taking into account the dependency, the Weibull parameters are calculated from the Gravity, Occurrence and Detection indices by the following formulas:

$$k = Gravity * Detection; \quad \lambda = \frac{1}{Occurrence} \tag{7}$$

- The analysis of the degrees of obsolescence for all system components was done at the same time.
- The rate of interaction depends on the state of obsolescence of the influencing component.
- Obsolescence is assumed to be unidirectional (No mutual interaction).

4 Case Study

4.1 Description of the Case

The example illustration used is an environment observation link to earth (EOLE) system (Fig. 3), a weather balloon system whose main purpose is to provide meteorological data to various scientific users. This system is used as a case study in various previous works on obsolescence, as in [12]. It is composed of two subsystems; the first represents the in-flight acquisition subsystem, it is composed of a Helium-filled balloon, a temperature sensor, a pressure sensor, a sensor carrier (nacelle) and a nanocomputer where the data provided by the sensors are collected. This computer will, in turn, transmit them to the processing subsystem on the ground.

In our first work, we dealt with the obsolescence of VHF transmission technology. It was pointed out that the upgrade from VHF to UHF will result in changes to the physical architecture of the system, in particular the replacement of the radio transmitter and receiver. We assume that the transmission technology and the transceiver are the most critical components of the system where the antenna is the influencing component and the transceiver is the affected component. The obsolescence interaction is manifested in the cumulative distribution functions of these interdependent components.

To show the impact of the interaction on the obsolescence process of the system, we will consider two simulations. In the first simulation, the model does not take into account the interactions between the components. While in the second simulation, the interactions between the components of obsolescence will be studied. After a first analysis FMECA_Obso, the estimates of the Gravity, Occurrence and Detection indices are listed in Table 2.

The components are presented by the probability density functions $f_{VHF}(t)$ and $f_{Radio}(t)$ quoted in (8), where k and λ are the Weibull parameters and to observation time.

$$f_{VHF}: \begin{cases} k_i = 9 \\ \lambda_i = \frac{1}{7} \\ t_o = 1.5 \end{cases} \quad f_{Radio}: \begin{cases} k_a = 6 \\ \lambda_a = \frac{1}{7} \\ t_o = 1.5 \end{cases} \tag{8}$$

Table 2. Obsolescence risk analysis FMECA_OBSO

Temporal Horizon: 2 years				Obso. value		
Entities	Availability or Suitability	Obsolescence classification	Effect	G	O	D
Technology VHF	Suitability	Technological	Syst. usability	9	7	1
Radio Emitter and Receiver	Suitability	Functional	Syst. performance	6	7	1

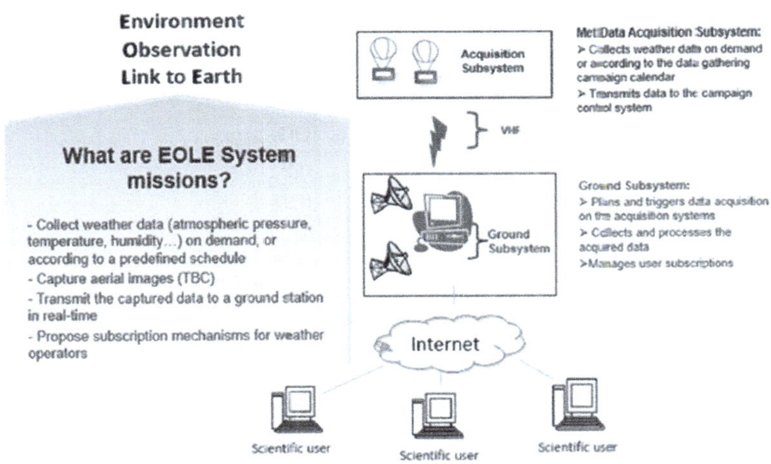

Fig. 3. Simplified specifications of the "EOLE" system [19]

According to Weibull's model, obsolescence is well modeled by the cumulative function F(t) as in Fig. 4. It is assumed that initially the interaction rate is equal to 1: $\rho_{i \to a} = 1$ which implies that the interactions between the components have not been taken into account. Generally, the rate of interaction depends on the state of obsolescence of the influencing component. It is very important when the state of obsolescence of VHF technology is serious. To study the impact of the interaction rate on the degree of obsolescence, we consider two levels for the interaction rate; $\rho_{i \to a} = 2$ when the obsolescence status of the VHF is critical and $\rho_{i \to a} = 3$ when the VHF is considered obsolete (see Fig. 5).

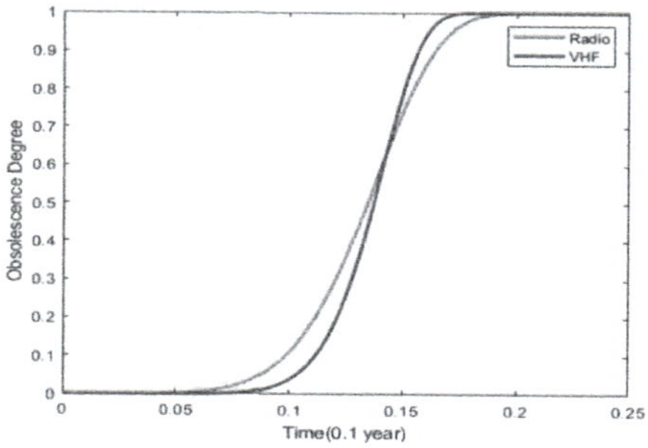

Fig. 4. CDF of the components

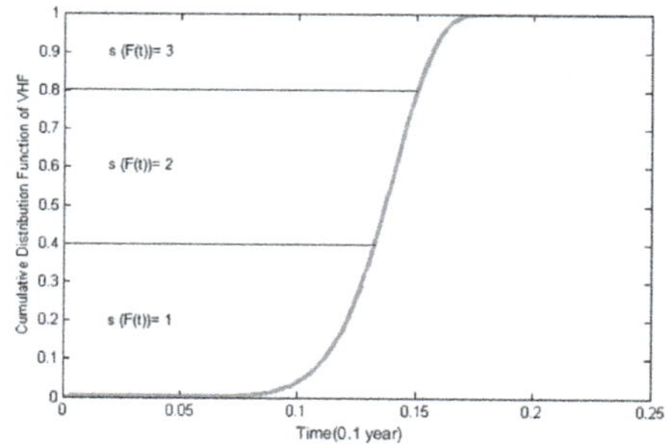

Fig. 5. Obsolescence states of VHF

4.2 Results and Discussions

The degree of obsolescence of the system increases as the rate of interactions increases and this is well illustrated in Table 3. Regardless of the inter-dependency, VHF technology is considered the most critical element that its obsolescence causes system obsolescence. However, considering the interactions between the components, the degree of obsolescence of the system will depend on the degree of obsolescence of the radio transceiver. Figure 6 shows the change in the degree of radio obsolescence.

Table 3. Simulation results

$\rho_{i \to a}$	DO_{VHF}	DO_{Radio}	DO_{System}
1	0.8	0.75	0.8
1.5	0.8	0.98	0.98
2	0.8	1	1

In this example, the Weibull distribution quoted in (6) was considered to vary the scale parameter as a function of the interaction rate. But really, the shape parameter also influences the variation in the obsolescence degree. Hence, in future work, we will consider that the shape parameter k will be affected by the interaction between the components.

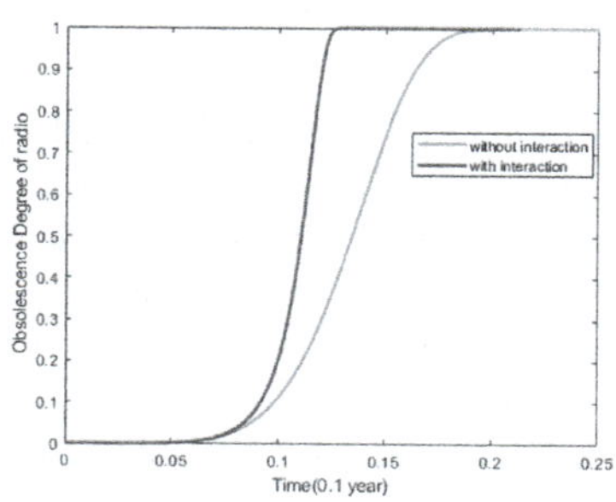

Fig. 6. Obsolescence degree of radio taking into account interaction

5 Conclusions and Outlook

In this paper, we presented FMECA-Obso for analyzing the risks of obsolescence. This tool consists of an in-depth analysis of the system to identify critical components and functions that can lead to system obsolescence. We also presented a model for predicting the obsolescence of a complex system where there are interactions between its components. From FMECA-Obso we can calculate both the degree of obsolescence and focus on the effect of the interaction between components on system obsolescence. The model is illustrated with a numerical example with a comparison between the different degradation models.

In this study, we considered that obsolescence is unidirectional, but in practice the interaction between the components could be mutual, i.e. obsolescence can propagate in both directions. Thus, not all components present the same risk of obsolescence and some are resilience, but they remain vulnerable. The challenge is to find a model for each component that integrates all these factors. These are our goals in future work to better align this obsolescence prediction using machine-learning techniques that could increase the prediction accuracy.

References

1. SD-22: Diminishing Manufacturing Sources and Material Shortages (DMSMS) A Guidebook of Best Practices for Implementing a Robust DMSMS (2016)
2. Sandborn, P.: Designing for technology obsolescence management. In IIE Annual Conference. Proceedings. Institute of Industrial and Systems Engineers (IISE), p. 1684 (2007)
3. Pecht, M.G., Das, D.: Electronic part life cycle. IEEE Trans. Compon. Packag. Technol. **23**(1), 190–192 (2000)
4. Rojo, F.J.R., Roy, R., Shehab, E.: Obsolescence management for long-life contracts: state of the art and future trends. Int. J. Adv. Manuf. Technol. **49**(9–12), 1235–1250 (2010)
5. IEC-International Electrotechnical Commission. IEC 62402 (2007)
6. Granberg, B.: The quality re-evaluation process: product obsolescence in a consumer-producer interaction framework, Swedish Environmental Protection Agency (1997)
7. Cooper, T.: Inadequate life? Evidence of consumer attitudes to product obsolescence. J. Consum. Policy **27**, 421–449 (2004)
8. Atterbury, R.: Component Obsolescence Group, United Kingdom; Minenfeld Obsolescence, A Guide to Tackling Disappearing Products, Issue 2 (2005)
9. Brewin, A.: The Pb-free minefield: a guide to mitigating risk during the transition to RoHS compliance (2005)
10. Bartels, B., Ermel, U., Sandborn, P., Pecht, M.G.: Strategies to the Prediction, Mitigation and Management of Product Obsolescence, vol. 87. Wiley, Hoboken (2012)
11. Glinz, M.: On non-functional requirements. In: 15th IEEE International Requirements Engineering Conference (RE 2007), pp. 21–26. IEEE (2007)
12. Soltan, A., Addouche, S.A., Zolghadri, M., Barkallah, M., Haddar, M.: System Engineering for dependency analysis-a Bayesian approach: application to obsolescence study. Procedia CIRP **84**, 774–782 (2019)
13. Zolghadri, M., Addouche, S.A., Boissie, K., Richard, D.: Obsolescence prediction: a Bayesian model. Procedia CIRP **70**, 392–397 (2018)

14. Meng, X., Thörnberg, B., Olsson, L.: Strategic proactive obsolescence management model. IEEE Trans. Compon. Packag. Manuf. Technol. **4**(6), 1099–1108 (2014)
15. Sandborn, P.: Design for obsolescence risk management. Procedia CIRP **11**, 15–22 (2013)
16. Pingle, P.: Selection of obsolescence resolution strategy based on a multi criteria decision model (2015)
17. Meyer, A., Pretorius, L., Pretorius, J.H.C.: A model to manage electronic component obsolescence for complex or long life systems. In: 2004 IEEE International Engineering Management Conference (IEEE Cat. No. 04CH37574), vol. 3, pp. 1303–1309, October 2004
18. Sandborn, P., Mauro, F., Knox, R.: A data mining based approach to electronic part obsolescence forecasting. In: Proceedings of the 2005 DMSMS Conference, 11–15 April, Nashville, TN (20052005)
19. Roques, P.: Systems Architecture Modeling with the Arcadia Method: A Practical Guide to Capella. Elsevier (2017)
20. Bian, L., Gebraeel, N.: Stochastic modeling and real-time prognostics for multi-component systems with degradation rate interactions. IIE Trans. **46**(5), 470–482 (2014)
21. Carmignani, G.: An integrated structural framework to cost-basedfmeca: the priority-cost fmeca. Reliab. Eng. Syst. Saf. **94**(4), 861–871 (2009)
22. Weibull, W.: Wide applicability. J. Appl. Mech. **103**(730), 293–297 (1951)

i-DATAQUEST: A Proposal for a Manufacturing Data Query System Based on a Graph

Lise Kim[1(✉)], Esma Yahia[1], Frédéric Segonds[2], Philippe Véron[1], and Antoine Mallet[3]

[1] Arts et Metiers Institute of Technology, LISPEN, HESAM Université, Aix-en-Provence, France
{lise.kim,esma.yahia,philippe.veron}@ensam.eu

[2] Arts et Metiers Institute of Technology, LCPI, HESAM Université, Paris, France
frederic.segonds@ensam.eu

[3] CapGemini DEMS, Toulouse, France
antoine.mallet@capgemini.com

Abstract. During the manufacturing product life cycle, an increasing volume of data is generated and stored in distributed resources. These data are heterogeneous, explicitly and implicitly linked and they could be structured and unstructured. The rapid, exhaustive and relevant acquisition of information from this data is a major manufacturing industry issue. The key challenges, in this context, are to transform heterogeneous data into a common searchable data model, to allow semantic search, to detect implicit links between data and to rank results by relevance. To address this issue, the authors propose a query system based on a graph database. This graph is defined based on all the transformed manufacturing data. Besides, the graph is enriched by explicitly and implicitly data links. Finally, the enriched graph is queried thanks to an extended queries system defined by a knowledge graph. The authors depict a proof of concept to validate the proposal. After a partial implementation of this proof of concept, the authors obtain an acceptable result and a needed effort to improve the system response time. Finally, the authors open the topic on the subjects of right management, user profile/customization and data update.

Keywords: Graph database · Query system · Information retrieval · Manufacturing data · Manufacturing industry

1 Manufacturing Data Query

Leveraging the data product generated during its life cycle is a main issue for manufacturing industry. Manufacturing can be qualified as either discrete – i.e., the production of discrete items (e.g., cars, aircraft and appliances) – or continuous process, i.e., the production process that lends itself to an endless flow of non-discrete product (e.g., pharmaceutical, food and beverage, chemicals and cosmetics) [1, 2]. In this paper, our proposal is mainly dedicated to discrete manufacturing but could be enlarged to

F. Nyffenegger et al. (Eds.): PLM 2020, IFIP AICT 594, pp. 227–238, 2020.
https://doi.org/10.1007/978-3-030-62807-9_19

other domains. It requires collecting and managing data that are heterogeneous (including structured and unstructured data), explicitly and implicitly linked. Data are stored in distributed resources. One part is stored in information systems (PLM, ERP, MES etc.) databases which are supported by different data models and the other part are mainly unstructured and semi-structured data such as target tracking in spreadsheets, note taking in a text editor, reporting written in e-mail, etc. All this data are generated by different actors, using different languages, codifications and vocabulary.

The rapid, exhaustive and relevant acquisition of information in this complex context is difficult. There is no unique point of access to get the requested information and this information is often difficult to access. The time spent searching for information represents a non-negligible part of the employee's working time estimated to 19% [3].

When considering the relational nature of manufacturing data, the authors directed the work towards a graph-database query system. This choice allows the exploitation of all data relationships when searching. Besides, the authors have chosen to prioritize the search in all the textual content of the data (which can come from metadata, text files, but also images and tables). Indeed, the authors consider that textual content is of all other types (3D, schematic, etc.) the one that contains the most useful information for different people. The use of geometric content, images, diagrams, videos or any other type of non-textual content is therefore excluded from this paper to limit the study.

The authors present the main issues to be solved and deduce their main function required for a solution in Sect. 2. A detailed state of the art by function is presented in Sect. 3. The authors detail in Sect. 4 the proposal and its partial validation and conclude with a discussion in Sect. 5.

2 Key Challenges and Associated Functions

A retrieval information system is defined by three main functions which are: data pre-processing, query pre-processing and relevance evaluation of the data according to the query. Beyond the main requirements of a retrieval information system, which are fast time response, completeness and relevance of results, retrieving information in a manufacturing company context involves many other challenges. To answer these challenges, the authors proposed to enrich the three main functions of any query system with four supplementary functions derived respectively from each identified challenge, which are:

1. *Data exploitation despite its syntactic heterogeneity:* Data can be recorded in databases or in documents as text files. In order to optimize search capabilities, the system must be able to exploit the specifications of each type of data and return, as required, either a file list, a record list from a database, data linked to another through a relational database, a metadata value, a table cell value or a specific sentence in a text content. To answer this challenge, the authors define a function that integrates each searchable element in the graph data model. This concerns the metadata of the records in the databases, the metadata of semi and unstructured files, explicit relationship between database tables, the textual content of the text files,

image files and tables. This function is called: **"Function A – Process syntax specifics of data"**.

2. *Data exploitation despite vocabularies and languages heterogeneity:* Data contains textual content defined by a wide variety of actors, especially in an extended enterprise. In order to optimize the query results displayed to the user, it is necessary to return all the relevant results, even if the language or the vocabulary used in the data content differs from the language or vocabulary used in the query. A new function is then needed to extend the search for query keywords to all its semantically related terms. For example, if the term *battery* is used in the query, results must contain those with the battery translation as *batterie* in French and the *battery* synonyms as *accumulator*. This function is called: **"Function B - Search by Semantic Proximity".**
3. *Exploitation of implicit links between data:* One impact of the distributed nature of data is the lack of links between data. For example, if the user searches for the price of a part using its functional reference but the price is associated with the supplier reference in another database, the search system must be able to detect the link between the two references in order to obtain the expected result. To answer this challenge, a function is then needed to detect implicit links between data. This function is called: **"Function C - Detect implicit links between data".**
4. *Displaying results by relevance:* The ranking of results by relevance is essential to any query system that provides a significant number of results. It is therefore necessary to present the result according to a degree of relevance. The authors propose to define a system function called: **"Function D – Rank the results in relevance order".**

3 Related Works

The authors conduct a general state of the art considering several works that proposing query or analysis systems based on graph databases to deal with distributed and heterogeneous data source issues. In Table 1, the authors identify some works where each function consideration is evaluated.

Table 1. Related work evaluation according to the expected functions.

References	Function A Process syntax specifics of data	Function B Search by Semantic Proximity	Function C Detect implicit links between data	Function D Rank the results in relevance order
[4]	Yes	No	Yes	No
[5]	Yes	No	No	No
[6]	No	No	Yes	No
[7]	No	Yes	Yes	Yes
[8–13]	No	No	No	No

The treatment of syntactic heterogeneity is achieved by using a meta-model to be instantiated at each new information source in the work of [4] and by integrating as many plug-ins as necessary transformations in the work of [5]. The works described in [4] and [7] deal with the automatic detection of non-existent links mentioning the use of various analytics such as text mining and the use of Levenshtein distance. The work describes in [6] integrates the detection of links between data to be unified by rules involving the relationships and common properties between the data. Finally, the authors of [7] integrate the notion of semantic search thanks to semantic annotation via bio-ontologies and result classification according to a model specific to biology. The authors of [8–13] don't integrate any of the functions mentioned, notably because the sources of the data involved are known and limited in number, which makes processing ad hoc.

As none of these works encompasses all the manufacturing industry challenges, the authors define a specific state of the art by function. It allows deeply defining the possible orientations transcribed in the scientific literature for each specific function. This study is described in the bullet list below.

- **Function A – The treatment process of data syntactic specificity.** The transformation of relational database schema into a graph database schema is a well-proven field. For some graph database, the transformation is conducted by ETL (Extraction Transformation and Load) tools plug-in[1]. This transformation allows the relationships retrieval between tables (with foreign keys) to generate graph links. Whereas, text extraction from document is possible with parser tools. Supported by natural language processing algorithms [14], the specific sentence detection according to language specificities such as grammatical rules can be done. Besides, property extraction from documents is possible with standard computer operation. Finally, spreadsheet syntax exploitation has already been done in papers like [15] but the transformation is limited by adaptability of the different array formats.
- **Function B – Search by enabling semantic proximity.** Since the Latent Semantic Indexing proposed by the Information Retrieval field [16], the tendency is rather to exploit knowledge resources of semantic relation between terms supported by ontologies [17] or knowledge graph [18]. Two orientations are then taken, query expansion or enrichment of indexed descriptors.
- **Function C – Detect implicit links between data.** Record Linkage is the task of finding two records referring to the same entity through different sources. Two objects can be associated if they have a common key. The typographical variations problems in this key are to be considered and can be solved by the comparison of common character strings (Levenshtein distance for example [19]). The link can be accentuated according to the number of common labels, and according to the labels involved, which can be weighted based on a revelation criterion [20]. On the other hand, it is also possible to use a knowledge graph and the user browsing history to detect link between data [21]. Besides, link prediction is an important research area in social network analysis where the existing link analysis allows to the new links prediction [22].

[1] https://neo4j.com/developer/neo4j-etl/.

- **Function D – Rank the results in relevance order.** The results ranking is carried out using several criteria. In the Information Retrieval field, the vector model used the number of terms occurrences. Other methods used by web search engines in the field of Search Engine Optimization should be considered [23]. These methods use for example the popularity of the sites (are they often browsed or searched?), the page freshness (are they regularly updated?) and the pages authority (do other sites refer to them?) etc.

4 I-DATAQUEST, a Proposal for a Manufacturing Data Query System

4.1 Proposal Description

The authors define the proposal for a manufacturing data query system based on a graph in Fig. 1. The main object of the proposal is to offer to any manufacturing stakeholder the possibility to query all the company data. The back end of the proposed system contains three areas presenting the system main functions: data pre-processing, query pre-processing and relevance evaluation of the data according to the query. Each of these parts was then enriched by sub-blocks allowing to respond to the specific functions listed in Sect. 2 and thus to the key challenges related to the study context. The details of the proposal implementation are briefly presented below.

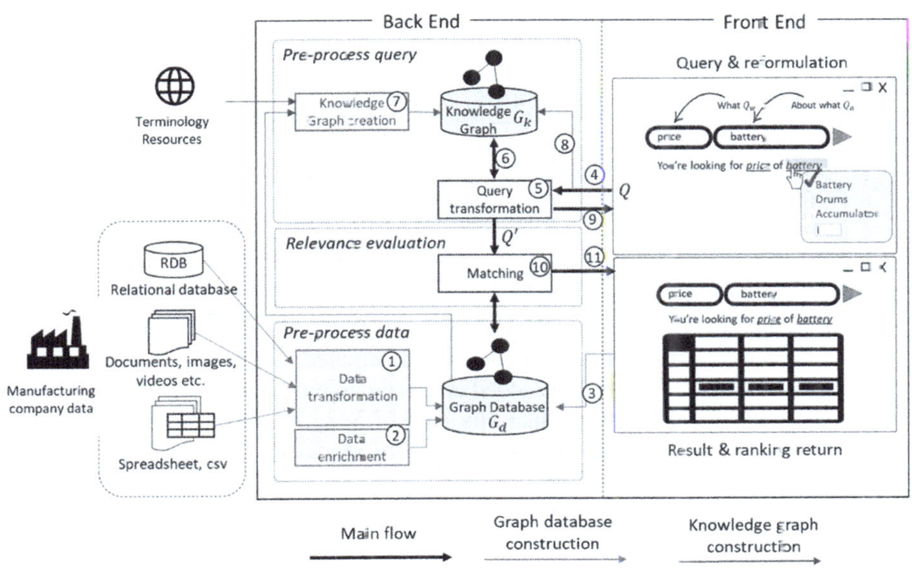

Fig. 1. I-DATAQUEST – Architecture proposal for a manufacturing data query system

1. *Heterogeneous data transformation.* As in the ETL transformation rules and the spreadsheet-specific transformation rules set out in Part 3, heterogeneous data are transformed to the unified graph data model of G_d as shown in Fig. 2. (a) The node represents a document, a relational database record or a table row. (b) The nodes have relationships between them carried by the foreign keys of relational databases. (c) The nodes carry labels with a name and value that represent properties of documents, metadata of relational databases or columns value of a table content. (d) The label 'contents' integrating the textual content of the documents is added to each node concerned. (e) The 'relevance' label including a relevance score is added to each node.

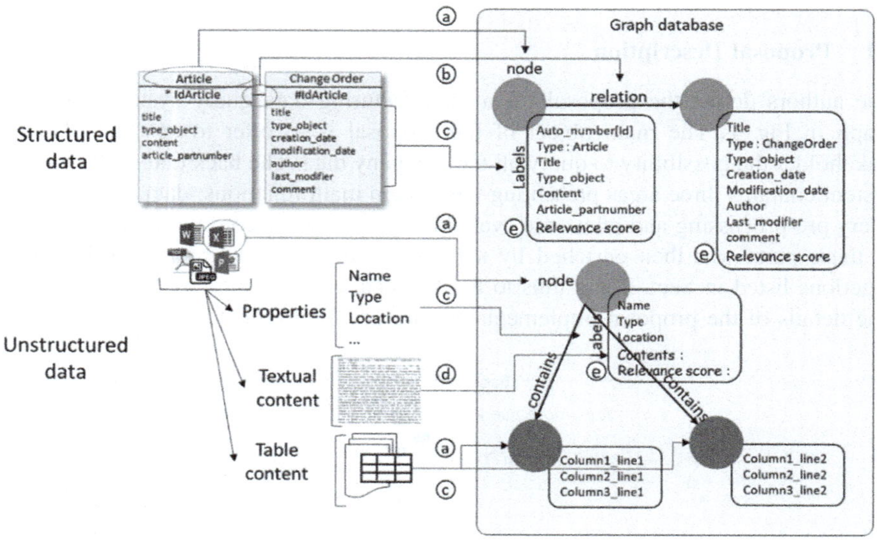

Fig. 2. Transformation of heterogeneous data to the graph data model

2. *Data enrichment.* Implicit links between nodes are added to G_d. In line with the record linkage domain, these relationships are detected if a main label value (e.g. title, reference, name etc.) of a node A is mentioned in a label of a node B. The weighting of this relationship is added according to the presence of versioning label values (e.g. version, revision, maturity etc.) of node A in the labels of node B.
3. *Relevance return.* As in popularity ranking methods for websites, when the user selects a query result, the value of the label 'relevance score' of the associated node in G_d is increased.
4. *Query Q integration.* The query Q integration is carried out by a graphical user interface represented in Fig. 1. The user expresses his need for information in two parts: $Q = Q_w \cdot Q_a$ with Q_w terms representing the information type sought ('what') and Q_a terms contained in the information sought ('about what'). In addition to the 'about what' field, the use of the 'what' field allows searching for the value of a specific node label (for example the search for the 'price' label of a

node whose title is 'battery' is thus allowed when $Q_w = 'price'$ and $Q_a = 'battery'$).

5. *Transformation of the query Q to Q'*. The Q query is translated into the query language adapted to the graph database and it is adapted according to the values of Q_w and Q_a. For example, if Q_w is not null, Q' will integrate the query of all named or approximately named Q_w and return the values as results. In addition, Q' will query all textual content and return specific sentences based on the terms of Q and using natural language processing algorithms. For example, in a requirement search query, it is then possible to search for all sentences expressing a requirement because they contain specific verbs and modals as 'require', 'must' etc. The query is also divided into several sub-queries to evaluate the ranking of the results. For example, the sub-query querying only the labels named 'title' will return results of high relevance.
6. *Query expansion*. The terms used in query are extended to the relevant terms. The relevant terms defined with a knowledge graph G_k and according to a relevance score. This relevance score is calculated based on the frequency of the term use in previous queries. For example, in a car manufacturer context, if the user uses the term 'batterie' in French, which means both the musical instrument and the energy storage element, the English translation 'battery' and not 'drums' will by preferred because it is more often used.
7. *Knowledge graph G_k creation*. Merging both ontology and knowledge graph concepts, G_k is built using external resources such as [24] to obtain synonymous, related and translating terms used in G_d.
8. *Knowledge graph G_k enrichment*. When the user submits a query, the relevance score S_r between the query terms t_q and the terms selected in reformulation contained in G_k is increased. Conversely, when terms are deselected, the relevance score S_r is decreased.
9. *Query reformulation*. A cross-reference of the terms used in Q and all terms in relationship in G_k are proposed to the user as shown in Fig. 1. The user can select or deselect the terms to be included and thus reformulate the query.
10. *Graph database querying*. The query Q' is applied to the graph database G_d.
11. *Results displaying*. The results of the query of G_d according to Q' are displayed to the user in an order of relevance established by steps 2 and 9.

4.2 Proposal Validation

The authors checked that necessary functions defined in Sect. 2 are taken into account in the proposal. The authors have transcribed the result in Table 2.

A validation concerning the main requirements of a query system such as the fast response time, completeness and relevance of results must be conducted. This validation has been so far partially achieved. Indeed, only the first four functions in Table 2 has been developed for the moment (including step 1, 2, 5, 6, 7) and by excluding the automation of data transformation step.

Table 2. Functions consideration in the proposal.

Step	Query pre-processing	Data pre-processing	Relevance evaluation	Function A	Function B	Function C	Function D
1, 2, 4	X						
7, 8, 9		X					
5			X				
7				X			
3, 10, 11					X		
8						X	
6							X

The proof of concept developed by the authors uses different tools among the Python language, Apache Tika[2] to extract the textual content of documents, Tesseract[3] for the characters recognition in images documents and Neo4J[4] as graph databases. Py2neo[5] was selected to conduct the query to Neo4j with Python language and DashByPloty[6] generates a web interface suitable for data analysis. Figure 3 shows the different tools used for each layer of the proposition.

The dataset used to validate the author's approach, comes from a digital model of a drone project and enriched. It contains 686 elements, 47% of which are unstructured data, 22% tree structure data and 17% from a relational database. The authors identified 19 queries to meet the requirements of innovative uses in the manufacturing company and from its various departments. The expected answers per query were evaluated manually by browsing through each object in the dataset. For time measurement, the aim is to achieve less than one second between the submission of the query by the user and the display of the result according to [25].

The measures used to evaluate the Information Retrieval system are the recall (number of relevant documents found according to the number of relevant documents in the database) and the precision (number of relevant documents found according to the total number of documents display in result). A system returning all relevant results without displaying irrelevant results will have these two measurements equal to 1.

The results obtained are in Table 3. The results are compared to a first step where only node and labels without processing of texts and tables content, have been integrated in the graph database.

[2] https://tika.apache.org.

[3] https://opensource.google/projects/tesseract.

[4] https://neo4j.com.

[5] https://py2neo.org/v4.

[6] https://plot.ly/dash/.

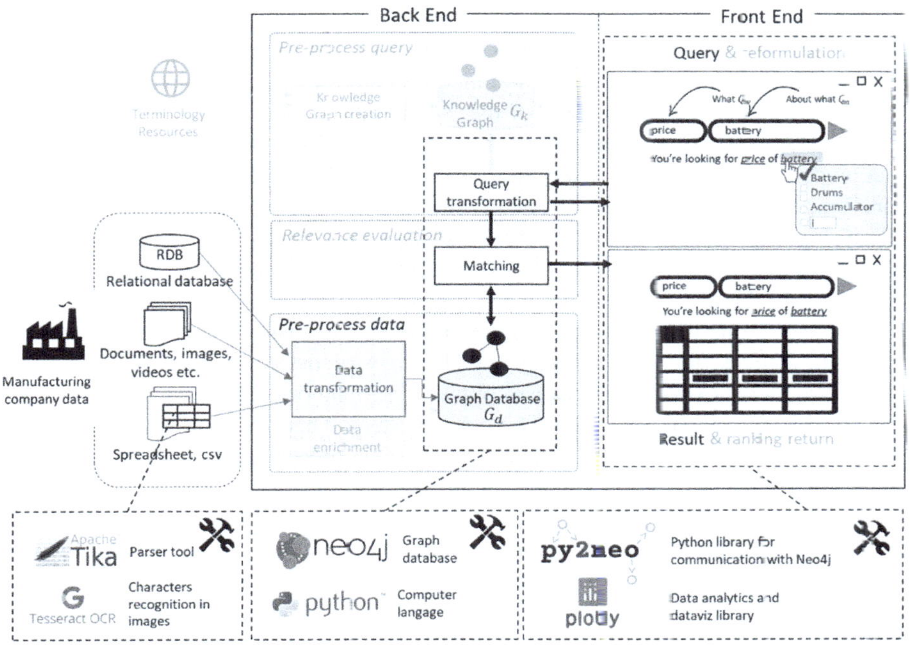

Fig. 3. Proof of concepts tools

Table 3. Partial evaluation of the proposal

Stage	Response time (s)	Precision	Recall
First step: Only metadata	25	1	0.01
Second step: With function A	79	0.60	0.45

Evaluation of the results shows a degraded query time. An important waste of time is due to the search for sentences in the textual content. There are ways to improve time such as the search for sentences on demand only but also by the integration of text content descriptors rather than the entire content, the reduced selection of labels to be used in a search, and the table content extracts on demand. It will therefore be necessary to evaluate each option according to the degradation of the other requirement values. However, the recall measurement improves and precision decreases with the increase in the number of results.

5 Perspectives

In order to address the issue of information retrieval in the context of manufacturing industry, the authors have highlighted the key challenges related to the manufacturing context and specifies the functions to be developed. These challenges have been defined according to the nature of the manufacturing data. These characteristics may be common to other domains, so it will be interesting to study the applicability of the solution to other domains in the future. A graph-based query system proposal was presented in this paper with three main functions and four specific functions. A proof of concept has been conducted for 4 of the 7 functions. This proposal responds to key challenges by first transforming the syntactic specificities of the data into a graphical data model, by extending the query terms to semantically close terms, by detecting and transforming the implicit links between the data into explicit links, and finally by classifying the results according to their relevance. It is therefore necessary to develop the integration of the remaining functions in order to complete the evaluation of the proposal. In addition to this work, some topics can be discussed.

The user rights management is an important security issue. Indeed, unifying multiple data sources, the system integrates a variety of heterogeneous rights matrices, particularly in the extended enterprise context. The main orientation is then the creation of a specific rights management to the query system. This right management required the same complexity as the existing one, which is a greatest remaining challenge.

Beyond the management of user rights, the user profile information (who, what profession, with what history of use) is an important asset to improve the results relevance. One of the questions is whether knowledge graphs by profile or user is needed. If so, its feasibility will have to be assessed while still meeting the requirements.

Updating source data is also a feature to be considered in this proposal. This paper does not present the automation of data extraction from their sources but one orientation was taken in the creation and the update by batch. So the features to be considered are the creation, modification and deletion of nodes and relationships.

Finally, the authors wish to consolidate the detection of implicit links between data. This allows a better follow-up in change management as presented in [26] with graphs and ontology.

References

1. International Organization for Standardisation (ISO): ISO 15531-1:2004 Industrial Automation Systems and Integration – Industrial Manufacturing Management Data – Part 1: General Overview, Geneva (2004)
2. Pinquié, R., Rivest, L., Segonds, F., Philippe, V.: An illustrated glossary of ambiguous PLM terms used in discrete manufacturing. Int. J. Product Lifecycle Manage. **8**(12), 142–171 (2015). https://doi.org/10.1504/IJPLM.2015.070580
3. Chui, M., et al.: The social economy: unlocking value and productivity through social technologies. McKinseyGlobal Institute (2012). http://www.mckinsey.com/industries/high-tech/our-insights/the-social-economy. Accessed 27 Mar 2020
4. Gröger, C., Schwarz, H., Bernhard, M.: The deep data warehouse: link-based integration and enrichment of warehouse data and unstructured content. In: 2014 IEEE 18th International Enterprise Distributed Object Computing Conference (2014). https://doi.org/10.1109/edoc.2014.36
5. Martínez-Bazan, N., Muntés-Mulero, V., Gómez-Villamor, S., Nin, J., Sánchez-Martínez, M.-A., Larriba-Pey, J.-L.: DEX: High-Performance Exploration On Large Graphs For Information Retrieval. In: International Conference on Information and Knowledge Management, Proceedings (2007). https://doi.org/10.1145/1321440.1321521

6. Touré, V., et al.: STON: exploring biological pathways using the SBGN standard and graph databases. BMC Bioinform. **17**(1) (2016). https://doi.org/10.1186/s12859-016-1394-x
7. Henkel, R., Wolkenhauer, O., Waltermath, D.: Combining computational models, semantic annotations and simulation experiments in a graph database. Database 1–16 (2015). https://doi.org/10.1093/database/bau130
8. Lysenko, A., Roznovăţ, I.A., Saqi, M., Mazein, A., Rawlings, C.J.: Representing and querying disease networks using graph databases. BioData Min. **9**(11), 23 (2016). https://doi.org/10.1186/s13040-016-0102-8
9. Yoon, B.-H., Kim, S.-K., Kim, S.-Y.: Use of graph database for the integration of heterogeneous biological data. Genomics Inform. **15**, 19–27 (2017). https://doi.org/10.5808/gi.2017.15.1.19
10. Bonnici, V., Russo, F., Bombieri, N., Pulvirenti, A., Giugno, R.: Comprehensive reconstruction and visualization of non-coding regulatory networks in human. Front. Bioeng. Biotechnol. **2**, 69 (2014). https://doi.org/10.3389/fbioe.2014.00069
11. Messina, A., Fiannaca, A., La Paglia, L., La Rosa, M., Urso, A.: BioGraph: a web application and a graph database for querying and analyzing bioinformatics resources. BMC Syst. Biol. **5**(112), 75–89 (2018). https://doi.org/10.1186/s12918-018-0616-4
12. Noel, S., Harley, E., Tam, K. H., Gyor, G.: Big-data architecture for cyber attack graphs representing security relationships in NoSQL graph databases. In: IEEE Symposium on Technologies for Homeland, Boston (2015)
13. Schabus, S., Scholz, J.: Spatially-linked manufacturing data to support data analysis. J. Geogr. Inf. Sci. **15**(11), 126–140 (2017). https://doi.org/10.1553/giscience2017_01_s126
14. Chowdhury, G.G.: Natural language processing. Ann. Rev. Inf. Sci. Technol. 51–89 (2003). https://doi.org/10.1002/aris.1440370103
15. Zhu, Z., Zhou, X., Shao, K.: A novel approach based on Neo4j for multi-constrained flexible job shop scheduling problem. Comput. Ind. Eng. **130**, 671–686 (2019). https://doi.org/10.1016/j.cie.2019.03.022
16. Dumais, S.T.: Latent semantic indexing (LSI) and TREC-2. In: The Second Text Retrieval (TREC2), pp. 105–116 (1994)
17. Kyriakakis, A., Koumakis, L., Kanterakis, A., Iatraki, G., Tsiknakis, M.: Enabling ontology-based search: a case study in the bioinformatics domain. In: IEEE 19th International Conference on Bioinformatics and Bioengineering (BIBE) Enabling (2019). https://doi.org/10.1109/bibe.2019.00048
18. Xiong, C., Power, R., Callan, J.: Explicit semantic ranking for academic search via knowledge graph embedding. In: 26th International World Wide Web Conference, WWW, pp. 1271–1279 (2017). https://doi.org/10.1145/3038912.3052558
19. Navarro, G.: A guided tour to approximate string matching. ACM Comput. Surv. **33**(1), 31–88 (2001). https://doi.org/10.1145/375360.375365
20. Fellegi, I.P., Sunter, A.B.: A theory for record linkage. J. Am. Stat. Assoc. **64**(1328), 1183–1210 (1969). https://doi.org/10.1080/01621459.1969.10501049
21. Hakkani-Tür, D., Heck, L., Tur, G.: Using a knowledge graph and query click logs for unsupervised learning of relation detection. In: ICASSP, IEEE International Conference on Acoustics, Speech and Signal Processing – Proceedings (2013). https://doi.org/10.1109/icassp.2013.6639289
22. Cukierski, W., Hammer, B., Yang, B.: Graph-based features for supervised link prediction. In Proceedings of International Joint Conference on Neural Networks, San Jose, California, USA (2011). https://doi.org/10.1109/ijcnn.2011.6033365
23. Xing, W., Ghorbani, A.: Weighted PageRank algorithm. In: Proceedings. Second Annual Conference on Communication Networks and Services Research (2004). https://doi.org/10.1109/dnsr.2004.1344743

24. Speer, R., Chin, J., Havasi, C.: ConceptNet 5.5: an open multilingual graph of general knowledge. In: Proceedings of the Thirty-First AAAI Conference on Artificial Intelligence (AAAI 2017) (2017)
25. Arapakis, I., Bai, X., Cambazoglu, B.: Impact of response latency on user behavior in web search. In: SIGIR 2014 - Proceedings of the 37th International ACM SIGIR Conference on Research and Development in Information Retrieval, pp. 103–112 (2014). https://doi.org/10.1145/2600428.2609627
26. Mordinyi, R., Shindler, P., Biffl, S.: Evaluation of NoSQL graph databases for querying and versioning of engineering data in multi-disciplinary engineering environments. In: IEEE International Conference on Emerging Technologies and Factory Automation, ETFA (2015). https://doi.org/10.1109/etfa.2015.7301486

Ontologies for Interoperability

Supporting Linked Engineering Data Management of Smart Product Systems Through Semantic Platform Services

Jonas Gries(✉), Thomas Eickhoff, Andreas Eiden, and Jens Christian Göbel

Institute of Virtual Product Engineering, TU Kaiserslautern, Gottlieb-Daimler-Str. 44, 67663 Kaiserslautern, Germany
gries@mv.uni-kl.de

Abstract. The increasing industrial relevance of connected smart product systems, enhanced individualized customer requirements, regulatory boundary conditions as well as advanced value networks and volatile international markets determine a new level of engineering complexity. Current engineering processes are enabled by a large number of IT applications, which are partially orchestrated by product lifecycle management solutions. Considering the dramatically increasing complexity, the IT applications are often not adequately connected as a whole, leading to interruptions in the process chains and finally resulting in quality problems, time expenditure, and additional costs.

To support seamless engineering processes, a sufficiently linked information system structure is necessary. Due to the often-existing best-of-breed solutions and historically grown IT infrastructures, the direct point-to-point coupling of IT systems among each other requires disproportionately high efforts. As an approach to improve the existing situation, integration platforms utilizing loose coupling of individual heterogeneous engineering IT applications by semantic web technologies could be used to create a comprehensive, linked engineering data structure.

This paper presents a conceptual IT-Service approach that utilizes this linked data structure to address problems in the area of information retrieval, data exchange, and data quality. A fundamental service function enables easy access to the information scattered throughout the whole organization. This approach could contribute to a high level of transparency within the company's internal processes and relationships between data across individual engineering IT applications. The proposed concepts for IT platform services facilitate the exchange of data between different software applications and the standardized checking and documentation of data quality.

Keywords: Semantic services · Linked engineering data · Smart products · Product lifecycle management

Published by Springer Nature Switzerland AG 2020
F. Nyffenegger et al. (Eds.): PLM 2020, IFIP AICT 594, pp. 241–255, 2020.
https://doi.org/10.1007/978-3-030-62807-9_20

1 Introduction

Smart products, which are composed of a multitude of interdisciplinary subsystems and including smart connected IT services based on the Internet of Everything [1] confront engineers with fundamentally new challenges. Also, increasing demand for customer-specific individualization determines a strong increase in the number of product variants. Consequently, interdisciplinary engineering in globally distributed dynamic value networks requires enhanced communication throughout all phases of the product lifecycle.

Product Lifecycle Management (PLM) approaches try to address this problem by managing business processes and associated data, which are generated by a large number of individuals using software applications distributed over the entire product life cycle [2]. Due to the high amount of existing best-of-breed solutions and historically grown IT infrastructures, many software applications are not linked to the PLM infrastructure, which in turn causes disruptions in the process chains through missing interoperability.

The conceptual approach for a basic set of platform-based IT services presented in this paper utilizes linked engineering data to support cross-product-lifecycle and interdisciplinary collaboration. To define basic needs for these IT-Service concepts, an engineering process requiring a high degree of interdisciplinary cooperation due to a large amount of data and specific engineering knowledge involved is exemplarily considered. This exemplary use case scenario includes a Noise, Vibration, and Harshness (NVH) simulation of the powertrain form a modern hybrid vehicle.

Based on the generalized needs derived from the use case scenario, a concept for three IT services addressing information retrieval, data exchange, and data quality has been developed using our metadata repository for semantic product lifecycle management SP^{2}IDER, which has been developed in our research group since 2016 [3].

2 Use Case Scenario and Needs for Conceptual IT Services

Considering the problem-solving cycle of systems engineering, simulation is a part of the search for solutions and involves the four steps of mission definition, model structure building, simulation runs, and solution recommendation [4]. The use case scenario of Noise, Vibration, and Harshness (NVH) processes includes Multi-Body Simulation (MBS), Finite Element Method (FEM) and Statistical Energy Analysis (SEA), which are used in combination to investigate vibrations and noises caused by oscillations [5]. These simulation methods, nowadays are part of the methodical standard repertoire in the automotive industry, which is especially crucial for new challenges in the context of the electrification of the drivetrain [6].

The simulation process begins with the mission definition. In the considered use case, there is suddenly a higher torque requested to accelerate a hybrid vehicle (Tip-In) where in consequence the internal combustion engine is started by engagement to the electric motor. A proper tuning of the electrical and mechanical components as well as a capable control system are necessary. Otherwise, an unexpected, noticeable longitudinal shake in the vehicle could occur [7]. After the mission has been defined, the engineer is responsible for acquiring the necessary data for the simulation model. An MBS simulation is carried out for the low-frequency examination, which requires the locations and masses of the components for the model assembly. However, the engineer responsible for this task is not necessarily aware of which software application the data can be found in. Studies like [8, 9] show that engineers today spend over 50% of their working hours searching for information.

Once the necessary data is found, it has to be transferred into the simulation application. In the considered use case scenario, non-existing connections between the data management application like PLM and simulation application lead to uncontrolled data exchange, e.g. via e-mail. As a result, it is no longer possible to trace the development stage on which the data is based and a large source of potential errors is created. Since the accuracy of a simulation is correlated directly with the quality of the input data [10], data quality assurance is crucially important. However, the scope and complexity of the data make manual data quality monitoring unfeasible for the responsible engineer.

As soon as the data is available in the simulation application, the engineer builds up the simulation model. When the assembly is completed, the correctness of the model can be checked. For this purpose, either known historically test data or, if available, physical experiments are used. Now that the pre-processing is completed, the actual calculation and solving of the simulation takes place. In subsequent post-processing, the results of the simulation must be interpreted and evaluated with the help of in-depth specialist knowledge. The simulation model and results are then incorporated into a simulation data management (SDM) solution to enable reusability. However, simulation applications often are not necessarily connected to an SDM solution. As a consequence, the simulation models and results are often only persisted locally.

A detailed analysis of the mentioned use case scenario lead to following needs developing conceptual IT services for the semantic engineering platform SP²IDER:

N1 Software application can be linked with a low as possible effort
N2 Data can be retrieved from different source systems centrally
N3 Data can be exchanged between different source systems
N4 Data Quality can be determined and monitored

3 Current State of Linked Engineering Data Management Solutions

Product Lifecycle Management and Enterprise Resource Planning (ERP), existing over decades, have been applied to a multitude of use cases across the product lifecycle. However, these solutions often coexist as separate information technical and organizational ecosystems within the corresponding departments of a company [11]. As a result, these solutions typically manage data such as requirement data, product models, and source code, supplemented by numerous authoring software applications, which are specific to a particular life cycle phase or engineering discipline. The data from these software applications could be managed in a single, consistent data model across the whole product lifecycle. In reality, however, there are often several redundant and inconsistent data models that are often synced manually or using ad hoc processes [12]. Smart, connected products further increase the data management effort by providing more and more data from the product use phase. This also enables new data usage scenarios (e.g. availability-oriented business models) that would not be possible without a coherent view of both product instance-specific and generic product development data. However, for these use cases, the data must be gathered, prepared, and made available across the whole product lifecycle and different departments [13]. Also, processes often require access to data which is scattered across a variety of software applications, which in turn requires knowledge about the existence and structure of all data sets. This need for data and process integration has led to several industrial IT solutions supporting the mentioned use case scenarios. Solutions can be classified according to their strategy for providing a unified view of data from different source systems. Systems like Intercax Syndeia [14] enable the synchronization of several databases. Similarly, platforms like eQube BI [15] or the Semantic Data Management Integration Platform [16] add an additional layer on the top of existing systems to enable centralized access to all required data. In all approaches, a unifying data model or ontology provides the required information for mapping the data. These approaches are primarily based on data integration rather than the processes using the data. Also, the mentioned approaches are only considering particular areas of the product lifecycle and have to be tailored to exactly address the problem.

The Open Services for Lifecycle Collaboration (OSLC) provide a decentralized approach towards data integration by using open web technologies based on linked data instead of integration or synchronization [17]. According to the principles of linked data, the data is represented by URIs that refer to objects. Information about these objects is provided in the form of RDF [18]. OSLC currently provides just a small core and several specific application profiles that could undermine interoperability. Using OSLC for data integration requires all connected systems to support the required profiles in a compatible way, which will be a challenge for such solutions in the short term. Similar approaches like OPC-UA exist in the context of manufacturing and production [19].

There is no general common consensus on comprehensive IT solutions which could serve as the primary source of information in these models. Based on the previous examples this could either be PLM, ERP, an IoT platform, a common dashboard that connects to all these platforms or a common data model that is deployed across different systems and synchronized automatically. However, the analyzed approaches show several trends: Building on (open) standards enables interoperability, graph-based representations allow the modeling of highly connected data and the various source systems are largely being left intact. Other aspects like the question of whether to synchronize, to add a central system or to link data in a decentralized architecture, do not seem to have been addressed yet by obvious solutions. Additionally, all the mentioned approaches are built on the assumption that data is available and correct. Managing data in a realistic industrial scenario requires processes for managing and requesting access rights to data as well as ways to ensure the consistency and quality of data objects stored in the various IT systems.

4 Conceptual Framework for Semantic Platform Services

To address the basic needs analyzed in Sect. 2, a capable Linked Engineering Data Management solution is mandatory and serves as a prerequisite for the needs N2, N3, and N4. Previous research projects also show that effective collaboration requires data exchange across systems [20] as well as a holistic view on all relevant aspects of the system in question [21]. Additionally, redundant data stored and often inconsistent data across multiple systems have to be handled systematically.

To address these challenges, the Semantic Product and Process Information and Digitized Engineering Repository (SP²IDER) platform has been developed since 2016 by a team of researchers at the Chair of Virtual Product Engineering at the University of Kaiserslautern in Germany [3]. The approach is based on loose coupling of source systems to a central core using lightweight application-specific wrappers built on open web technologies. Similar to OSLC, the concept is based on RESTful API and Linked Data but in contrast offers a superordinate (data) layer to provide a comprehensive knowledge base. A code generator for the wrappers allows new source systems to be connected to the core with manageable effort, thus ensuring interoperability.

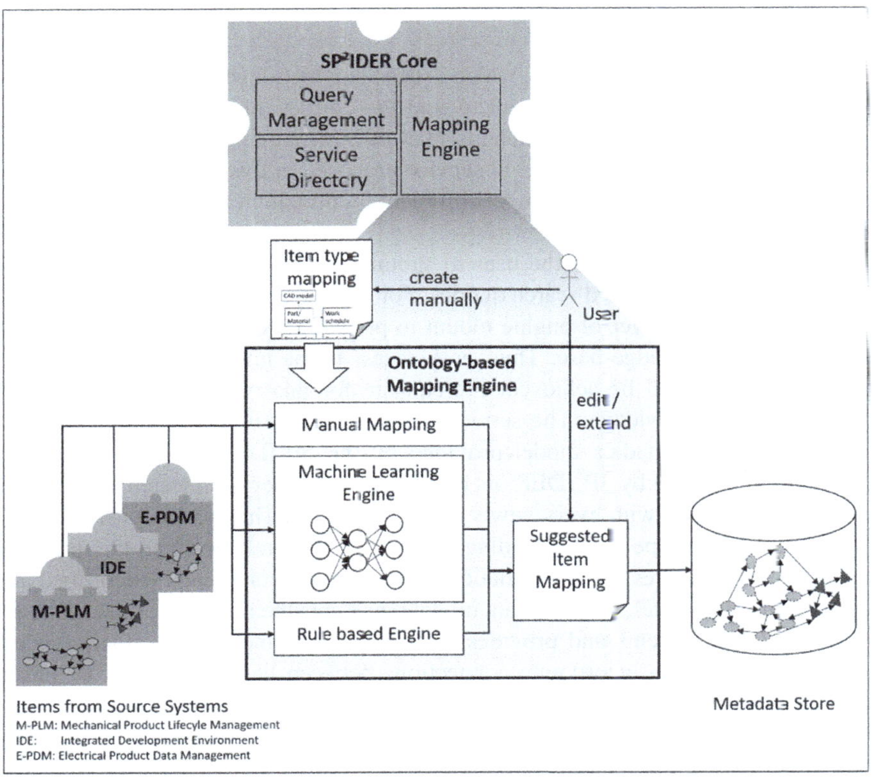

Fig. 1. SP²IDER data mapping engine according to [3]

The SP^{2}IDER Metadata Store does not store deep copies of data objects, but instead, it stores only metadata about the objects in a graph repository. Due to the possibility of performing create, read, update, and delete (CRUD) operations by HTTP methods, the core can fetch required data through the wrappers on the fly.

Managing the unified metadata model requires the unification of synonymous objects and identical objects stored in different source systems. These are data objects existing in different source systems representing an identical logical unit, for example, a part which is held in a PLM system for product development processes and in an ERP system for economic business or manufacturing processes. Responsible for this task is the SP^{2}IDER mapping engine as shown in Fig. 1. Identical objects from different source systems can be merged into one graph node using a combination of imperative rules, probabilistic mappings using machine learning algorithms which are subsequently checked by the user, and manual mapping to cover exceptions. The merged graph nodes contain the necessary metadata to enable processes like information retrieval or data exchange requests. Beside the mapping engine, the SP^{2}IDER core includes a query management as well as a service directory thus supporting workflows.

Based on the technological foundations of the SP^{2}IDER platform, we propose three conceptual IT services that are introduced in the following.

4.1 Information Retrieval

A keyword-based search approach, which is used at a high level of maturity by internet search engines, is often not sufficient to find the correct information across different engineering IT systems due to problems like different naming conventions or hierarchies [22]. The **information retrieval service** proposed in this paper will use semantic search technologies as a solution to this problem by utilizing knowledge described in a formal and machine-interpretable way.

This approach will enable the user to submit queries for which he lacks explicit knowledge in keyword-based search queries. For instance, search queries such as "Who is the sub-project manager of engine mount in project engine 2025?" will be possible with the fitting knowledge-base. Thus, easy access to the information scattered across the value network will be achieved. Prerequisite for this type of search is a formal representation of knowledge. The service therefore will utilize the semantically enriched, graph-based metadata model provided by the SP^{2}IDER Metadata Store. This metadata model is built by SP^{2}IDER out of the data from every connected source system and will be expanded with every newly attached system. The model consisting out of two layers: the data type level providing classes and their relations and the data object level providing instances and their relations. Using the mapping engine described at the beginning of this chapter, the metadata model represents the relations of data across the connected source systems and provides the needed machine-interpretable knowledge base. That allowing to incorporate connections between the data objects in question across all connected source systems and tracing located information as well as relations back to a single source system. Thus, retrieving primarily metadata, SP^{2}IDER can additionally fetch further detailed information if required, by supporting HTTP methods like 'get' through the wrapper on each source system.

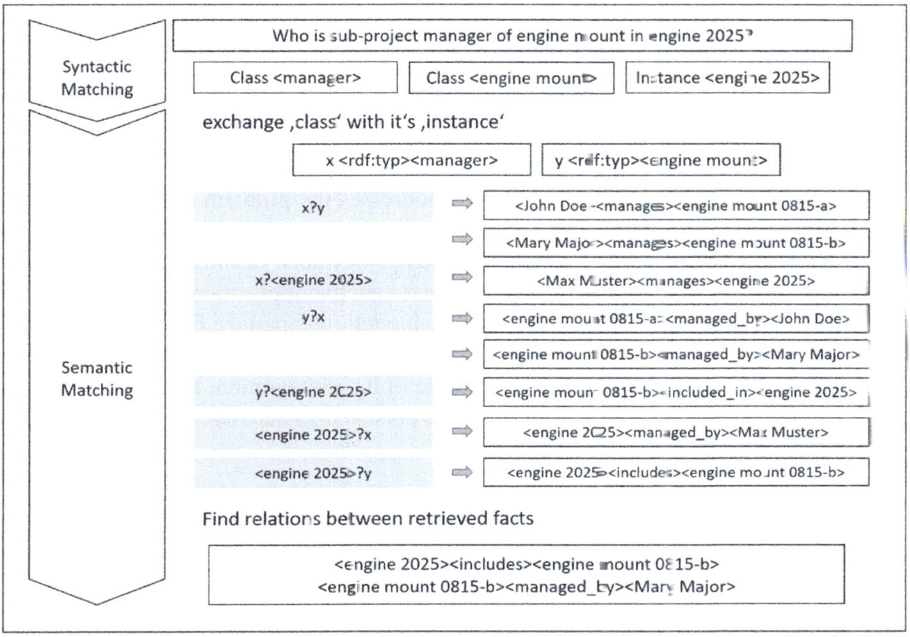

Fig. 2. Procedure of semantic information retrieval service by a statement-based approach

According to Dengel [23], semantic processing can take place in three different phases: in query processing, the search algorithm itself, or the processing and presentation of the results. There are different methods like reasoning, traversing on graphs, or statement-based approaches available for semantic-based search algorithms. Concerning SP^{2}IDER, we recommend a statement-based algorithm due to the graph-based metadata model. Because of the wide range of users informal, natural language free-text search queries are intended. The query will be first subjected to a syntactic comparison with the textual content of the knowledge base to identify any fitting concepts (see Fig. 2 syntactic matching). Concepts can be classes, instances, or properties from the SP^{2}IDER metadata model. Subsequently, semantic processing will take place by exploring the ontological context of the concepts found and searching for related instances [23]. Therefore, SPARQL-Queries are built out of <subject, predicate, object> triples where subjects and objects being classes or instances and predicates being properties retrieved in the previous step (see Fig. 2 semantic matching). While a traditional retrieval only exploits the syntactic matching, the here proposed approach uses the machine-interpretable relations within the metadata model to consider the meaning of the search terms and provide fitting, precise results. The search result is finally presented to the user in a way that facilitates the transparency and traceability of the information and its structure.

Besides, an explorative search will be provided based on the retrieval results. Therefore, the user can limit or generalize the search result by using facets. The selected retrieval results will be visualized in a graph, in which the search results are nodes and the relations between them are edges. This provides the user with a clear overall view of the information structure across the boundaries of individual software applications and organizational units.

4.2 Data Exchange

The conceptual approach for data exchange addresses the problem of transferring data defined in one system deploying a certain source schema to an instance of another system in a target schema [24]. Computer science has been dealing with this problem for quite some time and coming up with context-specific application protocols bundled under the ISO 10303 accompanied by the data modelling language EXPRESS [25]. But due to the increasing number and diversity of the software applications in recent years, the complexity is rising. As well as in the case of data integration, the problem of data exchange arises from the management of data persisted in heterogeneous formats [24].

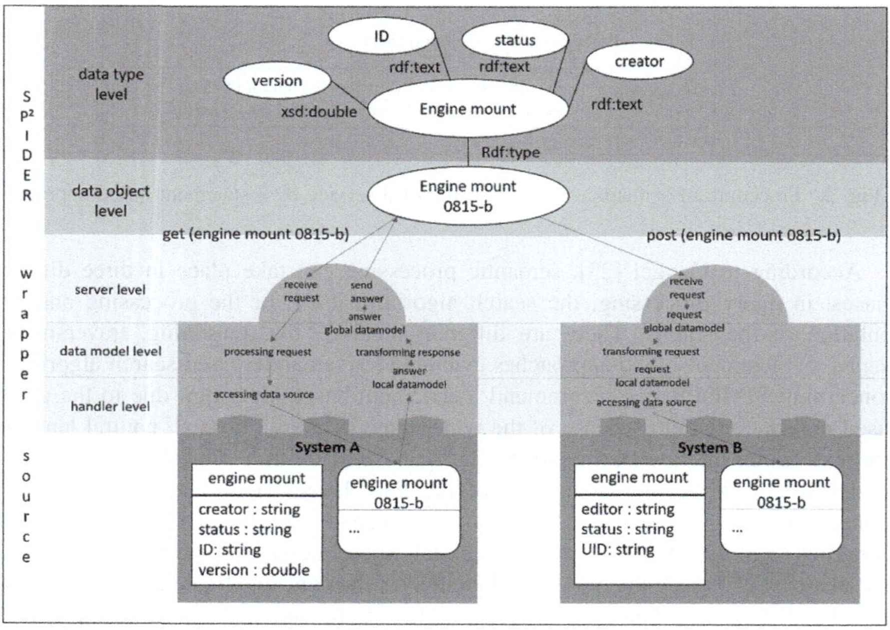

Fig. 3. Procedure of data exchange service between two source systems connected to SP²IDER

In times of digitized engineering processes strongly driven by computer-aided technologies (CAx), data exchange has become dramatically more crucial. The downstream processes require data from the previous steps, associated with a costly, centrally coordinated data provision [10]. A linked engineering data management solution like SP²IDER proves to be a promising technical basis for enabling seamless engineering using a comprehensively controlled data exchange. Since the source and target schemata as well as relationships are known by SP^{2}IDER through the metadata model and CRUD operations are supported by HTTP Protocols and a REST API wrapper on top of the source system, a **data exchange service** is possible without much additional effort.

After a successfully executed information retrieval like described in Sect. 4.1, this service will enable the user to transfer the retrieved data object into an instance of a desired connected source system. A data object can take any form known to SP^{2}IDER. For example, it can be a geometric model from a PLM system as well as a single data set from an SQL database. By using the graph-based metadata model, a compatibility check is carried out to determine whether the selected data object can be transferred to the desired target schema. Therefore, the data type level of the metadata model is used to check whether the corresponding class of the source system instance exists in the target system. If the exchange is possible at the schema layer, the service will check whether a matching instance exists in the target system. In case of matching, the user can decide to update the instance data or not. In the other case, a new instance in the target system is created and the data is transferred. The service therefore will fetch the data using an HTTP get method towards the source system and creates the new instance with an HTTP put method in the target system (see Fig. 3). If the instance already exists and the user confirmed the update, an HTTP post method will be used.

4.3 Data Quality

An important step to master data quality in the long term is measuring and monitoring the data quality to create transparency. Despite its high relevance, it has not yet been possible to find generally applicable and accepted metrics for measuring data quality [26]. Most approaches originate from the Total Data Quality Management by Wang [27] where data quality is considered over the entire life cycle of data. For this purpose, the steps following the Plan-Do-Check-Act cycle of defining, measuring as well as evaluating quality and finally taking appropriate measures for a sustainable increase in quality are continuously carried out.

The complexity and amount of data make an automated checking of the quality necessary. For this reason, we propose a **data quality service**, which will measure data quality by using executable rules. The rules can range from rather simple tasks like checking if values range in an interval to complex mathematical examinations of a simulation result. Depending on the data and use case, the rules can vary significantly, whereby we recommend the six primary dimensions for data quality assessment by the DAMA [28] as a guideline for the rule development. The rules will be embedded into executable processes, which allows the modeling of triggers and subsequent events along with an implementation of the rule logic. The processes will be developed in Business Process Execution Language for Semantic Web Services (BPEL4SWS), which extends BPEL 2.0 by the ability to use semantic information for describing activity implementations [29]. The independence from the interface description thus achieved in conjunction with the data mapped in ontologies will enable semantic reasoning and reusability of the process models. As an appropriate engine, we propose a customized version of the open-source Apache ODE to fit the BEPL4SWS extensions.

Every user, data producer as well as data consumer, can define quality checking rules and associated process within a dedicated development environment. This allows to address the intrinsic interest of the data producer in high-quality results of his work as well as the quality requirements from the perspective of the data consumer. The usage of the XML-based BPEL4SWS for rules and processes facilitates the application of an intuitive, graphical development environment like a customized Eclipse BPEL Designer. The process containing the rule has to be associated with a certain data class and is always executed when an instance of this class is transferred via the service presented in Sect. 4.2. After development, the processes have to be approved and activated by a central reviewing instance.

Whenever the data exchange service sends a get request to a source system, a quality check will be initiated. Therefore, the quality service will determine the class of the instance to be exchanged and cache all rules associated with that class. Subsequently, the cached rules will be executed with the data instance as input and the results will be logged. Finally, a quality report consisting of every executed rule and the corresponding result will be generated. The data consumer thus always will receive a quality report for his data with the help of which he can evaluate the given data quality. As a simple aggregated quality index, the percentage of failed rules will be provided. The user will be able to drill down to single rules and results and browse or filter the report. This transparency enables conscious handling of the data and if needed taking appropriate measures to improve quality in the long term.

5 Use Case Study Including the Semantic Platform Services

The presented IT-service concepts have been applied in the use case scenario introduced in Sect. 2. Supporting the considered use case by the proposed IT services, a significant difference can be noted in retrieving the required data. Instead of searching for data in an unstructured and haphazard way, the engineer uses the information retrieval service, which provides a central user interface to search for data from different source systems (see Fig. 5 step 1).

Figure 4 provides an early graphical user interface mockup of the information retrieval service. According to the search string and the active filters, the data is visualized in the form of a graph, which transparently shows the relation between the concerning project, a single part, and the responsible manager. In the example shown, the engineer is looking for the manager responsible for a component, the engine mount, of the engine 2025 project, e.g. to clarify any detailed questions. This shows the superiority of the semantic search, which determines the concrete engine mount of the project and the corresponding manger using the semantic network within the SP^{2}IDER Metadata Store. Beside the relation, further meta-information for the retrieved data will be given as well as a jump-off point to respective source systems.

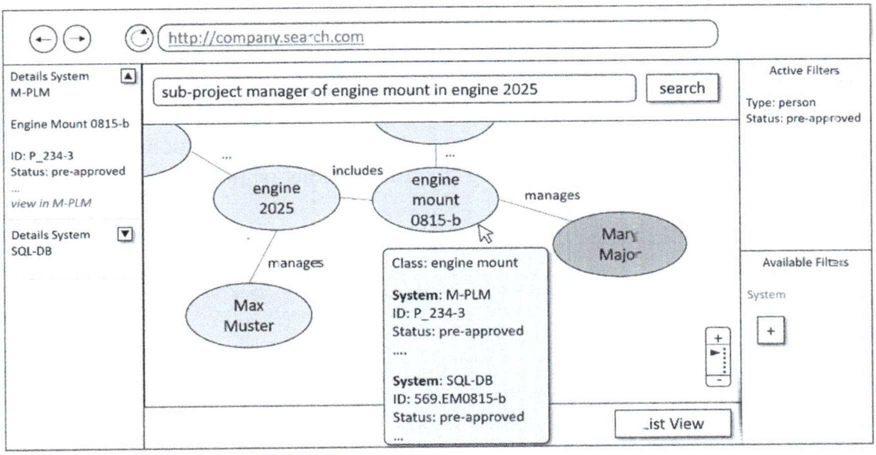

Fig. 4. Mock-up of the information retrieval service

Once the required data has been found, the information retrieval service offers a starting point for the data exchange service. The mass and location of the engine mount required for the simulation were found in the company's M-PLM system. Because both, the M-PLM and the simulation tool, are connected to SP^{2}IDER, the exchange service can transfer data between the systems after a compatibility check is carried out (see Fig. 5 step 2). In the course of this process, the third service automatically checks the data quality. The assigned rules check, for example, whether the stiffness of the engine mount is within a plausible range. The engineer receives a quality report for his data, which contains the executed test rules and the respective test results (see Fig. 5 step 3). It is now up to the engineer to evaluate whether the quality of the data is sufficient for his purpose or not. If there is a sufficient data quality, the model building and simulation run processes can follow. Finally, the models and results are incorporated into an SDM solution. Assuming that the SDM solution is connected to SP^{2}IDER, the data exchange service enables the direct transfer of models and results into the SDM (see Fig. 5 step 4).

With regard to the Linked Engineering Data Management solutions introduced in Sect. 3, we try to assess the performance increase for the engineering process of this use case. The superordinate layer, provided by the metadata model of SP^{2}IDER, provides the necessary foundation for the services presented in this paper. In contrast to commercial solutions, SP^{2}IDER offers a flexible open-source platform that enables easy connection of source systems throughout the entire product life cycle as well as the development of further specialized services if needed. In contrast, completely decentralized approaches do not have this superordinate layer and therefore do no provide the knowledge base needed for services like the information retrieval. The services themselves promise to significantly shorten process runtimes and at the same time create a consistent quality standard through transparency and documentation. The time required to gather information will be shortened by the information retrieval service. Furthermore, a largely independence from individual knowledge carriers in the information retrieval will be achieved. The data exchange service reduces the manual steps for data exchange to a minimum and thus reduces potential sources of error. In addition, the data quality service reveals quality problems in the data at an early stage in the process and documents the present quality. Thus, it is possible to take measures in time and avoid carrying problems further down the process, which in turn leads to the repetition of larger, time-consuming process sections or poor decisions.

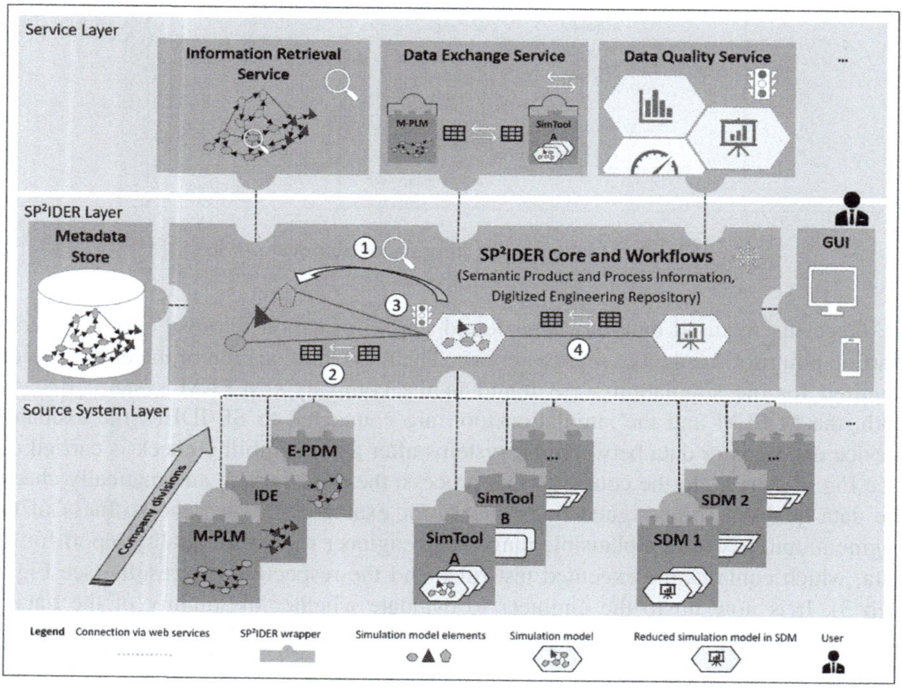

Fig. 5. The SP^{2}IDER system architecture with semantic platform services

6 Conclusion

To enable semantic engineering management IT services are introduced. Based on a linked engineering data management solution like SP^{2}IDER, we designed three IT services as a conceptual solution. A semantic search service allows the retrieval of information scattered through many software applications and departments. Based on this, a second service enables the exchange of data across the boundaries of individual applications. Using a data quality service, data quality can be measured and monitored, and thus more transparency is achieved.

The potential of such a combined solution of a linked engineering data management and IT services is huge, as the need for findable high-quality data spreads all over the product life cycle. Potential use case scenarios include e.g. engineering change management. With the help of SP^{2}IDER and connected IT services, the impacts of a design change can easily be traced into downstream processes. Engineers can find change-affected items at an early stage and trigger the necessary adjustments allowing simultaneous engineering and shorter lead times. Especially disruptive and unpredictable changes from external triggers require a solid knowledge base concerning product and process information for an effective collaboration even in heavily fragmented and decentralized engineering activities. Another possible scenario is the development of a new product. Hence many new product development projects are based on previous product generations, SP^{2}IDER and the connected IT services allow for the search of life cycle data from previous product generations, saved inter alia in so-called digital twins. This enables the engineers to learn from data and adjust their designs accordingly. During the new product development, engineers can use a platform like SP^{2}IDER and the connected IT services to gather the necessary information for the initial configuration of a digital twin (see [30]).

References

1. Abramovici, M., Herzog, O. (eds.): Engineering im Umfeld von Industrie 4.0. Einschätzungen und Handlungsbedarf. Acatech Studie. Herbert Utz Verlag GmbH; acatech, München (2016)
2. Bruno, G., Villa, A.: The exploitation of an ontology-based model of PLM from a SME point of view. IFAC Proc. Vol. (2013). https://doi.org/10.3182/20130619-3-RU-3018.00141
3. Eickhoff, T., Eiden, A., Göbel, J.C., Eigner, M.: A metadata repository for semantic product lifecycle management. Procedia CIRP **91**, 249–254 (2020)
4. Acél, P.P.: Methode zur Durchführung betrieblicher Simulationen: effiziente Optimierung der diskreten Simulation, ETH Zurich (1996)
5. Zeller, P.: Handbuch Fahrzeugakustik. Grundlagen, Auslegung, Berechnung, Versuch, 2nd edn. ATZ/MTZ-Fachbuch. Springer, Wiesbaden (2012). https://doi.org/10.1007/978-3-8348-8657-6
6. Ruschmeyer, S.: Herausforderungen bei der NVH-Entwicklung von Hybrid- und Elektrofahrzeugen. In: Möser, M., Schulte-Fortkamp, B., Ochmann, M. (eds.) Fortschritte der Akustik. 36. Deutsche Jahrestagung für Akustik, 15. bis 18. März 2010 in Berlin, pp. 319–320. Deutsche Gesellschaft für Akustik e.V, Berlin (2010)
7. Graf, B., Brandl, S., Rust, A.: Vehicle NVH optimization by interdisciplinary drivetrain development. ATZextra Worldw (2016). https://doi.org/10.1007/s40111-016-0011-3
8. Robinson, M.A.: An empirical analysis of engineers' information behaviors. J. Am. Soc. Inf. Sci. (2010). https://doi.org/10.1002/asi.21290
9. Skoogh, A., Perera, T., Johansson, B.: Input data management in simulation – industrial practices and future trends. Simul. Model. Pract. Theory (2012). https://doi.org/10.1016/j.simpat.2012.07.009
10. Zimmer, M.: Durchgängiger Simulationsprozess zur Effizienzsteigerung und Reifegraderhöhung von Konzeptbewertungen in der Frühen Phase der Produktentstehung. Springer, Wiesbaden (2015). https://doi.org/10.1007/978-3-658-11500-5
11. Lentes, J., Eckstein, H., Zimmermann, N.: A platform to integrate manufacturing engineering and product lifecycle management. IFAC Proc. Vol. (2012). https://doi.org/10.3182/20120523-3-RO-2023.00425

12. Schuh, G., Dölle, C., Schmitz, S., Koch, J., Höding, M., Menges, A.: Data-based determination of the product-oriented complexity degree. Procedia CIRP (2018). https://doi.org/10.1016/j.procir.2018.03.293
13. Matsas, M., Pintzos, G., Kapnia, A., Mourtzis, D.: An integrated collaborative platform for managing product-service across their life cycle. Procedia CIRP (2017). https://doi.org/10.1016/j.procir.2016.09.009
14. Bajaj, M., et al.: Graph-based digital blueprint for model based engineering of complex systems. In: INCOSE International Symposium (2017). https://doi.org/10.1002/j.2334-5837.2017.00351.x
15. Sinha, A.K., Weaver, M., Morgan, S.G.: Visualising, analysing, and managing the design factory. In: Volume 3: Engineering Systems; Heat Transfer and Thermal Engineering; Materials and Tribology; Mechatronics; Robotics. ASME 2014 12th Biennial Conference on Engineering Systems Design and Analysis, Copenhagen, Denmark, 25 July 2014–27 July 2014. American Society of Mechanical Engineers (07252014). https://doi.org/10.1115/ESDA2014-20393
16. Abramovici, M., Göbel, J.C., Dang, H.B.: Semantic data management for the development and continuous reconfiguration of smart products and systems. CIRP Ann. (2016). https://doi.org/10.1016/j.cirp.2016.04.051
17. Johnson, D., Speicher, S.: Open Services for Lifecycle Collaboration Core Specification Version 2.0 (2013). https://archive.open-services.net/bin/view/Main/OslcCoreSpecification.html. Accessed 5 Mar 2020
18. Schreiber, G., Raimond, Y.: RDF 1.1 Primer (2014). https://www.w3.org/TR/rdf-primer/. Accessed 28 Mar 2020
19. Senington, R., Baumeister, F., Ng, A., Oscarsson, J.: A linked data approach for the connection of manufacturing processes with production simulation models. Procedia CIRP (2018). https://doi.org/10.1016/j.procir.2018.03.243
20. Franke, M., Klein, K., Thoben, K.-D.: Interoperable information exchange as enabler of NFF related TES. Procedia CIRP (2017). https://doi.org/10.1016/j.procir.2016.08.037
21. Oks, S.J., Jalowski, M., Fritzsche, A., Möslein, K.M.: Cyber-physical modeling and simulation: a reference architecture for designing demonstrators for industrial cyber-physical systems. Procedia CIRP (2019). https://doi.org/10.1016/j.procir.2019.04.239
22. Yao, Y., Lin, L., Dong, J.: Research on ontology-based multi-source engineering information retrieval in integrated environment of enterprise. In: 2009 International Conference on Interoperability for Enterprise Software and Applications China. 2009 International Conference on Interoperability for Enterprise Software and Applications China (IESA), Beijing, China, 21 April 2009–22 April 2009, pp. 277–282. IEEE (2009). https://doi.org/10.1109/I-ESA.2009.25
23. Dengel, A.: Semantische Technologien. Spektrum Akademischer Verlag, Heidelberg (2012). https://doi.org/10.1007/978-3-8274-2664-2
24. Fagin, R., Kolaitis, P.G., Miller, R.J., Popa, L.: Data exchange: semantics and query answering. Theor. Comput. Sci. (2005). https://doi.org/10.1016/j.tcs.2004.10.033
25. ISO: Industrial automation systems and integration — Product data representation and exchange. Part 11: Description methods: The EXPRESS language reference manual (ISO 10303-11:2004) (2004). https://www.iso.org/standard/38047.html
26. Ehrlinger, L., Rusz, E., Wöß, W.: A survey of data quality measurement and monitoring tools (2019). http://arxiv.org/pdf/1907.08138v1
27. Wang, R.Y., Kon, H.B.: Toward total data quality management (TDQM). In: Information Technology in Action: Trends and Perspectives, pp. 179–197 (1993)
28. Henderson, D., Earley, S. (eds.): DAMA-DMBOK. Data Management Body of Knowledge. Technics Publications, Basking Ridge, New Jersey (2017)

29. Nitzsche, J., van Lessen, T., Karastoyanova, D., Leymann, F.: BPEL for semantic web services (BPEL4SWS). In: Meersman, R., Tari, Z., Herrero, P. (eds.) OTM 2007. LNCS, vol. 4805, pp. 179–188. Springer, Heidelberg (2007). https://doi.org/10.1007/978-3-540-76888-3_37
30. Göbel, J.C., Eickhoff, T.: Konzeption von Digitalen Zwillingen smarter Produkte. ZWF - Zeitschrift für den wirtschaftlichen Fabrikbetrieb (2020)

Ontology Matching for Product Lifecycle Management

Alexander Smirnov(✉) and Nikolay Teslya

SPIIRAS, 14th Line 39, 199178 St. Petersburg, Russia
{smir, teslya}@iias.spb.su

Abstract. Every product goes through many stages of the life cycle from manufacturing through usage to utilization. Some stages can change its properties, which in turn changes its description. To describe the product and its life cycle many ontologies have been created with varying levels of detail. Ontologies usage at different product lifecycle management (PLM) stages provides a better match to these stages since they provide properties of the product important only for this stage. During the transition between stages, the data should be integrated across all systems in manufacturing domain to provide semantic interoperability. Therefore, an issue arises of matching descriptions presented with ontologies of lifecycle stages. This is especially critical if ontologies for different stages are created by various specialists (for example, designer, technology engineer, retailer, maintainer, etc.). The paper proposes the method of matching ontologies for the formation of a common PLM ontology based on the automatic matching of ontologies referred to PLM stages. It allows to overcome heterogeneity and ensure interoperability in the process of tracking the product through the PLM stages. The matching process is based on the identification of common concepts by which ontologies will be combined into one. To identify common concepts, the ontology matching method is used, based on a combination of a context-based matching with neural network to find similarities of concepts (name, characteristics names and their string values) and study the ontology structure to identify common design patterns.

Keywords: Product · Ontology · Alignment · Lifecycle · Matching · Heterogeneity

1 Introduction

Most of knowledge management systems for the production network provide ontology-based description of products and lifecycle stages for semantic-based operability between participants on the various stages [1]. The management of product lifecycle can be viewed in two possible directions: based on product instances or product types lifecycles [2]. For the first direction the main attention is paid to product items that can be produced, used and recycled. The second direction corresponds to the product development process. In this work the main focus will be concentrated on the first direction – product instances.

Published by Springer Nature Switzerland AG 2020
F. Nyffenegger et al. (Eds.): PLM 2020, IFIP AICT 594, pp. 256–269, 2020.
https://doi.org/10.1007/978-3-030-62807-9_21

Every product goes through many stages of the lifecycle from planning and producing through usage to utilization or recycling. Some stages can change its properties, which in turn changes its description. However, the data should be integrated across all systems in manufacturing domain. Production network as well as management systems have to be scalable and adaptable for their environment changes and variability of participants' knowledge. A method of ontology matching for participants of the production network has to be developed to automate matching of the ontologies of several participants for their interoperability. It allows to increase efficiency of the future interaction during joint operational management in product lifecycle.

During the product transition between lifecycle stages, the issue arises of matching descriptions presented with ontologies and the transferring of product properties between stages. This is especially critical if ontologies for different stages are created by various specialists (for example, designer, technology engineer, retailer, maintainer, etc.).

For supporting production network scalability and adaptability to changes in business environment the paper proposes an original method of ontology matching. Method is based on the combination of several matching strategies:

- Pattern-based matching. For the patterns the ontology design patterns are used.
- Context-based matching (including neural network usage [3]). The context of ontology concept includes neighboring concepts, relation types, semantic of concept term.
- Community-driven matching. To increase accuracy and quality of matching experts can be involved. They provide expertise on the stages of product lifecycle to find better correlations between product ontology and stage ontology.

This combination provides analysis on ontology concepts from the various points of view. Usage of multiple matchers is widely spread practice [4, 5]. The main advantages of such kind of approach is that it allows to take into account various aspects of ontology concept's semantics and increase accuracy of matching.

The rest of the paper is structured as follows. Section 2 provides overview of ontology matching methods, using for product lifecycle management. Section 3 provides architecture description of proposed matching method. Section 4 describes implementation from the technologies point of view. Section 5 shows an evaluation using the example of ontologies from the same project on the different

2 Overview of Ontology Matching for Product Lifecycle Management

In developing ontologies for managing the product life cycle, various techniques are used. As a rule, for each stage of the life cycle, its own ontology is developed that most fully describes the characteristics of the product that are important in this cycle. These private ontologies are designed by experts using top-level ontologies and using design patterns. To ensure the knowledge sharing between the stages of the life cycle in this case, the use of a mechanism for ontology matching is required. The purpose of this mechanism is to identify concepts that are common to different ontologies and to align or merge ontologies into one large ontology, based on general concepts.

Another technique is the formation of a large ontology, which describes the product at several or all stages of the life cycle [6, 7]. This approach requires combining knowledge from different problem domains and their reduction into a common knowledge base. This process is carried out by experts. In fact, experts manually or semi-automatically apply methods for ontology matching to form a common ontology from private ones. The quality of the alignment using this technique is higher due to the use of experience and implicit knowledge of experts in the subject area.

Automation of the process of creating and matching ontologies in both cases is possible using ontology matching methods. These methods are specially designed to identify concepts that are of similar meaning in different ontologies. The basis for matching may be the semantic meaning of terms describing ontologies, their context, the structure of the concept (general characteristics and domains of the value of characteristics), the structure of the ontology. In this regard, in the classification of methods, several groups are identified that correspond to the parameters on the basis of which a comparison is made [8]. Of this work, of all the available classes, context-based, pattern-based and community-based techniques are of particular interest.

While using the context-based ontology matching the relation between ontology with its environment is used [9]. This environment can be upper level ontology that is using as an external source of common knowledge about concepts of matching ontologies, as well as a problem area [10]. Also, the semantics of concept can be utilized for estimating concept similarity. It can be done by dictionaries, like WordNet that can compare concept by their meaning, or by neural networks [11]. Two approaches are existing on neural network utilization for ontology matching. The first one is a classification of ontology concept that allows to find similar concept based on the neural network training to classify concept between ontologies based on the set of parameters, i.e., characteristics, relations, and terms [12, 13]. The second approach is based on the linguistic analysis of concepts within the vector model of language. The vector model can be based on Word2Vec [14, 15] or BERT model [16]. It reflects the word meaning by concept vector. Words that describes similar concepts are described by vectors that are close to each other in vector space. It can be used in ontology matching by additional training the existing models on ontology concepts and further estimation of similarities between ontology concepts.

Using design patterns when creating an ontology can also help with their subsequent comparison. The ontology design patterns are meant as aligned groups of linked ontology concepts (ontology fragments) [6, 17, 18]. These patterns are used as templates to create ontologies describing similar concepts. Patterns can relate to separate connection of classes (relations between concepts) and classes with their relation, or to complex interconnection of classes, etc. When a pattern is detected in different ontologies, it can be stated with a high degree of certainty that concepts corresponding to the pattern will have similar meaning in ontologies.

When using the first two techniques, situations are possible where the algorithm cannot determine with high certainty the similarity of ontology concepts. In this case, the best way is to contact the experts to resolve the ambiguous situation. For each problem area the community of professionals is forming from the employees of production network participants [19]. They have different roles and competences that allows to engage experts of problem area to ontology matching process. It also allows to share alignment through the network, discuss it and reusing. All of that allows to increase alignment completeness and quality, but requires significant time consuming from the side of community members.

Professional community also resolves controversial situations that raises when alignment coefficient belongs to the controversial range. Recommendation of the professional community provides adjusting of the alignment coefficients ranges boundaries, creating of the new matching patterns or modification (adaptation, adjustment) of existing matching patterns.

3 Architecture of Ontology Matching for PLM

The proposed ontology matching method includes the following main steps.

1. The ontologies of problem domains are formed from the ontologies of production network and its' participants that have to be matched. Problem domain ontologies include abstract and operational contexts which are structure of domain and current situation correspondingly [20, 21].
2. Specific problem domains are defined using the abstract context. Problem domain defines set of ontology designing patterns that can be used in matching process in it. The result of pattern-based matching is a matrix containing align coefficients of ontologies concepts.
3. The context-based matching of operational context ontology models is performing. During the context-based matching, the instances of ontology concepts are matching. The result is matrixes that contain align coefficients of concept instances. The results are using to clarify coefficients in ontologies alignment matrix. For example, the value of align coefficient can be increased in the case of the value of align coefficient of concept instances is higher that the value of concept alignment coefficient.
4. Checking of the alignment coefficients is performed for each problem area. For this purpose, the values ranges are used. The ranges define are separate concepts aligned, not aligned or controversial. Concepts are controversial if the alignment cannot be defined automatically. Range boundaries are set by experts with highest ratings among users with similar roles from the professional community before the matching process.

To provide semantic interoperability between the entities of product lifecycle management system it is proposed to develop a special method for ontology matching. Architecture of the method is presented on the Fig. 1. It describes required modules and links between them to provide the ontology matching.

Architecture can be conditionally divided into three major components related to the ontology matching in the product lifecycle management system. The first one is related to the entities of the system, which needs to have support for semantic interoperability. Also, among these entities there are a *community of experts* who participate in the process of ontologies matching, providing their knowledge and experience to adjust the alignment obtained automatically. The entity of the system that request semantic interoperability support provides ontologies in form of OWL and the corresponding context to the *ontology matching method.*

The received ontologies and context are divided into abstract and operational contexts in the ontology matching method, according to the approach described in the previous section. Abstract contexts are matched in the module *"Patter-based matcher"*, which uses background knowledge in form of ontology design and correspondence patterns from public *pattern libraries*. Operational contexts are used in the *"Context-based matcher"*, which, in addition to ontologies' own context, refers to sources of background knowledge for additional information while calculating the correspondence. These sources are upper level ontologies and lexical databases.

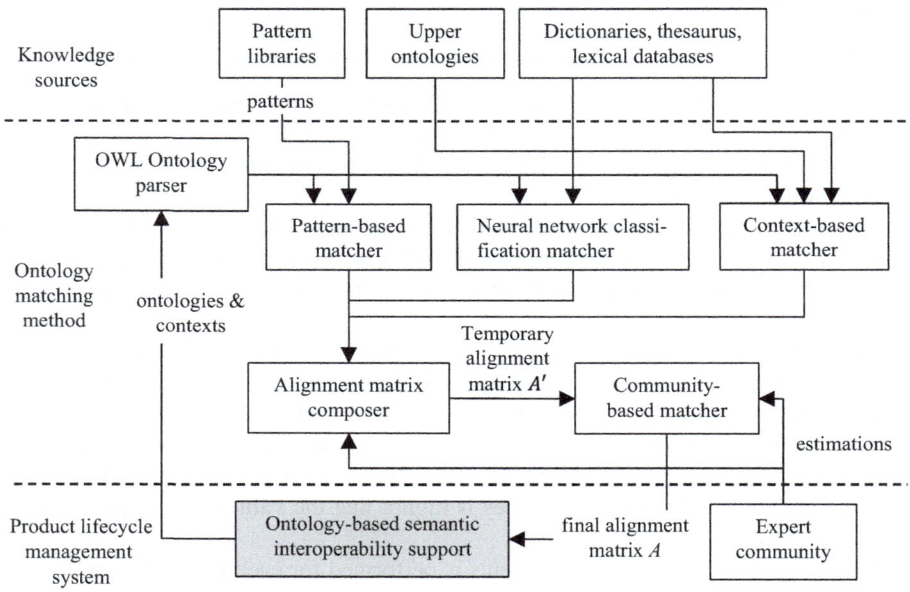

Fig. 1. Architecture of ontology matching method for product lifecycle management system

Also, ontology concepts are transferred to the input of the neural network, where the training and further classification is carried out. The results of the work of all matchers are combined according to the formula (1) in the module *"Alignment matrix composer"*. The intermediate result of the matching (temporary alignment matrix A') is transferred to the *"Community-based matcher"*, where it can be adjusted by the community of experts that are part of the product lifecycle management system. Decisions of experts can also influence to the work of *"Alignment matrix composer"*, by changing the coefficients in formula (1). The result is transferred to the entity of the product lifecycle management system, which initiated the process of ontology matching.

3.1 Context-Based Matching

When considering comparisons based on contextual information, two stages are distinguished. The first stage involves comparing the names of ontology concepts and is based on the fuzzy string comparison algorithm presented in [22]. The result of this comparison is the matrix $A_{context}$, which contains similarity coefficients of ontology concepts, among which are concepts that exceed the lower threshold of concept comparison $b_1 = 0.6$, at which concepts can still be considered coincident. The rows of the matrix correspond to the concepts of ontology O_1, and the columns correspond to the concepts of ontology O_2.

The upper threshold, $b_2 = 0.9$, defines the boundary above which the concepts are considered to coincide. Pairs of concepts for which the similarity coefficient falls into the interval $[b_1, b_2]$ are transferred to the community for a final decision. The thresholds values b_1, b_2 can be defined manually by expert who match ontologies, or automatically based on the analysis of average values from be other matching cases from the problem domain.

The second stage of contextual matching is comparing concept instances. Here we will consider instances for fragments of ontologies limited by the classes organization (company), product, consumer (customer), supplier, process.

To compare operational contexts, the measure of inclusion of sets composed of instances of ontology concepts is analyzed. Each individual set includes instances of a separate concept. The inclusion measure is asymmetric and shows to what extent one set is included in another and vice versa. In this paper, the following measures of inclusion is used.

$$K(A, B) = \frac{n(A \cap B)}{n(A)} \tag{1}$$

$$K(B, A) = \frac{n(A \cap B)}{n(B)}, \tag{2}$$

corresponding to a symmetric measure of Sørensen similarity [23] (the latter is obtained by averaging the presented asymmetric measures), where A and B are the sets under consideration. To determine the same elements of a set, the fuzzy string comparison method used earlier to compare the names of concepts is used. We compare the elements of one set with the elements of another set using the fuzzy string comparison algorithm, summarize the results and divide by the number of elements in the first set. Repeat the procedure for the second set. We choose the maximum of two measures:

$$\mathrm{k} = \max(K(A, B), K(B, A)). \tag{3}$$

3.2 Neural Network for Concept Matching

In the proposed approach the neural network is used to analyze ontology concepts and cross-search for similar concepts in matching ontologies. The network is based on the

Word2Vec model and uses pre-trained English language model. The neural network consists of three layers: the input, the hidden and the output layer. The input layer corresponds to the dimension of the word vector in Word2Vec model. The hidden layer of the neural network stores a vector model of titles, and can be represented by a matrix of size [m; n], where m is the number of words in the model dictionary, and n is the size of the word vector. The dimension of the output layer corresponds to the size of the dictionary. The neurons of this layer implement the sigmoid activation function [24], which activates neurons depending on the value of the vector in hidden layer. Neurons with the maximum value of the activation function will contain the names of the concepts that are as close as possible to the provided vector of the ontology concept.

Neural network can be trained with any pre-cleaned text corpora. Text can be obtained from encyclopedias articles, electronic libraries, and news or messages archives. A previously trained word model can be used instead of training. It can be general model of language or specific model for a problem area of the ontologies under consideration. The model used can be further trained on the context of ontology concepts (neighboring concepts, relationships between concepts, characteristics of concepts), to provide better reflection of the semantics for a specific ontology.

The method accepts the ontologies in the OWL format and returns the result as an alignment matrix for ontology concepts A. The basic scheme of the method includes use of entities labels and the context of the concepts of these ontologies (see Fig. 2).

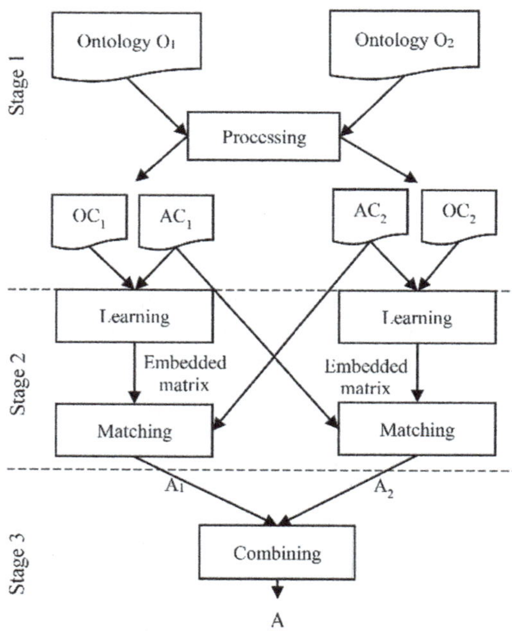

Fig. 2. Ontology matching scheme with neural network

The work of the method can be divided into three stages: processing of input ontologies; the mapping of processed ontologies; the composition of intermediate correspondence matrices. During the processing if input ontologies, abstract (AC_1, AC_2) and operational (OC_1, OC_2) contexts are identified, as well as the problem area of each ontology is extracted. The mapping is based on methods using matching patterns and concept contexts takes place. Through the composition the final matrix is forming, which is the result of the work of the ontology matching method.

3.3 Pattern-Based Matching

The proposed approach allows using the ontology design patterns to identify matching classes. It is assumed that the coincidence of classes and relations between them, according to the provided pattern, indicates the coincidence of specific instances of the concept class. The pattern can be selected from existing pattern libraries, for example, W3C, the ontologydesingpatterns.org portal and the Manchester ODP catalog according to the criteria for matching the problem area of the ontologies under consideration or specified by the community. It is proposed to search for a pattern in each ontology based on the method proposed in the article [22]. To obtain a result, a complete ontology fragment must be fully consistent with the presented pattern. The example of patter in presented on Fig. 3. This pattern can be used to describe relations between customer and supplier, that are actors, where supplier provides prerequisite and basis for creating product that further is utilized by customer.

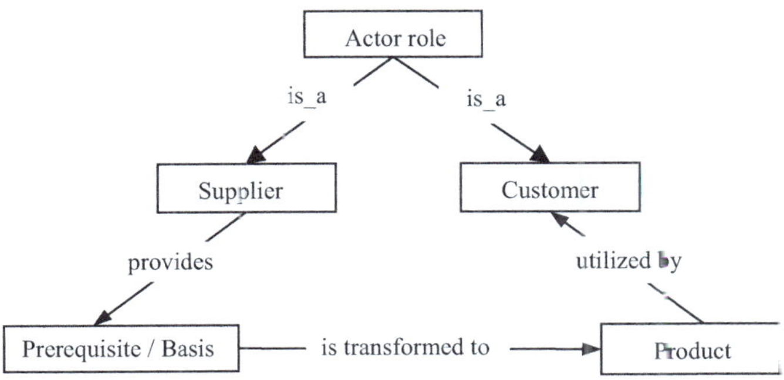

Fig. 3. Example of a pattern

The matrix A_{patt} of pattern-based concept correspondence contains unambiguous correspondences between ontology classes that correspond to a given pattern. This result can be used to obtain the final comparison matrix. To do this, it is necessary to select from the matrix A_{patt} the submatrix A^2_{patt} (it is believed that the dimension of the correspondence matrix for the template cannot exceed the dimension of the correspondence matrix for the context method), the matrix $A_{context}$ corresponding in dimension and the rows and columns included in it, and apply the composition function

$$A' = f\left(A_{\text{context}}, A^*_{\text{patt}}\right) = \alpha_1 A_{\text{conntext}} + \alpha_2 A^*_{\text{patt}}, \quad (4)$$

where $\alpha_1, \alpha_2, \sum_{i=1,2} \alpha_i = 1$ are weight coefficients that allow changing the effect of the intermediate results of each of the comparison methods (based on the use of ontology templates and based on the analysis of the context of concepts) on the final result. Subsequently, the matrix A' is combined with the matrix A_{patt} with the replacement of the elements in the corresponding rows and columns and we obtain the final matrix A containing the ontology matching model.

3.4 Community-Based Matching

For elements of the matrix A', threshold values b_1, b_2 are defined that define sets corresponding to three similarity states of the concepts o_1, o_2 of the ontologies O_1 and O_2, respectively.

$$f\left(o_{1i}, o_{2j}\right) = \begin{cases} 0, a'_{ij} \in [0, b1) - \textit{merging not found} \\ 0.5, a'_{ij} \in [b_1, b_2] - \textit{merging questionable} \\ 1, a'_{ij} \in [b_2, 1] - \textit{merging found} \end{cases}$$

A couple of concepts for which the value of the function $f\left(o_{1i}, o_{2j}\right) = 0.5$ are sent for analysis to a community made up of experts - employees of the organization who are specialists in the problem domain to which the ontology belongs. Experts make the final decision in determining which of the ontology concepts are similar. In addition to working with specific pairs of concepts, experts can change threshold values b_1, b_2 and edit the templates used.

4 Implementation

To verify the proposed method, two ontologies were used that describe the process of creating and maintaining a product in different companies (Fig. 4 and Fig. 5). When organizing a joint production cycle, organizations should exchange knowledge about the product life cycle, each providing information based on its own ontology. Accordingly, for the organization of interaction, life cycle ontologies for organizations should be compared.

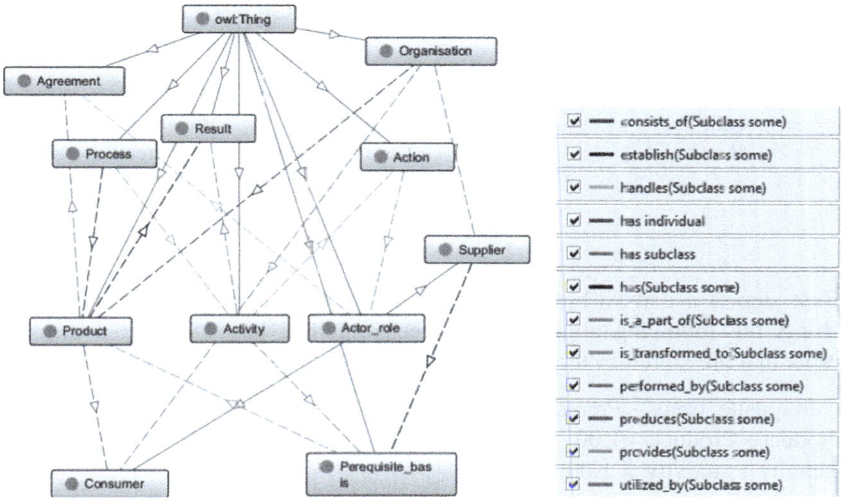

Fig. 4. Example ontology O_1

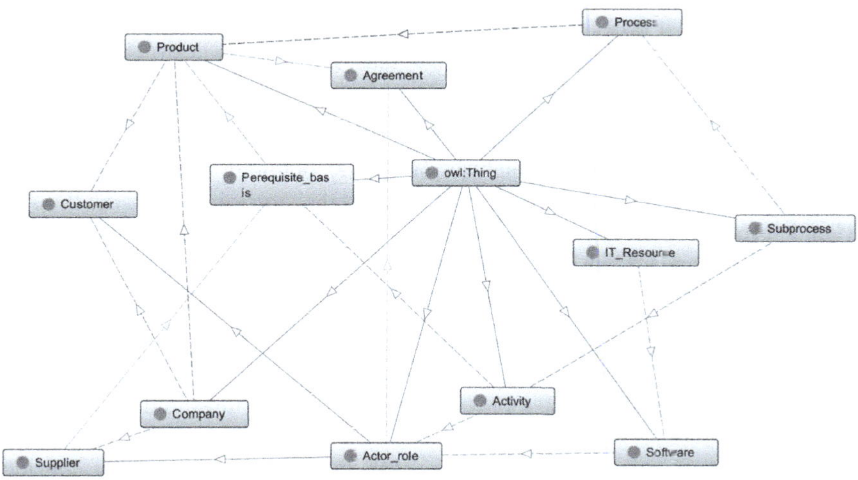

Fig. 5. Example ontology O_2

These ontologies have been initialized with the following instances of concepts (see Table 1 and Table 2). These operational contexts correspond to supply chain of three companies for car manufacturing. The first one, OC includes O_1 ontology concepts instances for supplying products for consumers. Two last (OC_1 and OC_2) are based on the same ontology O_2 and describe processes that corresponds to product creation in companies.

Table 1. Examples of OC instances for fragment of O_1 ontology

OC			
Organization	Consumer	Product	Supplier
Lear Bosch	GM Volvo Volkswagen Subaru	Seating Car multimedia Steering system	WeSupply DataStream

First step is a context-based matching of ontology concept. After performing a matching, the following alignment has been obtained based on the names of the concepts that are stored in the matrix $A_{context}$:

- Prerequisite_basis – Prerequisite_basis = 1.00
- Product - Product = 1.00
- Activity - Activity = 1.00
- Actor role - Actor role = 1.00
- Agreement - Agreement = 1.00
- Supplier - Supplier = 1.00
- Process - Process = 1.00
- Thing - Thing = 1.00
- Process concepts - Subprocess = 0.76 => must be shared with the community.

According to pattern-based matching the following results was obtained. In the O_2 ontology, a complete match is found for the presented P pattern, including the connections between the concepts. Analysis of the O_1 ontology for matching with the P pattern allows us to determine the coincidence of the structure and, using the "Actor role" and "Product" concepts common to both ontologies, to assume the coincidence of the "Customer" and "Consumer" concepts, which ultimately gives the diagonal alignment matrix A_{patt}. So, the result is as follows:

- Company (1) - Organization: $k = 1$ (full match)
- Company (2) - Organization: $k = 1$ (match)
- Customer (1) - Consumer: $k = 0.5$ (less than the lower threshold, not considered further)
- Customer (2) - Consumer: $k = 0.5$ (less than the lower threshold, not considered further)

Table 2. Examples of OC_1 and OC_2 instances for fragment of O_2 ontology

OC_1			
Company	Customer	Product	Process
Lear	Ford Toyota GM Volvo BMW Nissan Porsche	Seating Interior trim Electrical power management system	Production
OC_2			
Company	Customer	Product	Process
Bosch	Volkswagen BMW Ford Toyota Porsche Subaru	Gasoline system Diesel system Electrical drive Starter motor Generator Car multimedia Steering system	Production Design Research

As a result, a coincidence of ontology concepts was found, the coincidence of which was not revealed by other methods: Company and Organization, which is entered into the intermediate alignment matrix A_{patt}.

Moreover, the measure of inclusion defined for Customer - Consumer exceeds the value of the similarity coefficient in the matrix A_{patt} for the corresponding concepts, which indicates the need to increase the similarity coefficient in the matrix A_{patt} to 0.5, based on the similarity of operational concepts for the concepts.

The result of context-based and community-based alignment is combined using the Eq. (4). For the given example, the coefficients $\alpha_1 = \alpha_2 = 0.5$, which means the equal contribution of each of the methods to the result of the comparison.

Alignment matrix A' is evaluated by the following threshold values: $b_1 = 0.6, b_2 = 0.9$. The interval $[b_1, b_2]$ includes pairs of concepts:

- Process - Subprocess = 0.76
- Consumer - Customer = 0.75

These pairs should be analyzed by the community, after which a joint decision is made whether the concepts under consideration coincide and a matrix A is formed from the matrix A', containing coefficients only for the matching concepts.

5 Conclusion

One of the ways to support semantic-based interoperability in a product lifecycle management system is the ontology management technology. Development of efficient methods of ontology matching could significantly improve the knowledge processing and interoperability between various stages of production.

To utilize ontology matching in product lifecycle management system an approach has been proposed that combines four models of ontology matching: pattern-based, context-based, neural network based on natural language model, and community-driven matching. The results from first three methods are composed to temporal alignment matrix that is adjusted by experts of production lifecycle.

The architecture of service for ontology matching method has been also proposed in the paper. The architecture allows to combine various modules for ontology matching by adding or removing any of them and adjusting the function that calculates the temporal alignment matrix. The usage of community-based matcher after the automated matching allows to utilize knowledge and experience of the product lifecycle management system's experts if autonomous matchers cannot find correspondences for the problem domain. It is expected that community-based matcher will be used in the cases of strong uncertainty, when the most of alignment coefficients calculated by autonomous matchers will belong to the ranges of ambiguous alignment coefficient values.

The future work will be aimed on studying of method appropriateness for industrial practice for close integration of a new supplier or new stage to the product lifecycle. More of real cases will be gathered and tested in order to estimate performance and accuracy of the proposed method.

Acknowledgments. The reported study was funded by RFBR, project number 20-07-00904 for Sect. 3 of ontology matching methods and by Russian State Research No. 0073-2019-0005 in the other sections.

References

1. Mohd Ali, M., Rai, R., Otte, J.N., Smith, B.: A product life cycle ontology for additive manufacturing. Comput. Ind. **105**, 191–203 (2019). https://doi.org/10.1016/j.compind.2018.12.007
2. Nyffenegger, F., Hänggi, R., Reisch, A.: A reference model for PLM in the area of digitization. In: Chiabert, P., Bouras, A., Noël, F., Ríos, J. (eds.) PLM 2018. IAICT, vol. 540, pp. 358–366. Springer, Cham (2018). https://doi.org/10.1007/978-3-030-01614-2_33
3. Teslya, N., Savosin, S.: Matching ontologies with Word2Vec-based neural network. In: Misra, S., et al. (eds.) ICCSA 2019. LNCS, vol. 11619, pp. 745–756. Springer, Cham (2019). https://doi.org/10.1007/978-3-030-24289-3_55
4. Otero-Cerdeira, L., Rodríguez-Martínez, F.J., Gómez-Rodríguez, A.: Ontology matching: a literature review. Expert Syst. Appl. **42**, 949–971 (2015). https://doi.org/10.1016/j.eswa.2014.08.032
5. Ngo, D., Bellahsene, Z.: YAM ++: a multi-strategy based approach for ontology matching task. In: ten Teije, A., et al. (eds.) EKAW 2012. LNCS (LNAI), vol. 7603, pp. 421–425. Springer, Heidelberg (2012). https://doi.org/10.1007/978-3-642-33876-2_38
6. Schönteich, F., Kasten, A., Scherp, A.: A pattern-based core ontology for product lifecycle management based on DUL. In: CEUR Workshop Proceedings, pp. 92–106 (2018)
7. Bruno, G., Antonelli, D., Villa, A.: A reference ontology to support product lifecycle management. Procedia CIRP **33**, 41–46 (2015). https://doi.org/10.1016/j.procir.2015.06.009
8. Euzenat, J., Shvaiko, P. (eds.): Ontology Matching. Springer, Heidelberg (2013). https://doi.org/10.1007/978-3-642-38721-0_13

9. Raad, E., Evermann, J.: The role of analogy in ontology alignment: a study on LISA. Cogn. Syst. Res. **33**, 1–16 (2015). https://doi.org/10.1016/j.cogsys.2014.09.001
10. Hecht, T., Buche, P., Dibie, J., Ibanescu, L., dos Santos, C.T.: Ontology alignment using web linked ontologies as background knowledge. In: Guillet, F., Pinaud, B., Venturini, G. (eds.) Advances in Knowledge Discovery and Management. SCI, vol. 665, pp. 207–227. Springer, Cham (2017). https://doi.org/10.1007/978-3-319-45763-5_11
11. Lin, F., Sandkuhl, K.: A survey of exploiting WordNet in ontology matching. In: Bramer, M. (ed.) IFIP AI 2008. ITIFIP, vol. 276, pp. 341–350. Springer, Boston, MA (2008). https://doi.org/10.1007/978-0-387-09695-7_33
12. Manjula Shenoy, K., Shet, K.C., Dinesh Acharya, U.: NN based ontology mapping. In: Das, V.V., Chaba, Y. (eds.) Mobile Communication and Power Engineering. CCIS, vol. 296, pp. 122–127. Springer, Heidelberg (2013). https://doi.org/10.1007/978-3-642-35864-7_18
13. Ganesh Kumar, S., Vivekanandan, K.: Odmm - an ontology based deep mining method to cluster the content from web servers. J. Theor. Appl. Inf. Technol. **74**, 162–170 (2015)
14. Jayawardana, V., Lakmal, D., De Silva, N., Perera, A.S., Sugathadasa, K., Ayesha, B.: Deriving a representative vector for ontology classes with instance word vector embeddings. In: 7th International Conference on Innovative Computing Technology, INTECH 2017, pp. 79–84 (2017). https://doi.org/10.1109/INTECH.2017.8102426
15. Wohlgenannt, G., Minic, F.: Using word2vec to build a simple ontology learning system. In: CEUR Workshop Proceedings, pp. 2–5 (2016)
16. Devlin, J., Chang, M.-W., Lee, K., Toutanova, K.: BERT: pre-training of deep bidirectional transformers for language understanding. In: Proceedings of NAACL-HLT 2019, pp. 4171–4186 (2019)
17. Hammar, K.: Ontology Design Patterns in WebProtégé. In: 14th International Semantic Web Conference (ISWC-2015), Betlehem, pp. 1–4 (2015)
18. Scharffe, F., Zamazal, O., Fensel, D.: Ontology alignment design patterns. Knowl. Inf. Syst. **40**(1), 1–28 (2013). https://doi.org/10.1007/s10115-013-0633-y
19. Smirnov, A., Teslya, N., Savosin, S., Shilov, N.: Ontology matching for socio-cyberphysical systems: an approach based on background knowledge. In: Galinina, O., Andreev, S., Balandin, S., Koucheryavy, Y. (eds.) NEW2AN/ruSMART/NsCC -2017. LNCS, vol. 10531, pp. 29–39. Springer, Cham (2017). https://doi.org/10.1007/978-3-319-67380-6_3
20. Levashova, T., Lundqvist, M., Sandkuhl, K., Smirnov, A.: Context-based modelling of information demand: approaches from information logistics and decision support. In: Proceedings of the 14th European Conference on Information Systems, ECIS 2006. 171 (2006)
21. Teslya, N., Smirnov, A., Levashova, T., Shilov, N.: Ontology for resource self-organisation in cyber-physical-social systems. In: Klinov, P., Mouromtsev, D. (eds.) KESW 2014. CCIS, vol. 468, pp. 184–195. Springer, Cham (2014). https://doi.org/10.1007/978-3-319-11716-4_16
22. Seigerroth, U., Kaidalova, J., Shilov, N., Kaczmarek, T.: Semantic web technologies in business and IT alignment: multi-model algorithm of ontology matching. In: AFIN 2013, The Fifth International Conference on Advances in Future Internet, pp. 50–56 (2013)
23. Sørensen, T.: A method of establishing groups of equal amplitude in plant sociology based on similarity of species content and its application to analyses of the vegetation on danish commons. Det Kongelige Danske Videnskabernes Selskab Biologiske Skrifter **5**, 1–34 (1948)
24. Elfwing, S., Uchibe, E., Doya, K.: Sigmoid-weighted linear units for neural network function approximation in reinforcement learning. Neural Netw. **107**, 3–11 (2018). https://doi.org/10.1016/j.neunet.2017.12.012

An Ontology-Based Concept to Support Information Exchange for Virtual Reality Design Reviews

Stefan Adwernat(✉), Mario Wolf, and Detlef Gerhard

Institute for Product and Service Engineering, Digital Engineering Chair, Ruhr University Bochum, Universitaetsstr. 150, 44801 Bochum, Germany
stefan.adwernat@ruhr-uni-bochum.de

Abstract. The current change of traditional products towards intelligent, connected cyber-physical systems (CPS) increases the amount of heterogenous data and models generated throughout the products' life cycle stages, starting from their development and reaching as far as reconfigurations in the product use phase. As CPS are highly modular and often customizable by the user, the management and decision support regarding product variants is critical. Mastering the vast complexity of these product-type and product-instance-related information has become one of the main challenges in modern engineering.

In previous works, the authors presented different mixed reality (MR) approaches as suitable tools to integrate product-related information and facilitate the interaction with digital contents such as product manufacturing information (PMI) and inspection characteristics for design reviews or real-time sensor values to support maintenance tasks.

This contribution proposes an ontology-based concept to facilitate the information exchange from distributed data sources for mixed reality usage and vice versa. The goal of this paper is to improve the information provision and interaction within a collaborative Virtual Reality-driven design review process for CPS. The ability of ontologies for querying and reasoning of linked information supports the comparison of design variants and feedback integration from design reviews of previous or existing product generations as well as allocating relevant design review metrics such as requirements, simulation results, costs or product use data. The capability of CPS to call upon services from other Industrie 4.0 components opens up a way to implement said ontology to meet today's engineering challenges.

Keywords: Ontology · Interoperability · Virtual Reality · Design review · RAMI 4.0

1 Introduction

Throughout a product's life cycle, several validation and assessment tasks are performed on the product and its related processes and artifacts. Design reviews are essential for the quality assessment and troubleshooting in product engineering in this context, especially those using collaborative software approaches. According to IEC 61160 [1], design

F. Nyffenegger et al. (Eds.): PLM 2020, IFIP AICT 594, pp. 270–284, 2020.
https://doi.org/10.1007/978-3-030-62807-9_22

reviews are performed at different stages of the development process, mostly at project critical milestones to verify compliance with the previously defined requirements and aim to reveal potential deviations for correction at an early stage. The review usually involves an interdisciplinary team to address issues of all related departments in a collaborative process. Evaluated characteristics can be the product's overall impression, functionality, design and ergonomics, safety aspects, legal requirements, project timing, budgeting or production requirements and so on. In the end, a final status report documents the evaluation results along with possible countermeasures.

The radical change from traditional products towards "smart" products or more precisely cyber-physical systems (CPS) emphasizes the need for a unified data acquisition and traceability approach, which supports the fusion of real and virtual systems [2]. These cyber-physical systems have the ability to communicate and interact with their environment and other products by using Internet of Things (IoT) technologies and web-based services [3, 4], with the consequence of an increased amount and heterogeneity of product related information. This significantly complicates the information exchange and provision for later usage. Another relevant aspect in this context is the user interaction with the provided information. Virtual Reality (VR) is generally suitable to visualize digital contents (models or data) for multiple users at the same time and allows for intuitive interactions within a completely immersive virtual environment. Therefore, VR contributes to information transparency and facilitates collaborative interactions with this information. A core challenge in review processes, not only for VR utilization, is the provision or availability of relevant information. Regarding VR-supported design reviews, information on the characteristics to be evaluated must be available. However, this information is usually created in different engineering authoring systems and therefore often lies distributed in different models, documents or databases, which is further amplified in the case of CPS.

The persistent storage of performed user interactions within the immersive VR environment is another typical weak point of VR applications that needs to be addressed in the context of design reviews. As mandated by [1], observed errors during a design review and their countermeasures must be documented according to legal responsibility. Moreover, the general traceability of results and performed actions is compulsory when companies are certified following DIN ISO 9001 [5].

As a result, the goal of this paper is to propose a concept that accommodates the aspects of information and knowledge exchange, context-specific provisioning for VR usage from heterogenous data sources with a specific focus on characteristics of CPS (i.e. use data from products in the field), a CPS-compliant data model and an overarching ontology to connect the entities in this context semantically. Based on this concept, user interactions in a VR-based design review can be recorded and their entities linked to allow a persistent record and therefore a consistent process documentation and traceability of actions, results or decisions made during the design review.

2 Related Work

2.1 CPS in the Reference Architecture Model Industrie 4.0

Initiatives such as Reference Architecture Model Industrie 4.0 (RAMI 4.0) [6] of the National Platform Industrie 4.0, the Industrial Internet Reference Architecture (IIRA) of the Industrial Internet Consortium (IIC), among other things, are intended to solve the problems of model fragmentation and their lack of semantic descriptions in engineering [7]. Since 2016, these initiatives have been cooperating with each other, resulting in a functional mapping that ensures compatibility between the approaches and their implementations [8]. A prerequisite for the desired degree of interoperability in the context of VR design reviews using Industrie 4.0 methods is the introduction of a uniform digital representation for each product involved in the value creation process. The model of the asset administration shell (AAS) from RAMI 4.0 [6] can be used to achieve this functionality. Each so-called asset is subject to a life cycle in RAMI 4.0 according to the usual understanding but differentiated by the life cycles of the product type and the individual product instances. An asset is a tangible or intangible object with value for the organization, regardless of whether it is a tangible product, a software component or a service. The information about an asset is stored digitally in the associated asset administration shell and made available for human-machine and machine-machine communication, so that a so-called Industrie 4.0 (I4.0) component is created as a combination between an asset and its administration shell (cf. Fig. 1). The AAS comprises a "Header" with identifying details about the asset and its associated AAS as well as a "Body" with a large number of sub-models, representing different aspects of the asset. Depending on the kind of asset, these aspects could describe manufacturing capabilities (e.g. drilling, assembling), the lifecycle status, condition states or similar type- or instance-based information. As part of the particular sub-model, proprietary data models (CAD data, source code etc.) are managed by a component manager, which can also provide interfaces to other I4.0 components [9]. In this way, information can be interlinked between assets via the sub-models of their related AAS.

The combination of I4.0 components creates new I4.0 components, i.e. a new asset with its own administration shell. This results in a recursive asset description that is able to map any granularity level [9], from simple semi-finished products and individual parts to modules and components to complete systems and end products themselves, and to link them together by stored references. Recently, the National Platform Industrie 4.0 released a comprehensive guide on how to implement the asset administration shell in detail and with schema examples regarding (industrial) standards like XML, JSON, RDF, OPC-UA and AutomationML [10].

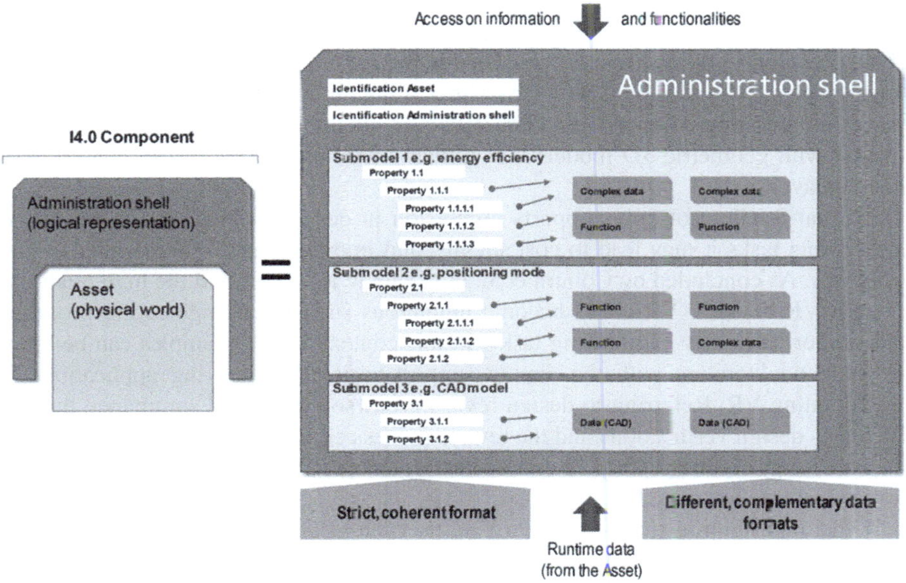

Fig. 1. Basic structure of the asset administration shell and I4.0 component - based on [10]

2.2 Knowledge Representation and Sharing

Several methods can be found in academic literature to represent and structure domain- or organization-specific knowledge. For example, Taxonomies are used to classify and categorize terms, whereas Thesauri additionally describe their relationship through synonyms, hypernyms or hyponyms [11]. Semantic networks map concepts, terms and their relations into a graph that consists of vertices (concepts and terms) and edges (relationships) that link vertices to each other [12]. Another common concept to represent knowledge are ontologies, which rest upon semantic networks, but are much stricter and more formal due to their axiomatic structure. Originally coined by Gruber [13], Studer et al. [14] define ontologies as "a formal, explicit specification of a shared conceptualisation". Therefore, ontologies are capable of modelling knowledge domains with complex, linked information structures as well as sharing and integrating heterogenous information originating from other domains. Due to axiomatic rules, ontologies allow for inferencing, i.e. new facts can be derived based on existing knowledge. In this context, the resource description framework (RDF) facilitates standardized data interchange through a textual formalization of resources and their properties expressed by statements in a triple structure (subject, predicate or property, object) [15].

Using ontologies or RDF stores for CPS data is encouraged by the fact that the asset administration shell schemata are now available in [10] and [16], so that a "common language" can be used between sub-models of different categories.

2.3 Virtual Reality Design Reviews

The motivation of the approaches described in the previous sections is to bridge the gap between physical and digital world by either bringing "intelligence" into products or linking information to products. Since VR is a suitable technology to visualize and interact with geometric 3D models in a virtual environment [17], it can contribute to this endeavor.

Virtual Reality not only supports immersion in design reviews but also for other engineering tasks it may lead to cost savings and improved and/or accelerated related processes. As concluded by Coburn et al. [18], due to low costs and the high quality of modern VR devices, VR could become ubiquitous for several engineering processes and support everyday engineering tasks. In this context, many examples can be found in academic literature with the aim to support various engineering applications by incorporating VR. Referring to design reviews, Lawson et al. [19] summarize that VR facilitates design verifications and the review process especially for physical prototypes and mock-ups can be replaced by its virtual counterpart, which in turn could lead to cost reductions for manufacturers.

Other contributions focus on improving user interactions within VR environments, such as Martini et al. [20], who developed a hardware and software-based user interface to simplify interactions in VR review processes. Freeman et al. [21] investigate tools and methods for CAD-software-like interaction and manipulation functionalities for 3D models in VR. The fact that interaction in VR environments is generally simple and intuitive is confirmed by Wolfartsberger [22]. Their study on VR-supported design reviews indicates that the participants are more likely to detect errors in a 3D model within an immersive VR scene compared to a traditional CAD software approach on a PC screen. Additionally, performing the design review and interacting with the 3D models is described to be more intuitive and "natural" for non-CAD experts due to the high degree of immersion using VR head mounted displays (HMD).

In our previous works, we presented different mixed reality (MR) approaches as suitable tools to integrate product-related information and facilitate the interaction with digital contents such as product manufacturing information (PMI) and inspection characteristics for design reviews [23] or real-time sensor values to support maintenance tasks [24]. Our most recent contribution [25] proposes a concept for a VR-supported design review process for CPS, taking their characteristics (e.g. use data of previous product instances) into account. This concept was prototypically implemented utilizing modern VR devices, with a clear focus on the collaborative review process, the visualization in VR and the intuitive user interaction.

In contrast to the approaches presented above, the paper at hand focusses on the aspects of information exchange and context-specific provisioning for VR-based design reviews in the light of CPS.

3 Approach

The main goal of this paper is to contribute to interoperability in the context of collaborative VR-based design reviews using the AAS of the relevant (virtual) components. Another focus is the persistent storage of the user operations within the immersive VR environment in order to comply with documentation and traceability requirements demanded by IEC 61160 [1] or ISO 9001 [5]. To accommodate this, this section presents a conceptual framework based on Industrie 4.0 methods, starting with potential use cases addressed by the concept.

3.1 Considered Design Review Use Cases

Design reviews serve as an instrument for quality inspection and assessment at different stages of a product's life cycle. The main intention is to evaluate product or process related characteristics, usually in a collaborative manner to address issues from all related stakeholders. In a generic design review process according to [1] the operative tasks are accompanied by several administrative processes such as planning, preparation, execution and follow-up. Depending on the pursued objectives of the design review various kinds of information are a prerequisite for discussion and decision making.

Based on the authors previous works [25], the considered use cases in this paper address VR-supported design reviews with a particular focus on cyber-physical systems, also known as smart products. As described above, CPS are characterized by the ability to communicate and interact with their environment and other products. Compared to traditional products, CPS therefore offer additional feedback information and services provided by the product instances and their "smart" components, as well as field reports from physical parts from a previous generation. This enhances evaluation possibilities for the product type under review especially for the development of an advanced product generation or when adapting existing designs.

In this context, the application of mobile VR technology with head mounted displays offers additional benefit. Firstly, it promotes the intuitive user interaction with the displayed information (textual or graphical) in virtual environments even across multiple sites and secondly, it allows for context-sensitive visualizations. As design reviews normally involve an interdisciplinary team, whose participants possess an individual role and function, specific content can and should be visualized for each individual user, for example mechanical simulations or cost overviews. The integrated visualization of relevant information can be used to simultaneously compare two design variants or to access real-time data from the product instances of a previous generation currently in the field.

Furthermore, individual user permissions can be derived, which restrict or allow user interactions during the design review. The same applies to a potential integration of external partners (customer or supplier), for example to clarify requirements or to take their feedback into account during agile review sessions. These participants should have only limited access for editing or viewing functionalities during the review process.

According to the standards ISO 9001 [5] and specifically IEC 61160 [1] regarding design reviews the documentation of organizational process is essential to maintain knowledge, make decisions reasonable and by this errors traceable. Therefore, the considered use cases also have to cover recording of user operation in VR, like adding a text note or highlighting individual parts.

3.2 Concept for Information Exchange in VR-Based Design Reviews

As detailed in the state-of-the-art section, initiatives like RAMI 4.0 or IIRA specify organizational frameworks and guidelines for these kinds of products or systems and introduce a uniform digital representation which contributes to interoperability. Therefore, this concept generally employs the model of the asset administration shell (AAS) from RAMI 4.0 [6]. According to their definition, an asset represents tangible or intangible objects and the respective information is stored digitally in the associated AAS. Transferred to this context, the main entities which have a specific AAS are the design review participants (user), the product to be reviewed (CPS 123) and the collaborative design review environment (VR-DR) as illustrated in Fig. 2.

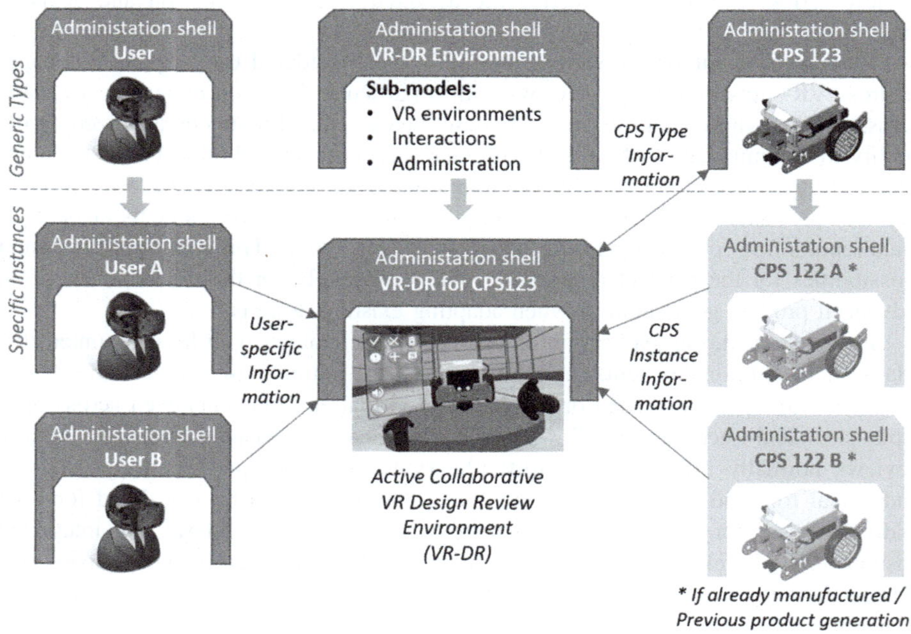

Fig. 2. Concept for information exchange in VR design reviews

Each asset is associated with its corresponding AAS, which describes the asset in the information world. According to [9], the AAS is composed of different sub-models, which represent different aspects of the asset (cf. Fig. 1). Here, the VR design review AAS (Fig. 2, top center) comprises specific sub-models to represent the general composition of the VR environment, available interactions with entities in VR as well as administrative capabilities to support the review process. In this regard, the differentiation between types and their instances must be noted. The type of an AAS (Fig. 2, top) serves as a structured template to derive an AAS instance with specific characteristics. For example, the AAS instances connected to the specific users "A" and "B" are created based on the generic user AAS type and holds individual information, such as identification, permissions and functions (see Fig. 2, left).

As described in our previous works [25], the immersive VR design review allows for user interaction, such as manipulating objects and giving feedback via text input, voice recordings, graphical highlights or interactive polls. During review execution, the information about an individual user (stored in its associated AAS) serves as an input for the AAS of the active VR-DR session (Fig. 2, center). This allows to identify a user and provide specific information and permitted interactions. At the same time, performed interactions during the review session can be stored together with the authoring information. This data is maintained in the respective sub-model of the VR-DR AAS and later referenced by the AAS of the reviewed product or system.

The various sub-models in the AAS of the reviewed product deliver additional input, that may benefit the review process. On the one hand, generic information related to the product type (e.g. 3D model, requirements associated with geometric features) have to be considered. In the case of developing advanced product generations or when adapting existing product designs, information of individual product instances in the field (operating or measurement data, maintenance data, fault reports etc.) can be additionally used during the design review, for example to discuss potential effects of operation conditions and agree on design alternatives.

3.3 Identification of Relevant Concepts and Terms

A prerequisite to build a comprehensive data model is the identification of key concepts and terms referring to the domain of interest. In this case, relevant terms of design reviews and collaborative VR environments in general have to be identified as well as specific terms derived from the considered use cases described above. In a first step, a taxonomy has been designed according to the subject areas. One goal of this paper is to establish a semantic connection of the entities representing VR-based design reviews for CPS. To achieve this, general categories for context-aware information supply were used to identify and allocate related terms. Shen et al. [26] propose a classification of context concerning location, time, identity (user role), task or activity, used devices, available interaction capabilities, the distribution (of data), the type of data and according to privacy and security settings. Based on this, three main categories are suitable to classify relevant concepts and terms in the context of this paper: user-specific, administrative and technical aspects.

The first category "user-specific aspects" summarizes terms which are related to the participants of VR-based design reviews and the considered use cases (cf. Fig. 3). At first, a distinction can be made between the different roles of a user, since participants may have different permissions in the review session, such as the moderator and guests. The same applies to the function of a user, which is linked to the respective department or if external participants (e.g. customer or supplier) are involved, too. The user's location delivers knowledge about the current time, which is an important aspect for distributed collaboration across multiple sites. Different permissions (e.g. create, read, update and delete) limit the user's access to objects or information within the VR environment. On top of that, a user's attendance, a name or identification may be attributed as well.

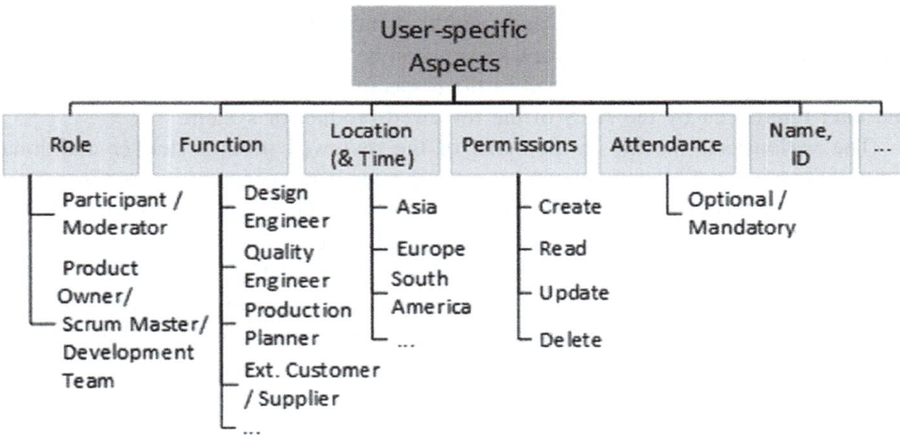

Fig. 3. Terms of user-specific aspects with exemplary characteristics

The second category "administrative aspects" addresses terms, which are connected to administrative characteristics of the design review. Among these, the collaboration type describes how the design review is performed. As mentioned in the use case description, the utilization of VR allows both, co-located and distributed collaboration as well as collaborating at the same time or asynchronously. The workflow progress captures the current stage of the design review, whereas the objectives have to be available as well (Fig. 4).

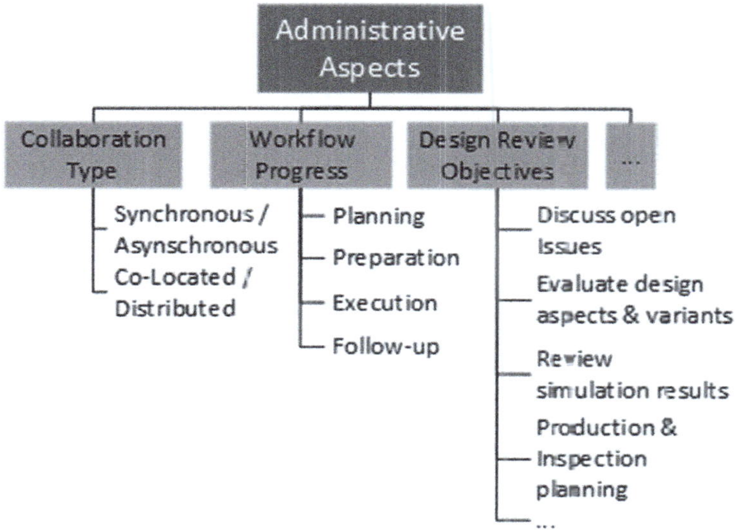

Fig. 4. Terms of administrative aspects with exemplary characteristics

The third category "technical aspects" contains essential information for conducting VR-based design reviews (cf. Fig. 5). They refer to the product, like its life cycle stage, related technical documents or engineering data as well as data from the product's use phase (field data). Apart from this, a large portion of relevant information is delivered by the VR environment itself. As already mentioned, a common weakness of existing VR approaches is the lacking persistence of actions performed in VR. Based on the authors previous works [25], the subcategories shown in Fig. 5 can be identified. The avatar related to a specific user is mainly described by its position in the virtual environment or room. This room in turn may have variable dimensions depending on the number of users in the review session, the scale of the reviewed part or even the amount of shared information during the review.

Further subcategories contain the used tools in review, such as text input, highlighting or redlining, as well as the objects for carrying the essential review information, e.g. the 3D model to be evaluated, virtual displays or free text for non-geometric information (including charts and figures), as well as symbols, curves or audio records for capturing annotations.

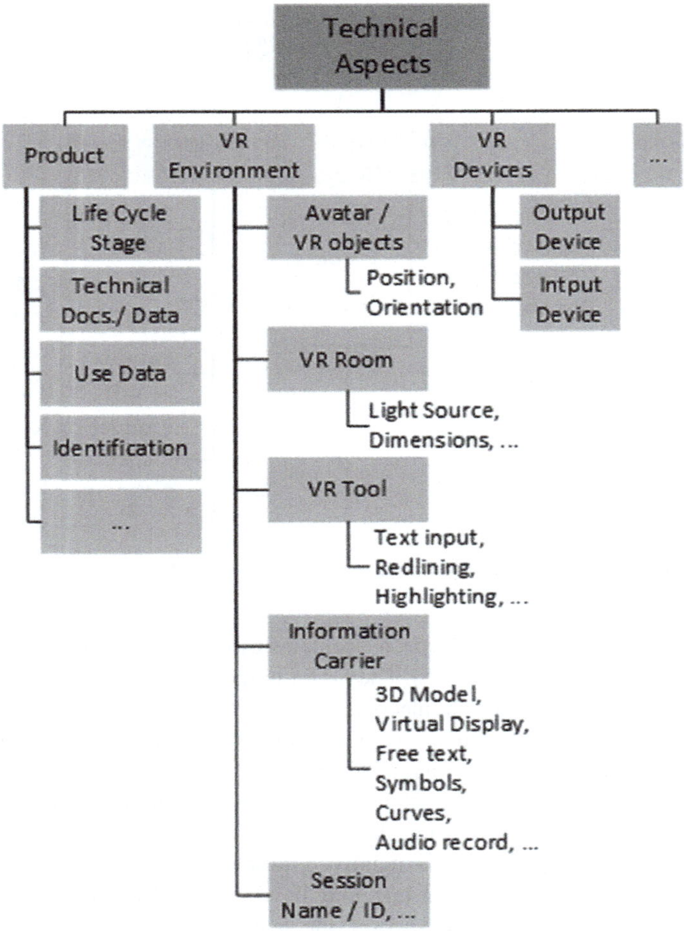

Fig. 5. Terms of technical aspects with exemplary characteristics

3.4 Semantic Data Model for VR-Based Design Reviews

The proposed concept (cf. Fig. 2) aims at facilitating knowledge exchange and context-sensitive provisioning for VR usage from heterogenous data sources with a specific focus on CPS characteristic. In order to guarantee a "common language", this concept generally employs the model of the asset administration shell (AAS) from RAMI 4.0 [6]. Recent activities related to the AAS introduced RDF- or ontology-based concepts to promote semantic interoperability of Industrie 4.0 components. In order to comply with this, the proposed concept also rests upon ontologies for knowledge representation and sharing in VR design reviews (VR-DR). Due to the general nature of ontologies being modular and reusable by other ontologies [14], an integration with the aforementioned ontologies is given.

Therefore, this ontology-based data model forms the basis to manage and exchange information between various data sources (engineering authoring systems, the products' operation data), the VR-based design review application and the participants of the review. This uniform data model serves as a reference for the integration of heterogenous information from and into the different systems.

In order to establish this data model, the identified concepts and terms in the presented taxonomies lay the foundation for modeling the VR-DR ontology by transferring concepts into classes or subclasses and related data properties. The main entities in the context of VR-based design reviews are the reviewed product, the VR-DR session itself and all participating users. These three entities build the top level class structure of the VR-DR ontology shown in Fig. 6. For reasons of clarity and comprehensibility, Fig. 6 illustrates only an excerpt of the complete ontology with exemplary classes and relationships.

According to the definition of RAMI 4.0 [6], the generic types of the three entities "product", "VR-DR" and "user" are associated with an AAS, which is inherited for the specific instances. As described in Sect. 2.1, the exchange of information between assets is performed via sub-models of their respective AAS (cf. Fig. 1). For example, the reviewed product is represented by a 3D CAD model, which can be part of a "Mechanical CAD" sub-model in the product's AAS. On the other side, the VR-DR is also associated with an AAS, where one of the sub-models represents the aspects of the

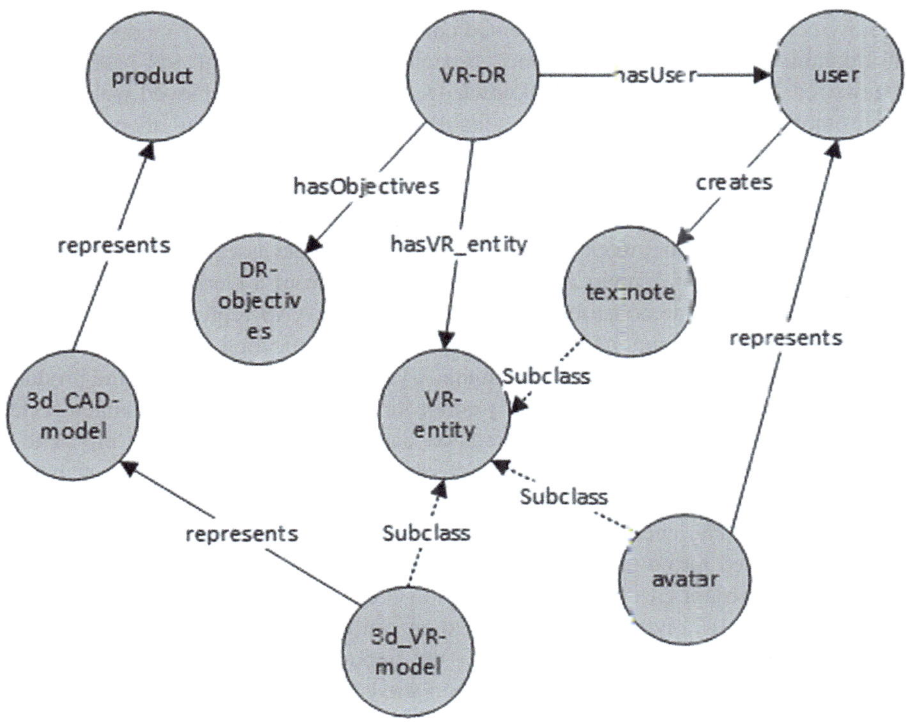

Fig. 6. Excerpt of the ontology implemented in Protégé

VR environment. One entity within the VR environment is the product's "VR model", which corresponds to the product's tessellated 3D CAD model, i.e. after conversion of the native model (cf. Fig. 6). This implies, that two different models are considered in each AAS, but a semantic mapping between them is established. The same applies to a VR avatar, which represents a user in the VR-DR session and a real person in the physical world. In this way, the entities of the respective sub-models can be connected according to their relation properties, for example a "USER" "creates" a "TEXT-NOTE" (see Fig. 6).

Based on this approach, the VR-DR ontology enables a common understanding for the mapping of different components or sub-models, when referring to the definition in RAMI 4.0 [6]. Finally, the ontology was implemented using the software Protégé.

4 Conclusion and Outlook

Today, VR is a common tool for several industrial tasks, which focus on immersive visualization and user interaction. Nevertheless, the necessary information is often integrated statically and isolated. The knowledge that is created during a VR session is also rarely available afterwards.

The current shift towards increasingly connected CPS in the era of Industrie 4.0 leads to ever larger amounts of information. RAMI and its AAS delivers a framework for a uniform digital representation of so-called assets, which contributes to interoperability between the assets. The presented concept employs the AAS model to support information exchange and persistence especially in the light of VR-based design reviews for CPS. As a first step, the knowledge formalization is achieved with the help of an ontology. Since ontologies are suitable for sharing knowledge about a specific area with other ontologies, the specific knowledge is not only limited to this concept, but can be reused at other stages of the product life cycle or for different applications as well.

Currently, the authors work on implementing a complete asset administration shell-based demonstrator of a smart factory training model from a German industrial education supplier. This demonstrator includes the holistic AAS representation of all the production system's components, organizing the communication between those components via OPC-UA through services in the AAS, tracking and tracing of the products via their administration shells and finally connecting both virtual and augmented reality frontends to monitor current and aggregated data directly on either the physical or virtual representation of production system or product. To facilitate the exchange of information between a variety of engineering authoring systems, the production system (representing a CPS) and the virtual or augmented reality applications, the ontology will be transferred into a graph database that supports reasoning of RDF stores.

This demonstrator case will then be used as a cyber-physical use case for the VR-based design review, giving us access to real operational data of the produced products and production system itself and yielding the opportunity to embed the VR design review data into existing asset administration shells.

References

1. International Electrotechnical Commission: Design review (IEC 61160:2005) (2005)
2. Monostori, L., et al.: Cyber-physical systems in manufacturing. CIRP Ann. Manuf. Technol **65**(2), 621–641 (2016)
3. Abramovici, M., Savarino, P., Göbel, J.C., Adwernat, S., Gebus, P.: Systematization of virtual product twin models in the context of smart product reconfiguration during the product use phase. Procedia CIRP **69**, 734–739 (2018)
4. Vajna, S., Weber, C., Zeman, K., Hehenberger, P., Gerhard, D., Wartzack, S.: CAx für Ingenieure. Springer, Berlin (2018). https://doi.org/10.1007/978-3-662-54624-6
5. DIN Deutsches Institut für Normung e.V.: Quality management systems - Requirements, DIN EN ISO 9001:2015. Beuth, Berlin (2015)
6. DIN Deutsches Institut für Normung e.V.: Referenzarchitekturmodell Industrie 4.0 (RAMI4.0), DIN SPEC 91345:2016-04. Beuth (2016)
7. Lin, S.W., et al.: The Industrial Internet of Things: Volume G1: Reference Architecture. Industrial Internet Consortium (2017)
8. Lin, S., et al.: Architecture Alignment and Interoperability - An Industrial Internet Consortium and Plattform Industrie 4.0 Joint Whitepaper. Industrial Internet Consortium (2017)
9. Plattform Industrie 4.0: Relationships between I4.0 Components – Composite Components and Smart Production, Working Paper. Federal Ministry for Economic Affairs and Energy, Berlin (2017)
10. Plattform Industrie 4.0: Details of the Asset Administration Shell: Part 1 - The exchange of information between partners in the value chain of Industrie 4.0 (Version 2.0). Federal Ministry for Economic Affairs and Energy, Berlin (2019)
11. International Organization for Standardization: Information and documentation - Thesauri and interoperability with other vocabularies - Part 1: Thesauri for information retrieval, ISO 25964-1:2011 (2011)
12. Quillian, M.R.: Semantic memory. In: Minsky, M. (ed.) Semantic Information Processing, pp. 227–270. MIT Press, Cambridge (1968)
13. Gruber, T.R.: A translation approach to portable ontology specifications. Knowl. Acquis. **5** (2), 199–220 (1993)
14. Studer, R., Benjamins, V.R., Fensel, D.: Knowledge engineering: principles and methods. Data Knowl. Eng. **25**, 161–197 (1998)
15. RDF Working Group: Resource Description Framework. https://www.w3.org/RDF/. Accessed 25 Mar 2020
16. Bader, S.R., Maleshkova, M.: The semantic asset administration shell. In: Acosta, M., Cudré-Mauroux, P., Maleshkova, M., Pellegrini, T., Sack, H., Sure-Vetter, Y. (eds.) SEMANTiCS 2019. LNCS, vol. 11702, pp. 159–174. Springer, Cham (2019). https://doi.org/10.1007/978-3-030-33220-4_12
17. Wolfartsberger, J., Zenisek, J., Sievi, C.: Chances and limitations of a virtual reality-supported tool for decision making in industrial engineering. IFAC-PapersOnLine **51**, 637–642 (2018)
18. Coburn, J.Q., Freeman, I.J., Salmon, J.L.: A review of the capabilities of current low-cost virtual reality technology and its potential to enhance the design process. J. Comput. Inf. Sci. Eng. **17**(3) (2017)
19. Lawson, G., Salanitri, D., Waterfield, B.: Future directions for the development of virtual reality within an automotive manufacturer. Appl. Ergon. **53**, 323–330 (2016)

20. Martini, A., et al.: A novel 3D user interface for the immersive design review. In: IEEE Symposium on 3D User Interfaces (3DUI), pp. 175–176 (2015)
21. Freeman, I.J., Salmon, J.L., Coburn, J.Q.: CAD integration in virtual reality design reviews for improved engineering model interaction. In: Proceedings of the ASME International Mechanical Engineering Congress and Exposition (2017)
22. Wolfartsberger, J.: Analyzing the potential of Virtual Reality for engineering design review. Autom. Constr. **104**, 27–37 (2019)
23. Adwernat, S., Neges, M., Abramovici, M.: Mixed Reality Assistenzsystem zur visuellen Qualitätsprüfung mit Hilfe digitaler Produktfertigungsinformationen. In: Stelzer, R.H., Krzywinski, J. (eds.) Entwerfen Entwickeln Erleben in Produktentwicklung und Design 2019, Dresden, pp. 67–74 (2019)
24. Abramovici, M., Wolf, M., Adwernat, S., Neges, M.: Context-aware maintenance support for augmented reality assistance and synchronous multi-user collaboration. Procedia CIRP **59**, 18–22 (2017)
25. Adwernat, S., Wolf, M., Gerhard, D.: Optimizing the design review process for cyber-physical systems using virtual reality. Procedia CIRP **91**, 710–715 (2020)
26. Shen, H., et al.: Information visualisation methods and techniques: State-of-the-art and future directions. J. Ind. Inf. Integr. **16**, 100102 (2019)

Initial Approach to an Industrial Resources Ontology in Aerospace Assembly Lines

Rebeca Arista[1,3](✉), Fernando Mas[2,3], and Carpoforo Vallellano[3]

[1] Airbus SAS, 31700 Blagnac, France
rebeca.arista@airbus.com
[2] M&M Group, 11500 Cadiz, Spain
[3] University of Sevilla, 41092 Seville, Spain
{fmas, carpofor}@us.es

Abstract. Industrial ontologies can support the Product Development Process (PDP) and the product and industrial system lifecycle, to have a seamless collaboration between actors. In this sense, an industrial resource ontology that supports an aerospace assembly line design process is key within the conceptual phase of the PDP. Industrial resources can have a different classification to support the design goal of the assembly line, in terms of process optimization, layout and space optimization, production time, costs, or even the assembly line capabilities definition. This work describes an initial approach to an industrial resources ontology, considering the notions that will describe these resources inside an assembly line design perimeter.

Keywords: Aerospace · Industrial resource ontology · Assembly line design · Knowledge-based systems · Models for Manufacturing

1 Introduction

A Product Development Process based on collaborative engineering between different domains, requires strong and interoperable process, methods and tools, to develop an aerospace product and industrial system. Lack of interoperable tools to support this process in the conceptual phase, has strong influence in the maturity of the industrial system during production ramp-up phase.

Formal engineering ontologies are emerging as popular solutions for addressing the semantic interoperability issue in heterogeneous distributed environments and for bridging the gap between the legacy systems and organizational boundaries [1].

The design process of an aircraft assembly line is similar to a product design process. Assembly line design methods are discussed in the literature [2], but only few address an aerospace product industrialization with its inherent and non-negligible constrains (e.g. product complexity, industrial system complexity, long lifecycle, among others).

One of the most difficult steps in the assembly line design is to choose among different resources for each assembly process so that the work is done within given

Published by Springer Nature Switzerland AG 2020
F. Nyffenegger et al. (Eds.): PLM 2020, IFIP AICT 594, pp. 285–294, 2020.
https://doi.org/10.1007/978-3-030-62807-9_23

performance requirements, like cycle time, quality and minimum cost. Industrial resources play therefore a major role, and have to be correctly addressed to enable reuse or reconfiguration of existing assets, or design considering flexibility and target performance parameters.

Due to product functional requirements, some industrial resources or mechanical equipment may have to be designed specifically for a product or process. Often, a company outsources the design of its assembly lines and is at the mercy of the vendor regarding types of equipment [3].

This paper defines an initial approach to an industrial resource ontology, to support the assembly line design process during the conceptual phase of a PDP, and enable early design trade-offs against performance requirements. Next sections are organized as follows: Sect. 2 highlights related work and describes the motivations for a new industrial resource ontology applied to the aerospace industry; Sect. 3 presents an initial approach of this ontology supporting the assembly line design process; Sect. 4 covers the conclusions and further work. The paper ends with an acknowledgements section.

2 Related Work

2.1 Concurrent and Collaborative Engineering. Models for Manufacturing

Aerospace industry was pioneer designing and industrializing aircrafts using Concurrent Engineering techniques starting in the 90s [4]. With the introduction of PLM methods, processes and tools and the need to reduce time-to-market the industry pursues new working methods. Traditional Engineering works sequentially, Concurrent Engineering overlaps tasks between teams and Collaborative Engineering promotes teamwork to develop product, processes and resources from the conceptual phase to the start of the serial production. The authors proposed to implement the industrial Digital Mock-Up (iDMU) concept and its exploitation to create shop floor documentation in a framework of a Collaborative Engineering strategy [5].

In parallel, targeting to improve multidisciplinary design and simulation of complex systems, MBSE (Model Based Systems Engineering) methodology use graphical modeling authoring tools to specify data and behaviors of the systems and simulation tests systems behavior of complex products. Using the MBSE approach and based on the existing research for modelling manufacturing systems for the aerospace industry and the functional and data models published and deployed proposed by the authors [6, 7], a new approach for modelling manufacturing systems has been coined. Models for Manufacturing (MfM) is based in a novel architecture based on 3-Layers Model (3LM): a Data layer, an Ontology layer and a Service layer. Ontology layer is the core of the 3LM. The Ontology layer defines Scope model, Data model, Behavior model and Semantic model [8, 9]. A software tool to manage MfM in the collaborative process [10] and a framework was presented by the authors in [11].

2.2 Resources Definition in the Assembly Line Design Process

Assembly processes, assembly planning and assembly system development are some of the elementary bricks of an Assembly Line Design Process. Most of the research efforts on this area have focused up to this day on the product and process definition, without a clear definition of the resources conforming the assembly system.

The term *"Resource"* has different definitions in the literature regarding the domain of applicability. For example, at enterprise level a "Resource" can be a mean to carry out an enterprise activity, at procurement level a mean to procure assets, and in different industries like telecommunications a node of a communications network. Some of the relevant work in the field of manufacturing is detailed next.

Resource is defined as *"Equipment"* by Graves [12] Rekiek [13]. Whitney [2] detail the equipment notion including tools, part presentation, sensors, transportation for the assemblies, and assembly aids like fluid dispensers, fixtures, and clamps.

One of the earliest manufacturing ontologies is the Process Specification Language (ISO 18629-1: PSL), designed to facilitate correct and complete exchange of process information among manufacturing systems [14]. With this goal, Lemaignan [15] proposes a preliminary upper ontology for manufacturing named MASON (Manufacturing's Semantics ONtology), with a *"Resource"* decomposition in geographical resource, human resource, and material resource.

ISO 15531 MANDATE, (ISO 15531-1) defines a *"Resource"* as any device, tool and means, excepted raw material and final product components, at the disposal of the enterprise to produce goods or services. Within it, the Resource Information model (ISO15531-31) defines a resource hierarchy (generic, specific, individual resource), resource characteristics (set of information about a resource), resource administration (administrative information), resource status (avail-ability or not of the resource), resource view (specific aggregation of resources), resource representation (physical values), resource configuration [16].

Mas [17] defined three different resource levels (line, station and basic), and within the basic level three types of resources: tools (ad-hoc mechanical equipment), industrial means (standard means or easily configurable that can be procured), and human resources (with defined set of skills).

The term *"Manufacturing Resource"* is used by several authors to clarify the scope of usage to manufacturing aspects. Manufacturing resource is defined by Chengying [18] as a 3D solid model composing three aspects: organization structure (5 levels each aggregating the lower level manufacturing behavior), capability status properties, and development activity. Manufacturing Service Description Language (MSDL) is an ontology developed for formal representation of manufacturing services primarily in mechanical machining domain [19].

Sanfilippo et al. [20], described a Manufacturing Resource as a physical object or amount of mater, which can be available/dedicated, agentive/non-agentive, or an input/output/mechanism. Järvenpää [1] defines a manufacturing resource as a device or factory unit as part of MaRCO ontology, with the goal of describing the capabilities and combined capabilities of manufacturing resources.

All the previous definitions suffer from lacks to have a holistic definition of industrial resources applicable to the aerospace industry. The assembly line design at conceptual phase, comprises strategic decisions of reconfiguration or redesign of industrial resources, which are different from operational decisions to be taken at production phase, where detailed capability information is needed to reconfigure in short time. This strategic decision level is poorly addressed in the literature.

Also, the aerospace industry has specific and non-negligible constrains for the Original Equipment Manufacturer and most of its Tiers (e.g. product size, complexity, long productive life of a same product), which drive the design of its industrial resources.

For example, the term *"Jig"*, widely used in the aerospace industry to refer to product dedicated industrial resources, seem not to be covered by the term *"Equipment"* used in other industries due to the complexity scale and associated costs.

Jigs can cover the full scale of aircraft (e.g. 75 m × 80 m × 25 m dimension of A380 aircraft) to assure aircraft functional surfaces or mechanical requirements, with very high costs (up to 70% of total costs of an aircraft program). Equipment in other industries, even if dedicated for a product, have relaxed tolerances associated to product functional or mechanical requirements, rather than the ones of an aerospace product.

These deficiencies motivates the development of an industrial resource ontology for aerospace assembly lines at conceptual design phase. An initial approach is presented in next section.

3 Initial Approach to an Industrial Resource Ontology

This section approaches the role of the industrial resources in the assembly line design process of an aerospace product, as an initial approach to an industrial resource ontology. The assembly line design process defined by Mas et al. [17] is used as starting point for this work.

In [21] the authors defined a preliminary ontology to support the activity in charge of generating an *"As-Planned"* Product structure and a *"Build Process"* at industrial system network level, at the conceptual design phase of the PDP.

The *"Build Process"* at industrial system network level, describes for a given aircraft product the top-level sequence of manufacturing, assembly and logistics between plants, in a worldwide industrial network. It considers the product workshare to be made between countries or partners, before make/buy decisions for supply chain definition. This top-level sequence is the highest point of the process structure.

For a mono-configured product, the *"As-Planned"* is the industrial view of the product breakdown structure, created from a common layer of elementary objects to the *"As-Designed"* product structure, being this last one the functional view of the product. The *"As-Planned"* defines the product workshare between partners/contractors and their responsibilities, defining the *"product work package"* of each one of them, meaning aircraft components, interfaces definitions and joints to perform.

After this activity, an assembly line design process is launched for each assembly node of the *"Build Process"* and its corresponding *"product work package"*. This is the starting point of the work detailed next.

3.1 Generate Assembly Line Activity - Black Box View

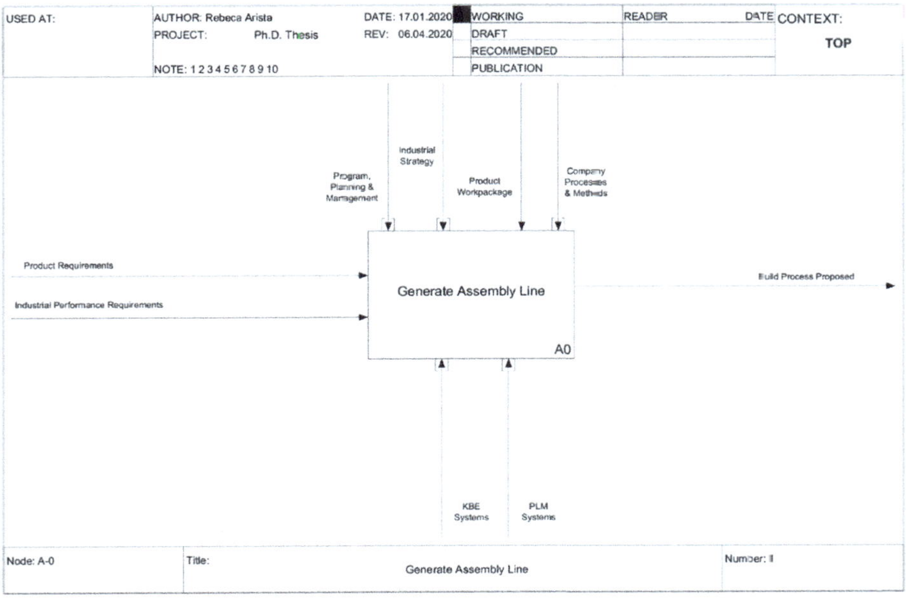

Fig. 1. Activity Generate Assembly Line – black box view

The assembly line design process is launched in the conceptual phase with the *"product work package"* definition, being controlled by the program planning & management, the industrial strategy and the company process, methods and tools. Figure 1 describes this activity in IDEF0, called A0 *"Generate Assembly Line"*.

This activity is in charge of generating a *"Build Process Proposed"* at assembly line level, which goes back to *"Define As-planned and Build Process"* activity to reevaluate both, the "As-Planned" product breakdown and "Build Process" at industrial system network level. This activity has as inputs: the product requirements (e.g. aerodynamic performance and weight), the industrial performance requirements (e.g. production time, costs and CO2 emissions), and supporting mechanisms KBE and PLM systems.

3.2 Generate Assembly Line Design Activity - White Box View

Figure 2 shows the activities inside A0 "Generate Assembly Line". A "Build Concept" is a work-in-progress "Build Process" at assembly line level, containing a general description of the assembly line with the aircraft components flow, an estimation of the number of stations and sequence between stations. It includes as well a preliminary sequence of the main activities to be performed at each station.

With the product work package (components and interfaces) and the product requirements, activity A1 "Generate Build Concept" defines a Build Concept containing the components flow, stations and main stations activities. It defines as well the first needs of industrial resources related to this Build Concept (e.g. logistic system between stations, positioning systems and test system), and specifies the product tolerances that have to be fulfilled by the given industrial resources (e.g. aerodynamic shape and functional interfaces).

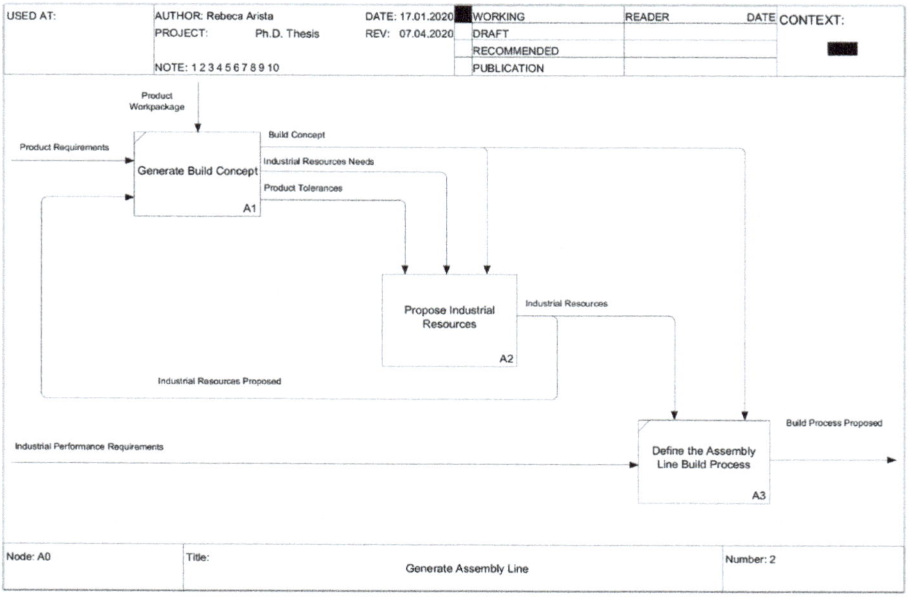

Fig. 2. Activity Generate Assembly Line – white box view

An example for a Final Assembly Line: a Build Concept is generated defining the joints between the components to be made one-by-one in different stations, and the flow of the aircraft components from one station to another. Taking the station where the wing and the fuselage joint will be made, in order to achieve the product requirements, the manufacture engineer defines the industrial resource needs at this station as a high precision positioning and alignment system for the components (wing and fuselage), a measurement system to check alignment and a machining system to perform the junction. The Build Concept would include the components flow in/out of this station from stations sequence with associated logistics resources needs, and the activities sequence, meaning positioning of component one, positioning of component 2, alignment of both components using alignment & measurement system, and perform joint with machining system.

The Industrial Resource Needs are then given to A2 *"Propose Industrial Resources"* activity, which proposes a set of possible industrial resources that could cover the needs defined, and with the given product tolerances. The Industrial Resources Proposed are given on a feedback loop to A1 "Generate Build Concept" activity, to review with it the Build Concept defined, adjust or change Industrial Resources Needs, and even change the Build Concept or the Product Tolerances if no industrial resource solution is found. This activity is described in detail in the following subsection.

Finally, the activity A3 *"Define the Assembly Line Build Process"* takes the Industrial Performance Requirements, analyzes the Build Concept and the Industrial Resources options with the parameters of each industrial resource (like cost, energy consumption and CO2 emissions), choosing the most suitable option that fulfills the Industrial Performance Requirements. The Build Concept and Industrial Resources chosen conform the *Build Process Proposed.*

3.3 Generate Industrial Resources Activity

Figure 3 shows the details of A2 *"Propose Industrial Resources"* activity. The first activity A21 *"Detail needs per resource type"* analyses the industrial resources needs defined in the activity A1, and details the Resource Needs per type, considering the flows and sequences defined in the build concept. Three types of industrial resources are proposed.

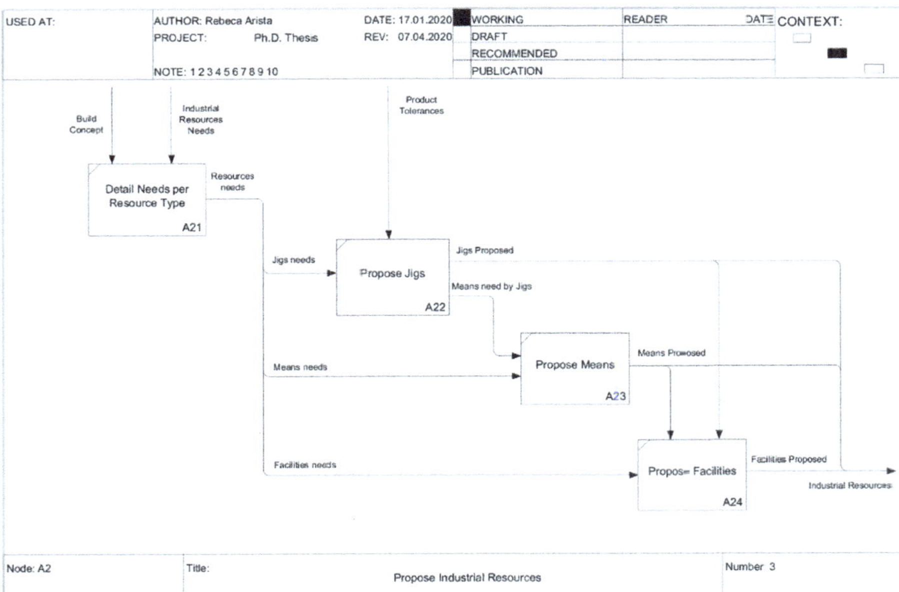

Fig. 3. Generate Industrial Resources

The term *"Jig"* is used to define an industrial resource specifically designed to fulfill an aerospace product functional and assembly tolerances (e.g. product functional requirements and aerodynamic shape). Jigs have no universal applicability, and can be dedicated (if its design parameters match to only one product tolerances), semi-dedicated (if some of its design parameters can be reconfigured for different products of a family), or flexible (if its design parameters can be reconfigured to achieve different product tolerances). Jigs can be among others: fixing or positioning elements, referencing elements, test elements, hoisting elements, transportation elements and machines.

The term *"Mean"* is defined as any element needed to complete the processes and activities defined in the Build Concept, which are not *"Jigs"* or *"Facilities"*. Means can be among others: grades, platforms, tools, test means, consumables, human resources, documentation and racks.

The term *"Facilities"* as defined in the facility ontology proposed by Tomašević et al. [22], is from a physical and topology perspective a site infrastructure, installations and supplies. Facilities can be among others: buffer areas, warehouses, buildings, hangars, water supply and power supply.

The Resource Needs per type, outcome of activity A21 *"Detail needs per resource type"*, will launch activities to propose as applicable industrial resources, which match the product and process requirements defined in the Build Concept: new industrial resources design, reconfigure existing in-house resources, and/or use standard resources form catalogs.

The activity A22 *"Propose Jigs"* proposes in a first step a set of Jigs, from the Jigs needs defined, and considering the product tolerances. It defines as well the needs of Means associated to these Jigs, like human resources skills, tools, among others.

Activity A23 *"Propose Means"* proposes different Means that can fulfill the needs from the Jigs and from the Industrial Resources requirements defined in the Build Concept.

The Jig Proposed and Means Propose control the last activity A23 *"Propose Facility"* where Facilities options are proposed considering the Jigs and Means constrains (like space and power/water supply) and the needs defined from the Build Concept (like logistic flow spaces, hangar accesses and warehouses).

4 Conclusions and Further Work

An initial approach to an industrial resource ontology to support the assembly line design process is presented, considering the specificities of the aerospace industry and aerospace products. An overview of related work is presented, describing the motivations for this industrial resource ontology.

An Assembly Line Design process is modelled in IDEF0, as continuity of the design activities defined by the authors in [21] at industrial system network level. The role of industrial resources in this process is emphasized; three types of industrial resources are defined. Further work will mature the industrial resource ontology, as well as its management and use in the conceptual phase of the Product Development Process.

Acknowledgements. The authors wish to express their sincere gratitude to University of Sevilla colleagues in Spain, to Airbus colleagues in France and Spain for their support and contribution during the development of this work.

References

1. Järvenpää, E., Siltala, N., Hylli, O., Lanz, M.: The development of an ontology for describing the capabilities of manufacturing resources. J. Intell. Manuf. **30**(2), 959–978 (2018). https://doi.org/10.1007/s10845-018-1427-6
2. Whitney, D.E.: Mechanical Assemblies: Their Design, Manufacture, and Role in Product Development. Oxford University Press Inc., New York (2004). ISBN 0-19-515782-6
3. Su, B.Q., Smith, S.S.: An integrated framework for assembly-oriented product design and optimization, J. Ind. Technol. **19**(2), 1–9 (2003)
4. Pardessus, T.: Concurrent engineering development and practices for aircraft design at Airbus. In: Proceedings of the 24th ICAS Meeting, Yokohama (2004)
5. Mas, F., Menendez, J.L., Oliva, M., Rios, J., Gomez, A., Olmo, V.: iDMU as the collaborative engineering engine: research experiences in Airbus. In: Proceedings of IEEE Engineering, Technology and Innovation International Conference (2014). https://doi.org/10.1109/ice.2014.6871594
6. Mas, F., Ríos, J., Gómez, A., Hernández, J.: Knowledge-based application to define aircraft final assembly lines at the industrialization conceptual design phase. Int. J. Comput. Integr. Manuf. **29**(6), 677–691 (2015)
7. Mas, F., Oliva, M., Rios, J., Gomez, A., Olmos, V.: PLM based approach to the industrialization of aeronautical assemblies. Procedia Eng. **132**, 1045–1052 (2015)
8. Mas, F., Racero, J., Oliva, M., Morales-Palma, D.: A preliminary methodological approach to Models for Manufacturing (MfM). In: Chiabert, P., Bouras, A., Noël, F., Ríos, J. (eds.) PLM 2018. IAICT, vol. 540, pp. 273–283. Springer, Cham (2018). https://doi.org/10.1007/978-3-030-01614-2_25
9. Mas, F., Racero, J., Oliva, M., Morales-Palma, D.: Preliminary ontology definition for aerospace assembly lines in Airbus using Models for Manufacturing methodology. In: Sanfilippo, E.M., Terkaj, W. (eds.). Formal Ontologies Meet Industry: Proceedings of the 9th International Workshop, within the Proceedings of the International Conference Changeable, Agile, Reconfigurable and Virtual Production (CARV) (2018)
10. Arista, R., Mas, F., Oliva, M., Racero, J., Morales-Palma, D.: Framework to support Models for Manufacturing (MfM) methodology. In: Proceedings of 9th IFAC Conference on Manufacturing Modelling, Management and Control, vol. 52, pp. 1584–1589 (2019). https://doi.org/10.1016/j.ifacol.2019.11.426
11. Arista, R., Mas, F., Oliva, M., Morales-Palma, D.: Applied ontologies for assembly system design and management within the aerospace industry. In: Proceedings of the Joint Ontology Workshops JOWO 2019, 10th International Workshop on Formal Ontologies meet Industry, vol. 2518 (2019). http://ceur-ws.org/Vol-2518/paper-FOMI1.pdf
12. Graves, S.C., Whitney, D.E.: A mathematical programming procedure for equipment selection and system evaluation in programmable assembly. In: Proceedings of the IEEE Decision and Control, pp. 531–536. IEEE Press (1979)
13. Rekiek, B., Alexandre., D., Del-Chambre, A., Bratcu, A.: State of art of optimization methods for assembly line design. Annu. Rev. Control **26**(1), 45–56 (2002)
14. Grüninger, M., Menzel, C.: The process specification language (PSL) theory and applications. AI Mag. **24**(3), 63–74 (2003)

15. Lemaignan, S., Siadat, A., Dantan, J.Y., Semenenko, A.: MASON: a proposal for an ontology of manufacturing domain. In: Proceedings - DIS 2006: IEEE Workshop on Distributed Intelligent Systems - Collective Intelligence and Its Applications, pp. 195–200 (2006)
16. Cutting-Decelle, A., Young, R., Michel, J., Grangel, R., Le Cardinal, J., Bourey, J.: ISO 15531 MANDATE: a product-process-resource based approach for managing modularity in production management. Concurr. Eng. **15**(2) (2007). https://doi.org/10.1177/1063293x07079329
17. Mas, F., Rios, J., Menendez, J.L., Gomez, A.: A process-oriented approach to modeling the conceptual design of aircraft assembly lines. Int. J. Adv. Manuf. Technol. **67**(1–4), 771–784 (2013). https://doi.org/10.1007/s00170-012-4521-5
18. Chengying, L., Xiankui, W., Yuchen, H.: Research on manufacturing resource modeling based on the O-O method. J. Mater. Process. Technol. **139**, 40–43 (2003). https://doi.org/10.1016/S0924-0136(03)00179-1
19. Ameri, F., Urbanovsky, C., McArthur, C.: A systematic approach to developing ontologies for manufacturing service modeling. In: Proceedings of the Workshop on Ontology and Semantic Web for Manufacturing (2012)
20. Sanfilippo, E.M., et al.: Modeling manufacturing resources: an ontological approach. In: Chiabert, P., Bouras, A., Noël, F., Ríos, J. (eds.) PLM 2018. IAICT, vol. 540, pp. 304–313. Springer, Cham (2018). https://doi.org/10.1007/978-3-030-01614-2_28
21. Arista, R., Mas, F., Vallellano, C., Morales-Palma, D., Oliva, M.: Towards manufacturing ontologies for resources management in the aerospace industry. In: 10th International Conference on Interoperability for Enterprise Systems and Applications I-ESA 2020, Tarbes, France (2020, in press)
22. Tomašević, N., Batić, M., Blanes, L., Keane, M., Vraneš, S.: Ontology-based facility data model for energy management. Adv. Eng. Inform. **29**(4), 971–984 (2015)

Tools to Support Early Design Phases

3D Sketching in VR Changing PDM Processes

Carsten Seybold([✉]) and Frank Mantwill

Helmut-Schmidt-University, Holstenhofweg 85, 22043 Hamburg, Germany
{carsten.seybold, frank.mantwill}@hsu-hh.de

Abstract. The use of PDM systems is especially in the late phases of product development state of the art. In fact, it is possible to integrate requirements for future products in the meaning of product lifecycle management into a PDM system. The following steps of product development like initial design sketches are almost not represented yet. Early design work is currently done without computer assistance. An integration of handcrafted sketches in PDM systems is in the case of digitalization possible, but further use is strongly limited. Concluding, in the early phases of product development a gap does still exist in computer assistance. 3D sketching in Virtual Reality (VR) helps to close this gap. Certainly, PDM systems are not prepared for integrating such content in present structures and processes. An approach to integrate these sketches into PDM systems is the main key to establish 3D sketches in product development. To evaluate the use of 3D sketches, a demonstrator in VR has been developed. 27 test subjects worked on two different tasks within this tool. An analysis of the working process and the created solutions shows that sketching in VR could be a possible assistance. In order to cater to these results, a process to handle sketches in PDM has been developed. This process allows preparing sketches with further information and preparing them for further use. The objective is to reach a traceability for the product from requirements via sketches to CAD models to complete the product lifecycle management approach in companies.

Keywords: PDM · VR · Sketching · Concept life cycle · Product development · Design

1 The Early Phases of Product Design

Product development is already been strongly affected by computer support for several years. Without computer support, many of the working methods used in product development are not possible [1]. Database systems, such as product data management (PDM) systems, provide continuous support to the product development process through all phases. However, the situation for support through concrete work applications is different. In the late phases, Computer Aided design (CAD) and other CAx-systems up to digital factory support design with dedicated applications. In the early phases, work steps are realized with office applications or even manually without digital support. As a result, the support possibilities of PDM systems cannot be used sufficiently in the early phases of product development. While requirements for products can be easily digitized and mapped in PDM systems, problems arise with hand-drawn sketches, handwritten notes or even physical models made of cardboard or

Published by Springer Nature Switzerland AG 2020
F. Nyffenegger et al. (Eds.): PLM 2020, IFIP AICT 594, pp. 297–310, 2020
https://doi.org/10.1007/978-3-030-62807-9_24

something else. Sketches and notes can indeed be digitized and stored in PDM. Further use of scanned documents is severely restricted by the few interaction possibilities. A model-based approach is the Sketch Port Model in Systems Engineering. The objective is to provide the product designer with a methodology that combines abstract functional models and 3D CAD models [2]. However, this approach focuses on the interface between the systems engineer and the product designer of the mechanical components.

In order to bypass this media break in PDM, the approach pursued is to develop a concept lifecycle that allows consistency in the development process within the PDM system in conjunction with 3D sketches from virtual reality environments. 3D sketches, annotations and further information can be integrated into PDM systems in a use-oriented way and build up a basis for the detailing in CAD. Figure 1 shows the current computer support in the product development process and the solution pursued here.

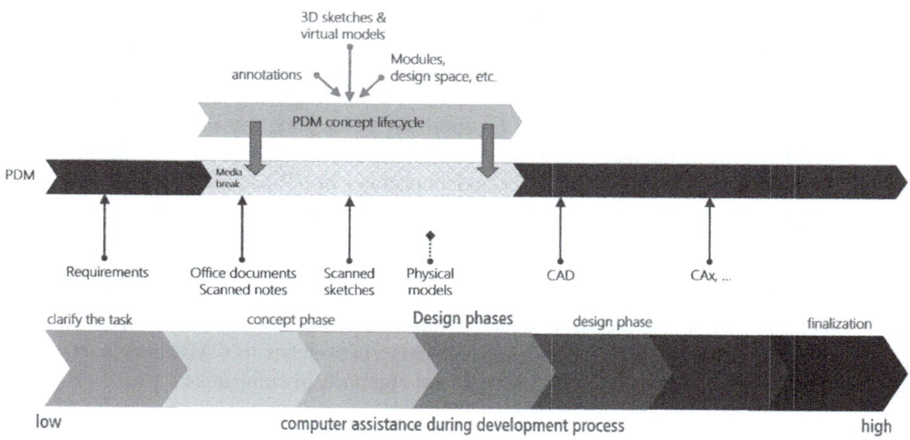

Fig. 1. Computer support in the product development process and the concept lifecycle approach

2 Sketches as External Support and the Connection to CAD and VR

However, why are sketches so important that further use in PDM systems is an objective? Sketches support intellectual activity [3]. They are used as analysis-, solution-, communication- and documentation support. In a few cases, they are also used as an assessment support, but typically here are other form of support used [4]. In addition, sketching has been proven to accelerate the work in product design [3]. In the past, the subsequent digitization of sketches created by hand and further processing has hardly been used [5]. Therefore, a change and support by digital tools seems to make sense. Proven CAD systems could offer a solution here. Among other things, CAD systems are suitable systems for visualization and communication - functions that are also very relevant for sketches [6]. In their use, CAD systems require the input of exact parameters, such as length dimensions or position conditions. However, sketches are deliberately kept imprecise. Individual sketched lines get not too much importance and there is space for change [7]. Therefore, common CAD software supports the early phases of product development not in a meaningful way [8]. In fact, it is not advised to use CAD-Systems in the early phases [6]. In addition, the use of CAD can even have a negative impact on creativity [7].

A platform for 3D sketching tools can be offered by virtual reality, or VR for short. The most common definition is formed by the three I, interaction, immersion and imagination. The user of virtual reality has the possibility to influence or change the virtual world (interaction). By appealing to the user's senses, the user is immersed in the environment (immersion) and how well the virtual environment works depends largely on the user's imagination [9]. A high level of immersion and imagination in virtual environments can only be achieved by a real-time capability of these environments [10]. Head Mounted Displays (HMD's) and CAVE systems (a projection based VR area) are regarded as such immersive VR systems [11]. The use of CAD or other CAx systems represent a special kind of virtual reality, called non-immersive virtual techniques. As a difference to non-immersive virtual techniques VR allow to display and interact with objects in a realistic environment and on a 1:1 scale. This is possible with the currently common HMD systems via stereoscopic immersion and intuitive interaction modalities. The interaction modalities in VR will allow a fast but relatively rough interaction. Working with high precision as in CAD is not intended in VR.

3 The Use of VR in Product Development

Looking at the literature published on VR in recent years, numerous use cases for VR in the product development process can be found:

- Design-Review processes [11, 12],
- Evaluation of design alternatives [14, 15],
- Realistic representation of vehicles without physical prototypes [16],
- Product presentation in the customer environment [16],
- Marketing [13],
- Visibility studies [12],
- Ergonomics studies [12, 15],
- DMU collision checks and assembly simulations [15],
- Assembly and installation studies [14, 15],
- Visualizations of FEM and CFD calculations [15],
- Wiring simulations [12],
- Studies on the virtual prototype [14],
- Testing of products for acceptance [15],
- Comparison of variants [15],
- Education and training [13, 17],
- Service measures (validation of work steps), tele maintenance (AR) [11].

In addition, research also include applications of VR in the field of communication [13, 18]. It is obvious that the VR technology is already used in various fields in product development. On a closer look at the use cases, it is clear that they partly overlap or cover very similar areas. In fact, VR is being used more and more in individual sectors such as the automotive industry - but these are individual applications. A comprehensive or even cross-industry use has not yet taken place. This applies to the area of product development, but also to the area of production or the digital factory, where very similar fields of application can be found [19].

It is also obvious that the applications are limited to the presentation and evaluation of mainly visual product properties [20]. Use cases such as the education of maintenance personnel, assembly simulations or training are used for simulations that are usually created outside VR in advance. Up to now, the industry uses Virtual Reality not to create new content. It is evident that the visualization of product functions in VR is most highly valued by companies. The support for communication is also gaining importance [10]. It is therefore appropriate to assume that VR will continue to increase its importance, especially in these areas.

However, VR technology has developed strongly in recent years, especially in the area of hardware. While for example in the automotive industry expensive CAVE systems are still often used for design review, low cost VR systems like HMD's are now available for the consumer and also for professional applications. In addition to the actual HMD viewing system, the most common systems have intuitive control units, which allow the VR user to interact with his environment and not only change the viewing angle. The low-cost hardware, development platforms from the gaming industry and the possibility of interacting more with virtual environments have reduced the barriers for the use of this technology in recent years.

It must be assumed that VR will spread further into other fields of application. Bruns (2015) even assesses VR as a key technology. The use of VR can offer opportunities for companies, such as competitive advantages. Risks resulting from high investments must also be taken into account. In fact, the significance of the opportunities offered by this technology is becoming increasingly secondary. The risk that arises from disregarding this key technology is increasing and companies must consider whether they can continue to disclaim VR technology [13]. To achieve a benefit the use of VR require certain conditions. The exchange of data between CAD and VR systems is still a problem [14]. Up to now, CAD models cannot be used in VR without further adaptations. In most cases, in addition to conversions, strong simplifications are necessary to achieve real-time capability for the geometric data. The future of VR requires a better integration of CAD, VR and also PDM. The connection of VR to PDM systems is getting an increasingly important role [14].

The same applies to VR support in the early phases of product development. If VR is used to provide an environment in which the product designer is supported in finding solutions by creating 3D sketches and models, it cannot be considered as a stand-alone software solution. In order to achieve a consistent digital product development, a connection to the PDM system must be established [14].

4 VR-Sketching as a New Approach

In order to investigate the support of the product development process during sketching, the Helmut Schmidt University (HSU) developed a demonstrator. Similar approaches are also available like SketchAR [21], Lift-Off [22], Napkin Sketch [23] and others. However, these methods focus on other problems, such as styling [21], transferring existing hand sketches into 3D [22] or projective 3D sketching [23]. For the demonstrator at HSU is the focus on providing a tool that support the product designer in finding and selecting alternative solutions and establishing a basis for further work in CAD. The hardware of the demonstrator is a common HMD, the Vive from HTC. In addition to the tracking of HMD and two control elements, it also allow a comparatively large movement area of 12 m^2. The software is created in the development environment Unity and provides the user with functions for sketching and modelling. These are for example, freehand sketching, drawing straight lines and circular arcs and sketching options such as changing the line width, color and line shape. The demonstrator provide also geometric basic bodies for modelling according to a modular system. In addition, the user can position, copy, group and manipulate objects freely in the virtual environment. Measuring distance and inserting audio comments are further supporting tools. These and other functions are available to the user in the form of a selection menu directly on one of the control elements, so that the user can select the function with the other control element and following use it in the virtual environment. In addition to the internal possibility to save and load work progress, it is also possible to export that work process as a .stl file. Further use in CAD is thus possible.

In order to determine the benefits of a VR sketching tool, such as the demonstrator developed at the HSU, two different design problems are developed, which were worked on by a total of 27 test subjects. The first task is to design an engine test bed. This test bed should be able to place and operate a car engine including all necessary attachments and further requirements have to be considered. In addition to this constructive task, the focus at the second task is placed on facility planning and workplace design. Here is the objective to redesign an area of test bench installations. In addition to the positioning of the test benches and the associated valve and pump units, the location of hydraulic tubes, escape routes and accessibility by crane also needed to be considered.

The tasks for the test subjects have their origin in real cases and they are oriented in the structure as closely as possible to the real working methods and the working environment of product designers and system planners. The test subjects had to finalize and prioritize the requirements based on the given information. It was also important that the test subjects required no special expertise in finding a solution. Otherwise, the task provided the necessary information or the problem was simplified. In addition, the objective was not to design a finished solution detailed in CAD, but a concept solution. The test subject should therefore create a design sketch or a design model, which enables further work and detailing in CAD. An example of creating a sketch in the VR demonstrator is shown in Fig. 2.

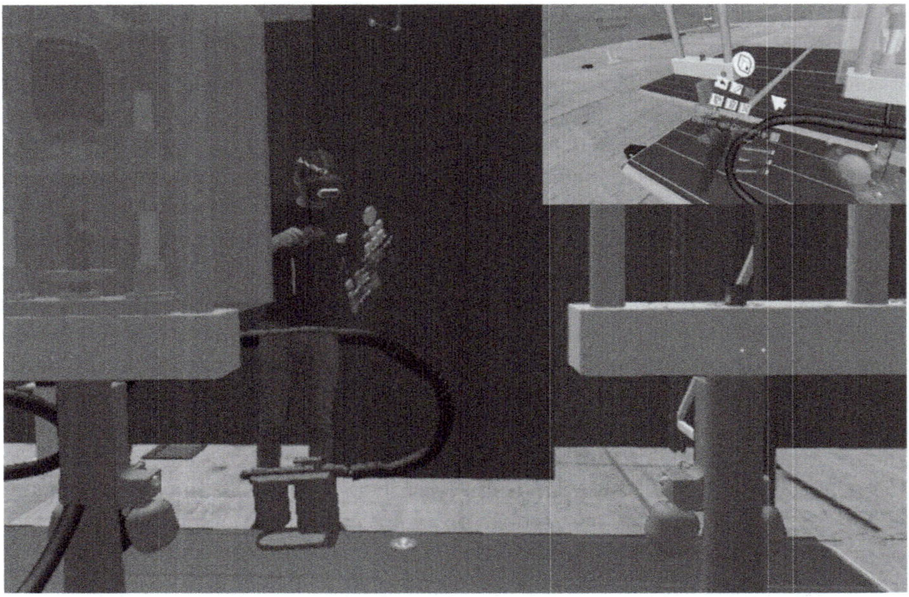

Fig. 2. Mixed reality view of a test subject during the solving of the task *test bed installation*, including the view of the test subject in the top right corner

Fifteen test subjects processed task 1 in VR, twelve test subjects processed task 2. The test subjects represented different ages. Eleven subjects have been 24 up to 29 years, 14 test subjects were at the age of 30–40 years. Two test subjects were significantly older with 46 and 59 years of age. The spectrum of professional experience is wide. Some of them had a professional experience of 10 to 19 years (3 subjects), but many were still students in technical master's degree courses without significant professional experience (11 subjects). In addition, there are different career paths, including a chief engineer and also design engineers and technical product designers without academic graduate (3 subjects). On the other hand, there is a conventionally created comparative solution for each task. The independent comparative test subject is at the age of 57 and is skilled with 30 years of professional experience as a designer. While creating the solution, the test subject used several hand-drawn sketches to visualize the solution and a CAD system to preposition given components in space.

A comprehensive evaluation of the test results is still pending. However, it is for example certain that the processing time of the task "engine test bed" in the VR sketching environment took averagely only 35.4% of the time compared to the conventionally created comparative solution. The average quality of the solutions remained the same. A more detailed chart is shown in Fig. 3. In addition, the comparative test subject could not represent safety aspects such as concrete protective devices and hose line routing like cooling and fuel in his manual sketches. These aspects are only considered in the later CAD detailing. In contrast the VR test subjects represented these aspects. An evaluation of the solutions created by the test subjects showed, that solutions created in VR get a higher ranking as hand-written sketches in aspects like the further usability.

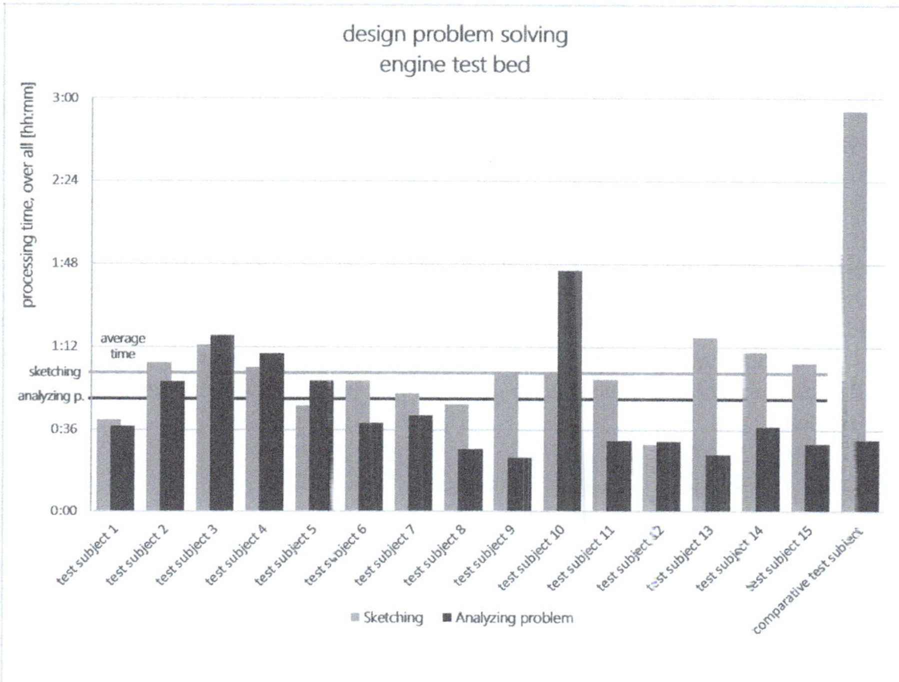

Fig. 3. Results test subjects for the problem "engine test bed" during the 3D sketch creation

In summary, 3D sketches and models are portable to VR and this technology has the potential to support the product development process in a medium or long term - even if 3D sketching should only complement the hand-drawn sketches and not completely replace it. But how should this new generation of data be integrated into the structure of product data management systems with the most possible benefit? PDM systems are not yet prepared for this. Although it is possible to store this kind of data resulting from the sketches easily, for example by assigning it to a project, to CAD data objects or as a separate independent data object. A process related assignment is not yet possible. This applies especially to 3D sketches created with the use of VR tools, but it is also valid for hand-drawn sketches. An assignment in PDM has to be found that is effective for all kinds of sketches.

5 Current Data Storage in PDM Systems

The functionality and the range of functions of PDM systems vary depending on the manufacturer. The implementation in companies is also individually different and adapted to the needs of the company [24]. Despite numerous differences and individualization options, PDM systems always follow the same approaches in their core functions. CAD data are stored as separate objects in the system, consisting of the actual CAD files and associated metadata. CAD objects pass a fixed status network, the object lifecycle, shown in its basic form in Fig. 4 [24]. Such lifecycle has proven itself and ensures that changes to CAD objects, which are located in the status "approved", are no longer possible. A defined status can be committed to production. If changes are necessary, it is only possible to deviate a new version of the CAD object [24]. Each relevant CAD component and each CAD assembly of a product is stored in the system as a CAD object and each object passes through individual states. This ensures that the processing advance of each component and each assembly can be read out directly. To assign CAD objects to a context, there are mostly project and product structures in PDM systems available. Accompanying documents can be displayed as attachments to CAD objects, as a separate object class assigned to a project or product structure, or linked to CAD objects. The same applies to requirements, which could also be mapped. This can be done as metadata in a project structure or as a separate object class. If requirements are created as a separate object, a link between projects and CAD objects is possible.

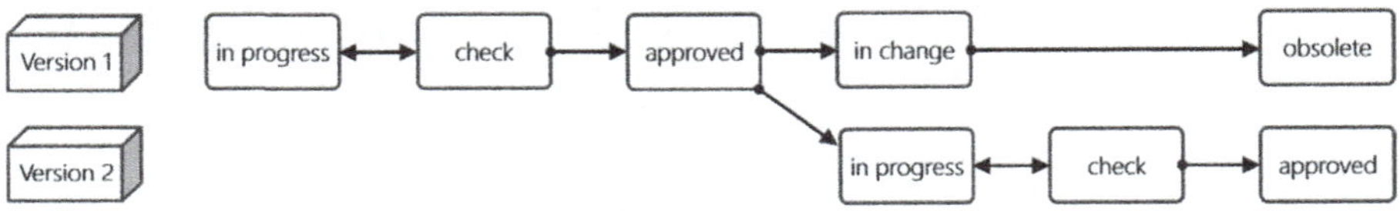

Fig. 4. Standard object lifecycle for CAD objects in PDM systems, based on [24]

It would be conceivable to store 3D sketches according to the same scheme in PDM systems: As a separate object class with a lifecycle based on the standard object lifecycle "concept creation - check - approved for CAD". Such a procedure is already used for technical drawings. The work on these drawings is located towards the work on CAD models. Of course, a CAD model does not have to be completely finished to start the work on the technical drawings. However, technical drawings are only released after the associated CAD models have been released. The prevention of further changes is an immediate requirement for production. Sketches, on the other hand, are a tool, an external form of support. Sketches are not a requirement for working in CAD or further steps in the product development process. In addition, fully complete sketches will not be reachable. Due to the fact that sketches rely on a lack of definition and simplifying aspects, complete sketches are neither possible nor intended favored.

6 The Status Network of Concept Models According to a Maturity Level Principle

How can the lifecycle of sketches be mapped in PDM systems if sketches cannot be fully CAD approved? One solution could be the status network developed below. After a initial status a flexible arrangement of further statuses follows. It is possible to switch from status to status as required. The steps do not have to be executed in a prescribed sequence. The product designer has the possibility to skip work steps and complete them later in the problem solving process. The status network is shown in Fig. 5.

The initial status "concept design" is taken directly when a sketch object is created in PDM. In this state, the 3D sketch and the relevant metadata must be created in the system. If there are several sketches of the same object, the product designer can also assign them to the same sketch object. Further 3D sketches of subassemblies or constructive details can be created as a separate sketch object below the main sketch structure with the possibility to transfer them to a later CAD structure. In this way, initial structural relationships can already be represented. The status and activity content in the middle section of the status network is structured as follows:

- Modularization (modular design): In this status, the product designer defines the future modules and therefore large parts of the future assembly structure. In the simplest case, this can be the entry of structural relationships in the metadata of the sketch object. Alternatively, the assignment of geometry elements of the sketches within a PDM-internal viewer or directly from VR to specific modules is possible. The objective is an automatic extraction of a product structure for further processing in CAD when work in CAD begins.
- Requirement assignment & verification (requirement mapping): If the product designer chooses this status, he gets the possibility to link geometric elements, modules (if already defined) or module sections with requirements for the product. This assignment can be done in VR or in a PDM-internal viewer, similar to common redlining functions. Of course, to do this, requirements must be represented in the project or product context in the PDM system. In addition, it would be conceivable to record new requirements in this status, which only arise after selecting a principle solution and during creating the sketch and are not based on the initial situation. It is only possible to assign requirements if they have a geometric reference, which is not necessarily the case for all requirements According to this, the existing requirements must be categorized. Later on, it is possible to link the further CAD models with the sketches and requirements. If certain sketch elements are not in line with the requirements, it can be noted accordingly and alternatives can be designed.
- Individualization check (clarification): The product designer must decide during his work whether individual components must be designed and manufactured as house parts in the company or whether purchased parts should be used. In this status, the objective is to prepare, evaluate and select several alternative solutions for these components if necessary. Information of selected alternatives can be directly reused for CAD, but also the information of the approaches not pursued further is retained and can therefore be reused later if necessary.

It is obvious that the intermediate statuses in concept lifecycle do not exclusively deal with sketch editing. Rather, the sketches are enriched with additional information to facilitate the change to the detailing phase in CAD. The status network is supported by a percentage maturity level, which is assigned to the sketch object, i.e. to the 3D sketch with its meta-information. This level of maturity should enable an evaluation of how much a 3D sketch with its metadata is suitable for further processing in CAD. This avoids a rigid status change to "approved for CAD" and therefore a rigid boundary between "suitable" and "unsuitable". Ideally, the product designer achieves a high level of maturity by completing and fulfilling the previous work steps before starting work in

CAD. However, it is also possible for the product designer to start early in CAD. In this case, he will be made aware of the work steps that are still open. As shown in Fig. 5, the maturity level of the concept model can be carried out across all lifecycle elements on a percentage basis. This means that subordinate sketch entities, such as detailed sketches of individual areas or sketches of subassemblies, influence the overall maturity level. In addition to a percentage calculation, other simplified representations of the maturity level are also possible, for example, using the Likert scale or a traffic light system.

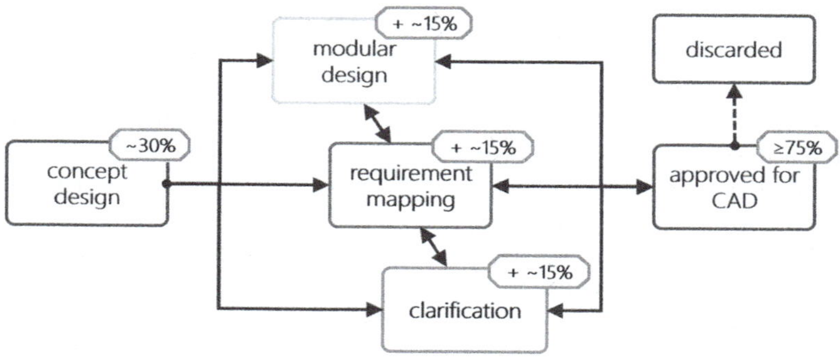

Fig. 5. Object lifecycle for concept models in PDM systems

Whenever the product designer is not working on one of the task packages of the intermediate work steps, the final status "approved for CAD" is taken. If a sketch is not in line with the requirements, it is also possible to change it to status "discarded" and, if necessary, upload a new sketch as a new version into the PDM system. A discarded sketch is no longer included in the maturity level calculation.

A possible procedure could look like the following: A product designer creates a 3D sketch for a new product "Test Bench for car engines" in VR and uploads it into the PDM system. The sketch object receives the status "concept design" and for example a initial maturity level of 25%. The product designer assigns in the status "modular design" a module to certain sketch elements in VR based on the initial thoughts during sketch creation. In the PDM, the assigned modules are hierarchically organized. Afterwards the product designer switches to the "requirement mapping" status to link the requirement "Mobility of the Test Bench" to the wheels in the sketch. This assignment could be done in a viewer integrated in the PDM system. Hereafter, the product designer assigns further requirements. During a break, the sketch object remains in the "approved for CAD" status. Therefore, the maturity level has increased due to the previous editing of the requirements. In a further processing step, the product designer decides to purchase the wheels and other components of the future test bench and not to manufacture them. These decisions are entered into the sketch object in the status "clarification". In this example, the concept model has now reached a maturity level of 68% as a result of processing. The product designer decides to transfer the structure created in the "modular design" step to a CAD object structure and to start working in CAD.

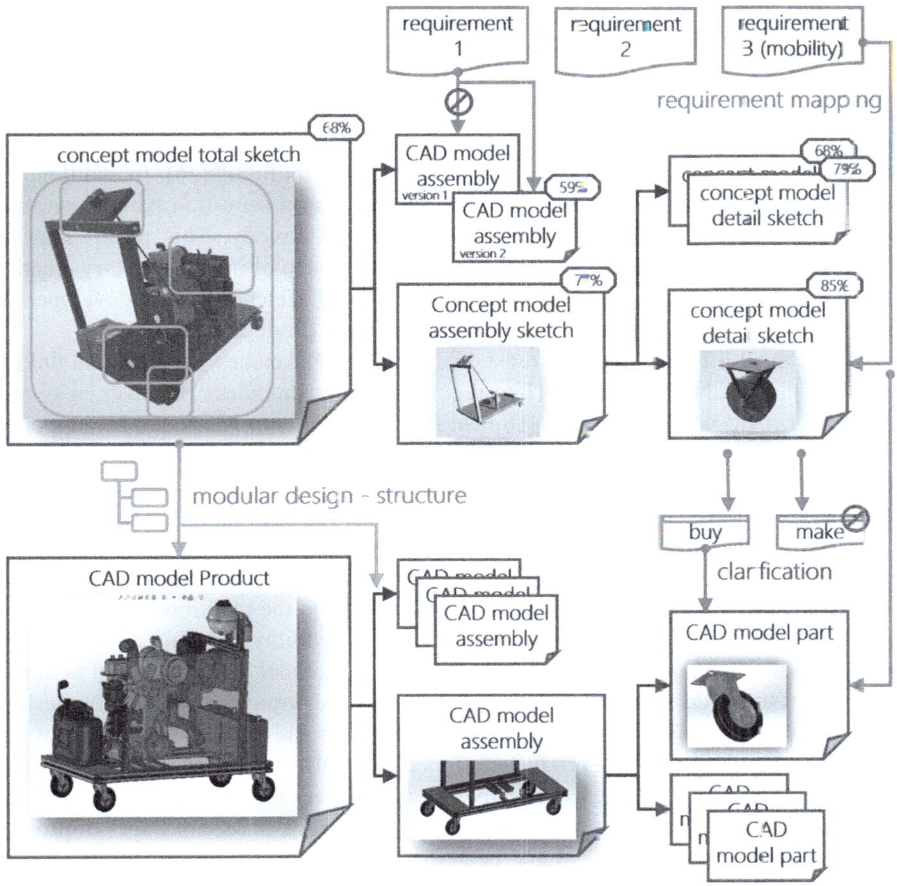

Fig. 6. Example of a concept model with selected functions within the PDM structure

This example shows what editing of the concept models might look like in future with the concept lifecycle. Throughout the process, the product designer can edit and complete metadata of the sketch object and makes changes or additions to the sketch as needed. However, if the product designer makes changes to the sketch, the system will create a new version of the sketch automatically. This ensures that older versions of the sketch can always be accessed. The relationships between the individual states and their effects on the concept model are shown in an example in Fig. 6.

7 Achievable Objectives with 3D Sketches and the Concept Lifecycle

With the implementation of such a concept model, the product designer has to deal with a corresponding amount of effort in the daily application in his work. This effort must be offset by a corresponding benefit. The use of 3D sketches and their integration into PDM systems generally provide a better possibility for further use in CAD detailing as handwritten sketches. 3D sketches are already available in a stereoscopic view, so there is no need to derive the 3D geometry from different views like in handwritten sketches. For the drawing of perspective representations, the product designer needs knowledge about the creation of projections in the area of hand sketches. This is not necessary when creating sketches directly in 3D [25]. In addition, the 3D sketch can be opened directly in CAD and used as a semi-transparent template. Proportions and positioning can partly be transferred directly. This means that the product designer can expect a quicker procedure in the area of initial geometry creation in CAD. It is also possible to create sketches or parts of sketches by non-developers in the future, which can then be further processed by the product designer.

The concept lifecycle model is most effective for 3D-sketches, especially in linking geometry and further information like requirements or modules. However, it is also suitable for hand written sketches. Typical operations in companies can be supported without the capital investment into VR technology. It is obvious that the model of a concept lifecycle does not support mainly the sketching itself. The concept lifecycle is styled to enrich the sketches with further information to support the following work in CAD. With the concept lifecycle, it is possible to archive consistency from the requirement via the sketch to the finished CAD component. This also applies to concept ideas that are not pursued further or are not in line to the requirements. Continuity is particularly important in industries where exact traceability is required. This can be extended with this approach. In principle, the concept model can be a useful addition. This applies to the development of new model series, subsequent products or to designs adapted to new requirements. Here, it is possible to fall back on sketches of the previous design, so that the product designer can reuse them. The reuse of partial solutions, which the company has already generated, saves time and effort. The concept model encourages the product designer to take a closer look at certain stages of product development after the sketches have been created. Especially inexperienced product designers are instructed so that important aspects are not left out. By guiding the product designer through the systematics of the product development methodology, problems or errors in the design implementation of the product can be identified and eliminated at an early stage, which is a main objective according to the "rule of ten" of error elimination costs [24].

8 Summary and Outlook

This paper has shown, that there is still a gap existing in computer assistance during product development. PDM systems could support all phases of product development, if sketches can be integrated in a beneficial way. The approach applied here was to close this gap by the use of 3D sketches in VR. During a study, test subjects solved two different design tasks with the use of a VR tool. Afterwards the designed solutions and the work itself have been rated. The result of the evaluation is that 3D sketching in VR has a positive influence on product development. The advantages are a comparatively fast creation and easier reusability as hand-drawn sketches. For the efficient and further use of 3D sketches, an integration of 3D sketches into the PDM-supported development processes is required. One solution can be the approach presented here, a concept lifecycle model for 3D sketches within PDM systems. This concept lifecycle model is not based on a rigid status network. It depends on a maturity level system to achieve the necessary level of flexibility. The concept lifecycle model achieves a consistency from the requirements to the sketches and up to the CAD models. This concept lifecycle model supports common hand-drawn sketches but also digital 3D sketches with benefits in linking objects. In addition, the model supports the product designer in the further processing of sketches and prepares for the next steps in the product design process. Further research is needed to analyze how the concept model can be extended to cover previous steps in the product development process and a cross-departmental approach in systems engineering. Subsequently, the optimized concept model is to be validated in a realistic application.

References

1. Feldhusen, J., Grothe, K.-H.: Pahl/Beitz Konstruktionslehre. Methoden und Anwendung erfolgreicher Produktentwicklung, 8th edn. Springer, Heidelberg (2013). https://doi.org/10.1007/978-3-642-29569-0
2. Grundel, M.: Skizzen-Port-Modell. Ein Modell zur Überbrückung der derzeitigen Lücke in der modellbasierten Konzeption mechanischer Systeme. Shaker, Aachen (2017)
3. Sachse, P., Leinert, S.: Skizzen und Modelle - Wieso Hilfsmittel des Denkens und Handelns beim Konstruieren? In: Winfried, H. (ed.) Denken in der Produktentwicklung. Psychologische Unterstützung der frühen Phasen, vol. 33, pp. 63–82. Hochsch.-Verl. ETH, München (2002)
4. Sachse, P., Hacker, W., Leinert, S., Riemer, S.: Prototyping als Unterstützungsmöglichkeit des Denkens und Handelns beim Konstruieren. Zeitschrift für Arbeits- und Organisationspsychologie **43**, 71–82 (1999)
5. Huet, G., McAlpine, H., Camarero, R., Culley, S.J., Leblanc, T., Fortin, C.: The management of digital sketches through PLM solutions. In: Proceedings of ICED 2009, the 17th International Conference on Engineering Design, vol. 8, pp. 239–250. Stanford (2009)
6. Robertson, B.F., Radcliffe, D.F.: Impact of CAD tools on creative problem solving in engineering design. Comput. Aided Des. **41**, 136–146 (2009)
7. Müller, F.D.: Intuitive digitale Geometriemodellierung in frühen Entwicklungsphasen. Dr. Hut, München (2007)
8. Römer, A., Pache, M.: Skizzieren und Modellieren in der Produktentwicklung. Hilfsmittel des Praktikers auch bei CAD-Arbeit? In: Winfried, H. (ed.) Denken in der Produktentwicklung. Psychologische Unterstützung der frühen Phasen, vol. 33, pp. 53–62. Hochsch.-Verl. ETH, München (2002)
9. Burdea, G., Coiffet, P.: Virtual Reality Technology. Wiley, New York (1994)
10. Decker, R., Bödeker, M., Franke, K.: Potenziale und Grenzen von Virtual Reality-Technologien auf industriellen Anwendermärkten. Inf. Manage. Consult. **17**(2), 72–80 (2002)
11. Dörner, R., Broll, W., Grimm, P., Jung, B. (eds.): Virtual und Augmented Reality (VR/AR). Grundlagen und Methoden der Virtuellen und Augmentierten Realität. Springer, Heidelberg (2013). https://doi.org/10.1007/978-3-642-28903-3

12. Ovtcharova, J.: Virtual engineering: principles, methods and applications. In: International Design Conference 11, pp. 1267–1274. Marjanović, Dubrovnik (2010)
13. Bruns, M.: Virtual Reality. Eine Analyse der Schlüsseltechnologie aus der Perspektive des strategischen Managements. Diplomica Verlag, Hamburg (2015)
14. Encarnacao, J., Benölken, P., Knöpfle, C.: Virtuelle Realität. Perspektiven für den Einsatz in der Produktentstehung. In: Virtuelle Produktentstehung: Inovationsforum Proceedings, pp. 287–302. Fraunhofer IGD, Berlin (2000)
15. Hausstädtler, U.: Der Einsatz von Virtual Reality in der Praxis. Handbuch für Studenten und Ingenieure, 2nd edn. Rhombos, Berlin (2010)
16. Schenk, M., Schumann, M. (eds.): Angewandte Virtuelle Techniken im Produktentstehungsprozess. AVILUSplus. Springer, Heidelberg (2016). https://doi.org/10.1007/978-3-662-49317-5
17. Schreiber, W., Zimmermann, P.: Virtuelle Techniken im industriellen Umfeld: Das AVILUS-Projekt. Technologien und Anwendungen. Springer, Heidelberg (2012). https://doi.org/10.1007/978-3-642-20636-8
18. Gräßler, I., Taplick, P.: Virtual Reality unterstützte Kreativitätstechnik: Vergleich mit klassischen Techniken. In: Wartzack, S., Krause, D., Peatzold, K. (eds.) Design for X. Proceedings to the 29. DfX-Symposium, pp. 215–226. Tutzing (2018). https://doi.org/10.18726/2018_3
19. Runde, C.: Konzeption und Einführung von virtueller Realität als Komponente der digitalen Fabrik in Industrieunternehmen. Jost-Jetter, Stuttgart (2007)
20. Rademacher, M.H.: Virtual Reality in der Produktentwicklung. Instrumentarium zur Bewertung der Einsatzmöglichkeiten am Beispiel der Automobilindustrie. Springer, Wiesbaden (2014). https://doi.org/10.1007/978-3-658-07013-7
21. Amicis, R.: SketchAR. Sketching in mixed realities. In: Gausemeier, J. (ed.) Paderborner Workshop Augmented & Virtual Reality in der Produktentstehung, pp. 145–156. HNI, Paderborn (2002)
22. Jackson, B., Keefe, D.F.: Lift-off: using reference imagery and freehand sketching to create 3D models in VR. IEEE Trans. Visual. Comput. Graph. **22**(4), 1442–1451 (2016)
23. Xin, M., Sharlin, E., Costa Sousa, M.: Napkin sketch - handheld mixed reality 3D sketching. In: Proceedings of the 2008 ACM Symposium on Virtual Reality Software and Technology, pp. 223–226 (2008)
24. Lindemann, U.: Handbuch Produktentwicklung. Carl Hanser, München (2016). https://doi.org/10.3139/9783446445819
25. Pache, M.W.: Sketching for Conceptual Design. Empirical Results and Future Tools. Dr. Hut, München (2005)

A Method to Formulate Problem in Initial Analysis of Inventive Design

Masih Hanifi[1,2](✉), Hicham Chibane[2], Remy Houssin[1], and Denis Cavallucci[2]

[1] Strasbourg University, 4 Rue Blaise Pascal, 67081 Strasbourg, France
remy.houssin@unistra.fr

[2] INSA of Strasbourg, 24 Boulevard de la Victoire, 67000 Strasbourg, France
{masih.hanifi,hicham.chibane,denis.cavallucci}@insa-strasbourg.fr

Abstract. Initial Analysis is one of the most important phases of Inventive Design, where designers apply the existing methods to formulate a problem. One of these methods is problem graph, which is a powerful tool to translate the knowledge, collected from available documents and data, into a graphical model. However, this graph, by considering today's competitive world, does not have the agility to present the essential information for applying in the next phase of Inventive Design. The aim of this article is to introduce a new method, which makes a designer able to formulate an appropriate problem, according to the objectives, without wasting time. This method, along with TRIZ, could create an agile design process. An example is done to illustrate better the process.

Keywords: Initial analysis · Complex problem · Inventive design · Problem graph · Root contradiction analysis · Root causes analysis

1 Introduction

Problem formulation, in the Initial Analysis phase of inventive design, has the greatest impact on the success of a company [2]. For this reason, the companies look for continuously good methods to formulate the problems. Among these methods, Problem Graph, Root Conflict Analysis play an important role, because they can illustrate the contradictions, which are inventive problems resulting from the conflict of the desired characteristics within a product life-cycle management (PLM) [14]. Theory of inventive problem solving or TRIZ provides the essential tools in the next phases of inventive design to solve these contradictions. The contradictions could be engendered by considering different phases of product life-cycle. Furthermore, our work provides the fist data in the first phase of the PLM. In TRIZ-based inventive design processes, the designers analyze the problem situation, and to solve it, they need to formulate the problems in the form of contradiction. However, the current methods, applied in the Initial Analysis phase, do not have suitable agility to respond to today's market requirements. Therefore, we needed a methodology, which could help to decrease the time consuming of the existing methods. This methodology is called Lean,

Published by Springer Nature Switzerland AG 2020
F. Nyffenegger et al. (Eds.): PLM 2020, IFIP AICT 594, pp. 311–323, 2020.
https://doi.org/10.1007/978-3-030-62807-9_25

and in our first article, we propose to apply it to Inventive Design Methodology. The proposed method in this article is the result of this application [12].

Lean theory was introduced in the early 1950s by Toyota Company to maximize value, decrease time, and reduce cost [7]. This theory provides tools and principles to eliminate non-value-adding activities within a process to achieve excellence.

In our research, we integrated the best features of Problem Graph, RCA+ into a new method. In addition, we apply Lean principles to this method, in order to introduce an agile and effective tool for initial analysis. This proposed method is able also to combine the proposed solutions to solve the contradiction with Initial Analysis phase of inventive design. This paper introduces this lean-based method to the readers. Furthermore, it discusses the differences, which distinguish it from other existing methods. 2 This paper is organized into five sections. In Sect. 2, we present the state of art of the existing methods for formulating problems and analyzing the initial situation of inventive. Section 3 presents the steps of our proposition (Inverse Problem Graph). We present the discussion in the Sect. 4, and the paper finishes by the conclusion in Sect. 5.

2 Literature Review

2.1 Existing Methods for Formulating a Problem in Initial Situation Analysis

Initial Analysis in inventive design is a phase to collect known knowledge, which comes from a) patent and company's internal documents, b) tacit know-how of expert, c) existing data related to a subject [5,6,8,27]. In the following, designers apply a wide range of methods to formulate problems. According to the state of the art, these existing methods for analyzing problems in innovation projects could be divided into two groups, first methods based on searching for causes, and second methods based on looking for the effects.

The first group related to those methods and techniques, which are applied to identify the causes creating the problems in an innovation project. It is possible to assign the available methods in this group into the two following categories. The first category includes the methods without the ability to demonstrate the contradiction and the second one related to the methods with the ability to show the conflicts. In the following, we describe the limitations related to the existing methods in each category.

A designer, by applying the existing methods in the first category, could search for the causes of a negative effect. However, these methods could not illustrate contradictions. In this category, we could find methods such as "Ishikawa", "5 Whys", and "CauseEffect Chain Analysis".

K. Ishikawa introduced "Cause and Effect" which merges mind Map and brainstorming, in order to explore the causes of the initial problem [19]. The designers, by applying this method, could classify the explored causes into the category, which makes them able to identify the areas where information should be collected for further study [15,26]. However, this method does not show the way of translating the discovered causes into contradictions [9]. In addition, it would be stopped in high-level of causes, and it could not demonstrate the causes at lower levels.

The "5 Whys", classical Root Cause Analysis, is a question-asking method which is applied to find the cause and effect relationships related to a particular problem [11]. The process of "5 Whys" starts with writing down a specific problem. Then, the designer should search for the reasons of the problems by asking the "Why" question and finding its answers. This asking-answering should be repeated until the identification of the root cause of the specific problem [11]. The application of the "5 Whys" method is easy to determine some causes of a specific problem [11]. Nevertheless, this method could not show the contradictions. Furthermore, it has a shortage to demonstrate the root causes related to a problem, and designers could not sometimes give answers to all "Why" question [11,20].

The "Cause-Effect Chain Analysis (CECA)" method has been successfully applied in many consulting projects of GEN3's Partners for developing new products [1,20]. This method is started with a selected problem, written in a box on top of the diagram. Then, the designers identify its underlying causes by asking, "What causes that problem?", and link them to the top problem [28]. "CECA" could reveal hidden causes of a target problem, which leads designers to more ideal solutions [15,26,28]. However, the shortage of revealing the contradictions still remains with this method. Accordingly, the designers, especially those who look for an innovative solution for their problems, need the existing methods in the second category, such as the method "RCA+".

The second category related to those methods with the ability to illustrate the contradictions. Among them, there are "Root Conflict Analysis", "Cause-Effect Chain Analysis Plus", which are described in the following. Because in inventive design, we need to overcome the contradiction in a complex problem. Our concentrate is on this category.

Root Conflict Analysis (RCA+), Fig. 1, eliminates difficulties in the extraction of contradictions [9,22,24]. Its process starts with a general expression by a statement of a negative effect [21]. Designers apply "What is a cause?" question to discover the related causes of the general problem [1,28]. The subsequent cause in the answer to "what" question could have a negative effect, and so forth. If the identified cause leads also to a positive cause, it is verified as a conflict in the RCA(+) diagram. Once the found cause, it has just a negative effect, the chain of the cause will be explored downward until an over-control or a conflict appears. [22]. Once the first chain has been completed, the process should be done for other negative effects in the diagram until all causes have been explored [11]. However, a designer, by applying "RCA+", should create all the chains of causes in the Initial Analysis phase of inventive design, which takes a long time, without paying attention to their utility in the solution step. Additionally, this method did not merge the solution part into its main structure.

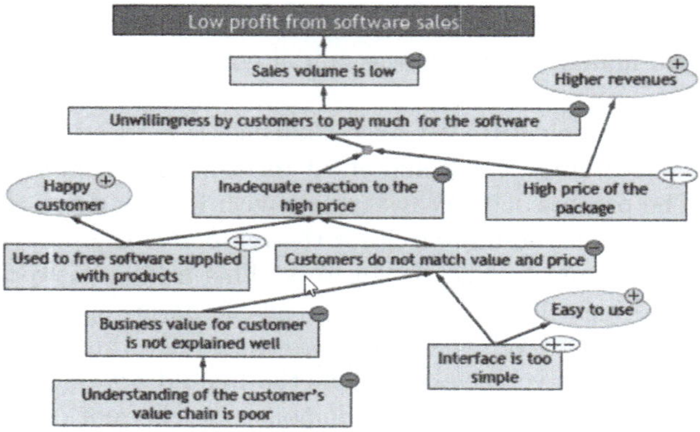

Fig. 1. A project, which applied Root Conflict Analysis to formulate problem [23]

The Cause-Effect Chain Analysis Plus has been introduced by Lee et al. [20]. This method has a development trend quite similar to "RCA+". In fact, designers choose a general problem and put it on the top of the diagram. Then, they start to create the chains of causes related to the first problem until they receive the cause with positive and negative effects in each chain, Fig. 2. This method could demonstrate the contradictions and add to solve them. However, loss of time for creating unusable chains of causes, like other discussed methods in this category, has been ignored. Furthermore, this proposed method cannot show the solutions, which could partially solve the negative effect. This drawback has been solved in the proposed methods in the second group.

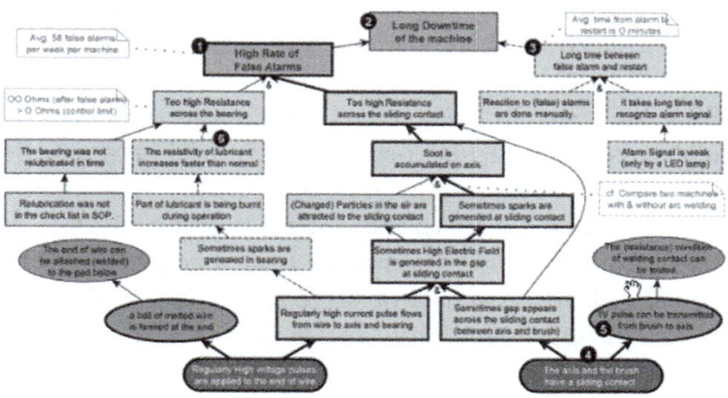

Fig. 2. Part of a Cause-Effect Chain Analysis Plus done for a project [20]

The second group is related to those techniques, which they are looking for the effects of the initial problems. In this group, we could find Network of Problems (NoP), and Problem Graph, which is an improved version of NoP.

Nikolai Khomenko developed the NoP in the framework of OTSM-TRIZ theory to decompose an overall problem to a set of sub-problems, which are easier to solve [3,4,10]. The network of problems can be defined as a graph, which includes nodes of problems, partial solutions or goals, Fig. 3. This graph is an illustration of the problem situation, which is derived from the collection and analysis of existing information of the initial situation. Its analysis could highlight a series of key problems of the whole problematic situation [17,18]. These key problems, which created the bottlenecks in the system, should be extracted. A series of contradictions are hidden in these bottlenecks, which are applied to construct the network of contradiction. However, The original version of NoP did not propose a clear definition for the nodes, problem and partial solution, forming its structure [4]. Additionally, a problem, which is considered a supper problem, is most of the time too general. This makes the network of problems in many cases too large and complex for designers. For solving drawbacks related to NoP, Problem Graph was proposed to solve some of them.

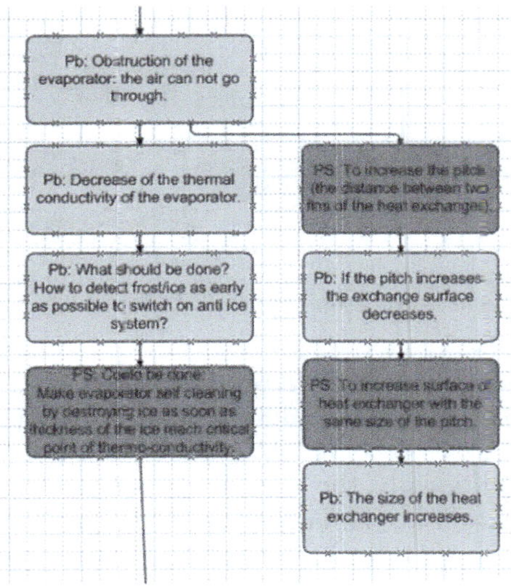

Fig. 3. Part of a NoP [16]

D. Cavallucci proposes Problem Graph by improving the original version of NoP. This graph also, like NoP, demonstrates a connection between a large set of problems and partial solutions, which are resulted from the main problem [13,19,25]. The process of problem graph's construction is like NoP. This process starts with a problem, which is the most critical for team members. Then, it is time to discover the immediate effect of the problem, which could be another problem or a partial solution, by asking the question "What is the effect of the problem?" and "What could initially solve this problem?". When a problem, results in an implementation of a partial solution to solve some of its aspects, a link between problem space and partial solution space has been created. A partial solution, which gives birth to a new problem, creates a relationship between partial solutions space and problem space. When a problem is resulted by another problem, a chain of interdependent problems has been created, Fig. 4. After creating a network of problems and partial solutions, the related parameters, including evaluation parameters and action parameters, should be extracted. These parameters are applied in the formulation of contradictions. Besides, they could connect the graph to the solution concept in TRIZ.

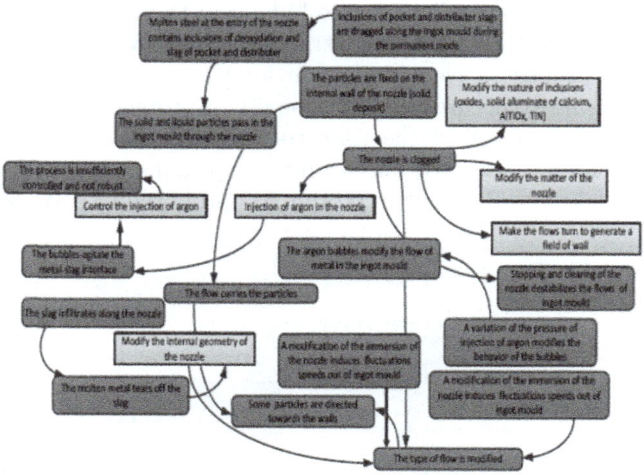

Fig. 4. Application of problem graph to formulate problem [25]

As we considered in the most important methods, which they can formulate the complex problems in the Initial Analysis step of inventive design, all of them did not pay attention to the usability of the created chains of causes and effects in the Solution step. Additionally, the amount of time that designers should assign to collect the information at the beginning of the project, without thinking if they are useful to receive the final solution or not. As a result, it was necessary to apply Lean to improve the agility and effectiveness of the process. Result of this application, it was a new agile method to formulate the problems. In the next section, we introduce this method.

3 Proposed Method: Inverse Problem Graph

3.1 Notions of Components of Inverse Problem Graph (IPG)

The Inverse Problems Graph is constructed with the following types of entities, which are shown graphically in Fig. 8:

1. Problem: In Inverse Problem Graph, a problem is a sentence, which describes a barrier, which prevents the achievement of what has to be done. There are 5 types of problems in IPG:
   (a) Initial problem: a problem that has been defined according to the objective of the project, and it is placed in the first level of the graph.

   (b) Harmful problem: A problem with harmfulness for the system.
   (c) Source of partial solution: A problem with harmfulness leading to the partial solution.
   (d) Harmful-useful problem: A problem with Harmfulness and Usefulness for the system (Problem with convertibility to partial solution).
   (e) Out-of-capacity problem
2. Partial solution: A phrase, which expresses knowledge of designers or members of the design team about a registered patent by the company or its rival and their experience.
3. Parameters: the existing parameters in IPG's structure are divided in two groups:
   (a) Evaluation parameters: they are the parameters, which gives to the designers the capacity of evaluating their design choice.
   (b) Action parameters: their nature lies in the capacity of state modification.
4. Level: the level precise the location of the problem and partial solution in the IPG, by considering initial problem.
5. Iteration: Number of entry to IPG, in order to choose a contradiction. This notion has been added to the structure of the proposed method, that we should create a flow of information.

3.2 Process of Inverse Problem Graph

In this section we present the steps of our methods using a case study of Food-Storage-Box design. For confidentiality reason we cannot explain more in detail this study.

1. Step1: Define the objective of the project: At the beginning, the objective of the project should be defined. For example, a Food-Storage-Box has been designed to store vegetables and fruits, but this product does not have the ability to help to save the stored material for a long time without using cooling electrical energy. The problem here is the short life of vegetables and fruits in the interior of Food-Storage-Box and the objective, as Fig. 5 shows, is to increase the life of them in the interior space of the box.

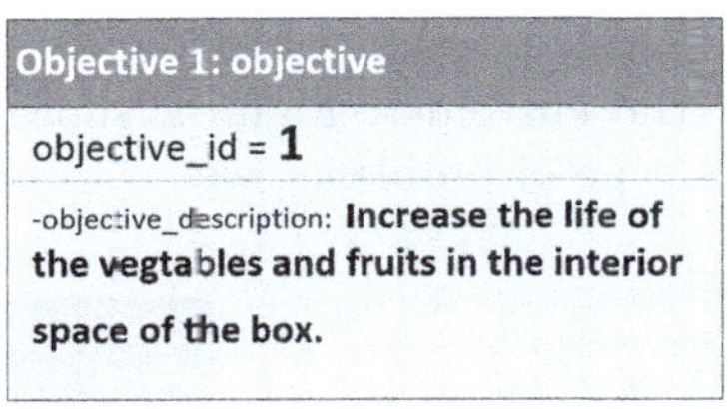

Fig. 5. Definition of objective in the example

2. Step 2: Write the initial problem of Inverse Problem Graph (IPG): Write the initial problem by considering the objective of the project in the first step of Inverse Problem Graph. In our example, the initial problem is "the vegetables have a short life in Food-Storage-Box".

3. Step 3: Find related problems to initial problems: In order to find all the problems and partial solutions, it should be asked "what in the Selected-Level cause the initial problem?" "This problem is the effect of what in the Next-level of graph, Fig. 6.

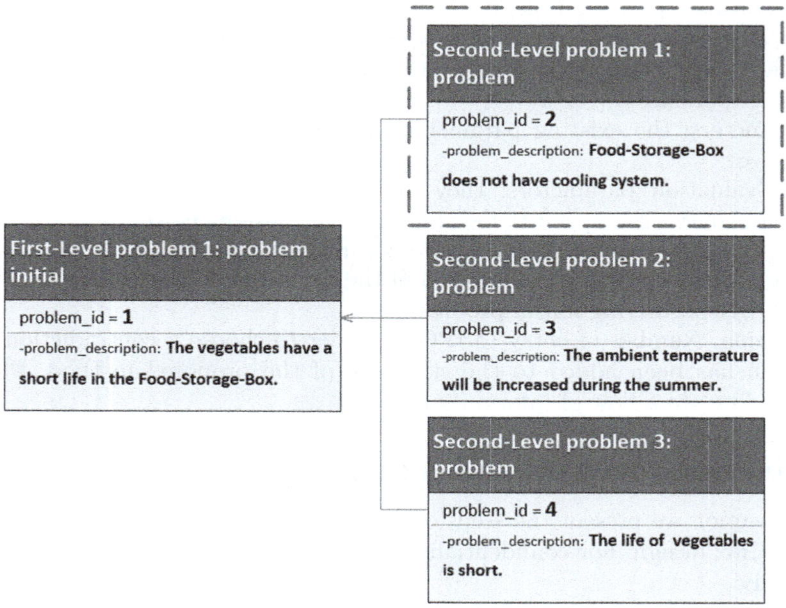

Fig. 6. Selection of the most important problem in the example

4. Step 4: Determine the type of the selected problem: For each second-level problem it should be identified, as a Harmful-Useful problem, or as a Harmful problem. This step includes the following sub-steps:
   (a) The Harmful-Useful problem should be converted to a partial solution. For ex-ample, the problem "Food-Storage-Box does not have a cooling system" has usefulness for the system, which could reduce electricity consumption for the customer. Figure 7 shows this conversion in our example. For this type of problems, we:

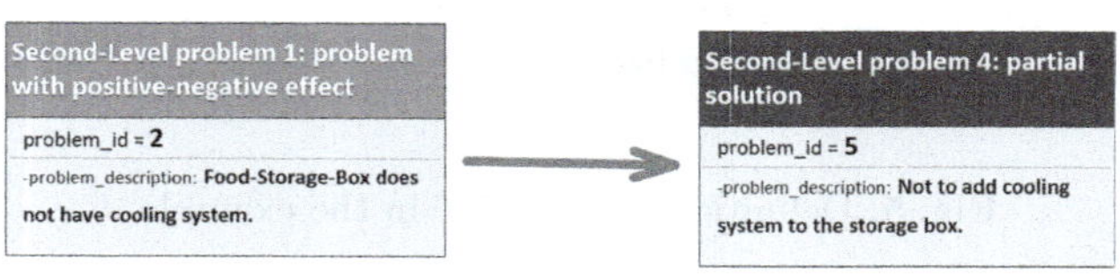

Fig. 7. Conversion of the problem to partial solution in the example

   i. Determine the source of the contradiction by asking the question "What problem in the Next-level of graph cause this partial solution?" "This partial solution is the effect of which problems in the Next-level of graph?". The result of this sub-step determines the source of contradiction.
   ii. Determine the cause of the source of the contradiction by asking this question "What problem in the Next-level of graph cause the source of the question?". This step might be done, if a designer needs to explore the root conflicts of the source of contradiction after evaluating the concept.

  (b) For a Harmful problem, it needs to ask this question "What problem in the Next-level of graph causes this problem?" "This problem is the effect of which problems in the Next-level of the graph?", Fig. 8.

5. Step 5: Extract the illustrated contradiction from the graph: extract the contradiction of the most important problem to solve. We should consider that in each iteration designer can select just one contradiction to receive to a flow of information. Figure 9 shows our extracted contradiction in our example.
6. Step 6: Allocate appropriate parameters: For the problems and partial solution in the selected contradiction, allocate the appropriate evaluation parameter, and the appropriate action parameter. In our example and for the first iteration, we created the allocation in Fig. 10.

4 Discussion

In order to make readers of this article more aware of the difference between Inverse Problem Graph and Network of Problem, it was necessary to visualize this difference, as Fig. 11 shows.

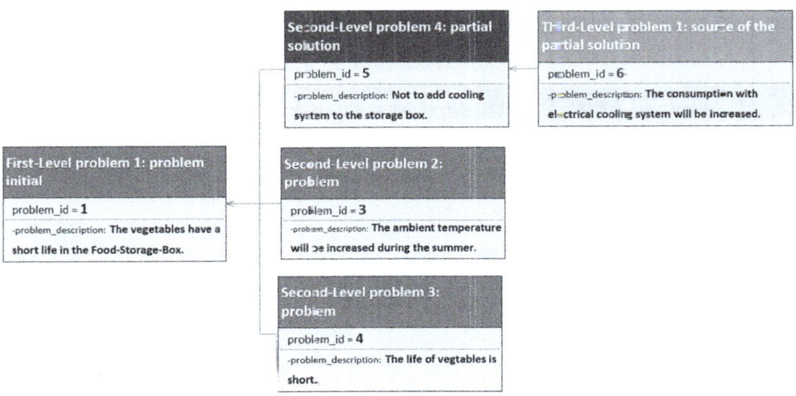

Fig. 8. Inverse Problem Graph of the example in the first iteration

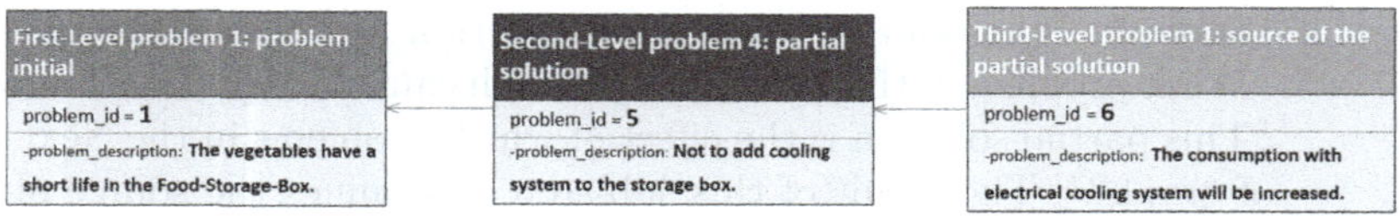

Fig. 9. Extraction of the contradiction in the example

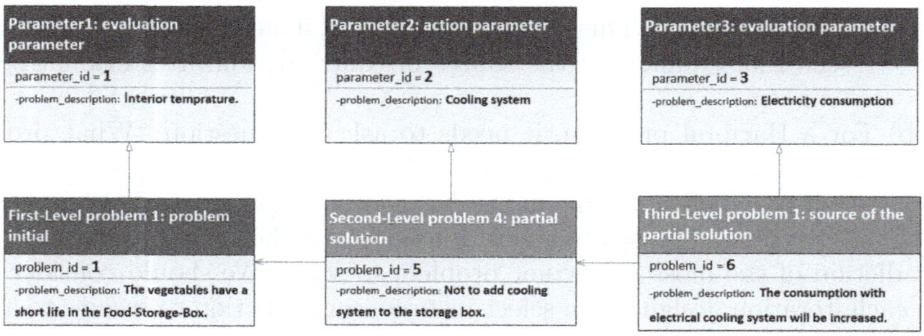

Fig. 10. Allocation of the parameters in the example

To verify the applicability and the advantage of our proposition, it is necessary to compare it with the discussed methods in the state of art section. The Table 1 shows a comparison between the reviewed methods in the literature and our proposed method. This comparison is built on the following criteria: contradiction structure, time agility of the process, and ability.

The contribution of this work to inventive design process is reflected on a number of aspects. First, our proposed method could reveal hidden root causes, as well as illustrate contradictions. Second, it could improve readability of the created chains by added iteration notion. As the third important contribution, our work could increase the agility of inventive design of process. Unlike other existing methods to formulate problems, we do not develop all chains at the

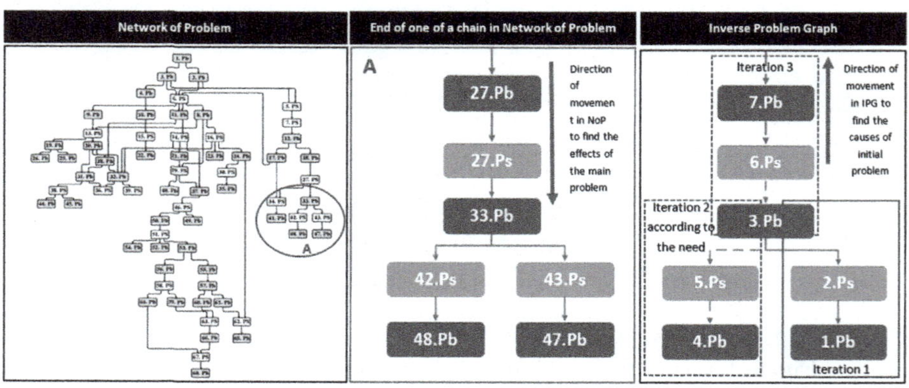

Fig. 11. Network of Problem and its difference with Inverse Problem Graph [18]

Table 1. Comparison of the existing methods of initial analysis phase with Inverse Problem Graph

Criteria	RCA+	CECA+	Problem Graph and Network of Problem	Inverse Problem Graph
Contradiction	The effects of a positive-negative problem help to illustrate the contradictions.	The effects of a positive-negative problem help to illustrate the contradictions	The contradiction is between the effect and the cause of a partial solution	The contradiction is between the effect and the cause of a partial solution
Development of the chains of causes and contradictions	Regardless of the need in concept solution step	Regardless of the need in concept solution step	Regardless of the need in concept solution step	Considering the needs in concept step
Time spending of the methodology	Significant to collect all information	Significant to collect all information	Significant to collect all information	Short because we collect only required information for an iteration
Agility of the process to introduce a contradiction to other stages of ID	Need to complete the initial analysis process	Need to complete the initial analysis process	Need to complete the initial analysis process	A designer can start other steps of ID after finding the contradiction related to the most important problem

beginning of the project. Instead, we start from a chain, which is more important for the designers. In the following, we develop the chains according to the needs in the solution step.

5 Conclusion

In this research, we analyzed the existing methods to formulate problems. We concluded that all the analyzed methods ignored time spent to collect useless information. Accordingly, we integrated the best characteristics of analyzed methods into a new method called Inverse Problem Graph. Besides, we applied

Lean principles to this proposed method to increase its agility. Finally, we compared this proposed method with the methods with the ability of illustrating the contradictions.

Further investigations are necessary in order to appreciate the proposed method and its application. One of the future investigations focuses on combining this proposed method in a process that, along with TRIZ tools, could connect faster the extracted contradiction in the initial analysis phase to the solution phase. This new process is called "Agile Inventive Design Process". The other investigation focuses on developing a software that, with the help of machine learning, could facilitate finding the innovative solutions.

References

1. Abramov, O.Y.: Triz-based cause and effect chains analysis vs root cause analysis. In: Proceedings of the TRIZfest-2015 International Conference, Seoul, South Korea, pp. 288–295 (2015)
2. Ang, T., Arnott, D., O'Donnell, P.: Problem formulation and decision support systems development. In: Proceedings of the Australian Conference on Information Systems, Melbourne, Australia (1994)
3. Becattini, N., Cascini, G., Rotini, F.: An OTSM-TRIZ based framework towards the computer-aided identification of cognitive processes in design protocols. In: Gero, J.S., Hanna, S. (eds.) Design Computing and Cognition '14, pp. 99–117. Springer, Cham (2015). https://doi.org/10.1007/978-3-319-14956-1_6
4. Becattini, N., Cascini, G., Rotini, F.: OTSM-TRIZ network of problems for evaluating the design skills of engineering students. Procedia Eng. **131**, 689–700 (2015)
5. Cavallucci, D.: Designing the inventive way in the innovation era. In: Chakrabarti, A., Blessing, L.T.M. (eds.) An Anthology of Theories and Models of Design, pp. 237–262. Springer, London (2014). https://doi.org/10.1007/978-1-4471-6338-1_12
6. Cavallucci, D., Strasbourg, I.: From TRIZ to inventive design method (IDM): towards a formalization of inventive practices in R&D departments. Innovation **18**(2) (2009)
7. Chen, H., Taylor, R.: Exploring the impact of lean management on innovation capability. In: PICMET'09-2009 Portland International Conference on Management of Engineering & Technology, pp. 826–834. IEEE (2009)
8. Chinkatham, T., Cavallucci, D.: On solution concept evaluation/selection in inventive design. Procedia Eng. **131**, 1073–1083 (2015)
9. Dobrusskin, C.: On the identification of contradictions using cause effect chain analysis. Procedia CIRP **39**(2016), 221–224 (2016)
10. Fiorineschi, L., Frillici, F.S., Rissone, P.: A comparison of classical TRIZ and OTSM-TRIZ in dealing with complex problems. Procedia Eng. **131**, 86–94 (2015)
11. Gîfu, D., Teodorescu, M., Ionescu, D.: Design of a stable system by lean manufacturing. Int. Lett. Soc. Hum. Sci. **17**(2), 61–69 (2014)
12. Hanifi, M., Chibane, H., Houssin, R., Cavallucci, D.: improving inventive design methodology's agility. In: Benmoussa, R., De Guio, R., Dubois, S., Koziołek, S. (eds.) TFC 2019. IAICT, vol. 572, pp. 216–227. Springer, Cham (2019). https://doi.org/10.1007/978-3-030-32497-1_18
13. Howladar, A., Cavallucci, D.: Analysing complex engineering situations through problem graph. Procedia Eng. **9**, 18–29 (2011)

14. Ilevbare, I.M., Probert, D., Phaal, R.: A review of TRIZ, and its benefits and challenges in practice. Technovation **33**(2–3), 30–37 (2013)
15. Ilie, G., Ciocoiu, C.N.: Application of fishbone diagram to determine the risk of an event with multiple causes. Manag. Res. Pract. **2**(1), 1–20 (2010)
16. Khomenko, N.: OTSM network of problems. https //otsm-triz.org/en/content/n-khomenko-otsm-network-problems-draft-discussion-and-improvements
17. Khomenko, N., De Guio, R.: OTSM Network of Problems for representing and analysing problem situations with computer support. In: León-Rovira, N. (ed.) CAI 2007. ITIFIP, vol. 250, pp. 77–88. Springer, Boston, MA (2007). https://doi.org/10.1007/978-0-387-75456-7_8
18. Khomenko, N., De Guio, R., Lelait, L., Kaikov, I.: A framework for OTSM? TRIZ-based computer support to be used in complex problem management. Int. J. Comput. Appl. Technol. **30**(1–2), 88–104 (2007)
19. Koripadu, M., Subbaiah, K.V.: Problem solving management using six sigma tools & techniques. Int. J. Sci. Technol. Res. **3**(2), 91–93 (2014)
20. Lee, M.G., Chechurin, L., Lenyashin, V.: Introduction to cause-effect chain analysis plus with an application in solving manufacturing problems. Int. J. Adv. Manuf. Technol. **99**(9–12), 2159–2169 (2018)
21. Souchkov, V.: Root conflict analysis (RCA+): structured problems and contradictions mapping. In: Proceedings of TRIZ Future Conference, Graz, Austria (2005)
22. Souchkov, V.: Application of root conflict analysis (RCA+) to formulate inventive problems in the maritime industry. Zeszyty Naukowe Akademii Morskiej w Szczecinie (2017)
23. Souchkov, V., Hoeboer, R., Van Zutphen, M.: TRIZ in business: application of RCA+ to identify and solve conflicts related to business problems. ETRIA TFC 9–11 (2006)
24. Souchkov, V.: A guide to root conflict analysis (RCA+). ICG training & consulting (2018)
25. Souili, A., Cavallucci, D., Rousselot, F., Zanni, C.: Starting from patents to find inputs to the problem graph model of IDM-TRIZ. Procedia Eng. **131**, 150–161 (2015)
26. Wong, K.C., Woo, K.Z., Woo, K.H.: Ishikawa diagram. In: O'Donohue, W., Maragakis, A. (eds.) Quality Improvement in Behavioral Health, pp. 119–132. Springer, Cham (2016). https://doi.org/10.1007/978-3-319-26209-3_9
27. Zanni-Merk, C., Cavallucci, D., Rousselot, F.: Use of formal ontologies as a foundation for inventive design studies. Comput. Ind. **62**(3), 323–336 (2011)
28. Zlotin, B., Zusman, A.: TRIZ software for creativity and innovation support. In: Carayannis, E.G. (ed.) Encyclopedia of Creativity, Invention, Innovation and Entrepreneurship. Springer, New York (2013). https://doi.org/10.1007/978-1-4614-3858-8_39

Using BSC and DEMATEL Method to Construct the Novel Product Concepts Evaluation System

Zhe Huang[1(✉)] and Mickaël Gardoni[1,2]

[1] École de technologie supérieure, Montréal, Québec, Canada
hz8018@outlook.com, mickael.gardoni@etsmtl.ca
[2] INSA de Strasbourg, Strasbourg, France
mickael.gardoni@insa-strasbourg.fr

Abstract. Concept assessment is a complex problem which needs to be evaluated comprehensively and multiple dimensions. This paper proposes a multi-dimensional concepts evaluation system based on Balanced Scorecard (BSC) and Decision-Making Trial and Evaluation Laboratory (DEMATEL) method. BSC provides a reference framework to select evaluation indicators. DEMATEL method can effectively analyze the mutual relationship and structure of components in the system. This methodology can help manager to evaluate from a holistic perspective. This paper identifies and constructs the causal relationships among the critical evaluation criteria. The cause and effect diagram analysis clearly indicate which aspect/criteria is more important to make continuous improvement, so as to enhance competitiveness.

Keywords: Concepts evaluation · Balanced Scorecard (BSC) · Decision-Making Trial and Evaluation Laboratory (DEMATEL)

1 Introduction

Innovation is a process of transforming concepts into useful products or services [1]. The concept evaluation has an important impact on the success and cost of innovation [2, 3]. Rietzschel et al. [4] proposed that it is necessary to clearly determine the concept evaluation criteria and optimize the evaluation process, in order to choose the best concept. Hart [5] emphasized that technical feasibility is the most commonly used criterion for evaluating concepts. Shortening the development time and choosing the right strategy are important factors to survive in the market [6]. Schwarz and Bodendorf [7] proposed that good concepts must be feasible, new, profitable, useful, very mature, and so on.

The concept evaluation is a complex issue, multiple factors need to be considered comprehensively [8]. The identification of key influencing factors is therefore significant to the reasonable concept evaluation. Our study aims to propose a multidimensional approach to conduct a comprehensive concept assessment. In view of the complexity of the evaluation issue, this paper identifies first the key influencing factors of concept evaluation based on Balanced Score Card (BSC) method. BSC provides a

Published by Springer Nature Switzerland AG 2020
F. Nyffenegger et al. (Eds.): PLM 2020, IFIP AICT 594, pp. 324–333, 2020.
https://doi.org/10.1007/978-3-030-62807-9_26

reference framework for us to select concept evaluation indicators [9]. However, the degree of mutual impact between key factors may be different [10]. This paper adopts Decision-Making Trial and Evaluation Laboratory (DEMATEL) method to identify the interdependence among criteria of evaluation system through a causal diagram. The proposed approach can aid decision makers to make decisions based on full consideration of the most relevant impact indicators for achieving goals. The next section presents the methodology used in this paper.

2 Methodology

2.1 Balanced Score Card (BSC)

Robert S. Kaplan and David P. Norton first proposed "balanced scorecard" (abbreviated to "BSC") in their article "Balanced Scorecard - measures to drive performance", which was published in Harvard Business Review in 1996 [9]. The BSC comprehensively takes into account a balance between short-term and long-term objectives financial and non-financial measures, and internal and external interests [11].

BSC provides a framework for thinking and acting sustainably [12]. This paper divides the concept evaluation system into four perspectives based on BSC method: Concept attractiveness perspective (P1), Financial perspective (P2), Market perspective (P3) and Innovative capabilities perspective (P4).

Concept Attractiveness Perspective (P1). Understanding of customer existing or potential needs is the starting point for innovation. The new concept shall be applicable to and effectively meet these needs [13, 14]. In addition, the concept should be clear, complete and well communicated (specificity) [15].

Financial Perspective (P2). The success of the enterprise must finally translate into financial success. Concepts evaluation must also take into account financial factors. The development of new concepts is a long process. Cooper [16] emphasizes that the shortening of R&D cycle and the acceleration of market access can provide a powerful guarantee for enterprises to seize market opportunities.

Market Perspective (P3). In research of Frishammar et al. [17], successful firms generally analyze the prospective and current product offerings of competitors. It is very important to assess market segments in which the business will compete.

Innovative Capabilities Perspective (P4). Not all new product concepts can be developed into new products. Some concepts may be very good, but if the enterprise lacks the corresponding resource conditions, the concept lacks the possibility of development. The Innovative capabilities perspective mainly measures the ability to achieve transformation of concept, so as to better meet the changing needs of customers and achieve sustainable growth.

16 evaluation criteria in 4 dimensions of the concept evaluation index system based on BSC method are summarized in Table 1, which will be set as P_{11}, P_{12}... P_{ij}.

Table 1. Evaluation index system.

Dimension	Criteria	Explication
Concept attractiveness perspective (P1)	Novelty (P_{11})	Original and uncommon
	Specificity (P_{12})	Clear, complete and explicit
	Workability (P_{13})	It does not violate known constraints or if it can be easily implemented
	Uniqueness (P_{14})	The degree to which the concept is unique
	Effectiveness (P_{15})	The degree to which the concept will solve the problem
Financial perspective (P2)	Investment cost (P_{21})	Financial resources required
	R & D cycle (P_{22})	R & D cycle
	Anticipated profitability (P_{23})	Anticipated profitability of an investment in development
Market perspective (P3)	Market need (potential) (P_{31})	Is it a growing market?
	Fôrward-looking (P_{32})	Does this concept match the current development, is it reasonable in the market?
	Competitive intensity (P_{33})	Market competition (number and intensity of competitors)
	Entry barriers (P_{34})	Obstacles that make it difficult to enter a given market
Innovative capabilities perspective (P4)	Access to technology (P_{41})	Measure complexity to master this technique
	Relevant capabilities and experience (P_{42})	Do we have the necessary skills and experience?
	Available physical resources (P_{43})	Difference between required and existing physical resources
	Strategic alignment (P_{44})	Consistency with the company's strategy

2.2 Decision-Making Trial and Evaluation Laboratory (DEMATEL)

In view of the different degree of interaction between criteria, this paper made an in-depth analysis of the relationship among criteria based on the Decision-Making Trial and Evaluation Laboratory (DEMATEL) method. DEMATEL method developed by Battelle Memorial Institute between 1972 to 1979 [18]. DEMATEL method can not only visualize the causal relationship among variables, but also identify the key factors. DEMATEL method has been successfully applied to the operation safety evaluation of urban rail stations [19], geographical environment evaluation and other fields. Here are the steps of DEMATEL [18, 20]:

Step 1: Generating the Initial Direct Relation Matrix A. An evaluation scale from 0 to 4 is used to measure the direct influence relationship among the indicators: 0 (no influence), 1 (low influence), 2 (medium influence), 3 (high influence), and 4 (very high influence), respectively. The initial direct relation matrix $A = \left(a_{ij}\right)_{n\times n}$ is then obtained,

$$A = \begin{bmatrix} a_{11} & a_{12} & \cdots & a_{1n} \\ a_{21} & a_{22} & \cdots & a_{2n} \\ \vdots & \vdots & \ddots & \vdots \\ a_{n1} & a_{n2} & \cdots & a_{nn} \end{bmatrix} \quad (1)$$

where a_{ij} denoted as the degree in which the factor *i* affects the factor *j* [20]. If factor *i* has a very strong influence on factor *j*, then define $a_{ij} = 4$.

Step 2: Normalizing the Direct-Relation Matrix D. Normalize matrix A according to Eq. (2).

$$D = \lambda * A \quad (2)$$

where $\lambda = Min\left(\frac{1}{Max\sum_{j=1}^{n} a_{ij}}, \frac{1}{Max\sum_{i=1}^{n} a_{ij}}\right)$; $1 \leqslant i \leqslant n$, $1 \leqslant j \leqslant n$.

Step 3: Construct the Total Relation Matrix T. Use the following Eq. (3) to calculate the total relation matrix T:

$$T = D * (I - D)^{-1} \quad (3)$$

Where I denoted as the identity matrix.

Step 4: Calculate (Eq. 4 and 5) the Sum of the Elements of Each Row (R) and Each Column (C) of the Total Relation Matrix T.

$$R_i = \sum_{j=1}^{n} t_{ij} (\mathrm{i} = 1, 2 \ldots \mathrm{n}) \quad (4)$$

$$C_j = \sum_{i=1}^{n} t_{ij} (\mathrm{j} = 1, 2 \ldots \mathrm{n}) \quad (5)$$

R_i represents the effects given by the factor *i* to other factors. C_j indicate the effect received by the factor *j* from other factors [21].

DEMATEL method can effectively show the complex causal structure. The relative importance degree among factors can be determined by calculating the value of (R + C) and (R − C). The causal diagram then can be draw. The sum (R + C) is horizontal axis, called "Prominence", which shows the relative importance of each index. The difference (R − C) is vertical axis called "Relation", which divides the indicator into cause group and effect groups [21]. When (R − C) is positive, the factor *i* belong to the cause group; if (R − C) is negative, the factor *i* is a receiver which belongs to the effect group.

3 Case Study

3.1 24 h of Innovation

"24 h of innovation" is an international innovation competition organized by ETS (www.24h.com). Participants must develop innovative solutions, within 24 h, to meet the challenges proposed by enterprises. The best solution for each site is ultimately evaluated by an international jury Committee from academia and industry to select the main winners of the year from local winners.

The goal of innovation competition is not only to encourage innovation, but also to help to find good concepts that can be transformed into efficient products. Varies evaluation factors coexist. This paper constructs the evaluation indicators system based on BSC and DEMATEL, in order to help select the promising concept which deserves further development. This system can effectively simplify the types and quantity of indicators and clarify the impact relationship between indicators, so as to help make decisions based on full consideration of various factors.

3.2 Proposed Methodology

On the basis of the above analysis, the procedure of concept evaluation index system with BSC and DEMATEL methods are presented as follows:

Identify the Influential Criteria for Concept Evaluation and Generate the Direct-Relation Matrix (A). The BSC method was used to identify the influential criteria for concept evaluation (Table 1), and DEMATEL was used to find out the influence degree among indicators. In this paper, the direct influence degree of criteria *i* on criteria *j* is divided into five grades (See Table 2). Three experts are invited to evaluate the interaction among criteria according to Table 2. The initial average direct relation matrix A (Table 3, Table 4) is generated by summing up all the scores separately and averaging them.

Table 2. Direct impact degree of criteria.

Direct influence degree of criteria *i* on criteria *j*	Score
No influence	0
Low influence	1
Medium influence	2
High influence	3
Very high influence	4

Table 3. Averaged direct-relation matrix A1 (Perspective)

A_1	P1	P2	P3	P4
P1	0.00000	2.66667	3.33333	2.66667
P2	1.66667	0.00000	1.00000	3.33333
P3	3.66667	3.66667	0.00000	2.00000
P4	4.00000	3.33333	2.66667	0.00000

Table 4. Direct-relation matrix A2 (Criteria)

A_2	P11	P12	P13	P14	P15	P21	P22	P23	P31	P32	P33	P34	P41	P42	P43	P44
P11	0.00000	1.00000	1.66667	2.00000	1.33333	1.00000	0.66667	1.66667	1.33333	2.33333	2.00000	0.33333	0.66667	0.66667	1.00000	1.00000
P12	1.00000	0.00000	3.00000	3.00000	3.66667	2.00000	1.00000	4.00000	3.33333	2.00000	3.33333	1.00000	2.66667	3.33333	2.00000	3.33333
P13	2.33333	2.66667	0.00000	2.00000	3.66667	2.00000	1.33333	2.33333	2.33333	1.00000	2.66667	0.33333	3.33333	1.33333	1.66667	3.00000
P14	3.66667	3.00000	3.00000	0.00000	2.00000	3.00000	3.00000	2.66667	3.66667	3.33333	2.66667	1.66667	4.00000	3.66667	3.00000	2.00000
P15	1.66667	3.66667	4.00000	2.00000	0.00000	3.00000	3.00000	2.33333	4.00000	2.66667	2.00000	0.33333	3.00000	3.00000	2.33333	3.00000
P21	2.00000	2.00000	3.00000	2.66667	2.00000	0.00000	2.33333	1.66667	1.00000	2.00000	3.00000	0.00000	4.00000	2.33333	3.00000	2.00000
P22	0.33333	1.66667	1.33333	1.00000	3.33333	3.66667	0.00000	3.00000	1.66667	0.66667	3.00000	0.66667	1.66667	2.00000	1.66667	1.00000
P23	0.00000	0.66667	1.00000	1.00000	0.66667	3.33333	2.66667	0.00000	2.33333	3.00000	3.00000	1.66667	2.66667	2.00000	1.33333	2.00000
P31	3.00000	4.00000	3.33333	3.66667	3.66667	3.33333	2.33333	4.00000	0.00000	2.33333	4.00000	1.33333	1.00000	2.66667	2.00000	1.66667
P32	4.00000	3.00000	0.66667	2.00000	0.33333	3.33333	3.00000	2.66667	3.33333	0.00000	3.33333	1.33333	2.00000	1.66667	2.33333	1.00000
P33	1.66667	1.33333	1.66667	2.00000	1.00000	2.66667	3.00000	3.00000	2.66667	2.33333	0.00000	0.33333	2.66667	3.00000	0.33333	0.66667
P34	1.33333	0.33333	2.66667	0.66667	0.00000	3.00000	2.00000	2.66667	0.33333	2.33333	3.33333	0.00000	4.00000	3.33333	2.00000	3.00000
P41	2.66667	3.33333	3.33333	3.00000	3.33333	3.66667	3.66667	2.66667	0.66667	3.00000	3.00000	1.66667	0.00000	1.66667	0.33333	2.66667
P42	2.33333	2.33333	3.66667	2.00000	3.00000	3.33333	3.66667	3.00000	0.66667	2.33333	1.66667	0.00000	3.00000	0.00000	1.66667	3.00000
P43	0.00000	1.00000	1.33333	1.00000	0.66667	2.66667	3.00000	2.00000	0.00000	0.33333	1.33333	0.00000	1.33333	1.33333	0.00000	2.66667
P44	3.00000	2.00000	2.00000	3.00000	2.00000	3.33333	3.00000	3.00000	0.00000	3.00000	1.00000	0.00000	2.00000	3.00000	2.00000	0.00000

Normalize the Direct-Relation Matrix and Construct the Total Relation Matrix (T). Equation (2) were used to normalize the matrix of direct relations A, and the total relation matrix (T) was calculated by using Eq. (3).

Calculate the Sum of the Elements of Each Row (R) and Each Column (C) of the Total Relation Matrix T. Equation (4) and (5) were used to calculate the sums of rows and columns of matrix T (Table 5, Table 6).

Table 5. Total relation matrix (T) of four perspective

T_1	P1	P2	P3	P4	R	C	R+C	R−C
P1	1.27115	1.53034	1.27565	1.37088	5.44803	5.64403	11.09206	−0.19600
P2	1.10136	0.98834	0.86727	1.12993	4.08689	5.86107	9.94796	−1.77418
P3	1.57574	1.63222	1.05522	1.37531	5.63849	4.54555	10.18404	1.09294
P4	1.69578	1.71017	1.34741	1.29175	6.04511	5.16787	11.21298	0.87723

Table 6. Total relation matrix (T) of criteria

T2	P11	P12	P13	P14	P15	P21	P22	P23	P31	P32	P33	P34	P41	P42	P43	P44
P11	0.07030	0.09999	0.11767	0.11780	0.10283	0.12272	0.10423	0.13033	0.09946	0.12761	0.13523	0.03461	0.10385	0.05513	0.08494	0.09226
P12	0.16098	0.15716	0.23228	0.21437	0.22937	0.24675	0.20356	0.27406	0.20808	0.19963	0.25419	0.07536	0.23624	0.23421	0.16831	0.19496
P13	0.16694	0.19018	0.14319	0.17234	0.20758	0.21414	0.18097	0.21051	0.16581	0.15521	0.21154	0.05225	0.22045	0.16760	0.14147	0.13576
P14	0.23374	0.23943	0.25229	0.17029	0.21564	0.29229	0.26548	0.27115	0.22866	0.24459	0.25586	0.09575	0.28349	0.25392	0.20465	0.20521
P15	0.18154	0.24287	0.25999	0.20291	0.16386	0.27586	0.25030	0.25000	0.22631	0.21748	0.23676	0.06283	0.24907	0.23334	0.18201	0.21470
P21	0.16101	0.17650	0.20589	0.18519	0.17409	0.17282	0.20406	0.19717	0.13746	0.17426	0.21917	0.04533	0.23583	0.18706	0.16935	0.15589
P22	0.10256	0.14574	0.14883	0.12804	0.17785	0.22125	0.12793	0.19688	0.13254	0.12463	0.19371	0.05165	0.16430	0.15898	0.12493	0.12449
P23	0.10157	0.12679	0.14114	0.13027	0.12306	0.21890	0.18827	0.13652	0.14451	0.17466	0.19764	0.07413	0.18571	0.16925	0.11917	0.11466
P31	0.21250	0.25248	0.25254	0.24034	0.24192	0.28946	0.24335	0.29053	0.15245	0.21907	0.28524	0.08625	0.21903	0.23538	0.18088	0.19242
P32	0.20060	0.19378	0.15675	0.17187	0.13737	0.24275	0.21498	0.21956	0.18564	0.13195	0.23045	0.07465	0.19324	0.17470	0.15661	0.14198
P33	0.14068	0.14732	0.16182	0.15645	0.13854	0.21060	0.19916	0.20665	0.15957	0.16697	0.14086	0.04885	0.19082	0.18503	0.10240	0.12201
P34	0.13715	0.12682	0.18505	0.13163	0.11816	0.22375	0.18603	0.20336	0.10750	0.17086	0.21305	0.04000	0.22502	0.19544	0.13850	0.17626
P41	0.19563	0.22594	0.23750	0.21385	0.22287	0.27955	0.25509	0.24623	0.15495	0.21940	0.24906	0.08871	0.18141	0.20028	0.13549	0.19937
P42	0.17566	0.19299	0.22972	0.18076	0.20515	0.25623	0.24123	0.23602	0.14030	0.19107	0.20418	0.04833	0.22755	0.14734	0.15161	0.19572
P43	0.06545	0.09581	0.10893	0.09423	0.09000	0.15670	0.15215	0.13433	0.06392	0.08214	0.11697	0.02463	0.11683	0.10610	0.06123	0.12655
P44	0.17756	0.17043	0.17935	0.18646	0.16764	0.23749	0.21180	0.21802	0.11389	0.19126	0.17345	0.04383	0.19081	0.19539	0.14819	0.11801
R	1.63997	3.28942	2.78603	3.72744	3.44982	2.81114	2.32373	2.36723	3.59386	2.82692	2.47772	2.57856	3.30584	3.02334	1.59813	2.72410
C	2.48388	2.78425	3.01294	2.69679	2.71592	3.66129	3.22858	3.42132	2.42106	2.79077	3.32735	0.94667	3.22366	2.93856	2.26976	2.60085
R+C	4.123849	6.073665	5.798971	6.424227	6.165741	6.472424	5.552312	5.788545	6.014918	5.617691	5.805078	3.525234	6.529498	5.962495	3.867886	5.324949
R-C	−0.84391	0.505173	−0.22691	1.030649	0.733895	−0.85015	−0.90485	−1.05409	1.172804	0.036145	−0.84963	1.631894	0.082179	0.08518	−0.67163	0.123243

4 Result Analysis

The analysis of causality is helpful to judge which evaluation dimensions are relatively important, which perspective needs continuous improvement [22]. DEMATEL presents the complex relationship among factors with cause and effect diagram.

4.1 Producing a Causal Diagram of Four Perspectives

According to Table 5, we can get the causal diagram of four perspectives (see Fig. 1).

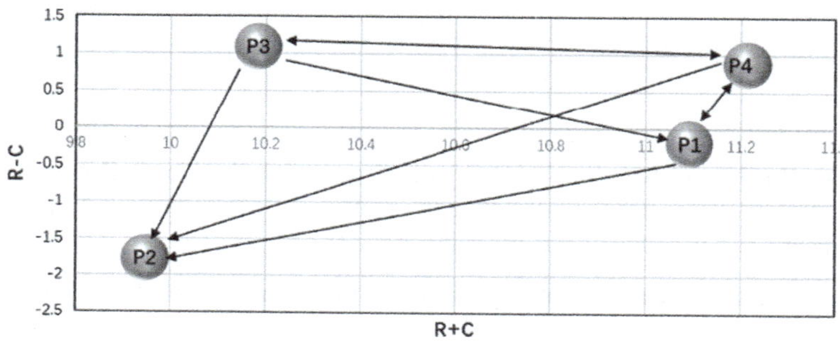

Fig. 1. Cause and effect diagram (Dimension relationship)

Perspectives was divided in cause group and effect group by the value of (R − C). Figure 1 shows that the perspective P1 and P2 belongs to the effect group which are influenced by the perspective P3 and P4. P3 and P4 constitute the cause group, which indicate that changes in the innovative capabilities dimension and the market dimension directly affect the concept attractiveness dimension and the financial dimension.

The horizon axis (R + C) indicates the importance degree of evaluation perspective. The greater the value of (R + C) is, the higher the importance is. As shown in Fig. 1, the (R + C) value of innovative capabilities perspective is the highest, which means that the impact of innovative capabilities perspective to other perspectives is the greatest. Innovative capabilities perspective affects the other three perspectives. Innovative capabilities perspective and concept attractiveness perspective affect also each other. Financial perspective is affected by concept attractiveness, market and innovative capabilities perspective. Compared with the concept attractiveness, financial or market perspective, improving innovative capabilities plays a crucial role to the success of innovation.

4.2 Producing a Causal Diagram of Indicators

According to Table 6, the cause and effect diagram among evaluate indicators was constructed as Fig. 2.

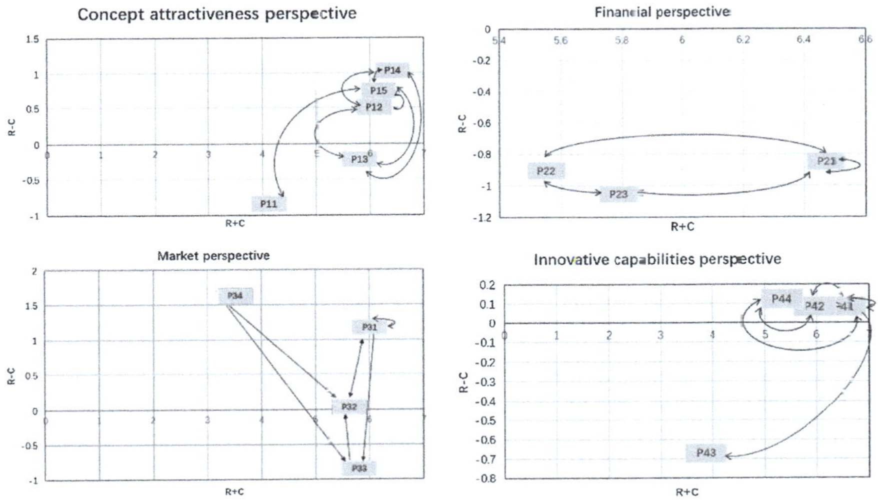

Fig. 2. Cause and effect diagram (Indicator relationship).

From Fig. 2, Uniqueness has a greater correlation with other factors of concept attractiveness perspective. Investment cost is the most critical within financial perspective; market need and access to technology are the most critical within market perspective and innovative capabilities perspective, respectively These factors have the greatest influence on other factors for each dimension. Enterprise managers should pay attention to these factors.

It can be seen from Fig. 2 that P12, P14, P15, P31, P32, P34, P41, P42 and P44 are cause factors according to their value of (R − C). P11, P13, P21, P22, P23, P33 and P43 are the result factors. The value of (R + C) shows the degree of importance of the factors. For example, in the concept attractiveness perspective, Uniqueness and Effectiveness have the greatest influence on other factors. Cause factors have great influence on other factors. Relatively, the factor in effect group are on the level of being affected, and there is no much room for improvement. If we want to improve the success rate of concept development/innovation, the cause index should be first focused on.

5 Conclusion

Concept evaluation is a complex problem, which is influenced by a number of factors. This paper establishes four dimensions and 16 specific evaluation criteria of the concept evaluation index system. BSC provides a reference framework to select performance indicators. DEMATEL method helps to analyze interrelationships of the criteria by dividing factors into cause and effect group. Cause factors are considered to be more influent in the decision. Managers should adjust and improve factors in cause group. The proposed integration approach can help to evaluate from a holistic perspective. This methodology identifies the most important aspect to enhance competitivity, so as to provide targeted basis for concept evaluation. In the future research, a priority of concepts will be reasonably identified in combination with other methods (such as ANP) to improve the accuracy of concept evaluation.

References

1. Robbins, S.P.: Organisational Behaviour: Global and Southern African Perspectives. Pearson South Africa, Cape Town (2001)
2. Cooper, R.G.: New products: what separates the winners from the losers and what drives success. In: PDMA Handbook of New Product Development, pp, 3–34 (2013)
3. Cooper, R.G., Kleinschmidt, E.J.: Screening new products for potential winners. Long Range Plan. **26**(6), 74–81 (1993)
4. Rietzschel, E.F., Nijstad, B.A., Stroebe, W.: The selection of creative ideas after individual idea generation: choosing between creativity and impact. Br. J. Psychol. **101**(1), 47–68 (2010)
5. Hart, S., Jan, H.E., Tzokas, N., Commandeur, H.R.: Industrial companies' evaluation criteria in new product development gates. J. Prod. Innov. Manag. **20**(1), 22–36 (2003)
6. Bandinelli, R., d'Avolio, E., Rossi, M., Terzi, S., Rinaldi, R.: Assessing the role of knowledge management in the new product development process: an empirical study. In: Fukuda, S., Bernard, A., Gurumoorthy, B., Bouras, A. (eds.) PLM 2014. IAICT, vol. 442, pp. 397–406. Springer, Heidelberg (2014). https://doi.org/10.1007/978-3-662-45937-9_39
7. Schwarz, S., Bodendorf, F.: Attributive idea evaluation: a new idea evaluation method for corporate open innovation communities. Int. J. Knowl. Based Organ. (IJKBO) **2**(1), 77–91 (2012)
8. Huang, Z., Ahmed, C., Mickaël, G.: A model for supporting the ideas screening during front end of the innovation process based on combination of methods of EcaTRIZ, AHP, and SWOT. Concurr. Eng. **29** (2020)
9. Kaplan, R.S., Norton, D.P.: The Balanced Scorecard: Translating Strategy into Action. Harvard Business Press, Boston (1996)
10. Falatoonitoosi, E., Ahmed, S., Sorooshian, S.: Expanded DEMATEL for determining cause and effect group in bidirectional relations. Scientific World J. **2014**, Article ID 103846, 7 pages (2014)
11. Yuan, F.C., Chiu, C.: A hierarchical design of casebased reasoning in the balanced scorecard application. Expert Syst. Appl. **36**, 333–342 (2009)
12. Fabio, D.F., Antonella, P.: Key success factors for organizational innovation in the fashion industry. Int. J. Eng. Bus. Manag. (2013). https://doi.org/10.5772/56882
13. Dean, D.L., Hender, J.M., Rodgers, T.L., Santanen, E.: Identifying good ideas: constructs and scales for idea evaluation. J. Assoc. Inf. Syst. **7**, 646–699 (2006)
14. Inoue, M., Yamada, S., Yamada, T., Bracke, S.: A design method for product upgradability with different customer demands. In: Fukuda, S., Bernard, A., Gurumoorthy, B., Bouras, A. (eds.) PLM 2014. IAICT, vol. 442, pp. 91–100. Springer, Heidelberg (2014). https://doi.org/10.1007/978-3-662-45937-9_10
15. Kudrowitz, B.M., Wallace, D.: Assessing the quality of ideas from prolific, early-stage product ideation. J. Eng. Des. **24**(2), 120–139 (2013)
16. Cooper, R.G.: Predevelopment activities determine new product success. Ind. Mark. Manag. **17**(3), 237–247 (1988)

17. Frishammar, J., Florén, H.: Where new product development begins: success factors, contingencies and balancing acts in the fuzzy front end. In: 17th International Conference on Management of Technology, Dubai, 5–8 April, p. 47 (2008)
18. Du, Y.W., Wang, S.S.: Fuzzy comprehensive evaluation on science fund project performance evaluation based on DEMATEL method. Bull. Natl. Nat. Sci. Found. China **18**(02), 161–169 (2018)
19. Li, X., Li, J.: A study on an assessment system on safe operation of urban rail stations based on DEMATEL and ISM. Railw. Transp. Econ. **40**(7), 115–121 (2018)
20. Amiri, M., Sadaghiyani, J., Payani, N., Shafieezadeh, M.: Developing a DEMATEL method to prioritize distribution centers in supply chain. Manag. Sci. Lett. **1**, 279–288 (2011)
21. Si, S.-L., You, X.-Y., Liu, H.-C., Zhang, P.: DEMATEL technique: a systematic review of the state-of-the-art literature on methodologies and applications **2018,** 33 pages (2018). https://doi.org/10.1155/2018/3696457
22. Zhang, S.X.: Fuzzy Multi - Criteria Evaluation Method and Statistics. Taiwan Wunan Book Publishing Co. LTD, Taiwan (2012)

Knowledge Graph of Design Rules for a Context-Aware Cognitive Design Assistant

Armand Huet[1(✉)], Romain Pinquie[2], Philippe Veron[3], Frédéric Segonds[1], and Victor Fau[4]

[1] Arts et Métiers Institute of Technology, LCPI, HESAM Université, 75013 Paris, France
{armand.huet, frederic.segonds}@ensam.eu
[2] Univ. Grenoble Alpes, CNRS, Grenoble INP, G-SCOP, Grenoble, France
romain.pinquie@grenoble-inp.fr
[3] Arts et Métiers Institute of Technology, LISPEN, HESAM Université, 13617 Aix-en-Provence, France
philippe.veron@ensam.eu
[4] Capgemini DEMS, Toulouse, France
victor.fau@capgemini.com

Abstract. [Context] The design of a system shall comply with many design rules that help industrial designers to create high quality design in an efficient way. Nowadays, design rules try to consider all product lifecycle's phases leading to an ever-increasing growth. This context makes the management of design rules a difficult but essential task. This is why many research and industrial works try to automate this task [1, 3, 4]. [Problem] The processing of design rules, which are natural language sentences stored in unstructured documents, requires expert software. Moreover, existing tools interrupt the design workflow and slow down the design process. [Proposition] We propose a Context-Aware Cognitive Design Assistant (CACDA) to support designers who have to satisfy some design rules among "Big Data". First, we describe the CACDA from the user's perspective. Second, we detail the process for modelling unstructured design rules into a computable knowledge graph that will feed the cognitive design assistant. [Future Work] Once our knowledge graph of design rules will be operational, we will concentrate on its processing to retrieve, recommend, and verify design rules. Experiments will also help to determine pros and cons of the design assistant.

Keywords: Design rules · Product design · Knowledge graph · Context awareness · Knowledge management · Cognitive assistant

1 Introduction

Context. According to Clakins et *al.* in [1], design rules synthesize the knowledge of a company and indicate how to create a proven design. They improve product quality, as well as decrease design time and costs. The definition and management of design rules is consequently a crucial design activity.

Published by Springer Nature Switzerland AG 2020
F. Nyffenegger et al. (Eds.): PLM 2020, IFIP AICT 594, pp. 334–344, 2020.
https://doi.org/10.1007/978-3-030-62807-9_27

Problem. The number of design rules is increasing due to the complexity of modern products (ElMaraghy et *al.* in [2]), legal constraints and DfX expectations. A designer has to search through a large collection of rules to find the ones to satisfy. The mushrooming of design rules makes their retrieval and exploitation laborious, all the more so that they are stored in unstructured documents of hundreds of pages [3].

Proposal. We propose a knowledge graph of design rules that will feed a Context-Aware Cognitive Design Assistant (CACDA). CACDA is a ubiquitous and intelligent cognitive assistant that uses the information of a design context to facilitate the exploitation (retrieval, recommendation, verification, automation, etc.) of design rules in a CAD environment. On the one hand, we present the services the CACDA provides to the end-users. On the other hand, we detail the knowledge graph that makes design rules computable by the CACDA.

2 Literature Review

Design Rules Checker. Design rules checking is an active subject in literature with two main tendencies, a procedural and a semantic approach. The procedural approach considers a fix set of design rules and try to ensure that a product respects these rules by detecting all design errors on the model. The rule is represented by a set of algorithms that detect geometric features in the digital mockup that do not respect the rule. The work of Huang et *al.* [4] and industrial tools [5–7] illustrate this approach. The main flaws are:

1. Many design rules are natural language statements, that is, an unstructured form of knowledge that is not directly computable. A procedural approach is therefore limited to some design rule types such as geometric constraints.
2. Algorithms representing design rules are complex, which makes their development and maintenance cumbersome.
3. Design rules information is stored in data silos, each representing a specific design context. For example, all rules for milling compliance will be in the silo "design for milling". Design is a multi-domain process and many design rules do not fit in a single pre-defined context.

Semantic Network. In [8], Sowa describes Semantic Networks (SN) as "a graph structure for representing knowledge in patterns of interconnected nodes and arcs". Languages for developing ontology (RDF, RDFS, OWL) and graph-databases (Neo4j, Grakn, Trinity RDF, Cayley) support the implementation of semantic networks. Such knowledge graphs break silos and focus on the interactions. SN are effective at modeling complex and unstructured knowledge, such as common [9] or specific design information [10]. Several strategies can be used to model design information. For example, MOKA methodology [11] for engineering design knowledge modeling can be used to capture design knowledge [12]. This structured information can then be used by knowledgeware tools. Instead of using a general design knowledge approach like MOKA, we can review specific knowledge modeling strategies for design rule application. Different research teams propose SN models for design rule application [13–15].

They use SN to structure CAD model information before performing reasoning on the semantic model in order to detect design errors.

However, this technique requires a lot of work to build a domain specific SN limited to a particular product type. Instead of describing a product type, we plan to use SN to model the information of a design context and create a user-centric cognitive agent that intelligently provides the right design rules to the right designer at the right time.

Context-Aware Systems. The context of a software user is: "*Any information that can be used to characterize the situation of an entity. An entity is a person, place, or object that is considered relevant to the interaction between a user and an application, including the user and applications themselves*" [16]. A context aware system uses context information to provide personalized services to the users. As explained by van Engelenburg et *al.* [17]: "*Context-aware systems are systems that have the ability to sense and adapt to the environment*". A context often contains different sub-context [18]. Each sub-context corresponds to a specific source of information that may serve to perform specific recommendation. The author argue that a social context is crucial for information retrieval "*where other people's preferences must be taken into account*". For example, when searching a new product to buy, other people advices can influence our expectations. The data model of a context depends on the application domain and the services it delivers. Dhuieb et *al.* propose a context-aware architecture to present manufacturing knowledge to workers in factories [19]. These technologies need to be adapted to our research problem. Pinquié et *al.* [20] paved the way for a graph-oriented data model of a design context. The data model consists in five sub-contexts: Social, Semantic, Operational IT, Engineering and Traceability contexts. This paper continues this work by presenting the actual implementation of the knowledge graph and the functional architecture of the Context-Aware Cognitive Design Assistant (CACDA) to facilitate the exploitation of design rules.

3 Capture Design Rule Data for an Efficient Management

This section will present the Context-Aware Cognitive Design Assistant from a user perspective before detailing the underlying knowledge graph that structures the design rules.

3.1 A Context-Aware Cognitive Design Assistant (CACDA)

The Context-Aware Cognitive Design Assistant (CACDA), which is an intelligent cognitive assistant, aims at supporting designers to provide computer-aided design solutions free of errors. Therefore, the CACDA needs to have access to a computable structure of design rules while being context-aware, that is, sensing and reacting based on the design context. So far, our CACDA focuses on four services provided to three stakeholders.

Knowledge Engineer. The knowledge engineer is responsible for the development and maintenance of the knowledge graph that structures the design rules. He performs the basic Create, Read, Update, and Delete operations on nodes and edges. Figure 1 illustrates that the CACDA shall enable the knowledge engineer to convert the unstructured manual designs into structured engineering and semantic sub-context. A sub-context is a sub-graph of the knowledge graph. The extraction of specific design information from unstructured documents is an entire and active field of research [10, 21, 22] but is out-of-scope in our research study. Indeed, we assume that the systematic digitalization of knowledge will lead to the disappearance of documents and knowledge engineers will directly enter the design rules in the CACDA. Therefore, the main function of the CACDA is to transform a list of unstructured design rules into a structured computable knowledge graph.

Fig. 1. CACDA service 1: transform a list of unstructured design rules into a knowledge graph.

Designer. The CACDA shall enable a designer to retrieve relevant design rules to be satisfied while designing in CAD environment. Path distances and semantic similarities applied to the knowledge graph [23] help to recommend design rules according to the design context. The designer can also query the knowledge graph to search for design rules (full-text search, faceted search, etc.). After their selection, design rules shall appear in the CACDA interface. Figure 2 and Fig. 3 present the service in which the design interact with the cognitive design assistant.

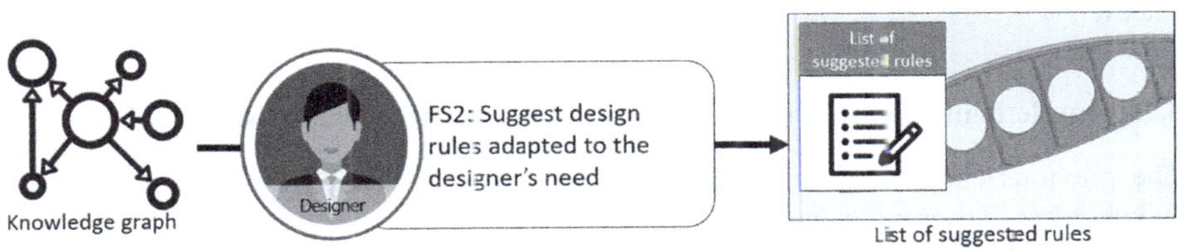

Fig. 2. CACDA service 2: suggest a design rule list to apply for knowledge graph analysis

Fig. 3. CACDA service 3: guide the designer in the application of suggested design rules.

Expert. The expert has a deep understanding of the domain and is consequently able to prescribe new design rules to consider as soon as possible in the design process. Figure 4 shows that he is the one who suggests new design rules to the CACDA and who appreciates the relevance of the recommendations.

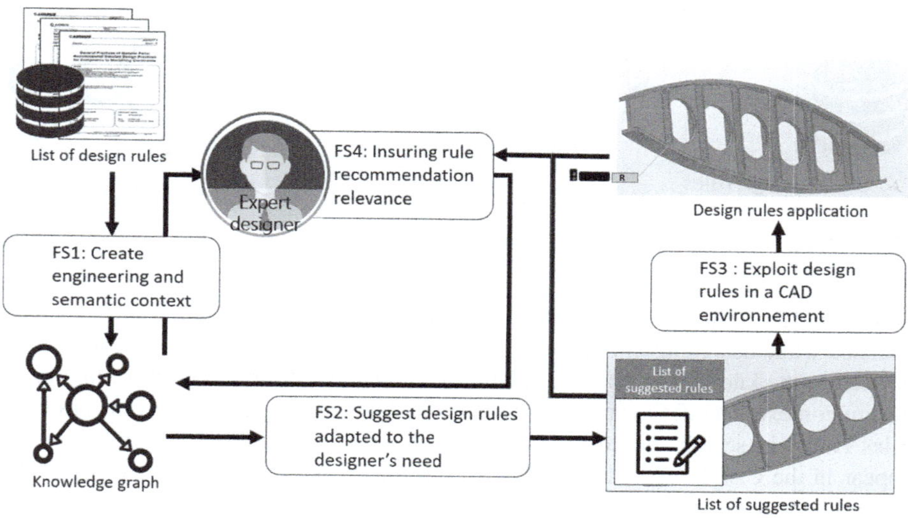

Fig. 4. CACDA service 4: insure that design rule suggestions are relevant to the designer's context

3.2 Implementation of Design Rules in the CACDA Demonstrator

The previous chapter described the main services the CACDA shall provide to the stakeholders. To provide such support, the CACDA needs design rules structured in a computable knowledge graph. In this section, we present how the processing of design rules and the design context leads to a computable knowledge graph. The CoreNLP toolkit [24] serves for the natural language processing. Ontologies such as ConceptNet

[25] and WordNet [26] are key linguistic and common knowledge that enriches the knowledge graph implemented with the NoSQL graph database Neo4J [27]. Python is the pivot language and Dash is the framework that facilitates the prototyping of the web-based user interfaces.

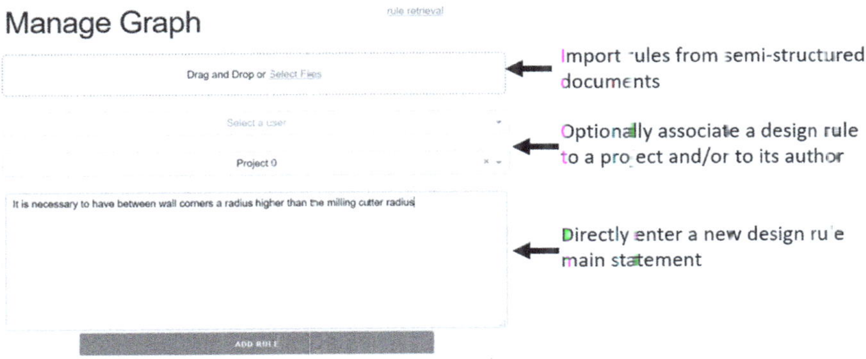

Fig. 5. CACDA knowledge engineer user interface for typing design rule

The knowledge engineer feeds the CACDA with raw design rules and extra knowledge, such as lists of acronyms, glossaries, etc. The semantic processing pipeline of the CACDA structures the knowledge into a computable graph. Figure 5 illustrates the knowledge engineer user interface from which he can input raw design rules or upload a document containing design rules. For instance, the knowledge engineer types the design rule: "*It is necessary to have between wall corners a radius higher than the milling cutter radius*", extracted from the chapter "*Standard value of wall corner*" of an aircraft design manual. We consider that the CACDA automatically captures the design rule as written in the source document. We will systematically reuse this design rule to illustrate the CACDA.

After entering the design rule, the semantic processing pipeline of the CACDA converts it into a structured graph representation. The graph of design rules forms the so-called semantic sub-context. Figure 6 shows that the semantic sub-context is a sub-graph of the knowledge graph that creates linguistic associations among keywords (nouns, verbs, adjectives, and adverbs). Thus, a full text search of the keyword "*wall*" would return two design rules.

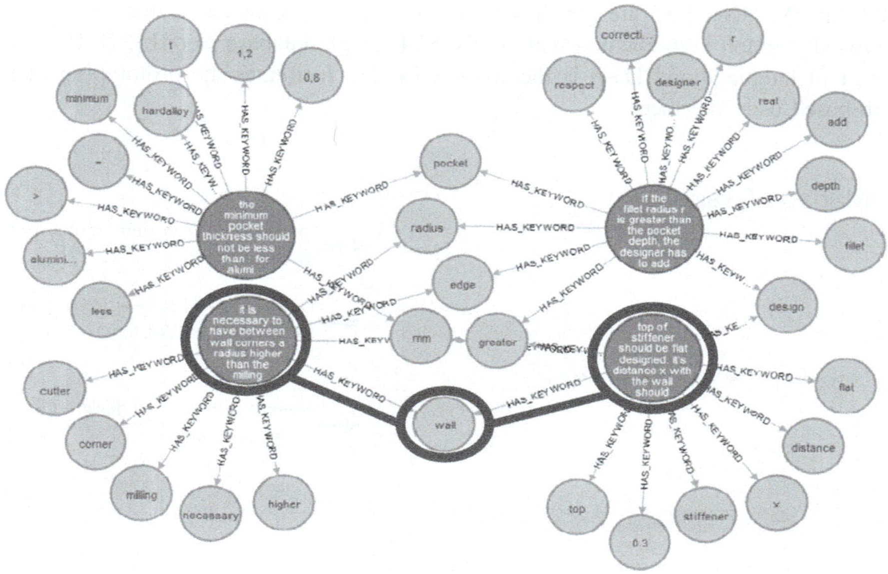

Fig. 6. Graph representation of four design rules (in red) with their keywords (in pink) (Color figure online)

Full text search is very limited as it supposes that the designer knows what to look for, whereas he does not really know what rules shall be satisfied. There is therefore a need to expand queries with relevant keywords and allow the navigation in the knowledge graph. State-of-the-art strategies for short statement analysis suggest enriching the data with external semantic resources [28–30]. To expand keywords with linguistic features (synonyms, homonyms, meronyms, etc.), we integrate the WordNet thesaurus [31]. Before expanding keywords with relevant terms, we disambiguate each keyword according to the existing semantic sub-context. Figure 7 represents the result of this process on the keyword "*corner*". By considering all the terms linguistically linked to the keyword "*corner*", the CACDA facilitates the retrieval of unmatched but relevant design rules. Moreover, the richer is the knowledge graph, the more pertinent will be the semantic exploration. For instance, if a designer consults a design rule, the CACDA can recommend similar rules that are very likely to be of interest.

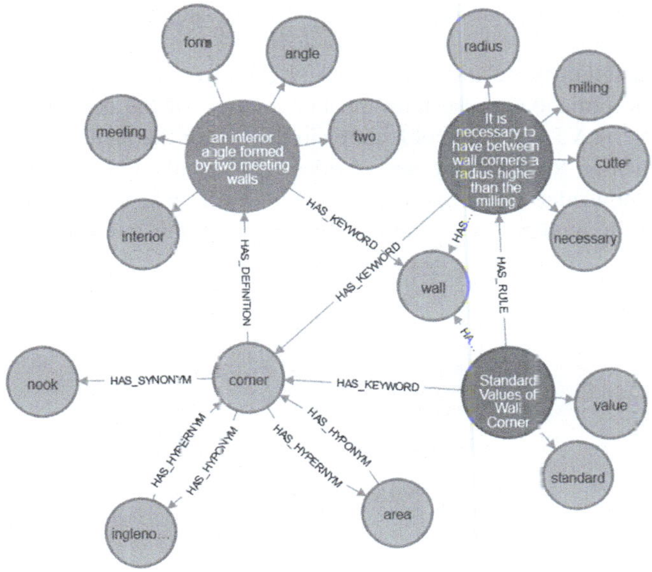

Fig. 7. Extract of a design rule's semantic sub-context with design rule (red), definition (grey), keywords (pink) and chapter (purple) (Color figure online)

The semantic sub-context is not enough to retrieve all relevant design rules according to a design context. Indeed, linguistic relationships help to navigate among rules but other aspects are of interest. For instance, as a designer, the CACDA can recommend me design rules because colleagues with a similar profile have satisfied some rules that I oversee. Figure 8 shows how to model the social context in the

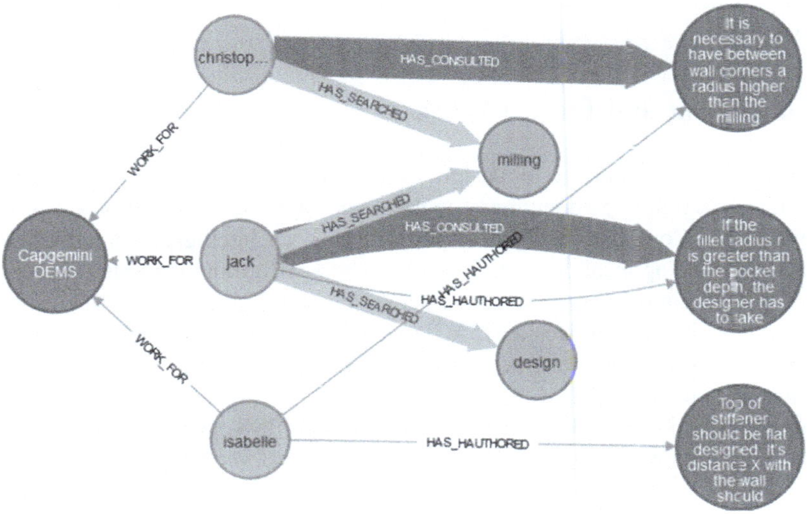

Fig. 8. Design rules with the relationships between the semantic and social sub-contexts. Design rules (red), keywords (pink), users (brown), company (purple) (Color figure online)

knowledge graph. By logging designer's activity, we can use collaborative filtering to suggest design rules.

Social and linguistic relationships are key elements for navigating across design rules, but IT information is also relevant. For instance, if the designer is designing a part using CATIA V5, the name of features in the tree or the name of CAD operations are key information for retrieving design rules. The so-called IT context is also a sub-graph of the knowledge graph that formally defines the current computer-aided design context (software, workbench, operation, etc.). Figure 9 illustrates an instance of an IT context.

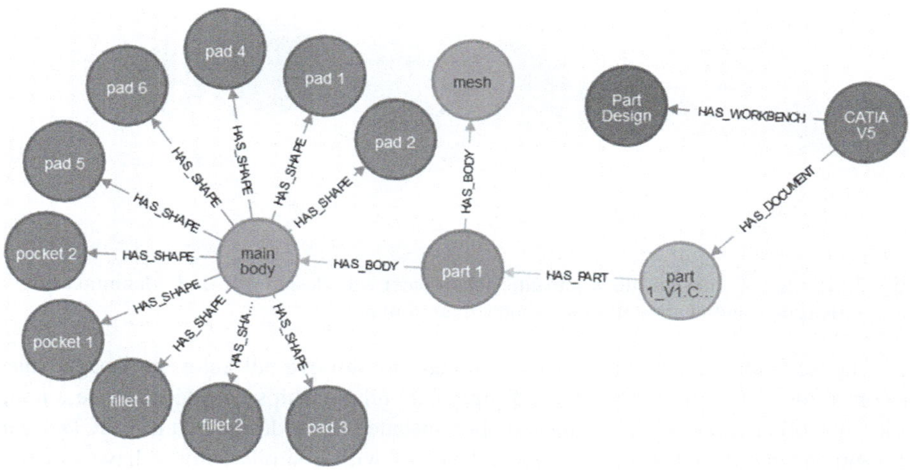

Fig. 9. IT sub-context of a CAD document opened in CATIA V5 with software (red), workbench (blue), document (brown), part (orange), bodies (green) and shapes (purple). (Color figure online)

4 Conclusion and Future Work

The ever-increasing number of design rules, which are multi-domain unstructured knowledge stored in large documents, makes their application laborious. We propose a Context-Aware Cognitive Design Assistant, that is, an intelligent cognitive assistant that facilitates the application of design rules while performing computer-aided design tasks. The assistant relies on a semantic network and design context awareness. In this paper, we describe the services the CACDA provides to the stakeholders and we detail how the processing pipeline structures the design rules and the design context into a computable knowledge graph.

In future work, we will continue the prototyping task, with an emphasis on the analysis of the knowledge graph for recommending and verifying design rules.

References

1. Calkins, D.E., Egging, N., Scholz, C.: Knowledge-based engineering (KBE) design methodology at the undergraduate and graduate levels. Development, 21 (1999)
2. ElMaraghy, W., ElMaraghy, H., Tomiyama, T., Monostori, L.: Complexity in engineering design and manufacturing. CIRP Ann. **61**(2), 793–814 (2012)
3. Kassner, L., Gröger, C., Mitschang, B., Westkämper, E.: Product life cycle analytics-next generation data analytics on structured and unstructured data. In: CIRP Conference on Intelligent Computation in Manufacturing Engineering, vol. 33, pp. 35–40 (2014)
4. Huang, B., et al.: An automatic 3D CAD model errors detection method of aircraft structural part for NC machining. J. Comput. Des. Eng. **2**(4), 253–260 (2015)
5. Dfmpro. https://dfmpro.geometricglobal.com/
6. Siemens NX Checkmate. https://www.plm.automation.siemens.com/en_us/Images/2504_tcm1023-11882.pdf
7. Dewhurst, B.: DFMA. https://www.dfma.com
8. Sowa, J.F.: Semantic networks. John_Florian_Sowa isi [2012-04-20 16: 51] > Author [2012-04-20 16: 51] (2012)
9. Wu, F., Weld, D.S.: Open information extraction using Wikipedia. In: Proceedings of the 48th Annual Meeting of the Association for Computational Linguistics, pp. 118–127. Association for Computational Linguistics (2010)
10. Cheong, H., Li, W., Cheung, A., Nogueira, A., Iorio, F.: Automated extraction of function knowledge from text. J. Mech. Des. **139**(11) (2017)
11. García, L.E.R., Garcia, A., Bateman, J.: An ontology-based feature recognition and design rule checker for engineering. In: Workshop "Ontologies come of Age in the Semantic Web" (OCAS2011) 10 th International Semantic Web Conference Bonn, Germany, 24 October 2011, p. 48 (2011)
12. Klein, R.: Knowledge modeling in design — the MOKA framework. In: Gero, J.S. (ed.) Artificial Intelligence in Design '00, pp. 77–102. Springer, Dordrecht (2000). https://doi.org/10.1007/978-94-011-4154-3_5
13. Skarka, W.: Application of MOKA methodology in generative model creation using CATIA. Eng. Appl. Artif. Intell. **20**(5), 677–690 (2007)
14. Moitra, A., Palla, R., Rangarajan, A.: Automated capture and execution of manufacturability rules using inductive logic programming. In: Twenty-Eighth IAAI Conference (2016)
15. Fortineau, V., Fiorentini, X., Paviot, T., Louis-Sidney, L., Lamouri, S.: Expressing formal rules within ontology-based models using SWRL: an application to the nuclear industry. Int. J. Prod. Lifecycle Manag. **7**(1), 75–93 (2014)
16. Dey, A.K.: Understanding and using context. Pers. Ubiquitous Comput. **5**(1), 4–7 (2001)
17. van Engelenburg, S., Janssen, M., Klievink, B.: Designing context-aware systems: a method for understanding and analysing context in practice. J. Log. Algebraic Methods Program. **103**, 79–104 (2019)
18. Ruthven, I.: Information retrieval in context. In: Melucci, M., Baeza-Yates, R. (eds.) Advanced Topics in Information Retrieval. The Information Retrieval Series, vol. 33, pp. 187–207. Springer, Heidelberg (2011). https://doi.org/10.1007/978-3-642-20946-8_8
19. Dhuieb, M.A., Laroche, F., Bernard, A.: Context-awareness: a key enabler for ubiquitous access to manufacturing knowledge. Procedia CIRP **41**, 484–489 (2016)
20. Pinquié, R., Véron, P., Segonds, F., Zynda, T.: A property graph data model for a context-aware design assistant. In: Fortin, C., Rivest, L., Bernard, A., Bouras, A. (eds.) PLM 2019. IAICT, vol. 565, pp. 181–190. Springer, Cham (2019). https://doi.org/10.1007/978-3-030-42250-9_17

21. Shi, F., Chen, L., Han, J., Childs, P.: A data-driven text mining and semantic network analysis for design information retrieval. J. Mech. Des. **139**(11) (2017)
22. Pinquié, R., Véron, P., Segonds, F., Croué, N.: Natural language processing of requirements for model-based product design with ENOVIA/CATIA V6. In: Bouras, A., Eynard, B., Foufou, S., Thoben, K.-D. (eds.) PLM 2015. IAICT, vol. 467, pp. 205–215. Springer, Cham (2016). https://doi.org/10.1007/978-3-319-33111-9_19
23. Strobin, L., Niewiadomski, A.: Recommendations and object discovery in graph databases using path semantic analysis. In: Rutkowski, L., Korytkowski, M., Scherer, R., Tadeusiewicz, R., Zadeh, L.A., Zurada, J.M. (eds.) ICAISC 2014. LNCS (LNAI), vol. 8467, pp. 793–804. Springer, Cham (2014). https://doi.org/10.1007/978-3-319-07173-2_68
24. Manning, C.D., Surdeanu, M., Bauer, J., Finkel, J.R., Bethard, S., McClosky, D.: The Stanford CoreNLP natural language processing toolkit. In: Proceedings of 52nd Annual Meeting of the Association for Computational Linguistics: System Demonstrations, pp. 55–60 (2014)
25. Speer, R., Chin, J., Havasi, C.: ConceptNet 5.5: an open multilingual graph of general knowledge, no. Singh 2002, pp. 4444–4451 (2016)
26. Miller, G.A.: WordNet: a lexical database for English. Commun. ACM **38**(11) 39–41 (1995). https://doi.org/10.1145/219717.219748
27. Miller, J.J.: Graph database applications and concepts with Neo4j. In: Proceedings of the Southern Association for Information Systems Conference, Atlanta, GA, USA, vol. 2324, no. 36 (2013)
28. Abdalgader, K.: Word sense identification improves the measurement of short-text similarity. In: The International Conference on Computing Technology and Information Management (ICCTIM), p. 233. Society of Digital Information and Wireless Communication (2014)
29. Shrestha, P.: Corpus-based methods for short text similarity (2011)
30. Yih, W.T., Meek, C.: Improving similarity measures for short segments of text. In: AAAI, vol. 7, no. 7, pp. 1489–1494 (2007)
31. Miller, G.A.: WordNet: An Electronic Lexical Database. MIT Press, Cambridge (1998)

New Product Development

Conceptual Reference Model for the Product Development Process Oriented by Design for Six Sigma

Marta Gomes Francisco[1,2], Osiris Canciglieri Junior[3(✉)], and Ângelo Márcio Oliveira Sant'Anna[4]

[1] Industrial and Systems Engineering Graduate Program - Polytechnic School, Pontifical Catholic University of Paraná (PPGEPS/PUCPR), Curitiba, Parana, Brazil

[2] Federal Institute of Education, Science and Technology of Paraná (IFPR), Campo Largo, Paraná, Brazil

marta.francisco@ifpr.edu.br

[3] Industrial and Systems Engineering Graduate Program (PPGEPS) - Polytechnic School, Pontifical Catholic University of Parana (PUCPR), Imaculada Conceição Street, 1155, Curitiba, Prado Velho CEP 80215-901, Brazil

osiris.canciglieri@pucpr.br

[4] Federal University of Bahia (UFBA), Salvador, Bahia, Brazil

angelo.santanna@ufba.br

Abstract. Changes in the world market and consumer expectations have changed the way organizations develop new products. Meeting these challenges means doing better from early stages of design, avoiding possible failures and adjustments at a late stage in the development process. Design For Six Sigma (DFSS) has been successfully applied in the product development process (PDP), with the purpose of ensuring convergence to customer specifications, ensuring reliability in product development, reducing or eliminating operational vulnerabilities and increasing product robustness with use of appropriate techniques and tools. This study showed that there is no systematic DFSS structure integrated with a reference model for the product development process that encompasses the entire process, from observing the consumer's need to discontinuing the product in the market. This paper proposes a conceptual model for the product development process oriented to DFSS, based on a systematic study of existing DFSS methods with the integration of a PDP reference model. The research strategy of this study sought to understand the phases of the existing DFSS methods, as well as to identify the factors that determine or contribute to the application of these methods in the product development process. The investigation of the theme showed a lack of standardization of a DFSS method integrated with a reference model for the product development process, which allowed the identification of 11 activities from each phase of the DFSS methods, which were aligned with the 14 activities proposed by the reference model for the MOP&D product development process. This study led to a consensus in the construction of an integrated conceptual model oriented to DFSS concepts with a friendly characteristic for application in the product development process of durable goods.

Published by Springer Nature Switzerland AG 2020
F. Nyffenegger et al. (Eds.): PLM 2020, IFIP AICT 594, pp. 347–356, 2020.
https://doi.org/10.1007/978-3-030-62807-9_28

Keywords: Design for Six Sigma methods · Reference models for product development · PDP · DFSS · Product development and manufacturing process

1 Introduction

The product development process transforms data and technical possibilities into a market opportunity and information, allowing the design of new products. The transformation of this market opportunity encompasses the quality of the product and process as well as competitive factors such as cost, development time, product, reliability and flexibility (Clark and Fujimoto 1991; Slack et al. 2002).

Developing new products is a systematic process that integrates different processes and people in an organization with the aim of identifying the needs of users and transforming them into valuable information for the design of a product capable of meeting market expectations. Thus, developing new products for commercial purposes is an important and necessary task for organizations, but they involve several steps, from the identification of the opportunity to the discontinuity of the product in the market, these steps being crucial for the success of the product (Pugh 1991; Rozenfeld et al. 2006).

To assist organizations in the product development process, several approaches to reference models are presented in the literature in order to assist organizations and professionals. PDP models can present specific approaches with a proposal for a creative process or sustainability, as well as product project management approaching engineering and design. Some reference models are well known in the literature such as Löbach's Model (2001), Baxter's Model (2011), El Marghani Model (2010), Ulrich and Eppinger Model (2012), Vezzoli Model, Kohtala and Srinivasan (2014), Platcheck et al. (2008), Asimow's Model (1968), Cooper's Model: Stage-Gate (1993), Pahl and Beitz Model (1996), Unified Model (Rozenfeld et al. 2006), Cascade Model (Coley Consulting 2010), Model V (Coley Consulting 2002), among others (Fernandes 2017; Pereira 2014; Sá 2017).

Incorporated in several product development strategies, we highlight Design For Six Sigma, with an approach that involves the use of engineering and statistical tools that are applied appropriately in each phase of product development. DFSS aims to integrate the principles of the six sigma concepts into product development, focusing on the robustness of the product design and process for the best functioning of the product under different conditions of use, identifying errors and problems likely to occur during the project and then outlining mechanisms of prevention.

Creveling et al. (2003) cite that Design For Six Sigma is guided by an integrated set of tools that are implemented in the phases of a product development process, providing qualitative results summarized in managerial performance indicators of the critical parameters of the product in question, related to a set of requirements obtained based on the customer's voice, in order to achieve 6 sigma standards in the product. DFSS encompasses many tools and best practices that can be selectively employed during the phases of a product development process in order to reduce cost, time and increase quality. In the literature there are several DFSS methods applied in order to develop new products, as well as to improve an existing product. However, DFSS methods do not cover the entire product development process, that is, from initialization to discontinuity of the product on the market.

In order to incorporate all the concepts that permeate the Design For Six Sigma methods applied to product development to a reference model for the integrated product development process, the authors had as a basic premise: How to integrate a product development reference model with the concepts of DFSS methods that is friendly and that meets the dynamics of organizations and consumer expectations?

This study aimed to build a reference model for the integrated product development process oriented to Design For Six Sigma, with the purpose of contemplating all the activities proposed by a reference model as well as the activities and concepts of Design For Six Sigma. The product development model oriented to Design For Six Sigma described, focuses on an integrative approach of the activities that make up the DFSS methods presented in the literature. The characterization of the 11 activities of each phase of the DFSS methods allowed a constructive convergence of the concepts of the DFSS methodology with the integration to a reference model for the product development process (Francisco et al. 2019). Thus, the reference model presented in this study aims to systematize the product development process since the product's initialization and discontinuity with synergy of the Design For Six Sigma concepts and a PDP reference model. The model presented, includes the phases and activities inherent to the manufactured product development process with its particularities within the product's life cycle in the market. This model allows an integration among the teams of different areas and roles of the organization, with activities being performed in parallel to provide a reduction in time and cost as well as improved product and process quality.

2 Design for Six Sigma and Reference Model for the Product Development Process

Developing new products is always a challenge for organizations as it is linked to their survival in the competitive market. Constant technological changes and a more observant and discerning consumer develop strategies capable of understanding and identifying potential for business expansion, which are in line with consumer expectations, lower manufacturing cost and quality, are important factors for the development process of product. Design For Six Sigma is an approach with great potential as a product development strategy, as it presents a phased structure that guides in the product development process, as well as the implementation of tools and techniques. DFSS can be defined as a global strategy of continuous improvement, leading organizations to concentrate efforts on systematic projects aiming at 6σ performance and allowing the products developed to be in line with consumer specifications (Awad and Shanshal 2017; Jenab and Moslehpour 2018).

Werkema (2005) mentions that Design for Six Sigma can be defined as a systematic methodological approach, characterized by the joint use of statistical and engineering methods. When properly applied, it allows the company to launch the right product on the market, in the shortest time and with minimal cost. Creveling et al. (2003) emphasize that DFSS is a prevention methodology, in which it seeks to do the right activity at the right time during the product development process, assists in the process of invention, development, optimization, incorporation of new technologies in the product and product verification before launching on the market.

The literature cites several DFSS methods that are applied in the product development process, some of which are better known and frequently applied by organizations, such as: Define, Measure, Analyze, Design and Verify (DMADV); Identify, Design, Optimize and Validate (IDOV); Define, Measure, Analyze, Design, Optimize and Verify (DMADOV); Define, Design, Optimize, Validate(DDOV); Identify, Characterize, Optimize, Validate (ICOV); Define, Measure, Explore, Develop, Implement (DMEDI); Define, Customer, Concept, Design, Implement (DCCDI); Invention and Innovation, Develop, Optimize, Verify(I^2DOV); Identify, Define, Develop, Optimize, Verify & Validate (IDDOV); Concept development, Design development, Optimization, Verify, Certification (CDOV) and Define, Characterize, Optimize, Verify (DCOV), among others (Sokovic et al. 2010; Ericsoon et al. 2009 and Shahin 2008). According to the authors Watson and DeYong (2010) the strength of DFSS is not in its independent performance, but comes from the integration of methods and concepts that were developed independently in a system of thought and work that results in product designs that serve customers better and generate attractive profits.

In this study, the authors observed in the theoretical line of investigation 11 activities that are performed by the different phases of the different DFSS methods. In this study, the authors observed in the theoretical line of investigation 11 activities that are performed by the different phases of the different DFSS methods. In this way, the authors were able to identify the similarities and gaps in the activities of the different phases of the existing methods (Francisco et al. 2019). Figure 1 seeks to summarize the 11 activities and gaps observed in the DFSS methods.

From the analysis of the activities of the DFSS methods, the authors sought to integrate these activities with a reference model for the Product Development Process. Thus, the reference model for the product development process applied in this integration of concepts was the model idealized by Pereira (2014), known as MOP&D. The MOP&D reference model was conceived through a careful analysis of the different approaches to development process models that are present in the literature. The MOP&D reference model presented in Fig. 2, contains in its structure 3 macrophases: Pre-development, Development and Post-development. These macrophases are broken down into six phases: Initiation, Planning, Design, Implementation, Production and Maintenance, being summarized in 14 different stages. Thus, the authors incorporated the 14 activities proposed by the reference model for the MOP&D product development process (Pereira 2014; Pereira et al. 2014; Pereira and Canciglieri 2014), with the 11 activities observed through the theoretical line of investigation of the DFSS methods.

ACTIVITIES / OBJECTIVES OF THE PHASES OF THE DFSS METHODS	DFSS METHODS	STEPS	DMADIC	DMADOV	DDOV	ICOV	DMEDI	DCCDI	I^2DOV	PIDOV	IDDOV	DIDES	CDOV	DCOV	IDEAS	DMADV	IDOV
	Define/identify/ plan the product design, the goals and constraints	1	✓	✓	✓		✓	✓		✓	✓	✓	✓		✓	✓	
	Generate new ideas-creating something new- Define innovation project	2							✓								
	Improve existing product	3															
	Identify/ measure the consumers necessities and translate them in functional requirements of the product	4	✓	✓		✓	✓	✓	✓	✓	✓			✓		✓	✓
	Conceptual idea of the product, selection and choice	5		✓		✓		✓					✓			✓	
	Project/development/execution of the product	6	✓	✓	✓	✓	✓	✓	✓	✓	✓	✓	✓	✓	✓	✓	✓
	Design / development of process concepts	7									✓						
	Optimize product and process design	8		✓	✓	✓	✓		✓	✓	✓			✓			✓
	Evaluation of the product in the production process in meeting the defined specifications	9		✓	✓	✓			✓	✓		✓	✓		✓	✓	
	Evaluation of process performance to identify best practices and correction of errors in production	10					✓	✓			✓			✓	✓		✓
	Maintain product control in the process to meet defined specifications	11	✓									✓			✓		

Fig. 1. Activities of DFSS methods.

Based on the study of the 11 activities of the DFSS methods and the 14 activities of the reference model for the MOP & D product development process, the authors proposed the integration of these activities by identifying the existing gaps, as shown in Fig. 3, in order to allow alignment of the concepts and the design of a conceptual reference model PDP oriented to DFSS.

Macro-phases	Phases	Stages	The MOP&D Model (Pereira, 2014)
Pre-Development	Initialization	1	Statement of Demand
	Planning	2	Scope Definition
		3	Project Planning
Development	Design	4	Study of Principles
		5	Conceptual Design
		6	Preliminary Design
		7	Detailed Design
		8	Refinement of the Design
	Implementation	9	Manufacturing Process Design
		10	Manufacturing and Finishing Product
		11	Marketing Planning
Pos-Development	Production	12	Product Launch
	Maintenance	13	Review Post Launch
		14	Discontinue Product

Fig. 2. Reference models for process development product

INTEGRATION OF THE ACTIVITIES/OBJECTIVES OF THE DFSS METHODS IN THE ACTIVITIES OF THE MOP&D MODEL (PEREIRA, 2014)		DFSS METHODS														
		DMADIC	DMADOV	DDOV	ICOV	DMEDI	DCCDI	I^2DOV	PIDOV	IDDOV	DIDES	CDOV	DCOV	IDEAS	DMADV	IDOV
Statement of Demand	1	✓	✓		✓	✓	✓		✓	✓			✓	✓	✓	✓
Scope Definition	2	✓	✓	✓		✓	✓	✓	✓	✓	✓	✓		✓	✓	
Product Planning	3															
Study of Principles	4															
Conceptual Design	5		✓		✓		✓					✓			✓	
Preliminary Design	6															
Detailed Design	7	✓	✓	✓	✓	✓	✓	✓	✓	✓	✓	✓	✓	✓	✓	✓
Refinement of the Design	8		✓	✓	✓	✓		✓	✓	✓			✓			✓
Manufacturing Process Design	9									✓						
Manufacturing and Finishing Product	10		✓	✓	✓			✓	✓		✓	✓		✓	✓	
Marketing Planning	11															
Product Launch	12															
Review Post Launch	13															
Discontinue Product	14															

Fig. 3. Activities of the DFSS methods contemplated in the reference model MOP&D

3 Results

Following with the analysis of the 11 activities of the phases and gaps observed in the DFSS methods by the authors Francisco et al. 2019, a constructive correlation of these activities was sought with the 14 activities presented in the reference model MOP&D idealized by Pereira (2014). That said, it was possible to outline the construction of a conceptual model for the product development process oriented to DFSS. In the DFSS-PDP conceptual model, the 3 macrophases of the product development process are being contemplated - Pre-development, Development and Post-development, and each macrophase is fragmented into 5 phases - Planning, Design, Implementation, Industrialization and Monitoring. The phases of the DFSS-PDP model are broken down into 8 stages, in which the activities relevant to each phase of the model will be performed, as well as the implementation of engineering tools and techniques. Therefore, the DFSS-PDP model emphasizes the deficiencies analyzed in the DFSS methods and incorporates with the integrated product development model MOP&D (Pereira 2014), idealizing a conceptual model for the process of developing a feasible product for application in the durable goods industry that can allow the organization a better performance of the quality of the product and process, promoting cost reduction and preventing failures during the manufacturing process.

Figure 4 summarizes the conceptual model DFSS-PDP conceived by merging the studies of the DFSS methods and the reference model MOP&D. A questionnaire to assess the structure of the proposed reference model, including the proposed phases, activities, tools and engineering techniques, summarized in Fig. 5, was directed to five specialists in the area of durable goods product development, working in national and multinational companies of different industrial segments. In the model evaluation questionnaire, the Likert Scale was applied with a variation from 1 to 5, with the following qualitative representation: Does not meet the expectation; meet the expectation a bit; partially meet the expectation; meet the expectation almost fully and meet the expectation fully was applied to analyze the degree of importance observed by the specialists. Through Cronbach's alpha reliability analysis, it was possible to guarantee the consistency of the questionnaire for the model, in which it was validated with an alpha value of 0,78. The result obtained was shown to be promising, since the coefficient value is above 0.70.

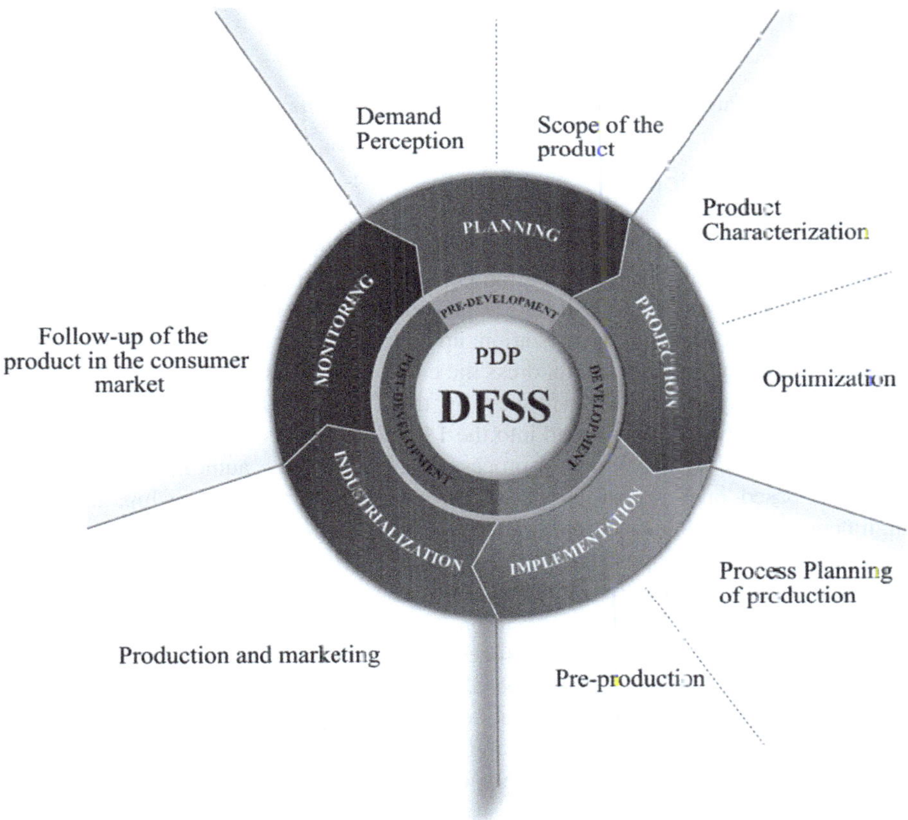

Fig. 4. Conceptual model for the product development process oriented to the Design For Six Sigma.

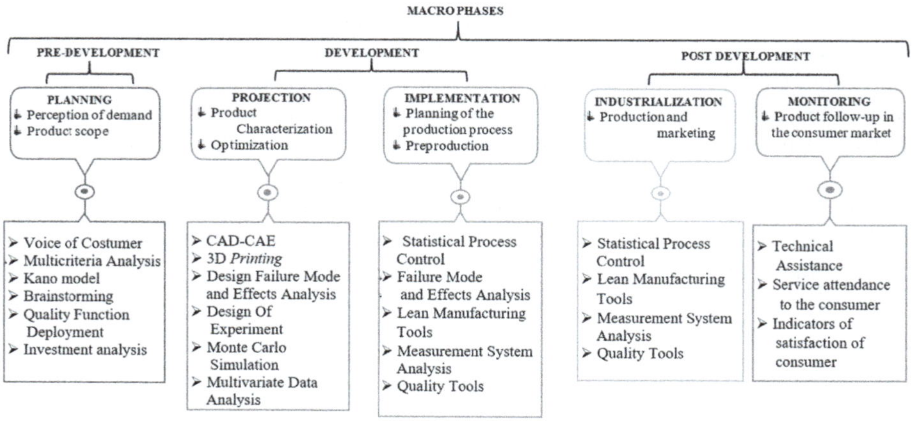

Fig. 5. Engineering tools and techniques suggested for the proposed model.

4 Final Discussion

The present study revealed that the application of Design For Six Sigma and its various methods allows to ensure reliability and convergence to product specifications during the development process. However, DFSS methods do not systematize a product development process from initialization up to product discontinuity PDP reference models seeks to systematize and address the entire product life cycle. Thus, the authors identified the key activities performed by the DFSS methods, summarized in 11 activities, which were incorporated into the 14 key activities of the reference model for the MOP&D product development processes. Therefore, the authors integrated these activities, based on a constructive and theoretical research relationship, led to the alignment of a conceptual reference model for the DFSS-oriented product development process. The model proposed by the authors, aims to ensure greater reliability and robustness to the product development process with reduction/elimination of operational weaknesses through the application of appropriate techniques and tools in all phases of the product development process, from initialization up to discontinuity of the product on the market. The proposal of the PDP-DFSS conceptual model is to provide a dynamic and friendly product development system capable of contemplating the expectations of the organization and the consumer in the product development process in less time, competitive price and cost reduction.

The PDP-DFSS conceptual model was evaluated by experienced professionals in the product development area, who, through a questionnaire, evaluated the structure of the conceptual model with the proposed phases, activities, tools and engineering techniques. In the analysis of the questionnaire's consistency, Cronbach's alpha coefficient was applied, presenting a value of 0,78. Therefore, the reliability of the results obtained was verified, ensuring greater robustness and relevance to the research. The object of exploration of future research, includes the application of the conceptual model PDP-DFSS in the development of a product.

Acknowledgements. The researchers would like to thank the Pontifical Catholic University of Paraná (PUCPR) - Polytechnic School – Industrial and Systems Engineering Graduate Program (PPGEPS) and National Council for Scientific and Technological Development (CNPq) for the funding and structure of this research.

References

Asimow, M.: Introdução ao projeto de engenharia. 1 edn. Edited by Jou, São Paulo (1968)

Awad, M.I., Shanshal, Y.A.: Utilizing Kaizen process and DFSS methodology for new product development. Int. J. Qual. Reliab. Manage. **34**, 378–394 (2017)

Baxter, M.: Projeto de produto: guia prático para o design de novos produtos, 3rd edn. Blucher, São Paulo (2011)

Clark, K.B., Fujimoto, T.: Product Development Performance: Strategy, Organization, and Management in the World Auto Industry, 1ª edn. Harvard Business School Press, Boston (1991)

Coley Consulting. From waterfall to v-model. http://www.coleyconsulting.co.uk/from-waterfall-to-v-model.htm. Accessed 25 Feb 2020

Coley Consulting. Waterfall model. Accessed 25 Feb 2020

Cooper, R.G.: Winning at New Products: Accelerating the Process from Idea to Launch, 1a edn. Basic Book, Wesley (1993)

Creveling, C.M., Slutsky, J., Antis, D., Slutsky, J.L.: Design for Six Sigma in Technology and Product Development, 1st edn. Prentice Hall PTR, New Jersey (2003)

El Marghani, V.G.R.: Design process model at the operational level (Doctorate Thesis). Aeronautics Institute of Technology. São José dos Campos (2010)

Ericsson, E., Närman, P., Lilliesköld, J., Sörqvist, L.: DFSS–evolution or revolution? A study of critical effects related to successful implementation of DFSS (2009)

Fernandes, P.T.: Reference model for sustainability oriented design process (doctorate Thesis). Industrial and Systems Engineering Graduate Program - PPGEPS at Pontifical Catholic University of Paraná (2017)

Francisco, M.G., Junior, O.C., Sant'Anna, Â.M.O.: Design for Six Sigma integrated product development reference model through systematic review. Int. J. Lean Six Sigma **11**, 767–795 (2019)

Jenab, K., Wu, C., Moslehpour, S.: Design for Six Sigma: a review. Manage. Sci. Lett. **8**, 1–18 (2018)

Löbach, B.: Desenho Industrial: base para configuração dos produtos industriais, 1st edn. Edgar Blücher, São Paulo (2001)

Pahl, G., Beitz, W.: Engineering Design: A Systematic Approach, 1a edn. Springer, Berlin (1996)

Pereira, J.A.: Integrated product development model oriented to P&D project of the Brazilian electric sector (doctorate Thesis). Industrial and Systems Engineering Graduate Program - PPGEPS at Pontifical Catholic University of Paraná (2014)

Pereira, J.A., Canciglieri Jr., O.: Product development model oriented for the R&D projects of the Brazilian electricity sector. Appl. Mech. Mater. **518**, 366–373 (2014)

Pereira, J.A., Canciglieri Junior, O., Lazzaretti, A.E., Souza, P.M.: Application of integrated product development model oriented to R&D projects of the Brazilian electricity sector. Adv. Mater. Res. **945–949**, 401–409 (2014)

Platcheck, E.R., et al.: Methodology of ecodesign for the development of more sustainable electro-electronic equipments. J. Clean. Prod. **16**, 75–86 (2008)

Pugh, S.: Total Design: Integrated Methods for Successful Product Engineering, 1st edn. Addison-Wesley, Harlow (1991)

Rozenfeld, H., et al.: Product Development Management: A Reference for Process Improvement, 1st edn. Saraiva, São Paulo (2006)

Sá, R.F.: Conceitual method for the application of biomimetics as support tool for the development process of sustainable products – BIOS (Masters Dissertation). Industrial and Systems Engineering Graduate Program - PPGEPS at Pontifical Catholic University of Paraná (2017)

Shahin, A.: Design for Six Sigma (DFSS): lessons learned from world-class companies. Int. J. Six Sigma Competitive Advant. **4**, 48–59 (2008)

Slack, N., Chambers, S., Johnston, R.: Administração da Produção, 2ª edn. Edited by Atlas, São Paulo (2002)

Sokovic, M., Pavletic, D., Pipan, K.K.: Quality improvement methodologies – PDCA cycle, radar matrix, DMAIC and DFSS. J. Achiev. Mater. Manuf. Eng. **43**, 476–483 (2010)

Ulrich, K.T., Eppinger, S.D.: Product Design and Development, 5th edn. McGrawHill, Boston (2012)

Vezzoli, C.; Kohtala, C., Srinivasan, A. Product-Service System Design for Sustainability, 1st edn. Greenleaf Publishing Limited, Sheffield (2014)

Watson, G.H., DeYong, C.F.: Design for Six Sigma: caveat emptor. Int. J. Lean Six Sigma **1**, 66–84 (2010)

Werkema, C.: Design for Six Sigma. 1ª edn. Edited by Werkema, Nova Lima (2005)

Implementing Secure Modular Design of Configurable Products, a Casestudy

Henk Jan Pels(✉)

Phi Knowledge Process Enabling B.V, Nuenen, The Netherlands
h.j.pels@outlook.com

Abstract. Secure modular design is a method to prevent failures in complex configurable product. After introducing the theory behind the method this paper describes a case study in implementing this method in a real mechanical engineering environment. Much attention has been paid to involving engineers and management in setting up the implementation process, especially in translating the abstract mathematical concepts in the theory to concrete mechanical concepts. Although the method requires serious additional effort in recording design constraints, the participants in the case study expressed confidence in the value of the method.

Keywords: Modular design · Product configuration · Module independence · Change management · Constraint management

1 Introduction

The market asks for ever increasing product variety to better meet individual customer needs [12]. Configure to order (CtO) production is an answer to this trend. A configurable product offers options with choices, such that the customer can configure his product by filling in his choice per option. Based on these choices the product configuration system generates the production information and the customer specific product can be produced. Often the product has a modular design, where each module implements specific options and choices. Each module is a product family where each set of choices specifies a module variant. Changing a choice can be seen as exchanging one module variant for another.

When developing the product, each module variant must be verified and tested. When there are 10 modules with 10 variants each, this means 100 module variants to be verified and tested. What makes it worse is that there may be unanticipated relationships between specific variants of different modules that may cause product failure if the combination of those two variants is selected, even when there is no direct interaction between those module variants. This means that to be sure that non of the possible configurations will cause failure during production or operation, each of the 10 ** 9 configurations should be verified individually, which clearly is not feasible. Because of this problem we see many failures of products during operation, caused by unforeseen interactions between modules. What makes the verification of modules in configurable products more complex is the problem of constraint propagation [13]: constraints can form chains through the product: a constraint between parameters A and

Published by Springer Nature Switzerland AG 2020
F. Nyffenegger et al. (Eds.): PLM 2020, IFIP AICT 594, pp. 357–368, 2020.
https://doi.org/10.1007/978-3-030-62807-9_29

B and a constraint between B and C infers a constraint between A and C. In this way long chains of relationships between design parameters may occur that reach from one far corner of the product to another.

The method for 'secure modular design of configurable products' as described in [1] proposes a theoretical solution for this problem. The method depends on formal rules for the specification of module interfaces depending on specified design constraints. The formal rules make the method rather abstract and difficult to introduce in engineering practice. Constraint management requires additional effort, which raises doubt on the effectivity of the method. This paper describes a case study of implementing the method in an engineering organization, where the focus is on translation of theoretical into practical concepts. For the theoretical description of the method we refer to [1].

The structure of the paper is as follows. Section 2 explains the environment of the case study and the expected problems. In Sect. 3 we present a summary of the theory behind the method, while Sect. 4 describes the case study. Sections 5 and 6 provide discussion and conclusion.

2 Research Question and Approach

In change management [8] it is known that every change in a product may have impact: intended impact in better properties of the product, as well as unintended impact in causing conflicts with elements of the product outside the changed part. Such conflicts may cause failure of the product during production or operation. Therefore, each change requires thorough impact analysis and serious verification and test before release. This implies that for configurable products each module variant must be verified and tested before it can be released for production, not in isolation, but in every possible configuration of the product. Breaking down the product into modules does not solve the problem because adding a module variant is not different from changing a part.

The Secure Modular Design Method, as described in [1], proposes a solution for the problem above by introducing the concept of module independence: an independent module needs only by verified against the specifications visible in its interface. A short description of the method is given in Sect. 3.2. Since the method is derived from information systems theory and based upon formal specification of design constraints, its application requires good understanding of some abstract concepts. Since most mechanical engineers are not trained in using such concepts there is a serious risk that it will take a lot of effort to implement the method in a mechanical engineering environment. This leads to the research question:

> *is it possible to implement the rather abstract secure modular design method in a very practically oriented engineering process?*

A Dutch company, designing and manufacturing trailers, was interested in implementing modular design. This company produces trailers in a CtO and EtO approach. To be more competitive they wanted to expand on product variety in the configure to order market and to reduce on ever growing engineering cost. In order to reduce production cost, this company had moved the production of their trailers to a factory in Bosnia. In order to reduce engineering cost, most order dependent engineering was moved to the Bosnian engineering department as well, leaving only new product development in the Netherlands.

Secure modular design seemed a promising approach, so they decided to implement the method. This enabled us to execute a use case in the company. Two main problems are foreseen in the implementation process:

1. Is it possible to explain the method in concepts that are close to the mechanical engineering profession?
2. The method requires elicitation, recording and management of all constraints in the product design. This is additional work and not immediately rewarding. Can a proper database tool help to reduce the effort to an acceptable level?

The approach of the case study is based upon principles to overcome resistance to change as proposed in [3]: first resolve differences in professional discourse between the parties involved and second create interactions between all operational and management levels involved.

3 Theory of Secure Modular Design

Before describing the case a short introduction of the theory behind secure modular design will be given.

3.1 Modular Design

What makes the difference between a module and a part? The generic meaning of module is "exchangeable component" [4, 5]. A basic requirement for exchangeability is compatibility of interfaces, so specification of interfaces is essential for modular design. The original aim of modular design is to enable the product to be adopted to changing needs of the user by exchanging modules [6, 7]. For decomposing a system into modules often the Design Structure Matrix method [10] is used: components with relatively more interactions are combined into one module, in order to minimize interactions between modules and to simplify interfaces. Other research aims at automation of the decomposition process, based upon mathematical theory of combinatorial engineering [9]. The importance of constraints in mechanical design is analyzed in [11]. All these methods provide guidance in how a product can be broken down into modules. However, they do not address the problem of how to make sure that a new module variant will not cause failure in other modules. To our knowledge the use of design constraints to manage change impact as proposed in [1] is unique until now.

Following database theory [2] a constraint can be understood as a predicate over one or more design parameters of the product. A design satisfies the constraint when the predicate is true. Requirements like 'payload <1000 kg' are constraints that are input for the design. Design considerations like 'diameter axle < diameter hole' are constraints that follow from engineering design considerations. Product failure occurs when during production or operation a product state occurs that violates a constraint e.g. when because of extreme temperature the axle fits gets stuck in the hole. The problem in complex products is that constraints can form chains via shared parameters, (constraint propagation) such that a change of state in one part can cause a conflict in another part, even if both parts have no direct relationships. The problem of constraint propagation is also discussed in the context of design compilers [13].

The purpose of the method described in [1] is to define a module in such a way that it can be designed and verified as an independent unit, without knowledge, other than specified in its interface, of the design of the system in which it is integrated. If a module can be specified in such a way, there is no need to test it in each individual configuration in which it can be applied. As a result, the risk of product failure could be largely reduced.

Because of the essential role of interfaces, the method uses the following definition of module:

A module is a part with a defined interface.

The interface contains the product specifications that the module shares with its environment. This interface can be split into two domains:

1. the *foreign domain* that contains the specifications of the product outside the part, that must be known to the designer of the part,
2. the *public domain* containing the specifications of the part that must be known by designers of other parts in the product.

In this definition the part is the artifact as specified in the CAD model. The set of its specifications is called the *own domain*. A good module has a small interface, meaning that the designer of the module only needs limited knowledge of the target product, making the module less sensitive to changes in its environment, while it shows only limited detail to its environment, giving the designer more freedom in changing his module without external impact.

3.2 Secure Modular Design

When changing a design parameter of a module, the designer must be able to check, all constraints that can possibly be violated by this change. Constraint propagation complicates this task. For secure design we need modules that:

can be verified and tested to operate secure in the intended product, without knowledge of that product other than specified in the module's foreign domain.

Such a module is called *independent in the product*. This concept of module independence has originally been developed for data-based information systems [2]. Such systems consist of a set of applications that operate on a common database.

Database constraints limit the allowed values of the data elements in the database. Because databases and their constraints can be specified in formal mathematical terms, database properties can be proven in a formal way. In this way it has been proven [2] that:

> *a module is independent in a database system, if every constraint in the database schema that refers to an element of the modules own domain, does not refer to any element outside the module.*

From this condition it follows that module independence depends on the specification of its interface in relation to the constraints that must hold for the product as a whole. For an independent module constraint chaines beyond its foreign domain can be ignored. Note that independence is not a property of the module on its own, but a property of the module in a specific product configuration. A module that is independent in one configuration may not be independent in another configuration. Replacing one module in a system may cause loss of independence of other modules.

Proving independence of a module depends on the constraints in the system. This means that for secure design all constraints must be explicitly known. Integration of a new module in a system implies:

1. Proving independence by checking all constraints that refer to the module,
2. Verifying the module against all constraints that refer to its own domain.

After these steps the module cannot cause any conflict with a constraint anywhere in the system. Note that in most modular design methods interfaces are viewed as gates for transfer of space, energy, information or material [1]. In our approach the interface is the windows through which the module and the system view each others specification.

If a mechanical product is specified in a 3D CAD system, each part is specified in terms of features with parameters (e.g. a cylinder with length and radius). In that sense a CAD model is like a database where each feature is an object in the database and each choice of parameter values a state of that object. Designing a part is then defining the proper features and choosing optimal values for their parameters. In this way the concept of module independence can be applied to mechanical systems and proven on basis of the condition for independence as formulated above.

Applying these steps in designing a modular product is the essence of "secure modular design". The main concepts used in the method are illustrated in the object diagram in Fig. 1. In the notation used each block is an object class with its attributes. Each line is a relationship between object classes that allows expressions over multiple objects. Unless explicitly labeled the link gets the name of the opposite class: if f is a Feature then f.Module is the module to which the feature belongs. An arrow at one end means a N:1 relationship. No arrows means an N:M relationship: f.Parameter is the set of parameters of Feature f.

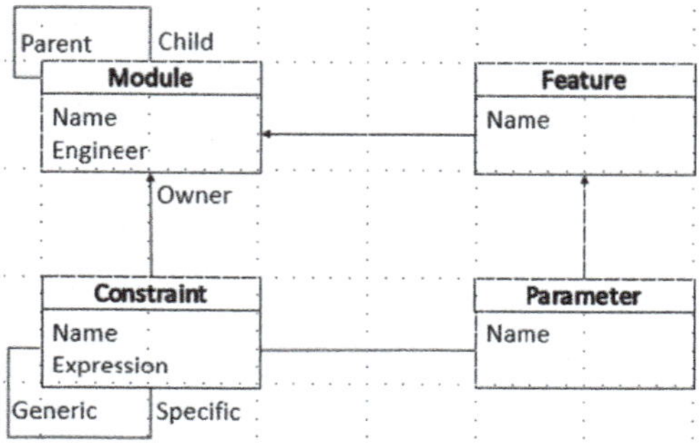

Fig. 1. Object diagram for secure modular design.

Figure 1 tells us that modules are structured in Parent-Child relationships: if m is a module then m.Parent contains the higher level modules of which m is a part. Note that a constraint can refer to many parameters and that the same parameter may occur in several constraints. There are constraints that are not specific for one module or even one product, but yet are relevant for the design. These are for instance legal rules, production rules, engineering rules, product requirements and customer order requirements. When designing his module, the designer will formulate module specific constraints to obey relevant generic rules. Therefore, a constraint can have a link to a generic constraint, meaning that the specific constraint is based upon that generic constraint. This construction also enables to trace where higher-level constraints are implemented in modules. Since requirements are constraints as well, this link provides an easy way to trace where changed requirements have impact. Generic constraints can be organized in generic modules that are not part of a product but serve as container for a group of constraints.

Also, constraints can be structured: if c1 and c2 are constraints and

$$\text{C2. Generic} = \text{c1},$$

then c2 is based upon c1. This can be the case when c1 is a legal requirement and c2 is this requirement expressed in the parameters of the design.

From this structure for each module a list can be derived of all parameters that occur in constraints that refer to at least one parameter of the module. After filtering out the constraints that are local for the module, this list shows exactly the minimum foreign domain to make the module independent. In formal notation the foreign domain of module m can be expressed as:

$$\{\text{p1} \in \text{Parameter} : \exists\, \text{c} \in \text{p1.Constraint} : \exists\, \text{p2}, \text{p3} \in \text{c.Parameter} : \\ \text{p2.Feature.Module} = \text{m} \wedge \text{p3.Feature.Module} \neq \text{m}\}.$$

Listing these parameters together with their module and features shows exactly the foreign domain of m, as required for module independence. If constraints are specified in formal language, then the tables Feature and Parameter can be derived by an algorithm.

4 Implementing Secure Modular Design: A Case Study

The method requires that all constraints in the product are specified explicitly. In mechanical engineering this is not common practice: only requirements are documented but design considerations are directly translated into design solutions without further documentation. Also, specification of mechanical constraints in formal language is not the core competence of most mechanical engineers. Further the condition for module independence seams simple in its abstract formulation but appears to be rather difficult to apply to a concrete design. This means that applying the method requires quite some intellectual exercise from the engineers which implies a large risk for non-acceptance of the method. Therefor the use case started with formulation of an implementation plan.

As mentioned in Sect. 2 changing the design process requires careful analysis of differences in the professional discourse of parties that propose the change and parties that are involved in the changed process. An implementation plan was conceived along the following steps:

1. Develop a Secure Modular Design course and take care for the professional language,
2. Present course to engineers and production management,
3. Initiate design project for a new modular configurable trailer,
4. Guide designers in applying the method,
5. Discuss, evaluate and improve method.

These steps will be discussed below.

4.1 Develop Secure Modular Design Course

The course has been developed in close cooperation between the researcher and the chief engineer. In the process it appeared that the formal mathematical concepts in which the method was defined, were difficult to explain in a mechanical context. Much effort was spent on translating mathematical concepts into mechanical terms. Also, the steps to introduce the abstract concept of module independence in mechanical terms, were carefully chosen. Since the essential part of the method is to identify and specify all relevant constraints, we found that a tool for managing constraints was needed. A prototype for such a tool was developed in Microsoft-Access. Where the description of the method in [1] focusses on formal and scientific explanation, the course should focus on ability to apply the method reliably in practice.

Before starting the course for the engineers, the course was presented to the company management. Since the method was new, also for the management, we found that the management should understand the method and be given opportunity to accept or reject the risk of engaging in such a novel approach. After the presentation, the management decided to fully support introduction of the method, which was felt to be important to motivate the organization to adopt it.

4.2 Present Course to Engineers and Production Management

The method was presented in Bosnia as a one-day course for engineering, production preparation, and quality management. Not only engineers, but also employees from other function related to production were invited in order to create the required common professional discourse. The participants were given exercises to identify and formulate constraints. From unstructured discussions during and after the course it appeared that the method was well accepted. Engineers from design as well as production stated that that errors due to neglected constraints often occurred. The quality control manager explicitly stated that he expected substantial reduction of quality cost from them method. Although these expressions of acceptance may partly have been motivated by politeness, they surely formed a basis for a positive attitude towards continuation of the project.

4.3 Initiate Design Project for New Modular Configurable Trailer

In order to apply the method in practice a design project was defined for a modular container carrier. A real design project was needed in order to give the engineers real budget to spend on the project. The container carrier (Fig. 2) was chosen for its relative simplicity.

Fig. 2. Container carrier trailer

The steps for a modular design project were defined as:

1. Module architecture design,
2. Issue design order per module
3. Support engineers in design process and evaluate method,
4. Verify module designs,
5. Release trailer,
6. Evaluate method.

The architecture design resulted in modules as shown in Fig. 3.

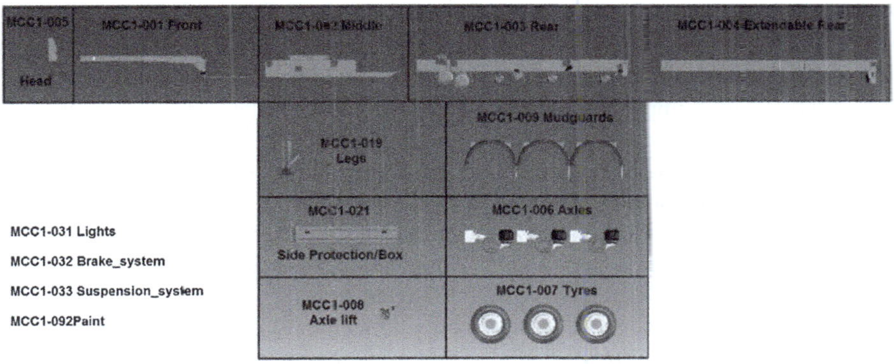

Fig. 3. Modular decomposition of trailer

This decomposition is based upon intuitive understanding of functional clusters. Also, constraints at product level, like commercial requirements en legal regulations were specified. Optimization for modularity criteria was postponed to a later phase.

4.4 Guide Designers in Applying the Method

A formal start of the project was made in a second one day course. Where the function of the first course was to introduce the concept of secure modular design and to create acceptance, the main goal of the second course was to introduce the engineers in using the constraint management tool. The tool, as presented in the first course, was largely conform the object model of Fig. 1. However, while developing the presentation for this second course we realized that the concepts used in the tool were still too distant from the current way of working of the engineers and thus required to many mental steps from the usual design task to specifying the constraints. Applying the formula at the end of Sect. 3.1 is quite an intellectual challenge indeed! Therefore, the tool was reshaped and simplified. Figure 4 shows the Ms-Access database structure of the improved constraint management tool.

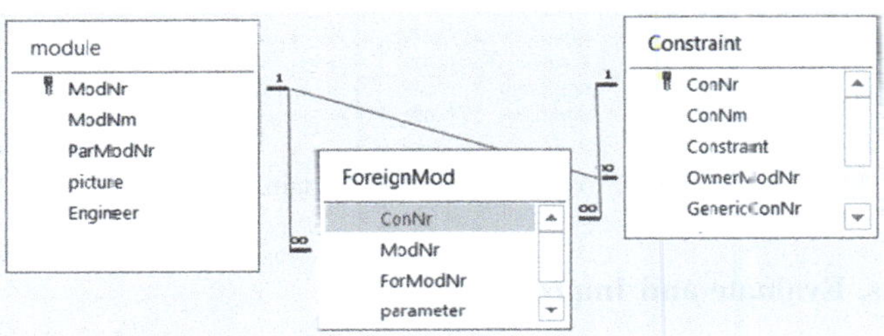

Fig. 4. Constraint management database structure

Modules and constraints are identified with a number. Although these numbers are not required in theory, it appeared that engineers are used to these numbers, so if the database offers no attribute for a number, they will integrate it in the name. The parent-child relationship is implemented in the ParModNr (parent module number) attribute. This implies that the same module can have only one parent module, but for the use case it was an acceptable simplification. Each module gets assigned a responsible engineer. Filling the module table is part of the architecture design.

Each engineer will have to specify the constraints owned by his module. Therefore, constraints can be entered per module using a subdatasheet. For this use case we allowed to formulate constraints in natural language.

To make a module independent, its foreign domain must contain all parameters that are referenced in any constraint that also references a prameter in the own domain of the module. Therefore, it is essential to know for each constraint to what modules it refers. This must be specified by the designer, using table ForeignMod. The object model (Fig. 1) requires that each parameter is assigned to a feature, but in practice most features will be identified only later in the design process. Therefore, the concept Feature has been left out of the tool. For each constraint that refers outside his module, the engineer must specify a ForeugnMod record in a subdatasheet. This specifies the other module and the referenced parameters. From the ForeignMod table the foreign domain per module can be derived in a query. Note that also constraints of other modules may induce foreign domain elements. These parameters form the foreign domain of the module and thus specify the interface that makes the module independent. Figure 5 shows the ForeignDomain query for some modules. Per module it shows the foreign module, the relevant constraints and the relevant parameters. This exactly shows for each module the foreign domain that makes it independent: the constraints that must be checked when verifying the module.

ForeignDomainQ

ModNr	ModNm	ForModNr	ForModNm	ConNr	ConNm	parameter	OwnerModN
MCC1-005	Head	MCC1-001	Front	C0009	Welding interface	Wgap5-1	Head
MCC1-005	Head	MCC1-001	Front	C0039	Module length	ml	Front
MCC1-005	Head	MCC1-002	Middle	C0005	CTC length twistlocks	head.twistlockl	Front
MCC1-005	Head	MCC1-003	Rear	C0005	CTC length twistlocks	head.twistlockl	Front
MCC1-005	Head	MCC1-004	Extendable Rea	C0005	CTC length twistlocks	CTCL	Front
MCC1-005	Head	MCC1-031	Lighting system	C0043	Pattern for sockets	sockettype	Head
MCC1-005	Head	MCC1-032	Brake system	C0042	Pattern for couplings	sockettype	Head
MCC1-006	Axles	MCC1-004	Extendable Rea	C0020	Height bumper	Angle_b	Extendable Rea
MCC1-007	Tyres	MCC1-004	Extendable Rea	C0020	Height bumper	Angle_b	Extendable Rea
MCC1-007	Tyres	MCC1-009	Mudguards	C0049	Radius mudguard	tyre.radius	Mudguards
MCC1-007	Tyres	MCC1-009	Mudguards	C0050	Width mudguard	tyre.width	Mudguards

Fig. 5. View on ForeignDomain query

4.5 Discuss, Evaluate and Improve Method

Because of the Corona crisis the use case temporarily got less priority. Thus, the design of the trailer could not yet be finished and evaluated.

5 Discussion

The main conclusion from this use case is that it is not impossible to convince an engineering organization of the potential of the Secure Modular Design Method. The second result is a prototype for a constraint management tool. Development of this tool learnt that the concepts of the theoretical background must and can be translated into a simplified structure as shown in Fig. 4.

Our expectation is that eliciting the constraints that touch a module is a good start for the module design process. Because constraints between two (or more) modules will probably be formulated by both engineers, the elicitation process will evoque effective discussion between engineers and ease the design process afterwards. Also, the tool will immediately show when a new of modified constraint touches other modules. This the responsiuble designers can be alerted to verify the new constraint.

Since the trailer design process is not finished, there are no trailers in production or operation, so it is not yet known whether the method actually reduces failure cost. However, the reactions of the staff on the introduction course showed that ignorance of constraints is a frequent source of failure, which indicates that the method has real potential to reduce failure cost.

The Generic-Specific relationship between constraints came up as a side effect of the use case. It was realized that recording all legal rules in the constraint database will be a huge effort which, however, can be spread over time by recording just the additional relevant rules per project. Since requirements are constraints as well, recording all constraint in the database will also be supportive to constraint management. The tool can show for each design detail on what constraints it is based and for each requirement it can be seen what design details in what products depend on this constraint. The constraint management tool will need integration with a requirement management tool, if in place.

In the tool as developed for the use case many details have been omitted that will be required for general use in a company. For instance, concepts for product, product family, customer order, design project will be needed. Also, constraint versioning related to module versioning will be needed. This means that integration with the PLM system will be required.

The method is based on the formal proof that an independent module that has been verified to obey all constraints in its interface, will not cause failure. However, this supposes that all relevant constraints have been identified and specified. In an information system, a constraint only exists if it is specified. In a mechanical system, constraints may follow from e.g. material properties and can be identified only as far as these properties are known. Therefore, there is always a possibility that a system with independent and properly verified modules will fail, because of an unforeseen constraint. Nevertheless, the method can strongly reduce the number of failures because in current practice constraints are used in design considerations, but not documented. Then in later changes the constraint is overlooked until it causes failure.

6 Conclusion

Although the Secure Modular Design Method is founded on abstract concepts that are quite distant from the mechanical design way of thinking, the use case shows that it is possible to make it accepted in an engineering department. By adapting the constraint management tool to the current wat of working, the additional effort for constraint management can be made feasible. The results so far are promising for better control of change impact in complex configurable products.

Acknowledgement. Execution of this use case was made possible in the context of the Dutch Government funded Private Sector Investment (PSI) Program 2014, project 'High End Engineering & Manufacturing Technology Bosnia', Group Jumbo Groenewegen & Eurometali. We also thank Group Jumbo Groenewegen, and the staff of the Hemtech Bosnia factory for their confidence and support in introducing the method in their organization.

References

1. Pels, H.J.: Secure modular design of configurable products. In: Ríos, J., Bernard, A., Bouras, A., Foufou, S. (eds.) PLM 2017. IAICT, vol. 517, pp. 450–461. Springer, Cham (2017). https://doi.org/10.1007/978-3-319-72905-3_40
2. Pels, H.J.: Geïntegreerde Informatiebanken, Modulair ontwerp van het conceptuele schema, Dissertation Eindhoven University of Technology, Stenfert-Kroese, Leiden (1988) (in Dutch)
3. Pieterse, J.: Service engineers in change: count your words, a case study into professional discourse and culture within three Dutch organizations, Dissertation Open Universiteit Nederland, 14 March 2014
4. Huang, C.C., Kusiak, A.: Modularity in design of products. IEEE Trans. Syst. Man Cybern. A **28**(1), 6677 (1998)
5. Gershenson, J.K., Prasad, G.J., Zhang, Y.: Product modularity: definitions and benefits. J. Eng. Des. **30**(3), 295–313 (2010)
6. Kusiak, A.: Integrated product and process design: a modularity perspective. J. Eng. Des. **13**(3), 223–231 (2002)
7. Pels, H.J.: Modularity in product design. In: Tichem M.E.A. (ed.) Proceedings of the 3rd WDK Workshop on Product Structuring, Jun 26027, Delft University of Technolgy, ISBN 90-370-0169-6 (1998)
8. Subrahmanian, E., Lee, C., Granger, H.: Managing and supporting product life cycle through engineering change management for a complex product. Res. Eng. Des. **26**(3), 189–217 (2015). https://doi.org/10.1007/s00163-015-0192-1
9. Levin, M.S.: Modular Systems Design and Evaluation. Springer, Heidelberg (1995). https://doi.org/10.1007/978-3-319-09876-0
10. AlGeddawy, E.: Reactive design methodology for product family platforms, modularity and parts integration. CIRP J. Manufact. Sci. Technol. **6**, 34–43 (2013)
11. Scudieri, P., Lilly, B.: A constraint-based model of the design process. In: Kovacevic, A., Ion, W., McMahon, C., Buck, L., Hogarth, P. (eds.) DS 69: Proceedings of E&PDE 2011, the 13th International Conference on Engineering and Product Design Education, London, UK, 08 September 2011–09 September 2011, pp 205–210 (2011)
12. Erens, F.J., Verhulst, K.: Architectures for product families. Comput. Ind. **33**(2–3), 165–178 (1997)
13. Ward, Allen C.: A theory of quantitative inference of artifact sets, applied to a mechanical design compiler. Technical report 1089 MIT Artificial Intelligence Laboratory (1989)

Addressing Obsolescence from Day One in the Conceptual Phase of Complex Systems as a Design Constraint

Sophia Salas Cordero[1,2(✉)], Rob Vingerhoeds[1,3], Marc Zolghadri[2,3], and Claude Baron[1,3,4]

[1] ISAE-SUPAERO, University of Toulouse, Toulouse, France
Sophia.Salas@isae-supaero.fr
[2] SUPMECA, Quartz Lab, Paris, France
[3] LAAS-CNRS, University of Toulouse, Toulouse, France
[4] INSA, University of Toulouse, Toulouse, France

Abstract. Obsolescence issues are one of the main costs in the life-cycle of sustainment-dominated systems, those that require support for many decades.

Obsolescence not only occurs when a system element becomes no longer available due to manufacturing updates or production interruption. It also includes the deterioration of the system or component capacity to operate as intended, since it is no longer suitable to fulfil its function, even if it still operates and can be manufactured and supported. As such, it also impacts on the "-ilities" (reliability, functionality, etc. ...) which can be even traced to legislation changes, for instance, the anti-pollution legislation updates for automotive.

Obsolescence has so far been mainly addressed from a reactive point of view. Around 70% of the total product cost is committed as a result of decisions in the early design stages. Late changes induce delays in the life-cycle plan and large increases in cost due to re-design and rework. Knowing the impact of the conceptual design phase on life-cycle cost, this paper intends to present a model-based systems engineering approach to proactively assess obsolescence risks.

The approach uses obsolescence considerations as constraints during the early design phases, to allow the identification of components potentially at risk of obsolescence. Presenting designers with this information allows them to improve the design, by making it robust and resilient, or to accept the risk and develop an obsolescence mitigation plan.

It will be illustrated with an example from the automotive industry.

Keywords: Obsolescence · Obsolescence management · Conceptual design · MBSE · Automotive

1 Introduction

Sustainment-dominated systems, those that require long-term support such as aircraft, ships, etc., have obsolescence issues that represent one of the main costs in the life-cycle [1]. For example, obsolescence costs up to $750 million per year to the US Navy [2].

The original version of this chapter was revised: the first author's name has been corrected. The correction to this chapter is available at https://doi.org/10.1007/978-3-030-62807-9_63

Published by Springer Nature Switzerland AG 2020
F. Nyffenegger et al. (Eds.): PLM 2020, IFIP AICT 594, pp. 369–383, 2020.
https://doi.org/10.1007/978-3-030-62807-9_30

Obsolescence has been mainly managed reactively, meaning that a solution is looked for only once a product discontinuance notice (PDN) has been received. Such an approach leaves little time for solutioning and may therefore be expensive [1]. Evidence [3, 4] shows that 70–80% of total product cost is decided during early design stages [5]. In an effort to address unplanned expenses and knowing the impact of the conceptual design on the life-cycle cost, this paper intends to present a model-based system engineering (MBSE) approach to proactively assess obsolescence risk as off the conceptual stage of design. Attempting to deal with obsolescence proactively means avoiding to wait until the release of a PDN, and to take precautionary measures to ensure the functionality of a system. Late changes in the design of a system cause delays in the life-cycle plan and large increases in cost due to re-design and the work that needs to be re-done.

In order to reduce costs and reduce waiting times, the use of Commercial off-the-shelf (COTS) components has become more and more common as a design solution. Nevertheless, a significant risk of using COTS is parts obsolescence [6]. COTS components frequently need to be adapted in order to fulfill system requirements. Such custom developments, need to be redone if the COTS vendor upgrades the component, making it an important factor to take into consideration. Whereas technology maturity is an important risk factor, product design adaptations do not seem to be always taken into account as a direct design risk of a system [7].

This paper intends to provide an analysis method that can be utilized since the early stages of design to raise and maintain awareness of what subsystems/parts of the system represent a bigger risk for the development of the system, and thus should be considered critical. Risk calculations will take into account the levels of technology readiness and the interfaces within system's elements, as well as the number of suppliers of a given technology; as a first approach for obsolescence mitigation in the conceptual stage of design.

The problem with most existing obsolescence management tools is that they are dedicated only to electronics [1] and do not evaluate the overall design of a system. The proposed method could be utilized as part of a proactive obsolescence management approach for the whole system, to help identify critical components prior to a PDN, considering that to avoid obsolescence the system elements should be available and suitable according to the requirements. The proposed approach is based on a structured way of assessing the risk involved in selecting certain components to fulfil a function.

The paper is structured as follows. Section 2 reviews the concept of obsolescence. Section 3 describes the risk analysis estimation methodology. Section 4 presents the case study and briefly introduces Design Structure Matrices (DSM), and why it was chosen as a modeling method to support this approach. Section 5 discusses the results obtained. In Sect. 6 the paper concludes with a recompilation of the achieved goals and a recommendation for further work on this topic.

2 Obsolescence and System Life Cycle

In this paper, the term of obsolescence goes beyond only the availability of a component from a supplier as in [8], referred to as logistical obsolescence in [9]. It intends to deal with functional and technological obsolescence. The former refers to when the "-ilities" become obsolete due to changes in the system requirements or changes in other parts of the system. The latter occurs when more technologically advanced components have become available and older parts are no longer supported. Also, in this paper, mitigation refers to "the measures taken to minimize the impact or likelihood of having an obsolescence problem" as in [1].

The strategy followed in obsolescence management is usually a combination of different mitigation measures. Obsolescence risk can be mitigated by taking actions in three main areas: supply chain, design and planning. While in general the decisions of a vendor do not depend only on one costumer, the design and planning are elements that can be controlled by the costumer from the moment when a product starts to be conceived. This is one of the reasons why it is important to address obsolescence proactively from the earliest stages.

At the design stage, it is essential to take into account the number of suppliers and manufacturers that are producing a particular component (implementing a particular technology) before including that component in the bill of materials (BOM). It may for example be necessary to make sure that the components included in the BOM can be provided by multiple suppliers to minimize the number of critical components [1].

Technology manufacturers regularly develop new versions of electronics, software and mechanical parts. These rapid changes lead to technology outpacing systems with long life times, which therefore require legacy parts support [6]. Technology production is a dynamic field that depends on market demand. A company may favor producing a part that brings high revenues and stop parts with lower revenues, or stop producing parts with higher production risks and/or outdated manufacturing technology. In addition, a company might stop the production of a part if they go out of business. The best case scenario would be for an upgraded version of a part to be designed with an open architecture, hence upgraded parts could normally replace previous ones without major issues. The worst case scenario would involve having to design new parts, because a system element abruptly left the market and only had one supplier.

Many authors [10–13] have pointed out how using open architectures and standard interfaces from the initial system design could help minimize the impact of technology insertion and integration due to the obsolescence or technological evolution of a system. The modularity that these approaches provide with, from a systems design point of view, is a plus. However, it could be seen as a disadvantage for the company that designed the system as more companies would possess the required knowledge to easily make changes to the system and compete for future contracts. Proprietary solutions may be favored over open architectures, so to maintain a competitive advantage, although it prevents designing for obsolescence avoidance.

Since open architectures are not compulsory, in the following sections an approach is presented to help estimate the impact of technology insertion and integration at the design phase, that could lead to obsolescence. A case study from the automotive industry will illustrate how the worst case scenario of stopping the production of a part could have been mitigated.

This paper intends to present MBSE analysis tools as an approach to track the status of a system since the early stages of design as part of the Obsolescence Management Plan (OMP) and to answer the following questions:

- How to address obsolescence since the conceptual design phase when there is barely detailed system information available?
- How to identify critical components?

As this paper advocates to address obsolescence from the earliest stages of design, this subsection aims at mentioning some of the standard life-cycles to position the conceptual design phase (Fig. 1).

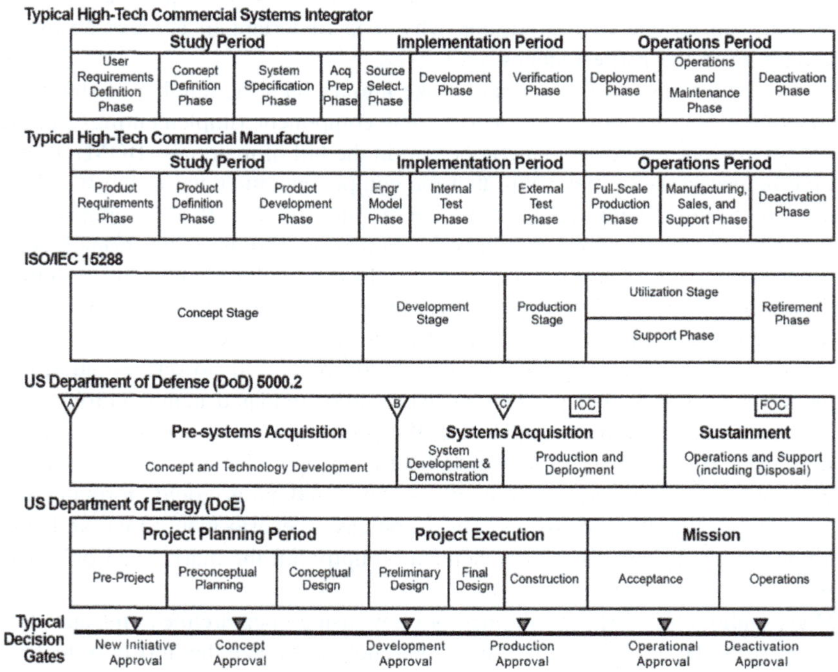

Fig. 1. Life cycle stages comparison of the ISO/IEC 15288 to other life cycle viewpoints [14].

ISO/IEC 15288 [15] identifies six life cycle generic stages: Concept, Development, Production, Utilization, Support and Retirement. The concept stage has a Pre-Concept Exploratory Research Stage which often identifies enabling technologies. The concept stage overall identifies stakeholders' needs, explores concepts and proposes viable and feasible solutions. As part of this stage mockups may be built (for hardware) or coded (for software), engineering models and simulations may be executed, and prototypes of critical components may be built and tested, to explore the feasibility and risks of the concepts. These studies include affordability assessment, environmental impact, failure modes, and hazard analysis [14]. Problems identified for individual hardware parts or software modules should be addressed early to minimize the risk that, when these entities are finally designed and verified, they fall short of the required functionality or performance.

As a next step, the development stage takes care of the integration and development, verification and validation (IV&V) activities. The following figure presents inherent design activities per life cycle stage. Concept design and Preliminary design are part of the concept stage, while the development stage comprehends detailed design (Fig. 2).

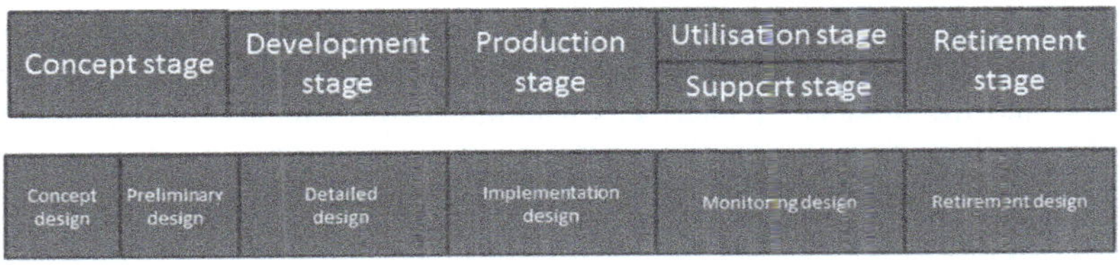

Fig. 2. Design activities per life cycle stage [16].

For NASA [17] as seen in Fig. 3 the early stages of the life cycle include pre-formulation and formulation phases: pre-phase A, Phase A and Phase B. These phases typical outcomes are:

- Pre-phase A (Concept Studies): Feasible system concepts in the form of simulations, analysis, study reports, models, and mockups.
- Phase A (Concept and Technology Development): System concept definition in the form of simulations, analysis, engineering models and mockups, and trade study definition.
- Phase B (Preliminary Design and Technology Completion): End products in the form of mockups, trade study results, specification and interface documents, and prototypes.

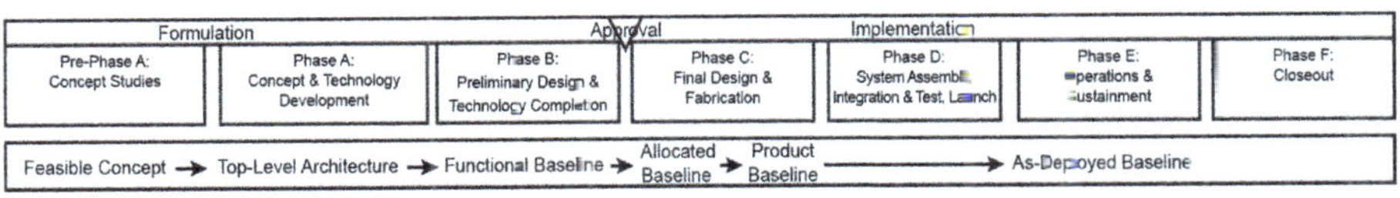

Fig. 3. NASA project life cycle phases [17].

Usually there is a confusion regarding what the conceptual stage comprises, versus what the development stage includes. This paper addresses these earliest stages when design decisions are taken.

3 Risk Estimation Methodology

When calculating risks, there has been an issue regarding the traditional risk calculation presented in the Eq. 1 [18].

$$\text{Risk} = \text{Likelihood} \times \text{Impact} \tag{1}$$

An important issue is how to objectively evaluate the likelihood and the impact. Both [19] and [7] use methodologies to avoid the subjectivity of risk likelihood and impact. They propose risk estimation frameworks that include systems architecture considerations for product development and technology integration programs. In this paper obsolescence is intended to be addressed since the early design stages; risk assessment is very important.

[19] and [7] manage to utilize an objective measure of risk likelihood and impact. The objective measurement parameters are technology readiness levels (TRLs) for the likelihood and the number of interfaces within system elements for the impact. The level of a product design adaptation, meaning the degree of certainty regarding the design, implementation and capabilities of a certain technology or part can be linked to TRLs as a system development risk, since it involves the aspects of integration and technology maturity. The more mature a system is, the less uncertainties there are on the design.

NASA's TRLs offer a well-documented and widely used scale for measuring the degree of maturity in a given component according to [7]. TRLs can be determined with the help of a Technology Readiness Assessment (TRA) [20]. TRA is a formal, systematic, metrics-based process and accompanying report that assesses the maturity of critical hardware and software technologies to be used in systems. The TRA is a document required in order to transition between phase B and C/D (NASA's life cycle). TRLs are defined as standardized levels ranging from 1 to 9 [6]. Their definitions are presented in Fig. 4, TRL 1 is the less mature level and the one that represents more risks while TRL 9 is the most mature and represents less risks as presented by [19].

TRL	Definition
TRL 1	Basic principles observed and reported.
TRL 2	Technology concept and/or application formulated.
TRL 3	Analytical and experimental critical function and/or characteristic proof-of-concept.
TRL 4	Component and/or breadboard validation in laboratory environment.
TRL 5	Component and/or breadboard validation in relevant environment.
TRL 6	System/subsystem model or prototype demonstration in a relevant environment (ground or space/target).
TRL 7	System prototype demonstration in a target/space environment.
TRL 8	Actual system completed and "flight qualified" through test and demonstration (ground or flight/target).
TRL 9	Actual system "flight proven" through successful mission operations.

Fig. 4. TRLs definitions from NASA systems engineering handbook [17].

Design/System changes propagate between components through their interfaces [3]. Hence the degree in which a change in the system will impact the system itself depends on the number of interfaces the system element has with other system elements. In this paper the interfaces taken into account are the first degree undirected interfaces. It takes into consideration if interfaces are present between the system's parts or not (which can be seeing as a simplified binary approach) and limits the approach to direct connections between the systems parts. They are undirected because the impact of the change of subsystem A on subsystem B is consider equal to the impact of the change of subsystem B on subsystem A. At the start of the conceptual design stage, a lot of system information is missing since a lot of design decisions have not been made. That is why as a first approach, first degree undirected interfaces are considered to be adequate. Subsequently, when in the next life-cycle stages more information is available, the estimations can be adapted and eventually extended to directed connections so to take it into account more precise and updated information.

Widely used in Systems Engineering (SE) and project management, Design Structure Matrices (DSM) were chosen to model the interfaces. The DSM is an NxN matrix that maps the interactions among the set of N elements, is a network modeling tool used to represent the elements comprising a system and their interactions, thereby highlighting the system's architecture or designed structure. DSMs are particularly well suited for applications in complex systems development and used more often in the area of engineering management [21].

In this paper, the convention used to represent the information on the DSM is inputs in rows (IR). As the name mentions it, the inputs of a discipline are the elements in its row, the elements of the DSM in this case are W, X, Y and Z (Fig. 5). For practical purposes in this work, the convention inputs in columns (IC) would look the same since as mentioned above, the interfaces taken into account are first degree undirected interfaces. This means that in the DSM example in Fig. 5, 'wy' = 'yw' and 'zx' = 'xz'. Since only undirected interfaces are being considered there is no difference between the inputs to Y from W or the inputs from Y to W. Naturally the value of 'zx' and 'xz' equals the number of interactions between X and Z.

	W	X	Y	Z
W			wy	
X				xz
Y	yw			
Z		zx		

Fig. 5. DSM example

The TRLs and number of interfaces are scaled from 1 to 5 as a risk input calculation in this paper, subsequently the risk is scaled for a maximum of 25 and minimum of 1, as in [19] with the following equation:

$$X_B = \frac{(L_B - U_B) \times X_A + U_B \times L_A - L_B \times U_A}{L_A - U_A} \tag{2}$$

Where:

X_A - Value in scale A,
X_B - Value in scale B,
U_A - Upper limit of scale A,
U_B - Upper limit of scale B,
L_A - Lower limit of scale A,
L_B - Lower limit of scale B.

For example, a TRL of 7 in a scale from 1 to 9 (scale A) needs to be recalculated in the scale from 1 to 5 (scale B) as a risk input calculation. Which would mean that: $X_A = 7$ (TRL level) and the TRL scale: $U_A = 1$, $L_A = 9$ and the new scale: $U_B = 5$, $L_B = 1$ and substituting in the Eq. 2 the value for X_B then equals to 2.

4 Case Study

Engine management, responsible for the control of the engine to so be able to provide the necessary torque for driving at the right moment, but also to provide energy for the other vehicle subsystems (climate control, etc.), is since the 1990's done with electronic control systems. A comprehensive set of sensors and actuators, and an electronic control unit, interpret the request of the driver, the current engine and vehicle conditions and allow for controlling several of the engine parameters.

Within engine management the detection and control of knock is an important functionality. Knock is an uncontrolled and unwanted self-ignition phenomenon for internal combustion engines with spark ignition that occurs when a high pressure is reached (close to the maximum torque) and that is triggered before or after the spark. Knock limits the good efficiency of internal combustion engines, that depends on high compression ratio and a proper spark timing. Knocking occurs when there is a spontaneous ignition of unburned air-fuel mixture that occurs after ignition by spark plug [22]. The very rapid heat release implied with this abnormal combustion generates shock waves. Knock consequences are harmful, from excessive emission of pollutants, efficiency decrease, to engine damage. Its detection and prevention are thus an important part of engine control.

For economic reasons, the direct method of measuring knock by in-cylinder pressure transducers is usually replaced by exploiting the vibration signal from one or more piezoelectric sensors mounted on the engine block surface. Knock being constituted of several resonances determined by cylinder geometry, the standard treatment is to apply a band-pass filter followed by computation of signal energy in a predefined time window. The result is compared to base engine noise to make a decision whether knock is present or not. Parameters of the treatment like the resonance to choose, filter frequency and time window are determined for each engine type during calibration phase.

Once knock has been detected, knock control algorithms can be used to bring the engine to safe operation mode. Usually, this control is accompanied by an adaptive control functionality that allows the engine management system to adapt its ignition set-up in function of changing parameters, such as the fuel type used.

Looking at the engine knock management functional diagram (Fig. 6), there are broadly four functions that can be identified:

- knock detection measurement (instrumentation)
- a knock signal pre-treatment (e.g. in smart ignition coils, before the signal goes via wiring to the engine management system)
- a knock signal hardware entry stage in the engine management system
- a knock detection

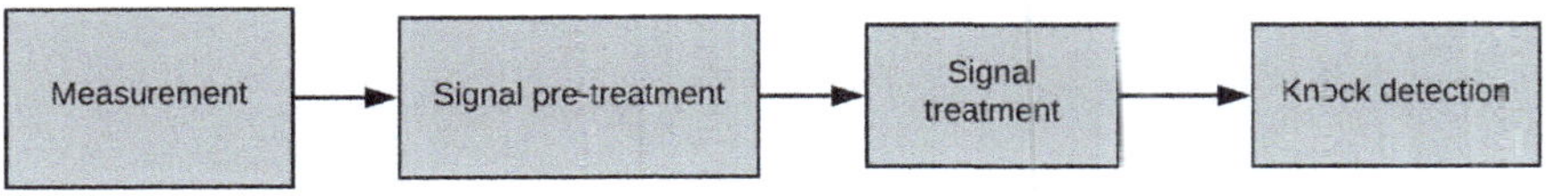

Fig. 6. Engine knock management functional diagram

For knock detection, different means can be envisaged: vibration detection as mentioned above, ionization current analysis, etc. In function of the choice of the instrumentation for the actual implementation, a knock signal pre-treatment may be necessary or not. For example, a piezoelectric transducer can undergo without such pre-treatment, whereas ionization current analysis may greatly benefit from such a pre-treatment with smart ignition coils. Of course, these options have different benefits and disadvantages.

For the hardware entry-stage different options can be thought of, like for example (see Fig. 7):

- dedicated Integrated Circuit (IC)
- general-purpose programmable IC
- software solution in the main microprocessor.

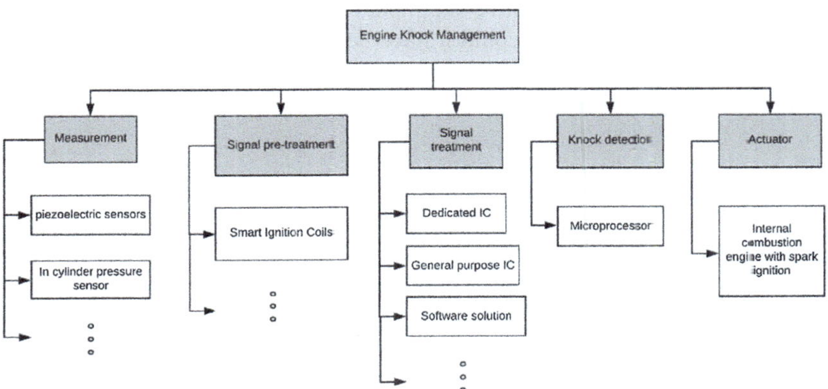

Fig. 7. Generic system architecture of the engine knock management system

In the current proposed case-study, the design of the knock detection functionality is explored and the data is based on a real industrial situation from the late 1990 – early 2000s. At the design stage of this system (some years earlier), several System Architectures (SA) were considered and finally one was selected. The selected SA includes a piezo-electric transducer, that was used for the actual measurement, no pre-treatment, a dedicated IC used for the hardware entry-stage and a regular software solution for the actual detection (see Fig. 8).

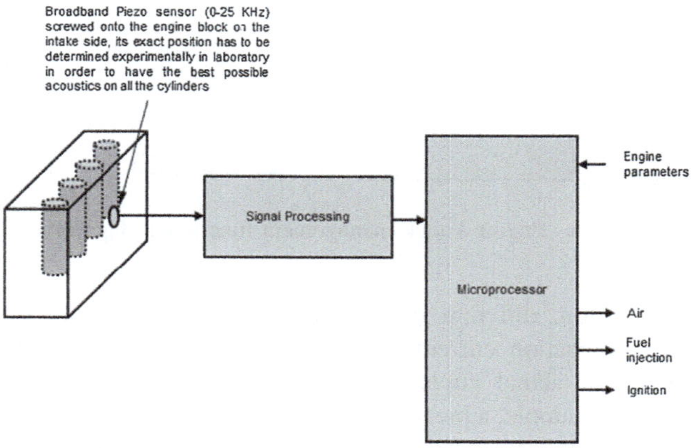

Fig. 8. Realization example of a knock detection functionality for a 4-cylinder in-line gasoline engine.

The dedicated IC was purchased from an external supplier. Because of the complex functionality inside the IC that was based on little by little outdated electronics, it was complex to produce and became costly. At some point, the supplier announced the stop of this IC's production and offered a last-time buy to all of its customers. As this particular IC bare-dies could not be stored for a long time and this last-time buy did not leave a lot of time to the automotive suppliers to find alternative solutions. The dedicated IC was a critical element; could it have been foreseeing earlier in the design of the system? As the design of the IC was proprietary to the manufacturer, no double sourcing had been possible.

5 Results and Discussion

Three architectures are presented here for consideration out of the many possible, for practical reasons they will be called Architecture A, B, and C:

a. Consists of a piezo-electric sensor, a microprocessor, an engine, and a dedicated IC as seen in the DSM (Fig. 9).
b. Consists of a piezo-electric sensor, a software solution (chosen as the signal treatment component), a microprocessor, and the engine (Figure 10).

c. Consists of an in-cylinder pressure sensor and smart ignition coils (that allow for data pre-processing), a microprocessor, an engine, and a dedicated IC (Figure 11).

	Piezo-electric sensor	Microprocessor	SI engine	Dedicated IC
Piezo-electric sensor			1	1
Microprocessor				1
SI engine	1			
Dedicated IC	1	1		

Fig. 9. DSM for Architecture A.

The results in Table 1 were calculated with the help of Eqs. 1 and 2 and the available information in the DSM for architecture A (Fig. 9). Firstly, the likelihood and impact component of the risk should be transitioned to the same scale (in this case from 1 to 5 with Eq. 2) as explained at the end of Sect. 3, and then the risk can be calculated per component (Eq. 1).

To calculate the impact as a risk input utilizing Eq. 2, the number of interfaces a component has is needed. This information is available in the DSM (Fig. 9). For instance, the dedicated IC and the piezo-electric sensor have 2 interfaces when the microprocessor and SI engine have 1. Therefore, the number of interfaces are a scale from 1 to 2 and need to be recalculated in the scale from 1 to 5 as a risk input calculation. Which would mean that: $X_A = 2$ (number of interfaces) and the interface scale: $U_A = 2$, $L_A = 1$ and the new scale: $U_B = 5$, $L_B = 1$ and substituting in the Eq. 2 the value for X_B then equals to 5.

Table 1. Impact versus likelihood per element Architecture A.

Component	Likelihood		Impact		Risk per comp.
	TRL	Risk input	N Connections	Risk input	
Piezo-electric sensor	7	2.0	2	5.0	10.0
Microprocessor	8	1.5	1	1.0	1.5
SI engine	8	1.5	1	1.0	1.5
Dedicated IC	4	3.5	2	5.0	17.5

	Smart Ignition Coils	Microprocessor	SI engine	Dedicated IC	In-cylinder pressure sensor
Smart Ignition Coils			1	1	1
Microprocessor				1	
SI engine	1				1
Dedicated IC	1	1			
In-cylinder pressure sensor	1		1		

Fig. 10. DSM for Architecture B.

Table 2. Impact versus likelihood per element Architecture B.

Component	Likelihood		Impact		Risk per comp.
	TRL	Risk input	N Connections	Risk input	
Microprocessor	8	1.5	1	1.0	1.5
SI engine	8	1.5	2	3.0	4.5
Dedicated IC	4	3.5	2	3.0	10.5
Smart Ignition Coils	8	1.5	3	5.0	7.5
In-cylinder pressure sensor	6	2.5	2	3.0	7.5

Table 2 and 3 were calculated correspondingly with the DSMs available in Fig. 10 and 11.

	Piezo-electric sensor	Microprocessor	SI engine	Software
Piezo-electric sensor		1	1	
Microprocessor	1			1
SI engine	1			
Software		1		

Fig. 11. DSM for Architecture C.

Table 3. Impact versus likelihood per element Architecture C.

Component	Likelihood		Impact		Risk per comp.
	TRL	Risk input	N Connections	Risk input	
Piezo-electric sensor	7	2.0	2	5.0	10.0
Microprocessor	8	1.5	2	5.0	7.5
SI engine	8	1.5	1	1.0	1.5
Software	7	2.0	1	1.0	2.0

In Fig. 12 the size of the bubble of the chart represents the risk of depending on solely one supplier for a component. Also in this figure in order to compare all the architectures in one chart, the initial scale for the impact was taken as 1 to 3 for all the architectures and transform to the scale of 1 to 5.

In the case of architectures A and B, the dedicated IC comes out as a critical component, with the highest likelihood of risk and only one supplier as it can be seen in Fig. 12. In addition, the TRL is estimated to be low, as at the time of developing the solution, the IC was not yet qualified for automotive applications, which meant an additional risk. A component designed for an environment different to the one in which is planned to be used automatically possesses a TRL of 4. The assumption that the TRL would be 9 in this case is not correct since the component was never validated in the automotive relevant environment.

The dedicated IC not only has the higher level of likelihood but also has only one supplier, which is a risk to consider as mentioned before. It may be necessary to make sure that components included in the BOM can be provided by multiple suppliers to minimize the number of critical components [1]. From this point of view Architecture A may not be a good option.

The components that integrate Architecture C have more than one supplier and hence the risk per component is not outgrowing the others The software solution would have been a good option, but at the time of developing the system due to technology constrains it would have not been possible to be applied because of economic reasons.

In Fig. 12 it can be observed also how when comparing several architectures, the impact index is intrinsic to the architecture it is in. Whilst the microprocessor possesses a TRL of 8 (likelihood of 1.5), the impact is proportionate to the number of connections which is higher for the microprocessor in Architecture C (Fig. 13).

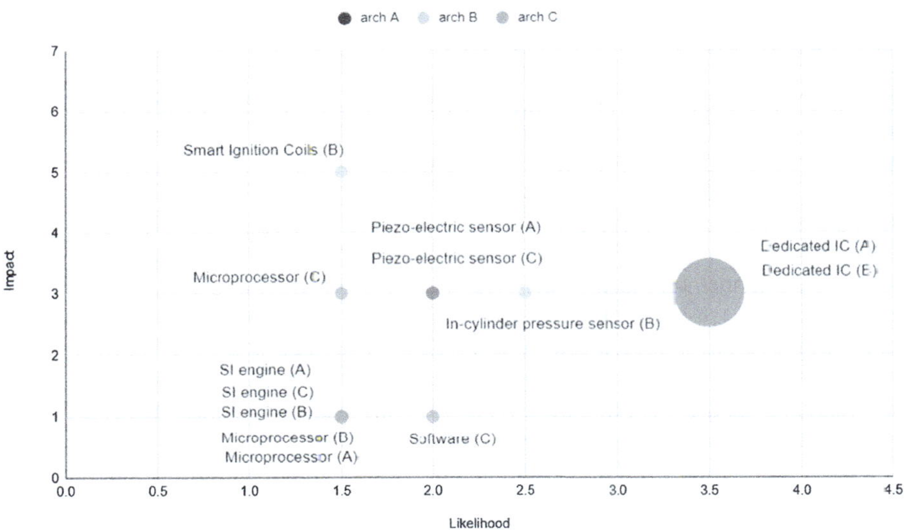

Fig. 12. Impact versus likelihood per element per architecture

Component	Risk factor	Risk %	More than one supplier	Cost
Dedicated IC (Arch A)	17.5	70	no	cheap
Smart Ignition Coils (Arch B)	7.5	30	yes	mic
Dedicated IC (Arch B)	10.5	42	no	cheap
Software solution (Arch C)	2	8	yes*	expensive

*Technology needed to implement the software solution was not available at the moment.

Fig. 13. Main architectures' element technology comparison.

6 Conclusions and Future Work

This paper presents an MBSE analysis method as an approach to track the status of a system since the early stages of design as part of obsolescence management, in order to maintain awareness of what subsystems/components of a system represent a bigger risk, and thus should be considered critical. The method is able to be used without detailed information about the types of interfaces within a system, and is able to compare possible architectures. This paper presents an example of a real-life case study, and illustrates how knowing a priori the risk that the dedicated IC represented for architecture A, the need for an obsolescence management plan could have been foreseen; and initiated at this phase as an obsolescence mitigation measure, in order to tackle the obsolescence proactively.

The presented method is accessible and feasible to implement. Nevertheless, this risk assessment as well as a formal TRA [20] complements but does not preclude the system's engineer and program manager's role to determine which trade-offs are considered acceptable in order to ensure the development of a system.

Technology Readiness Levels (TRLs) were used to rate the likelihood. While the number of interfaces represents the complexity and therefore the potential impact of the risk on the whole system. The likelihood and impact of the risk were objectively rated, for which this approach provides a good option to objectively obtain an evaluation of the risk a component might bring when developing a system.

System elements need to carefully be considered in order for a system not to become obsolete since the design phase. The so called heritage systems should be paid particular attention since they are normally used in architectures and environments different to the ones for which they were designed. Which is precisely the case of the dedicated IC, the assumption of it possessing TRL 9 would not be correct as the component was at the time of the concept stage of the function development, not yet validated in a relevant automotive environment, and therefore is TRL 4. It is also very important to consider if the component has only one supplier, because this constitutes a huge risk as mentioned above. Which was yet again the case of the dedicated IC.

DSMs were chosen as the modeling tool taking into account the possibility of expanding the approach in the future to take into consideration not only undirected interfaces but also directed, which could be possible when more system information is available.

During the early stages of design, alternative SA options and the results of technology maturation are reviewed. The technology maturation process can help identify requirements and development routes that are not feasible. While avoiding the use of high risk critical components can prevent from unnecessary unplanned expenses due to redesign and rework further down the life cycle.

As a recommendation for further work, it is advised to evaluate the impact of early risk analysis of the design on the life cycle of a system. To know if all the design decisions were made taking into consideration the future events that accepting a risk might signify. Another recommendation would be to observe how the design changes propagate when utilizing this method during the conceptual stage on the rest of the system development whilst actively tracking the risks for each design decision made.

References

1. Romero Rojo, F.J., Roy, R., Shehab, E.: Obsolescence management for long-life contracts: state of the art and future trends. Int. J. Adv. Manuf. Technol. **49**, 1235–1250 (2010). https://doi.org/10.1007/s00170-009-2471-3
2. Adams, C.: Getting a Handle on COTS Obsolescence - Avionics. https://www.aviationtoday com/2005/05/01/getting-a-handle-on-cots-obsolescence/. Accessed 15 Jan 2020
3. Clarkson, P.J., Simons, C., Eckert, C.: Predicting change propagation in complex design. J. Mech. Des. **126**, 788 (2004). https://doi.org/10.1115/1.1765117
4. Giffin, M., De Weck, O., Bounova, G., et al.: Change propagation analysis in complex technical systems. J. Mech. Des. (2009). https://doi.org/10.1115/1.3149847
5. Ullah, I., Tang, D., Yin, L.: Engineering change implications on product design: a review of the literature. In: Conference: International Conference on Education, Management and Computing Technology (ICEMCT 2015), pp. 1679–1691. Atlantis Press, Tianjin (2015)
6. Lebron, R.A., Rossi, R., Foor, W.: Risk-based COTS systems engineering assessment model: a systems engineering management tool and assessment methodology to cope with the risk of commercial off-the-shelf (COTS) technology insertion during the system life cycle (2001)
7. Garg, T., Eppinger, S., Joglekar, N., Olechowski, A.: Using TRLs and system architecture to estimate technology integration risk. In: Product, Services and Systems Design, pp. 301–310 (2017)
8. Dowling, T.: Planning for change with a holistic view of the system (2001)
9. Bartels, B., Ermel, U., Pecht, M., Sandborn, P.: Strategies to the Prediction, Mitigation and Management of Product Obsolescence, Wiley, Hoboken (2012)
10. Devereaux, J.E., Hale, P.: Obsolescence: a systems engineering and management approach for complex systems Massachusetts instift1te by of technology (2010)
11. Michael Ostrovsky, B., Asker, J., Bulow, J., et al.: Stability in supply chain networks. https://doi.org/10.1257/aer.98.3.897
12. Young, D.: New approaches to processor lifecycle management (2000)
13. Buratti, M., Del Brusco, D.: A strategies to mitigate obsolescence in defense systems using commercial components (2001)
14. INCOSE: Systems Engineering Handbook: A Guide for System Life Cycle Processes and Activities. International Council on Systems Engineering (INCOSE) (2007)
15. ISO/IEC/IEEE 15288:2015 - Systems and Software Engineering – System Life Cycle Processes (2015)
16. Brazier, F., van Langen, P., Lukosch, S., Vingerhoeds, R.: Design, engineering and governance of complex systems. Proj People – Mastering Success, pp. 34–59 (2018)
17. NASA: NASA Systems Engineering Handbook, SP-2016-6105 Rev2. 12th Media Services (2017)
18. ISO: 31000:2018 Risk management (2018)
19. Arroyo, I.H., Fortin, C.: Technological and complexity risk analysis for set based design evaluation. In: 2018 IEEE International Systems Engineering Symposium (ISSE), pp. 1–5. IEEE (2018)
20. Technology Readiness Assessment (TRA) Deskbook (2009)
21. Eppinger, S.D., Browning, T.R.: Design Structure Matrix Methods and Applications. MIT Press, Cambridge (2012)
22. Heywood, J.: Internal Combustion Engine Fundamental. McGraw Hill, New York (1988)

References

Business Models

Methodology for Designing a Collaborative Business Model – Case Study Aerospace Cluster

Mélick Proulx[(✉)] and Mickaël Gardoni

École de Technologie Supérieure, Montréal, Canada
melick.proulx.1@ens.etsmtl.ca,
mickael.gardoni@etsmtl.ca

Abstract. Innovation is a key skill of companies. The academic literature on innovation in product development is well documented and abundant. However, the one according to innovation at the level of collaborative business models is less available and rarely addressed. We are going to focus on innovation in terms of collaborative business model, more specifically on companies operating in a cluster. In 2020, it is necessary for companies to collaborate. However, when the time comes to carry out collaboration, they encounter different challenges. In order to act and try to resolve them, we will propose the design of a collaborative business model specifically for companies operating in a cluster. In this article, we will present the state of the art at the level of clusters as well as business models. We will then present our problematic relating to the need to collaborate between the companies belonging to a cluster. As an example, we will be referring to the Quebec aerospace cluster. We will end with the presentation of a proposal for a collaborative business model, which was developed by using three business model representations and performed validation interviews with key people. The model will be presented according to the Osterwalder and Pigneur business model canvas. Ultimately, the collaborative business model will allow clustered businesses not only to collaborate more effectively with one another, but also to distribute the gains to all businesses in the cluster.

Keywords: Business model · Collaboration · Cluster · SME

1 Introduction

Competition between companies is no longer just local but has become international. One of the solutions to overcome competition is co-evolution [20]. Local companies must no longer compete with each other but collaborate to overcome the various external threats. If they want to survive in the business world, it is important for them to develop their capacity to innovate, both in their technological ideas and in their business models [8].

We know from the outset that businesses operate on a business model. We also note that collaborative business models are booming in the accommodation sector with Airbnb or in the transportation sector with Uber for example [16, 26]. We acknowledge

Published by Springer Nature Switzerland AG 2020
F. Nyffenegger et al. (Eds.): PLM 2020, IFIP AICT 594, pp. 387–401, 2020.
https://doi.org/10.1007/978-3-030-62807-9_31

that it is often difficult to apply this model to several companies looking forward for mutual collaborations. In addition, by adding the concept of manufacturing companies, it further complicates the realization of the collaboration. In order to encourage collaboration between manufacturing companies, we propose the design of a collaborative business model adapted to companies operating in a cluster. The model's design contains certain challenges, especially the achievement of collaboration in an area that is culturally very competitive.

We believe that an interesting option is to offer collaboration by sharing resources, human or material, or by sharing knowledge within the network. Group members could trade on a peer-to-peer trading platform, where each party could find its addition and its gain in value.

The first section of the article will present the state of the art in terms of clusters and business models. The second section will present the Quebec aerospace cluster as well as the tool used to design the collaborative business model. The third and final section will present the development of the collaborative business model and will be followed by the conclusion.

2 State of the Art

2.1 Cluster

Let's start with the state of the art at the cluster level. Even if the term industrial cluster had no formal definition, we observe that competitive culture is the main reason why it is difficult to build a network [1, 4, 7, 12]. Trust is also a very important element in the formation and functioning of a network [1, 7, 13]. Cluster notion is often linked with the ecosystem notion. We can find a similarity between the ecosystems of fauna and flora and the industrial ecosystems [17]. Like animals, companies must co-evolve in order to survive in the business world [17]. We observe that there are four evolutionary stages of a business ecosystem such as birth, expansion, leadership and renewal. In case that there is no renewal, it is the death of the ecosystem [17]. We observe that the specialization of each company within a network allows it to reduce the overall transaction costs [12, 21].

As we go further, even if the term of industrial cluster is not clearly defined yet, we still observe that there are three reasons why companies participate in a network: collaboration in production channels, transfer of knowledge through human resources and partnerships with governments or different associations [1]. The first to propose a concrete definition of an industrial cluster is Porter who defined it as follows: "A geographic concentration of companies in a specific field" [23]. Porter also offers us a strategic agenda for a cluster, namely the choice of location, local engagement, improvement of the cluster and collective work [23]. We later observe that Porter spells out the advantages of clusters in a presentation to the international conference on technology clusters. Among the advantages, we find that clusters increase productivity, through access to resources, institutions and a faster diffusion of best practices [24].

Clusters stimulate and allow innovation by improving the detection of opportunities and bringing easier experimentation [14, 24]. There is one important aspect for members to believe in the network: members must understand that they cannot achieve their goals alone [13]. It is also essential for them to know that each member can bring value to the ecosystem [17]. We observe that there are four key tasks for managing a network. The first task is activation where members are chosen [14]. The second task is the definition of the framework, establishing the rules, values and standards of the network [14]. The third task is to bring separate entities into a collective entity [14]. The last task is the synthesis phase which allows relationships to be maintained within the network [14]. Barely a year later, we can see a three-step methodology for effective collaboration in the supply chain [10].

1. Create commitment and understanding.
2. To remove the resistant forces to the collaboration.
3. Constantly improve the capacities to collaborate.

Since 2008 and probably related with the recession, the authors state that the rules of competition are subject to change and that managers must learn to collaborate more easily [7]. According to Lee's article, the advantages of the network create the possibility to decrease time to the markets. The network gives access to additional resources and allows itself to increase its strength [18]. The case study involved Korean companies network and the authors noted an increase in sales, a decrease in costs and an increase in the utilization rate of resource [18]. These are some benefits that we may be able to observe as part of our research project. However, we observe that the financing of the network has been a problem.

The labor problem is not only recent. SMEs typically do not have the human resources, research and development capacity or financial resources to obtain knowledge from outside [11]. Sharing, creating and knowledge diffusion within the network is an important aspect [17]. Therefore, the factors that influence the sharing of knowledge within the network are trust between members, the leading firm in the grouping, the density of SMEs in the grouping and the absorption capacity of the members [17].

2.2 Business Model

Looking into business models, after our readings we established that the authors had different visions of business models. We are going to present the business model according to Chesbrough, to Christensen as well as to Osterwalder and Pigneur. We will then present the literature on collaborative business models and finish with the presentation of the chosen tool which is the business model canvas.

2.2.1 Business Model According to Chesbrough

According to Chesbrough and to S. Rosenbloom, there are differences between strategy and business models, the latter of which determine how value will be delivered to customers, while the strategy focuses on competition [7]. The authors describe the business model as the link between technical inputs and economic outputs, see Fig. 1. They also argue that making the link between the technical inputs and the economic outputs is the main difficulty in creating a business model. The ultimate goal of an innovative business model is to deliver value to customers.

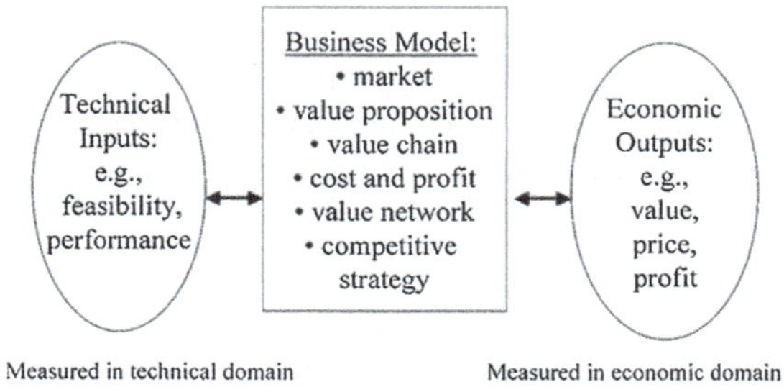

Fig. 1. Chesbrough business model

Still according to Chesbrough, poor technology combined with a good business model may prove to be more profitable than good technology combined with a poor business model [8]. The business model main components are listed above in Fig. 1, which refer to Chesbrough business model.

We note that these components are a more detailed version of the Business model box from the model presented in his 2002 article. They will certainly help us in the creation of our collaborative business model. Chesbrough says that companies must develop the capacity to innovate their business models as much as their ideas and technologies [8].

2.2.2 Business Model According to Christensen

Christensen, in an article written with two other authors, says that reinventing companies depends on their business model. The authors of this article argue that good business models can reshape an industry and lead to spectacular growth [27]. The authors believe that there is a lack of definition and understanding of business models. They believe there are four components to a business model [27]:

1. The client's value proposition: what work will the business model solve?
2. The profit formula: this combines the income model and the cost structure.
3. Key resources: the key assets of the business model, human resources, technologies, products, key elements that will create value for the customer.
4. The key processes: the operational and management processes which make it possible to deliver value to the customer such as the sales process, the manufacturing or financing processes.

The authors present their business model according to Fig. 2.

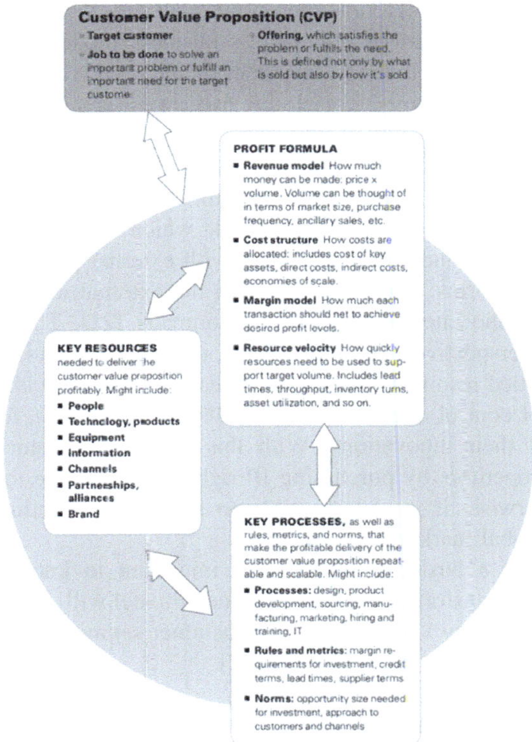

Fig. 2. Christensen business model

The authors emphasize that the new business model must inevitably meet an unmet need or the work of a client that has not yet been resolved. We believe that the elements of the Christensen model are a good complement to the Chesbrough business model.

2.2.3 Business Model According to Osterwalder and Pigneur

Here is how Osterwalder and Pigneur define a business model: "A business model describes how an organization creates, delivers and captures value" [21]. We find that the business model canvas is a tool that will allow us to design and present our collaborative business model. Section 4.2 presents each of the nine blocks making up the canvas.

There are a few patterns regarding business models. The long tail pattern seems to be interesting for our project, since it consists in selling less and in smaller volumes, but more frequently [21]. This model focuses on selling niche products to a targeted market [21]. The book publishing industry has used this model, formerly publishers were targeting large volumes to a very large market. Today, we see the emergence of a platform where publishers focus on small volumes offered to a niche market [21]. Another interesting pattern is the multi-sided platform. This brings together different groups of customers. A valuable platform for a group of customers is defined only if the other groups of customers are present [21]. We can observe the network effect through this pattern, the more people are on the platform, the more it will offer value [21]. An example of this pattern is Google's business model, it uses the keywords entered by users for free, in order to sell them by auction to advertisers or marketing people so that their advertisements reach the greatest possible number of people [21]. A sub-patron of the multi-sided platform is freemium. This model offers a basic service free of charge and a premium paid service [21]. Users paying for the premium service must at least cover all costs related to this business model [21]. The last pattern that seems interesting is the open business model, which translates into organizations creating and capturing value by collaborating with external partners [21]. This model can take mainly two forms, outside-in by using the external ideas of the company or inside-out by using the internal ideas of the company [21]. This model brings new concepts and new perspectives. With this model, the organization is no longer forced to hire the most qualified resources in the field, it can collaborate with external resources [21]. The notion of control over innovation is also set to change, formerly companies wanted to control their innovations. With this model, companies can acquire the innovations of competitors by purchasing IP rights, for example to freely use a technology [21]. Otherwise, it is also possible to sell the innovations, in order to be profitable to the global market [21].

In the design of a business model, it is important to know your epicenter to determine where the transformation of the business model will come from. Models can be driven by resources, by value supply, by customer segments, by costs, or by more than one of these centers at the same time [21].

2.2.4 Collaborative Business Model

We note that business models, the collaborative economy and business as a service models are increasing in the following sectors: accommodation, transportation, home supplies and designer clothing [25]. The typical structure of the collaborative economy is to connect thousands of suppliers and customers through a technological platform [16]. We find some examples of collaborative business models such as Airbnb for accommodation, Lyft or Uber for transportation, Eatwith for social dinners, 1000tools.com for rental of tools between members, SnapGood for household supplies [16, 26]. Formabilio is an example of a collaborative business model in the furniture manufacturing industry who was the link between SMEs, designers and customers [6]. Unfortunately, this company no longer seems to be in operation since its website is no longer accessible. We can observe in those specific cases, Airbnb as an example with accommodation or Uber with transportation, that this kind of collaborative business work well, specifically because they were well designed. We can see in those cases that the service provider and the customer are well connected via a platform. It would be interesting to see how the model can be applied to a cluster of manufacturing SME. We also note that this model is not a trend in the manufacturing sector, which represents an opportunity for us.

Creating an open or collaborative business model presents certain challenges. A high level of interdependence between the focal enterprise and the other players will result in a lower probability of BMI [2]. A lower level of heterogeneity in terms of incentives between the players concerned will increase the probability of BMI's success [2]. Finally, the greater the number of changes to a BMI for the actors involved, the less likely it is to succeed [2].

An important aspect that is often overlooked is the exchange of knowledge. These, the more they are exchanged within the network, the more the network has chances of success [2]. In addition, we note that rather than going towards contracts and lawsuits, it is a guarantee of success than moving towards trust, reciprocity, sharing of rich information [2]. This should be a huge incentive for the creation of our collaborative business model.

For Boons and Lüdeke-Freund, they claim that a business model, from a sustainable development point of view, consists of four components: the value proposition, the supply chain, the customer interface and the financial model [3].

The authors make connections between collaborative business models and vehicle or bike sharing. From a sustainable development perspective, the authors argue that each pillar of government must be involved in order to offer incentives to encourage the use of the collaborative model [9]. According to our project, we could ask the government to have incentives in the form of tax credits for participants in our project.

We note that it is possible for SMEs to benefit from the collaborative economy. According to an article on knowledge in a business network, here are some of the possible benefits [5]:

- Use assets effectively
- Increase the quality of goods or services to customers
- Reduce product development time
- Reduce expenses
- Reduce the risk of failure for the development of a new product
- Increase internal capacity

These are important selling points when we are at the stage of presenting the collaborative business model.

We note that according to an article on the circular economy, the social context and culture are important aspects that affect the success of a business model [15]. In addition, new consumption habits must create new business models by promoting sharing, sustainable development and ecology [15]. For us, apart from ecology, the other two components should be used in the formation of our collaborative business model.

3 Problematic

3.1 Need for Collaboration Between Companies

Within the framework of this project, we will use the case study of the Quebec aerospace cluster. An important aspect of this cluster is its supply chain, see Fig. 3. The principals are at the top of the chain, these are the companies that assemble complete aircraft or engines, while the Tier 4 company is at the bottom of the chain and is responsible for supplying the raw materials to it [19]. Before the 1990s, each client could interact with each of the different third parties, whether it be a Tier 1 or a Tier 4.

After the 1990s, a change of mentality took place and the objective was to reduce the number of suppliers to principals [19]. The supply chain offered a model where the OEM did business with Tier 1 organizations, Tier 1 organizations with Tier 2 organizations, and so on.

Not all OEM companies have adopted this change in their mentality since its appearance in 1990, which means that some of them are still going through this change today [19]. They are also concerned that with increasing orders from airlines, the supply chain may not be sufficiently strong to meet demand. Among the effects noted, we observe that the OEM and Tier 1 wish to reduce the number of suppliers. They want to outsource certain operations that were formerly carried out inside their facilities. The supply chain is currently short of Tier 2 companies, which means that it is undersupplied in response to demand. In terms of SMEs, resource needs are becoming more specialized and labor retention is also an issue. The Quebec aerospace cluster companies must collaborate to ensure their survival.

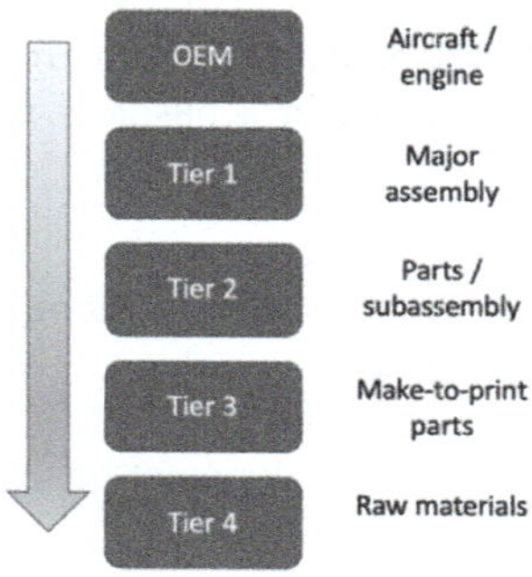

Fig. 3. Aerospace supply chain

3.2 It Is Time to Improve the Aerospace Supply Chain

The aerospace cluster is doing a good job. We are proposing to improve it and make it even more effective by promoting collaboration within it. From our readings, we observe some challenges related to the design of a collaborative business model during cluster operation. The competitive culture in the manufacturing sector and the trust between members are two important challenges who need to be considered within the design of our collaborative business model.

There is a lot of literature on the design of business models within the framework of a single business however, it is difficult to find any on the formation of a group of companies. The formation of this grouping based on collaboration brings other challenges. The grouping will undoubtedly promote innovation through collaboration, this implies that IP will be generated. We can consider the contribution of artificial intelligence during the realization of the project. Taking the collaboration through the sharing of resources as an example, we also believe that it will be difficult to change the culture and mentality of stakeholders. It will be important to address these challenges when designing our collaborative business model.

4 Collaborative Business Model Proposition

In this section, we will present the methodology chosen to determine the basic models, in order to design the collaborative business model. We will then present the tool used, in order to represent the collaborative business model and we will end with the detailed presentation of the collaborative business model.

4.1 Methodology to Choose Base Business Model

For the design of the collaborative business model during a cluster operation, we will start with an idea of generation phase where we identified the most popular business models. We started with a list of the 20 most used business models [22]. We used the following criteria to refine the list of business models:

- Collaboration: the business model must promote collaboration
- The level of application of the business model in service mode
- The level of trust generated by the business model
- The scalable level of the business model
- A certain level of innovation

We finished with a list of ten business models that may be useful in designing our business model. The table of business models and scores can be found in Table 1. The business model with a score of 4 or more will be used to help us design our collaborative business model.

Table 1. Scoreboard business model first sorting

Business models	Collaboration	Service applicable	Reliability	Scalable	Innovation level	Score
Affinity club	1	0	1	0	0	2
Brokerage	0	1	0	1	0	2
Bundling	1	1	1	1	1	5
Cell phone	0	1	0	1	0	2
Crowdsourcing	1	1	1	1	1	5
Disintermediation	1	1	1	1	1	5
Fractionalization, Fractionalized Ownership	0	0	1	0	0	1
Freemium	1	1	1	1	1	5
Leasing	0	1	1	1	1	4
Low-touch	0	1	1	1	1	4
Negative operating cycle	0	1	0	0	1	2
Pay-per-use	1	1	1	1	0	4
Razor and blades	0	0	1	1	0	2
Reverse razor blades	0	0	0	1	1	2
Reverse auction	0	1	1	1	1	4
Product to service	0	1	0	0	1	2
Standardization	1	0	1	0	0	2
Subscription	1	1	1	1	1	5
Vested Outsourcing	1	1	1	1	1	5

We designed the business model using the Osterwalder and Pigneur business model canvas, in order to properly represent the collaborative business model on one page. This model was designed iteratively by conducting interviews with our research director, Mr. Gardoni, the vice-president of innovation and infrastructure at the industrial partner, Groupe Meloche and others key people of the Quebec aerospace cluster. We used the literature on business models, as well as the book Business Model Generation to design the business model [21].

4.2 Tool Presentation

The most commonly used tool for representing a business model is the Osterwalder and Pigneur business model canvas found in Fig. 4. This model proposes the representation according to nine blocks that involve the pillars of a business model that we will briefly present one by one.

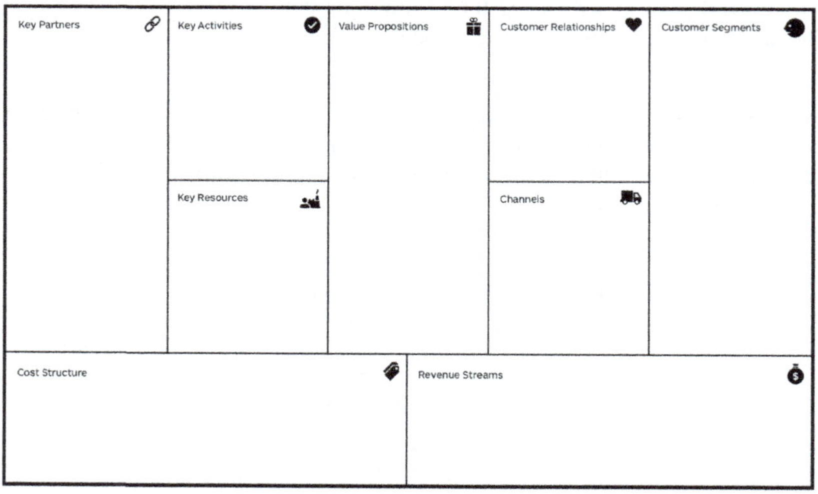

Fig. 4. Business model canvas

The value propositions is the core of the framework which is the heart of the business model. This value proposition offers problem solving and meeting customer needs. The value proposition can be perceived from the customer in a quantitative way, for example cost, speed of service or qualitative, through customer experience or design [21].

The customer segments are defined as the customer that is served by the organization. These are separated according to different needs, distribution channels or type of relationships. The customer segments can be a mass, a niche or a diversified type [21].

Channels are characterized as a method to deliver the value proposition to customer segments. Intimately linked a the marketing level, the channels can be direct, for example by organizing an online sales site or indirect by distributors. There are five phases linked to channels: awareness, evaluation, purchase, delivery and after-sales [21].

The customer relationship is the link between the organization and the different customer segments. This begins with the acquisition, retention and promotion of customers. Relationships can take many forms, personal assistance, communities, or co-creation to name a few [21].

The revenue structure is defined as a value proposition successfully delivered to customer segments. We can distinguish two possible income structures, transactions, linked to single payments per user, or recurring revenues which are payments linked to recurring value proposition transactions. The revenue structure can take the form of pay-per-use, rental or licensing. There are two mechanisms for determining prices: fixed, by a price list or dynamic, by negotiation or auction [21].

The key resources are the assets that will be used to deliver the items listed above. Key resources can take physical form like infrastructure or factories, intellectual like patents or other IP rights, or financial like bank loans or stocks [21].

Key activities are carried out by key resources, which can take the form of production of goods or services, problem solving, a platform or even a network [21].

The key partners are those who will carry out the key activities that will be outsourced by the organization. We can distinguish four types of partnerships, strategic alliances between non-competitors, coopetition, alliances between competitors, joint ventures or buyer-supplier relationships. We can also observe three motivations for forming partnerships, namely savings linked to volumes, risk reduction and the acquisition of specific resources [21].

The last block is the cost structure which totals the costs related to the entire business model. Costs must obviously be kept to a minimum, in order to facilitate the profitability of the organization. There are two main structures that are driven by costs or by value [21].

4.3 Business Model Within the Canvas

After meetings with our industrial partner, people in the industry, as well as our research director, we carried out four iterations of the collaborative business model. Of these four iterations, we were able to refine just one to get a collaborative business model. In our case, the model would be implemented by a focal company who will have to put more effort and involvement than any other members of the group. We established from the outset that one of the key activities of the business model will be the implementation of a peer-to-peer trading platform that will link supplying and consuming businesses. The model is shown in Fig. 5.

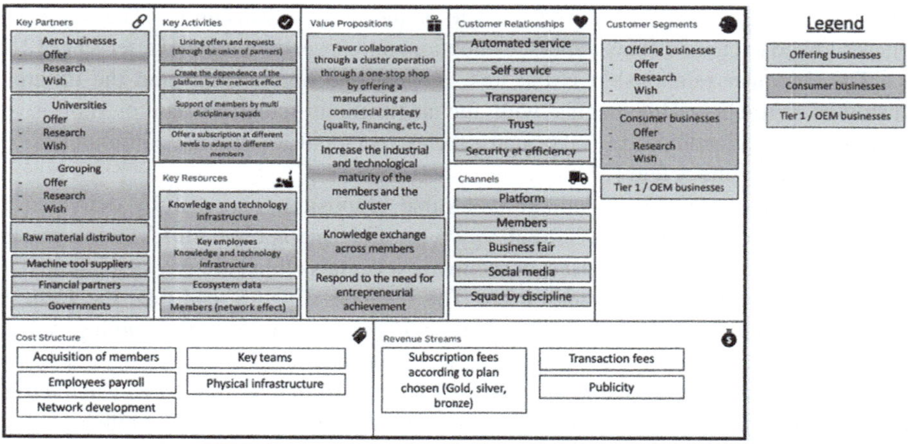

Fig. 5. Collaborative business model

The collaborative business model is based on four value propositions.

1. Encourage collaboration through a cluster operation with a unique counter by offering a manufacturing and commercial strategy. We can take the example of a quality or a commercial structure who would be shared by a mature member to another less mature member.
2. Increase the industrial and technological maturity of the members and the cluster. We can think of the accompaniment of a less mature member by a mature member on a given technology such as cyber security or automation. These technologies would be good subjects to be transfer from one member to another. We can also note that the accompaniment can be applied in different business processes such as marketing or manufacturing.
3. Exchange of knowledge through members. We can think that the exchange of knowledge will be as much at the technical level as commercial or at the level of business processes.
4. Respond to the needs of entrepreneurial achievement. According to our findings, we found that most of the SME owners were aging or that the next generation was not well prepared for the transition. We can think of an example of a franchise where the focal company would acquire the business for sale and position a person at the head of it and allow him to persue an entrepreneurial dream.

About the customer segments, we have divided the companies concerned into three: the offering companies, the consuming companies and ultimately we would like OEM and Tier 1 companies to be able to interact on the platform. These three customer segments will be able to put opportunity cards such as offer, research, wish or informative cards on the platform. We will further see what are the opportunity cards and their different types.

As mentioned above, one of the key activities of the business model is the implementation of a peer-to-peer trading platform. This will link customers and providers. The tiles eventually added to the platform will be called opportunity cards. On the platform, members will have the possibility to choose what type of card they want to add between offer cards, such as an offer of a project or an availability on equipment. Then, we will find the research choice, where members can search for any type of object. The wish cards is where members can express their wish for example to start a project related to a certain type of technology. The last choice, the informative card, could inform the members about good news and different challenges, so everyone stay well informed.

Partners are also an important part in achieving the collaborative business model. We note that aerospace companies from different tiers will have an absolute impact. We find universities that often have key skills for SMEs. Subsequently, we can think of regrouping whether it be Aéro Montréal or the CRIAQ. Distributors of raw materials may also have an impact, for example by offering discounts to members of the group due to the achievement of critical mass. Equipment suppliers could also offer discounts on base prices. The financial partners will also be a great help since sometimes the grouping does not work due to a lack of funding [18]. Banks dedicated to entrepreneurs like the BDC or the FTQ fund could be potential partners. The government could also be a partner of choice, which could offer tax credits to member companies of the grouping who would carry out collaborative projects of two or more companies.

Regarding the relationships with the different customer segments, we are looking forward to be able to offer secure, efficient and ultimately automated relationships with the help of artificial intelligence. For channels, we offer the platform, the members of the grouping as well as social media. One of the key activities will be to link the different customers and providers. We also offer a personalized subscription depending on the level of involvement of the group member. In terms of resources, we note that the data from the pool will be important as well as the knowledge infrastructure.

The level of collaboration will be evaluated by certains criterias. We will track the number of collaborative projects and meetings created. We will also track the number of opportunity card of any type placed on the platform during the experimentation phase, which will allow us to evaluate the card's success rate and the waiting time before a card get assigned.

The level of performance will be evaluated with the criterias previously announced. From those criterias, we will put quantitative bracket to be able to track the performance of the collaborative business model. Before the experimentation phase begins, we will decide if the bracket will be measured in percentage or in number. At the end of the experimentation phase, we will evaluate every criterias and observe the different gap.

So far, we have not focused on the cost or revenue structure. We can however assume that the employees as well as the expenses related to the acquisition of members will be part of the costs. We note that subscription or transaction fees may be part of the revenue structure.

Even if we are at an early stage of our research project, here is the methodology that we think we will use for the project. We will try to find quantitative criterias that will help us to evaluate the collaboration throughout the experimentation phase. We will then choose a platform that will be suitable for our research project. We will have bi-monthly meetings with the industrial partner to have a close look at the project progression which will allow us to address issues and solve them quickly. We will conclude the experimentation phase by interviewing the industrial partner, in order to get his feedback and to be able to adjust the collaborative business model according to the experimentation phase. We will validate the collaborative business model with some key people outside of our project from different enterprise size. We will conduct interviews with these people to question them about our collaborative business model. To conclude the validation phase, we will adjust our model based on the comments that we received from the interviews.

5 Conclusion

This article context is based on the problem of the aerospace supply chain of Quebec in term of collaboration. We propose to develop a business model with the framework of the business model canvas, in order to stimulate collaboration. One of the key activities of this collaborative business model will be the implementation of a peer-to-peer trading platform that could link the offering and consuming companies. The collaborative business model will allow the capacity of the aerospace supply chain to be increased, to allow a full use of resources and more efficient collaboration between members of the group. In the next articles, we will discuss the experimentation phase, as well as the validation of the collaborative business model.

References

1. Doeringer, P.B., Terkla, D.G.: Business strategy and cross-industry clusters. Econ. Dev. Q. **9** (225), 225–237 (1995). https://doi.org/10.1177/089124249500900304
2. Berglund, H., Sandstrom, C.: Business model innovation from an open systems perspective: structural challenges and managerial solutions. Int. J. Product Dev. **18**(3/4), 274–285 (2013)
3. Boons, F., Lüdeke-Freund, F.: Business models for sustainable innovation: state-of-the-art and steps towards a research agenda. J. Clean. Prod. **45**, 9–19 (2013)
4. Braun, P.: SME networks: clustering for regional innovation purposes. In: Small Enterprise Association of Australia and New Zealand 16th Annual Conference, pp. 1–8 (2003)
5. Cagnazzo, L., Tiacci, L., Rossi, V.: Knowledge management system in SMEs within stable enterprise networks. In: WSEAS Trans. Bus. Econ. **11**, 155–174 (2014)
6. Carida, A., Colurcio, M., Melia, M.: Designing a collaborative business model for SMEs. Sinergi Ital. J. Manage. **33**(98), 233–253 (2015)
7. Chesbrough, H., Rosenbloom, R.S.: The role of the business model in capturing value from innovation: evidence from Xerox corporation's technology spin-off companies. Ind. Corp. Change. **11**(3), 529–555 (2002)
8. Chesbrough, H.: Business model innovation: opportunities and barriers. Long Range Plann. **43**, 354–363 (2010)
9. Cohen, B., Kietzmann, J.: Ride on! Mobility business models for the sharing economy. Organ. Environ. **27**(3), 279–296 (2014)
10. Fawcett, S.E., Magnan, G.M., McCarter, M.W.: A three-stage implementation model for supply chain collaboration. J. Bus. Logistics **29**(1), 93–112 (2008)
11. Gumilar, V., Zarnic, R., Selih, J.: Increasing competitiveness of the construction sector by adopting innovative clustering. Inzinerine Ekonomika-Eng. Econ. **22**(1), 41–49 (2011)

12. Jarillo, J.C.: On strategic networks. Strateg. Manage. J. **9**, 31–41 (1988)
13. Keast, R., Mandell, M.P., Brown, K., Woolcock, G.: Network structure: working differently and changing expectations. Public Adm. Rev. **64**(3), 363–371 (2004)
14. Keast. R., Hampson, K.: Building constructive innovation networks: role of relationship management. J. Constr. Eng. Manage. **133**, 364–373 (2007)
15. Korhonen, J., Honkasalo, A., Seppala, J.: Circular economy: the concept and its limitations. Ecol. Econ. **143**, pp 37–46 (2018)
16. Laamanen, T., Pfeffer, J., Rong, K., Van de Ven, A.: Business models, ecosystems and society in the sharing economy. Acad. Manage. Discov. **2**, 218–221 (2016)
17. Lan, W., Zhanglui, W.: Research on interactive learning, knowledge sharing and collective innovation in SMEs cluster. Int. J. Innov. Manage. Technol. **3**(1), 24–29 (2012)
18. Lee, S., Park, G., Yoon, B., Park, J.: Open innovation in SMEs – an intermediated network model. Res. Policy **39**(2010), 290–300 (2010)
19. Michaels, K.: Key trends in commercial aerospace supply chains. In: Global Supply Chain Summit, Montréal, Canada (2017)
20. Moore, J.F.: Predators and prey: a new ecology of competition. In: Harvard Business Review, May–June, pp. 75–86. Harvard Business Publishing (1993)
21. Osterwalder, A., Pigneur, Y.: Business Model Generation. Wiley, Hoboken (2010)
22. Ovans, A.: What is a business model? Harvard Bus. Rev. (2015). https://hbr.org/2015/01/what-is-a-business-model
23. Porter, E.M.: Clusters and the new economics of competition. Harvard Bus. Rev. **60**(9), pp 77–90 (1998)
24. Porter, E.M.: Clusters and regional competitiveness: recent learnings. In: International Conference on Technology Clusters, Montréal, Canada (2003)
25. Sundararajan, A.: From Zipcar to the sharing economy. Harvard Bus. Rev. **1**, 1–2 (2013)
26. Sundararajan, A.: Peer-to-peer businesses and the sharing (collaborative) economy. In: The Power of Connection: Peer-to-Peer Businesses, held by the Committee on Small Business of the United States House of Representatives (2014)
27. Johnson, W., Christiensen, M.C., Kagermann, H.: Reinventing your business model. Harvard Bus. Rev. **86**, 57–68 (2006)

Rapid Sales Growth Mechanisms and Profitability for Investment Product Manufacturing SMEs Through Pay-Per-X Business Models

Mikko Uuskoski(✉), Hannu Kärkkäinen, and Karan Menon

Tampere University, Tampere, Finland
{mikko.uuskoski,hannu.karkkainen,karan.menon}@tuni.fi

Abstract. Manufacturing small and medium enterprises (SMEs) are recognized as a major driving force economically in the European Union (EU). However, manufacturing companies and SMEs have often met with major difficulties in digitalization, and more specifically, in the implementation of novel industrial internet-enabled business models, such as pay-per-X (PPX) type business. The overall aim of this study is to understand how manufacturing companies (especially SMEs) can make use of PPX business models largely in capital product markets, and how this impacts rapid sales growth and profitability for these investment product manufacturers. The studied two investment product manufacturing companies experienced rapid sales growth and there was an impact on the overall profitability for the companies. Sales growth was significant in both companies and PPX business models opened various new opportunities to extend company businesses. We found four main mechanisms that enabled rapid sales growth through PPX business models: strategic, pricing, financing and risk management mechanisms. Both the SME companies also experienced a negative impact on profitability despite rapid sales growth through PPX business models because of issues related to financing the investment product.

Keywords: Industrial Internet of Things · Industry 4.0 · Business models · Pay-per-X · IIoT · IoT · Rapid sales growth · Profitability

1 Introduction

Manufacturing companies in general, and more specifically, manufacturing small and medium enterprises (SMEs) are recognized as a major driving force in European Union (EU) and elsewhere. However, manufacturing companies and SMEs have often met with major difficulties in digitalization, and more specifically, in the implementation of novel industrial internet-enabled business models, such as pay-per-output type business. It has been noted that manufacturing companies and especially SMEs (that have limited financial, technological and knowledge-related resources, and smaller tolerance towards risks derived from extensive business-related decisions, such as changes and modifications in business models) struggle with the implementation of novel types of

Published by Springer Nature Switzerland AG 2020
F. Nyffenegger et al. (Eds.): PLM 2020, IFIP AICT 594, pp. 402–415, 2020.
https://doi.org/10.1007/978-3-030-62807-9_32

PPU services and related business. For instance, the tire manufacturer, Michelin, after having found that its high product quality and lifecycle cost advantages allowed a new competitive pricing model (pay-per-kilometer), the company reconfigured its sales competences to sell pay-per-kilometer services. However, it struggled for many years to become commercially successful. Michelin's pay-per-kilometer services became first successful, when it was able to implement technological novel possibilities to monitor the tire wear put, and to re-design its pay-per-kilometer services into a specialized PPU solution [1].

Even though in the above example, the company was a very large company, similar problems are common many PPU/PPX business model implementations, and they are common with manufacturing SMEs. While known that existing academic research concentrates almost solely on large companies in the topics of digitalization, Industrial Internet of Things (IIoT) and Industry 4.0 [2], the produced generic research or large-company-related research cannot be used as such by SMEs due to the special characteristics of SMEs [2, 3].

The actual strategic benefits of pay-per-X and especially pay-per-output type business models in manufacturing companies (especially in SME-companies) are very little studied and reported in academic literature. It is not yet properly understood how PPX BMs enable various strategic benefits, such as sales growth, and whether the BMs enable the created new business to be profitable, as well as how the investment product companies implement such advanced business models in such a manner that significant strategic benefits are achieved. Furthermore, it is possible that even if for instance the PPX models would allow sales growth, this sales growth might not be feasible in terms of sufficient profits and profitability. It is not yet properly understood in academic research which types of mechanisms related to the BM implementation help to create such feasible strategic benefits (here, especially sales growth and related profitability).

There are existing recent studies for instance on novel IIoT supported or enabled services and advanced non-ownership business models, including pay-per-use (PPU) and pay-per-performance (pay-per-output/outcome (PPO)) business models (BMs). However, existing studies very rarely consider the specific viewpoint of capital goods manufacturing companies or SMEs, and have provided practically no managerial implications to such companies (e.g. [4]). We aim to address this recognized research gap in this study by studying through detailed case studies manufacturing SMEs which have made use of PPX/PPO business models largely in their business. And in particular, in increasing rapid sales growth and profitability and seem to benefit from such BMs in various ways in investment product manufacturing.

The overall aim of this study is to understand how manufacturing companies (especially SMEs) can make use of PPX BMs largely in capital product markets, and how this impacts rapid sales growth and profitability for these investment product manufacturers. The main research questions are as follows:

1. How is the rapid sales growth achieved by PPX BMs for investment product equipment manufacturing SMEs?
2. How does the rapid sales growth enabled by PPX business models impact overall profitability for investment product equipment manufacturing SMEs?

The studied two investment product manufacturing companies can be considered as at least somewhat pioneering companies in their own investment product businesses, in making use of pay-per-output business models in the SME company category. The structure of this study is as follows: we first review existing research and the research gap in more detail. Second, we introduce the methodology of this paper, describe the cases and explain the questionnaire themes. Third, we present the results, and discuss them, leading finally into the conclusions and managerial implications.

2 Theoretical Background

2.1 Pay-Per-X Business Models

Non-ownership services can be defined as *services in which customers acquire some property rights to an asset and are offered a certain degree of freedom in using this asset for a specified period of time while the burdens of ownership remain with the supplier (owner)* [5].

The advanced nonownership types of business models can be divided into pay-per-use (PPU), pay-per-output and pay-per-outcome (both previous: PPO) models (the jointly so-called PPX business models). Pay-per-use model means that the customer pays for the use of the machine, and usually the other aspects related to the machine, i.e. ownership, installation, maintenance, upgradation, recycling is taken care of by the manufacturer. Pay-per-output models focus on the result of the machine use, which is normally demonstrated in monetary terms, and Pay-per-outcome models on the value derived by the customer after using the machine provided by the manufacturer.

It has been demonstrated in recent literature that advanced PPX business models are significantly enabled and facilitated by Industry 4.0 technologies, and e.g. [6–9] have studied the role of IoT technologies in PPX BMs.

2.2 Business Models and SMEs

Many studies have noted important differences between SMEs and large companies. For instance, [2] provide a good condensed description of major SME characteristics compared to large multinational enterprises: they sum up these characteristics to include 8 overall characteristic groups, including the following: finance, technical resource availability, product specialization, standards, organizational culture, employee participation, alliances and collaboration. Furthermore, various studies, e.g. [1] show that research on Industry 4.0/IIoT focuses strongly on large enterprises [16], and only marginally on SMEs [17].

There are studies that focus on servitization and advanced business models in manufacturing, which study the topic of service business and business models from the SME perspective [2, 3], and note the importance of business model studies specifically from SME perspective, due to the above various special characteristics of SMEs. Furthermore, some studies also take at least somewhat into consideration the context of capital goods/investment product sector while studying SMEs [4, 10].

Thus, we can draw the conclusion that business models, including advanced servitization business models such as PPX models, should be studied specifically from the perspective of SMEs for them to be useful, and furthermore, in addition to merely studying SMEs in this context (like some recent studies have done, e.g. [4]), the studies should also provide implications and guidelines for SMEs in particular.

2.3 Servitization, PPX Models and Profitability in Manufacturing Companies

In overall, research shows that servitization in general has a positive impact on the performance of manufacturing companies, and furthermore, it increases manufacturing companies' profitability (e.g. [11]). However, while some rather recently popularized services like advanced Pay-per-X type of services may have a positive impact on companies' profitability, it has been noted in literature that there can also be risks in the PPX implementation that require novel capabilities from companies, and may negatively impact profitability unless the implementation is planned carefully (e.g. [12]). Thus, the topic of profitability should be considered when studying the feasibility of advanced BMs, such as PPX models.

2.4 PPX Business Models and Their Strategic Impacts in Manufacturing Companies

There are a few studies which have relatively recently addressed the topic of PPX business model uses in the B2B and partly also in more detail in the investment product sector [4, 13]. They found, in general, first, that in this context, companies have been able to receive important strategic benefits from PPX services. The main focal point of these studies were specifically PPU services, not so much the PPO services and business models, which have been very little studied in the investment product sector companies, and which are focused on in our study. These found benefits were related to three distinct strategic objectives: rapid sales growth, market share expansion, and new market creation. They also found that PPU models accelerated market penetration and impacted rapid sales growth often in the early lifecycle phases of industries, and with relatively novel technologies, such as solar and wind power industries. Also other benefits have been found, including more steady and predictable cash flows, sustainability in terms of both environment and business, etc. [4, 14, 15].

We identified several major mechanisms from recent literature [4, 16] to reflect impacts to the rapid sales growth with PPX BMs in manufacturing companies. Some of the commonly addressed ones were related to sales strategy, pricing, financing, and risk management mechanisms. Sales strategy impacts sales growth, because customers do not necessarily evaluate lifecycle costs and companies are losing business to competitors, which are less expensive in short term, but more expensive in long term. A well-known basic intrinsic advantage of PPU is that it can be offered to customers who do not desire a large number of uses of the product. Another advantage of the PPU lies in the firm's flexibility toward incomplete information about customers' usage needs: if the usage quantities are imperfectly known to the firm beforehand, the seller needs to hedge in its pricing against this uncertainty in usage. One more advantage of the PPU business model stems from the ability to vary the “level of service” by making the product more or less available to the consumers. Varying services affect the customer’s benefit but also the service total costs [16].

However, there are also potential risks and downsides noticed from PPX/PPU services: for instance, companies have to cope with the threat that amortizing product costs can take longer through PPU revenues, compared to selling the product directly, and furthermore, the uncertainty about maintenance costs can impact the profitability of PPU services (see [12]).

Thus, we find that there should be more research to better understand the strategic benefits of PPX in the specific context of B2B companies and especially the manufacturing investment product sector companies, also considering the important aspect of profitability of PPX models, and the generic mechanisms behind the strategic benefits and profitability from PPX BMs.

2.5 PPX Business Models and Profitability

There are various existing studies that address PPX pricing and business models in the context of software products. For instance, [17] study the profitability of adopting PPU for a digital good, compared with a fixed-price one-time purchase business model. However, there are limitations in making use of software-related PPX research in manufactured products, especially in the context of investment products and project business/manufacture-to-order products, because of huge differences in production and logistics costs, as well as the related scalability of earnings and the business model to a large quantity of customers. [12] found that regarding PPU profits, uncertainty about a product’s maintenance costs can threaten the profitability of PPU services. [16] present a model explaining why PPU business models have become profitable alternatives to traditional selling models across a wide range of goods. In more detail, they identify three situations where a PPU BM can be more profitable than selling: first, when the logistics costs of goods are not too high (new technologies such as Industry 4.0 have been found to reduce logistics costs, making the PPU models more profitable); second, when companies have little information about customer usage profiles, PPU’s effective pricing that takes into consideration customers’ varying usage offers an advantage over selling; and third, when service providers can vary their service level (in the form of the good’s availability), they further increase their advantage because they attract even the high usage consumers. In such a case, the PPU model performs more profitably even for higher levels of logistics costs.

2.6 Research Gaps Addressed by This Study

In overall, there are very few studies that aim to understand the role of PPX, especially the little studied PPO business models in investment product sector companies, which differ significantly in many respects from the much studied PPX services and BMs in the software sector, as well as the relatively much studied PPX in the consumer mass product sector. The latter ones (PPX in software and mass consumer product industries) differ significantly from investment products in the respect of e.g. the economies of scale that can be made well use of in their PPX business models, as well as considering the very different supplier risk profile compared to the investment/make-to-order products, that this study concentrates on.

We have found no detailed case studies on the mechanisms behind sales growth and profitability in the context of PPX models in SMEs and investment products; we have recognized few more overall multi-company case studies studying PPU BMs (e.g. [4]), which do address PPU business models from the perspective of strategic objectives, but they do not study specifically PPO BM's, like we do in this study, and they do not go into very much detail behind sales growth and profitability mechanisms, and in particular, current studies that exist have not provided implications specifically to SMEs like our study aims to do.

Furthermore, to our best knowledge, our study is also the first or at least among the very first to consider SME company size in somewhat more depth while studying the strategic objectives of PPX business models, and particularly so in understanding the strategic opportunities of PPX BMs in manufacturing SMEs in the specific context of investment product manufacturing companies.

3 Methodology

The aim of this research is to understand how SME companies can make use of PPX business models largely in investment product markets, and how these impact rapid sales growth and profitability for the investment product manufacturers. To study this, we have used case study methodology, by selecting pioneering SME investment product manufacturing companies that have been doing business using the PPX business model for few years. In order to answer the research questions appropriately, we designed a selection criterion, under which we selected companies that were investment product manufacturing SMEs, pioneering in their business, B2B businesses, companies that had already implemented PPX business models.

Based on the above selection criteria, we selected two companies, Company A and Company B based in Europe. Both the companies make complex machines equipped with Industry 4.0 based technologies. We have signed a confidentiality agreement with the companies, that does not allow us to mention their names and details of their businesses. On a broader level, they are B2B investment product manufacturing SMEs, pioneering in their business and have implemented the PPX business models with many of their customers.

Company A

Company A manufactures investment products and have been using a variety of PPX business models to sell the investment product to their customers, who in turn use the investment product to manufacture the end-product. Company A has been selling the machines under PPX business models for the last 3 years and approximately 40% of their business comes from PPX business models. Company A works with a third party that buys the machine as assets from Company A and Company A is able to provide the same machine via PPX contract to the end customer. This way Company A offloads the ownership of the asset to the third party. Because of the non-disclosure agreement between the researchers and the Company A, we cannot provide more details about the third party.

The various PPX business models Company A uses are as follows:

1. pay per availability – customer pays for the uptime
2. pay per output (with a minimum payment threshold) – customer pays for the output that the investment product generates. As per the agreement, the customer agrees to pay a minimum per month irrespective of the output.
3. pay per savings (investment part paid partly) – This is a PPX business model which is not implemented but very close towards implementation. The logic of this business model is that the customer pays partly for the product and both the customer and the manufacturer agree to share the savings created by the use of the product.
4. extended warranty – This is more of a "Hybrid" PPX business model. The earning logic behind this business model is of the hybrid nature, as in, the customer pays a reduced price for the investment product and purchases regular maintenance contract where the manufacturer guarantees the performance and any savings made because of the machine's usage will be shared between the manufacturer and the customer.

Company B

Company B manufactures investment products and via distributor sells it to the customers (B2B) using PPX business models. The PPX business model contracts are made and controlled by the distributors. Hence, the distributors act as the third party between the manufacturer and the end customer, as far as the PPX business models are concerned. Company B's distributors have been selling Company B's machines via PPX contracts for the last 2 years. The distributors are selling Company B's machines under the pay-per-output PPX business model to the end customer. Company B guarantees the performance of the machine to the distributor in order to make sure the PPX business model contracts are successful. Approximately 15% of their business comes from the above arrangement with the distributor via PPX business models.

We conducted a qualitative interview session with both the companies that lasted for about 2 h each. In both Company A and Company B we interviewed senior vice presidents, who understood the strategy behind PPX business models for their respective companies in detail. As there is lack of space, we are not able to attach the entire interview questionnaire, but we will describe the major interview themes in the following paragraph. We designed a semi-structured questionnaire with a few open questions and some specific structured questions. All the questions are categorized under the following categories:

1. Background questions
2. Questions about strategic objectives towards PPX business models from rapid sales growth point of view
3. Impact of PPX business models enabled rapid sales growth on the overall profitability
4. SME related opportunities and limitations that impact the rapid sales growth because of PPX business models.

We recorded the interview using a recording device and then transcribed it manually in order to extract the data for the result section.

4 Results and Findings

1. *Rapid sales growth because of the PPX business models*

Both companies stated that the PPX business models are very important for the rapid sales growth. They have grown during last two years significantly because of PPX business models.

Company A stated,

"We started implementation in 2017 and last year (2019) 35–40% of produced machine are sold via PPX business models."

Company B stated,

"For us, more than half of the growth, in the last two years is attributed to PPX business models via distributors. We have doubled our turnover during last two years because we are able to sell more machines through the PPX business model contracts."

2. *Rapid sales growth PPX BMs, mechanisms*

Rapid sales growth has come through different mechanisms. We identified four different mechanisms from interview data: strategic, pricing, financing and risk management mechanisms. According to our results gaining new customers and extending business with existing customers were important for the sales strategy mechanism. Pricing mechanism sets the balance between sales growth and profitability. Partnering with financial institutes is essential to get enough financial resources for growth, and PPU BM is impacted by risks related to sales growth and profitability. Research results showed that financing was experienced as important in PPX BM implementation. Interviewed companies emphasized risk management's important role when implementing PPX BMs.

Table 1 above describes the mechanisms that enable rapid sales growth by PPX business models. Both the companies have described the mechanisms under the factors of strategy, pricing, financing the product and risk management.

3. *Impact of PPX business models on overall profitability of the companies*

For company A PPX business models related rapid sales growth start impacting the profitability of the company once the cost of manufacturing the machine is amortized. The machine manufactured by Company A is complex and uses novel technologies, which makes it high-end and expensive, resulting into a negative impact on profitability via traditional selling based business model, whereas, PPX contracts guarantee additional profits based on the X (i.e. use, output or outcome of the machine).

Company A stated,

"In short term profitability is not impacted much, but in long term when the fleet is massive and bigger part of the investment is amortized then profits are prominent."

Table 1. Mechanisms for rapid sales growth by PPX business models.

Factors impacting rapid sales growth	Company A	Company B
Strategic mechanisms	- PPX business models allowed selling to new customers, who found the machine very expensive otherwise. - Reason for high price is better technology, which leads to the significant lower operation costs. - Absolute turnover depends on the contract type, where, capital can be in company A's own balance sheet, 3rd party's balance sheet or end customer's balance sheet or all combinations	- Machines are sold to the distributors who in turn sell it to the end-customer by PPX business models. - Threshold to order reduces. - Reduction in investment cost for the distributors if they buy fleets. - Increase in the maintenance contract to accommodate PPX related issues. - Dynamic business for the end-customer, hence, PPX provides required capacity to them via the distributor
Pricing mechanisms	High cost of machine limits the sales, but PPX business models allow flexible pricing reducing the customer's threshold for purchase	Company B reduced the investment cost for the distributors and increased the service contract (to accommodate PPX). This allowed the distributor to sell the machines as PPX contracts
Financing mechanisms	Usage of third part financing is enabling PPX BM. But it is also limiting and capturing part of the profit	Current system allows the distributor to extract maximum benefits of PPX contracts
Risk management mechanisms	For both the companies, their customers can change the machine supplier, because of PPX business models in case of unforeseen circumstances (such as bankruptcy for company A and B)	

Company A internally calculated that the investment amortization time is much shorter than expected lifetime of the machine. Moreover, they are also earning during amortization time after paying the financing cost to the third-party company. In company A amortization time is about seven years, but because the product operation cost is very low compared to the competitors, they were able to set a relatively better (and higher) PPX business model contract price. Hence the cumulative profit accrual during the machine lifetime is much higher than if the machine was sold under the traditional selling-based business model.

For company B, the presence of distributors dilutes the additional profits to some extent, but overall profitability is positively impacted because of increased sales (by reducing investment cost) and higher service contracts.

Company B stated,

> *"As of now we share the profits of PPX business models with the distributor, but it would be ideal if we can keep the ownership of the machines and customers pay using the PPX business models, without the distributor presence"*

4. *Size (SME) impact to the implementation of PPX BM*

Company A saw size of the company (SME) as an advantage in a manner that they can be flexible and fulfil customers specific and customized requirements without much of an internal resistance. PPX business models allow them to approach and sell the machines to bigger customers based on the X (use, output or outcome) even if the cost of the machine is high.

Company B stated,

> *"Because we are SME, hence there is an advantage from low hierarchy, fast decision making, and capabilities to modify contract according to customers' requirements (resulting into more deals)."*

Both stated that significant disadvantage is that in overall, financing needs of PPX model limit the PPX BM implementation and growth, which also resulted into involving various third parties (financing the machines, distributors).

5 Discussion and Conclusions

We will next draw major conclusions on the basis of our results, and thus aim to answer to our main research questions.

Responding to RQ1 (How is the rapid sales growth achieved by PPX BMs for investment product equipment manufacturing SMEs?). On basis of the results we find that the sales growth of both the studied companies could be significantly impacted because of PPX business models. Investment product manufacturing companies that manufacture high-end machines from the technological perspective (Industry 4.0 technologies) do not usually achieve rapid sales growth through traditional selling-based business model because of a high threshold to buy from the customers. PPX business models seemed to lower the threshold significantly by allowing the customers to pay for the use, output or the outcome instead of the machine itself. This resulted in rapid sales growth for these kind of manufacturing companies.

We can infer that there were several different types of important mechanisms, described in more detail in Table 1 of Sect. 4 (Results and findings), which enabled or facilitated the rapid sales growth in the studied SMEs. In overall, these mechanisms were related to pricing, financing, risk management and strategic sales decisions as mentioned in Table 1. For larger customer companies, trust (in terms of reliability and performance of the machine) is often a major roadblock while buying expensive high-end machines from SMEs such as company A and company B. PPX business models were found to lower this threshold to buy and to allow the customer to experience the performance as well as the reliability that the machine offers, without a significant risk. Customers were able to get these machines to their respective factories via PPX contracts and pay for the result or performance of the machine. This, in turn, introduced a major risk for the manufacturing companies in terms of capital, while somebody has to bear the cost of manufacturing the machine. Both the case companies were found to have created interesting approaches to mitigate the risks related to capital in PPX model implementation. Company A did this by selling the machines to a third party that provided the needed capital and allowed company A to sell the machine to the end-customer through PPX business models. Company B, in turn, sold the machine to a distributor (also a third-party in this case) and the distributor sold the machines to the end-customers via PPX business models. This eventually led to rapid sales growth for both the companies. PPX business models also lowered the risk for the customers in case of unforeseen circumstances such as bankruptcy of the SME manufacturing companies, which had only a limited capability to carry such risks by themselves, due to their relatively small size and own resources. Customers were able to change the supplier of the machine by terminating the PPX contract and thus, they did not have the burden of a non-performing asset in their company. These mechanisms together led to rapid sales growth for the SME case companies (company A and company B).

Responding to RQ2 (How does the rapid sales growth enabled by PPX business models impact overall profitability for investment product equipment manufacturing SMEs?). We can infer that the studied companies were able to make use of PPX models for rapid sales growth, the PPX models ultimately impacting positively the overall profitability. Results related to the overall profitability clearly demonstrate that because of the different mechanisms for rapid sales growth, the positive impact on profitability was different for both companies. For company A, they saw an immediate impact on their profitability even during the amortization time, after paying of the agreed sum to the third party. More importantly, they estimated that this positive impact on profitability will be grow exponentially once the amortization period is done. For company B, the impact on profitability was also positive but rather limitedly so, because of the distributors. It was essential for them to work towards a situation where they could replace the distributor with a financing third party like company A, and thus start getting a bigger share on profits from PPX business model implementation. In general, rapid sales growth enabled by PPX business model did impact positively the overall profitability of the companies, but there were other factors, such as third parties, that had their at least temporarily limiting impact to the profitability.

We also found that the small SME size and related limited resources (financial, technological and expertise- related) seemed to impact clearly many of the studied decisions and mechanisms in both the SME companies, which were related to the strategically beneficial and profitable implementation of PPX BMs. SME size advantages such as faster decision making, and flexibility seemed to allow the companies to provide customized solutions to the end-customers making the PPX business model even more attractive for the customers. On the other side, financing the equipment under the PPX business model was a major SME size related downside for both companies. Both the companies dealt with the issue of financing via the third-party mechanism, either engaging with a third party that bought the equipment as an asset and let the company (company A in this case) to figure out the PPX contract terms, or by selling the equipment (and an extensive service contract) as a fleet to the distributor, who in turn sold the equipment to the end-customer via PPX business models.

The need for involving such third parties, again, seemed to decrease the profitability of PPX at least in the short term.

Academic Contribution. This study contributed to the academic understanding of the major strategic benefits of advanced BMs, especially the very little studied PPX models, through increasing the understanding of the generic mechanisms behind the rapid sales growth in especially in manufacturing companies that produce investment products for the use of other companies in their production processes, which has been studied earlier e.g. in [4]. We add especially by analyzing in more detail a) some major mechanisms towards sales growth in particular, and b) mechanisms behind the profitability of PPX business model implementation. Some interesting recognized and analyzed ones here are related to the varied use of third parties that provide additional resources (expertise, financing, networks and contacts) to studied SMEs, which cannot find it not feasible to acquire such resources feasibly by themselves.

Furthermore, we add the academic understanding of the strategic benefits realization (especially rapid sales growth and related profitability) of PPX business models, in the context of investment product companies and SMEs in particular. Earlier studies have not provided implications especially to SMEs in this context. We have demonstrated that the SME perspective mattered significantly in studied SMEs e.g. in the manner of the third part involvement, faster decision making as well as flexibility to provide best suited PPX business model contracts to the end customer.

Managerial Implications. Managers of the investment product manufacturing SMEs should take into consideration various strategic objectives especially rapid sales growth while implementing PPX models. The cases in this paper have demonstrated various mechanisms that can enable rapid sales growth through PPX business models. It is important that the managers take into account these mechanisms in order to successfully implement PPX BMs, and achieve rapid sales growth through them. One of the key outcomes for strategic objectives is to impact profitability and both the studied cases demonstrate what the managers should take into account while strategizing profitability impacts via rapid sales growth enabled by PPX business models. Managers of SMEs should think about the role of third parties from the financing perspective in order to achieve rapid sales growth and create an immediate impact on profitability.

Limitations of the Study. The conclusions are somewhat limited by this study's approach to studying two case companies, and as such, it does not allow the direct generalization of results to other companies. The results and conclusions are important, however, already in this case study format because there are very few studies that focus on SMEs in the field of advanced BMs (such as PPX business models) and industry 4.0. It seems viable, however, to make the claim that also other SMEs will very probably find both similar types of strategic benefits and related mechanisms viable and useful in their attempts to make use of advanced business models like PPX model.

Future studies can explore in more depth the role of third parties to achieve rapid sales growth and eventually impact profitability through PPX business models, especially for SMEs. This paper presented rapid sales growth mechanisms through PPX business models from SME perspective. Future studies can compare the mechanisms for SMEs and larger companies and identify similarities as well as differences in the mechanisms.

One of the objectives of this paper is to study the impact on profitability through rapid sales growth enabled by PPX business models. Future studies can take into account other strategic objectives presented by [4], such as market share expansion and new market creation and study their impact on profitability from investment product SME manufacturing companies. Future studies can focus on pricing of the PPX business model contracts and analyze the impact of pricing on overall profitability.

References

1. Ulaga, W., et al.: From product to service: navigating the transition. Insights@ IMD. 1–4 (2013)
2. Müller, J.M., Buliga, O., Voigt, K.-I.: Fortune favors the prepared: how SMEs approach business model innovations in Industry 4.0. Technol. Forecast. Soc. Change. **132**, 2–17 (2018). https://doi.org/10.1016/j.techfore.2017.12.019
3. Mittal, S., Khan, M.A., Romero, D., Wuest, T.: A critical review of smart manufacturing & Industry 4.0 maturity models: Implications for small and medium-sized enterprises (SMEs). J. Manuf. Syst. **49**, 194–214 (2018). https://doi.org/10.1016/j.jmsy.2018.10.005
4. Gebauer, H., Saul, C.J., Haldimann, M., Gustafsson, A.: Organizational capabilities for pay-per-use services in product-oriented companies. Int. J. Prod. Econ. **192**, 157–168 (2017). https://doi.org/10.1016/j.ijpe.2016.12.007
5. Wittkowski, K., Moeller, S., Wirtz, J.: Firms' intentions to use nonownership services. J. Serv. Res. **16**, 171–185 (2013). https://doi.org/10.1177/1094670512471997
6. Ehret, M., Wirtz, J.: Unlocking value from machines: business models and the industrial internet of things. J. Market. Manage. **33**, 111–130 (2017). https://doi.org/10.1080/0267257X.2016.1248041
7. Ardolino, M., Rapaccini, M., Saccani, N., Gaiardelli, P., Crespi, G., Ruggeri, C.: The role of digital technologies for the service transformation of industrial companies. Int. J. Prod. Res. **56**, 2116–2132 (2018). https://doi.org/10.1080/00207543.2017.1324224
8. Metallo, C., Agrifoglio, R., Schiavone, F., Mueller, J.: Understanding business model in the Internet of Things industry. Technol. Forecast. Soc. Change **136**, 298–306 (2018). https://doi.org/10.1016/j.techfore.2018.01.020
9. Bock, M., Wiener, M.: Nonownership business models in the manufacturing industry: the role of uncertainty and the industrial Internet of Things. In: ICIS 2018 Proceedings (2018)
10. Gebauer, H., Edvardsson, B., Gustafsson, A., Witell, L.: Match or mismatch: strategy-structure configurations in the service business of manufacturing companies. J. Serv. Res. **13**, 198–215 (2010). https://doi.org/10.1177/1094670509353933
11. Crozet, M., Milet, E.: Should everybody be in services? The effect of servitization on manufacturing firm performance. J. Econ. Manage. Strategy **26**, 820–841 (2017). https://doi.org/10.1111/jems.12211
12. Cusumano, M.A., Kahl, S.J., Suarez, F.F.: Services, industry evolution, and the competitive strategies of product firms. Strateg. Manage. J. **36**, 559–575 (2015). https://doi.org/10.1002/smj.2235
13. Gebauer, H., Saul, C.J., Haldimann, M., Gustafsson, A.: Organizational capabilities for pay-per-use services in product-oriented companies. Int. J. Prod. Econ. (2015). https://doi.org/10.1016/j.ijpe.2016.12.007
14. Sundin, E., Lindahl, M., Ijomah, W.: Product design for product/service systems: design experiences from Swedish industry. J. Manuf. Technol. Manage. **20**, 723–753 (2009). https://doi.org/10.1108/17410380910961073

15. Sundin, E., Bras, B.: Making functional sales environmentally and economically beneficial through product remanufacturing. J. Clean. Prod. **13**, 913–925 (2005). https://doi.org/10.1016/j.jclepro.2004.04.006
16. Ladas, K., Kavadias, S., Loch, C.H.: Product selling versus pay-per-use services: a strategic analysis of competing business models. Available at SSRN 3356458 (2019)
17. Jiang, B., Chen, P., Mukhopadhyay, T.: Software licensing: pay-per-use versus perpetual. Available at SSRN 1088570 (2007)

An Analysis of Flexible Manufacturing on the Support of the Development of Smart Product-Service Systems

Athon F. C. S. de M. Leite[1(✉)], Matheus B. Canciglieri[1], Anderson L. Szejka[1(✉)], Yee Mey Goh[2], Radmehr P. Monfared[2], Eduardo de F. R. Loures[1], and Osiris Canciglieri Junior[1]

[1] Industrial and Systems Engineering Graduate Program, Pontifical Catholic University of Paraná, Curitiba, Paraná, Brazil
{athon.moura, anderson.szejka, osiris.canciglieri}@pucpr.br

[2] School of Mechanical, Electrical and Manufacturing Engineering, Loughborough University, Loughborough, Leicestershire, UK

Abstract. Currently, changes in the customer's mindset and increased flexibility in manufacturing shifted competition between companies to focus on the product's value rather than its cost. In this context, Product-Service Systems (PSSs) are an alternative to traditional value propositions (i.e. pure products, pure services) by combining services with products and providing an experience to customers. In recent decades, PSSs were expanded from solely business aspects to engineering aspects and technical considerations in their scope, such as the paradigms of Technical PSS, Industrial PSS, Digitalized PSS and Cyber-Physical PSS. More recently, due to the application of Industry 4.0 concepts, there is a significant increase of "smart technologies", i.e. sensors; connectivity; mobile application, in PSSs, naming it a new paradigm on the field, known as Smart PSSs. In this context, this research aims to explore and discuss current issues related to the integration of flexible manufacturing processes and Smart PSSs through a literature review and analysis, regarding information sharing, traceability and system reconfiguration based on customer's requirements. Found literature points to gaps in the theme related to semantic issues and design issues regarding the dynamic reconfiguration of the manufacturing process and the Smart PSS. The modern approaches to the theme, as found in literature, are still not able to cope with the semantic barriers and high volume of heterogeneous information in a holistic manner. Conclusions point that further investigation of the cited issues is required in a systematic manner, as well as the development of models that can cope with the presented issues.

Keywords: Smart PSSs · Process flexibility · Semantic heterogeneity · Dynamic system reconfiguration

Published by Springer Nature Switzerland AG 2020
F. Nyffenegger et al. (Eds.): PLM 2020, IFIP AICT 594, pp. 416–425, 2020.
https://doi.org/10.1007/978-3-030-62807-9_33

1 Introduction

In past decades, the increased competitiveness in markets was characterised mostly by a competition related to product's cost instead of product's value, due, in part, to the massification of manufacturing of consumer goods [1]. With the trend shift to flexible manufacturing and new market needs, an alternative to improve the value offer of the product was to add services to increase it, a phenomenon known as Servitisation, which can be represented as the origin of the Product-Service Systems (PSSs) [2–4]. These systems are achieved through a combination of products and services to better fulfil user's needs, by a single organisation or a joint effort between organisations [4]. In recent decades, research found on [5] points to further increase of "smart technologies" in Industry 4.0 scenarios, i.e. sensors; connectivity; mobile applications; e-services, in PSSs, naming it a new paradigm on the field, known as Smart PSSs.

The Smart PSSs development are characterised as a combination, in different degrees of depth, of Smart Products and E-Services [4, 6]. Due to the current development scenarios being shorter than before, more methodologies and technologies are being combined to improve the 'time and resources' management on those types of system [6]. This can be exemplified in the increasing connections between the development of the concept of Smart PSSs and the current trends on integrated and flexible manufacturing systems, smart factories, and Service 4.0 [5–7].

In another aspect, the systems' interoperation in the Fourth Industrial Revolution tends to generate a large amount of data and dynamic requirements during development cycles, in order to attend more needs from stakeholders [8]. In this context, Smart PSSs, aided by flexible manufacturing techniques, need to cope with dynamic stakeholder's needs, which contributes to the aspect of a Co-creative Value Proposition in it, but increases the number of unclear information and ambiguous interpretations, reducing the interoperability capability on its development [4, 6].

This research has as its main goal to study and analyse literature on the current issues regarding the development of Smart PSSs with the aid of flexible manufacturing techniques, and analyse, in a qualitative manner, some of the gaps and areas of interest approaching the research themes.

1.1 Materials and Methods

The research is considered to have a basic nature, with a qualitative approach. Its scientific objectives are exploratory, using as procedure an introductory literature review, followed by an analysis based on synthesis and reflection.

The expected result of the review is a discussion on the themes, represented through a schema, which serves as the starting point to expose the current issues on the continuous development and flexibilization related to Flexible Manufacturing in the context of Smart PSSs. A summarization of the method for the Literature Review is depicted in Fig. 1.

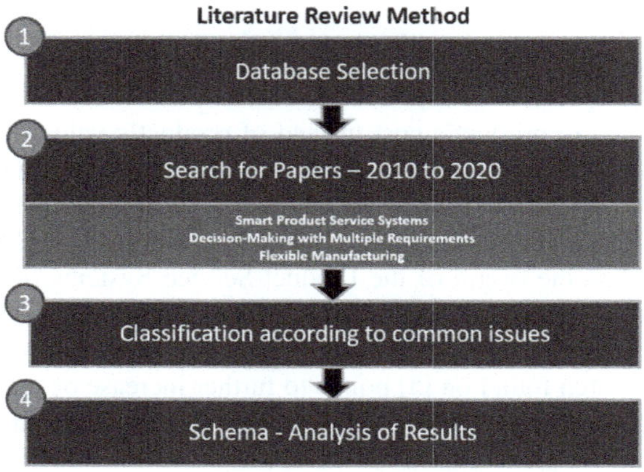

Fig. 1. Method for the literature review

The research has as its starting point the definition of the scientific database (Detail 1 of Fig. 1) in which the review will be conducted, followed by the search (Detail 2 of Fig. 1) and categorisation of the research in found issues (Detail 3 of Fig. 1). The review focuses on establishing a conceptual link for the themes, as well as to improve understanding of the areas and their intricate relations. The final analysis will be represented in a schema that represents the issues in the domains of research (Detail 4 of Fig. 1).

2 Literature Review

As the starting point for the literature review, this research defined the main database for research as the Brazilian CAPES scientific database (an aggregator of more than 519 research databases, including the bases from Elsevier, IEEE, Emerald, Taylor & Francis, Springer, among others). In sequence, papers from 2010 to 2020 were searched, using the keywords of:

- Smart Product-Service Systems
- Decision-Making with Multiple Requirements
- Flexible Manufacturing.

As Smart PSS is a recent theme, later research found on PSS and its varieties were also considered, as some of the issues are common between the different terminologies. The topic of Decision-Making with Multiple Requirements was also approached as Multi-Criteria Decision-Making, which turned out as a more fruitful search in terms of available literature.

The selected literature for this research were classified in a content analysis based on the nature of issues and current solutions in the context of Smart PSSs and Flexible Manufacturing, as follows, (i) Issues on Semantic Interoperability, (ii) Issues on Decision-Making Process with Multiple Requirements and (iii) Issues on Flexibility on System's Development.

2.1 Issues on Semantic Interoperability

The occurrence of semantic issues in the development of products, services and systems, as pointed out by literature, relates to the representation of requirements by developers [9]. Specialists tend to focus on a single phase of development; single domain; and/or single way to represent knowledge, based on self-expertise. Three aspects compose the Semantic Interoperability issues, as defined by [8, 10, 11], detailed as follows:

i. Domain: reflects multiple knowledge domains, necessary to develop products, services and systems, and their particularities;
ii. Knowledge Representation: represents the taxonomies and modelling of knowledge from different requirement sources (Design, Manufacture, ISO, among others). This difference has a significant impact on a programming level, as there are different notations to represent these requirements (XML models, RDF schema, for instance) and their conceptual structure (representation of product's features) across different phases and domains;
iii. Development: reflects the whole process of development. Each phase may approach different domains of knowledge and their representations.

The different kinds of knowledge of multiple domains imply in heterogeneous information that may cause semantic inconsistencies along the development process. In another perspective, the communication between different phases of development might present divergent information, resulting in semantic issues related to information transfer, its uniqueness and traceability, among others [11].

Within a domain and a phase of development, there are various notations of representing knowledge, presenting semantic interoperation issues on conceptual and computational levels [8]. Furthermore, semantic issues related to knowledge structures communicating without any similarity, which imply in lack of trustworthy, verifiable, unique, coherent, complete and traceable information [8].

Currently, ontologies are one of the most popular tools for representing and sharing knowledge across different systems and domains [5, 12, 13], being a viable solution on the formalization of common information models and sharing of the formal information throughout the stages of the development process, which, consequently, provides increased knowledge in the domains of application [14–16].

In [17], the author affirms that with the rapid advance and development of semantic technologies based on ontologies, there has been a shift towards more complex and better semantic modelling of manufacturing processes. This process culminates in the insertion of machining features in the semantic technologies to retrieve the considerable machining knowledge and shape semantics presented in these features.

In [18], the authors assert that ontology technology has great advantages in improving the semantic consistency of multi-source heterogeneous data. However, for complex dynamic decision-making problems, there are some limitations in the mining of ontology relations and the establishment of inference rules.

2.2 Issues on Decision-Making Process with Multiple Requirements

The complexity of current stakeholders' needs demands the participation of specialists from multiple backgrounds, providing a holistic view that ensures the best solution to fulfil customers' needs [19]. Although this approach increases value, it ends up generating a set of heterogeneous information, which may not have the same meaning, representing interests and the background of different groups of stakeholders. As globalization, collaboration, and cooperation contribute to a more connected and integrated competitive environment for the manufacturing industries, they have also made the decision-making process more complex whilst reducing the time for the decision to be made [15].

Recently, few models consider the consistency of requirements and performance in dynamic environments. In [15], the authors explain a design framework for cyber-physical systems, based on Design Rationale, connecting different design parameters and requirements from varied sources. In [9], the authors explore the Manufacturing domain and requirement's gathering from different domains. Both pieces of research have combined different models to achieve verifiably and validated information within the context of dynamic requirements, but still, there is a significant presence of specialist's decisions during the process of translating the requirements.

In another aspect, prioritization of criteria is of high importance, as demonstrated in [20]. To aid in an environment that is dynamic and has multiple requirements, research has been made on the use Multi-Criteria Decision Making (MCDM) algorithms, aiding in the decision-making process [20–22]. Furthermore, current trends on the theme, as shown by [23, 24], present the use of machine learning techniques and algorithms to solve multi-criteria problems. This happens due to the inherent ability of these methods to judge different alternatives through several criteria (attributes or requirements) to provide the most suitable alternative.

Over the last decades, several MCDM methods have been proposed, the most popular of which are AHP (Analytic Hierarchy Process), ANP (Analytic Network Process), TOPSIS (Technique for Order of Preference by Similarity to Ideal Solution), ELECTRE (ELimination and Choice Expressing REality), and PROMETHEE (Preference Ranking Organization METHod for Enrichment Evaluations) [21, 25, 26]. For some recent developments, it is possible to cite the Superiority and Inferiority Ranking (SIR) method, Stepwise Weight Assessment Ratio Analysis (SWARA), multi-attribute evaluation using Imprecise Weight Estimates (IMP), among others [16, 27, 28].

2.3 Issues on Flexibility on System's Development

The complexity of market requirements and the different configuration of systems not always accompany each other, since deep changes in system's structure need to consider a significant number of factors and usually take time to be implemented [29]. According to [30] the possibility to the reconfiguration of a system is essential to maintain it agile and flexible in the industrial scenario, but there is still little consensus on which architectures are the most effective in general.

In the scenario of Smart Product-Service Systems, few models formalise development methods for application, as pointed out by [6]. According to the same author,

Smart PSSs are in a verge of a challenge regarding adaptable systems, attributing it to the different contexts that a system is a part of. Furthermore, the author also comments about the implementation challenges related to sustainable applications of Smart PSSs, which received a lesser focus on research. According to [31], main issues on the flexibilization of the design of Smart PSSs can be related to the intense synergy that is demanded on the development of a complex system, in comparison to other kinds of system.

In another aspect, the development of the Smart Product component of Smart PSSs still deals with traditional manufacturing techniques that are not in synergy with the dynamic requirements in the development scenario. Currently, to improve that, the choice of advanced manufacturing technologies is made, based on operational criteria such as productivity and performance, which can offer a competitive advantage and more flexible [23, 32].

Advanced manufacturing systems are systems that use mechanical, electronic and computational subsystems to operate and control production, encompassing a large set of machines that execute, monitor and connect the production processes [20]. According to [20], the adoption of advanced manufacturing technologies is a key condition for maintaining the company's competitiveness in the long term. Nevertheless, many advanced manufacturing implementation projects fail to be more significant in small and medium-sized companies, as the managers of these companies are the ones who most want to implement these technologies, but they do so from instinct or information from similar companies. Yet, authors in [33] and [34] states in his research that small and medium-sized companies do not wish to implement, or do not understand how these technologies could assist them in improving customer satisfaction and market results. The author also states that these companies have limited financial and human resources, preventing these companies from implementing complex technological systems.

Over the past two decades, there have been reports of improvements in flexibility, quality and productivity in industries caused by advanced manufacturing technologies. As shown in [5, 12, 13, 32], advanced manufacturing technologies can effectively assist the length of manufacturing objectives and simultaneously consider competitive objectives and manufacturing decision areas, being considered resources mobilized for the construction of competencies.

3 Analysis of Results

At first glance, through the identification and representation of current issues on the flexibilization of Smart Product-Service Systems and reconfigurable manufacturing processes, it can be implied that a systemic approach would be necessary to cope with all those issues at once, but modularity in the system design is of great importance.

In addition, the mapping of the current issues revealed the limitations of an ontology-driven interoperable system when it is used in a highly mutable environment, and how the sharing of ambiguous information in such an environment can reduce the competitiveness of an enterprise as it will difficult the decision-making process, raising costs and diminishing the quality of the product. Figure 2 show the proposed schema for the main issues found on the literature review.

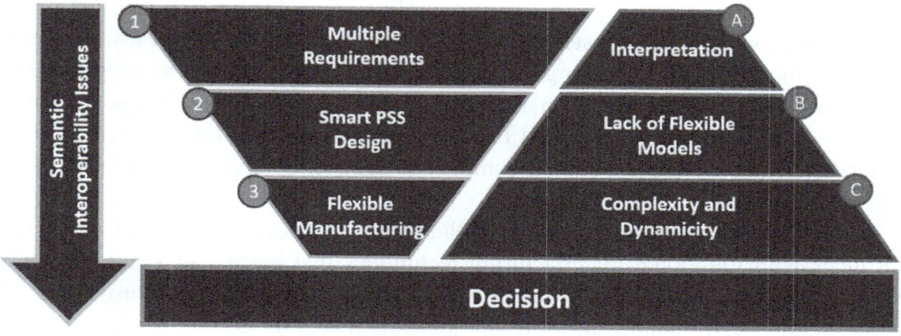

Fig. 2. Representation of current issues

The high dynamism of decision-making environment happens due to the numerous product and service requirements and their heterogeneous sources (Detail 1). These numerous and heterogeneous sources can cause information inconsistencies which can lead to wrong decisions (Detail A). The interpretation of these requirements is also subjective to the requirement analysis team which can cause non-optimal decisions to be made.

In the Smart PSS Design layer (Detail 2), the main issues identified were the lack of truly flexible PSS and manufacturing models that can solve the reconfiguration issue. There is also a lack of integrative methods between flexible manufacturing systems and services and Industry 4.0 technologies (Detail B). The industry 4.0 technology solutions identified, however, have their implementation too complex and not cost efficient.

In the last layer (Detail 3), it was identified as flexible manufacturing issues. These issues relate to the high complexity of flexible manufacturing systems and the numerous variables one must control to reconfigure the manufacturing process without losing product quality and increase process time and cost (Detail C).

All these layers of issues hinder the capacity of the real-time reconfiguration of a smart PSS and its manufacturing system. This makes it possible to note that the issues might have a significant impact on the success and longevity of the Smart PSS during its lifecycle. The concepts can be used integrated with ontology-based interoperability models to create a flexible decision-making environment that can aid in the reconfiguration of an advanced manufacturing system allowing for a more agile process and ensuring the product's quality.

The schema shows that semantic interoperability might have a significant impact on decision-making and consequently in themes of study, due to the necessity of keeping the semantical aspect of the requirements throughout the whole process of development.

4 Conclusion

This paper presented research that leads to the development of a model which shows some of the critical issues that hinder the development of flexible manufacturing on Smart PSSs. Results of the discussion showed that in an Industry 4.0 scenario, flexibilization demands that requirements from various sources must be considered and processed, as well as standardized for sharing across different phases of the system's development, without losing its content and context.

The research has identified that flexibilization of manufacturing in the context of Smart PSSs might have misinterpretation of information, heavily based on the heterogeneity of information and different sources of requirements.

In conclusion, the field and its associated domains have interesting exploration opportunities for the development of methods, approaches, and models to increase flexibilization while reducing semantic issues and improving the Smart PSSs by reducing development time and costs and improving the system quality dynamically.

The authors believe that key scientific topics to be explored in further works are:

i. A state-of-the-art literature review on the domains approached in this research, in order to refine the gap of study and provide more precise directions of improvement; and
ii. A model, approach, and/or architecture to handle the found issues in the application of flexible manufacturing in Smart PSSs.

Acknowledgements. Authors would like to acknowledge the Industrial and Systems Engineering Graduate Program of the Pontifical Catholic University of Paraná and the School of Mechanical, Electrical and Manufacturing Engineering of Loughborough University for the contribution and collaboration.

References

1. Wang, Z., Chen, C.H., Zheng, P., Li, X., Khoo, L.P.: A novel data-driven graph-based requirement elicitation framework in the smart product-service system context. Adv. Eng. Inform. **42**(100983), 1–15 (2019)
2. Aurich, J.C., Fuchs, C., Wagenknecht, C.: Life cycle oriented design of technical Product-Service Systems. J. Clean. Prod. **14**(17), 1480–1494 (2006)
3. Rese, M., Karger, M., Strotmann, W.-C.: The dynamics of industrial product service systems (IPS2)–using the net present value approach and real options approach to improve life cycle management. CIRP J. Manufact. Sci. Technol. **1**(4), 279–286 (2009)
4. Valencia, A., Mugge, R., Schoormans, J., Schifferstein, H.: The Design of Smart Product-Service Systems (PSSs): an exploration of design characteristics. Int. J. Design **9**(1), 13–28 (2015)
5. Qu, Y.J., et al.: Smart manufacturing systems: state of the art and future trends. Int. J. Adv. Manuf. Technol. **103**(9–12), 3751–3768 (2019)
6. Zheng, P., Wang, Z., Chen, C-H., Khoo, L.P.: A survey of smart product-service systems: key aspects, challenges and future perspectives. Adv. Eng. Inform. **42**, 100973 (2019)
7. Lerch, C., Gotsch, M.: Digitalized product-service systems in manufacturing firms: a case study analysis. Res. Technol. Manage. **58**(5), 45–52 (2015)
8. Leite, A.F.C.S.M., Canciglieri, M.B., Szejka, A.L., Junior, O.C.: The reference view for semantic interoperability in integrated product development process: the conceptual structure for injecting thin walled plastic products. J. Ind. Inf. Integr. **7**, 13–23 (2017)
9. Chungoora, N., et al.: A model-driven ontology approach for manufacturing system interoperability and knowledge sharing. Comput. Ind. **64**(4), 392–401 (2013)

10. Chungoora, N., Young, R.I.M.: Semantic reconciliation across design and manufacturing knowledge models: a logic-based approach. Appl. Ontol. **6**(4), 295–315 (2011)
11. Szejka, A.L., Canciglieri Jr., O., Panetto, H., Rocha Loures, E., Aubry, A.: Semantic interoperability for an integrated product development process: a systematic literature review. Int. J. Prod. Res. **55**(22), 6691–6709 (2017)
12. Qiao, L., et al.: An ontology-based modelling and reasoning framework for assembly sequence planning. Int. J. Adv. Manuf. Technol. **94**(9–12), 4187–4197 (2018)
13. Razia Sulthana, A., Subburaj, R.: Ontology and context based recommendation system using neuro-fuzzy classification. Comput. Electr. Eng. **74**, 498–510 (2019). https://doi.org/10.1016/j.compeleceng.2018.01.034
14. Wang, S., Wan, J., Li, D., Liu, C.: Knowledge reasoning with semantic data for real-time data processing in smart factory. Sensors (Switzerland) **18**(2), 1–10 (2018)
15. Moneva, H., Hamberg, R., Punter, T.: A design framework for model-based development of complex systems. In: 32nd IEEE Real-Time Systems Symposium 2nd Analytical Virtual Integration of Cyber-Physical Systems Workshop, Vienna (2011)
16. Peko, I., Gjeldum, N., Bilić, B.: Application of AHP, fuzzy AHP and PROMETHEE method in solving additive manufacturing process selection problem. Tehnicki Vjesnik **25**(2), 453–461 (2018)
17. Zhou, Q., et al.: Research on a configurable method for fault diagnosis knowledge of machine tools and its application. Int. J. Adv. Manuf. Technol. **95**(1–4), 937–960 (2018)
18. Hamdi, F., Ghorbel, A., Masmoudi, F., Dupont, L.: Optimization of a supply portfolio in the context of supply chain risk management: literature review. J. Intell. Manuf. **29**(4), 763–788 (2018)
19. Pereira, J.A., et al.: Application of integrated product development model oriented to R&D projects of the Brazilian electricity sector. In: Advanced Materials Research, pp. 401–409. Trans Tech Publications (2014)
20. Wang, L., et al.: Distributed manufacturing resource selection strategy in cloud manufacturing. Int. J. Adv. Manuf. Technol. **94**(9–12), 3375–3388 (2018)
21. Rezaei, J.: Best-worst multi-criteria decision-making method. Omega (United Kingdom) **53**, 49–57 (2015). https://doi.org/10.1016/j.omega.2014.11.0
22. Saeidlou, S., Saadat, M., Sharifi, E.A., Jules, G.D.: Agent-based distributed manufacturing scheduling: an ontological approach. Cogent Eng. **6**(1), 1–23 (2019). https://doi.org/10.1080/23311916.2019.1565630
23. Liu, K., El-Gohary, N.: Ontology-based semi-supervised conditional random fields for automated information extraction from bridge inspection reports. Autom. Constr. **81**, 313–327 (2017). https://doi.org/10.1016/j.autcon.2017.02.003
24. Saeidlou, S., Saadat, M., Jules, G.D.: Knowledge and agent-based system for decentralised scheduling in manufacturing. Cogent Eng. **6**(1), 1–19 (2019). https://doi.org/10.1080/23311916.2019.1582309
25. Alsina, E.F., Chica, M., Trawiński, K., Regattieri, A.: On the use of machine learning methods to predict component reliability from data-driven industrial case studies. Int. J. Adv. Manuf. Technol. **94**(5–8), 2419–2433 (2018)
26. Asghar, E., Zaman, U.K., Baqai, A.A., Homri, L.: Optimum machine capabilities for reconfigurable manufacturing systems. Int. J. Adv. Manuf. Technol. **95**(9–12), 4397–4417 (2018)
27. Navarro, I.J., Yepes, V., Martí, J.V.: A review of multicriteria assessment techniques applied to sustainable infrastructure design. Adv. Civ. Eng. **6134803** (2019)
28. Sevinç, A., Gür, S., Eren, T.: Analysis of the difficulties of SMEs in Industry 4.0 applications by analytical hierarchy process and analytical network process. Processes **6**(12), 1–10 (2018)

29. Igawa, H., Tajima, Y., Yamamoto, H., Sakikawa, S.: A design support method for automation system configuration using model-based simulation. In: 2017 IEEE 13th International Symposium on Autonomous Decentralized System (ISADS), pp. 84–89 (2017)
30. Qasim, L., Jankovic, M., Olaru, S., Garnier, J.L.: Model-based system reconfiguration: a descriptive study of current industrial challenges. In: Bonjour, E., Krob, D., Palladino, L., Stephan, F. (eds.) Complex Systems Design & Management (2019)
31. Maleki, E., et al.: Ontology-based framework enabling smart product-service systems: application of sensing systems for machine health monitoring. IEEE Internet Things J. **5**(6), 4496–4505 (2018)
32. Li, X., Zhang, S., Huang, R., Huang, B., Xu, C., Zhang, Y.: A survey of knowledge representation methods and applications in machining process planning. Int. J. Adv. Manuf. Technol. **98**(9–12), 3041–3059 (2018)
33. Zhao, Y., et al.: Dynamic and unified modelling of sustainable manufacturing capability for industrial robots in cloud manufacturing. Int. J. Adv. Manuf. Technol. **93**(5–8), 2753–2771 (2017)
34. Zhou, J., Yao, X.: Hybrid teaching–learning-based optimization of correlation-aware service composition in cloud manufacturing. Int. J. Adv. Manuf. Technol. **91**(9–12), 3515–3533 (2017)

Startup Definition Proposal Using Product Lifecycle Management

Bernardo Reisdorfer-Leite, Michele Marcos de Oliveira, Marcelo Rudek, Anderson Luis Szejka, and Osiris Canciglieri Junior(✉)

Polytechnic School, Industrial and Systems Engineering Graduate Program (PPGEPS), Pontifical Catholic University of Paraná (PUCPR), Rua Imaculada Conceição, 1155, Curitiba, Paraná 80215-901, Brazil
{bernardo.leite,marcelo.rudek,anderson.szejka, osiris.canciglieri}@pucpr.br, michele.m@grupomarista.org.br

Abstract. Innovative products and services remain the primary drivers in innovation ecosystems. New ventures emerge in these ecosystems, and the number grows by the day. The leading ecosystems actors appoint the new firms as startups, and usually academics, and young entrepreneurs design and establish these recent ventures. Many studies state that startups impact positively in the economy, contribute to its development, explore new market possibilities by investigating concrete exponential problems. Nevertheless, there is a missing concept of what a startup is, and even among practitioners, there are a plethora of definitions. As a result, it is an emerging standard without an explicit and universal meaning. This matter is also supported by the lack of definition in scientific literature, that does not define and delimit clearly the boundaries and the exact moments that may nominate an enterprise as a startup. Therefore, an explicit definition could support innovation ecosystems actors, like Policy Makers and University and Company Managers to improve the effectiveness of the establishment of startups as the main ecosystems' output. Hence, this study aims to propose a preliminary and generic definition of startups, using the PLM concept perspective as a starting point, since PLM seeks to improve innovation through managing company's products across their lifecycles, from the first idea until its discard. To initiate the discussion, we compare the startup and product lifecycles, specially the Beginning of Life (BOL) and Middle of Life (MOL) phases.

Keywords: Startup · Startup lifecycle · Product lifecycle management · Innovation ecosystems

1 Motivation

The current world economy is witnessing an increase in the amount of innovation in the market. New enterprises are being created around the world exponentially, and the number grows by the day. It is given to them a specific status: startups. Currently, startups represent an influential model in the innovation economy. Not only offering innovative products, but equally contributing to job creation and productivity growth

F. Nyffenegger et al. (Eds.): PLM 2020, IFIP AICT 594, pp. 426–435, 2020.
https://doi.org/10.1007/978-3-030-62807-9_34

[1]. At the same pace that the number of startups grow in quantity and variety, they are additionally becoming a complex issue. There are many actors involved in their creation and development. From universities to incubators and accelerators, from mature companies to governments, among others.

The fundamental activity of a startup is to transform ideas into products, measure how customers respond, and then learn whether to pivot or persevere [2]. Through trial and error, hiring and firing, successful startups all invent a parallel process to product development [3]. The enterprise has a learning process running at the same time as the product is being developed. While the learning process is engaged in customer-centric activities mainly happening outside the enterprise, product development is focused on the product-centric activities that are taking place internally [4]. Although many startups fail at the first stages (nine out of 10 startups [5]), an entrepreneurial society facilitates this entrepreneurial driven economic growth through an institutional context which is conducive to entrepreneurial activity [6].

Limited resources and pressure to achieve growth, startups focus on product development rather than complex management structures. Since there are no internal barriers, the response speed to changes are higher than in large and com-plex enterprises. The value creation process starts with an idea. People co-create and initiate its development. After the development stage, the enterprise starts manufacturing, distributing and promoting the product or outsourcing the manufacture and distribution and only selling the product. In due course, the enterprise achieves a rate of growth. When the product or service achieve its maturity, the enterprise will presumably represent an established company.

According to [7] startups are companies set up to test business models developed around new ideas, typically, proposed by a number of co-founders or team members. [2] defines startups as a human institution designed to create an innovative product or service under conditions of substantial uncertainty. Some authors define the features of startups. [8] describes startups as a dynamism of form and merit, which results from functioning in a very unstable, unpredictable environment. However, each author has its own understanding of the concept [7] and there is no unique definition in literature on what constitutes a startup [9]. The previously mentioned definitions are generic, and this situation represents the lack in scientific literature regarding the definition of startups.

Since enterprises are not profitable and do not survive in its initial stages; the expected growth is supported by its successful product; in due course, they achieve a maturity level which they do not maintain an increasing growth in revenue. The previous assertion leads to the research question, which is: “during the lifecycle of an innovative enterprise (often called as startup), when could they be named as startup?”.

From the research question, we have determined the aim of this paper suggesting the moment that an enterprise might be denominated as Startup; according to the stage in its lifecycle and the stage of its product based on Product Lifecycle Management (PLM) concepts.

2 Background

2.1 Startup Lifecycle

We have not found in scientific literature studies that directly assess the startup lifecycle. Authors have been using various lifecycles models and frameworks to support diverse applications. In our starting literature screening, we have observed some models that can support our goal.

We took into account that the sequence of activities and stages might vary among various startups [10]. Nevertheless, the findings contain similarities among the lifecycle stages.

Some initial frameworks were proposed regarding Small and Medium Enterprises (SMEs) in the 80 s [11, 12], and they seem applicable to the startup context. Table 1 compares the two initial models and more recent models found in recent grey and scientific literature. Some notable studies are equally identified on non-scientific literature: [13] and [2]. In the same way [7] summarize that the lifecycle begins with an idea and ends with an exit strategy (merger, acquisition, IPO, etc.).

Table 1. Startup lifecycle in scientific and non-scientific literature.

Author	Application	Lifecycle stages
Churchill and Lewis [11]	SMEs	Existence, survival, success, take-off, resource maturity
Scott and Bruce [12]	SMEs	Inception, survival, growth, expansion, maturity
Salamzadeh and Kesim [10]	Lifecycle and challenges	Bootstrapping, seed, creation
Picken [14]	Enterprise culture	Startup, transition, scaling, and exit
Mańkowska [15]	Internet of Things	Seed, start-up, early growth, expansion, mezzanine, exit
Paschen [16]	Crowdfunding	Pre-startup, startup, growth
Overall and Wise [17]	Customer development	Pre-seed, early stage, expansion, later stage
Startup Genome [13]	Startup ecosystems	Discovery, validation, efficiency, scale, sustain, maintain, decline

As stated in Sect. 1 the concept of startup is diverse in academia. However, among practitioners, the most acceptable startup lifecycle is the model related to the financing cycle (Fig. 1). As the reason for the existence of an enterprise is to generate profit, we corroborate with the affirmation as being the basic metric to commence this study. Therefore, we compare it with Product Lifecycle (PLC), since an enterprise make profit by selling its products and services. The startup lifecycle specificities are presented in Sect. 3.

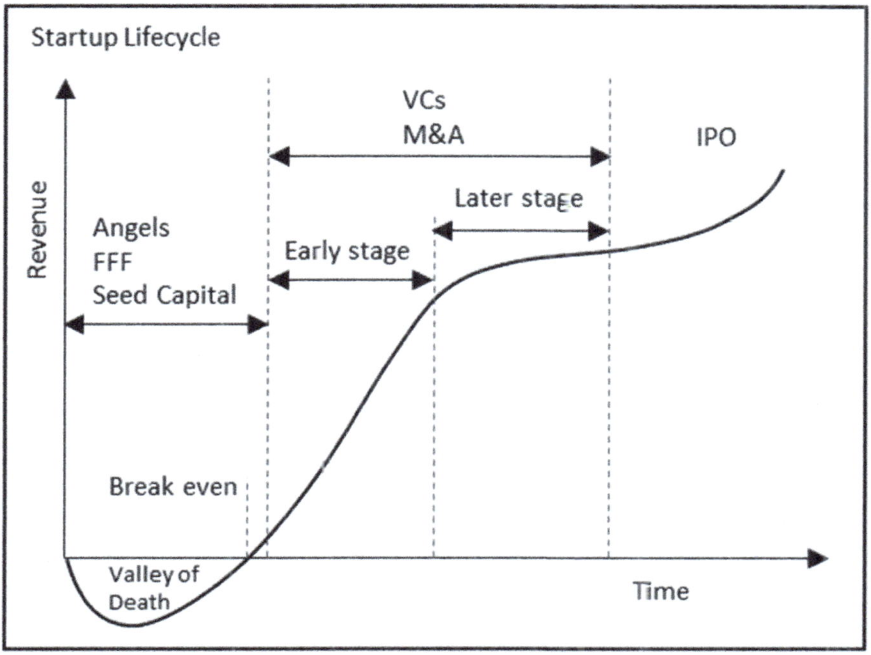

Fig. 1. Startup lifecycle. Adapted from [18]

2.2 Product Lifecycle Management

Product Lifecycle Management (PLM) is the business activity of managing, in the most effective way, a company's products, all the way across their lifecycles; from the very first idea for a product all the way through until it is retired and disposed of [19]. [20] define PLM as a strategic business solution for integrating people, information and processes across the extended enterprise through a common body of knowledge. The body of knowledge within an enterprise is comparable to a living organism which its health directly affects enterprise's ability to operate and compete effectively.

In modern product development, as the complexity and variety of products increase to satisfy increasingly sophisticated customers, so does the need for knowledge and expertise for developing products [20]. In this context, PLM aims at reintegrating the manufacturing organization by closing all the knowledge loops and positioning the product at the focal point of the whole organization. It is about reinventing and revitalizing the cobbler model for the information age [20].

Products generate a large amount of information during their lifecycles [21] and the PLM concept promises to provide support for the product's entire lifecycle; from the first conceptualization to the disposal of its latter instance. The volume, diversity, and complexity of information describing the product will increase correspondingly [22].

One of the advantages of adopting PLM is the knowledge base generated by the product in its lifecycle. A rich knowledge base, in turn, can potentially improve the efficacy of knowledge-intensive processes, thus resulting in better overall cash flow and competitive standing [20].

In general, the product lifecycle consists of three main phases: beginning of life (BOL), including design and production; middle of life (MOL), including logistics (distribution), use, service, and maintenance; and end of life (EOL), including reverse logistics (collecting), remanufacturing (disassembly, refurbishment, reassembly, etc.), reuse, recycle, and disposal [23] (Fig. 2).

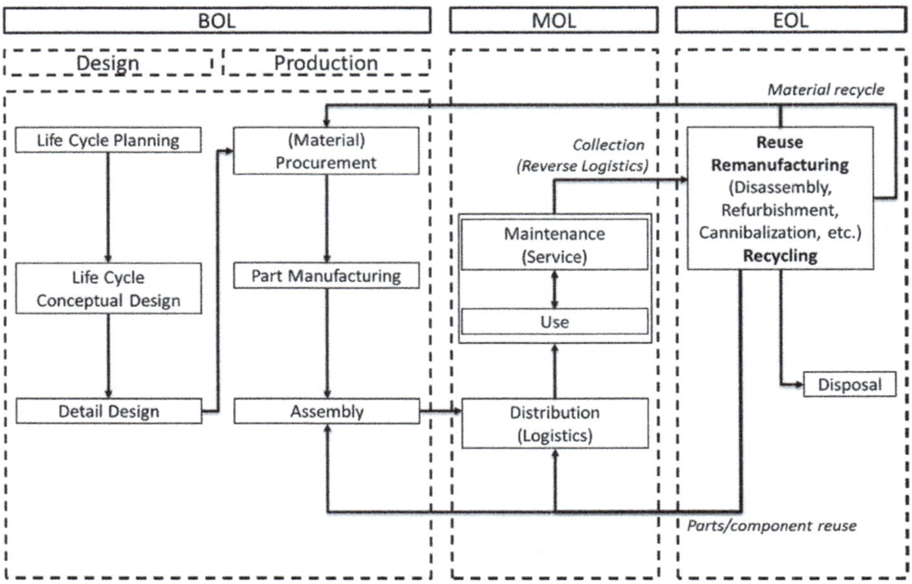

Fig. 2. Product lifecycle. Extracted from [22]

3 Application and Discussion

Our proposal encompasses the following concepts to explain when a new innovative firm should be called as startup. The first concept the knowledge base created across the three main stages of product lifecycle (BOL, MOL and EOL). The second concept is the startup lifecycle. Our basis represents the scientific literature regarding the startup lifecycle to propose the stage which an enterprise is a Startup. Figure 3 explains the concept model as well as the discussion below.

As described in Sect. 2.1, we suggest the enterprise revenue as the primary driver to explain the startup phases, since we suggest that is direct linked with its products and services.

When the enterprise initiates its operations, we presume the group of people do not develop any concrete innovative product. They start with an idea and must materialize into a product completely developed. Financial results are negatives due to costs of management and the initial stages of product development (BOL). The initial place of the enterprise in its lifecycle is designated the Valley of Death [24]. To survive the valley of death, the enterprises rely on financing from Friends, Family and Fools (FFF) [25], Angel Investors [26] and Seed-capital [27]. Many enterprises do not survive the Valley of Death [5]. We consider the point of surviving the Valley as the Mark nº 1 (M1).

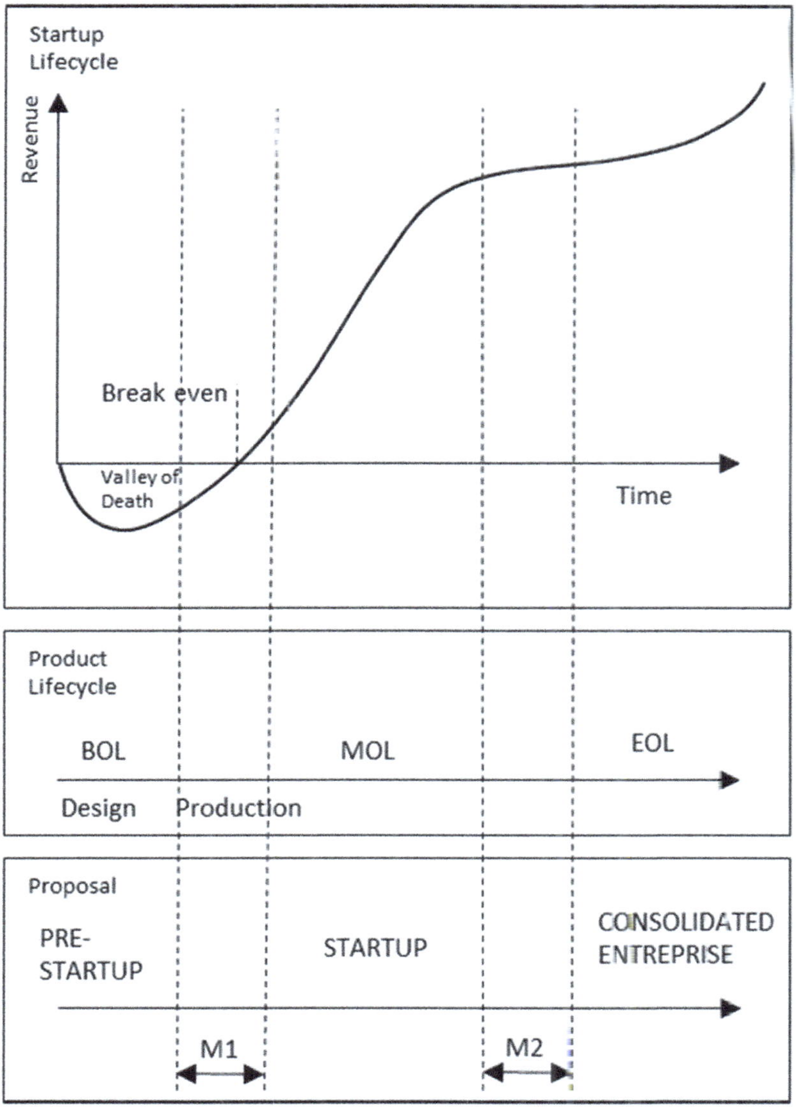

Fig. 3. Conceptual model proposition.

[3] suggests that through trial and error, hiring and firing, successful enterprises (startups) all invent a parallel process to product development. In particular, the winners invent and live by a process of customer learning and discovery. At this point the enterprise has likely generated a substantial knowledge base about the product BOL stage. Simultaneously, it has also developed management knowledge to start dealing with internal and external uncertainties, and probably the most significant achievement, it has reached the break-even point.

We suggest that enterprises situated in the stage before M1 might be called as PRE-Startups. Their key features are that they have not achieved enough revenue to swell, however they achieved a considerable knowledge base to learn with management and product commercialization. As the process is not linear nor precise, we determined a confidence level which the M1 might be located.

The enterprises that have survived to the Valley of Death and overpassed the M1, apparently will experience a rapid growth. The revenue growth is sustained in product BOL and MOL stages. The enterprise, in addition, receives resources from Venture Capital (VC) [28], Mergers and Acquisitions (M&A) [29], strategic alliances, etc. After rounds of investments, the firm achieve a plateau of revenue and rely on product updates and improved innovations.

When the product achieves its maturity on sales, its decline could be extended, or the enterprise launches an innovative product. Nevertheless, at this point the firm probably had already collected a substantial knowledge base regarding product MOL stage. With a consolidated product, uncertainties levels are low, allows the enterprise to know better about consumers, suppliers and competitors. When the enterprise achieves this stage, probably its revenue is with a low growth rate. We consider this point as Mark n° 2 (M2).

We suggest that from M1 to M2 the stage might be called as Startup. After M2, the enterprise achieves a maturity level, and it exits via Initial Public Offering (IPO), M&A. As mentioned earlier in M1, we suggest a confidence level which the M2 might be. Table 2 summarizes the proposition.

Table 2. Classification criteria of PLM and startup lifecycle.

Proposal	PLM stages	Investment sources	Revenue growth behaviour
Pre-startup	BOL	FFF, Angel Investors, Seed-capital	Negative until the break-even
Startup	BOL/MOL	VC, M&A, strategic alliances	Rapid growth
Consolidated enterprise	MOL	IPO, M&A	Low growth

4 Conclusion and Outlook

The present study is a preliminary proposition that aims to increase the entrepreneurship culture. The purpose of this paper was to propose an alternative conceptual definition of Startup stage in innovative enterprises (startups) using primarily BOL and MOL of PLM concepts. This paper does not intend decreasing entrepreneurial initiatives. On the contrary, we propose the study to incentive more entrepreneurs to launch their enterprises and obtain successful outcomes.

As new enterprises develop their products and gain management skills simultaneously, and both influence each other in a learning experience; it seems reasonable that an enterprise might be defined as Startup if it overpasses the M1; notably because it had survived to the Valley of Death, and is located before M2. Put differently, their product should be in MOL stage, and the enterprise must be experiencing growth in their revenue. The categorization of these enterprises in Pre-Startups and Startup are necessary because many Pre-Startups fail in the Valley of Death.

This proposal attends an initial discussion regarding this theme. Further studies are necessary especially the use of PLM as an alternative to allow entrepreneurs to develop better products that allow then to overpass the Valley of Death. A typical feature of innovative enterprises and SMEs represent the lack of resources; as in [30], Open Innovation strategies with PLM would be a compelling initiative to provide scientific evidence and body of knowledge to increase the successful rate of entrepreneurs. The introduction of the solution developed in the knowledge intensive collaborative environment proves to be very effective and efficient, leading to good results in terms of savings [31]. In parallel, to deal with management knowledge, enterprises have available several sources of knowledge like mentoring, accelerator programs, etc.

In addition, more criteria are necessary to enrich the discussion of defining when an enterprise is a Startup. It is explicit that not all SME is a Startup. It might be understandable in further studies to define when large companies once tagged as Startup should not have this label anymore.

Acknowledgements. The researchers would like to thank the Pontifical Catholic University of Paraná (PUCPR) - Polytechnic School – Industrial and Systems Engineering Graduate Program (PPGEPS) and National Council for Scientific and Technological Development (CNPq) for the funding and structure of this research.

References

1. Decker, R., Haltiwanger, J., Jarmin, R., Miranda, J.: The role of entrepreneurship in us job creation and economic dynamism. J. Econ. Perspect. **28**(3), 3–24 (2014)
2. Ries, E.: The Lean Startup: How Today's Entrepreneurs Use Continuous Innovation to Create Radically Successful Businesses. Crown (2011)
3. Blank, S.G.: The Four Steps to the Epiphany (2007)
4. Wang, X., Edison, H., Bajwa, S.S., Giardino, C., Abrahamsson, P.: Key challenges in software startups across life cycle stages. In: Sharp, H., Hall, T. (eds.) XP 2016. LNBIP, vol. 251, pp. 169–182. Springer, Cham (2016). https://doi.org/10.1007/978-3-319-33515-5_14

5. Krishna, A., Agrawal, A., Choudhary, A.: Predicting the outcome of startups: less failure, more success. In: IEEE International Conference on Data Mining Workshops ICDMW, pp. 798–805 (2016)
6. Audretsch, D.B.: From the entrepreneurial university to the university for the entrepreneurial society. J. Technol. Transf. **39**(3), 313–321 (2012). https://doi.org/10.1007/s10961-012-9288-1
7. Salamzadeh, A., Kawamorita Kesim, H.: The enterprising communities and startup ecosystem in Iran. J. Enterprising Commun. People Places Glob. Econ. **11**(4), 456–479 (2017)
8. Kopera, S., Wszendybył-Skulska, E., Cebulak, J., Grabowski, S.: Interdisciplinarity in tech startups development-case study of 'Unistartapp' project. Found. Manage. **10**(1), 23–32 (2018)
9. Paternoster, N., Giardino, C., Unterkalmsteiner, M., Gorschek, T., Abrahamsson, P.: Software development in startup companies: a systematic mapping study. Inf. Softw. Technol. **56**(10), 1200–1218 (2014)
10. Salamzadeh, A., Kawamorita Kesim, H.: Startup companies: life cycle and challenges. SSRN Electron. J. (2015)
11. Churchill, N., Lewis, V.: The five stages of small business growth. Harv. Bus. Rev. **61**(3), 30–50 (1983)
12. Scott, M., Bruce, R.: Five stages of growth in small business. Long Range Plann. **20**(3), 45–52 (1987)
13. Global Startup Ecosystem Report. Startup Genome LLC, San Francisco (2019)
14. Picken, J.C.: From startup to scalable enterprise: laying the foundation. Bus. Horiz. **60**(5), 587–595 (2017)
15. Mańkowska, N.: Startups in Poland on the internet of things market: development and life cycle. In: Proceedings of European Conference on Innovation and Entrepreneurship ECIE. 2 (Bartczak), pp. 621–628 (2019)
16. Paschen, J.: Choose wisely: crowdfunding through the stages of the startup life cycle. Bus. Horiz. **60**(2), 179–188 (2017)
17. Overall, J., Wise, S.: An S-curve model of the start-up life cycle through the lens of customer development. J. Priv. Equity. **18**(2), 23–34 (2015)
18. Understanding the enterprise startup lifecycle. https://www.zdnet.com/article/understanding-the-enterprise-startup-lifecycle/
19. Stark, J.: Product Lifecycle Management. Springer, Cham (2015). https://doi.org/10.1007/978-3-319-17440-2
20. Ameri, F., Dutta, D.: Product lifecycle management: closing the knowledge loops. Comput. Aided Des. Appl. **2**(5), 577–590 (2005)
21. Bruno, G., Antonelli, D., Villa, A.: A reference ontology to support product lifecycle management. Procedia CIRP **33**, 41–46 (2015)
22. Sudarsan, R., Fenves, S.J., Sriram, R.D., Wang, F.: A product information modeling framework for product lifecycle management. Comput. Des. **37**(13), 1399–1411 (2005)
23. Jun, H.B., Kiritsis, D., Xirouchakis, P.: Research issues on closed-loop PLM. Comput. Ind. **58**(8–9), 855–868 (2007)
24. Reagle, C., et al.: From idea to prototype: introducing students to entrepreneurship. In: ISEC 2017 - Proceedings of the 7th IEEE Integrated STEM Education Conference, pp. 71–75. IEEE (2017)
25. Kotha, R., George, G.: Friends, family, or fools: entrepreneur experience and its implications for equity distribution and resource mobilization. J. Bus. Ventur. **27**(5), 525–543 (2012)

26. Mitteness, C., Sudek, R., Cardon, M.S.: Angel investor characteristics that determine whether perceived passion leads to higher evaluations of funding potential. J. Bus. Ventur. **27**(5), 592–606 (2012)
27. Alves, S., Pimenta-bueno, J.A.: Quantifying the capital requirements of start-ups in early growth phase: exploratory evidence from a seed capital fund in Brazil. J. Private Equity **21** (3), 26–37 (2018)
28. Florida, R., Mellander, C.: Rise of the startup city. Calif. Manage. Rev. **59**(1), 14–38 (2016)
29. Pisoni, A., Onetti, A.: When startups exit: comparing strategies in Europe and the USA. J. Bus. Strategy **39**(3), 26–33 (2018)
30. Reisdorfer-Leite, B., Marcos de Oliveira, M., Canciglieri Junior, O.: A discussion about science, technology, engineering and mathematics education in the university R&D and its impact on the innovation and environment ecosystem. In: 8th IWACP international Workshop Advances in Cleaner Production, Sanya, pp. 75–76 (2019)
31. Ferreira, F., Faria, J., Azevedo, A., Marques, A.L.: Product lifecycle management in knowledge intensive collaborative environments: an application to automotive industry. Int. J. Inf. Manage. **37**(1), 1474–1487 (2017)

Circular Economy

Exploring How Design Can Contribute to Circular Economy Through Design for X Approaches

Claudio Sassanelli(✉), Paolo Rosa, and Sergio Terzi

Department of Management, Economics and Industrial Engineering, Politecnico di Milano, Piazza Leonardo da Vinci, 32, 20132 Milan, Italy
{claudio.sassanelli,paolo1.rosa, sergio.terzi}@polimi.it

Abstract. Design plays a strategic role for companies in addressing servitization and Circular Economy (CE) paradigms, to deliver either products, or services or Product-Service Systems (PSSs). Design for X (DfX) practices, belonging to concurrent engineering approach, have revealed great effectiveness in enriching products with functionalities as service supportability and circularity. They have been also used to systematize PSSs components along the design process, enabling and easing design knowledge creation and sharing between product and service designers. Nevertheless, notwithstanding the abundance of DfX approaches related with the End of Life (EoL) stage, they still lack of a CE perspective. Therefore, this paper wants to explore how design can contribute to CE through the use of DfX approaches.

Keywords: Circular design · Design for X · Circular economy · End-of-life · Design guidelines · Knowledge management

1 Introduction

Two upcoming factors are affecting product manufacturers. Firstly, Circular Economy (CE) [1], highlights the always more worrying natural resources scarcity. Secondly, servitization [2], leads towards a more sustainable economy [3], through the advent of the sharing economy and the delivery of product-related services [4]. Going ahead with this transition, companies have also to enact a business model shift [5, 6], leading hurdles [7] and potential benefits [8]. However, the integration of product-services under a circular perspective still need suitable methods and tools. Specifically, Design for X (DfX) guidelines [9], belonging to the concurrent engineering context, can enable the design of products/service/systems to address requirements (e.g. features, performance, constraints, etc.) pursuing specific DfX abilities. DfX approaches are very successful in improving competitiveness measures and rationalizing design decisions in product development [9]. They have been also used to systematize PSSs components along the design process, enabling and easing design knowledge creation and sharing between product and service designers [10, 11]. Furthermore, several DfX methods and tools already focus on the End of life phase, but lack of a CE focus [12]. The aim of this

Published by Springer Nature Switzerland AG 2020
F. Nyffenegger et al. (Eds.): PLM 2020, IFIP AICT 594, pp. 439–447, 2020.
https://doi.org/10.1007/978-3-030-62807-9_35

work is understanding the role of design along the CE transition through the use of DfX approaches. The paper is organized as follows. Section 2 describes the adopted research methodology. Section 3 presents results coming from the literature review and Sect. 4 discusses them. Section 5 provides conclusions and future research trends.

2 Research Methodology

A literature review [13, 14] on scientific articles published up to the third quarter of 2019 and gathered from Science Direct® and Scopus® has been carried out. The keywords "Circular Economy" and "end of life" have been combined with either "Design for X", "DfX" or "design guideline" and searched without any time/document restriction. Searches led to 741 results. Furthermore, 25 documents were found through cross-referencing and 4 by hand search. 15 additional documents have been recommended by experts and serendipity. After having excluded: i) grey literature, ii) non-English contributions, iii) redundancies, iv) unfitting papers (by title/abstract check) and v) unfitting papers (by full-text check), a total of 31 articles have been selected. An assessment of results unveils that about 60% of these papers have been published from 2015 onwards. European experts contributed more in this context (71%), followed by North Americans (16,1%) and Southeast Asian/Chinese ones (12,9%). Most of the selected contributions provided a theoretical perspective of the context. Indeed, more than half of the documents (19 of 31) provided just a theoretical interpretation of the link between DfX approaches and the circularity paradigm. Instead, 12 of them proposed case studies and application cases to strengthen their researches from an empirical point of view. Here, the most cited products/industries where circular DfX have been applied are Electrical and Electronic Equipment and automotive sectors.

3 Results: DfX Approaches Supporting CE Adoption

The literature review led to the understanding of relationships among DfX abilities and CE. Contributions have been grouped according to 3 different drivers (Table 1):

- DfX purposes supporting CE, grouped in 5 categories (circular design improvement, circular design metrics and evaluation, circular design decision support, design driving circular transition, circular design knowledge management), to understand how design contributes to the circular transition through the adoption of DfX approaches;
- Ability/ies addressed (Supply Chain (SC), Resource/energy efficiency, Reliability, Multiple Lifecycle, Sustainability), detailed in Table 1,
- Triple Bottom Line (TBL) perspective (economic, environmental, social).

Table 1. Categorization by DfX purposes, DfX Abilities, TBL perspective

DfX purposes	Authors	Main Abilities														TBL		
		SC	Res/En Eff	Rel		Multiple Life Cycle (MLC)						Sustainability			Other	Eco	Env	Soc
		C/S SC; SysC	REf&C	SLC; LLUoP; Ma; PLExt	Rel & Sa	MLC; FPD; TecC; BioC; CLPSS; EofC/S/A	D&Rea	Rem; Rema; Reco	Recy	EoL	Ad; St; Com; Mo; Upg	Su	E	SR				
Circular design improvement	Bakker et al. (2014)		x	x				x	x	x						x	x	
	Ceschin and Gaziulusoy (2016)											x				x	x	x
	Go et al. (2015)					x											x	
	Moreno et al. (2016)	x	x	x		x											x	
	Pigosso and McAloone (2017)					x									x	x	x	
	van der Laan and Aurisicchio (2019)					x										x	x	
	Vanegas et al. (2018)						x									x	x	
	Favi *et al.* (2019)						x		x							x	x	
	Wahab et al. (2018)				x			x								x	x	
	Sundin (2004)							x					x				x	
	Hultgren (2012)						x		x			x	x				x	
	Allwood et al. (2011)							x									x	
	Rose (2000)												x				x	
	Peeters *et al.* (2012)						x										x	
	Arnette, Brewer and Choal, (2014)	x										x	x	x		x	x	x
Circular design metrics and evaluation	Bovea and Pérez-Belis (2004)						x	x	x	x			x				x	
	Mendoza et al. (2017)			x		x	x				x						x	
	Rocha et al. (2019)											x				x	x	x
	Rossi et al. (2016)		x				x	x									x	
	Van den Berg and Bakker (2015)			x		x	x	x									x	
	Shu and Flowers (1999)							x								x		
	Desai and Mital (2003)						x									x		
	Mayyas et al. (2012)											x				x	x	x
Circular Design Decision-Support	Gould et al. (2017)	x						x				x		x	x	x	x	x
	Kuo et al.(2019)				x		x				x				x	x	x	
	Pozo Arcos et al. (2018)						x			x								
Design Driving Circular Transition	De Los Rios and Charnley (2016)					x							x		x		x	
	Bhamra (2004)											x				x	x	
	Rahito, Wahab and Azman (2019)							x							x		x	
Circular Design KM	Favi et al. (2016)						x	x	x								x	
	Toxopeus et al. (2018)		x	x		x	x		x								x	

- SC= Supply Chain; C/S SC=Circular/Sustainable SC; SysC=System Change;
- Res/En Eff= Resource/Energy Efficiency;
- Ref&C= Resource Efficiency and Conservation;
- Rel= Reliability; SLC= Slowing Life Cycle; LLUoP=Long Life Use of Products; Ma=Maintenance; PLExt=Product Life Extension; Rel &Sa= Reliability and Safety;
- MLC= Multiple Life Cycle; FPD= Future Proof Design; TecC= Technical Cycle; BioC= Biological Cycle; CLPSS= Closed-loop PSS; EofC/S/A= Ease of Cleaning/Storage/Access; D&Rea= Disassembly and Reassembly; Rem= Remanufacturing; Rema= Remake; Reco= Recovery; Recy= Recycling; EoL= End of Life; Ad= Adaptability; St= Standardization ; Com= Compatibility; Mo= Modularity; Upg= Upgradability;
- Su= Sustainability; E= Environment; SR=Social Responsibility; TBL=Triple Bottom Line; Eco=Economic; Env= Environmental; Soc= Social.

Circular Design Improvement

[12] evaluated how product life extension and product recycling can be addressed by product design. To decide when to apply a specific strategy (prevention, reuse and recycling), they presented a methodology defining the optimal product lifespan and applied it to two case studies on a domestic refrigerator and a laptop. [16] explored how Design for Sustainability (DfSu) approach grew, gathering design approaches in four innovation levels: Product, Product-Service System (PSS), Space-Social and Socio-Technical System. To this aim, they assessed DfX guidelines and toolkits suitable with sustainable attitudes. [17] presented a framework for CE design strategies, assessing the literature on DfSu and circular business models and finding five main circular design strategies plus ten circular design recommendations. [18] defined Design for Multiple Lifecycle (DfMLC) as a mix of eco-design strategies. They provided the main guidelines of all the DfX approaches considered, promoting their concurrent adoption for the circular design application. [19] detected three main design topics in the CE context. Among them, PSS seems to be a strategic for CE adoption, especially if coupled by design guidelines and sustainability evaluation methods. [20] formulated 10 guidelines for the design of closed-loop PSSs. [21] proposed a method, "eDiM" (ease of Disassembly Metric) to measure ease of disassembly and recoverability and compare design alternatives. An LCD monitor case study was conducted. [15] created a Design for Disassembly method and tool to support the implementation of re-design improving product de-manufacturability and EoL performances. The LeanDfD package can assess design decisions, store and classify disassembly data (standard times and corrective factors of each disassembly liaison and operation) to create valuable knowledge. [22] detected Design for Remanufacturing as the enabler for life cycle reliability and safety. A relevant issue related to this work is to predefine the useful life of products already in

the development phase to further assess the reliability and safety of the product along their MLCs. [23] proposed the RemPro-matrix, studied Design for Environment and Design for Remanufacturing, identifying the most important related product properties and their relationship with the remanufacturing process phases. Several application cases with remanufacturers were conducted. [24] formulated, through application cases in consumer electronics industry, 4 guidelines and 14 design strategies on recyclability to help engineers in designing products that are easier to recycle. [25] proposed four strategies for managing material demand through material efficiency, trying to provide directions for this research context through a list of 20 open questions: the main one was to verify the possibility for companies/industries/countries to raise competitiveness and prosperity through improving material efficiency. [26] proposed a design tool, End-of-life Design Advisor, leveraging on designers' and product managers' recycling experiences to take EoL strategy decisions. By conducting 37 case studies, she detected six final technical product characteristics (wear-out life, technology cycle, level of integration, number of parts, design cycle, reason for redesign). [27] grouped design guidelines for the demanufacturing strategies and categorized three types of products to be considered in the remanufacturing process: PSS-based products; electronic products; products to be not repaired, remanufactured or refurbished. [28] highlighted that PSS's product components lead manufacturers or retailers to implement demanufacturing improvements and grouped DfX approaches in four categories under the DfSu umbrella.

Circular Design Metrics and Evaluation

[29] organized, from a CE lens in five circular design groups, 46 design guidelines derived from them the eco-design framework and DfX approaches, also proposing new guidelines. A methodology was proposed to check if a product design meets the design guidelines required from a CE perspective. The methodology was applied on twelve case studies, defining two main criteria to define circularity degree (margin of improvement and relevance). [30] categorized product design and business model strategies in two main actions, slowing and closing resource loops. They also identified several gaps related to the adoption of DfX approaches related to design sustainable and circular products. [31] proposed an analytical framework for DfSu models. They found that several are the attempts to support companies in implementing DfSu, either for products or service or PSS development. However, the link between this approach and CE has still to be adequately studied, as suggested by the majority of the political agendas to foster environmental sustainability without compromising economic growth. [32] conducted a review of eco-design methods and tools to allow CE industrial application. DfX approaches, usually used by the design team to manage product-specific solutions, are suggested to be strongly considered in the field of eco-design. [33] proposed a CE framework from a product design perspective performing a review of the extant CE terminology. They defined five most design-relevant topics and detected two main streams (futureproof and disassembly). A B2B indoor LED lighting was used as a case study in the tools development. [34] explored remanufacturing and its conflicts with other DfX approaches, detecting six processes to ease this process and proposed a framework to quantify costs. The framework has been tested on photocopiers and toner cartridges. [35] proposed a methodology performing calculations that

allow the detection of disassembly anomalies, design modifications and finally also disassemblability improvement. They tested the effectiveness of the methodology to verify the disassemblability of an electric drill. [36] made a review of the literature on vehicles' life cycle, disposal and end of life analyses, declining DfSu into 4 main groups.

Circular Design Decision-Support
[37] proposed a decision-support prototype to select design strategies, defining them through a literature review in six main groups. [38] developed a decision-making model to assess and implement sustainable PSSs, tracking both product design and life-cycle cost analysis. A heat-pump water heater case study was conducted to generate product selling and leasing model design suggestions and facilitate sustainable servitization through development considerations. [39] proposed a categorization of functional recovery guidelines for product design based on the need to plan for recovery at early design stages. Guidelines have been grouped in 4 main classes: ease of cleaning, ease of diagnosis, disassembly and reassembly, ease of storage.

Design Driving Circular Transition
[40] classified the DfX/methods considered successful for sustainable and CE practices under three typical design strategies umbrella terms: Design for life-cycle, Design for the environment, Whole-system design. [41] identified several factors impelling companies, internally and externally, to pursue eco-design. [42] focused on the potential of Direct Energy Deposition technology for repair and restoration of remanufacturable components. They suggested the development of design guidelines for restoration of remanufacturable products using Additive Manufacturing.

Circular Design Knowledge Management
[43] evaluated the link between product design and EoL phase. They propose a method to gather knowledge and expertise from dismantler and remanufacturing centers with a focus on the disassembly processes to be used during the product design phase [44] proposed a design support tool to cater designers and engineers with design guidelines for development decisions. They linked product characteristics and reverse cycle processes through a disassembly level to support the resource circulation strategy.

4 Discussions

From the analysis of the article selected in this review, DfX main purpose to address circularity is the enhancement of the design of solutions. In addition, the most adopted DfX abilities to sustain CE belong to the MLC domain, impelling the concept of lifecycle from a single cycle to multiple circular ones. It has also to be highlighted that most of the contributions gave evidence to several gaps hindering the corroboration of this twofold DfX-CE research context. Indeed, first of all they claimed that the extant DfX tools and methods should be revitalized since companies have difficulties in practically use eco-design tools and methods. New tools are requested to:

- better support designers and engineers to take decisions and actually implement the circular product/service BM, and a combined quantitative assessment to measure how the circular design is applied to different products and BMs;
- support the reduction of product environmental impact through MLC design;
- provide detailed design guidelines and strategies for engineers to address recycling and close the materials loop in a easy to apply and evaluate way;
- provide strategic directions linked to environmental performance;
- integrate and rank the several DfX strategies;
- define a preference among the abilities/guidelines considered and find the best trade-off between product requirements;
- revolutionize the way in which products and services are developed;
- strengthen the connections between the product design and EoL phase.

From a strategic and BM perspective, the main issues were:

- to understand how to integrate obsolescence,
- to develop design strategies to foster take-back services and reverse logistics;
- to understand the value of resources used in PSSs (that change over time);
- to define which type of products need a specific EoL ability;
- to align the product development with supply chain and BM to exploit CE.

Instead, under a technological lens, there is a lack of a robust information system, leveraging on a single input data sheet, to make product design information, provided by OEMs, available along the supply chain to pursue a certain circular BM, to optimize the EoL process and simultaneously gauge multiple eco-design performances. Also the knowledge management domain needs strongly improvements. Among all, it has to be highlighted the urgent need to integrate the circular design guidelines aiming at extending life span with those related with component reuse. In particular, extant DfX guidelines and techniques do not foster the use of product design information along business planning and decision-making processes at systems-level. All these issues, calling for a more effective transition from linear to circular design through the adoption of DfX approaches, could be better analysed and grouped with the aim to be addressed in a more effective way. Wrapping up, the main gap seems to be the necessity of new DfX methods and tools. Their provision would solve different issues along the design process: to aid design decision-making process (also through quantitative KPIs), to balance out the heterogeneous DfX abilities (also revealing their proper shortcomings and limits), to re-enact the design process itself and focus its attention on specific perspective, service supportability and circularity. This would help also under several perspectives (knowledge management, competences, Technology, strategic). Indeed, new methods could be useful to create new knowledge (structured in design guidelines), to coalesce the different DfX abilities needed and to fully take advantage of the technology used (information systems and unique input data sheet).

5 Conclusions and Further Researches

This research operated a literature review to evaluate how DfX practices can contribute to the design of circular solutions. This research context is still very limited, since only 31 contributions were selected, and the majority of the contributions are either theoretical assessment or literature reviews (providing frameworks, models, classification or design guidelines pertaining the DfX abilities involved). The author of this research detected five main purposes of using DfX in the CE research context: *Circular Design Improvement, Circular Design Metrics and Evaluation, Circular Design Decision-Support, Design Driving Circular Transition, Circular Design KM.* Among them, the first two are the most recurrent, confirming the traditional roles of DfX approaches. This research confirms that circular design can be addressed only addressing several abilities in a hybrid way. A high number of DfX approaches was detected, leading to their gathering in five macro areas (representing the main functionalities to be considered in a product/service/PSS if circularity has to be addressed): *Supply Chain, Resource/Energy Efficiency, Reliability, MLC, Sustainability.* Among them, the last three are those more considered by researchers to prolong or slow the linear product lifecycle. While, the first two need more investigations. Moreover, DfX abilities and their purposes have been assessed under the TBL perspective: confirming what presented in recent literature reviews on CE, the social aspect still needs to be further explored. Finally, several gaps have been revealed in these research contexts, revealing that there is room for future investigations. Among them, new hybrid DfX methods and tools can address several problems concerning the design process, either in the design decision-making process or in balancing the several DfX abilities required. An interesting case is revealed by the PSS research context, recognized as one of the most important BM to apply CE but where DfX approaches are rarely used by experts. The five macro areas of abilities can be the basis to select the DfX approaches that could foster a circular PSS design process.

Acknowledgements. This work has received funding from the European Union's Horizon 2020 research and innovation programme under grant agreement No 760792.

References

1. The Ellen MacArthur Foundation: Towards a Circular Economy: Business Rationale for an Accelerated Transition (2015)
2. Kowalkowski, C., Gebauer, H., Oliva, R.: Service growth in product firms: past, present, and future. Ind. Mark. Manag. **60**, 82–88 (2017)
3. Bocken, N.M.P., de Pauw, I., Bakker, C.A., van der Grinten, B.: Product design and business model strategies for a circular economy. J. Ind. Prod. Eng. **33**(5), 308–320 (2016)
4. Goedkoop, M.J., Van Halen, C.J.G., te Riele, H.R.M., Rommens, P.J.M.: Product service systems, ecological and economic basics. Report for Dutch Ministries of environment (VROM) and economic affairs (EZ), vol. 36, no. 1, pp. 1–122 (1999)
5. Rosa, P., Sassanelli, C., Terzi, S.: Towards Circular Business Models: a systematic literature review on classification frameworks and archetypes. J. Clean. Prod. **236** (2019)

6. Sanasi, S., Ghezzi, A., Cavallo, A., Rangone, A.: Making sense of the sharing economy: a business model innovation perspective. Technol. Anal. Strateg. Manage. 1–15 (2020)
7. Brax, S.: A manufacturer becoming service provider – challenges and a paradox. Manag. Serv. Qual. An Int. J. **15**(2), 142–155 (2005)
8. Rosa, P., Sassanelli, C., Terzi, S.: Circular business models versus circular benefits: an assessment in the waste from electrical and electronic equipments sector. J. Clean. Prod. **231**, 940–952 (2019)
9. Huang, G.Q.: Design for X - Concurrent Engineering Imperatives. Springer, Dordrecht (1996). https://doi.org/10.1007/978-94-011-3985-4
10. Sassanelli, C., Pezzotta, G., Pirola, F., Rossi, M., Terzi, S.: The PSS design GuRu Methodology: guidelines and Rules generation to enhance product service systems (PSS) detailed design. J. Des. Res. **17**(2/3/4), 125–162 (2019)
11. Sassanelli, C., et al.: Using design rules to guide the PSS design in an Engineering Platform based on the Product Service Lifecycle Management (PSLM) paradigms. Int. J. Prod. Lifecycle Manag. **11**(2), 91–115 (2018)
12. Bakker, C.A., Wang, F., Huisman, J., Den Hollander, M.: Products that go round: exploring product life extension through design. J. Clean. Prod. **69**, 10–16 (2014)
13. Smart, P., Hemel, S., Lettice, F., Adams, R., Evans, S.: Pre-paradigmatic status of industrial sustainability: a systematic review. Int. J. Oper. Prod. Manag. **37**(10), 1425–1450 (2017)
14. Sassanelli, C., Rossi, M., Pezzotta, G., Pacheco, D.A.D.J., Terzi, S.: Defining Lean Product Service Systems (PSS) features and research trends through a systematic literature review. Int. J. Prod. Lifecycle Manage. **12**(1), 37–61 (2019)
15. Favi, C., Marconi, M., Germani, M., Mandolini, M.: A design for disassembly tool oriented to mechatronic product de-manufacturing and recycling. Adv. Eng. Inform. **39**, 62–79 (2019)
16. Ceschin, F., Gaziulusoy, I.: Evolution of design for sustainability: from product design to design for system innovations and transitions. Des. Stud. **47**, 118–163 (2016)
17. Moreno, M., De los Rios, C.I., Rowe, Z., Charnley, F.: A conceptual framework for circular design. Sustainability **8**(9), 937 (2016)
18. Go, T.F., Wahab, D.A., Hishamuddin, H.: Multiple generation life-cycles for product sustainability: the way forward. J. Clean. Prod. **95**, 16–29 (2015)
19. Pigosso, D.C.A., McAloone, T.C.: How can design science contribute to a circular economy?. In: International Conference on Engineering Design, ICED, vol. 5, no. DS87-5, pp. 299–307 (2017)
20. van der Laan, A.Z., Aurisicchio, M.: Designing product-service systems to close resource loops: circular design guidelines. Procedia CIRP **80**, 631–636 (2019)
21. Vanegas, P., et al.: Ease of disassembly of products to support circular economy strategies. Resour. Conserv. Recycl. **135**, 323–334 (2018)
22. Wahab, D.A., Blanco-Davis, E., Ariffin, A.K., Wang, J.: A review on the applicability of remanufacturing in extending the life cycle of marine or offshore components and structures. Ocean Eng. **169**, 125–133 (2018)
23. Sundin, E.: Product and process design for successful remanufacturing. Linköpings Universitet (2004)
24. Hultgren, N.: Guidelines and design strategies for improved product recyclability: how to increase the recyclability of consumer electronics and domestic appliances through product design. Chalmers University of Technology (2012)
25. Allwood, J.M., Ashby, M.F., Gutowski, T.G., Worrell, E.: Material efficiency: a white paper. Resour. Conserv. Recycl. **55**(3), 362–381 (2011)
26. Rose, C.M.: Design for environment: a method for formulating product end-of-life strategies. Stanford University (2000)

27. Peeters, J.R., Vanegas, P., Dewulf, W., Duflou, J.R.: Design for manufacturing: a life cycle approach. In: i-SUP2012, pp. 9–13 (2012)
28. Arnette, A.N., Brewer, B.L., Choal, T.: Design for sustainability (DFS): the intersection of supply chain and environment. J. Clean. Prod. **83**, 374–390 (2014)
29. Bovea, M.D., Pérez-Belis, V.: Identifying design guidelines to meet the circular economy principles: a case study on electric and electronic equipment. J. Environ. Manage. **228**, 483–494 (2004)
30. Mendoza, J.M.F., Sharmina, M., Gallego-Schmid, A., Heyes, G., Azapagic, A.: Integrating backcasting and eco-design for the circular economy: the BECE framework. J. Ind. Ecol. **21** (3), 526–544 (2017)
31. Rocha, C.S., Antunes, P., Partidário, P.: Design for sustainability models: a multiperspective review. J. Clean. Prod. **234**, 1428–1445 (2019)
32. Rossi, M., Germani, M., Zamagni, A.: Review of ecodesign methods and tools. Barriers and strategies for an effective implementation in industrial companies. J. Clean. Prod. **129**, 361–373 (2016)
33. Van den Berg, M.R., Bakker, C.A.: A product design framework for a circular economy. In: PLATE (Product Lifetimes and the Environment) Conference Proceedings, June, pp. 365–379 (2015)
34. Shu, L.H., Flowers, W.C.: Application of a design-for-remanufacture framework to the selection of product life-cycle fastening and joining methods. Robot. Comput. Integr. Manuf. **15**(3), 179–190 (1999)
35. Desai, A., Mital, A.: Evaluation of disassemblability to enable design for disassembly in mass production. Int. J. Ind. Ergon. **32**(4), 265–281 (2003)
36. Mayyas, A., Qattawi, A., Omar, M.A., Shan, D.: Design for sustainability in automotive industry: a comprehensive review. Renew. Sustain. Energy Rev. **16**(4), 1845–1862 (2012)
37. Gould, R., Lagun Mesquita, P., Bratt, C., Broman, G.: Why choose one sustainable design strategy over another: a decision-support prototype. In: Proceedings of International Conference on Engineering Design, ICED, vol. 5, no. DS87-5, pp. 111–120 (2017)
38. Kuo, T.-C., Chiu, M.-C., Hsu, C.-W., Tseng, M.-L.: Supporting sustainable product service systems: a product selling and leasing design model. Resour. Conserv. Recycl. **146**, 384–394 (2019)
39. Pozo Arcos, B., Balkenende, A.R., Bakker, C.A., Sundin, E.: Product design for a circular economy: functional recovery on focus. In: International Design Conference - Design 2018, pp. 2727–2738 (2018)
40. De los Rios, I.C., Charnley, F.J.S.: Skills and capabilities for a sustainable and circular economy: the changing role of design. J. Clean. Prod. **160**, 109–122 (2017)
41. Bhamra, T.A.: Ecodesign: the search for new strategies in product development. Proc. Inst. Mech. Eng. Part B J. Eng. Manuf. **218**(5), 557–569 (2004)
42. Rahito, S.W., Wahab, D.A., Azman, A.H.: Restoration of remanufacturable components using additive manufacturing. In: 5th International Conference on Sustainable Design and Manufacturing, SDM 2018, vol. 130, pp. 193–198 (2019)
43. Favi, C., Germani, M., Mandolini, M., Marconi, M.: Disassembly knowledge classification and potential application: a preliminary analysis on a washing machine. Procedia CIRP **48**, 401–406 (2016)
44. Toxopeus, M.E., van den Hout, N.B., van Diepen, B.G.D.: Supporting product development with a practical tool for applying the strategy of resource circulation. Procedia CIRP **69**, 680–685 (2018)

An Innovative Methodology to Optimize Aerospace Eco-efficiency Assembly Processes

Manuel Oliva[1(✉)], Fernando Mas[2,3], Ignacio Eguia[3], Carmelo del Valle[3], Emanuel J. Lourenço[4], and Antonio J. Baptista[4]

[1] Airbus, Avenida del Aeropuerto s/n, 41020 Seville, Spain
manuel.oliva@airbus.com
[2] M&M Group, 11500 Cadiz, Spain
[3] University of Sevilla, 41092 Seville, Spain
{fmas,ieguia,carmelo}@us.es
[4] Institute of Science and Innovation in Mechanical and Industrial Engineering, Porto, Portugal
{e.lourenco,a.baptista}@inegi.pt

Abstract. Sustainability and eco-efficiency have been researched in multiple scientific papers since the last years. However the literature is not so abundant when applying those concepts to industrial assembly processes. This paper presents an innovate methodology to optimize aerospace assembly processes. Authors propose the introduction of a new element, the eco-efficiency, along with the traditional criteria, cost and time, currently used for optimization. Using a large Aero-Structure as an industrial case of study, the methodology analyzes the eco-efficiency of an assembly process in connection with a Life Cycle Assessment (LCA) to compute the environmental impact. Results are shown in a dashboard along with the relevant Key Process Indicator (KPI) to help the engineers to select the best assembly process.

Keywords: Eco-efficiency · Life Cycle Assessment (LCA) · Aerospace · Assembly processes · 3-Layers Model (3LM)

1 Introduction

In 1992 Schmidheiny [1] published an eco-efficiency concept defined as "The delivery of competitively priced goods and services that satisfy human needs and bring quality of life, while progressively reducing ecological impact and resource intensity throughout the life cycle, to a level at least in line with the Earth's estimated carrying capacity." Or defined in a more simplified way by Moreira et al. [2], "creating more with less".

When taking this definition to industry domain, it can be understood as reducing the consumption of resources, raw material, energy, waste and air emissions while keeping or reducing the costs for manufacturing a product. For an assembly process, it is a question of balance of environmental and economic benefits in an integrated way.

Published by Springer Nature Switzerland AG 2020
F. Nyffenegger et al. (Eds.): PLM 2020, IFIP AICT 594, pp. 448–459, 2020.
https://doi.org/10.1007/978-3-030-62807-9_36

There are several methods to measure impacts and evaluate environmental indicators and the authors selected Life Cycle Assessments (LCA), as it has been standardized according to the ISO 14040:2006 [3]. According to Ilgin et al. [4], "Life Cycle Assessment is a method used to evaluate the environmental impact of a product through its life cycle, encompassing extraction and processing of the raw materials, manufacturing, distribution, use, recycling, and final disposal". The author proposes starting by compiling an inventory of relevant inputs and outputs of a production system followed by an assessment of potential environmental impacts associated to those input and outputs and interpreting of the results. Applied to an assembly processes, LCA should respond to questions such as:

- What are the resources used in an assembly process and their consumption?
- What are the main potential effects of an assembly process over the environment?
- Where within the assembly are those potential effects on eco-efficiency?
- What elements in the process are mainly responsible for these potential effects?
- In which stage of the process can we potentially improve the eco-efficiency?

Life Cycle Assessment is commonly used for product system life cycle environmental analysis but requires high expertise that brings complexity for decision-making process. Selection of the best design among a set of alternatives is an important step in the industrial design of a product [5]. And when considering also the production environmental impact, the analysis for decision making needs to consider not only traditional cost and functional performance requirements, but also additional constrains such as eco-efficiency in product manufacturing. This approach was presented in [6] by analyzing the energy efficiency impact in the CNC machine design as an additional constrain versus traditional. Developments for sustainable manufacturing have been reported in [7, 8].

Most industrial companies' practices are currently focused on traditional cost/time/profit models, maximizing benefits, and keeping costs low while maintaining product quality. The work presented in this paper is a proposal to bring the ecoefficiency and traditional cost/time/profit analysis together in a framework for optimizing product industrialization. Some Aerospace companies like Airbus, Comlux and others are researching these innovative methodologies to assemble green products.

2 European Clean Sky 2 and DILECO Project

In the frame of the H2020 Framework Program, European Clean Sky 2 [9], DILECO (DIgitalization of ground-testing Life cycle with ECO design criteria) Project [10] aims to work on development and deployment of Product Lifecycle Management (PLM) tools for aircraft ground functional testing with eco-design criteria in order to improve the sustainability of the Final Assembly Lines (FAL) and the efficiency of the Ground System Tests (GST) process end to end.

DILECO research activities provide a comprehensive methodology and related software tools for the development, optimization and management of industrialization of aerospace assembly processes. The ultimate goal is to jointly improve productivity, cost-efficiency and eco-efficiency together.

During the conceptual design of products and assembly processes, most of the analysis are preliminary with low data definition. The current research will help, at conceptual development phase, to have a qualitative measurement of the eco-efficiency and influence the product industrialization decisions for a better environmental industrial design.

3 Eco-efficiency Framework

As part of the DILECO research activities a framework was developed to connect design-oriented tools, basically PLM tools, and lifecycle assessment cycle tools to help aerospace engineers in their decision-making.

The framework 3-Layers Model (3LM) is a novel model proposed by [11] in the Models for Manufacturing (MfM) methodology, proposed as a new approach to apply MBSE [12] concepts to Manufacturing: Ontology layer is the core of the 3LM. It holds all the company knowledge in terms of processes and scope, data and semantics, and the associated simulations. Data layer collects all the databases and interfaces and Service layer holds the software services.

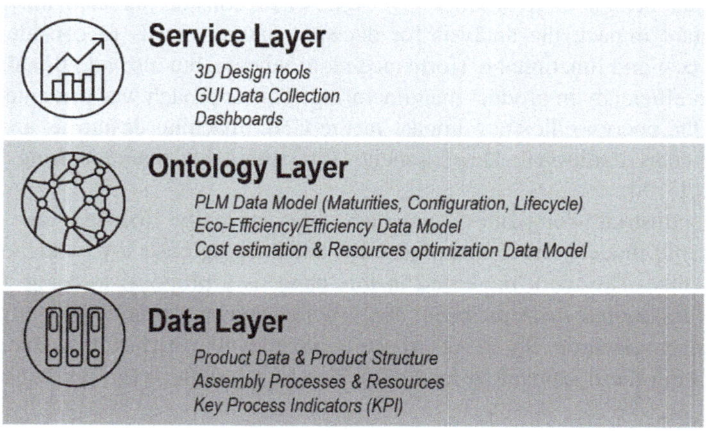

Fig. 1. Three Layer Model (3LM) framework

3LM framework is reused in this research and supports the prototype. It integrates the 3D engineering design environment with eco-efficiency and efficiency assessment. Framework 3LM is shown in the Fig. 1 particularized for the eco-efficiency approach and provides functionalities for:

- Design industrial assembly processes in 3D
- Manage eco-efficiency, efficiency and costs assessment for assembly processes
- Manage processes in a PLM
- Simulate and optimize.

4 Eco-efficiency Conceptual Model

The Conceptual Model supporting the framework is showed in Fig. 2. IDEF0 has been used as process analysis methodology. The following points explore in detail de different objects in the IDEF0 Conceptual Model.

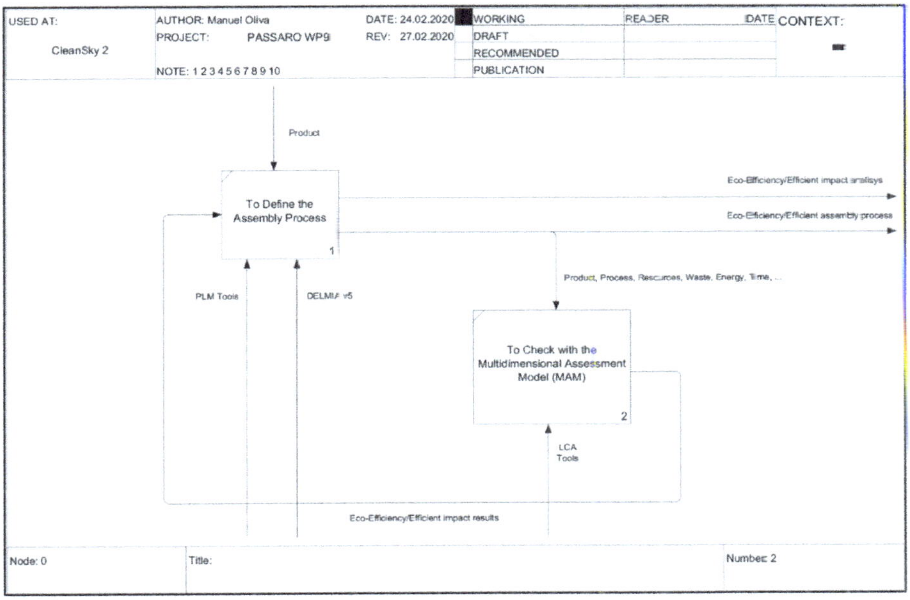

Fig. 2. Eco-efficiency aerospace assembly process assessment conceptual model

Define the Assembly Process: Development of the 3D assembly process is performed using Dassault Systèmes DELMIA v5 [13] creating an iDMU (industrial Digital Mock Up) [14] and the related links. Industrialization model breakdown starts with the build assembly process that is performed in a Final Assembly Line (FAL) [15]. An Assembly Line may have stations with one or more manufacturing solutions processes decomposed in operations and elementary tasks with detailed technical instructions. The 3D environment provides a main point of access for end-users through user interfaces, including capabilities for extending with additional developments required, such as the eco-efficient attributes needed to compute the environmental impact.

Check with the Multidimensional Assessment Model (MAM): The multidimensional design assessment model will allow an innovative practical integration of eco-efficiency analysis, including LCA and cost analysis component alongside with assembly efficiency. This is done from the perspective of Lean Manufacturing, thus implicitly evaluating "value added" and "non-value added" (waste) actions and resource usage. The MAM holds and computes the eco-efficiency, efficiency and costs for each required level of a build assembly process. A detailed description of the module has been published in [16]. Environmental impacts are provided by the LCA database.

Life Cycle Assessment (LCA) Tools: LCA is the database with the impacts for each one of the elements that are part of an assembly process. The development of a specific LCA for aerospace is a project being carried out in Clean Sky1 Life Cycle Assessment Database Improvement LCA DATIM [17]

Product Lifecycle Management (PLM): It provides the technical infrastructure for the data management. It contains the current information of an assembly process in development, historical data, constrains, and KPIs. It also controls the synchronous communication flow with the MAM module. Typical functionalities offered by a PLM, like vaulting, workflow, maturity states, are still used for the project. The tool selected for this research work is ARAS Innovator [18].

Eco Efficiency Impact and Results: A dashboard provides the comparative analysis of different versions for an assembly process: resource utilization, optimization, KPIs and visualization of results. The KPIs taken into consideration will mostly reflect eco-constraints. Inputs from the MAM will support the decision process, by simulating the potential evolution of relevant KPIs and allowing engineers taking decisions.

5 Eco-efficiency Data Model

The development of the Data Model requires the consideration of two conditions: the assembly process definition and the eco-efficiency/efficiency of it. The literature review shows many different solutions for a Data Model for aerospace assembly processes. In this research the authors take as input the proposed model in [19–21] and adapt it to the eco-efficiency requirements.

Aerospace assembly processes are characterized by intensive human labor with low automation. Several research work in eco-efficiency, efficiency and KPIs propose Data Model for single parts, but it not so much solutions for aerospace assembly with intense human labor. Main inputs used as starting point for the Data Model developed in this research are described in [22, 23].

Definition of the Data Model is shown in Fig. 3. The iDMU Data Model is extended to include the environmental concepts and is implemented in the PLM. Other additional functionalities are included such as vaulting and configuration management for assembly process development maturity.

Zone 1 (iDMU. Product, Processes and Resources): It holds most of the concepts commonly used in an iDMU structure with the particularity of adding the standard process and standard resources. The definition of standard processes and resources are functionalities developed to have a library of processes and resources commonly used in assembly. Such functionalities will help engineers to speed up the process definition and save on continually introducing the same information.

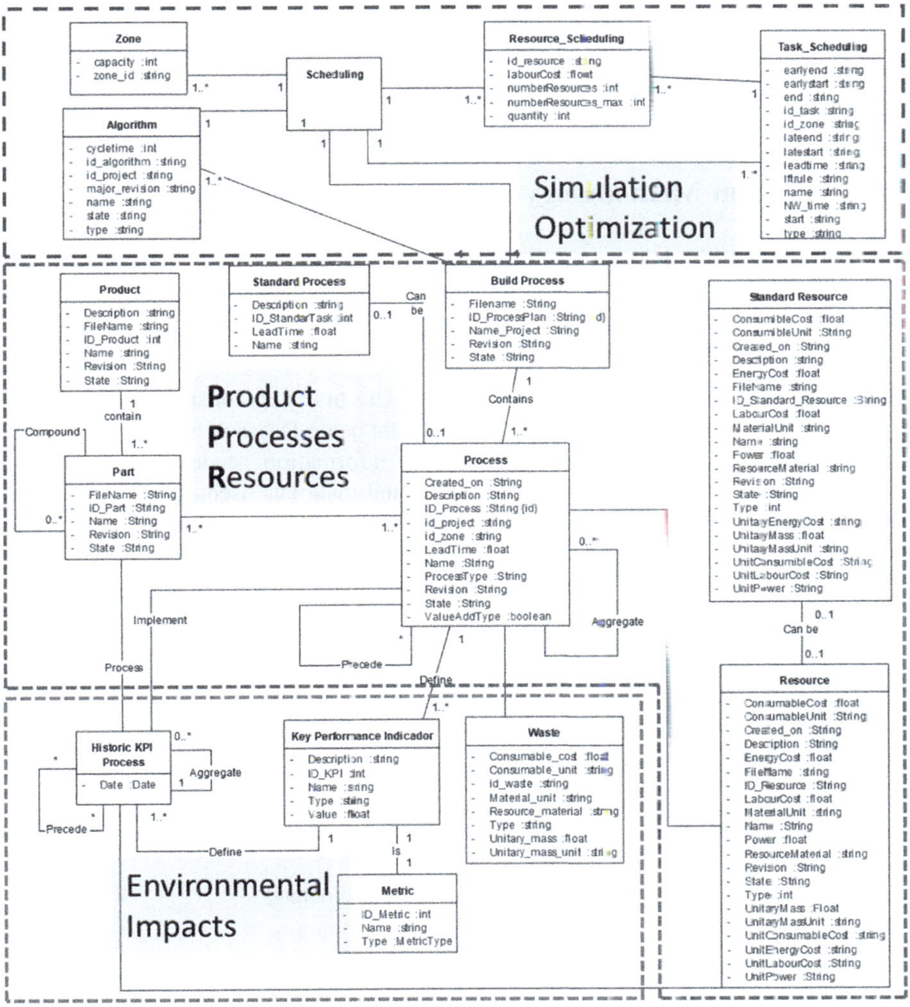

Fig. 3. Eco-efficiency data model

Zone 2 (Environmental Impacts): It includes the concepts needed to extend the iDMU with an environmental impact dimension, particularly the ones for eco-efficiency, and the associated metrics and KPIs. The *Key Performance Indicator* object defines every KPI for each process in the *Build Process*. The attribute value has the impact of the process for every KPI. Associated to each KPI, the *Metric* object defines the magnitude the KPI (meters, kg, liters, etc.). Additionally, the *Historic KPI Process* object holds the calculated value of different versions allowing decision-making comparing them.

Zone 3 (Simulation and Optimization): It contains the objects to help simulation and optimization; the *Algorithm* object associated to a build process together with the *Task*

Gantt and *Resource Gantt* objects are defined to apply the selected algorithm to an assembly process. The *Schedule* object together with the *Task Scheduling* and *Resource Scheduling* objects are defined to store the calculated schedule for a particular *Build Process*.

6 Application Methodology

The application methodology presents how to use the prototype software tool created to support the Conceptual Model and the Data Model presented. It follows the steps defined in the LCA methodology to create more value with less environmental impact. The main steps in the methodology are:

Compiling Inventory of Input and Outputs: The first step consists of defining the assembly process in a PLM 3D virtual environment using Dassault Systèmes DELMIA v5. The assembly process is modelled and all information needed to calculate the environmental impact is provided by resources and materials used during the process. Figure 4 shows assembly product structure and data entry interface window.

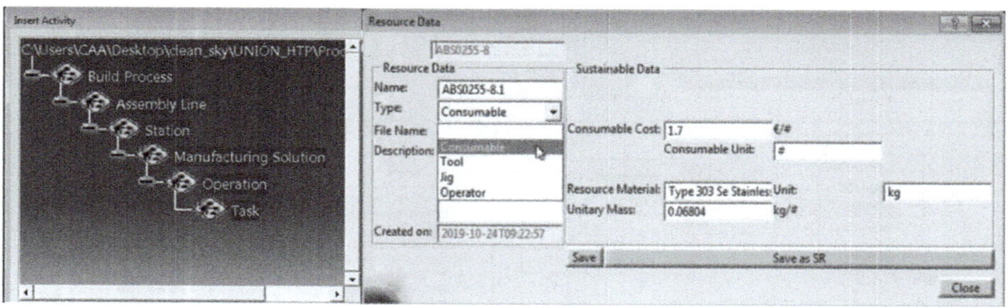

Fig. 4. Inventory of inputs and outputs

Assessment of Potential Environmental Impacts Associated to Input-Outputs: This event consists of the identification of all assembly means and their characterisation. Assembly processes data collected in the previous phase is sent to MAM to compute the eco-efficiency and efficiency. Most of the functionalities of this phase are developed in PLM. The process engineer inquires the application through the interface developed in Dassault Systèmes DELMIA v5, while most of the functionalities are orchestrated by ARAS Innovator. Communication to and from PLM and MAM to compute the process eco-efficiency is managed in this phase, and results are stored in the database.

Interpreting the Results: Following the characterization of the process, it is possible to create the assembly scenarios, and evaluate their global performance and performance for each domain in a virtual environment. After the virtual evaluation and comparison between the different assembly scenarios, the assembly sequence with better global performance takes place. This phase is performed in the Dassault Systèmes DELMIA v5 interface with the KPIs represented in a dashboard.

7 Aerospace Industrial Case of Study

The selected Case of Study to test and demonstrate the application methodology is based on the assembly processes for a large aerospace structure, a Horizontal Tail Plane (HTP), of a typical commercial aircraft. The structure is shown within the industrial environment in Fig. 5. below. This large aero-structure is composed by two main subassemblies, both HTP left box and right box, assembly together to produce the final product.

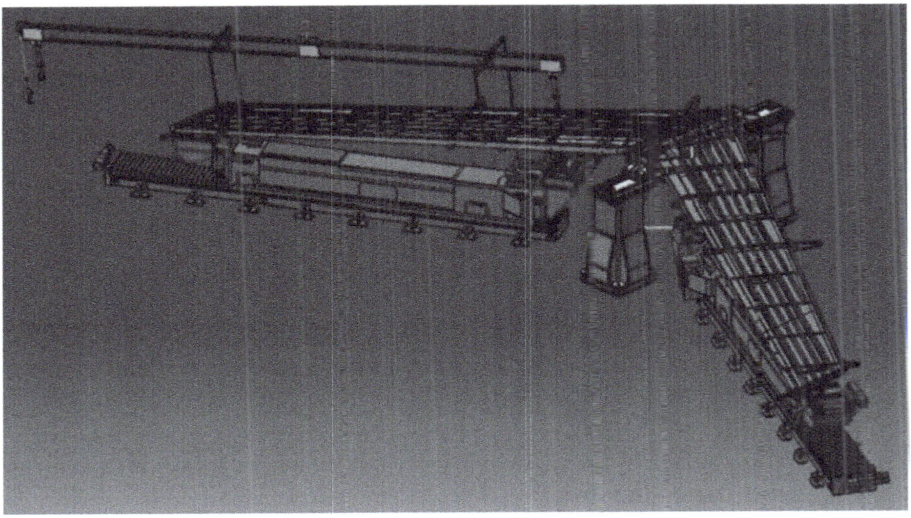

Fig. 5. HTP and manufacturing environment

The HTP assembly process is decomposed into manufacturing solutions and then in operations and elementary tasks. The Case of Study will be focused in the final assembly station dedicated to the assembly process between left box and right box. In the initial conceptual assembly process approach, five manufacturing solutions have been considered, with the associated resources and the related information: material, resources, energy, waste, etc. With the information collected, the MAM executed the impact analysis and returned the results.

Presenting the complete LCA data analysis results is very helpful for a specialist in LCA, but too complex for engineers and designers, since they need to consider many parameters to decide. The use of a representative emission of kg of CO_2 equivalent, which is easy to understand for engineers, is unsatisfactory since environmental problems can be obscured by redesigns which then shift the problem towards other classes of pollution.

The option selected is to keep one single indicator indicating points for emissions and waste. It can be done considering impact scores broken out into categories, with no weighting at all. To reduce complexity and to have an easily understandable and comparable environmental impact value the model considers a weighted single score. Such approach has the advantage of generating one, single and easy-to-communicate, impact number. The number is expressed as Eco-Points according to the ReCiPe method to normalization and weighting [24].

Different dashboards have been developed to present and manage the correct, most understandable information to the engineers and to help them in the decision-making for the selection of the best assembly process. The prototype incorporates a dashboard where the KPIs associated with assembly processes, used resources and associated products are displayed. Likewise, the dashboard allows comparisons between processes and variations showing versions or historical data of the same assembly process. The dashboard module shows KPIs previously computed in MAM.

The dashboard and graphics are intended to answer the initial questions from the introduction section of this paper; what are the elements that have an environmental impact, in what intensity and where during the assembly process. Since cost is one of the main drivers for an industrial company, the evaluation of the environmental improvement cost needs to be assessed.

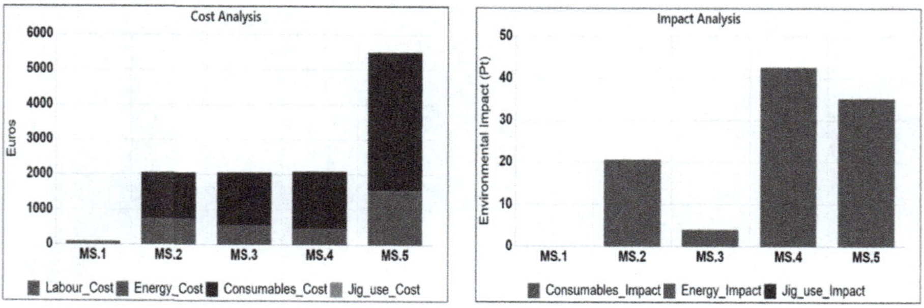

Fig. 6. KPI cost analysis and eco-points impact

The Fig. 6 represents the cost and eco-points for each of the five considered manufacturing solutions. In the cost analysis, a decomposition of the elements (labour, energy, consumables and jigs) which affect the cost of a manufacturing solution are depicted. Similarly, for the impact analysis, the elements with environmental impact (consumables, energy and jigs) are also depicted.

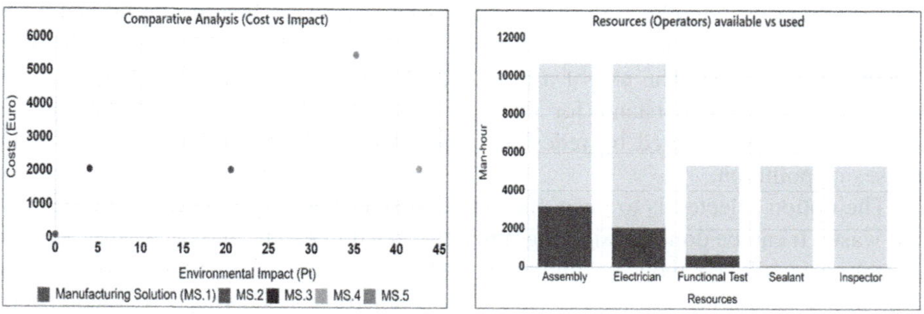

Fig. 7. Costs versus environment impact for manufacturing solutions and resources utilization

The dashboard also offers analysis to check cost versus impact and optimization of resources, like labor time. Figure 7 shows a first utilization for each operator skills used during the assembly process. During the optimization process is possible to smooth the curve of number of operators per assembly station.

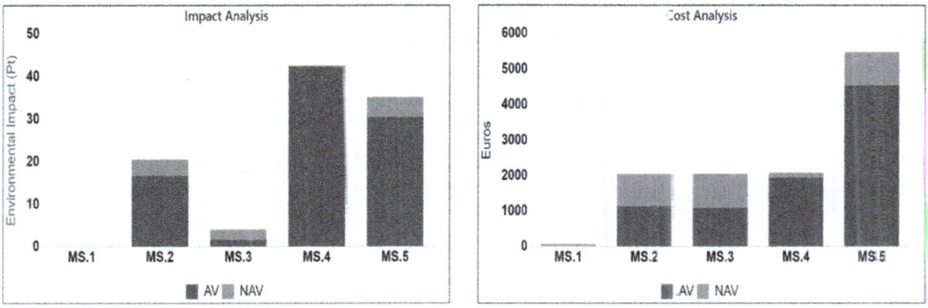

Fig. 8. Environmental impact analysis filtering AV versus NAV, and cost analysis

In terms of process efficiency and in relation to the environmental impact, Fig. 8 shows the eco-points for each manufacturing solution in relationship to Added Value (AV) versus Non Added Value (NAV) activities and similar comparison for the cost analysis.

8 Conclusions

The main conclusion of this research and the main results after the application can be resumed as:

- In this research the eco-efficiency analysis is proposed at the conceptual level, in a top-down approach, but the solution was also validated in performing detailed analysis in a bottom-up approach, gathering information at tasks level.
- The proposed framework solution and the methodology have been demonstrated in an industrial case study for a large aero-structure assembly process. Company organization should be aligned and software tools consolidated before including eco-efficiency as an additional criteria for selecting aerospace processes.
- The results in eco-points as a single measurement to ease the decision-making has become useful for process engineer although their first input was why not using CO_2 equivalent. This observation will be taking into consideration in the next development.
- It is necessary to make visible to process engineers that the assumptions taken when introducing data have direct impact in results. If design is at conceptual level with low detail, the impact can only be used as a first approach.

- The authors are still doing more tests to comprehend results in process engineering and how to be able to compare results of different versions of a build process. Although still in early tests of the solution, an extrapolation of results from the assembly of a product to other similar one for a new development can be of a high interest for industrial companies.

Acknowledgements. The authors wish to express their sincere gratitude to University of Sevilla colleagues in Spain, to INEGI and ISQ colleagues from PASSARO project in Portugal, to Airbus colleagues in France and Spain, and to Jordan Smith for their support and contribution during the development of this work.

DILECO is funded under Grant agreement ID: 785367 by H2020 Framework Programme, within Clean Sky 2 subprogram H2020-EU.3.4.5.4-ITD Airframe led by Airbus Defence and Space.

References

1. Schmidheiny, S.: Changing Course: A Global Business Perspective on Development and the Environment. MIT Press, Cambridge (1992)
2. Moreira, F., Alves, A., Sousa, R.: Towards eco-efficient lean production systems. In: Balanced Automation Systems for Future Manufacturing Networks, pp. 100–108 (2010). https://doi.org/10.1007/978-3-642-14341-0_12
3. ISO, 14040:2006: Environmental management - Life cycle assessment - Principles and framework. ISO – International Organization for Standardization, Geneva (2006)
4. Ilgin, M., Gupta, S.: Environmentally conscious manufacturing and product recovery (ECMPRO): a review of the state of the art. J. Environ. Manage. **91**(3), 563–591 (2010). https://doi.org/10.1016/j.jenvman.2009.09.037.PMID19853369
5. Mas, F., Ríos, J., Menéndez, J., Gómez, A.: A process-oriented approach to modeling the conceptual design of aircraft assembly lines. Int. J. Adv. Manuf. Technol. **67**(1–4), 771–784 (2012). https://doi.org/10.1007/s00170-012-4521-5
6. Nassehi, A., Imani-Ashari, R., Dhokia, V., Munoz-Escalona, P., Newman, S.T.: Energy efficiency analysis and evaluation of CNC machines. In: Proceedings of The 4th International Scientific Conference Management of Technology – Step to Sustainable Production, pp. 117–187 (2012)
7. Heilala, J., et al.: Collaborative product, process and service development with eco process engineering system. In: Proceedings of the 6th International Swedish Production Symposium (2014)
8. McEwan, W., Butterfield, J.: A digital methodology for the design process of aerospace assemblies with sustainable composite processes & manufacture (2011). https://doi.org/10.1063/1.3589758
9. Clean Sky 2 Core Partnership Program. https://www.cleansky.eu/. Accessed 22 Jan 2020
10. DILECO (DIgitalization of ground-testing Life cycle with ECO design criteria). https://cordis.europa.eu/project/id/785367. Accessed 22 Jan 2020
11. Mas, F., Racero, J., Oliva, M., Morales-Palma, D.: A preliminary methodological approach to models for manufacturing (MfM). In: Chiabert, P., Bouras, A., Noël, F., Ríos, J. (eds.) PLM 2018. IAICT, vol. 540, pp. 273–283. Springer, Cham (2018). https://doi.org/10.1007/978-3-030-01614-2_25

12. Holland, O.T.: Model-based systems engineering. In: Loper, Margaret L. (ed.) Modeling and Simulation In The Systems Engineering Life Cycle. SFMA, pp. 299–306. Springer, London (2015). https://doi.org/10.1007/978-1-4471-5634-5_23
13. Dassault Systèmes. https://www.3ds.com/. Accessed 22 Jan 2020
14. Mas, F., Menendez, J., Oliva, M., Rios, J., Gomez, A., Olmos, V.: iDMU as the Collaborative Engineering engine: research experiences in Airbus. In: 2014 International Conference on Engineering, Technology and Innovation (ICE) (2014). https://doi.org/10.1109/ICE.2014.6871594
15. Mas, F., Ríos, J., Gómez, A., Hernández, J.: Knowledge-based application to define aircraft final assembly lines at the industrialization conceptual design phase. Int. J. Comput. Integr. Manuf. **29**(6), 677–691 (2015). https://doi.org/10.1080/0951192X.2015.1068453
16. Lourenco, E., Oliva, M., Estrela, M., Baptista, A.: Multidimensional Design Assessment Model for eco-efficiency and efficiency in aeronautical assembly processes. In: 2019 IEEE International Conference on Engineering, Technology and Innovation (ICE/ITMC) (2019). https://doi.org/10.1109/ICE.2019.8792641
17. Life Cycle Assessment database improvement (LCA DATIM). https://cordis.europa.eu/project/id/267496. Accessed 22 Jan 2020
18. ARAS Innovator. https://www.aras.com/. Accessed 22 Jan 2020
19. Mas, F., Ríos, J., Menéndez, J.L., Hernández, J.C.: Information model for assembly line design at conceptual phase. In: 3rd Manufacturing Engineering Society International Conference, MESIC 2009, Alcoy, España (2009)
20. Mas, F., Gómez, A., Menéndez, J.L., Ríos, J.: Proposal for the conceptual design of aeronautical final assembly lines based on the industrial digital mock-up concept. In: Bernard, A., Rivest, L., Dutta, D. (eds.) PLM 2013. IAICT, vol. 409, pp. 10–19. Springer, Heidelberg (2013). https://doi.org/10.1007/978-3-642-41501-2_2
21. Gómez, A., Ríos, J., Mas, F., Vizán, A.: Method and software application to assist in the conceptual design of aircraft final assembly lines. J. Manuf. Syst. **40**, 37–53 (2016). https://doi.org/10.1016/j.jmsy.2016.04.002
22. Zhang, H., Zhu, B., Li, Y., Yaman, O., Roy, U.: Development and utilization of a Process-oriented Information Model for sustainable manufacturing. J. Manuf. Syst. **37**, 459–466 (2015). https://doi.org/10.1016/j.jmsy.2015.05.003
23. Zhang, H., Roy, U.: Development of an information model for the integration of product design and sustainability evaluation. In: Volume 1A: 34th Computers and Information in Engineering Conference (2014). https://doi.org/10.1115/DETC2014-34811
24. Goedkoop, M.J., Heijungs, R., Huijbregts, M., De Schryver, A., Struijs, J., Van Zelm, R.: ReCiPe 2008, a life cycle impact assessment method which comprises harmonized category indicators at the midpoint and the endpoint level; First edition Report I: Characterization, 6 January 2009. http://www.lcia-recipe.net. Accessed 22 Jan 2020

A Disassembly Line Design Approach for Management of End-of-Life Product Quality

Mohand-Lounes Bentaha(✉), Nejib Moalla, and Yacine Ouzrout

Université Lyon 2, DISP Laboratory, EA 4570, Lyon, France
{mohand.bentaha,nejib.moalla,yacine.ouzrout}@univ-lyon2.fr

Abstract. The purpose of this work is to efficiently design a disassembly line, as disassembly system, handling variability of End-of-Life (EoL) product quality as well as uncertainty of disassembly process operations and provides an optimal revenue of such a system. The main finding of this work is the development of a decision tool that allows decision-makers to choose the best disassembly process and disassembly depth, while assigning the corresponding tasks to the line workstations under precedence and cycle time constraints. Task times are assumed to be random variables with known normal probability distributions. Presence of hazardous material is considered and line cycle time constraints are to be jointly satisfied with at least a certain service (probability) level set by the decision-maker. The revenue of a product part depends explicitly on its EoL state or quality. Industrial applicability is shown using an industrial case focused on remanufacturing of mechatronic parts in the automotive industry.

Keywords: Sustainable manufacturing · Product recovery · Disassembly · Line design · EoL product quality · Uncertainty · Decision aiding

1 Introduction

This work develops a decision tool to optimize line design by minimizing the number of needed workstations and selecting optimal disassembly process and depth regarding line revenue. A line consists of an ordered sequence of workstations connected by a material handling system. At each workstation, an EoL product or one or more of its subassemblies are separated into their components and parts. The line revenue is defined as the difference between the revenue generated by recovered parts and the line operation cost. The latter includes the workstations operation cost and additional cost of workstations handling hazardous parts. In fact, certain parts or subassemblies may contain hazardous material and require a particular treatment incurring a supplementary cost.

The originality of the proposed approach is to consider the health state of the EoL product, its parts and sub-parts in the revenue estimation as random

Published by Springer Nature Switzerland AG 2020
F. Nyffenegger et al. (Eds.): PLM 2020, IFIP AICT 594, pp. 460–472, 2020.
https://doi.org/10.1007/978-3-030-62807-9_37

variables. The recycling decision requires a quantification of the part capacity to re-enter a cycle. For such a purpose, we use the Remaining Usage Potential (RUP) concept introduced in [8]. An extended literature review on disassembly lines can be found in [1,10].

The economical optimization of the disassembly line takes into account revenue gained from disassembled parts resale. The latter is highly dependent on the re-entering usage cycle whose decision is based on the RUP. The RUPs of a product and its parts are taken as distributions since we consider mass recycling. The novelty of the proposed decision tool as well is task processing times uncertainty management in the optimization approach. This is done by designing a line where cycle time constraints are jointly satisfied with at least a certain service level, $1-\alpha$, fixed by the decision-maker. In industrial terms, the probability level $(1-\alpha)$ reflects the level of the EoL product demand satisfaction; hence, it defines the level of customers satisfaction or the capability of the designed disassembly system to meet the demand.

This paper is structured as follows. A formal description of the studied problem is presented in Sect. 2. Section 3 presents the developed decision model along with the solution approach. Numerical experiments and optimization results are presented in Sect. 4. Section 5 concludes the paper with future research directions.

2 Problem Formal Definition

In this work, we study a disassembly process where the revenue from retrieved parts depends on the quality of the incoming return products. For an EoL product, the problem consists on the selection of a best disassembly process alternative, among all possible ones, taking into account its RUP and precedence relationships amongst all disassembly tasks and product parts obtained during the disassembly process. At the same time, selected disassembly tasks are optimally assigned to an ordered sequence of workstations, while satisfying cycle time constraints under uncertainty of the task processing times.

The goal is to design a line, as a disassembly system, providing the maximal revenue and resulting in a minimized number of stations. Cycle time (C_T) constraints for all workstations have to be jointly respected with at least a probability level $(1-\alpha)$ fixed by the decision maker; C_T is the amount of time allocated to each station to complete its assigned tasks. Line revenue is the difference between the profit generated by recovered parts and the line operation cost. Line cost includes the workstations operation cost and additional cost of workstations handling hazardous parts. Disassembly task processing times $t_i, i \in I$, are assumed to be random variables with known normal probability distributions; I represents the set of all possible disassembly tasks. In the case of task times assumed to be random variables following a different probability distribution, the resulted time of each workstation is not guaranteed to be normally distributed for any number of tasks assigned to it.

Each task time is noted as: $\tilde{t}_i, i \in I$. A disassembly task $i \in H \subset I$ is called hazardous if its execution generates a hazardous subassembly or component;

H is the set of hazardous tasks. The maximum disassembly level is the components level. A task can be performed at any workstation but cannot be split between two workstations. A fixed cost per operating a time unit of an opened workstation and an additional fixed cost per operating a time unit for treating a hazardous part are given. Each component or subassembly has a resale value which represents its revenue. This revenue depends on the quality of the corresponding component or subassembly. The state or quality of each subassembly is modeled using the concept of RUP which follows a probability distribution. This distribution models the variability of RUP of the input return products. In the optics of industrialized disassembly, i.e. a large number of products of the same category are returned, to obtain such a probability distribution, statistical studies on disassembled products can be conducted. The RUP concept is explained in detail in [2,8] and is summarized here in Subsects. 2.2 and 2.3.

2.1 Modeling of Disassembly Process and Precedence Relations

And/or graph models explicitly all possible disassembly process alternatives of an EoL product, as well as the precedence relationships among tasks and product subassemblies and components [2,5] (see Fig. 1).

Each subassembly is represented by a node labeled $A_k, k \in K$; K is the set of all generated subassemblies (only subassemblies). Each node labeled $B_i, i \in I$,

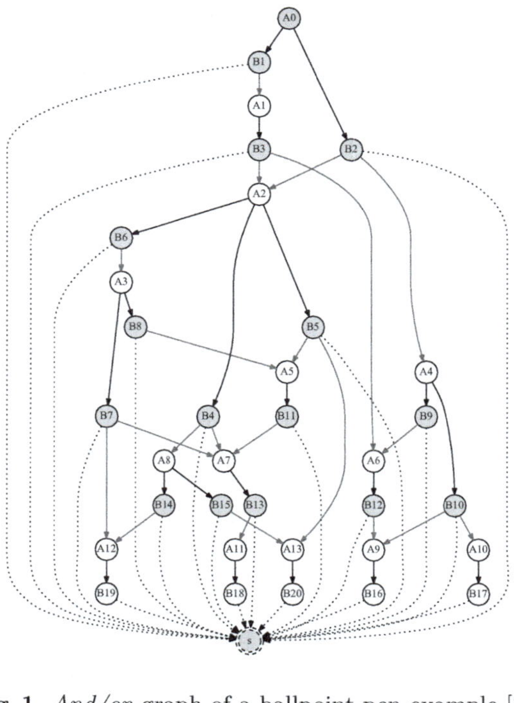

Fig. 1. *And/or* graph of a ballpoint pen example [3].

represents a disassembly task. For a more detailed description of the *and/or* graph modeling process, see our precedent work [4,7,8].

2.2 Idea of RUP Concept and Its PDF

The RUP is evaluated on a $[0,1]$ scale; 1 corresponds to the product state at the beginning of its life or exploitation (the product is at its maximal RUP); 0 means that the product/part has reached its end of life and has to be recycled as raw material. It is modeled as a normal Probability Density Function (PDF) truncated in 0 and 1. The RUP follows a truncated normal distribution on $[0,1]$ with μ and σ parameters: RUP $\rightsquigarrow \mathcal{N}_{[0,1]}(\mu,\sigma)$; μ and σ are respectively the mean and standard deviation of the original non truncated normal distribution. Figure 2 shows, over $[0,1]$ interval, 3 truncated normal distribution functions with parameters: $\mu = 0, \sigma = 0.3$; $\mu = 0.5, \sigma = 0.2$; $\mu = 1, \sigma = 0.3$.

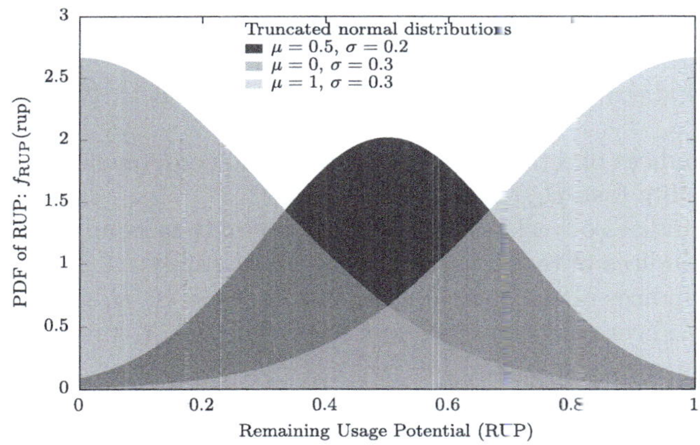

Fig. 2. RUP PDF examples as normal distributions truncated on [0, 1].

2.3 Part Revenue with Respect to Its RUP and Part Revenue PDF

All product items have not the same RUP, so their resale prices have to be considered as functions of their RUPs. The resale price represents the revenue (R_e) due to recycling recovery of disassembly items. The revenue R_e is defined as a function of the RUP: $R_e(\text{RUP})$. Three cases of $R_e(\text{RUP})$ are studied: (a) $R_e = (b-a)\cdot\text{RUP}+a$, affine function; (b) $R_e = (b-a)\cdot\sqrt[4]{\text{RUP}}+a$, root function; (c) $R_e = e^{\frac{1}{e-1}\left(e\ln(a)-\ln(b)\right)}e^{\frac{1}{e-1}\left(\ln(b)-\ln(a)\right)e^{\text{RUP}}}$, exponential function.

Here, $R_e(\text{RUP} = 1) = b$ and $R_e(\text{RUP} = 0) = a$, with $b > a > 0$; b and a are upper and lower bounds on resale prices, respectively.

Combining RUP probability density function with part revenue function gives part revenue probability density function. For the 3 R_e functions presented above, the corresponding probability density functions are defined in [2]. Again, three cases for the RUP distribution, i.e. RUP $\rightsquigarrow \mathcal{N}_{[0,1]}(\mu, \sigma)$, according to the part quality are studied: bad ($\mu = 0, \sigma = 0.2$), medium ($\mu = 0.5, \sigma = 0.3$) and good ($\mu = 1, \sigma = 0.2$).

3 Optimization Model and Solution Approach

The objective is profit maximization of the disassembly system to be designed. To model the defined problem, the following notations are introduced.

3.1 Parameters and Sets

I: set of disassembly task indices: $I = \{1, 2, \ldots, \mathsf{n}\}$, $\mathsf{n} \in \mathbb{N}^*$;
J: set of workstation indices: $J = \{1, 2, \ldots, \mathsf{m}\}$, $\mathsf{m} \in \mathbb{N}^*$, $\mathsf{m} \leqslant \mathsf{n}$;
H: set of hazardous disassembly task indices;
L: set of all product part indices (subassemblies and components): $L = \{1, 2, \ldots, \mathsf{l}\}$, $\mathsf{l} \in \mathbb{N}^*$;
K: set of indices for the generated subassemblies: $K = \{0, 1, \ldots, \mathsf{k}\}$, $\mathsf{k} \in \mathbb{N}$, $K \subseteq L$;
L_i: set of indices of retrieved subassemblies and components by the execution of disassembly task $B_i, i \in I$;
G_ℓ: set of indices of tasks generating subassembly or component $\ell, \ell \in L$;
D_ℓ: set of indices of tasks disassembling subassembly $\ell, \ell \in L$;
P_k: set of indices of A_k predecessors, $k \in K$: $P_k = \{i |\ B_i \text{ precedes } A_k\}$;
S_k: set of indices of A_k successors, $k \in K$: $S_k = \{i |\ A_k \text{ precedes } B_i\}$;
A_k: a subassembly, $k \in K$;
B_i: a disassembly task, $i \in I$;
$\mathtt{F_c}$: fixed cost per operating a time unit of a workstation, $\mathtt{F_c} > 0$;
$\mathtt{H_c}$: additional cost per time unit for stations handling hazardous parts, $\mathtt{H_c} > 0$;
$\mathrm{C_T}$: cycle time, $\mathrm{C_T} > 0$;
$\widetilde{t_i}$: processing time of task $B_i, i \in I$, where $\widetilde{t_i} \rightsquigarrow \mathcal{N}(\mu_i, \sigma_i), i \in I$;
$\widetilde{R_{e\ell}}$: revenue generated by a subassembly or component $\ell, \ell \in L$ (see subsection 2.3), where $\widetilde{R_{e\ell}}$ is a function of $\widetilde{\mathrm{RUP}_\ell}$: $\widetilde{R_{e\ell}}(\widetilde{\mathrm{RUP}_\ell})$, $\ell \in L$; $\widetilde{\mathrm{RUP}_\ell}$ represents the remaining use potential of a subassembly or component $\ell, \ell \in L$, as defined in Subsect. 2.2;
$1 - \alpha$: probability or line service level fixed by the decision-maker: cycle time constraints are jointly satisfied with at least this level value; α represents a risk and in general $\alpha \leqslant 10\%$.

3.2 Decision Variables

$$x_{ij} = \begin{cases} 1, & \text{if task } B_i \text{ is assigned to workstation } j; \\ 0, & \text{otherwise.} \end{cases} \qquad x_{sj} = \begin{cases} 1, & \text{if disassembly is finished at station } j, \text{ complete or partial;} \\ 0, & \text{otherwise.} \end{cases}$$

$$h_j = \begin{cases} 1, & \text{if a hazardous task is assigned to station } j; \\ 0, & \text{otherwise.} \end{cases} \qquad y_\ell = \begin{cases} 0, & \text{if } \sum_{i \in G_\ell} x_i = 1 \text{ and } \sum_{i \in D_\ell} x_i = 1, \ \ell \text{ subassembly;} \\ 1, & \text{otherwise.} \end{cases}$$

Variable $y_\ell, \ell \in L$ prevents to compute a subassembly revenue, in the objective function, when this latter is itself disassembled. Only revenues of its components or subassemblies (not disassembled) are used afterwards.

3.3 Set of Constraints and Objective Function

The decision tool proposed in this paper uses the optimization model defined below. This model allows to determine a disassembly process alternative with the maximum profit and assign its tasks to minimal number of workstations, while considering the quality or states of the subassemblies and components (generated during the disassembly process) and task processing times uncertainty. As mentioned in Subsect. 2.2, the state of a product (subassembly or component) is modeled using RUP. Thus, by taking the RUP of each subassembly and component, the optimization model allows to choose which components and subassemblies to retrieve in order to maximize the disassembly process profit. As explained in Subsect. 2.3, revenue R_e of each component or subassembly depends on its RUP, i.e. $R_e(\text{RUP})$. The objective function and associated constraints are formulated as follows.

$$\max \left\{ \sum_{i \in I} \sum_{j \in J} \sum_{\ell \in L_i} \widetilde{R}_{e\ell} \cdot y_\ell \cdot x_{ij} - \mathrm{C_T} \left(\mathtt{F_c} \cdot \sum_{j \in J} j \cdot x_{sj} + \mathtt{H_c} \cdot \sum_{j \in J} h_j \right) \right\} \tag{I}$$

s.t.

$$\sum_{i \in S_0} \sum_{j \in J} x_{ij} = 1 \tag{1}$$

$$\sum_{j \in J} x_{ij} \leqslant 1, \forall i \in I \tag{2}$$

$$\sum_{i \in S_k} \sum_{j \in J} x_{ij} \leqslant \sum_{i \in P_k} \sum_{j \in J} x_{ij}, \forall k \in K \backslash \{0\} \tag{3}$$

$$\sum_{i \in S_k} x_{iv} \leqslant \sum_{i \in P_k} \sum_{j=1}^{v} x_{ij}, \forall k \in K \backslash \{0\}, \forall v \in J \tag{4}$$

$$\sum_{j \in J} x_{\mathsf{s}j} = 1 \tag{5}$$

$$\sum_{j \in J} j \cdot x_{ij} \leqslant \sum_{j \in J} j \cdot x_{\mathsf{s}j}, \forall i \in I \tag{6}$$

$$h_j \geqslant x_{ij}, \forall j \in J, \forall i \in H \tag{7}$$

$$\text{If } \sum_{i \in D_\ell} x_i = 1 \text{ and } \sum_{i \in G_\ell} x_i = 1 \text{ then } y_\ell = 0, \forall \ell \in L \ (\ell \text{ subassembly}) \tag{8}$$

$$y_\ell = 1, \forall \ell \in L \ (\ell \text{ component}) \tag{9}$$

$$P\Big(\sum_{i \in I} \widetilde{t_i} \cdot x_{ij} \leqslant \mathrm{C_T}, \forall j \in J\Big) \geqslant 1 - \alpha \tag{10}$$

$$x_{\mathsf{s}j}, x_{ij}, h_j, y_\ell \in \{0, 1\}, \forall i \in I, \forall j \in J, \forall \ell \in L \tag{11}$$

Terms of the objective function represent, respectively, the earned profit of retrieved parts, the cost of operating workstations and the additional cost for handling hazardous parts. Constraint (1) models the fact that exactly one disassembly task, among all possible ones, must be chosen to start disassembling the EoL product, symbolized by A_0. Constraint set (2) indicates that a task is to be assigned to at most one workstation. Constraints (3) ensure that only one or-successor is selected. Constraint set (4) defines the precedence relationships among tasks and subassemblies. Constraint (5) imposes the assignment of the dummy task s to one workstation. Constraints (6) ensure that all disassembly tasks are assigned to lower or equal- indexed workstations than the one to which s is assigned. Constraints (7) ensure the value of h_j to be 1 if at least one hazardous task is assigned to a workstation j. Constraints (8), as previously mentioned, model an exclusion between the revenue of a subassembly (which is disassembled) and the revenue of its subassemblies and components. Constraints (9) are introduced in order to include in the retained disassembly process revenues that are generated by selected components. Constraints (10) enforce the workstation operating time to remain within the cycle time $\mathrm{C_T}$, for all opened workstations, jointly with at least a predefined probability $1 - \alpha$. Finally, set (11) represents the possible values of the decision variables.

In the next section, lower and upper bounding schemes will be defined in order to transform constraints (8) and (10) and optimally solve problem (I) with quadratically constrained program solvers, such as CPLEX.

3.4 Solution of the Problem

Upper Bounding Scheme for Program (I)

The optimal value of program (UMinI) below defines an upper bound of (I) [6,9].

$$\min \left\{ \mathrm{C_T}\Big(\mathtt{F_c} \cdot \sum_{j \in J} j \cdot x_{sj} + \mathtt{H_c} \cdot \sum_{j \in J} h_j\Big) - \sum_{i \in I} \sum_{j \in J} \sum_{\ell \in L_i} \widetilde{R_{e\ell}} \cdot z_{ij\ell} \right\} \tag{UMinI}$$

s.t.

$$v_j \leqslant \mathrm{C_T} - \mu^{\mathsf{T}} \cdot x_j, \forall j \in J \tag{12}$$

$$w_{ij} \geqslant \sigma_i \cdot z_{ij}, \forall i \in I, \forall j \in J \tag{13}$$

$$v_j \geqslant \|w_j\|, \forall j \in J \tag{14}$$

$$z_{ij} \geqslant a_k \cdot x_{ij} + b_k \cdot y_{ij}, \forall i \in I, \forall j \in J, k = 1, \ldots, m \tag{15}$$

$$\sum_{j\in J} y_{ij} = \sum_{j\in J} o_{ij}, \forall i \in I \tag{16}$$

$$o_{ij} \leqslant x_{ij}, \forall i \in I, \forall j \in J \tag{17}$$

$$o_{ij} \leqslant q_j, \forall i \in I, \forall j \in J \tag{18}$$

$$q_j + x_{ij} \leqslant 1 + o_{ij}, \forall i \in I, \forall j \in J \tag{19}$$

$$\sum_{j\in J} q_j = 1 \tag{20}$$

$$x \in X, v_j, q_j, y_{ij}, w_{ij}, o_{ij}, z_{ij} \geqslant 0, \forall i \in I, \forall j \in J \tag{21}$$

Where x is a vector of decision variables $x_{ij}, x_{sj}, h_j, y_\ell, \forall i \in I, \forall j \in J, \forall \ell \in L$, and $X = \{x|$ constraints (1)–(9), and (11) are satisfied$\}$; $z_{ij\ell} \leqslant y_\ell$, $z_{ij\ell} \leqslant x_{ij}$ and $z_{ij\ell} \geqslant y_\ell + x_{ij} - 1$, $\forall i \in I, \forall j \in J, \forall \ell \in L$.

Lower Bounding Scheme for Program (I)

Program (LMinI) here after defines a lower bound for (I); $\alpha_j, j \in J$ are parameters verifying $\sum_{j\in J} \alpha_j = \alpha$ [9,11].

$$\min \left\{ \mathrm{C_T}\left(\mathtt{F_c} \cdot \sum_{j\in J} j \cdot x_{sj} + \mathtt{H_c} \cdot \sum_{j\in J} h_j\right) - \sum_{i\in I}\sum_{j\in J}\sum_{\ell\in L_i} \widetilde{R_{e\ell}} \cdot z_{ij\ell} \right\} \tag{LMinI}$$

s.t.

$$v_j \leqslant \frac{1}{\Phi^{-1}(1-\alpha_j)} \cdot \left(\mathrm{C_T} - \mu^{\mathsf{T}} \cdot x_j\right), \forall j \in J \tag{22}$$

$$w_{ij} \geqslant \sigma_i \cdot x_{ij}, \forall i \in I, \forall j \in J \tag{13}$$

$$v_j \geqslant \|w_j\|, \forall j \in J \tag{14}$$

$$x \in X, v_j, w_{ij} \geqslant 0, \forall i \in I, \forall j \in J \tag{23}$$

In order to solve the defined problem, formulated as (I), using developed lower and upper bound models, (LMinI) and (UMinI), we consider different values of the revenue $\widetilde{R_{e\ell}}, \forall \ell \in L$, where ℓ represents a subassembly or a component. These values depend on: $\widehat{\mu_\ell}$ (mean of $\widetilde{R_{e\ell}}$) and $\widehat{\sigma_\ell}$ (standard deviation of $\widetilde{R_{e\ell}}$). Three values of $\widetilde{R_{e\ell}}, \forall \ell \in L$ will be studied: $R_{e\ell} = \widehat{\mu_\ell}$ and $R_{e\ell} = \widehat{\mu_\ell} \pm \widehat{\sigma_\ell}$, $\forall \ell \in L$.

4 Numerical Illustration

Models (LMinI) and (UMinI) as well as the nonlinear optimizations and numerical integrations are implemented in Linux using C++ on a PC with 8×CPU 2.80 GHz and 32 Go RAM. Nonlinear optimizations are done with ALGLIB, numerical integatons with Gauss-Legendre quadrature while models (LMinI) and (UMinI) are solved using CPLEX 12.6. All are applied to a remanufacturing industrial case product: a Knorr-Bremse EBS 1 Channel Module. It represents a real case study in the automotive part remanufacturing sector. Such a product is composed of at least 45 components [8].

Tables 1 and 2 and Fig. 3 summarize the obtained optimization results for different values of $\widetilde{R_{e\ell}}, \ell \in L$. Columns '(stat,hstat)' and 'time(s)' in Tables 1 and 2 indicate, respectively, the number of opened workstations of the disassembly system, the number of hazardous workstations, if there is any, and the resolution time in seconds. Table 1 presents the obtained optimization results for the lower bound of problem (I) and Table 2 presents those of the upper bound. Results of Tables 1 and 2 with Fig. 3 are analysed according to three main points: optimality of solved instances, obtained disassembly process alternatives and task assignment to defined workstations. They can be summarized as follows: the profit of the disassembly process, so task assignment to line workstations, depends not only on the sequence and level of disassembly but also on the state or quality of the product, subassemblies and components.

Table 1. Lower bound of problem (I): obtained disassembly alternative, opened workstations and corresponding line profit for each revenue function type

	$R_{e\ell} = \widehat{\mu}_\ell$	(stat,hstat)	time(s)	$R_{e\ell} = \widehat{\mu}_\ell - \widehat{\sigma}_\ell$	(stat,hstat)	time(s)	$R_{e\ell} = \widehat{\mu}_\ell + \widehat{\sigma}_\ell$	(stat,hstat)	time(s)	
Affine	63478.0	(2, 1)	2.6	54074.5	(2, 1)	3	72881.5	(2, 1)	2.5	EBS 1
Root	72638.5	(2, 1)	2.4	69630.2	(2, 1)	2.4	76040.2	(1, 1)	2.4	
Expo	26617.2	(2, 1)	2.7	6710.6	(2, 1)	3	46756.5	(2, 1)	2.8	
Mixture	71298.5	(2, 1)	2.5	68495.2	(2, 1)	3	75823.6	(1, 1)	2.4	

Table 2. Upper bound of problem (I): obtained disassembly alternative, opened workstations and corresponding line profit for each revenue function type

	$R_{e\ell} = \widehat{\mu}_\ell$	(stat,hstat)	time(s)	$R_{e\ell} = \widehat{\mu}_\ell - \widehat{\sigma}_\ell$	(stat,hstat)	time(s)	$R_{e\ell} = \widehat{\mu}_\ell + \widehat{\sigma}_\ell$	(stat,hstat)	time(s)	
Affine	63478.0	(2, 1)	45.9	54074.5	(2, 1)	101.5	72881.5	(2, 1)	104.9	EBS 1
Root	72638.5	(2, 1)	79.0	69630.2	(2, 1)	84.4	76040.2	(1, 1)	2.5	
Expo	26617.2	(2, 1)	3.15	6710.6	(2, 1)	3.0	46756.5	(2, 1)	2.8	
Mixture	71298.5	(2, 1)	48	68495.2	(2, 1)	3.3	75823.6	(1, 1)	2.5	

From optimality aspect of solved instances, as it can be seen in Tables 1 and 2, all instances of the EBS module are solved to optimality. In fact, for each instance the objective function value (that is line revenue) for both lower and upper bounds are equal.

From obtained disassembly process alternatives aspect, Fig. 3 illustrates in detail the sequence and the level of disassembly returned for each revenue function type of components and subassemblies. In order to identify easily disassembly alternatives in Fig. 3 one different color is assigned to each alternative. We can see that the disassembly sequence corresponding to the maximum profit depends on the revenue functions. It can be observed that the level of disassembly for the same alternative depends on the type of revenue functions. For example, tasks $B_1\ B_6\ B_{20}\ B_{34}\ B_{43}$ and $B_1\ B_6\ B_8\ B_{20}\ B_{34}\ B_{43}$ represent two different disassembly levels of the same disassembly alternative, see Fig. 3. The results show also that for the same alternative and the same level of disassembly, values of the corresponding profits depend on the type of the revenue functions considered. As example, for upper bound values and $R_{e\ell} = \widehat{\mu}_\ell - \widehat{\sigma}_\ell, \forall \ell \in L$, functions Affine, Root and Mixture define the same alternative $B_1\ B_4\ B_{15}\ B_{34}\ B_{43}$; but values of the objective functions are all different, see Table 2.

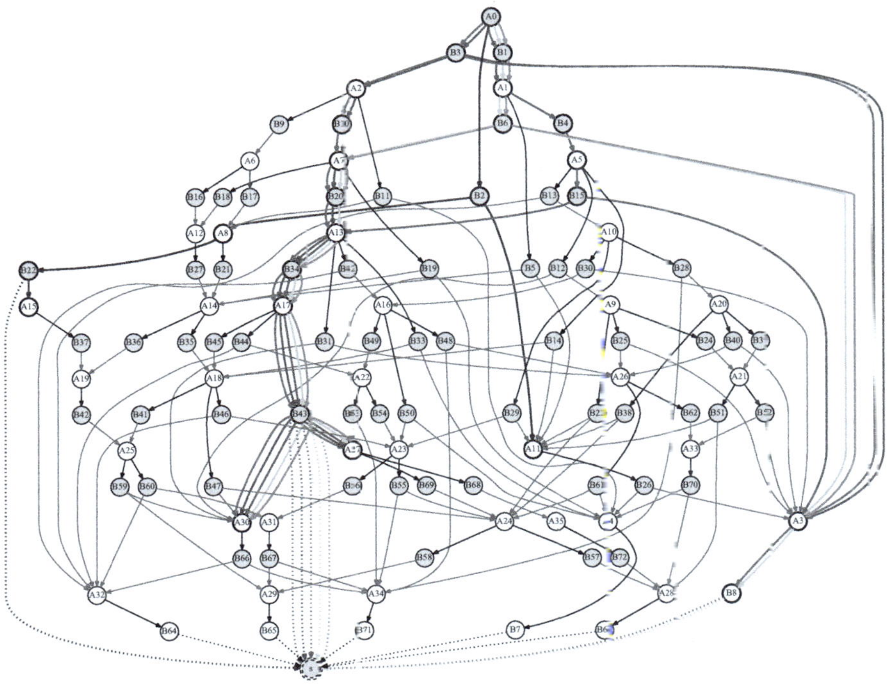

Fig. 3. Alternatives and disassembly levels returned according to the type of revenue functions: a Knorr-Bremse EBS 1 Channel Module

From task assignment to defined workstations aspect, we can deduce two main behaviours. The first one is the fact that for a same disassembly alternative and same number of workstations, task assignment is different. This is the case of alternative B_1 B_4 B_{15} B_{34} B_{43} (*a*: B_1 B_4 assigned to workstation 1 then B_{15} B_{34} B_{43} to 2, *b*: same but B_{15} assigned to workstation 1). The second one concerns solution with the same workstations number and same revenue but different disassembly alternatives are retained as optimal. Alternatives B_1 B_6 B_8 B_{20} B_{34} B_{43} and B_3 B_8 B_{10} B_{20} B_{34} B_{43} with objective value of 71298.5 present such an example. Furthermore, hazardous tasks are assigned to workstations in a manner to be, as possible, grouped in the same workstation and as possible such a workstation is located at the beginning of the designed line to minimize risk of hazardous material accidents and avoid accident risk propagation.

5 Discussion and Conclusion

The disassembly process plays a key role in the recovery of End-of-Life products. It allows, effectively, obtaining components and/or materials that can be reused or recycled with much more interesting recovery rates. To define effective disassembly and derive the economic benefits of the disassembly process, product quality and task processing times uncertainties must be taken into account. In order to provide an answer to this expectation, we presented in this work a decision tool on the disassembly process planning and line design handling the quality of the products to be disassembled and uncertainty of task times. The quality of a product is modeled using the Remaining Usage Potential (RUP) concept. RUP models the amount of use remaining before disassembling a product. At the beginning of the operation phase of a product, RUP has a value of 1; a value 0 of RUP means that the product must undergo a recycling of its material. The RUP is taken as a random variable with known normal probability distribution truncated on 0 and 1. Task processing times are also modeled as random variables with known normal distributions.

To model this problem, a stochastic program along with lower and upper bounding schemes are developed. The objective is to maximize the profit of the disassembly line to be designed. This is done by designing a line where cycle time constraints are jointly satisfied with at least a certain service level, $1 - \alpha$, fixed by the decision-maker. Line revenue is calculated as the difference between the revenue generated by recovered parts (subassemblies, components) and the line operation cost. The latter includes the workstations operation cost and additional cost of workstations handling hazardous parts. Subassemblies and components revenues are defined as functions of the RUP. All the possible disassembly alternatives of a product and the precedence relationships among tasks and subassemblies/components are modeled using an *and/or* graph.

The developed approach is evaluated and applied to an industrial instance: Knorr-Bremse EBS 1 Channel Module which represents a real case study, in the automotive part remanufacturing sector. The results show the applicability of the developed decision aiding tool in real disassembly context. In fact, the sensibility of results to the RUP, i.e. product quality, highlights 2 main points. First, the assessment of the product quality is mandatory for industrial issues, periodically not just ones, in order to re-optimize the disassembly level if it changes and, then, re-organize the disassembly line if required. Second, such assessment must be reliable and accurate. This requirement ensures the confidence in the results and thus in the industrial decision to be made.

Sensitivity of the results to the revenue leads, for industrial decision maker, to follow the resale price of the parts and raw materials. Disassembly level optimization should be redone when resale price evolves. The evolution of resale price is mainly market driven. Indeed, some market intelligence would allow anticipating resale price.

Finally, the computational time is short enough to give to the decision maker the opportunity to generate different disassembly alternatives and line configurations depending on the profit expected from the retrieved parts. The profit itself depends on the quality of the products. This model helps to make a decision on the disassembly alternative to be retained as disassembly process. Therefore, the choice between complete or partial disassembly can be made on the basis of economic arguments.

The modeling process and decision aiding tool presented can be easily adapted for more real life cases like End of Life Vehicles or Waste Electrical and Electronic Equipment. Undertaking such case studies is one of our future research objectives.

References

1. Bentaha, M.L., Battaïa, O., Dolgui, A.: A bibliographic review of production line design and balancing under uncertainty. IFAC-PapersOnLine **48**(3), 70–75 (2015)
2. Bentaha, M.-L., Voisin, A., Marangé, P.: Disassembly process planning under end-of-life product quality. In: Fortin, C., Rivest, L., Bernard, A., Bouras, A. (eds.) PLM 2019. IAICT, vol. 565, pp. 325–335. Springer, Cham (2019). https://doi.org/10.1007/978-3-030-42250-9_31
3. Bentaha, M.L., Battaïa, O., Dolgui, A.: Disassembly line balancing and sequencing under uncertainty. Procedia CIRP **15**, 239–244 (2014)
4. Bentaha, M.L., Battaïa, O., Dolgui, A.: A sample average approximation method for disassembly line balancing problem under uncertainty. Comput. Oper. Rese. **51**, 111–122 (2014)
5. Bentaha, M.L., Battaïa, O., Dolgui, A.: An exact solution approach for disassembly line balancing problem under uncertainty of the task processing times. Int. J. Prod. Res. **53**(6), 1807–1818 (2015)
6. Bentaha, M.L., Battaïa, O., Dolgui, A., Hu, S.J.: Second order conic approximation for disassembly line design with joint probabilistic constraints. Eur. J. Oper. Res. **247**(3), 957–967 (2015)
7. Bentaha, M.L., Dolgui, A., Battaïa, O., Riggs, R.J., Hu, J.: Profit-oriented partial disassembly line design: dealing with hazardous parts and task processing times uncertainty. Int. J. Prod. Res **56**, 1–23 (2018)

8. Bentaha, M.L., Voisin, A., Marangé, P.: A decision tool for disassembly process planning under end-of-life product quality. Int. J. Prod. Econ. **219**, 386–401 (2020)
9. Cheng, J., Lisser, A.: A second-order cone programming approach for linear programs with joint probabilistic constraints. Oper. Res. Lett. **40**(5), 325–328 (2012)
10. Deniz, N., Ozcelik, F.: An extended review on disassembly line balancing with bibliometric & social network and future study realization analysis. J. Clean. Prod. **225**, 697–715 (2019)
11. Galambos, J.: Bonferroni inequalities. Ann. Probab. **5**(4), 577–581 (1977)

Towards a Data Classification Model for Circular Product Life Cycle Management

Federica Acerbi(✉) and Marco Taisch

Department of Management, Economics and Industrial Engineering, Politecnico di Milano, via Lambruschini 4/b, 20156 Milan, Italy
{federica.acerbi,marco.taisch}@polimi.it

Abstract. Nowadays, due to the limited availability of resources, the adoption of sustainable practices is gaining importance, especially while dealing with the manufacturing sector that is considered one of the most resource greedy sectors. To cope with this issue, a new sustainable and industrial economy, called "circular economy" arisen. The diffusion of this economy can be eased by the advance management of data and information. Nevertheless, from the extant literature emerged some criticalities regarding information management flows while dealing with circular economy strategies adoption. Indeed, the present work aims to first identify the main criticalities in information management while adopting circular economy principles, and second to investigate the decisions, and the related data and information required to make these decisions, that manufacturers have to undertake to enable the circular product life cycle management. To achieve this goal, the present work relies on the scientific literature. This choice enables to grasp the widespread knowledge developed by scholars about these concepts, by individualizing the main decisions that should be taken by the company internal stakeholders, to manage circular products, being affected by external stakeholders' behaviours and decisions along product life cycle. Therefore, this work aims to support circular product life cycles management and, this objective has been achieved through the development of a data classification model.

Keywords: Circular economy · Product life cycle management · Decision-making process

1 Introduction

Nowadays, the huge increase in product demand by consumers is increasing the number of resources consumed, which leads to both municipal and industrial waste generation intensification [1]. To cope with this issue, some countermeasures have been proposed also by policymakers, among which the definition of the *sustainable development goals* that are urgent actions to be undertaken by the society as a whole [2]. Among these actions, it is stated the importance to promote a more responsible production and consumption, which is aligned with a new economy recently arisen. It is called "circular economy", being an industrial economy that is designed on purpose to be regenerative and restorative, is gaining importance for both scientific literature and

Published by Springer Nature Switzerland AG 2020
F. Nyffenegger et al. (Eds.): PLM 2020, IFIP AICT 594, pp. 473–486, 2020.
https://doi.org/10.1007/978-3-030-62807-9_38

industry [3]. Moreover, its adoption has been recently encouraged by policymakers too, in particular by the European Commission, through the promotion of new action plans [4]. Indeed, this economy aims to enable the efficient usage and restoration of resources by slowing, closing and narrowing resources loops [5] and, to address this goal, it is based on five main principles: (1) design out waste, (2) build resilience through diversity, (3) rely on energy from renewable resources, (4) think in systems and (5) waste is food [6].

To enable the successful implementation of this economy and fulfil the goal of regenerating resources at the end of their life cycle, manufacturers need to be aware about the importance to ensure an appropriate management of the entire product life cycle [7]. Product life cycle management is traditionally defined as "*the management of all the business processes and associated data generated by events and actions of various lifecycle agents (both human and software systems) and distributed along the product's lifecycle phases*" [8]. Under a circular economy perspective, even further, monitoring each stage of the product life cycle through adequate data gathering is gaining momentum. Indeed, considering that circular economy adoption is sustained also by appropriate information flows [9], the information and data required to be gathered should enable the producer to design the product in order to facilitate its subsequently circular management. Thus, by allowing, at the end of product life cycle, the wider possibility to reuse, remanufacture, recycle or regenerate somehow the product or its components. Indeed, in the present work, information and data considered to be gathered, should be made circulate with the objective to facilitate the closing of resource loops, and from this intention, the concept of "circular" product life cycle management.

Actually, in the extant literature, the most diffused barrier identified for the adoption of circular economy in manufacturing and thus, the appropriate management of product along their life cycles, regards data and information management [10]. Nevertheless, data and information are fundamentals to support an appropriate decision-making process [11], and in line with that are considered one of the most important resources in circular economy [9]. At the best of the authors' knowledge more narrowed researches have been performed to streamline information management, such as the ontological framework for Industrial Symbiosis [12] or for product life cycle management but without including circular economy considerations [13].

Being not yet developed a comprehensive work covering this barrier in circular economy, the present work aims to first envisage what are the main criticalities of information management while dealing with circular product life cycle management and second, it aims to identify the main decisions to be take and to clear out what are the most influencing stakeholders on the manufacturer decision process. All these findings will end up with the development of a preliminary data classification model. In particular, in the model are reported the most relevant decisions to be taken at the beginning of product life cycle which look towards the implications arising during the next stages of the product life cycle. Moreover, this contribution, with the model development, aims to put the basis for future researches towards the coverage of information management criticalities emerged in the extant scientific literature.

To conclude, the paper is structured as follows: (ii) Section 2 reports the main objective of the present work and, the used research methodology to address the objective, (iii) Section 3 presents the review developed about the major decisions required for the circular product life cycle management through which are highlighted the main information management criticalities, (iv) Section 4 the preliminary data classification model is proposed, explained and discussed as a result of the scientific literature review, (v) Section 5 figures-out suggestions for future researches and, the main limitations of the work.

2 Research Objective and Methodology

The present work aims to identify the main information management criticalities according to the extant scientific literature and to provide a first attempt of a data classification model, to put the basis to streamline information management and facilitate circular product life cycle management decision process. This objective is boosted by the barrier identified in the extant literature in terms of data and information management while adopting circular economy strategies.

This research objective has been addressed by relying on the scientific literature. In particular, Scopus was used as search engine, being it the most diffused engine in industrial engineering. It was queried by using the following keywords: ((("knowledge" OR "information" OR "data") AND "management") OR ("semantic*" OR "ontolog*" OR "data integr*")) AND ("circular economy" OR "close-loop") AND ("Remanufacturing" OR "Recycling" OR "Reuse" OR "Reduce" OR "Redesign" OR "Recover") AND "manufacturing". No-time frame was used and the only filter introduced was limiting the research on English-written documents. In the sample of papers identified, the ones selected for the analysis were those concerning products and their management under a circular economy perspective, the other were discarded being not coherent with the research focus.

Through the literature review it was possible to identify the most diffused criticalities regarding information management and to understand the knowledge, the information, and the data required to support the decision process in adopting circular economy strategies by manufacturing companies. Therefore, this review enabled to identify the major decisions that manufacturers have to take while dealing with circular product life cycle management and, to envisage the broad number of stakeholders involved along the product life cycle that concurrently affect the decision process. As it will be reported in the next sections, both external and internal stakeholders generally impact manufacturers decision process whenever circular economy strategies are adopted in manufacturing companies. In particular, internal stakeholders, e.g. business functions, need to take decisions at the beginning of the product life cycle by balancing their internal objectives and, by taking into account the external stakeholders' objectives and behaviours along the product life cycle.

Once these decisions had been defined and, the main stakeholders affecting these decisions were determined, it was possible to investigate what data were required in order to take the aforementioned decisions. Indeed, the decision process relies on specific knowledge, which requires to take into account the different behaviours and objectives of the stakeholders involved along the product life cycle. The key point ensuring to rely on the right knowledge is to have appropriate information that is gathered through specific data. This is the reason why data are gaining momentum in circular economy.

Last, through this review, a preliminary data classification model was developed to put the basis to cover the emerged criticalities, concerning information and data management, especially the semantic and the managerial ones.

3 A Review About Knowledge, Information, and Data Enabling Circular Product Life Cycle Management

In the extant scientific literature, one of the most diffused barriers, encountered by manufacturers in exploiting the potentialities of circular economy, concerns data and information management [10]. This is reflected in the creation, exchange, and exploitation of data and information [14], within and outside firms' boundaries, to support the manufacturers' decision-making process [11]. For years, end of life (EoL) strategies to enable resource loops have been addressed in the extant literature, since EoL it has been always considered the joint stage to ensure to close the loop. More recently, it has been understood how much the previous stages, Middle of Life (MoL) and Beginning of Life (BoL), influence the resource circularity potentialities [15]. Therefore, the appropriate management of the "end" of the product life cycle corresponds to the possibility to subsequently reintroduce waste, coming for the product, as a resource for a new cycle, but the product conditions at the EoL are affected by the design of the product [16] and the product usage [17]. From this, the importance to study the circular product life cycle management. This concept is close to the one of closed-loop product life cycle management [18] since, data are gathered from each stage of product life cycle to feedback the system, but in this case, the aim is to enable to facilitate the adoption of circular economy principles. Therefore, leveraging on the three standard moments of the product life cycle: BoL, MoL and EoL [19], from the extant literature it was observed the need to harness the knowledge gathered from each stage, to support the decision process of manufacturers by enabling them to design circular products and appropriate services [20] from the beginning. This would facilitate to empower the BoL towards product circularity, being this stage considered the one which determines most of the future environmental impacts [21]. Indeed, all the stakeholders impacting on the decision-making process of manufacturers should be considered from the foundation, to enable the producer to take adequate decisions [22], especially while dealing with the adoption of circular economy strategies in which the EoL is widely affected by the previous stages [15].

Starting from the product EoL, at this stage the product might be disposed becoming waste rather than reintroduced in a new cycle as a resource [23]. This latter requires to evaluate the product damage level and remaining useful life [24], once brought back, in order to decide whether it is possible its direct reuse or not. In case product direct reuse would not be possible, the second evaluation should concern the investigation about the possibility to disassemble the product together with the relative time and costs required [25]. In the case of a positive response, the evaluation is on the possibility to remanufacture the product and/or to recycle the product's components. These issues require respectively to find a supplier of substitute components to remanufacture the product ensuring the quality of the remanufactured product [26], and to find an industrial actor responsible to recycle the product components and materials. The reusability, re-manufacturability or recyclability of products might be affected by technical issues but also by consumers' demand for refurbished products [27], for this reason is required to be able to stimulate the market and thus, to create the demand of refurbished products through adequate marketing plans. All the choices taken at the EoL are also influenced by economic considerations, which are used to define whether a strategy could be adoptable or not and how the product could be designed in the future to ease its circularity [11, 28].

At the MoL stage, the product damage level and its remaining useful life are determined. Indeed, customers' behaviour impacts a lot on these issues. Nevertheless, customers' behaviours are affected on one side by their needs, expectations and personal income [21], but on the other side also by the services offered by the manufacturer itself to the user for extending the product life cycle [29]. The product quality maintenance is the target of the manufacturer actions while delivering maintenance services. Indeed, a deep analysis on the product, gathering data also from its life cycle, to investigate the potentialities to repair it or to substitute the ruined components is conducted in order to ensure its original conditions and extending its useful life [30].

Customers' behaviours at product MoL can be influenced by the right definition of product features and functionalities designed during the design phase [31] thus, defined at the BoL stage. To enable the uncontrollable disposal of still functional products, the product modularity should be designed to allow product updated and reuse. Moreover, to empower the product reverse flow, it is first necessary to design the appropriate closed-loop networks [32], but together with this, a successful outcome is also influenced by the product features. Indeed, specific features should be thought at the design phase, such as the possibility to disassemble the product [15] either to substitute not functioning components by remanufacturing the product [33] or to recycle the components [34]. This latter case depends also on the type of material used, recyclable and not toxic, that inevitably is reflected in the selection of the right supplier [35]. Indeed, at BoL, to enable the reverse flow of resources, the design and the procurement functions should be aligned with the other stakeholders' objectives, and in addition the decisions taken should be also coherent with the environmental regulations proposed by the governments and should encounter the relevant standards, such as the ISO [36]. Among the product features, also product dimensions should be designed to be aligned not only with customers' requirements, but also with logistics and transportation requirements, in order to reduce avoidable pollution generation by optimizing the transports [37]. Last, during the production process, the decisions to be taken regard the goal to sustain cleaner production processes. In line with that, the industrial waste generated should be analysed in order to evaluate whether to reuse waste [38] or sell it as a resource to someone else establishing for instance industrial symbiosis [39]. Wrapping up, at product BoL, product features should be thought to encounter all the next stages emerging requirements. Therefore, it is of relevant importance to ensure product high quality levels by adding appropriate services to support its maintenance after selling and to design appropriate spare parts to maximise the extension of the product life cycle. In addition, further efforts must be done in designing a product to enable its future refurbishment and its possible re-design, to allow the company to be always aligned with market needs.

To conclude, having analysed each stage of the product life cycle and having determined the most relevant decisions to be taken, it was possible to individualize the main criticalities related to information management according to the extant scientific literature. Indeed, due to these criticalities the decision processes is limited and this overall complex mechanism to ensure circular product life cycle is constrained. The criticalities emerged are: technical, managerial and semantic.

- Technical criticality: data and information integration inter- and intra- firms' information systems [24] along the product life cycle [40].
  Advanced technologies might support product and material traceability such as the blockchain [37], and also more traditional information systems should be designed to enable systems integration, for instance, the Enterprise Resource Planning (ERP) might be used to support product recovery [41]. In both of the cases, the integration with other systems is important to efficiently use them.
- Managerial criticality: data and information sharing inter- and intra-firms [39, 42]. Indeed, information sharing inter films requires that the entire company would be involved to efficiently embrace this new paradigm. In particular, the top management should promote a common direction, towards circularity, and all the other functions should be aligned with that. For instance, procurement should select the right materials in alignment with the business finance department budgetary constraints and the design department requests, which depend on marketing analysis. Moreover, in order to pursue the right direction, external industrial companies, affecting the business, need to be aligned with the company under analysis. For instance, the suppliers selected need to embrace common values of the supplied one.
- Semantic criticality: there is a lack of data and information standardization, which is reflected in the need to develop a common language sharable among different entities [39, 43]. This is a fundamental aspect to be considered in order to ensure efficient information sharing.

Some attempts to cover these criticalities, and structure these data, have been proposed by scholars. For instance, the ontology thought to develop an eco-industrial parks platform in order to manage input and output flows of resources through a standard language [44], and the knowledge management model for Product-Service System enabling to reuse and share explicit and tacit knowledge through knowledge standardization [45]. Nevertheless, for the discrete industry very few has been done [46] and further studies are required to be developed to encounter all the circular economy principles in discrete manufacturing companies, being heterogeneous the information and data regarding the discrete industry [43].

4 Results and Discussion: Data Classification Model for Circular Product Life Cycle Management

Based on the results of the literature review, summarized in Table 1, it is possible to highlight the main decisions to be taken and to derive the major data required to support the decision-making process of manufacturers in charge of the design and production process, thus involved at BoL of the product life cycle. This enabled to put the basis to cover the information management criticalities, especially regarding the managerial and semantic ones.

In line with the information management criticalities, the first result emerged from the extant scientific literature is related to the heterogeneity of the clusters of stakeholders involved along the product life cycle. These are not only internal to the company, such as the company's functions, but also external, as governments, customers and suppliers (see Fig. 1).

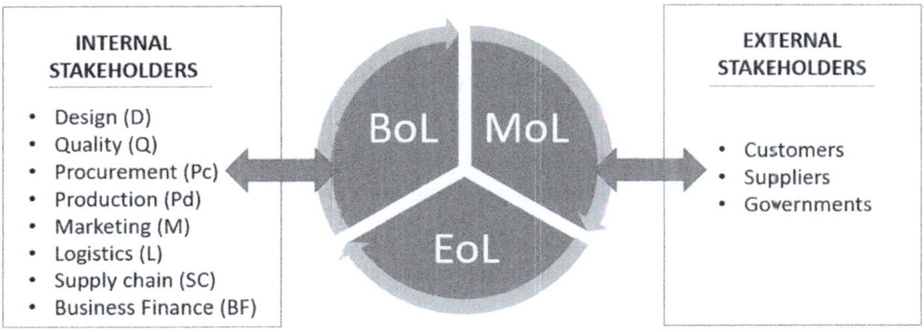

Fig. 1. Internal and external stakeholders impacting manufacturers decision process along the product life cycle

In particular, on the basis of what emerged from the review, the internal stakeholders involved in the circular product life cycle management are aligned with those already reported in the literature of product life cycle [47] but with a different shadow. In the present work, internal stakeholders are defined as follows:

- The *design department* is in charge of engineering and designing the product by defining product characteristics aligned with circular economy principles. This department is affected by customers' needs and requirements, economic constraints and governments regulations. Indeed, it must be highly aligned with marketing department and should direct the choices of procurement department.
- The *quality department* is in charge of monitoring the quality of materials and products, either just produced or turned back. It is influenced by the production, the feedbacks from the customers and thus, the data gathered by the marketing department.
- The *procurement department* is in charge of selecting appropriate suppliers and the related adequate materials or components in line with circular economy principles. This department is influenced by the design department and the business finance since it must be aligned with what defined by designers and its budget is constraints by economic objectives.
- The *production department* is in charge of producing the product by respecting environmental standards and circular economy principles. This department is influenced by the design and the governments.
- The *marketing department* is in charge of taking care of customers' expectations and demand. This department works highly close to the market and thus, it must be

aligned with what is requested by customers and has to boost they requests in terms of "circular" products.

- The *logistics department* is in charge of enabling all the transportations required to reach the customers and, also all the transportations required to enable the reverse flow of products and other resources.
- The *supply chain department* is in charge of establishing the right relationships with external companies. In particular, in the present work, this department is responsible for not only manage the relationships with the actors involved in the traditional supply chain but also establishing the right partnerships with other external actors in order to enable the exchange of waste, by-products and other resources.
- The *business finance department* is in charge of establishing the economic objectives and constraints to be set for all the other company's functions.

On the other side, in the present work, it is supposed to not have intermediaries, indeed the main external stakeholders are three and, are defined as follows:

- The *consumers* are the final end-users of the product. They are responsible to do not dispose the product once it has no more value according to them and to enable its reverse flow.
- The *suppliers* are those which provide the producer with the right materials and components to enable product development and ensure product circularity.
- The *governments* which dictate the most rigid rules and regulations to be respected. These are more than one since foreign markets might follow different regulations under different governments.

Considering the objective of enabling circular product life cycle management, both internal and external stakeholders emerged to be important to determine all the information required at BoL. Indeed, this enables to take into account all the implications, criticalities and requirements that might be encountered along the other stages of the product life cycle that could limit the closing of the resources loop.

In Table 1 are reported the most relevant decisions, emerged from the scientific literature, to be undertaken at BoL by the product producer thus, by its internal stakeholders. As visible, these decisions are taken internally by the different functions, which are influenced one another and need to be able to balance their choices due to the not always aligned objectives. Indeed, their objectives and choices are also affected by external stakeholders' behaviors, objectives, and decisions that are involved along the product life cycle. Therefore, the data classification model reported in Table 1 enables to envisage the decisions which, if not taken at the BoL, would arise subsequently in the next phases by limiting product circularity. Indeed, this enables to prevent the product to not be able to meet circular economy principles and thus, it allows to limit the product disposal whenever the product itself or its components are still valuable if appropriately managed. Moreover, this model is a preliminary attempt to face at least the semantic and the managerial criticalities that emerged from the extant literature.

Relying on what has been envisioned in the literature, each decisions to be made requires specific data and these data are reported in Table 1 too. In the present work, data collection concerns only product and part-product data required along each stage of the life cycle, with the ultimate goal to extend the product lifetime starting from the product BoL and thus, to facilitate "circular product life cycle management".

Table 1. Data collection to support the decision-making process enabling a circular product life cycle management

Product life cycle stage	Decisions	Data	Internal stakeholders	External stakeholders
BoL	Definition of product features	– Materials – Dimensions – Requirements and governments standards	D, Pd, M	Customers, Governments
	Definition of industrial waste management practices and possible partners	– Type of scrap generated – Quantity of scrap generated – Type of by-products generated – Quantity of by-products generated	Pd, SC	Governments
	Definition of product functionalities	– Customer needs and requirements	D, M	Customers
	Definition of circular product requirements	– Parts product to be disassembled – Recyclable material – Non-toxic material – Environmental governments requirement	D	Customers, Governments
	Sustainable supplier selection	– Material recyclability – Environmental standards of the supplier	Pc	Suppliers
	Definition of the final market	– Customers quantity demand	L, Pc, M	Customers
	Definition of standards to be adopted	– Environmental ISO	BF, M, Pc	Governments
	Definition of economic constraints	– Material costs – Production costs – Marketing costs		Customers, Suppliers
MoL	Definition of guidelines to help end-users to circularly manage products	– Part components description – Material compositions	M	Customers
	Definition of unsold products management practices	– Quantity of unsold products – Seasonality of unsold products	M	Customers
	Definition of after-sales services	– Spare parts characteristics – Repair activities description	M, D	Customers

(continued)

Table 1. (*continued*)

Product life cycle stage	Decisions	Data	Internal stakeholders	External stakeholders
EoL	Definition of end-of-life practice	– Quantity of products brought back – Quality of products brought back – Parts to be disassembled – Parts to be substituted – Parts to be remanufactured – Parts to be disposed – Costs of the different scenarios	L, Q, Pc, BF	Customers

5 Conclusions and Limitations

The present work aims to put the basis to streamline information management to enable circular product life cycle management. In particular, the paper identifies the major criticalities related to information management under a circular economy perspective and analyses the main decisions to be taken during the BoL of product, that emerged to be the most important stage in circular product life cycle management. This analysis enabled the development of a data classification model that has been designed to create the ground to face the criticalities that emerged from this review, especially the semantic and the managerial ones. Therefore, it represents the starting point to define a common language, at least exploitable within firm's boundaries, with the final goal to extend the model to finally standardize product data to ease circular product life cycle management.

Indeed, the main results of this contribution are the development of this data classification model and the identification of the role of the stakeholders involved along circular product life cycle management. The data reported in the model are the minimum requirements to be considered while dealing with circular product life cycle management. This is the first attempt that lays the foundation for a holistic data classification model, aiming to face the major criticalities that emerged from the review (e.g. technical, managerial and semantic) and thus, aiming to support the manufacturers complex decision process affected by heterogeneous stakeholders. Therefore, it has been highlighted that different company's functions necessitate to cooperate to enable the product final reintroduction in a new cycle and, many external stakeholders influence the circularity of the product. More in detail, design, quality, procurement, production, marketing, logistics, supply chain and business finance represent the most relevant functions covering a prominent position in the circular product life cycle management; while the most relevant external stakeholders are the customers, the suppliers and the governments. This requires to horizontally and vertically align the decision process in manufacturing companies and to include appropriate tools and to standardize information to enable the interoperability and the streamlining of the information flows also outside companies' boundaries.

In terms of limitations of the contribution, the focus of the present work is on product data, while the context in which manufacturers necessitate to operate is broader. This implies on one side to consider, for future researches, also process data and other sources of data thus, to take into account all the stakeholders along the entire supply chain, also externally to the firms, such as intermediaries between producers and final consumers. On the other side, it is required to include in future researches also other implications impacting the circular product life cycle decision process, such as the emissions generated to refurbish a product or to recycle the material, and the localization of the suppliers/retailers/consumers.

Moreover, to furtherly validate this primary result, concerning product data classification, this model should be applied on an empirical case and a performance indicator should be developed to demonstrate the benefits of the model.

Regarding future researches, first, being CE a driver for sustainable development, it must not be neglected to cover the three sustainable pillars (i.e. environmental, social and economic). Indeed, data sources and data requirements must be furtherly analyzed in light of this model to include all the pillars. In the reference literature, based on the above mentioned keywords, few contributions have investigated in detail economic issues and thus, further researches should be developed.

Second, as emerged from the scientific literature, one of the information management criticalities is the managerial one and, the decisions that the producers have to take might regard different levels within the organization such as strategic, tactical and operational. Indeed, in future researches, in order to provide a concrete tool exploitable by manufacturers, the sources of data must be analyzed looking at these three hierarchical levels.

Last, another criticality emerged is the technical one thus, more technologically oriented researches should be developed in order to identify what are the potentialities of traditional and more advanced technologies to support circular product life cycle management in light of this model. It is worth's to underline that an extensive literature has been already developed about Product Life Cycle Management systems, nevertheless, other traditional or industry 4.0 related technologies and software might be studied in light of these new circular requirements. Out of the possibilities, enterprise resource planning (ERP) and customer relationship management (CRM) systems might be integrated to streamline the information flows and facilitate resources loops. In addition, simulation and sensorized systems, if appropriately integrated, could even further support decision process relying on appropriate data gathering.

References

1. OECD: Global Material Resources Outlook to 2060. OECD (2019)
2. United Nations: About the Sustainable Development Goals - United Nations Sustainable Development. Sustainable Development Goals (2019). https://www.un.org/sustainabledevelopment/sustainable-development-goals/
3. The Ellen MacArthur Foundation: Towards the circular economy Economic and business rationale for an accelerated transition (2012)
4. European Commission: Circular Economy Action Plan (2020)

5. Bocken, N., Miller, K., Evans, S.: Assessing the environmental impact of new circular business models. In: "New Business Models" - Exploring a Changing View on Organizing Value Creation – Toulouse, France, 16–17 June 2016 (2016)
6. The Ellen MacArthur Foundation: Towards the circular economy-opportunities for the consumer goods sector, vol. 2 (2013)
7. Sassanelli, C., Rossi, M., Pezzotta, G., Pacheco, D.A.D.J., Terzi, S.: Defining Lean Product Service Systems (PSS) features and research trends through a systematic literature review. Int. J. Prod. Lifecycle Manage. 12, 37–61 (2019)
8. Matsokis, A., Kiritsis, D.: An ontology-based approach for Product Lifecycle Management. Comput. Ind. **61**(8), 787–797 (2010)
9. Valkokari, P., Tura, N., Ståhle, M., Hanski, J., Ahola, T.: Advancing Circular Business (2019)
10. Acerbi, F., Sassanelli, C., Terzi, S., Taisch, M.: Towards a data-based Circular Economy: exploring opportunities from Digital Knowledge Management Research context. In: Proceedings of the 6th European Lean Educator Conference (2019)
11. Nagiligari, B.K., Shah, J., Sha, Z., Thirugnanam, S., Jain, A., Panchal, J.: Integrated Part Classification for Product Cost and Complexity Reduction (2014)
12. Gómez, A.M.M., González, F.A., Bárcena, M.M.: Smart eco-industrial parks: a circular economy implementation based on industrial metabolism. Resour. Conserv. Recycl. **135**, 58–69 (2018)
13. Matsokis, A., Kiritsis, D.: An ontology-based approach for Product Lifecycle Management. Comput. Ind. **61**(8), 787–797 (2010)
14. Romero, D., Molina, A.: Reverse - green virtual enterprises and their breeding environments: closed-loop networks. In: IFIP Advances in Information and Communication Technology, vol. 408, pp. 589–598 (2013)
15. Marconi, M., Germani, M.: An end of life oriented framework to support the transition toward circular economy, vol. 5 (2017)
16. Lieder, M., Asif, F.M.A., Rashid, A., Mihelič, A., Kotnik, S.: Towards circular economy implementation in manufacturing systems using a multi-method simulation approach to link design and business strategy. Int. J. Adv. Manuf. Technol. **93**(5-8), 1953–1970 (2017). https://doi.org/10.1007/s00170-017-0610-9
17. Wastling, T., Charnley, F., Moreno, M., Wastling, T., Charnley, F., Moreno, M.: Design for circular behaviour: considering users in a circular economy. Sustainability **10**(6), 1743 (2018)
18. Guo, W., Zheng, Q., Zuo, B., Shao, H.: A Closed-loop PLM Model for Lifecycle Management of Complex Product (2018)
19. Dunque Ciceri, N., Garetti, M., Terzi, S.: Product lifecycle management approach for sustainability. In: Proceedings of the 19th CIRP Design Conference – Competitive Design (2009)
20. Ramanujan, D., Chandrasegaran, S.K., Ramani, K.: Visual analytics tools for sustainable lifecycle design: current status, challenges, and future opportunities. J. Mech. Design Trans. ASME **139**(11) (2017). American Society of Mechanical Engineers (ASME)
21. Laurenti, R., Sinha, R., Singh, J., Frostell, B.: Some pervasive challenges to sustainability by design of electronic products - a conceptual discussion. J. Clean. Prod. **108**, 281–288 (2015)
22. Baran, J.: Designing a circular product in the light of the semantic design areas (2017)
23. Bernon, M., Tjahjono, B., Ripanti, E.F.: Aligning retail reverse logistics practice with circular economy values: an exploratory framework. Prod. Plan. Control **29**(6), 483–497 (2018)
24. Gan, S.-S.: The Conceptual Framework of Information Technology Adoption Decision-making in a Closed-loop Supply Chain (2019)

25. Yang, Y., Chen, L., Jia, F., Xu, Z.: Complementarity of circular economy practices: an empirical analysis of Chinese manufacturers. Int. J. Prod. Res. **57**, 6369–6384 (2019)
26. Sitcharangsie, S., Ijomah, W., Wong, T.C.: Decision makings in key remanufacturing activities to optimise remanufacturing outcomes: a review. J. Clean. Prod. **232**, 1465–1481 (2019)
27. Kumar, S., Luthra, S., Haleem, A.: Customer involvement in greening the supply chain: an interpretive structural modeling methodology. J. Ind. Eng. Int. **9**, 6 (2013)
28. Hasegawa, S., Kinoshita, Y., Yamada, T., Bracke, S.: Life cycle option selection of disassembly parts for material-based CO2 saving rate and recovery cost: analysis of different market value and labor cost for reused parts in German and Japanese cases. Int. J. Prod. Econ. **213**, 229–242 (2019)
29. Liang, J.S.: A process-based automotive troubleshooting service and knowledge management system in collaborative environment. Robot. Comput. Integr. Manuf. **61**, 101836 (2020)
30. Zhang, Z., Liu, G., Jiang, Z., Chen, Y.: A cloud-based framework for lean maintenance, repair, and overhaul of complex equipment. J. Manuf. Sci. Eng. Trans. ASME **137**(4) (2015)
31. Chen, Z., Huang, L.: Application review of LCA (Life Cycle Assessment) in circular economy: From the perspective of PSS (Product Service System) Procedia CIRP **83**, 210–217 (2019)
32. Accorsi, R., Manzini, R., Pini, C., Penazzi, S.: On the design of closed-loop networks for product life cycle management: economic, environmental and geography considerations. J. Transp. Geogr. **48**, 121–134 (2015)
33. Tolio, T., et al.: Design, management and control of demanufacturing and remanufacturing systems. CIRP Ann. **66**(2), 585–609 (2017)
34. de Sousa Jabbour, A.B.L., et al.: Circular economy business models and operations management. J. Clean. Prod. **235**, 1525–1539 (2019)
35. Pal, R., Sandberg, E.: Sustainable value creation through new industrial supply chains in apparel and fashion. In: IOP Conference Series: Materials Science and Engineering, vol. 254, no. 20 (2017)
36. Shaharudin, M.R., Govindan, K., Zailani, S., Tan, K.C., Iranmanesh, M.: Product return management: linking product returns, closed-loop supply chain activities and the effectiveness of the reverse supply chains. J. Clean. Prod. **149**, 1144–1156 (2017)
37. Kouhizadeh, M., Sarkis, J., Zhu, Q.: At the nexus of blockchain technology, the circular economy, and product deletion. Appl. Sci. **9**(8), 1712 (2019)
38. Zhu, J., Chertow, M.R.: Greening industrial production through waste recovery: 'comprehensive utilization of resources' in China. Environ. Sci. Technol. **50**(5), 2175–2182 (2016)
39. Raabe, B., et al.: Collaboration platform for enabling industrial symbiosis: application of the by-product exchange network model. Procedia CIRP **61**, 263–268 (2017)
40. Ren, S., Zhang, Y., Liu, Y., Sakao, T., Huisingh, D., Almeida, C.M.V.B.: A comprehensive review of big data analytics throughout product lifecycle to support sustainable smart manufacturing: a framework, challenges and future research directions. J. Clean. Prod. **210**(10), 1343–1365 (2019)
41. Oltra-Badenes, R., Gil-Gomez, H., Guerola-Navarro, V., Vicedo, P.: Is it possible to manage the product recovery processes in an ERP? Analysis of functional needs. Sustainability **11**(16), 4380 (2019)
42. Masi, D., Day, S., Godsell, J.: Supply chain configurations in the circular economy: a systematic literature review. Sustainability (Switzerland) **9**(9), 1602 (2017). MDPI AG
43. Halstenberg, F.A., Lindow, K., Stark, R.: Utilization of product lifecycle data from PLM systems in platforms for industrial symbiosis. Procedia Manuf. **8**, 369–376 (2017)

44. Martín Gómez, A.M., Aguayo González, F., Marcos Bárcena, M.: Smart eco-industrial parks: a circular economy implementation based on industrial metabolism. Resour. Conserv. Recycl. **135**, 58–69 (2018)
45. Xin, Y., Ojanen, V., Huiskonen, J.: Knowledge management in product-service systems - a product lifecycle perspective. Procedia CIRP **73**, 203–209 (2018)
46. Nagiligari, B.K., Shah, J., Sha, Z., Thirugnanam, S., Jain, A., Panchal, J.: Integrated part classification for product cost and complexity reduction. In: Volume 1A: 34th Computers and Information in Engineering Conference (2014)
47. Terzi, S., Bouras, A., Dutta, D., Garetti, M., Kiritsis, D.: Product lifecycle management – from its history to its new role. Int. J. Prod. Lifecycle Manage. **4**(4), 360–389 (2010)

Maturity Implementation and Adoption

Preliminary Analysis of the Behavioural Intention to Use a Risk Analysis Dashboard Through the Technology Acceptance Model

Jean-Marc Vasnier[2](✉), Nicolas Maranzana[1], Norlaily Yaacob[3], Mourad Messaadia[2], and Ameziane Aoussat[1]

[1] Arts et Metiers Institute of Technology, LCPI, HESAM Université, 75013 Paris, France

[2] CESI, 1 Bd de l'Université, CS 70152, 44603 Saint-Nazaire, France
jmvasnier@cesi.fr

[3] Coventry University, Vancouver, UK

Abstract. In the age of the fourth industrial revolution, the competition between Small and Medium-sized Enterprises (SMEs) is fierce to operate efficiently and hold on to their customers. Due to lack of time and methodology, SME leaders are struggling to establish optimized strategies for their businesses. One way is by using dashboards that will proactively help to collect data, make decisions, facilitate the strategy implementation and keep the employees focused. This article aims at determining the suitability of the Technology Acceptance Model to the design of risk analysis dashboard and examining the influence between the model constructs.

Keywords: Technology acceptance model · Dashboard · SME · Partial least squares

1 Introduction

In the age of the fourth industrial revolution, Small and Medium-sized Enterprises (SMEs) are competing to improve their efficiency while retaining the interests of their customers. Unfortunately, many SME leaders have difficulties in establishing an optimized and coherent strategy due to lack of time, methodology and/or know-how. Too often, they react to changes in the environment by taking short-term actions, without worrying too much about their relevance to the overall strategy, or the consequences that such decisions can have on the future development of their business. Also, the growth of a business depends on its ability to identify and adapt to its environment risks, and then continuously measuring the performance of its key processes. However, this approach has little impact on a company's profitability unless employees interact with its performance dashboards and take actions based on the data collected (Grant et al. 2016; Velcu-Laitinen and Yigitbasioglu 2012). Hence, a good fit between the dashboard design features, its ease of use and its usefulness, should generate a positive predisposition among its users. The Technology Acceptance Model (TAM) has been used extensively in the last decades as the success of a new

F. Nyffenegger et al. (Eds.): PLM 2020, IFIP AICT 594, pp. 489–499, 2020.
https://doi.org/10.1007/978-3-030-62807-9_39

technology can be determined by its user acceptance, measured by three constructs: Perceived Usefulness (PU), Perceived Ease of Use (PEOU), and Attitude Towards Usage (ATU) of the system (Davis et al. 1989). Therefore, the purpose of this study is (i) to examine the relationship of employee' behavioural intention to use a risk analysis dashboard with the above constructs; and (ii) to develop a general model of risk analysis dashboard acceptance.

From these observations, emerged the following research question: *Does the Technology Acceptance model is appropriate to analyse the employees' behavioural intention to use a risk analysis dashboard?* In pursuit of this aim, this paper introduces the concept of dashboard, then presents the Technological Acceptance Model (TAM) with its relevance to the design of dashboard. The proposed research model is introduced, followed by the research methodology, data analysis, results and research findings. Finally, this paper concludes by pointing out the future research directions.

2 Outline

2.1 Dashboard

The term dashboard comes from the dashboard of a vehicle as it presents the metrics that the driver needs to know. Similarly, dashboards also presents information from which managers and employees can visually identify trends, patterns and anomalies about the company (Velcu-Laitinen and Yigitbasioglu 2012). Dashboards have three fundamental purposes: to monitor critical activities and processes using metrics that trigger alerts when performance falls short of established goals, to analyse the root causes of problems by exploiting relevant and timely data, to manage people and processes to improve decisions and lead the organization in the right direction (Eckerson et al. 2011). According to Tezel, the use of visual tools in a SME has multiple benefits such as improving transparency, facilitating routine job tasks, influencing people's behaviours, fostering continuous improvement, creating shared ownership, supporting management by facts, and removing organisational boundaries (Tezel et al. 2016).

2.2 Dashboard Design Features

Bititci et al. (2016) presents a classification for dashboards, depending on the level (strategic or operational) and the theme (planning or progress). Dashboard are characterised by two types of design features: functional and visual features. Functional features allow a cognitive adjustment with different types of users, while the visual features refer to how efficiently and effectively information is presented to the user. Table 1 summarizes the dashboard design features identified in the literature (Abduldae and Gravell 2019; Yigitbasioglu and Velcu 2012; Brandy et al. 2017; Rahman et al. 2017).

Table 1. Summary of dashboard design features

Functional features	Visual features
Drill-down capabilities	Display information on a single page
Scenario analysis	High data to ink ratio
Real-time notifications and alerts	Use of grid lines for 2D and 3D graphs
Format type (graphs vs tables)	Frugal use of colours (prefer intensity) and keep graphical icons sparse
Format flexibility and interactivity (to be able to display data in various formats and at different levels of aggregation)	Improve the context of metrics (performance state, trend and variance)

2.3 Technology Acceptance Model (TAM)

Technology Acceptance Model (TAM) was introduced by Fred Davis in 1986 and it is specifically tailored for modeling users' acceptance of information systems or technologies. Dashboards can be designed in a variety of ways, in our case the user wants to get specific piece of information about the results of the risk analysis and uses the dashboard to obtain it. As a result, the design and the visualization style must respond to some aspects of TAM (Janes et al. 2013). TAM is built on the Theory of Reasoned Action, positioning Perceived Usefulness (PU) and Perceived Ease Of Use (PEOU) as the main determinants of Behavioural Intention to Use (BIU) and Attitude Towards Usage (ATU) (as shown in Fig. 1). Perceived Usefulness is defined as "the degree to which a person believes that using a particular system would enhance his or her performance" (Davis et al. 1989). Perceived Ease Of Use refers to "the degree to which a person believes that using a particular system would be free of effort" (Davis et al. 1989). PU and PEOU have demonstrated high reliability, validity (Venkatesh 1996) and have received empirical support for being robust in predicting technology adoption for a variety of technologies such as ERP, e-book, smartwatch, E-payment, driving assistance systems or Dashboard Design (Janes et al. 2013).

TAM proposes that a higher level of PU and PEOU will lead to a higher level of positive Attitude Towards Usage (ATU) of that system, which finally indicates a higher degree of Behavioural Intention to Use (BIU) the system (Davis et al. 1989). Attitude Towards Usage refers to the "degree to which an individual evaluates and associates the target system with his or her job", while Behavioural Intention to Use is a "measure of the strength of one's intention to perform a specified behaviour" (Scholtz et al. 2016).

The literature review has revealed that the evaluation of dashboard using the Technology Acceptance Model is scarce (Rahman et al. 2017) hence the need to identify if the TAM framework is an appropriate tool for assessing employee's acceptance of a risk analysis dashboard (Vasnier et al. 2020).

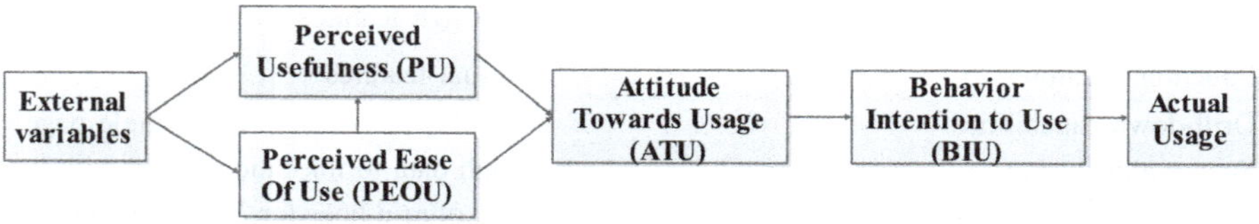

Fig. 1. Technology acceptance model (Davis et al. 1989)

3 Proposed Research Model and Hypotheses

In this section, we propose a research model that will analyse the employees' behavioural intention to use a risk analysis dashboard through the Technology Acceptance Model. In accordance with the research objectives and consistent with the related literature, this study examined the following hypotheses:

- H1: Dashboard Design Features positively affects Perceived Usefulness
- H2: Dashboard Design Features positively affects Perceived Ease Of Use
- H3: Dashboard Design Features affects Attitude Towards Usage
- H4: Perceived Usefulness positively affects Attitude Towards Usage
- H5: Perceived Ease of Use positively affects Attitude Towards Usage
- H6: Attitude Towards Usage has a positive affects on the Behavioural Intention to Use a risk analysis dashboard

Based on the Technology Acceptance Model (TAM), we derived our research model as shown in Fig. 2. The general hypothesis is that the Dashboard Design Features (DSF) have an impact on PU, PEOU and ATU of a risk analysis dashboard, which should indicates a strong impact on the Behavioural Intention to Use (BIU).

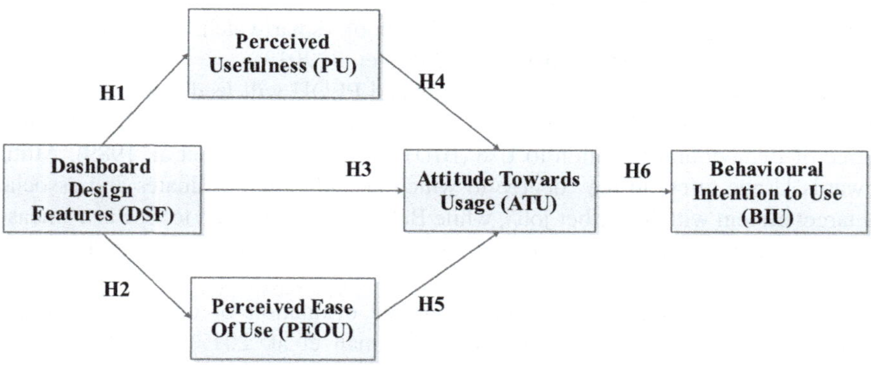

Fig. 2. Proposed research model

4 Case Study

4.1 Questionnaire Design

An internet-based survey[1] was conducted to explore the Attitude Towards Usage and Behavioural Intention to Use of a risk analysis dashboard. To limit the self-selection bias and conflict of interest, the survey was distributed to several groups of executives enrolled in postgraduate programmes (n = 90). A response rate of 57% (n = 51) was obtained (89% male, 11% female) with a mean age of 34 years ($\sigma \approx 9$ years). All respondents completed the survey based on the survey items shown in Table 2 and a proposed risk analysis dashboard (Fig. 3). This dashboard was derived from brainstorming activities carried out by a group of 14 mature students enrolled in a Master of Engineering (MEng) programme (86% male, 14% female) with a mean age of 37 years ($\sigma \approx 7.5$ years). This dashboard display the results of an assessment made by a SME management team on the impact of environment risk factors (either threats or opportunities) to the main strategic dimensions (Vasnier et al. 2020).

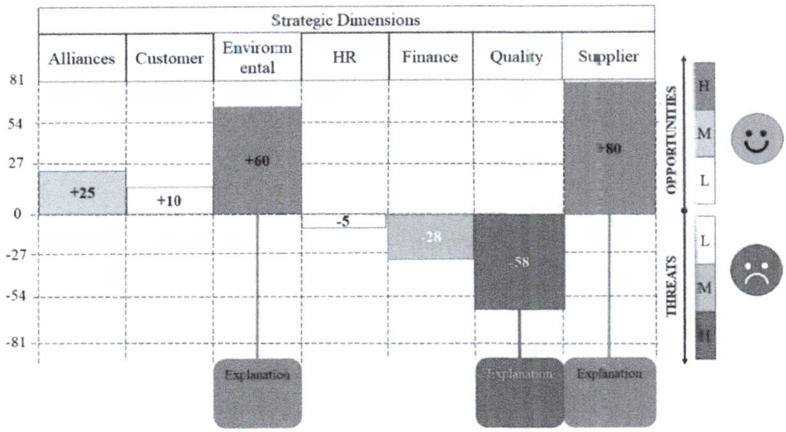

Fig. 3. The proposed risk analysis dashboard

The survey items are designed to capture the five constructs in the Proposed Design Dashboard Model (Fig. 2): Dashboard Design Features (DSF), Perceived Usefulness (PU), Perceived Ease Of Use (PEOU), Attitude Towards Usage (ATU) and Behavioural Intention to Use (BIU). Table 2 shows the grouping of the items under each construct. The TAM questionnaire was derived from Davis et al. (1989), Surendran (2012), Scholtz et al. (2016) and the Dashboard Design Features originated from the recommendations of Table 1.

[1] https://forms.gle/b43Eo5PMM92PA9V7.

Table 2. TAM questionnaire

Construct	Items	Survey items
Perceived Usefulness (PU)	PU1	This dashboard is effective in presenting the threats and the opportunities?
	PU2	Does the dashboard increase employee collaboration?
	PU3	The dashboard makes it possible to limit misunderstandings between the management and the employees?
	PU4	Does the dashboard increase the efficiency of employees?
	PU5	Overall, I find that the dashboard is useful?
Perceived Ease of Use (PEOU)	PEOU1	The dashboard is easy to understand and interpret?
	PEOU2	The interaction with the dashboard is simple and clear?
	PEOU3	The dashboard is easy to learn?
	PEOU4	The use of the dashboard requires little effort?
	PEOU5	Overall, the dashboard is easy to use?
Dashboard Design Features (DSF)	DSF1	Do the scores are prioritized?
	DSF2	Do the highest and lowest scores are explained?
	DSF3	Does each score is quantify by a number, a letter or other?
	DSF4	Does each score is strengthened by visual elements?
	DSF5	Does each score is interpretable using a global scale?
Attitude Towards Usage (ATU)	ATU1	I have a favourable attitude toward using those dashboards?
	ATU2	It will be a good idea to use these dashboards in my company?
	ATU3	Overall, I enjoyed using those dashboards?
	ATU4	I like the idea of using those dashboards?
Behavioural Intention to Use (BIU)	BIU1	I intend to use those dashboards in the future?
	BIU2	I intend to use those dashboards as often as possible?
	BIU3	I will recommend the use of those dashboards to my colleague?
	BIU4	If I had those dashboards in my company, I will adjust my priorities according to the information displayed?

All items were measured using a labelled seven-point Likert scale: Responses were coded from 1 (for 'Strongly Disagree') to 7 (for 'Strongly Agree'), so higher ratings indicated more positive attitudes.

4.2 Data Analysis and Results

The SmartPLS Version 3.0 software was used to analyse the data gathered from the survey. SmartPLS is one of the prominent software applications for Partial Least Squares Structural Equation Modeling (PLS-SEM). It has been deployed in many fields, such as behavioural sciences, marketing, business strategy and building information modelling (Enegbuma et al. 2015). Following the recommendations by other researchers (Chin 2010) the bootstrapping method (500 subsamples) was used to determine the significance levels of loadings, weights, and path coefficients.

The minimum sample size was identified at n = 55 by using the G*Power calculator with the setting as follows: effect size: $f^2 = 0.15$ (medium), $\alpha = 0.05$, number of predictors = 3 and a statistical power of 80% (Kwong and Wong 2013). The descriptive statistics of the five-construct items highlighted that all means are above the midpoint of 3.00 and the standard deviations ranged from 0.949 to 1.947.

Table 3. First-order constructs' reliability and validity

Constructs	CR	AVE
Perceived usefulness (PU)	0.896	0.635
Perceived ease of use (PEOU)	0.947	0.782
Dashboard design features (DSF)	0.760	0.397
Attitude Towards Usage (ATU)	0.971	0.894
Behavioural Intention to Use (BIU)	0.957	0.847

The Average Variance Extracted (AVE) and Composite Reliability (CR) measures of the five first order constructs are reported in Table 3. The measurements are acceptable if the AVE for each construct is greater than 0.50 and CR is greater than 0.70 (Hair et al. 2011). In this case, all items are loaded highly on their own latent variable, and thus all measurements have satisfactory levels of reliability.

The analysis of discriminate validity (Table 4) indicates a reasonably higher loading of each item on its intended construct than on any other constructs, to the exception of the very high correlation between DSF and PEOU (0,634), ATU and BIU (0,868). The calculation yielded Variation Inflation Factor (VIF) of 1.000 for both cases, which is less than 5. Therefore, it is confirmed that no multicollinearity exists among the constructs (Hair et al. 2011).

Table 4. Discriminate validity of first order constructs (Note: The diagonal represents the square root of AVE while the others entries represent le squared correlations)

	ATU	BIU	DSF	PEOU	PU
ATU	0.945				
BIU	0.868	0.920			
DSF	0.538	0.416	0.630		
PEOU	0.359	0.194	0.634	0.884	
PU	0.499	0.383	0.532	0.632	0.794

This study employed a structural equation modeling approach to develop a model that represents the relationships among the five constructs in this study: Perceived Usefulness (PU), Perceived Ease Of Use (PEOU), Dashboard Design Features (DSF), Attitude Towards Usage (ATU) and Behavioural Intention to Use (BIU) (Fig. 4).

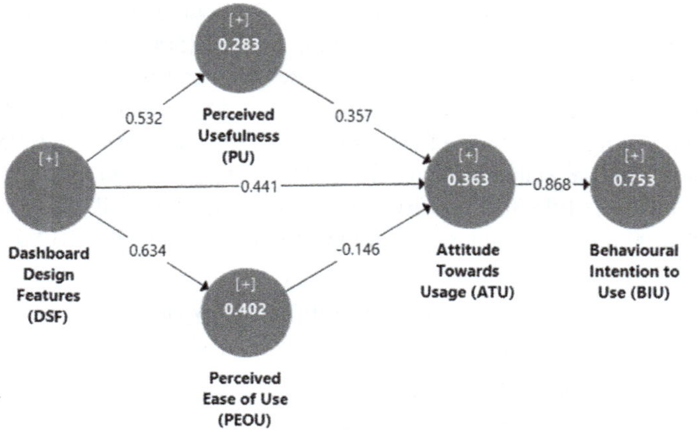

Fig. 4. Results of the proposed research model (from SmartPLS)

Table 5 presents the results of the hypotheses tests by confirming the presence of statistically significant relationship in the predicted axis of the proposed research model.

Table 5. Hypotheses testing results

Hypothesis	Relation	Path co-efficient	t value	p value	Result
H1	DSF → PU	0.532	6.436	0.000	Supported
H2	DSF → PEOU	0.634	7.546	0.000	Supported
H3	DSF → ATU	0.441	2.417	0.016	Supported
H4	PU → ATU	0.357	3.165	0.002	Supported
H5	PEOU → ATU	−0.146	0.655	0.512	Not supported
H6	ATU → BIU	0.868	17.651	0.000	Supported

Strong and statistically significant evidence were found in support of hypotheses H4 ($\beta = 0.357$, $p < 0.01$) and H3 ($\beta = 0.441$, $p < 0.01$). In addition, the results revealed that ATU strongly influences the users' BIU of risk analysis dashboard, with H6 ($\beta = 0.868$, $p < 0.01$) being supported. Hypothesis H2 ($\beta = 0.634$, $p < 0.01$) is supported which addresses the positive impact of the dashboard design features on PEOU. Statistically, significant support is found for H1 (DSF → PU, $\beta = 0.532$, $P < 0.01$), and this confirms previous studies reporting a positive effect of DSF on PU (Vasnier et al. 2020). However, H5 (PEOU → ATU, $\beta = -0.146$, $P > 0.05$) is not supported.

4.3 Findings and Discussion

The purpose of this study was to determine if the Technological Acceptance Model could be applied to the field of risk analysis Dashboard by examining the relationship between the five constructs: DSF, PU, PEOU, ATU and ultimately BIU.

- Consistent with prior research, PU has a significant effect on ATU. An explanation might be that when user perceive the risk analysis dashboard as one that is useful for their work, they have a positive attitude towards the usefulness of the tool.
- An interesting outcome of this research is the fact that the Dashboard design features have a strong effect on the Attitude Towards Usage of a risk analysis dashboard.
- The impact of PEOU on ATU was not found significant. This result is in correlation with the findings of Ramayah (Ramayah et al. 2017). This finding can be possibly attributed to the profile of the respondents that consists of mature and educated postgraduates. Presumably, the Perceived Usefulness and Dashboard Design Features are more critical to them than Perceived Ease of Use as they are decision makers.
- Hypothesis H2 is supported, i.e. the Dashboard Design Features (DSF) have a strong positive effect on PEOU.
- Furthermore, the role of ATU was found major in predicting the Behavioural Intention to Use a risk analysis dashboard. This provides support to the idea that the employees will use a risk analysis dashboard that is found useful and well designed.

5 Conclusion

This preliminary study has made several theoretical contributions to the use of the Technology Acceptance Model in the field of strategic dashboard application. Mainly, the statistical analysis validate the research question: Does the TAM is appropriate to analyse the employees' behavioural intention to use a risk analysis dashboard? It is interesting to note that the study showed that Attitude Towards Usage of a risk analysis dashboard is positively affected by the Perceived Usefulness and the Dashboard Design Features. Specifically, it identifies the strong influence of the construct Attitude Towards Usage towards the Behavioural Intention to Use a risk analysis dashboard. The "voice of the workers" in term of opinions about the design and use of a risk analysis dashboard was not the focus of this article. As a result, further research is required in assessing the workers' point of view, thus avoiding possible bias of employees from middle and top levels of management.

Finally, some further investigation are required to identify the strong effect of DSF on ATU by expanding the number of items investigated in the panel of functional and visual characteristics of a dashboard. Risk analysis dashboards sit at the crossroads of strategy formalization, data-capture, and decision-making. Carefully designed and deployed risk analysis dashboards can provide incisive strategic insight and enhance the alignment between the SME's strategy, its people, its organization and its processes.

References

Abduldaem, A., Gravell, A.: Principles for the design and development of dashboards: literature review. In: Proceedings of INTCESS 2019 - 6th International Conference on Education and Social Sciences, Dubai, 4–6 February 2019 (2019)

Bititci, U., Cocca, P., Ates, A.: Impact of visual performance management systems on the performance management practices of organisations. Int. J. Prod. Res. **54**, 1571–1593 (2016). https://doi.org/10.1080/00207543.2015.1005770

Brandy, A., Mantelet, F., Aoussat, A., Pigot, P.: Proposal for a new usability index for product design teams and general public. In: Proceedings of the 21st International Conference on Engineering Design (ICED17), Vol. 8, Human Behaviour in Design, Vancouver, Canada, 21–25 August 2017 (2017). https://doi.org/10.1080/09544820310001617711

Chin, W.W.: Bootstrap cross-validation indices for PLS path model assessment. In: Esposito Vinzi, V., et al. (eds.) Handbook of Partial Least Squares, pp. 83–97. Springer, Heidelberg (2010). https://doi.org/10.1007/978-3-540-32827-8_4

Davis, F.D., Bagozzi, R.P., Warshaw, P.R.: User acceptance of computer technology: a comparison of two theoretical models. Manage. Sci. **35**(8), 982–1003 (1989). https://doi.org/10.1287/mnsc.35.8.982

Eckerson, W.W.: Performance Dashboards: Measuring, Monitoring, and Managing Your Business, 2nd edn. Wiley, Hoboken (2011). https://doi.org/10.1002/9781119199984

Enegbuma, W.I., Ologbo, A.C., Aliagha, G.U., Ali, K.N.: Partial least square analysis of building information modelling impact in Malaysia. Int. J. Product Lifecycle Manage. **8**(4), 311–329 (2015). https://doi.org/10.1504/IJPLM.2015.075928

Grant, R.M.: Contemporary Strategy Analysis, Text and Cases Edition. Wiley, Hoboken (2016)

Hair, J.F., Ringle, C.M., Sarstedt, M.: PLS-SEM: indeed a silver bullet. J. Market. Theory Pract. **19**(2), 139–152 (2011). https://doi.org/10.2753/mtp1069-6679190202

Janes, A., Sillitti, A., Succi, G.: Effective dashboard design. Cutter IT J. **26**(1), 17–24 (2013)

Rahman, A.A., Adamu, Y.B., Harun, P.: Review on dashboard application from managerial perspective. In: 2017 International Conference on Research and Innovation in Information Systems (ICRIIS), pp. 1–5. IEEE (2017). https://doi.org/10.1109/icriis.2017.8002461

Ramayah, T., Yeap, J.A., Ahmad, N.H., Halim, H.A., Rahman, S.A.: Testing a confirmatory model of facebook usage in smartPLS using consistent PLS. Int. J. Bus. Innov. **3**(2), 1–14 (2017)

Scholtz, B., Mahmud, I., Ramayah, T.: Does usability matter? An analysis of the impact of usability on technology acceptance in ERP settings. Interdisc. J. Inf. Knowl. Manage. **11**, 309–330 (2016). https://doi.org/10.28945/3591

Surendran, P.: Technology acceptance model: a survey of literature. Int. J. Bus. Soc. Res. (IJBSR) **2**(4), 175–178 (2012). https://doi.org/10.18533/ijbsr.v2i4.161

Tezel, A., Koskela, L., Tzortzopoulos, P.: Visual management in production management: a literature synthesis. J. Manuf. Technol. Manage. **27**(6), 766–799 (2016). https://doi.org/10.1108/jmtm-08-2015-0071

Vasnier, J.M, Maranzana, N., Messaadia, M., Aoussat, A.: Preliminary design and evaluation of strategic dashboards through the technology acceptance model. In: International Design Conference–Design 2020, Dubrovnik, Croatia, 26–29 October (2020, to be published)

Velcu-Laitinen, O., Yigitbasioglu, O.M.: The use of dashboards in performance management: evidence from sales managers. Int. J. Digit. Account. Res. **12**, 36–58 (2012). https://doi.org/10.4192/1577-8517-v12_2

Venkatesh, V., Davis, F.D.: A model of the antecedents of perceived ease of use: development and test. Decis. Sci. **27**(3), 451–481 (1996). https://doi.org/10.1111/j.1540-5915.1996.tb01822.x

Yigitbasioglu, O.M., Velcu, O.: A review of dashboards in performance management: implications for design and research. Int. J. Account. Inf. Syst. **13**(1), 41–59 (2012). https://doi.org/10.1016/j.accinf.2011.08.002

Kwong, K., Wong, K.: Partial Least Squares Structural Equation Modeling (PLS-SEM) Techniques Using SmartPLS, Marketing Bulletin, vol. 24, Technical Note 1 (2013)

Challenges of Integrating Social Lifecycle Sustainability Assessment into Product Lifecycle Management - State of the Art -

Jing Lin[1](✉), Clotilde Rohleder[2], and Selmin Nurcan[3]

[1] Siemens PLM Software Inc., Digital Factory Division, Nuremberg, Germany
jinglin.nuernberg@yahoo.de

[2] Market Oriented Management, University of Applied Sciences, Constance, Germany
clotilde.rohleder@htwg-konstankz.de

[3] Centre de Recherche En Informatique, Université Paris 1 Panthéon-Sorbonne, Paris, France
nurcan@univ-paris1.fr

Abstract. Despite the importance of Social Life Cycle Sustainability Assessment (S-LCSA), little research has addressed its integration into Product Lifecycle Management (PLM) systems. This paper presents a structured review of relevant research and practice. Also, to address practical aspects in more detail, it focuses on challenges and potential for adoption of such an integrated system at an electronics company.

We began by reviewing literature on implementations of Social-LCSA and identifying research needs. Then we investigated the status of Social-LCSA within the electronics industry, both by reviewing literature and interviewing decision makers, to identify challenges and the potential for adopting S-LCSA at an electronics company. We found low maturity of Social-LCSA, particularly difficulty in quantifying social sustainability. Adoption of Social-LCSA was less common among electronics industry suppliers, especially mining & smelting plants. Our results could provide a basis for conducting case studies that could further clarify issues involved in integrations of Social-LCSA into PLM systems.

Keywords: Social Lifecycle Sustainability Assessment (S-LCSA) · Product Lifecycle Management (PLM) · Structured literature review · Social-LCSA integration into PLM system · Social-LCSA framework

1 Introduction

Increasingly pressure to improve sustainability comes from stakeholders such as society, non-profit-organizations (NPO), journalists, non-government-organizations (NGO), consumers and governments. Industries must respond, because production and products influence sustainability in at least three dimensions: economic, environmental and social. Industry must account for competition, changing markets that make the value

Published by Springer Nature Switzerland AG 2020
F. Nyffenegger et al. (Eds.): PLM 2020, IFIP AICT 594, pp. 500–513, 2020.
https://doi.org/10.1007/978-3-030-62807-9_40

chain a complex system, evolving laws and regulations. Manufacturing companies must undertake preventative approaches to environmental pollution within their manufacturing processes.

Consumers (C) and Government & Leadership (G) are playing increasingly active roles in achieving a sustainable world. Sustainability-driven manufacturing can provide a competitive advantage because it appeals to customers who value brand, image and reputation. Collaborative work increases the complexity of addressing sustainability. As shown in Fig. 1, Engineers & Designers (D), Manufacturer/Vendor (M) and Material Analyst (Ma), and other actors are involved in Sustainable World, cross-business functions. Globalization makes the situation more acute.

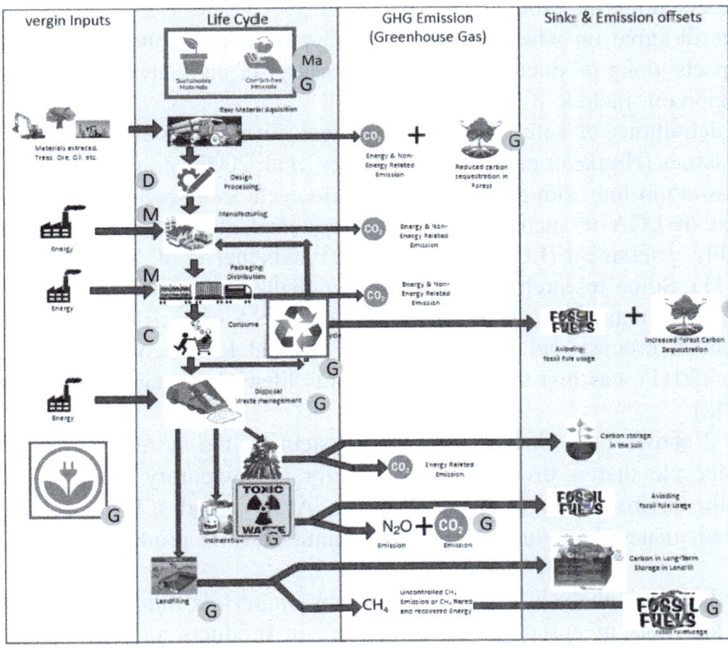

Fig. 1. Actors in sustainable world

A Life Cycle Assessment (LCA) tool can help determine impacts of products or systems over a range of environmental and resource issues. It measures all environmental impacts across the entire lifecycle. Currently, the most accepted framework and lifecycle-based approach for assessing a product's impacts on all three sustainability dimensions in an integrated way is Life Cycle Sustainability Assessment (LCSA). It is currently regarded as the only viable framework for comprehensive sustainability assessment of products. It can be understood as the evaluation of the combined positive and negative effects of a product over its entire lifecycle on the three dimensions of sustainability[1].

Life cycle sustainability assessment (LCSA) refers to the evaluation of all environmental, social and economic impacts in decision-making processes towards more sustainable products throughout their life cycles. This comprehensive assessment can be expressed by the following conceptual formula:[2]

$$[\mathrm{E-LCA}] + [\mathrm{S-LCA}] + [\mathrm{LCC}] = [\mathrm{LCSA}]$$

where E-LCA denotes the conventional environmental lifecycle assessment, Social-LCA (Social Life Cycle Assessment) represents the assessment of positive and negative social impacts along the product lifecycle.

Experts disagree on whether LCC (Life Cycle Costing), the assessment of economic impacts along product lifecycle, is necessary for an analysis. However, if cash flow is important, include it in the analysis [1].

Early definitions of Life Cycle Management covered environmental, social and economic issues (Hunkeler et al. 2004; Remmen et al. 2007) along a product lifecycle. These ideas are in line with developments in life cycle assessment that further expand the context of LCA to include social and economic elements under the life cycle sustainability assessment (LCSA) framework (Finkbeiner et al. 2010; Klöpffer 2008; UNEP 2011). Some researchers identified new challenges related to the criticality of materials (Sonnemann et al. 2015). Incorporating LCSA in decision-making processes at the product, process and individual organizational levels could maximize profit. Finkbeiner (2011) was first to describe the term "lifecycle sustainability management (LCSM)" [2].

Figure 2 shows LCA defines a product system by the system boundary and the product lifecycle that is divided into stages for the inventory analysis (LCI). LCI considers the environmental inputs and outputs. At the broadest level four stages may be identified: material production, product manufacturing, product use, and product disposal.

In the lifecycle analysis of product systems, *materials information* is necessary wherever materials are used in manufacturing, in products, or needed as ancillary inputs. Hence, materials data are essential to an LCI and to a full LCA. Materials should be selected in each PLM stage to enable tracking and sustainability checks along PLM. Figure 3 shows how we propose to align PLM with the material life cycle, since the product and materials cycles are parallel and intersecting. Some researchers have recommended enabling PLM for Material Selection because the potential of using PLM for material selection is great; e.g. Gabi…

---

[1] Source: UNEP (2012) Social Life Cycle Assessment and Life Cycle Sustainability Assessment.

[2] https://www.lifecycleinitiative.org/starting-life-cycle-thinking/life-cycle-approaches/life-cycle-sustainability-assessment/.

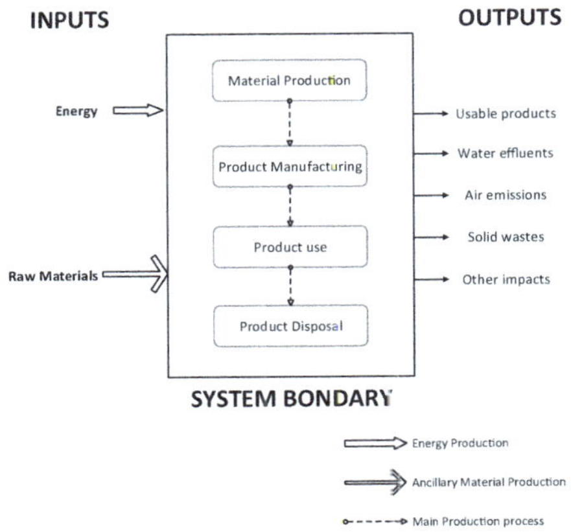

Fig. 2. Using LCA approach for material life cycle. Source: "Assessment of Environmental Lifecycle Approach for Industrial Materials and Products" by Steven B. Young

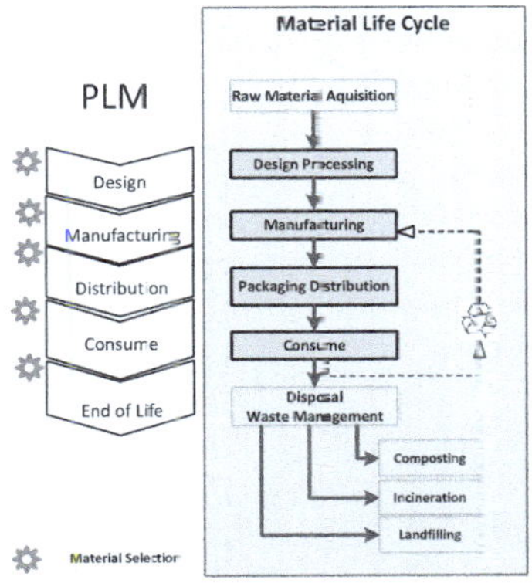

Fig. 3. PLM vs. material life cycle

Knowledge about the environmental performance is important in the LCA design process. Fortunately, a lot of information is available in this process, especially in modern, powerful PDM/PLM tools. Linking LCA and PLM therefore can be a good start[3], e.g. selecting recyclable materials, avoiding usage of fossil fuel, and tracking material flow from material extraction to final disposition.

Although the potential is great, little research has addressed how LCA can support PLM for Material Management. It is therefore worthwhile to discuss how LCA could be practiced to PLM in business contexts. For example, material selection is the prime concern of all engineering applications and design. This selection process can be defined by application requirements, possible materials, physical principles, and selection[4]. Selection of a material for engineering a new product involves several steps:

- Decide the requirements of the application, in terms of mechanical, thermal, environmental, electrical and chemical properties.
- Select materials for the application.
- Figure out what changes in the material properties are needed.
- Pick materials, which best fulfil the requirements of the application given possible changes in the material properties.

[3] Based on a survey of LCA practitioners carried out in 2006 LCA is mostly used to support business strategy (18%) and R&D (18%), as input to product or process design (15%), in education (13%) and for labeling or product declarations (11%).

[4] Retrieved from http://depts.washington.edu/matseed/mse_resources/Webpage/Bicycle/Material%20Selection%20Process.htm

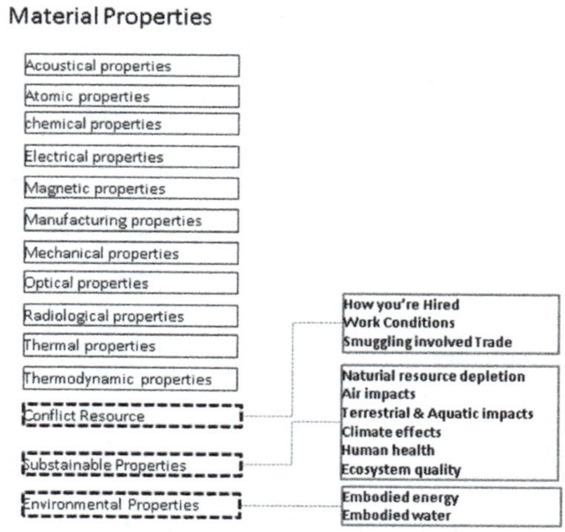

Fig. 4. Extension of the material property definition

This paper proposes to extend the definition of material properties to allow handling the conflict resource index (one of important social aspect) and sustainable properties that are remarked with a dotted line in Fig. 4. Furthermore, this paper aims also to organize the main references on Social-LCA to build a complete picture of the theoretical and practical implementation of this methodology in the electronics & electric sectors, especially with globalized supply chains. Also, it identifies needs for further research. The challenges and potential for Social-LCA at an electronic company will be identified to provide guidance for research into integrating Social-LCA with PLM and for managers attempting such integration. LCC is not covered in this paper because it is not essential to sustainability analysis in all situations.

The research has the following structure:

a. Literature review on Social-LCA with Integration into PLM to identify the main research needs.
b. Identification of recent lifecycle-based product sustainability assessments of electronic companies having globalized supply chains.
c. Findings about the challenges and potential of Social-LCA when integrated into PLM at an electronic company. These results could benefit decision-makers, stakeholders, enterprises and consumers.

2 Methods and Materials

2.1 Structured Literature Review of Social-LCA and PLM Integration

We structured our literature review to yield reproducible results - a reliable knowledge base without research bias – using the following steps [3]:

(I) Definition of review/check list; (II) Listing of research questions; (III) Identification of keywords; (IV) Selection of sources for literature search; (V) Define inclusion and exclusion criteria; (VI) Refining & finalizing keyword setting; (VII) Search of literature; (VIII) Evaluation and documentation of literature. Table 1 shows the review protocol.

Table 1. Review protocol

Review questions	"What are the thematic fields of research concerning social LCA with integration to PLM?" "What gaps exist in research?"
Keywords	Social Life Cycle Assessment LCSA sustainability Life cycle sustainability assessment (LCSA) "Social Life Cycle Assessment" + "PLM" "LCSA" + "Product lifecycle management"
Sources for literature search	Google Scholar | Semantic Scholar | Procedia CIRP[a]
Inclusion criteria	Title: same or similar as keywords mentioned above Abstract & Full Text: Social-LCA, or S-LCA framework, methods of PLM integration with any product lifecycle system
Exclusion criteria	Books; Non-English/non-German/non-Chinese publications; Application/analyses branch is other than electronic branch; Publication year earlier than 1990
Refining & finalizing keyword setting	Social Life Cycle Assessment + PLM
Evaluation/documentation	We will document the following important information in EXCEL Format: Publication Topic |Author | Publisher & Publication Year | Scope of Publication | Reference | Abstract

[a]Procedia CIRP is an open access product focusing entirely on publishing high quality proceedings from CIRP conferences, enabling fast dissemination so that conference delegates can publish their papers in a dedicated online issue on ScienceDirect.

Research Approach

- Type of study (empirical, theoretical, or both).
- Research application areas (industry sector).
- Sustainability dimension (which of the three dimensions of LCA the publication addresses).
- Type of case study (full case study or numerical example).
- Data for case study (extent to which real data was collected).
- Integration. Studies may be classified according to whether they address an integrated system, and if so, the kind of application of Social-LCA (Life Cycle Management (LCM); product lifecycle management (PLM), application life cycle management (ALM) for software, and data lifecycle management (DLM); information life cycle management (ILCM) [2].

2.2 Evaluation of Current Status in the Electronics and Electric Industries

This part of the research was conducted independently of the structured literature review on Social-LCA. Our approach resembled that of John W. Sutherland et al. [14], who explored social impacts identified by national-level social indicators, frameworks and principles. We also examined methodology development and various challenges for social life cycle assessment.

Martin Gerner found that "Quite a number of companies within the business segment are confronted with the dual challenge of both transforming their business models into future-proof concepts and paying tribute to an increase of sustainability awareness among customers simultaneously".

The gradual shift of business segments from hardware-related stationery and professional office supplies towards digitized media and IT business solutions addresses sustainability and corporate (social) responsibility as one core competence of related companies in a changing market environment (Altenburger 2013; Stanger 2017, p. 61; Zarnekow and Kolbe 2013). It is reasonable to focus upon corporate sustainability or sustainable entrepreneurship (Schaltegger and Wagner 2011, 225 et seqq.; Weidinger et al. 2014), interchangeably, examining subject plus contextual conditions. E.g. to analyze characters of industrial companies: are they "Innovation and business-model development" driven company, have a pivotal stake within the company's strategic development, e.g. heading for new product lines (eco-innovation), providing resourceful services, stretching brands etc.; or are they globally oriented companies, where cultural context plays important role.

2.3 Implications for Application at Electronic & Electric Company

In order to identify the most pressing challenges out of the ones identified by the two previous research steps to adopt Social-LCA, decision makers at electronic & electric company should be consulted. Interviews of experts and stakeholders should also reveal three types of knowledge for analysis: technical, procedural and interpretative. In reverse, an implementing concept will focus on the managerial aspects of corporate sustainability by returning analytically processed records to the case-presenting company [4].

3 Result and Decision

3.1 State of the Art of Social-LCA

The low amount of papers identified with our final keywords suggests that social Life Cycle Sustainability Assessment is still in an early stage of development. Our final set of 47 analyzed publications is consistent with the number of publications considered by other structured literature reviews [1, 4, 5].

3.1.1 Bibliometric Results

Figure 5 shows the chronic development of research in field of Social-LCA (with integration into PLM). It can be clearly seen that the majority of publications appeared after 2011, and the research is getting more and more attention. Publications peak in 2014, 2018 and 2019.

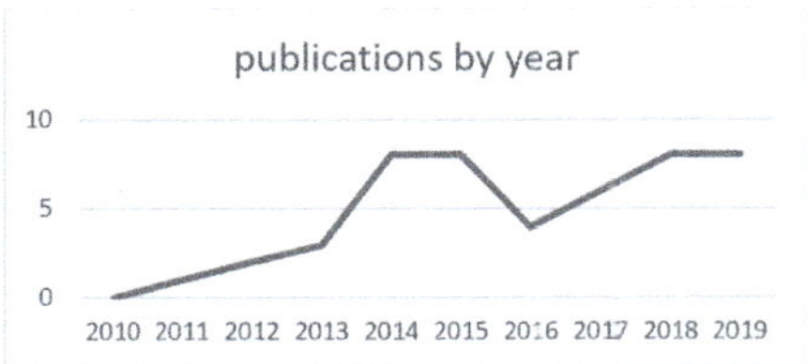

Fig. 5. Distribution of publications by year

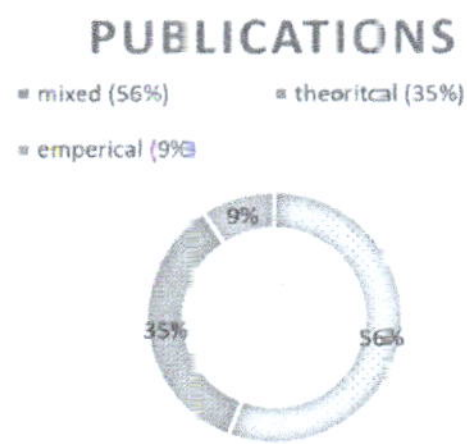

Fig. 6. Publications by type of study

Table 2 shows the distribution of publications by source. All sources that contributed only one publication were subsumed under "Rest" It is easily to see that Springer is the main medium in field of social LCA with integration into Life Cycle management. Other important journals for LCA include The International Journal of life Cycle Assessment or Journal of cleaner Production, Journal of remanufacturing, etc.

Table 2. Distribution of publications by source.

Publication by source	publications
Springer	13
Procedia CIRP	3
Journal of Industrial Ecology	5
semantic Scholar	6
Emerald Journals	3
Rest	11
total	41

Table 3. Publications by countries

Country	Publications	%
Switzerland	1	2
Czech	1	2
Germany	16	36
Finland	5	11
France	2	5
Italy	12	27
Korea	1	2
Nietherland	2	5
USA	4	9

The type of study or focus of research is also important for the evaluation of publications. Figure 6 shows that combined empirical and theoretical studies are mainly comprised of method developments that are subsequently tested by case study, which means the field of analyzed literature leans more strongly towards method development. Together with theoretical type of study, more than 90% of publications are about theorical and method development. This indicates also that the Social-LCA with integration into PLM is a new research area.

Table 3 show the distribution of publications by countries. Germany led (36%), followed by Italy (27%), Finland (11%), and USA (9%).

3.1.2 Classification of Literature by Thematic Fields

The maturity model was designed in such a way that a comprehensive capability analysis is possible in its application. It addresses the essential phases of the product lifecycle: planning, development, production planning, production, and operational and service tasks. The BABOK [6] explains the key terms used here as follows.

Framework: A generic lifecycle analysis or lifecycle assessment (LCA) explains the system structure. Most research into LCA has focused on the principle logic and improvements of the analysis framework or on empirical tests of conceptual frameworks. Klöpffer [7] and Finkbeiner et al. [8–10] defined the Life Cycle Sustainability Assessment framework. Martin Gerner (2019) [4] focused his research on LCA framework implementation strategy and applied the framework-implementation approach to corporate sustainability (Baumgartner and Rauter 2017, pp. 82–83). He also reported examples of applications of LCA framework implementation and provided recommendations. See Fig. 7 and Fig. 8.

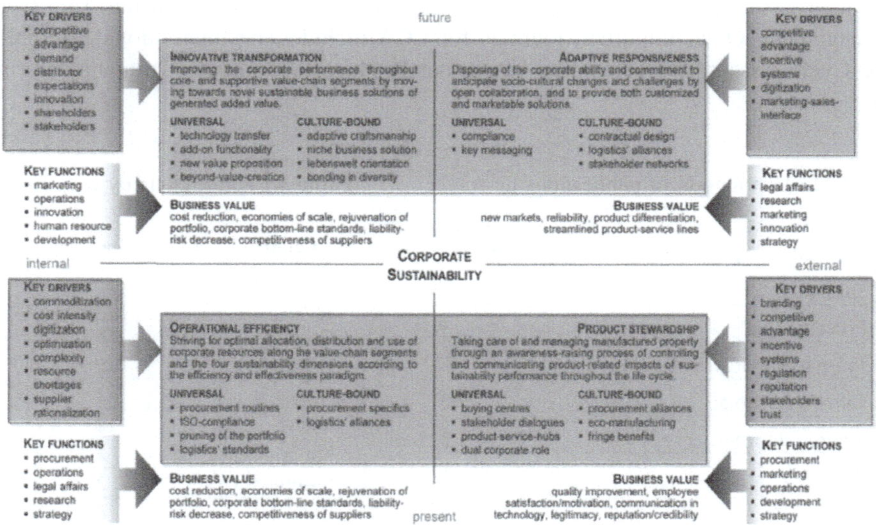

Fig. 7. Sample framework implementation strategy for corporate sustainability. Source: [4]

Given a dual character of defining strategy by referring to both identifying and assessing present and future comparative advantages and potential for success and deriving detailed implications for policies and plans of implementation, the framework strategy explicitly focuses on conceptual guidelines for realizing such business opportunity (Morioka and de Carvalho 2016; Rusnjak 2014, p. 48–50).

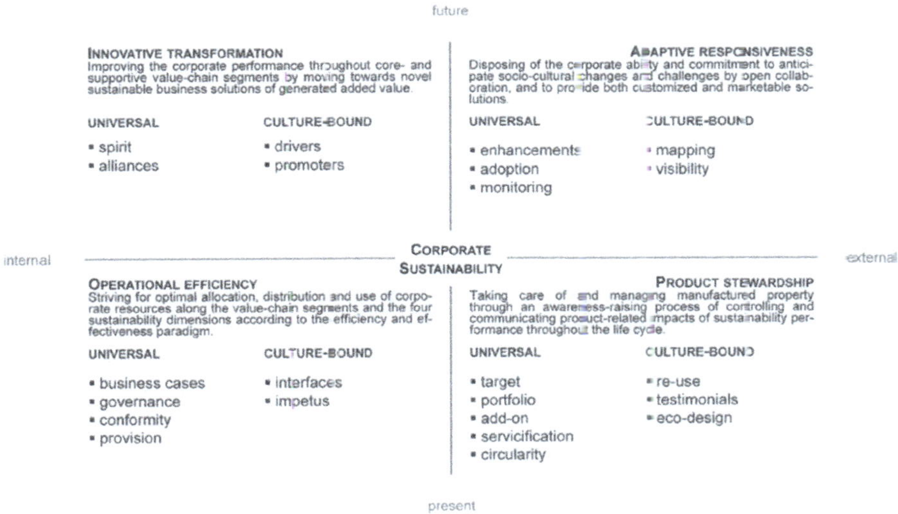

Fig. 8. Sample of implementing recommendations for corporate sustainability. Source: [4]

PLM is mainly a business management concept for sustainable products that can be applied in the industrial and service sectors with the aim of improving specific goods and services and enhancing the overall sustainability performance of the business and its value chains. PLM appeals to businesses that are ambitious and are committed to reduce their environmental and socio-economic burden while maximizing economic and social values. PLM is intended to create sustainable value rather than improve short-term success. So, PLM requires a holistic view and a full understanding of interdependency of businesses, environmental and social issues [11].

Method and Method Integration: Publications about methods proposed extensions of or changes to higher-level frameworks. Research into method integration focused on case studies, applications of methods, or methodological triangulation.

Case-related research is mainly exploring, including interpreting-inductive elements grounded in contested assumptions and referring to underlying theoretic frameworks and methodological concepts of relevant importance (Gioia, Corley and Hamilton 2013, 17 et seqq.; Jastram 2012, p. 53; Kromrey 2002, 58 et seqq.) [4].

Applications of methods addressed principles of qualitative content analysis (Atkinson 2017, pp. 122–123; Mayring 2014; Silverman 2013, 340 et seqq.) to understand applications of theories on corporate sustainability, take into account the leading theoretical concepts applied by scholars on selected corporate contexts, and to identify how to adequately embed the intended case study; collecting case-related characteristics to elicit elucidating, confidential up-to-date information through a status-quo-analysis of sustainability-related strategic approaches, activities and initiatives, means and instruments, examine underlying corporate perceptions through SWOT-analysis, including business analysis (internal) and environment analysis (external), and to benchmark performance targets and monitoring processes through an analysis of potential or opportunity assessment, respectively; and processing obtained findings in a strategic-directional way to adopt the value-chain-oriented reasoning based upon an extended lifecycle assessment (Frostell 2013, 842 et seqq.; Gauthier 2005) as structuring element, apply a multimethod approach of methodological triangulation, relying on stakeholder observation, expert interviews and company resources, and frame case-related characteristics as case study, including data collection, data analysis and data evaluation [4].

Methodological triangulation improves research validity through combining various techniques. The blend of multiple methods, not to be confused with mixed method, ensures best possible use of different sources of information, and thus generating sound and methodologically-grounded results, pertaining to qualitative research models, in particular (Bohnsack, Marotzki and Meuser 2006; Flick 2006, 2011; Kuckartz 2014, p. 19; Lamnek 2005; Mayring 2002, 73 et seqq., 2014, p. 8; Scholz and Tietje 2002; Silverman 2013, 199 et seqq., 2014, 22 et seqq.). (Prexl, 2010 301 et seqq.; Puls 2016) [6], Generally, this triangulation is evaluated by expert interviews, company resources and stakeholder observations.

Alternative Assessment Methods: Most researchers developed unique assessment methods but some incorporated parts of LSCA or LCSA frameworks. Luthe et al. [12] developed a tool that integrates LCA, Social-LCA, and economical aspects into product design, while Mjörnell et al. [13] integrated all three LCSA components into their sustainability assessment. Martin Gerner suggested integrating corporate sustainability into strategic management.

Case Studies: Most case studies tested applicability of the LCA framework and associated methods. Some case studies lacked effective ways of weighting sustainability dimensions and integrating all three dimensions., there are also some case studies and improving data availability addressed by examined publications, especially for Social-LCA [4, 8], were additionally identified as potential areas for improvement. E.g. A case study using LCSA framework with special focus on Social-LCA on mineral and compost fertilizers was conducted by Martínez-Blanco et al. [8] who used data from LCA databases (environmental impacts), LCC (purchase price), and Social-LCA to assess the sustainability impacts of fertilizers. Martin Gerner [4] focused upon corporate sustainability or sustainable entrepreneurship (Schaltegger and Wagner 2011, 225 et seqq.; Weidinger et al. 2014), interchangeably, these facets are to be elaborated by means of case study. in his case study Sustainability performance is related to [a] an extended lifecycle analysis (LCA), and [b] the triad of marketing in business-to-business relations, business segments in sustainability contexts, and culture bound/intercultural notions of sustainability.

His case study aimed at strengthening corporate sustainability with current and evolving culture-bound approaches. He provided guidelines for implementation at the operational level (Berns, Townend, Khayat, Balagopal and Reeves 2009, p. 7; Engert and Baumgartner 2016; Khalili 2011b, pp. 152–154) [4].

Data and Data Collection: Most researchers employed two approaches: (a) *Empirical Case Study*. Scholars used qualitative indicators of performance. Case-study research is most effectively carried out through combining multiple techniques simultaneously

(Gioia et al. 2013, p. 16; Jastram 2012, p. 58; Prexl 2010, p. 301; Scholz and Tietje 2002, 3–4, 9 et seqq., 14, 15 et seqq., 23–25) [4]; (b) *Theory-induced data collection*, stakeholder observation, expert interviews and company resources for research in industrial area.

3.2 Current Status in the Electronic and Electric Industry

Most European electronic & electric companies that have integrated LCA into the product development process have not effectively integrated social and economic impact assessment. First steps towards the operationalization of Social LCA have been taken by co-founding the Roundtable for Product Social Metrics, an industry-led initiative that produced a handbook on implementing product social impact assessment [4]. Environmental LCA is well-accepted and practiced throughout the world's top electric & electronics companies, like Siemens, Philips, GE, WAGO, BOSCH, etc., but few have employed comprehensive Life Cycle Sustainability Assessment of products. The immaturity of Social-LCA and the difficulty of gathering data on social impacts pose an additional barrier to implementing Social-LCA as part of an LCSA framework in industry. Most stake holders and experts consider an entire Social-LCA as too big a challenge, but many understand the importance of social risk assessment of supply chains in managing social risks.

There exists no universal strategy to integrate Social LCA into PLM (life Cycle Management). The strategy differs for each sub-cycle, including the following:

- Production management - Sustainability's focus is product stewardship, operational efficiency and/or innovative transformation
- Packaging/distribution management - Sustainability's focus is operational efficiency and/or adaptive responsiveness
- Service/use management - Sustainability's focus is product stewardship, innovative transformation and/or adaptive responsiveness
- End-of-life management - Sustainability's focus is product stewardship and/or innovative transformation

Industry is trending from corporate (social) responsibility towards an integrated concept of sustainability that is functionality-based and governance-oriented.

3.3 Implications for Applications at Electronic & Electric Industry

Our research determined the state of the art in the field of Social LCA and highlighted major areas for future research. We reported the status of product sustainability assessment in the electronic & electric industry and implications for the next steps towards the operationalization of Social-LCA. We identified several challenges for operationalization that hinder the adoption of LCSA at electronic & electric company.

We propose the following guidelines for further research.

Data Collection: Accessing internal, often confidential company information requires close interplay between academic and corporate entities [4]. Researchers should prepare to handle different languages across a company. Questions should be formulated ad hoc referring to pre-structured questionnaires. Interviewers should follow common routine of salutation, reciprocal introduction, question and answer, brief discussion and feedback, follow-up, and leave-taking (Bogner et al. 2014, 27–48, 58 et seqq.; Gläser and Laudel 2012, 83 et seqq.; Silverman 2013, 199 et seqq.) [4].

Data Analysis: In qualitative analysis, procedural arguments are to be granted priority over procedural arguments. Validity is of more importance than reliability.

Data Evaluation: Interpreting findings retrieving from qualitative data consequentially should follow the algorithms of qualitative content analysis

Comparatively Low Maturity of Social-LCA

- Ensure consistency of social topics with company specific strategy.
- Evaluate currently available databases and decide on a mode of data acquisition.

4 Limitations

We searched the literature using only three sources and narrowed down search terms to reduce the number of hits. Our narrow search focus may have overlooked some relevant publications, especially those that addressed only one method that could be a part of Social-LCA.

The research design included the social dimension in the lifecycle structure of analysis. Results of expert interviews, company resources and stakeholder observation revealed that assuming a generic, five-part lifecycle assessment represents a stylized or archetypal model of approaching corporate reality. Researchers must transfer or relate findings to the value-chain segments in the corporate structure. Without further research, our findings do not provide a basis for conclusions of a general nature. Our qualitative approach means findings pertain with certainty only to the cases studied [4].

5 Conclusion

This paper identified challenges and potential for implementing an integration of Social Life Cycle Assessment (Social-LCA) into Product lifecycle Management (PLM) at an electronic & electric company. The three-part structure of sustainability performance, sustainability opportunity and sustainability commitment made it possible to first, assess the status quo of corporate sustainability-related strategic approaches, activities and initiatives, means and instruments; second, identify universal and culture-bound drivers corresponding to industry-sector-specific characteristics; and third, deduce operational guidelines in view of stakeholder awareness, strategic options, projects and best practices [4].

Every sustainability dimension, i.e. environmental, societal, economic and cultural, should be studied individually and then correlated with the generic lifecycle category, i.e. supply chain, production, distribution/packaging, service/use, and end-of-life, and finally included into the afore mentioned three-step assessment.

References

1. Tarne, P., Traverso, M., Finkbeiner, M.: Review of life cycle sustainability assessment and potential for its adoption at an automotive company. J. Sustain. 9(4) (2017). https://doi.org/10.3390/su9040670
2. Sonnemann, G., Gemechu, E.D., Remmen, A., Frydendal, J., Jensen, A.A.: Life cycle management: implementing sustainability in business practice. In: Sonnemann, G., Margni, M. (eds.) Life Cycle Management. LCTCWLCA, pp. 7–21. Springer, Dordrecht (2015). https://doi.org/10.1007/978-94-017-7221-1_2
3. Pickering, C., Byrne, J.: The benefits of publishing systematic quantitative literature reviews for PhD, candidates and other early-career researchers. High. Educ. Res. Dev. **33**, 534–548 (2014)
4. Gerner, M.: Assessing and managing sustainability in international perspective: corporate sustainability across cultures – towards a strategic framework implementation approach. Int. J. Corp. Soc. Responsib. **4**(1), 1–34 (2019). https://doi.org/10.1186/s40991-019-0043-x
5. Sonnemann, G., Margni, M. (eds.): Life Cycle Management. LCTCWLCA. Springer, Dordrecht (2015). https://doi.org/10.1007/978-94-017-7221-1
6. Manda, B.M.K.: Application of Life Cycle Assessment for Corporate Sustainability: Integrating Environmental Sustainability in Business for Value Creation. Uitgeverij BOXPress, 's-Hertogenbosch (2014)
7. Klöpffer, W., Ciroth, A.: Is LCC relevant in a sustainability assessment? Int. J. Life Cycle Assess **16**(2), 99–101 (2011)
8. Martínez-Blanco, J., et al.: Application challenges for the social Life Cycle Assessment of fertilizers within life cycle sustainability assessment. J. Clean. Prod. **69**(15), 34–48. https://doi.org/10.1016/j.jclepro.2014.01.044. Accessed Jan 2014
9. Chang, Y.J, Nguyen, D., Finkbeiner, M., Krüger, J.: Adapting ergonomic assessments to social life cycle assessment. Science Direct (2016). https://doi.org/10.1016/j.procir.2016.01.064
10. Finkbeiner, M., Reimann, K., Ackermann, R.: Life cycle sustainability assessment (LCSA) for products and processes. In: Proceedings of the SETAC Europe 18th Annual Meeting, Warsaw, Poland, 25–29 May 2008
11. Sonnemann, G., et al. (eds.): Part of the Springer Open Book LCA Compendium – The Complete World of Life Cycle Assessment Book Series (LCAC). http://www.springer.com/series/11776
12. Luthe, T., Kägi, T., Reger, J.: A systems approach to sustainable technical product design. J. Ind. Ecol. **17**, 605–617 (2013). https://doi.org/10.1111/jiec.12000. Accessed 1 Mar 2013
13. Mjörnell, K., Boss, A., Lindahl, M., Molnar, S.: A tool to evaluate different renovation alternatives with regard to sustainability. Sustainability **6**, 4227–4245 (2014). https://doi.org/10.3390/su6074227. Accessed 8 July 2014
14. Sutherland, J.W., et al.: The role of manufacturing in affecting the social dimension of sustainability. CIRP Ann. **65**(2), 689–712 (2016)

A Comprehensive Maturity Model for Assessing the Product Lifecycle

Philipp Pfenning[1,2](✉), Hannes Christian Eibinger[1,2], Clotilde Rohleder[3], and Martin Eigner[4]

[1] Siemens Digital Industries Software, Munich, Germany
philipp.pfenning@siemens.com
[2] Siemens Digital Industries Software, Zurich, Switzerland
[3] University of Applied Sciences, Constance, Germany
[4] Technical University of Kaiserslautern, Kaiserslautern, Germany

Abstract. Digitalization is one of the most frequently discussed topics in industry. New technologies, platform concepts and integrated data models do enable disruptive business models and drive changes in organization, processes, and tools. The goal is to make a company more efficient, productive and ultimately profitable. However, many companies are facing the challenge of how to approach digital transformation in a structured way and to realize these potential benefits. What they realize is that Product Lifecycle Management plays a key role in digitalization intends, as object, structure and process management along the life cycle is a foundation for many digitalization use cases. The introduced maturity model for assessing a firm's capabilities along the product lifecycle has been used almost two hundred times. It allows a company to compare its performance with an industry specific benchmark to reveal individual strengths and weaknesses. Furthermore, an empirical study produced multidimensional correlation coefficients, which identify dependencies between business model characteristics and the maturity level of capabilities.

Keywords: Maturity model · Capability analysis · Digitalization · Product lifecycle management · Benchmark

1 Introduction

The product lifecycle refers to the processes of planning, designing, verifying, manufacturing and maintaining of products. In order to systematically manage all accruing product related information and to support engineering processes throughout the product lifecycle, the concept of product lifecycle management (PLM) raised [1].

The increasing demand for smart products and factories is forcing companies to rethink their product development process and thus also to adapt their PLM strategy. PLM plays a key role in the intended digitalization and represents an opportunity to make a company more efficient, productive and profitable. Maturity models have proven to be a valuable method for defining a future strategy, as they provide transparency on the strengths and weaknesses of a company. The goal of the model presented here is to create a standardized framework. The capabilities considered in the

Published by Springer Nature Switzerland AG 2020
F. Nyffenegger et al. (Eds.): PLM 2020, IFIP AICT 594, pp. 514–526, 2020.
https://doi.org/10.1007/978-3-030-62807-9_41

model cover both PLM core competencies as well as extended building blocks related to the use of new technologies (e.g. predictive maintenance through the Industrial Internet of Things). We will investigate and evaluate existing maturity models, introduce a novel holistic model and analyze the panel data in an empirical study.

2 State of the Art

Holistic maturity assessment approaches include elements of strategic guidance and roadmaps as those provided by Acatech [2] and Issa et al. [3] They propose guidelines for assessing Industry 4.0 maturity not only in the context of product lifecycle management. They rather emphasize the complete value creation process including horizontal and vertical integration. Most of the holistic maturity models focus on manufacturing and do not address product lifecycle management in detail.

Schumacher et al. [4] presented an Industry 4.0 realization model targeting industrial manufacturing companies. According to Schumacher et al. [5], their model accounts for 65 assessment items included in 8 maturity dimensions: Technology, Products, Customers and Partners, Value Creation Processes, Data & Information, Corporate Standards, Employees and Strategy & Leadership.

Besides holistic Industry 4.0 approaches, more specific maturity models are prevalent. Weber et al. [6] developed a maturity model for data-driven manufacturing, which helps companies to assess maturity of their IT regarding the requirements of vertical- and horizontal system integration.

Batenburg et al. [7, 8] worked on Product Lifecycle Management ‘s alignment and maturity using five business dimensions: 1) SP- strategy & policy, 2) OP - organization & processes, 3) MC - monitoring & control, 4) PC - people & culture, and 5) IT - information technology. Originally used for aligning CRM, these dimensions help visualize both the average PLM maturity and alignment using a radar plot.

Batenburg et al. [7] developed a PLM framework based on metrics. Batenburg et al. [8] showed how the PLM framework could be used by individual organizations to assess their current PLM maturity and alignment and use that as a starting point for defining their PLM Roadmap. Their findings suggest that PLM needs to be culturally embedded as an enterprise-wide system and concept.

Kärkkaeinen et al. investigated Batenburg et al.’s approach [9]. They claim that PLM implementation changes partners’ processes. Savino et al. [10] presented a PLM Maturity model based on an Analytical Hierarchy Process (AHP), a multi-criteria approach, which approach aims at helping companies analyze their requirements and identify the right PLM tools.

Bensiek and Kühn [11] introduced an approach for maturity-based process improvement that is suitable for SMEs (Small and Mid-sized Enterprise) and focused on virtual engineering. These components are maturity dimensions originally considered by Batenburg et al.’s model [7], Sääksvuori & Immonen’s model [12] and Bensiek & Kühn‘s model [11].

Paavel et al. [13, 14] combined the approach of Batenburg et al. [7] with the fuzzy logic method proposed by Zhang et al. [15]. Paavel et al.’s [13] model shows how these elements are combined for a PLM maturity model. Based on an assessment of benefits, the expert group evaluated readiness for different business dimensions. Paavel et al.'s PLM maturity model groups all PLM components into a TIFOS framework based on PLM functionalities, and proposes a PCMA maturity model to evaluate PLM components' strengths and weaknesses.

To provide companies an effective framework for identifying potential benefits along the entire product lifecycle, we believe that following requirements should be met by a maturity model.

- a) Holistic view on the product lifecycle (planning phase, definition phase, verification phase, production phase, service/operating phase)
- b) Reference data/benchmark of comparable companies
- c) Consideration of several dimensions (process, IT systems, employees, etc.)
- d) Clearly defined process for implementing the model
- e) Possibility to identify relevant topics – "Next Step"
- f) Clearly defined criteria behind the maturity levels
- g) Consideration of company characteristics (size, branch, strategy, etc.)
- h) Possibility to prioritize individual capabilities
- i) Graphical representation of the maturity levels

These criteria also build the foundation for our state-of-the-art review. Therefore, the already introduced models have been considered and evaluated, as depicted in Table 1.

Table 1. Evaluation of criteria for introduced maturity models

	Criteria								
Maturity Model	a)	b)	c)	d)	e)	f)	g)	h)	i)
Schumacher et al. 2019 [5]	◔	●	◕	●	◕	◔	◔	◔	◑
Zhang et al. 2018 [15]	◑	◑	◔	◑	◑	◑	◔	●	◕
Paavel et. al 2017 [14]	◑	◎	◕	◑	◑	◑	◔	●	◎
Weber et al. 2017 [5]	◔	◑	●	◑	◕	●	◎	◎	◎
Schumacher et al. 2016 [4]	◑	◔	◑	◑	◑	◔	◔	◑	◑
Bensiek & Kuehn 2012 [11]	◔	◔	◎	◑	◕	◎	◔	◎	◔
Savino & Mazza 2012 [10]	◑	◔	◑	◕	◑	◕	◔	◕	◎
Kärkkäinena et al. 2009 [9]	◑	◕	◑	◑	◕	◔	◕	◎	◑
Pels & Simons 2008 [16]	◔	◑	◑	◑	◑	◔	◕	◎	◑
Batenburg et al. 2006 [7]	◑	◕	◑	◑	◑	◕	◕	◎	◑
Batenburg et al. 2005 [8]	◑	◕	◑	◑	◑	◕	◕	◎	◑
Symbols: ● fully implemented and explicitly named, ◕ mostly implemented, ◑ partly implemented, ◔ only indirectly implemented, ◎not implemented									

As Table 1 displays, there are various maturity models available. However, none of them fits holistically to the introduced criteria. This circumstance encouraged us to define a maturity model addressing a company's capabilities along the entire product lifecycle. As already stated, the model does include core PLM capabilities, but also address other areas relevant from a digitalization perspective such as e.g. manufacturing planning, engineering and execution.

3 Maturity Model Description

3.1 Underlying Research Questions

The maturity model discussed was developed as part of research work that did focus on the following questions.

- Are there characteristics of strong PLM architectures that represent a Strategic Excellence Position for a company [17]?
- Does a company that aligns its PLM architecture with the company's business strategy achieve a competitive advantage?
- Can patterns be derived from the entrepreneurial or strategic characteristics of a company that require a specific PLM architecture?

A PLM Architecture in context of this work was understood as a firm's specific realization of Product Lifecyle Management within given boundary condition: Industry; industry segment; company characteristics such as business strategy (e.g. operational excellence); company size; structural and procedural organization enterprise role (e.g. contract manufacturer, tier 1, etc.); value chain and process design; order category (e.g. make-to stock, engineer to order, etc.); production type (e.g. one-off, serial or mass production); network of engineering, manufacturing and service locations; data/content managed; IT systems used; technology leveraged; etc.

Empirical investigation of these questions required a descriptive model. Creating that model, we built on proven techniques, methods or frameworks and used available practices wherever possible (see Sect. 3.2). The work finally led to the Maturity Model introduced in this paper.

3.2 Utilized Methods and Frameworks

Strategy Maps

Robert S. Kaplan's and David P. Norton's [18–20] framework of Strategy Maps [19] (based on the Balanced Scorecard (BSC) concept [18]) was identified as an appropriate approach to link PLM architectures to business strategies planning. The Strategy Map is based on the four perspectives known from the BSC, arranged in a cause-and-effect relationship: Learning and Growth, Business Process, Customer and Financial.

Kaplan and Norton [18–20] see the intangible assets of an organization anchored at the Learning and Growth level of the BSC. They are concerned with recognizing the value they add to the implementation of the corporate strategy. They differentiate between three aspects: human, information and organizational capital.

The Strategy Maps are a valuable advancement to the classic Balanced Scorecard because they show us how entrepreneurial success arises from intangible resources. The possibilities offered by PLM architectures allow companies to sharpen or develop comprehensive skills that address all three aspects of the Learning and Growth perspective. The maturity model focuses on selected operational capabilities, which are mapped by the interactions of the various information systems (Product Lifecycle Management, Enterprise Resource Planning, Supply Chain Management, Manufacturing Execution, etc.). The BABOK [23] explains the term Capability and Capability Analysis as follows.

Capability

- Capabilities are the abilities of an enterprise to perform or transform something that helps achieve a business goal or objective. Each capability is found only once on a capability map, even if it is possessed by multiple business units.
- Capabilities can identify explicit performance expectations. When a capability is targeted for improvement, a performance gap can be identified - the difference between the current performance and the desired performance, given the business strategy.
- At the strategic level, capabilities should support an enterprise in establishing and maintaining a sustainable competitive advantage and a distinct value proposition.

Business Capability Analysis
Identifying performance gaps helps prioritize investments. This analysis helps launch clearly focused initiatives that are coordinated with the various stakeholders. It creates a common understanding of the strategy adopted and the expected results. Analysis especially benefits I4.0 projects, which address the ability of the organization to either offer new products and services or improve operational excellence. This instrument promotes concerted cooperation across organizational boundaries. Capability analysis in a Maturity Assessment involves two challenges; company acceptance and acquiring a network of experts to apply this broad and cross-functional framework. We shall call Grading Models the listing of the capabilities to be analyzed and the development of the underlying assessment models. Siemens provided a good opportunity to apply the model because this company has a global network of subject matter experts and its portfolio covers almost all aspects of the product lifecycle.

3.3 The Maturity Model

The maturity model was designed in such a way that a comprehensive capability analysis is possible in its application. It addresses the essential phases of the product life cycle: planning, development, production planning, production, and operational and service tasks.

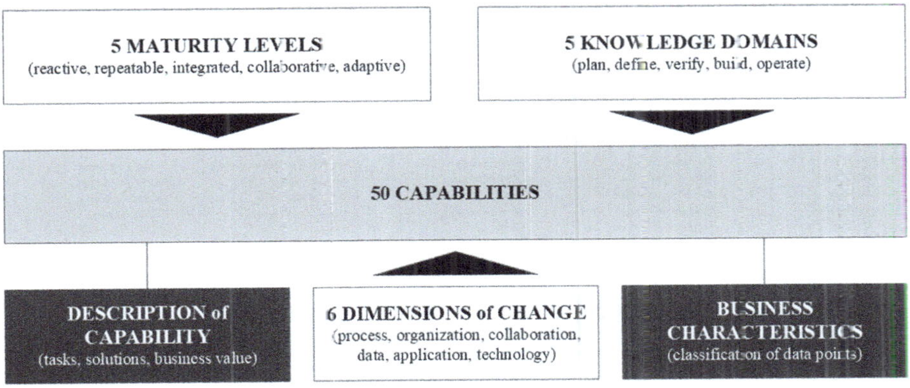

Fig. 1. Elements of the maturity model

As depicted in Fig. 1, at the heart of the model, we find a set of fifty recurring capabilities of companies designing and manufacturing products in various industries.

Any maturity model will cover only some aspects and will be subject to changes as new technologies push the boundaries of what is possible. Still, we found this model generic and stable enough to collect data, gain new insights, and draw conclusions. To enable benchmarks based on the model, it is necessary to maintain a time-stamp with every data point recorded. In this way, we ensure consideration of continuous improvements in the market by just comparing with other companies assessed within e.g. the last three years.

Description of Capability

A definition of terms is provided for each capability presented in the model in order to establish a common understanding or, where necessary, to define delimitations. Furthermore, business benefits, objectives, application examples and solutions are outlined.

Business Characteristics

In order for the model and the collected market data to be used for benchmarks, each company under consideration must be classified. A set of standard characteristics (e.g. industry, business strategy [25], size, target markets, etc.) allows taking a fingerprint of business characteristics. This data is relevant, when it comes to selecting datapoints for comparison with e.g. the Industry, firms of a similar size, firms within the same business strategy etc.

Five Knowledge Domains

The set of fifty capabilities has been clustered in five Knowledge Domains (see Fig. 2), which would typically see different roles or personas in the organization dealing with the topics. For example, skills in the areas of visualization, simulation and testing are summarized in the "Verify" section. This structure has proven valuable in planning and executing capability assessment workshops.

Domains				
PLAN	**DEFINE**	**VERIFY**	**BUILD**	**OPERATE**
Capabilities				
Ideation Mgmt.	E-BOM Mgmt.	Visualization	M-BOM Mgmt.	S-BOM Mgmt.
Requirements Mgmt.	Appl. Lifecycle Mgmt.	1D/Controls Simulation	Manuf. Process Mgmt.	Service Asset Mgmt.
Product Portfolio Mgmt.	Material Mgmt.	3D/CFD Simulation	Manuf. Resource Mgmt.	Service Planning
Program & Project Mgmt.	Substance Mgmt.	Physical Testing	Manufacturing Documentation	Service Forecasting
Document Mgmt.	Standardization	CAE Data Mgmt.	Shop-floor Integration	Service Scheduling
Content Mgmt.	Product Configuration	Human Simulation	Part Manufacturing	Factory Automation
Systems Engineering	Product Cost Mgmt.	Logistic Simulation	Robotic Engineering	Line Monitoring
Business Intelligence	Supplier Collaboration	Commissioning	Scheduling	Machine Data Analytics
Issue & Change Mgmt.	Revision & Release Mgmt.	Quality Mgmt.	Manuf. Execution Mgmt.	Safety Mgmt.
Advanced Planning	PLM/ERP Integration	Test Mgmt.	MES Integration	Security Mgmt.

Fig. 2. Capabilities covered by the maturity model

Five Maturity Levels

Maturity levels are based on the Gartner approach for Product Lifecycle Management presented by Dr. Marc Halpern [22] (Research VP, Engineering and Design Technologies, Gartner) at the Product Innovation Conference Munich (2016). This approach aligns in many aspects with the VDMA [23]. We use a five-step maturity model, as illustrated in Fig. 3.

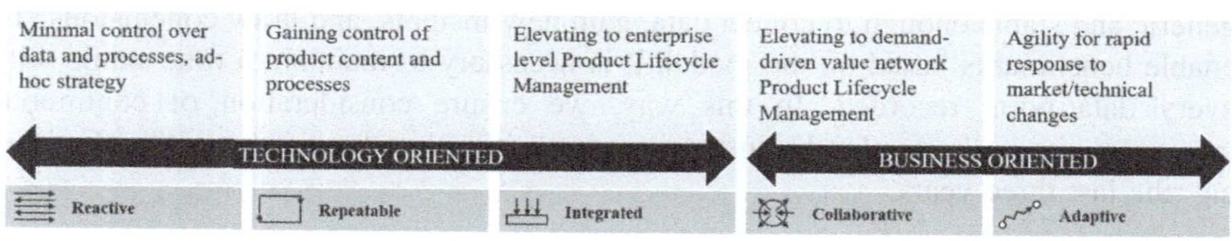

Fig. 3. Five-step maturity model based on Gartner Research; according to [22]

The individual stages build on one another. They represent a possible development path for the company. Reaching a higher level involves one-off (change project, IT costs) and recurring expenses (quality assurance, maintenance, administration). A company will therefore always strive to achieve the level of maturity that matches the operational requirements and makes a positive contribution to value. The necessary skills correspond to the fundamental tasks of product data management (PDM) up to expansion level two ("repeatable"). Upon reaching the "integrated" level, a company uses a cross-location or cross-product line PLM architecture. The necessary data models are harmonized, and working methods are based on standardized procedures [23]. Levels one to three have a strong technology orientation. At expansion stages four and five, a company has internalized the basic PLM principles as part of the corporate culture and is looking away from technical formalisms towards business benefits. A firm asks questions like. How can we optimize our processes in terms of vertical and horizontal integration? Where can we exploit further optimization potential using new technology?

Six Dimensions of Change

As a global provider of IT consulting and services, the company CSC[1] developed a comprehensive methodology kit under the title Catalyst. One of the cornerstones of this methodology framework was examination of a business problem and the impact of change from six perspectives, known as the domains of change. These are defined as Process, Organization, Location, Data, Application and Technology.

The Maturity Model did adopt this concept with one enhancement by replacing the Location perspective with Collaboration. This move still did include the CSC idea of understanding where a company was making business, but put more focus on how different sites, subsidiaries, suppliers and customers do interact with each other.

- **Process.** The business process dimension focuses on what the company does, how activities are carried out and in what sequence, what rules are followed, and the type of results obtained. Change in the business process domain is often a key driver for change in all the other domains.
- **Organization**. The organization dimension focuses on the people and organizations involved in the change: their culture, capabilities, roles, team structures, and organizational units.
- **Collaboration**. The collaboration dimension focuses on how stakeholders are interacting with each other and how communication is managed from an internal and external perspective. It may therefore include customer and vendor communication as well as with internal clients.
- **Data**. The data dimension focuses on the content, structure, relationships, and business rules for the data used by the business processes, applications, and organization. It also considers the transformations needed to result in information and knowledge that the company can use.
- **Application**. The application dimension focuses on the capabilities, structure, and user interface of software applications and application components used to support the change. Applications or components may be specific enterprise applications such as Product Lifecycle Management, Enterprise Resource Planning, Supply Chain Management, Manufacturing Execution, etc. or they may be general in nature, such as a data authoring system or even an electronic spreadsheet.
- **Technology**. The technology dimension focuses on the hardware, software, and communications infrastructure used to enable and support solutions and services. Change in the technology domain is often a key driver for change in other domains

3.4 Grading Model

Putting the six domains of change in context with the five levels of maturity results in a matrix as displayed in Fig. 4. This structure served as the basis for the development of

[1] The American company Computer Sciences Corporation (CSC) was founded in 1959 and grew a multinational corporation and globally important player in the IT-consulting and services business. In 2017 CSC merged with the HP Enterprise Service Line creating DXC Technology. With nearly 6,000 customers in over 70 countries, the company has an estimated annual turnover of $20 billion in 2020.

what we call Grading Models. In interviews with subject matter experts for each of the capabilities we discussed and documented the characteristics in each field of the matrix. The resulting, standardized framework allows companies to locate their individual skill levels. Grading models should be reviewed, updated and adjusted to market changes at least every three years.

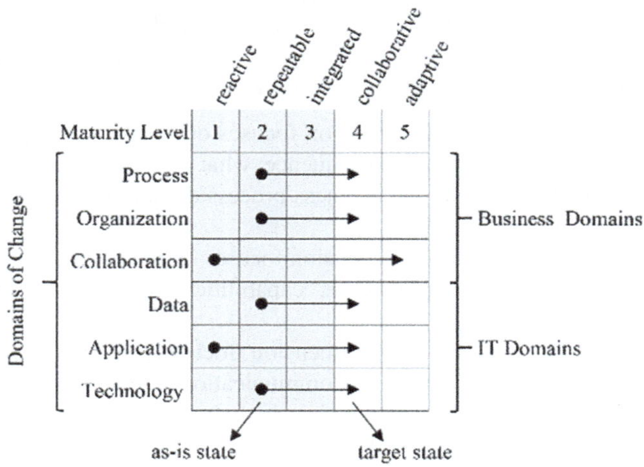

Fig. 4. Grading Model matrix

Figure 4 also illustrates generically (arrows) a detailed view on the as-is and target state discussed with firms. The gaps identified along the Dimensions of Change are valuable insights when it comes to planning transformation processes and required organizational change management.

3.5 Prioritization

In addition to assessing the maturity level, MoSCoW analysis is used to prioritize each capability. Following this principle each capability is prioritized via the values "Must", "Should", "Could" or "Won't". For a better guidance the prioritization system utilizes Porters value chain. If a capability contributes to a core competence of the organization, it shall be qualified as a "must have". If it contributes to primary activities in the value chain [24], it will be rated as a "should have". Whatever addresses support activities will be rated as a "could have". In case a capability is not relevant for a company it can be classified as "won't". By overlaying business priority and maturity, the model enables a qualitative view of hidden potential.

3.6 Example of Capabilities and Grading Models

Figure 5 finally gives an example for the capability Logistic Simulation. The generic representation shows how the model presents itself in case of an analysis, presenting description of capabilities, Grading Model along the 5 maturity levels and the possibility to prioritization. The image shows an excerpt of the expert's observation of how companies are operating today.

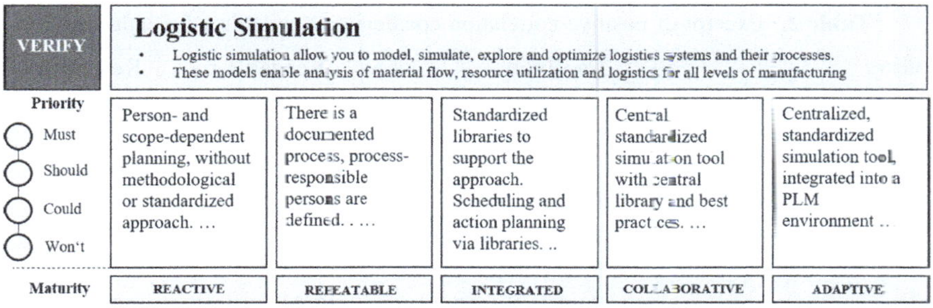

Fig. 5. Excerpt of specific grading model for Logistic Simulation

4 Empirical Study on Maturity Model Data

Besides capabilities with their priority and maturity levels, the model also utilizes several business characteristics (e.g. industry or country). In this paper we focus on the relations between industries and capabilities. The underlaying data panel consists of 189 companies. Most of them are in Machinery & Heavy Equipment Industry.

We examined the interdependencies between the introduced attributes by applying a correlation analysis. As part of the analysis the application "R" evaluates each classification feature with the corresponding maturity and priority stages. According to Puth et al. the Kendall or Spearman rank correlation are appropriate methods for the ordinate data values in the panel [26]. As the maturity and priority levels show a tied data behavior, which means that priority and maturity ranks can be assigned multiple times, the Kendall model offers a more resilient behavior and has therefore been chosen [26]. The correlation matrix consists of more than 30.000 coefficients, so only relevant dependencies have been evaluated in detail. The correlation coefficients can range from −1 to +1. A strong positive correlation takes a value close to +1, while a strong negative correlation takes a value close to −1. In case that the correlation coefficient shows a value around 0, no dependency between the characteristics exists.

According to Akoglu there are many interpretations of correlation coefficients. As most of the classification models confirm a fair correlation for coefficients larger than 0.3, this threshold has been used to identify relevant correlations [27].

Table 2 shows an excerpt of the calculated Kendall's rank correlation factor (τ) for different industries. Only four of the seven industries contain a positive correlation to at least one capability. Possibly there are so few because we had less than thirteen data points for the industries Electronics & Semiconductors, Energy & Utilities, and Medical Devices & Pharmaceuticals. In order to draw conclusions for these industries the panel data could be extended via further assessments. Additional to Kendall's τ the significance has been examined via p-values. At this point it should be mentioned that only correlations have been examined and that causality has not been proved.

Table 2. Excerpt of positive correlation coefficients/Kendall's τ for industries

Industry	Capability	Kendall's τ - priority	Kendall's τ - maturity
Automotive & Transportation	Program & Project Management	0.35	0.00
	Human Simulation	0.32	0.30
	Logistic Simulation	0.47**	0.21
	SBOM Management	–0,34	0.45*
	Service Scheduling	0.43	0.40**
Industrial Machinery & Heavy Equipment	Business Intelligence	0.30	–0.02
	Commissioning	0.38	0.13
	Scheduling	0.01	0.30*
	Service Scheduling	0.45	–0.23
Aerospace & Defense	Ideation Management	0.44**	0.04
	Systems Engineering	0.64	0.13
	Advanced Planning	0.31	0.24
	Application Lifecycle Mgmt.	0.43	0.10
	Substance Management	0.31	–0.02
	Visualization	0.32	0.22
	Quality Management	0.38**	0.29
	Test Management	0.43**	0.30**
	Manufacturing Documentation	0.39*	0.32
	Shop floor Integration	0.38	0.25
	Part Manufacturing	0.17	0.37**
	Line Monitoring	0.43	–0.06
	Safety Management	0.42	0.31
	Security Management	0.47	0.34
Consumer Products & Retail	Product & Portfolio Management	0.38	0.08
	Substance Management	0.47**	0.20
	Standardization	0.31	0.00
	Service Scheduling	0.44	0.34
	Factory Automation	0.31	0.06

*Correlation is significant at the 0.01 level (p-value < 0.01)
**Correlation is significant at the 0.05 level (p-value < 0.05)

Concerning the interpretation of the data, the positive coefficients show whether a capabilities' priority or maturity is explicitly larger for a specific industry segment compared to the remaining industries. A larger value shows a stronger correlation between the two classification features. Furthermore, some of the correlations display a level of significance under 5%. This indicates that the correlation exhibits a statistically significant behavior. For instance, the industry Automotive & Transportation reveals a correlation coefficient of 0.47 and a p-value under 0.05 for the priority of the capability Logistic Simulation. This potential coherence might be attributable to the often-prevalent mass production and the pursue to optimize the throughput in automotive industry. Another noteworthy correlation origin from the relationship between Aerospace & Defense industry to the capability of Quality Management. The correlation coefficient for the priority is 0.38 and shows that this industry ranks the capability Quality Management higher as the remaining industries. This may be since the industry is forced to follow aerospace and military standards demanding the traceability of manufacturing and quality information.

5 Results and Discussion

The new model allows companies to evaluate their maturity levels along fifty capabilities. It provides a standardized framework for the entire product lifecycle that allows rating, classifying, and comparing companies. The framework assists in defining potential filed of actions for improvement and it can drive the discussion of an appropriate digitalization strategy. The empirical study provides first insights into the current maturity and priority status of capabilities across various industries.

Future research could examine relationships between capabilities and business characteristics other than industry (e.g. strategy, operating processes, size of company or country). Companies could benefit from the development of a methodology to identify a suitable information technology and process architecture based on business characteristics.

References

1. Eigner, M., Stelzer, R.: Product Lifecycle Management - Ein Leitfaden für Product Development und Life Cycle Management. Springer, Heidelberg (2009). https://doi.org/10.1007/b93672
2. Schuh, G., Anderl, R., Gausemeier, M.: Acatech Study – Industrie 4.0 Maturity Index: Managing the Digital Transformation of Companies, Herbert Utz Verlag, Munich (2007)
3. Issa, A., Hatiboglu, B., Bildstein, A., Bauernhansl, T.: Industrie 4.0 roadmap: framework for digital transformation based on the concepts of capability maturity and alignment. Procedia CIRP **72**, 973–978 (2018)
4. Schumacher, A., Erol, S., Sihn, W.: A maturity model for assessing Industry 4.0 readiness and maturity of manufacturing enterprises. Procedia CIRP **52**(1), 161–166 (2016)
5. Schumacher, A., Nemeth, T., Sihn, W.: Roadmapping towards industrial digitalization based on an Industry 4.0 maturity model for manufacturing enterprises. Procedia CIRP **79**, 409–414 (2019)

6. Weber, C., Königsberger, J., Kassner, L., Mitschang, B.: M2DDM–a maturity model for data-driven manufacturing. Procedia CIRP **63**, 173–178 (2017)
7. Batenburg, R., Helms, R.W., Versendaal, J.: PLM roadmap: stepwise PLM implementation based on the concepts of maturity and alignment. Int. J. Product Lifecycle Manage. **1**(4), 333–351 (2006)
8. Batenburg, R.S., Helms, R.W., Versendaal, J.M.: The Maturity of Product Lifecycle Management in Dutch Organizations. A Strategic Perspective (2005)
9. Kärkkäinen, H., Myllärniemi, J., Okkonen, J., Silventoinen, A.: Assessing maturity requirements for implementing and using product lifecycle management. In: The 9th International Conference on Electronic Business, Macau, pp. 669–678, November 2009
10. Savino, M.M., Mazza, A., Ouzrout, Y.: PLM maturity model: a multi-criteria assessment in southern Italy companies. Int. J. Oper. Quant. Manage. **18**(3), 159–180 (2012)
11. Bensiek, T., Kuehn, A.: Maturity model for improving virtual engineering in small and medium-sized enterprises. In: Rivest, L., Bouras, A., Louhichi, B. (eds.) PLM 2012. IAICT, vol. 388, pp. 635–645. Springer, Heidelberg (2012). https://doi.org/10.1007/978-3-642-35758-9_57
12. Saaksvuori, A., Immonen, A.: Product Lifecycle Management. Springer, Heidelberg (2008). https://doi.org/10.1007/978-3-540-78172-1
13. Paavel, M., Karjust, K., Majak, J.: Development of a product lifecycle management model based on the fuzzy analytic hierarchy process. Proc. Est. Acad. Sci. **66**(3) (2017)
14. Paavel, M.: Product Lifecycle Management Maturity Model Development (2018)
15. Zhang, H., Bouras, A., Sekhari, A., Ouzrout, Y., Yu, S.: A PLM components monitoring framework for SMEs based on a PLM maturity model and FAHP methodology (2014)
16. Pels, H.J., Simons, K.: PLM maturity assessment. In: 2008 IEEE International Technology Management Conference (ICE), pp. 1–8. IEEE, June 2008
17. Puempin, C.: The Essence of Corporate Strategy. Gower Publishing Company Limited, Vermont (1987)
18. Kaplan, R., Norton, D.: The Balanced Scorecard - Translating Strategy into Action. Harvard Business Review Press, Harvard (1996)
19. Kaplan, R., Norton, D.: Strategy Maps - Der Weg von immateriellen Werten zum materiellen Erfolg. Schäffer-Poeschel, Stuttgart (2004)
20. Kaplan, R., Norton, D.: The Execution Premium - Linking Strategy to Operations for Competitive Advantage. Harvard Business Press, Harvard (2008)
21. International Institute of Business Analysis: BABOK v3. IIBA, Toronto (2015)
22. Halpern, M.: PLM maturity and usability - the steps to greater product success. In: PI Conference, Munich (2016)
23. Informatik, V.D.M.A.: Leitfaden zur Erstellung eines unternehmensspezifischen PLM-Konzeptes. VDMA Verlag GmbH, Frankfurt am Main (2008)
24. Porter, M.: Competitive Advantage: Creating and Sustaining Superior Performance. Simon & Schuster, New York (1998)
25. Treacy, M., Wiersema, F.: The Discipline of Market Leaders - A Common-Sense Map Toward Market Leadership. Perseus Publishing, Basic Books, New York (1995)
26. Puth, M.T., Neuhäuser, M., Ruxton, G.D.: Effective use of Spearman's and Kendall's correlation coefficients for association between two measured traits. Anim. Behav. **102**, 77–84 (2015)
27. Akoglu, H.: User's guide to correlation coefficients. Turk. J. Emerg. Med. **18**(3), 91–93 (2018)

PLM Functionalities in the Fashion Industry. Preliminary Results of a Classification Framework

Virginia Fani(✉), Romeo Bandinelli, and Bianca Bindi

Department of Industrial Engineering, University of Florence, Florence, Italy
{virginia.fani,romeo.bandinelli,bianca.bindi}@unifi.it

Abstract. As widely known, Product Lifecycle Management (PLM) is a set of business solutions and tools for the management of the entire lifecycle of a product, from its conception to its disposal. Despite PLM was born in traditional contexts, recently it is increasingly used in other sectors such as the fashion industry, even if it shows several features that distances it from the traditional approach to PLM deployment. Request for customized products, rapid changes in customer's preference and the consequent shorter product lifecycles make the fashion environment very complex. Within this scenario, PLM has the potential to enable fashion industry to reduce time to market and to increase competitiveness in the global scenario, but quite often clear guidelines are not available. Literature is not exhaustive, as we can't find articles covering the whole set of functionalities. Quite often only few features have been mentioned and the same functionalities have been differently called. To overcome this gap, the purpose of this research is the definition of a framework on PLM functionalities in fashion, classified according to the macro-processes where they are involved. The result is an overview of the PLM functionalities organized in macro-processes, moving from the development of the creative idea to the arrival in the stores, validated by experts of PLM software houses working within the fashion industry. From a managerial point of view, it represents a clear guideline to support companies and vendors to identify the whole range of PLM functionalities and the processes positively involved during their implementation.

Keywords: Fashion · Product lifecycle management · Framework · Functionalities

1 Introduction

PLM is a well-known software adopted into traditional industries, like the manufacturing one. In literature, several papers related to PLM functionalities, PLM adoption level in real case studies and advantages achievable by PLM software implementation can be found [1–3].

Due to its peculiarities, this paper is focused on the fashion industry, where PLM means clear visibility into the Product Development phase, sourcing, and pre-production processes and a more collaborative approach, through every phase of the lifecycle. In particular, several sectorial features make fashion and traditional industries

Published by Springer Nature Switzerland AG 2020
F. Nyffenegger et al. (Eds.): PLM 2020, IFIP AICT 594, pp. 527–537, 2020.
https://doi.org/10.1007/978-3-030-62807-9_42

different, such as the list and definition of the PLM functionalities to be adopted and the segment of the value chain where they should be implemented.

Going deeper into details, the fashion industry is characterized by not repetitive and standardized processes [4], often recognized as leaded by creativity, exclusivity and other qualitative criteria, different from the traditional principles of cost reduction and profit maximization. Thanks to the so-called "digital revolution", PLM systems can be used in fashion [5] since the beginning of the product lifecycle, integrated with 2D and 3D software, starting from the definition of samples and collection details to the retail level and further, involving user experience applications in the middle of life of the product. Every fashion item is highly customized and realized in small lots or, at least, as unique creation. Its, product lifecycle is very short (i.e. it may last up to six months) and, consequently, product details and catalogues are frequently updated, at least twice per year. Moreover, PLM users in the fashion industry are most of all designers and stylists, making the definition of dedicated software interfaces and functionalities suitable for these creative users, used to navigate on graphics and photo editing software, more challenging for the solution providers. In addition, a clear overview of the PLM functionalities available for the fashion companies will help them to better understand the benefits reachable through PLM solutions.

Therefore, the aim of this study is to present a comprehensive classification of PLM functionalities in the fashion industry, starting from a literature review and proposing a framework based on the SCOR model and validated by PLM software vendors.

The paper is structured as follows: in Sect. 2, the objective of the work and the adopted methodology are described; Sect. 3 collects the results coming from the literature review and the proposed framework; finally, main conclusions and future research directions are outlined in Sect. 4.

2 Objectives and Research Methodology

Even if PLM definition and related issues have been deeply analyzed in the literature, there is still a gap between industrial and academic point of view, especially in the definition of the key functionalities of a PLM software. During last years, the Industry 4.0 revolution has pushed PLM software houses towards the introduction of new functionalities that cover a wider range of supply chain (SC) processes, especially in the fashion industry. According to this, the main objective of this work is the identification of a framework to guarantee a well-structured overview of to the PLM functionalities commonly used within the fashion sector. In addition, each functionality has been linked to one or more macro-processes that characterize a fashion product SC, aiming to understand which company roles and departments should be involved during the implementation of a PLM solution.

In order to achieve the described results, two different steps have been carried out.

Firstly, a literature review on PLM functionalities has been conducted to identify the proposed PLM functionalities list. This step includes the rationalization of different nomenclatures found in literature for a single functionality according to its description, resulting on a complete and clear overview of the PLM functionalities available for the fashion industry. Secondly, the identified functionalities have been classified according to the processes where they are involved, then validated through the involvement of experts of PLM software houses.

3 Findings

3.1 PLM Functionalities

The literature review has been conducted on papers related to PLM functionalities with a specific focus on the fashion system, due to the evidence that there is a lack in a unique definition of the overall functionalities of a PLM software for that industry. More specifically, a single reference that exhaustively collects all the functionalities has not been found, while each paper is focused on a selection of them. In addition, a specific functionality is often differently named in different papers, making the identification of a complete and clear set of unique PLM functionalities for the fashion industry difficult to figure out.

Due to this evidence, the first goal of this work has been the definition of a comprehensive framework of the PLM functionalities in the fashion industry based on the literature review, as shown in Table 1. The description of every PLM functionality has not been reported due to space limit.

Table 1. Proposed classification of PLM functionalities based on literature review

PLM functionality	References	Description
Bill of Material Management	[6–8]	BOM management includes structured archiving of all the information, management and communication of change requests
Business Intelligence	[9, 10]	BI tools integrate all data into the PLM by creating interactive, easy-to-use boards and reports
Calendar Management	[7, 8, 11, 12]	Calendar Management allows to define the timing of the various phases of the life cycle of a product
Collaborative Tool	[6, 7, 9, 10, 13]	Collaborative Tools allow to manage all communication and sharing activities in a single connected digital space
Collection Book	[8]	Collection Book allows the creation of digital catalogues
Colour Management	[8–14]	The Color Management functionality has multiple goals: to define standards for the color definition, to manage the color-material association, to manage the color-product association
Composition and Care Label	[8]	Composition and Care Label is a functionality that allows the creation of labels, according to labeling regulations
Costing	[8, 9, 11, 12]	Costing functionalities allow to define a cost estimate from the early stages of product development to the production
Integration Software	[9–13]	Integration software functionalities allow the exchange of information with other business management systems and design tool

(*continued*)

Table 1. *(continued)*

PLM functionality	References	Description
Line Planning	[9, 12]	The line planning is the process where the number of products that will be sold is determined
Material Management	[8–14]	Material Management is the functionality that allows to define material libraries
Order Collection	[8, 11]	Order Collection collects all sales information into a one centralized location
Product Data Management	[6, 8–11, 13]	PDM is one of the core functionalities of the PLM, where all the data regarding the product are stored
Portfolio Management	[12]	Portfolio Management defines the criteria for selecting products and innovation projects to be carried out
Project Management	[12]	Project Management provides the functionalities to implement project management according to the principles of the PMI (Project Management Institute)
Quality Management	[11]	The product Quality Management and compliance with standards module assures the constantly evolving and updating of the standards
Range Planning	[11, 12]	The objective of this process is to assure that the product range is balanced in terms of styles, colors, sizes, price ranges and stocks
Report	[12]	Report features allows users to reorganize product and financial data into customized documents to be shared within the organization
Request For Quotation	[8, 9, 11]	RFQ defines standard supplier selection procedures
Size Range Management	[10, 11, 14]	Size Rage Management functionalities permit to interface PLM with CAD tools managing size-product association
Storyboarding	[8, 10, 11, 13]	It allows the creation of digital storyboards to be shared with stakeholders inside and outside the company
Supplier Auditing	[9, 12]	Supplier Auditing allows to keep up-to-date suppliers reports
Sustainability and Compliance	[10, 14]	This set of features guarantee the compliance with internal and external standards and regulations
Technical Sheet Management	[8, 10, 13]	Technical Sheet Management produce technical data sheet with production cycle specifications
Trend Analysis	[10, 12–14]	Trend Analysis allows to identify the trends in the specific company sector, considering the target audience
Visual Merchandising	[12]	Visual Merchandising allows brands and retailers to create virtual stores, visualizing the layout and generating interactive planograms
Workflow	[6, 7, 10, 12, 13]	Workflow module allows the definition of workflows and to define and execute stored procedures

3.2 Classification of PLM Functionalities Per SC Process

PLM software allows to manage processes along the entire product lifecycle. According to this, the PLM functionalities listed in Table 1 influence specific processes that characterize the fashion SC. In order to clarify which processes within this industry can be supported by PLM tools, a classification of functionalities by macro-processes has been developed.

To identify the macro-processes to be included, the SCOR (Supply Chain Operations Reference) model developed by the Supply Chain Council has represented the starting point for the framework definition. In fact, SCOR aims to create a reference model to describe the SC processes, independently of the specific industrial sector.

After an overview of the PLM functionalities in the fashion sector listed in Table 1, a first evidence is that they are quite relevant to support companies in managing their relationship with suppliers (i.e. "Source" phase in the SCOR model) and their production processes (i.e. "Make" phase in the SCOR model). On the other hand, the application of the same PLM functionalities does not cover the "Deliver" phase in the SCOR model related to internal and external logistics, but impacts the downstream processes related to the order collection and retail activities.

Table 2. Proposed classification of PLM functionalities per SC process

PLM functionality	Transversal	Design	Prototype, sampling & engineering	Sourcing	Production	Ordering & retail
Colour Management		x	x	x	x	
Line Planning		x				
Material Management		x	x	x	x	
Range Planning		x				
Storyboarding		x				
Trend Analysis		x				
Bill Of Material Management			x	x	x	
Size Range Management			x		x	
Technical Sheet Management			x		x	
Request For Quotation				x		
Supplier auditing				x		
Composition and Care Label					x	
Collection Book						x
Order Collection						x
Visual Merchandising						x

(*continued*)

Table 2. (*continued*)

PLM functionality	Transversal	Design	Prototype, sampling & engineering	Sourcing	Production	Ordering & retail
Business Intelligence	x					
Calendar Management	x					
Collaborative Tool	x					
Costing	x					
Integration Software	x					
Product Data Management	x					
Portfolio Management	x					
Project Management	x					
Quality Management	x					
Report	x					
Sustainability and Compliance	x					
Workflow	x					

In addition, the SCOR model focuses on operational processes, without taking into account the upstream SC related to the design phase, in which PLM solutions play a key role.

In fact, the implementation of tools that enable and support companies to innovate in order to rapidly react to market changes, realizing new products or customizing the existed ones, represents a critical success factor especially in dynamic industries such as the fashion one.

More specifically, fashion products are usually characterized by short lifecycles (i.e. from one week to a season), even if a small percentage of total production is usually represented by the carry-over products, which have a longer lifecycle. In this context, the complexity to be managed during the New Product Development (NPD) phase increases due to the need to reduce the time from conception to production. Following [15], they proposed to split the NPD process in the fashion industry into the following phases: Design, Prototyping, Sampling and Engineering.

For all these reasons, the macro-processes adopted to classify the identified PLM functionalities are *Design*, *Prototyping*, *Sampling and Engineering*, *Sourcing*, *Production*, *Ordering and Retail*. Table 2 shows the proposed framework, where each PLM functionality is clustered according to the macro-processes impacted by its implementation. *Transversal* column is selected for the PLM functionalities that impact on all the SC processes.

In the following paragraphs, the results shown in Table 2 are discussed, grouped by SC process.

Design

Design is the first SC process moving from upstream to downstream along the SC. It represents the initial point of the NPD phase, where creative idea starts.

Due to the fact that the decisions taken at this level can determine the success or failure of a product on the market, a crucial aspect of the Design process is to observe, store and share in a collaborative environment customers' needs, requirements and trends. This is the reason why *Trend Analysis* and *Storyboarding* are linked to this process. Moreover, in this phase *Line Planning* and *Range Planning* activities are used in order to simplify the forecasting and planning activities and to define the collection details in terms of product mix for each market. *Colour Management* and *Material Management* are other two PLM functionalities to be used starting from the Design process. The relevance of these two functionalities since the very early stages of the NPD is related to the evidence that just few years ago storyboards were realized by designers and stylists on polystyrene panels, where fabric cutouts of various colors were attached. Nowadays, this activity is usually digitized but the scope is the same: the only difference is that, instead of physical samples, digital contents are collected and stored. Moreover, colours managed through the Colour Management functionality can be selected starting from standard colour palette (e.g. Pantone), in order to guarantee the alignment between the brand owner and its suppliers.

Prototyping, Sampling and Engineering

Colour Management and *Material Management* are also used in the Prototyping, Sampling and Engineering processes. In fact, while the Design phase aims to define the range of colours and materials to be used in each collection, starting from the Prototyping process specific colours and materials will be associated to each item of the developed collection in order to realize prototypes and samples.

Under this macro-process can be found the functionalities of *Size Range Management*, *Technical Sheet Management* and *Bill Of Material (BOM) Management*. In fact, during these processes technical sheets are defined to provide guidelines for the realization of each collection item and the sizes per article to be produced are defined. Moreover, a first version of the BOM per item is developed, updated during the subsequent process after technical and functional controls and sales force feedback.

Sourcing

Within this group, the already mentioned functionalities of *Colour Management*, *Material Management* and *BOM Management* are also included. On the one hand, both the colour and material master data include the possibility to declare the preferred supplier per coloured material (e.g. black calfskin). On the other hand, information about the list of suppliers enabled to realize a specific item can be included within its BOM. Moreover, the unit consumption per coloured materials included in the BOMs crossed with the collected orders give to the sourcing department the exact quantities of coloured materials to be purchased.

Request For Quotation (RFQ) and *Supplier Auditing* functionalities are specific for the Sourcing process, supporting companies in suppliers' management and evaluation.

In fact, the first one supports the collection of the quotations per item of each supplier belonged to the company supply base, while the second one sums up the results of the assessment on suppliers' service levels.

Production

As the previous process, also the Production phase is covered by already mentioned functionalities, such as *Colour Management*, *Material Management*, *Technical Sheet Management, Size Range Management and BOM Management*. In fact, these functionalities are initially involved in previous SC processes but then updated according to the results of technical and functional controls and sales force feedback. For example, some coloured materials can result unfeasible for the realization of some collection articles or reviews to some samples are requested during the sales campaign.

Composition and Care Label functionality is used within the Production process to create the template and information to be included on the product labels, such as materials composition and other product-specific details.

Ordering and Retail

Collection Book and *Order Collection* features are classified into the Ordering and Retail macro-process, representing the workplace where all the information needed for the sales campaign are stored, pre-orders are filled and orders are collected, during trade fairs such as the Milan and Paris fashion weeks or directly in showrooms. These features are usually supported and integrated with digital catalogues and mobile apps. Moreover, the digital catalogues used in both the physical and digital store are based on the collection book developed in the PLM. In addition, retail managers' activities focused on making retail spaces more attractive and pleasing for customers, encouraging their impulse to buy, are supported by the *Visual Merchandise* functionality, related to the definition of store layout and items display.

Transversal

In addition to the ones described above, twelve functionalities are classified as "Transversal", highlighting that their adoption impacts on all the SC processes.

According to the evidence that one of the objectives of PLM software is to support the coordination of cross-functional teams, features such as *Collaborative Tool* allow different actors to manage updated information in a single digital space.

Another core element of PLM is *Product Data Management (PDM)*, that enables the data collection in a structured master data and allows to present product-related information in different views, according to the template configured for the logged user profile.

Integration Software is another transversal functionality, due to the fact that it impacts on different SC processes according to the software to be integrated with PLM. For example, it impacts on the NPD phase, interfacing PLM with CAD and CAM tools, on the Prototyping, Sampling, Engineering and Production processes, when PLM is interfaced with the company's ERP, on the Ordering and Retail macro-process where it is integrated with order collection software.

Another cross-process functionality is *Costing*, used from the Design phase, to support in a structured way the definition of the product target cost, to the Ordering and Retail process when the final price, based on the final production cost, has to be included in the collection catalogue. Using this PLM feature, cost analysis is carried out starting from the estimated material consumption calculated from CAD models crossed with the supplier pricing information stored within PLM software.

Quality Management and *Sustainability and Compliance* functionalities impact on the whole SC, as the compliance with quality standards, sustainability codes of practice and current regulations must be ensured at every stage of the process.

Workflow is the functionality used to define and apply automatic procedures with the aim to simplify and increase the productivity of the teamwork, reducing the occurrence of errors and the related costs. For example, automatic alerts can be sent to the involved users once some events occur, such as the formalization of the collection plan and the validation of the final version of the BOM. In the same way, BOM managers can be informed regarding the changing requests received and can be forced to approve or refuse them within a specific range of time.

Another functionality is the *Calendar Management*, that allows to schedule all the activities along the SC processes in order to meet the deadlines from the concept definition to the collection of the sales force feedback.

Portfolio Management enables the management of new product development projects. In fact, the existent product portfolio, such as the potential investment on innovative products, can be evaluated to establish the priorities based on objective decisional criteria. Moreover, this functionality supports the monitoring of sales growth and related ROI, considering each product or groups of them, in order to identify the best and worst performers.

The last two cross-process functionalities are *Report* and *Business Intelligence (BI)*. Reports feature supports users to collect, analyze and presents data in different formats, in order to be easily understood by different departments with different competences and focus. For example, reports can be used to analyze sales, production, raw material consumption, costs, comparing actual values with planned ones or data of previous years. On the other hand, BI functionality strongly supports in decision-making processes, enabling users to achieve information about the performance of different SC areas. An example of BI implementation is to identify which products receive the highest number of change requests in order to investigate the reasons behind and try to solve them. Moreover, this feature can be used in the Sourcing phase to identify similar components in order to choose, for example, the cheaper ones. For both these functionalities, customized dashboards can be configured by vendors through a deep business analysis.

4 Conclusions and Future Developments

The main result of the present study is a framework on PLM functionalities in the fashion industry, classified according to the SC processes they impact. The framework is based on the evidences collected from the literature and the review of the processes included in the SCOR model, readapted to a dynamic context such as the fashion one.

Once developed, the framework has been validated through structured interviews to experts from PLM software companies, both in terms of PLM functionalities nomenclature and classification per macro-process.

Among the identified functionalities, some of them are vertical in one process, while other cover more than one or, at least, the entire SC.

On the one hand, *Line Planning*, *Range Planning*, *Storyboarding* and *Trend Analysis* have a vertical impact only on the Design phase, such as *RFQ* and *Supplier Auditing* on Sourcing, *Composition and Care Label* on Production and *Collection Book*, *Order collection* and *Visual Merchandising* on Ordering and Retail macro-processes.

On the other hand, some functionalities, called "Trasversal" in the proposed framework, cover all the SC processes, mainly due to their nature. Examples of them are *Collaborative Tool* and *PDM*, based on the development of unique workspace and data library respectively, principles that can be applied by definition to all the SC processes. In the same way, *Reports* and *BI* modules can be used to analyse data coming from different departments, from style to sales offices.

Finally, other features occupy an intermediate position, covering more than one SC process but not all of them. These functionalities are *BOM Management, Colour Management*, *Material Management*, *Size Range Management* and *Technical Sheet Management*, that cover the Prototyping, Sampling and Engineering and the Production processes. This result is partially due to the fact that the realization of a fashion item includes a step-by-step evolution from the prototype, to the sample, to the final product, that forces to manage several versions of product-related documents, such as BOM and technical sheet, and their update along the SC.

From a scientific point of view, the proposed framework overcomes the gap in the literature related to a missing complete overview of all the PLM functionalities in the fashion industry, realized in the present work starting from the evidences coming from the literature review.

From a managerial point of view, the classification of the PLM functionalities by SC process included in the proposed framework represents a clear guideline to support companies and vendors during the implementation of PLM software, making the identification of the key users to be involved easier.

Future research will be focused on the development of an extended version of the proposed framework to investigate new challenges and features PLM software providers are working on, for example related to the Industry 4.0 (e.g. chatbots, AI, VR, AR). Updates and integrations to the present framework will be based on the evidences coming from secondary sources and semi-structured interviews to an experts' panel with members coming from fashion industries and software houses.

Moreover, the present work has constituted the starting point for an ongoing research related to the definition of a comprehensive framework for PLM adoption within fashion companies, starting from the analysis of the requirements up to the deployment of the selected software.

References

1. Rangan, R.M., Rohde, S.M., Peak, R., Chadha, B., Bliznakov, P.: Streamlining product lifecycle processes: a survey of product lifecycle management implementations, directions, and challenges. J. Comput. Inf. Sci. Eng. **5**(3), 227–237 (2005). https://doi.org/10.1115/1.2031270

2. Terzi, S., Bouras, A., Dutta, D., Garetti, M., Kiritsis, D.: Product lifecycle management - from its history to its new role. International Journal of Product Lifecycle Management **4**(4), 360–389 (2010). https://doi.org/10.1504/ijplm.2010.036489
3. Ronzulli, G., Garetti, M., Terzi, S.: Reference model for the evaluation of the performance of a PLM implementation. In: 2006 IEEE International Technology Management Conference, ICE 2006, art. no. 7477094 (2016). https://doi.org/10.1109/ice.2006.7477094
4. Brun A, et al.: Logistics and supply chain management in luxury fashion retail: empirical investigation of Italian firms. Int. J. Prod. Econ. 554–570 (2008). https://doi.org/10.1016/j.ijpe.2008.02.003
5. Liu, Y.-J., Zhang, D.-L., Yuen, M.M.-F.: A survey on CAD methods in 3D garment design. Comput. Ind. **61**(6), 576–593 (2010). https://doi.org/10.1016/j.compind.2010.03.007
6. D'Amico, S., Giustiniano, L., Nenni, M.E., Pirolo, L.: Product lifecycle management as a tool to create value in the fashion system. Int. J. Eng. Bus. Manage. **5**(SPL.ISSUE) (2013). https://doi.org/10.5772/56856
7. d'Avolio, E., Bandinelli, R., Rinaldi, R.: A process-oriented framework for PLM implementation in fashion companies. Int. J. Product Lifecycle Manage. **10**(3), 191–209 (2017). https://doi.org/10.1504/ijplm.2017.10008303
8. d'Avolio, E., Pinna, C., Bandinelli, R., Terzi, S., Rinaldi, R.: Analysing product development process and PLM features in the food and fashion industries. In: Ríos, J., Bernard, A., Bouras, A., Foufou, S. (eds.) PLM 2017. IAICT, vol. 517, pp. 509–521. Springer, Cham (2017). https://doi.org/10.1007/978-3-319-72905-3_45
9. Dalziel, A.: Product life cycle management in the textile and apparel industry. Text. Outlook Int. **140**, 12–35 (2009)
10. Segonds, F., Mantelet, F., Nelson, J., Gaillard, S.: Proposition of a PLM tool to support textile design: a case study applied to the definition of the early stages of design requirements. Comput. Ind. **66**, 21–30 (2015). https://doi.org/10.1016/j.compind.2014.08.002
11. d'Avolio, E., Bandinelli, R., Rinaldi, R.: The need for Product Lifecycle Management (PLM) in the fashion industry: a case study analysis. In: Proceedings of the Summer School Francesco Turco 09–12 September 2014, pp. 94–99 (2014). ISSN 22838996
12. d'Avolio, E., Bandinelli, R., Rinaldi, R.: Improving new product development in the fashion industry through product lifecycle management: a descriptive analysis. Int. J. Fashion Design Technol. Educ. **8**(2), 108–121 (2015). https://doi.org/10.1080/17543266.2015.1005697
13. Segonds, F., Mantelet, F., Maranzana, N., Gaillard, S.: Early stages of apparel design how to define collaborative needs for PLM and fashion? Int. J. Fashion Design Technol. Educ. **7**(2), 105–114 (2014). https://doi.org/10.1080/17543266.2014.893591
14. Vezzetti, E., Alemanni, M., Macheda, J.: Supporting product development in the textile industry through the use of a product lifecycle management approach: a preliminary set of guidelines. Int. J. Adv. Manuf. Technol. **79**(9-12), 1493–1504 (2015). https://doi.org/10.1007/s00170-015-6926-4
15. Soldani, E., Rossi, M., Bandinelli, R., Terzi, S.: New product development process in fashion industry: empirical investigation within italian companies. In: Bernard, A., Rivest, L., Dutta, D. (eds.) PLM 2013. IAICT, vol. 409, pp. 481–490. Springer, Heidelberg (2013). https://doi.org/10.1007/978-3-642-41501-2_48

Cross Industrial PLM Benchmarking Using Maturity Models

Philipp Steck[1(✉)], Felix Nyffenegger[1], Helen Vogt[2], and Roman Hänggi[1]

[1] Fachhochschule OST, Rapperswil, Switzerland
{philipp.steck, felix.nyffenegger, roman.haenggi}@ost.ch

[2] Zürcher Hochschule für Angewandte Wissenschaften (ZHAW), Winterthur, Switzerland
vogh@zhaw.ch

Abstract. Maturity models are commonly used to assess a company's position on a roadmap towards a defined mature PLM environment. The models focus mainly on an internal point of view, comparing a current state to a possible future state. The high level of adjustments in these models to the individual companies needed, make it difficult to compare companies across industries using existing maturity models.

The aim of this paper is to introduce a generic, cross-industrial maturity model suitable for the benchmarking of companies. The model uses an ability-based approach, similar to a case form report.

Using the model, a first benchmarking study has been conducted among ten Swiss companies. This initial study allowed to verify and discuss the suitability of the developed model. Furthermore, the actual results of benchmarking lead to interesting insights into potential success factors to achieve higher PLM maturity. This paper discusses both the maturity model and the actual results.

Keywords: PLM · Maturity model · Benchmarking

1 Introduction

Product lifecycle management (PLM) is a widely accepted practice in today's companies. In many places it has become a strategic initiative to support the overall goal of an enterprise. However, due to its complexity, it is hard to clearly explain the impact and value created by the implementation of PLM. Accordingly, arguing for investment into new PLM initiatives on top management level can be hard. Maturity models help to asses a company's current state and are able to show the potential next steps towards a higher maturity level. However, this is not enough to get a clear view on the added value to the company by this next maturity level. To better qualify such an investment, it would be interesting to do an industry wide comparison of the impact of maturity levels on a company's performance. Since companies in a particular economic system differentiate in very dimension (product, organization, business model, tools, …) the only way to achieve this is cross industrial benchmark. The initial question of the

F. Nyffenegger et al. (Eds.): PLM 2020, IFIP AICT 594, pp. 538–552, 2020.
https://doi.org/10.1007/978-3-030-62807-9_43

presented work was to evaluate weather maturity models can help to do a cross industrial benchmark and extract common success factors of PLM. As a result of this analysis a new assessment model was created and tested.

2 Related Works

The main goal of a PLM maturity assessment tool is to improve the PLM implementation process. This poses a great challenge for many companies [1]. PLM maturity models have been developed and used to assess the PLM implementation situations and determine the relative position of the enterprise by comparing PLM maturity levels with other enterprises [2]. Various frameworks for PLM maturity models have been described in literature [3] and been benchmarked [4]. As Vezzetti has shown, several important maturity models are worth analyzing: The Capability Maturity Model Integration (CMMI) is widely recognized within the PLM community [5] and has developed into an established model in the field of information systems development [6]. It is composed of five maturity levels: Initial, Repeatable, Defined, Managed and Optimized. Batenburg's model [7] focusses on the assessment of PLM implementations. The model applies four maturity levels: ad-hoc, departmental, organizational and interorganizational. Sääksvuori [8] determines the maturity of a large international corporation for a corporate-wide PLM development program and describes business and PLM related issues on the product lifecycle management. The origin of the model lies in the idea of phases or stages, which a company usually goes through as it adapts to new cultural issues, processes, management practices, business concepts and modes of operation [4]. In contrast to the previous models, which mainly focus on internal company processes, Kärkkäinnen [9] proposes a model that focuses on the customer aspects of PLM maturity. The authors distinguish between the following main levels, namely Chaotic, Conscientious, Managed, Advanced and Integration stages, and use elements such as level of proactivity, extent of coordination, extent of integration and quality and type of customer knowledge to characterize and measure these levels.

Most of these models have a clear scope on manufacturing companies and mainly focus on an as-is or a future state analysis. Hence, the models have primarily an intra-company view. They do not aim at comparing or benchmarking different companies. Furthermore, most models empathize the organizational perspective rather than a technical or functional point of view. The study carried out by Kärkkäinnen and Silventoinen analysed a broad spectrum of different models. Base on their analysis, it can be said that most maturity models do not have an indepth description of quantifiable factors that differentiate the different levels [10] Finally, the analyzed models evaluate maturity using open-ended questions or ask the participants to rank their own maturity based on a description of functionalities or of a use-case. The approach of using closed yes or no questions to verify whether a PLM system can fulfill a functionality is a more objective way of evaluating. It does not depend as much on the interviewee's personal opinion and in this way overcomes the typical limitations of a scale based questioning survey as described by Franzen [11].

The proposed model differs from the commonly used ones in the following points:

- Maturity is defined in this study as the capability of a company's PLM environment to fulfill a certain task. This allows a cross-industrial comparison of capabilities. Whether or not a certain capability is beneficial for a company depends on the market context.
- Main target of this model is the comparison of different companies for benchmarking purposes. Hereby the model helps companies to asses their level of maturity and compare themselves across indsturies. The models described in Sect. 2, on the other hand, have a mainly internal perspective and generally do not aim to compare companies.
- Industrial focus: The proposed model is applicable across industries. The models analysed all clearly focus on a limited number of industrial sectors.
- Survey format: The proposed closed yes or no questions focusing on PLM abilities and enable the exact analysis of the available functionalities within a a PLM environment. The analysed models use scale based ratings and ask the companies to rank their abilities in different areas.

This makes the proposed model and its application new and unique. It could help to quantify the influential factors for a successful PLM environment.

3 Method

To develop a cross-industry PLM maturity model, which is suitable for the benchmarking of companies, the methodology as proposed in the SPICE model has been used. SPICE is an international framework for assessment of software processes developed jointly by the ISO and the International Electrotechnical Commission (IEC). According to the literature search of Wangenheim et al. is it also one of the most commonly used approaches to develop maturity models for software products [12]. It describes the preconditions needed to conduct process analyses [13]. Additionally, it has been adapted in other industries (construction) and for other applications (elearnings) [14, 15].

The model was developed and validated along the process shown in Fig. 1.

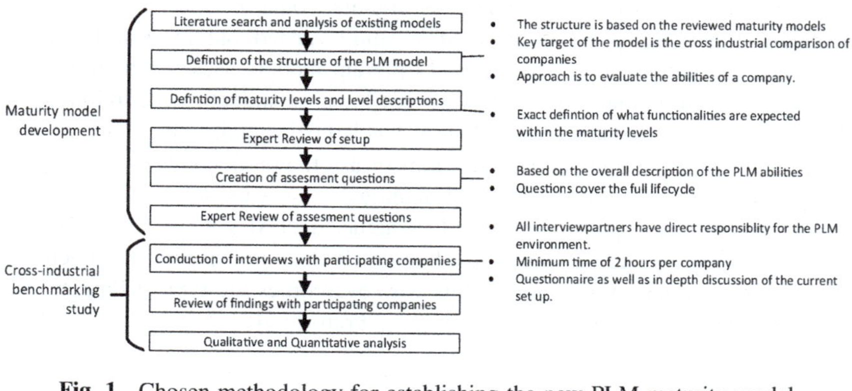

Fig. 1. Chosen methodology for establishing the new PLM maturity model

3.1 Maturity Model Development

Maturity models can be characterized by the number of dimensions (such as the 'process areas' in CMM), the number of levels, a descriptor for each level (such as the CMM's differentiation between initial, repeatable, defined, managed, and optimizing processes), a generic description or summary of the characteristics of each level as a whole, a number of elements or activities for each dimension, and a description of each element or activity as it might be performed at each level of maturity [16]. The introduced model distinguishes five levels of maturity (Initial, Low, Intermediate, Mature and Best Practice) as shown in Table 1. The five-level approach has been successfully used in similar application by Hchicha et al. [17]. Further is it also a recommended approach to asses processes on the base of ISO/IEC15504 [13]. For each of the five levels, Table 2 provides a brief description of the expected traits and abilities. The description is based on an interview with a PLM expert and on a literature review [18].

Table 1. Description of traits for the different levels in the maturity model

Level 1	Initial	• No data standards • Reactive approach • No master data plan • No clear strategy • Processes are not clearly defined • Processes are not transparent • Processes are not supervised • Process automation is not existing • All interfaces are handled manually
Level 2	Low	• Some processes are clearly defined • Processes are not transparent to all stakeholders • There is no systematic KPI tracking for key processes in place • Process automation is only implemented for a few processes/task • Processes are partially supervised • Some automated interfaces • No cross-supply-chain integration
Level 3	Intermediate	• Nominal data governance implemented • Some sort of MDM in place • Some KPI tracking regarding data quality in place • Most processes are clearly defined • Processes are not transparent to all stakeholders • There is no systematic KPI tracking for key processes in place • Processes are only partly supervised by tools • Multitool processes are not implemented • Automated interfaces widely used • Some cross-supply-chain integration

(continued)

Table 1. (*continued*)

Level 4	Mature	• MDM managing all companies meta data • Data layers implemented • Clearly defined data governance • Data models enable a smooth and quick exchange • All processes are clearly defined • Processes are transparent to operators and managers • There is systematic KPI tracking for key processes in place • Processes are supervised by tools • Multitool processes are implemented • Process engines are implemented for key processes • Automated interfaces widely used • Cross-supply-chain integration is standards
Level 5	Best-practice	• Scalable and easy to adjust data models • Data simplifies processes and is highly adjustable to different tools • Data is stored in a central database • Data objects are minimized • All processes are clearly defined • Processes are transparent to all stakeholders • There is systematic KPI tracking for all processes in place • Processes are supervised by tools • Processes enable a seamless workflow among the entire supply chain • Multitool processes are implemented • Process engines are implemented for all processes • Processes interact directly with customers and suppliers

3.2 Development of the Survey

For the creation of the survey, the decision was taken to create closed questions in binary form (yes/no). This approach is commonly used in medical examinations where a patient's symptoms are evaluated using case report forms. These forms mostly use closed yes or no questions. This approach helps to objectively evaluate the pattern of a possible illness based on the patient's description [19]. Transferring this to the field of PLM maturity, a questionnaire with a total of 64 closed binary questions was created.

The questionnaire was created using a five step approach.

1. Creation of a description of tasks for every phase of the lifecycle. Hereby the phases of beginning, mid and end of life defined by S. Terzi et al. were utilized [20].
2. For every task in each phase a description of functionalities that support or enable the task was created.
3. The functionalities were transformed into closed yes or no questions.
4. For validation of the questions, the model was pretested with a selected partner company.

Table 2. Questionaire and categorisation

ID	Question	Lifecycle phase	ID	Question	Lifecycle phase
1	Requirements for new products are collected systematically and transferred to R&D via a clearly defined process.		33	Bills of material can be generated automatically using configurators.	
2	Requirements are recorded directly in a process engine.		34	On the base of bills of material the system can automatically generate parameterized CAD models.	
3	Information about the current portfolio is provided systematically and can be sorted by properties.		35	There system enables the management of adjusted bills of materials for each end user according to the respective requirements.	
4	Within the process, resources are allocated and the planning is supported by an automated tool		36	The bill of material for service purposes is generated automatically.	
5	Findings from previous development projects are systematically incorporated into the definition of new development orders.		37	CAD models of assemblies are automatically checked for errors (e.g. collision check).	
6	Currently running development projects are tracked within a tool that enables sorting according to defined requirements.		38	The system checks the stored data for duplicates and completeness.	
7	Initial concepts to fulfil the requirements can be clearly assigned to requirements within the system.		39	The design review is carried out in a system-led process.	
8	The results of the product conception are systematically recorded and always according to the same procedure.		40	The system supports different roles and thus enables the systematic control of engineering data (example: developer and reviewer).	
9	Concepts and intial drafts are handed over to the development teams via a clearly defined release process.		41	If errors are detected during the review, any comments can be entered directly into the system and can be clearly assigned to a responsible.	
10	Documentation on first drafts can be clearly assigned to the final article in the system.		42	CAD data can be extracted directly from the system in a neutral CAD format.	
11	The system allows the search for modules that fulfill similar functions and requirements.		43	If CAD data is shared with a stakeholder, this happens in a clearly structured form (in terms of content) and following a processes based on clear guidelines.	
12	Articlenumbers are assigned automatically by the system.		44	In the event of a change, it is clear to the executing engineer whether the data has been shared externally or not.	
13	Numbering structures are clearly defined for standard and purchased parts.		45	Data is always exchanged via secure databases in which access can be monitored.	
14	The same article number is always used for all processes throughout the whole life cycle.	Beginning of life	46	All production relevant data for individual parts can be found in the CAD model.	Middle of life
15	While working in the CAD the engineer has access to information on tools / machines that are used in manufacturing. The engineer is using this information to adjust new product accordingly.		47	Manufacturing information is transferred to the production sites in a defined form and according to a clearly defined process	
16	Models are enriched with a defined set of metadata.		48	Manufacturing information is released fully automatically for the defined manufacturing locations and is automatically available after release.	
17	CAD models of individual parts are automatically checked for errors (e.g. incomplete definitions)		49	Production resources such as tools and machines are stored in the system and are accessible to the engineer during all development stages.	
18	Faulty CAD models cannot be transferred to the next process instance.		50	CAM-data is clearly to the actual CAD model and is considered a part of the change process.	
19	CAD models are the single source of truth and contain all relevant information for the whole life cylce (example: surface condition, material data, tolerances, surface treatment, raw material)		51	All manufacturing information regarding a product is stored in one consolidated database.	
20	The system enables the search for parts using technical traits of [illegible]		52	As built bills of materials are clearly assigned to the orders and can be called up at any time.	
21	Within the system one can systematically search for possible, suitable standard parts.		53	Visualizations can be generated automatically using the existing product parameters	
22	While selecting suitable standardparts the engineer gets imediate information about cost and availability		54	Change requests are systematically recorded and clearly assigned to the articles.	
23	If a new standard part would have to be introduced, the system allows a systematic search for possible alternatives.		55	Changerequests get systematically reviewed and categorized with system support.	
24	The system enables the systematic search for suitable purchased parts on the basis of technical parameters.		56	As part of a change order the required changes can highlighted directly in the CAD model.	
25	On the base of selected technical attributes and description the system is able to propose standard suppliers for certain parts.		57	Change orders are clearly assigned to a responsible.	
26	The creation of functional descriptions for tenders is supported by the system		58	In case of an index change, an overview of all affected articles is automatically generated.	
27	Simulation results and models are directly linked to all other product data.		59	Communication with stakeholders regarding changes is conducted through a clearly structured process.	
28	Transfer of the data to any special departments (example: simulation) is carried out in a clearly structured process, follwing clear guidelines.		60	The system supports the developer in deciding whether a new part number is necessary or not.	
29	Simulation results are sent back to the responsible development department via a clearly structured process.		61	If an article is discontinued, all data is automatically set to invalid..	
30	Bills of material are created in a clearly defined process, , follwing clear guidelines.	Middle of life	62	If a product is discontuined the system is able to deliver an overview of all interdependencies.	End of life
31	Bills of material are derived directly from the CAD-data.		63	The system supports communication if a product is discontinued to external stakeholders	
32	Bills of material are transferred to ERP without manual intervention.		64	Any successor products can be recorded within the system.	

5. The questionnaire was reviewed by PLM experts (more than 15 years of experience). The goal of this step was to ensure that all questions are unique and do not correlate with each other.

Table 2 shows the complete questionnaire. On the left hand side the current life cycle phase of the product is shown.

The following data can be extracted from the assessment questions:

- Sum of questions answered with yes
- Overall maturity level reflecting on the number of yes-answers
- Number of times a specific question got answered with yes
- Additional descriptive data about the participants and additional commentary and qualitative information

Using the sum of yes-answers the data can be used to create a benchmark of the companies and rank them. On this base the different PLM environments of the companies can be compared. On the base of the impact different factors can be estimated. Based on these factors, possible success factors for a mature PLM environment can be assessed using the qualitative data.

3.3 Crossindustrial Benchmarking Study

Using the questionnaire, a benchmarking study was conducted among potential best practice companies. The companies have been selected based on their potentially mature PLM-environment rather than industrial criteria. The following selection criteria were used:

i. Swiss headquarter
ii. Comparable product strategy
iii. Possible mature PLM-environment
iv. Similar manufacturing depth
v. Available during the required time period

Thus, the study does not represent an industrial benchmark. An overview of the different traits of all the participating companies can be found in the Table 3. Due to agreements with the participants, the data is displayed without any explicit description of the companies. The given categorical data will be used for further statistical analysis.

All interviews were conducted with company employees. The interviewees hold positions with direct responsibilities for the improvement of the IT-infrastructure and/or the PLM-environment in general. The interviews took place in the different locations. The minimum timeframe per interview was two hours. The interview followed hereby the following agenda:

1. Brief introduction of the research project (personal interview)
2. General questions about the PLM strategy and personal estimations (personal interview)
3. Interview using the assessment questions as shown in Sect. 3.3 (personal interview)
4. Immediate discussion of the results to gain a deeper understandign of the case at hand (personal interview)

5. Extended data analysis
6. Review of the findings by the participants
7. Creation of the final report.

Table 3. Participating companies of the benchmarking study

ID	Industries	Size	Last PLM change	Product strategy	Changes currently planned	Manufacturing locations	Engineering locations	Company age
A	Energy	Medium	2004	ATO	Yes	Multiple	Single	25 to 50 years
B	Energy	Medium	2019	ATO, ETO, MTS	Yes	Multiple	Multiple	50 to 100 years
C	Mechanical Engineering	Small	2019	ETO	Yes	Single	Single	>100 years
D	Building industries	Large	2017	ATO, ETO	Yes	Multiple	Multiple	>100 years
E	Building industries	Large	2014	MTS, ATO	Yes	Multiple	Single	50 to 100 years
F	Mechanical Engineering	Small	2019	ATO	Yes	Single	Single	<25 years
G	Mechanical Engineering	Large	2018	MTS, ATO	Yes	Multiple	Multiple	25 to 50 years
H	Mechanical Engineering	Small	2019	ETO	Yes	Multiple	Single	<25 years
I	Mechanical Engineering	Small	2010	ATO	Yes	Single	Single	25 to 50 years
J	Building industries	Large	2019	MTS, ATO	No	Multiple	Multiple	<25 years

4 Results

4.1 Overall Benchmarking Results

Using the developed questionnaire, the participating companies have been interviewed. The overall scores (amount of yes-answers) have been used to rank them. Figure 2 shows the results. The barplot on top shows the total sum of yes answers and the corresponding maturity levels. The matrix shows the individual answers of the participants of every question. The histogram on the right shows the amount of times a question has been answered with yes. The data is sorted in a ascending order using the sum of yes-answers from the lowest scoring to the highest one. For the further analysis, the overall PLM capability of a company is being considered. This means that only the sum of yes-answers is considered relevant, thus the answer to a single questions does not reflect the maturity of a company.

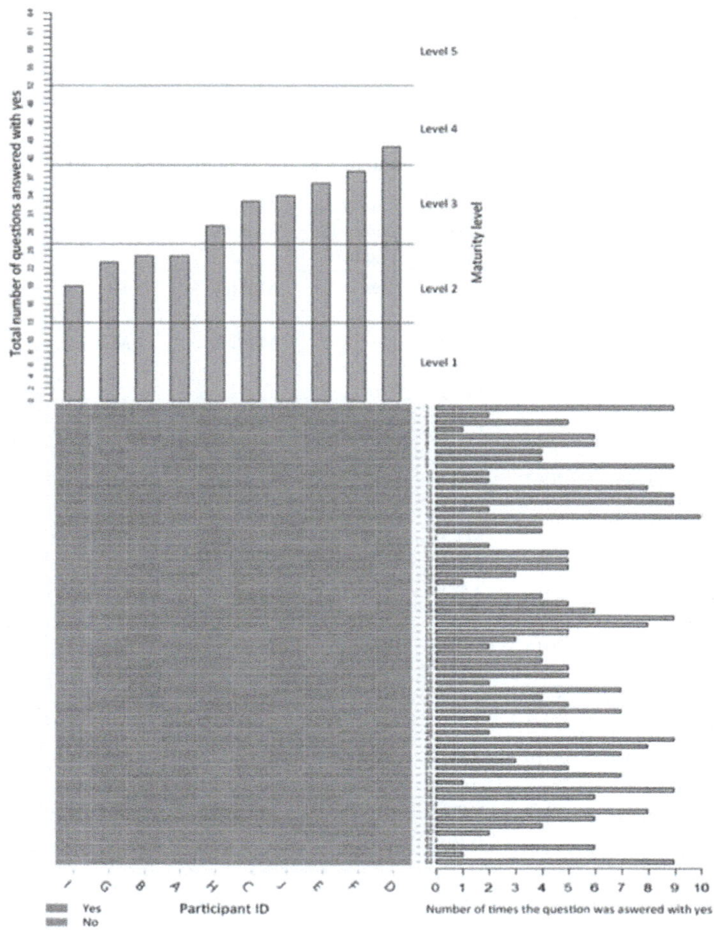

Fig. 2. Results benchmarking overall

4.2 Additional Insights from Top Performing Companies

Based on the results, the three top-scoring companies have been asked to describe organizational aspects that they felt were most critical in their opinion to the success of their PLM strategy and implementation. The following success factors were identified:

- Established a long-term road map regarding the system-landscape and the goals.
- Running smaller, but more frequent process improvement projects.
- Having designated teams working on the improvement of the PLM-environment.
- Frequent exchange with users on problems, possible ideas and upcoming projects.
- Frequent exchange with other companies and field experts.
- Implementing small changes on their own – this includes programming.
- PLM trainings are coordinated by designated specialists.
- Special tools implemented for PLM-users to propose changes.

4.3 Analysis of Influencing Factors

The further analysis focuses on the total number of yes-answers (scores) achieved by the companies. Table 4 shows the number of yes-answers given by the different companies and a summary of the basic statistical values.

Table 4. Number of yes-answers per company

ID	A	B	C	D	E	F	G	H	I	J
Score	24	24	33	42	36	38	23	29	19	34

Mean	Median	Variance	Standard deviation
30.2	31	6.84	7.54

A factor comparison of the mean values has been conducted. The analysed factors are shown in Table 5.

Table 5. Analysed factors

ID	Factor	Factor levels
1	Company size	Small, Medium, Large
2	Main product strategy	ATO, ETO, Mixed
3	Industries	Building, Energy, Machine
4	Manufacturing locations	Single, Multiple
5	Engineering locations	Single, Multiple
6	Company age	<25 years, 25 to 50 years, 50 to 100 years, >100 years
7	Termination of the last PLM Project	<1 year, >1 year

Figure 3 shows the results. The mean values are visualized as horizontal lines within the diagrams. All differences in the mean values that are greater than the standard deviation of the overall data set (6.84) were considered relevant.

This analysis shows that the following factors could be relevant for a high level of maturity:

- Company age
- Company size
- Industries
- Termination of the last PLM Project

Further analysis using a regression model would require a lager sample size.

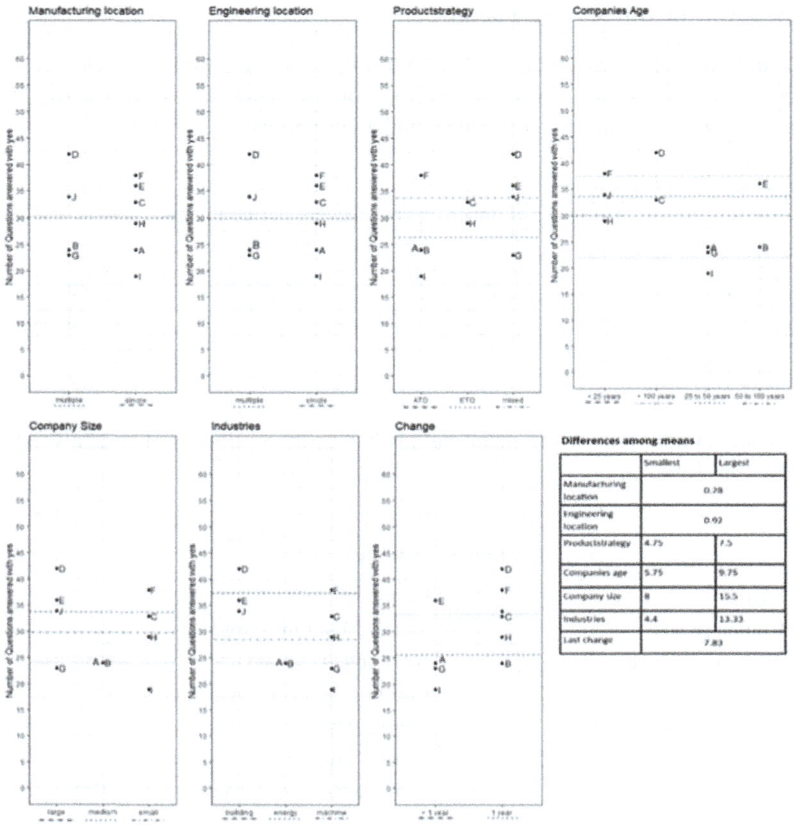

Fig. 3. Factorwise analysis

4.4 Sample Size Calculation

To gain representative results a larger sample group would be required. The minimum required sample size has been calculated on the base of the formula defined by Cochran [21]. The required number of participants is 247. For the calculation the following values have been used:

- Relevant population = 1956. The relevant population size has been defined as all European companies with at least 250 employees working in the sector of machine engineering [22, 23].
- Standard deviation relative to median = 0.24. This value has been transferred from the current sample.
- Margin of error of 5% and a z-value of 1.96 in accordance of a expected confidence interval of 95%.

5 Discussion

The overall results show a broad spectrum, ranging from the lowest score of 19 yes-answers to the highest value of 42. The maturity of five companies has been classified as intermediate (level 3). Four have been classified as low (level 2) and only one has achieved the level 4, which is described as mature. First, this distribution can interpreted as a validation of the assessment questions. This is due to the fact that the broad spectrum can only be achieved with a set of questions that is able to differentiate the companies on the base of their abilities. If the questions would be less generalistic, the expected distribution of the results would be either polarized or very strongly concentrated on a single score. Second, the distribution can be interpreted as a sign for possibly huge differences among the supported PLM functionalities within the companies. Some potential influential factors have been detected. These will be discussed in Sect. 5.1 and 5.2. Some of the questions never got answered with yes (19, 26 and 61). This may have two possible reasons. First, the questions simply may not reflect a relevant functionality of a PLM environment. Second, the participants may not be mature enough to achieve the required functionality. To ensure that the questions are relevant and realistic, a second round of review of the current questions may be needed.

5.1 Additional Insights from Top Performers

The measurements and approaches presented are mainly based on the discussion with the interviewees. Their influence on the actual PLM maturity has not been investigated as part of this study. At this point, the mentioned measurements can interpreted as factors that may contribute to a higher level of maturity.

However, the data has only been collected for the top three and not for all participants. For further research, a number of structured additional questions, targeting the chosen strategy and PLM tools utilized by these companies, would help to gain further insights. This data should definitely be collected for all participants, since the analysis of the chosen approaches of the low scoring companies could be just as insightfull as shown by Cooper [24].

5.2 Influecing Factors

The factor by factor by factor comparison of means clearly shows that certain factors lead to a larger difference among the means than others. Using the 6.84 threshold, the following relevant factors have been selected:

Company Size

Large and small companies scored higher than medium sized companies. The higher scores of the smaller companies can be explained by the expected lower level of organizational complexity. In contrast, the higher scores of the large companies would be due to the larger amount of ressources. The middle sized companies low scores could be caused by the increasingly complex set up without the right means to overcome this complexity.

- **Industries**: Companies from the building industry achieved significantly better results than companies from the machine engineering and energy industry. All three companies active in the building industry have a broad product portfolio with mixed product strategies. This is a clear sign of the comparatively high complexity of the overall PLM environment. This increased complexity may have led to a selection process within the industries, leaving only the mature companies.
- **Change:** The highest score was achieved by the companies that recently changed their environment. This is a clear sign, that PLM projects overall lead to an improvement in PLM maturity. Companies are capable to conduct such projects and gain benefits from them even if the change was only recently.
- **Companies age:** The highest mean was achieved by the oldest companies. The second highest by the youngest. These values are comparable close to one another and the difference to the companies older than 50 years is rather small. The companies older than 25 but younger than 50 years lag considerably behind. The root causes of this cannot be evaluated at this point. However, all companies scoring low in this category have the commonality that their last change in the PLM environment took place more than one year ago.

All the discussed results are based on a small sample group, the results are not statistically significant and the selected group is not representative for their corresponding industries. Additionally, the set of factors currently used is not comprehensive. As part of further research additional evaluation of factors would be required.

5.3 Sample Size Calculation

The calculated value of 247 European companies is based on the assumption, that the standard deviation of the current sample is transferable to a larger case group. Not all of the current participants would meet the criteria for the proposed study. This leads to the conclusion that the calculation has to be regarded as an estimation and a first indicator. Furthermore, any change in the assessment questions or the overall model would require a recalculation of the standard deviation on the base of a new study.

6 Conclusion

The chosen methodology can deliver meaningful results. Hereby, the frequent validation by experts and the review of the companies of the results have been proven to be crucial elements. The developed model is able to differentiate the companies and delivers a broad spectrum of results. Within these results certain patterns can be detected. These patterns lead to factors that may influence the maturity of a PLM environment of a company. The additional discussion of the results with the high scoring companies has been a useful approach to learn about measurements and approaches which may be beneficial for the maturity of the PLM environment. On the base of Cooper additional analysis of the low scoring companies would be beneficial. Conducting an additional study with a larger sample group would allow the data to be analyzed using statistical means and to quantify the effects of different factors. As part of this expanded study an expansion of the current set of questions could be beneficial to cover additional aspects of the PLM environment and get an even more holistic point of view.

References

1. Silventoinen, A.S., Pels, H.J., Kärkkäinen, H., et al.: PLM maturity assessment as a tool for PLM implementation process. In: Thoben, K.-D. (ed.) Product lifecycle management: Proceedings of the PLM10 Conference held at the University of Bremen, Germany, 12–14 July 2010. Inderscience Enterprises Ltd., Genève, pp. 369–379 (2013)
2. Zhang, H., Bouras, A., Sekhari, A., et al.: A PLM components monitoring framework for SMEs based on a PLM maturity model and FAHP methodology. J. Modern Project Manage. **2**, 108–119 (2014)
3. Paavel, M., Karjust, K., Majak, J.: PLM maturity model development and implementation in SME. Procedia CIRP **63**, 651–657 (2017). https://doi.org/10.1016/j.procir.2017.03.144
4. Vezzetti, E., Violante, M.G., Marcolin, F.: A benchmarking framework for product lifecycle management (PLM) maturity models. Int. J. Adv. Manuf. Technol. **71**(5-8), 899–918 (2013). https://doi.org/10.1007/s00170-013-5529-1
5. Wendler, R.: The maturity of maturity model research: a systematic mapping study. Inf. Softw. Technol. **54**(12), 1317–1339 (2012). https://doi.org/10.1016/j.infsof.2012.07.007
6. Fraser, P., Moultrie, J., Gregory, M.: The use of maturity models/grids as a tool in assessing product development capability. In: 2002 IEEE International Engineering Management Conference, pp. 244–249 (2002)
7. Batenburg, R., Helms, R.W., Versendaal, J.: PLM roadmap: stepwise PLM implementation based on the concepts of maturity and alignment. IJPLM **1**(4), 331–351 (2006). https://doi.org/10.1504/IJPLM.2006.011053
8. Saaksvuori, A., Immonen, A.: Product Lifecycle Management. Springer, Heidelberg (2008) https://doi.org/10.1007/978-3-540-78172-1
9. Kärkkäinen, H., Pels, H.J., Silventoinen, A.: Defining the customer dimension of PLM maturity. In: Rivest, L., Bouras, A., Louhichi, B. (eds.) PLM 2012. IAICT, vol. 388. pp. 623–634. Springer, Heidelberg (2012). https://doi.org/10.1007/978-3-642-35758-9_56
10. Kärkkäinen, H., Silventoinen, A.: Different approaches of the PLM maturity concept and their use domains – analysis of the state of the art. In: Bouras, A., Eynard, B., Foufou, S., Thoben, K.-D. (eds.) PLM 2015. IAICT, vol. 467, pp. 89–102. Springer, Cham (2016). https://doi.org/10.1007/978-3-319-33111-9_9
11. Franzen, A.: Antwortskalen in standardisierten Befragungen. In: Baur, N., Blasius, J. (eds.) Handbuch Methoden der empirischen Sozialforschung, pp. 701–711. Springer, Wiesbaden (2014). https://doi.org/10.1007/978-3-531-18939-0_51
12. García-Mireles, G.A., Ángeles Moraga, M, García, F.: Development of maturity models: a systematic literature review. In: 16th International Conference on Evaluation & Assessment in Software Engineering (EASE 2012), Piscataway, NJ, 14–15 May 2012. IEEE, pp. 279–283 (2012)
13. Wagner, K.W., Dürr, W.: Reifegrad nach ISO/IEC 15504 (SPiCE) ermitteln. Carl Hanser Verlag GmbH & Co. KG, München (2008)
14. Marshall, S., Mitchell, G.: Applying SPICE to e-learning: an e-learning maturity model? In: Lister, R. (ed.) Computing education 2004: Proceedings of the Sixth Australasian Computing Education Conference, Dunedin, New Zealand, January 2004, pp. 185–191 (2010)

15. Goulding, J., Haigh, R., Finnemore, M., et al.: SPICE: is a capability model applicable in the construction inddustry? In: Lacasse, M.A. (ed.) Information Technology in Construction: CIB W78 Workshop. NRC Research Press, Ottawa (1999)
16. Mettler, T.: Maturity assessment models: a design science research approach. IJSSS **3**(1/2), 81 (2011). https://doi.org/10.1504/IJSSS.2011.038934
17. Hachicha, M., Moalla, N., Fahad, M., Ouzrout, Y.: A maturity model to promote the performance of collaborative business processes. In: Bouras, A., Eynard, B., Foufou, S., Thoben, K.-D. (eds.) PLM 2015. IAICT, vol. 467, pp. 112–124. Springer, Cham (2016). https://doi.org/10.1007/978-3-319-33111-9_11
18. Stark, J. (ed.): Product Lifecycle Management: Volume 1: 21st Century Paradigm for Product Realisation. Decision Engineering, 3rd edn. Springer, Cham (2015). https://doi.org/10.1007/978-3-319-17440-2
19. Bellary, S., Krishnankutty, B., Latha, M.S.: Basics of case report form designing in clinical research. Perspect. Clin. Res. **5**(4), 159–166 (2014). https://doi.org/10.4103/2229-3485.140555
20. Terzi, S., Bouras, A., Dutta, D., et al.: Product lifecycle management – from its history to its new role. IJPLM **4**(4), 360 (2010). https://doi.org/10.1504/IJPLM.2010.036489
21. Cochran, W.G.: Sampling techniques. Charles E. Tuttle, Tokyo (1953)
22. Bundesamt für Statistik: Bestand aktiver Unternehmen. je-d-06.02.02.01.01 (2019). https://www.bfs.admin.ch/bfs/de/home/statistiken/industrie-dienstleistungen/unternehmen-beschaeftigte/unternehmensdemografie.assetdetail.10687098.html. Accessed 27 Mar 2020
23. EuroStat: Industrie nach Beschäftigtengrößenklassen (NACE Rev. 2, B-E) (2017). https://appsso.eurostat.ec.europa.eu/nui/submitViewTableAction.do. Accessed 27 Mar 2020
24. Cooper, R.G.: The dimensions of industrial new product success and failure. J. Market. **43**(3), 93 (1979). https://doi.org/10.2307/1250151

A Knowledge-Based Approach for PLM Implementation Using Modular Benefits Dependency Networks

Bas Koomen[1,2](✉)

[1] University of Twente, Enschede, The Netherlands
s.p.koomen@utwente.nl
[2] Cadmes B.V., s-Hertogenbosch, The Netherlands
bas@cadmes.com

Abstract. Industrial companies face significant challenges when they engage in the implementation of Product Lifecycle Management. Research has shown that organizations have difficulties in defining concrete and measurable goals and relating enabling technology to business benefits. Moreover, implementation service providers rely heavily on tacit knowledge when it comes to operational details. This paper proposes a conceptual framework as a methodology for implementation teams. It allows teams to reuse implementation knowledge on a detailed level, related to contribution to benefits and business goals. The methodology is derived from emerging, set-based product and process development methodologies and also from benefit management strategies for information systems. The goal of this methodology is to increase the probability that Product Lifecycle Management implementation contributes to the business benefits of organizations and therefore lower the economic risks. The paper describes the method and the result of two explorative case studies.

Keywords: Product Lifecycle Management · IT benefits management · Knowledge reuse

1 Introduction

Product Lifecycle Management (PLM) is a business practice to manage all product-related information and communication during the product's entire life, from concept to recycling [1–3]. PLM has become more important over the past years with the increasing complexity of products. Producing companies need to be more flexible in terms of product needs, volume, resource efficiency, adapt to (personalized) customer needs, and work in a networked supply chain [4].

PLM, as a business approach, is supported by PLM software. PLM software includes many applications, like Computer-Aided Design (CAD), Computer-Aided Manufacturing (CAM), and Product Data Management (PDM).

The implementation of PLM software is a challenge for many companies and many PLM implementation projects fail to achieve their goals [1, 5, 6]. In a review of published literature about PLM implementation [7], we found that structured guidelines for implementation projects exist. They mostly come down to four phases: 1) prepare

Published by Springer Nature Switzerland AG 2020
F. Nyffenegger et al. (Eds.): PLM 2020, IFIP AICT 594, pp. 553–562, 2020.
https://doi.org/10.1007/978-3-030-62807-9_44

the organization and define strategy and goals, 2) Analyze and measure the current state of the organization and processes, 3) Design a future state for the organization, processes, and ICT infrastructure, and 4) Implement and maintain the future state. It is a substantial investment for companies to perform all the tasks in each phase, and it requires process and management skills to perform them with sufficient quality. Large companies may have these skills in their organization, but Small and Medium-Sized Enterprises (SME) regularly don't.

In an empirical study on 9 PLM implementation projects in SME [8], we found that these companies are "cutting corners" in the hope that a technical software implementation will fix their business problems. Implementation service providers are likely to respond by delivering functionality that the company is requesting, with little evidence that the investment contributes to improved business processes.

Research on Enterprise Systems (ES) and Information Systems (IS)[1] shows that only the software itself does not bring value to an organization [10]. It is the way the organization can change its processes and culture that has the most influence on the value of an ES/IS investment. Therefore, they need to see the relation between enabling function, operational benefits, and business value [11]. Section 2.1 elaborates on the theory of IT Benefits Management.

Another valuable insight from our research is that the PLM implementation, as an organizational subject, is a design process. This insight is supported by the idea that an organization is an artifact, and therefore designed [12]. Furthermore, van Aken [13] has made the connection between the design of physical objects (products, buildings) and organizations. He also noted that in the design of physical objects, the designer, the maker, and the user can be separated. In organizations, this separation mostly absent.

Following these ideas, we looked into several product design methods. We found that Lean Product and Process Development (LPPD) [14] addresses issues that we recognized in our research on PLM implementation. This method emphasizes the contribution of functional and technical decisions to real customer value. Decisions should be delayed until evidence on value contribution is present. The concept of Set-Based Concurrent Engineering, as part of LPPD, enables the decision making process and efficient reuse of knowledge from previous projects. Section 2.2 contains more detailed background information on LPPD.

In this paper, we formulate a method that combines the principles of both IT Benefits Management and Lean Product and Process Development (Sect. 3). We explored elements of this new method in two case studies within a PLM implementation service provider (Sect. 4). The case studies showed promising results, and we gained information to improve the method. We believe that this method can help implementation service providers to improve their service and deliver better quality across all four phases of a PLM implementation. Moreover, it is likely that it lowers the implementation cost, particularly in the context of SME.

---

[1] Enterprise Systems and Information Systems are a generic descriptions of "means by which people and organizations, utilizing technology, gather, process, store, use and disseminate information." PLM can be classified as an Enterprise Systems or Information System [9].

2 Theoretical Background

This section describes the principal elements from Benefits Management and Lean Product and Process Development, upon which we based our implementation method.

2.1 Benefits Management

Benefits Management, as described by Ward and Daniel [9], is management in a way that benefits from the use of Information Systems (IS) are realized. "Benefits" are referring to business benefits: an advantage for a specific stakeholder or group of stakeholders that want to obtain value from an investment.

On the one hand, benefits are realized by organizational business changes, enabled by enabling changes and IS/IT enablers. On the other hand, benefits enable the achievement of investment objectives, derived from the company's business drivers. These interdependencies build a benefits dependency network (BDN). Figure 1 illustrates the interdependencies with arrows, pointing towards the business benefits. Each arrow represents an n-to-n relation. For example, multiple business changes can support a single benefit, and one single business change can support multiple benefits.

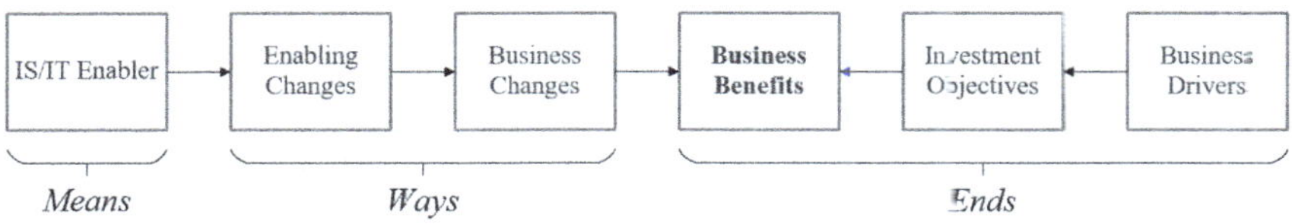

Fig. 1. Interdependencies within a BDN. Six categories in three areas of interest. Modified from [9]

Benefits Dependency Networks are used in various ways. Peppard, Ward, and Daniel [11] have investigated the use of BDNs in Customer Relationship Management (CRM) implementation projects. They found three starting areas of interest (Means, ways, or ends) in the BDN applicable in individual projects. In each scenario, the level of uncertainty increases with every step.

1. **Problem-based interventions**. In these cases, the project starts with a business driver to eliminate an existing problem or constraint. The event flow in this scenario:
   a. Define performance targets for the improved state (investment objectives and potential business benefits).
   b. Identify enablers and changes needed to achieve potential benefits.
   c. Decide which enablers and changes to implement, based on contribution to intended benefits.
2. **Innovation-based interventions, delivered from new ways of working.** Here, the focus is on the business and enabling changes. The flow of events:
   a. The start is a global vision about the future of the company.

   b. Describe new ways of working that would deliver benefits in the context of the vision.
   c. Determine how IT can enable these changes
   d. Evaluate the feasibility and the contribution to the benefits and the vision.
3. **IT innovation-based interventions.** These interventions start with the capabilities of IT enablers. The typical flow in this scenario:
   a. Understand the new capabilities of IT.
   b. Determine what changes to the ways of working are needed.
   c. Assess the benefits and the potential investment objectives that could be realized by the changes.

It is helpful to identify in which scenario a company is going to invest in IS/IT. We suspect that in many cases, a company is making investments based on scenario 3, but the project is managed as a scenario 1. In case of such a misinterpretation, evaluations are made on wrong arguments, and there is no evidence of the value contribution of IT enablers. A skilled application of a BDN can prevent these mistakes and let stakeholders focus on the right subjects. The research of Peppard et al. [11] have shown successes with this approach, delivering more proven benefits of IT investments.

2.2 Lean Product and Process Development

While investigating the design methodology at Toyota in the '90s, Ward, Liker, Cristiano, and Sobek II [15, 16] discovered set-based concurrent engineering (SBCE) as a key differentiator. As a design methodology, it was able to deliver more customer value in less time and effort. Rapid learning and reuse of existing knowledge are key elements in SBCE.

The term Lean Product and Process Development (LPPD) was introduced later by Ward and Sobek II [14]. It puts SBCE in the context of a specific design management concept. Based on their work, other researchers have refined some aspects of LPPD. For our method, we used a number of these elements:

Visual Management. In LPPD, it is essential to present information visually, in order to have all stakeholders maximally involved. Cloft and Kennedy [17] describe a method of causal mapping. These causal maps contain all relevant target parameters, input parameters, and internal parameters of a design problem.

Interdependencies of these parameters are presented as nodes, linking the parameters. The nature of these interdependencies is either known or unknown. In the case of unknown, there is a knowledge gap to be filled.

This visual approach helps to position reusable knowledge in context or narrow down on areas where research is needed. The research team can distribute tasks efficiently and publish the outcome in the causal map.

Set-Based Concurrent Engineering. SBCE includes the following practices, characteristic to its nature [18]:

- Requirements are not defined as exact point values but in ranges or sets. As the design progresses, these ranges can be refined based on knowledge acquired during the design process.

- Design limits and trade-offs between design parameters need to be explicit before design decisions are made.
- Sets of design alternatives are developed. The number of alternatives in the set gradually decreases as the design knowledge increases.
- (Sub-)system design and manufacturing development are done in parallel, with information shared between them. This helps to make better design decisions.

By developing multiple alternative solutions for sub-systems, the chance of success of the entire design project increases dramatically. Besides that, it generates a wealth of reusable knowledge for future design projects.

Structured Workflow. Kerga, Rossi, Taisch, and Terzi [19] have described a workflow to apply SBCE. This workflow consists of four steps:

1. Explore alternative solution sets for sub-systems, looking only at the sub-system itself.). Generate solution sets systematically by using existing knowledge (trade-off curves).
2. Eliminate incompatible solutions in the overlapping regions of the sets. Sets overlap when the sub-systems have design parameters in common. If the parameter value of one set does not exist in the other set, the solution is incompatible.
3. Narrow down the number of solutions by testing. Testing generates limit curves in the trade-off curve diagrams. Eliminate solutions that are outside the limits.
4. Select the final solution design from the remaining alternatives, based on optimal cost vs. performance.

A3 Methods to Reuse Knowledge. To solve problems, capture the acquired knowledge collaboratively, and reuse it visibly, Toyota uses the A3 method [20]. Nowadays, many companies have adopted various flavors of A3 problem-solving techniques (A3-thinking) as part of Lean Initiatives [21]. A3 methods guide teams through a structured process of reasoning to come up with solutions in a systematic way. The essential information of the problem-solving process is written down, supported by graphical information. Due to the standardized and structured approach, others who use the same structured approach can retrieve the information quickly. For our PLM implementation method, we focused on the following characteristics of A3 methods:

- A3s present information in a very compact way, lowering the barrier for users to use and maintain it.
- A3s are structured in a predefined way. It guides the thinking process of the readers and guides writers to put all essential details down in the same way and be complete in their input.

3 New Implementation Method

We derived our method from the two fields described in Sect. 2 They merge into a new method for repetitive PLM implementation in multiple companies. The method allows implementation service providers to link enabling technology to business improvements.

In this process, the method captures PLM implementation knowledge on a detailed level and in a modular way. Knowledge objects are reusable in future implementations in unique combinations that fit the specific customer's needs.

With this knowledge, an implementation service provider will be able to define and execute implementation projects that meet the real customer's requirements with higher quality and with less time and effort.

3.1 Visual Management

Where LPPD uses a causal map to visualize the interdependencies of the design parameters, we use a modified form of the BDN. We selected BDN, for its predefined context of IT implementation Initially, a BDN is made for a specific situation and describes a transformation from a current state to a future state of an organization. In our method, we want to reuse elements of the BDN. Therefore, our BDN has to present a possible future state instead of a change. The replacement for change is Use-Case in our method. Also, Operational Benefits should be described in absolute instead of relative terms.

We simplified the model based on the case study (Sect. 4.1) and merged the replacement for enabling change and business change into one category. Furthermore, we added more detail in the enabling technology by narrowing down on functions instead. These modifications resulted in the structure shown in Fig. 2. As with the BDN, described in Sect. 2.1, the arrows can describe n-to-n dependencies.

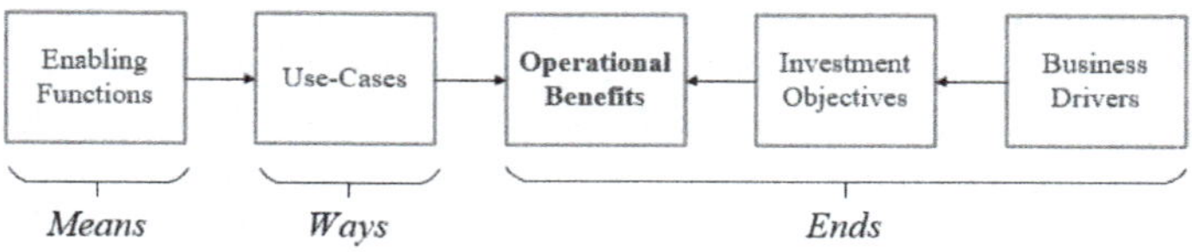

Fig. 2. Modified BDN as visual mapping for PLM implementations.

3.2 Set-Based Design

In our method, we subdivide the entire PLM implementation into PLM reference processes. PLM reference processes are common processes within the broader definition of PLM [22]. Examples are change management, project management, and product management. Potential benefits, related to a reference process, can be realized by multiple alternative Use-Cases: a set of solutions. How and how much each Use-Cases contributes to each benefit is information that is related to the dependency. In some cases, a Use-Case could be detrimental to a benefit, for example, when users have more administrative workload. This Use-Case then has a negative dependency on the benefit of "low workload". Benefits and Use-Cases can exist in multiple reference processes, creating an overlap between sets.

3.3 Workflow of the Method

In our method, we follow a similar workflow, as described in Sect. 2.2:

1. Find feasible alternative Use-Cases for Operational Benefits within a reference process.
2. Eliminate incompatible alternatives by evaluation of contribution to the benefits of overlapping sets.
3. Perform tests on remaining alternatives, based on the specific implementation requirement ranges. Measure the performance (contribution to Operational Benefits).
4. Select an optimal solution, based on cost vs. the estimated contribution to the achievement of the desired benefits.

3.4 Reuse Knowledge

In our method, we capture knowledge in predefined forms for each object (e.g., Enabling Function, Use-Case). The form contains a clear structure to guide the user. The structure varies per object class. For example, the Operational Benefit form currently contains a section for a description of the benefit (what is the advantage?), potential performance indicators (how can the benefit be measured?), and hyperlinks to related use-cases and investment goals.

The content should not exceed the amount of information that would fit on an A3. The form also includes references to other objects to represent potential dependencies. Physical A3 could be used for this purpose, but a digital method allows to hyperlink between forms. In our case study, we used an online wiki structure.

4 Explorative Case Studies

During the development of our method, we ran two explorative case studies to get feedback on elements of the method.

4.1 Explorative Case Study 1 – Modular Benefit Dependency Network

Our learning goal for this study was to observe if and how practitioners could apply our method in the early stage of development. We invited a technical and commercial consultant of a PLM implementation service provider to participate in this study.

First, we asked them to identify an industry segment within their SME customer base. Important was that they knew both operational and business contexts in this segment. Then, we trained them to use our modified BDN and let them create a potential Business Drivers, Investment Objectives, and other BDN obects that apply to this industry segment. The commercial consultant focused on the "ends" and the technical consultant on the "means" and "ways". They worked on the Benefits collaboratively. The knowledge was written down in wiki pages, using the wiki app in Microsoft Teams.

We gained several insights from this study. Both consultants were able to apply the method without much difficulty after some coaching in the first meetings. The commercial consultant claimed that this method helped him to structure a consultative conversation with customers. Instead of argumentation of the value of software products, he believes he can discuss value for the organization. Moreover, he believes he is better able to position more relevant solutions to help the customer to realize improvements. The technical consultant was also positive about the visibility of how technical enablers should be used to realize certain benefits. However, he suggests that more detail is needed in the enabling functions to make it usable as a detailed specification. With the current detail level, the deployment of a specified implementation still relies too much on the knowledge of the consultant in the project.

4.2 Explorative Case Study 2 – Alternative Enablers

In this study, we looked more deeply into the enabling functions. We participated in the early stage of a PLM implementation with an SME company that (among other subjects) was asking for a solution to manage design changes (reference process).

First, we engaged with the customer to ask for the desired Operational Benefits that they expect from change management and how they could measure them. The customer came up with eight potential benefits and realization criteria. Example: One Operational Benefit was “traceability of change” with the criterion “all changes must be traceable from origin to execution”.

After that, we made a list of potential Use-Cases to execute design changes. We found potential nine Use-Cases within the software platform of the customer, requiring various apps as Enabling Function.

Finally, we linked the Use-Cases to all Operational Benefits and rated the individual dependencies by estimated contribution. The rating is a five-point scale: strong negative, negative, neutral, positive, and strong positive. Figure 3 shows a simplified version of this rating.

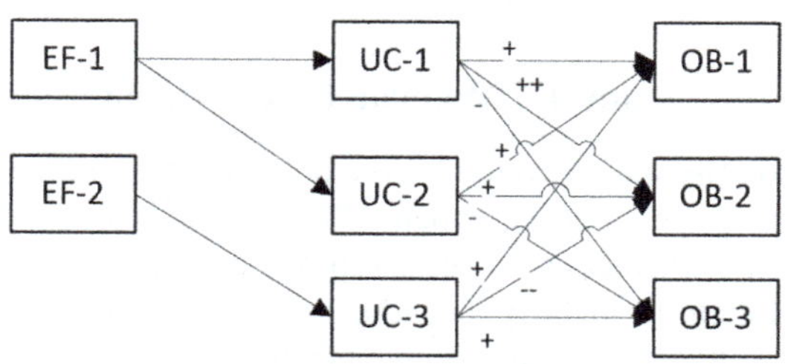

Fig. 3. Illustration of dependency rating for Use-Cases.

After the evaluation of the dependencies, three potential Use-Case remained feasible. They have to be evaluated with the stakeholders for final selection (yet to be performed).

We learned from this study that the method helps to make an objective selection of potential solutions to a problem. The customer shifted the attention from a request for functionality to a formulation of business outcomes. We expect to see more support from users when they are involved in the evaluation of the remaining Use-Cases.

5 Conclusion

In this paper, we described how we succeeded in forming a method for PLM implementation, based on LPPD and Benefits Management. The method can be used by PLM implementation service providers to find a match between enabling technology and their customers' business value. The explorative case studies gave encouraging feedback, growing confidence that the method improves the quality of PLM implementation. SME customers will benefit the most because, potentially, the reusable knowledge will replace costly business consulting.

We plan to make improvements to our method. Based on case study 1, we learned that we need to review the knowledge forms and improve them for clarity. We also need to write better instructions for the proper use of the method. Furthermore, the dependencies currently are only hyperlinks in a wiki system. The wiki system does not support meta-data on these links. In case study 2, we rated the dependencies manually in a spreadsheet. Another planned improvement is the ability to give priorities to Operational Benefits and make use of potential maturity levels to help organizations to formulate their ambition for individual reference processes [22].

To draw rigorous scientific conclusions about the effectiveness of the method, we have to perform a more extensive and a more formalized case study. This is planned for the next phase of this research after the refinement and formalization of the method.

References

1. Stark, J.: Product Lifecycle Management. Volume 1, 21st Century Paradigm for Product Realisation. Springer, Cham (2015). https://doi.org/10.1007/978-3-319-17440-2_1
2. CIMdata: About PLM (2017). https://www.cimdata.com/en/resources/about-plm. Accessed 2019 Jan 26
3. Gartner: IT Glossary - Product Lifecycle Management (2018). https://www.gartner.com/it-glossary/product-lifecycle-management-plm.. Accessed 2019 Jan 26
4. Smart_Industry: Dutch Smart Industry Report. Smart Industry Netherlands: Zoetermeer NL (2019)
5. Wognum, P.M., Kerssens-van Drongelen, I.C.: Process and impact of product data management implementation. Int. J. Product Dev. **2**(1), 5–23 (2005)
6. Siddiqui, Q.A., Burns, N.D., Backhouse, C.J.: Implementing product data management the first time. Int. J. Comput. Integr. Manuf. **17**(6), 520–533 (2004)
7. Koomen, B.: PLM in SME, what are we missing? An alternative view on PLM implementation for SME. In: Chiabert, P., Bouras, A., Noël, F., Ríos, J. (eds.) PLM 2018. IAICT, vol. 540, pp. 681–691. Springer, Cham (2018). https://doi.org/10.1007/978-3-030-01614-2_62

8. Koomen, B., Hoogeboom, M., Schellens, V.: PLM implementation success rate in SME. an empirical study of implementation projects, preliminary findings. In: Fortin, C., Rivest, L., Bernard, A., Bouras, A. (eds.) PLM 2019. IAICT, vol. 565, pp. 47–57. Springer, Cham (2019). https://doi.org/10.1007/978-3-030-42250-9_5
9. Ward, J., Daniel, E.: Benefits Management: Delivering Value from IS & IT Investments. Wiley, Hoboken (2005)
10. Carr, N.G.: IT doesn't matter. Harvard Bus. Rev. **81**(5), 41–49 (2003)
11. Peppard, J., Ward, J., Daniel, E.: Managing the realization of business benefits from IT investments MIS Q. **6**(1), 3 (2007)
12. Simon, H.A.: The Sciences of the Artificial. MIT, Cambridge (1969)
13. Aken, J.E.V.: Strategievorming en Organisatiestructurering : Organisatiekunde vanuit Ontwerpperspectief [Strategy Building and Organizational Structuring; Organization Science from a Design Perspective.], 2nd edn. Kluwer, Deventer (2002)
14. Ward, A.C., Sobek II, D.K.: Lean Product and Process Development, 2nd edn. The Lean Enterprise Institute, Cambridge (2014)
15. Ward, A., et al.: The second Toyota paradox: how delaying decisions can make better cars faster. Sloan Manag. Rev. **36**(3), 43–61 (1995)
16. Sobek II, D.K., Ward, A.C., Liker, J.K.: Toyota's Principles of Set-Based Concurrent Engineering in Sloan Management Review, pp. 67–84 (1999)
17. Cloft, P.W., Kennedy, M.N., Kennedy, B.M.: Success is Assured: Satisfy Your Customers On Time and On Budget by Optimizing Decisions Collaboratively Using Reusable Visual Models. Productivity Press, Cambridge (2018)
18. Kennedy, B.M., Sobek II, D.K., Kennedy, M.N.: Reducing rework by applying set-based practices early in the systems engineering. Process Syst. Eng. **17**(3), 278–296 (2014)
19. Kerga, E., et al.: A serious game for introducing set-based concurrent engineering in industrial practices. Concurrent Eng. **22**(4), 333–346 (2014)
20. Shook, J.: Managing to Learn: Using the A3 Management Process to Solve Problems, Gain Agreement, Mentor and Lead. Lean Enterprise Institute (2008)
21. Sobek II, D.K., Smalley, A.: Understanding A3 Thinking: A Critical Component of Toyota's PDCA Management System. Productivity Press, New York (2008)
22. Informatik, V.: Leitfaden zur Erstellung eines unternehmensspezifischen PLM-Konzeptes: Product-lifecycle-Management; transparente Prozesse und konsistente Informationen im Produktlebenszyklus [Guideline for creation of a company specific PLM concept: Product Lifecycle Management; Transparent Processes and Consistent Information in the Product Lifecycle]. Informatik. VDMA-Verl, Frankfurt (2008)

Enterprise Architecture Method for Continuous Improvement of PLM Based on Process Mining

Eugen Rigger[1(✉)], Thomas Vosgien[2], Samuel Bitrus[1], Piroska Szabo[2], and Benoit Eynard[3]

[1] V-Research GmbH, Digital Engineering, Dornbirn, Austria
eugen.rigger@v-research.at
[2] Hilti Befestigungstechnik AG, 9470 Buchs SG, Switzerland
[3] Department of Mechanical Systems Engineering, Université de Technologie de Compiègne, Compiègne, France

Abstract. The complexity and dynamics of IT landscapes and related PLM strategies of engineering enterprises are continuously growing due to trends such as Industry 4.0 and ever shorting product development cycles. To ensure interoperability, robustness, flexibility and efficiency of the IT systems and PLM, methods are needed that can handle these dynamics and complexities. In this paper, a method is presented that combines principles from enterprise architecture as well as business process mining to enable continuous improvement of PLM processes and the related IT systems. In particular, process mining is applied to validate the alignment of IT systems with related PLM processes. The method is demonstrated using an industrial case study that highlights the requirements from industrial practice and the applicability of the approach for PLM related processes. The method is shown to be particularly beneficial for the enterprise architects to support them with quantitative data as a basis for the design of continuous improvement cycles to make the PLM evolve. Future work will address the application of process mining for PLM related processes with distributed IT systems and the handling of the related complexity.

Keywords: PLM · Enterprise architecture · Process mining · Continuous improvement

1 Introduction

Digitalization of engineering companies [1] which builds upon trends such as Industry 4.0 [2] lead to increasing complexities in the IT landscape of engineering enterprises. In this context, Enterprise Architecture (EA) aims to ensure interoperability among IT applications as well as the related business processes and infrastructure satisfying the needs of an enterprise regarding robustness, flexibility and efficiency [3]. EA methods for modeling and management of architectures [3] have been proven to be beneficial in industrial practice with respect to monitoring and making enterprises evolve [4, 5] but are still subject to improvement with respect to new challenges stemming from the new opportunities in digital engineering and production [6].

F. Nyffenegger et al. (Eds.): PLM 2020, IFIP AICT 594, pp. 563–575, 2020.
https://doi.org/10.1007/978-3-030-62807-9_45

With respect to handling of data and applied tools among the lifecycle of a product, Product Lifecycle Management (PLM) is applied as a strategic management approach for product information, engineering workflows and related applications [7]. Hence, it can be governed and supported by enterprise architecture methods.

However, ever shortening product development cycles, the application of new technologies in industry such as Industrial Internet of Things or web-based technologies in general as well as the use of domain specific applications in engineering render the monitoring of enterprise architecture in a PLM context a challenge [1] calling for agile approaches to manage the continuous changes [8]. Hence, strategic approaches such as PLM and enterprise architecture require means to monitor and validate theoretically derived models of the enterprise architecture based on the actual operational use of applications. In this respect, process mining has been established as a means to validate and analyze business processes with respect to conformance based on analysis of event logs [9]. This enables to consolidate and optimize processes. Hence, the processes that are being applied in an enterprise, can be reengineered based on log data from the used systems. However, currently, process mining is applied to business processes with vast amount of data and single IT solutions which makes it difficult to be applied in a PLM context.

In response to these needs, this paper proposes a method enabling continuous PLM improvement combining principles from enterprise architecture as well as business process mining. The needs for this method are validated based on a use case reflecting the requirements from industrial practice and the actual method is illustrated using a reference process from PLM. Thus, this paper contributes by introducing a means that support business and operation excellence in the PLM area.

In the following, Sect. 2 reviews the state of the art and state of practice regarding business process mining. Following this, enterprise architecture methods are introduced and critically reviewed with respect to the applicability in agile and dynamic contexts. Section 2 is then summarized highlighting the research gaps that build the motivation and basis for derivation of the method that is presented in Sect. 3. Section 4 introduces case studies reflecting the current situation and application scenarios of the method in an industrial context. Section 5 comprehensively discusses these findings and Sect. 6 closes this paper by some concluding remarks.

2 Background

In this section the state of the art as well as state of practice of business process mining are discussed. Focus is put on currently applied industrial use cases of business process mining and its application in a context of product lifecycle management. Similarly, existing methodologies and supporting methods regarding enterprise architecture are reviewed. The background section is concluded by a summary highlighting the research gaps.

2.1 Business Process Mining vs. PLM

Process mining is a set of analysis techniques in the field of business process management [10] that applies machine learning and data mining to re-engineer and discover business process models using logs of information systems [9]. Correspondingly, the three main fields of application of business process mining refer to discovery, where a model is generated from event logs; conformance checking, where the data obtained from the model are compared to identify deviations from actual execution of a business process; and enhancement, where an existing process model is improved and optimized [11]. Recent reviews of the technology show that business process mining is an established technology [12] and multiple commercial platforms exist that address open research issues related to usability and understandability of the techniques with respect to non-experts.

In the context of PLM, reported applications of business process mining mainly focus on the improvement of manufacturing processes based on data from manufacturing execution systems [13–16] or decision making during operation of systems [17]. Considering the central data management systems that build the core of PLM such as the product data management system (PDM), only few works can be identified. The work presented in [18] claims PDM related process improvement. However, the work is available in Korean, only. Zhaoxia et al. [19] extends the attributes of the data format within the standardized Mining XML format [20] that enables mining of events related to data management in PDM systems such as the approval process of documents. Monitoring of process in PDM are particularly important due to the rapid evolution of new tools and technologies from fields such as CAx or design automation each interfacing with PDM.

2.2 Enterprise Architecture

Enterprise Architecture (EA) provides means to describe, analyze, represent and design different dimensions of an enterprise [3, 21]. EA aims to manage the organizational structure and related processes of an enterprise as well as the supporting information systems and infrastructure so to understand complexity and manage change [22, 23, p. 201]. Multiple EA methods and standards have emerged since the origins of enterprise architecture in the late 1980s [21], e.g. [24–27].

An essential part of PLM is concerned with the design process that is hard to formally model due to its situated [28] and iterative [29] character. Further, the engineering domain is characterized by domain specific tools featuring support for highly specific tasks, e.g. CAx [30] or design automation [31, 32]. Still, the works presented in [33, 34] have shown that the principles of enterprise architecture are also applicable in a PLM context. Hence, in this work methods of enterprise architecture are also used for the design and monitoring of PLM strategies.

Regarding the formal modeling of the enterprise architecture so to communicate and validate the knowledge about enterprise architecture, the ArchiMate graphical modeling language has been established as a standard [35]. Archimate features task precedence modeling in the three relevant layers for formalization of an enterprise architecture, namely business, application, and technology. The graphical modeling supports communication [36], participation and reengineering of enterprise architectures [37]. Archimate differentiates itself from other standardized notations for task precedence modeling, e.g. BPMN [38] or IDEF3 [39], by enabling modelling of the additional layers for applications and technologies.

2.3 Summary

Business process mining is an established technology that has gained recent interest in a PLM context due to the availability of structured data within the related information systems. However, there is a lack of methods with respect to systematic integration of business process mining in the context of the core applications of PLM such as the PDM to enable continuous improvement of the related business processes for data management. Existing EA methods need to be elaborated on to incorporate analysis and improvement cycles based on the monitoring capabilities provided by business process mining.

3 EA Method for Continuous Improvement of PLM

As highlighted in the review of the state of the art, existing methods from the field of enterprise architecture do not feature the continuous evolution process required to manage the dynamics of enterprise architecture within the field of PLM. Hence, in this work we propose a method featuring both the agility and flexibility required to account for the opportunities stemming from emerging technologies in the context of PLM as well as the monitoring capabilities required to guarantee streamlined application of these technologies based on process mining. The method is illustrated in Fig. 1.

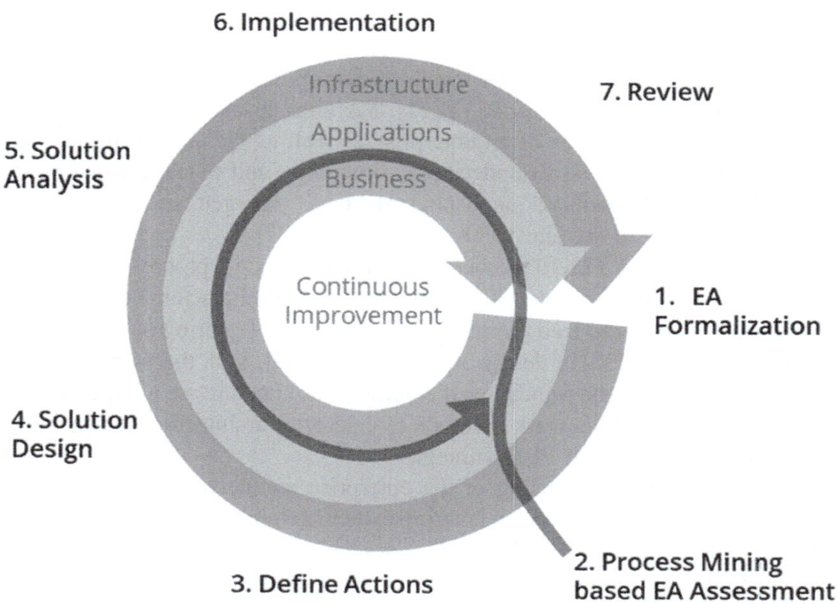

Fig. 1. Overview of the a method for continuous improvement of PLM

As can be seen in Fig. 1, the method presented in this work is based on the main principles of continuous improvement [40, 41] so that the dynamics of PLM can be taken into account. The method is constituted by the following steps:

1. The enterprise architecture is formalized using the ArchiMate modelling language. The business processes, related applications as well as the supporting infrastructure are captured holistically in one model repository. Each architecture artifact is then documented with additional metadata that will be used for the EA assessment.
2. The enterprise architecture is evaluated based on a comparison of the formalized EA with the practically applied PLM processes. The monitoring of processes as well as the evaluation of multiple dimensions of PLM maturity [42, 43] such as the level of IT alignment allow to draw a balanced scorecard indicating the maturity of a selected process.
3. Based on the yielded score card, informed decisions regarding the adaptation of the EA can be taken. Potential actions include the adaption of business processes, the inclusion/exclusion of specific application functions etc.
4. A potential solution reflecting the changes within the EA to realize the previously defined action is designed by the solution architects. Defining a potential solution follows basic software development principles as defined in ISO 25010 [44].
5. The potential solution is evaluated with respect to non-functional requirements reflecting the EA conformance.
6. When conformance is guaranteed, the solution is implemented and integrated to the enterprise IT systems.
7. The newly integrated IT solution is reviewed with respect to functional requirements and if necessary adapted.
8. The EA model is adapted to incorporate the newly integrated IT solutions.

Step 1 and step 8 encompass the same activity of EA modeling. Hence, these actions indicated the continuous character of the method that should be permanently applied to ensure robustness, flexibility and efficiency of modern engineering companies.

4 Case Study

In the following, the current state of application of the method in an engineering enterprise producing a large variety of high value-added manufacturing systems for the construction industry. In a first step, the challenges of this business with respect to EA are briefly introduced. Following this, the current state of application of the EA Method for continuous improvement of IT system is presented. Thereby, focus is put on assessment of the EA based on process mining as well as heat maps that enable multi-dimensional assessment of business processes and the related EA. Finally, an outlook including a representative PLM process is presented to highlight how the company wants to move towards comprehensive application of the method to fully grasp the potential of simultaneous application of enterprise architecture and business process mining.

4.1 Industrial Challenges for Applying EA in the PLM Area

The industrial case deals with products of large system complexity and like any other manufacturing industry product data is cross-functionally used among the various departments of the company, e.g. product data is shared and exchanged among the various disciplines involved in the design process. The IT systems that enable product data and configuration management processes require a stable and robust IT landscape where IT architecture guidelines and principles are fully applied. Contrarily, the cross-functionality and multidisciplinary character of the product development call for a variety of IT systems and authoring applications, which makes the PLM IT landscape particularly difficult to govern from an EA perspective. For example, the engineering business units ask for flexibility and efficiency in implementation of desired authoring applications without necessarily taking care of applying the company standards, whereas these standards are necessary for ensuring the full traceability and consistency of the processed product data. Eventually, this leads to data quality issues downstream the product life cycle.

From another perspective, the emergence of cloud solution for PLM enabling IT systems poses additional challenges to the enterprise architecture, since a mix of on-premise, desktop and cloud solutions needs to be integrated. This makes EA governance and EA principles difficult to apply and requires the definition of new integration patterns.

Finally, to align PLM enabling IT systems with the IT strategy of the company, costly and risky PLM transformation projects are necessary. However, complex PLM IT systems need to be validated regarding the operational usage in order to assess the alignment of the IT systems with the business process and eventually the IT strategy. This is particularly true for the PLM systems for product data management that need to cover many business use cases and are complex. This leads to gaps between the defined and applied processes. Therefore, potential future solutions need to be assessed with respect to the possibilities for setting up process mining cases for the application.

4.2 State of Practice of Application of Enterprise Architecture

This section shows how the EA Method for continuous improvement of PLM introduced in Sect. 3 is currently applied in practice to general business processes. Focus is put on the second step of the method, i.e. the EA assessment necessary to align the PLM IT systems with the EA strategy and principles of the company. The assessment itself consists of a compliance assessment with respect to EA architecture principles and also relies on a process mining solution to identify the state of application of a specific IT solution with respect to applied processes.

Assessment of Systems' Compliance and Maturity to EA Principles
Regarding the assessment of a systems maturity, the company introduced "assessment" metadata attributes for IT systems directly within modeling environment ADOit. Metadata comprises information such as the operating model (e.g. On Premise, XaaS), the mission criticality of a system, the level of customization of a system, the used integration patterns and technologies, lifecycle information, etc. This enables the

solution architects and enterprise architects to classify and assess the various software applications based on different IT strategy and principles criteria. Given the complete assessment of the corporate IT systems, a heatmap of IT systems maturity can be drawn as shown in Fig. 2 so that a comprehensive overview of the current state of IT system maturity is given. Alternatively, this data can also be visualized using balanced scorecards. One of the first principles which is checked is "A system is supporting and is aligned with business processes and avoids functional redundancy". Until now, this assessment was based on the qualitative and subjective evaluation of the architect and/or owner of the solution. In this paper, we propose now to complete this assessment by applying process mining to the respective supported business processes.

Software Systems	EA Score	A system is aligned with business processes and avoids functional redundancy	A system follows "best practice" architectures to foster reliability	A system has a managed lifecycle	A system has managed interfaces and follows interoperability standards
Principle Score		53.6	78.6	85.0	67.9
System A	65.9	P	M	M	M
System B	75.0	L	M	M	F
System C	68.2	M	L	F	L
System D	75.0	L	F	F	F
System E	54.5	P	M	M	P
System F	84.1	M	F	F	F
System G	72.7	M	M	M	P

Fig. 2. Excerpt of EA heat map report with columns indicating the different levels of IT system maturity. The systems are hidden for confidentiality reasons.

PLM Process Mining for Operational Alignment between PLM IT Systems and Processes

In the following, the application of process mining to assess the alignment of the used ERP/PDM system SAP S/4 HANA with applied engineering change management process. The case has been implemented using the Celonis process mining toolbox.

Whereas the company already applies the proposed method in the context of sales and marketing business processes (e.g. purchase-to-pay and order-to-cash), the PLM related processes are currently not yet operationally mined. One of the reasons is that the PLM environment is subject to current major changes and the engineering change management processes is currently involving several software applications which are currently not yet in the scope and roadmap of the process mining initiative. Moreover, each new process mining case requires additional costs, efforts and time, not only for integrating Celonis with other software systems but also for formalizing, setting up, implementing, executing the case and analyzing the results.

In the following, the data model of SAP S/4 HANA is investigated with respect to its capabilities to support and monitor the engineering change management process (ECM). ECM is taken as a representative PLM process since it is critical with respect to its impact on data quality and information traceability required in downstream engineering processes. Hence, misalignments between the software implementation and its usage by the end-users are critical and need to be avoided.

Figure 3 depicts the engineering change management reference process and the related data structure in SAP S/4 HANA as implemented in the company. This allows the identification of business processes based on the analysis of interrelations of the identified process activities. Given this information, the definition of process activities as required for setting up a process mining case can be performed.

Figure 4 shows some of the proof of concept results for the analysis of the ECM process. Even though the details cannot be provided due to confidentiality, it can be seen that multiple variants of processes are identified when tracking the data event logs for engineering change request/orders. This information can then be used to elaborate on the defined processes as well as to support the assessment of the IT system with regards to its capabilities alignment with their operational usage. In this specific case, the results of the process mining enabled the enterprise architect to adjust the EA assessment "A system is supporting and is aligned with business processes and avoids functional redundancy" so that a qualitative estimation is replaced by quantitative evaluations. Further, the setup of process mining cases right from the start of implementation of a new IT system in the PLM context, will be used to monitor the adoption of new systems so to enable continuous improvement of the IT systems also in a PLM context.

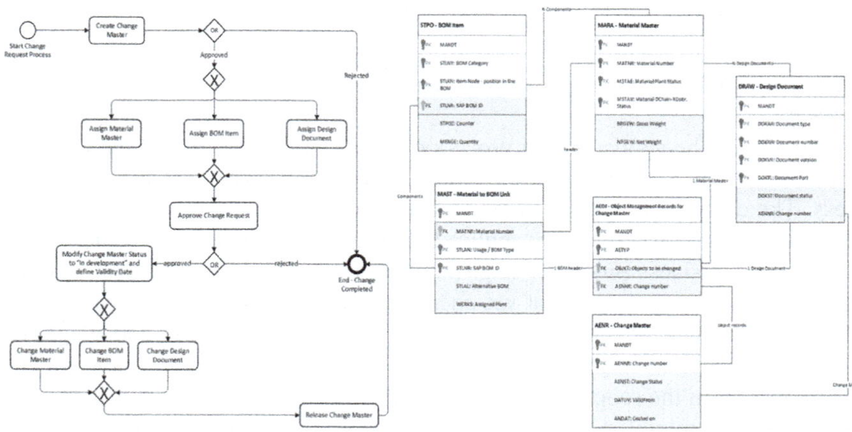

Fig. 3. Engineering change management process and related data structure in SAP S/4 HANA.

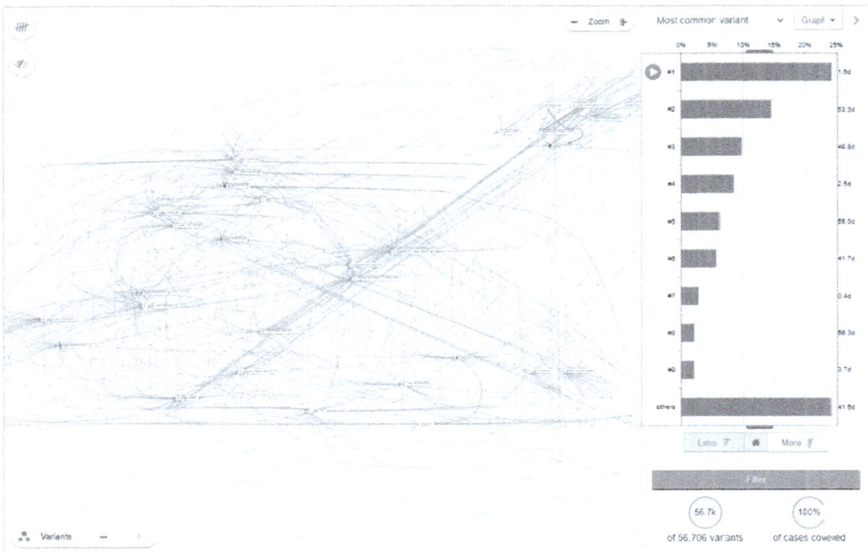

Fig. 4. Process deviations report in Celonis for the usage of SAP S/4 HANA.

5 Discussion

In the following, the work and results presented in this work are discussed with its impact with respect to industry as well as academia.

Regarding the contributions with respect to industry, the business case introduced in Sect. 4 summarizes the challenges of a manufacturing engineering enterprise with respect to PLM and EA adoption. Building upon these challenges, different dimensions of PLM/IT systems maturity are introduced to assess these challenges and enable continuous improvement of the PLM/IT systems. In this work, the application of process mining is proposed to support the assessment of PLM/IT systems also based on quantitative data stemming from the evaluation of data logs. In this respect, the results stemming from the process mining case can be used to rework the processes as well as the supporting IT systems and application functions. The enterprise architectures benefit from this data since it enables them to lead informed discussions with related stakeholders based on quantitative data rather than qualitative estimations. Further, the enhanced understanding of the As-Is state of the enterprise architecture also increases applicability and quality of the potential To-Be states since reality is reflected in more detail.

The introduced process mining case in Sect. 4 indicates how the ability to setup a process mining for a potential IT system can be an evaluation criterion for the evaluation of IT systems. Having the ability to conduct process mining for PLM related processes is key to improve the collaboration of the different engineering disciplines. Different disciplines have different requirements for product data management leading to potential misalignments in applied processes. Having the overview of different processes, established processes can be adapted eventually leading to a better data quality when PLM processes are well adopted by the different users. Considering the overview of the various instances of PLM processes from an applied process mining case, the origins of misalignments in data can be identified, e.g. when a discipline keeps ignoring specific process activities. Using this information, the related users can be identified and informed with respect to the effects of this misalignments. Thus, motivation of the related stakeholders can be increased to actively contribute to PLM and EA design and compliance. With regards to the number of observed process deviations, the real complexity of the case is much higher than expected. This leads to consider some limitations regarding the application of process mining in industrial practice. These great number of process deviations have been observed by analyzing the data logs of only one IT systems, whereas, in practice, the ECM process' actors generally uses several data management and authoring systems. Reflecting the operational reality would require more investigations and more process mining investments. On the other hand, by mining other data sources, the amount of data to analyze as well as the amount of process deviations would increase, leading to the risk of not being able to efficiently analyze these deviations. Therefore, industrialists must be careful when willing to apply process mining excessively. One of the challenges is to coordinate and align the process mining activities with the PLM transformation roadmap to avoid a negative perception or non-adoption of the approach by both management and process 'actors point of views.

With respect to academia, the proposed work contributes by the introduction of an EA framework that considers state-of-the-art technologies and puts a focus on the challenges stemming from the PLM domain. This work particularly takes into account the point highlighted in [23] that the future directions of EA need to push the boundaries of EA by integrating different field and pursue a multidisciplinary approach and therefore increase visibility and dynamics in the field.

The future work needs to focus on the actual implementation of PLM process mining cases and the development of a method to detect isolated (non-integrated) IT systems within PLM based on process mining.

6 Conclusion

This work contributes by introducing an enterprise architecture-based method for continuous improvement of PLM processes and the related IT systems. To quantitatively evaluate the As-Is state of PLM, the method applies process mining monitor the alignment of IT systems with the related PLM processes. The validation of the method based on an industrial case shows the applicability to support enterprise architects in the review of the As-Is state to enable continuous improvement of PLM. Further, the method contributes by merging different previously unconnected fields of research.

However, the industrial case also shows the complexity of process evaluation in a PLM context. Hence, future work needs to address the development of methods that enable the application of process mining for PLM related processes with distributed IT systems.

Acknowledgements. This work has been supported and funded by the Austrian Research Promotion Agency (FFG) via the "Austrian Competence Center for Digital Production" (CDP) under the contract number 854187.

References

1. Xin, Y., Ojanen, V.: The impact of digitalization on product lifecycle management: how to deal with it? In: 2017 IEEE International Conference on Industrial Engineering and Engineering Management (IEEM), Singapore, pp. 1098–1102 (2017). https://doi.org/10.1109/ieem.2017.8290062
2. Oztemel, E., Gursev, S.: Literature review of Industry 4.0 and related technologies. J. Intell. Manuf. **31**(1), 127–182 (2018). https://doi.org/10.1007/s10845-018-1433-8
3. Gampfer, F., Jürgens, A., Müller, M., Buchkremer, R.: Past, current and future trends in enterprise architecture—a view beyond the horizon. Comput. Ind. **100**, 70–84 (2018). https://doi.org/10.1016/j.compind.2018.03.006
4. Váchal, J., Straková, J.: Enterprise architecture within the process of permanent change. In SHS Web of Conferences, vol. 61, p. 01029 (2019). https://doi.org/10.1051/shsconf/20196101029
5. Shanks, G., Gloet, M., Asadi Someh, I., Frampton, K., Tamm, T.: Achieving benefits with enterprise architecture. J. Strateg. Inf. Syst. **27**(2), 139–156 (2018). https://doi.org/10.1016/j.jsis.2018.03.001
6. Saint-Louis, P., Morency, M.C., Lapalme, J.: Defining enterprise architecture: a systematic literature review. In: 2017 IEEE 21st International Enterprise Distributed Object Computing Workshop (EDOCW), Quebec City, QC, pp. 41–49 (2017). https://doi.org/10.1109/EDOCW.2017.16
7. Abramovici, M.: Future trends in product lifecycle management (PLM). In: Krause, P.D.-I.F.-L. (ed.) The Future of Product Development, pp. 665–674. Springer, Berlin Heidelberg (2007). https://doi.org/10.1007/978-3-540-69820-3_64
8. Gampfer, F.: Managing enterprise architecture in agile environments. In: Mikusz, M., Volland, A., Engstler, M., Fazal-Baqaie, M., Hanser, E., Linssen, O. (eds.) Projektmanagement und Vorgehensmodelle 2018, PVM 2018: der Einfluss der Digitalisierung auf Projektmanagementmethoden und Entwicklungsprozesse, Düsseldorf: Gesellschaft für Informatik e.V. (GI) (2018)
9. van der Aalst, W.: Process Mining: Discovery, Conformance and Enhancement of Business Processes. Springer, Berlin (2011). https://doi.org/10.1007/978-3-642-19345-3
10. van der Aalst, W.M.P., La Rosa, M., Santoro, F.M.: Business process management. Bus. Inf. Syst. Eng. **58**(1), 1–6 (2015). https://doi.org/10.1007/s12599-015-0409-x
11. van der Aalst, W.: Process mining: overview and opportunities. ACM Trans. Manage. Inf. Syst. **3**(2), 1–17 (2012). https://doi.org/10.1145/2229156.2229157
12. Cho, M., Song, M., Comuzzi, M., Yoo, S.: Evaluating the effect of best practices for business process redesign: an evidence-based approach based on process mining techniques. Decis. Support Syst. **104**, 92–103 (2017). https://doi.org/10.1016/j.dss.2017.10.004
13. Rozinat, A., de Jong, I.S.M., Gunther, C.W., van der Aalst, W.M.P.: Process mining applied to the test process of wafer scanners in ASML. IEEE Trans. Syst. Man Cybern. Part C (Appl. Rev.) **39**(4), 474–479 (2009). https://doi.org/10.1109/TSMCC.2009.2014169
14. Yang, H., Park, M., Cho, M., Song, M., Kim, S.: A system architecture for manufacturing process analysis based on big data and process mining techniques, pp. 1024–1029 (2014). https://doi.org/10.1109/bigdata.2014.7004336

15. Park, M., Song, M., Baek, T.H., Son, S., Ha, S.J., Cho, S.W.: Workload and delay analysis in manufacturing process using process mining. In: Bae, J., Suriadi, S., Wen, L. (eds.) AP-BPM 2015. LNBIP, vol. 219, pp. 138–151. Springer, Cham (2015). https://doi.org/10.1007/978-3-319-19509-4_11
16. Son, S., et al.: Process mining for manufacturing process analysis: a case study. In: Procedia of 2nd Asia Pacific Conference on Business Process Management, Brisbane, Australia, p. 5 (2015)
17. Es-Soufi, W., Yahia, E., Roucoules, L.: A process mining based approach to support decision making. In: Ríos, J., Bernard, A., Bouras, A., Foufou, S. (eds.) PLM 2017. IAICT, vol. 517, pp. 264–274. Springer, Cham (2017). https://doi.org/10.1007/978-3-319-72905-3_24
18. Lee, S.-I., Ryu, K.-Y., Song, M.-S.: Process improvement for PDM/PLM systems by using process mining. Trans. Soc. CAD/CAM Eng. **17**(4), 294–302 (2012). https://doi.org/10.7315/CADCAM.2012.294
19. Zhaoxia, W., Jianmin, W., Lijie, W., Yingbo, L.: Extracting real-life log with data perspective in PLM system for business process analysis. In: 2009 WRI World Congress on Computer Science and Information Engineering, Los Angeles, California USA, 2009, pp. 664–668. https://doi.org/10.1109/CSIE.2009.645
20. van Dongen, B.F., van der Aalst, W.M.P.: A meta model for process mining data. In: Proceedings of the CAISE 2005 Workshops, 2005, pp. 309–320 (2005)
21. Bernus, P., Nemes, L., Schmidt, G.J.: Handbook on Enterprise Architecture. Springer, Heidelberg (2003). https://doi.org/10.1007/978-3-540-24744-9
22. Lankhorst, M.: Enterprise Architecture at Work, 4th edn. Springer, Heidelberg (2017). https://doi.org/10.1007/978-3-662-53933-0
23. Lapalme, J., Gerber, A., Van der Merwe, A., Zachman, J., Vries, M.D., Hinkelmann, K.: Exploring the future of enterprise architecture: a Zachman perspective. Comput. Ind. **79**, 103–113 (2016). https://doi.org/10.1016/j.compind.2015.06.010
24. Zachman, J.A.: A framework for information systems architecture. IBM Syst. J. **26**(3), 276–292 (1987). https://doi.org/10.1147/sj.263.0276
25. The Open Group: The open group architecture framework (TOGAF), vol. 1. The Open Group, Reading (2009)
26. ISO/IEC/IEEE: ISO/IEC/IEEE 42010 - Systems and software engineering – Architecture description (2011)
27. Nightingale, D., Srinivasa, J., Mize, J.: Enterprise Transformation Roadmap. MIT Press, Cambridge (2010)
28. Gero, J.S., Kannengiesser, U.: The situated function–behaviour–structure framework. Des. Stud. **25**(4), 373–391 (2004). https://doi.org/10.1016/j.destud.2003.10.010
29. Wynn, D.C., Eckert, C.M.: Perspectives on iteration in design and development. Res. Eng. Design **28**(2), 153–184 (2016). https://doi.org/10.1007/s00163-016-0226-3
30. Vajna, S., Weber, C., Zeman, K., Hehenberger, P., Gerhard, D., Wartzack, S.: CAx für Ingenieure. Springer, Heidelberg (2018). https://doi.org/10.1007/978-3-662-54624-6
31. Rigger, E., Stanković, T., Shea, K.: Task categorization for identification of design automation opportunities. J. Eng. Des. (2018). https://doi.org/10.1080/09544828.2018.1448927
32. Rigger, E., Vosgien, T., Shea, K., Stankovic, T.: A top-down method for the derivation of metrics for the assessment of design automation potential. J. Eng. Des. 1–31 (2019). https://doi.org/10.1080/09544828.2019.1670786
33. McKendry, D., Whitfield, R.I., Duffy, A.H.B.: Business and information management architectures for delivering Product Lifecycle Management (PLM) in Engineering To Order (ETO) products. In: Proceedings of ICCAS 2015, Bremen, Germany, pp. 1–9 (2015). https://doi.org/10.3940/rina.iccas.2015.16

34. Vosgien, T., Rigger, E., Schwarz, M., Shea, K.: A federated enterprise architecture and MBSE modeling framework for integrating design automation into a global PLM approach. In: Ríos, J., Bernard, A., Bouras, A., Foufou, S. (eds.) PLM 2017. IAICT, vol. 517, pp. 36–48. Springer, Cham (2017). https://doi.org/10.1007/978-3-319-72905-3_4
35. The Open Group: ArchiMate 3.1 Specification. The Open Group, Reading (2019)
36. Wynn, D.C., Clarkson, P.J.: Process models in design and development. Res. Eng. Design **29**(2), 161–202 (2017). https://doi.org/10.1007/s00163-017-0262-7
37. Melao, N., Pidd, M.: A conceptual framework for understanding business processes and business process modelling. Inf. Syst. J. **10**(2), 105–129 (2000). https://doi.org/10.1046/j.1365-2575.2000.00075.x
38. White, S.A., Miers, D.: BPMN Modeling and Reference Guide: Understanding and Using BPMN; Develop Rigorous Yet Understandable Graphical Representations of Business Processes. Future Strategies Inc., Lighthouse Point (2008)
39. Mayer, R.J., Menzel, C.P., Painter, M.K., Dewitte, P.S., Blinn, T., Perakath, B.: Information integration for concurrent engineering (IICE). Process description capture method report, Knowledge Based Systems Inc., College Station, TX (1995)
40. Taghizadegan, S.: Essentials of Lean Six Sigma. Butterworth-Heinemann, Oxford (2010)
41. Pyzdek, T., Keller, P.A.: The Six Sigma Handbook. McGraw-Hill Education, New York (2014)
42. Stark, J.: Product Lifecycle Management. DE. Springer, Cham (2015). https://doi.org/10.1007/978-3-319-17440-2
43. Probst, M.: Anwendung eines PLM Reifegradmodells als strategisches Instrument. Intelliact AG (2016)
44. ISO/IEC: ISO/IEC 25010: Systems and software Quality Requirements and Evaluation (SQuaRE) — System and software quality models (2011)

Blockchains: A Conceptual Assessment from a Product Lifecycle Implementation Perspective

Abdelhak Belhi[1,2](✉), Abdelaziz Bouras[1], Masood Khan Patel[1], and Belaid Aouni[3]

[1] Computer Science and Engineering, College of Engineering, Qatar University, Doha, Qatar
{abdelhak.belhi,abdelaziz.bouras,mp1912826}@qu.edu.qa
[2] DISP Laboratory, University Lumière Lyon 2, Lyon, France
[3] College of Business and Economics, Qatar University, Doha, Qatar
belaid.aouni@qu.edu.qa

Abstract. PLM systems are heavily distributed collaborative platforms resulting in multiple challenges related to the integrity and reliability of the exchanged information. Such issues are usually difficult to address using traditional software solutions. However, since the introduction of blockchains, such challenges are currently being effectively addressed. On the one hand, traditional PLM systems design philosophy was mainly about centralized proprietary systems that have difficulty to cope with new distributed and open environments imposed by the extensive use of IoT platforms and other Industry 4.0 tools. On the other hand, blockchains address data integrity issues by design, and mitigate some of the trust concerns found in collaborative platforms. Through this paper, we study and evaluate the integration of blockchain technology with PLM systems highlighting the different advantages, challenges, and issues that this integration might induce.

Keywords: Product lifecycle management · Blockchain · Supply Chain management

1 Introduction

PLM systems are the swiss knives behind product manufacturing. Their original design philosophy was to integrate all the processes related to the product lifecycle into a single centralized solution. This promised a lot of improvements to all product lifecycle stages and attracted a lot of interest. By nowadays standards, product information is distributed across multiple stakeholders and traditional PLM systems have a hard time coping with Industry 4.0 standards which stress on openness, the use of cyber-physical systems, IoT, AI, cloud-based solutions, etc. [1]. Usually, companies are often not ready for this transition as it may alter with their business logic and can result in major failures in their security policies. In fact, having their intellectual property (IP) in cloud environments can lead to it being compromised and stolen. However, it is really difficult to avoid these transformations especially in a time where companies have to

Published by Springer Nature Switzerland AG 2020
F. Nyffenegger et al. (Eds.): PLM 2020, IFIP AICT 594, pp. 576–589, 2020.
https://doi.org/10.1007/978-3-030-62807-9_46

manage information across multiple remote sites or to deal with multiple international stakeholders such as suppliers, etc. The vulnerabilities of traditional systems and the constant need to shift to Industry 4.0 processes are pushing for finding new ways to secure PLM systems while enabling new processes paradigms [2, 3].

These applications among others demonstrate the potential of blockchain technology is revolutionizing the way we collaborate. As a result, through this paper, we aim at studying the PLM-Blockchain integration while evaluating its added benefits, potential drawback, added value and challenges yet to be addressed.

The rest of this paper is organized as follows. In section two, we give a general overview of PLM systems. This is followed in Sect. 3 by a series of selected questions that we elaborated to shape the integration of PLM and blockchain. In Sect. 4 we present supply ledger which is a new project aiming at integrating the blockchain technology in the context of supply chains. Our conclusions and final thoughts are depicted in Sect. 5.

2 Product Lifecycle Management Systems

PLM systems encompass a set of business software tools used in an enterprise context to manage the entire lifecycle and activities related to products and assets from their design, manufacturing, iterations until it is discontinued and disposed of. The goal of such systems in the design phase for instance is to empower the efficiency of product design by accelerating the processes, improving the communication between the different actors, reducing costs, and allowing for effective iterative design [4]. One of the main PLM systems' features is the ability to efficiently integrate the data of the different product's stages. Since the rise of the Internet and with increasing performance of information technologies, PLM systems were adapted to involve stakeholders and diverse collaborators in the whole lifecycle process [5] (see Fig. 1). Usually, these stakeholders may be collaborating on different life cycle stages: design, prototyping, testing, validation, manufacturing, distribution, maintenance and recycling. PLM is the go-to tool for companies seeking improvements to their product quality, their collaboration as well as their competitiveness [6].

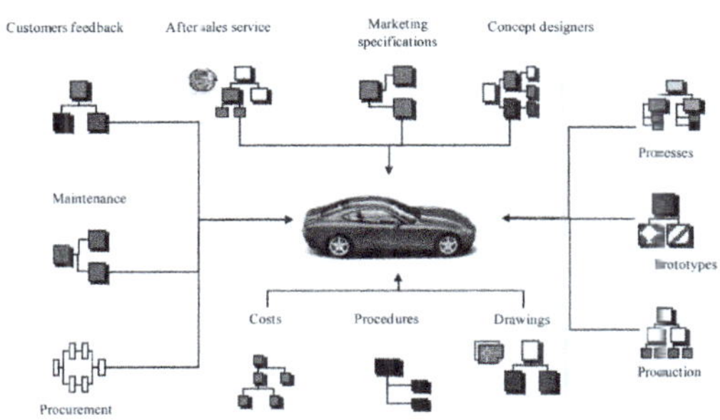

Fig. 1. The Product data managed by PLM systems (a case of care manufacturing) [5]

By nowadays standards, and with Industry 4.0 challenges, several challenges related to security and data integrity have arisen with the introduction of IoT and cloud infrastructures. The blockchain technology and a collaboration infrastructure are good candidates to tackle such challenges.

3 Blockchain in PLM Systems

There is a great deal of complexity associated with data exchanges around PLM systems due to the iterative processes where multiple internal and external stakeholders are involved [7]. Nowadays products are made collaboratively. Think of any product you use, and you will see that it requires the involvement of multiple companies that manufacture a certain part of it. In such a scenario, it is usually the manufacturer or the assembler who is the chief of the orchestra and has to coordinate all the data exchanges between the network of stakeholders. The complexity of such networks grows up exponentially which raises concerns about security, integrity of data, etc.

The blockchain is a decentralized collaboration platform that was proven to solve such concerns. Blockchains have been adapted to multiple applications. To study its adaptation to PLM systems, we have highlighted hereunder a list of points that will help understanding how to integrate blockchain and PLM systems.

3.1 What Is a Blockchain?

Blockchain refers to a new evolving collaboration technology that is considered disruptive by many experts. Blockchains are shared ledgers used to log transactions in an append-only fashion (see Fig. 2). These ledgers are usually stored across a decentralized environment. The data that they stored is secured and chained using different cryptographic techniques. Cryptocurrencies are one of the first applications relying fully on the blockchain technology. As awkward as it seems, blockchains are not managed by any third party. In blockchains, there is no space for a regulatory body, or managing authority. Trust is achieved by consensus and by design. Blockchain gained in popularity following the introduction of the bitcoin cryptocurrency in 2008. For cryptocurrencies such as bitcoin, the blockchain contains all the transaction data [8].

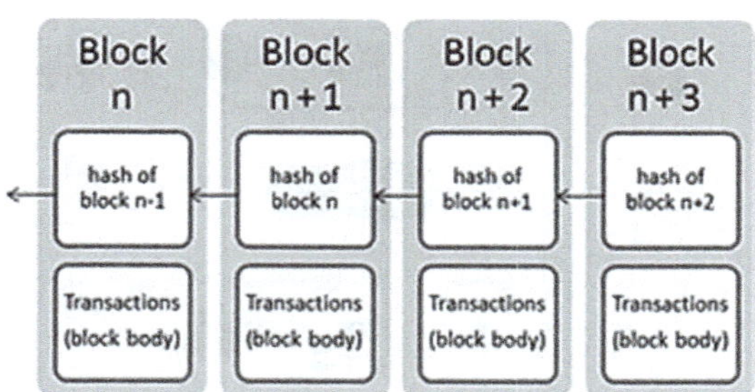

Fig. 2. Blockchain diagram highlighting the hashing of blocks

3.2 How Disruptive Is the Blockchain?

The disruption that blockchain made in the tech industry can be comparable to the one made by the internet. It revolutionized the financial industry and its concepts are being adapted to other sectors [9]. The revolutions introduced by the blockchain can be summarized as follows:

- Secure shared tamperproof storage: Data is shared through a decentralized architecture where each node holds a copy. Each block of data is linked to the previous one.
- Consensus Trust: Trust is not achieved by a managing party but rather through a census where a proof-of-work algorithm is used to validate new blocks and transactions (See Fig. 3).
- P2P transactions: no third party is required to certify a transaction or to monitor it.
- Smart contracts: a new way of transactions using the concept of pre-conditions and action. A smart contract is a script that resides in the blockchain and executed upon the satisfaction of a set of pre-conditions. As an example, think of a payment issued once tracking shows delivered, etc. These contracts are enforced automatically without any third party.

Through these concepts, the blockchain-inspired multiple fields such as health care, supply chain, voting, etc. thanks to all the benefits related to transparency in a peer-to-peer network.

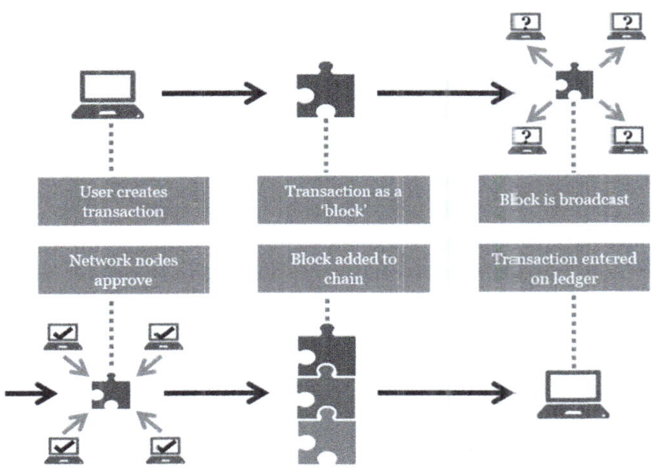

Fig. 3. The consensus in peer-to-peer blockchains https://digital.pwc.com/en.html

3.3 What Benefits Does the Blockchain Bring to PLM Systems?

The benefits of the blockchain are linked to its key features. Through these features, the blockchain can bring additional benefits to most collaborative applications including

PLM [10]. In the following, we highlight the key features of the blockchain technology and their benefits in the PLM context.

- Decentralized: By nowadays standards and with the massive use of IoT and cloud-based solutions, decentralized architecture can be used to solve issues related to reliability and uptime eliminating points of failures such as servers, etc. Blockchain relies on multiple nodes which can store and handle the data.
- Immutable: Blockchain is an append-only database where data is secured by hash chains and other strong cryptographic concepts. PLM systems can benefit from these concepts in all forms of critical data such as maintenance logs, etc.
- Transparency: depending on the implementation and the targeted application, blockchain can enforce transparency constraints as the data is shared publicly in multiple sources and cannot be tampered with. In PLM systems, this can be useful whenever information needs to be publicly available while being able to verify its authenticity.

3.4 Is the Blockchain Successful in Other Fields Related to PLM Systems?

The blockchain technology which is the backbone of cryptocurrencies did not stop flexing its muscles as one of the most secure and resilient peer-to-peer information exchange platforms. Thanks to their proven advantages such as security, availability, tamper-proofness, etc., blockchains have been adapted to multiple applications in healthcare, supply chains, finance, … In the supply chain, many blockchain-powered applications are currently being deployed for real-world use especially in the logistics industry. For the logistics supply chain, IBM and Maersk presented the first real-world scenario of using the blockchain as the main data exchange platform to ship a container from Lyon, France to Newark, USA. The challenge, in this case, was not the physical movement of the container itself but rather related to all the documents that are exchanged between the different stakeholders (shipper, banks, customs, carrier port authority, forwarder, etc.). By using blockchain in the scenario, all the information was exchanged using one platform which made it more transparent, effective to track, and added the ability to quickly identify and solve any issues which resulted in a boost in terms of performance.

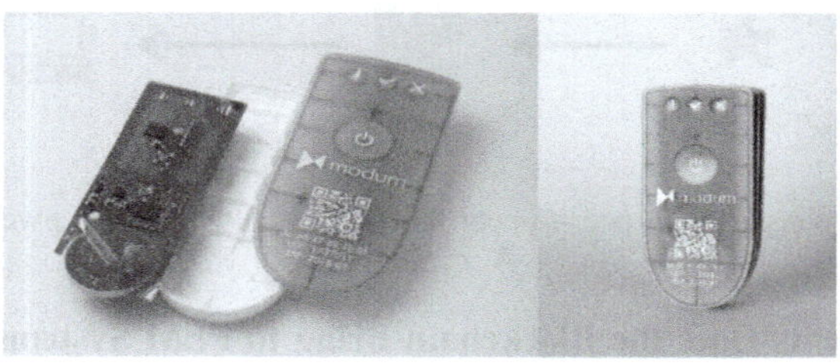

Fig. 4. The Modum IoT tracking device [11]

The pharmaceutical industry is facing many challenges related to transparency, conformity, and reliability of pharma products. The blockchain start-up Modum [11] is working on ensuring drug and medical product safety with blockchain technology. Their product 'Mod' (see Fig. 4), which is an IoT sensor, is revolutionizing asset tracking. The 'Mod' device is added by the shipper or the pharmaceutical factory to packages of pharmaceutical and medical products prior to their shipment. During the transportation of the package, the device monitors the temperature and the humidity conditions of the package autonomously. When the receiver, a pharmacist, for instance, accepts the package, all the data is transferred to the blockchain where a smart contract is executed to check if the product always complied with the temperature and humidity regulations. Once in the blockchain, this data can't be changed and is publicly accessible. The result is immediately reported back to the end consumer as well as to the distributor. This tool is currently in use in many European countries as new GDP regulations (European commission Good Manufacturing and Distribution Practices) require the reporting of temperature deviation and humidity levels to both the distributor and the recipient of the medical product.

3.5 How Can Blockchain Be Applied in PLM Systems?

In the context of industrial applications beyond the fintech context, Internet of Things (IoT) seems to be the most targeted application for the huge amount of interaction between sensors and edge devices with the cloud. This imposes challenges related to infrastructure reliability, security, and data integrity. In this context, a blockchain-based IoT platform was presented in [12], the authors presented a proof-of-concept of a sensor network in an industrial application interacting in a trustless environment through the blockchain. The authors of [13] investigate how to implement an open manufacturing architecture through a cross-enterprise service and knowledge exchange framework based on edge computing and blockchain. In the same context, in [10], a blockchain-based business management framework is presented. The authors highlighted the fact that Business Process Management (BPM) is one of the pillars of Industry 4.0 and one of the critical bottlenecks to proceed with BPM systems is related to data integrity. The proposed solution is based on the blockchain technology and aims at addressing the highlighted issues. Another application presented in [14] targets the challenge of securing smart grids through the design and implementation of a blockchain securing machine-to-machine interactions in the context of electricity trading.

In the supply chain management context, numerous applications were proposed such as [15] where the authors proposed a conceptual model to integrate the blockchain technology with supply chains. The authors of [16] explored the use of ontologies and a design tool for blockchain-based supply chains where they translated some traceability representation from an ontology to smart contracts to enforce constraints. An aircraft parts supply chain case was studied in [17] where a blockchain is used not just for traceability but also for performance monitoring and parts usage which positively impacts data integrity and safety. An architectural design scenario of industrial platforms based on blockchain-powered product-centric information management platform using the blockchain technology was presented in [18].

The following table represented a set of industrial application based on the blockchain. We highlight the type of blockchain used and the benefit of integration in each type (Table 1).

Table 1. A table of some blockchain-based industrial applications highlighting the benefit of blockchain use in each case.

Industry	Type of Blockchain [19]	Benefits of using blockchain	References
Supply chain management	Private or consortium	• Help reduce time delays, management costs, and human errors • Facilitate faster and more efficient agreements between companies involved in logistics activities • Securely and efficiently support planning, scheduling, coordinating, monitoring, and validating logistics activities	[20, 21]
Real estate	Public or consortium	• Transparency and real estate data accessibility • Reduced transfer/transaction costs • Tokenization of properties, a piece of real estate can be a stock holding • Technical efficiency and reduced red tape	[22, 23]
Financial settlement	Public or consortium	• Reduce financial activities costs • Reduce transactional and operational errors • Enable the use of digital currencies • Enhance insurance policies and related activities such as negotiations, agreements and claims handling • Enable stock exchanges without involving a third party • Enable financial settlements without involving a third party	[24, 25]
Healthcare	Consortium	• Enable controlled sharing of EMRs among multiple healthcare providers and related industries • Facilitate patients' ownership of their EMRs, while inhibiting their ability to alter them • Allow patients to control and securely share their health data while maintaining their privacy • Enhance pharmaceutical supply chain management processes • Facilitate fine grain analysis of patients' data, medical innovations and research results	[26, 27]

(*continued*)

Table 1. (*continued*)

Industry	Type of Blockchain [19]	Benefits of using blockchain	References
Insurance	Private or Consortium	• Efficient claims handling • Promotes reinsurance practices • Enhanced KYC (Know your customer) and AML (anti-money laundering) procedures • Enabling insurance on any asset • Settle transactions automatically by reducing human intervention	[28, 29]
Stock trading	Consortium	• Speed up the settlement of trades • Reduce the time taken by intermediaries, operational trade clearance, and regulatory processes • Tracing ownership and automatic dividend sharing	[24, 30]
Intellectual property	Public or consortium	• Easy licensing and signature process • Enhance the sharing and transfers of IP • Direct royalties and reduced intermediaries • Digital rights management	[31, 32]

Despite the appealing advantages that blockchain promises in PLM environments, several challenges are still present to achieve good integration. Most of these challenges are usually not standard as every company has with one or more of the following issues:

- Resistance to change: the stakeholder of a certain platform may refuse to use a blockchain based solution.
- Information security: making the data for public use may lead to leaks if the solution is not designed correctly.
- Potential impact: In the best-case scenario, the integration of the blockchain may boost the performance and secure the data exchanges which can be the opposite if the risks of misintegration are not handled correctly.
- Regulations: Blockchain can be restricted for public use is some countries for financial or non-financial applications.

Overall, any integration of blockchain and PLM systems needs to be evaluated and its performance should be monitored to ensure that this integration is solving problems, not creating new ones. This may be achieved using a set of Key Performance Indicators (KPIs) and performance indicators evaluated upon the testing stage of such platform integration.

3.6 What Information to Put on the Blockchain and How?

Blockchain is an append-only database that is heavily secured using hash chaining and other cryptographic concepts. Blockchain was designed for many things and interaction performance is not one of them. This can be seen as a potential drawback as if one wants to put a large file on the blockchain, this may result in a very important computational burden that can lead to platform failure. Blockchains are not storage platforms, blockchains are not fast interaction relational databases that are used for information retrieval and online queries. Instead, blockchains can be considered as a secure interaction platform that can be used to exchange critical data securely.

Having this in mind, we need to evaluate concretely what to store on the blockchain in the case of PLM systems. Additionally, to ensure that the information is available for all stakeholders without compromising confidentiality on Intellectual Property (IP), what are the data encapsulation solutions can we use to enforce these rules?

Blockchain provides the stakeholders with an open platform, tamper-proof traceability data, regulatory-compliance checking, etc. However, there are 3 different types s of implementation (See Fig. 5): fully public, private and consortium (hybrid). The security and performance aspects vary with each type which makes architecture choices not trivial.

Property	Public blockchain	Consortium blockchain	Private blockchain
Consensus determination	All miners	Selected set of nodes	One organization
Read permission	Public	Could be public or restricted	Could be public or restricted
Immutability	Nearly impossible to tamper	Could be tampered	Could be tampered
Efficiency	Low	High	High
Centralized	No	Partial	Yes
Consensus process	Permissionless	Permissioned	Permissioned

Fig. 5. Type of blockchain depending on their property [18]

In private blockchains, we can select a group of users from an institution or organization to view and/or edit data. This makes it easy to tamper with the data depending on the implementation as the blockchain will be mostly managed by a single entity and can only be used inside an organization. Public blockchains such as the one used by cryptocurrencies, allow everyone to view and access the data. They are more secure, however, their performance low as usually the validation of transaction takes a considerable amount of computational resources. In hybrid blockchains, some peers can see all the data while others can see only selections; or all can see all the data, but only some can add new data. It depends on how it is defined by the system designer.

4 The SupplyLedger Project Approach to Blockchain Integration

Traditional business process management systems rely on the client/server centralized architecture. Several issues arise in these kinds of systems such as downtime, lack of transparency and security flaws. Even though business risk management strategies can address these issues, however, that comes usually with a set of compromises. In the context of Supply Chain management, businesses rely on mutual trust and own ledgers to track and manage their exchanged assets. Nowadays, blockchain technology is proliferating into every field that uses record-keeping and assets exchange. Several companies and researchers are trying to convince businesses to adopt this decentralized approach and show its benefits. Its new features are considered as a revolution in business management to generate value and revenue. However, in reality, it is really hard to make a revolution in something that was established for decades [33].

In an effort to secure supply chain networks, in light with the recent international events and challenges, the blockchain has been successfully used in many fields. In the context of supply chains and PLM, SupplyLedger is a new project that aims at integrating the blockchain technology with supply chain frameworks.

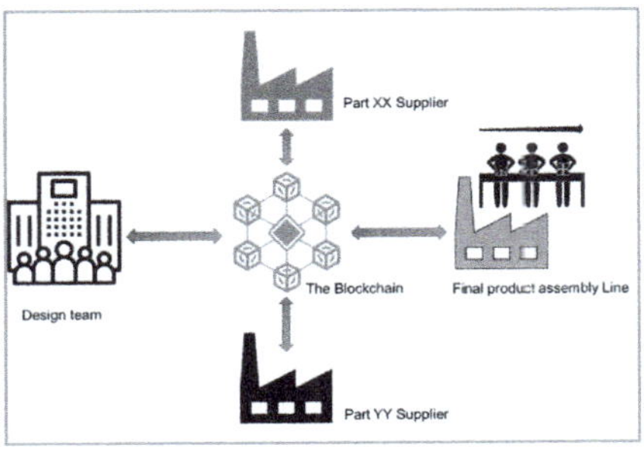

Fig. 6. A blockchain linking a manufacturing supply chain

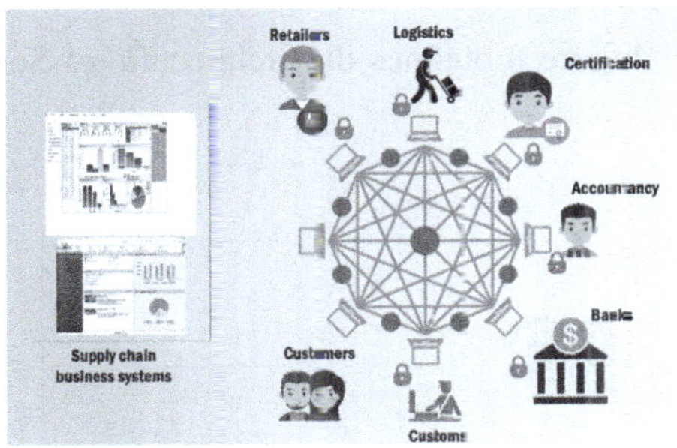

Fig. 7. Blockchain-based/SC interoperability

To improve the business process of Supply Chain management and to leverage the benefits of the blockchain technology, the blockchain should be able to integrate with numerous business systems such as Customer Relationship Management (CRM), Enterprise Resource Planning ERP), etc. (See Fig. 6 and 7). The benefits of integrating these systems with the blockchain are: transparency, improved reporting, and tracking cost reduction [34]. More specifically the benefits include:

- The blockchain makes the transactions generated by these systems transparent and reliable.
- Integration with the blockchain reduces the costs incurred by disputes on invoices and other transactions between the different parties in the Supply Chain.

- The blockchain stores a copy of the information generated by the different activities in the Supply Chain (tracking, shipping products, etc.) that is tamper-proof and can be referred to at any time.
- Integration with the blockchain provides better transparency in terms of the origin and the current possession of the product.
- The blockchain may improve the tracking of faulty parts that can affect an entire assembly line.

The SupplyLedger team aims at designing and implementing a blockchain-based architecture for supply chain management. The project team is studying existing Supply Chain Management platforms and identifying the functional and nonfunctional requirements captured from end-users focusing on a specific case study. The main focus points are as follows:

- Development of design principles for transforming an existing supply chain model to a smart contract-based blockchain model.
- Interoperability of blockchain-based supply chain management platform with traditional platforms
- Implementation and evaluation of the performance of the proposed blockchain-based system for supply chains
- Mining supply chain data in blockchain architectures.

Figure 8 outlines the architecture of SupplyLedger.

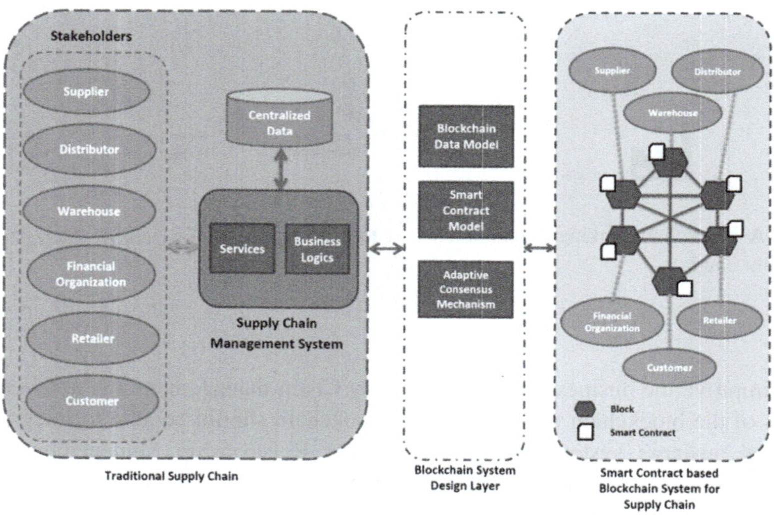

Fig. 8. SupplyLedger architecture

SupplyLedger is an impact-driven project that aims at making a significant contribution towards meeting the Qatari strategic vision of creating a sustainable "Smart Nation" in which its economic sector's knowledge is promoted and shared securely, safely and transparently through a blockchain-based logistics SC management architecture. The project impact will be achieved through a number of enabling factors that will be realized through:

- Creation of innovative techniques and effective methods for understanding the impact of the blockchain on supply chain management in Qatar. The global objective of SupplyLedger is to specify and develop a blockchain-based solution adapted to the logistics SC management activities.
- The system to develop in the course of the SupplyLedger project will enable a blockchain-based solution that ensures trust, transparency, and security in SCs in Qatar. The goods entering and transiting through the country will be fully annotated with their lifecycle information starting from their origin. This will drastically improve consumer satisfaction not only in the industry sector but also in the community as a whole. The time and cost will also be optimized especially in case of disputes or irregularities as all the information regarding the payment transaction and its physical location are publicly and transparently available on the blockchain in real-time. Refunds will be issued immediately, and products will be delivered securely. Furthermore, counterfeiting will be effectively reduced.
- The SupplyLedger project will provide training for researchers in Qatar higher education institutions such as universities and research centers. This will further enhance the Qatari researchers' understanding of blockchain adaptation to other domains besides the classical financial technologies (Fintech) domain. Thereby allowing them to reap the benefits of the blockchain architecture. Moreover, the project will develop new blockchain business and enterprise integration techniques. This will enable interested stakeholders in Qatar to adopt the blockchain technology.

5 Conclusion

Blockchain is a new innovative way of collaboration that went beyond its original application in cryptocurrencies to disrupt multiple fields. PLM systems are collaborative platforms that manage a wide variety of resources. New industry 4.0 requires new ways of interaction with the abundance of sensor data coming from IoT devices and new ways of collaboration through cloud computing. This induces multiple challenges related to reliability, security and data integrity which can be addressed using blockchain technology. Blockchains address data integrity issues by design and mitigate some of the trust concerns found in collaborative platforms. In this regard, we studied how we can integrate the blockchain technology with PLM systems through a series of selected questions that we elaborated to shape the integration of PLM and blockchain. Additionally, we presented SupplyLedger which is a new project aiming at integrating the blockchain technology with supply chain management systems.

Acknowledgement. This publication was made possible by NPRP grant NPRP11S-1227-170135 from the Qatar National Research Fund (a member of Qatar Foundation). The statements made herein are solely the responsibility of the authors.

References

1. Li, J., Tao, F., Cheng, Y., Zhao, L.: Big data in product lifecycle management. Int. J. Adv. Manuf. Technol. **81**, 667–684 (2015)
2. Lasi, H., Fettke, P., Kemper, H.-G., Feld, T., Hoffmann, M.: Industry 40. Bus. Inf. Syst. Eng. **6**, 239–242 (2014)
3. Tao, F., Zuo, Y., Da Xu, L., Zhang, L.: IoT-based intelligent perception and access of manufacturing resource toward cloud manufacturing. IEEE Trans. Industr. Inf. **10**, 1547–1557 (2014)
4. Saaksvuori, A., Immonen, A.: Product Lifecycle Management. Springer, Cham (2008). https://doi.org/10.1007/978-3-540-78172-1
5. Terzi, S., Bouras, A., Dutta, D., Garetti, M., Kiritsis, D.: Product lifecycle management-from its history to its new role. Int. J. Product Lifecycle Manage. **4**, 360–389 (2010)
6. Stark, J.: Product lifecycle management. In: Product Lifecycle Management. Decision Engineering. Springer, London (2011). https://doi.org/10.1007/978-0-85729-546-0_1
7. Ferreira, F.D., Faria, J., Azevedo, A., Marques, A.L.: Product lifecycle management enabled by industry 4.0 technology (2016)
8. Nofer, M., Gomber, P., Hinz, O., Schiereck, D.: Blockchain. Business & information. Syst. Eng. **59**, 183–187 (2017)
9. Underwood, S.: Blockchain Beyond Bitcoin. ACM, New York (2016)
10. Viriyasitavat, W., Da Xu, L., Bi, Z., Sapsomboon, A.: Blockchain-based business process management (BPM) framework for service composition in industry 4.0. J. Intell. Manuf. **30**, 1–12 (2018)
11. Bocek, T., Rodrigues, B.B., Strasser, T., Stiller, B.: Blockchains everywhere-a use-case of blockchains in the pharma supply-chain. In: 2017 IFIP/IEEE Symposium on Integrated Network and Service Management (IM), pp. 772–777. IEEE (2017)
12. Bahga, A., Madisetti, V.K.: Blockchain platform for industrial internet of things. J. Softw. Eng. Appl. **9**, 533–546 (2016)
13. Li, Z., Wang, W., Liu, G., Liu, L., He, J., Huang, G.: Toward open manufacturing. Industr. Manage. Data Syst. **118**, 303–320 (2018)
14. Li, Z., Kang, J., Yu, R., Ye, D., Deng, Q., Zhang, Y.: Consortium blockchain for secure energy trading in industrial internet of things. IEEE Trans. Industr. Inf. **14**, 3690–3700 (2017)
15. Francisco, K., Swanson, D.: The supply chain has no clothes: technology adoption of blockchain for supply chain transparency. Logistics **2**, 2 (2018)
16. Kim, H.M., Laskowski, M.: Toward an ontology-driven blockchain design for supply-chain provenance. Intell. Syst. Account. Financ. Manage. **25**, 18–27 (2018)
17. Madhwal, Y., Panfilov, P.B.: Blockchain and supply chain management: aircrafts'parts'business case. In: Annals of DAAAM & Proceedings, vol. 28 (2017)
18. Mattila, J., Seppälä, T., Holmström, J.: Product-centric information management: a case study of a shared platform with blockchain technology (2016)
19. Andreev, R., Andreeva, P., Krotov, L., Krotova, E.: Review of blockchain technology: Types of blockchain and their application. Intellekt. Sist. Proizv. **16**, 11–14 (2018)
20. Saberi, S., Kouhizadeh, M., Sarkis, J., Shen, L.: Blockchain technology and its relationships to sustainable supply chain management. Int. J. Prod. Res. **57**, 2117–2135 (2019)
21. Hackius, N., Petersen, M.: Blockchain in logistics and supply chain: trick or treat? In: Digitalization in Supply Chain Management and Logistics: Smart and Digital Solutions for an Industry 4.0 Environment. Proceedings of the Hamburg International Conference of Logistics (HICL), vol. 23, pp. 3–18. epubli GmbH, Berlin (2017)

22. Krupa, K.S., Akhil, M.S.: Reshaping the real estate industry using blockchain. In: Sridhar, V., Padma, M.C., Rao, K.A.Radhakrishna (eds.) Emerging Research in Electronics, Computer Science and Technology. LNEE, vol. 545, pp. 255–263. Springer, Singapore (2019). https://doi.org/10.1007/978-981-13-5802-9_24
23. Spielman, A.: Blockchain: digitally rebuilding the real estate industry. Massachusetts Institute of Technology (2016)
24. Tapscott, A., Tapscott, D.: How blockchain is changing finance. Harvard Bus. Rev. **1**, 2–5 (2017)
25. Yoo, S.: Blockchain based financial case analysis and its implications. Asia Pacific J. Innovation Entrepreneurship **11**, 312–321 (2017)
26. Engelhardt, M.A.: Hitching healthcare to the chain: an introduction to blockchain technology in the healthcare sector. Technol. Innovation Manage. Rev. **7**, 22–34 (2017)
27. Mettler, M.: Blockchain technology in healthcare: the revolution starts here. In: 2016 IEEE 18th International Conference on e-Health Networking, Applications and Services (Healthcom), pp. 1–3. IEEE (2016)
28. Cohn, A., West, T., Parker, C.: Smart after all: blockchain, smart contracts, parametric insurance, and smart energy grids. Georgetown Law Technol. Rev. **1**, 273–304 (2017)
29. Crawford, M.: The insurance implications of blockchain. Risk Manage. **64**, 24 (2017)
30. Lee, L.: New kids on the blockchain: how bitcoin's technology could reinvent the stock market. Hastings Bus. LJ **12**, 81 (2015)
31. Gürkaynak, G., Yılmaz, İ., Yeşilaltay, B., Bengi, B.: Intellectual property law and practice in the blockchain realm. Comput. Law Secur. Rev. **34**, 847–862 (2018)
32. Wang, J., Wang, S., Guo, J., Du, Y., Cheng, S., Li, X.: A summary of research on blockchain in the field of intellectual property. Procedia Comput. Sci. **147**, 191–197 (2019)
33. Wu, H., Li, Z., King, B., Ben Miled, Z., Wassick, J., Tazelaar, J.: A distributed ledger for supply chain physical distribution visibility. Information **8**, 137 (2017)
34. Abeyratne, S.A., Monfared, R.P.: Blockchain ready manufacturing supply chain using distributed ledger (2016)

Model Based Systems Engineering

Analysis of MBSE/PLM Integration: From Conceptual Design to Detailed Design

Yaroslav Menshenin[1(✉)], Dominik Knoll[2], Yana Brovar[1], and Clement Fortin[1]

[1] Skolkovo Institute of Science and Technology, Bolshoy Boulevard 30, bld. 1, Moscow 121205, Russia
{y.menshenin, yana.brovar, c.fortin}@skoltech.ru

[2] Babeş-Bolyai University, Mihail Kogalniceanu 1, Cluj-Napoca 400084, Romania
dominik.johannes.knoll@scs.ubbcluj.ro

Abstract. Model-Based Systems Engineering (MBSE) approaches guide complex system/product design and development from the very early stages of the product development process. Its full-scale integration into the Product Lifecycle Management (PLM) would allow to facilitate a better data flow from conceptual design to detailed design. In this paper we discuss such data flow focusing on three core models: Object-Process Methodology (OPM), Core product model (CPM), and STEP. We describe core artefacts of these models and those entities in which they overlap, thus we define which data is critical throughout the entire system/product development. We demonstrate that the fundamental problem associated with the integration of MBSE and PLM is due to the fundamental essence of systems, which needs both explicit representations of time and space to represent completely the system form and behavior throughout the product/system life cycle. An analysis for a CubeSat mission is also presented to illustrate the data correspondences between the various models.

Keywords: MBSE · PLM · Conceptual design · Ontology · Data flow

1 Introduction

A "Vision for the European industry for 2030" [1] makes a special emphasis on how industry will be transformed through the digitization of manufacturing, products, and data-driven services. While the Product Life cycle Management (PLM) approach is core to support such transformation, one of the key issues arising is a need to integrate conceptual information from a very early stage of the product development process with the data at later stages of design. In [2] authors highlighted a difficulty associated with "…the necessity to operate not only with different terminologies but also with different formalisms…" while building a multi-aspect PLM ontology to engage inter-operability support across PLM processes. Data integration is also required with the early phases of conceptual design, with Model-Based Systems Engineering (MBSE) [3, 4] which supports the development of complex systems and products. The integration of MBSE with PLM solutions is still very limited in practice and major barriers remain between these two worlds of the digital chain.

Published by Springer Nature Switzerland AG 2020
F. Nyffenegger et al. (Eds.): PLM 2020, IFIP AICT 594, pp. 593–603, 2020.
https://doi.org/10.1007/978-3-030-62807-9_47

In this paper we analyze three important components of the digital chain from conceptual to detail design in order to clearly identify the misfits which prevent a proper integration between MBSE and PLM.

MBSE is an evolution of the Systems Engineering approach, which is a well-established discipline for the development of complex systems in the space industry in the later part of the 20th century. MBSE core idea is to shift a paradigm of system/product design from a document-centric to a model-centric approach. For this, conceptual modelling languages are used – to allow the representation of both - space and time – explicitly in a model. Thus, the MBSE approach allows modeling not only of a static reality, but also of system/product behavior and functions.

To analyze the MBSE to PLM data integration, we propose to use the Design Structure Matrix (DSM). DSM has been developed by Steward [5] and over time proved its effectiveness as a tool to manage interconnections within a complex system or product [6]. Hereby, the system designers can determine the relationships between the various systems elements [7, 8]. DSM has such capabilities that make it a universal approach to not only analyze the architecture, but also the data integration between different models. In our work we use DSM to map the core entities from conceptual to detail design. Doing this, we identify the overlaps and gaps in the digital engineering information exchange [9].

In the following Sect. 2, we discuss MBSE and PLM Data Modeling strategies based on three models – OPM (Subsect. 2.1), CPM (Subsect. 2.2), and STEP (Subsect. 2.3). In Sect. 3, we present an analysis of digital constructs between MBSE and PLM, mapping the entities of conceptual design with entities of detailed design. After this, in Sect. 4, we demonstrate how the proposed approach could be applied to a CubeSat's Earth Observation Mission to represent the digital engineering information from conceptual design to detailed design. We discuss the results of our work and conclude in Sect. 5.

2 MBSE and PLM Data Modeling

A well-integrated chain between MBSE and PLM is essential to facilitate the data flow from the conceptual design to the detailed design. Such a chain would allow a product design team to store the design heritage and keep track of how the systems architecture transforms through the design process.

There are a number of different conceptual modeling languages and semantics that could be used to represent conceptual design. The system modeling language (SysML) has a grammar of 9 types of diagrams that support specification, analysis, design, verification, and validation of systems [10]. SysML which has been derived from the Unified Modeling Language (UML) for computer programming applications is currently widely used in industry. However, it has clear weaknesses, including those related with the correspondence between these 9 types of diagrams, that can be divided into Structure and Behavior categories, and there is currently a substantial effort to develop a new version called SysML 2.0. Another solution, is to use the Object-Process Methodology (OPM) [11], which is based on solid fundamental knowledge of systems and is now standardized in ISO 19450 [12]. Since OPM is able to represent the essence of systems well, we take this standard as a basis for the analysis at the conceptual design phase and study its integration with the later stages mainly supported by PLM systems. We will discuss OPM in Subsect. 2.1.

For the PLM data structure, we used the CPM data model (Subsect. 2.2), which was developed by NIST; and the STEP standard (Subsect. 2.3), which is used extensively in current PLM systems. CPM has been proposed as an advanced PLM framework, which includes behavioral and functional information, as well as geometry.

2.1 Object-Process Methodology (OPM)

OPM specifies the core elements of a system as the objects and processes, and related states. OPM provides both graphical (Object-Process Diagram) and linguistic (Object-Process Language) representations that allow documenting and modeling the core information about a system. The key data that is contained at the conceptual design phase in OPM includes the information about objects, represented by rectangles, processes, denoted as ovals and states, represented as rounded corner rectangles. OPM also includes a number of specific relationships between these objects, processes and states, which provide a powerful representation language of complex cyber-physical systems and all complex systems. The idea behind OPM is that the combination of these entities and relationships allow a systems designer to effectively represent a complex system of any nature, its function and behavior particularly at the conceptual design level.

2.2 Core Product Model (CPM)

The Core Product Model (CPM) was developed through the synthesis of various related artifacts to create a representation of the design information [13, 14]. CPM is a model allowing to describe key characteristics of PLM information by using generic semantics, that is based on two principles. First, the key entity in the core model is the artifact and not the geometric model as in STEP. Second, the focal point is the representation are artifacts that includes form, corresponding function and product behavior.

The core model is aimed to be applied as the informational support mechanism to create reliable representations of all data that are relevant to the continuous design process covering the whole range of PLM activities. Consequently, for the early conceptual design stage reasoning on the requirements of the product could be supported by the entity "function", and the product behavior in the post-design stages can be modeled by the behavior entity.

2.3 STEP

The STEP format, based on the widely used ISO 10303 – STandard for Exchange of Product model data, aims to provide a representation of product information and to exchange and interoperate product data between Computer-Aided Design, Manufacturing, Analysis, and Inspection software, independent from any particular system [15, 16].

STEP consists of several Application Protocols that satisfy the scope and informational requirements for many industry specific applications and use the same terminology. In the aerospace and automotive industries, ISO 10303 AP 214 and ISO 10303 AP 203 are widely implemented to support the exchange of CAD and PDM information with suppliers and other PLM applications. To support subsequent stages of product development, STEP AP 224 has been adopted for product data exchange for process planning. It contains all the necessary information to enable modern Computer Aided Manufacturing Planning systems including materials definition, parts geometry, dimensions and tolerances.

To achieve greater benefits, these AP 214 and AP 203 were combined into a single convergent information model that was formulated in AP 242, that covers all main technical requirements contained in AP 203 and AP 214 and extended them with some of the needed complementary capabilities. It defines a single integrated ISO standard that covers product information interoperability capabilities for: Product Data Management, 3D Model-based design with Product Manufacturing Information (PMI), Mechanical, Composite, Electrical harness design, 3D parametric and geometric constraints design, tessellation and kinematics [17]. A new version of AP 242 was recently published in April 2020.

3 Analysis of Digital Constructs Between MBSE and PLM

The following approach was selected to represent the data flow from conceptual design to detailed design. We start this process by extracting key entities associated with OPM, CPM, and STEP models. Following the models' descriptions in the corresponding literature, we list the selected entities in the DSM matrix presented in Fig. 1. In total, 23 entities have been chosen: 3 for the OPM model, 10 for the CPM model, and 10 for the STEP model. The key entities are then mapped to each other through the DSM-based methods. The cells at the intersection of different rows and columns indicate that two entities are corresponding fully (denoted by F) or partially (denoted by P).

It is also important to note that in our work we only consider the transfer from conceptual design to detailed design, therefore only these downstream correspondences are included in Fig. 1 and relate to those below the diagonal. The DSM presented in Fig. 1 should be read "from column to row". For example, we have taken the first column "(1) object" and have checked the presence of this entity in other models, starting from entity "(4) artifact" to the entity "(23) process plan".

Figure 1 contains important information about the digital engineering model integration from conceptual design to detailed design. It is also important to note that we have not mapped entities within each model, shown as grey blocks in Fig. 1 in order to highlight the correspondences and misfits between the models.

In OPM, the essential entities of a system are summarized as "object" (entity №1 in Fig. 1), "process" (entity №2), and "state" (entity №3). As defined by Dori [11], any system can be represented by a combination of these entities, plus their relationships. A "state" links an entity "object" (space representation) and an entity "process" (time representation). Thus, time is explicit in OPM models and "objects" can be defined as stateful objects, as described by Dori [11] and Crawley et al. [19], meaning that they carry both space and time in their essence. This is thus a very important characteristic of systems and thus of MBSE by extension. This integrated space and time domains, allow proper modeling of behavior and functions that are critical to represent requirements and also product/systems architectures.

However, CPM and STEP models are geometry-centric; they are PLM representations that are very much focused in the space domain, so time is generally implicit in PLM data structures. CPM proposes to include the time domain explicitly in its data model by inserting the entities "function" (entity №6) and "behavior" (entity №8) as shown in Fig. 1.

		OPM			CPM										STEP AP 242								
		(1) Object	(2) Process	(3) State	(4) Artifact	(5) Feature	(6) Function	(7) Form	(8) Behavior	(9) Geometry	(10) Material	(11) Specification	(12) Requirement	(13) Flow	(14) Product	(15) Assembly	(16) Shape	(17) Feature	(18) Material	(19) Product specification	(20) Geometry	(21) Action	(22) Process plan
OPM	(1) Object																						
	(2) Process																						
	(3) State																						
CPM	(4) Artifact	F																					
	(5) Feature	P																					
	(6) Function		P																				
	(7) Form	P																					
	(8) Behavior	P	P																				
	(9) Geometry	P																					
	(10) Material	P																					
	(11) Specification																						
	(12) Requirement																						
	(13) Flow	P	P																				
STEP AP 242	(14) Product	F			F					P													
	(15) Assembly	F			F					P													
	(16) Shape	P						F		F													
	(17) Feature	P				F				P													
	(18) Material	P						P			F			P									
	(19) Product specification											F	F										
	(20) Geometry	P						P		F													
	(21) Action	P	F				P		P					P									
	(22) Process plan	P	F																				

Fig. 1. A DSM-based information representation of important MBSE and PLM entities.

To better illustrate the importance of these entities in terms of frequency of their appearance we summarized the information in Fig. 2. From this Figure, we may conclude that largely there are three categories of entities. The first category contains the physical and informational entities. The entities of this category are the most frequently appearing ones in Fig. 2. Among these entities are "object", "artifact", "feature", "form", "geometry", and "material". This result has some rationale, as the physical/informational entities are the universal entities that all product developers are working on, since these entities are tangible and are dealing with space representation. The second category of entities are the time-related entities: "process", "function", "behavior", "specification", "requirement", "flow". These entities appear less frequently, dealing with time representation, which is generally implicit in PLM systems. Finally, the third category is represented by one entity – "state" We have not found any correspondence of this entity with other entities in Fig. 1. This result has some rationale. "State" links both – space and time – together. Since we have a frequent representation of space, a less frequent representation of time, it is logical that a space to time relationship is even less frequently considered by engineers in PLM systems. We argue that this is one of the core results of our analysis of the problem in integration of MBSE and PLM approaches, since there is clearly a major gap in representations between these domains.

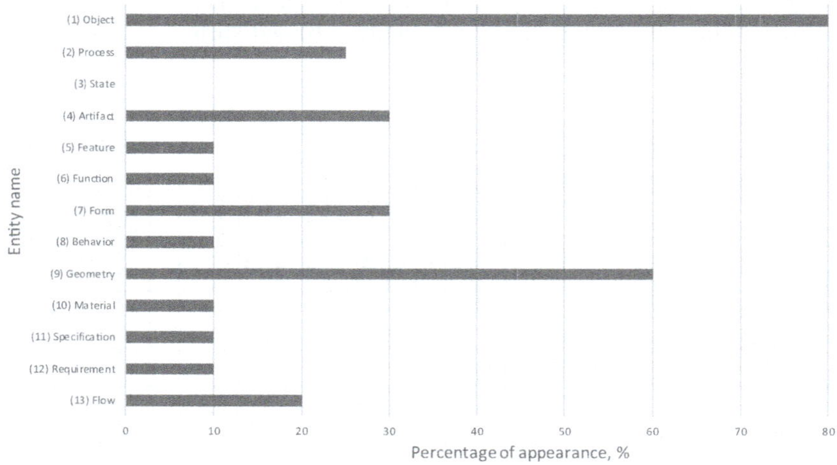

Fig. 2. A frequency of OPM entities appearance in CPM and STEP models; and CPM entities appearance in STEP model.

Note that in Fig. 2, because we analyzed the frequency of appearance of OPM entities in CPM and STEP, and the frequency of appearance of CPM entities in STEP, we only listed the first 13 entities related to OPM and CPM models. This is due to the underlying idea of our analysis: to analyze the unidirectional data flow from conceptual design to detailed design.

4 Earth Observation Mission Representations

To illustrate the information flow from conceptual to detailed design, we chose to represent a technical system by various modeling approaches typical for the different phases of development. As an example of a technical system, we chose a small satellite. The mission to be fulfilled by the satellite is to observe the earth surface and transmit the recorded images to the ground, where the data will be processed in order to generate meaningful information. The concept of the satellite mission can be described with an OPM diagram. As shown in Fig. 3, the satellite mission is described with objects and processes. The satellite consists of a number of subsystems, namely an Optical Instrument, a Power System, a Structure, a Communications System, a Thermal Control System, and an Attitude Determination and Control System (ADCS). The satellite system handles the process of observing the earth. The process of observing the earth can be broken down into subprocesses, each of them requiring a subsystem. The process "recording images" is supported by "relaying data" and "pointing instrument". Following the OPM approach, we can zoom-in on the thermal control system, to represent and design its structure and behavior.

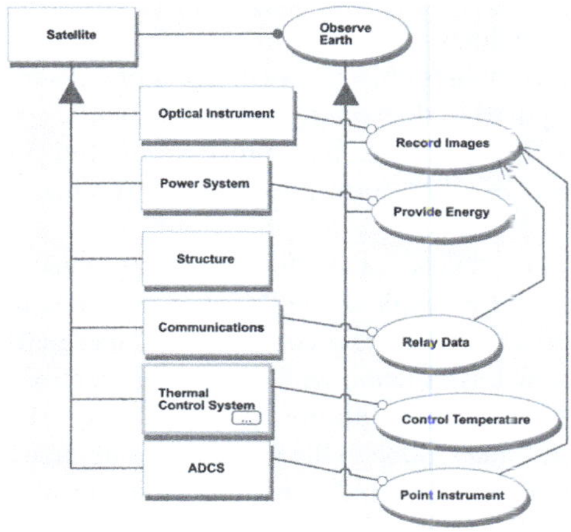

Fig. 3. OPM representation of CubeSat mission.

Figure 4 shows the details of the object "Thermal Control System", that is required for the process "Control Temperature". This subsystem is made of a heater, sensors, a radiator and a controller. The controller handles the two processes "heating" and "cooling", and they require the heater, sensors, and the radiator. The Thermal Control System can be in one of the three possible states depending on the measured temperatures. The heating process will change the state from "temp <= Tlow" to "temp > Tlow and temp < Thigh", whereas the cooling process, does the opposite.

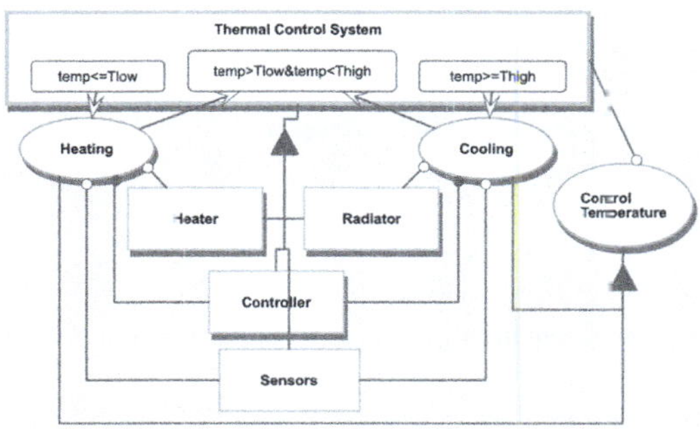

Fig. 4. OPM representation of simple CubeSat mission's thermal system

To present an understandable representation of CPM entities and clear comparison with the OPM approach, Fig. 5 shows the structure of the CubeSat's Thermal Control System as an instance of the "Artifact" class, which matches the "object" entity in the OPM representation. This instance is linked through "subArtifact" relationships to a set of other instances representing subartifacts of the Thermal Control System. The figure also shows instances of the "feature", "function", "form", "behavior", "flow", "geometry" and "material" entities.

The entity function combines object modeling and process modeling, as it describes what the artifact is supposed to do, so it has a strong relation with the entity "process" in the OPM diagram. For example, the "process" of Temperature control, that is described as a "process" in OPM corresponds to the Thermal Control System "function" in CPM.

The entities "feature", "flow" and "form", which consists of "geometry" and "material", are shown in the example of the Radiator. As it could be seen by comparing Fig. 4 and Fig. 5, there is no complete conformity of these CPM entities with OPM entities, but there is partial association with the "object" entity. The "Flow" entity, as well, could be partially compliant with the "process" entity. However, CPM does not allow the description of "states", due to the fact that this approach was created from the purpose of geometry representation and is less focused on the representation of artifacts throughout their life cycle.

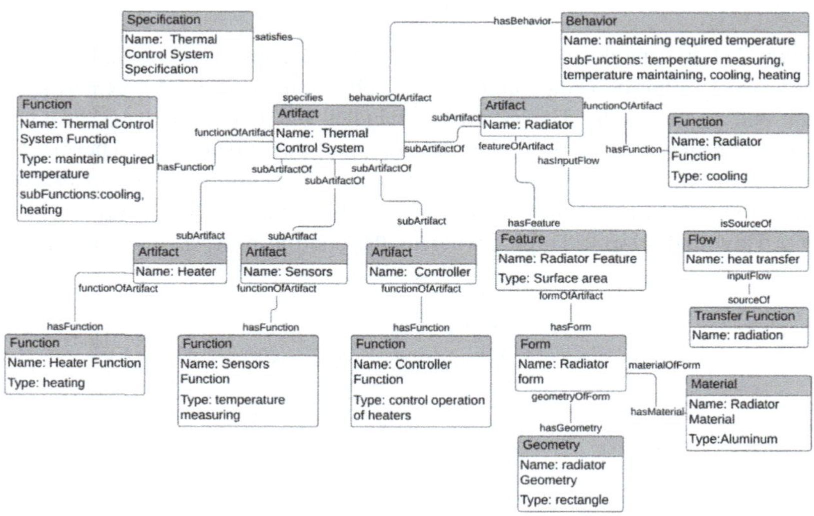

Fig. 5. CPM representation of simple CubeSat mission's thermal system

To analyze the information of the CubeSat representation in AP 242, a spreadsheet of all entity and attribute information was created in the STEP analyzer and viewer (SFA) tool [18] developed by NIST. Table 1 shows key entities and their count in the corresponding STEP file, based on the SFA tool. Information related to "process plan" and "action" entities are specified in parts of ISO that are related to manufacturing information, so there are absent in AP 242 representation.

All information related to the entities "specification", "features", and "materials" are absent in this simplified assembly; however, their presence depends on the chosen 3D model construction.

The "product" count represents the number of components of the simple CubeSat 3D model. All entities that are related to geometry of those components were counted, and due to the fact that main capability of AP 242 is geometry representation, the number of those entities is the greatest.

Table 1. CubeSat entity information of STEP 242 file

Entity	Count
Product / part	69
Assembly_definition	13
Product_definition_shape	354
Feature_definition	0
Material	0
Product specification	0
Geometry	86229
Action	0
Process plan	0

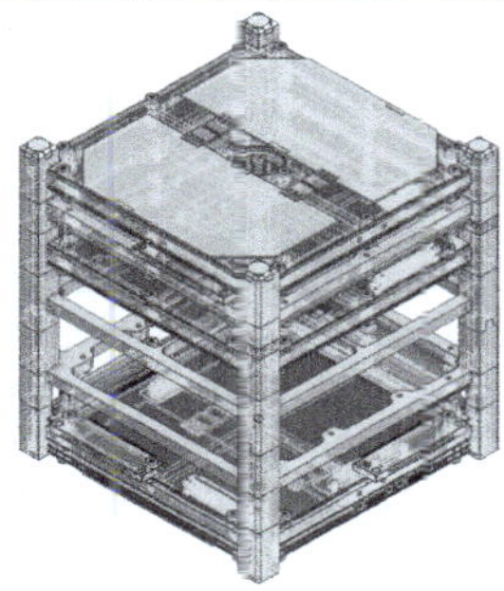

5 Discussion and Conclusion

In this paper, we presented the results of an analysis of MBSE to PLM systems integration, focusing on the integration associated with a unidirectional data flow from conceptual design to detailed design.

We extracted the core entities and some relationships that are present in OPM, CPM, and STEP models. Through a DSM-based approach, we mapped these entities to each other in order to identify their presence at different stages of product development. Additionally, we analyzed the frequency of appearance of OPM entities in CPM and STEP models; as well as the frequency of appearance of CPM entities in STEP model.

From the data presented in Fig. 1 we realized that the fundamental problem associated with the integration of MBSE and PLM is due to the fundamental essence of systems. This difficulty arises from the need to explicitly represent time and space to completely define the system form and behavior throughout the product/system life cycle. Current PLM systems explicitly represent space in great detail but leave the time domain mostly as an implicit dimension, except in particular modules like kinematics, simulation and manufacturing systems, making it difficult to properly integrate the digital chain from conceptual to detail design and further along the product life cycle.

Future work will further explore the relationships within and between these models with a potential engagement of additional models, such as SysML [10].

Another specific result of our analysis is that there are essentially three categories of entities associated with the data flow from conceptual design to detailed design. The first category deals with space representation and is extensively present in PLM systems; the second category represents time, and is less frequently appearing in digital integration but is strongly present in MBSE; the third category, namely "state" is very present in all systems representations but is essentially not present in PLM systems.

The limited but revealing analysis is only a first step to better understand the fundamental principles and current flaws of the digital chain integration. For future work, we see the extension to other product development and lifecycle phases, the inclusion of other types of entities and also an analysis of the relationships between the entities of each domain.

References

1. Vision for the European industry until 2030, European Commission (2020). https://ec.europa.eu/docsroom/documents/36468. Accessed 28 Oct 2020
2. Smirnov, A., Shilov, N., Parfenov, N.: Building a multi-aspect ontology for semantic interoperability in PLM. In: IFIP 16th International Conference on Product Lifecycle (2019)
3. Walden, D.D., Roedler, G.J, Forsberg, K.: INCOSE Systems Engineering Handbook, Version 4 (2016)
4. Spangelo, S.C., et al.: Applying model based systems engineering (MBSE) to a standard CubeSat. In: IEEE Aerospace Conference, pp. 1–20 (2012)
5. Steward, D.V.: The design structure system: a method for managing the design of complex systems. IEEE Trans. Eng. Manage. **3**, 71–74 (1981)
6. Eppinger, S.D., Browning, T.R.: Design Structure Matrix Methods and Applications. MIT Press, Cambridge (2012)
7. Browning, T.R.: Applying the design structure matrix to system decomposition and integration problems: a review and new directions. IEEE Trans. Eng. Manage. **48**, 292–306 (2001)
8. Menshenin, Y., Crawley, E.: DSM-based methods to represent specialization relationships in a concept framework. In: 20th International DSM Conference, pp. 151–157 (2018)
9. INCOSE: Digital Engineering Information Exchange. https://www.incose.org/incose-member-resources/working-groups/transformational/digital-engineering-information-exchange. Accessed 10 Feb 2020
10. Friedenthal, S., Moore, A., Steiner, R.: A Practical Guide to SysML: The Systems Modeling Language. Morgan Kaufmann, Burlington (2014)
11. Dori, D.: Object-Process Methodology: A Holistic System Paradigm. Springer, Berlin (2002). http://dx.doi.org/10.1007/978–3-642-56209-9
12. ISO 19450, Automation systems and integration - Object-Process Methodology
13. Szykman, S., Fenves, S.J., Keirouz, W.T., Shooter, S.: A foundation for interoperability in next-generation product development systems. Comput. Aided Des. **33**(7), 545–559 (2001)
14. Fenves, S.J.: A core product model for representing design information. National Institute of Standards and Technology, NISTIR 6736, Gaithersburg, MD 20899, USA (2001)
15. Kemmerer, S.J.: STEP: The Grand Experience. NIST Special Publication 939 (1999)

16. ISO 10303-1 Industrial automation systems and integration—Product data representation and exchange—Part 1: Overview and fundamental principles
17. White Paper: Development of STEP AP 242 ed2 – Managed Model Based 3D Engineering, Version 1.0, 30 Mar 2014
18. NIST STEP File Analyzer and Viewer. https://www.nist.gov/services-resources/software/step-file-analyzer-and-viewer
19. Crawley, E., Cameron, B. Selva, D.: System Architecture: Strategy and Product Development for Complex Systems. Prentice Hall Press, Upper Saddle River (2015)

Issues on Introducing Model-Based Definition - Case of Manufacturing Ecosystem

Pekka Uski[1], Antti Pulkkinen[2(✉)], Lasse Hillman[3], and Asko Ellman[4]

[1] Etteplan Finland Oy, Juhana Herttuan Puistokatu 21, 20100 Turku, Finland
pekka.uski@tuni.fi
[2] VTT Technical Research Centre of Finland Ltd., Visiokatu 4, 33720 Tampere, Finland
antti.pulkkinen@vtt.fi
[3] Tampere University of Applied Sciences, Kuntokatu 3, 33520 Tampere, Finland
lasse.hillman@tuni.fi
[4] Tampere University, Korkeakoulunkatu 6, 33720 Tampere, Finland
asko.ellman@tuni.fi

Abstract. The benefits of Model-Based Definition (MBD) are well known. Considering this there is a need to understand the reasons why MBD is utilized rarely in the manufacturing ecosystems of low volume, customized products. For studying MBD, manufacturing ecosystems and their mutual relations a literature study and a case study of manufacturing ecosystem were applied. It was noticed that there are differences between the maturities of digital product processes between the actors of the ecosystem, while MBD itself is a matter affecting the whole ecosystem. Investing in education and renewing, integrating and harmonizing processes, legacy data and software lower barriers towards adopting MBD. The motivation of the actors of an ecosystem has to ensure investments and commitment to change. The investment decisions require an ecosystem wide value definition and business case for each actor. The role of an actor within an ecosystem, how common or niche the utilized product and production technology is and the economic situation of a company appear to impact companies' willingness to change into MBD. Also, the motivation to adopt MBD depends on the amount of legacy data and the complexity of manufactured parts. Adopting PMI-data can increase the efficiency of manufacturing processes, such as quality control.

Keywords: Model-Based Definition · Model-Based Enterprise · MBD · MBE · Ecosystem · Manufacturing ecosystem · PMI

1 Introduction

Automotive, aerospace and military industries have been the forerunners in developing digital methods to seamless information flow from design engineering to production. For example, Toyota Motorsport announced already in 2004 that they were involved in a drawing-less project where the conception, manufacturing and inspection of engine

Published by Springer Nature Switzerland AG 2020
F. Nyffenegger et al. (Eds.): PLM 2020, IFIP AICT 594, pp. 604–617, 2020.
https://doi.org/10.1007/978-3-030-62807-9_48

components were carried out in a digital environment. In addition, Boeing was one of the first aircraft builders to utilize a complete digital definition in one of its aircrafts [1].

1.1 Objective of the Article

Manufacturing industry has not been an early adopter of digital thread. However, the practices of managing engineering data and used IT support for industries appear to be similar. Thus, the presentation and the use of information content can be a differentiating factor. In this paper, we study the reasons that prevent a manufacturing ecosystem from adopting digital methods integrating engineering design and manufacturing operations. The purpose of the paper is to increase understanding how digital functionality may come true in the ecosystem of the case.

Motivation. Our motivation to study and promote new ways to define and communicate product design comes from experience and practical cases. For example, an obvious need for the reconsideration of the means for product definition was noticed when a mechanical engineer was preparing manufacturing drawings for a certain steel construction project. The drawing sheet was finally a size of A0X5! One can ask how to utilize this size of a drawing in a manufacturing company as well as on a construction site. Of course, this leads to need to make more drawings in a smaller sheet due to part manufacturing processes. Furthermore, it is common to type annotations, including a bill of material (BOM), manually in the documents of large assemblies instead of getting them from the properties of a 3D model. Manual work and the redundancy of information causes a threat of inconsistencies and errors. Yet, 3D model is the mandatory source for 2D drawings, but manually typed several rows of BOM may cause mistyping and in a hurry, the checking of final documentation can be careless. Although it is inconvenient to study a large 3D PDF, one can zoom the view and to recognize details.

Even today, documents are the dominant means of communication in manufacturing and often files are a kind of digital twin of the paper-based documentation, but not the part or product itself. Therefore, the means of digital thread do exist at least in engineering design, but the manufacturing has not caught up in the potential of digital definition. We argue that MBD is one of the key enablers for the creation of a Digital Twin of a manufactured product.

Despite the obvious benefits of Model-based Definition (MBD), industrial companies still rarely utilized it [2]. Reasons for this are worth understanding. The Model-Based Definition is a basis for the wider term Model-Based Enterprise (MBE). In practise, MBE means that all or most of the functionalities of an enterprise rely on information in a form of a 3D model.

Research Approach. We study the adoption of MBD in a manufacturing ecosystem with a triangulation of the findings of three sources. First, we carry out a literature study (Sect. 2). Second, we interviewed a sample of case companies in a manufacturing ecosystem, and finally, we tested the benefits of MBD in a case study, replicating the actual operations of a subset of the ecosystem parties (Sect. 3) The research method is qualitative, and the aim is to provide answers to question, what are the factors preventing from and promoting for the adoption of MBD in a manufacturing ecosystem?

As the research approach, we adopt critical realistic approach that was adopted by Fox [3] for revealing that the hype about Building Information Model (BIM) underplays many inter-related causal requirements. Although MBD and BIM are used in different technical contexts, they are conceptually similar and the critical realistic approach appears feasible.

2 Literature Review

A reliable answer to the research question requires a definition of the topics that are the concepts related to MBD as well as the benefits and barriers of adopting MBD in industry. In addition, we define the role of product definition in a manufacturing ecosystem and the ecosystem itself.

2.1 Product Definition in Engineering Design and Manufacturing

Typically, a design engineer creates the product data with Computer Aided Design (CAD) and stores it in a product lifecycle management (PLM) system for the use of e.g. manufacturing operations. The data is comprised of models and documents, such as the drawings of parts, the structures of products and metadata. The drawings represent the characteristics of the part and structures represent the composition of a product, i.e. the bill of materials (BOM). Characteristics are geometric and alphanumeric data, such as dimensions, tolerances, surface qualities, material properties, etc.

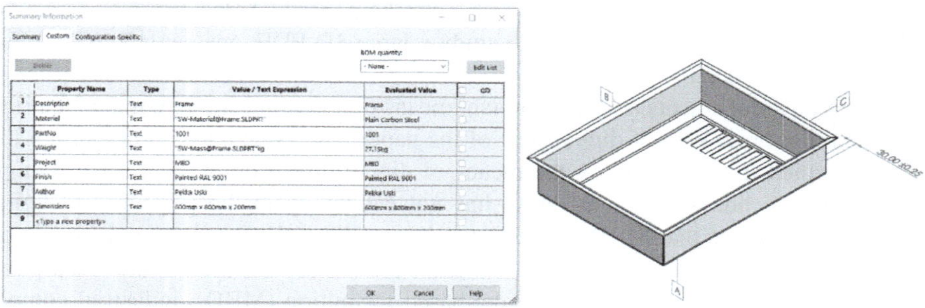

Fig. 1. Typical properties chart i.e. data card of 3D model. The model includes 3D annotations (datums A–C and dimensions).

Modern CAD software have possibilities to include part data, such as material, mass, dimensions, stock codes, color and engineer ID, to model's properties by filling the data card. The data card is usually included in PLM systems and so part or assembly properties can be inserted to a drawing's title block and bill of material (BOM). The properties chart includes 3D CAD's characteristics too and a separate PLM system may not always be needed (Fig. 1). Utilizing the potential of the data card of 3D model varies in companies. Some use many possibilities of 3D and some trusts manual methods, even if 3D modelling is relevant part of product design and manufacturing.

2.2 Model-Based Definition

Model-Based Definition (MBD) [1] can serve as an integrated presentation of a part and replace the datasets of models and drawings [4, 5]. Thus, MBD embraces the idea of a "single source of truth", by combining the different and potentially inconsistent sources of information [6]. Model-Based Definition (MBD) is an annotated 3D model and its associated data elements that fully define the product. The MBD includes all tolerances, dimensions, surface quality, material information as well as process specifications annotations that are needed for downstream users in a company and its networks. A MBD may include a Bill of Material (BOM) and product life-cycle management attributes, when it constitutes an authoritative, single source of master, product definition data completely without 2D drawings [2]

Quintana [1] points out that Model-Based Definition means the 3D product model is the most appropriate vehicle for the delivery of all the detailed product information necessary for downstream organizations to perform their portion of the product delivery cycle. MBD is a thing, a digital representation (artefact) of a physical object or system and all its attributes is used to communicate information within various MBx activities in model-based enterprise [7]. Ruemler et al. [7] means by MBx model-based manufacturing (MBm), model-based sustainment (MBs) and any other model-based activities (MBx) are categories of activity within the model-based enterprise. Adamski [8] defines Model-based Definition (MBD) as a process that allows the design team to input all their information into the 3D model, thus eliminating the need to create a drawing.

Product and Manufacturing Information. According to Herron [9] Product and Manufacturing Information (PMI) conveys non-geometric attributes in 3D Computer Aided Design/Manufacturing/Inspection/Engineering (CAx) systems necessary for manufacturing product components. PMI may include Geometric Dimensions & Tolerances (GD&T), 3D annotation (text) and dimensions, surface finish, and material specifications. CAx application literature may also refer to PMI synonymously with Geometric Dimensions and Tolerances (GD&T) or Functional Tolerancing and Annotation (FT&A).

Model-Based Enterprise. Model-based Enterprise (MBE) is a fully integrated and collaborative environment founded on 3D Model-based product definition constructed and shared across the enterprise to enable the deployment of products from a concept through delivery [10]. MBE is an environment, e.g. an organization that has transformed itself to leverage model-based information in its various activities and decision-making processes [11].

2.3 The Benefits of MBD

Model-Based Definition speeds the product ramp-up and lowers quality defects [1]. Apparently, there are separate mechanisms for this, as some of effects caused by MBD associate to information management and processes in general, while other effects are distinct benefits that appear in the separate activities of process. The essential purpose of MBD is to accelerate and to improve communication between the parties of product development. According to the author's experience, every product development and engineering project has difficulties due to deficiencies of communication. The single-source principle is the key general benefit of the MBD [9], because the same 3D model can be utilized in the several process phases of an enterprise. Another general aspect of utilizing the MBD is that, 2D drawings can be avoided, which means it is not anymore needed to control whether there are correct paper-revisions in a production or not. This presumes the shared source of information and persistent processes of MBE.

Automatic toolpath generation is a distinct, but repeatedly gained benefit enabled by MBD. The use of MBD datasets can be useful also in quality control as the geometry and associated attributes, such as dimensions, geometric tolerances, datums and surface qualities, are part of a MBD. Unlike Quintana et al. [1] noticed, path planning for Coordinate Measuring Machine (CMM) based on part geometry, can incorporate the use of tolerance data. We noticed this during the measuring test that we describe later in this article. Zhu [12] introduced that MBD enables the intelligent manufacturing of parts. This is possible through a feature machining and Coordinate Measuring Machine (CMM) control technologies.

2.4 Barriers of MBD

According to Ruemler et al. [7], large capital investment, lack of business pulls, and legacy designs are the biggest barriers of utilizing MBD and MBE. The study revealed that the lack of workforce skilled in MBD or the lack of training opportunities were less regarded issues. All these are general barriers against the use of MBD. Quintana et al. [1] categorized the barriers towards utilizing the MBD into three main categories: technical issues, process issues and legal issues [1].

Technical Issues. Problems may occur when there is different software in delivering than in receiving systems. Consequently, a receiving system cannot open the files. Difficulties may come also when the maturity level of MBE is different in delivering and receiving organizations. For example, a customer sends separate 3D STEP files to the sheet metal manufacturing subcontractor that can utilize only 2D DXF files. In that case, the customer may need to make traditional, redundant 2D drawings, including all necessary dimensions, tolerances and annotations. The 2D drawings will be saved as PDF and/or DXF/DWG files and the subcontractor often prints them on paper. Technical issues are distinct barriers preventing the efficient use of MBD, even though they may appear repeatedly.

Process Issues. *Data accessibility and visualization* can be a distinct, key issue preventing the use of MBD, because most downstream users (including suppliers and customers) do not have access to CAD software. Therefore, visualization tools that enable the users to access and present the MBD datasets are vital. *Data content* is another process issue, because downstream users need to be confident that the MBD datasets will carry the core of a drawing and the required management elements.

The single sourcing and use of data are important for manufacturing operations and production planning, e.g. computer aided manufacturing. Users need that an MBD dataset is in machine-readable form, a representation of product definition. This approach can ensure the seamless single source of product definition and minimize unnecessary, distinct errors due to human intervention e.g. in off-line programming of toolpaths.

Version management means that an appropriate method must be available in order to manage and record revisions of MBD datasets. *Data security* is another issue, because a mechanism that incorporates security features (confidentiality, authentication, integrity and non-repudiation) when accessing, exchanging and interacting with MBD datasets will be required. Both of the issues appear to be general barriers against MBD.

Data retention is another general issue against the use of MBD, because usually only 2D data is stored and used for legal or business purposes. The distinct examples of this are:

- A request for quote
- Validation and release
- Manufacturing
- Inspection
- Certification
- Engineering change management (ECM)
- Long-term storage

Traditionally, drawings are considered as the controlling contract document with customers and suppliers. Drawings, electronic, printed or microfilmed, are the usual medium to safely and securely preserved the product definition, which allows for product maintenance and data reuse.

Legal Issues. Governments control very strictly some products and industries such as medical, military, construction, aircraft and vehicle industries. All products and processes of them, need to be done very properly. Herron [9] has found five main barriers to overcome on the road to adopting MBE:

1. Decision makers need more information about Model-Based Engineering
2. Holes appear in the technology tapestry of Model-Based Enterprise.
3. Standards do not address large-scale assembly integration into MBE.
4. Agreement on authoritative sources needs to be determined.
5. Change is hard, that causes often change resistance.

All the legal issues cause a general barrier against the adoption of MBD, even though they may appear distinct issues alone.

Summary of Barriers. For a company, transition to MBD is an investment and each investment must pay off in a form or another. Change from traditional product definition to MBD is a project, which must result with a higher benefit than the investment. Thus, the business case for a MBD project is necessary.

A company has usually invested in the legacy processes and archives of designs in files and models. The legacy product data is an illiquid asset and a company usually cannot convert it easily into another format. Getting rid of or the re-design of a large set of designs into a new format may not be appealing. The amount of legacy data can be large in a company that has to manage it along with new data. Some companies have stored legacy data to different databases or systems than the new data. It may not a viable option to combine old drawings and 3D models to a new system. Eventually, the size of the new database can be much larger than the legacy data.

When adopting MBD an organisation is not only changing technology but also making changes in engineering design and manufacturing engineering processes. If the technology and the processes do not comply with each other, it may be difficult to motivate the change. However, the technology has to provide seamless digital thread for computer-integrated processes. The business and legal processes contain distinct issues that as a whole cause a barrier against the utilization of MBD.

2.5 Product Definition in an Ecosystem

A single enterprise is hardly responsible of both design and manufacturing of all the parts and product definition is a matter of inter-organizational communication. Organizations must exchange product definition, either in a form of MBD or traditional document-oriented definition, between engineering and manufacturing organizations.

Digital Extended Enterprise. A whole supply network may form a digital extended enterprise, if the given conditions on e.g. business development, processes, metrics, and information sharing are met [13]. The interconnected infrastructure, environment, and methodology (process, methods, and tools) used to store, access, analyze, and visualize evolving systems' data and models to address the needs of the stakeholders [14]. Developing a digital extended enterprise requires development activities in many fields and product definition is one of them. However, the development should occur with a balanced manner, because the key development areas are interrelated [15]. The utilization of a digital extended enterprise can lead to remarkable improvements for example in the reliability of suppliers' deliveries and quality. The concept of single sourcing is essential in the digital extended enterprise, because in it the up-to-date digital definition is shared, version management enhanced and access to consistent product definition ensured throughout the extended enterprise [13].

Ecosystems. An ecosystem is always a unique concept, which has a unique set of actors and interactions [16]. The ecosystem has borders and each actor has a certain role, which may differ from roles in other ecosystems. The borders can be set by geographical scope, by temporal scale, by permeability, as well by types of flows (material, knowledge, value) [16]. As well as the ecosystem, have actor's common target and purpose to act to serve the whole ecosystems benefit. Typically, the manufacturing ecosystem, which is one type of business ecosystems, consists of a keystone, a niche, a commodity and a physical dominator (PD) [17]. The keystone is the company, which dominates the value of the ecosystem. It also protects the ecosystem against other ecosystems, and it provides rules and standards for other actors in the ecosystem. Niche is the actor that has special skills and technology. Physical dominator occupies a wide range of technology and services in the ecosystem. However, the physical dominator results a low level of innovation. The commodity competes with price and volumes by producing components with a large series.

Collaborative networks as well as an outsourcing, according to the standard ISO 44001 [18] belong also to business relationships. They have similarities with business ecosystems like common target with each actor but also differences. The collaborative network and the outsourcing may function between two companies only. The other company sells products and/or services to the other and each company develop its business individually. Each actor in a business ecosystem needs to develop business on the ecosystems' point of view.

3 A Case of a Product Definition in the Manufacturing Ecosystem

Several manufacturing companies and three research institutes are carrying out a joint development and research project under the title "Intelligent Manufacturing Ecosystem" (IME) during 2019–2020. The companies presented in this chapter are part of the project consortium, but not the whole consortium. The project IME has three themes focusing on intelligent materials, engineering and manufacturing, and ecosystem.

Table 1. Characteristics of case companies (values from 2018)

Position	Turnover (M€)	Result/ (M€)	Specialization	Personnel	Actor/role
Customer	1 000	155.6	Dedicated mobile machinery	2009	Keystone
Supplier A	15.7	1.8	Bearing sleeves, material expert	85	Niche
Supplier B	12.5	0	ETO Gears	62	Niche
Supplier C	9.4	0	Subcontractor machine shop	50	PD
Supplier D	7.6	0.3	Subcontractor machine shop	40	PD
Inspector			Measuring		Niche

This case study is part of work package the integration of engineering design and manufacturing and it focuses on five industrial companies of the IME (see Table 1). One of them was the customer company for the other four companies, i.e. suppliers. The customer has outsourced part manufacturing and the suppliers deliver components and subassemblies that the customer designs and assembles in its products. In the case, the customer acts as a keystone, the suppliers A and B can be described as a niche and the suppliers C and D are typical physical dominators. Albeit, the nature of the ecosystem in this research is kind of niche itself and the size of product series is relatively small, the Suppliers C and D represent a commodity in this ecosystem and context.

In addition, the sixth organization acted as a niche actor for the manufacturing ecosystem by replicating the measurement operations in the laboratory of the university (Inspector). The laboratory has the digitalized, integrated measurement facilities, such as similar CAx environment than the Customer and coordinate measurement machine (CMM). During the case, the Inspector made measurement tests to find out how feasible the PMI-model is when measuring a part without engineering drawings.

3.1 The Ecosystem Members

The Customer – A keystone. The customer company of the ecosystem is manufacturing mobile machinery for a dedicated, niche purpose. The international corporation, the customer is part of, is investing 18 M€ on developing an R&D center in Finland. The company has recognized that it must update the technology of the key module of the product offering and at the same time modernize the factory that produces the module. While the factory is undergoing a large modernization and automation project, also the processes and management of product definition, production, supply chain collaboration and information exchange must be re-considered. The objective is to enhance information and material flow, radically increase agility and to reduce throughput time in both product development and in production processes. Simultaneously, the company must maintain or improve the high level of quality. The role of networks and manufacturing ecosystems is critical in the achieving of the objective, while the company is solving many issues on production, engineering and collaboration. For all this, the company has launched a manufacturing ecosystem project with selected supplier companies, IT-vendors, consultants and researchers from different institutions.

In the project, the customer company is aiming at Model-Based Definition internally and in the ecosystem where it is collaborating with its key suppliers. However, the company must recognize how far the suppliers are able to go with MBD. In the beginning of the ecosystem project, the company recognized that drawings were still a master of product definition for it even though drawings always accompany a part model in the native format of the CAD system (NX by Siemens). The intent of the company is to change this so that a model will be a master file, sometimes accompanied by a drawing. Along with this, the company will take into use MBD and derive drawings when needed. In the beginning most of the suppliers relied solely on part drawings, while some received the geometry in STEP- or JT-files. The aim is to study the potential of sharing MBD files with the selected suppliers.

Supplier A - Niche. The supplier A has also a long history of manufacturing machined products as parts for the machinery. Typically, the parts are sleeve bearings for large installations in demanding conditions. On top of only machining parts, the company also casts the blanks of bronze for products. The material is mostly re-cycled from outside and within the company. Typically, the parts are axially symmetric, and the geometries are quite simple, and invariant. The number of customers is large and stable, when the company's ability to deliver bearings and gaskets with special alloys at a short notice is an asset. In addition, material management is a competitive asset for the company.

The product documentation is typically in the format of part drawings, stored either in paper archives or in PDF files. The company did not indicate a need to change the way of managing product definition, because the geometries of products are rather simple and persistent. In addition, changes in the way of work for just one customer do not pay off in the case of many customers. Instead, automation and managing the flow of material and the management of materials in general may be more appealing investments for the company.

Supplier B – Niche. The company manufactures components for gear installations with high performance requirements. An asset for the company is the ability manufacture specialized gears with high precision and to sustain the high quality of products. Therefore, the geometries of the parts do not follow standardized modules of part geometries. Therefore, the company has specialized grinding tools for the special gear geometries. When considering the routing of the parts and products, the management recognized that the company would benefit from the MBD only in the very first stages of production or in the final inspection of parts, which sums up only about 20% of the whole production. Thus, investing in MBD is not an intention of the company and the focus is on enhancing the production management and flow of production. None of the suppliers had already a dedicated manufacturing execution system, but supplier B was implementing a system for manufacturing operations planning, simulation and management.

Supplier C – Physical Dominator. The case company has a history of 50 years of part manufacturing with more than 30 machining systems such as NC controlled lathes and machining centers, robots for tool and part exchange as well as a dumbwaiter and a CMM. The clientele is quite large, comprising of both many national and some international customers, who deliver part documents in PDF-files and sometimes the geometry of parts in native CAD or STEP format. The products are prismatic and axially symmetrical machined parts and a team of few experts does the toolpath programming of parts. The variations of parts and part geometries exhibit in complex part documentation. The flexibility and the expertise of the CAM team are assets for the company. Typically, a new, complex part geometry takes one day of offline programming.

The company has automated part and tool exchange to certain extent, but due to the small series of products, full automation is not feasible. A typical set size, the company reported in an interview is approximately 40 pieces. A separate unit does the inspection of machining and the set of tools such as CMM system deliver measurement reports in PDF format. The labelling of products and document management is manual.

An asset for the company is the expertise in heavy machining and the continuous modernization of equipment. The company is aiming at streamlining the computer aided manufacturing of parts. For this purpose, the company has been introducing the same NX CAM as some of the main customers of the company have already. Therefore, the company expects that the use of MBD is going to replace part drawings, in some cases. The company may also invest in managing the data from quality assurance, i.e. the CMM data, so that the customers investing in MBD would be served better than drawing oriented customers.

Supplier D – Physical Dominator. The manufacturing company focuses on subcontracting machined parts for a limited set of customers. The company delivers more than 75% of production value to two main customer companies. Typically, the toolpath generation relies on part geometry in STEP-file, and the drawings indicating the tolerances and surface qualities of the parts. The company makes part inspection with CMM's, but statistical process control is not possible due to a small series (less than 40) of production.

One of the assets of the company is the marking of the parts so that the traceability of the parts is possible. In general, the company is rather development oriented, and it is investing in MBD as well as in automation.

Inspector-Niche. Tampere University of Applied Sciences (Tampere UAS) had a pilot project in Intelligent Manufacturing Ecosystem, with supplier and its customer. The target was to find out the benefits of using PMI data with coordinate measuring machine comparing measuring by traditional way (Fig. 2).

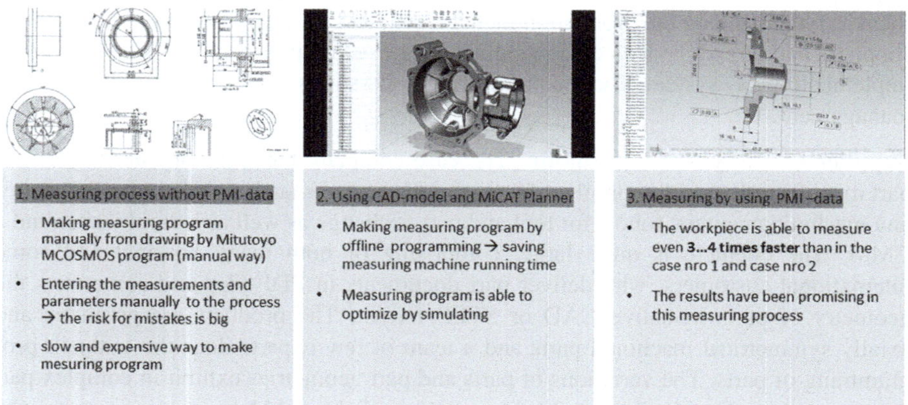

Fig. 2. Three ways to measure the workpiece by using coordinate measuring machine (CMM).

The laboratory set up resembled the actual situation within Supplier D, but the Inspector utilized the MBD instead of traditional part definition in the measurement operations. Thus, the Inspector's laboratory tests provided a comparable empiric evidence on the utilization of different forms of product definition.

The empiric research brought forth several direct benefits:

- Measuring by using PMI-data is 3…4 times faster than in traditional way
- The more features there are to measure, the more evident the difference between the traditional way and using PMI-data becomes
- Applying PMI, improves the lead time of production
- The benefit is bigger, if production batch is small

- Measuring process with PMI-data is simpler, so it is easier to teach more people in the production to use measuring machine

One may regard the benefits above as distinct benefits that Supplier D can gain within the quality control operations of the company Likewise, the supplier C might have similar benefits in quality control, although the replication did not include data from it.

4 Results and Discussions

In this article, we have studied several barriers and issues in introducing model-based product definition with a literature research as well as by studying the case of manufacturing ecosystem. On top of the qualitative assessment of literature and material from interviews, researchers conducted an empiric study replicating the measurement operations of a company. Some of the results of the empiric study are quantitative.

It is noteworthy that companies can solve many of the technical challenges and MBD is a feasible option to represent product information within a manufacturing ecosystem. Moreover, MBD is a specific topic for a manufacturing ecosystem, because its' members add value to the ecosystem with different means. For example, single sourcing is a mutual, general interest that can benefit the whole ecosystem, but often with an indirect manner.

A decisive challenge for the adoption of MBD in an ecosystem is the community nature of MBD as it is a means of communication and, thus, requires that both sides of the communication, which are the maker and the users of documentation, agree upon the means. Within the challenge, a general issue that both Ruemler et al. [6] as well as we acknowledged is the reasoning of business investment in MBD. In an ecosystem, the mutual, comprehensive model of ecosystem business case is needed in order to balance the investment and value added. There, the concept of dispositions by Andreasen & Olesen [19] may a viable option to represent the relations between the members of manufacturing ecosystems.

The second issue to acknowledge is the co-existence and the need of several ecosystems. Along with business ecosystem there is a need for knowledge ecosystem that will enhance the knowledge on MBD. For example, to a manufacturing service provider or a supplier the potential of MBD and the ways of presenting e.g. geometric tolerances with MBD require often the introduction of new knowledge. Investing in education on utilizing Model-Based Definition [20] can lower the barrier to adopt new methods. Also, the versions of software brands support certain standards of MBD representation while other versions do not.

The software and the related standards form an innovation ecosystem that runs according to its own rules. Being aware and solving the issues of interoperability requires knowledge on the rules. In practise, companies can avoid the incompatibility issues between systems and software by using similar systems or file transferring formats. Nowadays several 3D CAD software include smart tools for file transferring and Model-Based Definition. Standards, such as ISO 16792 and ASME Y14.41, have been supporting digital product definition for a long time.

Revision management, data retention, data accessibility and visualization all can be managed by modern systems, but they require the adoption of mutually operated processes. In a business ecosystem the setting of the rules for digitally enhanced processes is another topic worth noticing. When considering manufacturing ecosystems as well as supply chain networks, to be able to act in digital process, it is fundamentally important for all actors in ecosystems and networks to have similar abilities of digital processes. In addition, all actors must have high motivation to change way to work. For a single company, adopting MBD is a long-term investment and therefore requires strategic collaboration between the members of a manufacturing ecosystem. Like we have noticed in the case, Suppliers C & D have challenges in business profit as niche actors. However, they are motivated to develop processes, such as MBD, and consequently they are investing in the new way to work. However, the dominant actors, such as Suppliers A and D, find the mentioned barriers, such as lack of recognized benefit and legacy data, as inhibitors for adopting MBD. The empirical study proved there are leapfrog benefits using PMI-data in measurement process. To be able to prove benefits can be found in whole operations processes product lifecycle, more research need to be done.

Acknowledgements. The research organizations have received financial support from Business Finland for the project IME and the authors of the paper acknowledge the support. Authors are grateful for the collaboration with the companies.

References

1. Quintana, V., Rivest, L., Pellerin, R., Venne, F., Kheddouci, F.: Will model-based definition replace engineering drawings throughout the product lifecycle? A global perspective from aerospace industry. Comput. Ind. **61**, 497–508 (2010)
2. Action-Engineering, 3D Model Based Definition (2019a). https://www.action-engineering.com/dictionary/#3d_model%20based%20definition. Accessed 25 Nov 2019)
3. Fox, S.: Getting real about BIM: critical realist descriptions as an alternative to the naïve framing and multiple fallacies of hype. Int. J. Manag. Projects Bus. **7**(3), 405–422 (2014). https://doi.org/10.1108/IJMPB-12-2013-0073
4. Camba, J., Contero, M., Johnson, M., Company, P.: Extended 3D annotations as a new mechanism to explicitly communicate geometric design intent and increase CAD model reusability. Comput. Aided Des. **57**, 61–73 (2014)
5. Alemanni, M., Destefanis, F., Vezzetti, E.: Model-based definition design in the product lifecycle management scenario. Int. J. Adv. Manuf. Technol. **52**(1–4), 1–14 (2011). https://doi.org/10.1007/s00170-010-2699-y
6. Schuh, G., Rudolf, S., Riesener, M.: Design for Industrie 4.0. In: International Design Conference-Design 2016, Dubrovnik (2016)
7. Ruemler, S.P., Zimmerman, K.E., Hartman, N.W., et al.: Promoting model-based definition to establish a complete product definition. J. Manuf. Sci. Eng. Trans. ASME **139**(5) (2017). https://doi.org/10.1115/1.4034625. American Society of Mechanical Engineers (ASME)
8. Adamski, W.: Adjustment and implementation of CAD/CAM systems being used in Polish aviation industry. J. Mach. Eng. **10**(3), 37–47 (2010)
9. Herron, J.: Re-Use Your CAD. The Model-Based Handbook. CreateSpace Independent Publishing Platform, Scotts Valley (2013)

10. Action-Engineering, 3D Model Based Enterprise (2019b). https://www.action-engineering.com/dictionary/#3d_model%20based%20enterprise. Accessed 25 Nov 2019
11. Hartman, N.W.: Establishing a lexicon for the Model-Based Enterprise. West Lafayette (2017)
12. Zhu, W., Bricogne, M., Durupt, A., et al.: Implementations of model based definition and product lifecycle management technologies: a case study in Chinese aeronautical industry. IFAC-PapersOnLine **49**(12), 485–490 (2016). https://doi.org/10.1016/j.ifacol.2016.07.664
13. Pulkkinen, A., Anttila, J-P., Leino, S-P.: Assessing the maturity and benefits of digital extended enterprise. Procedia Manuf. **38**, 1417–1426 (2019). https://doi.org/10.1016/j.promfg.2020.01.146
14. Action-Engineering, Digital Engineering Ecosystem (2019c). https://www.action-engineering.com/dictionary/#digital_engineering%20ecosystem. Accessed 25 Nov 2019
15. Pulkkinen, A., Vainio, V., Leino, S.-P., Anttila, J.-P.: Modelling of digital extended enterprise. In: 20th International Dependency and Structure Modeling Conference, DSM 2018-Trieste, Italy (2018)
16. Valkokari, K.: Business, innovation, and knowledge ecosystems how they differ and how to survive and thrive within them. Technol. Innov. Manage. Rev. **5**(8), 17–24 (2015)
17. Paulus-Rohmer, D., Schatton, H., Bauernhansl, T.: Ecosystems, strategy and business models in the age of digitization - how the manufacturing industry is going to change its logic. In: Westkamper, E., Bauernhansl, T. (eds.) 49th CIRP Conference on Manufacturing Systems (CIRP-CMS 2016), vol. 57, pp. 8–13. Elsevier B.V. (2016)
18. ISO 44001:2017 Collaborative business relationship management systems—Requirements and framework, Mar 2017. https://www.iso.org/standard/72798.html. Accessed 29 Feb 2020
19. Andreasen, M.M., Olesen, J.: The concept of dispositions. J. Eng. Des. 1(1), 17–36 https://doi.org/10.1080/09544829008901640. (31 January 2007 Taylor & Francis Online)
20. Garland, N., Wade, R., Glithro, R., et al.: Model based definition: finally, the engineering drawing killer? In: International conference on engineering and product design education, Strathclyde. University of Strathclyde (2019)

A New Agile Hybridization Approach and a Set of Related Guidelines for Mechatronic Product Development

Sagar Mule[1(✉)], Regis Plateaux[2], Peter Hehenberger[1], Olivia Penas[2], Stanislao Patalano[3], and Ferdinando Vitolo[3]

[1] University of Applied Sciences Upper Austria, Wels, Austria
sagarmule20@gmail.com, peter.hehenberger@fh-wels.at
[2] Supméca, Laboratoire QUARTZ, EA7393 Paris, France
{regis.plateaux,olivia.penas}@supmeca.fr
[3] Fraunhofer J-Lab IDEAS, University of Naples Federico II, Naples, Italy
{patalano,ferdinando.vitolo}@unina.it

Abstract. In industry 4.0, the growing incorporation of cyber-physical systems (CPS) into manufacturing facilities composed of mechatronic products brings forth the need of reducing development cost while maintaining the quality and in parallel the need to adapt changes along the lifecycle of the product development. Most of the traditional development methods fail to solve such new challenges. However, some agile methods, widely used in the software industry, could meet these requirements. It is then essential to identify the criticalities of agile methods regarding mechatronic system development specificities.

As a result, our research work focuses on combining traditional and agile approaches to improve mechatronic products development in a changing market context. The development of hybrid approach is based on the analysis of traditional, agile methods and consideration of challenges in the development of mechatronic products. To illustrate the advantages of such hybridization, we propose a first hybrid approach consisting of some elements of the Scrum method (the most popular agile approach) into the V-Model. Differentiating advantages of this new approach, compared to other agile methods, include the freedom to propagate necessary changes in product architecture during the development of its different modules.

This new approach focuses on the hybridization of traditional and agile methods and the required guidelines to adopt and use for enhanced mechatronic products development. These guidelines are the base for changing the organizational culture and values which were previously associated with traditional development approaches.

Keywords: Mechatronic products development · Hybrid approach · Agile approach · Scrum · V-Model

Published by Springer Nature Switzerland AG 2020
F. Nyffenegger et al. (Eds.): PLM 2020, IFIP AICT 594, pp. 618–633, 2020.
https://doi.org/10.1007/978-3-030-62807-9_49

1 Introduction

The new era of industry 4.0 requires us to use various information technologies in order to fulfil the goal towards automation and smart factories. In order to reach that goal, industries demand a new approach for more efficient product development, especially for the mechatronic products as they can be backbones of IoT and CPS. A common goal of industry 4.0 steers everyone towards the most effective interaction of the machine, internet and human for creating a better environment for production. Which also make us stumbled upon to the problems like the uncertainty of the market, complexity, continuous change in the requirements. The traditional approach, which provides rigidity to the product development based on sequential processes, usually in a top-down framework and with a fixed team structure [1], has been inefficient, thus the need for more flexible product development methods leads industries towards agile approaches. The research issue is then how to take a result, the aim of this research is to provide hybrid approaches to develop mechatronic systems by combining agile and traditional product development methods. Extensive literature research and semi-structured interview method allows extracting the information on agile methods, its use in the development of mechatronics product development and its crucial aspects for adoption as well as the use of a hybrid approach. This research helps to break down the steps during mechatronic product development and to assign the agile approach to relevant phases. Finally, in order to provide flexibility in product architecture and modules design, the hybridization of the V-Model with Scrum is presented.

1.1 Industry 4.0

Industry 4.0 arises from the increased complexity in the product, the market customization, the drive towards digitization, the ubiquitous internet and the global competition to produce a better product in less time while reducing the human interaction with the production facility. This term was coined in Germany in 2011 to revolutionize the production system with the help of the internet, rapid prototyping techniques, artificial intelligence and cloud computing [2]. Other reasons to focus on industry 4.0 was to improve the communication between machines and humans. The fascination for this aspect is to reduce human errors, maximizing the efficiency of the machines with human skills in problem-solving and strategic decision making [3].

Two crucial elements of industry 4.0 are the Internet of Things (IoT) and cyber-physical system (CPS).

Internet of Things (IoT). Development of various technologies such as sensors, internet, Radio Frequency Identification (RFID) technique, computers can be utilized for realizing dynamic interactions between machine to machine and human to machine [4]. Transparent sharing of information while providing security and using one common language are the important issues of IoT which need to be addressed [5].

Cyber-Physical Systems (CPS). Using mechatronic systems to automate the production facilities using a network will help reduce human error [6] and support the concept of a dark factory with full automation [7]. Modelling of this complex system requires a communication across various disciplines and a more flexible development method in order to reduce uncertainty and cost of detailed modelling [8].

1.2 Traditional Product Development Methods

Traditional product development methods provide sequential, plan-driven and organized approach and are well suited for the product development when requirements are fixed. Traditional product development methods affect project management activities too such as strict scheduling, fixed budget allocation, documentation and tracking [9]. Here are two of the most common traditional product development methods.

Stage-Gate Method and Waterfall. The Stage-gate method, also known as a Waterfall method (referred to in the IT sector) has a linear structure with definite stages. Each stage requires inputs from the previous stage. Over the past two decades, the Waterfall method has been criticized for being too rigid. While for software product development, the incremental output is essential to know the unforeseeable problems which arise in the middle of the development process, the waterfall model fails to provide this incremental output [1, 10, 11].

V-Model. V-Model was encouraged to be used in mechatronic product development. The difference between the V-Model used for software product development and V-Model for mechatronic is the disintegration of function for development purpose and again integrating it in the testing phase [12]. This difference is due to the multiple domains in the mechatronic system. Though it is known for its plan-driven approach, it contains iterations for refining the results [12]. An example of the V-Model is shown in Fig. 1.

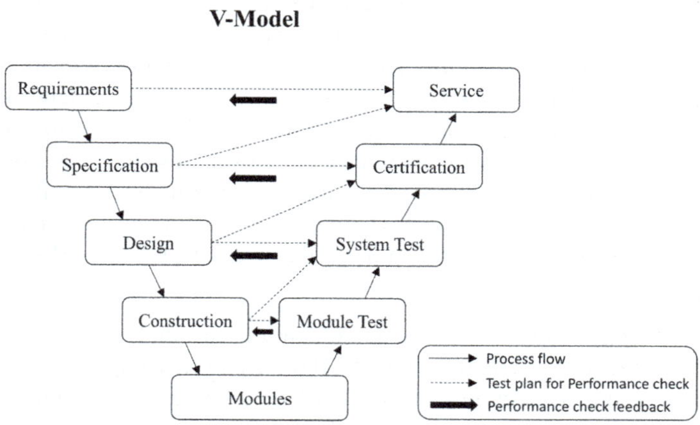

Fig. 1. V-Model [6, 13]

Unlike an agile approach where product requirements are not entirely fixed, in a traditional approach, detailed requirements are given by customers in advance before planning the project. This approach is linear and process-oriented with exceptional long iterations. Organizational structure is also hierarchical; centralized authority steers the project by keeping control to most of the activities. Communications are mostly formal, which needs to go through proper channel and keeping authorities in the loop. Formal statements are crucial while transferring the knowledge which makes knowledge transfer process too bureaucratic. Also, reporting of work progress to the only manager and not the whole team creates misunderstanding within the team about work. Another difference is that the traditional approach is a document-based [14, 15].

1.3 Limits of Traditional Product Development Methods

Though traditional product development methods have served the industries well in the last few decades, they failed to fulfil an essential requirement to avoid uncertainty and to provide flexibility during product development [1]. Few disadvantages of the traditional approach are, not suitable for breakthrough innovation, governance of the project cannot be changed over a long period, change in requirements cannot be adapted, tangible product can only be seen at the end, the consideration for uncertainty is null or very low, no measure of performance is available in the middle of the process, cost and time for each stage is not definable, the feedback from testing can be generated only at the end [1, 13, 16–19].

2 State-of-the-Art

In order to provide a hybrid framework comprised of different methods it is essential to study specific methods and their important aspects. This chapter describes the agile methods. It also explains the criticalities in mechatronic product development which will be used for deriving requirements for creating a hybrid approach for multidisciplinary product development.

2.1 Agile Methods

Based on the values of agility such as individuals and interactions over processes and tools, working software over comprehensive documentation, customer collaboration over contract negotiation and responding to change over following a plan, [20] software industries have been successfully developing products in a flexible manner. Customer integration within the product development process and iterative development cycles are the backbones of the agile methods. Some of the agile methods are as follows:

Scrum. Scrum is the most popular method in product development [21], as it provides an easy adaptable framework in any industry and its features are not just limited to software development [22]. Application of Scrum for hardware product development starts with changing the mindset included in traditional approaches, and instead of keeping complete internal control over the process and outcome, customer has to be involved in each iteration to provide feedback and eventually propose some requirements changes. Instead of a hierarchical structure of a team, self-organizing team and transparent organization need to be provided [22]. While implementing Scrum for hardware product development, few constraints need to be considered and worked on such as definition of the "done" (deliverable), multidisciplinary team structure and integration of different developed modules from different disciplines in case of Scrum of Scrum.

Kanban. Kanban is an agile product development method with no iterations but only increments in the product. This term has migrated from the logistic application, where it was used to show the availability of material and keeping the inventory at an optimum level. Kanban method works on a continuous run of completing the task in a to-do list. Kanban has no specific framework, which makes it ideal to use it in any phase of an innovation process [23].

The backbone of this method is its tool, Kanban board. This tool helps the team visualize the progress at each phase. It uses cards with tasks written on it, in a column which describes the status of that task.

Other agile methods are Feature Driven Development (FDD), Design Thinking, Extreme Programming and Hackathon [23]. Most of the agile methods are not suitable for hardware or mechatronic product development as well as for the mass production [24]. Along with this, a change from traditional to agile is difficult as the employees have the mindset developed from traditional approach. For Scrum, framework is easy to understand but hard to follow due to lack of self-discipline [22].

2.2 Hybrid Approach

Many academics in this field have researched about hybrid approach along with the creation of a framework. One research paper has described the Scrum method with Model-Based System Engineering (MBSE) to make MBSE more reliable and flexible. It is a Scrum method with the addition of three main aspects: black-box analysis, white box analysis and physical prototype increment. In this framework, black-box analysis is used for an analysis to build the requirements by exploring all the views in agreement with the customer. This analysis is included to reduce the further changes in the product backlog, which is an essential point as changes occurred later in hardware or mechatronics product development are costly. White box analysis recognizes the architecture of the system with the prioritized set of functions which are defined in the black-box analysis. In this analysis, components are allocated for connecting the architecture with those functions. In the end, those incorporated components are validated as per the requirement set in black box analysis [25].

Another research in hybrid approach is a vertical agile approach which focuses on the development of mechanics with traditional method and informatics and electronics with agile method simultaneously. Integration of the outcome of each cycle from the agile approach into the traditional one is challenging and requires efforts in communicating [12].

2.3 Criticalities in Mechatronic System Development

Combining constraints, knowledge and more importantly, teams from more than three different domains is difficult. Technological advancement in each segment is at a different pace from other segments. There are many challenges in the field of mechatronic which are categorized into two areas, product development and organizational. Few authors have described the challenges in mechatronic which are listed as follows [6, 26–29].

Product and Development Process Related: Long development duration, product complexity, large number of modules, technological innovation at a different rate in a different segment, fast pace of innovations in software and electronics, life of each element is different, upgrades frequently needed, product customization, changes in requirements, ineffective product development process, challenges of adopting agile, verification of physical prototype is expensive, computational analysis in the design phase is expensive, dependency on a supplier for design affects virtual testing, one design tool to integrate the design of each element, meeting design requirements in the final product, unpredictable behaviour of a virtual prototype.

Organizational Related: communication within a multidisciplinary team, synergy of cross-functional teams, information flow from different departments, difficult to find experts in the field, failing to comprehend the effect of design change over all disciplines, lack of knowledge about all elements of mechatronic, low market penetration, teams structure becomes complex, ownership of individual segment, complex internal and external stakeholder dependency.

3 Proposal for an Agile Hybridization Approach

From the past few decades, the traditional approach was dominant in the mechatronic industry, but it fulfills very few of the current challenges faced in product development. Using traditional product development exclusively have advantages and disadvantages. Agility in mechatronics is beneficial to support continuous integration within the teams from different domains and reduce the lead time to introduce new product or updated versions of it [30]. But, the change could be overwhelming to transform the organizational culture from traditional to fully agile. As a result, this proposal is focused on a hybrid approach including a more agile mindset. All the criticalities have been studied and taken into consideration while preparing this hybrid agile framework. Hybrid approach can provide flexibility in designing the product along with the rigidity in the phases of product development where changes could be costly and disrupt the timeline of project.

3.1 Requirements Derived from Criticalities

Criticalities mentioned in Sect. 2.2 have been translated into requirements for building an effective product development method by following MBSE methodology. This methodology includes a black-box analysis with various views (from an external point of view) that generate all the derived requirements that the system has to fulfil. It is more described later, as it has also been used in the hybrid approach. Those requirements are as follows:

Product and Development Process Related:

- Faster product development
- The method should be able to handle complex modelling
- To provide a well-defined and iterative way to develop product architecture
- Focused on the development of each module with iteration
- Possibility to adapt changes in product architecture and module at any point in the product development
- Suited for product customization
- Should minimize the cost of development and of the related physical prototyping
- Should follow values of agility
- Use of virtual prototyping
- Evaluation of product, based on the product requirements

Organization Related:

- Efficient communication within the development team
- Well-formed cross-functional team
- Improvement in knowledge sharing capabilities between cross-functional departments
- Size of the involved team should be between 5 and 9 in one team
- Well established decision-making system to convey changes in the product requirement
- Need of involving supplier
- Regularly involving customers in the review process
- Involvement of a market research team in product development
- Simple team structure
- Single owner of the product to solve documentation in the product development management
- Effective change management

An efficient product development method for mechatronic products requires certain qualities mentioned above. Most important requirements are based on the use of iterations which can provide a better quality product. In order to create a cheaper complex product, a product development approach should consist of a state-of-the-art virtual testing technologies and involvement of different stakeholders in it. The proposed method also demands a well-defined team structure that efficiently supports communication between internal as well as external stakeholders.

3.2 An Illustration of a Hybrid Approach: V-Model with Scrum

To illustrate the benefits of such agile hybridization, we present here an example of a way to hybridize tradition and agile approach for mechatronic products development.

Due to the merits of Scrum to prioritize the backlog, iterate the development, with a full development workflow during each sprint and high compatibility with the development of product architecture and modules of product, it has been selected for this first hybrid approach. This hybrid framework consists of Scrum in the first half of the V-Model. The basic idea behind the framework is shown in Fig. 2.

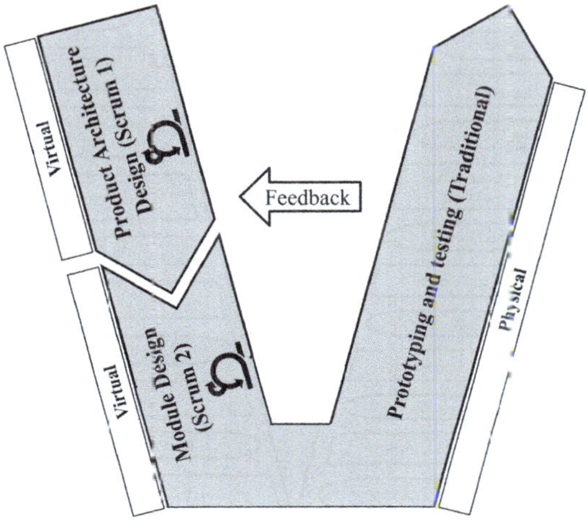

Fig. 2. Basic idea of a hybrid framework- V model with Scrum

This V-Model is divided into three phases, product architecture design, module design and prototyping along with testing. Among which, product development in the first two phases will be done in iteration using the Scrum method. The output of these first two phases will be carried as an input for the next phase once the review has been done by the team, as well as customer. Physical prototyping and testing will be done with a traditional approach as virtual product development have undergone many iterations which would resolve most of the issues with module design. This way, the cost associated with the physical prototyping can be reduced, and it also reduces the possibility of any uncertainty which might arise in the physical prototype building.

The detailed framework of V-Model with Scrum is shown in Fig. 3. As shown in the figure, the requirement gathering and analysis stage is carried out with a black-box analysis. An analysis to build the requirements by exploring all the views in agreement with the customer is a black-box analysis [31]. This analysis aims at increasing the comprehensiveness of the product backlog and limit late costly changes. It is performed through the identification of its life cycle, system context and system-environment interaction. This analysis includes the definition of external interfaces, which are introduced as requirements and finally can define the product backlog [25]. In the traditional approach, more in-depth analysis is carried out by dealing exhaustively with all the requirements in order to avoid further changes. In the agile approach, the customer can change the requirements to be quickly taken into account.

The stage of building a product architecture goes through white-box analysis with the Scrum method. It defines the architecture of the system, starting by its functions and then logical and physical modules. At the end, product architecture is validated regarding the requirements whole set defined during the black box analysis [25].

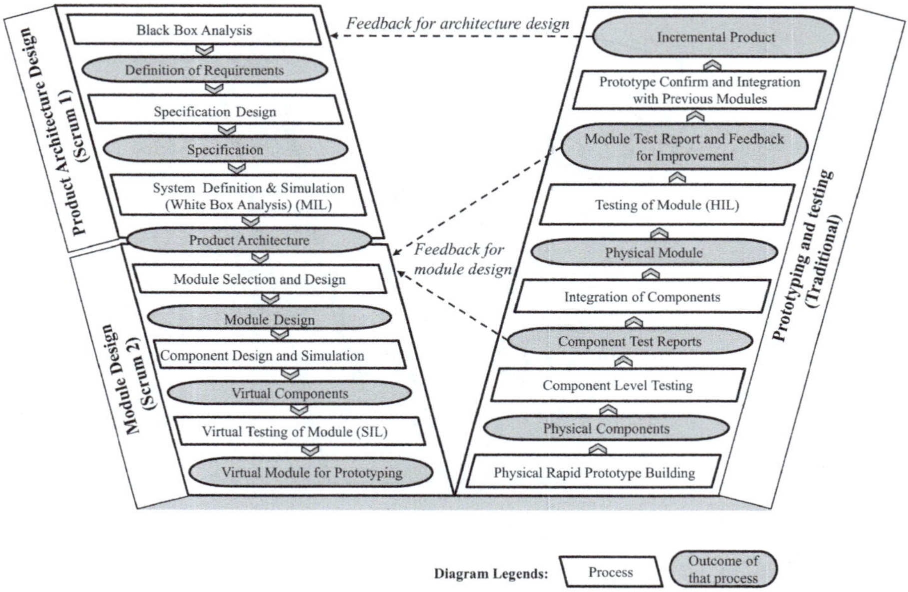

Fig. 3. Detailed hybrid framework- V model with Scrum

Then a series of N Scrum Sprints can be carried out. For each sprint, some requirements are prioritized and put in the Sprint backlog to develop a particular module allocated to a specific function. When enough virtual testing of modules has been verified, the traditional physical prototyping can then be performed.

Virtual testing has been introduced to test the module design in the second phase of this framework, as it provides flexibility to test and ask for feedback to customers in less time and with no investment in a physical prototype. At the beginning of the third phase, artifacts of this framework are referred from the conventional V-Model with few changes at the physical prototyping, testing and integration phase. The use of rapid prototyping method is highly recommended as it could provide physical components in short duration without investing into a conventional way to produce a prototype from suppliers. The most popular rapid prototyping method is the additive manufacturing which is also known as 3D printing.

In order to test product architecture, virtual design of modules and hardware prototype, simulation techniques from a model-based design approach are used. Functions of the product are tested with model-in-loop (MIL) simulation technique and software of the respective ECU will be later checked by software-in-loop (SIL) simulation technique. In order to test each module or increment in the absence of the full product, hardware-in-loop (HIL) simulation technique is used as it can provide test results before the final assembly and flexibility to iterate the development of that particular module instantly.

A benefit of this framework is that, product architecture can be altered even after building modules also, if asked by a customer in a review at the end of the second or third phase. This framework has been built to solve the critical problems in mechatronic product development, yet with the simple use of Scrum, which makes it easy to adopt and use.

3.3 Analysis of the Adequacy of This Proposal with Respect to the Requirements

Requirements described in Sect. 3.1 for the development of a hybrid approach are cross-verified with the proposal. It has been found that some of the requirements are fulfilled in the hybrid framework. Analysis of the adequacy of the hybrid approach is explained briefly below.

The Framework Is in Compliance with the Following Requirements:

- Faster product development: due to the inclusion of virtual testing and rapid prototyping techniques, development time can be reduced.
- A method should be able to handle complex modelling: iterative approach of designing product architecture as well as modules (enabling architecture changes) provides an efficient way to handle complexity.
- A well-defined and iterative way to develop product architecture: the use of Scrum in the first phase to allow modification in product architecture if necessary.
- Focused on the development of each module with iteration: use of Scrum in second phase.
- Possibility to adapt changes in product architecture and module at any point in the product development: customers are involved at the end of each phase and even after testing of a physical prototype changes can be done in a product architecture.
- Should minimize the cost of development and of the related physical prototyping: the use of virtual testing and 3D printing reduces uncertainty in the prototyping phase and then the associated cost.
- Should follow values of agility: the agility values interpreted in context of hardware product development explained by [32], are fulfilled. Regarding the necessity of documentation, it is an organization's decision to define the requisite list of documents for their use.
- Use of virtual prototyping: possible at the end of the second phase.
- Involving customer in the review process: permitted at the end of each phase, and after each sprint in the first and second phase.
- Evaluation of product based on the product requirements.

Requirements Not Specifically Addressed:

- Efficient communication within the development team.
- Well-formed cross-functional team.
- Improvement in knowledge sharing capabilities between cross-functional departments.

- Size of the involved team should be between 5 and 9 in one team and efficient team structure with decision making ability of each member.
- Involving supplier and market research team in the process.
- Suited for product customization.
- Effective change management.

Most of the essential requirements, such as the method should be flexible to adapt changes at any point, involving the customer in the development process, and an iterative method, are fulfilled. This approach will also result in the reduction of the cost and duration of the development. Use of rapid prototyping techniques and virtual commissioning have solved problems with time and cost and provided practical and easy manoeuvring while iterating the development cycle. Requirements from the organizational aspect are not completely fulfilled, they will be taken as a reference for the future development of this hybrid agile framework.

3.4 Guidelines for the Implementation and Use of Hybrid Approach

Before adopting the hybrid approach for the multidisciplinary product development, it is crucial to mention certain key structure or guidelines an organization should follow. Requirements to adopt agility, use agility, requirements or change in current product development processes and an organizational structure are mentioned in Fig. 4. These requirements are extracted from literature research and interviews.

The four core values of agility have been found efficient and useful in software industry. Here, it has been explained how agile values from software industry could be adopted for multidisciplinary/hardware product development.

- Mechatronic product development requires an effective communication channel within the involved team that consists of experts from multiple domains. Increasing complexity within a product requires complex interactions between many experts and stakeholders [32].
- Comprehensive documents which are not necessary while the development of product should be omitted except documents such as the documentation for the concept development, technical specification, drawings and interface description [32].
- Customer involvement at early stage in order to prepare a product architecture, features and interfaces is beneficial instead of a signing of a contract only and deliver the product directly [32].
- Adopting changes over following plan provides the assurance of meeting market requirements more accurately. Customer differentiation is a continuous process till the end, based on a iterative approach, allowing for the adoption of any changes to the product throughout the development process [32].

According to a four stage adoption process [33], to confirm the adoption of agility, an organization needs to assess its competency. In the pre-assessment phase, the factors which can resist this change are being identified. Those factors are: (i) no necessity of agility, (ii) lack of funds to support the adoption process, (iii) unavailability of executive support. If these factors are pre-assessed, it will save the organization's time, cost and efforts in adoption.

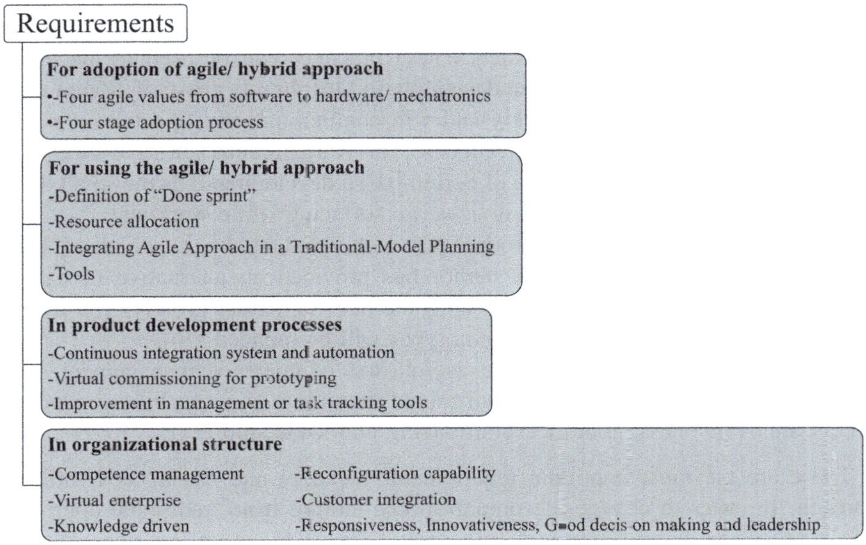

Fig. 4. Guidelines for implementation of a hybrid agile approach

Other guidelines to adopt and use agile method for mechatronic product development are as follows,

- Specify a "Done Sprint": unlike software, it is not possible every time to produce a working prototype in hardware product development. Sometimes working prototype is achieved only after the final iteration. The organization must decide what could be the outcome of each iteration in order to provide an incremental product to the customer [34].
- Resource Allocation: in the hardware product development, procurement, prototyping and testing activities which are dependent on different teams and stakeholders can have waiting times. During these waiting periods, a team can neither finish the sprint which includes prototyping nor go forward with the next sprint without the outcome of the previous sprint. Cooper et al. have provided a solution for teams to work on different tasks in the meantime [34]
- Integrating Agile Approach in a Traditional-Model Planning: coupling of traditional agile process with traditional approach can be difficult [34]. Required skillset should be generated within teams throughout the product development processes to support the agile approach adopted at one particular stage or all stages.
- Tools of agile methods: it is the responsibility of an organization to find and practice the tools which are suitable for them. With conventional methods of tracking the progress and managing the development is quite complicated and inefficient. For tracking the progress, new tools should be incorporated within the system, such as

JIRA. JIRA tool helps track the tasks, make boards for Scrum and Kanban, effective communication by notification feature, project timeline, performance check of a team and report handling [35].

- A continuous integration system and automation: in order to respond faster to changes in the software product development, continuous integration of codes into the server for testing is automated. These practices can be used in mechatronic product development and system design phase [36]. In this phase of system design, the work is done daily or weekly and will continuously get updated on a virtual prototyping platform for quick feedback. This way, a team can save time by one complete iteration (sprint in case of Scrum-based development) as the small defects, which will be found in a sprint review, are surfacing while working.
- Unlike software, mechatronic product possesses substantial parts which are hard to deliver after each iteration. An author has provided an alternative to hardware prototype: the virtual prototyping. With the help of virtual prototyping, time and cost associated with incremental prototypes will be reduced [36].
- Few organizational guidelines are as follows: competence management, virtual enterprise, knowledge-driven organization, reconfiguration capability, responsiveness, innovativeness, good decision making and leadership [37].

These are the most important requirements to adopt and use in an hybrid agile approach. In order to change the organizational culture from traditional approach to agile approach or hybrid approach, organization must focus on the steps of change management which can be a topic for future work in this area.

4 Conclusion

V-Model has proven to be an efficient method in both software and mechatronic industry. Even though a product can be developed in iteration with V-Model, it was restricted and needed a full cycle to be completed before the next iteration. The proposed hybrid approach of the V-Model with Scrum for developing the product architecture and each module, has provided freedom of iterating specific phase within one cycle of V-Model. Also, the proposed approach has explained the use of a rapid prototyping technique and virtual testing to improve the efficiency of the product development method. The proposed method has addressed the most critical issue such as the need of iterations within a traditional method, need of reduction in time as well as the cost of the development process and adapting the changes gathered from the continuous customer differentiation, in the product through iterations.

Along with the hybrid approach, essential guidelines for implementing and using the hybrid agile approach are discussed. Four values of agility have guided the software product development throughout these years. Now, their interpretation for mechatronic product development will be beneficial to understand the agility for mechatronic product development. Remaining guidelines have stated the importance of the "definition of done", resources, tools, the coupling of the two approaches and virtual prototyping.

With the use of these guidelines and the proposed method, better quality product is expected with less development time and cost, and most importantly, complying with the current market needs. Further development to the present work will deal with the application of the proposed approach to a set of industrial use-cases, in order to validate the actual results of the research. Also, presented results will be applied in a pedagogical context for the design of a mechatronic system, modular robot.

Acknowledgments. The presented research was conducted between three universities, University of Applied Sciences Upper Austria, Wels, Austria, Supméca, Laboratoire QUARTZ, EA7393, Paris, France and Fraunhofer J-Lab IDEAS, University of Naples Federico II, Naples, Italy. The research for few sections was also conducted during the preparation of a master thesis at University of Applied Sciences Upper Austria.

References

1. Beaumont, M., Thuriaux-Alemán, B., Prasad, P., Hatton, C.: Using agile approaches for breakthrough product innovation. Strateg. Leadersh. **45**, 19–25 (2017). https://doi.org/10.1108/SL-08-2017-0076
2. Erboz, G.: How to define industry 4.0: main pillars of industry 4.0. In: 7th International Conference on Management (ICoM 2017), Nitra, Slovakia (2017)
3. Gorecky, D., Schmitt, M., Loskyll, M., Zühlke, D.: Human-machine-interaction in the industry 4.0 era. In: 2014 12th IEEE International Conference on Industrial Informatics (INDIN), pp. 289–294, Porto Alegre (2014). https://doi.org/10.1109/INDIN.2014.6945523
4. Li, C.H., Lau, H.K.: A critical review of product safety in industry 4.0 applications. In: 2017 IEEE International Conference on Industrial Engineering and Engineering Management (IEEM), pp. 1661–1665, Singapore (2017). https://doi.org/10.1109/IEEM.2017.8290175
5. Patel, K.K., Patel, S.M.: Internet of Things-IOT: definition, characteristics, architecture, enabling technologies, application & future challenges. Int. J. Eng. Sci. Comput. **6**, 6122–6131 (2016). https://doi.org/10.4010/2016.1482
6. Bricogne, M., Le Duigou, J., Eynard, B.: Design processes of mechatronic systems. In: Hehenberger, P., Bradley, D. (eds.) Mechatronic Futures, pp. 75–89. Springer, Cham (2016). https://doi.org/10.1007/978-3-319-32156-1_6
7. Bassi, L.: Industry 4.0: hope, hype or revolution? In: 2017 IEEE 3rd International Forum on Research and Technologies for Society and Industry (RTSI), pp. 1–6, Modena (2017). https://doi.org/10.1109/RTSI.2017.8065927
8. Hehenberger, P., Howard, T.J., Torry-Smith, J.: From mechatronic systems to cyber-physical systems: demands for a new design methodology? In: Hehenberger, P., Bradley, D. (eds.) Mechatronic Futures, pp. 147–163. Springer, Cham (2016). https://doi.org/10.1007/978-3-319-32156-1_10
9. Chan, F.K.Y., Thong, J.Y.L.: Acceptance of agile methodologies: a critical review and conceptual framework. Decis. Support Syst. **46**, 803–814 (2009). https://doi.org/10.1016/j.dss.2008.11.009
10. Agarwal, A., Garg, N.K., Jain, A.: Quality assurance for product development using Agile. In: ICROIT 2014 – Proceedings of the 2014 International Conference on Reliability Optimization and Information Technology, pp. 44–47 (2014). https://doi.org/10.1109/ICROIT.2014.6798281
11. Ajmal, S., Ali, S.: Agile-waterfall hybrid model for software development processes. Sci. Int. **28**, 5165–5170 (2016)

12. Feldmüller, D.: Usage of agile practices in mechatronics system design potentials, challenges and actual surveys. In: Proceedings of the 2018 19th International Conference on Research and Education in Mechatronics, REM 2018, pp. 30–35 (2018). https://doi.org/10.1109/REM.2018.8421803
13. Zheng, C., Hehenberger, P., Le Duigou, J., Bricogne, M., Eynard, B.: Multidisciplinary design methodology for mechatronic systems based on interface model. Res. Eng. Design **28** (3), 333–356 (2016). https://doi.org/10.1007/s00163-016-0243-2
14. Gausemeier, J., Dumitrescu, R., Kahl, S., Nordsiek, D.: Integrative development of product and production system for mechatronic products. Robot. Comput. Integr. Manuf. **27**, 772–778 (2011). https://doi.org/10.1016/j.rcim.2011.02.005
15. Bianchi, M., Marzi, G., Guerini, M.: Agile, Stage-Gate and their combination: Exploring how they relate to performance in software development. J. Bus. Res. 1–16 (2018). https://doi.org/10.1016/j.jbusres.2018.05.003
16. Barringer, B.B., Gresock, A.R.: Formalizing the front-end of the entrepreneurial process using the stage-gate model as a guide an opportunity to improve entrepreneurship education and practice. J. Small Bus. Enterp. Dev. **15**, 289–303 (2008). https://doi.org/10.1108/14626000810871682
17. Kannan, V., Jhajharia, S., Verma, S.: Agile vs waterfall: a comparative analysis. Int. J. Sci. Eng. Technol. Res. **3**, 2680–2686 (2014)
18. Hehenberger, P., Poltschak, F., Zeman, K., Amrhein, W.: Hierarchical design models in the mechatronic product development process of synchronous machines. Mechatronics **20**, 864–875 (2010). https://doi.org/10.1016/j.mechatronics.2010.04.003
19. Yadav, R.S.: Improvement in the V-Model. Int. J. Sci. Eng. Res. **3**, 2229–5518 (2012)
20. Beck, K., et al.: Manifesto for agile software development. Agile alliance. http://agilemanifesto.org/. Accessed 20 May 2019
21. Ghani, I., Bello, M.: Agile adoption in organizations. KSII Trans. Internet Inf. Syst. **9**, 3231–3248 (2015). https://doi.org/10.1201/b13085-13
22. Böhmer, A.I., Hugger, P., Lindemann, U.: Scrum within hardware development insights of the application of scrum for the development of a passive exoskeleton. In: 2017 International Conference on Engineering, Technology and Innovation (ICE/ITMC), pp. 790–798 (2017). https://doi.org/10.1109/ICE.2017.8279965
23. Böhmer, A., Beckmann, A., Lindemann, U.: Open innovation ecosystem - makerspaces within an agile innovation process. In: ISPIM Innovation Summit, pp. 1–11, Brisbane (2015)
24. Cho, J.: Issues and challenges of agile software development with scrum. Issues Inf. Syst. **9**, 188–195 (2008)
25. Mabrouk, A., Penas, O., Plateaux, R., Barkallah, M., Choley, J.Y., Akrout, A.: Integration of agility in a MBSE methodology for multidisciplinary systems design. In: 4th IEEE International Symposium on Systems Engineering, ISSE 2018 – Proceedings, pp. 1–5. IEEE (2018). https://doi.org/10.1109/SysEng.2018.8544425
26. Böhmer, A.I.: When digital meets physical – agile innovation of mechatronic systems (2018). http://mediatum.ub.tum.de/doc/1430507/1430507.pdf
27. Böhmer, A.I., et al.: Towards agile development of physical products. In: 23th International Conference on Engineering, Technology and Innovation, vol. 17, pp. 78–85 (2017). 978-1-5386-0774-9/17
28. Boucher, M., Houlihan, D.: System design: new product development for mechatronics (2008)
29. Torry-Smith, J.M., Qamar, A., Achiche, S., Wikander, J., Mortensen, N.H., During, C.: Challenges in designing mechatronic systems. J. Mech. Des. **135**, 1–11 (2013). https://doi.org/10.1115/1.4007929

30. Eklund, U., Berger, C.: Scaling agile development in mechatronic organizations - a comparative case study. In: Proceedings - IEEE/ACM 39th International Conference on Software Engineering: Software Engineering in Practice Track, Buenos Aires, Argentina, pp. 173–182. IEEE Press (2017). https://doi.org/10.1109/ICSE-SEIP.2017.25
31. Mhenni, F., Choley, J., Penas, O., Plateaux, R., Hammadi, M.: A SysML-based methodology for mechatronic systems architectural design. Adv. Eng. Inform. **28**, 218–231 (2014). https://doi.org/10.1016/j.aei.2014.03.006
32. Fuchs, C., Golenhofen, F.J.: Agile for mechatronics and hardware. Mastering Disruption and Innovation in Product Management. MP, pp. 147–162. Springer, Cham (2019). https://doi.org/10.1007/978-3-319-93512-6_8
33. Sidky, A., Arthur, J., Bohner, S.: A disciplined approach to adopting agile practices: the agile adoption framework. Innov. Syst. Softw. Eng. **3**, 203–216 (2007). https://doi.org/10.1007/s11334-007-0026-z
34. Cooper, R.G., Sommer, A.F.: The agile–stage-gate hybrid model: a promising new approach and a new research opportunity. J. Prod. Dev. Manag. Assoc. **33**, 513–526 (2016). https://doi.org/10.1111/jpim.12314
35. Tutorialspoint: JIRA Tutorials point- simply easy learning, https://www.tutorialspoint.com/jira/index.htm. Accessed 01 Oct 2019
36. Johnson, N.: Agile hardware development – nonsense or necessity ? In: DESIGN West 2012, pp. 1–7, San Jose, California (2012)
37. Kettunen, P.: Adopting key lessons from agile manufacturing to agile software product development-a comparative study. Technovation **29**, 408–422 (2009). https://doi.org/10.1016/j.technovation.2008.10.003

A Study of Behavior and State Representation Methods in Modern PLM Systems

Petr Mukhachev(✉) and Clement Fortin

Skolkovo Institute of Science and Technology, Bolshoy Boulevard 30, bld. 1, Moscow 121205, Russia
petr@mukhachev.me, c.fortin@skoltech.ru

Abstract. Increasing product complexity and the growing importance of software components poses challenges for PLM systems in modern companies and extended enterprises. Today product behavior and its processes drive product value, so companies use sophisticated software to accurately predict it before its manufacture. In this work we argue that states are a natural atomic part of any product, system or process. Then we briefly review and compare current methods for behavior and state representations in domain engineering and systems engineering practices. We show that the support provided to the engineer by PLM systems in managing and sharing behavioral and state product properties across an extended enterprise is insufficient in comparison to their significance for successful product development and its complete life cycle.

1 Introduction

Growing product complexity continues to be one of the hardest challenges facing design and manufacturing today. Many vendors developed systems to help the designer save his time and effort during the design. One of the earliest efforts was to build modeling tools, i.e. tools to aid in representing and viewing the designer's work. In order to support system evaluation, tools for simulation were developed as well as tools for manufacturing support. Today, PLM systems cover many engineering and management domains. However, the introduction of software intensive systems, IoT, Industry 4.0, Cyber-Physical systems concepts set additional challenges to interoperability, modeling and simulation capabilities of the software.

Modern cyber-physical and automated systems blend the distinction between physical and computer systems. The development of these systems and their components requires physical as well as behavioral product information. The physical representation includes typical CAD structures, like form and material. Behavioral product specification is related to its functionality, possible interactions with other systems or their parts in different domains, like structural, electrical or informational. Sophisticated simulation of system behavior at the

Published by Springer Nature Switzerland AG 2020
F. Nyffenegger et al. (Eds.): PLM 2020, IFIP AICT 594, pp. 634–644, 2020.
https://doi.org/10.1007/978-3-030-62807-9_50

detail product development phase and its interaction with the environment has become essential for predicting and ensuring commercial product success.

Furthermore, in a highly connected world, companies often need to simulate their target system interacting with other systems across the extended enterprise, so advanced means for change management, collaboration and model reuse between disparate simulation and modeling systems are required.

Despite the diversity of simulation software, any digital process simulation uses some kind of event model: continuous event model, or discrete event model, or a mixed one. In any of these cases, the system of interest could be represented by a set of variables that evolve over time in a continuous or discontinuous way. The domain of these variables is called state space and their values at any particular point in time define the state of a simulated system. This way state is a fundamental concept for systems behavior simulation and analysis.

In spite of their fundamental meaning for product development, system states still could not be effectively reused and handled by software solutions. Geometry modeling and solid object representation serves as a backbone for version control and collaboration, which do not provide sufficient support for product state control.

In this work we will underline the importance of the system state concept for product development. We will concentrate on system state definition as a fundamental block of product representation at all stages of the life cycle. We will discuss with examples current practices for state and behavior representation from the systems engineering and PLM point of view and underline the importance of explicit management of stateful objects for complex system development.

2 Defining Processes and Product States

Fundamentally, the work of a designer is to create the definition of products and systems as objects. An object can be defined as a thing that exists or might exist. Real objects can be transformed in various ways: they can be heated, deformed or wear out during the operations. A process is something that transforms objects: consumes, creates, or modifies its state. The function is the main process of the system, which is designed to deliver value—benefit at cost—to the system beneficiary.

The Webster dictionary [1] proposes the following definitions of "state", any of which is applicable in the scientific and engineering domain:

"State", noun:

- a condition or stage in the physical being of something
- any of various conditions characterized by definite quantities (as of energy, angular momentum, or magnetic moment) in which an atomic system may exist

There are several important implications of that definition:

- there are no stateless objects. A CAD solid object has at least a single state: it is an abstraction which does not change in time and can only change its position. Real objects are much more complex and could be potentially decomposed into many states. Thus, a state is a natural part of any physical object in a system, which defines the object at some point in time or in a time frame;
- the notion of state effectively allows us to describe only some of the parameters of a condition in which the system may exist. Indeed, the designer considers only those variables which are essential for product definition, ignoring others. Moreover, he narrows the set of variables to a minimal set that appropriately, i.e. to a degree that allows to solve a problem at hand, describe the product or system. Even the information that does not allow appropriate system description could be useful, e.g. at early project stages, when the system is not yet sufficiently defined;
- a state is a natural primitive constituent of any process within a system. A process in a system can be defined as a change of state over time.

Sometimes the change in system parameters can be insufficient for our senses or instruments to capture the difference with the adjacent state. This idea leads us from a continuous state space to a discrete state space. A discrete state space is also useful to intentionally simplify a system behavior representation.

Valid states for a kettle are: hot and cold; a landing gear of an aircraft can be retracted or extended; a tablecloth can be clean or dirty, etc. These states are characterized by parameters, such as temperature, gear position, or color respectively. Usually the designer defines his or her product for being "good enough" in some state, such as cruise state for an aircraft, or for changing the state of other objects, such as "making the water hot" in case of a kettle.

3 Representations

Knowledge representation and reasoning are deeply intertwined. It was argued by Davis [4] that by choosing a particular representation, one chooses a character of answers and method of reasoning it could provide by its ontology, which inevitably captures only a part of the underlying phenomenon.

Many systems for reasoning about processes and states are used in industry. Even more are developed in academic literature, but none of them surprisingly are explicitly present in PLM systems. The next section briefly reviews some of existing methods for state and process representation.

Discrete event systems and continuous event systems are a part of modeling and simulation theory. It is an active field of research, which formalizes modeling concepts for complex systems. System states play an essential role in the formalism by defining the event as a transition from one state to another. Currently this theory could be considered as a backbone for different simulation engines and softwares used by engineering community [3].

Process Specification Language [8,11] is a comprehensive ontology developed by NIST, which was designed to provide unified means for software semantic interoperability and formal reasoning about business and manufacturing processes. The ontology is based on extended and modified situation calculus, which provides formal reasoning mechanisms. The state extension supports definitions of states before and after certain activities through their attribution to changeable properties of the objects. Many kinds of properties and their connections to processes and other properties are defined for formal reasoning support.

The SAPPHIRE model was originally proposed by Venkataraman and Chakrabarti [14] to support conceptual product design. In Fig. 1 it is shown in the form proposed by McSorley in [10]. The model underlines causal relationships between objects, processes and states. The function of an object could be attributed to an *"affect"* link to components of other models. In other words, it represents the reality that the function of a system affects its environment. The model allows to describe in detail and track product behavior. In this causality model, states have a central role as a causal connector between physical phenomena and other entities in a system.

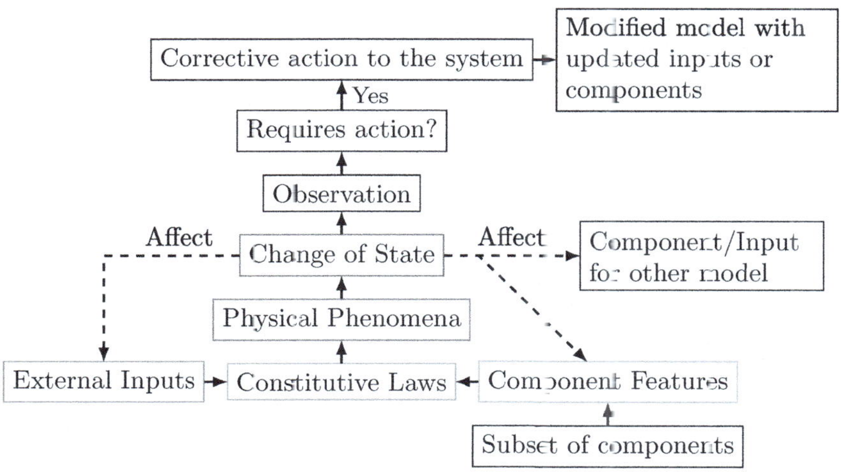

Fig. 1. SAPPHIRE model structure

3.1 Systems Engineering

Systems engineering could be defined as a methodical multi-disciplinary approach for the design, realization, technical management, operations and retirement of a system. A significant overlapping exists between PLM and Systems Engineering. PLM scope of application is larger and can be applied independently of Systems

Engineering methods. Systems Engineering is more concerned with engineering methods and processes from the very beginning of the system development, as well as with enhancing communication and interoperability between multidisciplinary teams, as it was described by Vosgien in [15]. So, in contrast to domain modeling and analysis in PLM systems, for systems engineering the semantic representation is essential, especially at the conceptual design stage, when the system may be not yet sufficiently defined to run precise simulations.

From this point of view, states are important to define concept of operations and requirements for a product to accurately convey system functionality description to system's stakeholders. According to NASA Systems Engineering Handbook [12], top-level requirements define constraints and scope for a technical system. The concept of operations and functional requirements describe them on subsequent stages. These documents prescribe how the system will be used and define its functional and behavioral expectations, that is, they loosely define states and transitions of the considered system and product. For example, consider two excerpts from James Webb Space Telescope (JWST) Mission Operations Concept [13], which defines possible states of the telescope and its subsystems and transitions between them:

- MO-44. The JWST Mission will be divided into 5 operational phases: Prelaunch, Launch, Deployment and Trajectory Correction, Cruise and Commissioning, and Normal Operations.
- MO-226. A generic sequence of events in a typical science observation with a JWST instrument would be:
  1. The spacecraft slews to a new target field.
  2. The FGS (Fine Guidance Sensor) performs a guide star acquisition and the spacecraft fine points the Observatory.
  3. etc....

Each mission phase will have different requirements, corresponding to various mission states, and different types of verification procedures for the same physical products and parts. In other words, the designer has to consider that an object of interest has more than one potential state. In early product development stages, the designer doesn't know all the details to precisely specify state variables values, so he is forced to hide some complexity by specifying only high-level system states, in fact representing subsystem states as indistinguishable.

Traditional ways of delivering the information to the stakeholders is to use documents and natural language. However, currently, many graphical and formal notations have appeared to partially substitute natural language in order to make the information more expressive and compact. As a result, Model-Based Systems Engineering (MBSE) concept emerged. One of the earliest attempts to formalize systems engineering was performed by Wymore [17]. He used system state as one of fundamental building blocks in his formalism. However, modern MBSE to a large extent adopted state and process concepts as well as their representations from software engineering practices. Harel state machine is adopted in SysML and very popular among systems engineers. A review of different kinds of state machines is presented in [16] by Wach.

The Object Process Methodology developed by Dori [5] provides a simple, but powerful vocabulary for system representation in a holistic way. It is standardized as ISO19450-2015 and gains popularity in different domains. It has only three fundamental objects: object, process and state, along with different types of relations between them. OPM defines both graphical and textual language representations which can be used to model any complex system and offers zoom-in capabilities in its proposed application OPCloud, to represent any subsystems or components in greater detail particularly for the system architecture definition. Dov Dori proposes [6] to use the term *stateful objects* in OPM to articulate states as a natural constituent of an object. With this definition he effectively integrates changeability into any physical object or system, and proposes that all complex systems representations must include this fundamental characteristic to be appropriately defined (Fig. 2).

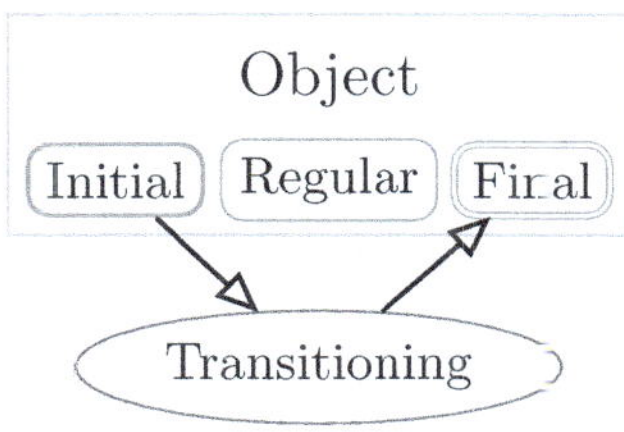

Fig. 2. OPM object, process and state representations

As an atomic structure, the state of the object is defined as a "possible situation or position of an object". The state of the system is derived as a "snapshot of the system model taken at a certain point in time, which shows all the existing object instances, current states of each stateful object instance, and the process instances, with their elapsed times, executing at the time the snapshot occurs".

At every point in time, a stateful object is in one of its states or in transition between two of its states as a consequence of a process currently affecting that object. Rounded-corner rectangle with a label placed inside the object denotes an object state. Initial, final and default states could be visually distinguished. The classification of state within a value range is also supported.

OPM authors argue that stateful objects, processes and relationships constitute a minimal universal ontology, meaning that any system in any domain could be modeled using that ontology.

SysML standardized by OMG, is a collection of diagrams for visual systems representation. SysML has a pretty rich tool set for behavior representation that includes statecharts, sequence charts, activity diagrams and functional flow diagrams. SysML was originally designed to replace classic documents and was not meant to provide simulation capabilities. UML and SysML adopt Harel statecharts as one of the means for behavior representation.

First published in 1984, and later adopted in UML and SysML, Harel statecharts [9] are a broad extension of the state machine formalism. They were at first aimed for software systems description, but eventually gained popularity for physical systems and now are adopted in UML2 and SysML languages. They are easy to read, require no prior training and are widely used in different areas.

Statecharts can be concisely described as state diagrams with hierarchy, orthogonality and broadcast communication support. An example of a statechart is shown on Fig. 3. Here states B and C are orthogonal, i.e. could coexist simultaneously. They are triggered from state A by event1. State B has one sub-state D, which is entered right after event1. State C has two sub-states E and F, which are switched by event2 and event3.

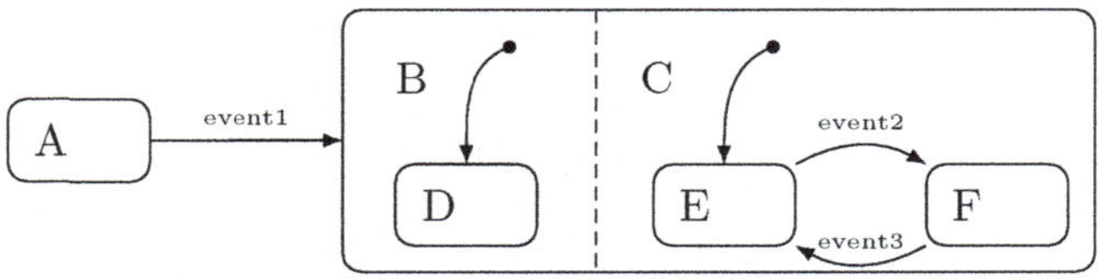

Fig. 3. Statechart example

In statecharts, events are considered to be external inputs and should be provided for execution. Some tools, like MagicDraw use events generated by activity diagrams in order to trigger the transitions. Many tools try to provide some simulation capabilities to SysML, integration with different simulation software, etc. However, modern SysML still remains to be a graphical language with 9 diagrams representing the structure and behavior of a system, rather than its simulation.

3.2 Domain Modeling

Electrical, mechanical, hydraulic and many other mature engineering domains have developed many types of simulation software with readable graphical processes representations and dynamic system simulation support. They are capable to calculate the values of state variables in any particular point in time by solving algebraic and differential equations or using discrete event systems. The heterogeneous and multidisciplinary nature of today's products often demands interoperability with specialized or locally used software as well as other large PLM systems.

In-house solutions are often implemented using general-purpose modeling software like Matlab and Simulink, or programming languages: Python, Java, and C++ are among the most widely used now. For these solutions engineers share system behavior using Excel or plain text "csv" formatted files, because they afford relatively easy to read and write system independent interface. For more complex interactions the Functional Mock Up (FMI) is a powerful tool which was developed by the MODELISTAR consortium and the Modelica Association Project [2], which is now supported by more than 100 tools. Time-continuous as well as time-discrete process descriptions are supported by FMI as well as feedback loops and many more features.

A time series representation can be easily considered as a representation of state evolution in time of discrete state or continuous state system, but for the FMI interface between systems this kind of mapping is not always possible, because it implements direct simulation of a process with its inputs and outputs.

Software and robotics engineers also frequently use state machines for description of logic in their systems. Many variations of state machines are used for computer systems representations, protocol modeling, etc.

Work of the engineer frequently requires the use of simulation software to check whether the requirements for the product are met or not. Some vendors of simulation software afford integrations with requirements management software. As we have seen, requirements are deeply connected with system states. PLM system support for system state could significantly enhance interoperability between these products.

It could be seen that despite the need to explicitly share and manage information about operational states, current PLM software capabilities mostly concentrate on geometry description and its change management. There is little or no support for managing engineering and software changes for these systems.

Space Systems Design Example. In the European Space Agency, a data model for information exchange in concurrent design facilities is described in technical memorandum ECSS-E-TM-10-25A [7]. It is generally designed to facilitate data exchange during the earliest stages in the product lifecycle, thus the standard aims for simplicity of specification with less precise definitions, which are appropriate for this task. Product states are implemented to store several instances of a single variable. This interface is mainly designed to exchange discrete state variables rather than continuous ones and very actively used during space mission design. Typical examples comprise the specification of power consumption of an instrument, different torques of attitude control system, etc. in different operational modes.

4 Discussion

A complex electromechanical system is operating in various states throughout its life cycle and change its state during operations, e.g. for the whole aircraft—taxiing, taking-off, climb, cruise or descent, while for its subsystems it could be retracted/extended gear, retracted/extended flaps or slats, different operation states of the engine, etc. Each system state may be a subject to different requirements that have to be properly implemented in the design, e.g. size of retracted undercarriage might be more constrained than that in an extended position, certain safety requirements may be applied only to engine in operation, etc. A difficulty that can be foreseen in a sold modeler is the coherency of all the states that needs to be maintained with options and version control.

To illustrate the above, in Fig. 4 different deployment states of James Webb Space Telescope are shown. While the spacecraft essentially consist of the same structural elements in all of its states, each of them could be a subject to different requirements and thus different simulation scenarios. Different people could be in charge of product design and its functionality in different states, so state coherency may become a big issue.

Fig. 4. JWST states: inside rocket fairing (left) and deployed (right)

Cyber-physical systems and Industry 4.0 make the problem of maintaining state coherency even more demanding by increased number of interactions with other systems in an extended enterprise. These systems mix software, electronic, and physical parts making system state management increasingly important.

Systems Engineering has developed many languages with rich vocabulary and expressivity for more formalized description of behavior, concept of operations, requirements, and architecture in comparison to natural language. Besides being machine interpretable, they tend to be stricter and clearer than natural languages. During system development they are primarily used for information exchange between stakeholders, for requirements and functional specifications. In many graphical languages for process specification and representation, states play a key role.

On the other hand, simulation tools that provide extensive support for numerical simulation operate with time series, which can be seen as continuous state change in time. Simulation usually serves as preliminary verification to ensure requirements compliance. In that sense, state representation could help in generating simulation procedures as well as tracing requirement to concrete simulation results and verification procedures. For example, it could be possible to explicitly define single procedure and run it on a number of system states to check system compliance to the requirement in every considered case.

There is an intrinsic connection of state management with configuration management for simulation purposes. For analysis purposes that do not involve state change, an object in some state could be regarded as one of its configurations. For example, an aircraft with retracted landing gear could be treated similarly to one of its configurations. This aspect is quite important for integration with Simulation Data Management software, proper design of experiments and numerical simulation for verification. However, PLM systems have generally evolved from solid modeling tools through Engineering Data Management tools and much of their functionality is still constrained by data structures from solid modeling heritage and thus, single state data structure.

5 Conclusion

The importance of states is shown by their explicit presence in the most significant documents in the project, such as concept of operations and requirements definition documents. During detail design, they are used to define simulation procedures and during the verification and validation stages states are used to define physical and numerical experiments.

Despite the importance of states for product development, product data management systems still heavily rely only on solid models and solid product part representations. Solid object by definition has a single state, and that fact may sufficiently limit the capabilities for cyber-physical and complex systems design support. Objects in a real world are fundamentally stateful and we should represent this feature in design support systems in order to support full product life cycle.

Our study clearly shows that states are explicitly present in software design practices, mission requirements definition, simulation procedures for verification and validation, since behavior is so pervasive in these processes. However, mechanical design and its corresponding PLM systems with their phenomenal solid modeling capabilities have so far maintained implicit state representations apart from their simulation modules; their formal representation of behavior, process and states remains limited, and therefore limits their capability to support the complete development of complex cyber-physical systems.

References

1. Definition of STATE. https://www.merriam-webster.com/dictionary/state
2. Functional Mock-up Interface. https://fmi-standard.org/
3. Zeigler, B., Muzy, A., Kofman, E.: Theory of Modeling and Simulation. Elsevier, Amsterdam (2019). https://doi.org/10.1016/C2016-0-03987-6
4. Davis, R., Shrobe, H., Szolovits, P.: What is a knowledge representation? AI Mag. **14**(1), 17–17 (1993). https://doi.org/10.1609/aimag.v14i1.1029
5. Dori, D.: Object-process methodology. In: Encyclopedia of Knowledge Management, 2nd edn., pp. 1208–1220 (2011). https://doi.org/10.4018/978-1-59904-931-1.ch116

6. Dori, Dov: Conceptual modeling: purpose and context. Model-Based Systems Engineering with OPM and SysML, pp. 75–96. Springer, New York (2016). https://doi.org/10.1007/978-1-4939-3295-5_9
7. ESA: ECSS-E-TM-10-25A Engineering Design Model Data Exchange (CDF). ESA Requirements and Standards Division (2010)
8. Gruninger, M., Menzel, C.: The process specification language (PSL) theory and applications. AI Mag. **24**(3), 63–63 (2003). https://doi.org/10.1609/aimag.v24i3.1719
9. Harel, D.: Statecharts: a visual formalism for complex systems. Sci. Comput. Program. **8**(3), 231–274 (1987). https://doi.org/10.1016/0167-6423(87)90035-9
10. McSorley, G., Fortin, C., Huet, G.: Modified SAPPHIRE model as a framework for product lifecycle management. In: DS 77: Proceedings of the DESIGN 2014 13th International Design Conference (2014)
11. Pouchard, L.C., Cutting-Decelle, A.F., Michel, J.J., Grüninger, M.: ISO 18629 PSL : a standardized language for specifying and exchanging process information. IFAC Proc. Volumes **38**(1), 37–45 (2005). https://doi.org/10.3182/20050703-6-CZ-1902.01525
12. Shea, G.: NASA Systems Engineering Handbook Revision 2, June 2017
13. Space Telescope Science Institute: JWST Mission Operations Concept Document. Technical Report JWST-OPS-002018 (2006)
14. Venkataraman, S., Chakrabarti, A.: Sapphire – an approach to analysis and synthesis. In: DS 58-2: Proceedings of ICED 09, the 17th International Conference on Engineering Design, vol. 2, Design Theory and Research Methodology, Palo Alto, CA, USA, 24 August 2009–27 August 2009 (2009)
15. Vosgien, T.: Model-based system engineering enabling design-analysis data integration in digital design environments: application to collaborative aeronautics simulation-based design process and turbojet integration studies. Ph.D. thesis, Paris (2015)
16. Wach, P., Salado, A.: Can Wymore's mathematical framework underpin SysML? An initial investigation of state machines. Procedia Comput. Sci. **153**, 242–249 (2019). https://doi.org/10.1016/j.procs.2019.05.076
17. Wymore, A.W.: Mathematical Theory of Systems Engineering. Wiley, Hoboken (1967)

Artificial intelligence in CAx, MBE, and PLM

Data Analytics and Application Challenges in the Childrenswear Market - A Case Study in Greece

Evridiki Papachristou[1(✉)] and Nikolaos Bilalis[2]

[1] Department of Creative Design and Clothing, International Hellenic University, 14 Km Thessaloniki - N.Moudania, 57001 Thermi, Thessaloniki, Greece
epapachristou@isc.tuc.gr
[2] School of Production Engineering and Management, Technical University of Crete, Kounoupidiana, 73100 Chania, Greece

Abstract. Integrating technology solutions like PLM, 3D Prototyping, digital printing, automatic cutting, AR & VR into the fashion product development process can deliver continuous improvement in everyday business and empower fashion companies navigate the challenges and opportunities of Industry 4.0 Leveraging powerful artificial intelligence capabilities that guide the discovery of next-generation - in popularity- fashion product designs, can improve innovation and conceptual design exploration to the clothing companies. This study focuses in the market of childrenswear which is the fastest-growing and one of the most lucrative markets in the garment industry; a growth that had overtaken both menswear and womenswear. At the same time, childrenswear product consumers are fashion conscious, demanding more fashionable designer clothing. Predicting the best appealing and selling product maybe the recent demand of applying AI tools in the design generation phase or decision making process, however comfort, fit for play, rest and safety most of all, are requirements that childrenswear must comply with. This paper aims to identify the challenges that AI technology applications face regarding childrenswear, due to safety restriction and standards by taking into consideration a Greek childrenswear manufacturer and retailer.

Keywords: Childrenswear · Data analytics · Machine learning · Safety standards

1 Introduction

Integrating technology solutions like PLM, 3D Prototyping, digital printing, automatic cutting, AR & VR into the fashion product development process can deliver continuous improvement in everyday business and empower fashion companies navigate the challenges and opportunities of Industry 4.0. Leveraging powerful artificial intelligence capabilities that guide the discovery of next-generation - in popularity- fashion product designs, can improve innovation and conceptual design exploration to the clothing companies. This study focuses in the market of childrenswear which is the

Published by Springer Nature Switzerland AG 2020
F. Nyffenegger et al. (Eds.): PLM 2020, IFIP AICT 594, pp. 647–658, 2020.
https://doi.org/10.1007/978-3-030-62807-9_51

fastest-growing and one of the most lucrative markets in the garment industry; a growth that had overtaken both menswear and womenswear. At the same time, childrenswear product consumers are fashion conscious, demanding more fashionable designer clothing. Predicting the best appealing and selling product maybe the recent demand of applying AI tools in the design generation phase or decision making process, however comfort, fit for play, rest and safety most of all, are requirements that childrenswear must comply with. This paper aims to identify the challenges that AI technology applications face regarding childrenswear, due to safety restriction and standards by taking into consideration a Greek childrenswear manufacturer and retailer. It is organized in six main sections.

Section 2 addresses the importance of childrenswear market in the clothing sector, the interest that this segment shows in fashionability which leads to fashion conscious and demanding fashionable product consumers, and the product safety restrictions and standards that designs must comply with. Section 3 summarizes the latest projects on artificial intelligence technology applications in the clothing industry, and more specifically in fashion product design, with aim to predict future market preferences and high buy rates. Section 4 presents not only the academic work conducted in the distinct domain of the fashion and apparel industry but a literature review focusing on the supply chain stage of the design of new products. Section 5 illustrates how a Greek childrenswear manufacturer and retailer develops fashion products taking into consideration comfort, fit for play, rest and safety regulations and restrictions. Finally, the research concludes with the challenges that arise when applying AI technology methods in the design process of such specialized products and the potential of new approaches rising from these challenges.

2 The Childrenswear Market

Childrenswear and babywear are outperforming the overall apparel market in Europe, presenting exciting opportunities for exporters from developing countries. The childrenswear market is the fastest-growing and one of the most lucrative markets in the garment industry [1], and in 2016 this growth had overtaken that of both menswear and womenswear [2]. Especially in Europe, this segment market shows interesting fashionability since the influence of social media and celebrities on younger children – and their parents – has caused children's clothing to evolve into a trend leader, with kids more aware than ever of trends [1].

Parents may be eager to give their children the best possible appearance but children's clothing basic requirements are comfort, fit for play and rest as well as safety. Product safety is one of the legal requirements that childrenswear must comply with, to be allowed on the European market. However, designers, when developing a child's garment, keep in mind special characteristics like growth features. Children grow rapidly, therefore features that allow for growth are important. Design for this specifications usually include sleeveless designs, adjustable shoulder straps, elasticised waistlines or wrap styles. Closures, which are on the front of the garments so children can see the fasteners and manipulate them easily, are carefully selected by the designers based on the age and the ease of manipulation by the wearer (child). Zippers, buttons, hooks and loop fastener tape, gripper snaps are not only functional but sometimes decorative. Enhancing a basic design style with decorative trims and accessories like motifs, ribbons, buttons and zippers trying sometimes to imitate an adult's style, is a usual practice. Adding value to a clothing product with decorative accessories is as much a commodity in modern children clothing as are the guidelines on the standards of such items for safe use.

Das [3], discussed the importance of safety issues and possible hazards associated with the application of different accessories in children garment and the guidelines on the standards of such items for safe use. Indeed, assisting the suppliers with the right guideline through the product development process, helps not only to establish the required safety standards, but also to produce apparel products that will limit potential hazards. Children's' safety through clothing has been the research focus also of Esrafilian & Nazari [4], who considered simultaneous and stable design of colourful diversity and announcement of protective alarms on child's garment against ultraviolet utilizing photochromic dyes.

To prevent children from (fatal) incidents, children's clothes must meet the requirements on cords and drawstrings laid down in the EU standard EN 14682:2007 [5]. Another voluntary, ASTM F1816-18 [6], is the current Standard Safety Specification for Drawstrings on Children's Upper Outerwear.

According to the studied Greek childrenswear company and to the study of Chatterjee [7], the value-added works in children garments mostly consist of:

1) Embroidery
2) Patchwork
3) Attachment of accessories
4) Printing and decorative painting

Trim can make a garment special to a child. Decorative machine stitching, embroidery, smocking, ribbons, braid, appliqués, ruffles, lace, and bias binding are some trimming possibilities [7].

Below, in the Fig. 1 we explain the restrictions on embroidery and accessories

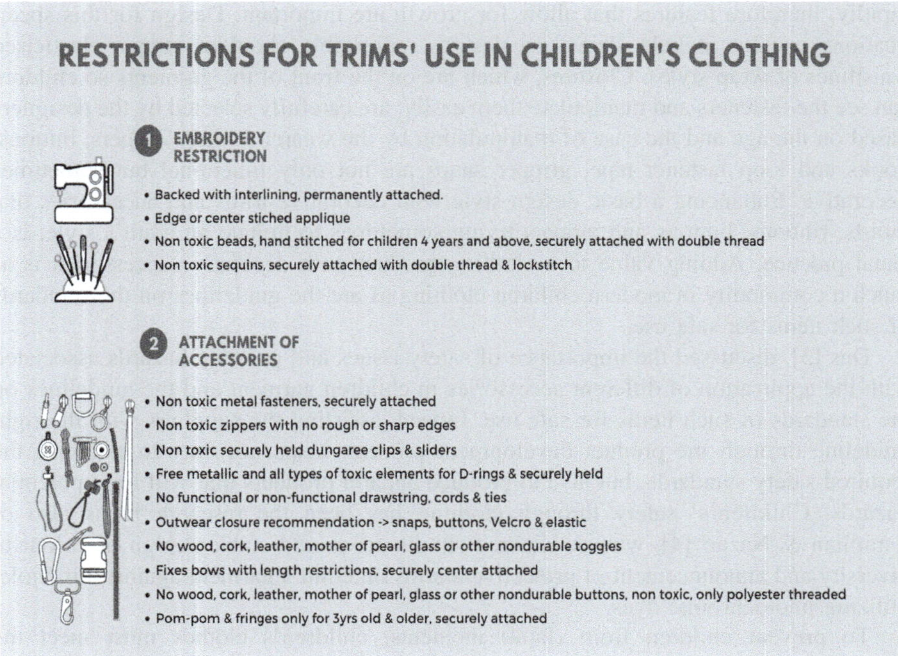

Fig. 1. Restrictions for trims' use in children's clothing

3 AI Technology Applications in the Clothing Industry

Since childrenswear product consumers are fashion conscious, demand more fashionable designer clothing. They also follow the adult apparel trends and as a result, brands and manufacturers need to analyse customer's intentions, so as to determine the trend of future products and business development direction [8]. Most of the production and distribution processes of clothing product cycle have been automated in a high level, based on customer preferences and new trends. Lately however, we see several projects that combine Artificial Intelligence technology in fashion product design, since it can effectively enhance the product development process, which is long and high in cost., being difficult to grasp the market's preference. Zalando a on-line fashion platform, team-up with Google who trained a neural network of 50.000 datasets, to analyse the style preferences of 600 fashion influencers, and predicted what kind of fashion people might like and created designs that match them [9]. Amazon's Lab126 [10], has developed an algorithm that learns about a particular style of fashion from images, and can then generate new items in similar styles from scratch—essentially, a simple AI fashion designer. Reimagine Retail, a project from Tommy Hilfiger, IBM and Fashion Institute of Technology, uses natural language understanding, computer vision as well as several deep learning techniques trained specially with fashion data, to create completely new designs by incorporating the trends of other designs into the ones already existing in the Tommy Hilfiger database [11]. Stitch Fix, an upstart e-commerce service, uses data science and combine popular attributes from past items to create pieces that will have predictably high profit margins and buy rates [12] Gap Inc. [13], in order to shorten the cycle from design to sale and find the right trends, utilizes a data mining approach to extract the market trend for the next season's collections instead of relying solely on the Creative Director's vision [14].

4 Academic Relative Work

In the last decade, the fashion and apparel industry has drawn the attention of AI academic researchers and specialists to not only respond quickly to constant change of consumer demands and behaviour, but also to predict the best trend, colour combination, fabric and fit. Guo et al., [15] identified 95 research issues for AI application in apparel industry, with 26 of them in apparel design and more specifically in apparel CAD system, fabric-related issues, color-related issues, pattern design and garment evaluation. The work of Ngai et al. [16], although a review of 77 papers related to the application of decision support and intelligent systems in the textile and apparel supply chains, showed only 4 in product design and development. The study of Hsiao et al. [17], chose grey theory and used Fuzzy C-Means algorithm to investigate fashion colour prediction, by automatically recognising colour clusters among digital images. The same year, Mok et al. [18], developed a customised fashion design system to create fashion designs and make corresponding patterns by using interactive generic algorithms and fuzzy set theory to model design knowledge. Researchers from UC San Diego and Adobe [19] have outlined a way for AI to learn an individual's style and create customised computer-generated images of new items that fit that style; a first step towards building systems that go beyond recommending existing items from a product corpus, but which can be used to suggest styles and aid the design of new products [20]. Yildirim et al. [21], presented a survey on how Data Mining methods can help the decision making processes, but it was restricted in textile applications and not in apparel or fashion design. Hong et al., [22] presented a knowledge-based open performance measurement system (KBOPMS) in big data environment, in order to support complex industrial decision-making for new product development to address the current market pressures that drive firms to adapt new design process in product development (PD) processes. Zhu et al. [23], proposed a new approach to discover popular fashion product styles from product images and transaction history without supervision by training a CNN-based deep attribute model. In the second phase, new "must-have" fashion products are automatically designed by Variational Autoencoder with images of discovered popular styles. Generating new products based on popularity information with AI technology, may have not been considered in previous fashion design studies using generative models [24], but a forecasting model which was trained to represent fashion trends over time and predict their popularity in the future was introduced by Al-Halal et al. [25].

Colour and material decision is every season's designer's headache. AI Color Trend, a database on color fashion trend analysis and guidance, was released in 2017. [26] analysed data from international fashion weeks, brands as well as the most popular colours and fabrics in the domestic market of China. More recently, Google Arts &

Culture unveiled a machine learning project, in partnership with Business of Fashion, called Runway Palette. The tool, open to the public, maps out 144.000 runway looks of almost 1000 designers from the past four years, and allows users to upload their own photos to find dozens of similar runway outfits [27]. With this experiment, designers from clothing brands can discover not just the seasons, but also the trends that come from fashion weeks worldwide.

The latest development of Li et al. [8], introduced MixNMatch, a conditional generative model that learns to disentangle and encode background, object pose, shape, and texture factors from real images with minimal human supervision. Although not applied to fashion design yet, its proposed applications show many potentials.

Despite valuable contributions to the previous literature reviews, when observed, the reviews studied show several limitations (in total or separately):

1) The studies are restricted to specific product categories like T-shirts [23] or skirts [18]. T-shirt clothing in manufacture, in particular, is considered the most basic clothing product. Our case study childrenswear brand usually develops 180 initial T-shirt designs and 14 skirt designs, out of which 156 and 11 respectively, go to production.
2) The above mentioned studies of Sect. 3 are not applied in the real world of fashion retail sales or are not proposed for nonprofessional users, therefore the effectiveness and accuracy of the proposed model and method is not verified
3) Materials or decorative items are not considered separately as they do in the design phase
4) Safety factors of used accessories and components in children apparel are not considered either in any of the pro-mentioned academic research

5 Children Clothing Manufacturer and Retailer - A Greek Case Study

In order to produce and deliver safe, sustainable, and environmental friendly products to the customer, adherence to the appropriate specification, standard, law and regulation applicable for the merchandise is important [3]. The primary purpose of this research was to explore the complexity of today's fast-fashion product development process in the childrenswear market and the challenges that the creative team behind new product development face keeping in mind restrictions on safety. This section investigates how the childrenswear brand company in our case study, tries to be successful by achieving that. The researchers conducted field observation and interviews with 10 professionals who work in the Greek childrenswear brand. It was stated that the research and development of new production procedures are directed towards three main goals:

- Quality improvement
- Cost reduction in favour of the consumer
- Respect towards the client

A special focus was given to identify the product development model of a kidswear company with 500 selected children's clothing stores in Greece, Cyprus and other

European countries. Our investigation resulted that it follows a traditional push system where:

- the new product development department —> develops the designs and technical specifications of the fabrics and the garments to be produced (Fig. 2)
- the sales department along with the managers —> provide the manufacturers in Asia with information of the above as well as the volume of the products and sizes in which the garment is to be produced.
- the manufacturer —> follows the instructions to create multiple samples, which upon approval by the company, are converted into finished products and are transported to the company's headquarters in Greece. Figure 2 shows an example of a boys-set design accompanied with all the relevant instructions that reassure the construction of the garments based on the safety measures according to EU 14682. The company is also certified for ISO 9001:2008 by TUV.

The company, acts as a wholesaler and as a retailer. In the case of the wholesaler, the garments are sold through:

- an intermediate to brick-and-mortar stores of multi brand retailers
- an intermediate to four (4) retail stores with consignment stock arrangements
- one (1) shop-in-shop retail point in a department store
- company's web store in retail price
- company's owned brick-and-mortar stores in Greece and abroad (13 stores)

The designers employed by the company, are responsible for creating collections based on the current market and trend analysis [28], international trade show visits and participations, market research, previous collections sales etc. The Fig. 3, shows a collection of brand logos where the designers collect their inspiration data from.

Importantly, based on the industry challenges and the opportunities that technology, and in particular AI, represents, the company is currently attempting to add smart applications into their existing product lifecycle. This AI approach will be similar to the one presented in the study of Pinquié et al. [29], which utilizes a graph-oriented data structure that defined a design context based on its sub-elements: social, semantic, engineering, operational IT and traceability.

However, the company's approach will only be considering the semantic, engineering and traceability aspects of [29], and in contrast to the original work that uses the property graph to create proof designs that satisfy specific design rules, will utilize the application to derive design rules recommendation, and in association with its product lifecycle management (PLM) software, also produce as output similar items, that can be the basis of inspiration for new products. This will be done via natural language processing and machine learning text mining to obtain relevant keywords for the semantic context, data in terms of the engineering context directly derived from the PLM, and manual input in terms of the items as to the origin of the existing design items' inspiration by the product designers, as to the traceability context.

This will allow the company to obtain new designs in a structured way, faster than previously, as well produce designs that meet their clients' criteria and previous preferences, based on a semi-automated AI process.

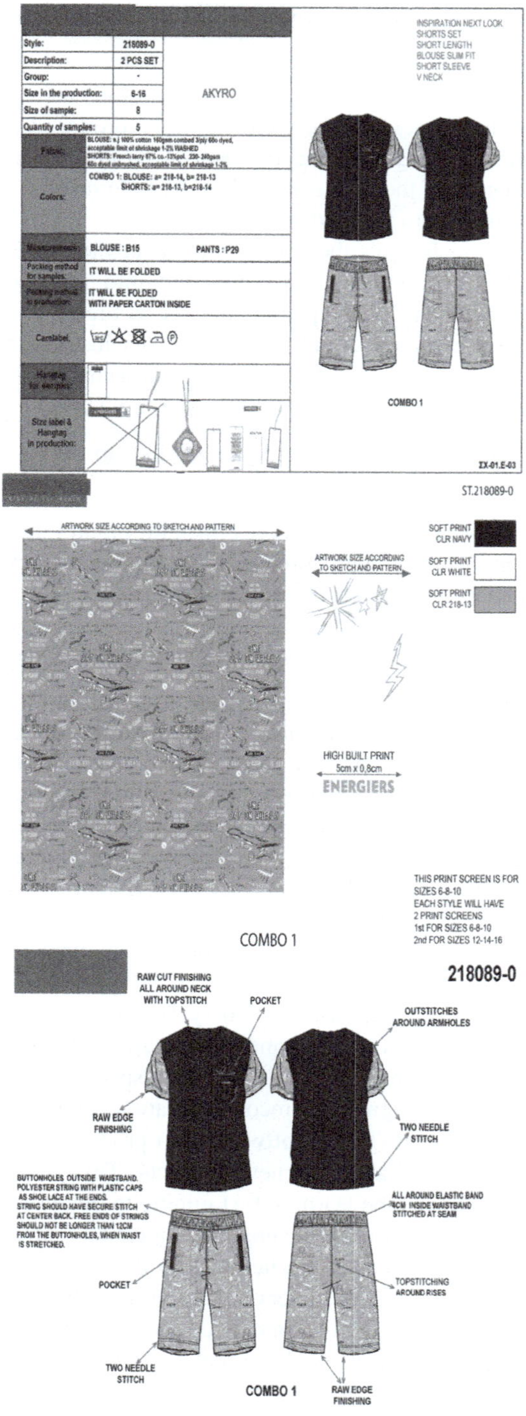

Fig. 2. Design & technical specifications of a boy's clothing set

Fig. 3. Designers' inspiration sources

6 Conclusion

Enhancing a basic design style with decorative trims and accessories like motifs, ribbons, buttons and zippers trying sometimes to imitate an adult's style, is a usual practice especially for childrenswear. However, while selecting accessories for children's wear, special attention should be given to the safety of the kids. Quality inspection and evaluation are required before purchasing any accessories by the garment industry [7]. At the same time, reports like the one of McKinsey [30], state that companies with the greatest overall growth in revenue and earnings receive a significant proportion of that boost from data and analytics. Yet, up to our knowledge, no research has been found on the application of Artificial Intelligence technology in the product development of children's clothing identifying, at the same time, critical indicators for achieving apparel safety. When applying AI techniques in decision making process in the design stages of apparel, safety technical regulations/standards related to apparels are not included. According to Chen et al. [31], the introduction of apparel safety evaluation in apparel design and manufacturing process has the potential to minimize recall rates, and a further shift to pro-action and to prevention of losses will be made possible.

Acknowledgements. This research has been co-financed by the European Regional Development Fund of the European Union and Greek national funds through the Operational Program Competitiveness, Entrepreneurship and Innovation, under the call RESEARCH – CREATE – INNOVATE (project code: T1EDK-03464).

References

1. CBI Centre for the Promotion of Imports. Childrenswear in Europe. CBI Ministry of Foreign Affairs (2018)
2. Abnett, K.: The childrenswear market comes of age. Retrieved 20 Mar 2019, from Business of Fashion, 21 June 2016. https://www.businessoffashion.com/articles/intelligence/the-childrenswear-market-comes-of-age
3. Das, S.: Product Safety and Restricted Substances in Apparel. Woodhead Publishing India Pvt. Ltd., New Delhi (2013)
4. Esrafilian, M., Nazari, A.: Simultaneous and durable design of colourful diversity and protective alarms against ultraviolet on child's apparel. Int. J. Appl. Arts Stud. **3**(4), 61–70 (2018)
5. EN 14682. European Standard Through Decision 2011/196/EU. European Commission, Brussels (2007)
6. ASTM F1816-18. Standard Safety Specification for Drawstrings on Children's Upper Outerwear. ASTM International, West Conshohocken (2018)
7. Chatterjee, K.N., Jhanji, Y., Grover, T., Bansal, N., Bhattacharyya, S.: Selecting garment accessories, trims, and closures. In: Nayak, R., Padhye, R. (eds.): Garment Manufacturing Technology, pp. 129–184. Woodhead Publishing Series in Textiles (2015)
8. Li, Y., Singh, K.K., Ojha, U., Lee, Y.J.: MixNMatch: multifactor disentanglement and encoding for conditional image generation. ArXiv abs/1911.11758 (2019)
9. Project Muse. Fashion inspired by you, designed by code. Retrieved from Google, 02 September 2016. https://blog.google/around-the-globe/google-europe/project-muze-fashion-inspired-by-you/
10. Amazon Lab126 (n.d.). Accessed from Wikipedia. https://en.wikipedia.org/wiki/Amazon_Lab126

11. Wright, B.: Just-Style. Retrieved from FIT and IBM to accelerate AI in the fashion industry, 25 April 2019. https://www.just-style.com/news/fit-and-ibm-to-accelerate-ai-in-the-fashion-industry_id136063.aspx
12. Smiley, L.: Stitch Fix's radical data-driven way to sell clothes–$1.2 billion last year–is reinventing retail. Retrieved 20 Feb 2019, from Fast Company, 19 February 2019. https://www.fastcompany.com/90298900/stitch-fix-most-innovative-companies-2019
13. Gap. Retrieved from Gap Inc (2019). https://www.gapinc.com/content/gapinc/html.html
14. Du, Y.: Data Analytics and Applications in the Fashion Industry: Six Innovative Cases. Retrieved Dec 2019, from Digital Commons, University of Rhode Island (2019). https://digitalcom-mons.uri.edu/cgi/viewcontent.cgi?article=1007&context=tmd_major_papers
15. Guo, Z., Wong, W., Leung, S., Li, M.: Applications of artificial intelligence in the apparel industry: a review. Text. Res J. **81**, 1871–1892 (2011)
16. Ngai, E., Peng, S., Alexander, P., Moon, K.K.: Decision support and intelligent systems in the textile and apparel supply chain: an academic review of research articles. Expert Syst. Appl. **41**(1), 81–91 (2014)
17. Hsiao, S.-W., Lee, C.-H., Chen, R.-Q., Yen, C.-H.: An intelligent system for fashion colour prediction based on fuzzy C-means and gray theory. Colour Res. Appl. **42**(2), 273–285 (2016)
18. Mok, P., Xu, J., Wu, Y.: Fashion design using evolutionary algorithms and fuzzy set theory e a case to realize skirt design customizations. In: Choi, T.-M. (ed.) Information Systems for the Fashion and Apparel Industry, pp. 163–197 (2016). Woodhead Publishing Series in Textiles
19. Kang, W.-C., Fang, C., Wang, Z., McAuley, J.: Visually-aware fashion recommendation and design with generative image models. In: Proceedings of IEEE International Conference on Data Mining (ICDM 2017), New Orleans (2017)
20. Papahristou, E.: AI: the Antidote to Fashion's Fear of Change. Retrieved from WhichPLM, 23 April 2018. https://www.whichplm.com/ai-antidote-fashions-fear-change/
21. Yildirim, P., Birant, D., Alpyildiz, T.: Data mining and machine learning in textile industry. Wiley Interdisc. Rev. Data Min. Knowl. Disc. **8**(1), e1228 (2017)
22. Hong, Y., Wu, T., Zeng, X., Wang, Y., Yang, W., Pan, Z.: Knowledge-based open performance measurement system (KBO-PMS) for a garment product development process in big data environment. IEEE Access **7**, 129910–129929 (2019)
23. Zhu, J., Yang, Y., Cao, J., Mei, E.C.F.: New product design with popular fashion style discovery using machine learning. In: Wong, W.K. (ed.) AITA 2018. AISC, vol. 849, pp. 121–128. Springer, Cham (2019). https://doi.org/10.1007/978-3-319-99695-0_15
24. Deverall, J., Lee, J., Ayala, M.: Using generative adversarial networks to design shoes: the preliminary steps. CS231 (2017)
25. Al-Halah, Z., Stiefelhagen1, R., Grauman, K.: Fashion forward: forecasting visual style in fashion. In: IEEE International Conference on Computer Vision (ICCV), Venice, pp. 388–397. IEEE (2017)
26. Huo, M., Tang, J., Kim, C.S.: Research on application prospect of artificial intelligence technology in clothing industry. Adv. Soc. Sci. Educ. Humanit. Res. **329**, 925–928 (2019)
27. Catheleen, C.: Google Unveils Machine Learning Project, in Partnership with BoF. Retrieved from Business of Fashion, 21 November 2019. https://www.businessoffashion.com/articles/news-analysis/voices-talk-cyril-diagne-google-tool-fashion-palette
28. Giri, C., Jain, S., Zeng, X., Bruniaux, P.: A detailed review of artificial intelligence applied in the fashion and apparel industry. IEEE Access, **7**, 95376–95396 (2019)

29. Pinquié, R., Véron, P., Segonds, F., Zynda, T.: A property graph data model for a context-aware design assistant. In: Fortin, C., Rivest, L., Bernard, A., Bouras, A. (eds.) PLM 2019. IAICT, vol. 565, pp. 181–190. Springer, Cham (2019). https://doi.org/10.1007/978-3-030-42250-9_17
30. McKinsey Analytics. Catch them if you can: How leaders in data and analytics have pulled ahead. McKinsey & Company (2019)
31. Chen, L., Yan, X., Gao, C.: Developing an analytic network process model for identifying critical factors to achieve apparel safety. J. Text. Inst. **107**(12), 1519–1532 (2016)

Trusted Artificial Intelligence: On the Use of Private Data

Norbert Jastroch(✉)

MET Communications, 61352 Bad Homburg, Germany
norbert.jastroch@metcommunications.de

Abstract. Artificial Intelligence has come into focus anew in the context of digitization and global competition. So has the tension between human ethics, regulation, and the potential gains this technology field offers for economic and societal progress. This paper is intended to contribute to the ongoing debate about opportunities and uncertainties in particular with respect to the use of private data in AI. We discuss the status of AI outcomes in terms of their validity, and of AI input as to the quality of data. In a first order approach we distinguish between the commercial, public, industrial, and scientific data spheres of AI systems. We resume the ethical and regulative approaches to the utilization and protection of massive private data for AI. Regarding the currently favoured ways of organizing the collection and protection of data we refer to respective ruling and denominate distributed ledger systems and open data spaces as functional means. We conclude by arguing that governing data privacy and quality by distinguishing different AI data spheres will enable a reasonable balance of these two aspects.

Keywords: Artificial Intelligence · Data privacy · Data quality · Ethics · Regulation · Open data spaces

1 Introduction

While the concept of Artificial Intelligence has been introduced into the technological evolution decades ago already, it has gained novel interest by taking up recent developments in the context of the digital revolution. Significant progress in computing power and communication technology, in advanced sensor capabilities, and in large scale data generation and distribution drive research into and the application of systems incorporating hardware, software and data for the purpose of automated information analysis and synthesis. In particular, systems that allow for software controled decision making leading to the automated performance of related action are gaining focus attention. Such systems are currently highly promoted worldwide, and the term Artificial Intelligence has become a widely used label, comprising a variety of concepts like data reasoning, robotics, and machine learning, to name a few. In [5] the AI HLEG provide a comprehensive description and suggest a sound definition of Artificial Intelligence (AI). For reasons of methodological clarity, and to avoid the vagueness that is often inherent to the talking about Artificial Intelligence, we employ this terminology.

Published by Springer Nature Switzerland AG 2020
F. Nyffenegger et al. (Eds.): PLM 2020, IFIP AICT 594, pp. 659–670, 2020.
https://doi.org/10.1007/978-3-030-62807-9_52

Artificial Intelligence is expected to offer new and powerful economic potential, contribute to scientific progress, and support sustainable societal development. In the wider context of digitization, Körner et al. [12] present a discussion of chances and fears that go with the economic and socio-economic consequences as far as these can be foreseen from today's perspective. Körner [13] also takes a look onto societal implications and political challenges, where, on a global scale, various and sometimes conflicting systems of constitutional principles create significant differences in the uptake of AI, hence in potential opportunities and threats related with its application.

Intrinsic to AI is the lack of transparency this technology bears not only for those lacking the required technical expertise, but also for those who make use of it or have to deal with its implications. Embedded algorithmic reasoning can produce unforeseeable results and lead to unexpected action, as could be observed in various examples. In the economic sphere, however, the proprietary character of algorithms is often considered a crucial competitive element, hence the interest in transparency is limited. Trustworthiness of AI applications, nevertheless, is regarded an essential requirement to ensure acceptance of AI systems which, in turn, impacts their successful implementation. The European Commission therefore has put transparency on a prominent place in the list of ethical principles to address in AI [6]. But there are far more ethical reflections needed. With respect to the use of data in AI, Floridi and Taddeo [4] suggest 'data ethics' as a comprehensive approach to understand ethical implications that come with the combination of hardware, software and data, as is the case in applied AI.

The availability of data is fundamental to successful utilization of AI. Data is often called the new resource, the novel raw material of the economy in the digital age. In the industrial field, the use and flow of data are core features of digitized applications. Manufacturing intelligence, under the headline of e.g. Industry 4.0 or Smart Manufacturing, has become subject to research and development programs throughout the world [19], and may to certain extent be subsumed under the concept of artificial intelligence. In a wider context, Wellsandt et al. [21] identified characteristics of information and data feedback in product development and product lifecycle management. While the quantity of data to be processed in these industrial applications rises, the quality of data is getting higher attention as a key feature of their relevance. With focus on product lifecycle management, Wuest et al. [22] suggested an approach to the analysis of information quality in the context of a specific production process, based upon a framework of fifteen dimensions of information quality.

The prominent role of data and information is valid likewise in the field of public administration, as well as in science. While most of these data originate from the private sphere of individuals here, need is there to reflect upon the use of data and the limitations that must be addressed. It is out of the scope of this paper to present a deep and comprehensive investigation of the related questions for all fields or AI applications. We therefore focus, in the following, on basic reflections, with a look on specific sectors like e.g. health only to exemplify particular consideration.

First question we address, in Sect. 2, is the status of the outcome AI systems generate when they use empirical data as their input. In Sect. 3 we discuss the utilization of massive data for applied AI for commercial, administrative, industrial, or scientific purposes. An overview of principles intended to govern the use of private data follows in Sect. 4. Then we present promising approaches for the collection and protection of private data from a technical perspective in Sect. 5, and end up with the formulation of concluding remarks, Sect. 6.

2 Pattern Recognition, Data Reasoning and Knowledge Generation

Beyond the question of what intelligence does mean and if it is valid to attribute this concept to an artificial device, there are two aspects that call for clarification of the status of AI systems' output. These are machine learning, and automated decision making and action taking. The AI HLEG [5] provided comprehensive specifications of both these we are using as reference.

Be it robotics, big data applications, or sensor driven actuation, AI systems typically work with empirical or statistical data as their input. These are processed by embedded algorithms to detect patterns of interest (that are also used to advance the experience base of the system) and suggest or initiate a certain decision or action, according to predefined goals. While in human intelligence these mental processes involve evaluative attributes like 'good' or 'right', and include deductive assessments of theoretical nature, these are missing in artificial intelligence systems. Results generated by an AI application are correlation based and have an empirical status. They do not comply with the scientific concept of epistemics. The term machine learning, however, suggests that an AI system generates a kind of knowledge. While, from a functional point of view, it may be reasonable to talk about AI in these terms, one must bear in mind that a specific dimension of knowledge is meant (compare also [9], and for a more detailed discussion with regard to the medical sector, compare [15]). In [10] we have made explicit different dimensions of knowledge and discussed some implications for their externalization and internalization. It is essential, however, to consider the special status of AI generated 'knowledge' if it is to be used for scientific purposes or in scientific theory. AI systems produce probabilistic results. Epistemics calls for cause-effect analyses and deductive syntheses[1].

In pointing out this distinction, attention is drawn to the issue of reliability of applied AI, with regard to both input data and output decision or action. This issue is a principal, not a gradual one. E.g., facial recognition delivers probabilistic identification of a person, with probabilistic matching getting better, the higher the number of measured parameters is – but the matching remains probabilistic. This implies the possibility of false-positive as well as false-negative identification. If such a technique is integrated into an application that enacts a pre-defined action, it bears the principal risk of error. This risk of error is problematic (the more, the higher the impact of the action is), as the question of responsibility is an open issue. Here again, the AI HLEG's

[1] As an illustration of this distinction, think of a right-angled triangle. An AI system may well be able to recognize that every triangle it has analyzed where the square over the longest side and the sum of the squares over the two other sides are equal is right angled, and vice versa. And it may reason that this is the case with a new triangle it comes across with. But it will not be able to deduce, formulate and prove that this equivalence is true in general for any triangle - what the ancient hellenic mathematicians successfully did.

Guidelines [6] offer some helpful orientation. What remains, though, is the fundamental dependence of AI systems on the quality not only of their algorithms, but in particular of their data used.

The reflections made in this chapter advise to differentiate the level of data quality that is held sufficient for an AI application in accordance with the status of the application. The following chapter is intended to shed some more light on this.

3 Utilizing Massive Data

At the current stage of development in AI, frequently no real distinction of AI and, say smart IT systems, or digitization, is made. Any attempt to specify distinguishing features must relate to the machine learning aspects of an AI system, which lie basically in the dynamics of the empirical data used, expanded throughout operation by feeding in more input data and by the use of former patterns as the experience base for the generation of improved patterns. In [9] we provided an illustration of the learning process from data to information to knowledge to competence, in a general sense, the principles of which are also applicable to the special case of AI.

Hence there are two aspects of central relevance: the elicitation of new input data and the algorithms for pattern detection and generation. Both aspects contribute to the added value to be realized by an AI application and are fundamental to the innovative potential of AI. In this paper, focus is on the input data aspect, the one affecting individuals and institutions more or less directly and therefore being subject to a wide public debate about chances and risks. We leave the investigation into and discussion of the functional algorithmic aspect to further work.

3.1 Data as Knowledge Objects

Data, understood as the formal representation of quantitative or qualitative features of a something that is knowledgeable, is basically not free of intentionality, nor of context.[2] Referring to an analysis provided in [11], we consider data a knowledge object, as such made of the core content, fixed in its syntax and semantics, and embedded in an environment of aspects useful for abstraction, translation, and interpretation (Exhibit 1). Such aspects are *glossary*, providing semantic support by clarifying terms used, *notation*, providing information regarding syntax and structure employed, and *purpose* and *view,* standing for the observational perspective. They also include reference to specific conceptual domains, like *ontologies*, and to systemic abstractions, like process *models*.

[2] A terminological clarification can be drawn from the example of the in-flight collection of weather data by aircraft: *data* measured are e.g. temperature, time, and location; their linking provides *information* regarding the atmospheric state at a specific point in space and time; feeding multiple of such empirical objects into an appropriate 'weather application' delivers *information* about the meteorological processes in the atmosphere we call weather. All this is *knowledgeable*, i.e. can be internalized by one's mind.

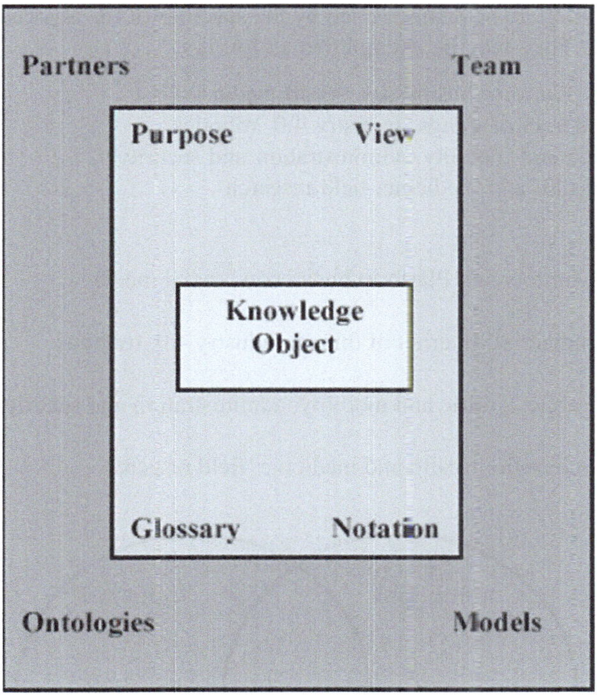

Exhibit. 1. Data as contextual knowledge objects (Source: [11])

Meaningful data hence has to be considered bound to such aspects. In fact, e.g. location data is, as to its meaning, tied to the specification – be that explicit, or implicit – of these aspects. That makes what we call Data Spheres. In the example of in-flight weather data collection, location data of the measuring sensor will be GPS coordinates including height. In the context of intelligent manufacturing, location data of a part to be used in the production process will be some warehouse specification. In the case of public traffic management, it will be GPS data of vehicles (eventually enriched by data from the measurement of distance to other vehicles, when we think of assisted driving). For commercial purposes, location data will involve GPS coordinates, or cell identification of a smart phone.

The concept of data spheres described so far is similar to that of data spaces for e.g. certain industries, which are subject to a number of initiatives currently, while it is of lower level of specificity. It is useful, though, as it allows for the investigation and evaluation of data quality and likewise of data privacy interference issues.

3.2 Data Spheres

Data used as input to AI systems originate from different sources and are used within various spheres. For our considerations here, we take four major spheres into view that are predominant in the current discourse on AI: commercial, industrial, public, and scientific (Exhibit 2), to be distinguished by the specifics of the aspects denominated in Sect. 3.1 above. They may be exemplified as follows:

Commercial: Platform businesses, social media
Industrial: Internet of things, Industry 4.0, robotics
Public: Traffic and mobility, administration and security
Scientific: Health and medicine, field research

Commercial: Platform businesses, social media

Industrial: Internet of things, Industry 4.0, robotics

Public: Traffic and mobility, administration and security

Scientific: Health and medicine, field research

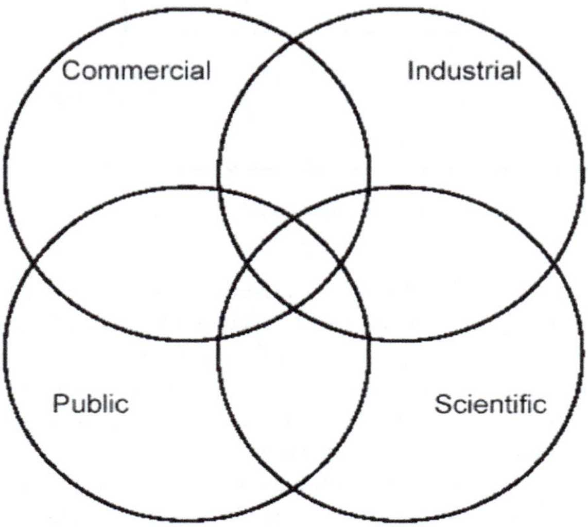

Exhibit. 2. Major data spheres relevant to AI applications

These spheres are obviously not mutually exclusive but overlapping. Their distinction enables separate perspectives with regard to the collection and utilization of data in terms of quality and privacy.

3.2.1 Commercial

Main purpose of data utilization here is to influence individual behaviour, in particular buying behaviour. The concept behind is targeted advertising. Massive data collection enables the detection of preference patterns which in turn are used to generate personalized advertisement. Web based platforms for this business model of digital commerce have two functional elements: Collecting private data of users and addressing individuals by personalized advertisement and product offers. As the correlation of private attributes of users and certain product preferences is stronger, the more information about the user is available, there is the clear interest of platform business operators to dig for as much private user data as possible. Personalization, on the other hand, creates individual information spaces for users, by setting the information focus while excluding other information that is assumed to be of no interest to the user. These functions are basically in-transparent for users.

3.2.2 Industrial

Within the concept of digitization, the relevance of data for the industry, in particular manufacturing, lies in the optimization of processes, where optimization includes both the automization, especially machine-to-machine linking, and flexibilization, in essence on demand production. Control of these processes requires high quality of data in terms of reliability and precision. Sensors must provide data with adequate precision, and the communication with actuators has to be robust and reliable. This calls for high functional quality of the technical devices applied, including software as in AI systems. In the context of connected processes between different sites or enterprises, privacy and sovereignty of data becomes an issue of conflicting interest, as it is a competitive element in general and, in particular, can have significant value as potential input to machine learning in AI applications.

3.2.3 Public

The public sphere, where public administration plays the leading role, comprises the control of traffic on land, air and water, the organization of public services including democratic procedures, and the societal aspects of security and safety. Apparently, constitutional principles and government practices differ to a large extent between nations. So does the availability of private data in established administrative structures and the collection of such data by surveillance of public and private life. AI applications like facial recognition, automated traffic surveillance and control or personalized political influencing mechanisms can be very powerful means of effective governance. And they are the more powerful in realizing the potentials in these areas, if they are implemented on a massive scale, and intrude the private sphere of citizens deeply. Data privacy then tends to dissolve in favour of data quality.

3.2.4 Scientific

Science, as mentioned in Sect. 2 above, is founded in agreed methodological principles that are bound to guarantee validity of insights in a general sense, invariant to specific settings or a select empirical base. Nevertheless, many hypotheses in science are initially generated from empirical data and then made subject to methodological investigation aiming at epistemically valid results. AI can definitely be a worthwhile source for the detection of data patterns that allow for the formulation of research hypotheses. Their relevance must be expected to depend on the quality of input data. Hence the need for high quality of data on the one hand. On the other hand, the worth of input data ideally is independent from its being anonymous or attributed to personal or private features. The latter holds true even if data used for scientific purposes in this sense may be most private, personal data, as is the case e.g. in medicine or the health sector. Car et al. [2] investigated examples of the use of big data studies to stimulate medical research. They concluded taking a positive position, while remaining concerned about ethical issues like interference with data privacy.

4 Data Privacy, Ethics and Regulation

The utilization of massive data affects both data privacy, the origin of data, and data sovereignty, the control of data. These are subject to a wide discourse addressing the tension between individual rights and economic (or public) interest. Not surprisingly, there is no globally agreed concept of their balancing. Moreover, even the assessment of risks and chances are disputed, although it is clear the potential impact of the novel technology AI will not be constrained regionally but have its effects globally. The lines of conflict appear similar to those showing up in other fields, like genomics and bioengineering, or climate change and action, to name two prominent ones only. The question therefore is how to approach this dilemma adequately.

Europe, more precisely the EU, have chosen to develop their position from start on by taking into consideration ethical principles, societal values, and regulative means. The High Level Expert Group on AI, set in charge by the European Commission, elaborated on Ethical Guidelines for Trustworthy AI and presented their final report early 2019 [6]. Therein four principles are stated which developers, deployers, users, and regulators should follow in order to uphold the purpose of human-centric and trustworthy AI. These are the principles of respect for human autonomy, prevention of harm, fairness, and explicability [6, page 12 ff]. They are intended to build an ethical fundament for AI that is aimed to guarantee this new technological field to be trustworthy. Like the Oviedo Convention for the Protection of Human Rights and Dignity in the Biomedical field, the ethical guidelines for AI are an ambitious attempt to set limits to what shall be done in research (and development) into a technology which is bound to entail transformations of potentially deep impact to human lives and societal constituencies.

While it is far from being likely that these guidelines will become globally accepted easily, they contribute to the debate about ethics and regulation of AI as opposed to innovation and competitiveness. Consensus is that regulation is contrafactual to innovation. The question comes down to how far regulation goes. The central problem, that of the balance between regulation and innovation in AI, appears to be one of different perspectives, the economic versus the societal one. This is similar to a problem discussed in [17] on the subject of organ donation. The issue there in the context of organ allocation for transplantation is that of fundamentally diverging perspectives which make a specific question unresolvable in a general sense. The argument is that instead of trying to force obligatory political decision, it is more promising to organize an institutionalized permanent ethical reflection on the subject under consideration. Taking such an approach and transferring it to the problem of balancing regulation and innovation in the field of AI offers a way how to deal with the fundamental perspective differences here. Floridi [3] suggests a likewise approach when he distinguishes soft and hard ethics, putting focus on the implications of a soft ethical perspective.

With a view on the current state of AI in general, and of the utilization of private data in particular, one can expect these issues to remain disputed. Nevertheless, need is there to set standards proactively in order to ensure the basic principles of human autonomy and the prevention of harm will be kept (cf. Floridi [3], and the comprehensive discussion by Morley et al. regarding the health sector in [16]). Having put in place the General Data Protection Regulation GDPR, Europe took such an important step after a long public debate. As AI technology evolves, adjustments may follow. These should well be addressing various spheres by different levels of regulation, taking into account considerations like those made in Sect. 3 above.

5 Organizing the Collection and Protection of Private Data

The relevance of massive data for AI applications is uncontested. E.g. platform businesses realize a major part of their value creation by collecting data from their users and analyzing these with respect to individual preferences. These can be used for commercial purposes like personalized advertising, but also for other ways of influencing individual behaviour or opinion. Facial recognition, another example, produces more reliable results, the larger the quantity of data in the experience base is. The nature of these data is private, their collection and utilization interfere with data privacy. These are examples from the commercial resp. public sphere, where probabilistic results generated by AI algorithms in general are sufficient. Hence these spheres allow for lower data quality without having to accept low validity of the results.

In the industrial or scientific sphere, the need for highly reliable data is much more relevant. This is immediately evident for applications regarding the autonomous car which are frequently subsumed to AI. A number of examples in the recent past have revealed the consequences of deficient input data, which caused fatal dysfunctionalities, affected severely the acceptance of these applications in the public opinion, and had significant impact on the economic assessment of R&D in this sector. Science, as is easy to understand, needs even higher quality of data as useful input e.g. to systems in the medical, pharmaceutical, or, generally, the health sector. For these spheres, in most cases it is feasible to use anonymous input data, what keeps the interference with data privacy on a low level.

Exhibit 3 depicts the localization of the data spheres of AI we take into view according to the respective levels of interference with data privacy and the quality of data, as exemplified. Resuming what has been considered in Sects. 2, 3 and 4 above allows to suggest a twofold approach to the way the collection and protection of input data for AI can be organized.

The basic principle to guide the privacy of data is human dignity, one of the fundamental rights of humans as laid down in the declaration of human rights, reflected in the German constitution as the right of informational self-control, and on European level in the GDPR. Extended and broadly elaborated, it has been incorporated into the Ethical Guidelines [6], which are the source of the Policy and Investment Recommendations for Trustworthy AI [7]. Beyond the regulative ruling following the GDPR in Europe, and further to encryption methods used to protect data (for a medical sector

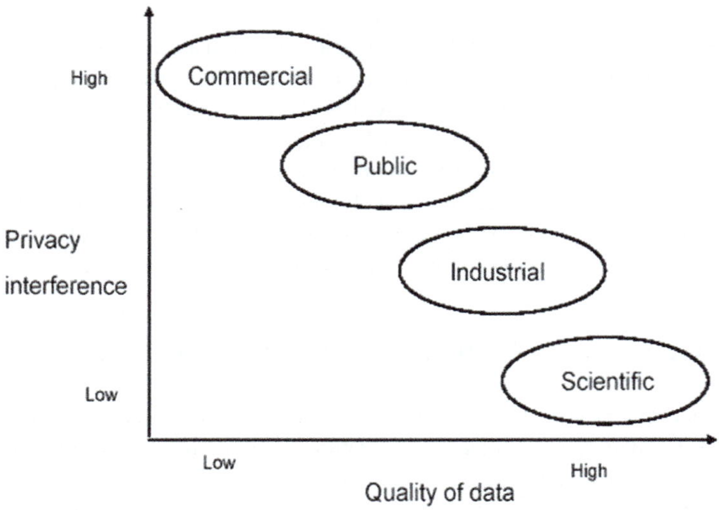

Exhibit. 3. Level of data quality and privacy interference in different AI spheres

focused suggestion cf. [20]), for the organization of the collection of data there are two major concepts currently discussed: blockchain based distributed ledger technology, and (industrial) open data spaces.

A blockchain concept for the health sector has been proposed by Koscina et al. [14]. Within the architecture they develop, it is the health care institutions that hold blockchain contracts which control shared data and make it traceable. One could consider extending such a concept even to the commercial or public sphere, however, it is far from being realistic this point in time to see private users become blockchain contractors in a distributed data sharing system. The, from a privacy point of view, ideal situation of keeping individuals in full control of their private data under the blockchain concept thus seems out of sight for the time being. Furthermore, even a concept like this has restrictions to data protection, as it is subject to the considerations presented by Hittmeyer et al. [8] on the possibility of identity disclosure by powerful analyses of individual attributes from synthetic data.

For the industrial, but also for the scientific sector, the concept of shared (industrial) data spaces (or multi-sided platforms) offers a promising approach that is put into focus by several initiatives in Europe. The idea is to create open data systems that are made accessible for third parties within an alliance for commercial or scientific use. Bohlen et al. [1] present a respective position paper of the IDS association, describing their approach to an Open Data Ecosystem where trust and security are realized based upon a certification concept. Otto and Jarke [18] provided a resume of the findings from a case study in the IDS association with regard to the design of a multi-sided platform for data sharing. There are various similar initiatives on European level (European Data Space) or in an industry specific setting, for example for the automotive sector. Initiatives like these are intended to make high quality data available by adhering to the limitations data privacy principles and respective regulation may impose.

6 Conclusion

The need for data privacy is undeniable, as human dignity and individual autonomy are most basic principles of human rights. Individual freedom, furthermore, is an acknowledged source of innovative progress, not only, but also in economic context. With regard to the novel technologies expected to evolve under the label Artificial Intelligence, the utilization of massive data provides a second source of innovation, the value of which becomes higher, the better their quality is. However, privacy and quality of data tend to be in mutual conflict. This calls for prudent balancing of these two aspects of the utilization of massive data.

In order to enable this balancing, we distinguish various data spheres that let show different levels of privacy interference and quality of data. The purpose is to tailor adequate governance of data protection for each of the spheres of commercial, public, industrial, and scientific data utilization. Exhibit 2 illustrates our first order approach to a useful specification of data spheres, while Exhibit 3 suggests a reasonable assessment of these spheres according to the level of data privacy interference and data quality.

We have made explicit the fundamental principles of ethics, the regulation as it is in place in Europe or being discussed elsewhere, and currently pursued concepts of data privacy protection. On this background we argue for the governance of protection and usability of private data to be adjusted to different fields of AI application (thus taking up economic and scientific motivation), and to be dynamically adapted as AI research and development progresses.

References

1. Bohlen, V., Bruns, L., Menz, N., Kirstein, F., Schimmler, S.: Open Data Spaces – Towards the IDS Open Data. Fraunhofer Institute FOKUS (2018). https://www.internationaldataspaces.org/wp-content/uploads/2019/07/Open-Data-Spaces-IDSA.pdf. Accessed 02 Feb 2020
2. Car, J., et al: Beyond the hype of big data and artificial intelligence: building foundations for knowledge and wisdom. BMC Med. **17**, 143 (2019). https://doi.org/10.1186/s12916-019-1382-x
3. Floridi, L.: Soft ethics, the governance of the digital and the general data protection regulation. Phil. Trans. R. Soc. A **376**, 20180081 (2018). http://dx.doi.org/10.1098/rsta.2018.0081
4. Floridi, L., Taddeo, M.: What is data ethics? Phil. Trans. R. Soc. A **374**, 20160360 (2016). http://dx.doi.org/10.1098/rsta.2016.0360
5. High Level Expert Group on Artificial Intelligence (AI HLEG): A definition of AI: Main capabilities and scientific disciplines. European Commission, Brussels (2018)
6. High Level Expert Group on Artificial Intelligence (AI HLEG): Ethics Guidelines for Trustworthy AI. European Commission, Brussels (2019)
7. High Level Expert Group on Artificial Intelligence (AI HLEG): Policy and Investment Recommendations for Trustworthy AI. European Commission, Brussels (2019)
8. Hittmeyer, M., Mayer, R., Ekelhart, A.: A baseline for attribute disclosure risk in synthetic data. In: Proceedings of the Tenth ACM Conference on Data and Application Security and Privacy (CODASPY 2020), New Orleans, LA, USA, 16–18 March 2020. ACM, New York (2020). 11 pages . https://doi.org/10.1145/3374664.3375722

9. Jastroch, N., Neumann, M.: Innovation im wissensintensiven Umfeld. In: LNI, vol. 35, pp. 351–358 (2003)
10. Jastroch, N.: Wissensmanagement – Darstellung und Transfer von Wissen – Potenziale und Grenzen. In: GI Lecture Notes in Informatics, Bonn, vol. P-28 (2003). http://CEUR-WS.org/Vol-85/
11. Jastroch, N.: Advancing adaptivity in enterprise collaboration. J. Syst. Cybern. Inform. JSCI **7**(6), 7–11 (2009)
12. Körner, K., Schattenberg, M., Heymann, E.: Digitale Wirtschaft - Wie künstliche Intelligenz und Robotik unsere Arbeit und unser Leben verändern. DB Research (2018). https://www.dbresearch.de/MAIL/RPS_DE-PROD/PROD0000000000468838.pdf. Accessed 02 Feb 2020
13. Körner, K.: Digitalpolitik – KI, Big Data und die Zukunft der Demokratie. DB Research (2019). https://www.dbresearch.de/MAIL/RPS_DE-PROD/PROD0000000000499444.pdf. Accessed 02 Feb 2020
14. Koscina, M., Manset, D., Negri, C., Perez Kempner, O.: Enabling trust in healthcare data exchange with a federated blockchainbased architecture. In: IEEE/WIC/ACM International Conference on Web Intelligence (WI 2019 Companion), Thessaloniki, Greece, 14–17 October 2019. ACM, New York (2019). 7 pages. https://doi.org/10.1145/3358695.3360897
15. Morley, J., Floridi, L.: An ethically mindful approach to AI for health care, vol. 395. 25 January (2020). www.thelancet.com
16. Morley, J., et al.: The Debate on the Ethics of AI in Health Care: a Reconstruction and Critical Review (2019). https://digitalethicslab.oii.ox.ac.uk/wp-content/uploads/sites/87/2019/11/The-Debate-on-the-EThics-of-AI-in-Health-Care-pre-print-.pdf
17. Nassehi, A., et al: The strength of weak procedures. Zeitschrift fuer Soziologie **48**(3) (2019). https://doi.org/10.1515/zfsoz-2019-0015
18. Otto, B., Jarke, M.: Designing a multi-sided data platform: findings from the international data spaces case. Electron. Mark. **29**(4), 561–580 (2019). https://doi.org/10.1007/s12525-019-00362-x
19. Thoben, K.-D., Wiesner, S., Wuest, T.: "Industrie 4.0" and smart manufacturing. a review of research issues and application examples. Int. J. Autom. Technol. **11**(1), 4–16 (2017)
20. Vitiziu, A. et al.: Privacy-preserving artificial intelligence: application to precision medicine. conference. In: Proceedings of the 41st Annual International Conference of the IEEE Engineering in Medicine & Biology Society (EMBC), pp. 6498–6504 (2019). https://doi.org/10.1109/embc.2019.8857960
21. Wellsandt, S., Thoben, K-D., Klein, P.: Information feedback in product development: analysing practical cases. In: International Design Conference - DESIGN 2018 (2018). https://doi.org/10.21278/idc.2018.0379
22. Wuest, T., Wellsandt, S., Thoben, K.-D.: Information quality in PLM: a production process perspective. In: Bouras, A., Eynard, B., Foufou, S., Thoben, K.-D. (eds.) PLM 2015. IAICT, vol. 467, pp. 826–834. Springer, Cham (2016). https://doi.org/10.1007/978-3-319-33111-9_75

Real-Time Detection of Eating Activity in Elderly People with Dementia Using Face Alignment and Facial Landmarks

Mhamed Nour[1](✉), Mickaël Gardoni[2], Jean Renaud[2], and Serge Gauthier[3]

[1] Laboratoire NUMERIX, Département du Génie de la Production Automatisée, GPA, ETS, Montréal, Canada
mhamed.nour.1@ens.etsmtl.ca
[2] Professeur associé au département du Génie de la Production Automatisée, GPA, ETS, Montréal, Canada
[3] Research Centre for Studies in Aging, Professeur au McGill University, Montréal, Canada

Abstract. The aim of this research is to automatically detect the intake of meals for elderly people with dementia living alone by using the product lifecycle management concepts (PLM). We use it to create a service based on an Artificial Intelligence product which will reduce the need for a caregiver or a person as medical support, hence less travel (Co2, etc.), less time spent by a third party on a verification/monitoring task, greater autonomy and therefore improve quality of life. Thus, overall, for society, this service based on an AI product is a win-win approach for pollution and an increase in the value of the tasks of the caregiver and the person as a medical support.

The choice of appropriate AI assistive technology was done to satisfy both the elderly people with neurodegenerative disorders and the caregiver, to verify the ethical aspect, simplify design, optimize code and improve user friendly aspects. During all this process of design of the new service based on an AI product, the PLM concepts were fruitfully applied by involving the different experts concerned (medical, ethical, technological, etc.) and taking into account all the characteristics of the environment of the product from the beginning to the end

Keywords: Automatic detection · Human activity · Eating detection · Neurodegenerative disorders · Assistive technology

1 Introduction

Dementia and its related diseases strike very strongly [1]. With alarming statistics and a lack of curative and preventive solutions to date. However, the non-mediated approach improves patients' quality of life by allowing them to regain more autonomy, memory, etc. and thus to delay the progression of the symptoms of the disease.

The current challenge in treating patients with mental disabilities is whether the patient has eaten perfectly, especially if the patient lives alone. Another challenge is when assistance techniques to identify eating without ethical conflict, using these

Published by Springer Nature Switzerland AG 2020
F. Nyffenegger et al. (Eds.): PLM 2020, IFIP AICT 594, pp. 671–679, 2020.
https://doi.org/10.1007/978-3-030-62807-9_53

assisting technologies, how could one influence the person being followed to induce them to stop eating or encourage him to eat.

Recognizing human activities from video footage using assistive technology is a difficult task due to problems, such as background clutter, partial occlusion, scale changes, point of sight, lighting and appearance and accompanying noise. Many applications, including patient video monitoring systems, require a multiple activity recognition system.

In this article, we provide a detailed review of recent progress in research in the area of human activity classification [2–6]. Then include the ethical aspect in the classification because the majority of current proposals for recognition of activities are carried out only in laboratories.

The aim is to develop an automatic real-time meal-taking detection project in elderly people with early dementia living alone to ensure that they eat their meals normally. Our work will be distinguished by the practical application of the ethical aspect that will surely reduce the options but with a practical realization, will be better suited as a solution to the detection of meal-taking in patients at the beginning of dementia because there will be no object attached to the patients and with a respect of the autonomy and privacy of the patient.

2 Artificial Intelligence Modeling

Eating Activity Detection is part of the Human activity recognition (HAR) which aims [7] to recognize activities from a series of observations on the actions of subjects and the environmental conditions. The vision-based HAR research is the basis of many applications including video surveillance, health care, and human-computer interaction (HCI).

The challenges of the HAR domain are:

- the intraclass variation and interclass similarity,
- the recognition under real-world settings:
  - complex and various backgrounds.
  - multisubject interactions and group activities.

The paper reviews a list of papers in the Domain. They don't take into account the ethical aspect of the assistive technology utilization and the respect the patient privacy.

The objective of this paper is the provide an approach for the Eating activity detection using assistive technology without the violation of the ethical aspect.

2.1 Assistive Technology for Person with Dementia Review and Ethical Related Issues

Paper [8] lists a series of AT methods to detect eating activity but all of them are still at the testing level in the LAB and they don't take into account the ethical aspect. The following are methods to detect eating using Assistive technology:

- Dietary Assessment Methods include food frequency questionnaires with limitations: forget, underestimate or overestimate portion sizes
- Automated Dietary Monitoring includes oral sensors, wearable systems, on-body sensing approaches, crowdsourcing techniques, neckband wearable.
- Sensing with Objects, places and Artifacts include dining table, smart surface table, camera on dining ceiling light, sensor-embedded fork & interface mobile applications.
- Acoustic Sensing for Eating Detection include sound detection, bathroom sounds recorded with microphone.
- Recognizing Eating with On-body Inertial Sensing include small wearable accelerometers and gyroscope.
- Identifying Daily Routines and Patterns include the collection of data of many mobile phones over certain period on time.
- Techniques for Estimating Ground Truth in Real World Settings include the use of statistical machine learning for interference & modeling.

The objective of this paper is to use an assistive technology that respect the ethical aspect of the patient.

2.2 Artificial Intelligence and Machine Learning

Human activity recognition is a challenging problem [9] given the large number of observations produced each second, and the lack of a clear way to relate accelerometer data to known movements. Deep learning methods such as recurrent neural networks and one-dimensional convolutional neural networks or CNNs have been shown to provide state-of-the-art results on challenging activity recognition tasks with little or no data feature engineering.

The following steps have been followed in order to build our Deep learning eating detection Model:

Step 1—Data Pre-processing
Step 2—Separating Your Training and Testing Datasets
Step 3—Transforming the Data
Step 4—Building the Artificial Neural Network
Step 5—Running Predictions on the Test Set
Step 6—Checking the Confusion Matrix
Step 7—Making a Single Prediction
Step 8—Improving the Model Accuracy
Step 9—Adding Dropout Regularization to Fight Over-Fitting
Step 10—Hyperparameter Tuning

2.3 Product Lifecycle Management Concepts

Product lifecycle management (PLM) [10] is the process of managing the entire lifecycle of a product from its conception, through design and manufacture, to service, and disposal. PLM integrates people, data, processes, and business systems and provides a product information backbone for companies and their extended enterprise. It can be represented as shown in Fig. 1.

The conception of the Eating Activity Detection product is using the following steps of the PLM steps (Fig. 1) to build our solution (building a prototype that grow up with the time):

- Manage and Collaborate during the whole project.
- Plan (Innovate and Specify the technology to be used for this project)
- Define (Develop and Validate the application)
- Build (Produce and Deliver. In the testing steps now.)
- Support (Service and Sustain)

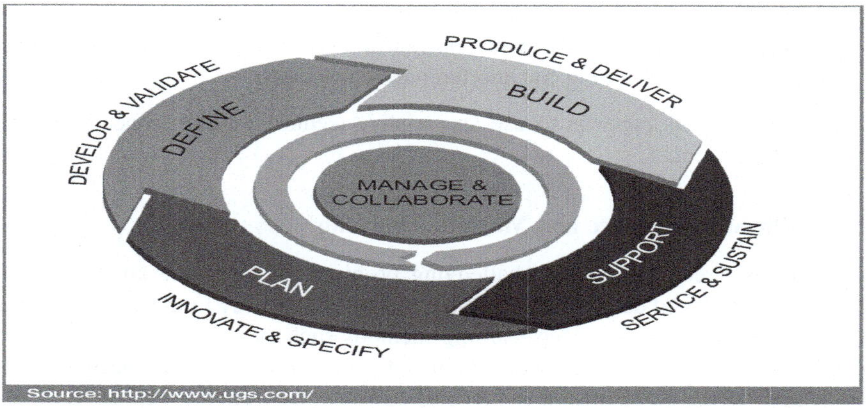

Fig. 1. The PLM processes

3 Artificial Intelligence Modeling of the Real-Time Eating Activity Detection

TensorFlow is an open-source software library for machine learning. It works efficiently with computation involving arrays; so, it's a great choice for the model. Furthermore, TensorFlow allows for the execution of code on either CPU or GPU, which is a useful feature especially when you're working with a massive dataset.

3.1 Facial Landmarks Detection

Facial landmarks [11] are used to localize and represent salient regions of the face, such as: Eyes, Eyebrows, Nose, Mouth, Jawline. Facial landmarks have been successfully applied to face alignment, head pose estimation, face swapping, blink detection and much more.

The shape predictor algorithm [11] implemented in the dlib library comes from Kazemi and Sullivan's 2014 CVPR paper, The paper (Algo) addresses the problem of Face Alignment for a single image. The paper shows an ensemble of regression trees can be used to estimate the face's landmark positions directly from a sparse subset of pixel intensities, achieving super-Realtime performance with high quality predictions.

Our solution will use the facial landmarks detection to detection positions of the patient's face and store these positions in a database. In order to respect the patient's privacy, no pictures of the patients will be stored.

Figure 2 shows the Visualizing of the 68 facial landmark coordinates from the iBUG 300-W dataset. If the execution time of the solution is not acceptable, we may use another version of the facial landmarks that will use just for instance 5 facial landmark coordinates from the iBUG 300-W dataset.

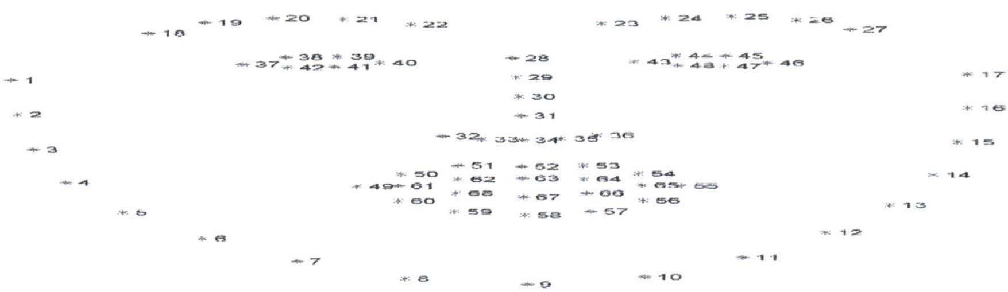

Fig. 2. Visualizing the 68 facial landmark coordinates from the iBUG 300-W dataset [11].

3.2 Face Alignment

In order to have accurate data while recording the positions of multiple points of the face, a new procedure has been added to align the face of the patient. The face alignment procedure will be used during the data collection to train the model and during the track procedure.

Figure 3 shows the original picture on the right and the aligned picture on the left, the two eyes are aligned.

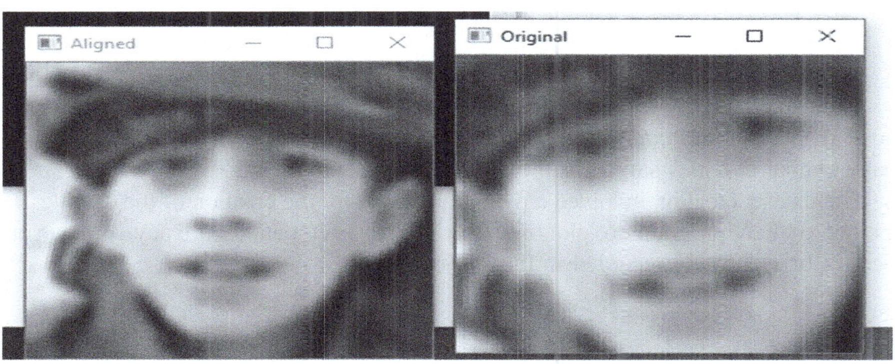

Fig. 3. Shows the aligned procedure of the picture.

3.3 Data Collection

Detecting the Jawlines and store their coordinate on csv files during the eating activity for many times. To verify the patient privacy, there is no video recording at all. For now, only two activities will be stored (eating and speaking), more activities will be added in the future. Figure 4 shows the corresponding plots of these eating activities.

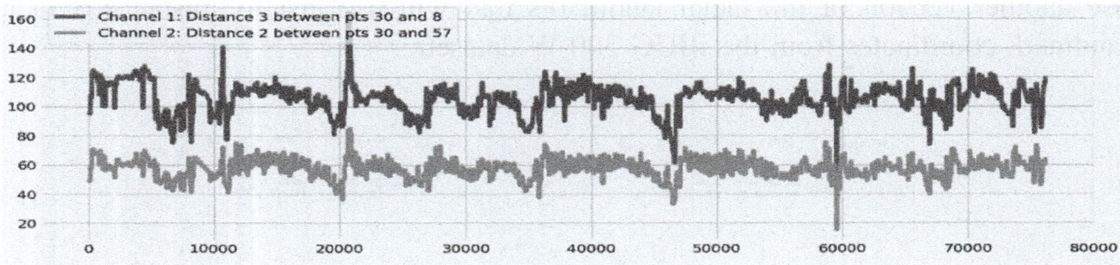

Fig. 4. The corresponding plots of these eating activities.

In order to distinguish between eating and speaking, we will record these two profiles and train the model to distinguish them. Figure 5 shows the patterns of these two activities. These patterns are repeated for many times and recoded using a data collection script.

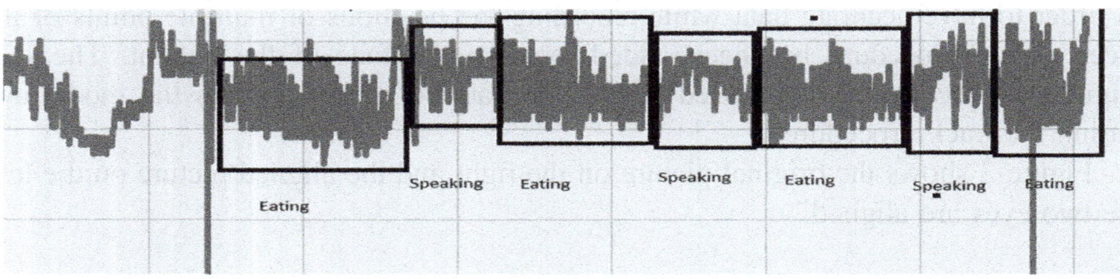

Fig. 5. The plots of these eating and speaking activities.

The eating activity form a specific pattern. Figure 6 Shows the Coordinates of the facial points and the content of the csv file created by the Python Script. There are many similar csv files saved for the data training process.

The dataset creation involved a python program for the creation of the csv files and another python program to plot the data. To respect patient privacy, no personal pictures or videos are recorded in this project.

	A	B	C
1	x_value	total_1	total_2
2			
3	1	99.08078	56.0803
4			
5	2	99.08078	56.0803

Fig. 6. Coordinates of the facial points and the content of the csv file created by the Python Script.

3.4 Data Training

Datasets (training data) has been created which involves collecting data and labeling it. Having a high-quality labeled data is the key to develop good ML solutions.

The goal of the training is to build a classifier to be able to distinguish between these types of HAR activities. The fast Fourier transform (FFT) was used to obtain frequency characteristics.

After running FFT on the data, the Principal Component Analysis (PCA) was used to reduce the number of dimensions.

The windows size was 40, the number of trials used for training was 30, the rest was used for validation, the number of the PCA Components was 25 and the number of dimensions in the IMU Data was 6.

Four classes have been defined for this project: classes = [‘Eating’, ‘Speaking’, ‘Smile’, ‘relaxing’].

The processed data becomes a set of 40-dimensional functionalities. An SVM (which is a Supervised Machine Learning algorithm) classifier was built using these feature sets in order to use an algorithm for classification. The SVM uses a kernel trick to transform data in order to found an optimal boundary between possible outputs.

The two models classifier.pkl and pca.pkl are the output of the train data program.

3.5 Real Time Activity Tracking

A qualified classifier was used to track activities in real time. Data is collected in real time and a classification program is run continuously every 10 s.

Figure 7 provides a live activity tracking with the above trained model and shows live tracking result. It also shows the position values, their diagram plots and eating activity detection.

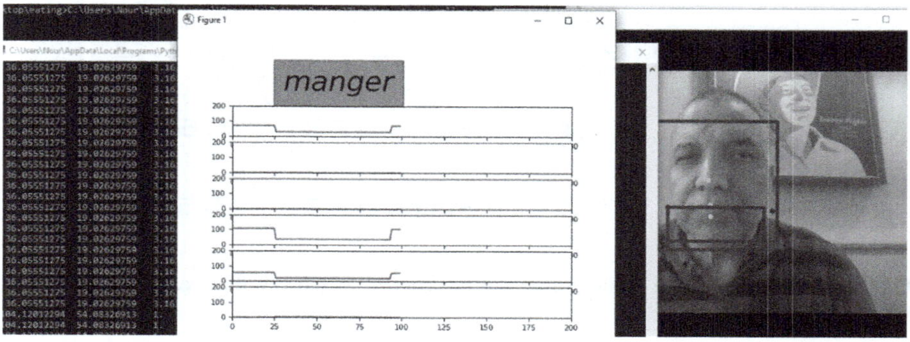

Fig. 7. Output of the track python script detecting eating activity.

3.6 Methodology Validation

A validation process is currently installed in order to evaluate the prototype. This process need improvement with a configuration of parallel programming to speed up the execution of the real-time tracking activity. Then a real-time evaluation process can be done taking into account the variability of the PCA components.

4 Conclusions and Future Works

This paper proposes a new approach for human activity detection specially the eating detection for elderly with data collection and tracking. At this stage optimizing performance and increasing classification accuracy is not the main goal of this project.

Most of the work in literature are still at the lab level and most of them use wiring assistive technology which may violate the ethical values of the patients. Our next step will be the optimization of the approach by adding a parallel computation.

References

1. Source Fondation pour la recherche médicale. https://www.frm.org/alzheimer/ampleur-maladie.html
2. https://www.pyimagesearch.com/2017/04/03/facial-landmarks-dlib-opencv-python/
3. One Millisecond Face Alignment with an Ensemble of Regression Trees Vahid Kazemi and Josephine Sullivan KTH, Royal Institute of Technology Computer Vision and Active Perception Lab Teknikringen 14, Stockholm, Sweden
4. Real Time Activity Recognition with accelerometer and gyroscope sensor (MYO). https://medium.com/softmind-engineering/real-time-activity-recognition-with-accelerometer-and-gyroscope-sensor-myo-663cda8536e6
5. https://github.com/hiukim/myo-activity-track?files=1
6. Bennett, B., et al.: Assistive technologies for people with dementia: ethical considerations. Bull. World Health Organ. **95**, 749–755 (2017). http://dx.doi.org/10.2471/BLT.16.187484

7. Zhang, S., Wei, Z., Nie, J., Huang, L., Wang, S., Li, Z.: A review on human activity recognition using vision-based method. J. Healthc. Eng. **2017**. https://doi.org/10.1155/2017/3090343. Article ID 3090343, 31 pages
8. Vu, T., Lin, F., Alshurafa, N., Xu, W.: Wearable food intake monitoring technologies, a comprehensive review. Computers **6**, 4 (2017). https://doi.org/10.3390/computers6010004
9. https://www.digitalocean.com/community/tutorials/how-to-build-a-deep-learning-model-to-predict-employee-retention-using-keras-and-tensorflow
10. Javvadi, L.: Product life cycle management an introduction. https://www.researchgate.net/publication/285769844

Participative Method to Identify Data-Driven Design Use Cases

Simon Rädler and Eugen Rigger(✉)

V-Research GmbH, Dornbirn, Austria
{simon.raedler,eugen.rigger}@v-research.at

Abstract. Paradigms such as smart factory and industry 4.0 enable the collection of data in enterprises. To enhance decision making in design, computational support that is driven by data seems to be beneficial. With this respect, an identification of data-driven use cases is needed. Still, the state of practice does not reflect the potential of data-driven design in engineering product development. With this respect, a method is proposed addressing the business and data understanding in industrial contexts and corresponding Product Lifecycle Management (PLM) environments. This allows to identify use cases for data-driven design taking into account business processes as well as the related data. In the proposed method, first the main process tasks are analyzed using a SIPOC analysis that is followed by a process decomposition to further detail and highlight corresponding applications using Enterprise Architecture principles. Following this, value stream mapping and design process failure mode effect analysis are used to identify sources of waste and the related causes. With this, a feature analysis of given data is proposed to identify use cases and enable to further use standard data science methods like CRISP-DM. The method is validated using the infrastructure of the Pilotfabrik at TU Vienna. The use case shows the applicability of the method to identify features that influence the cost of a product during the manufacturing without changing the functional specifications. The results highlight that different methods need to be combined to attain a comprehensive business and data understanding. Further, a comprehensive view of the processes is yielded that enables to further identify use cases for data-driven design. This work lays a foundation for future research with respect to data-driven design use cases identification in engineering product development.

Keywords: Data-driven-design · PLM · Enterprise architecture · ArchiMate · SysML

This work has been partially supported and funded by the Austrian Research Promotion Agency (FFG) via the "Austrian Competence Center for Digital Production" (CDP) under the contract number 854187.

Published by Springer Nature Switzerland AG 2020
F. Nyffenegger et al. (Eds.): PLM 2020, IFIP AICT 594, pp. 680–694, 2020.
https://doi.org/10.1007/978-3-030-62807-9_54

1 Introduction

Approximately 70% of the product costs are determined during the design stage, making it crucial to come to informed decisions at this stage of product development [2,9,10]. In this respect, the use of computational methods and tools has shown to be an enabler to increase design performance [14] regarding efficiency and effectiveness of product development [29,33]. Nevertheless, state of practice still does not reflect the opportunities computational methods provide in the early stages of engineering design [28]. Still, recent trends such as Industry 4.0 [1,23,24] push enterprises towards implementation of smart factories that enable collection of data from Industrial Internet of Things (IIoT) [12] devices during the manufacturing process [7]. Furthermore, the advancement of mechanical engineering products towards smart cyber physical systems [37] due to the integration of IoT (Internet of Things) technologies provides information about the usage and status of a product in use [20]. The resulting sets of data from IIoT and IoT can be considered relevant data from the product lifecycle and can be used as an enabler for data-driven technologies in the design stage such as data-driven design. Data-driven refers to the application of computational methods that support decision-making in design based on data instead of intuition [5]. Hence, applications of data-driven design can rely on previous design revisions and related PLM data or other designs that feature similar characteristics. However, there is a lack of methods supporting the identification and formalization of use cases for data-driven design in the context of established product lifecycle management (PLM) strategies [32].

In response to this need, this work presents a method that enables the identification and formalization of data-driven design use cases in engineering companies based on participative workshops with the designers to analyze engineering processes and its supporting technological environments. It builds upon a PLM process decomposition by using Enterprise Architecture methods [4] tool and applies lean engineering methods for design process analysis [22]. In order to contextualize data artefacts with design features, a detailed analysis of the systems and data features is performed based on the Systems Modelling Language (SysML) [35]. The method is validated with a case study focusing on design and manufacturing of chess figures like in Fig. 1 using the infrastructure of the Pilotfabrik [15]. This paper is structured as follows: Sect. 2 analyzes the related literature with respect to existing case studies for data-driven design, methodologies to derive requirements for data mining and finally highlight research gaps in a summary. Section 3 proposes the new method which is evaluated in Sect. 4. Finally, a critical discussion with respect to validation and limitations is given which is finalized in Sect. 6 that highlights the conclusion and future work.

2 Background

In the following subsections, recent case studies with respect to data-driven design are reviewed. Following this, the state of the art for methodologies to enable data-driven applications in engineering companies is analyzed. Next, an overview of modelling languages is given in order to support process and data mining. Finally, the state of the art is summarized and research gaps are highlighted.

2.1 Case Studies for Data-Driven Applications

Fig. 1. 3D Model of a bishop chess figure

Recent scientific publications show different use cases according to the use of data-driven design with different level of details. The use cases comprise reports from variable selection over knowledge acquisition to decision modelling techniques. The data-driven design use case given in [18] shows a study that uses parameterized numerical simulation models and surrogate models to enable optimization based on a genetic algorithm. Since this approach not suggest a variable selection approach, the selection use case study of [17] is applicable. Here, all available high speed train design variables are analyzed each with respect to the relative importance based on previous engineering designers knowledge. For a more systematic approach to acquire the knowledge of a designer and formalize it for an impact estimation, [42] proposes to use focus groups studies. If the domain expert assignment of influence variables is not sufficient enough, an indication- and pattern-based method could be additionally used [13]. Since the data amount grows through the design process and data is rare at initial design steps, [21] recommends to start data-driven approaches in later design stages caused by the transformation from knowledge to data during the design process. The proposed framework support to numeralize different types of available variables and derive a decision tree based on subjective knowledge and previous data. As well, [8] suggests to build a decision tree based on geometrical behaviour to define the design space and reduce the complexity. The resulting decision tree builds a basis for rule based design tool support. A similar approach is given by [30], which focuses on minimizing the influence of uncontrollable (noise) variables. Here, a meta-heuristic is used to optimize the controllable variables to minimize the influence of the noise ones. The literature shows that case studies have been realized indicating the potential of data-driven design methods. However, these studies lack by using methodologies driving decisions with respect to data-driven design use cases, selection of data and traceability. Further, there is a lack of systematic evaluation of data-driven approaches in industrial practice based on metrics/key performance indicators.

2.2 State of the Art for a Data-Driven Methodology

An open standard process for data mining is Cross-industry standard process for data mining, known as CRISP-DM [40] is shown in Fig. 2. The methodology guides data mining project in industrial projects from the business understanding until the implementation of an application. More specifically tailored towards

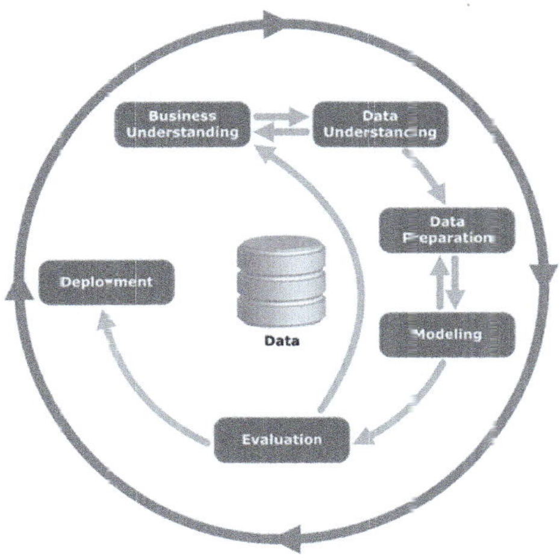

Fig. 2. CRISP-DM standard process [27]

data science in the context of digital factories, the DMME builds an extension to CRISP-DM and proposes methods for data acquisition to detail the understanding of how machine, material, tools and product properties are related. Thereby, focus is put on identification and interrelation of different sources of data, e.g. sensor and machining data [16,39]. A similar approach for the usage of data from manufacturing can be found in [31]. The methodology proposes to use a failure mode analysis combined with a quality function deployment to preselect influencing variables. However, the methodologies support on some points for data science projects while a comprehensive methodology for engineering design considering PLM, data back propagation and different types of sources is missing.

2.3 Modelling Languages

With respect to the process of CRISP-DM, business structure and processes needs to be collected to increase the business understanding. According to literature, enterprise architecture (EA) seems to be beneficial [19,34]. One of the main advantages of EA is the visual interrelation between the business and the application layer. However, the benefit of EA models is given, but a detail level selection is needed to reduce the amount of elements that needs to be drawn.

In order to model systems in the context of software applications, Systems Modeling Language (SysML) is widely used [35]. SysML is defined as an extension for Unified Modeling Language (UML) which is also an project by the object management group (OMG) [11]. One of the aims of SysML is to support the communication between interdisciplinary workers. Additionally, diagrams like the data-flow diagram supports in a validation process whether all needed interfaces are implemented.

2.4 Summary

The review of related literature shows that use cases are investigated for data-driven design applications in industrial contexts. However, the reviewed works do not highlight the applied methodology pursued for development of the use case. Hence, the presented use cases of data-driven design are difficult to trace and lack systematic evaluation of the potential in industrial contexts. In this respect, the application of methodologies to guide the integration and implementation of data-driven methods in design practice would lead to better comparability of published results and more comprehensive decision making in the evaluation of potential use cases for data-driven design. To reduce these shortcomings, this work further elaborates on the CRISP-DM methodology and refines it with respect to the details required for identification of use cases for data-driven design in established PLM environments. More specifically, focus is put on the formalization of the initial steps "business understanding" and "data understanding" of the CRISP-DM to provide the necessary context to comprehensively evaluate use cases for data-driven design. The refined steps apply methods stemming from enterprise architecture and systems engineering domains to leverage comprehensive analysis on both the (PLM) process as well as the system levels.

3 Method

In response to the needs highlighted in Sect. 2, this section proposes a participative method for identification of data-driven design use cases in engineering design while comprehensively taking the PLM into account with its technological environments as well as related data. The method builds upon the CRISP-DM methodology and extends its first two steps for business and data understanding as illustrated in Fig. 3 in order to make it applicable in an engineering design context.

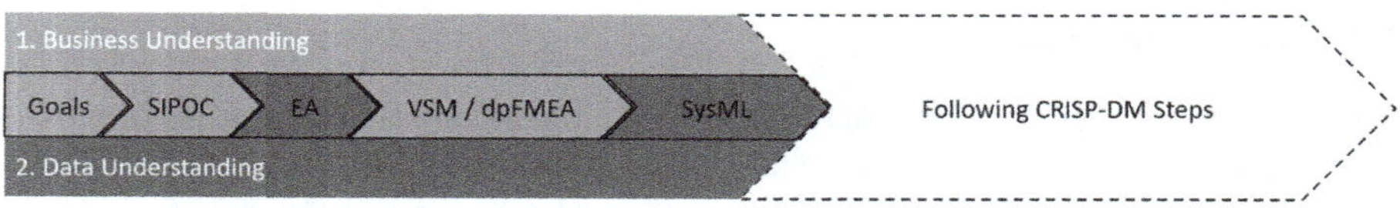

Fig. 3. Method embedding in the CRISP-DM methodology

According to the figure shown in Fig. 3, the definition of goals is proposed as a first step to establish a business understanding and formalize the needs for design performance improvement. Further, goals are building the basis for the subsequent steps of identification and evaluation of data-driven design use cases. Next, one or multiple SIPOC analysis need to be conducted within participative workshops to define the scope of the investigated aspects of PLM. The workshops are conducted with engineers, designers and a workshop leader who guides the re-engineering of the product lifecycle process steps and is familiar with the method that is presented in this paper. The yielded SIPOCS are then further refined using EA modelling to investigate the processes as well as the supporting technological environments and related data. Therefore, the relevant aspects of PLM can be comprehensively analyzed. In this respect, design process value stream mapping (VSM) [22] is applied to identify potential shortcomings that can be resolved using data-driven design, e.g. a lack of information back-flow. Additionally, design process failure mode effect analysis (dpFMEA) [6] is used to guide metrics derivation as proposed in [28]. Based on these sources of information, relevant data objects can be identified and contextualized with the initially identified goal. In particular, the SysML is used to link features of the data to the goals. Therefore, the necessary data understanding can be achieved which is required for the subsequent steps of the CRISP-DM methodology that address the mathematical modelling and identification of respective computational methods. In the following, the newly proposed steps are detailed.

3.1 Goals - Definition of Operative Goals

Once a system or a process to optimize is selected, a goal needs to be defined in order to guide the subsequent steps for identification of use cases for data-driven design. This is well aligned with existing approaches for metrics definition that state that goals need to be defined prior to selection of metrics and corresponding actions, e.g. the Goal-Question-Metric method [3]. Hence, goals can refer to specific design artefacts such as "improve lifetime of feature XY" or more generally to (parts of) the design process, e.g. "use less narrow tolerancing in detail design without losing functionality". Additionally, the desired goal specifies whether data-driven design can rely on previous design revisions and related PLM data or other designs that feature similar characteristics.

3.2 SIPOC

The second step comprises the identification of the processes that are related to the previously identified goal. More particularly, all aspects of the product lifecycle that impact or are impacted by the investigated design artefact/process need to be comprehensively assessed. To acquire the knowledge about the related processes, a Supplier-Input-Process-Output-Customer (SIPOC) [41] is applied within participative workshops with the related engineers to gain a high-level overview of the processes and define the scope of investigations. Graphical modelling is applied to enable direct validation of the generated models by the participants. The SIPOC process captures the process in three to five main tasks (P), the related input (I) and output data (O). The main suppliers (S) and recipients (C) are connected considering read and/or write access with the input/output data. Figure 4 shows a generic example process with two tasks structured according to the SIPOC schema. Depending on the formalized goals, multiple SIPOC analysis might be needed to capture all related processes of the product lifecycle.

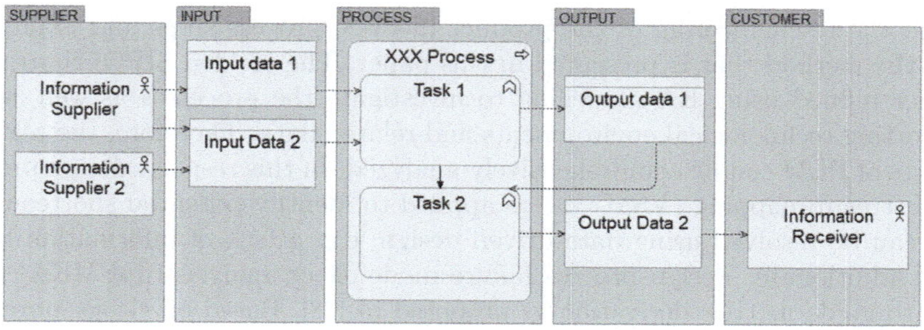

Fig. 4. SIPOC schema

3.3 EA - Detailed Process Modelling

The results from the SIPOC analysis are used as a basis to further detail the processes by decomposition of the tasks to yield single (design) activities [14]. In this respect, the ArchiMate modelling language [36] is applied to graphically model the specifics of the business processes, the related applications as well as the infrastructure including all the interrelations. The modelling expert guides the workshops by successive detailing of the main tasks from the SIPOC analysis based on a directed question-answer-talk. After modelling the design and business processes, the related applications are mapped to the activities. In particular, the main tasks are split up so to yield distinct design activities that are supported by a single application, e.g. "define initial 3D layout" that is supported by the CAD modelling application. Following this, the infrastructure needs to be modelled so that a comprehensive model of the enterprise architecture [19] is yielded. Particular focus is put on identification of data sources including its specific formats and accessibilities. Within this model, data artefacts and related tools can be directly contextualized with the business processes.

3.4 Value Stream Mapping/dpFMEA

To further strengthen the business understanding, information wastes are identified within the previously yielded model of the enterprise architecture using a design process value stream mapping [22]. Using a design process FMEA [6], effects and causes can be associated to the identified sources of information waste, e.g. redundant data generation that causes time to maintain and synchronize. This allows to derive related metrics [29] that can be used to validate the initially defined goal. In addition, the identified sources of waste permit to narrow down the amount of relevant data that needs to be investigated, e.g. when engineers identify unused information within artefacts.

3.5 SysML - Identification of Data Enabling Data-Driven Design

Based on the established business understanding and the yielded information about available data artefacts within the derived enterprise architecture model, relevant sources of data can be identified so to potentially enable data-driven design. In particular, data attributes are identified and visualized using SysML block-definition diagrams [35]. Dependencies within the data can be highlighted based on data dependency interrelations that are used to focus explicitly on semantic dependencies within data objects, e.g. depth of a drilling hole and length of the selected drill. These data interrelations are visualized by adding information flows using the SysML "Item flow" relationship to the block-definition diagram. This data analysis based on decomposition and association of data artefacts to goals yields a comprehensive view of relevant data attributes. Hence, the data understanding is established. After an SysML expert modelled the diagram, another participative workshop is conducted to double check the results and to complete the interrelations. With the yielded results, influencing data sources can be identified to build the basis for systematic implementation of data-driven design. Building upon these findings, methodologies like CRISP-DM can be followed to support data preparation, modelling etc.

4 Validation

In this section, the method validation is presented with a use case taking design and manufacturing of bishop chess figures into account. The case study is conducted at the Pilotfarik of the TU Vienna [15].

In the following, the results of each step are presented:

4.1 Goals - Definition of Operative Goals

The goal of the investigations for application of data-driven design is defined as to reduce the manufacturing time of a bishop chess figure during the turning process without changing its functional specifications or changing the chess figure shape. The desired data-driven design support has to affect the design attributes of a product and not the manufacturing parameters. Since the tolerance of a feature is not design specific, data is usable from other designs as well. Consequently, data is collected from multiple designs and revisions.

4.2 SIPOC

Since the Pilotfabrik corresponds to the prototype of a smart factory for demonstration scenarios, the supporting PLM processes such as the adaptive design process are not formalized. Hence, in this work, a generic design process according to [25] is assumed. Figure 5 indicates the corresponding SIPOC with In/Outputs and Suppliers and Customers as given in the context of the Pilotfabrik. The adaptive design process describes the optimization of an already existing design.

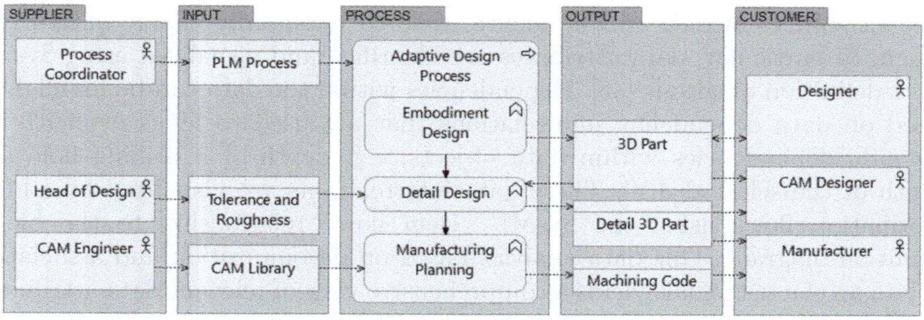

Fig. 5. SIPOC containing the main tasks of the adaptive design process

4.3 EA - Detailed Process Modelling

To accomplish a detail process model, first, a workshop was conducted visiting the shopfloor and analyzing the processes of a design expert. The main process tasks and the related tools were identified and the subjective worker view was modelled using a EA. Next, the process manager further detailed the EA model process tasks. The result of the two workshops yields in a EA model describing the current adaptive design process with the related application. Following this, the EA expert post processed the EA model with respect to readability and additionally annotated open questions, e.g. "Where is the CAD file stored?". Finally, a workshop was conducted to answer the identified questions and to double check the model correctness. Figure 6 shows a subsection of the yielded workshops results. It shows the main design process tasks with its relation to the used applications and corresponding manufacturing data. The identified applications are SolidWorks for CAD, HyperMill for CAM and Centurio.works for data logging and orchestration usin Business Process Model and Notation (BPMN) [26,38] (blue) which are both stored on the network drive (green).

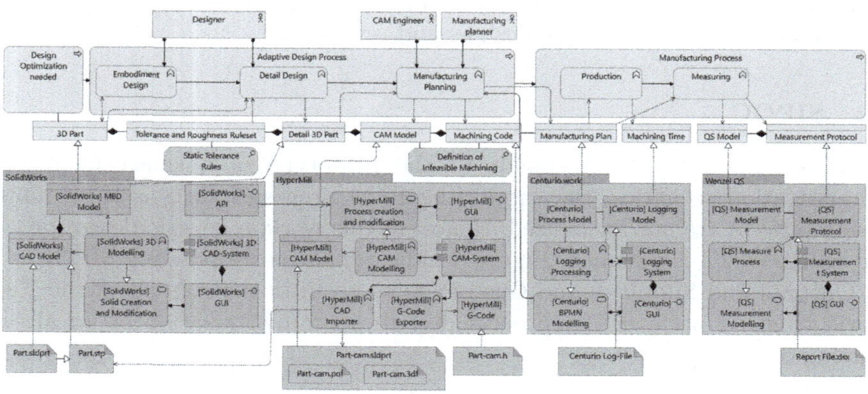

Fig. 6. Detail PLM process with respect to the SIPOCs (Color figure online)

4.4 Value Stream Mapping/dpFMEA

The EA expert, the design expert and the process manager participated in a workshop to identify sources of waste using a value stream mapping. With respect to this, the EA expert used to ask questions and guided the workshop to yield the result that is visualized (purple) in the EA model Fig. 6. Thus, a dpFMEA was conducted during the workshop to identify causes and effects. The method to acquire the causes and effects was equal to the value stream mapping method, based on a question-answer-talk.

The result of the workshop yields in two sources of waste. The details according to the cause and effects are visualized in Table 1.

Table 1. dpFMEA result to identify further method steps

Activity	Failure mode	Effects	Causes
Detailing the design	Static tolerance rules	Increase in cost caused by narrow tolerances or roughness, time waste caused by missing tolerance selection support, additional iterations because of not manufacturable tolerances	Lack of tool support for dynamic tolerance and roughness rules
CAM programming	Definition of infeasible machining code	Inefficient machining code, additional iterations on failing machining code, no tolerance evaluation according to manufacturability	Lack of tool support for NC Code simulation

4.5 SysML - Identification of Data Enabling Data-Driven Design

Based on the previous findings, the detail data understanding is improved during a analysis of data attributes. The findings of the dpFMEA is used to limit the amount of data objects from the EA process. The SysML model was created by analyzing the data object on a data format level by reviewing the API documentation of SolidWorks. The result was a comprehensive model on an attribute level without interrelations including possible redundancies. Next, a participative workshop was conducted to successively check attributes according to relevance and interrelations with other attributes. The result is presented in Fig. 7. The grey blocks are passive influencing the data-driven design. The yellow data block (dimension) is the object that mainly influences the desired data-driven design goal. The tolerance is influencing (red dashed arrow) the tool and corresponding turn feature specific parameters. The BPMN model and the QS model are both generated during the manufacturing task and are used for further implementation of the data-driven design support following further CRISP-DM steps.

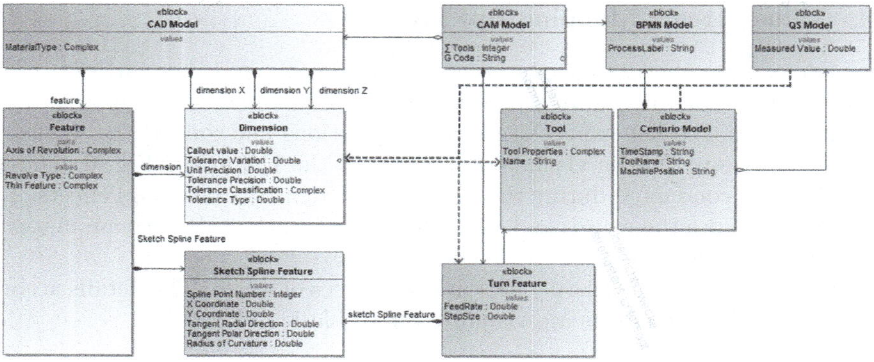

Fig. 7. System analysis to identify interrelations of feature (Color figure online)

5 Discussion

In this section the findings of this paper are discussed and assessed. The introduced method aims to be applicable in different engineering fields and validated based on a case study in the Pilotfabrik. The validation shows, that the method is valid for the identification and formalization of data-driven design use cases in mechanical engineering, more specific, with a turned part. The goal definition was beneficial to guide the participative workshops and sharpen the aim of the data-driven design approach. Additionally, a first idea of how the data-driven design use case might look like is given. The conducted SIPOC showed to be beneficial to share the business understanding between domain experts with different engineering background. During the workshops the graphical modelling of the main process tasks was helpful since all participants were able to follow the task modelling process and assess whether another process task is missing. Further, the EA modelling to create a more detailed view of the process and the related applications helped to introduce a first consolidated data understanding between the EA expert and the design expert. The question-answer-talk was useful to identify the detail tasks and related applications and the corresponding IT infrastructure. However, the modelling without EA templates caused difficulties in the level of detail which depends on the experience of the EA expert. The templates have to provide a generic process step with its corresponding application, functions and interface on the infrastructure level and a Information supplier and consumer on a business level. Next, the model proved to be a solid basis for the subsequent design process value stream mapping. The participants were able to identify information waste based on the diagram without further details that proved the aim of the EA model to increase the data understanding. Further, the dpFMEA was used to identify effects and causes with respect to the specific goal defined in method step one. This enabled to derive metrics to quantify the potential benefit of data-driven design and to narrow down the amount of relevant data that needs to be investigated in the following SysML step. With the yielded result from the previous steps, the data understanding on a data level is improved during a data object decomposition with SysML. Feature of the data are identified with a data object analysis and, again, the visualization was beneficial to communicate between different domain experts. Still, a more detailed guidance of how to conduct the data object analysis with SysML is needed. Therefore, an abstraction of different data attributes needs to be introduced due to the possibly complicated interpretation of attributes which needs to be seen in context with other attributes. This work shows that a PLM processes decomposition is beneficial to generate a comprehensive view to identify data-driven design use cases. Corresponding, enterprises are able to introduce different applications that support the design process. From a scientific point of view, this work contributes by the introduction and evaluation of a new method to identify and formalize data-driven design use cases in engineering enterprises. More specific, knowledge is consolidated from different scientific communities like data science, engineering and lean management. The method contributes to industry by supporting the identification and formalization of data-driven design use cases while taking the experience of different domain experts into concern and giving the opportunity to derive metrics. Even though the validation highlights the beneficial effects of the method in a case study focusing on manufacturing of turned parts, the method requires further validation in different industrial contexts.

6 Conclusions

This paper contributes by presenting a new method to identify data-driven design use cases in engineering companies. The method is presented and validated with a case study in a smart factory with respect to design and manufacturing of turned chess figures. The method builds upon a systematic decomposition of related PLM processes using SIPOC analysis and enterprise architecture modelling to analyse business processes and the related infrastructure. To identify sources of waste and increase the business understanding, design process value stream mapping and dpFMEA are used. Additionally, a systematic analysis of systems and related data features is conducted using the graphical modelling language SysML. This supports the identification of data interrelations required to establish a profound data understanding to implement a data-driven method. The validation with experts with different engineering background that were involved in the case study shows that this method establishes a shared business and data understanding required to successfully identify and implement data-driven design in industry. Future work will focus on further industrial validation to validate the genericity of the approach for different domains and PLM strategies. Further, additional work needs to focus on development of templates and supporting tools to enhance usability of the method.

References

1. Andelfinger, V.P., Hänisch, T. (eds.): Industrie 4.0: Wie cyber-physische Systeme die Arbeitswelt verändern. Gabler Verlag (2017). https://doi.org/10.1007/978-3-658-15557-5
2. Barton, J.A., Love, D.M., Taylor, G.D.: Design determines 70% of cost? A review of implications for design evaluation. J. Eng. Des. **12**(1), 47–58 (2001). https://doi.org/10.1080/09544820010031553
3. Basili, V.R., Caldiera, G., Rombach, H.D.: The Goal Question Metric Approach (1994)
4. Bernus, P., Laszlo, N., Schmidt, G. (eds.): Handbook on Enterprise Architecture. Springer, Heidelberg (2003). https://doi.org/10.1007/978-3-540-24744-9
5. Brynjolfsson, E., Hitt, L.M., Kim, H.H.: Strength in numbers: how does data-driven decision making affect firm performance? SSRN Electron. J. (2011). https://doi.org/10.2139/ssrn.1819486
6. Chao, L.P., Ishii, K.: Design process error proofing: failure modes and effects analysis of the design process. J. Mech. Des. **129**(5), 491 (2007). https://doi.org/10.1115/1.2712216
7. Chen, B., Wan, J., Shu, L., Li, P., Mukherjee, M., Yin, B.: Smart factory of Industry 4.0: key technologies, application case, and challenges. IEEE Access **6**, 6505–6519 (2018). https://doi.org/10.1109/ACCESS.2017.2783682
8. Du, X., Zhu, F.: A new data-driven design methodology for mechanical systems with high dimensional design variables. Adv. Eng. Softw. **117**, 18–28 (2018). https://doi.org/10.1016/j.advengsoft.2017.12.006
9. Ehrlenspiel, K., Kiewert, A., Lindemann, U.: Cost-Efficient Design. Springer, Heidelberg (2007). https://doi.org/10.1007/978-3-540-34648-7
10. Ferreirinha, P., Hubka, V., Eder, W.: Early cost calculation - reliable calculation, not just estimation. In: Design for Manufacturability, ASME DE, vol. 52, pp. 97–104 (1993), https://www.researchgate.net/publication/279998839
11. Fisher, D.: OMG | Object Management Group (1989). https://www.omg.org/. Library Catalog: www.omg.org
12. Gilchrist, A.: Introduction to the industrial Internet. In: Industry 4.0, pp. 1–12. Apress, Berkeley (2016). https://doi.org/10.1007/978-1-4842-2047-4_1
13. Gröger, C., Niedermann, F., Mitschang, B.: Data mining-driven manufacturing process optimization. In: Proceedings of the World Congress on Engineering 2012 Vol III, vol. 3 (2012)
14. Haffey, M., Duffy, A.: Design process performance management support (2003)
15. Hennig, M., Reisinger, G., Trautner, T., Hold, P., Gerhard, D., Mazak, A.: TU Wien Pilot Factory Industry 4.0. Procedia Manuf. **31**, 200–205 (2019). https://doi.org/10.1016/j.promfg.2019.03.032
16. Huber, S., Wiemer, H., Schneider, D., Ihlenfeldt, S.: DMME: data mining methodology for engineering applications - a holistic extension to the CRISP-DM model. Procedia CIRP **79**, 403–408 (2019). https://doi.org/10.1016/j.procir.2019.02.106

17. Jiang, J., Ding, G., Zhang, J., Zou, Y., Qin, S.: A systematic optimization design method for complex mechatronic products design and development. Math. Probl. Eng. **2018**, 1–14 (2018). https://doi.org/10.1155/2018/3159637
18. Knight, D.: Data driven design optimization methodology a dynamic data driven application system. In: Sloot, P.M.A., Abramson, D., Bogdanov, A.V., Gorbachev, Y.E., Dongarra, J.J., Zomaya, A.Y. (eds.) ICCS 2003. LNCS, vol. 2660, pp. 329–336. Springer, Heidelberg (2003). https://doi.org/10.1007/3-540-44864-0_34
19. Lankhorst, M., Proper, H., Jonkers, H.: The anatomy of the archimate language. Int. J. Inf. Syst. Model. Des. **1**(1), 1–32 (2010). https://doi.org/10.4018/jismd.2010092301
20. Lee, J., Bagheri, B., Kao, H.A.: A Cyber-Physical Systems architecture for Industry 4.0-based manufacturing systems. Manuf. Lett. **3**, 18–23 (2015). https://doi.org/10.1016/j.mfglet.2014.12.001
21. Liu, C., Chen, X.: Data-driven design paradigm in engineering problems. Proc. Inst. Mech. Eng. Part G J. Aerosp. Eng. **231**(8), 1522–1534 (2017). https://doi.org/10.1177/0954410016653502
22. Mcmanus, H.: Product Development Value Stream Mapping (PDVSM) Manual Release 1.0 (2005). https://www.semanticscholar.org/paper/Product-Development-Value-Stream-Mapping-(PDVSM)-Mcmanus/5349ab84748e957cd05c9dfe5eede8307c07be02
23. Müller, J.M., Voigt, K.I.: Sustainable industrial value creation in SMEs: a comparison between Industry 4.0 and made in China 2025. Int. J. Precis. Eng. Manuf. Green Technol. **5**(5), 659–670 (2018). https://doi.org/10.1007/s40684-018-0056-z
24. Mutlu, B., Yamaoka, F., Kanda, T., Ishiguro, H., Hagita, N.: Nonverbal leakage in robots: communication of intentions through seemingly unintentional behavior. In: Proceedings of the 4th ACM/IEEE International Conference on Human Robot Interaction - HRI 2009, La Jolla, California, USA, p. 69. ACM Press (2009). https://doi.org/10.1145/1514095.1514110
25. Pahl, G., Beitz, W.: Pahl/Beitz Konstruktionslehre Methoden und Anwendung erfolgreicher Produktentwicklung. Springer, Heidelberg (2013). https://doi.org/10.1007/978-3-642-29569-0
26. Pauker, F., Mangler, J.: centurio.work - higher productivity through intelligent connectivity. In: Wiener Produktionstechnik Kongress, vol. 4. New Academic Press OG (2018)
27. Riepl, W.: CRISP-DM: Ein Standard-Prozess-Modell für Data Mining (2012). https://statistik-dresden.de/archives/1128. Library Catalog: statistik-dresden.de
28. Rigger, E., Vosgien, T.: Design automation state of practice - potential and opportunities. In: DS 92: Proceedings of the DESIGN 2018 15th International Design Conference, pp. 441–452 (2018). https://doi.org/10.21278/idc.2018.0537. https://www.designsociety.org/publication/40462
29. Rigger, E., Vosgien, T., Shea, K., Stankovic, T.: A top-down method for the derivation of metrics for the assessment of design automation potential. J. Eng. Des. 1–31 (2019). https://doi.org/10.1080/09544828.2019.1670786
30. Sadati, N., Chinnam, R.B., Nezhad, M.Z.: Observational data-driven modeling and optimization of manufacturing processes. Expert Syst. Appl. **93**, 456–464 (2018). https://doi.org/10.1016/j.eswa.2017.10.028

31. Stanula, P., Ziegenbein, A., Metternich, J.: Machine learning algorithms in production: a guideline for efficient data source selection. Procedia CIRP **78**, 261–266 (2018). https://doi.org/10.1016/j.procir.2018.08.177
32. Stark, J.: PLM implementation strategy and plan. Product Lifecycle Management (Volume 2). DE, pp. 555–565. Springer, Cham (2016). https://doi.org/10.1007/978-3-319-24436-5_29
33. Stjepandić, J., Wognum, N., Verhagen, W.J.C. (eds.): Concurrent Engineering in the 21st Century: Foundations, Developments and Challenges. Springer, Cham (2015). https://doi.org/10.1007/978-3-319-13776-6
34. Tamm, T., Seddon, P.B., Shanks, G., Reynolds, P.: How does enterprise architecture add value to organisations? Commun. Assoc. Inf. Syst. **28** (2011). https://doi.org/10.17705/1CAIS.02810
35. The Object Management Group: OMG SysML Home | OMG Systems Modeling Language (1989). https://omgsysml.org/
36. The Open Group: ArchiMate® 3.1 Specification (2019). https://pubs.opengroup.org/architecture/archimate3-doc/
37. Wang, L., Törngren, M., Onori, M.: Current status and advancement of cyber-physical systems in manufacturing. J. Manuf. Syst. **37**, 517–527 (2015). https://doi.org/10.1016/j.jmsy.2015.04.008
38. White, S.A., Miers, D.: BPMN modeling and reference guide: understanding and using BPMN; develop rigorous yet understandable graphical representations of business processes. Future Strategies Inc., Lighthouse Point, Fla (2008)
39. Wiemer, H., Drowatzky, L., Ihlenfeldt, S.: Data mining methodology for engineering applications (DMME) - a holistic extension to the CRISP-DM model. Appl. Sci. **9**(12), 2407 (2019). https://doi.org/10.3390/app9122407
40. Wirth, R., Hipp, J.: CRISP-DM: towards a standard process model for data mining. In: Proceedings of the 4th International Conference on the Practical Applications of Knowledge Discovery and Data Mining (2000)
41. Yang, K., El-Haik, B.S.: Design for Six Sigma: A Roadmap For Product Development, 2nd edn. McGraw-Hill, New York (2009)
42. Zhang, J., Ding, G.F., Zhou, Y.S., Jiang, J., Ying, X., Qin, S.F.: Identification of key design parameters of high-speed train for optimal design. Int. J. Adv. Manuf. Technol. **73**(1–4), 251–265 (2014). https://doi.org/10.1007/s00170-014-5822-7

PLM Migration in the Era of Big Data and IoT: Analysis of Information System and Data Topology

Piers Barrios[1,2], François Loison[2], Christophe Danjou[3], and Benoit Eynard[1(✉)]

[1] Université de technologie de Compiègne, Compiègne, France
{piers.barrios,benoit.eynard}@utc.fr
[2] Gfi Informatique, Saint-Ouen, France
francois.loison@gfi.world
[3] Polytechnique Montréal, Montréal, Canada
christophe.danjou@polymtl.ca

Abstract. As product lifecycle management is starting to be a standard information system in most companies, a data manipulation issue starts to emerge. Indeed, the information contained in a system often needs to be accessible or even transferred to another one to exploit a new software's functionalities. With the Big Data era, new methods of analysis start to emerge, and the graph visualisation of data enables a better human understanding of the data itself. We propose to address the PLM migration issues with a new approach based on analysis of information system and data topology. The data is passed onto a graph and bundles are made thanks to clustering algorithms; this bundling enables a better understanding of the data and ease migration. However, PLM has links between links which complicate the transition to graphs. Finally, the described use-case proves that data bundling eases the data migration and prevents some usual pitfalls and delays.

Keywords: Product lifecycle management · Internet of Things · Data package · Group clustering

1 Introduction

Information and communication technology (ICT) systems are in constant evolution to manage more information, improve the user interface or enable new features. However, data migration remains a core problem when going from one software package to the next. It can be mitigated by keeping the same software editor and doing regular updates, but this is too costly compared to keeping the system intact for many years and doing a brutal upgrade. An upgrade often means a major change in the data model in between the source and the target. To address this complexity, most of ICT systems' upgrades are conducted by three main actors: the industrial, client of this upgrade; the software editor of the target system and the integrator, the company that makes sure that the software will fit the industrial's needs. In the context of Big Data [1] and emergence of Internet of Things (IoT) [2], PLM data needs to be easily accessible in

Published by Springer Nature Switzerland AG 2020
F. Nyffenegger et al. (Eds.): PLM 2020, IFIP AICT 594, pp. 695–708, 2020.
https://doi.org/10.1007/978-3-030-62807-9_55

the context of a data migration to be efficiently used by these emerging technologies. However, until now this is not the case and we aim to reduce the gap in this domain by proposing a method to ease data migration.

An upgrade process can be split up into multiple streams (Fig. 1):

- The applicative stream concerns the user interface, the behaviour and the data model.
- Data migration stream produces a method to migrate data as well as executing it.
- Interfaces stream ensures the link with external applications.
- Infrastructure stream tackles the IT infrastructure needs for the app to function.
- User experience and acceptance stream manages the change and the user acceptance of the new system.
- Finally, pilot and system engineering stream ensure the constraints and interactions in-between the different streams.

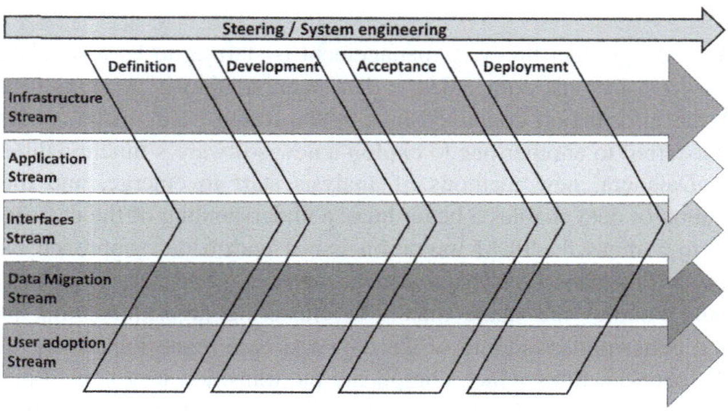

Fig. 1. ICT system upgrade decomposition into streams

Managing a product's lifecycle is quite a tenuous task as it goes from its ideation to its disappearance. In this regard, Terzi [3] defines Product Lifecycle Management (PLM) as follows: "PLM can be broadly defined as a product centric – lifecycle-oriented business model, supported by ICT, in which product data are shared among actors, processes and organisations in the different phases of the product lifecycle for achieving desired performances and sustainability for the product and related services"».

Nevertheless, ICT, only being there to support the PLM process and methodologies, has gained an increasing impact in recent years to the point where vendors are now providing "PLM software" aiming to encapsulate all the necessary components for a properly functioning process and even methodologies.

Compared to other ICT systems such as MES or ERP, PLM data migration is fundamental in PLM systems as the data needs to be available throughout the existence of the product's instances. In some cases, such as major aircraft companies, the legacy PLM system needs to remain available causing huge impact on IT costs. Indeed, the knowledgeable personnel tends to retire earlier than some of the products on the market; hence the resource gets rarer and incidentally more expensive.

In this regard, one could easily conclude that it would be cheaper for a company to do a migration than to keep legacy systems up and running. However, going from a legacy system to a top-of-the-pop system implies the successful migration of the existing data.

Overall, implementation of a data migration process is challenging because:

- The data migration strategies are plenty and dimensioning for any project. Unfortunately, theoretical reality that can be far from data's reality. To our knowledge, there is no specialised software to evaluate data migration strategy.
- Initial resource estimation tends to underestimate the complexity of data migration because of no direct or visible added value for the trade and users.
- Data migration stream has a transient state – i.e. data migration elaboration -followed by a steady state. During elaboration, complexity is very high because of impact of other streams and organisational make or buy choices. A tooled-up method intended to reduce this complexity is needed.
- Finally, the triptych of application, data migration and user acceptance are strongly interdependent and tends to destabilise the project and the global system.

Most often, the migration isn't going from one legacy system to one target system but from multiple sources to one target associated with important data volumetry. Data extraction may require to only migrate part of a system's data as that data is not relevant anymore or should be migrated towards another system. Also, on the data migration stream, there are no established methodologies to tackle such a complex task as there would be on other streams; e.g. Waterfall, Scrum.

Therefore, to address this issue, our article will be structured as follows: we will focus our state of the art on interoperability and PLM data migration. The methodology proposition will underline the issues faced and the choices made to attain a usable solution. This proposition will be illustrated by use cases inspired by our industrial experience. Finally, discussion, conclusion and future works will complete this paper.

2 State of the Art

2.1 Interoperability

The European interoperability framework [4] defines three dimensions for interoperability: technical, semantic and organisational. Technical interoperability is composed mostly of all the communication protocols and infrastructure that enable various systems to communicate. Semantic interoperability is the key one here; it "is the ability to automatically interpret the information exchanged meaningfully and accurately in order to produce useful results as defined by the end users of the systems under consideration" [5]. Finally, organisational interoperability is concerned with people that wish to exchange information and may have different internal structures and processes.

PLM's ICT systems are, until now, made to address semantical interoperability as they add sense to data for the various trades working on the products; people within the same company may achieve semantic interoperability through their access to PLM. ISO 14258 [6] says that semantic interoperability can be achieved in three ways:

- Integrated: "With integrated models there is a standard model form." The main limit there is the standardisation of models.
- Unified: A meta-model exists to represent all existing models. Hence, one can establish correspondence between the various models.
- Federated: Models are diverse and rely on the establishment of dynamic correspondence.

PLM migration from multiple initial systems to one target system can be considered as one way to achieve integrated semantic interoperability. Hence, enabling a better understanding of data migration could enable, in a near future, the transition of integrated systems towards a unified or even a federated ICT system. However, we need to better understand what has already been done concerning PLM data migration.

On data exchange and interoperability, one might look towards one of the following for extended state of the art: Rachuri et al. [7], Fortineau et al. [8] and Sriti et al. [9].

2.2 PLM Data Migration

Research review through Scopus and Web of Science highlights the following:

- In Müller et al. [10], "PLM migration project" is only in the abstract; in the rest of the articles, the authors talk about "PLM deployment". Unfortunately, data migration is not mentioned throughout this article. However, project management in interestingly discussed in one paragraph, providing precious insight about the management of such projects: Even if led by equal rights between the business unit and IT, PLM upgrade still had been perceived as a pure IT project.
- Singh [11] challenges only the transition to the cloud and does not address data migration itself. It is understood that this is an isomorphic migration and that systems are unlikely to evolve between on-premise PLM and cloud PLM. Unfortunately, experience has proven otherwise as PLM migration always implies upgrade.
- Renji Kuncheria [12] stresses out key points of data migration, without however tackling them, in these terms: "Migration of data from legacy enterprise data-systems is one of the important and challenging tasks for most PLM implementations. [...] Moreover, the dependency of production activities on data, that is complete and accurate, stresses the importance for error free data migration. Translating data stored in formats as required or limited by legacy systems to conform to the PLM system specifications only adds to the complexity". However, throughout the article the actual data migration process is neither explicated, nor detailed.

In order to address product development, Guérineau et al. [13] proposes a four-level categorisation for product development. However, none of the listed artefacts enables us to tackle the data migration stream of an ICT system upgrade from the multiple source applications into a unified target application.

3 Methodology Proposition: Data Systemizer

To challenge the previously cited challenges, we propose a standard reusable methodology for data migration stream. The applied approach consists in decoupling a complex problem into several simpler problems, while controlling the interdependencies between the sub-problems. Applied to data transformation issues, this principle amounts to breaking down the dataset into the most independent data islands possible.

First, we will explore the data model before exploring the data clustering and the existing interface.

3.1 Concise and Generalised Data Model

As PLM systems try to encompass as much information on the product as possible, the number of entities and number of attributes per entity is staggering. As a global understanding is key to making accountable choices, only a few elements are useful to understand the system from one point of view. For a decisional tool such as Data Systemizer, the model must be restricted to entities and attributes that are mandatory for analysis, i.e. entities and attributes driving data clustering. Therefore, we will base ourselves on a concise part of the data model.

PLM software tends to consider the various instances of an object separately. For instance, one may consider that a part is spread over several entities such as engineering part and manufacturing part for instance. In this case there is no such thing as a part by itself. To better approach a model, we proceed to a reification meaning that we consider all the parts as actual parts and process information on them: all parts attributes are now considered similar. Generalising the model eases the analysis a great deal and the definition of analysis rules.

3.2 Data Model Structuring Choice

Indeed, the PLM data is more than often stored in a relational database for speed and reliability purpose. However, graph databases take benefit from these similarities to propose full-featured graph applications with interfaces including real world object/link-based data.

In this regard, we consider switching the data stored into PLM towards a graph. In the graph theory, everything is either a vertex or an edge and an edge is necessarily between two vertices. In PLM, any artefact is either an object or a link. An object is a standalone entity holding attributes and a link is an entity relaying objects, generally 2 objects identified by their role; links can hold attributes. As one may realise, PLM data model systems have strong similarities with graph theory models. However, PLM application usually push-up the limit by considering links on links. When including these, the model is no longer comparable with the graph theory as a vertex cannot connect a node and a vertex.

Figure 2 illustrates data model. It shows a Printed Circuit Board (PCB) accepting a Surface Mount Device (SMD) chip. Both are objects. PCB contains pads for SMD chip, it is materialized by a structure link. To prevent component shortage issues, PCB has a dual option loading, its pads can accept a SMD chip or a Dual Inline Package

(DIP) chip. The ability of replacing SMD chip by DIP chip is not global but is constrained by a validation. Equivalence link enables replacement for the specific PCB/SMD chip association. This is a "link on link" as DIP chip is connected to structure link. Replacement is enabled only for this specific PCB/SMB chip assembly.

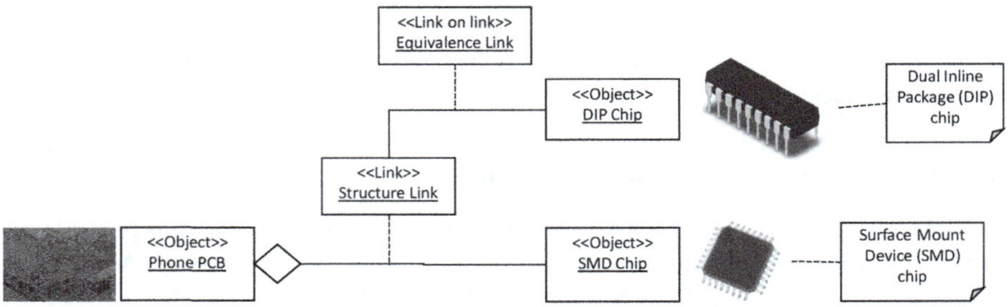

Fig. 2. Data Model illustration

Gutwenger et al. [14] and Farhadian [15] propose solutions to convert such "links on links" model to a graph. However, it requires a virtual node splitting the vertex in two, the "link on link" vertex being connected to this virtual node. This approach is suitable for presentation (sketching the model into a graph). At this point, it is not compatible with clustering as the virtual node does not belong to any cluster. However, to enhance analytics on the data, clustering is essential.

We therefore shift towards an Entity/Link model: Entity is either an object or a link and Link is a link between 2 entities. This model allows implementing links on links between objects. Recursive definition of link allows more sophisticated constructions: "links on links between objects and links" for example. The Entity/Link model has an impact on clustering and tree traversal consolidation processes (Breadth-first search, Depth-first search) needed, for example, to apply metrics on clusters; e.g. counting entities. Basically, clustering allocates entities to lots, while remaining links are stored into a link between lots called a Lot Dependency. Lots and lot dependencies are also entities that can be processed by a further clustering pass.

In the end, everything is an entity. We can distinguish different classes of entities depending on the sophistication; as follows:

Element	Entity class
Object or Link	$\text{Entity}^{[0]}$
Lot or Lot Dependency containing $\text{Entities}^{[0]}$	$\text{Entity}^{[1]}$
Lot or Lot Dependency containing $\text{Entities}^{[1]}$	$\text{Entity}^{[2]}$
…	…
Lot or Lot Dependency containing $\text{Entities}^{[N-1]}$	$\text{Entity}^{[N]}$

In the case where there are no links on links, lot dependencies allocation calculation and tree traversal processes are nominal. In the case of links on links, issues are raised because nominal algorithms raise precedence problems; e.g. entity accessed but not yet initialised.

We define an ordering metric called LinkLevel such as:

$$\text{LinkLevel (object)} = 0 \tag{1}$$

$$\text{LinkLevel(link)} = \text{LinkLevel(edge A entity)} + \text{LinkLevel(edge B entity)} + 1 \tag{2}$$

Links are sorted by increasing LinkLevel and are processed one after the other, starting by LinkLevel 1. This approach sorts out the precedence issues explained previously. Our model also contains Virtual Entities which are not taken into consideration by the clustering process. As circuits (loops of directed vertices) are an issue, we isolate them as such. These are present in the final graph, while clustering remains unchanged [16].

To summarise:

- We implement an Entity/Link data model which is not a graph model
- The model is completed to allow further lot clustering by a meta-model containing lots and lot dependencies; a lot is an entity and a lot dependency is a lot link
- Bridges to graph model exist for clustering entities into lots and lot dependencies & sketch graphs for presentation
- Entity/Link data model raises tree model traversal precedence issues, a metric called LinkLevel allows to correctly order links processing

3.3 Clustering

Zhong et al. [17] explored the possibilities of putting part of the PLM data into clusters in order to increase relevancy and flexibility. However, PLM data migration was not addressed. The most important success factor of PLM migration is choosing the right data transformation strategy. Successful data transformation strategies go as follows:

- Loosely coupled data lots to allow to parallelise data lot processing.
- Most possible functionally significant data lots: a data lot and its dependencies should contain a business product to foster validation tests. On the contrary, a lot dividing strategy based on bottom/up layers such as bolt & nuts, assemblies, modules and end items is not acceptable because it's testable only at the end of migration.
- Lots should be decomposed in a loosely coupled lot tree in order to recourse this process at lot level and build efficient test lots given a size and error rate.

Clustering is the key to achieve these needs. The clustering is realised by a "Lot Divider" which takes entities as input and output lots and lot dependencies partitioning entities. There are two categories of Lot Dividers:

- Business Lot Divider: driven by functional parameters available from data. For example divide data by program name, divide data by site name.

- Mathematical Lot Divider: driven by graph topology, requires no business parameters. E.g. Metis Lot Divider partitions a graph in sub-graphs while reducing sub-graphs dependencies; Adherence Lot Divider creates sub-lots to understand and measure lot adherence; Bill of Material (BOM) Lot Divider groups entities until an entity is re-used.

Both dividers produce lots who have a type that could be Business or Technical. Lot type drives further passes of dividing as explained in next chapters. By default, Business Lot Dividers produce Business Lots and Mathematical Dividers product Technical Lots but this default settings can be overridden by parameterization depending on clustering strategy needed.

Metis [18] is a graph partitioning tool taking as input a graph and desired number of partitions N. It produces N sub-graphs optimised to reduce number of cross-partition vertices. Metis is used by "Better than Big Bang Divider" intended to split data in most possible number of independent lots, to reduce data migration complexity.

The experimental approach is based on scenarios. A scenario is a pipe of Lot Dividers that allocates data entities$^{[0]}$ (objects, links) to entities$^{[M]}$ (lots and lot dependencies), M being the number of clustering passes. Scenario outcomes are evaluated by verifying they are compliant to rules enounced previously. Data Systemizer defines a lot type: business or technical. Whatever the Lot Dividers execution sequence is and their numbers, the lot aggregation chain is always a business lot chain followed by a technical lot chain:

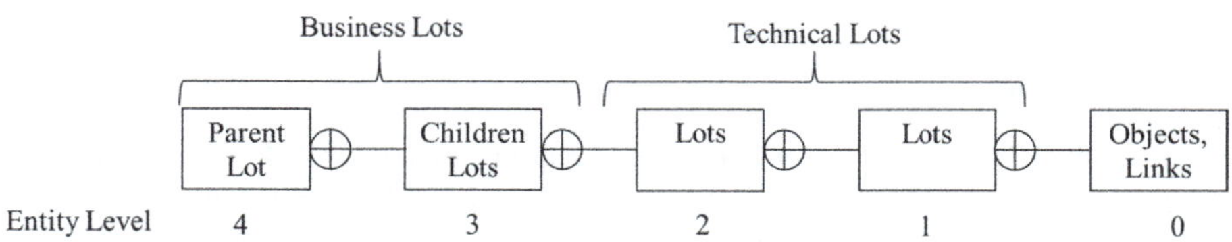

Fig. 3. Example of sequence of processing

Figure 3 introduces lot inclusion chains given the Entity Level (EL). In this example four levels are retained. Each lot is noted as included (UML) in the previous one. The deducted properties are as follows:

$$\text{Entity}^{[\text{EL}]} = \{\text{Object, Links}\}\text{for EL} = 0 \quad (3)$$

$$\text{Entity}^{[\text{EL}]} = \{\text{Lot, Lot dependency}\} \text{ for EL} \geq 1 \quad (4)$$

$$\text{An entity with EL} = \text{N} + 1 \text{ contains entities EL} = \text{N}: \text{Entity}^{[\text{EL}+1]} = \left\{\text{Entity}^{[\text{EL}]}\right\} \quad (5)$$

The clustering pipe is then executed as following:

1. Identify min($EL_{Business}$) and max($EL_{Technical}$), the EL directly preceding (business/technical lots) break. From example: min($EL_{Business}$) = 3, max($EL_{Technical}$) = 2
2. For each Business $Lot^{[min(ELBusiness)]}$:
   a. Allocate to a dedicated working space (bench) the Lot Divider with $Entities^{[max(ELTechnical)]}$ belonging to current Business Lot
   b. Run the Lot Divider algorithm using bench entities as input. Lots produced by Lot Divider are either Business or Technical (functional parameter of scenario). They are attached as direct children of current business lot.
3. Run the Lot Divider with $Entities^{[max(ELTechnical)]}$ as input

Throughout this section, we set out all the necessary artefacts and tools necessary to dive into PLM systems' data; we shall now consider the use cases this methodology can be applied to.

Needless to say, Data Systemizer is data format agnostic. I.e. a data format such as XML imposes a structure whereas the analysis detailed here is agnostic and able to explore multiple structures. Hence, the flatter the format, the better. The contribution of a format such as XML in this case is grammar and completeness verification, which is nice but remains optional.

4 Use-Case

4.1 Optimizing an ETL Data Load

ETL (Extract/Transform/Load) tools aim to migrate data from source to target system by applying a pattern. However, it is flow driven and unaware of data topology, e.g. decomposition of data in loosely coupled lots. Some approaches to ETL processes such as [19] in the data warehouse and big data contexts might be graph-based and semantic however these do not fit the PLM needs as expressed here.

During ETL elaboration, loading error rate may be dramatic for PLM data structures because of the re-use object factor - an object is re-used by other objects through a link. If the re-used object loading is broken, all dependent links and all recursively dependent links will fail, a.k.a. explosive errors spreading. As a result, data is not business testable and the error analysis task is complex because valuable error root causes are flooded by useless dependent errors. Data Systemizer can extract a "successful transformation data strategy" and drive ETL.

Figure 4 presents interfaces in the black-box manner. Data is input via CSV or XML files, clustered by Data Systemizer and then output. On this interface, the various clusters are going to have their own files; hence enabling smooth input to ETL solution for the new PLM system. ETL is fed by data lots respecting the original data format, not full data from the input. After lot loading is processed by ETL, Data Systemizer gets objects, link errors and inspects impacts of errors. If explosive errors spreading phenomena are detected, loading is stopped for dependent lots while independent lots continue to load.

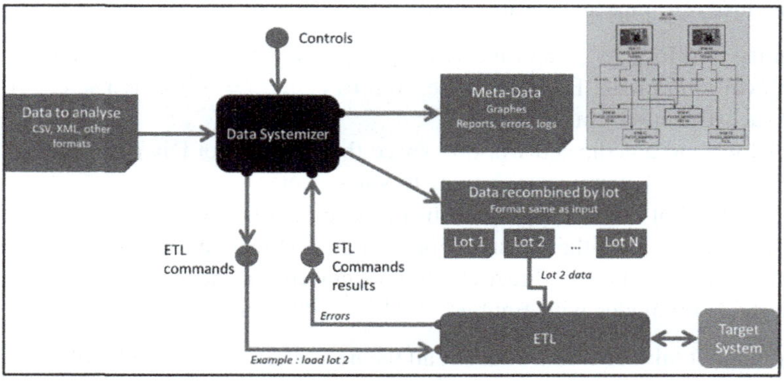

Fig. 4. Interfaces of Data Systemizer in the ETL Use-case

Moreover, output can be a graph; this is helpful as it enables meaningful insight of data; it enables company and project leaders to understand and anticipate possible issues; they will be able to evaluate the right complexity of the data transfer. Also, it sometimes underlines the fact that the theoretical truth about the data is far from reality.

4.2 Optimizing a Migration Strategy

A data migration project needed to evaluate migration strategy of data package containing 10 million objects and links. ETL direct approach had failed because of "explosive errors spreading" phenomenon and the duration of a test increment which was too long to bear iterative development mode.

Data is extracted from a PLM source system. Data extraction has been made by source object types into a set of CSV flat files. Files data sets are not organized by programs nor any business organization. Loading data type by type in a Big Bang migration strategy is not acceptable because this loading strategy would be testable only at end of process and subjected to cascading errors phenomenon. The question raised was: Is there a more optimal than the Big-Bang migration strategy?

Data Systemizer was parameterised to perform two BOM Dividing and Metis BOM Dividing:

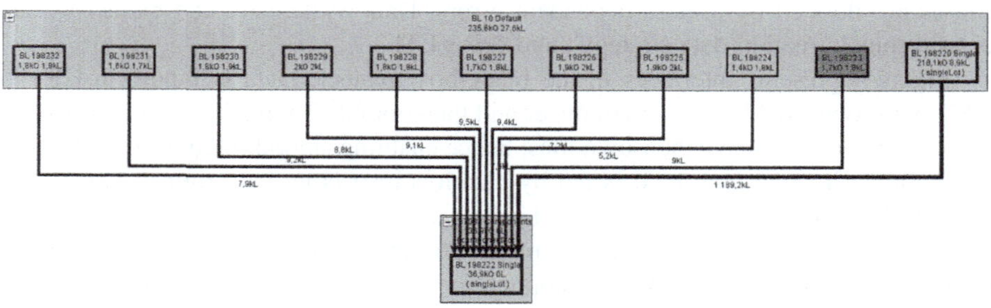

Fig. 5. Result of Data Systemizer application: data is separated in 12 different lots

Figure 5 shows input data which has been clustered into 12 lots; 11 separated lots all depending on a single component lot. Data Systemizer can restitute this monolithic data package in 12 lots. The lot in orange contains some data referential integrity errors; i.e. orphan links. Some elaboration specific test data lots can be provided given needed volumetry and error rate. Test data lots are functionally significant, they contain testable end-to-end business data.

4.3 Choosing Right Migration Strategy

An aircraft company needs to migrate a certification application from a PLM system to an ERP system. Volumetry is low but data model is complex. Drastic system changes and model complexity requires important end users testing hence big-bang migration is not acceptable because on one hand, it would retain tests at the end of the migration project and on the other end, users would redo costly tests.

To enable a fine-grained migration strategy, two lot dividing strategies are studied: at Family level (top level) and at Baseline level (middle level). Business users would like to know what level is best.

As data model is complex, some specific algorithms have been developed to extract Family and Baseline information. Two graphs are produced to compare both migration strategies.

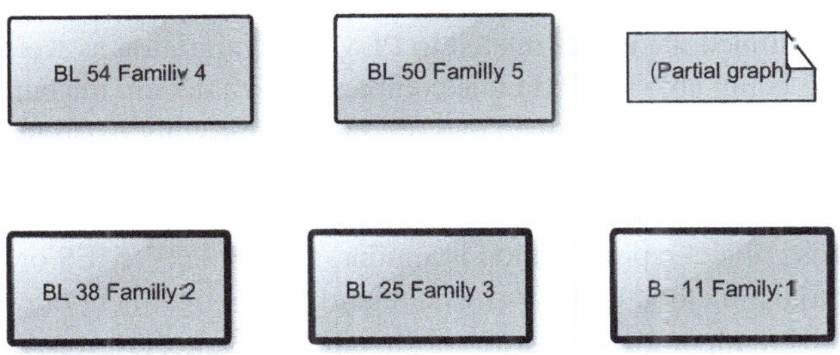

Fig. 6. Partial graph of Family level migration strategy

Figure 6 shows graph corresponding to Family level migration strategy. Family lots are totally separated, this migration strategy is efficient.

To see if data could be split at lower level, the baseline level analysis has been run.

Figure 7 shows partial graph corresponding to Baseline level migration strategy. Outer box is a family lot, inner boxes are baseline lots contained in this family lot. Clearly baseline lots are highly coupled. Baseline lots should be migrated altogether, but this wastes the benefit of baseline-level migration strategy. In this case, the study shows that Family level migration is best choice.

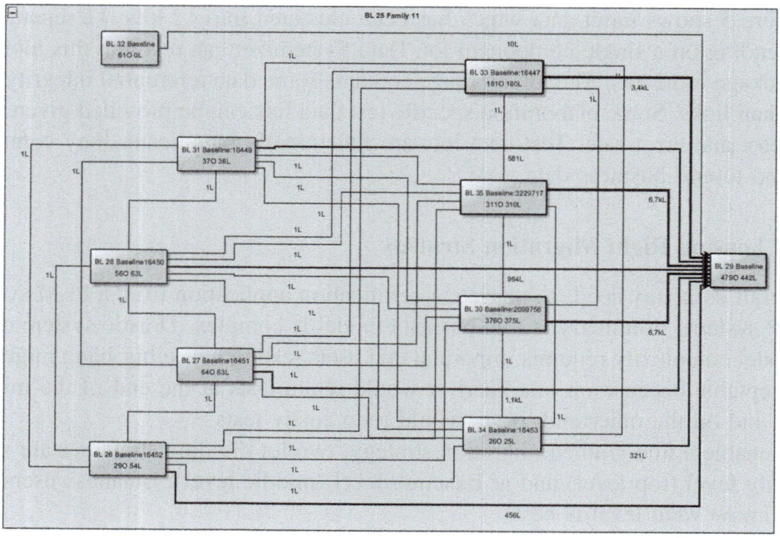

Fig. 7. Partial graph of Baseline level migration strategy

5 Conclusion and Future Work

This article has outlined the issues related to PLM data migration as well as why this is crucial regarding being able to tackle one company's own data in the current context of Big Data. Methodology was described and use cases improving existing were outlined.

Discussion focus on possible reusability of the underlined methodology as well as possible improvements. Indeed, the method outlined could be reused in any information system whose object representation is similar, such as ERP, MES or IoT platforms. Improvements to the method could be made regarding the treatment of circuits. Indeed, they are currently temporarily put away to avoid blocking the process. However, in some scenarios, their number would be too non-negligible, and one would need to tackle them head on. Also, improvements would be made on the implementation and focus on enabling user-friendly interfaces.

Future works should tackle measuring the effectivity increase thanks to the use of this method which would be necessary to leverage further deployments.

Current work could we improved according to the following directions:

- Some real-life examples such as Fig. 7 show data graphs with lots highly coupled. The raw question is to know whether highly coupling is intrinsic to data topology or to weakness of clustering algorithm. A tooled-up method able to inspect graph coupling quality would be helpful.
- This article deals with data loading use cases. They are other interesting use cases: modification and purge/archive. Modification use case implies a 2 ways data analysis: data to process versus data present in the system. Purge/archive use case is interesting in PLM systems because data are highly linked to other data. Scoping the purge/archive target is challenging, executing purge/archive is even more

complicated. Deletion use case is a simpler subcase of purge/archive, still not achievable manually.

- Data verification after migration. Current industry practice is based on end users' tests. This practice should be improved. Current directions are: probability and statistics-based method to provide a more controlled confidence level to tests executed, mode-based approaches relaying entity counts to reconciliate number of entities before and after migration, brute force export after migration and comparison with source data.

References

1. Dekhtiar, J., Durupt, A., Bricogne, M., Eynard, B., Rowson, H., Kiritsis, D.: Deep learning for big data applications in CAD and PLM – research review, opportunities and case study. Comput. Ind. **100**, 227–243 (2018). https://doi.org/10.1016/j.compind.2018.04.005
2. Barrios, P., Eynard, B., Danjou, C.: Towards a digital thread between industrial internet of things and product lifecycle management: experimental work for prototype implementation. In: Fortin, C., Rivest, L., Bernard, A., Bouras, A. (eds.) PLM 2019. IAICT, vol. 565, pp. 273–282. Springer, Cham (2019). https://doi.org/10.1007/978-3-030-42250-9_26
3. Terzi, S., Bouras, A., Dutta, D., Garetti, M., Kiritsis, D.: Product lifecycle management - from its history to its new role. Int. J. Prod. Lifecycle Manag. **4**, 360 (2010)
4. Chen, D., Doumeingts, G., Vernadat, F.: Architectures for enterprise integration and interoperability: past, present and future. Comput. Ind. **59**, 647–659 (2008)
5. Özacar, T., Öztürk, Ö., Ünalır, M.O.: ANEMONE: an environment for modular ontology development. Data Knowl. Eng. **70**, 504–526 (2011)
6. ISO 14258: Industrial automation systems — concepts and rules for enterprise models. International Organisation for Standards, Geneva (1998)
7. Rachuri, S., Subrahmanian, E., Bouras, A., Fenves, S.J., Foufou, S., Sriram, R.D.: Information sharing and exchange in the context of product lifecycle management: Role of standards. Comput. Aided Des. **40**, 789–800 (2008)
8. Fortineau, V., Paviot, T., Lamouri, S.: Improving the interoperability of industrial information systems with description logic-based models-the state of the art. Comput. Ind. **64**, 363–375 (2013)
9. Sriti, M.F., Assouroko, I., Ducellier, G., Boutinaud, P., Eynard, B.: Ontology-based approach for product information exchange. Int. J. Prod. Lifecycle Manag. **8**, 1 (2015)
10. Müller, P., Muschiol, M., Stark, R.: PLM-based service data management in steam turbine business. In: Rivest, L., Bouras, A., Louhichi, B. (eds.) PLM 2012. IAICT, vol. 388, pp. 170–181. Springer, Heidelberg (2012). https://doi.org/10.1007/978-3-642-35758-9_15
11. Singh, S., Misra, S.: Migration of PLM systems to cloud. Int. J. Commun. Syst. **31**, e3815 (2018)
12. John, R.K.: PLM implementation at MAN diesel A/S: a case study. In: Garetti, M., Terzi, S., Ball, P., Han, S. (eds.) Product Lifecycle Management. Assessing the Industrial Relevance, Inderscience, Geneva, pp. 199–204 (2007)
13. Guérineau, B., Rivest, L., Bricogne, M., Durupt, A.: Agile and project-planned methods in multidisciplinary product design. In: Harik, R., Rivest, L., Bernard, A., Eynard, B., Bouras, A. (eds.) PLM 2016. IAICT, vol. 492, pp. 108–118. Springer, Cham (2016). https://doi.org/10.1007/978-3-319-54660-5_11

14. Gutwenger, C., Mutzel, P., Weiskircher, R.: Inserting an edge into a planar graph. Algorithmica **41**, 289–308 (2005)
15. Farhadian, A.: A coordinate system for graphs. arXiv:1701.02443 [math]. (2018)
16. Johnson, D.: Finding all the elementary circuits of a directed graph. SIAM J. Comput. **4**, 77–84 (1975)
17. Zhong, H., Yan, G., Lei, Y.: Evolution supporting class-cluster data model for PLM. In: Jin, D., Lin, S. (eds.) Advances in Electronic Commerce, Web Application and Communication. Advances in Intelligent and Soft Computing, vol. 148, pp. 191–196. Springer, Heidelberg (2012). https://doi.org/10.1007/978-3-642-28655-1_30
18. Abou-Rjeili, A., Karypis, G.: Multilevel algorithms for partitioning power-law graphs. In: Proceedings 20th IEEE International Parallel & Distributed Processing Symposium, Rhodes Island, Greece, p. 10 pp. IEEE (2006)
19. Simitsis, A., Vassiliadis, P., Terrovitis, M., Skiadopoulos, S.: Graph-based modeling of ETL activities with multi-level transformations and updates. In: Tjoa, A.M., Trujillo, J. (eds.) DaWaK 2005. LNCS, vol. 3589, pp. 43–52. Springer, Heidelberg (2005). https://doi.org/10.1007/11546849_5

Building Information Modelling

A Quantitative Evaluation Framework for the Benefit of Building Information Modeling for Small and Medium Enterprises Leveraging Risk Management Concepts

Christoph Paul Schimanski[1,2(✉)], Giada Malacarne[2], Gabriele Pasetti Monizza[2], and Dominik T. Matt[1,2]

[1] Faculty of Science and Technology, Free University of Bozen-Bolzano, Piazza Università 5, 39100 Bolzano, Italy
christophpaul.schimanski@natec.unibz.it
[2] Fraunhofer Italia Research, Via A.-Volta 13a, 39100 Bolzano, Italy

Abstract. Building Information Modeling plays an increasingly important role in today's construction sector due to its growing prevalence among practitioners and the increasing legal obligation to use it in public projects. The general and most obvious benefits such as improved communication/coordination or rapid generation of various planning alternatives are widely accepted. However, there is a lack of a generic framework to quantify these benefits. This is especially important from the perspective of small and medium sized enterprises because larger investments - as they may occur through software and training when implementing BIM - should be balanced against a traceable return-on-investment. With a few exceptions, other research focuses on qualitative or non-monetary assessment parameters to evaluate these benefits. Such an approach may be too vague in the context of small and medium-sized enterprises to justify the necessary strategic decisions on a BIM changeover. In this study we propose a generic framework for quantitative evaluation of the BIM benefit. This evaluation is based on the BIM-impact on contingency estimation in construction risk management relying on Monte Carlo simulations. Semi-structured interviews and questionnaires with practitioners are used to evaluate how risk factors and subsequently contingencies can differ from each other in BIM-projects and Non-BIM projects.

Keywords: BIM benefits · SMEs · Risk factors · Monte-Carlo simulation

1 Introduction

1.1 BIM and the Assessment of its Benefits

Building Information Modeling (BIM) is a process for creating and managing information throughout the lifecycle of a building or an infrastructure [1]. This process results in a Building Information Model, a digital representation of the built asset, developed collaboratively by designers, construction firms and clients. Collaboration is the key aspect of the BIM methodology since it enhances decision making, increases

Published by Springer Nature Switzerland AG 2020
F. Nyffenegger et al. (Eds.): PLM 2020, IFIP AICT 594, pp. 711–723, 2020.
https://doi.org/10.1007/978-3-030-62807-9_56

productivity resulting in a greater whole life value for the asset [2]. For this reason, BIM plays an increasingly important role in today's AEC sector and its adoption is growing faster, year after year. E.g., in the United Kingdom, the number of practitioners using BIM has increased from 13% in 2011 to 69% in 2019 [3]. This exponential trend addresses also the incremental demand for BIM from the client's side and especially from public organizations. In fact, since the introduction of BIM in the European Directive on Public Procurement (24/14/EU) in 2014, several governments across Europe are pushing the mandatory use of BIM in public works with the aim of reducing waste, delays and costs, while increasing the quality of their built environment [4].

Beyond strategic expectations from the AEC community on BIM, its use has already evidenced many benefits also at both project and company level, such as: better communication, coordination and rapid generation of design alternatives [5, 6]. However, even if these benefits are widely accepted, previous research in this field still consists in observations from singular case studies [5] and, as stated by [7], no unified nor global approach has been proposed so far. Since implementing BIM in organizations is a strategic investment, the lack of a framework to quantitatively measure its benefits is critical especially from the perspective of small and medium sized enterprises (SMEs) [6], where investments have to be balanced against a clear return-on-investments (ROI).

Measuring the ROI of BIM has different finalities: (i) understanding the impact on the organization performance; (ii) measuring benefits; (iii) considering the risks associated to the benefits; (iv) collecting data useful for the IT investment analysis [8]. While previous research investigated the relationship between benefits and how these effects ROI, to our best knowledge there are no scientific studies that are concerned with the relationship between potential risk factors in a construction project and the mitigation improvements achievable using BIM. This interplay might affect ROI considerations when thinking of BIM implementations.

1.2 Problem Statement

As being outlined above the benefit of the BIM approach for implementing companies – especially for SMEs – is not reliably measurable in a direct way. One reason for this is that there is little long-term experience with the use of BIM, and it is not sufficiently widespread within the construction industry. Secondly, the BIM impact on the performance of a construction project is difficult to relate to a reference or benchmark of a traditional approach. This is due to the unique characteristics of buildings: Two identical buildings with identical boundary conditions (same subsoil conditions, neighboring buildings, weather, team of project participants, contractor and subcontractors, etc.) would have to be built in order to compare the two approaches. However, even in this case, no direct comparability would be guaranteed, as the project team would probably learn from the first realization, and the second one would therefore run better and faster in any case, which would dilute the assessment of the BIM influence.

Therefore, we follow an indirect way to potentially assess the impact of BIM by considering different BIM functionalities and their impact on risk management in construction projects.

More precisely, we use methods of probabilistic risk management. In the field of probabilistic risk management there are numerous known risk factors (such as poor communication and coordination. Their influence on the monetary contingency to be made available in case of risk occurrence is sufficiently described in the literature. However, what is not described in the literature is the potential influence of BIM on these risk factors. This paper aims at contributing to fill this gap.

We further hypothesize that several BIM functionalities have a positive influence on certain risk factors, both in terms of the likelihood of its occurrence and financial impact. Consequently, the contingency to be held available would be reduced compared to non-BIM projects. Using this indirect way, we attempt to describe the BIM benefit quantitatively. Accordingly, this paper investigates two aspects of research, namely (i) the quantitative evaluation of the BIM approach and (ii) the BIM influence on known risk factors in construction.

2 State of the Art: Risk Management in Construction

According to the PMBOK® Guide [9], risk management plays a crucial role in project management and is defined therein as "systematic process of identifying, analyzing, and responding to project risks".

The extent of a risk is determined by two factors The "likelihood of occurrence" and the "impact" of a risk. Both determinants have different probabilities. The first specifies the likelihood of the risk occurring, while the second quantifies the probable magnitude of the financial impact in case of occurrence [10] Two approaches are used here: Qualitative and quantitative risk assessment strategies.

Within the existing frameworks for qualitative risk assessment, the respective risk impact and the likelihood of occurrence are classified merely trough few levels (high, medium, low) and within this classification, percentage supplements in terms of budget are added on the estimated production costs [11].

Quantitative risk assessment on the other hand requires a more detailed consideration from an economic and financial perspective. The individual risks are assigned a potential impact range in monetary units accompanied by probability distributions as well as binomial distributed likelihoods of occurrence. A resulting quantitative measure of the overall risk impact of a project is the *value at risk* as a loss-oriented risk measure. This value is estimated with the aid of numerical simulation methods such as the Monte Carlo simulation (MCS) method.

The MCS method is used as a computer-supported, mathematical instrument for solving complex tasks. In general, the Monte Carlo method is understood as the use of random numbers for the solution of stochastically describable problems, even if these problems are not stochastic in their origin [12, 13].

It is possible to distinguish two fields in which MCS is typically used: The first field contains deterministic problems, where also exact analytical solutions exist. MCS is used here when simulation results, as an approximate solution, can describe the actual solution with enough accuracy. The loss of accuracy that is associated with MCS is consciously accepted and part of a trade-off with simplicity and velocity within the process of finding a solution. This trade-off yields frequently to the selection for MCS, as analytical solutions, in these fields, are often very computationally and resource intensive. This use of MCS has a high significance within the natural sciences and mathematics. Application examples for deterministic problems that can be solved with MCS are the calculation of integrals and the solution of ordinary and partial differential equations [13].

The second problem area comprises stochastic problems. These are characterized by the fact that the input parameters and the resulting target variables are to a certain extent subject to chance. In stochastic problems, MCS can be used to investigate situations where either no analytical solution exists or input parameters comprise random variables [14]. In the area of risk analysis, MCS can be used to aggregate individual risks to form an overall risk, multi-scenario simulations as well as for decision optimization.

3 Research Strategy

The research strategy followed in this paper is a combined approach of (i) elaborating a probabilistic risk model containing risk factors in accordance with [15]. The calibration of the risk model is performed by analyzing literature, results from a questionnaire as well as findings of semi-structured interviews with construction experts. Secondly (ii), the research strategy consists of performing the MCS to assess the impact of BIM on contingency estimation in construction from the risk management perspective. By doing so, we aim to measure the added value of BIM in an indirect way. While the use of MCS for contingency estimation in construction is widely described in research [15–17], the analysis of the BIM influence within such a probabilistic system is new to our best knowledge.

This evaluation is based on the framework for benefit evaluation of Target Value Design (TVD) on construction costs by [18]. TVD is a method from Lean Construction management to create more value for the client. One dimension of value in Lean Construction consists in staying on budget. In the mentioned evaluation framework, a theoretical cost-breakdown model was postulated, which divides the individual cost components for construction projects into cost of work, contingency and profit.

Their findings on the statistical analysis of TVD and non-TVD projects impose a reduction of contingency in TVD projects. The authors denominate the drivers for contingency as "forces" that drive up total construction costs. These forces are identified by the authors as e.g. poor communication and coordination, lack of trust, change orders etc. They argued further that in TVD projects, these negative drivers can be reduced and hence the required contingency is likely to be reduced, too.

Drawing a line back to this research, these mentioned "forces" can be also considered risk factors in construction. The implementation of BIM might affect some of these risk factor positively. However, it remains unclear to which extent BIM affects these risk factors, and what effects this has on contingency considerations.

Therefore, the proposed framework for quantitative BIM benefit evaluation is based on a probabilistic risk model to determine the effect of BIM on contingency estimation.

The underlying assumption, that BIM can actually contribute to contingency reduction through the mitigation of risk factors is shown in Fig. 1 as adaptation of TVD projects by [18].

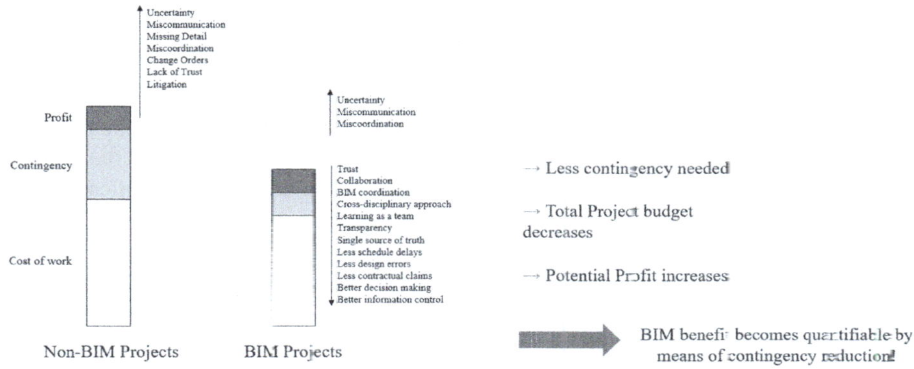

Fig. 1. Potential contingency reduction through BIM, graphic adapted from [18]

For the purpose of BIM benefit assessment, we attempt to determine a so-called BIM-based contingency delta (BIM-C-Δ), which might be caused by certain risk factors. Thus, the BIM-C-Δ does not represent the potential overall BIM benefit in that regard, since we are not going to consider all factors that might have an impact on contingency estimation, but only the top risk factors which might be affected through the use of BIM. This means, the potential overall BIM-benefit could be even higher if all risk factors were examined.

Consequently, this study aims to examine the following hypotheses:

1. Null-Hypothesis H_0: $\mu_d \leq 0$
   The implementation of BIM has no positive impact on the required contingency in cost estimation.
2. Alternative-Hypothesis H_A: $\mu_d > 0$
   The implementation of BIM has a positive impact on the required contingency in cost estimation.

For assessing these hypotheses, we elaborate a risk register that contains a total five risks factors which might be affected by BIM. The elaboration of this risk register is described in detail in Sect. 4.1. The risks contained therein are transferred into a questionnaire that is handed out to selected local construction experts to evaluate the extent to which the likelihood of occurrence varies under BIM application. In this study, we analyze a total of 22 responses to this questionnaire.

To test the presented hypotheses, we conducted a paired t-test on the questionnaire results. The test results are discussed in Sect. 4.2.

Presuming a statistically significant difference of risk perception in the two scenarios (rejection of H_0), we apply MCS to simulate the needed contingency for a defined project scenario (residential construction in the order of magnitude up to 10

Mio.€ contract volume), taking into account the questionnaire's results for configuration of the probabilistic risk model in terms of likelihoods, impacts and dispersion.

4 Proposal for Quantitative BIM Benefit Evaluation

4.1 Elaborating the Risk Register

The risk register used in this study is based on the overall top 10 risks identified in a literature review of the most common risks in construction [19]. These are the risks that occur most frequently according to that study. We contrast these risks with the 10 risks that are most significant according to [20]. The assessment criteria for significance here are the likelihood of occurrence and the potential financial risk impact in case of occurrence.

We have made an intersection of these two lists and we have neglected all those risks which are not clearly influenced by BIM in terms of likelihood of occurrence with regard to the mentioned BIM benefits in Sect. 1.1. We have given the five remaining risks an aggregate name and assigned them to risk categories in line with [17]. Additionally, we ranked them according to their relative likelihood of occurrence and financial impact as reported by [21]. The resulting list is shown in Table 1 and forms the basis for the probabilistic risk model in this study.

Table 1. Considered risk factors

Risk factor	Category according to [17]	Risk ID	Rel. likelihood rank	Rel. impact rank
Slow decision-making process	Managerial	M1	3	2
Frequent change orders by client	Technical	T1	2	4
Errors and omissions in design drawings	Technical	T2	1	1
Unavailability or shortage in specified material	Resource-related	R1	4	2
Delay in response to requests for information (generalized)	Managerial	M2	5	5

4.2 Expert Questionnaire and Hypotheses Testing

We elaborated a questionnaire for the configuration of the probabilistic risk model. The questionnaire goals are two-fold: (i) to evaluate how the likelihood of occurrence of the risk factors changes under BIM usage from the experts' point of view for the purpose of hypotheses testing, and (ii) to find out which dispersion parameters are appropriate for the impact distribution for MCS in the case the Null-Hypothesis has to be rejected. A total of 22 responses have been analyzed when this study was conducted.

As an example, out of these risk factors, the first risk factor (M1) is concerned with whether a project can be delayed due to decisions not taken or taken too late because the information needed was not (sufficiently) available. The experts were asked to express their opinion on the likelihood of the occurrence of this risk factor on a 4-point Likert-scale with the options (i) very likely; (ii) likely; (iii) unlikely and (iv) very unlikely in the two scenarios of traditional and BIM-based project delivery. By BIM project delivery, we mean a full use of all available functionalities (e.g. collision check, common data environment, automatic plan derivations, model-based quantity take-off etc.) by all project participants. The results are presented in Fig. 2.

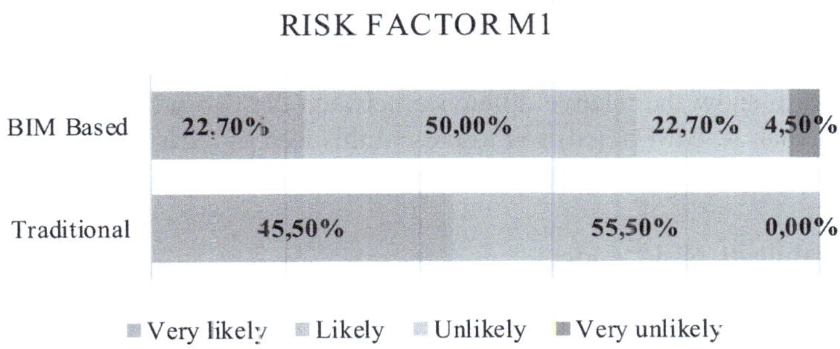

Fig. 2. Risk factor M1

These results show a change in the perception of risk occurrence from *very likely* to *unlikely*. In fact, the number of votes for *very likely* has been halved, which in turn increased the votes of an unlikely risk event in the BIM-based case. The number of votes for *likely* have approximately remained the same.

Furthermore, the respondents were asked to estimate the potential financial impact of the considered risk factors. For the risk factor M1 it has been estimated in the range from *significant* (68%) to *critical* (23%) with a medium degree of statistical dispersion, meaning that the financial impact of this risk factor is subject to uncertainties (not shown in the graphic).

The findings for the other four considered risk factors are of similar appearance, so that a detailed description of those is omitted at this point.

Subsequently, and in accordance with [22], who studied probability related terms and their corresponding values as percentages, the different options of the Likert-scale of the questionnaire have been assigned the following percentages as a numerical likelihood of occurrence as an assumption: (i) *Very likely* = 65%; (ii) *Likely* = 50%; (iii) *Unlikely* = 7,5%; (iv) *Very Unlikely* = 2,5%.

As a next step, we calculated the mean of the responses by creating ordinal data through assignment of numbers from 1 to 4 to the answer options (1 = *Very unlikely*; 2 = *Unlikely*; 3 = *Likely*; 4 = *Very unlikely*). The mean here is used to find out general tendency of the responses with respect to the numerical likelihood as percentages and eventually for hypotheses testing, making use of a paired t-test. The question to be analyzed with this paired t-test is whether BIM does impact the required project budget positively or not. Hence, the difference of the mean in both cases is in question, hypothesizing that $\mu_d \leq 0 (= H_0)$.

The paired t-test with an α-level of 0,1 and under t-distribution with 4 degrees of freedom has shown that the null hypothesis H_0 is to be rejected and the alternative hypothesis is to be accepted, which means that BIM has a statistically significant (positive) effect on the risk occurrence according to the questionnaire findings given the considered risk factors. It remains to be analyzed whether this discrepancy in perception on the effect on construction risks between traditional and BIM-based projects is also measurable trough numerical simulation of risk events.

The next section presents the probabilistic risk analysis framework to quantify this effect in terms of required contingency of a given project budget. In this study, the project budget is assumed to be 10 million € (project scenario: residential construction). Simulation results do not claim to be reliable or valid in terms of absolute numbers but are intended to show the relative difference between the two project delivery approaches (traditional vs. BIM-based) and to present this idea of measuring the BIM benefit in an indirect way to the scientific community.

4.3 Probabilistic Risk Model

This list of risk factors given in Table 1 is the fundamental element of the probabilistic risk model for performing the MCS for contingency estimation. Figure 3 shows the risk model in the BIM-based configuration exemplarily.

Risk Register												Total project budget [€]	€10.000.000,00
Risk factor					Financial impact								
								Distribution form parameters					
Risk_ID	Risk Event	Description	Likelihood with BIM [%]	Simulated occurrence [0/1]	Impact	Rough Order Impact (€)	Impact probability distribution function	Mean Impact [€]	Standard Deviaton (genau/ungenau?)	Simulated Impact [€]	Strong Correlation to Other(s)	Resulting contingency allowance [€]
M1	Slow decision-making process	The project is delayed due to decisions not taken or taken too late because the information needed was not (sufficiently) available.	47,24%	0	Significant	€500.000,00	Log-normal	€500.000,00	€150.000,00	€701.489,24	M2	€0,00
T1	Frequent change orders by client	Frequent requests for changes from the client require time-consuming revision of all planning documents and cause uncertainty about the approval status of plans during execution.	47,97%	0	Significant	€500.000,00	Log-normal	€500.000,00	€150.000,00	€678.061,21	T2	€0,00
T2	Errors and omissions in design drawings	Defective planning or collisions that are not detected or are detected too late lead to delays.	43,60%	1	Significant	€500.000,00	Log-normal	€500.000,00	€150.000,00	€626.206,23	T1	€626.206,23
R1	Unavailability or shortage in specified material	Incorrect quantity take-offs from planning results in material shortages and thus delays on the construction site.	39,93%	1	Critical	€1.000.000,00	Log-normal	€1.000.000,00	€300.000,00	€790.923,46	-	€790.923,46
M2	Delay in response to requests for information	The response to requested planning deliverables or detailed specifications is not always immediate and thus causes "bottlenecks" in the planning or execution process and thus also delays.	42,84%	1	Critical	€1.000.000,00	Log-normal	€1.000.000,00	€300.000,00	€763.583,83	M1	€763.583,83
											SUM Contingency	€2.180.713,52

Fig. 3. Risk model BIM-based project delivery

It is conceptually derived from the risk register presented by [23] and composed of (i) the risk factors themselves and a short description; (ii) a quantitative likelihood of occurrence as derived from the questionnaire results; (iii) a qualitative impact in the range from *negligible* to *crisis*; (iv) a rough financial order of impact in terms of euros [€] as agreed with local construction experts; (v) the type of probability distribution for that impact and form parameters for stochastic analyses (mean and standard deviation) as well as (vi) the presumed correlation of the single risk factors.

In both cases, traditional and BIM-based project delivery, we assume a lognormal distribution for the probability density function (PDF), since only mathematically positive values for the financial impact are allowed (even though risk occurrence would create a negative impact on the project budget). Moreover, this selection is in line with other research on cost estimation and risk management in construction which argues that lognormal distributions fit construction cost components generally the best [17].

Regarding the estimation of form parameters of the PDF, we abstracted the screened literature and findings of semi-structured interviews with representatives of a total of five enterprises from the South Tyrolean construction sector. These enterprises comprise SMEs from the fields of timber construction, civil engineering, shell construction and HVAC. Their representatives were asked to roughly estimate the given risk factor's impact in case of occurrence. Together with literature indications [21] as well as the questionnaire results, we configured the risk model for both cases, traditional project delivery approach and BIM-based project delivery approach. The likelihood of occurrence was modelled as binomial distribution with form parameters according to the percentage values according to [22].

In construction cost estimation, simulation-based analysis is highly affected by potential correlations of single cost factors [24]. The cited author demonstrates a slight to medium positive correlation of cost components which was confirmed in expert discussions for the considered risk factors and incorporated accordingly in the probabilistic risk model.

5 Preliminary Simulation Results

The Monte Carlo simulation was run 10000 times in both cases. Figure 4 shows the simulation results in a histogram. It can be seen that the maximum (2,56% discrepancy) and the standard deviation (1,12% discrepancy) differ only slightly from each other, while the mean (μ) and median ($\tilde{x}$) show a relatively large discrepancy: In the BIM-based case, the mean is more than 20% below the traditional project delivery. The BIM-based median is even 28,21% lower than in the traditional case.

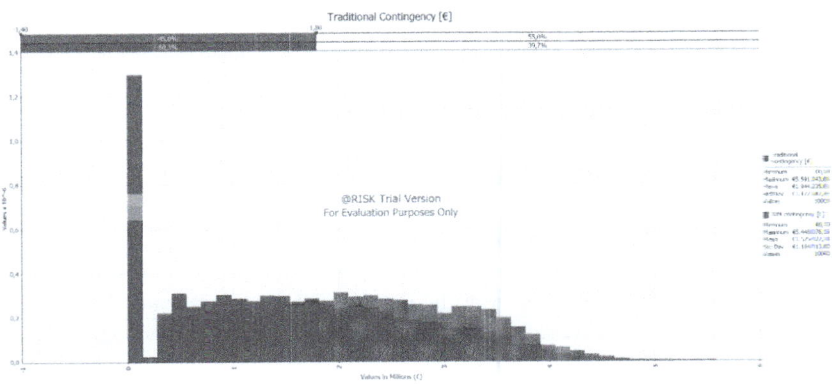

Fig. 4. Histogram of simulation results

In both cases the distributions can be considered as approximately symmetric. Only a slight skewness to the right in the BIM-based distribution can be noted (0,39). Given the kurtoses of 2,12 (traditional) and 2.24 (BIM-based), both resulting distributions can be considered as platykurtic and thus having relatively low and broad central peaks compared with the normal distribution. The mode corresponds in both cases to 0€. However, in the BIM-based case the value of 0€ for the required contingency occurs almost twice as often as in traditional project delivery.

6 Inferences from Results and Discussion

The simulation results for the selected configuration of the risk model and the resulting descriptive statistics allow the following statements: There are relatively large differences in the mean (μ) and median ($\tilde{x}$) between traditional and BIM-based project delivery (21,52% and 28,21%, respectively), while the minima and maxima, as well as the standard deviation σ_x, are relatively close to each other. The standard deviation itself appears as approx. 60% respectively 76% of the mean. Within two standard deviations there are more than 95% of all simulated values, and within three standard deviations there are more than 99,7% of all simulated values which is an indication for normal distribution. A high standard deviation indicates many outliers, which means that the median is the more appropriate single value to describe the whole sample with only one value. From this background, the median difference of almost 30% indicates a significantly positive effect of the BIM approach on contingency estimation.

However, these results should only be interpreted as a general tendency, since on the one hand the modeling and simulation results are associated with some limitations (see Sect. 7) and on the other hand the results from the mere histogram analysis with the usual confidence percentile of, for example, P90, only shows relatively small differences. Since these high confidence intervals are usually the ones on the basis of which strategic decisions are made (such as investment decisions), it remains to be checked whether the proven relative differences between traditional and BIM-based project delivery are sufficient to justify such - especially for SMEs drastic - changes as a complete BIM changeover.

7 Limitations, Conclusion and Outlook

This study has some worth mentioning limitations: only few risk factors have been considered in the probabilistic risk model, thus, the underlying risk register should be expanded in further studies. Furthermore, the assumed financial impact is only a rough estimation by the construction experts surveyed with reference to a hypothetical project scenario. These impacts would have to be determined for a larger number of different project scenarios and in a more robust manner - for example, by evaluating historical project data - which is out of scope of this study, since the focus is on presenting the benefit evaluation concept itself.

Even if this were to be done in the future, it could still be argued with the criticism that every project in the construction industry is different and it is therefore difficult to make general statements about the BIM impact. This criticism would still be justified - as explained in the section on related work in other examples - but in our view, the Monte Carlo simulation approach helps to refute this counter-argument, because this type of numerical simulation aims to play through as many random scenarios as possible in order to derive general inferences.

With respect to the chosen probability distributions there is also uncertainty, especially since the choice of the distribution has a considerable influence on the simulation results as explained by [25]. However, the presented probabilistic risk model aims at providing reasonable assumptions for the final choice of the log-normal distributions, which are explained in Sect. 4.1. In addition, this benefit assessment framework aims at providing an example of the relative difference in contingency requirements comparing a traditional and BIM-based project delivery approach, which we believe is possible even if the absolute numbers are not sufficiently reliable.

In the light of future questionnaire extensions, this study represents an invitation to the research community to evaluate the influence of BIM on risk factors in a supra-regional context in order to obtain a more complete picture of the appropriateness of the suggested indirect evaluation approach.

To conclude the results of this study, the initially stated research objectives of (i) formulation of a quantitative BIM-benefit evaluation framework and (ii) analysis of the BIM influence on known risk factors in construction have been both addressed and validated respectively through the simulation and questionnaire results.

Given the reference to TVD in this study, it may also be useful to examine projects where both BIM and TVD have been used for the combined impact on contingency determination. This could lead to a contribution to the body of knowledge in the area of practical BIM benefits, as well as new BIM-Lean synergies that have not yet been explored.

Future considerations using this BIM benefit evaluation framework should be also put in relation to the incurred costs, which require a changeover to BIM-based project delivery. In the area of BIM implementation, these costs mainly concern the investment in software, training, process changeover and personnel. Only in this overall context, quantitative BIM evaluation can provide reliable information about strategic management investment decisions of SMEs.

Acknowledgements. This work is part of BIM Simulation Lab – FESR 1086 a research project financed by the European Development Fund (ERDF) Südtirol/Alto Adige.

References

1. NBS: What is building information modelling (2019). https://www.thenbs.com/knowledge/what-is-building-information-modelling-bim. Accessed 9 Mar 2020
2. Eastman, C.M., Teicholz, P., Sacks, R., Liston, K.: BIM Handbook: A guide to Building Information Modeling for Owners, Managers, Designers, Engineers and Contractors, 1st edn. Wiley, Hoboken (2008)
3. NBS: National BIM Report 2019 (2019). https://www.thenbs.com/knowledge/national-bim-report-2019. Accessed 9 Mar 2020

4. Government H: Construction 2025 (2013). https://assets.publishing.service.gov.uk/government/uploads/system/uploads/attachment_data/file/210099/bis-13-955-construction-2025-industrial-strategy.pdf. Accessed 9 Mar 2020
5. Azhar, S.: Building information modeling (BIM): trends, benefits, risks, and challenges for the AEC industry. Lead. Manag. Eng. **11**, 241–252 (2011). https://doi.org/10.1061/(ASCE)LM.1943-5630.0000127
6. Ghaffarianhoseini, A., Tookey, J., Ghaffarianhoseini, A., et al.: Building information modelling (BIM) uptake: clear benefits, understanding its implementation, risks and challenges. Renew. Sustain. Energy Rev. **75**, 1046–1053 (2017). https://doi.org/10.1016/j.rser.2016.11.083
7. Guerriero, A., Kubicki, S., Reiter, S.: Building information modeling in use: how to evaluate the return on investment? In: eWork and eBusiness in Architecture, Engineering and Construction - Proceedings of the 11th European Conference on Product and Process Modelling, ECPPM 2016, pp 537–544 (2016)
8. NRC: NRC Publications Archive (NPArC) Archives des publications du CNRC (NPArC) (2012)
9. Snyder CS: A guide to the project management body of knowledge: PMBOK (®) guide (2014)
10. Girmscheid, G., Busch, T.A.: Unternehmensrisikomanagement in der Bauwirtschaft, Bauwerk Verlag (2008). (in German)
11. Haid, N., Schneidewind, A.: Risikomanagement in Bauunternehmen: risiken beherrschen, nicht ertragen. Straßen- und Tiefbau **7**, 5–9 (2010). (in German)
12. Johnson, P.E.: Monte carlo analysis in academic research. In: Little, T.D. (ed.) The Oxford Handbook of Quantitative Methods in Psychology, vol. 1, pp. 1–67. Oxford University Press, Oxford (2011)
13. Lemieux, C.: Monte Carlo and Quasi-Monte Carlo Sampling, 1st edn. Springer, New York (2009)
14. Rider, G., Milkovich, S., Stool, D., et al.: Quantitative risk analysis. Inj. Control. Saf. Promot. **7**, 115–133 (2000). https://doi.org/10.1002/9780470924860.ch5
15. Allahi, F., Cassettari, L., Mosca, M.: Stochastic risk analysis and cost contingency allocation approach for construction projects applying Monte Carlo simulation. In: Lecture Notes in Engineering and Computer Science, vol. 2229, pp. 385–391 (2017)
16. Medgenberg, J., Nemuth, T.: Potential der Monte-Carlo-Simulation für Risikoanalyse im Projektmanagement. In: 1. Internationaler BBB-Kongress, pp 153–171 (2011). (in German)
17. Peleskei, C.A., Dorca, V., Munteanu, R.A., Munteanu, R.: Risk consideration and cost estimation in construction projects using Monte Carlo simulation. Management **10**, 163–176 (2015)
18. Do, D., Chen, C., Ballard, G., Tommelein, I.D.: Target value design as a method for controlling project cost overruns. In: 22nd Annual Conference of the International Group for Lean Construction, vol. **1**, 171–181 (2014)
19. Siraj, N.B., Fayek, A.R.: Risk identification and common risks in construction: literature review and content analysis. J. Constr. Eng. Manag. **145** (2019). https://doi.org/10.1061/(ASCE)CO.1943-7862.0001685
20. Jarkas, A.M., Haupt, T.C.: Major construction risk factors considered by general contractors in Qatar. J. Eng. Des. Technol. **13**, 165–194 (2015). https://doi.org/10.1108/MBE-09-2016-0047
21. Chileshe, N., Boadua Yirenkyi-Fianko, A.: An evaluation of risk factors impacting construction projects in Ghana. J. Eng. Des. Technol. **10**, 306–329 (2012). https://doi.org/10.1108/17260531211274693

22. Hillson, D.A.: Describing probability: the limitations of natural language dimensions of risk. Risk Manag., 1–7 (2005)
23. Dziadosz, A., Rejment, M.: Risk analysis in construction project - chosen methods. Procedia Eng. **122**, 258–265 (2015). https://doi.org/10.1016/j.proeng.2015.10.034
24. Yang, I.T.: Simulation-based estimation for correlated cost elements. Int. J. Proj. Manag. **23**, 275–282 (2005). https://doi.org/10.1016/j.ijproman.2004.12.002
25. Arnold, U., Yildiz, Ö.: Economic risk analysis of decentralized renewable energy infrastructures - a Monte Carlo Simulation approach. Renew. Energy **77**, 227–239 (2015). https://doi.org/10.1016/j.renene.2014.11.059

Cross-Pollination as a Comparative Analysis Approach to Comparing BIM and PLM: A Literature Review

Hamidreza Pourzarei(✉), Louis Rivest, and Conrad Boton

École de Technologie Supérieure, Montréal, Canada
hamidreza.pourzarei.1@ens.etsmtl.ca,
{louis.rivest, conrad.boton}@etsmtl.ca

Abstract. Comparison is at the center of many research studies that leads to the interaction between different objects and mostly resulted in significant improvements. Especially, comparing business/technological approaches, such as building information modeling (BIM) and product lifecycle management (PLM), is an activity that is often difficult and complex, and requires particular methodological approaches. One of the biggest challenges through such a comparison is to identify the most effective methodological approach. Previous research studies have introduced cross-pollination as an interesting comparative analysis approach. However, it is important to mention that it remains a relatively untapped approach in the literature. This article provides a review of the cross-pollination variants and related terms and steps. Research findings of comparative analysis methods and approaches are evaluated to demonstrate the similarities and differences. This evaluation leads this research to represents the lessons learned of the existing methods and approaches.

Keywords: BIM · PLM · Comparison · Comparative analysis · Cross-pollination

1 Introduction

Comparison is fundamental to human thought and ever present in world observation, which makes thinking without comparison unthinkable [1]. Many research studies focus on comparing two or more objects with different aims, such as benchmarking, interaction and inspiration. Furthermore, various research studies have focused on comparing objects in different domains, such as BIM and PLM [2–10], two business/technological approaches [11] and [12], two systems [11], two perspectives [12], and two business models [13]. The comparison can possibly bring the improvement of productivity between the intended objects. Accurate comparison is usually a difficult task, and it comes with different types of challenges, two of the most significant of which are how to compare objects and how compared objects can learn from and interact with each other.

A variety of methods and approaches have been proposed to address these two challenges, such as statistical and mathematical methods, and modeling techniques [13–15]. However, these techniques are not sufficient for the comparison of two holistic

Published by Springer Nature Switzerland AG 2020
F. Nyffenegger et al. (Eds.): PLM 2020, IFIP AICT 594, pp. 724–737, 2020.
https://doi.org/10.1007/978-3-030-62807-9_57

approaches involving multiple components and dimensions (e.g. BIM and PLM). One possible avenue for the comparison of such approaches is cross-pollination. While it has been mentioned a few times in the literature, it remains relatively uncommon and seems far from being clearly formalized as an effective comparison approach. This article presents the first steps of a more comprehensive research project that aims to compare BIM and PLM approaches, from the standpoint of the engineering change management. It reviews the dedicated literature in order to define cross-pollination as a comparison method, and to analyze how it has been used in different research studies.

This article is followed into five sections. Section 2 reviews the selected literature; we identify the cross-pollination and its different terms. Section 3 represents an investigation of how these methods and approaches have been used through different research studies, as well as what are the methods and steps for effective cross-pollination. In Sect. 4, this article analyzes the various types of pollination (cross-pollination and its equivalent terms). The fifth section discusses the results. Finally, the last part wraps up the article with the conclusion and future works.

2 Terms and Variations of Cross-Pollination

This section aims at defining the cross-pollination as well as identifying its related terms and variants. Generally, when referring to the concept of cross-pollination or its different terms, we thought of a method or approach that can let two or more objects to interact and/or compare with each other. More precisely, several research studies have used cross-pollination to compare objects and find common and transferable characteristics for improvement. Interestingly, the term "cross-pollination" in the context of comparison is inspired by the pollination mechanism of plants [16, 17]. Pollination can be described as pollen transmission in the same plant or between plants from one flower to another [17]. There are two types of pollination mechanisms:

- *Self-pollination* – When the pollen from a flower pollinates the same flower or another flower on the same plant [18].
- *Cross-pollination* – When pollen grains are moved to a flower on another plant [18].

Although most research studies used the term "cross-pollination" for comparison, some others used different terms and variants, such as "cross-fertilization" and "bi-directional coordination and interaction." While there are many different terms in use to refer to cross-pollination, the following four were selected from the literature because they were used in the context of comparative analysis:

- *Flower pollination* – This is the earliest of the terms used to define the pollination mechanism. Xin-She Yang [19] proposed a flower pollination algorithm that was inspired by the pollination mechanism used by plants [19]. The flower pollination algorithm is proposed for many design applications in engineering and industry.
- *Cross-pollination* – This is one of the terms most commonly used in research studies. It has been used in different research domains, such as software development [20], optimization [21], comparative studies in education [22] and the comparison of BIM and PLM [2, 3], the oil & gas industry and space & satellite sector [23], partnerships in healthcare [24].

- *Cross-fertilization* – This term is commonly used when focusing on interaction. It is used when comparing objects and enables collaboration, such as in the case of the research of Piètre-Cambacèdès and Bouissou [25], to identify potential common characteristics between safety and security engineering. It is also used for comparing building design and engineering design [26] as well as the construction industry and manufacturing [27].
- *Bi-directional coordination and interaction* – This is another term that is used when focusing on interaction, for example, in the research of Wiesner et al. [11]. The authors used this term for comparing service lifecycle management (SLM) and product lifecycle management (PLM) and finding potential for collaboration.

These terms and variants will be analyzed further in the next section by investigating how they were used in different domains.

3 Use of Cross-Pollination as a Comparative Analysis Approach

Now that cross-pollination and its equivalent terms and variants have been defined, this section goes on to investigate how these terms have been used in various research studies. Here is a sampling of the research studies:

- *Cross-pollination for BIM and PLM comparison* – Boton et al. [2, 3] compared BIM and PLM from a product structure (PS) standpoint and indicated that cross-pollination between BIM and PLM could benefit both the construction and shipbuilding industries in terms of knowledge transfer. The authors investigated further by conducting a practical study in the construction and shipbuilding industries to provide an in-depth understanding of these two industries. They aimed to identify equivalent notions in the construction and shipbuilding industries from a product structure standpoint, and mentioned "comparing BIM and PLM is a useful endeavor that could help improve both domains through cross-pollination" [2]. In addition, this comparison facilitated cross-pollination between the technological approaches of the two domains, so as to interact and benefit from the knowledge transferred between the two industries.

Flower pollination algorithm (FPA) – One of the initial research studies that used "cross-pollination" or more precisely "pollination" is that of Xin-She Yang [19]. Their research suggests that in many design applications for engineering and industry, under highly complex constraints, we will try to find the optimal solution to a given problem. Such unique optimization problems are often highly nonlinear, and finding the optimal solution is often a very difficult, if not impossible, task. Xin-She Yang [19] introduced a new algorithm, the FPA inspired by flowers' pollination process. The algorithm was later developed and used by other researchers in different domains [28]. Kaur and Kumar [17] used the concept of cross-pollination and the FPA for selecting the optimum number of base stations and optimizing site locations in wireless communication. Valenzuela et al. [18] used a fuzzy inference system to improve the FPA to solve complex optimization problems. Moreover, the work of Deepa and Rasi [29] used the FPA to resolve color image segmentation.

- *Cross-pollination between critical pedagogy and democratic education* – The research of Edwards [22] compares and contrasts the potential of connecting democratic education and critical pedagogy for cross-pollination. Three steps were proposed in this research to achieve cross-pollination: 1) investigate critical pedagogy and democratic education, 2) conduct a comparative analysis (of similarities and differences, using both theoretical and empirical studies), 3) identify the possibilities for cross-pollination.
- *Cross-pollination for software development* – The research of Hantos and Gisbert [20] aimed to introduce a framework for cross-pollination between software development and alternative disciplines. The research illustrated that cross-pollination can fosters improvements in software development relatively inexpensively, providing subtle benefits in individual and group settings [20]. The proposed framework has three steps:
  - *Selection* – Select a case study from another discipline that offers potentially relevant problem solving or process improvement examples.
  - *Analysis* – Analyze the case study, record observations and debate the case study issues in their context. In the end, this part classified the results of observations into one of the three categories: people, process or technology.
  - *Mapping, evaluation and emulation* – This step systematically maps the collected solutions or process improvement ideas to practical solutions and improvement approaches in the target discipline and then devises methods to emulate and implement these techniques.

It is important to mention that the case study proposed compares observations as well as unique challenges in the construction and software domains based on the proposed categories—people, process, and technology [20]. In the end, they evaluated and rated the results to identify the potential for cross-pollination.

- *Cross-pollination for optimization* – Soni et al. [21] proposed a unified (algorithm) approach to enable the cross-pollination of ideas between established communities, which would help with the mapping of sequential decision-making problems (SDMP). The interesting point of this approach is that it required both theoretical and experimental research on algorithm performance.
- *Cross-pollination between the oil and gas industry and space and satellite sector* – Over the years, experts from both the upstream oil and gas industry and the space and satellite sector have noticed many striking similarities between the two domains, resulting in many direct media and industry press correlations [23]. Despite the fact that the two sectors have also intersected in academic literature, little sharing or cross-pollination has occurred in terms of asset maintenance. The research of Perrons and Richards [23] argues that the oil and gas industry could significantly improve the maintenance of its assets by selectively applying some aspects of the maintenance strategies and philosophies used in space and satellite sector [23]. The authors considered maintenance as the standpoint for their comparison to facilitate cross-pollination.
- *Cross-pollination for partnerships in healthcare* – Partnerships are a common approach to delivering healthcare [24]. Despite evidence from various settings of

the challenges of putting partnerships into practice, there has been little cross-pollination between literature from different fields [24]. These problems led Aveling and Martin [24] to evaluate partnerships through a comparative analysis of two case studies of multi-level partnerships in different contexts in the UK National Health Service and an internationally funded health program in Cambodia. Two points were of particular interest in this research: first, using partnering as the comparison standpoint facilitated both comparison as well as cross-pollination, and second, the authors analyzed both theoretical and empirical studies.

- *Cross-fertilization between building design and engineering design* – It is important to use design models to promote information exchange between engineering designers in both the construction industry and manufacturing [26]. It could be assumed that the use of design models varies between the two fields and that the models used in building design are more suitable for integrating discipline-specific perspectives than those used in engineering design. Based on these assumptions, the objective of the study of Eisenbart and Blessing [26] was to investigate the reasons for using different design models for cross-fertilization. Building design and engineering design were comparatively analyzed based on three categories of comparison: 1) comparison of the development process, 2) comparison of communication within the development process, and 3) comparison of the use of design models within the development process.
- *Cross-fertilization between safety and security engineering* – Safety and security developed over many years as two distinct disciplines, led by discrete communities to develop their own tools and methodologies [25]. The research of Piètre-Cambacédès and Bouissou [25] aimed to highlight the potential for cross-fertilization between safety and security engineering by evaluating related initiatives and outcomes in scientific literature and industry practices. The authors sought to identify commonalities and distinguishing features of safety and security through different perspectives to facilitate their comparison. Cross-fertilization was well implemented in this research by organizing how safety and security interact with each other. The authors classified the characteristics of these objects that interact into three groups:
  - Existing characteristics for cross-fertilization, with interactions divided into two sub-classes: 1) from safety to security, and 2) from security to safety.
  - Potential characteristics for cross-fertilization, ones that have the potential to interact, divided into two sub-classes: 1) from safety to security, and 2) from security to safety.
  - Characteristics for safety and security integrated tools – the authors thought that in some cases, combining the characteristics of both domains could be more efficient [25].
- *Cross-fertilization between the construction industry and manufacturing* – The research of Sanvido and Medeiros [27] used the term "cross-fertilization" to investigate ways and approaches to develop an integrated process model for construction and manufacturing. The comparison in their research was followed by two perspectives—first, comparing the process modeling approaches used in both construction and manufacturing, and second, comparing the integrated process

model in construction and manufacturing. From their investigation, they proposed potential candidates for cross-fertilization.

- *Bi-directional coordination and interaction* – The research of Wiesner et al. [11] used this term for the interaction between service lifecycle management (SLM) and product lifecycle management (PLM). They aimed to "combine PLM and SLM approaches to support the lifecycle of integrated product-service systems" [11]. According to their research, the collaboration consists of four cooperative processes in the phases in which PLM and SLM are not yet fully integrated: coordination, the exchange of information, negotiation and conflict resolution [11].

Table 1 summarizes the terms and variants as well as their intended domain.

Table 1. Terms and variants of pollination and their intended domain

Author(s)	Term used	Intended domain
Boton et al. [2]	Cross-pollination	Comparing BIM and PLM
Xin-She Yang [19]	Flower pollination algorithm	Solving optimization problems
Kaur and Kumar [17]	Cross-pollination (+ flower pollination algorithm)	Optimizing site locations in wireless communication
Valenzuela et al. [18]	Flower pollination algorithm	Solving optimization problems, with a fuzzy inference system
Deepa and Rasi [29]	Flower pollination algorithm	Resolving color image segmentation
Edwards [22]	Cross-pollination	Comparing educational systems
Hantos and Gisbert [20]	Cross-pollination	Comparing different software development disciplines
Soni et al. [21]	Cross-pollination	Comparing algorithms in decision-making problems
Perrons and Richards [23]	Cross-pollination	Comparing the oil and gas industry and space and satellite sector
Aveling and Martin [24]	Cross-pollination	Comparing partnerships in healthcare
Eisenbart and Blessing [26]	Cross-fertilization	Comparing building design and engineering design
Piètre-Cambacédès and Bouissou [25]	Cross-fertilization	Comparing safety and security engineering
Sanvido and Medeiros [27]	Cross-fertilization	Comparing the construction industry and manufacturing
Wiesner et al. [11]	Bi-directional coordination and interaction	Comparing SLM and PLM

The following section evaluates the aforementioned terms and variants and their intended domain to extract the similarities and differences between them.

4 Analysis of Various Types of Pollination

This part aims to analyze the results and identify the similarities and differences between different types of pollination (cross-pollination and its equivalent terms). Interestingly, most of the research studies used the same three-phase structure for comparison: compared concepts and defined terms, comparative analysis and pollination. In some cases, the order varies or one step is skipped (but still considered indirectly). The structure is summarized in Table 2.

Table 2. Comparative analysis structure for different types of pollination

Author(s)	Compared concepts and defined terms	Comparative analysis	Pollination
Boton et al. [2]	PLM, BIM, BOM, product structure, discrete manufacturing	• Comparing product Beginning-of-life (BOL) in shipbuilding and construction • Analyzing Bill of Materials (BOM) and Product Structure (PS) concepts in shipbuilding and identifying equivalent notions in construction • Comparing PLM in shipbuilding and BIM in construction from different perspectives	• Demonstrate which equivalent elements distinguish BIM in construction and PLM in shipbuilding
Wiesner et al. [11]	PLM; PDM; SLM; various phases of the product lifecycle (BOL, Middle-of-life (MOL) and End-of-life (EOL)) and service lifecycle (service creation, service engineering and service operations)	• Identifying the occurring interaction pattern between PLM and SLM through four case scenarios: 1) SLM follows PLM, 2) PLM follows SLM, 3) SLM is aligned with PLM, 4) SLM is integrated with PLM	• Determine the patterns that exist in terms of interaction between PLM and SLM • Identify areas in which PLM and SLM are not completely integrated (coordination, the exchange of information, negotiation and conflict resolution)

(*continued*)

Table 2. (*continued*)

Author(s)	Compared concepts and defined terms	Comparative analysis	Pollination
Piètre-Cambacèdés and Bouissou [25]	Safety, security, related concepts such as risk	• Comparing the similarities and differences between safety and security from different perspectives, such as similarities in design and operation principles, and differences in the rating of consequences • Comparing the existence of the interactions between safety and security	• Propose characteristics for cross-fertilization between safety and security
Perrons and Richards [23]	–	• Identifying best practices from space and satellite industry • Comparing two domains from the standpoint of maintenance	• Recommend four research questions to accelerate the rate of learning and sharing (pollination) between two industries
Aveling and Martin [24]	Partnership in healthcare	• Comparing instrumental and transformative partnerships • Comparing partnerships from different perspectives (i.e., partnership in high- and low-income countries) • Comparing partnerships in two practical studies	• Identify opportunities for improvement in partnerships

(*continued*)

Table 2. (*continued*)

Author(s)	Compared concepts and defined terms	Comparative analysis	Pollination
Eisenbart and Blessing [26]	Design models in product development and building design	• Comparing the design models used in product development and building design • Comparing the development process used in building design and engineering design • Comparing communication in both industries	• Identify opportunities for cross-pollination between the design models used in building and product development
Edwards [22]	Critical pedagogy and democratic education	• Comparing critical pedagogy and democratic education from different perspectives (i.e., classroom, government)	• Propose opportunities for cross-pollination between critical pedagogy and democratic education
Hantos and Gisbert [20]	Cross-pollination	• Comparing two practical studies in the construction and software domains using the proposed framework	• Propose a framework for cross-pollination that has three steps: 1) selection, 2) analysis, and 3) mapping, evaluation and emulation • Address three categories (people, process and technology) in the analysis step

On one hand, some research studies used a single standpoint, such as *maintenance* [23], *product structure* [2] and *partnership* [24], for their comparative analysis. On the other hand, multiple standpoints are used to identify similarities and differences, for instance, "similarities in design and operation principles" or "differences in the rating of consequences" [23].

In the literature, the researchers classified two types of pollination characteristics [25]: 1) characteristics of the first object that are mapped and used on the second object to convey its benefits, and 2) potential characteristics that can be transferred to the other object or combined to create the new characteristics that can be applied to both objects.

These types of pollination characteristics are mapped and explained briefly in the following section.

5 Discussion

After reviewing the selected literature on comparative analysis methods and approaches, the next step is to identify the lessons learned that can be used to compare BIM and PLM, considered here as holistic objects involving multiple components.

The first issue is to consider the comparative analysis structure used in most types of pollination and it has three phases: compared concepts and defined terms, comparative analysis and pollination. This structure was presented briefly in Table 2. The structure can help to organize the comparison. On the other hand, several standpoints have been used to organize and facilitate comparison, for instance, maintenance for comparing space and satellite sector with oil and gas industry [23], product structure for comparing BIM and PLM [2], and partnership for comparing two healthcare systems [24]. Therefore, using a standpoint can be considered as the other lesson learned.

Three pollination patterns were extracted from the literature review and definitions are proposed here after: self-pollination, cross-pollination (transposition) and cross-pollination (combination).

- *Self-pollination* – This type of pollination aims to create or improve the components that are the result of self-pollinating. Self-pollinating means self-improvement or self-learning that one holistic object can learn from itself.
- *Cross-pollination (transposition)* – This type of pollination aims to create or improve the components of one holistic object by transposing and adapting some components from another holistic object in order to extend the capabilities of this holistic object.
- *Cross-pollination (combination)* – This type of pollination aims to create a new holistic object by combining components from other holistic objects, in order to build on the strengths and mitigate the weaknesses of the parent holistic objects.

Figure 1 illustrates three patterns of pollination: self-pollination, cross-pollination (transposition), and cross-pollination (combination), which represents the holistic objects and their components before and after pollinating.

Digital Twin in both manufacturing and construction is an example of self-pollination that can result in different types of improvements such as optimizing the processes and virtual control. Since both the physical and the virtual component that are being compared belong to the same universe (be it BIM or PLM), it is considered as self-pollination.

A common idea for the BIM and PLM comparison is that the mature functionalities of PLM could be tailored to the specific context of the construction and infrastructure industry to effectively manipulate complex BIM models (transposition) [6]. In addition, several research studies [2], and [30] suggest that BIM and PLM cross-pollination would be more beneficial and provide an opportunity to improve efficiency and productivity in both BIM- and PLM-supported industry (transposition).

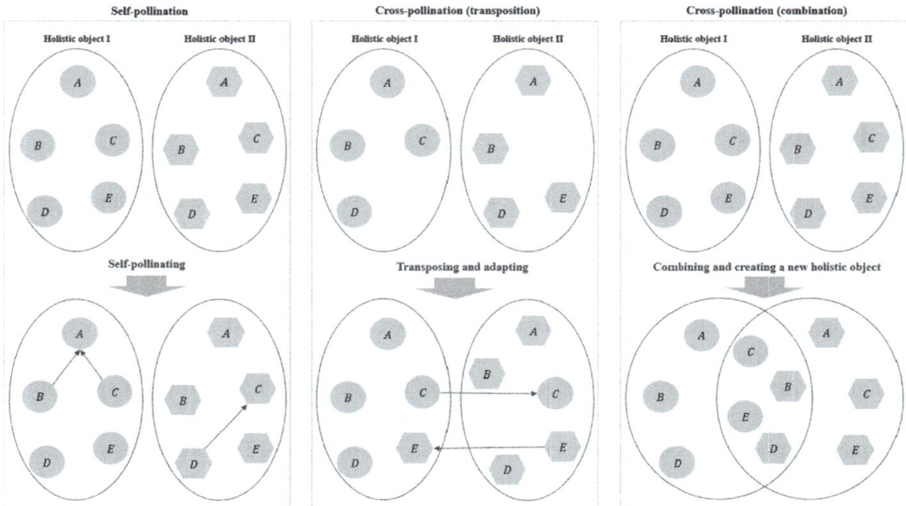

Fig. 1. Three patterns of pollination

Some research work studied cross-pollination in BIM and PLM either by mentioning the term cross-pollination or not, such as the research of Aram and East-man [31] that discussed "the potential benefits of adopting the PLM solution in the AEC industry" (transposition) as well as proposing a conceptual model for integrating PLM solutions with BIM servers (combination). Jupp and Singh [32] and Jupp [33] investigate the opportunities that PLM can address in BIM (transposition). The work by Biccari et al. [9] and Boton et al. [2] also studied these types of improvement between BIM and PLM by considering, respectively, configuration view and product structure as a standpoint (transposition and combination).

Hence, various investigations between BIM and PLM can be considered as belonging to the different types of pollination such as self-pollination—do the improvement by self-learning, cross-pollination (transposition)—transposing and adapting components from another holistic object, and cross-pollination (combination) —create a new holistic object by combining components from other holistic objects.

As mentioned, the cross-pollination (combination) can create a new holistic object by integrating or combining the components that can be used in different domains. For instance, in the research of Cheutet et al. [7], the characteristics and functionalities of BIM and PLM are integrating together to be used in the nuclear facility decommissioning.

6 Conclusion and Future Works

The concept of cross-pollination in research refers to the influence of interaction between two objects that can lead to a gain by comparative analysis. This article aimed to review the dedicated literature about cross-pollination as a comparison method and to analyze how it has been used in different research studies.

This investigation resulted in three achievements. First, the comparative analysis structure used in most types of pollination has three phases: compared concepts and defined terms, comparative analysis, and pollination. Second, comparing complex objects could be better performed according to a specific standpoint. Third, three pollination patterns were extracted from the literature review and definitions are proposed here after: self-pollination—do the improvement by self-learning, cross-pollination (transposition)—transposing and adapting components from another holistic object, and cross-pollination (combination)—create a new holistic object by combining components from other holistic objects.

Globally, this preliminary investigation reveals that literature uses the concept of cross-pollination as an approach to compare two holistic objects. However, cross-pollination does not appear as a carefully defined mechanism for comparison. For instance, some research studies proposed 2, 3, or 4 phases for doing cross-pollination, and do not propose an accurate comparison framework. Hence, authors will decide either using cross-pollination, by proposing a more accurate version of cross-pollination, or investigating more for other approaches.

References

1. Rihoux, B., Ragin, C.C.: Configurational Comparative Methods: Qualitative Comparative Analysis (QCA) and Related Techniques, vol. 51. Sage Publications, Thousand Oaks (2008)
2. Boton, C., Rivest, L., Forgues, D., Jupp, J.R.: Comparison of shipbuilding and construction industries from the product structure standpoint. Int. J. Prod. Lifecycle Manag. 11(3), 191–220 (2018)
3. Boton, C., Rivest, L., Forgues, D., Jupp, J.: Comparing PLM and BIM from the product structure standpoint. In: Harik, R., Rivest, L., Bernard, A., Eynard, B., Bouras, A. (eds.) PLM 2016. IAICT, vol. 492, pp. 443–453. Springer, Cham (2016). https://doi.org/10.1007/978-3-319-54660-5_40
4. Jupp, J.R., Singh, V.: Similar concepts, distinct solutions, common problems: learning from PLM and BIM deployment. In: Fukuda, S., Bernard, A., Gurumoorthy, B., Bouras, A. (eds.) PLM 2014. IAICT, vol. 442, pp. 31–40. Springer, Heidelberg (2014). https://doi.org/10.1007/978-3-662-45937-9_4
5. Jupp, J.R.: Cross industry learning: a comparative study of product lifecycle management and building information modelling. Int. J. Prod. Lifecycle Manag. 9(3), 258–284 (2016). https://doi.org/10.1504/ijplm.2016.080502
6. Mangialardi, G., Di Biccari, C., Pascarelli, C., Lazoi, M., Corallo, A.: BIM and PLM associations in current literature. In: Ríos, J., Bernard, A., Bouras, A., Foufou, S. (eds.) PLM 2017. IAICT, vol. 517, pp. 345–357. Springer, Cham (2017). https://doi.org/10.1007/978-3-319-72905-3_31
7. Cheutet, V., Sekhari, A., Corbeaux, N.: PLM and BIM approach to support information management in nuclear decommissioning: a synthesis. In: Chiabert, P., Bouras, A., Noël, F., Ríos, J. (eds.) PLM 2018. IAICT, vol. 540, pp. 104–114. Springer, Cham (2018). https://doi.org/10.1007/978-3-030-01614-2_10
8. Chen, Yu., Jupp, J.: Model-based systems engineering and through-life information management in complex construction. In: Chiabert, P., Bouras, A., Noël, F., Ríos, J. (eds.) PLM 2018. IAICT, vol. 540, pp. 80–92. Springer, Cham (2018). https://doi.org/10.1007/978-3-030-01614-2_8

9. Di Biccari, C., Mangialardi, G., Lazoi, M., Corallo, A.: Configuration views from PLM to building lifecycle management. In: Chiabert, P., Bouras, A., Noël, F., Ríos, J. (eds.) PLM 2018. IAICT, vol. 540, pp. 69–79. Springer, Cham (2018). https://doi.org/10.1007/978-3-030-01614-2_7
10. Jupp, J.R., Nepal, M.: BIM and PLM: comparing and learning from changes to professional practice across sectors. In: Fukuda, S., Bernard, A., Gurumoorthy, B., Bouras, A. (eds.) PLM 2014. IAICT, vol. 442, pp. 41–50. Springer, Heidelberg (2014). https://doi.org/10.1007/978-3-662-45937-9_5
11. Wiesner, S., Freitag, M., Westphal, I., Thoben, K.-D.: Interactions between service and product lifecycle management. Procedia CIRP **30**, 36–41 (2015)
12. Brotheridge, C.M., Grandey, A.A.: Emotional labor and burnout: comparing two perspectives of 'people work'. J. Vocat. Behav. **60**(1), 17–39 (2002)
13. Gordijn, J., Osterwalder, A., Pigneur, Y.: Comparing two business model ontologies for designing e-business models and value constellations. BLED 2005 Proc., 15 (2005)
14. Van Reijswoud, V., Lind, M.: Comparing two business modelling approaches in the language action perspective. In: Proceedings of the Third International Workshop on Communication Modelling: LAP, vol. 98 (1998)
15. Law, N., Chow, A., Yuen, A.H.: Methodological approaches to comparing pedagogical innovations using technology. Educ. Inf. Technol. **10**(1–2), 7–20 (2005)
16. Panawala, L.: (3) (PDF) Difference Between Self and Cross Pollination. ResearchGate. https://www.researchgate.net/publication/316616996_Difference_Between_Self_and_Cross_Pollination. Accessed 15 Dec 2019
17. Kaur, R., Kumar, A.: An approach for selecting optimum number of base stations and optimizing site locations using flower pollination algorithm. Int. J. Comput. Appl. **133**(10), 34–39 (2016)
18. Valenzuela, L., Valdez, F., Melin, P.: Flower pollination algorithm with fuzzy approach for solving optimization problems. In: Melin, P., Castillo, O., Kacprzyk, J. (eds.) Nature-Inspired Design of Hybrid Intelligent Systems. SCI, vol. 667, pp. 357–369. Springer, Cham (2017). https://doi.org/10.1007/978-3-319-47054-2_24
19. Yang, X.-S.: Flower pollination algorithm for global optimization. In: Durand-Lose, J., Jonoska, N. (eds.) UCNC 2012. LNCS, vol. 7445, pp. 240–249. Springer, Heidelberg (2012). https://doi.org/10.1007/978-3-642-32894-7_27
20. Hantos, P., Gisbert, M.: Identifying software productivity improvement approaches and risks: construction industry case study. IEEE Softw. **17**(1), 48–56 (2000)
21. Soni, A., Lewis, Peter R., Ekárt, A.: Synergies between reinforcement learning and evolutionary dynamic optimisation. In: Lewis, P.R., Headleand, C.J., Battle, S., Ritsos, P.D. (eds.) ALIA 2016. CCIS, vol. 732, pp. 91–96. Springer, Cham (2018). https://doi.org/10.1007/978-3-319-90418-4_7
22. Edwards, D.B.: Critical pedagogy and democratic education: possibilities for cross-pollination. Urban Rev. **42**(3), 221–242 (2010)
23. Perrons, R.K., Richards, M.G.: Applying maintenance strategies from the space and satellite sector to the upstream oil and gas industry: a research agenda. Energy Policy **61**, 60–64 (2013)
24. Aveling, E.-L., Martin, G.: Realising the transformative potential of healthcare partnerships: insights from divergent literatures and contrasting cases in high-and low-income country contexts. Soc. Sci. Med. **92**, 74–82 (2013)
25. Piètre-Cambacédès, L., Bouissou, M.: Cross-fertilization between safety and security engineering. Reliab. Eng. Syst. Saf. **110**, 110–126 (2013)

26. Eisenbart, B., Blessing, L.: Application of design models in mechatronic product development and building design–reflections of researchers and practitioners. In: DFX 2011: Proceedings of the 22nd Symposium Design for X, Tutzing nr. Munich, Germany, 11–12 Oct 2011, pp. 87–98 (2011)
27. Sanvido, V.E., Medeiros, D.J.: The cross fertilization of construction and manufacturing through computer integration. In: Proceeding 6th ISARC San Francisco, pp. 73–79 (1989)
28. Yang, X.-S., Karamanoglu, M., He, X.: Flower pollination algorithm: a novel approach for multiobjective optimization. Eng. Optim. **46**(9), 1222–1237 (2014)
29. Deepa, S.N., Rasi, D.: Global biotic cross-pollination algorithm enhanced with evolutionary strategies for color image segmentation. Soft. Comput. **23**(8), 2545–2559 (2019). https://doi.org/10.1007/s00500-018-03720-7
30. Chen, Yu., Jupp, J.: BIM and through-life information management: a systems engineering perspective. In: Mutis, I., Hartmann, T. (eds.) Advances in Informatics and Computing in Civil and Construction Engineering, pp. 137–146. Springer, Cham (2019). https://doi.org/10.1007/978-3-030-00220-6_17
31. Aram, S., Eastman, C.: Integration of PLM solutions and BIM systems for the AEC industry. In: ISARC. Proceedings of the International Symposium on Automation and Robotics in Construction, vol. 30, p. 1 (2013)
32. Jupp, J.R., Singh, V.: A PLM perspective of BIM research initiatives. Int. J. Prod. Lifecycle Manag. **9**, 180–197 (2016)
33. Jupp, J.R.: Incomplete BIM implementation: exploring challenges and the role of product lifecycle management functions. In: Bernard, A., Rivest, L., Dutta, D. (eds.) PLM 2013. IAICT, vol. 409, pp. 630–640. Springer, Heidelberg (2013). https://doi.org/10.1007/978-3-642-41501-2_62

Enhancement of BIM Data Representation in Product-Process Modelling for Building Renovation

Janakiram Karlapudi[1(✉)], Karsten Menzel[1], Seppo Törmä[2], Andriy Hryshchenko[3], and Prathap Valluru[1]

[1] Institute for Construction Informatics, Technische Universität Dresden, Dresden, Germany
janakiram.karlapudi@tu-dresden.de
[2] VisuaLynk, Espoo, Finland
[3] School of Engineering, University College Cork, Cork, Ireland

Abstract. Building Information Modelling (BIM) has the potential to become a technology which will help to use a holistic information repository to generate and represent relevant information in different building life-cycle stages (BLCS) to dedicated groups of stakeholders. However, the scope of model components of BIM data (e.g., IFC meta-data) is limited and some parts of it are not modelled in a manner that supports the diversity of engineering use cases. This paper aims to address this deficit by identifying the capability to formulate inference rules as one of the major benefits in the ontology-based information modelling approach. However, before one can formulate inferencing rules a detailed and in-depth understanding is required on how stakeholder information needs are defined in different BLCS and on how available, open-BIM meta-data models support these information requirements. Therefore, the research progressed initially on existing definitions for Level of Detail (**LOD**) and selected process-modelling standards (**BLCS**). In the subsequent part, different renovation **Activities** and the **Stakeholder** involvements are analysed. **Use cases** are defined and used as a grouping mechanism for selected scenarios. Based on these grouping mechanisms, a methodology of how components of a **BIM-model** could be classified to support automated inferencing in the future. The outcome of this research is an established 6-dimensional intercommunication framework (LOD, BLS, Scenarios, Stakeholders, Use Cases, BIM model data) based on the Linked Building Data approach and focusing on renovation processes optimization. Based on the framework, a renovation Product-Process Modelling ontology is developed to connect existing components and to support new interoperable applications.

Keywords: BIM model · Building life-cycle stages · Ontology for Product-Process modelling (OPPM) · Stakeholder scenarios · Linked building data · Interoperability

Published by Springer Nature Switzerland AG 2020
F. Nyffenegger et al. (Eds.): PLM 2020, IFIP AICT 594, pp. 738–752, 2020.
https://doi.org/10.1007/978-3-030-62807-9_58

1 Introduction and Background

In an ideal case, buildings are managed and renovated systematically throughout their whole life cycle. The basis is the execution of the maintenance strategy of the building owners, which ensures that there are always up-to-date condition surveys made by professionals with long-term planning and budgeting based on them. Unfortunately, the ideal case rarely exists and resulting to the renovation debt and the poor documentation of buildings' present conditions and maintenance history. There are many reasons behind the lack of efficient approaches and this results in the overall slow implementation of renovation in the residential building stock, for example [1]:

- lack of understanding of the long-term planning and its importance;
- the need to save in housing costs in the short run, especially in the privately-owned apartment buildings;
- the non- or semi-professional ownership of the residential buildings;
- involvement of various actors along the stages of the building life cycle and misunderstandings between them [2, 3].

The BIM4EEB-project [4] aims to tackle these challenges by presenting the fast mapping to ground the initial stage quickly and produce an enriched BIM - either the building has been ideally maintained or not. This approach creates the basis for the cost-efficient renovation planning, implementation and seamless hand over for the post-renovation phase. The further process or phase in building construction and renovation requires the integrated communication and interchange of information between the involved stakeholders and tools along the building's complete lifecycle [5]. Many kinds of research progressed on data interoperability in the AEC domain either by the use of the IFC schema or other data transfer techniques. The diversity of AEC information and the complex interpretation of it among different stakeholders makes those efforts complex and challenging [6–8]. Research on the application of semantic web technologies in the AEC industry represents an approach to connect diverse alternative information modelling techniques to OpenBIM (IFC) concepts and enable knowledge generation, representation and sharing [9].

This paper presents a framework supporting renovation process using a Product–Process ontology, which clearly describes the different activities, tasks, sequences, their interrelations to stakeholders involved, the required information, resources, etc. Additionally, it supports the establishment of standardized collaboration protocols between stakeholders, uninterrupted communication flows and sharing of relevant information represented in BIM models when required. An explanation of parameters for the related Product-Process ontology and the development methodology is presented in this paper as well. The result of this paper is an ontological framework for BIM data representation on different levels of detail corresponding to renovation process modelling.

2 Renovation Framework

The project's [4] research idea is to bridge the current gap between renovation planning tools and their inherent process models with BIM authoring tools and their native models. The concept of integrated Product-Process Modelling is adopted to map stakeholders' basic needs and requirements with related application strategies to achieve the research aim. We have identified the major credentials for the development of an integrated Product-Process ontology framework (see Fig. 1). It comprises of six different aspects, such as BIM-objects (product data), Building Life-Cycle Stages (time context), Activities (process data), Use Cases (processes in their context), LOD (specification of integrated Spatio-temporal context), and Stakeholders (execute processes on BIM-objects).

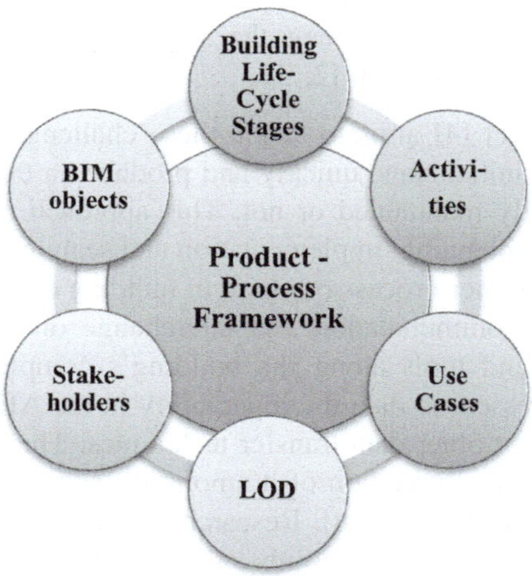

Fig. 1. Components of Product-Process Modelling

Building Information Modelling (BIM) is an advanced information technology that should be adopted by relevant Stakeholders. These stakeholders are performing their activities with the use of BIM for managing the information produced during the renovation processes throughout all BLCS. Going through the BLCS, an additional BIM-content (e.g. classes and attributes of classes) need to be populated which means the BIM-model growth. The early BIM models are broader when covering entities at the upper levels of breakdown structures and focused on constraints between those entities. This information refinement process is defined through the concept of LOD. Moreover, to simplify the understanding of the renovation process and to provide a methodology for the development of LOD-related Product-Process ontologies with general applicability. The concept of Use Cases as a dynamic combination of those activities is defined. The subsequent sections focus on the above-mentioned individual variables and enrich their internal framework with further information.

2.1 Level of Detail (LOD)

The LOD of BIM should be generally defined for key stages of projects when data sharing takes place. This would allow stakeholders to verify that project information is detailed enough to meet their requirements, enabling them to decide whether to proceed to the next project stage or not.

Since 2004, different countries have developed dedicated LOD standards generating a complex situation at an international level. A single, unified approach for the definition of LOD is pending. The abbreviation "LOD" is used in various meanings in different countries, such as USA - BIMForum Specification [10], UK - BS 1192-1 and PAS 1192-2, 3 [11, 12], and Italy UNI 11337 part 4 [13] (see also Table 1).

Table 1. LOD system according to the different national specifications.

Country	LOD means	Sub-type	Scale
USA	Level of Development	LOD: As Designed	LOD 100, LOD 200, LOD 300, LOD 350, LOD 400
		LOD: As Built	LOD 500
UK	Level of Definition	LOD: Level of Detail	LOD 1, LOD 2, LOD 3, LOD 4 LOD 5, LOD 6
		LOI: Level of Information	LOI 1, LOI 2, LOI 3, LOI 4, LOI 5, LOI 6
Italy	Level of Development of Objects	LOG – Geometrical Objects	LOG A, LOG B, LOG C, LOG D, LOG E, LOG F, LOG G
		LOI – Information Objects	LOI A, LOI B, LOI C, LOI D, LOI E, LOI F, LOI G

With the publication of ISO 19650 Parts 1 [14] and 2 [15] a consolidated structure for LOD is being proposed with the introduction of the LOIN concept (Level of Information Need). The LOIN [16] aims to replace the model of predefined scales and to switch into a gradual, incremental, milestone-free system with relevant points established beforehand. However, the LOIN concept is under development.

Based on the above analysis of different LOD frameworks, an ontology schema has been developed as illustrated in Fig. 2. Since different renovation projects can adopt different LOD systems, the developed ontological representation of the proposed LOD framework can accommodate the different representations summarized in Table 1.

The methodological idea is to represent LOD frameworks and its levels as classes, which can then be instantiated on a project-to-project basis. The class oppm[1]: LODFramework can be instantiated with the frameworks called USA BIMForum, UK LOD, Italian LOD (refer Table 1). Similarly, the levels in different frameworks are

[1] The word 'oppm' called prefix for Product-Process Ontology, which generally represents the IRI of the ontology. PREFIX oppm <https://w3id.org/digitalconstruction/oppm#>.

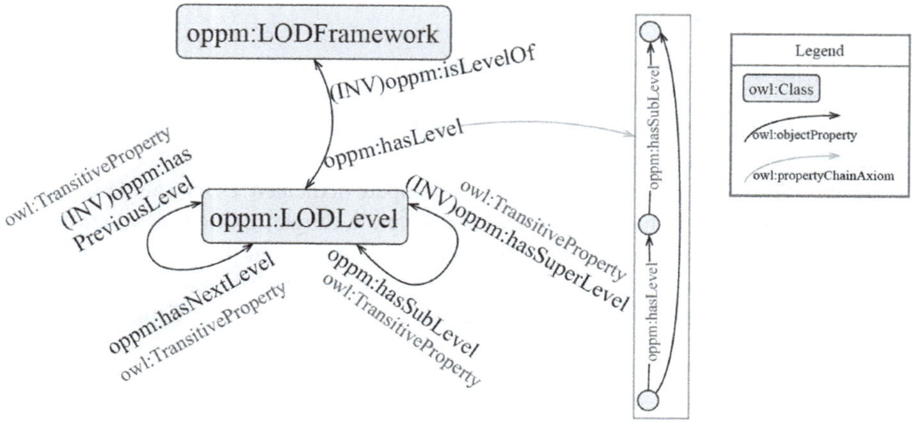

Fig. 2. Ontological representation of LOD framework

added as instances to the class oppm:LODLevel. Later on, the link between framework and its respective levels are generated using the object property oppm:hasLevel and its inverse property oppm:isLevelOf. As represented in Fig. 2 these two relationships are inversed to each other to provide bi-lateral compatibility for the relationship or the link.

Furthermore, relationships between the levels of a framework are indicated using the object properties oppm:hasNextLevel, oppm:hasSubLevel and their inverse properties oppm:hasPreviousLevel, oppm:hasSuperLevel respectively. A property characteristic called owl:TransitiveProperty is defined for these properties in-order to represent aggregation relationship between levels. For example, an individual inst[2]: LOD100 has next level inst:LOD200, and inst:LOD200 has next level inst:LOD300, then the ontology can infer that inst:LOD100 has also its next level inst:LOD300. Another way of defining semantic interpretation of the levels is with the use of axioms. In the LOD Framework (represented in Fig. 2), a subproperty of chain axiom (`oppm: hasLevel o oppm:hasSubLevel subPropertyOf: oppm:hasLevel`) is assigned to oppm:hasLevel object property. This axiom infers that all the sublevels (inst:LOD100, inst:LOD200, etc.) defined within the main levels (inst:AsDesigned or inst:AsBuilt) are also been the levels of specific LOD framework.

2.2 Building Life-Cycle Stage

An intense analysis is carried on the BLCS framework according to the different standards of specifications for categorization of the building renovation process. The specification of BLC stages is necessary for each construction project to manage and assess engineering services. However, the standard stages in the project differ from country to country and may also be subjected to differences in legislation. Some of those specified standards and the publications are listed below:

[2] The prefix 'inst' is used to represent some example individuals in the explanation.

- BS EN 16310:2013 – Engineering services terminology to describe engineering services for buildings, infrastructure and industrial facilities [17],
- HOAI – Official Scale of Fees for Services by Architects and Engineers [18],
- RIBA – RIBA (Royal Institute of British Architects) Plan of Work 2013 [19],
- ISO 22263:2008 – Organization of information about construction work – Framework for management of project information [20].

The developed ontological structure of the LOD framework can accommodate different standards for BLCS representation. A process of mapping between those standards was carried out and comprehensibly detailed in Table 2. This mapping process intends to distinguish the difference between the standards in terms of their life-cycle stage information and vocabulary notation. The application or the usage of these standards in building construction and management projects is based on the locality, requirements and legislation regulations, etc. Thus, a newly proposed ontological schema for a BLCS framework should be capable to represent all these standards more comprehensively. Similar to the LOD framework, an ontological BLCS framework is proposed to denote different life-cycle stages as shown in Fig. 3.

Table 2. BLCS in different standards and publications.

Stages	Standards				
	BS EN 16310:2013		HOAI	RIBA	ISO 22263
1	Initiative	Market study	Establish the base of the project	Strategic definition	Inception
		Business case			
2	Initiation	Project initiation		Preparation and brief	Brief
		Feasibility study			
		Project definition			
3	Design (D.)	Conceptual D.	Preliminary design	Concept design	Design
		Preliminary D.			
		Developed D.	Final design	Developed D.	
		Technical D.	Bldg. execution drawing	Technical design	
		Detailed D.	Prepare contract award		
4			Bldg. permission applic.		
5	Procurement	Procurement	Assist award proc.		
		C. Contracting			
6	Construction (C.)	Pre-construction	Project supervision (C. Supervision)	Construction	Production
		Construction (C.)			
		Commissioning	Project control & documentation	Handover and Close out	
		Hand over			
		Regulatory approval			
7	Use	Operation		In use	
		Maintenance			
8	End of life	Revamping			Demolition
		Dismantling			

The proposed ontology framework is more generic and capable to represent the BLCS framework according to different standards, publications, user-defined or project-based specifications. The adopted methodology is similar to the LOD framework ontology in terms of assigning the stages as a class (oppm:BLCStage). It provides the relationship between the stages using the object properties called oppm:hasSubstage, oppm:hasNextStage and their respective inverse properties oppm:hasSuperStage, oppm:hasPreviousStage. Similarly, the transitive character of the properties is enabled by assigning owl:TransitiveProperty to each object property which further enables the aggregated relationships between the stages.

In addition to the property characteristics, some axioms are defined to achieve the complete semantic meaning of BLCS stages into an ontological framework. These defined axioms are clearly illustrated in Fig. 3. In an example scenario of BS EN 16310 framework, each stage is comprised of many sub-stages and technically these substages are also stages to that framework. This semantic meaning is inferred in ontology with the help of the subProperty chain axiom (`oppm:hasStage o oppm:hasSubStage subPropertyOf: oppm:hasStage`) defined to the object property oppm:hasStage. Similarly, in the same scenario, the main stage inst:Design (refer Table 2) have a next stage relation with the substage called inst:Maintenance (refer Table 2) or vice versa. These complex relations are modelled in the ontology by using axioms `oppm:hasNextStage o oppm:hasSubStage subPropertyOf: oppm:hasNextStage`, `oppm:hasPreviousStage o oppm:hasSubStage subPropertyOf: oppm:hasPreviousStage` assigned to properties oppm:hasNextStage, oppm:hasPreviousStage respectively.

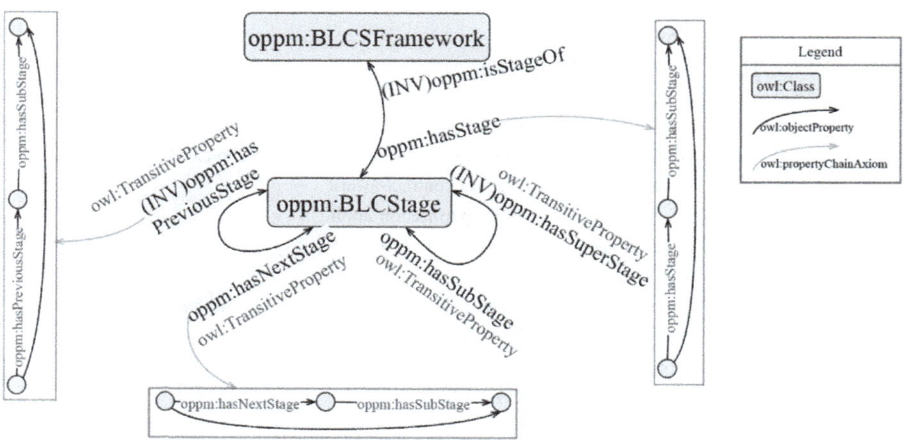

Fig. 3. Ontological representation of BLCS framework

2.3 Activity and Stakeholder

The term Activity indicates the task to be carried out in the process of building renovation. In general, these activities are performed by the different stakeholders involved in the project at different BLCS based on the available information. When a renovation process takes place, different stakeholders are responsible for several activities. For mapping a renovation process, considering the experience of the main author and through a literature review [1, 19, 21] and [22], the list of involved stakeholders has been produced in the BIM4EEB project [4].

To overcome possible inefficiencies due to the incorrect or redundant data exchange among stakeholders, it is necessary to rationalize the information flow. This can be reached by adequate management of information during the different renovation process stages (BLCS) and by the appropriate connection of various stakeholders involved (e.g. inhabitants/end-users, clients/owners, designers, surveyors, etc.) [23].

2.4 BIM Object (Product Information)

BIM is a process of managing the physical and functional characteristics of building objects. The BIM process results in the digital representation of a different aspect of the project and supports decision making through the project life-cycle. Several international and national standards [11, 12, 14, 15] and [24] were published to support the data management and data transfer capabilities within the AEC domain and between the domains. The standard ISO 16739 (2018) [24] proposes a vendor-neutral meta-data model called Industry Foundation Classes (IFC) to manage the information of all physical, functional and process objects involved within the project. In this research, the IFC entities are considered to represent the buildings physical and functional characteristics within the ontology and are related to other variables (BLCS, LOD, Stakeholder, Use Case).

Product, System and Control Elements

Among building core-and-shell elements, it is necessary to describe services, processes, and control elements (for services and/or processes) within enriched BIM models. These developed BIM data entities are listed below as used in the development of the product-process ontology for building renovation.

- Building core-and-shell elements (e.g. wall, slab, window, door, shading, beam etc.);
- Distribution and flow elements (in terms of control processing, e.g. actuator, alarm, sensor, flow control device, flow fitting device, etc.);
- Spatial and feature elements (i.e. building, storey, site, space, opening);
- Element and Furnishing components (e.g. furniture, fasteners, tendon, etc.).

Properties and Quantities

The definition of related properties and quantities for each component or element in the building is necessary to enrich the BIM model and make it more informative. There are different attributes related to associated building systems within the IFC schema. All of this complex information is incorporated into the building objects by using property sets and quantity sets parameters. Additionally, the IFC schema allowed us to attach the user-defined property sets to building elements. The developed ontology schema is considering these capabilities and incorporating a specific adaptive mechanism.

2.5 Use Cases

Within the development of the product-process ontology for renovation, the aspect of Use Cases is considered as an additional feature to represent grouped activities involved in renovation process modelling. The list of pre-defined activities was taken from the D2.1 [1] of the BIM4EEB project. All of them were clearly defined and distinguished according to the life cycle phases of the built asset. Based on the above factors (see credentials in Fig. 1), we have outlined the three main Use Cases as a dynamic combination of selected activities performed by related stakeholders during the renovation processes. The purpose of these Use Case definitions is to narrow down the scope of the work concerning the development of the product-process ontology. The specified three Use Cases in the project are as following:

- Use Case 1 (UC1): Data acquisition for HVAC Design, Operation and Efficiency Management;
- Use Case 2 (UC2): HVAC Design, Operation and Efficiency Management;
- Use Case 3 (UC3): Fast Track Renovation Operation.

3 Product-Process Ontology

The development goal of an integrated renovation Product-Process ontology is to clearly describe the different activities, tasks, and sequences, their interrelations to stakeholders involved, the required information, other resources, etc. Figure 4 represents the methodological approach adopted for ontology development. The developed

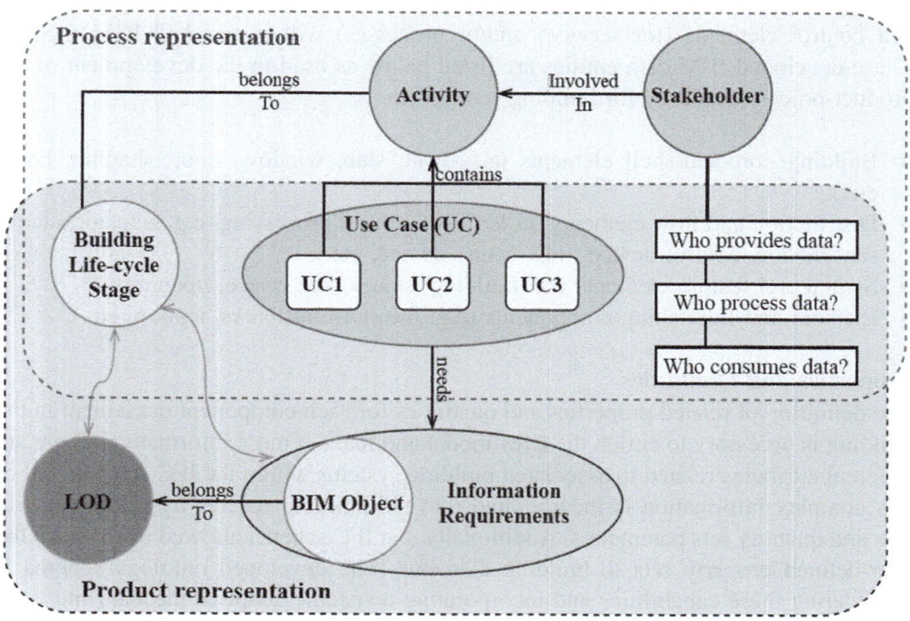

Fig. 4. Product-process ontology framework

methodological schema results in the 6-dimensional intercommunication framework including Activity, Stakeholder, BLCS, LOD, BIM data and Use case (see Fig. 1). The clear understanding of these aspects is presented in the Renovation Framework section of this document. The represented methodology in Fig. 4 also expresses the relationship between these six aspects of the building renovation process.

A major step towards the development of an ontology is the development of a precise understanding of the scope, the content and the relations between the constituent elements of the ontology. The complete methodology is represented in two stems called Product representation and Process representation. The Product representation indicates the relation between BIM objects and their level of detail needed in building life-cycle stages through the involved activities in it. The ontological representation of these interrelations between activities, BIM data and its level of detail is comprehensively elaborated in Fig. 5.

Similarly, the Process representation describes the role of different stakeholders involved in the renovation interventions or activities. According to the framework definition, represented in Fig. 4, the stakeholder roles are categorized dependent on data development, process and consumption activities. As described in the above sections, all the activities are grouped into different use cases needed for the specific tools or domain tasks involved in the renovation process. Based on the developed framework, the ontology for the renovation process is explained in the subsequent sections.

3.1 Activity – BIM Data – LOD

The developed ontological schema in Fig. 5 aims to establish relationships between Activities, BIM object data and its LOD for a specific activity in the project. A difficult representational challenge in RDF is how to represent the values of the same properties of objects at multiple different levels. The most typical approaches are to use objectified properties or named graphs of RDF datasets. In the following, the former approach objectified properties is adopted. Existing work on Ontology for Property Management (OPM) [25], Building Topology Ontology (BOT) [26] in the Linked Building Data (LBD) community and ifcOWL ontology [27] is used. In the OPFM ontology, a class oppm:BuildingObject is produced to hold the information of the objects and is aligned to classes of existing ontologies (bot[3]:Element, bot:Space and ifcowl[4]:IfcObject) using rdf:subClassOf property. This oppm:BuildingObject is further interrelated to the Activities (oppm:Activity) in the project using the object property oppm:requires and its inverse property oppm:wasNeededFor.

The classes opm[5]:Property and opm:PropertyState in OPM ontology make it possible to add an ultimate number of properties to building objects and their growth of accuracy throughout the project life-cycle. Additionally, it supports for defining metadata attributes for each property (e.g. role or quantity kind) and each property state (e.g.

3 PREFIX bot: <https://w3id.org/bot#>.

4 PREFIX ifcowl: <https://standards.buildingsmart.org/IFC/DEV/IFC4/ADD2_TC1/OWL#>.

5 PREFIX opm: <https://w3id.org/opm#>.

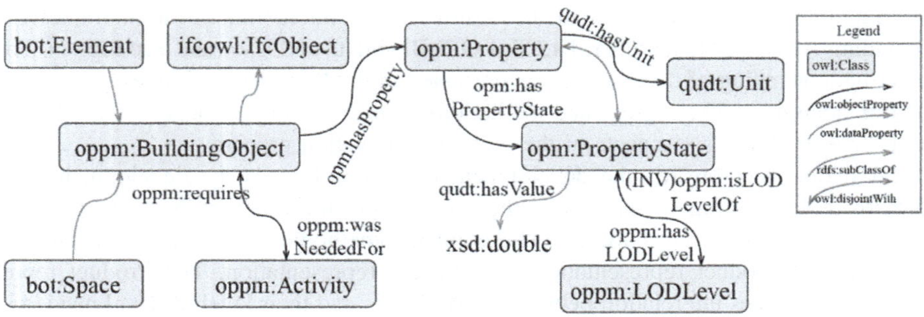

Fig. 5. An ontology representing the relation between activity, BIM data and LOD

source, timestamp, etc.). Figure 5 indicates these capabilities for instances of OPM classes. The developed ontology also supports the modelling of relationships between LOD and BIM attributes by using the object property oppm:hadLODLevel and its respective inverse property oppm:isLODLevelOf.

3.2 BLCS – Activity – Stakeholder

The next phase of the ontology development is to enable modelling of the data flow between Agents (either Stakeholder or Actor in a project) according to their requirements and involvement in the activities specified by the BLCS. In the ontology for Product-Process-Modelling the class oppm:Agent specifies all actors/stakeholders involved in the building renovation process. As represented in Fig. 6, the list of identified actors/stakeholders are instances of the class oppm:Agent. A role is assigned to them based on their involvement in the specific activity (oppm:Activity). A class oppm:Role accommodates different roles (oppm:InformationConsumer, oppm: InformationProcessor, oppm: InformationProvider) as its subclasses and is assigned to the agent through the object property dice[6]:hasRole and its inverse property dice:isRoleOF.

A simple relationship is defined between activity and the agent in terms of agent oppm:carries activity and vice-verse activity oppm:wasCarriedBy agent. Furthermore, the object property oppm:carries is categorized into three sub-properties oppm:consumesFrom, oppm:providesTo and oppm:processFrom, which are used based on the role of the agent. In common practice, the activities are listed according to the BLCS of the project and the same is represented in the ontology using the object property called oppm:wasRepresentedIn and its inverse property oppm:represents. The class oppm: Activity is also directly related to the BIM object data (see Fig. 5).

The use case (UC1, UC2, and UC3) variable defined in the methodological framework in Fig. 4 represents the grouping of the activities. In general, these are mostly application-oriented and can be defined by the user and relates to the ontology.

[6] PREFIX dice: <https://w3id.org/digitalconstruction/Entities#> [28].

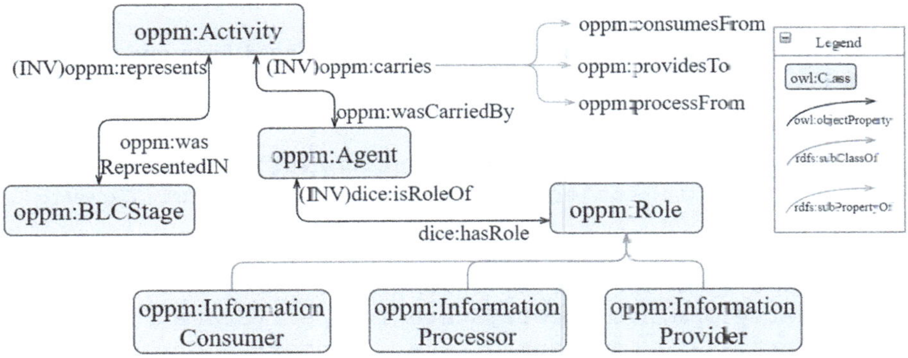

Fig. 6. An ontology representing the relation between BLCS, activity and stakeholder

4 Validation

This research is still not at the stage to enable a proper validation with models populated with significant amounts of data or with data gathered over the construction lifecycle. Validation work is, however, ongoing in the BIM4EEB project, first focusing on LODs and limited scopes of data and initially concerning particular renovation measures. The validation method is to formulate competency questions for the OPPM-ontology complemented by SPARQL queries. Some examples are provided below.

 # CQ1. What contexts precede this context?

```
SELECT ?context ?predecessor
WHERE
{ ?context
oppm:hasSuperLevel*/oppm:hasPreviousLevel+/oppm:hasSubLev
el*  ?predecessor }
```

 # CQ2. What are the attributes of an entity in a given context?

```
SELECT ?context ?subject ?property ?value
WHERE
{ ?subject opm:hasProperty ?property .
  ?property opm:hasPropertyState ?propertyState .
  ?propertyState oppm:hasLODLevel ?context .
  ?propertyState oppm:hasValue ?value }
```

 # CQ3. How has the data properties of an entity changed from one context to another?

```
PREFIX dicv:
<https://w3id.org/digitalconstruction/Variables#>
SELECT ?context ?subject ?value ?previousContext ?previ-
ousValue
WHERE
{ ?subject opm:hasProperty ?property .
  ?property opm:hasPropertyState ?propertyState .
  ?propertyState oppm:hasLODLevel ?context .
  ?propertyState oppm:hasValue ?value .
  ?property dicv:limitedBy ?previousPropertyState .
  ?previousPropertyState dicv:applicableIn ?previousCon-
text .
  ?preivousPropertyState dicv:hasValue ?previousValue }
```

5 Conclusion

The presented research results in a modelling approach based on a six-dimensional intercommunication framework for process modelling to support building renovation interventions. The established integrated Product-Process Modelling ontology for building renovation is capable to describe activities and their sequences in different phases of the building life-cycle along with the involvement of stakeholders and the required information to execute these activities. From the development process of the Product-Process Modelling ontology for building renovation, it becomes clear, that one can specify the roles and responsibilities of project partners on the level of activities for specific BLCS and related LOD. The Ontology for Product-Process Modelling is an instrument which will support the flexible, automatic generation of "filters" or "queries" against a holistic BIM-repository. When available, it will simplify the work and lead to efficiency gains through time-savings. Moreover, it also supports automated quality checking of BIM-files, since it provides information on attribute level about the information content to be shared.

6 Future Work

The underlying ontologies – OPPM, ifcOWL, BOT – are still going through refinements, especially related to harmonization with existing ontologies and ease of understanding for human readers. The greatest significance of future work is to progress on the enhancement of either inclusion of already used vocabulary in the BIM4EEB ontologies or the range of the emerging ontology standards by ISO, CEN, or W3C. Harmonization is a principal mechanism to promote wide-spread usage and applicability of ontologies by building connections to the expanding linked data and ontology ecosystem. This process needs to be carried out using alignment and evaluation techniques for ontologies.

Moreover, refinements in the technical capabilities of the ontologies to support efficient information management may also become possible through alternative approaches, especially concerning the way how to capture multi-context data, e.g. by utilizing the mechanism of named graphs for RDF databases. Furthermore, a demonstration use case is planned to provide a clear understanding and to prove the practical applicability of the OPPM Ontology presented in this paper. A basic example of extracting data concerning the activity, level of information needs and so on is organized based on the implementation of different SPARQL queries.

Acknowledgement. This research is part of the EU project entitled "***BIM4EEB – BIM-based fast toolkit for the Efficient rEnovation in Buildings***" which is **supported and funded by EU's H2020 research and innovation program**. The authors gratefully acknowledge the support and funding from the European Union.

References

1. WP2: D2.1 Definition of relevant activities and involved stakeholders in actual and efficient renovation processes, BIM based toolkit for Efficient rEnovation in Buildings (BIM4EEB), H2020. https://www.bim4eeb-project.eu/reports.html. Accessed 10 Mar 2020
2. Dainty, A., Moore, D., Murray, M.: Communication in Construction. Theory and Practice. Taylor & Francis, New York (2006)
3. Schweigkofler, A., et al.: Development of a digital platform based on the integration of augmented reality and BIM for the management of information in construction processes. In: Chiabert, P., Bouras, A., Noël, F., Ríos, J. (eds.) PLM 2018. IAICT, vol. 540, pp. 46–55. Springer, Cham (2018). https://doi.org/10.1007/978-3-030-01614-2_5
4. BIM4EEB: BIM based fast toolkit for Efficient rEnovation of residential Buildings, funded by European Union's H2020 research and innovation program. https://www.buildup.eu/en/news/bim4eeb-bim-based-fast-toolkit-efficient-renovation-buildings-definition-requirements-efficient. Accessed 10 Mar 2020
5. Tauscher, E., Mikulakova, E., Beucke, K., König, M.: Automated generation of construction schedules based on the IFC object model. In: International Workshop on Computing in Civil Engineering. ASCE, Austin, pp. 666–675 (2009). https://doi.org/10.1061/41052(346)66
6. Karlapudi, J., Shetty, S.: A methodology to determine and classify data sharing requirements between OpenBIM models and energy simulation models, 31, pp. 331–338. Forum Bauinformatik, Berlin (2019)
7. Karlapudi, J., Menzel, K.: Gap analysis on automatic generation of BEPS model from the BIM model. In: Proceedings of Building Simulation 2020, IBPSA, Graz (2020 in press)
8. Giannakis, G.I., Lilis, G.N., Garcia, M.A., Kontes, G.D., Valmaseda, C., Rovas, D.V.: A methodology to automatically generate geometric inputs for energy performance simulation from IFC BIM models. In: Building Simulation Conference, Hyderabad (2015)
9. Pauwels, P., De Meyer, R., Van Campenhout, J.: Interoperability for the design and construction industry through semantic web technology. In: Declerck, T., Granitzer, M., Grzegorzek, M., Romanelli, M., Rüger, S., Sintek, M. (eds.) SAMT 2010. LNCS, vol. 6725, pp. 143–158. Springer, Heidelberg (2011). https://doi.org/10.1007/978-3-642-23017-2_10

10. BIMFORUM: Level of Development (LOD) Specification Part I & Commentary For Building Information Models and Data, BIMFORUM (2019)
11. PAS 1192-2: Specification for information management for the capital/delivery phase of construction projects using building information modelling, BSI Standards Limited (2013)
12. PAS 1192-3: Specification for information management for the operational phase of assets using building information modelling, BSI Standards Limited (2014)
13. UNI 11337-4: Building and civil engineering works – Digital management of building information process – Part 4: Evolution and development of information within models documents and objects, UNI (2017)
14. BS EN ISO 19650 – 1:2018: Organization and digitization of information about buildings and civil engineering works, including building information modelling (BIM) – Information management using building information modelling – Part 1: Concepts and principles, BSI Standards Limited (2019)
15. BS EN ISO 19650 – 1:2018: Organization and digitization of information about buildings and civil engineering works, including building information modelling (BIM) – Information management using building information modelling – Part 1: Delivery phase of the assets, BSI Standards Limited (2019)
16. prEN 17412:2019: Building Information Modelling – Level of Information Need (LOIN) – Concepts and principles, Technical Committee CEN/TC 442 (2019)
17. BS EN 16310:2013: Engineering services – Terminology to describe engineering services for buildings, infrastructure and industrial facilities, BSI Standards Limited (2013)
18. HOAI: Official Scale of Fees for Services by Architects and Engineers, 3rd edn. Der Vieweg & Sohn verlag/GWV Fachverlage GmbH (2004)
19. RIBA: Royal Institute of British Architects (RIBA) Plan of WORK. In: Sinclair, D. (ed.) RIBA, 66 Portland Place, London (2013)
20. ISO 22263: Organization of information about construction works – Framework for management of project information, International Organization for Standardization (ISO), ISO (2008)
21. Global Buildings Performance Network, what is a deep renovation definition. http://www.gbpn.org/reports/what-deep-renovation-definition. Accessed 10 Mar 2020
22. California Commissioning Collaborative, California Commissioning Guide: Existing Buildings. https://www.cacx.org/resources/commissioning-guides.html. Accessed 10 Mar 2020
23. Sanchez, A.X., Hampson, K.D., London, G.: Integrating Information in Built Environments. Routledge, Abingdon (2017)
24. ISO 16739-1: Industry Foundation Classes (IFC) for data sharing in the construction and facility management industries - Part 1: Data schema (2018)
25. Ontology for Property Management (OPM). https://w3c-lbd-cg.github.io/opm/. Accessed 12 Mar 2020
26. Building Topology Ontology (BOT). https://w3c-lbd-cg.github.io/bot/. Accessed 27 May 2020
27. ifcOWL Ontology (IFC_ADD2_TC1). https://standards.buildingsmart.org/IFC/DEV/IFC4/ADD2_TC1/OWL/index.html. Accessed 27 Mar 2020
28. Digital Construction Entities (DICE). https://digitalconstruction.github.io/Entities/. Accessed 27 Mar 2020

Towards AR/VR Maturity Model Adapted to the Building Information Modeling

Ahlem Assila(✉), Djaoued Beladjine, and Mourad Messaadia

LINEACT CESI Engineering School, 51100 Reims, France
{aassila,dbeladjine,mmessaadia}@cesi.fr

Abstract. The challenge of improving the efficiency of the different phases of a building or infrastructure life demands considerations of innovative technologies such as Augmented Reality (AR) and Virtual Reality (VR). During this last decade, AR/VR systems for construction started to be emerged. These applications aim to virtualize or augment in real time the content of the Building Information Modeling (BIM) in order to support continuous improvement. To ensure the maturity of these applications, implementing a maturity model is needed. Based on literature, several maturity models for BIM have been proposed. However, it stays generic and needs to be adapted to the AR and VR technologies in the BIM context. To that end, we started in this paper by proposing an adapted AR/VR maturity model for BIM that aims to evaluate the maturity of these technologies according to the BIM lifecycle. This model has been conceived based on a mapping between three existing maturity models corresponding to AR, VR and BIM technologies from the most adapted existing works that deal with our goal. As a result of this mapping, three maturity levels have been identified and a detailed description of each level has been established. This model will be proposed to construction companies in order to evaluate their maturities on the use of AR/VR technologies.

Keywords: Virtual reality · Augmented reality · BIM · Maturity · Model

1 Introduction

In a world where technology is used in every sector of the industry, the Architecture, Engineering, and Construction (AEC) sector is no exception. The building information modeling (BIM) is a set of interacting policies, processes, and technologies that allow the creation of infrastructures' models during and across their complete lifecycle [1, 2]. This process assists teams in taking the best decisions in construction projects by helping them on conceive, visualize, run simulations, and collaborate easily [3]. The challenge of improving the efficiency of the different phases of a building or infrastructure life demands considerations of innovative technologies. Virtual tools are considered as a part of Smart Working as they support the decision-making process. The emergence of these new technologies has changed the industry from mechanical systems adoption to highly automated assembly lines. Augmented Reality (AR) and Virtual Reality (VR) are two emerging technologies in this field that create partial and complete virtual environments [4, 5]. In the context of next-generation building design,

Published by Springer Nature Switzerland AG 2020
F. Nyffenegger et al. (Eds.): PLM 2020, IFIP AICT 594, pp. 753–765, 2020.
https://doi.org/10.1007/978-3-030-62807-9_59

these two technologies can improve the BIM by allowing users to visualize the data of the developed 3D model and to connect to its data in real-time [3]. The earliest functional of VR and AR systems were developed in the 1990s, and these technologies are used today as one of the most promising technology in the industry 4.0 context [6]. It is increasingly used in many application fields, such as industry, construction, maintenance, engineering, and education [7].

Today these technologies have started to be used with the BIM and need to be further developed. Thus, as a first step, we are interested in this article to study and determine if these technologies meet the needs and expectations of BIM. To this end, we are studying the maturity of the AR and VR technologies compared to BIM in order to determine the quality of the services and processes offered by these technologies and to identify possible improvements. In the literature, there are many maturity models for evaluating BIM, however, they are generic and must be adapted to AR and VR technologies in the BIM context. To the best of our knowledge, no work has defined an AR/VR maturity model adapted to BIM.

Looking for this scenery, we proposed in this paper, an adapted AR/VR maturity model for BIM based on existing and the best-known maturity models adopted in the literature. This model is designed based on a mapping between three existing maturity models corresponding to AR, VR and BIM technologies.

This article is organized as follows: Sect. 2 introduces a brief background about AR, VR, BIM and maturity models concepts and the previous works about our subject. Section 3 describes our proposed AR/VR maturity model for BIM in order to evaluate the maturity of these technologies with BIM according to model maturity levels. Finally, Sect. 4 concludes the paper, presents a discussion that highlights some limits of our proposal and outlines some future perspectives.

2 Background

This section presents the background of our research. First, we define the concepts related to VR, AR, BIM and maturity models. In the following, we present recent research works proposed in literature.

2.1 BIM, Maturity Models, VR, AR Concepts

Building Information Modeling (BIM) is an intelligent 3D model-based process that gives Architecture, Engineering and Construction (AEC) professionals the insight and tools to improve efficiency when building plans, designing and managing buildings and infrastructure [3]. It implies the creation of 3D models and a significant amount of information, both geometric and semantic, related to the modeled infrastructure and buildings [1]. Although BIM is not used universally by the entire construction world because it is not a standard and it has a high implementation cost as well, it is usually implemented in large projects, including 3D views. Therefore, it allows the visualization of projects in four, five or six dimensions, integrating the notions of time, money, and human resources [8].

BIM in the construction sector is considered a break technology since it leads to a paradigm shift. It encourages companies to abandon their traditional practices and adopt emerging practices. The implementation of BIM generally results in a redefinition of practices and processes in order to increase the efficiency and the consistency of BIM collaborative design and enhance the quality of information delivered to stakeholders involved in a project lifecycle [9, 10]. However, BIM technologies in companies are often integrated in a less structured way [11, 12]. Thus, BIM maturity models are proposed as a solution to identify and prescribe good practices in order to manage technological, procedural and organizational changes [13–15]. Maturity models are tools used to measure and evaluate organization maturity according to defined KPIs. These models are presented as per levels ranging from basic level until to mastery and high performance [16]. The set of proposed models brings together good BIM implementation practices around three main dimensions: Technology, Organization and Processes or Protocols [17]. Thus, the maturity assessment aims for capturing the actual state of organization according to model maturity levels.

In the context of construction or building operations, Augmented and Virtual reality technologies prove to be effective, immersive and/or real-time tools allowing visualizing complex situations in the workplace, to reinforce risk prevention knowledge [18].

Augmented Reality (AR) is an innovative technology allowing superimpose virtual objects on real-world images for user interaction [19]. It has made leaps and bounds over the past few years. With the explosion in power of mobile devices, AR now allows the use of glasses or a smartphone to create a virtual layer that the user can see through, showing actual data, in our case BIM data [20]. While virtual reality is a technology that allows users to have total immersion and navigate in a virtual environment, in order to explore it and interact with 3D objects [21]. This technology is generally carried out via advanced display devices, such as immersive headsets (HMD - Head Mounted Displays).

By providing an immersive or real-time virtual environment, stakeholders can gain a better view of the physical context of the construction activity, task or structure on site in order to make more informed and precise design decisions [22]. In addition, the deployment of these technologies allows a gain in productivity and an efficient presentation of the future building to customers [23].

2.2 Related Work

Maturity Models for BIM. Today, the countries, which use BIM in a developed way, had adopted maturity models in accordance with the needs of their company. The maturity models were built to meet a specific context and needs. Most models are built from the Capability Maturity Model CMM [9, 24, 25]. Its objective is to qualify companies so as to know if they have the capacities to meet the objectives of an IT project.

To date, around ten BIM maturity models have been developed. The main models published in the literature are often compared in relation to their country of origin, organizational scale, year of publication, type of models and style of evaluation [26, 27]. The work of Succar [28, 29] is one of the most cited authors on the subject of

BIM maturity. It had built its maturity model by distinguishing between BIM capacity and maturity.

The evolutionary character of its concept can however be underlined since the first publications of this same author [28] dating from 2009, proposed three phases of maturity BIM which were then reconsidered and replaced by the concept of capacity [30, 31]. This is to apprehend the implementation of BIM in stages, since it is by nature doomed to create innovative breakthroughs and gain momentum within companies [29].

More recently, Dakhil et al. [32] have proposed a model inspired by the model of Succar et al. [28] (see Fig. 1).

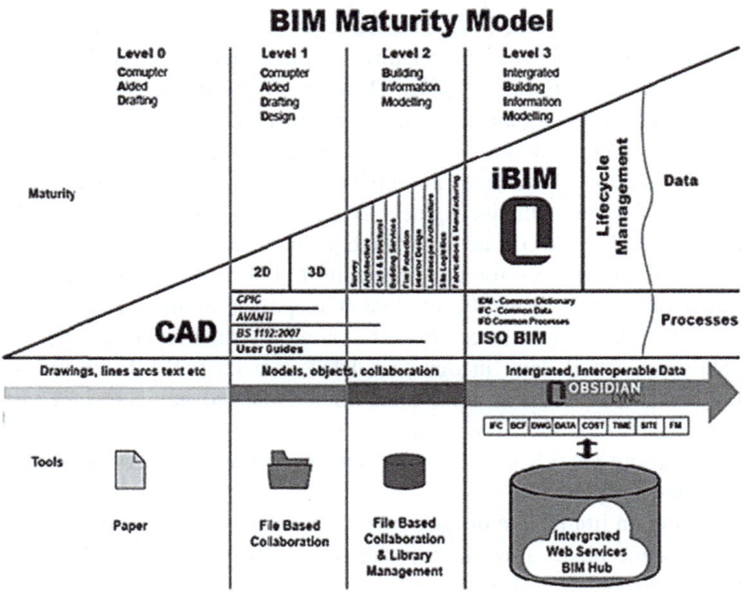

Fig. 1. BIM maturity model proposed by Dakhil et al. [32]

The latter offers maturity levels that correspond to the gradual and continual improvement of processes, technologies and strategies within each BIM stage. As illustrated in the Fig. 1, this model proposed four main levels from level 0 to level 3. The level 0 is based on the use of unmanaged Computer Aided Design (CAD) to create drawings. The level 1 allows to manage the CAD in 2D or 3D format where the company engaged industry standards within the modeling process such as BS1192 with commercial data and is managed by stand-alone finance and a cost management package. In addition, this level allows combining the 2D drafts with 3D models in a common Data Environment. The level 2 allows to manage 3D environment held in separate discipline tools with parametric data and commercial data managed by Enterprise Resource Planning. Thus, several additional dimensions such as time calculation are added. Furthermore, this level ensure a full collaboration and partial interoperability using distinct CAD models. During this stage, integration occurs based on proprietary interface or bespoke middleware. While the level 3 is based on a full collaboration and a full integration in a cloud based environment. It is based on a fully open interoperable process and data integration enabled by IFC. This level, named integrated BIM, allows managing the data and information by a collaborative model server.

Maturity Models for Augmented and Virtual Reality Technologies. Based on literature, only one work has been proposed on this subject. In this work, Hammerschmid [33] has proposed a first draft of virtual and augmented reality maturity model. It aims supporting companies in deciding for or against VR and/or AR. Two maturity models have been proposed concerning respectively virtual and augmented reality where each one is composed by five levels. The VR maturity levels are defined as follows: The first level is to view 3D model in virtual word. The second is to adjust background to 3D model. The third level is the interaction in the virtual world. The fourth level is the configuration of the 3D models, and the level 5 is the total immersion. While the five AR maturity levels are described as follows, the first level indicates that products or environment are tracked and recognized by AR devices. The second level indicates that objects and information are displayed. The third level mentions that the objects and information can be configured. The fourth level concerns connecting other people to share information and presentations. The fifth level indicates that problem areas are automatically recognized and suitable solution suggestions are displayed. This model has been tested in four companies based on the focus group discussions to evaluate their maturity in the use of virtual and augmented reality. As a result, analyses show firstly that all companies wanted to deal more attention with the technologies by applying the VR/AR application in more products before enhancing the application itself. Further, the finding show that the majority of these companies have already in application in the field of marketing and sales, and all of them have high potential in the field of customer service and human resources. Moreover, all four companies were able to handle the model and need just slightly changes of the levels to fit their needs.

Summary. Based on these related works, two conclusion are drawn. The first concerned the AR/VR maturity model [33] which remains a first draft that needs to be tested in other companies working on other fields, in our case, the building field. The second concerned the existing BIM maturity models. Despite their diversity, these models have no empirical confirmation and no model has been identified as a universal model to impose on the entire construction industry.

Since some companies, whatever their fields of application implement augmented and virtual technologies without analyzing their own needs, it is necessary to use a more adaptable maturity model, which helps them to visualize and determine the benefits of these technologies. In the field of building, BIM solution aims to generate a data model containing the maintain building information along the whole lifecycle of a building project. The model offers different information extracted from different data relating to different steps of lifecycle. Today, both the augmented and virtual reality are integrated in the building design process. Yet, to our knowledge, there is currently no AR/VR maturity model suitable for BIM. Thus, we argue that the integration of the existing maturity models are essential to obtain better refined AR/VR maturity model adapted for BIM.

3 Augmented Reality/Virtual Reality Maturity Model for BIM

Considering the limited number of researches, the analysis of the maturity of AR/VR in the construction field (especially in BIM) is today in these early stages. The aim of this work is to define an adapted AR/VR maturity model for BIM based on the existing and the best-known maturity models in the literature. Those includes the BIM Maturity Model proposed by Dakhil et al. [32] and the AR/VR maturity model proposed by [33] (see Sect. 2.2).

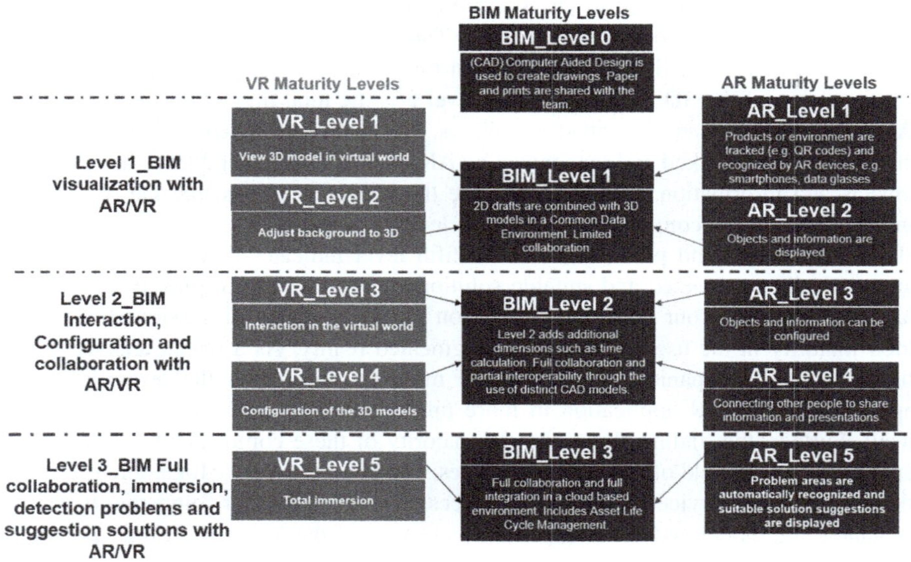

Fig. 2. The proposed AR/VR maturity model for BIM

As illustrated in the Fig. 2, our proposed model is conceived based on a mapping between these two models according to their maturity levels. It includes three maturity levels. The level 1 is named BIM Visualization with AR/VR. The level 2 is named BIM Interaction, Configuration and Collaboration with AR/VR, and the level 3 is the BIM Full collaboration, Full immersion, detection problems and suggestion solutions with AR/VR. In the following, we present the features introduced in each level.

3.1 Level 1: BIM Visualization with AR/VR

As illustrated in the Fig. 2, we decided firstly to eliminate the level 0 from the BIM model since it is based on the use of the CAD (computer Aided Design) to create, prints and shared 2D models on paper, which means that this level is overtaken by the AR/VR technologies.

The first level, called BIM visualization with AR/VR, is the result of a mapping between the first two maturity levels of AR/VR model and the first maturity level of BIM model. This mapping comes from two sub-mappings. The first concerns the virtual reality and BIM and the second concerns the augmented reality and BIM. As illustrated in the Fig. 2, the level 1 of BIM allows combining the 2D drafts with 3D models in a common Data Environment. This means that this level allows only visualizing the 3D model.

By integrating the AR/VR technologies, this first level of BIM corresponds, on the one hand, with the first two levels of VR maturity model relating respectively to the visualization of the 3D model in virtual word and the background adjustment to 3D model. On the other hand, this level corresponds with the level 1 of AR maturity model that indicates that object or environment are tracked and recognized by AR devices and the level 2, which indicates that objects and information are displayed.

Consequently, these two sub-mapping allow us to identify two main functionalities on which this level is based, respectively:

- The visualization of the BIM model in virtual word and the adjustment of its content in virtual reality; Several VR devices can be used to visualize the BIM content, among them we quote Samsung Gear VR[1] [34], Oculus Rift[2] [35].
- The tracking, the recognition and the display of the BIM model based on AR device. There are two significant ways to track and recognize a BIM model with AR. The first is based on location-based systems, using physical sensors to position objects and users such as Bluetooth Low Energy (BLE) beacons [2] or Wi-Fi positioning [19]. The second way concerns vision-based systems, by using feature points put on site and detected by cameras, such as markers [19, 36] or natural features tracking [20, 36]. Thus, in this case, users place two markers on the construction site and capture the scene, and the augmentation can be accurately and automatically achieved, by computing a "projective space" of two-selected reference images [37]. Regarding display techniques, AR is introduced on the construction site, firstly, using a headset that is worn on-site to allow the display of 3D models on the real world as done by [36]. In this way, the worker can see the BIM components directly over the real world. In a second way, using smartphones or other mobile devices [2, 36].

3.2 Level 2: BIM Interaction, Configuration and Collaboration with AR/VR

This level integrated three main components respectively, the interaction, configuration and collaboration. It is the result of a mapping between the third and fourth maturity

[1] Samsung Gear VR is a virtual reality device that allows exploring virtual worlds at the construction site or during meetings [34].

[2] Oculus Rift is a real-time viewer application with interactive capacities, developed by the Oculus Company, and can be implemented as a plugin in Revit [35]. These VR glasses are handling to visualize and experience 3D model, 360° panorama picture, and virtual mock-up over a BIM model [38].

levels of AR/VR model and the second maturity level of BIM model. As a result, two sub-mapping are defined. The first concerns the virtual reality and BIM and the second concerns the augmented reality and BIM (see Fig. 2). Those later have two main functionalities, respectively: (1) BIM interaction and configuration with AR/VR and (2) BIM collaboration with AR/VR.

- *BIM Interaction and Configuration with AR/VR.* In an AR environment, building information can be generated and represented as 3D virtual models; those can then be viewed in 3D, performed virtual interactions with the real environment, or extracted and inserted into the multi-disciplinary users' views of a real-world scene (i.e. the actual building site). AR devices (for examples, headset, smartphones or other mobile devices) can be used for interacting with the application to change the type of data to be visualized [20]. The AR can also support tangible interactions. Further, the coupling of BIM and AR can open up potential opportunities for exploring alternative approaches to data representation, organization and interaction for supporting seamless collaboration in BIM. VR offers to the user an interaction with the virtual building and its environment, which considers the virtual world, immersion, sensory feedback, and interactivity. The users must be able to change/move virtually some elements like doors, windows or walls. The transformation of objects in VR must be instantaneous; otherwise, the effect of immersion is heavily impaired. In this context, updates in the Revit[3] model can take from milliseconds to multiple seconds depending on database and geometry complexity. VR requires devices for interaction with the virtual environment of the building and the construction space. The interaction with the virtual environment of the building and the construction space required the use of head-mounted displays (HMDs) devices such as Oculus Rift, Samsung Gear VR, HTC Vive [39].
- *BIM Collaboration with AR/VR.* Collaboration in building design projects is very important, as they bring together a large number of diverse disciplines, supply chain stakeholders who have not worked together before. To establish clear and effective collaboration practices, it is imperative to manage a large amount of information and procedures involving complex tools and systems. As defined in [40], the collaborative environment in VR is "multiple users interacting within a virtual world that enables interaction among participants" where collaborative visualization is the most used. The collaborative visualization can be through Large Volume Displays (LVD), which allow the simultaneous collaboration of several individuals [41]. While for AR, as defined by Renevier and Nigay [42], a collaborative AR system is "one in which augmentation of the real environment of one user occurs through the actions of other users and no longer relies on information pre-stored by the computer". In the building industry, it is still common for R&D teams to use 2D models and documents to explain and exchange with the project owner, client and stakeholders.

[3] Revit is building information modelling software for architects, landscape architects, structural engineers, mechanical, electrical, and plumbing (MEP) engineers, designers and contractors [35].

However, the lack of knowledge in engineering or industrial design makes the exchange or understanding of plans difficult and may lead to misunderstandings.

With the VR integration into the building field, these technologies support design applications, and used for collaborative visualization and construction processes improvement. The 3D visualization, provided for users by VR, allows a real time collaboration during different stages of the construction process. The collaboration platform BIM, through its server allows the interaction of different stakeholders by data management. According to access rights, the platform allows building data storage, modification, export/import of different files, viewing and modifying. Thus, during the whole building life cycle, the augmented or virtual 3D model can be viewed and updated or modified.

During design phase, the AR offers to users (architect, engineers and contractors, etc.) a collaborative design review through usage of AR technologies with BIM. Engineers can work on augmented drawings or 3D models in real-time and can have an overview about samples or types of materials. In this case, the AR coupled to the VR allows the BIM design review, communicate, modify at distance or office in virtual world. During construction phase, the AR allows the construction information management through examining work process check and validate the working process. Thus, users (project manager, workers, engineers, architects and contractors, etc.) can interact, confirm, inspect, review, and add changes in a shared database in real time at job site, office or any place. During maintenance phase, AR can be used for tasks and process efficiency according to the fact that information can be available in real time and in the real context. Using AR enables maintenance teams to reduce errors and be guided during their maintenance actions. The usage of HMD gives to technician the possibility to focus in the task, visualize and interact with the related information at the same time [43].

The solution needs the deployment of technologies such as mobile devices (mobile, tablets), mixed environment (MRCVE), identification systems (barre code, RFID) and geo tracking solutions (GPS. WPS) [44].

3.3 Level 3: BIM Full Collaboration, Full Immersion, Detection Problems and Suggestion Solutions with AR/VR

This level presents the highest level of AR/VR maturity of applications for BIM. It is the result of a mapping between BIM/AR and BIM/VR maturity levels as illustrated in Fig. 2. It includes two sub-levels: the first concerns the use of VR and BIM. We called it BIM full collaboration, full immersion, detection problems and suggestion solutions with VR. The second concerns the use of AR and BIM; we named it BIM full collaboration, detection problems and suggestion solutions with AR. These two sub-levels are the results of a mapping between BIM/AR and BIM/VR maturity levels.

In this level three, different functionalities characterize each sub-level. They can be summarized as follows:

– *BIM Full Collaboration, Full Immersion, Detection Problems and Suggestion Solutions with VR.* The VR brings together the actors of the construction around a single BIM model hosted in a full collaborative platform, which allows ensuring a full collaboration. This Platform allows different collaborators to fully immerse themselves in real time, to meet together in virtual and to navigate inside the digital model, learn about all of its data and interact with its components. In addition, the use of the VR is much more useful in the design phase because it can detect and report upstream anomalies and catch up before starting the construction. This technology can be considered as a mean that allows proposing solutions and recommendations to the team workers in order to resolve the construction problems detected. Thus, in order to facilitate their collaborative work, the project actors must be equipped with VR tools with the same performance (resolution, sound, interaction, haptic, etc.).

- *BIM Full Collaboration, Detection Problems and Suggestion Solutions with AR.* During the works phase, when using the AR, the site team uses the BIM model, which is in the collaborative platform to display it in the real environment of the site. This technology will help field teams to carry out precise monitoring of the site in real time. The augmented elements give the impression of an almost natural presence of the building in the real environment. Therefore, the full collaboration will help the site team, in interaction with the BIM model in real time, to follow and simply enter the progress of the site, annotate and share the added information, report and detect problems, as well as offer a way to repair these anomalies.

The collaboration process allows a more fluid flow of exchanges between the different project stakeholders throughout the building life cycle (from design to exploitation).

The AR/VR allow access to the database of the digital model via mobile devices remotely or on site. The workers will have the same level of information (geotagged photos, text or audio notes, showing a design flaw or any unforeseen event, etc.) and can handle heterogeneous data.

In addition, this level allows access to the BIM on site and the management, in real time, of the differences between the work as planned and the actual construction: the coherence between the "As built" object and the virtual model "as planned".

4 Conclusion and Perspectives

This paper presents the first step towards the specification of an AR/VR maturity model for BIM. The proposed model has been conceived based on the most known existing maturity models according to BIM and AR/VR technologies. Three main maturity levels have been identified based on a mapping between the selected existing maturity models. This preliminary study gives us some relevant findings. First, we can say that the specification of this model can benefit the construction industry; both in the design, construction and maintenance phases to evaluate identify their maturity levels and therefore enhance their systems. Thanks to the three maturity levels proposed, this model allows us identifying the main aspects characterizing the AR/VR systems for BIM, which are the visualization, interaction and configuration, collaboration, full collaboration, full immersion and detection problems and suggestion solutions.

However, this subject is only in its infancy. The proposed maturity model should be, firstly, tested to be validated. To that end, we envisage performing a theoretical evaluation of the proposed conceptual model with experts and then performing a case study with companies specializing in BIM, AR/VR. Secondly, a reflexion about the model implementation within company is needed in order to facilitate its integration. Eventually, this conceptual model did not deal with the transition from one maturity level to another. For this, we plan to integrate the transition mechanisms for moving from one maturity level to another in order to allow companies to develop their maturities.

References

1. Carneiro, J., Rossetti, R.J., Silva, D.C., Oliveira, E.C.: BIM, GIS, IoT, and AR/VR integration for smart maintenance and management of road networks: a review. In: 2018 IEEE International Smart Cities Conference (ISC2), pp. 1–7. IEEE (2018)
2. Schweigkofler, A., et al.: Development of a digital platform based on the integration of augmented reality and BIM for the management of information in construction processes. In: Chiabert, P., Bouras, A., Noël, F., Ríos, J. (eds.) PLM 2018. IAICT, vol. 540, pp. 46–55. Springer, Cham (2018). https://doi.org/10.1007/978-3-030-01614-2_5
3. Karji, A., Woldesenbet, A., Rokooei, S.: Integration of augmented reality, building information modeling, and image processing in construction management: a content analysis. In: AEI 2017, pp. 983–992 (2017)
4. Elia, V., Gnoni, M.G., Lanzilotto, A.: Evaluating the application of augmented reality devices in manufacturing from a process point of view: an AHP based model. Expert Syst. Appl. **63**, 187–197 (2016)
5. Gilchrist, A.: Introducing Industry 4.0. In Industry 4.0, pp. 195–215. Apress, Berkeley (2016)
6. Michele, G., Scurati, G.W., Michele, F., Uva, A.E., Ferrise, F., Bordegoni, M.: Towards augmented reality manuals for Industry 4.0: a methodology. Robot. Comput. Integr. Manuf. **56**, 276–286 (2019)
7. Quandt, M., Knoke, B., Gorldt, C., Freitag, M., Thoben, K.D.: General requirements for industrial augmented reality applications. Procedia CIRP **72**(1), 1130–1135 (2018)
8. Calderon-Hernandez, C., Brioso, X.: Lean, BIM and augmented reality applied in the design and construction phase: a literature review. Int. J. Innov. Manag. Technol. **9**(1), 60–63 (2018)
9. Kassem, M., Succar, B., Dawood, N.: Building information modeling: analyzing noteworthy publications of eight countries using a knowledge content taxonomy. In: Building Information Modeling: Applications and Practices (2015)
10. Kassem, M., Succar, B.: Macro BIM adoption: comparative market analysis. Autom. Constr. **81**, 286–299 (2017)
11. Oraee, M., Hosseini, M.R., Papadonikolaki, E., Palliyaguru, R., Arashpour, M.: Collaboration in BIM-based construction networks: a bibliometric-qualitative literature review. Int. J. Proj. Manag. **35**(7), 1288–1301 (2017)
12. Chan, A.P., Ma, X., Yi, W., Zhou, X., Xiong, F.: Critical review of studies on building information modeling (BIM) in project management. Front. Eng. Manag. (2018)
13. Yılmaz, G., Akçamete Güngör, A.S.L.I., Demirörs, O.: A review on capability and maturity models of building information modelling (2017)

14. Abdirad, H.: Metric-based BIM implementation assessment: a review of research and practice. Arch. Eng. Des. Manag. **13**(1), 52–78 (2017)
15. Tranchant, A., Beladjine, D., Beddiar, K.: BIM in French smes: from innovation to necessity. WIT Trans. Built Environ.WIT Trans. Built Environ. **169**, 135–142 (2017)
16. Schumacher, A., Erol, S., Sihn, W.: A maturity model for assessing Industry 4.0 readiness and maturity of manufacturing enterprises. Procedia Cirp **52**(1), 161–166 (2016)
17. Pilehchian, B., Staub-French, S., Nepal, M.P.: A conceptual approach to track design changes within a multi-disciplinary building information modeling environment. Can. J. Civ. Eng. **42**(2), 139–152 (2015)
18. Li, X., Yi, W., Chi, H.L., Wang, X., Chan, A.P.: A critical review of virtual and augmented reality (VR/AR) applications in construction safety. Autom. Constr. **86**, 150–162 (2018)
19. Chen, H.M., Chang, T.Y.: Integration of Augmented Reality and indoor positioning technologies for on-site viewing of BIM information. In ISARC Proceedings of the International Symposium on Automation and Robotics in Construction, vol. 31, p. 1 (2014)
20. Chionna, F., Argese, F., Palmieri, V., Spada, I., Colizzi, L.: Integrating building information modeling and augmented reality to improve investigation of historical buildings. Conserv. Sci. Cult. Herit. **15**(1), 133–163 (2015)
21. Assila, A., Plouzeau, J., Merienne, F., Erfanian, A., Hu, Y.: Defining an indicator for navigation performance measurement in VE based on ISO/IEC15939. In: De Paolis, L.T., Bourdot, P., Mongelli, A. (eds.) AVR 2017. LNCS, vol. 10324, pp. 17–34. Springer, Cham (2017). https://doi.org/10.1007/978-3-319-60922-5_2
22. Gheisari, M., Foroughi Sabzevar, M., Chen, P., Irizzary, J.: Integrating BIM and panorama to create a semi-augmented-reality experience of a construction site. Int. J. Constr. Educ. Res. **12**(4), 303–316 (2016)
23. Wang, J., Wang, X., Shou, W., Xu, B.: Integrating BIM and augmented reality for interactive architectural visualisation. Constr. Innov. **14**(4), 453–476 (2014)
24. Crowston, K., Qin, J.: A capability maturity model for scientific data management: evidence from the literature. Proc. Am. Soc. Inf. Sci. Technol. **48**(1), 1–9 (2011)
25. Martin, P., Beladjine, D., Beddiar, K.: Evolution within the maturity concept of BIM. WIT Trans. Built Environ. **192**, 131–142 (2019)
26. Giel, B., Issa, R.R.: Quality and maturity of BIM implementation in the AECO industry. Appl. Mech. Mater. **438**, 1621–1627 (2013)
27. Giel, B., Issa, R.R.: Framework for evaluating the BIM competencies of facility owners. J. Manag. Eng. **32**(1), 04015024 (2016)
28. Succar, B.: Building information modelling framework: a research and delivery foundation for industry stakeholders. Autom. Constr. **18**(3), 357–375 (2009)
29. Succar, B., Sher, W., Williams, A.: Measuring BIM performance: five metrics. Arch. Eng. Des. Manag. **8**(2), 120–142 (2012)
30. Succar, B., Sher, W.: A competency knowledge base for BIM learning. Australas. J. Constr. Econ. Build. Conf. SERIES **2**, 1–10 (2014)
31. Succar, B., Kassem, M.: Macro-BIM adoption: conceptual structures. Autom. Constr. **57**, 64–79 (2015)
32. Dakhil, A., Alshawi, M., Underwood, J.: BIM client maturity: literature review. In: Proceedings of 12th International Post-Graduate Research Conference (2015)
33. Hammerschmid, S.: Developing and testing of a virtual and augmented reality maturity model. In: Larrucea, X., Santamaria, I., O'Connor, R.V., Messnarz, R. (eds.) EuroSPI 2018. CCIS, vol. 896, pp. 279–288. Springer, Cham (2018). https://doi.org/10.1007/978-3-319-97925-0_23
34. Gear VR. https://www.samsung.com/us/mobile/virtual-reality/gear-vr/gear-vrwith-controller-sm-r324nzaaxar. Accessed 20 Feb 2020

35. Rift, Oculus Rift. https://www.oculus.com/experiences/rift. Accessed 20 Feb 2020
36. Yokoi, K, Fukuda, T, Yabuki, T, Motamedi, A.: Integrating BIM, CFD and AR for thermal assessment of indoor greenery. In: 22nd International Conference on Computer-Aided Architectural Design Research in Asia, pp. 85–94 (2017)
37. Jiao, Y., Zhang, S., Li, Y., Wang, Y., Yang, B.: Towards cloud augmented reality for construction application by BIM and SNS integration. Autom. Constr. **33**, 37–47 (2013)
38. Mirzaei, M.A., Chardonnet, J.R., Merienne, F., Genty, A.: Navigation and interaction in a real-scale digital mock-up using natural language and user gesture. In: Proceedings of the 2014 Virtual Reality International Conference, pp. 1–4 (2014)
39. Sampaio, A.Z.: 4D/BIM model linked to VR technology. In: Proceedings of the Virtual Reality. International Conference-Laval Virtual, pp. 1–4 (2017)
40. Sherman, W.R., Craig, A.B.: Understanding Virtual Reality: Interface, Application, and Design. Elsevier, Amsterdam (2002)
41. Mengoni, M., Raponi, D., Ceccacci, S.: A method to identify VR-based set-up to foster elderly in design evaluation. Int. J. Intell. Eng. Inform. **4**(1), 46–70 (2016)
42. Renevier, P., Nigay, L.: Mobile collaborative augmented reality: the augmented stroll. In: Little, M.R., Nigay, L. (eds.) EHCI 2001. LNCS, vol. 2254, pp. 299–316. Springer, Heidelberg (2001). https://doi.org/10.1007/3-540-45348-2_25
43. Love, P.E., Edwards, D.J., Irani, Z., Walker, D.H.: Project pathogens: the anatomy of omission errors in construction and resource engineering project. IEEE Trans. Eng. Manag. **56**(3), 425–435 (2009)
44. Kim, M.J., Lee, J.H., Gu, N.: Design collaboration for intelligent construction management in mobile augmented reality. In: International Symposium on Automation and Robotics in Construction (2011)

Developing BIM Thinking: Fundamental Objectives and Characteristics of BIM to Think Critically About in BIM Research and Implementation

Vishal Singh(✉)

Indian Institute of Science, Bangalore 560012, Karnataka, India
singhv@iisc.ac.in

Abstract. This article proposes pathways towards developing BIM thinking as a set of objectives and characteristics that allow revisiting the grounds and principles on which one can reason about BIM, irrespective of the specific applications or tools. The article looks into questions such as– Why do we need BIM thinking, and why now? What should we look for in BIM thinking, and how? The research applies abductive reasoning for qualitative grouping and classification of the preprocessed data collected from the existing literature review articles and BIM glossaries, combined with peer feedback from workshops and discussions. The fundamental objectives and characteristics to be considered in BIM thinking include representation, documentation, transactions and exchange, decision support, standardization, knowledge and information management, automation, and ecosystem and systems. Since the hope of the future transformation of the construction industry is largely pinned on a range of digital technologies, BIM thinking should facilitate informed decisions about the ways forward.

Keywords: BIM thinking · BIM framework · Fundamental objectives

1 Introduction

Building Information Modeling (BIM) has been one of the most popular topics in the literature on digitalization and construction management in the last decade or more. BIM still remains at the centre of the projected future of digital construction e.g. [1]. Despite this growing BIM research and development, and barring the seminal foundational works of the pre-BIM era from 1970s to 1990s [2–6], BIM research has predominantly been applied research, with numerous application areas and pilot studies, but with limited fundamental or theoretical discussion. In addition, some authors have questioned the extent of realized benefits of BIM in practice [7, 8]. Thus, it appears that the applied BIM research could benefit from a revisit of the theoretical foundations of BIM, as a step towards 'BIM thinking'. Therefore, this article focuses on the propositions and pathways towards developing BIM thinking as a set of objectives and characteristics that form the contemporary theoretical understanding of BIM.

Published by Springer Nature Switzerland AG 2020
F. Nyffenegger et al. (Eds.): PLM 2020, IFIP AICT 594, pp. 766–782, 2020.
https://doi.org/10.1007/978-3-030-62807-9_60

1.1 Why Do We Need BIM Thinking? And, Why Now?

During the pre-BIM research, when early conceptualization and prototyping of building product models was in progress, the leading researchers [2–6] investigated diverse theoretical approaches, conceptual frameworks and requirements of the desired system, including database theories, ontological frameworks, product data modelling, geometric modelling– space boundaries, topological networks, class hierarchies, knowledge-based systems, programming language theory, abstraction principles, system architecture and process modelling.

Though the pre-BIM literature built the theoretical and conceptual foundations that led to the conception and development of BIM tools and applications, the mainstream BIM literature since 2004 has not shown adequate theoretical review and reflection from the applied research and practice to revisit and improve our conceptual understanding of BIM, barring a few noticeable exceptions. For instance, Succar's [9] highly cited article that emphasized the need for a research framework went on to identify conceptual dimensions of the BIM research landscape, including research fields, stages, steps and lenses. Though this conceptual and theoretical work made a significant contribution in 'scene-setting' to understand and guide BIM research trends, the discussed concepts pertain to research areas and trends, and do not adequately deal with underlying foundations of BIM itself. This is further reflected in the follow-up articles of Succar and colleagues [9, 10], which focus on conceptual dimensions of BIM macro-adoption patterns [10], maturity models and capability matrix [11]. In a similar context, there is considerable effort in developing BIM guidelines and execution plans, with more recent focus on structured classification of the various factors and use cases towards developing a common language of BIM purposes and objectives [12]. Thus, the theoretical focus of these researchers pertains to what Singh and colleagues [13, 14] term as the BIM ecosystem, and not BIM itself. That is, rather than seeking the underlying foundations on which the workings of BIM applications can be explained, these articles discuss the conceptual frameworks related to the products, processes, people and policies that determine adoption, execution and growth of BIM [9].

In contrast, the discussions around BIM applications and tools have mostly continued around data models, ontologies, geometrical modeling, information exchange and semantics, but there have been limited attempts at theory building. Nonetheless, with greater maturity and hands-on experience with BIM, questions confronting the future of BIM are beginning to emerge e.g. [15], which necessitates a relook at the basics. For instance, Turk [15] recently wrote about the ten key questions confronting the future of BIM research, framing his discussion around the Function-Behaviour-Structure (FBS) ontology [16]. Turk [15] puts emphasis on the need to understand the chain of reasoning from the functions of BIM; the structure of BIM, i.e. the way it is realized, and; the behavior of BIM, i.e., how it works in different contexts. Turk further discusses how the context in which BIM is used will influence the future directions, implicitly noting the connection between BIM and the BIM ecosystem.

The effort towards BIM thinking or 'how to critically think about BIM' should be seen as an indicator of maturity in evolution of BIM as a discipline, analogous to other thinking paradigms in complementary disciplines such as engineering design, computation and systems engineering, where we have recently seen the emergence of

'Design thinking', 'Computational thinking' and 'Systems thinking' frameworks that capture the understanding of the key objectives and characteristics underpinning the respective disciplines. This article has similar objectives, recognizing that by now we have adequate practical experience with BIM applications and tools to critically reflect on and outline the key characteristics that underpin BIM applications and tools. Such a reflective, abductive theory building process should help improve and complement the conceptual and prescriptive theoretical foundations built in the pre-BIM era.

1.2 What Should We Look for in BIM Thinking? And, How?

Given that BIM research has expanded across several themes and areas [17], there are various potential pathways to approach BIM thinking. Nonetheless, before we look into the potential pathways, it is desirable to establish the process, the requirements, and the goals and objectives. What should BIM thinking help us with? How should we go about developing BIM thinking? What do we start with?

BIM thinking should provide the grounds and principles on which one can reason about the fundamental objectives and characteristics of BIM, irrespective of the specific application. For instance, as an analogy, Fig. 1 shows different machine tools - a pair of scissors, a wheelbarrow and a tongue, which share the same underlying principle of Lever design. That is, irrespective of the use cases and applications of a lever, we can reason the design and working of the system in terms of the force applied, fulcrum, and the force produced following established computable principles. While it may be challenging to reach this level of precise theoretical working principle for BIM, given that it goes beyond physical laws to socio-cognitive aspects of human interaction, at least the endeavor should be to identify the key objectives and characteristics that are fundamental across all BIM applications.

Fig. 1. Fundamental principles of lever design, independent of the use case and application area.

2 What Should Be the Research Approach and Methodology?

There is a set of prescriptive theoretical foundations and concepts from the pre-BIM era. In contrast, a complementary approach should independently build on the observations and findings from practical implementation and usage of BIM tools and applications. Such observations and findings are reported in the BIM literature, guidelines and execution plans, reviews, and community forums. In addition, users and experts can provide feedback and insights. Therefore, this research builds on the existing literature, BIM glossaries, as well as feedback from workshops and group discussions.

In order to conduct a thematic grouping and classification of the data to identify BIM objectives and characteristics, instead of collecting the data through another comprehensive literature review, the author builds on a preprocessed dataset by aggregating the findings from existing review articles [17–20] and other sources (e.g. [12], www.bimexcellence.org) that have systematically identified the keywords and themes associated with BIM. In addition, some of the notable articles that list the benefits of BIM [21–24] were also reviewed for keywords.

Since the thematic grouping and classification of the dataset was done qualitatively, the author relied on abductive reasoning to infer and trace each of the keywords and themes in the dataset to their fundamental objectives and characteristics. Abductive reasoning allows best possible explanation and inference when the observations cannot be inferred with deductive certainty.

The identified objectives and characteristics have also been informed by group discussions and peer feedback via workshops and lectures over the last four years, including lectures and workshops in international BIM Summer Schools (2016–2019).

3 What Are the Objectives and Characteristics Identified So Far?

Based on the qualitative grouping and classification, eight fundamental objectives and characteristics of BIM are identified– representation, documentation, transactions and exchange, decision support system (DSS), standardization, knowledge and information management (KIM), automation, and ecosystem and systems.

Figure 2 uses the identified objectives and characteristics to group and classify some of the commonly posited benefits of BIM, such as visualization, coordination and clash detection, consistent drawings, building design, as-built model, building assembly, construction sequencing, spatial program and massing studies, quantity take-offs, model based estimation, feasibility studies, design options and alternative development, direct fabrication, environmental analysis, code review, facilities management, forensic analysis, logistics and supply chain, and retrofitting and recycling [21–24].

Similar to the classification of BIM benefits shown in Fig. 2, the BIM related terms and themes listed in other notable sources were found to be classifiable according to the eight BIM objectives and characteristics proposed in this paper. Figure 3 shows how many terms in these sources primarily associate with which objective or characteristic. For the purpose of this paper, the distribution patterns seen in Fig. 3 will not be discussed any further, but it suffices to show that the identified objectives and characteristics seem adequate to classify all the BIM related terms and themes.

The Penn State BIM Execution Plan [12] originally listed twenty-five use cases while the BIMe Initiative (www.bimexcellence.org) lists fifty-two general model uses and seventy-three domain model uses. The authors of the Penn state Execution Guide also noted the need for more structured approach to identifying the BIM uses, classifying BIM uses in terms of the BIM Use purposes (gather, generate, analyze, communicate and realize) and characteristics (facility element, facility phase, discipline, and level of development) [12]. On the other hand, Succar et al. in the BIMe initiative (www.bimexcellence.org) have put together a list of more than seven hundred keywords and terms in the BIM glossary. In addition, numerous BIM topics and themes have been identified through systemic literature reviews [17–20]. For example, [17] identified BIM research themes and areas at different levels of granularity.

Thus, it can be seen that the keywords and themes associated with BIM, as identified by authors who have previously conducted systemic and comprehensive review of the BIM literature, can be grouped and classified according to the eight objectives and characteristics. This supports the claim that these are the fundamental objectives and characteristics of BIM.

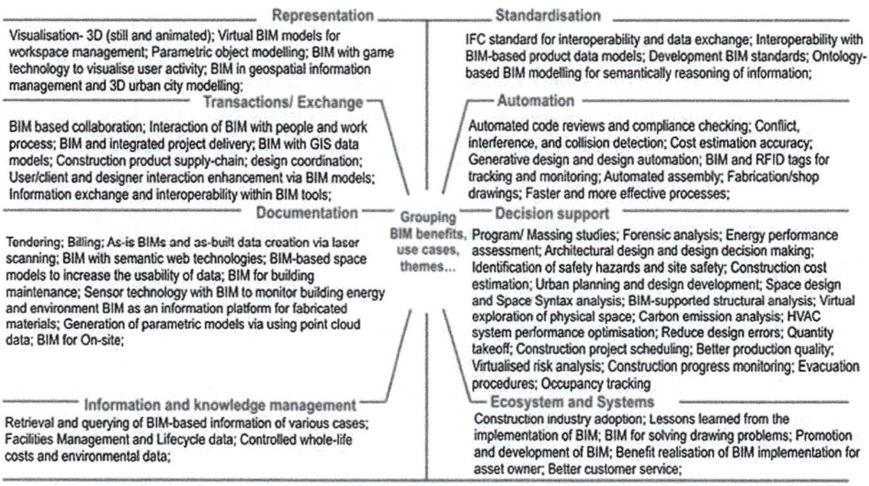

Fig. 2. Fundamental objectives and characteristics of BIM based on qualitative clustering

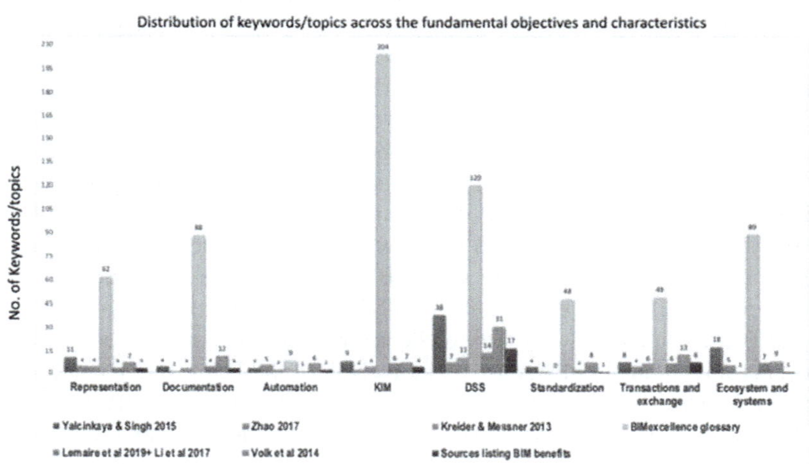

Fig. 3. Distribution of keywords/topics across the fundamental objectives and characteristics

Before we expand on each of the objectives and characteristics, it is useful to go back to some of the notable definitions of BIM to identify the keywords in these definitions.

The National Institute of Building Sciences (NIBS) defines BIM as "a digital representation of physical and functional characteristics of a facility. As such it serves as a shared knowledge resource for information about a facility forming a reliable basis for decisions during its lifecycle from inception onward". The NIBS definition of BIM remains broad, putting emphasis on digital representation, information and knowledge sharing, and decision making, rather than going into specifics of how these functional characteristics are realized and for what use cases. Nonetheless, in the NIBS documents the text that follow do outline specific prerequisites and purposes such as digital database, intelligent data including product data and other specifications, 2D drawings to 3D elements, animations, and 4D-5D capabilities such as scheduling, estimation, etc.

Similarly, [23] define BIM as modeling technology and associated set of procedures to produce, communicate, and analyze building models. The definition is further qualified to state that the building models are characterized by (1) building components represented with intelligent digital representations (objects) with computable graphics, data attributes, and parametric rules (2) components that include data needed for analyses and work processes such as takeoff and energy analysis (3) consistent and non-redundant data, and (4) coordinated data. This definition also puts emphasis on the characteristics and objectives, rather than the specific purposes. The additional statements highlight the basic technical criteria of an intelligent object-based representation with attributes, parametric relationships and rules.

In contrast, the Penn State guide [12] defines BIM as "the act of creating an electronic model of a facility for the purpose of visualization, engineering analysis, conflict analysis, code criteria checking, cost engineering, as-built product, budgeting and many other purposes". The guide also defines BIM Use as "a method of applying BIM during a facility's lifecycle to achieve one or more specific objectives". Thus, the Penn State guide, aimed at practitioners, defines BIM in terms of its purposes and use cases rather than its underlying characteristics.

The keywords in the three representative definitions are captured within the identified fundamental characteristics and objectives of BIM. However, it is notable that some aspects of BIM have dominated the narrative in practice rather than a more fundamental understanding of BIM. For example, though the definitions emphasize digital representation, the dominant discussion in practice is specific to 3D Visualization and 3D models. It is not uncommon among practitioners to think of BIM synonymously with 3D models and 3D visualization. Similarly, others consider 'I' as the single most important aspect of BIM, underplaying the other characteristics.

Therefore, it is proposed that we need a course correction in the common narrative and understanding of BIM to foster a more fundamental and broader way of thinking about BIM such that the wider potential of BIM can be realized in practice. Figure 4 illustrates how each of the objectives and characteristics of BIM hold multiple dimensions and aspects to consider.

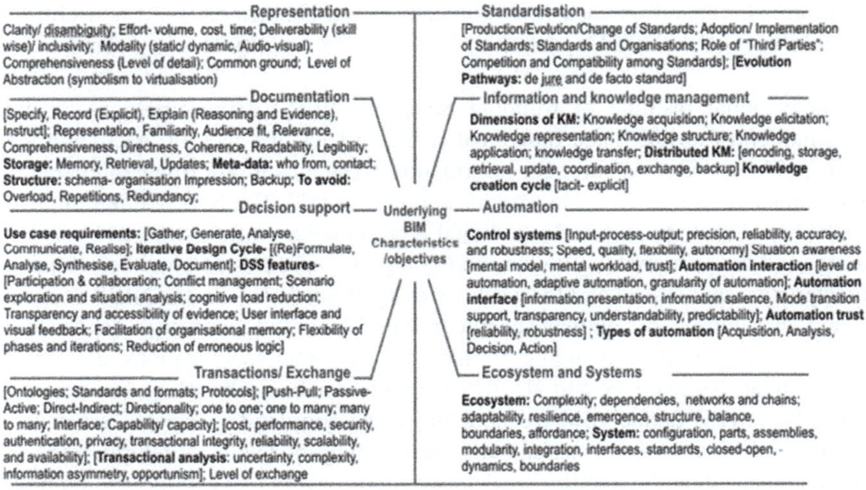

Fig. 4. Some aspects and dimensions to consider for the identified objectives and characteristics

3.1 What Is Desired in a Representation? And, What Does It Mean in the Context of BIM?

Representation goes beyond visualization and 3D or 2D discussions. Representation can be for communication of ideas, for externalization of ideas, for documentation, etc e.g. [25–28]. The attributes and requirements of the representation may vary with the purpose, but in general it can be stated that:

- Representation should be clear and disambiguous, which requires adequate level of detail. Typically, the less abstract a representation, the greater is the clarity. While symbolic representations such as drawings are abstractions, object-based 3D representations and virtual models are less abstract or ambiguous.
- In a typical resource-constrained work environment, creating representations should require as little effort as possible in terms of cost, volume and time without compromising on the clarity and required level of detail [29].
- In a team environment, the mode of representation should be inclusive such that the stakeholders are able to create, understand and share the representations. The more demanding a representation gets in terms of the skills and competence required to work with, the greater will be the challenge to diffuse and use it across the team.
- On one hand representations should be as comprehensive as needed, but at the same time require as little effort, time, skills and cost to produce and use. There is a trade-off between the level of detail and how well the details serve the intended purpose.
- One of the factors determining the level of detail and the extent of abstraction in a representation is common ground held between producers and consumers of the representation and the context [30]. Standards provide one such mechanisms for

creating a common ground. Languages are a good example of symbolic representations that work well because of common ground shared within a society. The further we move away from abstraction to virtualization, the easier it is to have a common ground. Nonetheless, such a move would typically require higher volume, effort, cost, time and skill.

For example, in Fig. 5, from left to right we move from a 2D symbolic representation to 3D perspective view to an object-based model with object attributes.

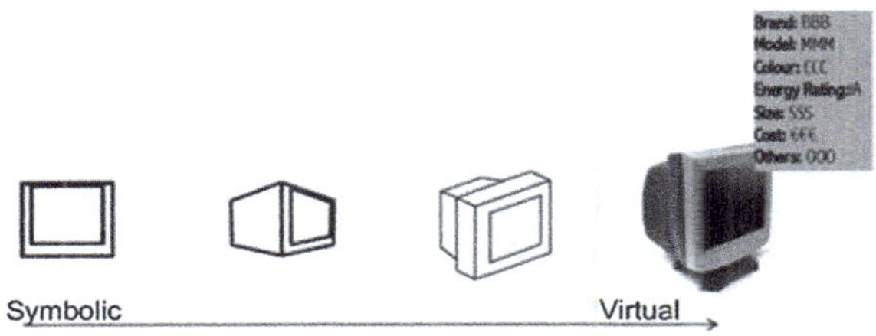

Fig. 5. Evolution of digital representation from symbolic drawings to virtual models

As evident in Fig. 5, the representations on the right are less ambiguous. This shift from symbolic to virtual representation is akin to the evolution of digital representation in construction from 2D drawings to BIM. Nonetheless, as we move from left to right, the representations increasingly become more demanding in terms of the time, volume, skills and cost of production. Creating a 2D rectangle is easier and faster for most people when compared to creating a 3D perspective. Thus, unless it is necessary and significant value add to create a very detailed representation, a simpler representation will typically save cost, time, and effort. This is where the evolution of BIM has played a critical part. If the details of an object exist apriori in the object library, producing a detailed 3D representation is just a click away. At the same time, the processing power and data storage in computers have grown significantly to process high volumes of data, allowing the production of all this detailed data without much concern for volume. Consequently, the factors determining the choice of representation have gradually shifted from the challenges in production of the representation to the purpose and consumption of the representations. The questions have shifted from how to why, for whom, and for what? Traditionally the representations were meant for human-to-human (H2H) communication of intent or for instructions or for interpretation and feedback. The designers produced representations for the clients to understand the design and for the engineers to build. As we move towards automation, representations may not only be intended for H2H communication, but also for human-to-machine (H2M), machine-to-machine (M2M), and machine-to-human (M2H) communication. The role of representation is growing beyond the communication of intent to include computational processing and the command for production. As a result, aspects such semantics, machine readability and accuracy of the representation are becoming critical [31].

3.2 What Is Desired in Documentation? And, What Does It Mean in the Context of BIM?

Documentation is another primary objective of BIM applications. Turk [15] suggests that the primary function of BIM is to serve as a database. Intelligent documentation of the data across different representational modes allow consistency, history tracking, and archiving. Following are some of the key aspects of documentation

- Documentation should provide specifications, explicit records, adequate explanation to facilitate reasoning and evidence, and instructions relevant to the activities and tasks. The record should have content, structure and context [32].
- Some of the aspects to consider in documentation include, the type of representation, familiarity of audience with the content, relevance of the content to the purpose, and characteristics such as comprehensiveness, directness, coherence, readability and legibility of the content [33, 34].
- From the perspective of data management and organization, factors include storage related aspects such as memory, retrieval and updates; meta-data such as authors details; representational and structural issues such as schema; and, backup.
- Documentation should not have information overload, repetitions and redundancy.

Several aspects of documentation listed above are already noted in the BIM literature. There is extensive discussion on meta-data, representation and schema e.g. [35]. Issues on information requirements, specifications and archiving have been emphasized in execution plans and guidelines. Thus, this line of BIM thinking from documentation perspective can provide useful insights. Who is the documentation for? Who requires what meta-data, explanation and reasoning? Documentation can also be for human users as well as for automated reasoning by machines, in which case machine readability and semantics is once again important.

3.3 What Is Desired in BIM as a Decision Support System (DSS)?

Given the range of BIM tools and applications, BIM means different things to different stakeholders [36], but in almost all cases it is more than just a database. From the early design phase to the facilities management and operations phase, BIM is envisioned to support one or more of the decision-making activities, ranging from clash detection, cost analysis, energy simulations and analysis, other performance analyses to assessing construction deviations, tracking building performance, and condition monitoring. That is, broadly speaking, one of the primary objectives of BIM is to serve as a DSS. Therefore, following are some of the desired aspects of BIM as a DSS

- Kreider et al. [12] summarize the use cases broadly under the objectives of gathering, generating, analysing, communicating, and realising.
- BIM should support the iterative design decision process, including problem formulation and reformulation, analysis, synthesis, evaluation, and documentation [16].
- From a groupware and organizational perspective, DSS should have features that support participation and collaboration, conflict management, scenario exploration and situation analysis, reduction of cognitive load, transparency and accessibility of

evidence, user interface and visual feedback, facilitation of organisational memory, flexibility of phases and iterations, and reduction of erroneous logic [37–39].

Several aspects of DSS are already noted in the BIM literature, ranging from conflict management, collaboration and visual feedback. Other aspects such as cognitive load and facilitation of organizational memory have not been adequately investigated.

3.4 How Is Transaction and Exchange Fundamental to BIM? What Is Expected in Terms of Transaction and Exchange?

Facilitating communication, collaboration and exchange is often emphasized as one the main objectives of BIM e.g. [36]. This has been articulated in several ways, including the emphasis on exchange formats on one hand [40] to the shift in perspective from lonely BIM to social (collaborative) BIM [41]. While the emphasis on collaborative BIM and exchange is unquestionable in a team environment, unlike traditional design and drafting tools, BIM also provides an interactive media where the designer also collaborates and transacts with the tool, which can provide feedback, highlight human errors, auto-correct and auto-complete actions, etc. That is, collaboration and exchange is not limited to H2H interactions, but there is collaboration between the tools and the users as well [42, 43]. Thus, transactions and exchange are also fundamental to BIM applications. Following are some of the key aspects to consider:

- Transactions and exchange are facilitated by agreed protocols and established standards, formats and ontologies e.g. [40].
- Transactions can be evaluated in terms of cost, performance, security, authenticity, privacy, transactional integrity, reliability, scalability and availability [44].
- Transactional analysis also includes a review of uncertainty, complexity, information asymmetry and opportunism [45]. For example, information asymmetry and directionality of transactions can be assessed in terms of interfacing mechanisms, push and pull, passive and active, etc.

While aspects such as protocols, formats, standards, etc are some of the most commonly discussed topics in the BIM literature, a more fundamental transactional analysis dealing with aspects such as information asymmetry, opportunism, etc can provide further insights into BIM applications and processes.

3.5 In What Ways Is Standardization Fundamental to BIM?

Plenty has been written about BIM standards and standardization [35, 40, 46–48]. Following are some of key aspects to consider

- Standards exist in all socio-technical systems, ranging from informal norms to formal specifications– equally applicable to products, processes, people and policies e.g. [49–52].
- Standards tend to reduce uncertainly by regularizing things. There is a trade-off between routine and non-routine, determining the degrees of freedom and flexibility.

- In a complex system, standards are particularly critical at the interfaces to facilitate transactions, scalability, flexibility and cross-functionality [53].
- Factors that determine the impact of a standard include the production and evolution of standards, the adoption and implementation of standards, the number of competing and compatible standards [51, 54, 55].

Some aspects of standardization such as data formats and exchange standards have dominated the BIM discourse. Object libraries and standard components may influence standardization and uniformity in the design outcomes. In contrast, with increasing integration of generative design systems with BIM applications, there is more to think about the roles and opportunities for BIM standards in routine and nonroutine design.

3.6 How Is Information and Knowledge Management (KIM) Fundamental to BIM? And, What Is Expected?

Several experts and practitioners argue that BIM should be seen as 'Building Information Management'. Information management (IM) is evidently one of the fundamental objectives of BIM [56]. Since BIM applications are meant to have object attributes, rules and relationships, capturing domain knowledge is also integral to BIM e.g. [57–61]. Hence, following are some of the points to consider from an information and knowledge management (KIM) perspective

- From the perspective of IM, aspects such as Create-Read-Update-Delete (CRUD) operations, storage and retrieval of information are also related to documentation.
- Dimensions of KM to consider include knowledge acquisition, elicitation, representation, structure, application and transfer e.g. [62, 63].
- Sociotechnical systems typically involve distributed KIM, comprising of activities related to encoding, storage, retrieval, update, coordination, exchange and backup for data, information, and knowledge [64, 65].
- While the tacit-explicit knowledge creation cycle provides continuous improvement, there is continuing need for updates and upgrades [66].

Several aspects of KIM are commonly considered in the BIM literature. Nonetheless, some aspects such as the CRUD operations, knowledge structure, application and transfer have dominated the discourse. Some factors related to distributed KIM such as coordination and exchange have been extensively discussed [36]. However, further insights can be gained by looking deeper from the perspective of KIM e.g. [25, 67]. For example, what role does BIM play in the knowledge creation cycle?

3.7 How Is Automation Fundamental to BIM? What Does It Mean?

Automation is subsumed in multiple BIM features and use cases. From intelligent documentation to clash detection to performance analyses to generative design to the creation of as-built models, automation is ingrained in BIM with the objective to reduce manual labour and human error. Thus, automation remains one of the fundamental objectives of BIM. Some of the key aspects to consider in terms of automation include

- Automation from a control systems perspective takes into account the Input-process-output activities. Some of the measures and performance indicators are precision, reliability, accuracy, and robustness, besides process measures such as speed, quality, flexibility, and autonomy [68].
- Automation design considerations include the assessment of interaction in terms of the level of automation (how much?), adaptivity of automation (when?), and the granularity of automation (for what tasks?) [68].
- Factors to consider with respect to automation interface include information presentation, information salience, mode transition support, transparency, understandability, and predictability [68, 69].
- In terms of situation awareness, the types of automation goals include acquisition, analysis, decision, and action [68–70].

Automation is integral to BIM applications, both as a requirement and as an objective. BIM should also support automation in the production and construction process.

3.8 Why Is Ecosystem and Systems View Fundamental to BIM?

BIM should be seen from an ecosystem perspective with a range of products, processes and people that co-evolve [13, 14, 71]. Therefore, if we are seeking the fundamentals of BIM thinking, the systems and ecosystem perspective must be considered.

- Structure and links between the constituents and parts of the system.
- Dependencies and relationships between the pats and constituents of the system.
- System boundaries, which can be analyzed at micro to macro levels.
- Adaptability, resilience, flexibility and stability of the ecosystem.
- Emergence, whereby unexpected and new opportunities continue to emerge.

The ecosystem perspective of BIM has been discussed extensively, ranging from BIM adoption models and frameworks, execution plans and maturity models, to tools matrix and product suites, the recognition of BIM ecosystem is widespread.

4 What Can We Conclude, and What Next?

The qualitative analysis revealed a set of objectives and characteristics that can be claimed to be fundamental to BIM thinking. One of the ways to work with these objectives in any BIM research or implementation scenario is to ask the 5Ws1H (Who? Why? What? When? Where? and How?) questions for each, Fig. 6. For example, who needs the representation or who has to produce it? Why and what for? When is it needed and where? And, how is it going to be produced, delivered and consumed? It is also important that the questions not only consider the human actors but also the non-human actors including software applications, machines and smart equipment and devices.

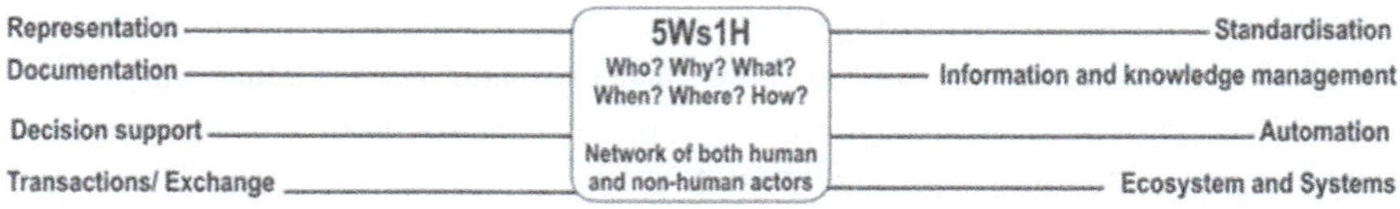

Fig. 6. Working with the fundamental objectives using the 5Ws1H questions

In addition, following points must be noted:

- Some of the basic requirements for a system to be considered within the purview of BIM such as object-based model with attributes, parameters, rules and relationships is considered as technical prerequisites and requirements, rather than objectives or characteristics. A significant part of the pre-BIM theoretical and conceptual work fall in this category. However, a comprehensive comparison and theoretical benchmarking of where we are (based on observations and inferences) and what was conceived in the pre-BIM and early development stages of BIM is still to be done.
- The identified objectives and characteristics identified are not mutually exclusive. For example, there is evidently close relationships between representation and documentation, or representation, documentation and KIM. While we have identified a set of fundamental objectives and characteristics in BIM thinking, we need further research to understand and establish the relationships between them.
- While a set of objectives and characteristics have been identified, further research is needed to assess if these are the 'necessary and sufficient' set of fundamental objectives and characteristics to think about BIM or not.
- Since the set of objectives and characteristics are identified through abductive grouping and classification, without a theoretical or conceptual framework to begin with, it will be useful to benchmark and assess these aspects of BIM thinking against complementary thinking paradigms of design thinking [72], computational thinking [73] and systems thinking [74] to get further insights. Design thinking broadly views design as a problem-solving approach independent of the nature of the problem. Thus, design thinking is relevant when we approach BIM as a solution to the varied problems that are derived from the use cases. Since BIM is inherently based on a computational foundation, computational thinking is relevant because it involves a set of problem-solving approaches that express problems and solutions in ways that a computer can aid. And finally, BIM can be seen from a systems perspective, which means we can also adopt systems thinking which provides a holistic approach that focuses on the way that a system's constituent parts interrelate and how systems work over time and within the context of larger systems.

References

1. Gerbert, P., Castagnino, S., Rothballer, C., Renz, A., Filitz, R.: Digital in Engineering and Construction, The Transformative Power of BIM. The Boston Consult, Boston (2016)
2. Eastman, C., Fisher, D., Lafue, G., Lividini, J., Stoker, D., Yessios, C.: An Outline of the Building Description System, Res. Report No. 50. Inst. of Phys. Planning, CMU (1974)

3. Eastman, C., Augenbroe, G.: Product modeling strategies for today and the future. In: Proceedings of CIB W78 Workshop on the Life-Cycle of Construction IT Innovations, Sweden, pp. 191–208, 3–5 June 1998
4. Björk, B., Penttila, H.: A scenario for the development and implementation of a building product model standard. Adv. Eng. Softw. **11**(4), 176–187 (1989)
5. Björk, B.: A conceptual model of spaces, space boundaries and enclosing structures. Autom. Constr. Autom. Constr. **1**(3), 193–214 (1992)
6. Björk, B.: A unified approach for modelling construction information. Build. Environ. **27**(2), 173–194 (1992)
7. Barlish, K., Sullivan, K.: How to measure the benefits of BIM—a case study approach. Autom. Constr. **24**, 149–159 (2012)
8. Herva, M., Singh, V.: Assessing gaps and opportunities in measuring the benefits of BIM in infrastructure design projects: what can we consider before, during and after the project? Int. J. Prod. Lifecycle Manage. **11**(4), 326–349 (2018)
9. Succar, B.: Building information modelling framework: a research and delivery foundation for industry stakeholders. Autom. Constr. **18**(3), 357–375 (2009)
10. Succar, B., Kassem, M.: Macro-BIM adoption: conceptual structures. Autom. Constr. **57**(9), 64–79 (2015)
11. Succar, B.: Building information modelling maturity matrix. In: Underwood, J., Isikdag, U. (eds.) Handbook of Research on BIM and Construction Informatics: Concepts and Technologies, pp. 65–103. Information Science Reference, IGI Publishing (2010). https://doi.org/10.4018/978-1-60566-928-1.ch004
12. Kreider, R.G., Messner, J.I.: The Uses of BIM: Classifying and Selecting BIM Uses. Version 0.9. PennState, Univ. Park, PA, USA (2013). http://bim.psu.edu
13. Singh, V.: BIM ecosystem research: what, why and how? Framing the directions for a holistic view of BIM. In: Harik, R., Rivest, L., Bernard, A., Eynard, B., Bouras, A. (eds.) PLM 2016. IFIPAICT, vol. 492, pp. 433–442. Springer, Cham (2016). https://doi.org/10.1007/978-3-319-54660-5_39
14. Gu, N., Singh, V., London, K.: BIM ecosystem: the coevolution of products, processes, and people. In: Kensek, K., Noble, D. (eds.) BIM in Current and Future Practice, pp. 197–211. Wiley, Hoboken (2014)
15. Turk, Ž.: Ten questions concerning building information modelling. Build. Environ. **107** (2016). https://doi.org/10.1016/j.buildenv.2016.08.001
16. Gero, J.S.: Design prototypes: a knowledge representation schema for design. AI Mag. **11**(4), 26–36 (1990)
17. Yalcinkaya, M., Singh, V.: Patterns and trends in building information modeling (BIM) research: a latent semantic analysis. Autom. Constr. **59**(11), 68–80 (2015)
18. Li, X., Wu, P., Shen, G.Q., Wang, X., Teng, Y.: Mapping the knowledge domains of Building Information Modeling (BIM): a bibliometric approach. Autom. Constr. **84**(10), 195–206 (2017)
19. Zhao, X.: A scientometric review of global BIM research: analysis and visualization. Autom. Constr. **80**(4), 37–47 (2017)
20. Lemaire, C., Rivest, L., Boton, C., Danjou, C., Braesch, C., Nyffenegger, F.: Analyzing BIM topics and clusters through ten years of scientific publications. J. Inf. Technol. Constr. (ITcon) **24**, 273–298 (2019)
21. Azhar, S.: Building Information Modeling (BIM): trends, benefits, risks, and challenges for the AEC industry. Leadersh. Manage. Eng. **11**(3), 241–252 (2011)
22. Becerik-Gerber, B., Jazizadeh, F., Li, N., Calis, G.: Application areas and data requirements for BIM-enabled facilities management. J. Constr. Eng. Manage. **138**(3), 431–442 (2012)

23. Eastman, C., Teicholz, P., Sacks, R., Liston, K.: BIM Handbook: A Guide to Building Info. Modeling for Owners. Managers, Architects, Engineers and Contractors (2011)
24. Hergunsel, M.F.: Benefits of Building Information Modeling for Construction Managers and BIM-based scheduling, Worcester Polytechnic Institute (2011)
25. Dossick, C.S., Anderson, A., Azari, R., Iorio, J., Neff, G., Taylor, J.E.: Messy talk in virtual teams: achieving knowledge synthesis through shared visualizations. J. Manage. Eng. **31**(1) (2015)
26. Yalcinkaya, M., Singh, V.: Exploring the use of Gestalt's principles in improving the visualization, user experience and comprehension of COBie data extension. Eng. Constr. Archit. Manage. **26**(6), 1024–1046 (2019)
27. Kirsh, D.: Thinking with external representations. AI Soc. **25**(4), 441–454 (2010)
28. Schön, D.A.: The Reflective Practitioner: How Professionals Think in Action, NY (1983)
29. Russell, D.M., Stefik, M.J., Pirolli, P., Card, S.K.: The cost structure of sensemaking. In: ACM/IFIPS InterCHI 1993 Conference on Human Factors in Software, pp. 269–276. ACM, New York (1993)
30. Stalnaker, R.: Common ground. Linguist. Philos. **25**(5–6), 701–721 (2002)
31. Pauwels, P., Zhang, S., Lee, Y.-C.: Semantic web technologies in AEC industry: a literature overview. Autom. Constr. **73**, 145–165 (2016)
32. Waller, R.: What makes a good document? The criteria we use. From the Simplification Centre. The University of Reading (2011)
33. Forward, A., Lethbridge, T.C.: The relevance of software documentation, tools and technologies: a survey. In: Proceedings of ACM Symposium on Document Engineering, pp. 26–33. ACM Press (2002)
34. Lethbridge, T.C., Singer, J., Forward, A.: How software engineers use documentation: the state of the practice. IEEE Softw. **20**(6), 35–39 (2003)
35. BuildingSMART. Model View Definition Summary. http://www.buildingsmarttech.org/specifications/ifc-view-definition. Accessed 12 Apr 2019
36. Singh, V., Gu, N., Wang, X.: A theoretical framework for BIM-based multi-disciplinary collaboration platform. Autom. Constr. **20**(2), 134–144 (2011)
37. Pretorius, C.: Exploring procedural decision support systems for wicked problem resolution. S. Afr. Comput. J. **29**(1), 191–219 (2017)
38. DeSanctis, G., Gallupe, R.B.: A foundation for the study of group decision support systems. Manage. Sci. **33**(5), 589–609 (1987)
39. Sprague, R.H.: A framework for the development of decision support systems. MIS Q. **4**(4), 1–26 (1980)
40. East, E.W., Nisbet, N., Liebich, T.: Facility management handover model view. J. Comput. Civil Eng. **27**(1), 61–67 (2012)
41. Kuiper, L., Holzer, D.: Rethinking the contractual context for building information modelling in the Australian built environment industry. Aust. J. Constr. Econ. Build. **13**, 1–17 (2013)
42. Singh, V., Gu, N.: Towards an integrated generative design framework. Des. Stud. **33**(2), 185–207 (2012)
43. Oxman, R.: Theory and design in the first digital age. Des. Stud. **27**(3), 229–265 (2006)
44. Papazoglou, M., Georgakopoulos, D.: Service-oriented computing. Commun. ACM **46**(10), 25–28 (2003)
45. Love, P.E.D., Tse, R.Y.C., Holt, G.D., Porverbs, D.G.: Transaction costs, learning, and alliances. J. Constr. Res. **3**(2), 193–207 (2002)
46. Björk, B.C., Laakso, M.: CAD standardisation in the construction industry—a process view. Autom. Constr. **19**(4), 398–406 (2010)

47. Laakso, M., Kiviniemi, A.: A review of IFC standardization—interoperability through complementary development approaches. In: Proceedings of the CIB W78–W102, pp. 25–28 (2011)
48. Shin, D.H., Kim, H., Hwang, J.: Standardization revisited: a critical literature review on standards and innovation. Comput. Stand. Interfaces 38, 152–157 (2015)
49. Hanseth, O., Monteiro, E., Hatling, M.: Developing information infrastructure: the tension between standardization and flexibility. Sci. Technol. Hum. Values **21**(4), 407–426 (1996)
50. Park, S.: Standardization and network externalities. Adv. Top. Inf. Technol. Stand. Stand. Res. **1**(1), 251 (2005)
51. Söderström, E.: Formulating a general standards life cycle. In: Persson, A., Stirna, J. (eds.) CAiSE 2004. LNCS, vol. 3084, pp. 263–275. Springer, Heidelberg (2004). https://doi.org/10.1007/978-3-540-25975-6_20
52. Xie, Z., Hall, J., McCarthy, I.P., Skitmore, M., Shen, L.: Standardization efforts: the relationship between knowledge dimensions, search processes and innovation outcomes. Technovation **48–49**, 69–78 (2016)
53. Sosa, M.E., Eppinger, S.D., Rowles, C.M.: Identifying modular and integrative systems and their impact on design team interactions. J. Mech. Des. **125**(6), 240–252 (2003)
54. Crargil, C.F.: Information Technology Standardization: Theory, Process, and Organization. Digital Press, Bedford (1989)
55. De-Vries, H.J.: IT standards typology. Adv. Top. IT Stand. Stand. Res. **1**, 1–26 (2006)
56. Demian, P., Walters, D.: The advantages of information management through building information modelling. Constr. Manage. Econ. **32**, 1153–1165 (2013)
57. Deshpande, A., Azhar, S., Amireddy, S.: A framework for a BIM-based knowledge management system. Procedia Eng. **85**, 113–122 (2014)
58. Holzer, D.: BIM and parametric design in academia and practice: the changing context of knowledge acquisition and application in the digital age. Int. J. Archit. Comput. **13**(1), 65–82 (2015)
59. Meadati, P., Irizarr, J.: BIM – a knowledge repository. In: Associated Schools of Construction - Annual International Conference, Massachusetts, USA, 7–10 April 2010
60. Motamedi, A., Hammad, A., Asen, Y.: Knowledge-assisted BIM-based visual analytics for failure root cause detection in facilities management. Autom. Constr. **43**, 73–83 (2014)
61. Motawa, I., Almarshad, A.: A knowledge-based BIM system for building maintenance. Autom. Constr. **29**, 173–182 (2013)
62. Alavi, M., Leidner, D.: Knowledge management and knowledge management systems: conceptual foundations and research issues. MIS Q **25**(1), 107–136 (2001)
63. Argote, L.: Reflections on two views of managing learning and knowledge in organizations. J. Manage. Inq. **14**(1), 43–48 (2005)
64. Choi, S.Y., Lee, H., Yoo, Y.: The impact of information technology and transactive memory systems on knowledge sharing, application, and team performance: a field study. MIS Q. **34**(4), 855–870 (2010)
65. Wegner, D.M.: Transactive memory: a contemporary analysis of the group mind. In: Mullen, B., Goethals, G.R. (eds.) Theories of Group Behavior, pp. 185–208. Springer, New York (1987). https://doi.org/10.1007/978-1-4612-4634-3_9
66. Nonaka, I., Takeuchi, H.: The Knowledge-Creating Company: How Japanese Companies Create the Dynamics of Innovation. Oxford University Press, New York (1995)
67. Holmström, J., Singh, V., Främling, K.: BIM as infrastructure in a Finnish HVAC actor network: enabling adoption, reuse, and recombination over a building life cycle and between projects. J. Manage. Eng., A4014006 (2014). https://doi.org/10.1061/(asce)me.1943-5479.0000305

68. Endsley, M.R.: From here to autonomy: lessons learned from human–automation research. Hum. Fact. **59**, 5–27 (2016)
69. Endsley, M.R.: Automation and situation awareness. In: Parasuraman, R., Mouloua, M. (eds.) Automation and Human Performance: Theory and Applications, pp. 163–181. Lawrence Erlbaum, Mahwah (1996)
70. Parasuraman, R., Sheridan, T., Wickens, C.: Situation awareness, mental workload, and trust in automation: viable, empirically supported cognitive engineering constructs. J. Cogn. Eng. Decis. Making **2**, 140–160 (2008)
71. Singh, V., Holmström, J.: Needs and technology adoption: observation from BIM experience. Eng. Constr. Archit. Manage. **22**(2), 128–150 (2015)
72. Brown, T.: Design thinking. Harv. Bus. Rev. **86**, 84–92 (2008)
73. Wing, J.: Computational thinking. Commun. ACM **49**(3), 33–35 (2006)
74. Senge, P.M.: The Fifth Discipline. Doubleday, New York (1990)

Industrial Technical Contributions

Engineering IT Management on End-to-End PLM Structure in Automotive Sector

Kaan Doga Ozgenturk[1,2](✉), Buse Isil Elmali[1,2], and Semih Otles[2]

[1] BMC Automotive Company, 35060 Izmir, Turkey
{kaan.ozgenturk, buse.elmali}@bmc.com.tr
[2] Ege University, 35100 Izmir, Turkey
semih.otles@ege.edu.tr

Abstract. As of today, PLM infrastructure has key role on companies' processes with respect to their end-item quality whereas it also practically determines the company culture, validness of the data, complexity, singularity and most of all profitability. Moreover, in order to give birth to these integrated processes, systems of PLM are needed which are administrated by solution architects who are experts on both IT and engineering solutions. Occasionally, single tool is not capable of handling processes from beginning to end. For that reason, there occurs a demand in multiple softwares. These diverse programs have characteristic powerful aspects coming with their weaknesses as well and they determine companies' way of work. Nevertheless, they have tendency on creating complex flows on data and process. In order to avoid these interruptions and provide a single source of data, it is necessary to create end-to-end process on a single platform within the company. This is where the solution architects must lead this PLM journey for all departments according to their needs. Particularly in automotive sector, the journey starts with the requirements, which are then driven to functional and logical objects. The further phases are designing, manufacturing, planning and work instructions, which must be led by allocating the resources. It can be understood that all these functions require different expertise; however, traceability can only be handled on a linear flow so that the impact analysis and change management can work smoothly. In order to stand to those needs, solution architects should handle both IT and engineering requirements in order to create end-to-end process flow.

Keywords: End-to-End · PLM · Engineering IT · Cad · Change

1 Introduction

This study presents a different perception on automotive sector in management of PLM and Engineering IT services. In order to define these concepts, the terminology behind PLM and Engineering IT should be understood preliminary.

Product lifecycle management (PLM) is a methodological approach for managing complex product information, engineering and manufacturing workflows and orchestrating them with each other. Product data management (PDM) and product lifecycle management (PLM) systems provide support in companies by integrating and

Published by Springer Nature Switzerland AG 2020
F. Nyffenegger et al. (Eds.): PLM 2020, IFIP AICT 594, pp. 785–797, 2020.
https://doi.org/10.1007/978-3-030-62807-9_61

automating complex operational activities; mainly on design and change processes. Significantly, in a dynamic environment like automotive where time is of the essence, this approach is supported by engineering and business softwares which includes a PLM software as well. The construction and deployment of these programs require multidisciplinary and comprehensive approach where engineering and information systems (IT) start to merge.

PLM system tools are used for handling a variety of product definitions to manage workflow of development activities, and to measure relational properties such as cost and performance [1].

The most significant service to manage this orchestration is Engineering IT, which can be considered as a division including a group of solution architect professionals who can understand these requirements and provide solutions to all, including IT systems management, PLM and process designations. This topic will be covered in Sect. 3 comprehensively.

Using all these approaches and techniques, the ultimate goal is to maintain a linear flow on processes in PLM starting from the first until the last. This concept can be called "end-to-end process management". Mainly in automotive sector, the most suitable way is to achieve this ultimate goal is by collaborating the main departments below:

- Program Management
- System and Configuration Management
- Process Planning
- Design and Engineering
- Production

In Sect. 2, construction of this end-to-end collaboration will be explained in details. However, it should not be forgotten that even though these departments have different solutions to problems with different softwares, they can always be collaborated with the required database and process solutions. The single platform should always be the answer but when it is not possible to do that, methods have to be created for managing these bottlenecks between departments.

On a very high-level point of view, end-to-end PLM strategy in companies with related people and divisions will be an asset mainly on four points [2]:

- Cost reduction
- Quality improvement
- Time saving
- Traceability

Figure 1 shows a general perspective of PLM in automotive sector. In product life cycle process, it is necessary to supply different kinds of models with appropriate modules depending on departments. This the most challenging point in process deployment.

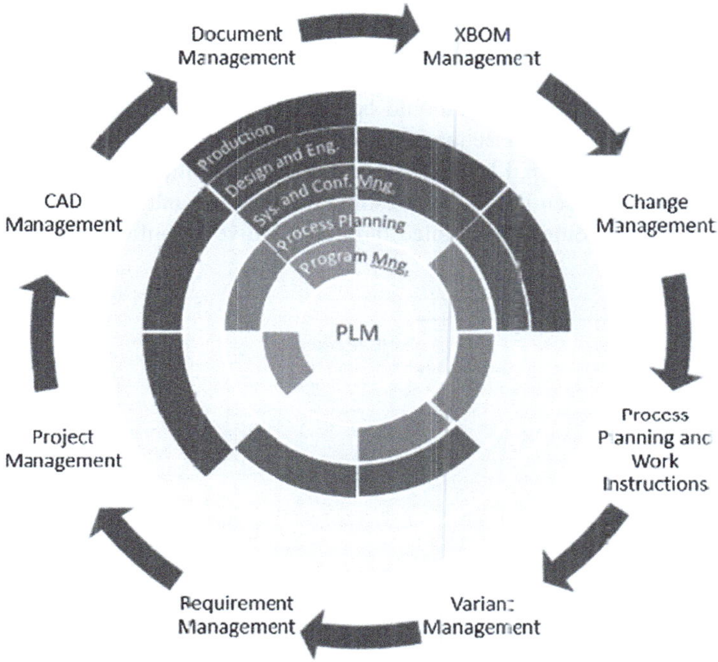

Fig. 1. PLM vision

2 End-to-End PLM Structure

In traditional management way of thinking, there are many ongoing methods to simplify and maintain workflows in a company to get suitable and desired outcomes and metrics. For instance, lean management can be adapted, which supports the continuous improvement in a company. Basic targets in a lean concept are used in order to eliminate the unnecessary time, excess effort and particularly excess money. This can only be done by analyzing a business process and revising it accordingly to make it suitable. Example of a lean model can be seen in Fig. 2 [3].

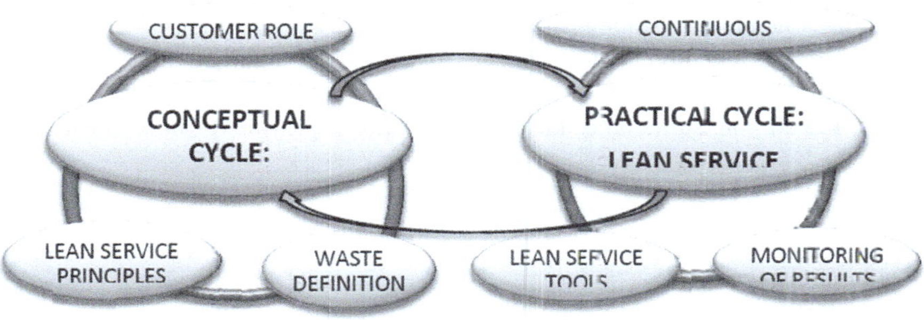

Fig. 2. Lean service conceptual model [3]

Furthermore, there are many agile methods for characterizing the companies' way of work for adapting business flows more accurately with less effort. All these different methods have to be used since companies' have many different divisions with many employees of expertise and they should be collaborated with respect to the business that they are involved in. Consequently, there is no doubt that when business models are being created, end-to-end business structure must be aimed.

Another model is seen in Fig. 3 for estimating the time and costs of the end-to-end process to deliver a component printed through additive manufacturing [4].

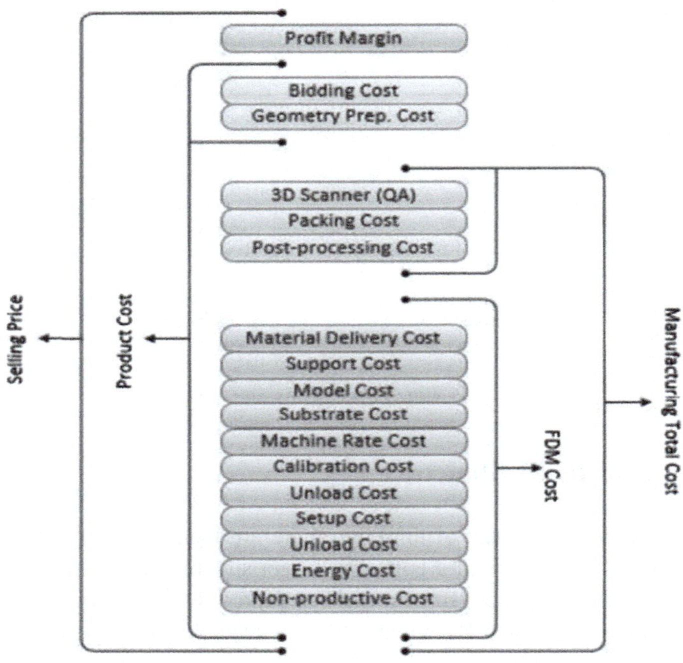

Fig. 3. Cost model to estimate the time and costs of the end-to-end process to deliver a component printed through additive manufacturing [4]

The big dilemma in adapting traditional ways for capturing end-to-end processes comes from its difficulty in deployment. Especially in automotive where dynamic changes are daily routine, most of the time it requires a very deep knowledge of impact analysis. In addition, some other factors for difficult deployment can be mentioned as below:

- Resistance to change
- Lack of agility in softwares
- Cultural change
- Fear of huge transformation and adaptation process
- Legacy data

For this reason, PLM can make a high difference in constructing an end-to-end process. In this section, a study will be taken to define end-to-end process of an automotive company including the bottlenecks of the data and workflow in a PLM platform. Table 1 defines the certain modules of a PLM software versus the departments in the company respectively;

Table 1. Modules of PLM and related departments

Modules vs. departments	Program management	Process planning	System and configuration management	Design and engineering	Production
Change management		x	x	x	
CAD management		x		x	
Document management	x	x	x	x	x
Requirement management			x		
XBOM management			x	x	
Project management	x			x	
Process planning and work instructions		x			
Variant management		x	x		

The need of the departments in a single PLM platform is constructed as a matrix in Table 1. This is the most important vision to see the exact requirements with respect to departments so that the required steps can be taken. An example CAD model of an end-item product (defense vehicle) in BMC is shown in Fig. 4 where the study will be based on.

Fig. 4. Defense vehicle data model

Related departments in a company, PLM modules and external inputs are shown in Fig. 5 in end-to-end structure. Significantly, in automotive industry, the life cycle of a product launches with requirements and carries on with project management and designing stages. Starting with requirements, this cycle should be able to reach the production stage without any interruption (even by adding more data at each stage). Requirements are evaluated and turned into project tasks. In project stage, EBOM (Engineering Bill of Materials) is constructed as an output of the design stage and operation sheets and assembly instructions are prepared by process planning department. Moreover, EBOM evolves into MBOM (Manufacturing Bill of Materials) and the data smoothly flows into ERP system by integrations, which means that the product is ready for production. Document management has a role in being every stage in the process; however, change management and variant management have major effects on the process even though they are not mastered in every step.

In this process flow, traceability is essential because it allows changes to be propagated efficiently while implications can be detected easily based on relations between multiple artefacts [5].

Because of the insufficient abilities of the system and end users' traditional working methods, there might be external inputs coming from different sources on whole process. These external inputs are mostly requirements (eg. it may be necessary to use applications deemed appropriate by the national defense ministry in the defense industry), outputs of project management tools and outputs of other design tools. To cope up with this complexity, use of engineering IT tools for computer-aided anything (CAx) is spreaded throughout the entire process [6].

Although the most accurate method to prevent bottlenecks and ensure traceability in the process is the management of the data in the single platform, in some cases, data flow and traceability can be ensured through the integrations between applications or customizations [7].

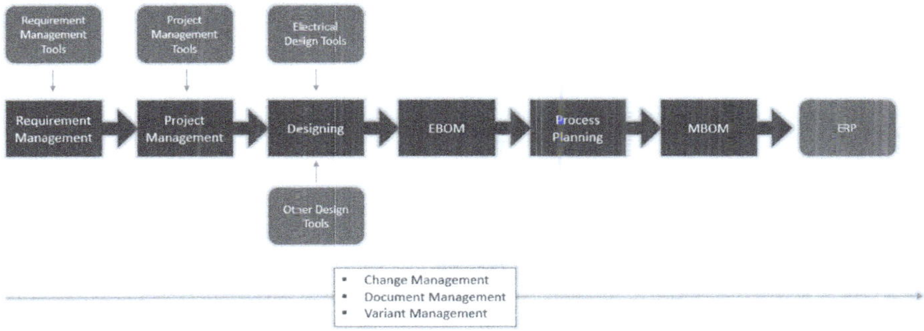

Fig. 5. End-to-End PLM process

End-to-end PLM process aims to provide traceability of the data and to create singularity of it. In order to make this manageable, various aspects of data management must be consistently implemented. The main issues of 'Single Source of Truth' are the relationships between data and dependencies and system conditions for workflows and interfaces [8].

It is proposed that increasing the role of information technologies in systems, traceability and sustainability will be supported, and in parallel, it will facilitate the cooperation of stakeholders in engineering and production processes [9].

3 Engineering IT Management on Business Process

This section aims to define how to best serve when building and deploying PLM and IT structures in a company to achieve end-to-end standards. The term "Engineering IT (Information Technologies)" can be considered as a service that is given to all engineering processes; particularly engineers on conceptual and theoretical phases as well as on technology and IT management aspect. This is not widespread in most of the companies however, in order to manage and understand processes and systems, IT and engineering point of view and expertise should not be taken apart from each other. Hence, solution architects that are responsible for Engineering IT department and concept should be willing to give solutions with both engineering and IT systems administrator approach. Success on processes' agility might only come with this understanding from internal or external customer. Moreover, this comprehensive insight of the requirement can be transformed and reflected into the system professionally.

A common known example of this kind of failure is examined in "Redafi Research and Development Africa Initiative" where Airbus A380 project was delayed for many years with a loss of billions of dollars due to:

- Configuration and change management insufficiency,
- Lack of collaborative environment [10]

Regarding this complex IT management systems, a defined vision of PLM in engineering networks is given in Fig. 6 [11].

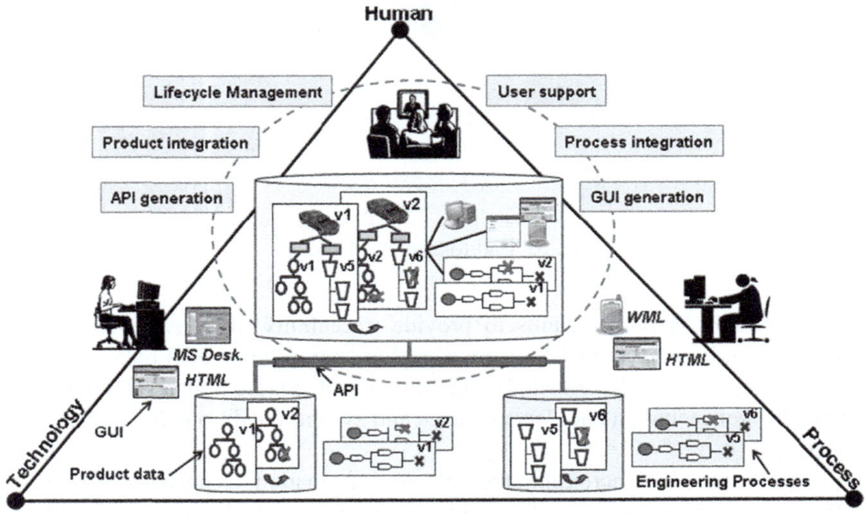

Fig. 6. Vision of PLM in engineering networks

Continuously, the major areas of Engineering IT and its methods that are applied by solution architects in automotive sector are listed in following sub-sections:

3.1 Solution Consultancy on Conceptual and Technical Phases of PLM and IT

The most important function of Engineering IT is the solution consultancy to different departments in a company. The requirements of departments might come with dependency to others and the system whereas sometimes they can be independent. In order to manage this; impact analysis should always be done and be prioritized accordingly. Most of the time; these requirements need collaborative management and the response times get extended because of the conflictions in between. This is why the solution architect has to have vast knowledge on business solutions so that he/she can lead the team to a common goal. During the conceptual idea growth phase, the technical feasibility must always be analyzed simultaneously by the solution architect. Otherwise, there emerges a risk on implementing the solution to PLM systems which then might lead to failure. This is the other major attribute of the solution architect that he/she must be fully capable of managing the services that he/she is responsible for.

A mapping of integrated multidisciplinary way is given in Fig. 7 where the complexity between the departments and services can be seen [6].

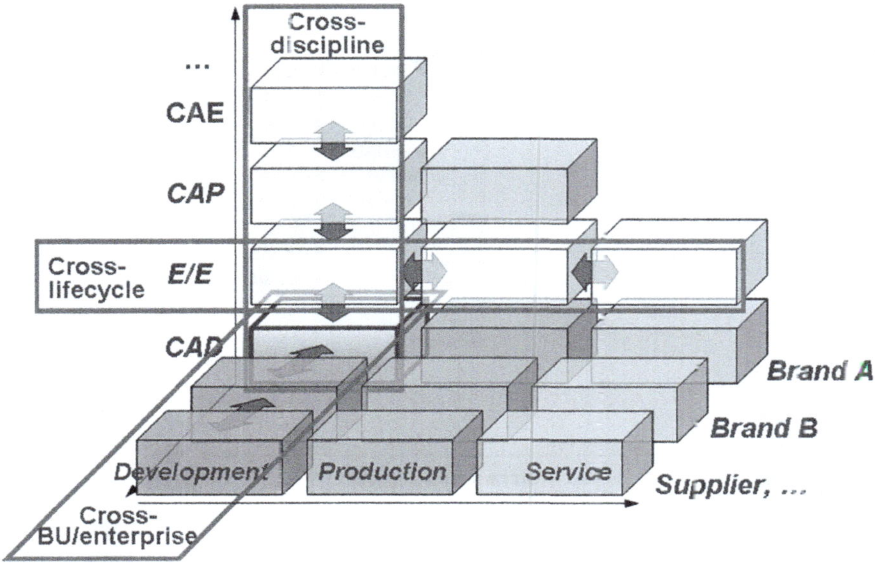

Fig. 7. Cross-x engineering in design dimensions [5]

3.2 Systems Architecture and Management

Another major responsibility of Engineering IT is to manage and administrate PLM and related IT systems and servers. The systems must always be up and they should be controlled and reported by SLAs (Service Level Agreement). On the other hand, based on customer requests and enhancements, daily and planned administrative activities should be done for improving systems' performance and agility. In addition, for maintaining an uninterrupted service to end users, high availability should always be taken into consideration supported by SPOFs (Single point of failure). Figure 8 shows the basic PLM system server architecture in BMC Automotive Company.

3.3 Business Solutions by Configuration and Code Deployment

As it can be interpreted from many cases, the platforms generally cannot satisfy the needs of the customer, therefore, many customizations on tool is done by solution architects. Some of them might be web-based adjustments whereas others might be done by scripts and batches. On a higher level, there are cases that require third part integrations with other business softwares and unique programs where code development and deployment stages become vital. Hence, Engineering IT is responsible for those processes as well.

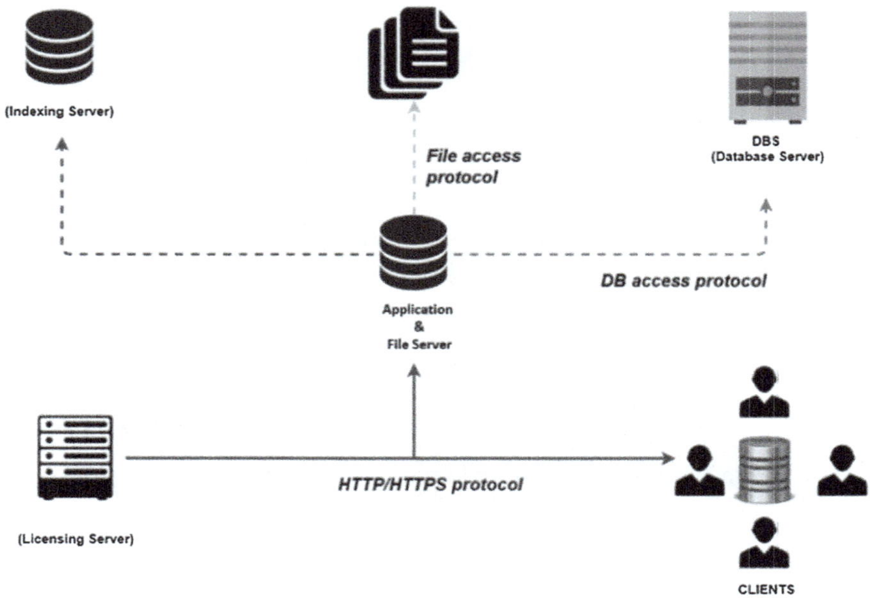

Fig. 8. PLM system server architecture

3.4 Technical Support on IT Side (Helpdesk)

This section might be covered with a typical example of a change management process where configurative mistakes are mostly done by designers and product engineers. Some of these mistakes are caused by rule violations of PLM software's change management module and some are caused by hardware issues. These different feedbacks from end users can only be managed by helpdesk tools within the company. An example of this management can be seen in Fig. 9.

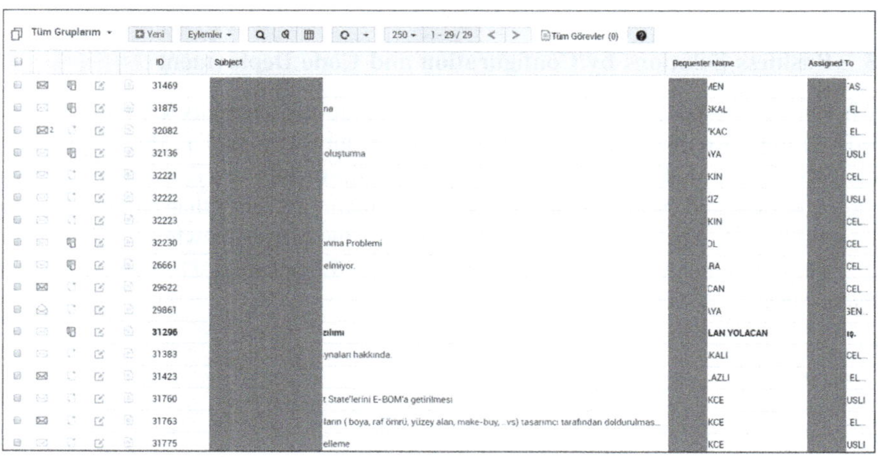

Fig. 9. Helpdesk management of Engineering IT

3.5 Knowledge Base, Lectures and Trainings

In order to provide a living mechanism of Engineering IT ideology, documents must always be created and revised accordingly for:

- Trainings
- Having a technical database (Knowledge base)
- Sustainability

3.6 Digital Mockup (DMU) Support on Vehicle Designing

Due to the fact that the Dynamic DMU runs along throughout the product lifecycle, it is linked to existing PDM/PLM structures [12]. At this point, it is very important that DMU support is provided by the engineering IT team due to having a comprehensive knowledge of the entire product design, privileges and ensuring cleanliness of data (Fig. 10).

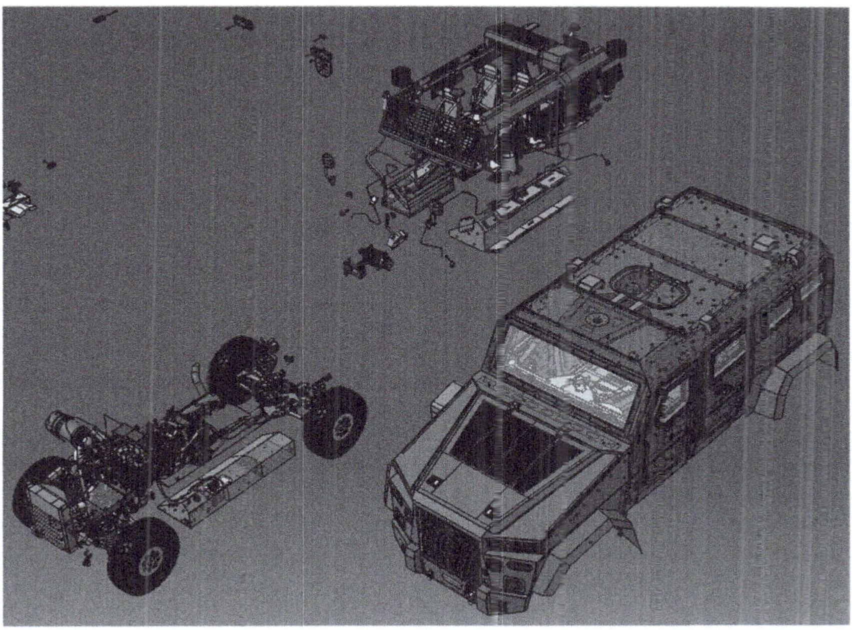

Fig. 10. Sub-components of a defense vehicle

3.7 Implementing New Software or Methods from Scratch to Be Used by Engineering Teams

One of the main responsibilities of solution architects is to implement new software for engineering teams. Demands and problems should be collected from the teams, benchmarking should be done, and the best practices should be presented by analyzing the requirement.

An attempt to introduce a new application stagnates because it's linked to changes in processes and working procedures. It calls for new skills and interfaces, and it has a tendency on changing old habits [13]. Therefore, being in touch with teams from start to finish will help in successful commissioning.

4 Conclusion

This study examines how engineering IT approach works on end-to-end PLM structure in a company. Furthermore, it is intended to be a guide for administrative structure that needs to be established for end-to-end collaborated processes, which has a key role on information technologies and product lifecycle management.

On the other hand, PLM applications in automotive industry have direct effect on whole process and products; therefore, it affects company profitability severely. End-to-end process can be considered as a key factor in successful PLM implementation where traceability is ensured by smooth functioning of change management and impact analysis. Solution architects who are devoted to maintain sustainability of all these systems and provide continuous improvements are responsible for these systems. On engineering point of view, support is handled mainly in solution consultancy, digital mockup, implementation of new applications and trainings whereas on IT point of view, it is handled by system administration, software customization for business processes and helpdesk management.

As a conclusion, it is beneficial to take this study as a guide on reaching successful implementations on PLM and engineering applications.

References

1. Bruun, H., Mortensen, N., Harlou, U., Wörösch, M., Proschowsky, M.: PLM system support for modular product development. Comput. Ind. **67**, 97–111 (2015)
2. Paavel, M., Kaganski, S., Lavin, J., Sonk, K.: Optimizing PLM implementation from vision to real implementation in Estonian SMEs. In: 9th International DAAAM Baltic Conference, Tallinn, Estonia (2014)
3. Andrés-López E., González-Requena I., Sanz-Lobera A.: Lean service: reassessment of lean manufacturing for service activities. In: The Manufacturing Engineering Society International Conference, Madrid, Spain (2015)
4. Busachi, A., et al.: A system approach for modelling additive manufacturing in defence acquisition programs. In: 11th CIRP Conference on Intelligent Computation in Manufacturing Engineering (2017)
5. Königs, S., Beier, G., Figge, A., Stark, R.: Traceability in systems engineering – review of industrial practices, state-of-the-art technologies and new research solutions. Adv. Eng. Inform. **26**, 924–940 (2012)
6. Bergsjö, D., Vielhaber, M., Malvius, D., Burr, H., Malmqvist, J.: Product lifecycle management for cross-x engineering design. In: International Conference on Engineering Design, Paris, France (2007)

7. Müller, P.: Configuration management – a core competence for successful through-life systems engineering and engineering services. In: 2nd International Through-life Engineering Services Conference, Bremen, Germany (2013)
8. Hertwig, M., Trippner, D., Lentes, J.: Certification of Openness – Corner Stone of an Agile PLM Strategy. In: 25th International Conference on Production Research Manufacturing Innovation: Cyber Physical Manufacturing, Chicago, Illinois, USA (2019)
9. Belkadi, F., Bernard, A., Laroche, F.: Knowledge based and PLM facilities for sustainability perspective in manufacturing: a global approach. In: The 22nd CIRP conference on Life Cycle Engineering, Nantes, France (2015)
10. Redafi Research and Development Africa Initiative: Why Projects Fail Case Study of Airbus- A380. Nairobi, Kenya (2017)
11. Eigner, M., Fabrice, M.: Conceptual modeling and generator framework for multidisciplinary and collaborative product lifecycle management. In: 13th International Conference on Computer Supported Cooperative Work in Design, Santiago, Chile (2009)
12. Gerhardt, F.J., Eigner, M.: Dynamic and conceptual DMU. In: International Design Conference, Dubrovnik, Croatia (2008)
13. Stark, J.: Product Lifecycle Management, Decision Engineering. Springer, London (2011). https://doi.org/10.1007/978-0-85729-546-0

Continuous Engineering Through ALM-PLM Integration

Purnima Rao[1(✉)] and Kandhasami Palaniappan[2]

[1] Colorado State University, Fort Collins, CO 80523, USA
Purnima.rao@in.bosch.com
[2] Bharathiar University, Coimbatore 641004, TN, India
Kandhasami.Palaniappan@in.bosch.com

Abstract. "A techno-domain-driven approach will in all likelihood revolutionize how a product development organization resonates with changing end-user demands and, its vendors in a collaborated and continuous engineering setup, and thereby driving transformational change".

The increasing convergence of markets and smart products, shifting business models as well as increased customer expectations have created an unprecedented level of complexity for product development organizations. Particularly, in the automotive industry, complexity has literally exploded in the four dimensions of **product**, **processes, tools** and **compliance**. Thereby, product development organizations are under tremendous stress to adopt stringent processes thus, leading to complex tools usage to meet the target compliance. In order to be in a position to cope with this dilemma of new complexity and to safeguard sustainable competitiveness, it is vital for organizations to implement an integrated, holistic approach to manage the different dimensions of product development. As current product development involves hardware, electrical & mechanical (PLM) components and software components (ALM), their respective lifecycle management processes also throw challenges of coordinated and continuous engineering. This means we need a paradigm shift from the traditional practice of disparate lifecycle management to an innovative concept like **S**leek **L**ifecycle Integration & **M**anagement (**SLIM**).

Keywords: Lifecycle · Integration · ALM · PLM · Exchange · Synchronization · Traceability · Disparate systems · Continuous engineering · Connected automation · Lean lifecycle management · Lean lifecycle integration

1 Preface [1–3]

Studies in the recent past indicate that organizations are serious about software and technology as their products are worthwhile only if it is smart. Smart products comprise not just HW[1], but also embedded SW[2]. This indicates that the integration of disparate

[1] Hardware
[2] Software

ALM—Application Lifecycle Management.PLM—Product Lifecycle Management.

Published by Springer Nature Switzerland AG 2020
F. Nyffenegger et al. (Eds.): PLM 2020, IFIP AICT 594, pp. 798–811, 2020.
https://doi.org/10.1007/978-3-030-62807-9_62

HW and SW lifecycles becomes the core essential in product development. Added to this, market expectations are value for money, shorter launch cycles, etc. This means cost of engineering and predictive maintenance too become essential for the organizations to keep their product costs competitive (Fig. 1).

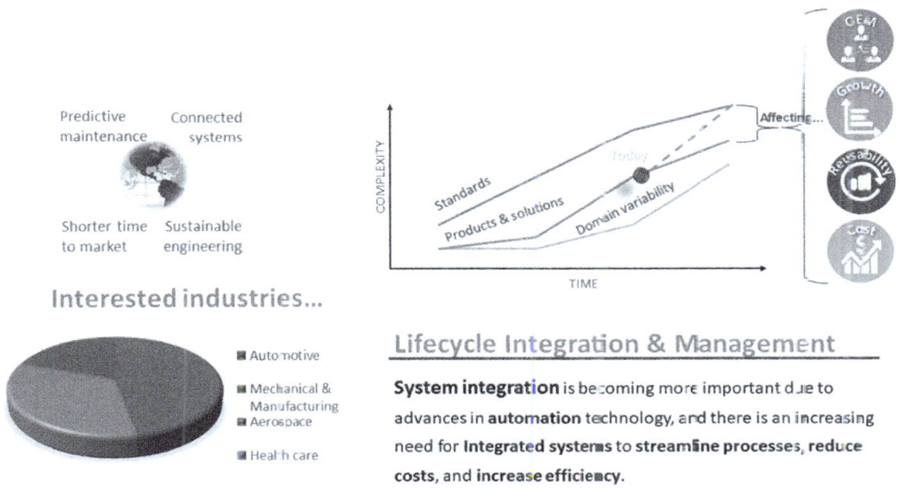

Fig. 1. Author's derivation based on the pulse of industries and market

---

SNIPPET

As per the market study by independent blogger Mr. Oleg Shilovitsky, smaller companies are better and faster in adopting the digital thread. Most of these companies are "digital native (see Footnote 1)" and they have urgent needs in solutions capable to connect engineering and downstream processes. The need of the hour for them is to have quick deployable engineering solutions (targeting the core engineering functions).

We see that software and technology is a critical element, and it is important to know what they comprise. Software and technology comprise tools, solutions, domain and standards. The core challenges of industries will resolve when standards, technology (products & solutions) and domain variability converge at some point. Otherwise, the gap will continue to affect OEM-supplier integration, growth of the organization, cost of engineering and reusability. Hence, lifecycle integration & management become core mantra going forward.

The core essential problem is integrating these lifecycles for a coordinated and continuous engineering while solving cross-domain traceability and smart KPI reporting.

> "What got us till here, will not take us there; unless, we digitally transform by changing the definition of integration in the world of product engineering'

2 Market Trends [1–3]

The Product development in any industry is continuously evolving. It is all about innovation, being different, getting to market first and keeping up with consumer demand. Additionally, today's conventional approach of product development is being constantly challenged for its sustenance with new advances in AI and IoT. Below is a snapshot of market trends gathered from different sources (Fig. 2).

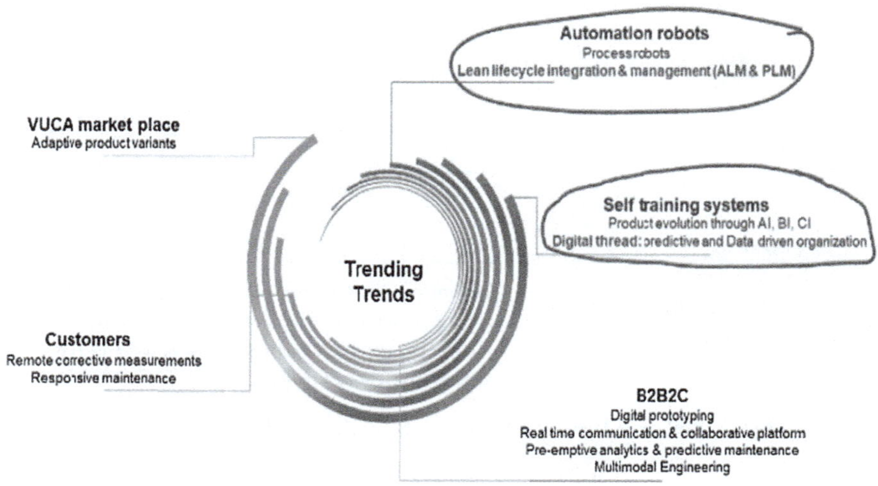

Fig. 2. Author's perception based on market trends

Digital Thread manages the complexity of the product development. A product may have hundreds of individual components or assemblies, some of which the manufacturer may produce and others that are sourced from a range of suppliers (or suppliers' suppliers). This chain can become incredibly complex to manage, as a single design change can affect the manufacturing of multiple components. By providing a "single version of the truth," the Digital Thread helps manage this complexity. In a MBE[3], the structured way of handling the information happens via the Digital Thread (such as 3D model, meta-data information for MBM[4], MBQ[5], etc.)

[3] Model Based Enterprise.

[4] Model Based Manufacturing.

[5] Model Based Quality.

In the face of these intricacies, **ALM-PLM**[6] **is emerging as an innovation platform** that enables the digital thread, providing traceability, agility, and customization. While doing so, it is important to remember the following four major objectives:

- Identifying and incorporating customer needs
- Understanding and improving customer experience (i.e., UX[7])
- Completely closing the loop in the product design & development (CLLM[8])
- Infusing the insights from the sample field data collected from connected products

Connected products enable the concept of a closed loop lifecycle and bring the data back to the design and development team. With the data flowing back (to the design teams), the teams will not only be able to run the predictive design but also build smarter products (Fig. 3).

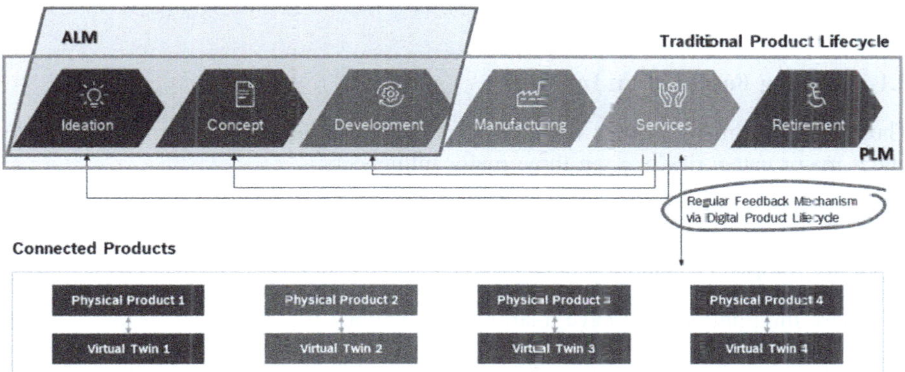

Fig. 3. Data driven product development involving ALM-PLM (Digital Thread)

Top Drivers of Digital Thread:

1. Collaboration and better configuration management
2. Unification of software and hardware in the product
3. Product Development and Manufacturing Integration focusing on **traceability of product artifacts**[9]

---

[6] ALM & PLM integrated.

[7] User eXperience.

[8] Closed Loop Lifecycle Management.

[9] One of many engineering tangible objects used in product development. Ex: requirement, UML models (use case, class diagrams, etc.), test case, documents, etc.

4. Product lifecycle development & Servitization[10]
5. End of cycle & compliance management
6. Circular economy[11]

INSIGHTS

- Overall PLM market has grown by 9.9% to USD 48b in 2018 (including ALM, PLM, and Digital Manufacturing). Share of PLM is USD 16.2b and ALM is USD 5b
- Product data on digital thread & traceability (ALM + PLM + IoT + Digital Twin)
- Adoption of PLM on the cloud with micro services (with DevOps)
- While data is the crude oil, the governance of the data is the key to have a 'refined' oil (Master data governance)
- PLM + Additive Manufacturing
- PLM + Blockchain
- Digital Thread

2.1 Driving Forces of an Industry

There could be many drivers or influencers for a business. When broadly classified under major categories, we see three major influencers –

- Customer brand loyalty
- Holding maximum market share
- Being futuristic – adopting technology

These three influencers have a strong correlation.

- While the customer is always looking for something new from a product, business sees a way to capture maximum market share of that product.
- Customer expects continued support from the product while the business wants to focus on evolution of its family of products.
- Customer never wants to move away from a brand unless the business has nothing more to offer that is trendy.

It is also on the business to see how to match this demand vs supply or be a trendsetter by thinking "first in business". Technology is the underlying fact that helps enliven collaborated, continuous and integrated product development (Fig. 4).

---

[10] Servitization is a transformation journey - it involves firms (often manufacturing firms) developing the capabilities they need to provide services and solutions that supplement their traditional product offerings.

[11] A circular economy is an economic system aimed at eliminating undesirable product cost by continual reuse of product features.

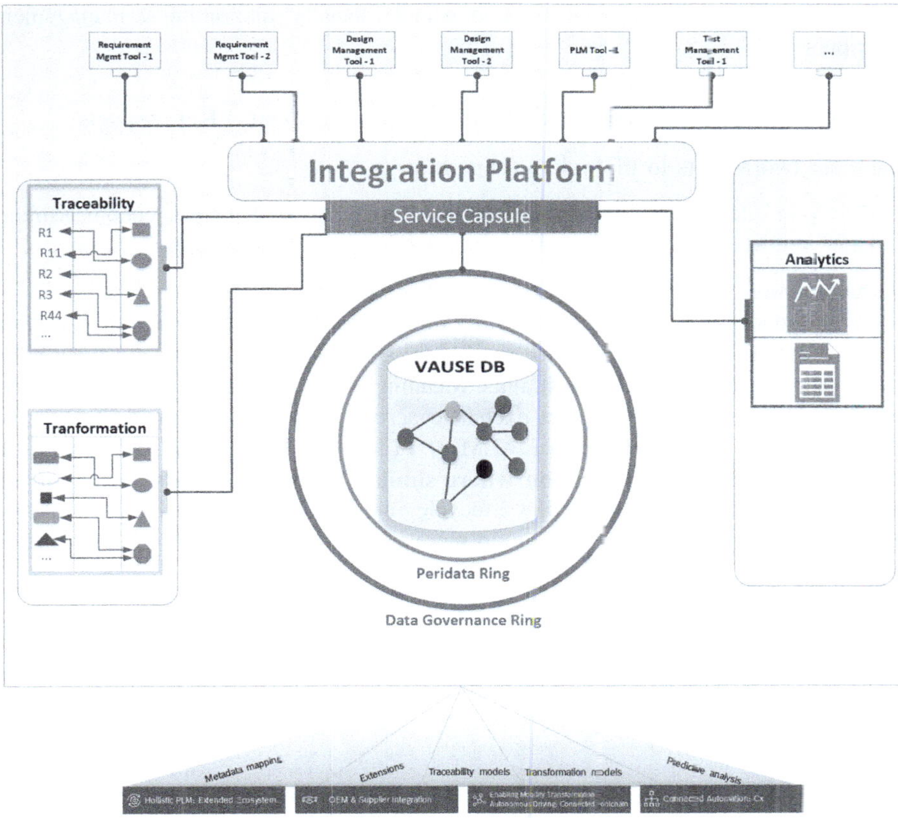

Fig. 4. Tool agnostic integration view

The above depiction shows that no matter what the category of tools are; whether they are requirements or testing of model management tools; they all can seamlessly integrate as long as the engineering can be centrally persisted. This also gives us an opportunity to apply AI/ML, ASPICE, cross-domain reference KPIs and transformations, etc.

Having understood so far, the bottom-line indication is continuous engineering. What we need for an efficient future is a concept that will allow software (ALM) and hardware (PLM) to seamlessly integrate, communicate and thus exchange product-engineering artifacts keeping product traceability in focus (to meet ISO/IEC 15504[12] and ASPICE[13]).

[12] A standard for Information technology – Process assessment.

[13] Automotive Software Performance Improvement and Capability dEtermination.

This now becomes important to understand lifecycle integration & management concepts.

2.2 Relevance of Lifecycle Integration and Management – Key Aspects

There are two aspects to lifecycle management

- Lifecycle Integrations - Landscapes having homogeneous & heterogeneous artifacts
- Lifecycle Management - Process standardization and Automations

Homogeneous[14] Lifecycle Integration & Management

When an organization has limited visibility of its need for lifecycle integration, it often goes for a short-term investment for a solution; a solution that specifically focuses on solving the requirement with constraints. Meaning, let us say your organization wants to solve a specific issue of defect exchange across engineering units, following the same discipline of lifecycle (either ALM or PLM). **Therefore, this terms to be a homogeneous lifecycle integration where similar lifecycle artifacts are involved**. This leads to simple, point-to-point lifecycle integration. This is termed as classic approach of the pre-millennium. A good representation of this scenario is seen below (Fig. 5).

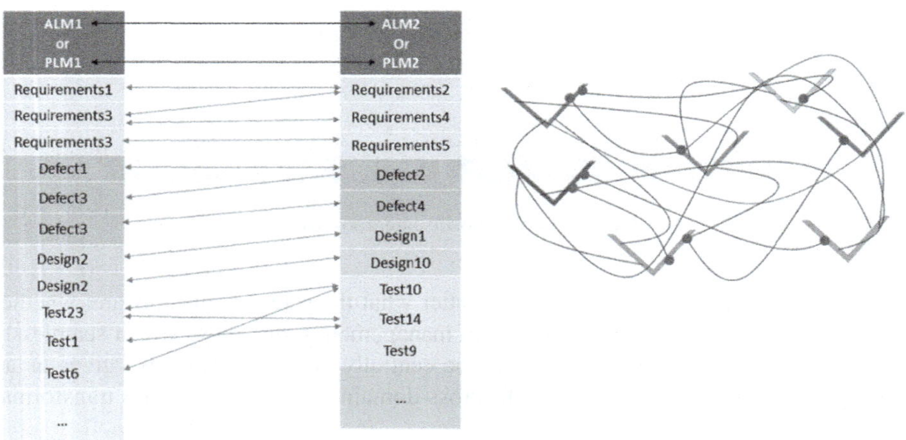

Fig. 5. Homogeneous lifecycle integration

Achievement

- Simple and straightforward tool integration
- A limited lifecycle integration

[14] All of same kind.

Continued challenges

- Frequent tool customization needed in order to maintain the integration through upgrades, etc.
- Cross lifecycle/tool integration is a challenge due to the incompatibility in the nature of data contained by the tool
- Changing a tool is a challenge, as it would break the integration mechanism
- Data non-transparency due to no cross tool integration (Ex: no integration possibility between requirements and design tools)
- Underlying technology of tools

Heterogeneous[15] Lifecycle Integration & Management
When an organization aspires to achieve high degree of traceability and audit compliance, it often goes for a long-term investment for a solution; a solution that specifically focuses at integration of lifecycles at a product development level (ALM-PLM). Having said this, we can straightly assume the involvement of many engineering and non-engineering tools and technology to achieve such a high degree of compliance. This also means that the best way to achieve the compatibility is to use tools that are mutually compatible for lifecycle integration. Ex: requirements module in ALM has to ensure that it is compatible with requirements module in PLM. This means, the two disparate sets of tools following heterogeneous lifecycles are brought together via a mutually compatible interface. A good representation of this scenario is as seen below (Fig. 6).

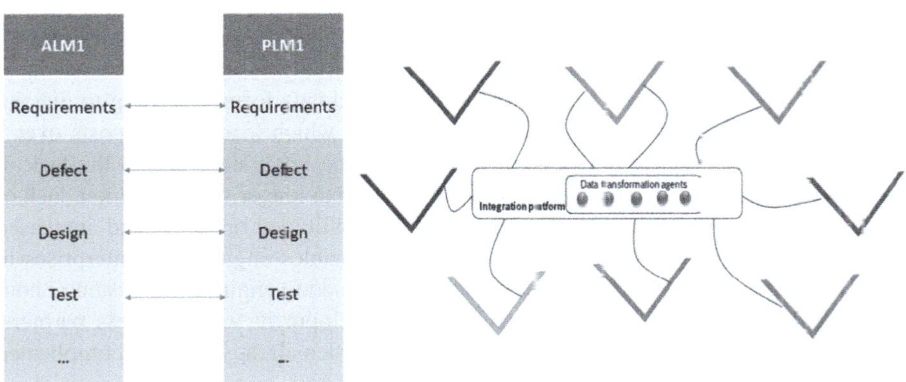

Fig. 6. Heterogeneous lifecycle integration

Achievement

- Wider scope of lifecycle integration achieved with mutually compatible interface provided by a licensed vendor

[15] Diverse in character and content.

- Some amount of traceability achieved among compatible toolchains on either sides of the lifecycles

Continued Challenges

- Organizations are still forced to adopt usage of compatible tools for the sake of lifecycle management
- The above constraint offers limited tool flexibility to engineering units
- Technology and tool upgrade continues to be difficult
- Maintenance and business aspects of closed loop lifecycle management or multi-modal engineering is still a far dream

Therefore, the bottom line issues and challenges of sustainable and continuous engineering, a trustworthy lifecycle management solution and achieving some of the critical business KPIs remain to exist. Organizations are now realizing that what we have until now is not sufficient to match the pulse of the market demands.

3 SLIM: RBEI's[16] Proposal for a Solution

The key to building a Sustainable and Trustworthy multimodal[17] engineering establishment is to enable interoperability between disparate systems and processes involving varied standards and data formats. Product development organizations need and use these disparate tools and lifecycle processes resulting in a complex mesh of point-to-point connectivity that in turn becomes inefficient and unmanageable over a period. Technological compulsions and the varied cycle speeds of development make it cumbersome for an ecosystem of disparate tools and lifecycle processes to dovetail.

Product Development Organizations have traditionally struggled with islands of heterogeneous systems that use different standards and data formats leading to disjoint system or tightly coupled point-to-point integrations, which lead to high costs over a long run. Lack of efficient data exchange and lifecycle integration add to the lack of interoperability and maintenance. These problems lead to longer time to market, lack of traceability for product issues, unmanageable variability of products and increased costs. The need of the future is for a solution that enables engineering enterprises to collaborate efficiently using well-integrated heterogeneous engineering systems, coupled with lifecycle processes that enable easier development with business partners, and yet not introducing another tooling solution to burden already existing complicated engineering tooling landscapes (Fig. 7).

We do have many brands that offer lifecycle integration platforms to manage product and application lifecycle. What we have often experienced is that these available solutions work well only when our engineering systems integrate with them. This is the catch. Our engineering tooling landscape is so diverse with homegrown and proprietary tools that it simply becomes impractical to invest once again in another

[16] Robert Bosch Engineering and Business Solutions Private Limited. https://Www.Bosch-India-Software.Com/En/Index.Html.

[17] Application of multiple types of activities on the same medium.

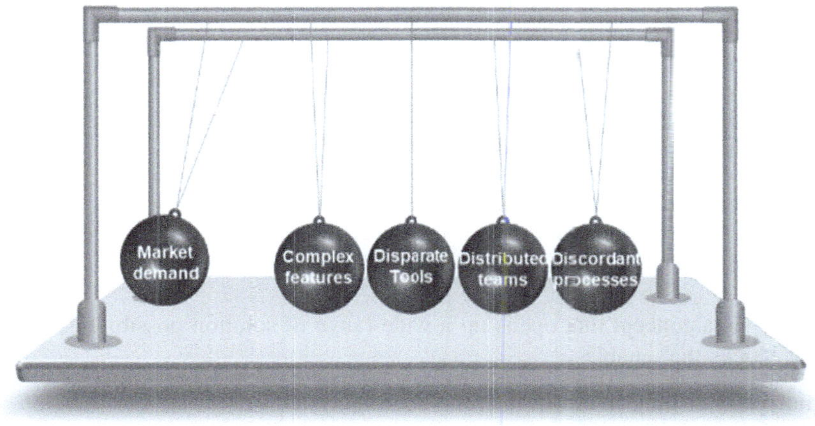

Fig. 7. Market demand and its influence on the systems

solution, just to get on to the chosen platform. In spite of doing so, we are still not certain if we can completely integrate with the platform in order to achieve **traceability** and **variability**.

Therefore, what we really need is a solution that will let us continue to use age-old tried-and-tested engineering tools and yet bind them together to exchange data and provide traceability and variability. Not stopping at this, we would also like if the same solution can extend to provide us an opportunity to apply AI/ML[18] & BI[19] to achieve predictability in our engineering (Fig. 8).

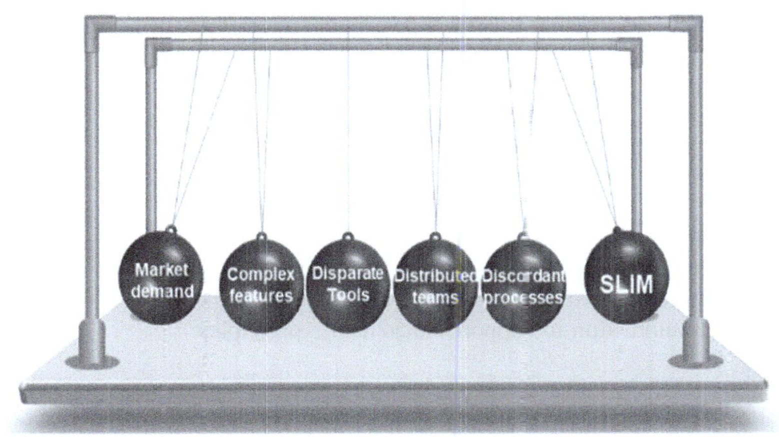

Fig. 8. SLIM to solve market demands

[18] Artificial Intelligence/Machine Learning.

[19] Business Intelligence.

SLIM HIGHLIGHTS
• Integrate any PLM to any ALM. • Provide abstraction from multiple tools, data formats and standards. • Support easier integration of new tools/systems by providing a configuration over programming approach – Integration Platform • Model your business logic and data exchange rules into reusable templates • Efficient transformation and traceability of heterogeneous engineering artifacts • Provides multi-standard transformation compliance – VAUSE™ • Cross platform reporting and analytics – smart KPI dashboards

SLIM[20] is a concept that opens up a wide range of solution possibilities with key building blocks that enable

- rapidly establishing interoperable engineering systems
- well connected lifecycle processes and secure data sharing ecosystem with OEMs, suppliers and engineering units
- predictable engineering

While SLIM enables you the above, it yet does not force another tool to an already existing complicated engineering tooling landscape. SLIM uses a combination of products like any integration platform and VAUSE™ [21] to establish a feasible and elegant process that makes exchange mechanism between any PLM systems to any ALM system seamless. This relieves product development organizations that often find it arduous to establish such an integration, considering their complex and heterogeneous engineering practices. Below is a representation of such a concept where tools from any PLM system can communicate with tools from any ALM system (Fig. 9).

Having said this, the only next thought that comes to our minds is to **define a minimum basic exchange protocol that is tool agnostic**. Staying tool agnostic is the key differentiator. This is where SLIM uses integration platform products and VAUSE™ to achieve a tool agnostic lifecycle integration and management solution.

SLIM – A Detailed View

The above solutions serves multiple purposes such as (Fig. 10):

- Lifecycle synchronization
- Migration
- SW exchange
- Partner integration
- Connected toolchain
- Connected automation to support blockchain[22] principles

[20] **S**leek **L**ifecycle **I**ntegration & **M**anagement.

[21] Vault of Archetypes for Unified Systems Engineering.

[22] Chain of growing block of data and records that are linked using cryptography.

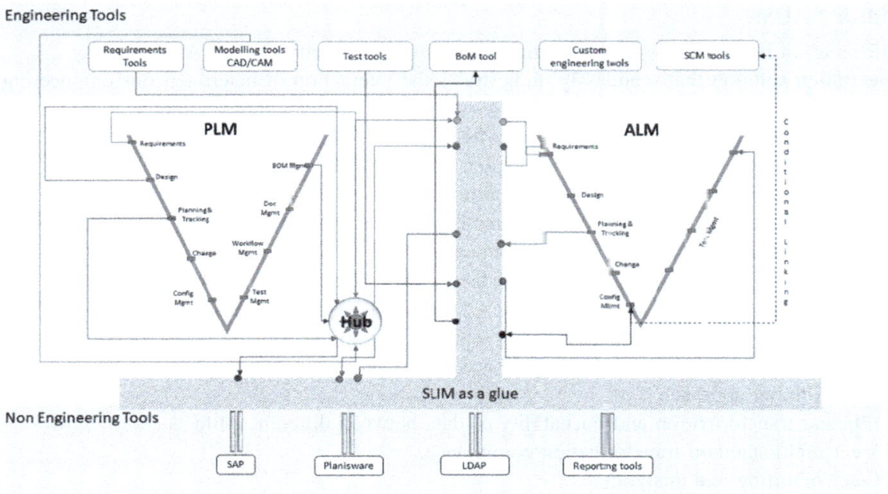

Fig. 9. Any ALM-PLM integration through SLIM as a glue

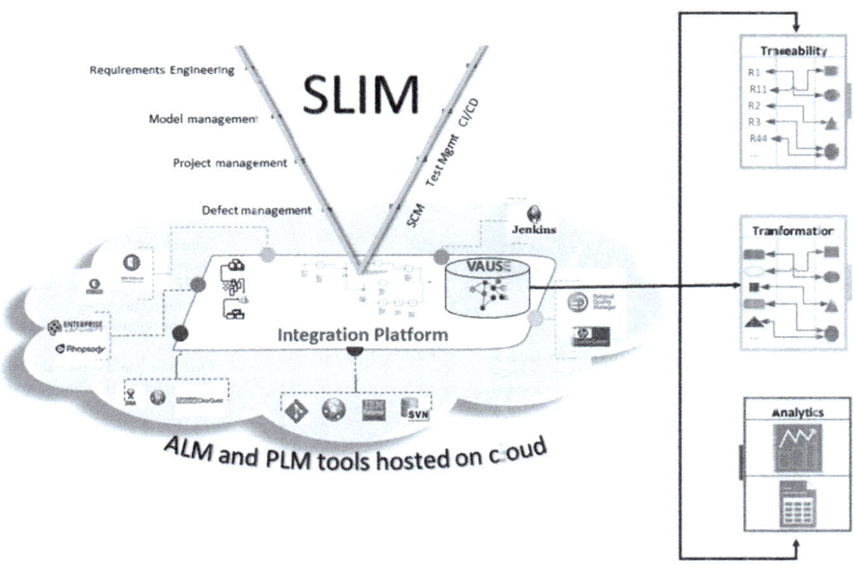

Fig. 10. Detailed view of SLIM

BIP & VAUSE
BIP is an in-house developed integration platform solution enabling an Any-to-Many integration solution that seamlessly orchestrates the interaction of heterogeneous engineering systems with transactional integrity. BIP – • Provides integration platform to connect heterogeneous lifecycle tools • Work Flow Modeler feature help construct lean protocols for integration • Exposes extensions for transactional data reflection Note: any integration platform solution enabling the basic minimum needs mentioned above could also be a good candidate for experimenting VAUSE – is a vault of engineering artifacts references that makes SLIM tool agonistic integration solution. This solution provides the needed building blocks to • Provide abstraction from multiple tools, data formats and standards. • Support easier integration of new tools/systems by providing a configuration over programming approach • Efficient transformation and traceability of data between different artifacts • Meet multi-standard transformation compliance. • Cater reporting and analytics

Some of the benefits one may explore to realize (Fig. 11):

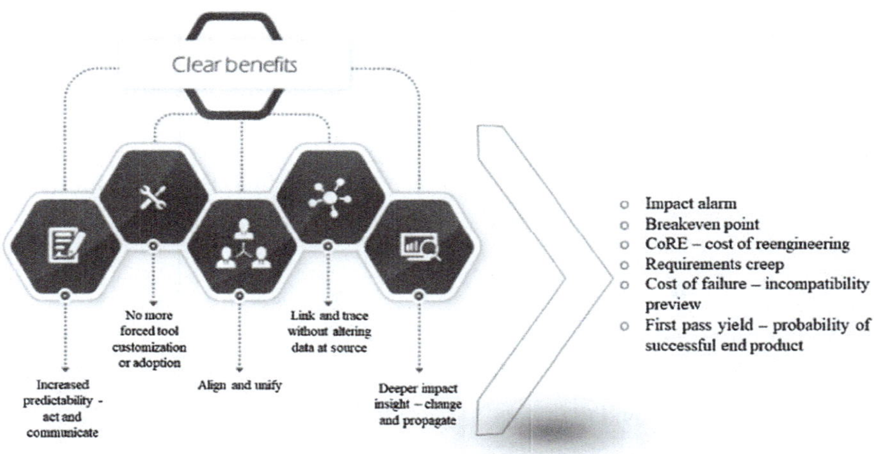

Fig. 11. Benefits of SLIM

4 Conclusion

It is evident that organizations are in dire need of harmonizing product development to stay relevant in today's market. SLIM not only focusses on process automation and tools specific integration but also holistic product engineering enabling organizations to achieve this harmony by; involving software, hardware and product lifecycle as a whole, thereby giving an opportunity to bring any PLM to integrate with any ALM.

RBEI thus firmly believes that SLIM is the future of connected and continuous engineering that can help build an integrated ecosystem for a sustainable and trustworthy engineering.

References

1. https://www.mckinsey.com/~/media/mckinsey/industries/automotive%20and%20assembly/our%20insights/monetizing%20car%20data/monetizing-car-data.ashx
2. https://www.gartner.com/smarterwithgartner/staying-on-track-with-connected-car-security/
3. https://www.gartner.com/en/newsroom/press-releases/2019-10-23-gartner-says-global-it-spending-to-grow-3point7-percent-in-2020
4. http://beyondplm.com/

Correction to: Addressing Obsolescence from Day One in the Conceptual Phase of Complex Systems as a Design Constraint

Sophia Salas Cordero, Rob Vingerhoeds, Marc Zolghadri, and Claude Baron

Correction to:
Chapter "Addressing Obsolescence from Day One in the Conceptual Phase of Complex Systems as a Design Constraint" in: F. Nyffenegger et al. (Eds.): *Product Lifecycle Management Enabling Smart X*, IFIP AICT 594, https://doi.org/10.1007/978-3-030-62807-9_30

The original version of this chapter was revised. The last name of the author Sophia Salas Cordero was incorrectly tagged. Her last name has been corrected to Salas Cordero.

The updated version of this chapter can be found at
https://doi.org/10.1007/978-3-030-62807-9_30

Published by Springer Nature Switzerland AG 2021
F. Nyffenegger et al. (Eds.): PLM 2020, IFIP AICT 594, p. C1, 2021.
https://doi.org/10.1007/978-3-030-62807-9_63

Author Index

The manufacturer's authorised representative in the EU is Springer Nature Customer Service Centre GmbH, Europaplatz 3, 69115 Heidelberg, Germany. If you have any concerns regarding our products, please contact ProductSafety@springernature.com

Printed and bound by CPI Group (UK) Ltd, Croydon, CR0 4YY
30/09/2026
02225505-0020